I0818367

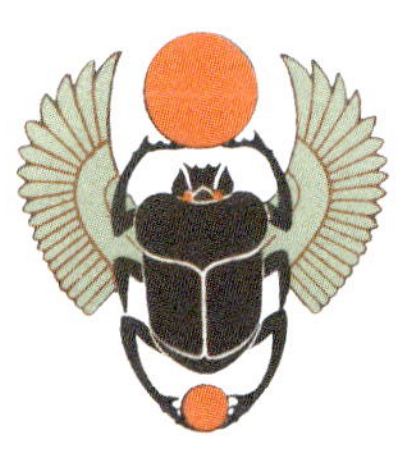

MONUMENTS EGYPTIENS.

BAS-RELIEFS, PEINTURES, INSCRIPTIONS &c.

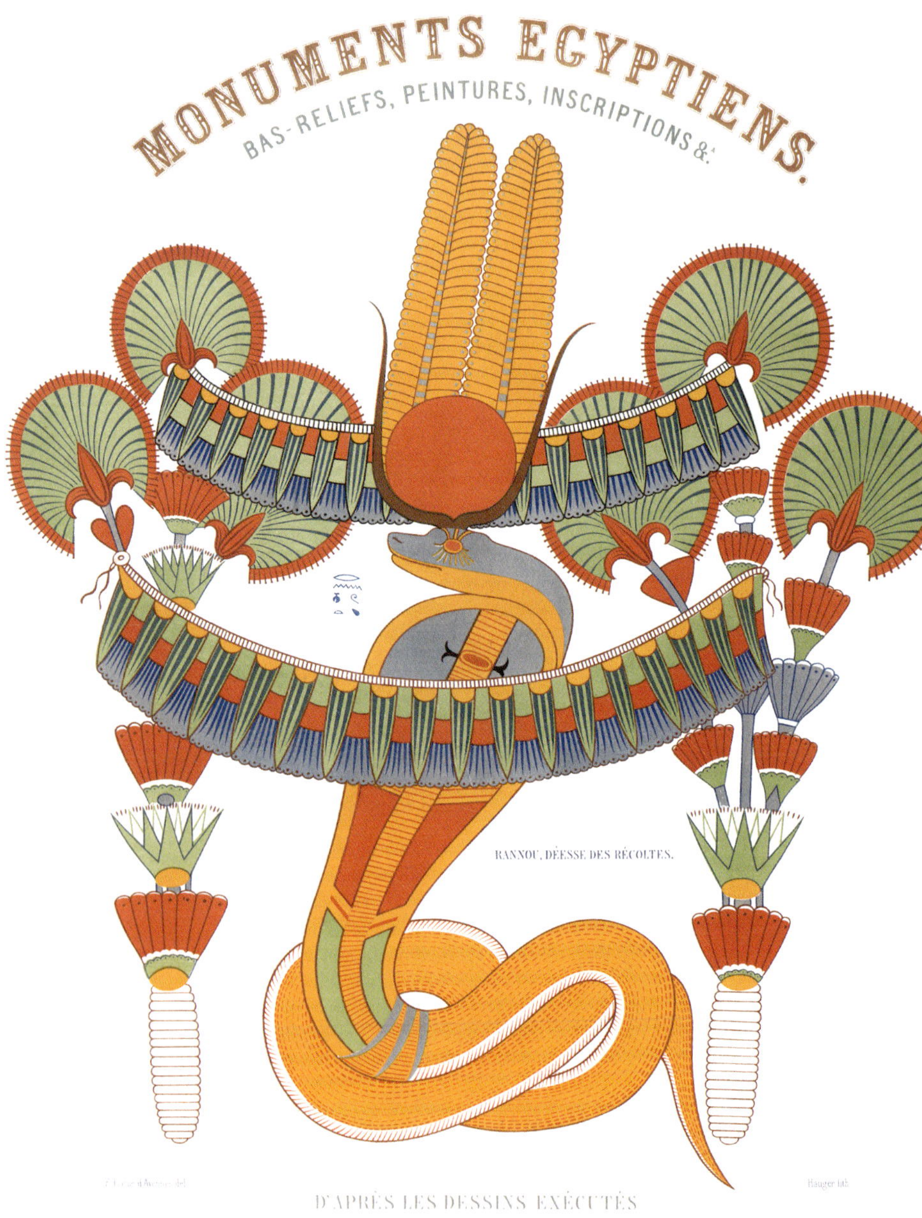

D'APRÈS LES DESSINS EXÉCUTÉS

PAR

E. PRISSE D'AVENNES.

IMPRIMÉ EN COULEURS PAR LEMERCIER À PARIS

ÉMILE PRISSE D'AVENNES

EGYPTIAN ART

Ägyptische Kunst — L'Art égyptien

The complete plates from
Monuments égyptiens & Histoire de l'art égyptien

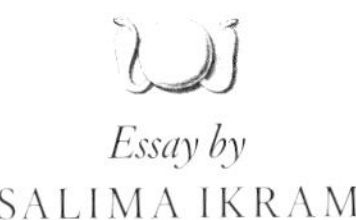

Essay by
SALIMA IKRAM

The copies used for printing belong to
NIEDERSÄCHSISCHE STAATS-
UND UNIVERSITÄTSBIBLIOTHEK GÖTTINGEN
UNIVERSITÄTSBIBLIOTHEK HEIDELBERG

With a selection of original texts by
ÉMILE PRISSE D'AVENNES

Directed and produced by
BENEDIKT TASCHEN

TASCHEN
Bibliotheca Universalis

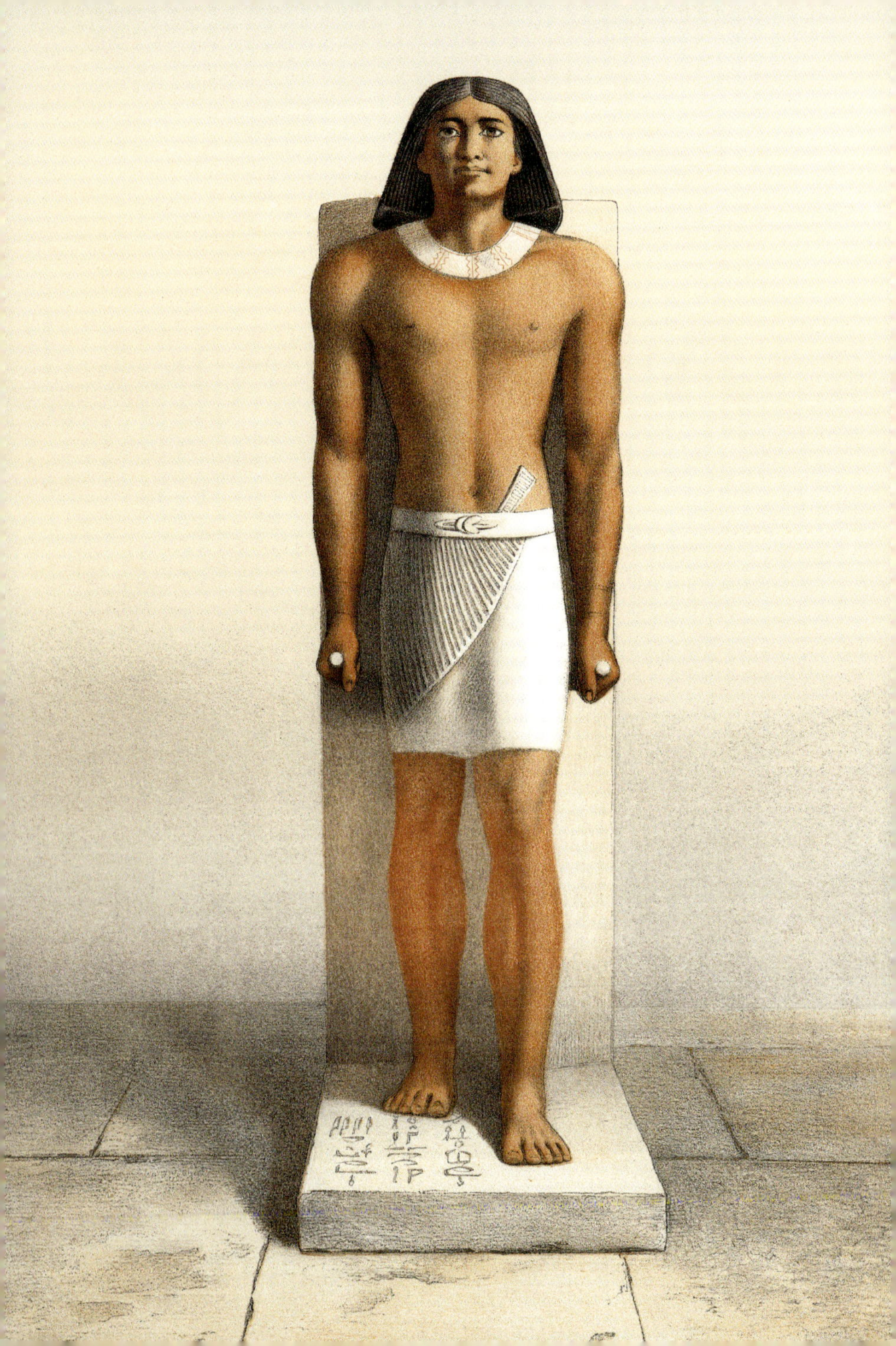

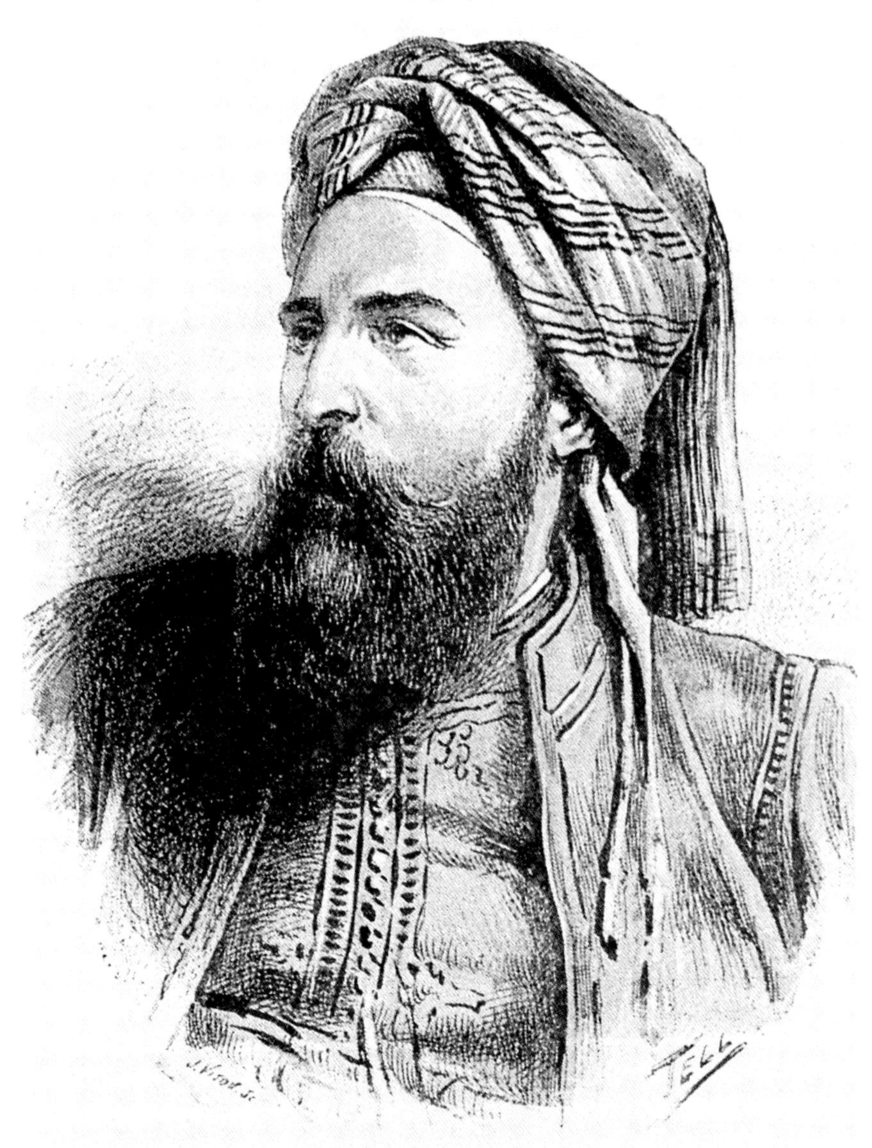

D'après Deveria.

Émile Prisse d'Avennes and Ancient Egypt

SALIMA IKRAM

Egyptology owes a tremendous debt to the many travellers to Egypt in the 19th century who were seduced by its monuments and recorded all that they saw, thus becoming the earliest Egyptologists, long before the discipline was properly established. Achille Constant Théodore Émile Prisse d'Avennes (1807–1879) was one such traveller, who not only visited and documented many sites throughout the Nile Valley but also made one of the earliest studies of Egyptian art, thereby laying the foundation for specialised studies in this field (ills. 1, 9). Prisse is unusual in that he did not limit his interests to ancient Egypt: his regard for Egyptian art and architecture extended to the Islamic period, and thus his two great œuvres, *Histoire de l'art égyptien, d'après les monuments, depuis les temps les plus reculés jusqu'à la domination romaine* (Paris, 1878/79; History of Egyptian Art) and *L'Art arabe d'après les monuments du Kaire, depuis le VIIe siècle jusqu'à la fin du XVIIIe siècle* (Paris, 1869–1877; Arab Art), span almost the entire length of Egyptian art history. One can but wish that he had devoted a similar amount of time and space to Coptic art, thereby ensuring a thorough record of many monuments that have since been lost to posterity.

Until recently little was known of Prisse save for his works, which speak eloquently for themselves, and only a handful of other publications that mention his name. Chief amongst these are a biography (or hagiography, rather) written by his son Émile that was intended to elevate his father's reputation and defend his memory against the published and publicised libellous remarks of Maxime du Camp in his *Souvenirs littéraires* (1888). These last were unfortunately repeated in the encyclopaedic *Voyageurs et écrivains français en Égypte* (1932) by the historian Jean-Marie Carré, although for the most part Carré discredited du Camp's statements. The period from the 1980s on saw a marked rise in interest in the history of Egyptology, including a few publications pertaining to Prisse (and others) by Michel Dewachter that help provide a more balanced view of this

Ill. 1
Achille Devéria
Prisse d'Avennes, dressed as an Arab, 19th century / Prisse d'Avennes, in arabischem Gewand / Prisse d'Avennes, vêtu en arabe
Lithograph, 13 x 10 cm (5 1/8 x 3 7/8 in.). Paris, Bibliothèque nationale de France

extraordinary man. Most recently, the work by Prévost (et al., 2011) and Volait (2013) goes a long way to reviving interest in Prisse, correcting misapprehensions about his work, as well as shedding fresh light on his life. With the current republication of Prisse's two major works, on Pharaonic and Islamic art, he is once more in the limelight, a spot that he well deserves.

Prisse's Early Life

Prisse was born on January 27, 1807, in the modest French town of Avesnes-sur-Helpe (Nord) to a family that, according to its own traditions, was of British origin, from Aven in Wales. The spelling "d'Avennes" was adopted, after some earlier variations, in 1690, and would seem to be a tribute to both the original and adopted cities of the family. After training at the École d'Arts et Métiers at Châlons-sur-Marne (1822–1825) the 19-year-old Prisse, who had a thirst for adventure, left France to fight in the Greek War of Independence. After a very brief time there he travelled to India and thence to Palestine, where he stayed for a short period. There, he became involved with the sacred sites, earning him the title of Knight of the Sepulchre. Prisse's desire to explore the East and its ancient treasures led him on to Egypt in 1826. He then had the good fortune to be hired by Muhammad Ali Pasha (r. 1805–1848) and his son, Ibrahim, who acted as regent for his father briefly at the end of his rule. Prisse worked in a variety of capacities, including teaching at various military institutions, and even doing a brief stint as tutor to the princes. During this time he took the name Idris Effendi, ostensibly converted to Islam (although this was probably a matter more of politics than faith), learnt Arabic, and became adept in hieroglyphs – insofar as it was possible to do this at the time (ill. 13). Prisse remained in the employ of the Pasha for some ten years before finding his true calling: the study and recording of the monuments of Egypt, which culminated in his encyclopaedic publications.

In the early 19th-century Egypt was the focus of European antiquarian, political and economic interest. To a large extent this was due to Napoleon Bonaparte's politically ill-fated, but intellectually and artistically triumphant expedition to Egypt (1798–1801) that resulted in the publication of the multi-volume *Description de l'Égypte*, which took nearly two decades to publish (1809/10–1828; ills. 2, 3, 19). The first edition consisted of nine quarto volumes and 11 enormous volumes of plates, a total of some 837 copperplate engravings, and over 3,000 drawings. The *savants* who had accompanied Napoleon on his expedition explored all aspects of Egypt, including antiquities, natural history, modern history and topography. These volumes further piqued the interest of Europeans and shaped the course of European (and Egyptian) scholarship. They also influenced architectural and artistic styles and tastes, created an apparently insatiable demand for Pharaonic antiquities and, by virtue of their completeness, contributed to fuelling the transition of Egyptology from an antiquarian hobby to a formal discipline. Indeed, one of the most important and active artists who took part in the mission and later became director-general of the Louvre, Vivant Denon (1747–1825), published his experiences as part of the team of *savants*, in his *Voyage dans la Basse et la Haute Égypte* (1802), which attracted a great deal of attention and became an immediate bestseller throughout Europe.

Prisse's craving for adventure and attraction to the East might well have been fuelled by the *Description* as well as other popular books published by the individual *savants* who accompanied Napoleon. Indeed, Jean-François Champollion's (1790–1832) lectures and publications on the Rosetta Stone, a crucial artefact recovered by the French, and on Egyptian grammar apparently were one of the main reasons for Prisse's interest in Egypt. Early illustrated travelogues, such as Frédéric Norden's *Voyage d'Égypte et de Nubie* (1755); Bishop Pococke's *A Description of the East and some other Countries* (1743–1745), which was translated into French from 1772 to 1773; Comte Constantin-François Volney's *Voyage en Syrie et en Égypte, pendant les années 1783, 1784, et 1785* (1787); and Claude Étienne Savary's *Lettres sur l'Égypte* (1786) also might have captured the young draughtsman-engineer's imagination and encouraged him to pursue a life in the East. Western travellers, scientists and adventurers flooded into Egypt in the wake of the Napoleonic expedition and Muhammad Ali's demand for experts. The Pasha seems to have been particularly welcoming to the French, and already had the talented architect Pascal Coste (1787–1879) on his staff. Coste is known for his studies on Islamic architecture, particularly in Cairo, but also shared with Prisse an enthusiasm for the Pharaonic past, which is evident in his many notebooks and sketches. It is quite possible that the two men met in Cairo or Alexandria.

The Context of Prisse's Work

Some of those who travelled to Egypt were lured by romantic ideas of the Orient and its antiquities, whereas others went with the more prosaic intention of making a profit. Regardless of their initial reasons for going there, many of these individuals were beguiled by the wonders of ancient Egypt, and turned their attention to exploring ancient Egyptian sites, discovering, gathering and recording antiquities.

The French proconsul to Egypt, Bernardino Drovetti (1776–1852), and his arch-rival, the British Consul-General Henry Salt (1780–1827), were two of the many men who, together with their other duties, focused on acquiring Egyptian antiquities for their respective governments. Tales of their feuds and subterfuges as they struggled to acquire colossal statues, papyri and almost entire tombs and temples make for gripping reading, and are but another manifestation of the endless rivalries between the two nations.

Amongst Salt's employees was one Giovanni Battista Belzoni (1778–1823), a giant of a man (he had been a circus strongman in England), who originally went to Egypt as an engineer but, following a series of chance developments, had become an antiquarian. A large portion of the British Museum's holdings was secured thanks to the combined efforts of Belzoni and Salt. In addition to working for Salt, Belzoni explored Egypt and dealt in antiquities on his own account. His archaeological triumphs include the exploration of Abu Simbel and Giza – afterwards also explored by Prisse (ill. 4) – and Belzoni was the first modern person to enter the pyramid of Khafre at Giza, in 1818, leading the way for future Egyptological inquiry. Like Prisse, Belzoni made copies, casts and squeezes of scenes from tombs and temples, particularly those in Thebes. Squeezes, made by dampening special

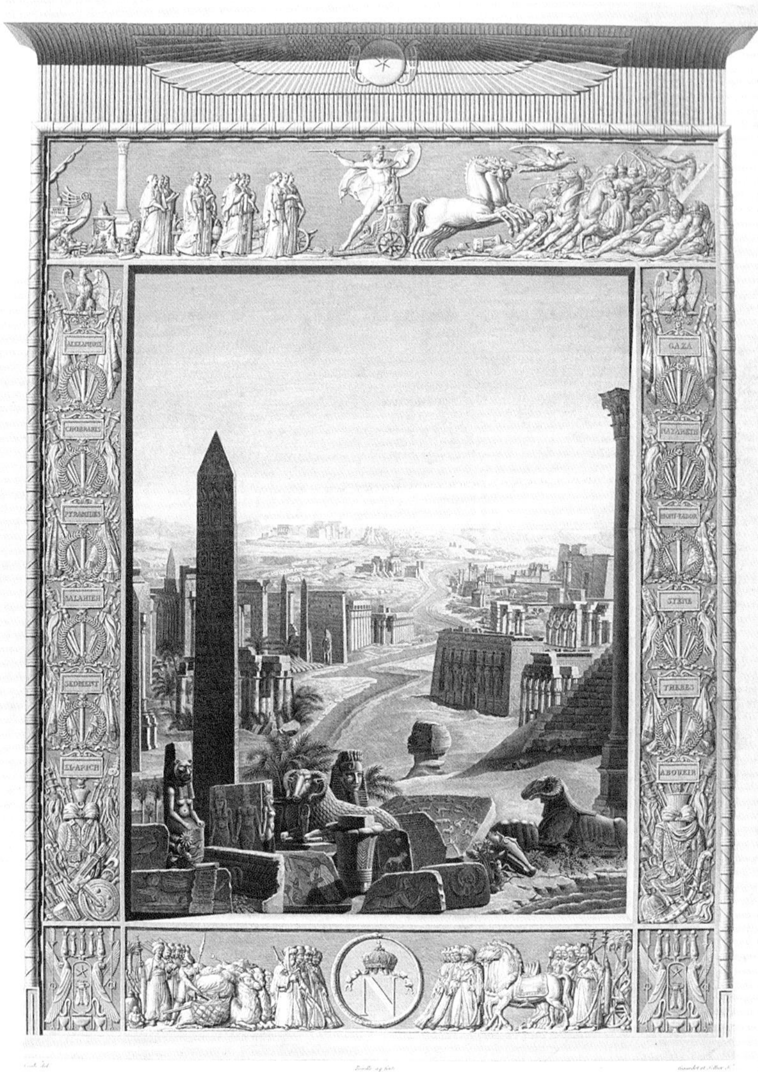

Ill. 2

Frontispiece / Frontispiz / Frontispice

in: *Description de l'Égypte ou recueil des observations et des recherches qui ont été faites en Égypte*, vol. IV ("Antiquités – Planches"), Paris, 1817

Lithograph, 55 x 41 cm (21 5/8 x 16 1/8 in.). Weimar, Herzogin Anna Amalia Bibliothek

paper, similar to blotting paper, and rubbing it vigorously to take the form of the relief beneath, were a popular, albeit destructive means of accurately recording relief decoration, and also used by Prisse. Drovetti's employees and companions were less colourful than Belzoni, but equally successful when it came to the acquisition of objects, as is attested by their collections which are now scattered throughout France and in Turin and Berlin. Two of Drovetti's most notable companions, Jean-Jacques Rifaud (1786–1852) and Frédéric Cailliaud (1787–1869), explored Egypt and Nubia and published extensively on these areas, making a lasting contribution to Egyptology. Rifaud's five-volume *Voyage en Égypte, en Nubie et lieux circonvoisins, depuis 1805 jusqu'en 1827* (1830–1844) was illustrated with colour lithographs, as were his other multi-volume works. However, none of these publications was a study in art history, as was the work of Prisse.

Some of the young Cailliaud's publications had something in common with the work of Prisse's *Oriental Album: Characters, Costumes and Modes of Life, in the Valley of the Nile* (London, 1848; texts by James Augustus St. John). Cailliaud documented the manners and customs of contemporary Egyptians as well as the more ancient inhabitants of the Nile Valley in his 1831–1837 publication *Recherches sur les arts et métiers, les usages de la vie civile et domestique des anciens peuples de l'Égypte, de la Nubie et de l'Éthiopie*. The description of the manners and customs of the Egyptians, both ancient and modern, was a popular field. A pair of Englishmen, Sir John Gardner Wilkinson (1797–1875) and Edward William Lane (1801–1876), provided an even more comprehensive overview of the daily life of the ancient and modern Egyptians than Cailliaud did. Wilkinson, who had arrived in Egypt in 1821, resided there for 12 years or so, returning there regularly until 1856. Like Prisse, he was fascinated by hieroglyphs, adopted an Arabic name, learnt the language and dressed like an Arab. Unlike Prisse, he even took an Egyptian wife, whom he later, sadly, abandoned. Wilkinson travelled through Egypt, collecting information and copying texts and scenes from both tombs and temples that contributed to the decipherment and study of the language of the pharaohs. He discovered, explored and numbered many Theban tombs, excavated a host of antiquities and ultimately published his *magnum opus*, the three-volume *Manners and Customs of the Ancient Egyptians* (1837), which chronicled the daily life of the ancient Egyptians using tomb reliefs as the basis of his interpretation (ill. 5). Throughout much of his later years in Egypt, Prisse corresponded regularly with Wilkinson, exchanging ideas and passing along information gleaned from his new discoveries. Although it is uncertain whether the two scholars ever met, they managed to establish and maintain a close working relationship for many years.

Presumably Prisse was also familiar with Lane. Lane was a brilliant Arabist and, like some of his contemporaries, spoke the language fluently, dressed in local attire, married (and took to England) an Egyptian woman, explored Egypt and wrote in detail about what he saw and understood of local customs of that era. His work resulted in the publication of *Manners and Customs of the Modern Egyptians* (1836), a companion to Wilkinson's work, and doubly fitting as both men were friends as well as colleagues.

The era of Prisse's activities in Egypt was not just one in which individuals plumbed the depths of Egypt's antiquities; indeed, entire nations sent large-scale scientific expeditions to Egypt to document and collect Egyptian antiquities. Naturally much of this activity was the consequence of the rivalry amongst European nations to possess the finest and largest Egyptian collections as a palpable manifestation of their wealth, erudition, power and control. However, the people who took part in these expeditions did so not just for the glory of their country and themselves, but also out of a genuine desire to unravel the complex culture of ancient Egypt. One of the earliest such expeditions was that led by Champollion, who is best known for his work on deciphering hieroglyphs. In 1828, under the aegis of the French king, Champollion, together with his pupil Ippolito Rosellini (1800–1843), embarked on a joint Franco-Tuscan mission to collect, examine and record the antiquities of Egypt. A team of artists, architects, organisers and doctors accompanied them as they travelled the length of Egypt and into Nubia, copying texts, acquiring antiquities and, in some cases, leaving their names carved on various monuments. This expedition yielded a prodigious amount of information as it was the first time that someone who could read hieroglyphs had made such a collection, and worked to translate all that had been gathered. In addition to bringing back large collections of Egyptian antiquities, Champollion and Rosellini assembled a large body of drawings of texts, monuments and artefacts which were published in several volumes that are invaluable to the study of ancient Egypt; they also served to inspire Prisse, who was a great admirer of Champollion (ill. 7). These works include *Monuments de l'Égypte et de la Nubie* (1833); *Lettres écrites d'Égypte et de Nubie en 1828 et 1829* (1833); and *I monumenti dell'Egitto e della Nubia, disegnati dalla spedizione scientifico-letteraria Toscana in Egitto* (1832–1844).

The other great scientific expedition of the 19th century was a Prussian undertaking led by Karl Richard Lepsius (1810–1884). In 1827 Friedrich Wilhelm III, King of Prussia, had acquired a large collection of Egyptian items for his royal art collection. This gave him a taste for Egyptian antiquities, and the scholarship associated with them, and led to the formal establishment of the Ägyptisches Museum in Berlin. Shortly after his accession, Friedrich Wilhelm IV, with the blessing of his scientific advisers, sponsored Lepsius's expedition from 1842 to 1845 to visit and collect monuments and collect and record the antiquities of Egypt. This was probably the best-equipped scientific expedition ever to be sent to Egypt, with the possible exception of that of Napoleon; however, Lepsius's expedition was certainly far better funded and planned. It included a large staff of skilled draughtsmen, engineers and scholars, all with some familiarity with Egypt. Lepsius and his team collected 15,000 objects, many of which he had excavated himself, although Prisse had trumped him in the acquisition of the Karnak King List (see below), and took them back to Berlin. All the drawings, maps and plans compiled in Egypt by Lepsius and his team were published in the massive 12-volume *Denkmaeler aus Aegypten und Aethiopien* (1849–1859; ill. 6). The five text volumes were

Ill. 3

Thebes, Memnonium: Interior View of the West Temple (detail)

Theben, Memnonium: Innenansicht des Westtempels (Detail)

Thèbes, Memnonium: Vue perspective intérieure du temple de l'ouest (détail)

in: *Description de l'Égypte ou recueil des observations et des recherches qui ont été faites en Égypte,*
A, vol. II ("Antiquités – Planches"), Paris, 1817, plate 37. Lithograph, 58 x 42 cm (22 7/8 x 16 1/2 in.)
Göttingen, Niedersächsische Staats- und Universitätsbibliothek

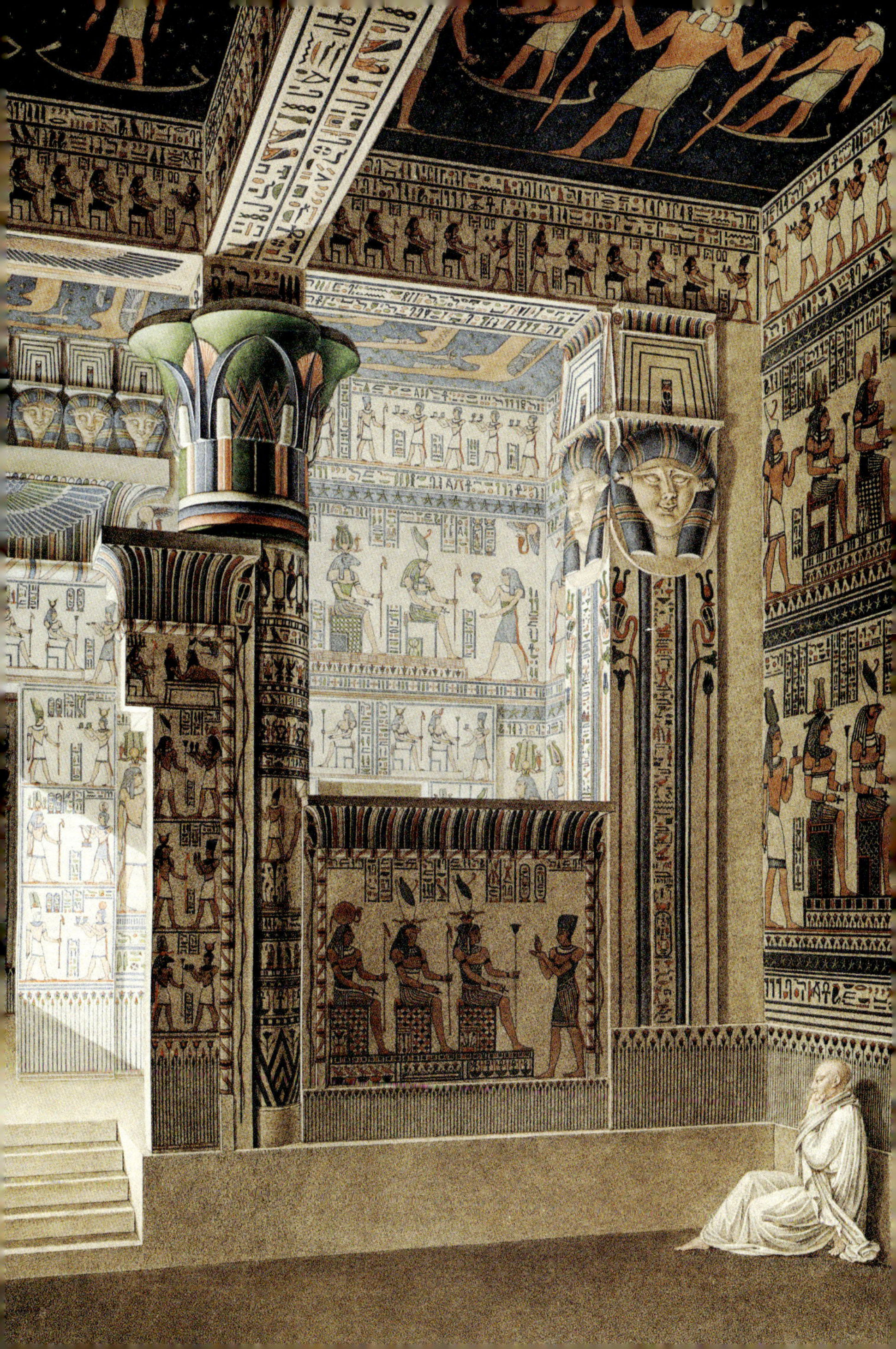

published long after Lepsius's death, between 1897 and 1913. Lepsius's *Denkmaeler*, along with his other publications, doubtless inspired the establishment of the earliest journal dedicated exclusively to Egyptology, the *Zeitschrift für ägyptische Sprache und Altertumskunde*, which was founded in Berlin in 1863. The *Denkmaeler*, together with the French *Description*, continue to form the foundations of current Egyptological research.

In addition to the scientific recorders of antiquities, many able artists travelled through Egypt, presenting a romanticised view of both Pharaonic and Islamic Egypt that makes a pleasing foil to the more technical and exact representations of the scholars. Most significant amongst their number is the Scottish painter David Roberts (1796–1864), known for his paintings and lithographs, which are still amongst the most popular images of Egypt ever to have been produced (ills. 8, 10). Numerous other painters have depicted Egypt, but John Frederick Lewis (1805–1876), Jean-Léon Gérôme (1824–1904) and William Holman Hunt (1827–1910) stand out amongst them.

The Work of Prisse d'Avennes

The rich backdrop against which Prisse played out his time in Egypt was thus peopled with pashas, politicians, plunderers, scholars, intellectuals, artists and adventurers. After severing official ties with the royal family in 1836, following a disagreement with the commanding general of the School of Infantry where he was then employed, Prisse set about exploring Egypt and the Near East until 1839. In Cairo he became fast friends with Dr Henry Abbott (1807–1859), and together in 1842 they founded the short-lived Association littéraire d'Égypte, a group that met and discussed Egyptian art and history, sponsored lectures and established a research library. This institution put both Abbott and Prisse in contact with many of the artists and scholars who passed through Egypt. Prisse had a great fondness for founding organisations and for being a member of learned societies; later on, in France, he established two occasional journals, *Le Miroir de l'Orient* and the *Revue orientale et algérienne*, both of which tied in with his love of the contemporary East.

During his travels Prisse drew incessantly, whilst collecting antiquities through both excavation and purchase. In this endeavour he was little different from a host of others engaged in the same occupation, although his geographical range was wider than that of many of his contemporaries, including the Delta and some far-flung sites within the Nile Valley, such as Shenhur, and his precision in recording was often better than that of his contemporaries. His interest in ancient Egypt was, however, spurred on by Champollion's scholarly work, and Prisse's own knowledge of hieroglyphs was surprisingly good for the time. His correspondence reveals that he was in contact with Champollion, Wilkinson, Mariette and other scholars. Were it not for Prisse's identifying and recording, many objects, buildings, scenes and inscriptions, such as a rare Claudian inscription in Latin, found reused in a mosque in Aqfahs, south of Beni Suef, and the Amarna material in Thebes, these would have been lost, and the history of Egypt the poorer for it.

In 1839 Prisse moved to Luxor to study the treasure trove of monuments located in that city. There he made friends with the Welsh botanist George Lloyd (1815–1843) and established a base from which to work. He spent nearly six years there acquiring antiquities for the glory of France (such as the Stele of Bakhtan now in the Louvre), drawing temples and their plans, copying scenes from tombs and temples, collecting squeezes and undertaking a thorough study of Egyptian art and the grammar of ornament employed by the ancient Egyptians (ill. 17). Quite possibly Prisse would have stayed in Thebes indefinitely had it not been for two occurrences. The first was the tragic death of his friend George Lloyd, who was fatally shot when his rifle accidentally discharged. The second was Prisse's dubious acquisition of part of the Karnak King List, also known as the *Chambre des Ancêtres*, or Chamber of the Ancestors (ills. 11, 12).

The Karnak King List is a key document in the study of ancient Egyptian history. King lists provide the names of rulers by succession, and thus are useful in establishing the chronology of a large part of Egyptian history. Frequently, however, certain rulers and even entire dynasties are left out of these lists, thus a complete list can be obtained only by combining several of them. The Karnak list is particularly valuable as it provides the names of the rulers of the troubled First (2181–2040 BC) and Second (1782–1570 BC) Intermediate Periods, which are ill-attested elsewhere. The list was carved by order of king Thutmosis III (1504–1450 BC) and erected in the southwest corner of the Akh-Menu (Festival Hall) pavilion in Karnak Temple (ill. 14). Sixty-one kings were listed on the stone, starting with one Neferkare, although the first fully preserved name is that of Snefru of the Fourth Dynasty. Prisse recognised the importance of this monument for Egyptology. According to his notes and letters he decided to remove the list as he feared that this portion of the temple, like many other monuments (such as some of the temples at Esna, Elephantine, el-Kab, and even Thebes), was going to be demolished and burnt for lime. Certainly, this was a common enough problem; in 1841 George Glidden, the former United States consul at Cairo, had issued what was perhaps one of the earliest pleas to scholars to help stop the destruction of antiquities by copying and, in some cases, removing them. Glidden lauded Prisse for his efforts to copy and thereby preserve extant Pharaonic monuments, and the speed at which he tried to rescue, or at least record, what he could of threatened monuments.

Other scholars have suggested that Prisse had heard that Lepsius was on his way to Thebes and, as a point of national pride, wanted to ensure that the French owned this prize antiquity and not the Prussians. Perhaps it was a combination of both these reasons, coupled with letters from Wilkinson urging Prisse to copy and/or protect the monument somehow, that led Prisse to act as he did. Under cover of darkness, in the course of 18 nights, he and his workers dismantled the wall upon which the King List was inscribed and boxed up the reliefs, storing them in his large tent nearby. Soldiers were sent by the local governor of Luxor to try to remove the boxes but Prisse invoked his French citizenship and the protection of his government. Temporarily safe, and after paying hefty

Ill. 4
Émile Prisse d'Avennes
The Giza Plateau, 1832 / **Das Gizeh-Plateau** / **Le plateau de Gizeh**
Watercolour on textured paper, 30.5 x 47.5 cm (12 x 18 3/4 in.)
Paris, Bibliothèque nationale de France

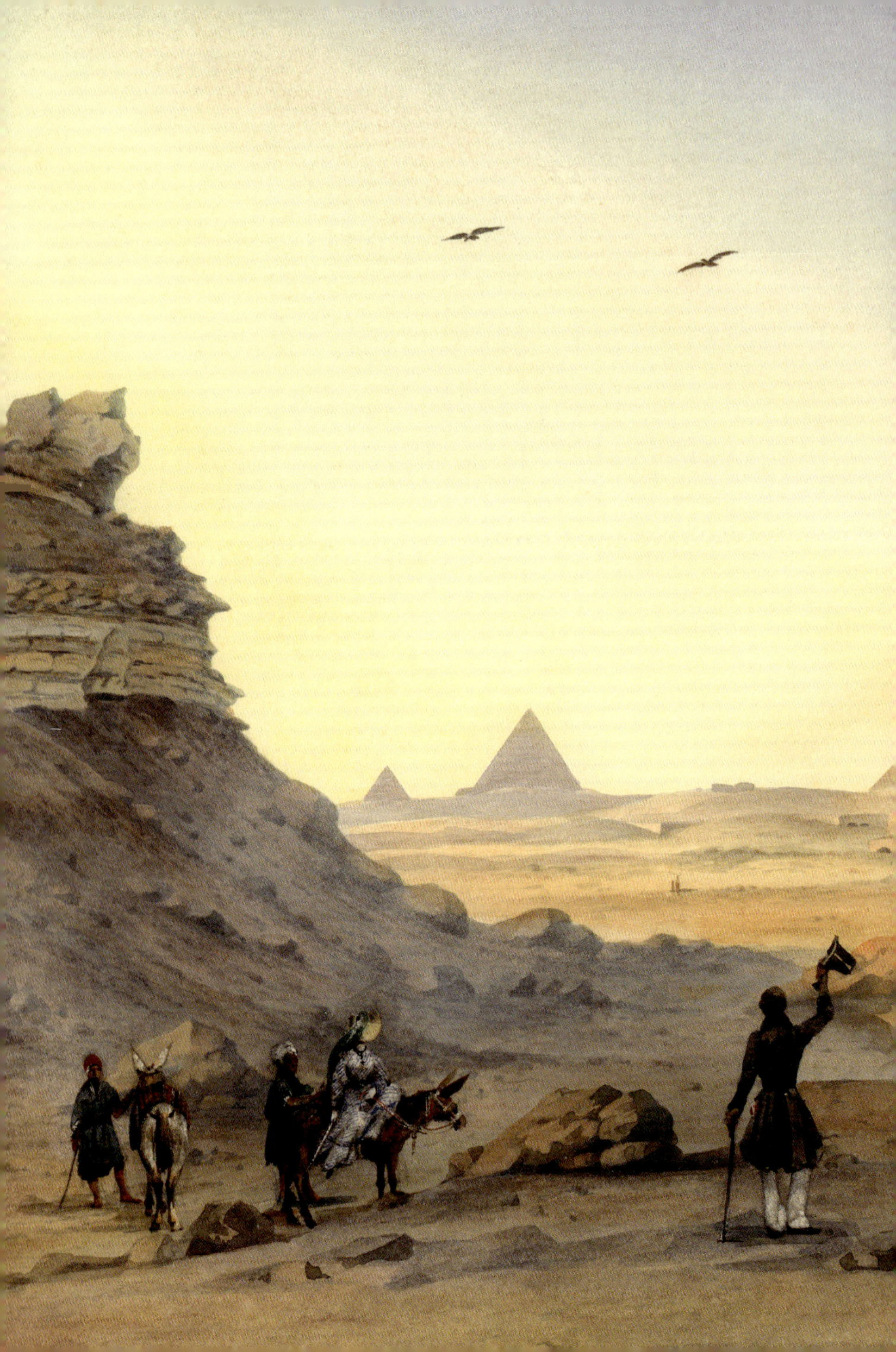

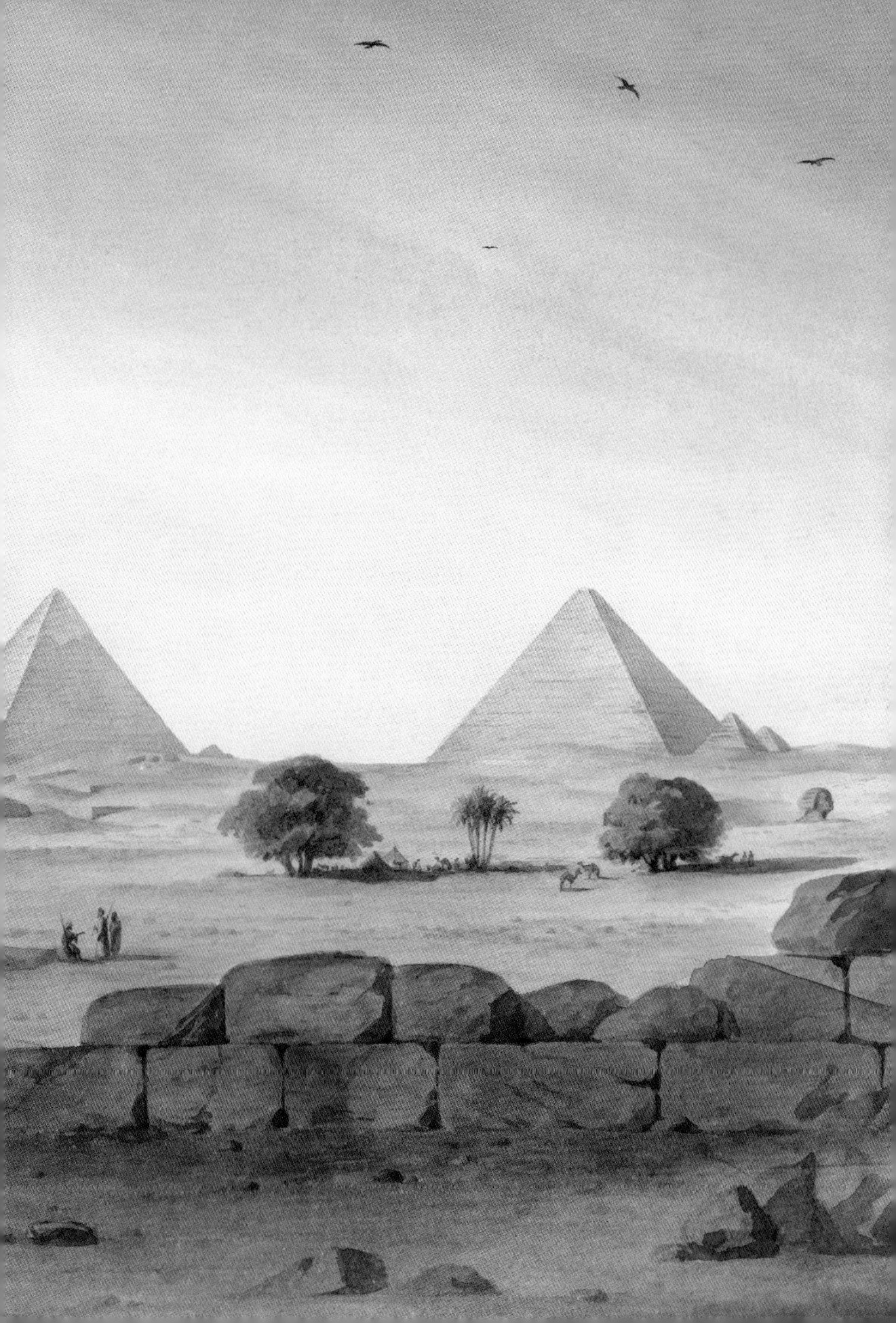

bribes to all and sundry, he smuggled the 27 large boxes containing the inscriptions on to a narrow, fast-moving local boat, called a *cange*, at night and made his way northward over six days. In Alexandria he received no real support from his government, so by dint of further bribery, braggadocio and bullying, he managed to load his precious cargo on board *Le Cerbère* on May 15, 1844, labelled as natural-history specimens for the Musée de Paris. Once in France he gave the blocks to the state. They were first kept in the Bibliothèque Nationale de France, with a plan for their conservation and display worked out by Prisse. Sadly, the installation took place in his absence and consequently many of the blocks were damaged. Later the King List was moved to the Louvre, where it is still on display. Thanks to Prisse this most important artefact can be studied in the Louvre as well as in libraries, owing to the very precise copy that he made.

The circumstances of Prisse's ignominious (and almost certainly illegal) departure from Egypt necessitated a longer stay in Europe than he had originally envisioned. However, there was a great deal of work to be done. Besides planning the installation of the Chamber of the Ancestors, he had to work on its preservation, and the completion of its copying and translation. In addition, he also presented the Bibliothèque Nationale with the Prisse Papyrus (pBN 183–194; ill. 16). This papyrus together with the Chamber of the Ancestors are the two most important artefacts that Prisse brought back from Egypt. The papyrus dates from the Middle Kingdom and is inscribed with a series of Wisdom Texts. This genre of ancient Egyptian literature consists of moral and practical advice for a virtuous, fulfilled and successful life. Prisse's papyrus, which he probably purchased in Thebes, contains part of the *Instructions Addressed to Kagemni*, as well as the only complete surviving copy of the *Instructions of Ptahhotep*. The papyrus was heralded as the oldest surviving piece of literature and is of crucial importance not only to the study of philology but also to the understanding of ancient Egyptian mores and beliefs. Prisse lovingly copied and published it in 1847 *(Fac-similé d'un papyrus égyptien)*, thereby making it available to scholars all over the world.

In recognition of these gifts and his research into ancient Egypt, France awarded Prisse the Légion d'honneur for his services. His acquisition of the Karnak List was celebrated in the press, particularly in the *Revue archéologique*, while scholars rushed to study the Prisse Papyrus.

While in France Prisse started to collate his notes, drawings and squeezes. The result was the publication of *Monuments égyptiens* (Paris, 1847), containing 50 plates, a foretaste of his more ambitious work on all of Egyptian art. In a way, this work was a tribute to Champollion, whom Prisse admired enormously. The book was supposed to supplement Champollion's *Monuments de l'Égypte et de la Nubie* by presenting 100 chromolithographs of drawings Prisse had made during his last six years in Egypt. The book did not appear quite as planned because of financial constraints, for which Prisse apologised to his readers in the book's introduction. Despite its truncation, it was a major work of scholarship. It included a great deal of hitherto unavailable material dating from the reign of Akhenaten, originating from Tuna el-Gebel and Tell el-Amarna (*Monuments*, see pp. 95–99), as well as Thebes. Indeed, Prisse is perhaps the first person to have made an extensive record of Akhenaten's building activities in Thebes. He recognised the distinctive artistic style of the period and identified a group of small sandstone blocks *(talatat)* that had come to light when Karnak's third pylon was dismantled to be burnt for lime as belonging to the reign of Akhenaten. He brought these to the attention of Wilkinson and Nestor l'Hôte (1804–1842), an artist who had participated in Champollion's expedition and was himself the author of a three-volume book of letters from Egypt, as well as to Jacques-Joseph Champollion-Figeac (1778–1867), the elder brother of Jean-François Champollion. Prisse's letter to the latter was published, but he never wrote a formal article connecting the different monuments that dated from the time of Akhenaten.

Despite its modest size, Prisse's *Monuments* met with considerable popular acclaim and was lauded by intellectuals and artists on both sides of the Channel. In fact, Théophile Gautier (1811–1872) claimed that his *Le Roman de la momie*, perhaps the earliest work of fiction based on ancient Egypt, was inspired by Prisse's publication. Gautier also lauded the work's artistic quality, and was a staunch supporter of Prisse.

By the late 1850s Prisse was restless to return to Egypt to collate, correct and complete his earlier work, to continue recording and studying the monuments and to gather more antiquities for France. This time he went not as a young adventurer with little to his name, but as an established authority on Egypt and the head of a small official mission to collect and copy Egyptian antiquities for France. The expedition was sponsored by Napoleon III, financed by the Ministry of Education, and lasted for three years, from 1858 to 1860. Two young men accompanied Prisse: Willem de Famars Testas (1834–1896), a Dutch artist and a distant relative, and Édouard Jarrot (1835–1873; ill. 15), a French photographer.

The Egypt of 1858 was a very different place from the Egypt of a decade before. Just prior to Prisse's arrival in Egypt, Saïd Pasha had established an antiquities service as well as a museum, headed by the Frenchman Auguste Mariette (1821–1881). Mariette, a relative of Nestor l'Hôte, strictly enforced pre-existing regulations concerning the treatment and removal of antiquities and added further regulations himself. This meant that Prisse was unable to remove the number and type of antiquities that he had originally wanted. Undaunted by this reverse, Prisse and his companions travelled through Egypt, Nubia and Arabia, collecting an increasing body of plans, sketches, squeezes, rubbings, notes and photographs (ill. 20). The use of photography at such a relatively early date in the development of this technology is significant.

In the case of the documentation of the architecture of Cairo, Prisse relied on the work of the daguerreotypist Joseph-Philibert Girault de Prangey (1804–1892), as well as, to a lesser extent, Jarrot, and was no doubt pleased to have his own photographer. Prisse was a hard taskmaster and both his young protégés suffered to the point that an exhausted Jarrot had to leave early, soon followed by Prisse and Famars Testas.

Prisse returned to France in 1860 with 300 folio drawings of paintings and reliefs from different monuments (ill. 18), each up to seven or eight metres (23 to 26 feet) long, 400 metres (1,300 feet) of squeezes and 150 photographs of architectural and ornamental details, as well as plans, sections and elevations, together with his enormous collection of sketches and notes. He also managed to bring back, and later donated to the Louvre, some antiquities, as well as the skulls of 29 mummies that he had identified by era, position and individual name. This haul, together with his earlier work, formed the basis of his *magnum opus* on ancient Egyptian art, which he compiled, together with its Islamic complement, over the following years using the facilities of the Faculté des Sciences de Lille.

Histoire de l'art égyptien, published in its entirety in 1879, consisted of two volumes containing 159 plates. This, however, represented only a portion of Prisse's work. A text volume based on his notes, and written by P. Marchandon de la Faye, was published in 1879, the year of Prisse's death. Had Prisse lived longer, perhaps more volumes would have been forthcoming; as it is, the lion's share of his scientific archive (drawings, photographs, squeezes, notes) is held at the Bibliothèque Nationale, with a portion of his personal papers stored in the archives of the Société archéologique et historique d'Avesnes-sur-Helpe.

Prisse's *Histoire de l'art égyptien* is an extraordinary work, even when compared to the products of the great state-sponsored expeditions. It is the largest single-handed series of illustrated records of Egyptian art, and truly a complete survey of Egyptian art when taken in conjunction with *L'Art arabe*. It covers architecture, drawing, sculpture (including bas-relief), painting and industrial art (minor arts), lavishly illustrated with examples. Interestingly, the section on architecture consists not only of images of buildings but ancient Egyptian depictions of buildings, particularly those found on the walls of the tombs at Amarna (*Histoire de l'art égyptien* [*Hist.*], see pp. 274–281). The particular situation whereby a single person executed all the final illustrations and oversaw the production of the publication gives the work a harmonious unity lacking in other compendia of the 19th century. Prisse's hand, although criticised by some as being too "pretty", does justice to the scenes carved and painted by the ancient Egyptians.

Indeed, most of his versions are far closer to the "truth" than those of other artists or his predecessors, contemporaries, and even successors – such as the copy of a sketch depicting foreigners in a Theban tomb of the 18th Dynasty (*Hist.*, see p. 333), which is exemplary, although his copy of a scene from Amarna (*Hist.*, see pp. 390–392) does warrant criticism. His work is a great leap from that of the artists of the *Description*, amongst others, who persisted in putting a Classical stamp on the images from ancient Egypt (ill. 19), or who painted images in an overly naïve way, despite the rather more sophisticated reality, a trait shared by other artists as well (ills. 21, 22). These variations in the quality of drawings are shared by the *Denkmaeler*, in part owing to the various talents of the different artists enlisted to produce the images, as well as their own views of ancient Egyptian art (ill. 23). Prisse's work is clean, but not overly prettified and more true to the images made by the ancient Egyptians.

The architectural drawings in the *Histoire* are superb and are a testament to Prisse's early training. Sections, plans, architectural details and surface decoration of the façade of each monument – such as the plan and section of the tomb of the High Priest Petamenophis (*Hist.*, see p. 211), or the Temple of Dendur (*Hist.*, see p. 213), now in the Metropolitan Museum of Art in New York – are perfectly documented and depicted. Indeed, it is unlikely that these renditions have been surpassed even today.

Prisse's study of ornamental patterns found in friezes and on ceilings (*Hist.*, see pp. 250–267) is extremely thorough and valuable as he shows variations through time and evokes the idea of

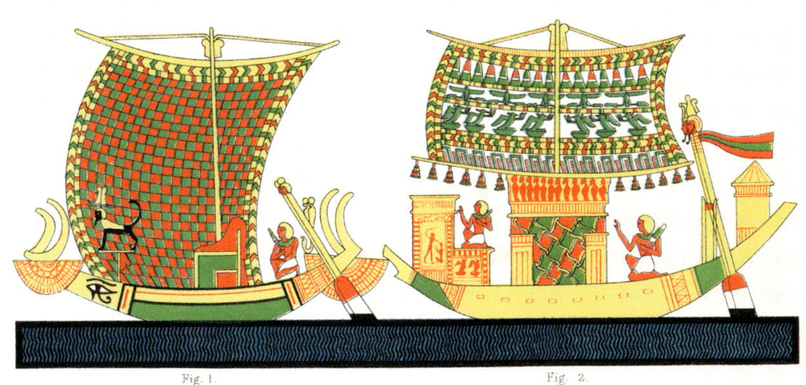

Ill. 5

Boats with coloured sails, from the tomb of Ramesses III at Thebes
Boote mit bunten Segeln, aus dem Grab Ramses' III. in Theben
Bateaux avec de petites voiles colorées, provenant du tombeau de Ramsès III à Thèbes
in: John Gardner Wilkinson, *Manners and Customs of the Ancient Egyptians*, vol. II, London, 1878, frontispiece
Göttingen, Niedersächsische Staats- und Universitätsbibliothek

ancient pattern-books. These images certainly influenced the European minor arts and design in Prisse's time, and may also have influenced the late 19th- and early 20th-century Arts and Crafts movement as well as Art Nouveau. Certainly, some of the work in Owen Jones's widely circulated *The Grammar of Ornament* (1856) echoes the Egyptian motifs documented by Prisse.

As with other publications of the period that are still in use today, Prisse's work provides us with a record of what once existed at certain sites. This is particularly important as many of them have been devastated by the hands of time, and more often, at the hands of the *sebbakhin*, who dug up and destroyed sites in their quest for fertiliser. The greed of collectors who, despite the attempted regulation of the removal of antiquities, continued to rip out relief blocks from their contexts, and even of scholars who have removed objects or "squeezed" to extinction reliefs from all over Egypt, have made Prisse's works invaluable to modern Egyptology. Prisse's keen eye and devotion to recording accurately all he saw has preserved many an object that would be unknown to us today. His watercolour of King Menkaure's sarcophagus is a rare record of this unique object and a case in point. The sarcophagus was taken from Menkaure's (2493–2475 BC; *Hist.*, see p. 205) pyramid at Giza and shipped off to England, only to sink in the Bay of Biscay during a storm. Prisse's work was so fine that many other scholars specially commissioned him to illustrate their books, or used his

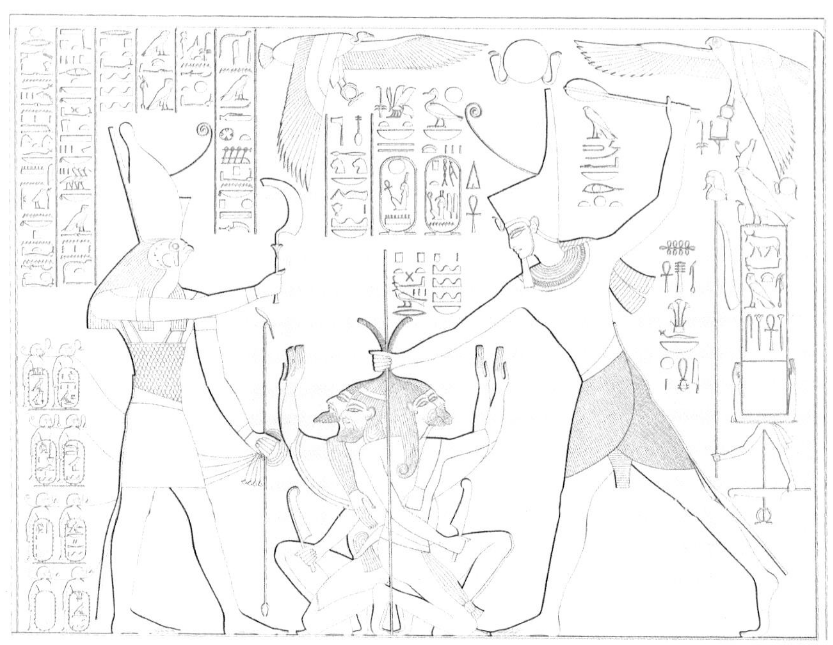

Ill. 6

Ramesses II smiting his enemies / Ramses II. erschlägt seine Feinde / Ramsès II tue ses ennemis

in: Karl Richard Lepsius, *Denkmaeler aus Aegypten und Aethiopien*, Berlin, 1849–1859, Abth. III, pl. 140a
Göttingen, Niedersächsische Staats- und Universitätsbibliothek

images as they were superior to any others available at the time. His coloured images impart a sense of what Egyptian wall paintings were like when freshly painted (*Hist.*, see p. 483). Prisse's artwork has continued to endure and be a source of illustrations. It graces many a book, both scholarly (such as those of the great Egyptologist Gaston Maspero and the renowned art historian Jean Capart) and popular (including the massive tome *Ancient Egypt or Mizraïm* by Samuel Augustus Binion), as well as appearing in more mundane settings, such as on postcards or T-shirts sold in Egypt today.

Prisse's understanding of Egyptian art was profound—he was one of the earliest scholars to have noticed and accurately recorded the Egyptian grid system (e.g. *Hist.*, see pp. 329, 331). This was the canon of proportions adhered to by the ancient Egyptians in their representations of scenes and portraits; in its most classical phase it constituted, for the main figure in a scene, 18 "fists" or squares from the sole of the foot to the hairline (*Hist.*, see p. 329). Other figures were produced as halves, quarters etc. of the main figure, depending on their relative significance. The grid system

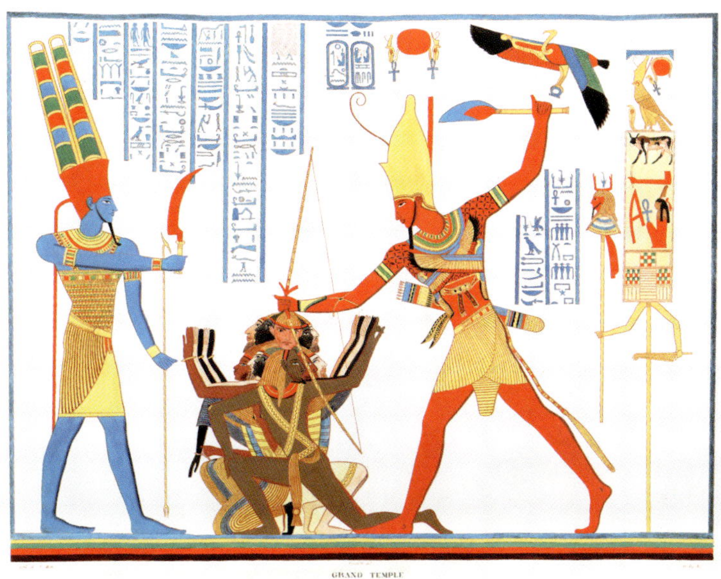

Ill. 7

Ramesses II smiting his enemies, temple of Abu Simbel / Ramses II. erschlägt seine Feinde, Tempel von Abu Simbel / Ramsès II tue ses ennemis, temple d'Abou Simbel

in: Jean-François Champollion, *Monuments de l'Égypte et de la Nubie*, vol. I, Paris, 1835, pl. XI

Göttingen, Niedersächsische Staats- und Universitätsbibliothek

underlies all of Egyptian art, and its identification and recording are amongst the most important of Prisse's scholarly contributions to this area of study. Such an understanding of the grid system may also have enabled Prisse to make more faithful copies of the originals than his contemporaries ever did. His use of colour is sensitive and, indeed, is relied upon today to get a sense of the ancient originals. Additionally, his use of photography enabled him to increase the accuracy of recording the monuments and these images are an invaluable source of information for long-destroyed scenes and buildings. As most of the monuments that he recorded are now gone, his work remains as often the sole testament to these buildings and the artistry of the ancient Egyptians.

Prisse's accurate and sensitive recording of Egyptian art throughout the 3,000 years of Egyptian history (and beyond) has provided us with a record and an unparalleled understanding of ancient Egyptian architecture, sculpture, painting and even industrial arts. In addition to his skill as an artist, this is the result of his understanding of the historical, social and religious setting that engendered it, rendering his encyclopaedic works invaluable to the study of ancient Egypt.

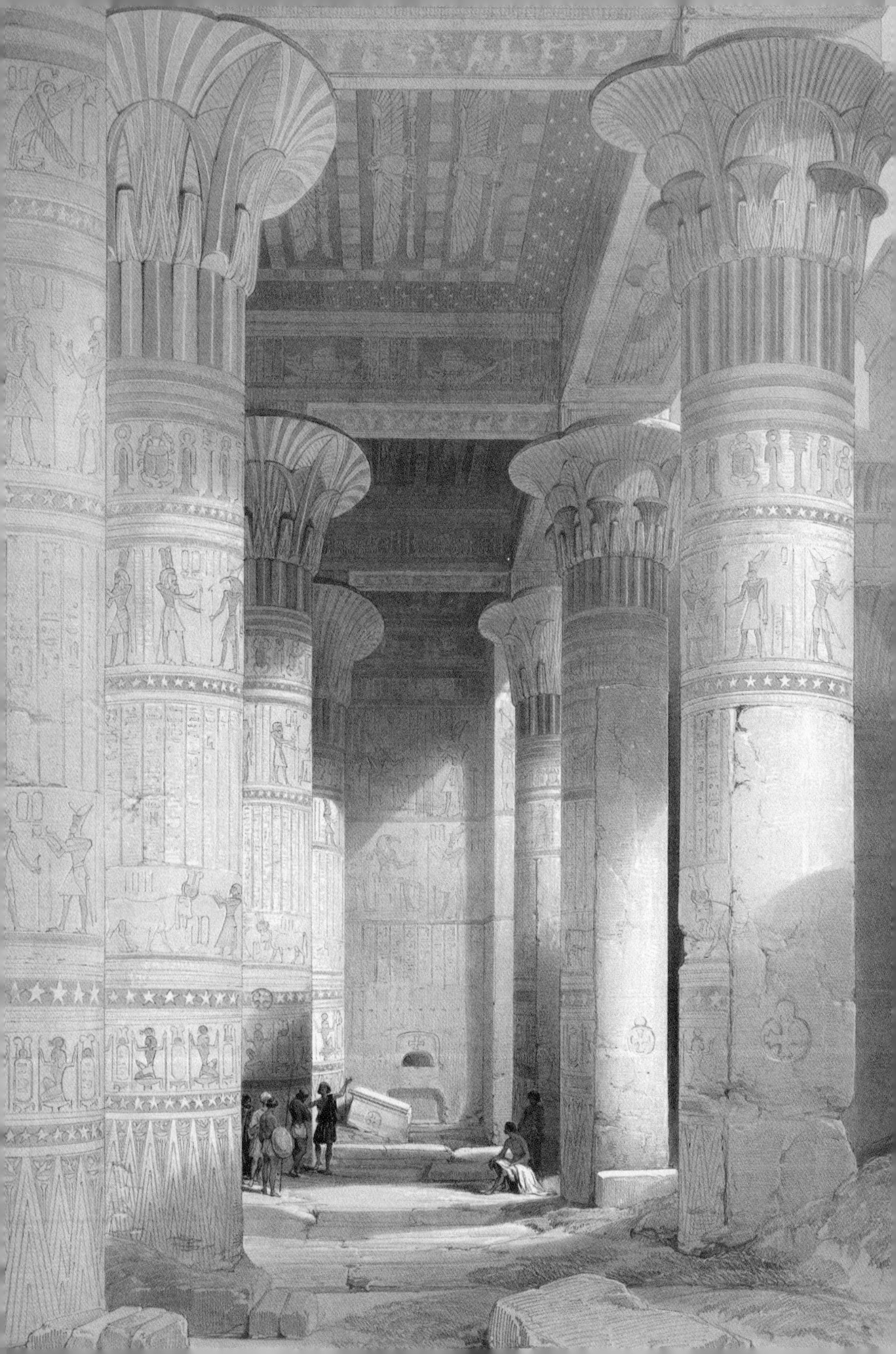

Émile Prisse d'Avennes und das Alte Ägypten

SALIMA IKRAM

Die Ägyptologie steht tief in der Schuld der zahlreichen Ägyptenreisenden des 19. Jahrhunderts. Angelockt von den dortigen Monumenten, dokumentierten sie alles, was sie sahen, und wurden so – lange bevor sich diese Wissenschaft etablierte – zu den ersten Ägyptologen. Einer dieser Reisenden war Achille Constant Théodore Émile Prisse d'Avennes (1807–1879), der nicht nur zahlreiche antike Stätten im gesamten Niltal besuchte und dokumentierte, sondern auch eine der ersten Studien zur ägyptischen Kunst vorlegte und damit die Grundlage für eingehende Forschungen auf diesem Feld schuf (Abb. 1, 9). Prisse zeichnet sich dadurch aus, dass sich sein Interesse nicht auf das Alte Ägypten beschränkte; vielmehr reichte seine Wertschätzung der ägyptischen Kunst und Architektur bis in die islamische Zeit. Seine beiden großen Werke *Histoire de l'art égyptien, d'après les monuments, depuis les temps les plus reculés jusqu'à la domination romaine* (Paris, 1878/79) und *L'Art arabe d'après les monuments du Kaire, depuis le VIIe siècle jusqu'à la fin du XVIIIe siècle* (Paris, 1869–1877) umfassen somit nahezu die gesamte ägyptische Kunstgeschichte. Wie bedauerlich, dass er der koptischen Kunst nicht ähnlich viel Zeit und Raum widmete, sonst wären zahlreiche weitere, mittlerweile für die Nachwelt verlorene Monumente dokumentiert.

Bis vor Kurzem war über Prisse kaum etwas bekannt – abgesehen von seinen Werken, die beredt für sich selbst sprechen, und einer Handvoll weiterer Publikationen, in denen sein Name auftaucht. Von besonderer Bedeutung ist eine Biografie (oder vielmehr Hagiografie), die sein Sohn Émile schrieb, um das Ansehen des Vaters zu heben und sein Andenken gegen die öffentlichen Schmähungen Maxime du Camps zu verteidigen, die sich in dessen *Souvenirs littéraires* (1888) finden. Unglückseligerweise wiederholte der Historiker Jean-Marie Carré sie in seinem enzyklo-

Ill. 8
David Roberts
View under the Grand Portico, Philae (detail), *c.* 1840
Grand Portikus des Tempels von Philae (Detail) / **Le grand portique du temple de Philæ** (détail)
Lithograph, 50.4 x 34.8 cm (19 7/8 x 13 3/4 in.), in: David Roberts, *The Holy Land. Syria, Idumea, Arabia, Egypt & Nubia*, vol. "Egypt & Nubia", lithographed by Louis Haghe, London, 1847
Weimar, Herzogin Anna Amalia Bibliothek

pädisch angelegten Werk *Voyageurs et écrivains français en Égypte* (1932), wenngleich er die Ausführungen du Camps großenteils widerlegte. Seit den 1980er-Jahren ist ein deutlich gestiegenes Interesse für die Geschichte der Ägyptologie zu beobachten; so verfasste Michel Dewachter einige Schriften über Prisse (und andere), die zu einem ausgewogeneren Urteil über diesen außergewöhnlichen Mann beitrugen. Zuletzt hat das weitreichende Werk von Prévost (u.a., 2011) und von Volait (2013) das Interesse an Prisse neu belebt, Missverständnisse über seine Arbeit korrigiert und sein Leben neu beleuchtet. Mit dem nun vorgelegten Reprint der beiden Hauptwerke über die pharaonische und die islamische Kunst steht Prisse verdientermaßen wieder im Licht der Öffentlichkeit.

Die frühen Jahre

Prisse wurde am 27. Januar 1807 in dem französischen Städtchen Avesnes-sur-Helpe (Département Nord) geboren. Die Familiensaga berichtet von einer britischen Herkunft – aus Aven in Wales; nach einigen frühen Varianten entschied sich die Familie 1690 für die Namensschreibweise „d'Avennes", offenbar um dem Ursprungsort und der Wahlheimat Tribut zu zollen. Nach seiner Ausbildung an der École d'Arts et Métiers in Châlons-sur-Marne (1822–1825) packte den 19-jährigen Prisse die Abenteuerlust, sodass er Frankreich verließ, um im griechischen Unabhängigkeitskrieg zu kämpfen. Nach kurzer Zeit reiste er weiter nach Indien und dann nach Palästina. Während seines kurzen Aufenthalts dort widmete er sich den heiligen Stätten, was ihm den Titel „Ritter vom Heiligen Grab" eintrug. Sein inniger Wunsch, den Orient und seine antiken Schätze zu erforschen, führte ihn 1826 nach Ägypten. Dort fand er zu seinem Glück eine Anstellung bei Muhammad Ali Pascha (reg. 1805–1848) und seinem Sohn Ibrahim, der zum Ende der väterlichen Herrschaft kurzfristig die Regentschaft innehatte. Prisse arbeitete in diversen Funktionen, etwa als Dozent in einigen militärischen Einrichtungen und für eine kurze Zeit sogar als Privatlehrer der Prinzen. Während dieser Zeit nahm er den Namen Idris Effendi an, gab vor, zum Islam zu konvertieren (obwohl es dabei wahrscheinlich eher um Politik als um den Glauben ging), lernte Arabisch und wurde zum Experten für Hieroglyphen – soweit eine Kennerschaft damals möglich war (Abb. 13). Prisse blieb rund zehn Jahre in Diensten des Paschas, bevor er zu seiner wahren Berufung fand: dem Erforschen und Dokumentieren der Monumente Ägyptens, eine Beschäftigung, die in seinen enzyklopädischen Werken ihren Gipfelpunkt erreichte.

Anfang des 19. Jahrhundert stand Ägypten bei den Europäern im Brennpunkt archäologischen, politischen und wirtschaftlichen Interesses. Dazu hatte vor allem Napoleon Bonapartes Expedition nach Ägypten (1798–1801) beigetragen, die politisch zwar im Desaster, intellektuell und künstlerisch jedoch im Triumph endete. Ergebnis war das vielbändige Werk *Description de l'Égypte*, dessen Veröffentlichung sich über fast zwei Jahrzehnte hinzog (1809/10–1828; Abb. 2, 3, 19). Die Erstausgabe bestand aus neun Quartbänden und elf Bildfolianten mit insgesamt 837 Kupferstichen und mehr als 3000 Zeichnungen. Jene Gelehrten, die Napoleon auf seinem Feldzug begleiteten, erforschten das Land in allen Aspekten, so auch dessen Altertümer, Naturgeschichte,

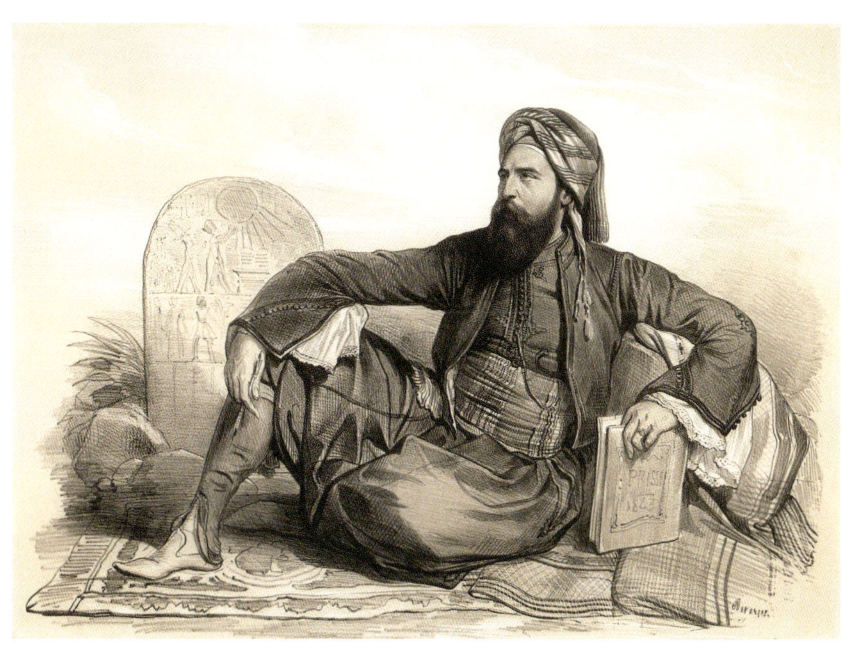

Ill. 9
Achille Devéria
Prisse d'Avennes in Oriental Costume, 1844 / **Prisse d'Avennes in orientalischer Tracht** / **Prisse d'Avennes en costume oriental**
Lithograph, 29.2 x 39.7 cm (11 1/2 x 15 5/8 in.). Annecy, Musée-Château d'Annecy

moderne Geschichte und Topografie. Das Werk beförderte das Interesse der Europäer und prägte den Fortgang der europäischen (und ägyptischen) Forschung. Außerdem prägte es architektonische und künstlerische Stile und Moden – und schuf eine scheinbar unstillbare Nachfrage nach altägyptischen Objekten. Durch seinen umfassenden Ansatz beschleunigte es die Entwicklung der Ägyptologie vom bloßen Steckenpferd zur vollwertigen Forschungsdisziplin. Vivant Denon (1747–1825), einer der bedeutendsten und aktivsten der an der Mission beteiligten Künstler und später Direktor des Louvre, veröffentlichte seine Erlebnisse als Mitglied des Gelehrtenteams in seinem Buch *Voyage dans la Basse et la Haute Égypte* (1802), das viel Aufsehen erregte und in ganz Europa sogleich zum Bestseller wurde.

Prisse' Abenteuerlust und Begeisterung für den Orient mag durchaus durch die *Description* und andere populäre Bücher angestachelt worden sein, die einzelne Gelehrte aus Napoleons Geleitzug verfassten. Auch Jean-François Champollions (1790–1832) Vorträge und Schriften über den Stein von Rosetta, ein bedeutendes, während der französischen Ägypten-Expedition geborgenes Artefakt, und über die ägyptische Grammatik trugen maßgeblich dazu bei, Prisse' Interesse an Ägypten zu wecken. Frühe illustrierte Reisebeschreibungen wie Frédéric Nordens *Voyage d'Égypte et de Nubie* (1755), Bischof Pocockes *Description of the East and some other Countries* (1743–1745), dessen französische Übersetzung 1772/73 erschien, Comte Constantin-François Volneys *Voyage en Syrie et en Égypte, pendant les années 1783, 1784, et 1785* (1787) und Claude Étienne Savarys *Lettres sur l'Égypte* (1786) haben womöglich die Fantasie des jungen Zeichners und Ingenieurs ebenfalls beflügelt und ihn ermutigt, sich im Orient niederzulassen. Im Fahrwasser des napoleonischen Feldzugs und aufgrund von Muhammad Ali Paschas Bedarf an Experten strömten zahlreiche westliche Reisende, Wissenschaftler und Abenteurer nach Ägypten. Besonders willkommen waren dem Pascha offenbar Franzosen, zumal der talentierte Architekt Pascal Coste (1787–1879) bereits in seinen Diensten stand. Coste ist für seine Studien zur islamischen Architektur, vor allem in Kairo, bekannt; mit Prisse verband ihn aber auch die Begeisterung für die pharaonische Vergangenheit, von der seine zahlreichen Notizbücher und Skizzen zeugen. Es ist durchaus möglich, dass die beiden einander in Kairo oder Alexandria begegnet sind.

Prisse' Werk im Kontext

Einige der Europäer, die nach Ägypten reisten, ließen sich von romantischen Vorstellungen vom Orient und seinen antiken Schätzen anlocken; andere indes kamen in der eher prosaischen Absicht, Profit zu machen. Ungeachtet dessen, was sie anfangs dorthin führte, ließen sich zahlreiche Reisende von den Wundern des Alten Ägypten betören. Ihre Aufmerksamkeit wandte sich der Erkundung altägyptischer Stätten zu, und so begannen sie – aus finanziellem wie akademischem Interesse – Altertümer aufzuspüren, zusammenzutragen und zu dokumentieren.

Bernardino Drovetti (1776–1852), der französische Prokonsul in Ägypten, und sein Erzrivale, der britische Generalkonsul Henry Salt (1780–1827), stehen für jene zahlreichen Männer, die sich neben ihren anderweitigen Verpflichtungen darauf konzentrierten, ägyptische Altertümer für ihre jeweiligen Regierungen zu erwerben. Die Geschichten über ihre Fehden und Winkelzüge beim Kampf um Kolossalstatuen, Papyri und ganze Grabmäler und Tempel sind spannend zu lesen – ein weiterer Beleg für die kein Ende findenden Rivalitäten zwischen den beiden Nationen.

Für Salt arbeitete auch ein gewisser Giovanni Battista Belzoni (1778–1823), ein Riese von einem Mann, der in Großbritannien als Kraftprotz im Zirkus aufgetreten war. Ursprünglich als Ingenieur nach Ägypten gekommen, war er durch eine Reihe von Zufällen zum Sammler von Altertümern geworden. Die Bestände des British Museum verdanken sich zu einem großen Teil den vereinten Bemühungen von Belzoni und Salt. Neben seiner Arbeit für Salt erkundete Belzoni Ägypten auf eigene Faust und betrieb auf eigene Rechnung Handel mit Altertümern. Zu seinen archäologischen Triumphen zählt die Erkundung von Abu Simbel und Gizeh – der sich später auch Prisse widmete (Abb. 4). Belzoni betrat 1818 als erster Mensch der Moderne die Chephren-Pyramide von Gizeh, was der weiteren ägyptologischen Erforschung den Weg bereitete. Wie Prisse fertigte auch Belzoni Kopien, Abgüsse und Frottagen von einzelnen Szenen der Grabmäler und Tempel, hauptsächlich in Theben. Solche Frottagen, bei denen eine Art Löschpapier angefeuchtet und kraftvoll berieben wird, damit es die Form des darunter liegenden Reliefs annimmt, waren ein beliebtes Mittel, um ein Reliefdekor präzise zu dokumentieren, ließen dieses jedoch nicht unbeschädigt; auch Prisse nutzte dieses Mittel.

Drovettis Mitarbeiter und Weggefährten waren nicht so auffällige Erscheinungen wie Belzoni, doch nicht minder erfolgreich im Erwerb von Objekten. Das bezeugen ihre Sammlungen, die sich heute an verschiedenen Orten in Frankreich sowie in Turin und Berlin befinden. Zwei seiner bemerkenswertesten Gefährten, Jean-Jacques Rifaud (1786–1852) und Frédéric Cailliaud (1787–1869), erkundeten Ägypten und Nubien und leisteten mit ihren zahlreichen Veröffentlichungen über diese Regionen einen bleibenden Beitrag zur Ägyptologie. Wie seine anderen mehrbändigen Werke ist auch Rifauds *Voyage en Égypte, en Nubie et lieux circonvoisins, depuis 1805 jusqu'en 1827* (1830–1844) mit Farblithografien illustriert. Allerdings kann man keine dieser Publikationen als kunstgeschichtliche Studie bezeichnen, wie sie Prisse' Werk darstellt.

Einige Veröffentlichungen des jungen Cailliaud zeigen Gemeinsamkeiten mit Prisse' *Oriental Album: Characters, Costumes and Modes of Life, in the Valley of the Nile* (London 1848, Texte von James Augustus St. John). In seinen 1831–1837 erschienenen *Recherches sur les arts et métiers, les usages de la vie civile et domestique des anciens peuples de l'Égypte, de la Nubie et de l'Éthiopie* dokumentierte Cailliaud die Sitten und Gebräuche der Ägypter seiner Zeit und der früheren Bewohner des Niltals. Die Beschäftigung mit dem Brauchtum der alten und der modernen Ägypter war seinerzeit sehr beliebt. Das englische Autorenteam Sir John Gardner Wilkinson (1797–1875) und Edward William Lane (1801–1876) bot eine noch umfassendere Darstellung des Alltagslebens der alten und zeitgenössischen Ägypter. Wilkinson war 1821 in Ägypten eingetroffen, ließ sich dort für rund zwölf Jahre nieder und kehrte bis 1856 regelmäßig dorthin zurück. Wie Prisse war auch er von Hieroglyphen fasziniert, nahm einen arabischen Namen an, erlernte die Sprache und kleidete sich wie ein Araber. Im Gegensatz zu Prisse nahm er sogar eine Ägypterin zur Frau, die er allerdings später verließ. Bei seinen Reisen durch Ägypten sammelte Wilkinson Informationen und kopierte Texte und Szenen aus Gräbern und Tempeln, die zur Entschlüsselung und Erforschung der Sprache der Pharaonen beitrugen. Er entdeckte, erkundete und nummerierte zahlreiche thebanische Gräber, barg eine gewaltige Zahl von Altertümern und veröffentlichte schließlich sein Hauptwerk, das dreibändige *Manners and Customs of the Ancient Egyptians* (1837) – eine Darstellung des Alltagslebens der alten Ägypter, basierend auf der Deutung von Grabreliefs (Abb. 5). In späteren Jahren seines Ägypten-Aufenthalts korrespondierte Prisse regelmäßig mit Wilkinson, ein Gedankenaustausch, bei dem er auch Informationen über eigene Entdeckungen weitergab. Wenngleich nicht sicher ist, ob sich die beiden Gelehrten jemals begegnet sind, gelang es ihnen doch, über viele Jahre eine enge Arbeitsbeziehung aufrechtzuerhalten.

Vermutlich stand Prisse auch mit dem Orientalisten Edward William Lane in Kontakt. Lane, ein brillanter Arabist, sprach wie einige seiner Zeitgenossen fließend Arabisch. Er kleidete sich in die ortsübliche Tracht, ehelichte eine Ägypterin (die ihn später nach England begleitete), erkundete Ägypten und beschrieb ausführlich die lokalen Gebräuche jener Zeit. So entstand *Manners and Customs of the Modern Egyptians* (1836), Lanes Gegenstück zum Werk seines Kollegen und Freundes Wilkinson.

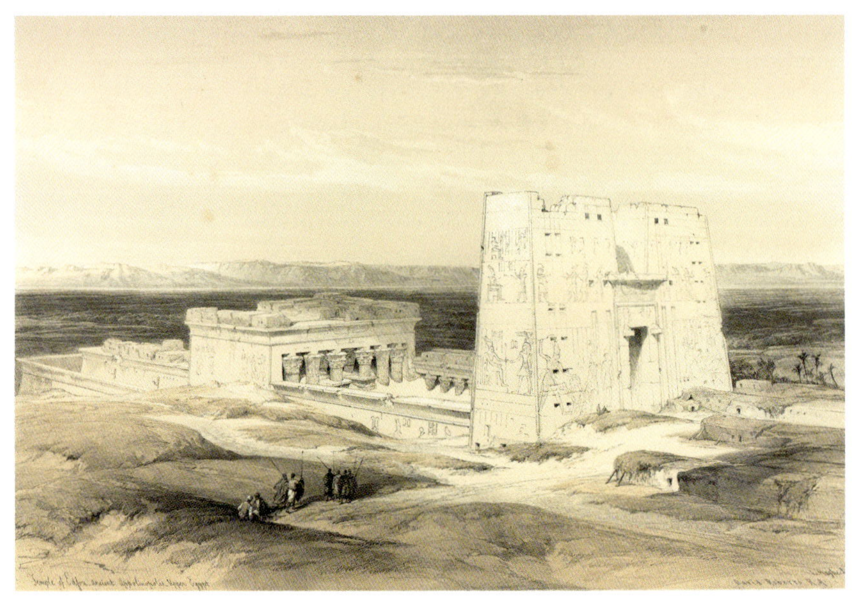

Ill. 10
David Roberts
The Temple at Edfou, Upper Egypt, *c.* 1840 / **Der Tempel von Edfu, Oberägypten** / **Le Temple d'Edfou, Haute-Égypte**
Lithograph, 33.7 x 50.2 cm (13 1/4 x 19 3/4 in.), in: David Roberts, *The Holy Land. Syria, Idumea, Arabia, Egypt & Nubia*, vol. "Egypt & Nubia", lithographed by Louis Haghe, London, 1847
Weimar, Herzogin Anna Amalia Bibliothek

Zu der Zeit, als Prisse in Ägypten tätig war, gruben nicht nur Einzelpersonen nach verborgenen Altertümern, vielmehr entsandten ganze Nationen große wissenschaftliche Expeditionen dorthin, um altägyptische Objekte zu dokumentieren und zu sammeln. Diese Aktivitäten waren natürlich vor allem vom Wettstreit der europäischen Nationen um den Besitz der größten und besten Ägyptensammlung getragen, die Wohlstand, Gelehrsamkeit, Macht und Einfluss augenfällig dokumentieren sollte. Doch die an diesen Expeditionen teilnehmenden Menschen arbeiteten nicht allein für ihren eigenen Ruhm oder den ihres Vaterlandes, sondern sie hegten auch den aufrichtigen Wunsch, die komplexe Kultur des Alten Ägypten zu enträtseln.

Eine der ersten dieser Expeditionen wurde von Champollion geleitet, der vor allem für seine Entzifferung der Hieroglyphen bekannt ist. Unter der Schirmherrschaft des französischen Königs startete Champollion 1828 mit seinem Schüler Ippolito Rosellini (1800–1843) eine französisch-toskanische Gemeinschaftsmission, um ägyptische Altertümer zu sammeln, zu erforschen und zu dokumentieren. Ein Team von Künstlern, Architekten, Logistikern und Ärzten begleitete sie, als sie Ägypten bis nach Nubien hinunter abreisten, Texte kopierten, Altertümer erwarben und bisweilen ihre Namen in diverse Monumente ritzten. Da hier erstmals ein Hieroglyphenkundiger eine Sammlung ägyptischer Altertümer zusammentrug und sich systematisch an die Arbeit des Übersetzens machte, führte die Expedition zu einem immensen Wissensgewinn. Champollion und Rosellini brachten nicht nur eine große Sammlung mit nach Hause, sie veröffentlichten auch in mehreren Bänden die Zeichnungen, die sie von Texten, Monumenten und Artefakten angefertigt hatten. Ihre Arbeiten, die für die Erforschung des Alten Ägypten von unschätzbarem Wert sind, inspirierten auch Prisse, einen großen Bewunderer Champollions (Abb. 7); dazu gehören *Monuments de l'Égypte et de la Nubie (1835), Lettres écrites d'Égypte et de Nubie en 1828 et 1829* (1833) und *I monumenti dell'Egitto e della Nubia, disegnati dalla spedizione scientifico-letteraria Toscana in Egitto* (1832–1844).

Die andere große wissenschaftliche Expedition des 19. Jahrhunderts war eine preußische Unternehmung unter der Leitung von Karl Richard Lepsius (1810–1884). Der preußische König Friedrich Wilhelm III. hatte 1827 für seine königlichen Kunstsammlungen eine große Sammlung ägyptischer Objekte erworben. Sie gab ihm eine Kostprobe ägyptischer Altertümer und der damit verbundenen Forschungen und legte den Grundstock für das bald darauf gegründete Ägyptische Museum in Berlin. Bald nach seiner Thronbesteigung finanzierte Friedrich Wilhelm IV. mit dem Segen seiner wissenschaftlichen Berater Lepsius' Expedition, damit diese in den Jahren 1842 bis 1845 Monumente besuchte und die Altertümer Ägyptens sammelte und dokumentierte. Hierbei handelte es sich vermutlich um die bestausgestattete Expedition, die jemals nach Ägypten entsandt wurde – vielleicht mit Ausnahme der napoleonischen; allerdings war Lepsius' Unternehmung mit Sicherheit weitaus besser geplant und verfügte über größere finanzielle Mittel. Mit von der Partie waren zahllose versierte Zeichner, Ingenieure und Gelehrte, die allesamt auf die eine oder andere Weise mit Ägypten vertraut waren. Lepsius und sein Team brachten 15 000 Objekte nach Berlin; viele hatte er selbst ausgegraben (wenngleich ihn Prisse beim Erwerb der Königsliste von Karnak ausstach; siehe unten). Sämtliche von Lepsius und seinem Team in Ägypten geschaffenen Zeichnungen, Karten und Grundrisse erschienen in dem gewaltigen zwölfbändigen Werk *Denkmaeler aus Aegypten und Aethiopien* (1849–1859; Abb. 6). Die fünf Textbände wurden zwischen 1897 und 1913, lange nach Lepsius' Tod, in Paris veröffentlicht. Womöglich führten Lepsius' *Denkmaeler* und seine anderen Publikationen 1863 in Berlin zur Gründung der *Zeitschrift für ägyptische Sprache und Altertumskunde*, des ersten Periodikums, das sich ausschließlich der Ägyptologie widmete. Zusammen mit der französischen *Description* bilden die *Denkmaeler* bis heute eine Grundlage der ägyptologischen Forschung.

Neben den Wissenschaftlern, die die Altertümer dokumentierten, reisten auch viele talentierte Künstler durch Ägypten; sie schufen ein romantisierendes Bild des Landes in pharaonischer und islamischer Zeit, ein ansprechendes Gegenstück zu den eher technischen, exakten Darstellungen der Gelehrten. Der bedeutendste unter ihnen ist der Schotte David Roberts (1796–1864), dessen Gemälde und Lithografien sich bis heute größter Beliebtheit erfreuen (Abb. 8, 10). Unter den zahlreichen Malern ägyptischer Szenen verdienen außerdem John Frederick Lewis (1805–1876), Jean-Léon Gérôme (1824–1904) und William Holman Hunt (1827–1910) Beachtung.

Das Werk Prisse d'Avennes'

Während der Zeit, die Prisse in Ägypten zubrachte, beherrschten also Paschas, Politiker, Raubgräber, Gelehrte, Intellektuelle, Künstler und Abenteurer die Szene. Nachdem er 1836 aufgrund einer Meinungsverschiedenheit mit dem kommandierenden General der Infanterieschule, an der er damals beschäftigt war, die offizielle Verbindung zur Königsfamilie beendet hatte, machte er sich auf, um bis 1839 Ägypten und den Nahen Osten zu erkunden. In Kairo schloss er Freundschaft mit Dr. Henry Abbott (1807–1859), mit dem er 1842 die kurzlebige Association littéraire d'Égypte gründete – einen Zirkel, der über ägyptische Kunst und Geschichte diskutierte, Vorträge finanzierte und eine Studienbibliothek einrichtete. Über diese Institution kamen Abbott und Prisse in Kontakt mit vielen jener Künstler und Gelehrten, die damals in Ägypten unterwegs waren. Prisse hatte ein Faible dafür, Organisationen ins Leben zu rufen und gelehrten Gesellschaften anzugehören. Später in Frankreich gründete er den *Miroir de l'Orient* und die *Revue orientale et algérienne*, zwei unregelmäßig erscheinende Zeitschriften, die von seiner Begeisterung für das orientalische Leben seiner Zeit zeugen.

Auf seinen Reisen zeichnete Prisse nicht nur unaufhörlich, er sammelte auch Altertümer, sei es durch Ausgrabungen oder Ankauf. Hierin unterschied er sich kaum von unzähligen seiner Zeitgenossen, obwohl er geografisch weiter ausgriff als viele andere und auch im Nildelta und einigen abseits gelegenen Stätten im Niltal, wie Schenhur, aktiv war. Außerdem waren seine Aufzeichnungen häufig präziser als die seiner Zeitgenossen, und er kannte sich für die damalige Zeit überraschend gut mit Hieroglyphen aus, schließlich hatten die wissenschaftlichen Arbeiten Champollions sein Interesse für das Alte Ägypten beflügelt. Aus seiner Korrespondenz ist ersichtlich, dass er mit Champollion, Wilkinson, Mariette und weiteren Gelehrten in Kontakt stand. Hätte er sie nicht identifiziert und dokumentiert, wir wüssten nichts über zahlreiche Objekte, Bauwerke, Szenen und Inschriften, und entsprechend ärmer wäre unsere Kenntnis der ägyptischen Geschichte; zu nennen sind etwa das Amarna-Material in Theben und die seltene claudianische Inschrift auf Lateinisch, die er in neuer Verwendung in einer Moschee in Akfahs, südlich von Beni Suef, aufspürte.

Im Jahr 1839 übersiedelte Prisse nach Luxor, jener Schatzkammer altägyptischer Monumente. Hier freundete er sich mit dem walisischen Botaniker George Lloyd (1815–1843) an und richtete sich einen Arbeitsstützpunkt ein. Prisse verbrachte fast sechs Jahre in Luxor, er erwarb Altertümer, um Frankreichs Ruhm zu mehren (wie die Stele von Bechten, heute im Louvre), zeichnete Tempel und ihre Grundrisse, kopierte Szenen aus Gräbern und Tempeln, fertigte Frottagen und befasste sich intensiv mit der ägyptischen Kunst und der „Grammatik des Ornaments" im Alten Ägypten (Abb. 17). Prisse wäre womöglich dauerhaft in Theben geblieben, hätten nicht zwei Ereignisse ihn daran gehindert: zum einen der tragische Tod seines Freundes George Lloyd bei einem Schießunfall und zum anderen seine eigene, höchst zweifelhafte Aneignung eines Teils der Königsliste von Karnak, auch bekannt als *Chambre des Ancêtres* oder Kammer der Ahnen (Abb. 11, 12).

Für die Erforschung der altägyptischen Geschichte ist die Königsliste von Karnak ein Schlüsseldokument. Königslisten führen Herrschernamen auf und sind somit von Nutzen, um für einen großen Teil der ägyptischen Geschichte eine Chronologie aufzustellen. Oft aber werden in diesen

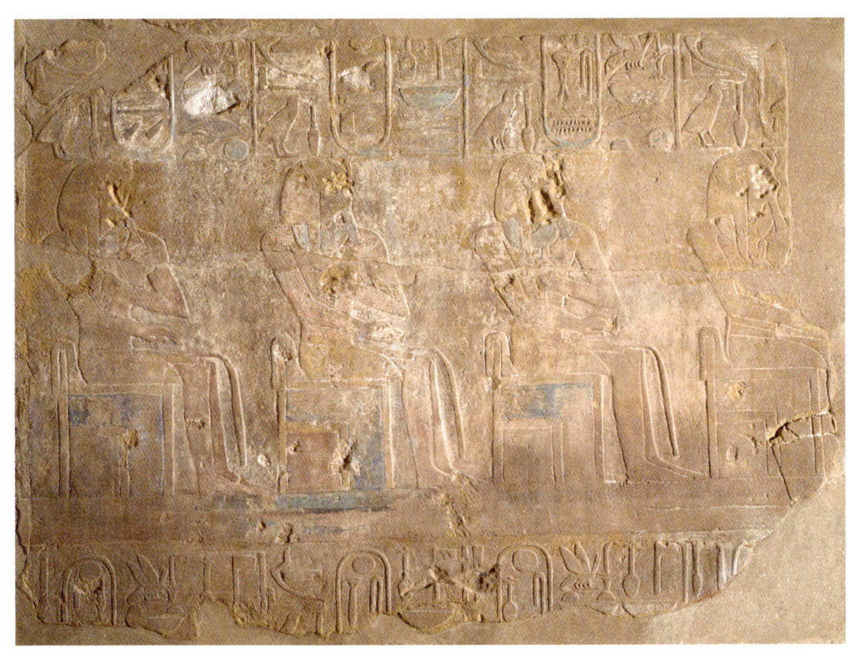

Ill. 11
The Karnak King List (Chamber of the Ancestors, detail), 1479–1425 BC
Die Königsliste von Karnak (Kammer der Ahnen, Detail)
La liste des rois de Karnak (La Chambre des Ancêtres, détail)
Sandstone, right wall. Paris, Musée du Louvre, inv. E 13481 bis

Listen bestimmte Herrscher oder sogar ganze Dynastien ausgelassen, sodass sich eine vollständige Aufzählung nur durch die Kombination mehrerer Listen gewinnen lässt. Die Karnak-Liste ist insofern von besonderem Wert, als sie die Namen der Herrscher aus der unruhigen Ersten (2181–2040 v. Chr.) und Zweiten (1782–1570 v. Chr.) Zwischenzeit enthält, die andernorts nicht belegt sind. Die Steinliste wurde auf Geheiß von König Thutmosis III. (1504–1450 v. Chr.) geschaffen und in der südwestlichen Ecke des Festtempels Ach-menu in der Tempelanlage von Karnak (Abb. 14) errichtet. 61 Könige waren in Stein verewigt, beginnend mit einem Neferkare, obwohl der erste vollständig erhaltene Name der von Snofru aus der Vierten Dynastie ist. Prisse wusste um die Bedeutung dieses Monuments für die Ägyptologie. Seinen eigenen Aufzeichnungen und Briefen zufolge fasste er den Entschluss, die Liste abzutragen, weil er fürchtete, dieser Teil des Tempels könnte bald abgerissen und zur Kalkgewinnung verbrannt werden, wie viele andere Monumente (etwa einige Tempel von Esna, Elephantine, el-Kab und sogar Theben). Da es solche Probleme häufiger gab, hatte George Glidden, der ehemalige US-Konsul in Kairo, sich 1841 mit einem Appell – vielleicht einem der ersten überhaupt – an die Gelehrtenwelt gewandt, die gefährdeten

Altertümer zu kopieren und in manchen Fällen ganz abzutragen, um so der Zerstörung Einhalt zu gebieten. Glidden lobte Prisse für seine Bemühungen, noch vorhandene pharaonische Monumente zu kopieren und damit für die Nachwelt zu erhalten, und für das Tempo, mit dem er möglichst viele gefährdete Monumente zu retten oder zumindest zu dokumentieren versuchte.

Manchen Forschern zufolge wusste Prisse, dass Lepsius auf dem Weg nach Theben war, und wollte in seinem Nationalstolz dafür sorgen, dass die Franzosen und nicht die Preußen in den Besitz dieses begehrten Objekts gelangten. Womöglich ließ er sich in seinem Handeln von beiden Gründen – und vom brieflichen Drängen Wilkinsons, das Monument zu kopieren und/oder irgendwie zu schützen – leiten: In 18 Nächten trugen Prisse und seine Arbeiter im Schutz der Dunkelheit die Wand mit der Königsliste ab und verpackten die Reliefs in Kisten, die sie nahebei in seinem großen Zelt lagerten. Der Gouverneur von Luxor entsandte Soldaten, um die Kisten beschlagnahmen zu lassen, doch Prisse berief sich auf seine französische Staatsbürgerschaft und den Schutz seiner Regierung. Einstweilen in Sicherheit, verteilte er saftige Bestechungsgelder an alle und jeden und schmuggelte die 27 großen Kisten mit den Inschriften des Nachts auf ein schmales, schnelles Boot, eine sog. *cange*, und fuhr über sechs Tage lang gen Norden. In Alexandria erfuhr er durch seine Regierung keine rechte Unterstützung, und so gelang es ihm nur durch weitere Schmiergelder, Aufschneiderei und Einschüchterung, seine kostbare Fracht am 15. Mai 1844 an Bord der *Cerbère* zu bringen, gekennzeichnet als naturgeschichtliche Objekte für das Musée de Paris. In Frankreich angelangt, übereignete er die Steinblöcke dem französischen Staat. Aufbewahrt wurden sie zunächst in der Nationalbibliothek, doch Prisse hatte bereits einen Plan für ihre Aufbewahrung und Präsentation entworfen. Bedauerlicherweise war er beim Aufbau nicht zugegen, sodass viele Blöcke beschädigt wurden. Später wurde die Königsliste in den Louvre transferiert, wo sie auch heute noch ausgestellt ist. Dank Prisse kann man dieses überaus bedeutsame Artefakt dort studieren, und da er eine höchst exakte Kopie davon gefertigt hat, ist dies auch in Bibliotheken möglich.

Die Begleitumstände von Prisse' unrühmlicher (und höchstwahrscheinlich auch illegaler) Abreise aus Ägypten erforderten einen längeren Aufenthalt in Europa als ursprünglich vorgesehen. Doch es gab viel zu tun. Neben den Vorbereitungen für den Aufbau der Ahnenkammer galt es, diese zu konservieren und die Kopie und ihre Übersetzung abzuschließen. Prisse schenkte der Nationalbibliothek neben der Königsliste auch den Papyrus Prisse (pBN 183–194; Abb. 16) und damit die beiden bedeutendsten Artefakte, die er aus Ägypten herausgeschafft hatte. Der aus dem Mittleren Reich datierende Papyrus enthält eine Reihe von Weisheitstexten. Dieses Genre der altägyptischen Literatur enthält moralische und praktische Ratschläge für ein tugendhaftes, erfülltes und erfolgreiches Leben. Prisse' Papyrus, den er vermutlich in Theben erworben hatte, enthält einen Teil der *Lehre für Kagemni* sowie das einzige vollständig erhaltene Exemplar der *Lehre des Ptahhotep*. Der als das älteste erhaltene literarische Zeugnis präsentierte Papyrus ist nicht nur philologisch, sondern auch für das Verständnis der altägyptischen Sitten und Glaubensvorstellungen von entscheidender Bedeutung.

Durch eine von Prisse mit Hingabe gefertigte, 1847 veröffentlichte Kopie *(Fac-similé d'un papyrus égyptien)* wurde er der akademischen Welt zugänglich gemacht. Der französische Staat dankte

Prisse für diese Geschenke und seine Forschungen über das Alte Ägypten mit der Aufnahme in die Ehrenlegion. Während die Presse, vor allem die *Revue archéologique*, die Beschaffung der Karnak-Liste feierte, eilten die Gelehrten herbei, um den Papyrus Prisse zu studieren.

In Frankreich begann Prisse mit dem Ordnen seiner Notizen, Zeichnungen und Frottagen. Dies führte zur Veröffentlichung des Buchs *Monuments égyptiens* (Paris 1847), das 50 Tafeln enthielt und einen Vorgeschmack auf sein ambitionierteres Werk über die gesamte ägyptische Kunst gab. In gewisser Weise war *Monuments égyptiens* eine Ehrenbezeugung gegenüber Champollion, den Prisse sehr verehrte. Mit seinen 100 Farblithografien nach Zeichnungen, die Prisse während seiner letzten sechs Jahre in Ägypten gefertigt hatte, sollte das Buch Champollions *Monuments de l'Égypte et de la Nubie* ergänzen. Aufgrund knapper Finanzen konnte das Buch nicht ganz so erscheinen wie geplant, wofür sich Prisse in der Einleitung bei den Lesern entschuldigt. Doch auch in der gekürzten Fassung handelt es sich um ein maßgebliches wissenschaftliches Werk. Es erhielt in erheblichem Umfang bis dahin unzugängliches Material aus der Regierungszeit Echnatons, das aus Tuna el-Gebel und Tell el-Amarna (*Monuments*, siehe S. 95–99) sowie aus Theben stammte. In der Tat hat Prisse – womöglich als Erster – die Bautätigkeit Echnatons in Theben ausführlich dokumentiert. Er hatte einen Blick für den unverwechselbaren Kunststil jener Zeit und datierte in die Herrschaftszeit Echnatons auch eine Gruppe kleiner Sandsteinblöcke *(talatat)*, die ans Licht gekommen waren, als man Karnaks dritten Pylon abriss, um ihn zur Gewinnung von Kalk zu verbrennen. Hiervon berichtete er Wilkinson und Nestor l'Hôte (1804–1842), einem Künstler, der an Champollions Expedition teilgenommen und selbst ein dreibändiges Werk mit Briefen aus Ägypten verfasst hatte, und auch Jacques-Joseph Champollion-Figeac (1778–1867), dem älteren Bruder Jean-François Champollions. Zwar wurde Prisse' Brief an Letzteren veröffentlicht, eine echte Abhandlung, in der er die verschiedenen aus der Zeit Echnatons datierenden Monumente in Beziehung zueinander setzte, existiert jedoch nicht.

Trotz des bescheidenen Umfangs fanden Prisse' *Monuments* große Resonanz und wurden von Intellektuellen und Künstlern in Frankreich und Großbritannien gerühmt. Théophile Gautier (1811–1872) behauptete gar, sein *Roman de la momie*, vielleicht das erste im Alten Ägypten spielende literarische Werk, sei durch Prisse' Veröffentlichung inspiriert. Zudem pries Gautier die künstlerische Qualität des Werks, so wie er generell ein treuer Anhänger des Autors war.

Ende der 1850er-Jahre drängte es Prisse, nach Ägypten zurückzukehren. Er wollte seine früheren Arbeiten ordnen, korrigieren und abschließen, seine Studien und Dokumentationen der Monumente fortsetzen und weitere Altertümer für Frankreich zusammentragen. Nun indes kam er nicht mehr als junger namenloser Abenteurer, sondern als anerkannter Ägypten-Experte und Leiter einer kleinen offiziellen Mission mit dem Auftrag, ägyptische Altertümer für Frankreich zu sammeln und zu kopieren. Die von Napoleon III. unterstützte und vom Bildungsministerium finanzierte Expedition dauerte drei Jahre (1858–1860). Prisse wurde von zwei jungen Männern begleitet: dem niederländischen Künstler und entfernten Verwandten Willem de Famars Testas (1834–1896) und dem französischen Fotografen Édouard Jarrot (1835–1873; Abb. 15). Ägypten hatte sich innerhalb der letzten zehn Jahre stark verändert. Unmittelbar vor Prisse' Ankunft hatte Said Pascha einen Altertümerdienst und ein Museum eingerichtet, die unter der Leitung des

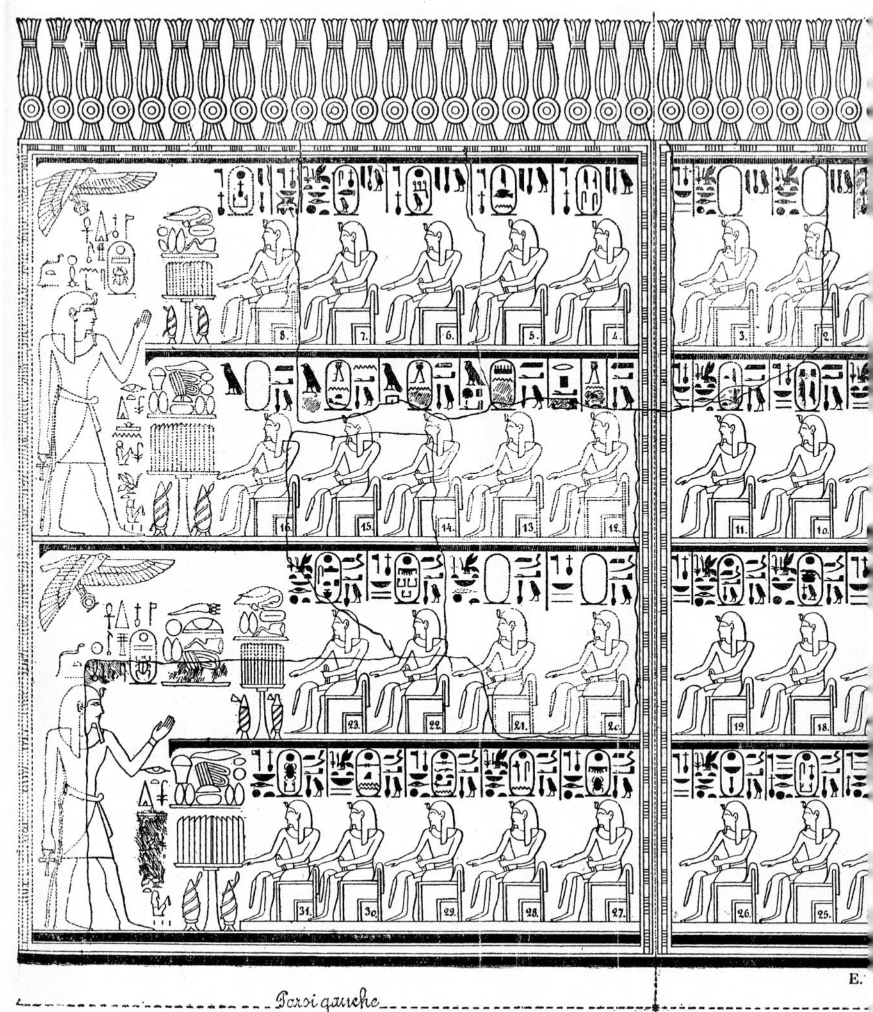

Ill. 12

Émile Prisse d'Avennes

Drawing of the Karnak King List / Zeichnung der Königsliste von Karnak / Dessin de la liste des rois de Karnak

Lithograph, 16.7 x 33 cm (6 5/8 x 13 in.), in: Émile Prisse d'Avennes (Jr.), *Le Papyrus à l'époque pharaonique*, Avesnes, 1926, p. 64. Paris, Bibliothèque nationale de France

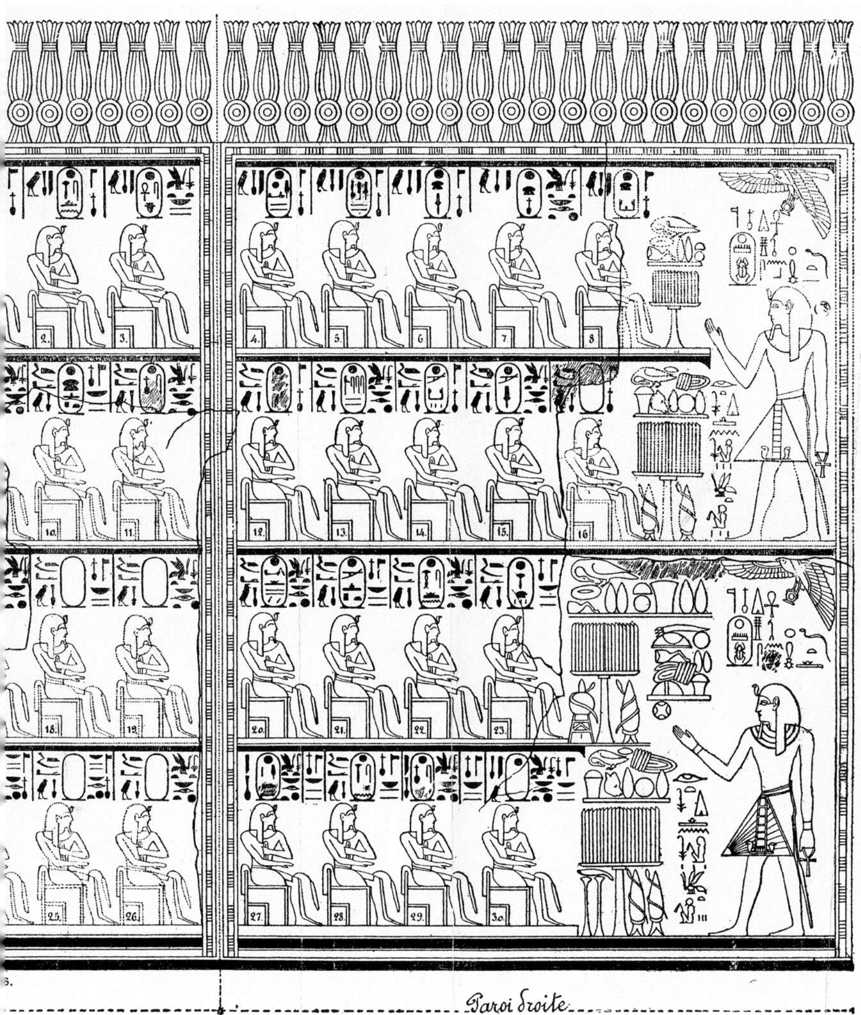

Franzosen Auguste Mariette (1821–1881) standen. Mariette, ein Verwandter von Nestor l'Hôte, verschärfte bereits existierende Bestimmungen hinsichtlich der Behandlung und Entnahme von Altertümern und ergänzte sie um weitere. Für Prisse bedeutete dies, dass er nicht im ursprünglich geplanten Umfang und in der gewünschten Qualität Objekte bergen konnte. Unbeeindruckt von diesem Rückschlag reisten Prisse und seine Begleiter durch Ägypten, Nubien und Arabien, um eine stetig wachsende Zahl von Grundrissen, Skizzen, Frottagen, Abrieben, Notizen und Fotografien zusammenzutragen (Abb. 20). Bemerkenswert ist dabei der Rückgriff auf das noch vergleichsweise junge Medium der Fotografie.

Bei der Dokumentation der Architektur Kairos vertraute Prisse auf die Arbeit des Daguerreotypisten Joseph-Philibert Girault de Prangey (1804–1892) und in geringerem Umfang auch auf Jarrot; er war gewiss froh, über einen eigenen Fotografen zu verfügen. Doch Prisse war ein strenger Meister, und seine beiden jungen Schützlinge litten so sehr, dass Jarrot wegen Erschöpfung vorzeitig abreisen musste, bald gefolgt von Prisse und Famars Testas.

Prisse kehrte 1860 mit 300 bis zu sieben oder acht Meter langen Folio-Zeichnungen von Malereien und Reliefs aus verschiedenen Monumenten nach Frankreich zurück (Abb. 18), mit 400 Metern Frottagen, 150 Fotos von Bau- und Dekordetails sowie Grundrissen, Längsschnitten und Ansichten, neben einer gewaltigen Sammlung von Skizzen und Notizen. Außerdem hatte er einige Altertümer und die Schädel von 29 Mumien im Gepäck, die er zeitlich, hierarchisch und namentlich identifiziert hatte; beides schenkte er später dem Louvre. Zusammen mit seinen älteren Arbeiten bildete diese Ausbeute die Grundlage für sein Hauptwerk über die altägyptische Kunst, das er zusammen mit dem Pendant zur islamischen Kunst in den folgenden Jahren unter Nutzung der Einrichtungen der Faculté des Sciences von Lille zusammenstellte.

Sein 1879 vollständig erschienenes Werk *Histoire de l'art égyptien* bestand aus zwei Bänden mit 159 Tafeln. Doch dies war nur ein Teil seiner Arbeiten, denn 1879, in seinem Todesjahr, erschien ein auf seinen Aufzeichnungen basierender, von P. Marchandon de la Faye verfasster Textband. Hätte Prisse länger gelebt, wären womöglich noch weitere Bände erschienen. Derzeit wird der größte Teil seines wissenschaftlichen Archivs (Zeichnungen, Fotografien, Frottagen, Notizen) in der französischen Nationalbibliothek aufbewahrt und ein Teil seiner persönlichen Papiere in den Archiven der Société archéologique et historique d'Avesnes-sur-Helpe.

Selbst im Vergleich mit den Resultaten der großen staatlich finanzierten Expeditionen ist Prisse' *Histoire de l'art égyptien* ein herausragendes Werk, bietet es doch die größte aus einer Hand stammende Serie illustrierter Darstellungen ägyptischer Kunst und im Zusammenspiel mit *L'Art arabe* eine wirklich umfassende Übersicht über die Kunst Ägyptens. Behandelt werden, jeweils mit zahlreichen Beispielen illustriert, Architektur, Zeichnung, Bildhauerei (mitsamt Flachreliefs), Malerei und Kunstgewerbe. Interessanterweise enthält der architektonische Teil nicht nur Bilder von Bauwerken, sondern auch altägyptische Darstellungen von Bauten, vor allem jene, die man an den Wänden der Gräber von Amarna fand (*Histoire de l'art égyptien* [*Hist.*], siehe S. 274–281).

Der Umstand, dass eine einzelne Person sämtliche Illustrationen in der Endfassung schuf und den Publikationsprozess beaufsichtigte, verleiht dem Werk eine Einheitlichkeit und Harmonie, die anderen Kompendien des 19. Jahrhunderts fehlt. Prisse' Künstlerhand wird, wenngleich bisweilen als zu „gefällig" kritisiert, den von den alten Ägyptern gemeißelten und gemalten Szenen gerecht. In der Tat kommen die meisten seiner Wiedergaben der „Wahrheit" weit näher als die anderer Künstler oder seiner Vorgänger, Zeitgenossen und sogar Nachfolger. Dies gilt etwa für seine mustergültige Kopie einer Skizze mit Fremden in einem thebanischen Grab aus der 18. Dynastie (*Hist.*, siehe S. 333), wohingegen seine Kopie einer Szene aus Amarna (*Hist.*, siehe S. 390–392) durchaus

Kritik verdient. Sein Werk bedeutet jedenfalls einen großen Schritt nach vorn, vergleicht man es etwa mit den Abbildungen der *Description*, deren Schöpfer den Bildern aus dem Alten Ägypten durchgängig ein klassizistisches Gepräge gaben (Abb. 19) oder mit ihrer allzu naiven Wiedergabe der raffinierteren Vorlage nicht gerecht wurden, was auch für andere Künstler gilt (Abb. 21, 22). Eine solche schwankende Qualität der Abbildungen findet sich auch in den *Denkmaelern*, sei es wegen der unterschiedlichen Talente der beteiligten Künstler oder abweichender Auffassungen zur altägyptischen Kunst (Abb. 23). Prisse' Werk ist sauber ausgeführt, zugleich nicht übermäßig geschönt und wird den Bildnissen der alten Ägypter eher gerecht.

Die hervorragenden Architekturzeichnungen in der *Histoire* zeugen von Prisse' früher Ausbildung. Jedes einzelne Monument ist durch Schnitte, Grundrisse, Baudetails und Fassadenschmuck perfekt dokumentiert und wiedergegeben; das gilt für den Grundriss und Längsschnitt des Grabes des Hohepriesters Petamenophis (*Hist.*, siehe S. 211) ebenso wie für die des Tempels von Dendur (*Hist.*, siehe S. 213), die sich heute im Metropolitan Museum of Art in New York befinden. Diese Darstellungen dürften bis heute unübertroffen sein.

Prisse' Studien zu den ornamentalen Mustern von Friesen und Decken (*Hist.*, siehe S. 250–267) sind höchst genau und auch deshalb von einigem Wert, weil sie zeitliche Abwandlungen dokumentieren – man fühlt sich an alte Musterbücher erinnert. Diese Abbildungen haben zweifellos bereits zu Prisse' Lebzeiten das europäische Kunstgewerbe und Design beeinflusst, eventuell auch gegen Ende des 19. und Anfang des 20. Jahrhunderts die Arts-and-Crafts-Bewegung und den Jugendstil. Sicher ist, dass einige Illustrationen in Owen Jones' weit verbreitetem Werk *The Grammar of Ornament* (1856) die von Prisse dokumentierten ägyptischen Motive widerspiegeln.

Wie andere bis heute herangezogene Veröffentlichungen aus jener Zeit bietet auch Prisse' Werk eine Bestandsaufnahme dessen, was einst an bestimmten Örtlichkeiten vorhanden war. Dies ist von besonderer Bedeutung, da viele Stätten im Fortgang der Zeit, häufiger jedoch unter den Händen der *sebbakhin* gelitten haben, die auf der Suche nach Dünger alles freilegten und zerstörten. Prisse' Werke sind auch deshalb für die moderne Ägyptologie unverzichtbar, weil gierige Sammler – ungeachtet aller Bemühungen, die Entnahme von Altertümern strengen Regeln zu unterwerfen – weiterhin ganze Reliefblöcke aus dem Kontext herausbrachen und auch Wissenschaftler überall in Ägypten Objekte abtrugen und Reliefs bis zur Unkenntlichkeit „frottierten". Sein waches Auge und seine stets präzise, nichts auslassende Dokumentation haben uns zahlreiche Objekte überliefert, von denen wir sonst heute nichts wüssten. Ein Beispiel ist sein Aquarell des Sarkophags von König Menkare (*Hist.*, siehe S. 205), eine seltene Darstellung dieses einzigartigen Objekts. Der Sarkophag wurde aus der Pyramide des Menkare in Gizeh (2493–2475 v. Chr.) geborgen und nach Großbritannien verschifft, ging dann aber bei einem Unwetter im Golf von Biscaya unter. Prisse' Darstellungen waren so gelungen, dass viele Gelehrtenkollegen ihn mit Illustrationen für ihre eigenen Bücher beauftragten oder seine Bilder verwendeten, da sie alles damals Verfügbare übertrafen. Seine Farbillustrationen lassen erahnen, wie eine eben erst geschaffene ägyptische Wandmalerei aussah (*Hist.*, siehe S. 483). Prisse' Kunst hat weiterhin Bestand und ist Quelle für Illustrationen. Sie ziert noch heute so manche Bücher, Forschungsliteratur (etwa die des großen Ägyptologen Gaston Maspero oder des renommierten Kunstkritikers Jean Capart) ebenso wie populärwissenschaftliche Werke (wie den gewaltigen Band *Ancient Egypt or Mizraïm* von Samuel Augustus Binion). In eher profanem Rahmen erscheint sie zudem auf den heute in Ägypten angebotenen Postkarten und T-Shirts.

Prisse' tiefes Verständnis für ägyptische Kunst zeigt sich auch darin, dass er als einer der ersten Forscher das ägyptische Gittersystem erkannte und präzise dokumentierte (z.B. *Hist.*, siehe S. 329, 331). Die alten Ägypter hielten sich bei ihren Zeichnungen an diesen Kanon der Proportionen; in der klassischen Kernphase hieß dies, dass die Hauptfigur einer Szene vom Scheitel bis zur Sohle 18 „Fäuste" oder Quadrate maß (*Hist.*, siehe S. 329). Die übrigen Figuren waren je nach Rang als Hälften, Viertel etc. der Hauptfigur angelegt. Das Gittersystem liegt der gesamten ägyptischen Kunst zugrunde. Seine Identifizierung und Dokumentation zählen zu den bedeutendsten Beiträgen, die Prisse in diesem Forschungsbereich geleistet hat. Die Kenntnis des Gittersystems hat Prisse womöglich auch in die Lage versetzt, genauere Kopien anzufertigen als seine Zeitgenossen. Prisse traf eine derart einfühlsame Farbauswahl, dass man noch heute darauf vertraut, um ein Gespür für die altehrwürdigen Originale zu bekommen. Sein Rückgriff auf die Fotografie ermöglichte ihm zudem eine noch akkuratere Dokumentation der Monumente; für seit Langem zerstörte Szenerien und Bauwerke stellen diese Bilder eine unschätzbare Informationsquelle dar. Viele der von Prisse dokumentierten Monumente existieren nicht mehr, sodass seine Arbeiten als einziges Zeugnis dieser Bauten und der Kunstfertigkeit der alten Ägypter bleiben.

Prisse' akkurate und kluge Dokumentation der ägyptischen Kunst für die gesamten 3000 Jahre ägyptischer Geschichte (und mehr) bietet uns eine Bestandsaufnahme und eine beispiellose Einsicht in Architektur, Bildhauerei, Malerei und sogar Kunstgewerbe der alten Ägypter. Neben Prisse' künstlerischen Fähigkeiten verdankt sich dies auch seinem Verständnis des jeweiligen historischen, sozialen und religiösen Kontexts, weshalb seine enzyklopädischen Werke für die Erforschung des Alten Ägypten von unermesslichem Wert sind.

Ill. 13
Andrzej Mniszech
Émile Prisse d'Avennes, 1872
Photograph, approx. 33 x 25 cm (approx. 13 x 9 3/4 in.)
Paris, Bibliothèque nationale de France

Ill. 14
Émile Prisse d'Avennes
Karnak, the great forecourt with the Taharqa column, *c.* 1836–1844 / **Karnak, der große Vorhof mit der Säule des Taharqa** / **Karnak, la première cour avec la colonne de Taharqa**
Watercolour on vellum paper, 34.6 x 48.9 cm (13 5/8 x 19 1/4 in.) Paris, Bibliothèque nationale de France

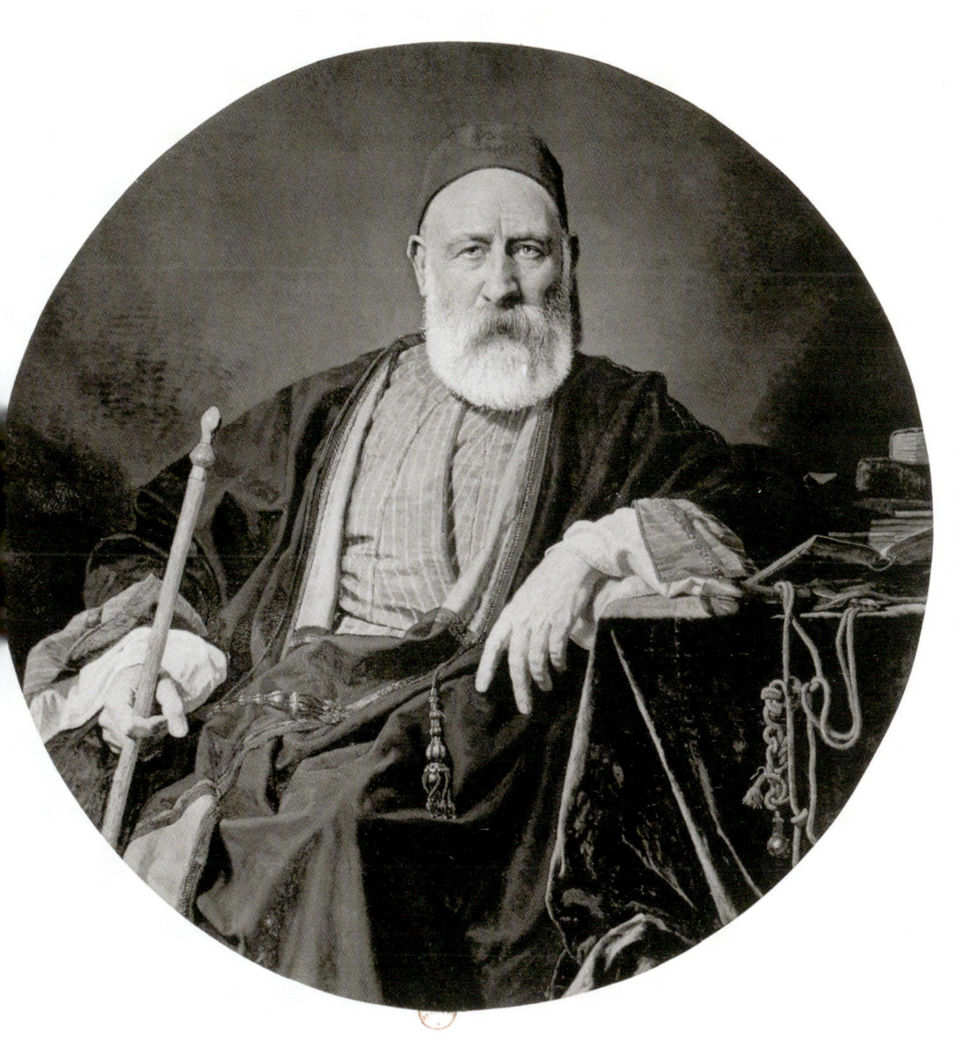

Prisse d'Avennes

Achille, Constant, Théodose, Emile.

1807 – 1879.

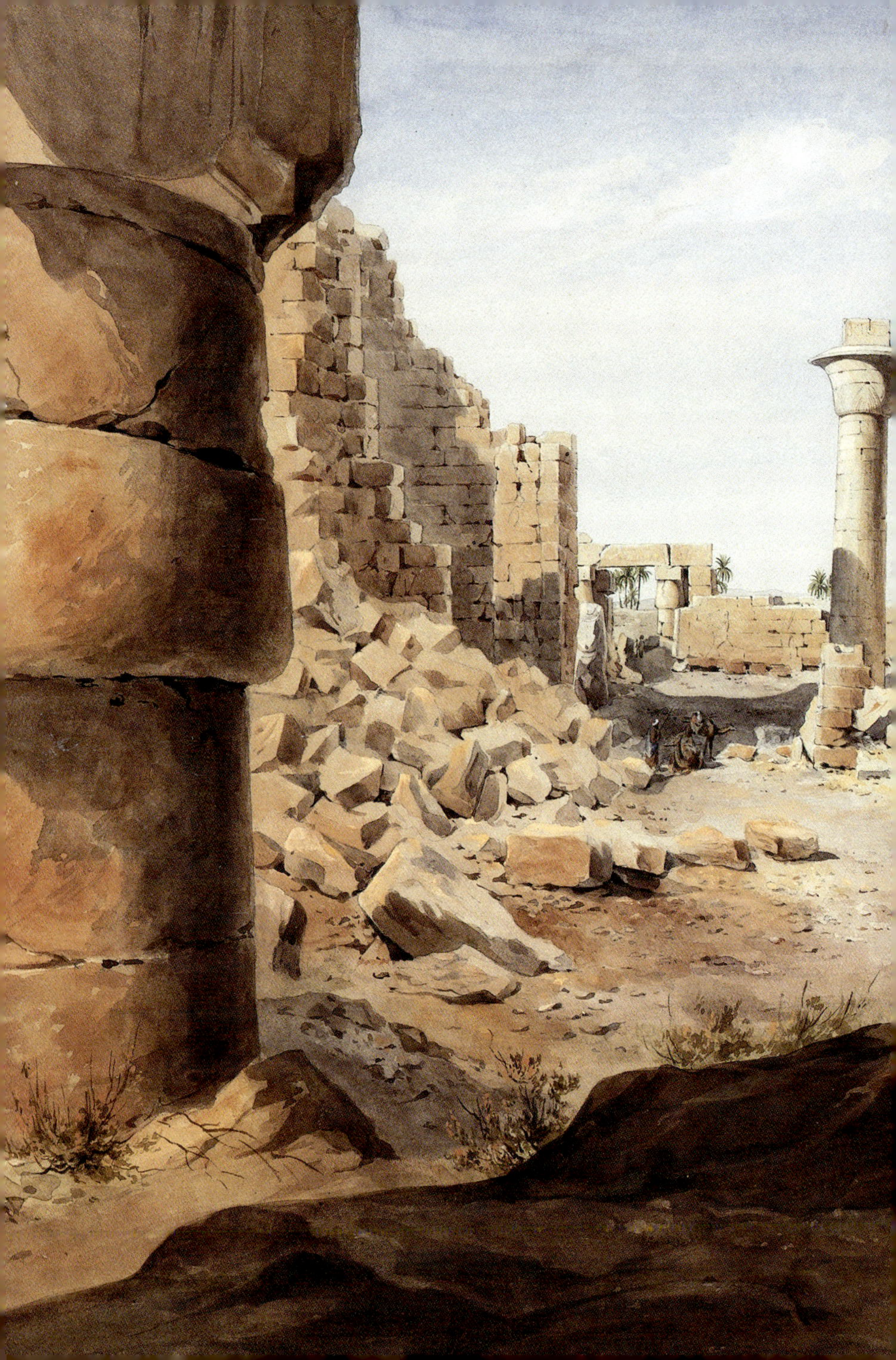

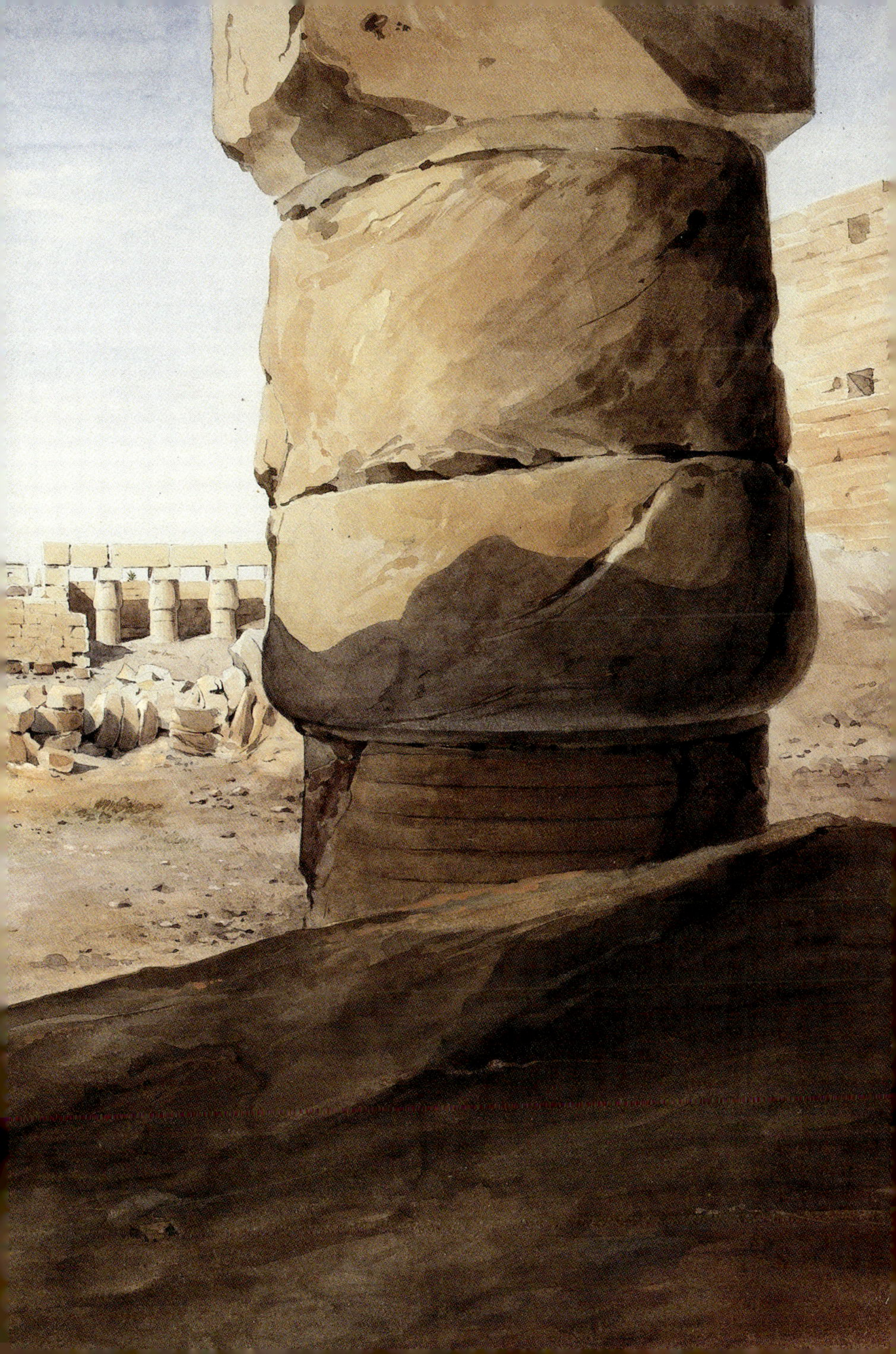

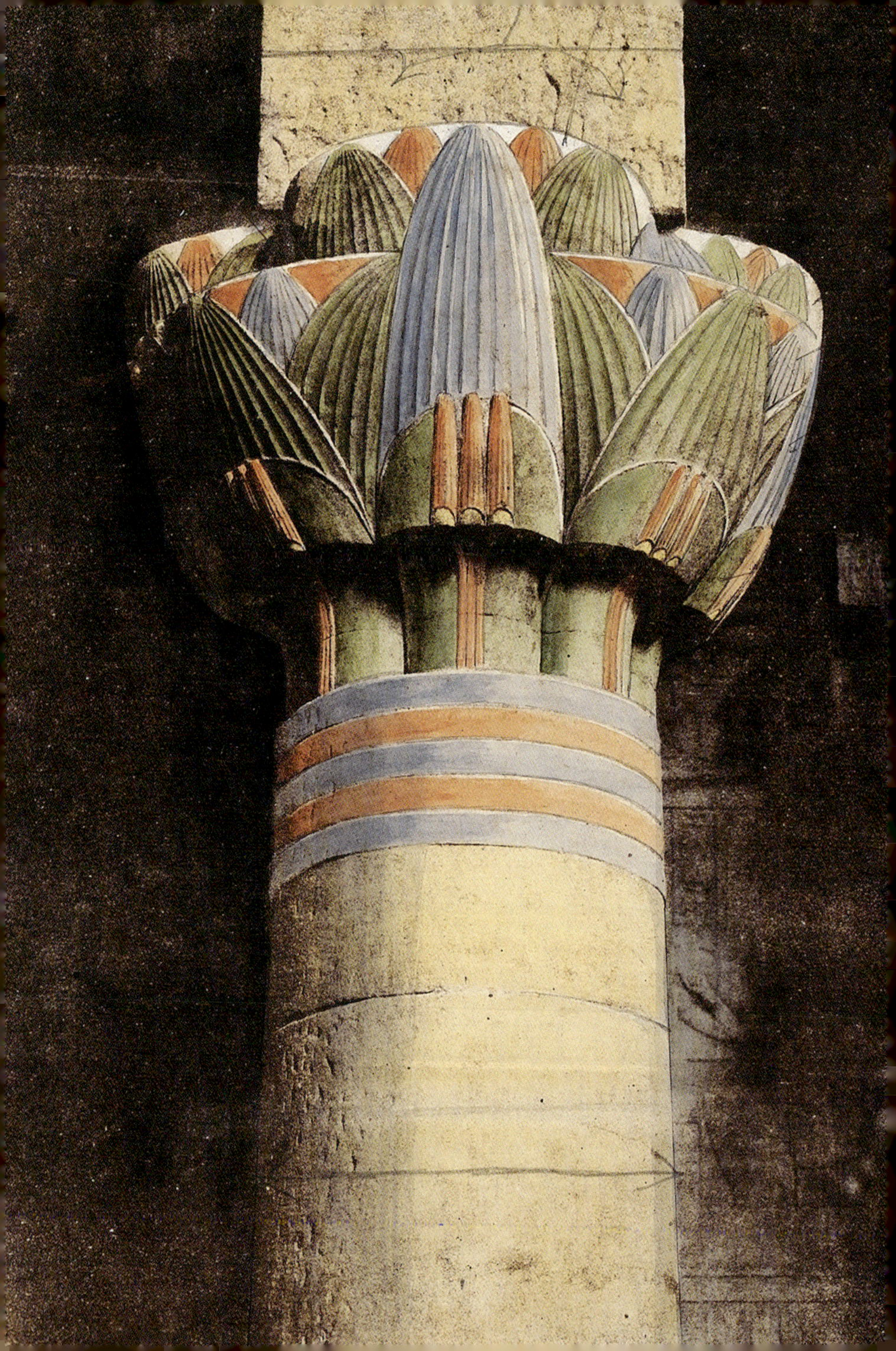

Émile Prisse d'Avennes et l'Égypte ancienne

SALIMA IKRAM

L'égyptologie a une dette considérable à l'égard des nombreux visiteurs de l'Égypte qui, au XIXe siècle, furent séduits par ses monuments et gardèrent la trace de tout ce qu'ils y avaient vu, devenant les premiers égyptologues, bien avant la création officielle de cette discipline. L'un d'eux, Achille Constant Théodore Émile Prisse d'Avennes (1807–1879), ne se contenta pas de visiter les nombreux sites de la vallée du Nil et d'en rendre compte, mais il est également l'auteur de l'une des toutes premières études consacrées à l'art égyptien et, par là même, l'un des fondateurs des études spécialisées dans ce domaine (ill. 1, 9). Prisse ne s'intéressa pas qu'à l'Égypte ancienne, et c'est ce qui fait toute son originalité ; il se passionna pour l'art et l'architecture de l'Égypte de la période islamique. Ses deux grandes œuvres – *Histoire de l'art égyptien d'après les monuments depuis les temps les plus reculés jusqu'à la domination romaine* (Paris, 1878/79) et *L'Art arabe d'après les monuments du Kaire depuis le VIIe siècle jusqu'à la fin du XVIIIe siècle (Paris, 1869–1877)* – couvrent quasiment toute l'histoire de l'art égyptien. On ne peut que regretter qu'il n'ait pu consacrer le même temps à l'art copte et établir ainsi un compte rendu détaillé des nombreux monuments qui ont disparu depuis.

Il y a encore peu, on connaissait mal Prisse d'Avennes, à l'exception de ses œuvres qui parlent si bien d'elles-mêmes et d'une poignée de publications qui citent son nom. Parmi ces dernières, il existe une biographie (qui relève plutôt de l'hagiographie), rédigée par son fils Émile dans le but de redorer le blason de son père et de défendre sa mémoire face aux commentaires diffamatoires publiés et amplement diffusés par Maxime du Camp dans ses *Souvenirs littéraires (1888)*. Malheureusement, ces propos furent repris dans l'ouvrage encyclopédique de l'historien Jean-Marie Carré, *Voyageurs et écrivains français en Égypte* (1932), même si Carré discrédite pour l'essentiel les remarques de Du Camp. À partir des années 1980, l'histoire de l'égyptologie a connu un net regain d'intérêt et suscité

ILL. 15
Édouard Jarrot
Crateriform capital, Philae, 1859 / Kraterförmiges Kapitell, Philae / Chapiteau cratériforme, Philæ
Watercoloured photograph, 38.2 x 31.8 cm (15 x 12 ½ in.). Paris, Bibliothèque nationale de France

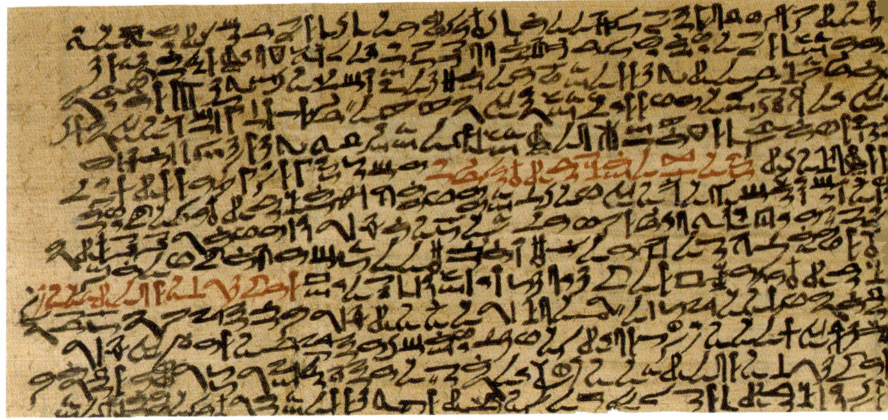

quelques ouvrages consacrés à Prisse (et à d'autres égyptologues), que l'on doit à Michel Dewachter, lequel a su dresser un portrait plus nuancé de cet homme extraordinaire. Plus récemment, l'ouvrage de Prévost (et al., 2011) et de Volait (2013) a largement contribué à raviver l'engouement pour Prisse en rectifiant les malentendus concernant son œuvre tout en jetant une lumière nouvelle sur sa vie. Grâce à la réédition de ses deux grandes œuvres, sur l'art pharaonique et l'art islamique, Prisse revient, de droit, en pleine lumière.

Les premières années

Prisse est né le 27 janvier 1807 dans la petite ville d'Avesnes-sur-Helpe (Nord), au sein d'une famille à laquelle la légende familiale donne des ancêtres britanniques (originaires d'Aven, au Pays de Galles ; après avoir connu quelques variantes, l'orthographe « d'Avennes » fut adoptée en 1690 afin, semble-t-il, de rendre un hommage simultané aux villes d'origine et d'adoption de la famille). Après des études à l'École d'Arts et Métiers de Châlons-sur-Marne (1822–1825), Prisse, assoiffé d'aventures, quitta la France à dix-neuf ans pour combattre dans la guerre d'indépendance grecque. Il ne resta que très brièvement en Grèce, puis il se rendit jusqu'en Inde et en Palestine où il effectua un court séjour. Il s'intéressa aux sites sacrés de Palestine, ce qui lui valut le titre de chevalier du Saint-Sépulcre. C'est son désir d'explorer l'Orient et ses trésors antiques qui mena Prisse en Égypte en 1826. Il eut ensuite la chance d'être engagé par Méhémet Ali Pacha (qui régna de 1805 à 1848) et par son fils, Ibrahim, devenu régent pendant une courte période à la fin de son règne. Prisse occupa diverses fonctions, notamment celles de professeur dans plusieurs institutions militaires et même, brièvement, de précepteur des princes. Il prit le nom d'Edris Effendi, se convertit ostensiblement à l'islam (pour des raisons sans doute plus politiques que religieuses),

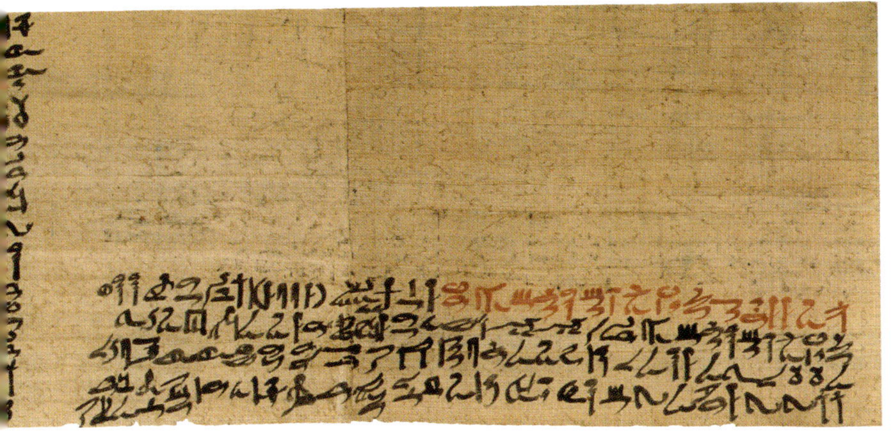

apprit l'arabe et devint expert en hiéroglyphes, pour autant qu'il était possible de les déchiffrer à l'époque (ill. 13). Prisse resta au service du pacha pendant une dizaine d'années avant de découvrir sa véritable vocation, l'étude et la recension des monuments égyptiens dont ses publications encyclopédiques furent le couronnement.

Au début du XIXe siècle, l'Égypte attisa les convoitises des amateurs d'antiquités et des milieux politiques et économiques, principalement en raison de l'expédition napoléonienne dans le pays (1798–1801), malheureuse sur le plan politique, mais triomphale dans les domaines intellectuel et artistique, et qui donna naissance à la publication en plusieurs volumes de la *Description de l'Égypte*, dont la réalisation nécessita près de vingt ans (1809/10–1828 ; ill. 2, 3, 19). La première édition comprenait neuf volumes in-quarto et onze volumineux tomes de planches, pour un total de 837 gravures en taille-douce et plus de 3000 dessins. Les savants qui avaient accompagné Napoléon dans sa campagne étudièrent tous les aspects de l'Égypte : antiquités, histoire naturelle, histoire moderne et topographie. Ces volumes piquèrent l'intérêt des Européens et façonnèrent l'érudition européenne (et égyptienne) en la matière. Ces publications eurent aussi une grande influence sur les styles et les goûts architecturaux et artistiques, provoquèrent une demande apparemment insatiable en antiquités pharaoniques et contribuèrent à transformer en discipline savante ce loisir d'antiquaire qu'avait été jusqu'alors l'égyptologie. D'ailleurs, Vivant Denon (1747–1825), l'un des artistes les plus importants et les plus actifs ayant participé à cette mission, et qui allait devenir

Ill. 16

The Prisse Papyrus (detail: verses 1–73), *c.* 1900–1800 BC

Der Papyrus Prisse (Detail: Verse 1–73) / **Le Papyrus Prisse** (détail : verses 1–73)

Black and red ink on papyrus, 14.5 x 68 cm (5 ¾ x 26 ¾ in.)

Paris, Bibliothèque nationale de France, mso Égyptien 186

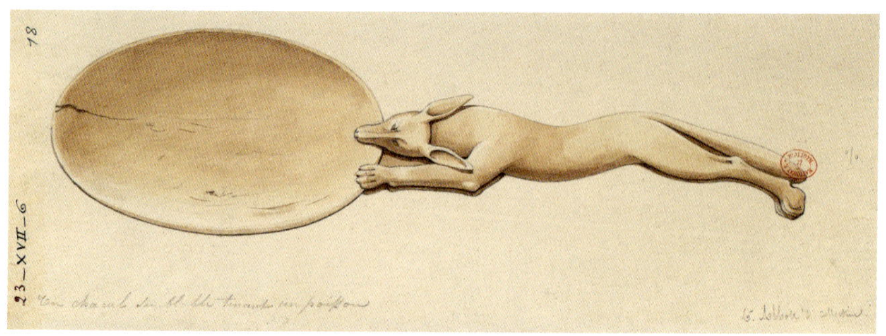

Ill. 17
Émile Prisse d'Avennes
Spoon with jackal-shaped handle, 1836–1844 / **Löffel mit schakalförmigem Griff** /
Cuillère à manche figurant un chacal
Pencil and watercolour on vellum paper, 10.7 x 30.8 cm (4 1/4 x 12 1/8 in.)
Paris, Bibliothèque nationale de France

conservateur au Louvre, relata son expérience au sein de l'équipe de savants dans son *Voyage dans la Basse et Haute Égypte* (1802), ouvrage qui suscita une grande attention et devint aussitôt un best-seller dans toute l'Europe.

Il est possible que le désir d'aventure et l'attirance pour l'Orient soient nés, chez Prisse, de la lecture de la *Description* et d'autres ouvrages célèbres publiés par ces savants de la campagne napoléonienne. L'intérêt de Prisse pour l'Égypte provient essentiellement des conférences et des publications de Jean-François Champollion (1790–1832) consacrées à la pierre de Rosette, objet d'importance considérable découvert par les Français, et à la grammaire égyptienne. Les premiers récits de voyage illustrés – parmi lesquels *Voyage d'Égypte et de Nubie* (1755) de Frédéric Norden ; *A Description of the East and some other Countries* (1743–1745) de l'évêque Pococke, traduite en français de 1772 à 1773 ; *Voyage en Syrie et en Égypte, pendant les années 1783, 1784, et 1785* (1787) du comte Constantin-François Volney ; et les *Lettres sur l'Égypte* (1786) de Claude Étienne Savary – ont pu également stimuler l'imagination du jeune dessinateur et ingénieur et l'inciter à s'installer en Orient. Voyageurs, scientifiques et aventuriers affluèrent d'Europe à la suite de l'expédition napoléonienne et pour répondre à la demande en experts de Méhémet Ali. Particulièrement accueillant pour les Français, le pacha avait déjà à son service le talentueux architecte Pascal Coste (1787–1879). Ce dernier est connu pour ses études sur l'architecture islamique, notamment celle du Caire, mais partageait l'enthousiasme de Prisse pour le passé pharaonique, ce dont témoignent ses nombreux carnets et dessins. Il est fort possible que les deux hommes se soient rencontrés au Caire ou à Alexandrie.

Le contexte du travail de Prisse

Certains visiteurs de l'Égypte étaient séduits par une vision romantique de l'Orient et de ses monuments antiques, tandis que d'autres s'y rendirent avec l'intention plus prosaïque de gagner de l'argent. Quelles qu'aient été leurs motivations initiales, beaucoup furent fascinés par les merveilles de l'Égypte ancienne et se consacrèrent à l'exploration des sites antiques ; c'est ainsi qu'ils découvrirent, recueillirent et recensèrent des antiquités, tant pour le lucre que pour l'érudition.

Bernardino Drovetti (1776–1852), proconsul français en Égypte, et Henry Salt, consul général britannique (1780–1827) et rival acharné du Français, sont deux des nombreux Européens qui, outre leurs fonctions, se consacrèrent à l'acquisition d'antiquités égyptiennes pour leurs gouvernements respectifs. On est captivé par la lecture des récits de leurs querelles et de leurs subterfuges pour s'approprier des statues colossales, des papyrus, des tombeaux et des temples presque entiers – manifestation supplémentaire de la rivalité éternelle entre les deux nations.

Salt avait à son service un certain Giovanni Battista Belzoni (1778–1823), de taille gigantesque (il avait été homme fort dans un cirque en Grande-Bretagne), parti en Égypte comme ingénieur, mais qui, après une suite de hasards, était devenu antiquaire. Les efforts conjugués de Belzoni et de Salt permirent au British Museum d'obtenir une grande partie des pièces détenues par cette institution. C'est aussi pour son propre compte que Belzoni explora l'Égypte et se fit antiquaire. L'exploration d'Abou Simbel et de Gizeh (ill. 4) figure parmi les victoires archéologiques de Belzoni ; il est aussi le premier homme de l'ère moderne à avoir pénétré dans la pyramide de Khafrê à Gizeh, en 1818, ouvrant la voie aux futures investigations égyptologiques. À l'instar de Prisse, Belzoni fit des copies et des moulages, notamment au papier, des scènes représentées dans les tombeaux et les temples, en particulier à Thèbes. Le moulage au papier consistait à humidifier un papier spécial, semblable au buvard, et à le frotter vigoureusement pour qu'il prenne la forme du relief, méthode répandue, mais destructrice, pour répertorier avec précision une ornementation en relief. Moins hauts en couleur que Belzoni, les employés et compagnons de Drovetti eurent néanmoins tout autant de succès dans l'acquisition d'objets, comme l'attestent leurs collections, aujourd'hui dispersées un peu partout en France, ainsi qu'à Turin et à Berlin. Deux de ses compagnons les plus remarquables, Jean-Jacques Rifaud (1786–1852) et Frédéric Cailliaud (1787–1869), explorèrent l'Égypte et la Nubie et publièrent de très nombreux ouvrages sur ces régions, contribuant ainsi durablement à l'égyptologie. Le *Voyage en Égypte, en Nubie et lieux circonvoisins, depuis 1805 jusqu'en 1827* en cinq volumes de Rifaud (1830–1844) était illustré de lithographies en couleur, de même que ses autres publications en plusieurs volumes. Toutefois, aucun de ses ouvrages ne relève de l'histoire de l'art, contrairement aux œuvres de Prisse.

Certaines publications du jeune Cailliaud ont des points communs avec l'*Oriental Album* (Londres, 1848 ; texte par James Augustus St. John) de Prisse. Cailliaud rend compte des us et coutumes des Égyptiens contemporains, ainsi que des anciens habitants de la vallée du Nil, dans sa publication *Recherches sur les arts et métiers, les usages de la vie civile et domestique des anciens peuples de l'Égypte, de la Nubie et de l'Éthiopie* (1831–1837). La description des mœurs et des coutumes des Égyptiens était un thème répandu. Deux Anglais, John Gardner Wilkinson (1797–1875) et Edward William Lane

(1801–1876), ont rendu compte, de façon encore plus détaillée que Cailliaud, de la vie quotidienne aux époques antiques et contemporaines. Arrivé en 1821, Wilkinson résida en Égypte pendant une douzaine d'années et y retourna régulièrement jusqu'en 1856. Comme Prisse, il était fasciné par les hiéroglyphes, adopta un nom arabe, apprit la langue et s'habilla comme un Arabe. Mais, contrairement au Français, il alla jusqu'à épouser une Égyptienne que, malheureusement, il finit par abandonner. Sillonnant l'Égypte, Wilkinson recueillit des renseignements et recopia des textes et des scènes de tombeaux et de temples, données qui contribuèrent au déchiffrement et à l'étude de la langue des pharaons. Il découvrit, explora et répertoria un grand nombre de tombeaux de Thèbes, exhuma de très nombreux objets, avant de publier son grand œuvre en trois volumes *Manners and Customs of the Ancient Egyptians* (1837), chronique de la vie quotidienne des habitants de l'Égypte ancienne s'appuyant sur l'interprétation des reliefs des tombeaux (ill. 5). Durant la majeure partie de ses dernières années en Égypte, Prisse eut une correspondance régulière avec Wilkinson, dans laquelle il lui faisait part de ses idées et lui donnait des renseignements recueillis à l'occasion de ses nouvelles découvertes. Il n'est pas certain que les deux hommes se soient rencontrés ; toutefois, ils parvinrent à créer et à entretenir des rapports professionnels pendant de nombreuses années. Il est vraisemblable que Prisse a eu connaissance de l'orientaliste Edward William Lane. Brillant arabisant, Lane parlait, comme certains de ses contemporains, l'arabe couramment, s'habillait à l'égyptienne, épousa (et emmena en Angleterre) une Égyptienne, explora l'Égypte et consigna par écrit, et avec force détails, ce qu'il avait vu et compris des coutumes locales de l'époque. Son travail donna lieu à la publication de *Manners and Customs of the Modern Egyptians* (1836), pendant de l'ouvrage de Wilkinson.

L'époque durant laquelle Prisse œuvra en Égypte ne fut pas seulement celle d'individus se consacrant à la recension systématique des antiquités du pays ; des nations entières y envoyèrent des expéditions scientifiques de grande envergure pour effectuer la description et la collecte d'objets. Naturellement, cette activité était essentiellement due à la rivalité entre des nations européennes désirant s'approprier les collections égyptiennes les plus belles et les plus importantes, afin d'exhiber leur richesse, leur érudition, leur puissance et leur autorité. Néanmoins, ceux qui participèrent à ces expéditions ne le firent pas uniquement pour la gloire de leur pays et leur gloire personnelle, mais aussi en raison d'un désir authentique de déchiffrer la culture complexe de l'Égypte ancienne. L'une des toutes premières expéditions du genre fut celle menée par Jean-François Champollion, surtout connu pour son travail de déchiffrement des hiéroglyphes. En 1828, sous l'égide du roi de France et accompagné de son disciple Ippolito Rosellini (1800–1843), Champollion mit sur pied une mission franco-toscane destinée à collecter, étudier et recenser les antiquités de l'Égypte. Une équipe d'artistes, d'architectes, d'ordonnateurs et de médecins se joignit à eux pour parcourir toute l'Égypte et la Nubie et recopier des textes, acquérir des objets et, parfois, graver les noms de ses membres sur divers monuments. Cette expédition produisit une quantité prodigieuse d'informations, car c'était la première fois qu'une personne capable de lire les hiéroglyphes avait effectué pareille collecte et travaillé à la traduction de tout ce qui avait été réuni. Ne se contentant pas de rapporter d'immenses collections d'objets antiques, Champollion et Rosellini publièrent leurs dessins reproduisant des textes, des monuments et des objets dans plusieurs volumes extrêmement

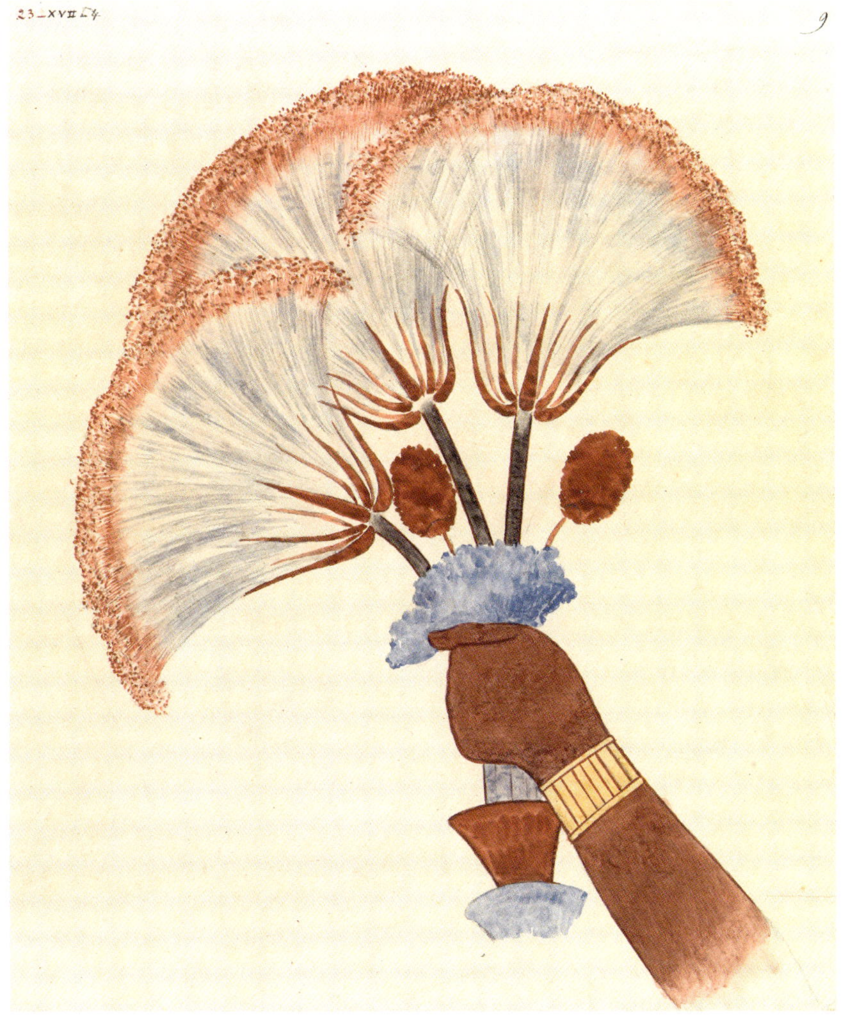

Ill. 18
Émile Prisse d'Avennes
Bouquet of papyrus, tomb of Nebamun, Qurna, 1859? / Papyrusstrauß, Grab des Nebamun, Qurna / Bouquet de papyrus, tombe de Nebamon, Gournah
Pencil and watercolour on tracing paper, 42.7 x 36.9 cm (16 3/4 x 14 1/2 in.)
Paris, Bibliothèque nationale de France

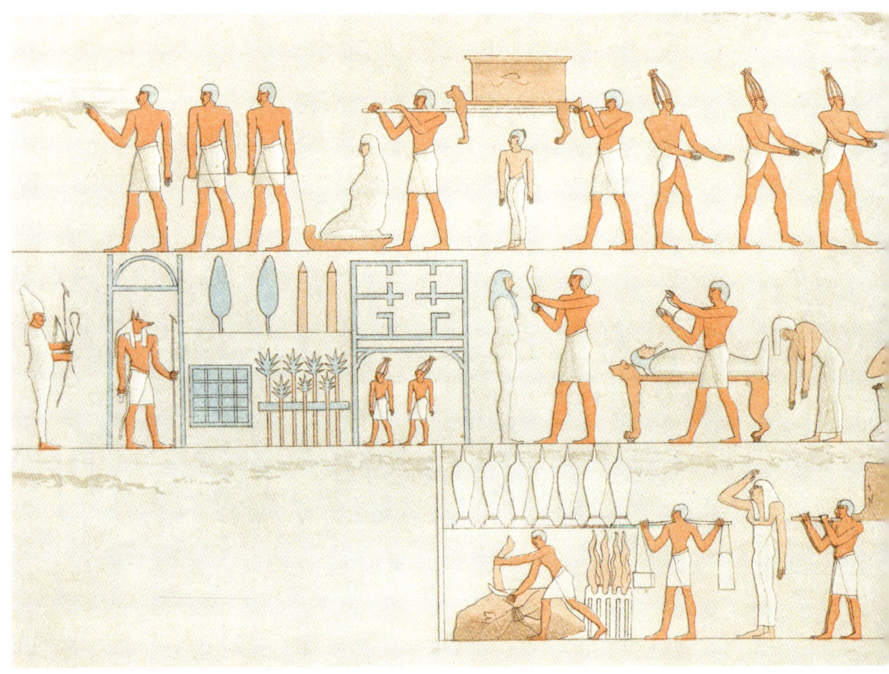

précieux pour l'étude de l'Égypte ancienne. *Monuments de l'Égypte et de la Nubie* (1833), *Lettres écrites d'Égypte et de Nubie en 1828 et 1829* (1833) et *I monumenti dell'Egitto e della Nubia, disegnati dalla spedizione scientifico-letteraria Toscana in Egitto* (1832–1844) inspirèrent Prisse, grand admirateur de Champollion (ill. 7).

L'autre grande expédition scientifique du XIXe siècle fut dirigée par le Prussien Karl Richard Lepsius (1810–1884). En 1827, Frédéric-Guillaume III de Prusse avait acquis une grande collection égyptienne. C'est ainsi qu'il s'intéressa aux antiquités égyptiennes et aux études qui leur étaient consacrées, et que l'Ägyptisches Museum vit le jour à Berlin. Peu après son accession au trône, Frédéric-Guillaume IV, avec la bénédiction de ses conseillers scientifiques, devint donc, de 1842 à 1845, le mécène de l'expédition de Lepsius, chargé de visiter et répertorier des monuments, puis de répertorier et de recenser les antiquités de l'Égypte. Cette expédition scientifique est sans doute celle qui fut le mieux équipée pour partir en Égypte, peut-être à l'exception de celle de Napoléon ; toutefois, l'expédition prussienne fut la mieux financée et la mieux organisée. Elle était composée d'un grand nombre de dessinateurs, d'ingénieurs et de savants, tous très compétents et familiers de l'Égypte. Lepsius et son équipe réunirent 15 000 objets, dont bon nombre avaient été exhumés par Lepsius en personne, bien que Prisse ait obtenu avant lui la Chambre des Ancêtres (voir ci-dessous), et les rapportèrent à Berlin. Tous les dessins, cartes et plans réunis en

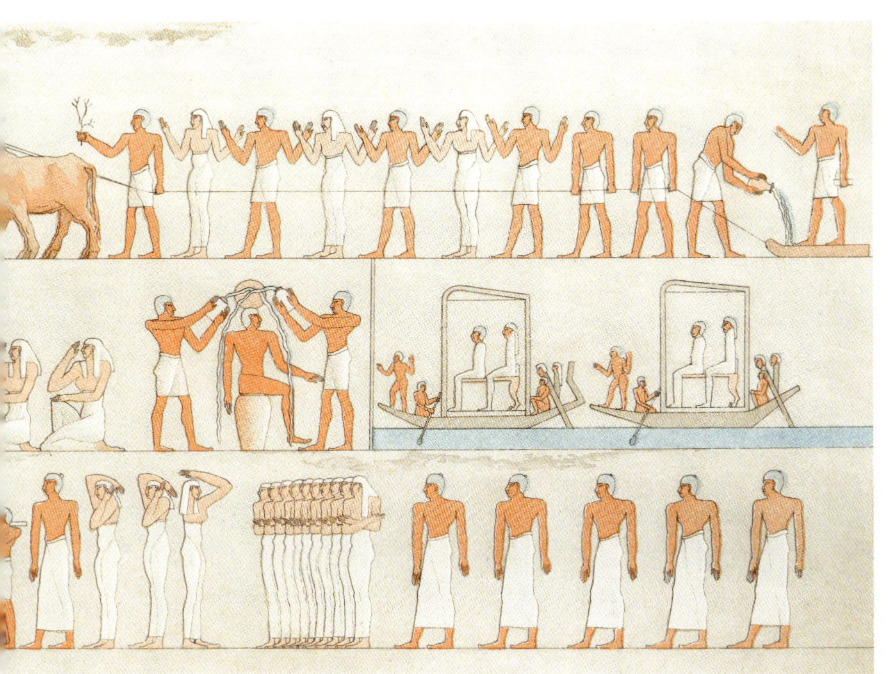

Égypte par Lepsius et son équipe furent publiés dans l'ouvrage monumental en douze volumes *Denkmaeler aus Aegypten und Aethiopien* (1849–1859 ; ill. 6). Les cinq volumes de textes furent publiés bien après la mort de Lepsius (1897–1913). Il est possible que ce soient le *Denkmaeler* et d'autres publications de Lepsius qui aient inspiré la création de la toute première revue scientifique exclusivement consacrée à l'égyptologie, la *Zeitschrift für ägyptische Sprache und Altertumskunde*, fondée à Berlin en 1863. La *Description* et le *Denkmaeler* constituent aujourd'hui encore les fondements de la recherche en égyptologie.

Outre les savants recenseurs d'antiquités, de nombreux artistes talentueux parcoururent le pays et donnèrent de l'Égypte pharaonique et islamique une vision romantique, contrepoint plaisant aux représentations plus techniques et plus précises des érudits. David Roberts (1796–1864) est le plus

Ill. 19

Funeral scene, tomb of Paheri at el-Kab, 1809

Beerdigungsdarstellung, Grab des Paheri in el-Kab / Scène funéraire, tombe de Pahéri d'el-Kab

Lithograph, 15.3 x 41 cm (6 x 16 ⅛ in.), in: *Description de l'Égypte ou recueil des observations et des recherches qui ont été faites en Égypte*, vol. I ("Antiquités – Planches"), Paris, 1809, pl. 70 (detail)

Weimar, Herzogin Anna Amalia Bibliothek

important de ces artistes ; il est célèbre pour ses tableaux et ses lithographies qui figurent encore parmi les images de l'Égypte les plus connues qu'on ait jamais produites (ill. 8, 10). Bien des peintres ont représenté l'Égypte, mais John Frederick Lewis (1805–1876), Jean-Léon Gérôme (1824–1904) et William Holman Hunt (1827–1910) sortent du lot.

L'œuvre de Prisse d'Avennes

Ainsi Prisse a-t-il séjourné en Égypte dans un environnement peuplé de pachas, de politiciens, de pillards, de savants, d'intellectuels, d'artistes et d'aventuriers. Après avoir rompu les liens officiels qui le liaient à la famille royale en 1836, à la suite d'un désaccord avec le commandant en chef de l'École d'infanterie qui l'employait à cette époque, Prisse partit explorer l'Égypte et le Proche-Orient jusqu'en 1839. Au Caire, il devint très ami avec le docteur Henry Abbott (1807–1859). Ensemble, ils fondèrent en 1842 l'éphémère Association Littéraire du Caire, dont les membres se réunirent pour discuter de l'art et de l'histoire de l'Égypte, organisèrent des conférences et mirent sur pied une librairie destinée aux chercheurs. Grâce à cette institution, Abbott et Prisse purent rencontrer nombre des artistes et des savants qui visitèrent l'Égypte. Prisse se plaisait à créer des associations et à appartenir à des sociétés savantes ; plus tard, en France, il fonda deux revues aux parutions irrégulières, *Le Miroir de l'Orient* et la *Revue orientale et algérienne*, toutes deux associées à son amour pour l'Orient contemporain.

Au cours de ses voyages, Prisse ne cessait de dessiner et de collectionner des objets, trouvés lors de fouilles ou achetés. En cela, il se distinguait peu de tous ceux qui se livraient à la même activité, mais son aire géographique, incluant le Delta et quelques sites reculés au cœur de la vallée du Nil comme Chenhour, était plus vaste que celle de la plupart de ses contemporains et la précision de ses recherches surpassait souvent celle de ces derniers. En revanche, son intérêt pour l'Égypte ancienne fut aiguisé par le travail d'érudition réalisé par Champollion. Prisse possédait une connaissance des hiéroglyphes surprenante pour l'époque. Sa correspondance révèle qu'il était en contact avec Champollion, Wilkinson, Mariette et d'autres savants. Sans les identifications et les inventaires effectués par Prisse, de nombreux objets, constructions, scènes et inscriptions – tels qu'une rare inscription claudienne en latin, recyclée dans une mosquée d'Aqfahs, au sud de Beni Suef et les objets du site de Tell el-Amarna à Thèbes – auraient été perdus et l'histoire de l'Égypte s'en serait trouvée amputée.

En 1839, Prisse s'installa à Louxor pour étudier le véritable trésor de monuments qui s'y trouvait. Il y devint l'ami du botaniste anglais George Lloyd (1815–1843) et y établit son quartier général. Il passa près de six ans sur place et acquit des objets antiques pour la gloire de la France (comme la Stèle de Bakhtan, conservée au Louvre), fit des dessins de temples et en dressa les plans, recopia des scènes visibles dans les tombeaux et les temples, recueillit des moulages au papier et réalisa une étude exhaustive de l'art égyptien et de la grammaire ornementale employés par les Égyptiens de l'Antiquité (ill. 17). Prisse aurait pu rester indéfiniment à Thèbes si deux événements ne s'étaient pas produits. Ce fut d'abord le décès tragique de son ami George Lloyd, mortellement blessé par son propre fusil. Le second tient aux conditions douteuses dans lesquelles Prisse obtint une partie de la liste des rois de Karnak, ou tables de Karnak, aussi connues sous le nom de « Chambre des Ancêtres » (ill. 11, 12).

Les tables de Karnak constituent un document essentiel pour l'étude de l'Égypte ancienne. Répertoriant les noms des souverains selon les successions, les listes de rois sont précieuses pour établir la chronologie d'une grande partie de l'histoire égyptienne. Mais il arrive souvent que certains rois et même des dynasties entières ne figurent pas dans ces listes. Il n'est alors possible de constituer une liste complète qu'en réunissant plusieurs listes distinctes. Les tables de Karnak sont d'autant plus précieuses qu'elles donnent les noms des souverains des époques troublées que furent les Première (2181–2040 av. J.-C.) et Deuxième (1782–1570 av. J.-C.) Périodes intermédiaires, noms difficilement attestés ailleurs. Cette liste fut gravée sur l'ordre du roi Thoutmôsis III (1504–1450 av. J.-C.) et érigée dans l'angle sud-ouest du pavillon de l'Akh-Menou (salle de réception) du temple de Karnak (ill. 14). Soixante-et-un rois furent répertoriés sur la pierre, en tête desquels figure un Néferkarê bien que le premier nom entièrement conservé soit celui de Snéfrou, roi de la IVe dynastie. Prisse reconnut l'importance de ce monument pour l'égyptologie. La lecture de ses archives révèle qu'il décida de retirer les tables du temple car il craignait que cette partie du bâtiment, comme bien d'autres monuments – certains temples d'Esna, d'Éléphantine, d'el-Kab et même de Thèbes, par exemple –, ne fût démolie pour fabriquer de la chaux. C'était, en effet, un problème courant ; en 1841, George Glidden, ancien consul des États-Unis au Caire, avait lancé un des tout premiers appel aux savants pour qu'ils contribuent à empêcher les destructions d'objets antiques en les copiant et, dans certains cas, en les emportant. Glidden félicita Prisse pour son travail de copie et de préservation des monuments pharaoniques existants, et pour la vitesse avec laquelle il avait tenté de sauver, ou du moins de recenser, ce qu'il pouvait.

Selon d'autres savants, Prisse aurait appris que Lepsius était sur le point d'arriver à Thèbes et, par fierté nationale, il voulait s'assurer que cette pièce de choix reviendrait à la France et non à la Prusse. Si Prisse a agi comme il l'a fait, c'est peut-être pour ces deux raisons, auxquelles s'ajoutent des lettres que lui envoya Wilkinson pour lui demander instamment de copier et/ou de protéger les monuments d'une manière ou d'une autre. À la faveur de l'obscurité, pendant dix-huit nuits, il démonta, avec ses ouvriers, le mur sur lequel étaient gravées les tables royales, il emballa les reliefs dans des caisses et les entreposa dans la grande tente qu'il avait installée non loin de là. Le gouverneur de Louxor envoya des soldats qui tentèrent de reprendre les caisses, mais Prisse invoqua sa nationalité française et la protection de son gouvernement. Pendant qu'il était temporairement protégé, et après avoir versé des pots-de-vin considérables tous azimuts, il fit transporter clandestinement, de nuit, les vingt-sept grandes caisses contenant les inscriptions sur un *cange*, bateau étroit et rapide de la région, et entreprit un voyage de six jours vers le nord. À Alexandrie, ne recevant guère de soutien de la part de son gouvernement, il se livra à nouveau au versement de pots-de-vin, à des fanfaronnades et à des brutalités qui lui permirent de charger sa précieuse cargaison à bord du *Cerbère*, le 15 mai 1844. Les caisses portaient des étiquettes mentionnant des spécimens d'histoire naturelle destinés au Musée de Paris. À son arrivée en France, il remit les tables à l'État. Elles furent d'abord conservées à la Bibliothèque Nationale de France. Prisse avait élaboré un projet de conservation et de présentation. Malheureusement, l'installation eut lieu en son absence et beaucoup de tablettes furent endommagées. Par la suite, les tables furent transférées au Louvre où elles sont aujourd'hui exposées. Grâce à Prisse, cette liste de la plus haute importance peut être étudiée au Louvre, comme à distance, car Prisse en avait fait une copie très précise.

Les circonstances du départ ignominieux (et presque certainement illégal) d'Égypte l'obligèrent à rester en Europe plus longtemps que ce qu'il avait envisagé initialement. Or il y avait tellement à faire. Outre l'installation de la Chambre des Ancêtres, il lui fallait continuer à travailler. Il présenta également à la Bibliothèque Nationale le Papyrus Prisse (pBN 183–194 ; ill. 16). Avec la Chambre des Ancêtres, ce papyrus représente l'un des deux objets les plus importants que Prisse rapporta d'Égypte. Le papyrus date du Moyen Empire et comporte toute une série de préceptes moraux. Ce genre de textes de l'Égypte ancienne est composé de conseils moraux et pratiques nécessaires pour mener une vie vertueuse, accomplie et réussie. Sans doute acheté à Thèbes par Prisse, le papyrus contient une partie des *Instructions pour Kagemni*, ainsi que la seule copie complète encore existante des *Maximes de Ptahhotep*. Présenté comme l'œuvre littéraire égyptienne la plus ancienne parvenue jusqu'à nous, ce papyrus est d'une importance capitale non seulement pour l'étude philologique, mais aussi pour la compréhension des mœurs et des croyances de l'Égypte ancienne. En le recopiant soigneusement et en le publiant en 1847 *(Fac-similé d'un papyrus égyptien)*, Prisse l'a rendu accessible aux savants du monde entier.

En reconnaissance de ces dons et des recherches de Prisse sur l'Égypte ancienne, la France le décora de la Légion d'honneur. Son acquisition de la Chambre des Ancêtres fut applaudie par la presse, notamment par la *Revue archéologique*, tandis que les savants se précipitèrent pour étudier le Papyrus Prisse.

Durant son séjour en France, Prisse commença à rassembler ses notes, ses dessins et ses moulages au papier, ce qui lui permit de publier ses *Monuments égyptiens* (Paris, 1847), contenant 50 planches avant-goût de son œuvre plus ambitieuse consacrée à l'ensemble de l'art égyptien. *Les Monuments égyptiens* sont une sorte d'hommage à Champollion, pour lequel Prisse avait une immense admiration. Cet ouvrage aurait dû être un complément aux *Monuments de l'Égypte et de la Nubie* de Champollion, en comprenant cent chromolithographies de dessins qu'il avait réalisés au cours des six années précédentes sur place. Mais les contraintes financières en décidèrent autrement, ce dont Prisse s'excuse auprès du lecteur dans son introduction. Les suppressions dont il fit l'objet ne l'empêchent pas d'être un important ouvrage d'érudition. Il contient beaucoup d'éléments jusqu'alors indisponibles, datant du règne d'Akhénaton et provenant de Tounah el-Gebel et de Tell el-Amarna (*Monuments*, voir pp. 95–99), ainsi que de Thèbes. Prisse est peut-être le premier à avoir établi un répertoire quasi complet des constructions réalisées par Akhénaton à Thèbes.

Ill. 20
Émile Prisse d'Avennes
Portrait of Khaemhat found in his tomb, Qurna, 1859/60 / Bildnis des Chaemhat aus seinem Grab, Qurna / Portrait de Khâemhat relevé dans son tombeau, Gournah
Embossing on vellum paper, 35.5 x 17 cm (14 x 6 3/4 in.). Paris, Bibliothèque nationale de France

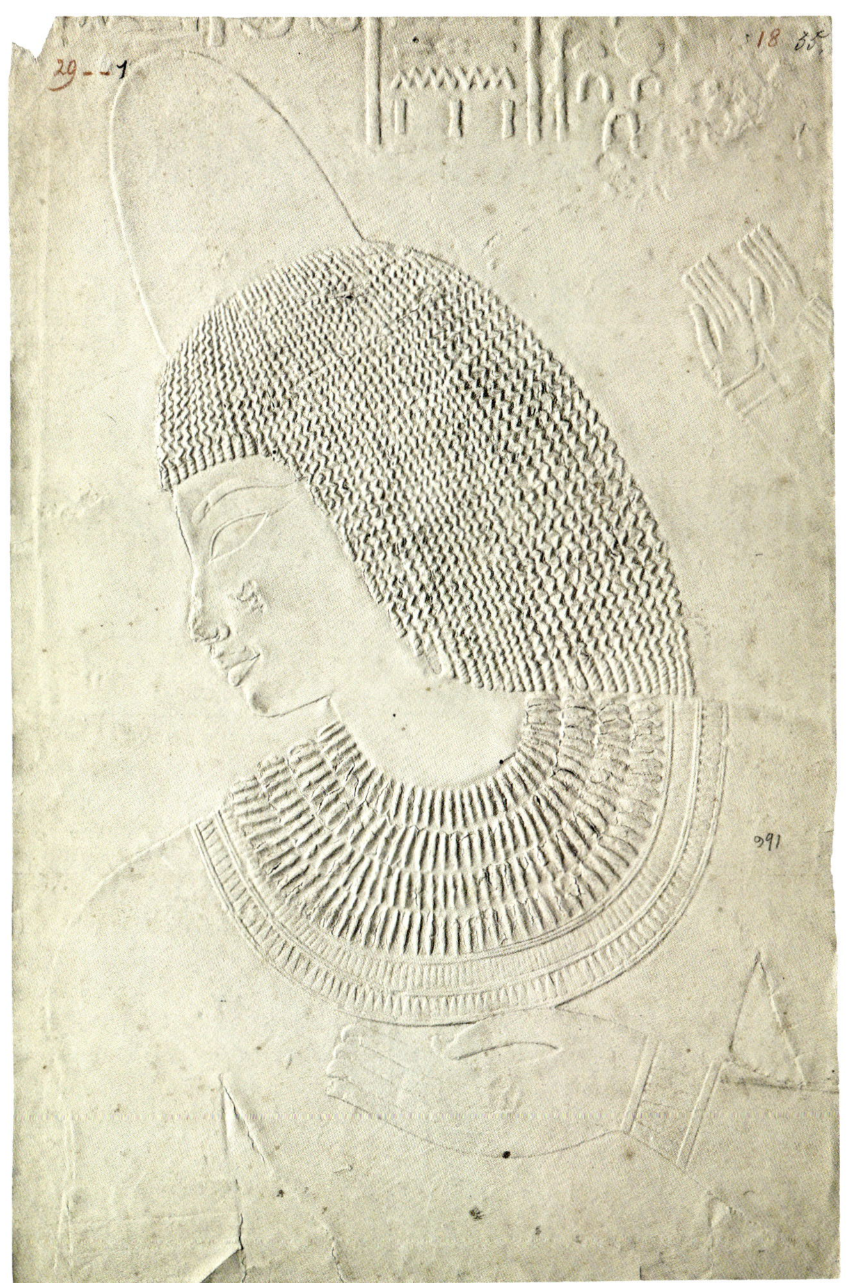

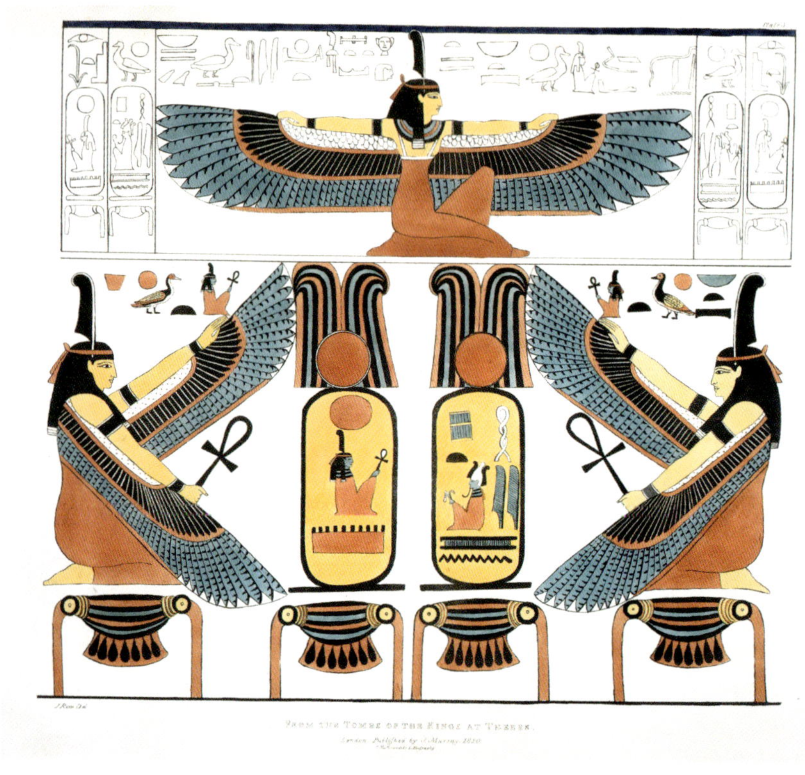

Ill. 21
J. Ricci
Mural from the Tombs of the Kings at Thebes (discov. by G. Belzoni), 1822
Wandgemälde aus den Königsgräbern in Theben (entdeckt von G. Belzoni)
Peinture murale des tombes royales à Thèbes (découverte par G. Belzoni)
Lithograph, 42.5 x 55.2 cm (16 3/4 x 21 3/4 in.). Private collection

Il sut reconnaître les différents styles de cette période et dater du règne d'Akhénaton un petit ensemble de blocs de grès *(talatat)*, mis au grand jour lorsque le troisième pylône de Karnak fut démonté pour être brûlé et transformé en chaux. Il signala ces pièces à Wilkinson et à Nestor l'Hôte (1804–1842), artiste qui avait participé à l'expédition de Champollion et auteur d'un livre épistolaire en trois volumes composé de lettres d'Égypte, ainsi qu'à Champollion-Figeac (1778–1867), frère aîné de Jean-François Champollion. La lettre de Prisse à ce dernier fut publiée, mais Prisse ne rédigea jamais d'article scientifique établissant les rapports entre les différents monuments de l'époque d'Akhénaton.

Malgré sa taille modeste, les *Monuments* de Prisse rencontrèrent un accueil très enthousiaste et furent salués par les savants et les artistes des deux côtés de la Manche. Théophile Gautier (1811–1872) affirma même que son *Roman de la momie*, sans doute la première œuvre de fiction dont le cadre est l'Égypte ancienne, fut inspiré par l'ouvrage de Prisse. Ardent avocat de Prisse, Gautier salua également la qualité artistique de son œuvre.

À la fin des années 1850, Prisse s'impatientait de retourner en Égypte pour rassembler de nouveaux objets, corriger et compléter ses travaux antérieurs, poursuivre le recensement et l'étude des monuments et rapporter de nouvelles antiquités en France. Ce n'est plus en jeune aventurier sans renom qu'il regagna l'Égypte, mais en savant reconnu, à la tête d'une petite mission officielle devant collecter et copier des antiquités égyptiennes pour la France. Parrainée par Napoléon III et financée par le ministère de l'Éducation, cette expédition dura trois ans, de 1858 à 1860. Prisse était accompagné de deux jeunes hommes, Willem de Famars Testas (1834–1896), artiste et lointain parent, et Édouard Jarrot (1835–1873 ; ill. 15), photographe.

L'Égypte de 1858 ne ressemblait guère à celle que Prisse avait connue dix ans auparavant. Peu avant son arrivée, Saïd Pacha avait créé un service des antiquités et un musée, dirigé par le Français Auguste Mariette (1821–1881). Parent de Nestor l'Hôte, Mariette faisait appliquer strictement les réglementations déjà existantes sur le traitement et le déplacement des antiquités et en édicta de nouvelles. Prisse fut donc dans l'impossibilité d'emporter le nombre et les catégories d'objets qu'il avait prévu de prendre. Loin d'être abattus par ce revers, Prisse et ses compagnons parcoururent l'Égypte, la Nubie et l'Arabie et réunirent un ensemble de plus en plus important de plans, de croquis, de moulages au papier, de frottages, de notes et de photographies (ill. 20). Le recours à la photographie est significatif, à un moment où cette technique en était encore à ses débuts. La présence d'un photographe fut très précieuse pour Prisse. Pour documenter l'architecture du Caire, Prisse s'appuya sur les travaux du daguerréotypiste Girault de Prangey (1804–1892), ainsi que, dans une moindre mesure, sur Jarrot ; en tout cas, il était ravi d'avoir son propre photographe. Menés à la baguette par Prisse, ses deux jeunes protégés furent tellement épuisés que Jarrot dut quitter le groupe rapidement, bientôt suivi de Prisse et de Testas.

En 1860, Prisse rapporta en France 300 dessins reproduisant des peintures et des reliefs issus de divers monuments (ill. 18), mesurant chacun jusqu'à sept ou huit mètres de long, 400 mètres de moulages au papier et 150 photographies de détails architecturaux et ornementaux, ainsi que des plans au sol, des plans de coupe et des élévations, sans compter une collection considérable de croquis et de notes. Il rapporta également plusieurs objets antiques, dont il fit ensuite don au Louvre, ainsi que les crânes de vingt-neuf momies dont il avait identifié l'époque, la position et le nom. S'ajoutant à ses recherches précédentes, cette récolte constitua le fondement de son grand œuvre consacré à l'art égyptien qu'il compila, avec son pendant sur l'art islamique, au cours des années suivantes, grâce aux installations de la Faculté des Sciences de Lille.

Publiée dans son intégralité en 1879, l'*Histoire de l'art égyptien* comprend deux volumes contenant 159 planches. Ceci ne représente pourtant qu'une partie de l'œuvre de Prisse. Un volume de textes, rédigés par Marchandon de la Faye à partir des notes de Prisse, parut en 1879, l'année de la disparition de ce dernier. D'autres volumes auraient peut-être été publiés si Prisse en avait eu le temps ;

en l'état, la part du lion de ses archives scientifiques (dessins, photographies, moulages au papier, notes) est conservée à la Bibliothèque Nationale, une partie de ses documents personnels se trouvant aux archives de la Société archéologique et historique d'Avesnes-sur-Helpe.

L'Histoire de l'art égyptien est une œuvre extraordinaire, même lorsqu'on la compare aux productions des grandes expéditions soutenues par l'État. Il s'agit du plus grand ensemble de comptes rendus illustrés consacrés à l'art égyptien par une seule et même personne, et, lorsqu'on l'associe à *L'Art arabe*, d'un véritable panorama complet de l'art de l'Égypte. Il y est question d'architecture, de dessin, de sculpture (bas-reliefs compris), de peinture et d'artisanat (arts mineurs), richement illustrés d'exemples. Il est intéressant de souligner que la section dévolue à l'architecture contient non seulement des images d'édifices, mais aussi des représentations antiques de bâtiments, notamment celles trouvées sur les murs des tombeaux de Tell el-Amarna (*Histoire de l'art égyptien* [*Hist.*], voir pp. 274–281). Prisse a entièrement réalisé les illustrations définitives et dirigé la fabrication de l'ouvrage, ce qui lui confère une unité et une harmonie dont d'autres compilations du XIXe siècle sont dépourvues. Parfois critiquée pour sa « joliesse », la patte de Prisse rend néanmoins justice aux scènes gravées et peintes par les artistes de l'Égypte ancienne.

La plupart de ses illustrations sont d'ailleurs beaucoup plus fidèles à la « vérité » que celles d'autres artistes ou de ses prédécesseurs, contemporains ou disciples. C'est le cas d'un croquis exemplaire, représentant des étrangers dans un tombeau de Thèbes de la XVIIIe dynastie (*Hist.*, voir p. 333) ; toutefois, sa reproduction d'une scène d'Amarna (*Hist.*, voir pp. 290–292) justifie la critique. Son œuvre se démarque nettement des illustrations des artistes de la *Description*, entre autres, qui persistaient à donner une touche de classicisme aux images de l'Égypte ancienne (ill. 19), ou qui avaient recours à un style pictural exagérément naïf, en dépit d'une réalité plus subtile, caractéristique commune à d'autres artistes (ill. 21, 22). Le *Denkmaeler* est victime de pareilles variations de qualité dans ses illustrations, notamment en raison des styles divers des artistes engagés pour les réaliser et de leur vision personnelle de l'art égyptien antique (ill. 23). Si les illustrations de Prisse sont nettes, elles n'ont rien de léché et sont plus fidèles aux images des Égyptiens de l'Antiquité.

Les magnifiques dessins d'architecture de l'*Histoire* témoignent de la formation initiale de Prisse. Plans au sol, plans de coupe, détails architecturaux et ornementation de la façade de chaque monument – comme le plan au sol et le plan de coupe du tombeau du grand prêtre Padiamenopé (ou Pétamounôph, selon Prisse ; *Hist.*, voir p. 211) ou le temple de Dendour (*Hist.*, voir p. 213), conservés au Metropolitan Museum of Art de New York – sont parfaitement documentés et représentés.

Il est même peu probable que l'on puisse faire mieux aujourd'hui. L'étude effectuée par Prisse des motifs ornementaux visibles dans les frises et sur les plafonds (*Hist.*, voir pp. 250–267) est extrêmement détaillée et précieuse : ses illustrations donnent, en effet, à voir les variations au fil du temps et font penser à des albums d'échantillons. Ces images ont eu une grande influence sur les arts mineurs et la décoration en Europe à l'époque de Prisse, ainsi que, probablement, sur les mouvements Arts and Crafts et Art Nouveau, au tournant des XIXe et XXe siècles. Certaines œuvres de *The Grammar of Ornament* d'Owen Jones (1856), qui connut une grande diffusion, rappellent les motifs égyptiens réunis par Prisse.

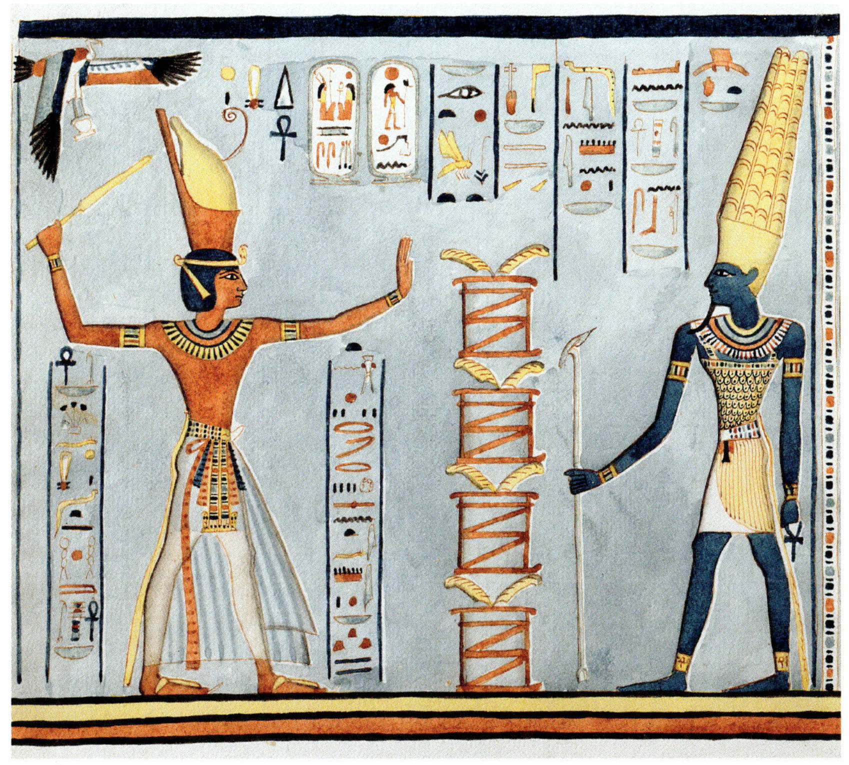

Ill. 22
Linant de Bellefonds (attr. earlier to A. Ricci)
Ramesses II offering boxes to Amun-Ra, 1819 / **Ramses II. bietet Amun-Re Gaben dar** / **Ramsès II offrant des boîtes à Amon-Rê**
Copy of a wall painting from the Great Temple at Abu Simbel for William Bankes
Watercolour on paper, 21 x 18 cm (8 1/4 x 7 1/8 in.). Dorset (UK), Kingston Lacy

Comme d'autres ouvrages de cette période toujours en usage aujourd'hui, l'œuvre de Prisse présente ce qui existait alors sur certains sites. C'est un document d'autant plus important que de nombreux sites ont été dévastés par le travail du temps et, plus fréquemment, par celui des *sebbakhin* qui les ont creusés et détruits en quête d'engrais. Poussés par la cupidité et malgré les tentatives de réglementation du déplacement d'objets antiques, les collectionneurs ont continué à extraire des reliefs de leur contexte ; les savants eux-mêmes ont retiré des objets ou abîmé irrémédiablement des reliefs à force de les mouler au papier, et ce, dans toute l'Égypte. Ce qui rend les œuvres de Prisse plus précieuses encore pour l'égyptologie moderne. La finesse d'observation et le dévouement dont il a fait preuve pour enregistrer avec précision tout ce qu'il voyait ont permis de conserver bien des objets dont, sans lui, nous n'aurions aucune connaissance aujourd'hui. Son aquarelle du sarcophage du roi Menkaourê (*Hist.*, voir p. 205) constitue une trace unique d'un objet exceptionnel, ainsi qu'un parfait exemple. Retiré de la pyramide de Menkaourê à Gizeh (2493–2475 av. J.-C.), ce sarcophage devait être transporté par bateau jusqu'en Grande-Bretagne, mais sombra dans le golfe de Gascogne lors d'une tempête. La peinture qu'en fit Prisse est l'une des rares représentations de cet objet. Son travail était d'un tel raffinement que beaucoup d'autres savants lui confièrent les illustrations de leurs ouvrages ou utilisèrent les siennes, de qualité bien supérieure à tout ce que l'on pouvait trouver à l'époque. Ses illustrations en couleur évoquent de façon tangible l'impression que pouvaient produire, dès leur achèvement, les peintures murales égyptiennes (*Hist.*, voir p. 483). Aujourd'hui encore, l'œuvre artistique de Prisse perdure comme source d'illustrations et embellit bien des ouvrages, qu'ils soient savants (comme ceux du grand égyptologue Gaston Maspero et du célèbre historien de l'art Jean Capart) ou vulgarisation (comme le volumineux *Ancient Egypt or Mizraïm* de Samuel Augustus Binion). On les trouve aussi reproduites sur des supports moins nobles, les cartes postales et les T-shirts qui se vendent actuellement en Égypte.

Prisse avait acquis une compréhension très complète de l'art égyptien ; il est l'un des tout premiers savants à avoir remarqué le système de quadrillage égyptien et à en avoir rendu compte avec précision (p. ex. *Hist.*, voir pp. 329, 331). Il s'agit du canon des proportions observé par les Égyptiens pour leurs dessins ; dans sa période la plus classique, la figure principale d'une scène mesure dix-huit « poings », ou carrés, de la plante du pied à la racine des cheveux (*Hist.*, voir p. 329). Les autres figures représentent des moitiés, des quarts, etc., de la figure principale, selon leur importance relative. Ce système constitue le fondement de tout l'art égyptien ; en l'identifiant, Prisse a réalisé l'une des contributions savantes les plus cruciales pour son étude. La compréhension de ce système lui a peut-être aussi permis d'effectuer des copies plus fidèles que celles de ses contemporains. Son utilisation de la couleur est d'une grande sensibilité et nous est précieuse aujourd'hui pour avoir une idée des pièces antiques originales. En outre, grâce à la photographie, Prisse a pu rendre compte des monuments avec une précision accrue ; ses prises de vues constituent une source d'information inestimable pour la connaissance de scènes et de bâtiments détruits depuis longtemps. Il est étonnant qu'en dépit des excellents résultats produits par cette technique visuelle, la photographie n'ait pas été mise plus tôt au service de l'égyptologie savante. Une grande partie des monuments répertoriés par Prisse, grâce à la photographie, au dessin ou au moulage au papier, a aujourd'hui disparu ; son œuvre demeure le seul témoignage de ces constructions et du savoir-faire des Égyptiens de l'Antiquité.

Prisse nous a laissé une recension précise et fine de l'art égyptien sur trois millénaires d'histoire de l'Égypte (et au-delà de l'Égypte), nourrie par une compréhension sans précédent de l'architecture, de la sculpture, de la peinture et de l'artisanat de l'Égypte ancienne. Le savant fait preuve non seulement de son talent d'artiste, mais aussi d'une connaissance parfaite des contextes historiques, sociaux et religieux dans lesquels sont nées ces productions. Les œuvres encyclopédiques de Prisse d'Avennes en sont d'autant plus fondamentales pour l'étude de l'Égypte ancienne.

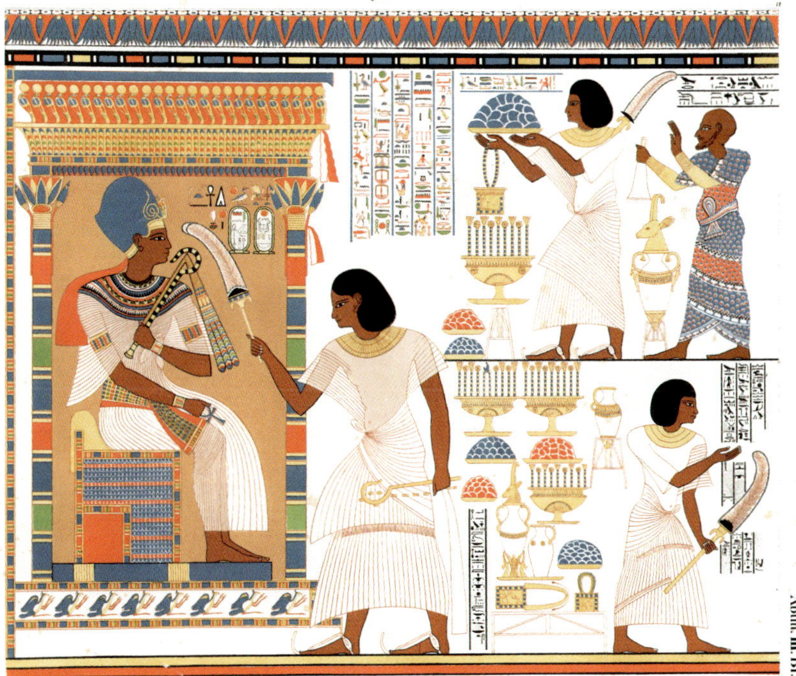

Ill. 23

Tutankhamun and Huy, Theban Tomb at Qurnet Murai / Tutanchamun und Huy, thebisches Grab in Qurnet Murrai / Toutânkhamon et Houy, tombe thébienne à Gournet Mourraï

in: Karl Richard Lepsius, *Denkmaeler aus Aegypten und Aethiopien*, Berlin, 1849–1859, vol. III, pl. 115

Göttingen, Niedersächsische Staats- und Universitätsbibliothek

Egyptian Monuments

Ägyptische Baudenkmäler / Monuments égyptiens
(Paris, 1847)

Page/Seite 66

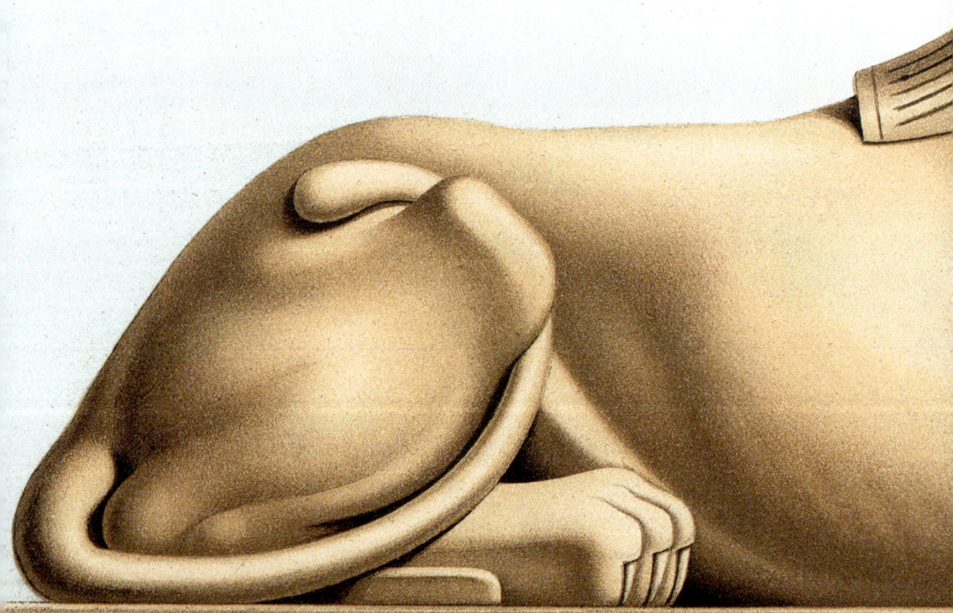

History of Egyptian Art

Geschichte der ägyptischen Kunst / Histoire de l'art égyptien
(Paris, 1878/79)

Page/Seite 192

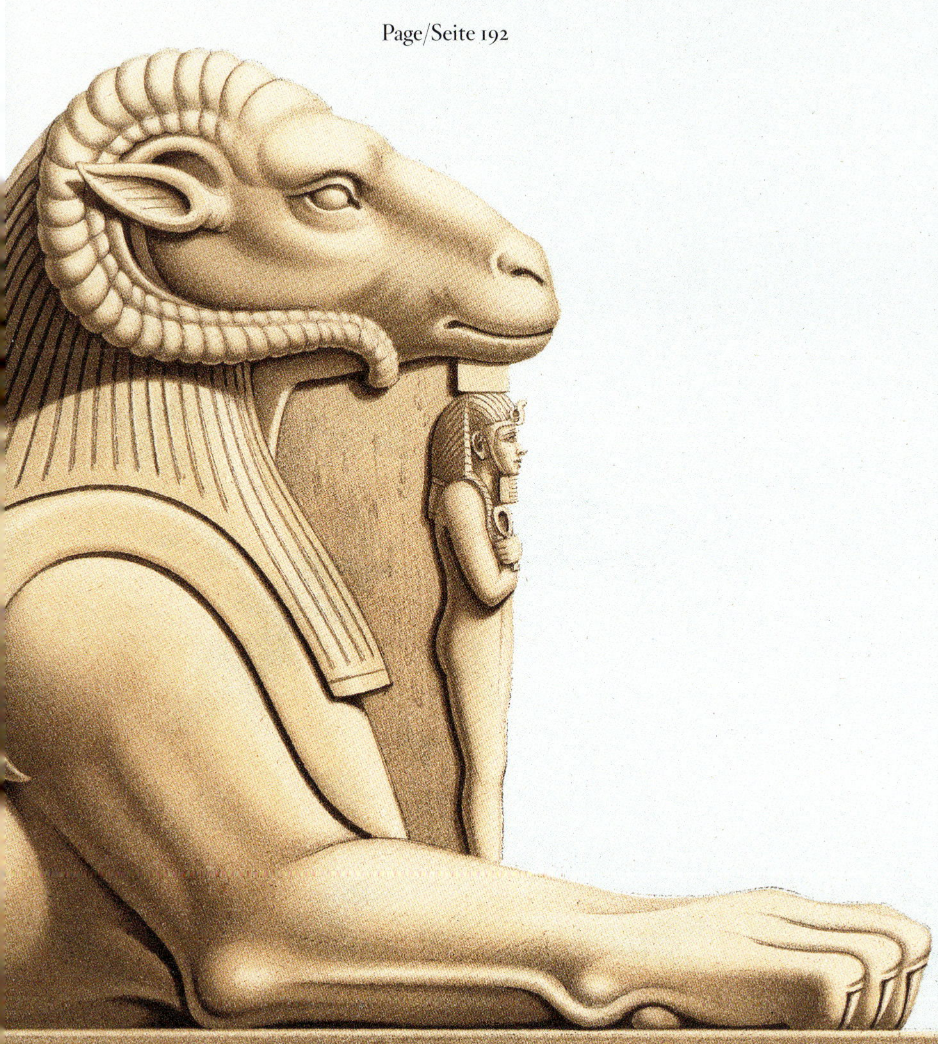

THÈBES. PA

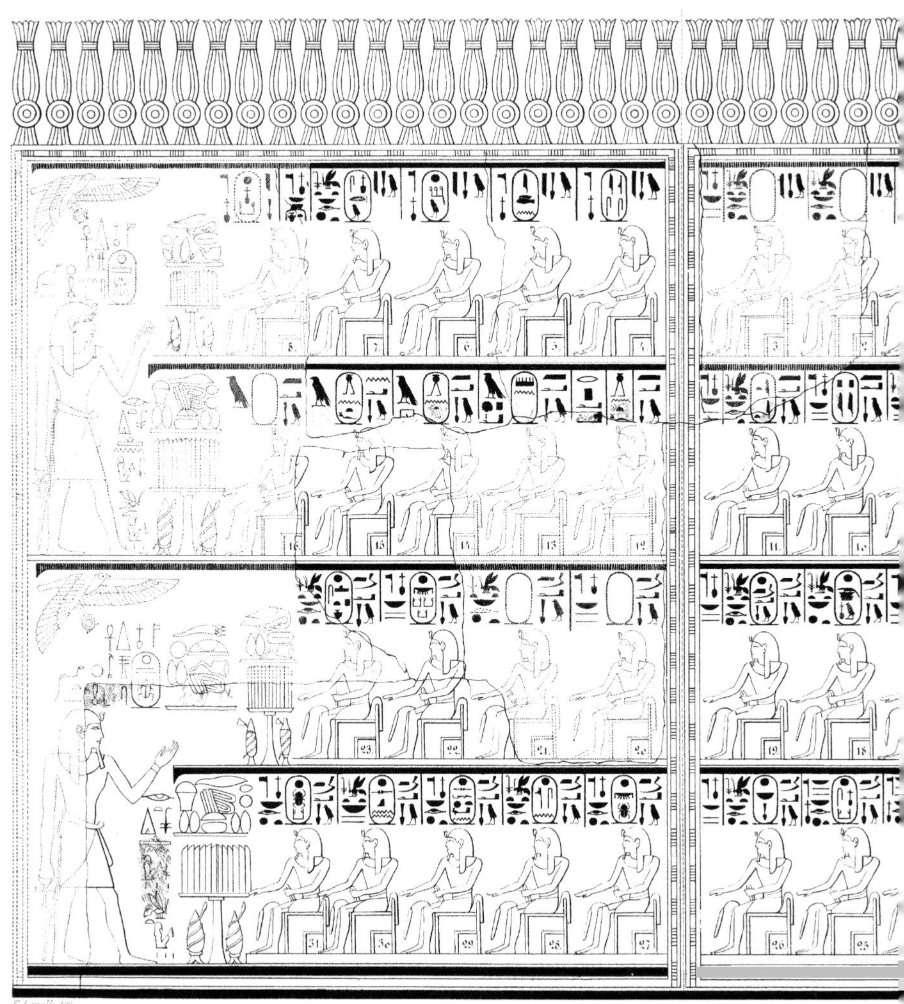

F. Lepelle lith.

SALLE DES ANCÊTRES OU

Transportée à la

EURS DE THOUTMES III.

ale de Paris?.

ABYDOS (HARA

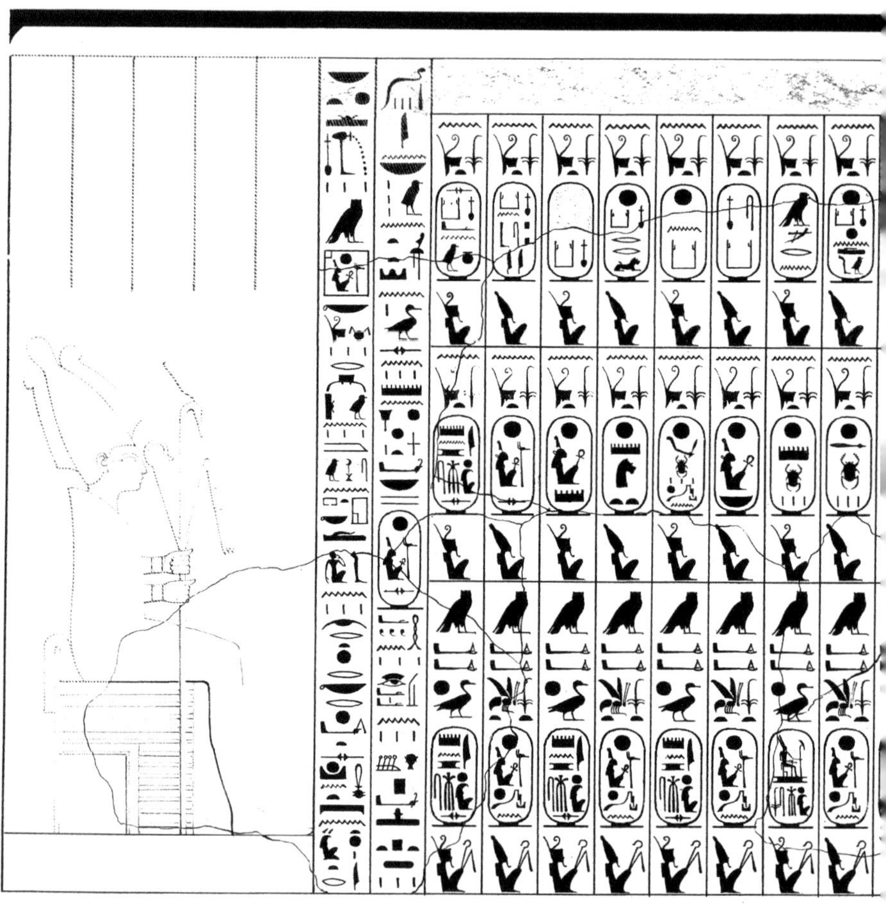

G. Barry, lith.

TABLEAU DES ANCÊTRES

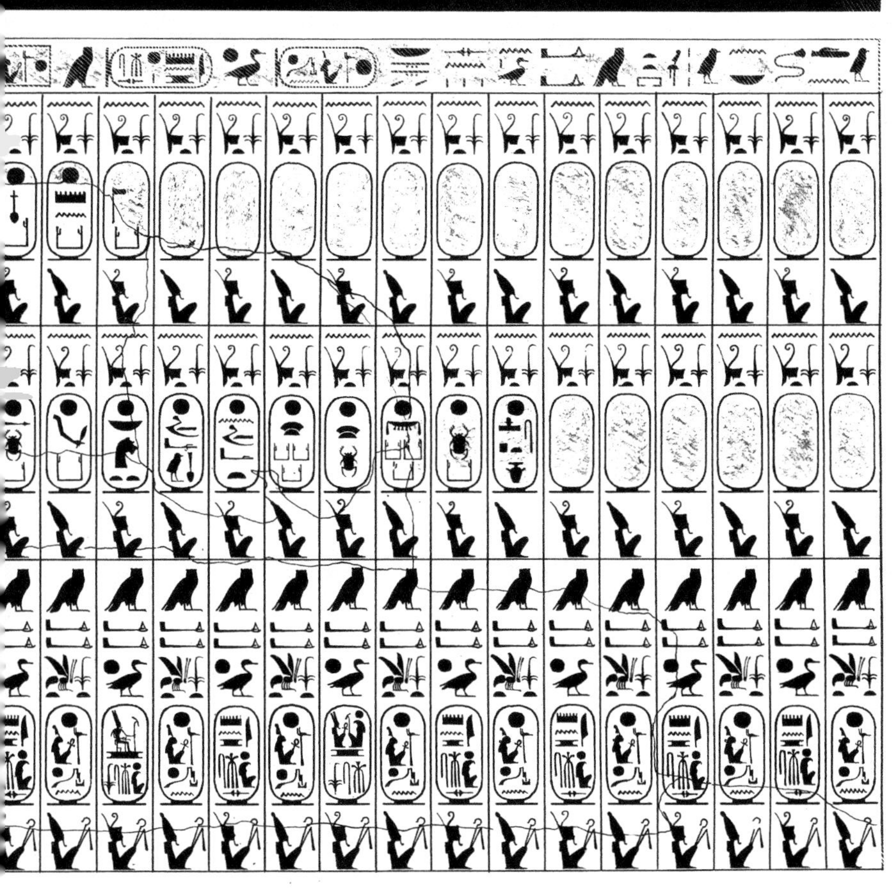

Imp. Kaeppelin & Cie

CESSEURS DE RAMSÈS II.

(Pages/Seite 66/67)

THEBES. PALACE OF KARNAK

Chamber of the ancestors or predecessors of Thutmosis III

Drawing worked from three walls in the chamber of the ancestors or predecessors of Thutmosis III, in the palace of Karnak in Thebes. I transported this precious document to France in 1844 and presented it to the Bibliothèque Royale in Paris. The stippled parts are missing in the original and have been restored in character with stamps, figures and inscriptions found nearby, with the exception of the cartouches, which have been left empty.

THEBEN. PALAST VON KARNAK

Saal der Ahnen oder Vorgänger von Thutmosis III.

Rekonstruktionszeichnung der drei Wände aus dem Saal der Ahnen oder Vorgänger von Thutmosis III. im Palast von Karnak in Theben. Im Jahre 1844 habe ich dieses wertvolle Dokument nach Frankreich verbracht und es der Königlichen Bibliothek von Paris zum Geschenk gemacht. Im Original fehlen die gestrichelten Bereiche, die – mit Ausnahme der von uns leer gelassenen Kartuschen – nach Abklatschen, Zeichnungen und benachbarten Hieroglypheninschriften rekonstruiert sind.

THÈBES. PALAIS DE KARNAC

Salle des ancêtres ou prédécesseurs de Thoutmès III

Développement des trois parois de la salle des ancêtres ou prédécesseurs de Thoutmès [Thoutmôsis] III, dans le palais de Karnac, à Thèbes. J'ai transporté ce précieux document en France en 1844, et j'en ai fait don à la Bibliothèque royale de Paris. Les parties pointillées manquent dans l'original, et ont été restituées d'après les estampages, les figures, et les légendes voisines, à l'exception des cartouches qu'on a laissés vides.

(Pages/Seite 68/69)

ABYDOS. EL ARABA EL-MADFUNA

Table of the ancestors or predecessors of Ramesses II

Table of the ancestors or predecessors of Ramesses II, taken from the temple of Osiris in el Araba el-Madfuna, the ancient Abydos. This inscription was part of a bas-relief which filled the entire width of one wall of a small chamber situated close to the adytum. To obtain the drawing which I have published here, I have collated with the copy I made of the original those documents as provided by the plate published by M[onsieur] F[rédéric] Cailliaud and that published by Sir G[ardner] Wilkinson. I have combined these three copies with some fragments collected on site. I have carefully marked all the characters which are no longer visible on the original, so that these characters can be judged solely on their own merit.

ABYDOS. EL ARABA EL-MADFUNA

Tafel der Ahnen oder Vorgänger von Ramses II.

Tafel der Ahnen oder Vorgänger von Ramses II. aus dem Osiris-Heiligtum in El Araba el-Madfuna, dem ehemaligen Abydos. Diese Inschrift war Bestandteil eines Flachreliefs, das die ganze Breite der Mauer eines kleinen, in der Nähe des Adytons gelegenen Raumes einnahm. Um die hier vorgelegte Zeichnung zu erhalten, habe ich die am Original angefertigte Kopie mit den Unterlagen kombiniert, die durch die Veröffentlichung der Tafeln von M[onsieur] F[rédéric] Cailliaud und von Sir G[ardner] Wilkinson verfügbar wurden. Ich habe die drei Kopien durch einige vor Ort aufgesammelte Bruchstücke ergänzt. Besondere Sorgfalt habe ich darauf verwendet, alle im Original nicht mehr vorhandenen Schriftzeichen zu stricheln, um den Buchstaben nur die Aussagekraft zu verleihen, die ihnen tatsächlich zukommt.

ABYDOS. HARABAH EL-MADFOUNEH

Tableau des ancêtres ou prédécesseurs de Ramsès II

Table des ancêtres ou prédécesseurs de Ramsès II, tirée du temple d'Osiris, à Harabah el-Madfouneh, l'ancienne Abydos. Cette inscription faisait partie d'un bas-relief qui occupait toute la largeur du mur d'une petite salle située près de l'adytum. Pour obtenir le dessin que je publie, j'ai réuni à la copie faite sur l'original les documents que me fournissaient la planche publiée par M[onsieur] F[rédéric] Cailliaud et celle de sir G[ardner] Wilkinson. J'ai combiné ces trois copies avec quelques débris recueillis sur les lieux. J'ai eu soin de ponctuer tous les signes qui n'existent plus sur l'original, afin de donner seulement à ces caractères l'autorité qu'ils méritent.

NÉCROPO

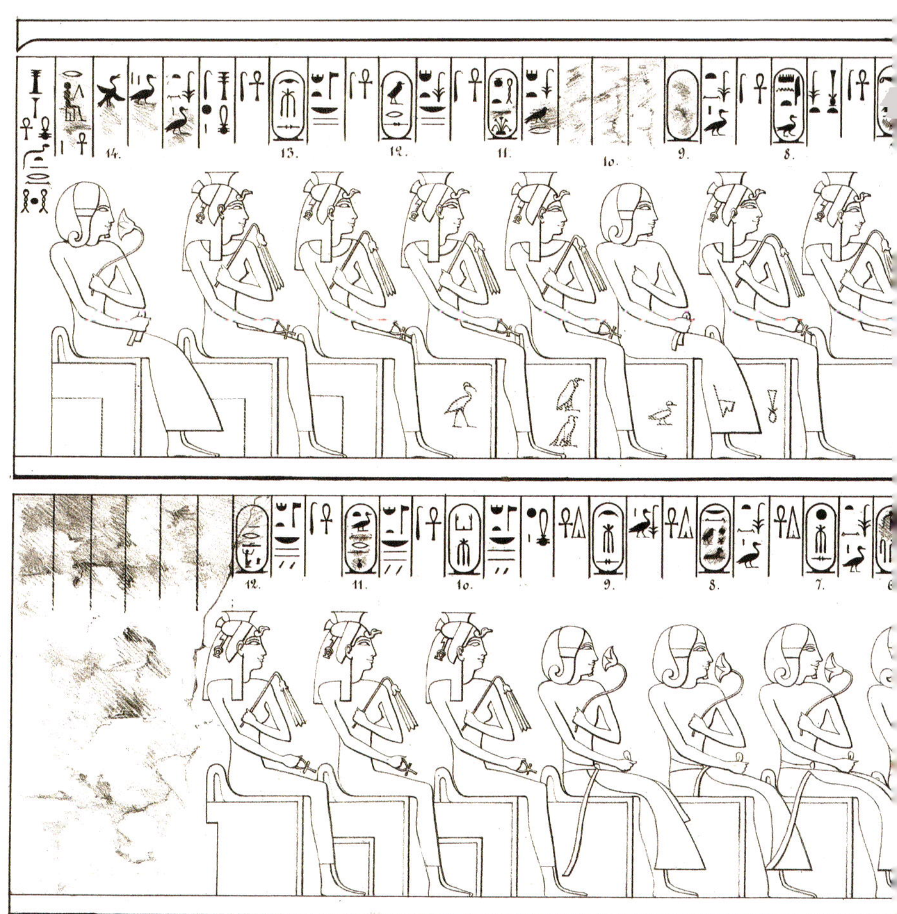

F. Lepelle lith.

TABLEAU DE LA I

tiré du tombeau de Souhem

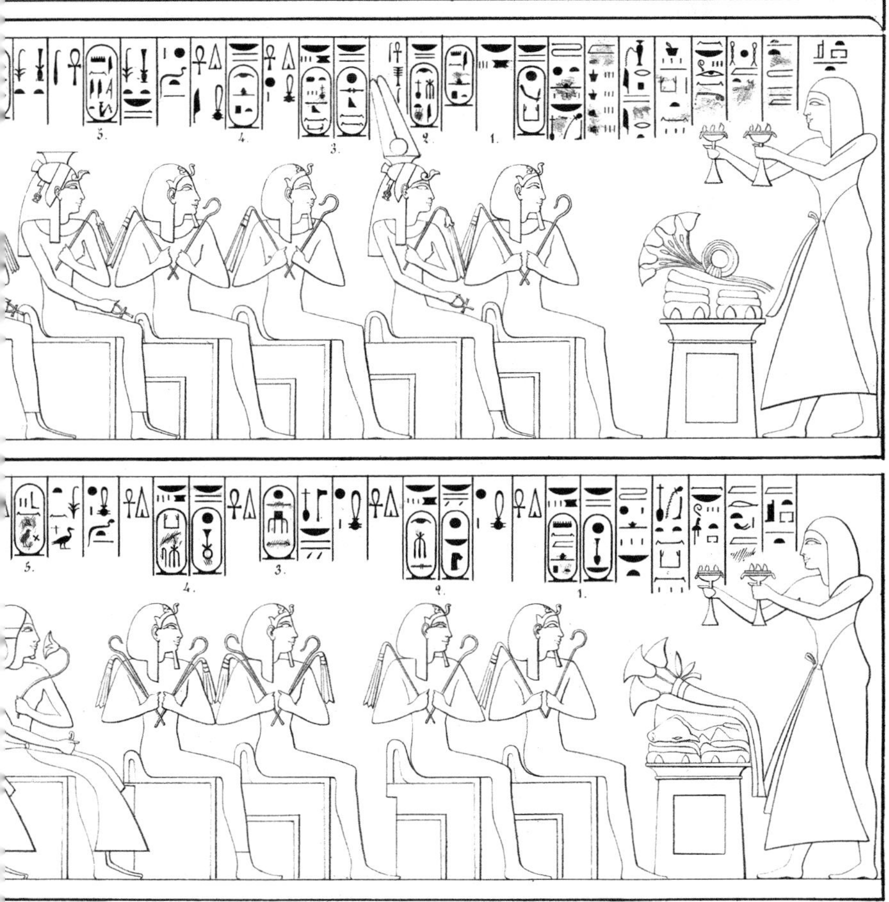

Imp. Kaeppelin & Cie

AMOUNÔPH 1ER.

otice dans la salle du trône.

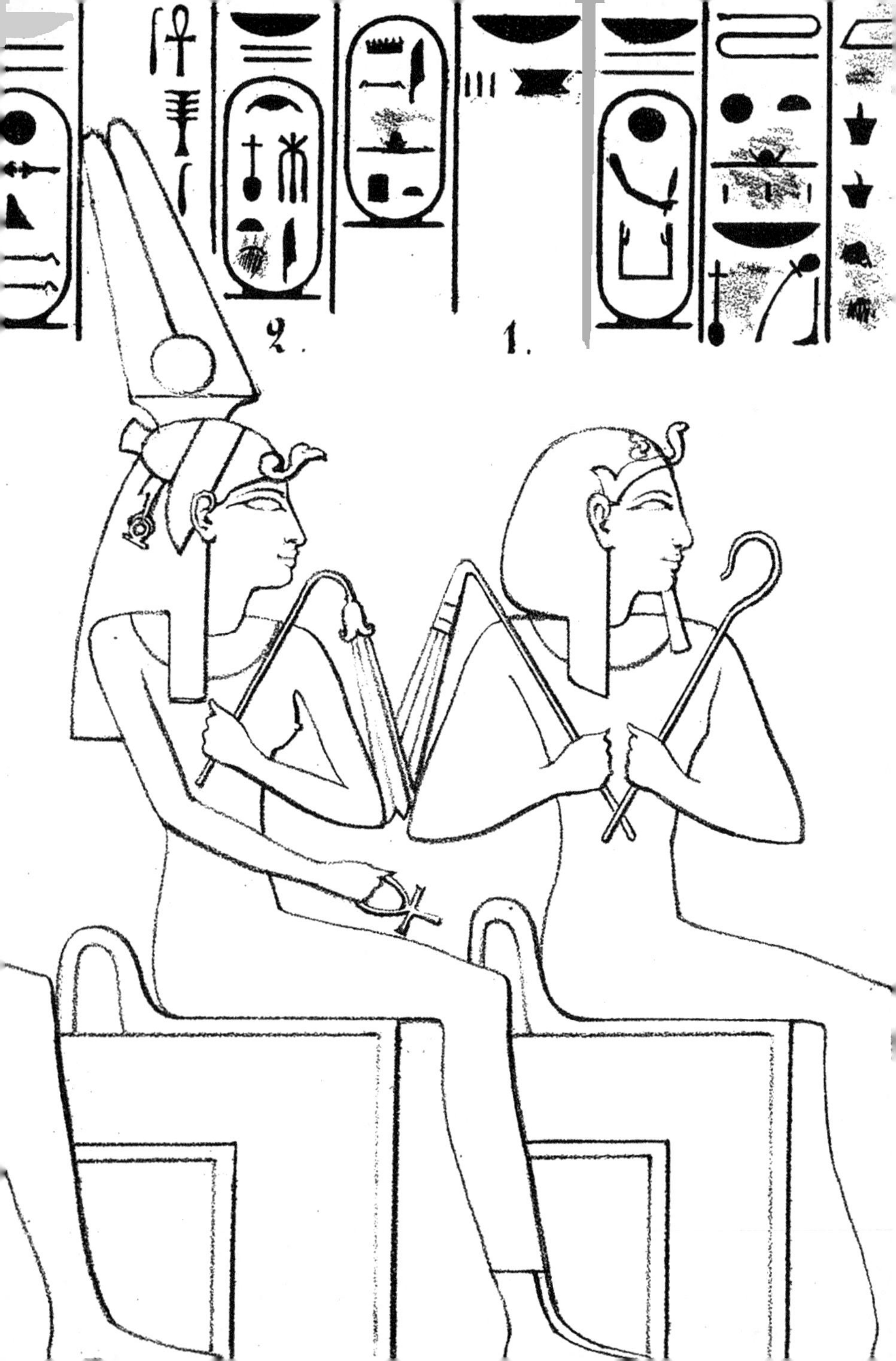
2.
1.

(Pages/Seite 72/73)

NECROPOLIS OF THEBES

Tableau of the family of Amenophis I

Tableau showing the family members of Amenophis I and of a number of his predecessors, taken from the tomb of Sonhem [Khabekhnet, temp. Ramesses II], the legal auditor of the throne-room. The hypogeum of this high-ranking functionary is situated in Thebes, in the small valley which leads from the temple of Maat and Hathor to the palace of Medinet Habu. This family list is extremely interesting: it gives not only the names of the wives and children of Amenophis but also makes it possible to see how Ahmose I, founder of the 18th Dynasty, was linked by a series of alliances to Menemhotep-Ranebtu [Mentuhotep II Nebhepetre], while the first wife of Amenophis, who succeeded the first of these princes, is placed immediately beside Sekenenra, who appears to be the predecessor of Ahmose. This table offers a striking exception to the general rule that the names of princes who have never reigned or of princesses who were never wives of kings are never enclosed in a cartouche.

NEKROPOLE VON THEBEN

Bild der Familie von Amenophis I.

Bild der Familienmitglieder und einiger Vorgänger von Amenophis I. aus dem Grab von Sonhem [Khabekhnet, Regierungszeit von Ramses II.], dem Rechtsvorsteher im Thronsaal. Das Hypogäum dieses hohen Beamten befindet sich in einem kleinen Tal in Theben, das vom Tempel der Maat und der Hathor zum Palast von Medinet Habu führt. Diese Auflistung der Familie ist äußerst aufschlussreich: Sie enthält nicht nur die Namen der Ehefrauen und Kinder von Amenophis I., sondern sie zeigt auch, wie sich Ahmose I. – der Begründer der 18. Dynastie – durch eine Reihe von Schwägerschaften mit Ménémotp-Ranebtou [Mentuhotep II. Nebhapetre] verband, während die erste Gemahlin von Amenophis I. – der auf den ersten der genannten Prinzen folgte – direkt neben Sekenenra dargestellt ist, der somit als Vorgänger von Ahmose I. erscheint. Dieses Bild stellt eine bemerkenswerte Ausnahme von der allgemeinen Regel dar, nach der die Namen von Prinzen, die nicht regiert haben, oder von Prinzessinnen, die keine königlichen Gemahlinnen waren, niemals in einer Kartusche erscheinen.

NÉCROPOLE DE THÈBES

Tableau de la famille d'Amounôph Ier

Tableau des membres de la famille d'Amounôph [Aménophis] Ier et de plusieurs de ses prédécesseurs, tiré du tombeau de Sonhem [Khâbekhnet, sous le règne de Ramsès II], auditeur de justice dans la salle du trône. L'hypogée de ce haut fonctionnaire est situé à Thèbes, dans la petite vallée qui conduit du temple de Tmei [Maât]et Hathor au palais de Medineh-Tabou [Médinet Habou]. Cette liste de famille est fort intéressante : elle donne non-seulement les noms des épouses et des enfants d'Amounôph, mais elle fait voir comment Ahmès [Amôsis], chef de la XVIIIe dynastie, se rattachait par une suite d'alliances à Ménémotp-Ranebtou [Montouhotep II Nebhépetrê], tandis qu'Amounôph, qui succéda au premier de ces princes, placé immédiatement – à côté de sa première épouse – Ra-Skenn [Séqénenrê], qui paraît être le prédécesseur d'Ahmès. Ce tableau offre une notable exception à la règle générale, à savoir que les noms de princes qui n'ont point régné, ou ceux des princesses qui n'étaient point épouses de rois, ne sont jamais enfermés dans un cartouche.

EGYPTIAN MONUMENTS

Documents relating to the 18th Dynasty

No. 1. Stele in fine-grained limestone, whose workmanship and style belong to the finest period of Egyptian art. It portrays king Menkheperre (throne name of Thutmosis III), followed by a princess whose name is Mauthirites who is described as priestess of the goddesses Mut and Hathor, worshipping with her father the first of these two divinities. Nos. 2 and 3. Fragments of two inscriptions in the same style and engraved on similar stone, which undoubtedly both belong to the same monument. They contain cartouches of the early kings of the 18th Dynasty, amongst whom one whose name is Ahmose takes part in a number of military expeditions in various countries.

ÄGYPTISCHE DENKMÄLER

Belege zur 18. Dynastie

Nr. 1. Stele aus feinkörnigem Kalkstein, die in Stil und Ausführung der besten Zeit der ägyptischen Kunst zugehört. Sie stellt den König Menkheperre (Thronname von Thutmosis III.) dar, gefolgt von einer Prinzessin namens Mauthirites, die als Priesterin der Göttinnen Mut und Hathor bezeichnet wird und gemeinsam mit ihrem Vater die erste der genannten Gottheiten anbetet. Nr. 2 und 3. Fragmente zweier Inschriften, die in übereinstimmendem Stil in zwei ähnliche Steine eingraviert sind und zweifellos zu ein und demselben Denkmal gehörten. Sie weisen Kartuschen der ersten Könige der 18. Dynastie auf, unter denen einer namens Ahmose an mehreren Feldzügen in verschiedenen Ländern teilgenommen hat.

MONUMENTS ÉGYPTIENS

Documents relatifs à la XVIIIe dynastie

N° 1. Stèle en calcaire d'un grain fin, d'un travail et d'un style qui appartiennent au plus beau temps de l'art égyptien. Elle représente le roi Rementor ([Menkhéperrê] prénom de Thoutmès [Thoutmôsis] III), suivi d'une princesse nommée Mauthirites, qualifiée de prêtresse des déesses Mauth [Mout] et Hathor, adorant avec son père la première de ces divinités. N°s 2 et 3. Fragments de deux inscriptions d'un même style, gravées sur des pierres semblables, et qui appartenaient incontestablement à un même monument. Elles contiennent des cartouches des premiers rois de la XVIIIe dynastie, sous lesquels un nommé Ahmès [Amôsis] prit part à plusieurs expéditions militaires, faites en divers pays.

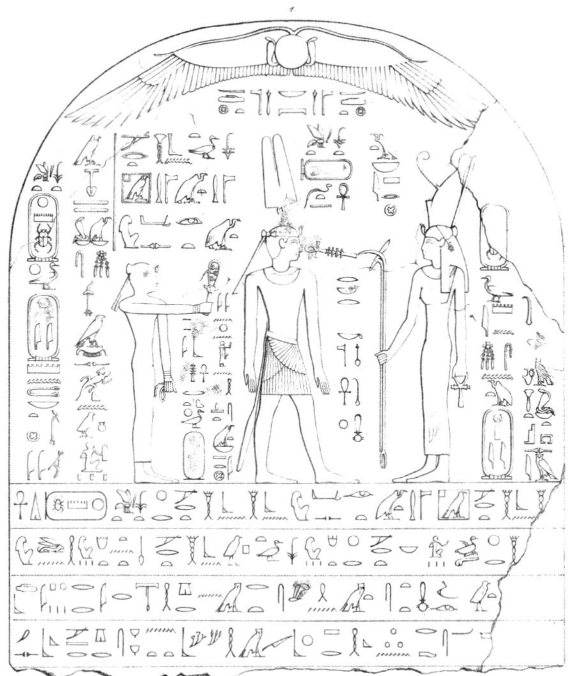

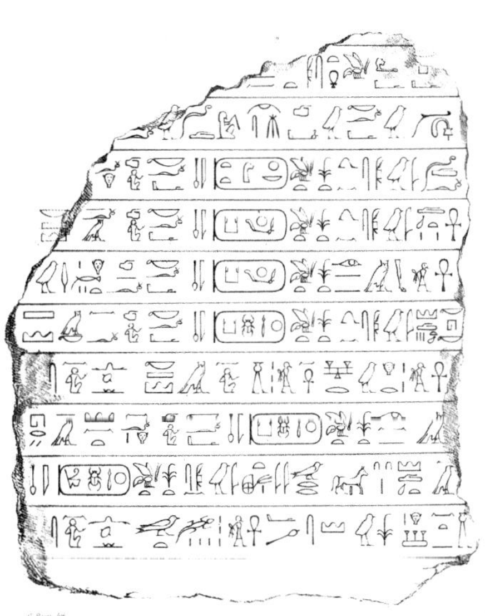

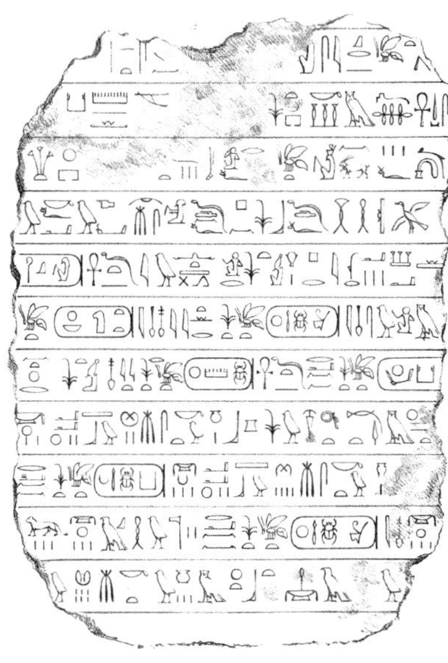

G. Barry lith. F. Prisse Imp. Kaeppelin & Cie.

DOCUMENTS RELATIFS A LA XVIIIe DYNASTIE.

HYPOGEA OF QASR EL-SAID. CHENOBOSKION

1. Worship scene engraved at the entrance to the main hypogeum. 2. Plan of this hypogeum. 3. & 4. Inscriptions

Scene of worship and inscriptions from the hypogea at Qasr el-Said, the Chenoboskion of the Greeks. No. 1. Worship scene engraved at the entrance of the hypogeum, whose plan is given below. No. 2. Plan of the main hypogeum. No. 3. Inscription engraved inside the tomb. From this we learn that Tjauti must have lived during the reigns of three pharaohs, [Pepi I] Meryre, Merenre and [Pepi II] Neferkare. No. 4. Inscription engraved on the surround of the door into another hypogeum. The characters inside the cartouche can be read as Pepi.

HYPOGÄEN VON KASR ES-SAYAD. CHENOBOSKION

1. In den Eingangsbereich des Haupt-Hypogäums eingravierte Proskynema. 2. Grundriss des Hypogäums. 3. & 4. Inschriften

Proskynema und Inschriften aus den Hypogäen von Kasr es-Sayad, dem griechischen Chenoboskion. Nr. 1. In den Eingangsbereich des Hypogäums, dessen Grundriss nachfolgend abgebildet ist, eingravierte Proskynema. Nr. 2. Grundriss des Haupt-Hypogäums. Nr. 3. Im Inneren des Grabes eingravierte Inschrift. Aus dieser geht hervor, dass Tjauti unter drei Pharaonen gelebt haben muss: [Pepi I.] Merire, Merenre und [Pepi II.] Neferkare. Nr. 4. In die Zarge der Eingangstür eines anderen Hypogäums eingravierte Inschrift. Die in der Kartusche befindlichen Schriftzeichen lesen sich Pepi.

HYPOGÉES DE QASR-ESSAYD. CHÉNOBOSCION

1. Proscynème gravé à l'entrée de l'hypogée principal. 2. Plan de cet hypogée. 3. & 4. Inscriptions

Proscynème et inscriptions des hypogées de Qasr-Essayd, la Chénoboscion des Grecs. N° 1. Proscynème gravé à l'entrée de l'hypogée dont le plan est figuré au-dessous. N° 2. Plan de l'hypogée principal. N° 3. Inscription gravée dans l'intérieur du tombeau. Elle nous apprend que Tiouta a dû vivre sous trois pharaons, [Pépi I] Maïré [Méryrê], Réméran [Mérenrê] et [Pépi II] Nofrekaré. N° 4. Inscription gravée sur le chambranle de la porte d'entrée d'un autre hypogée. Les caractères qui entrent dans ce cartouche peuvent se lire Papi [Pépi].

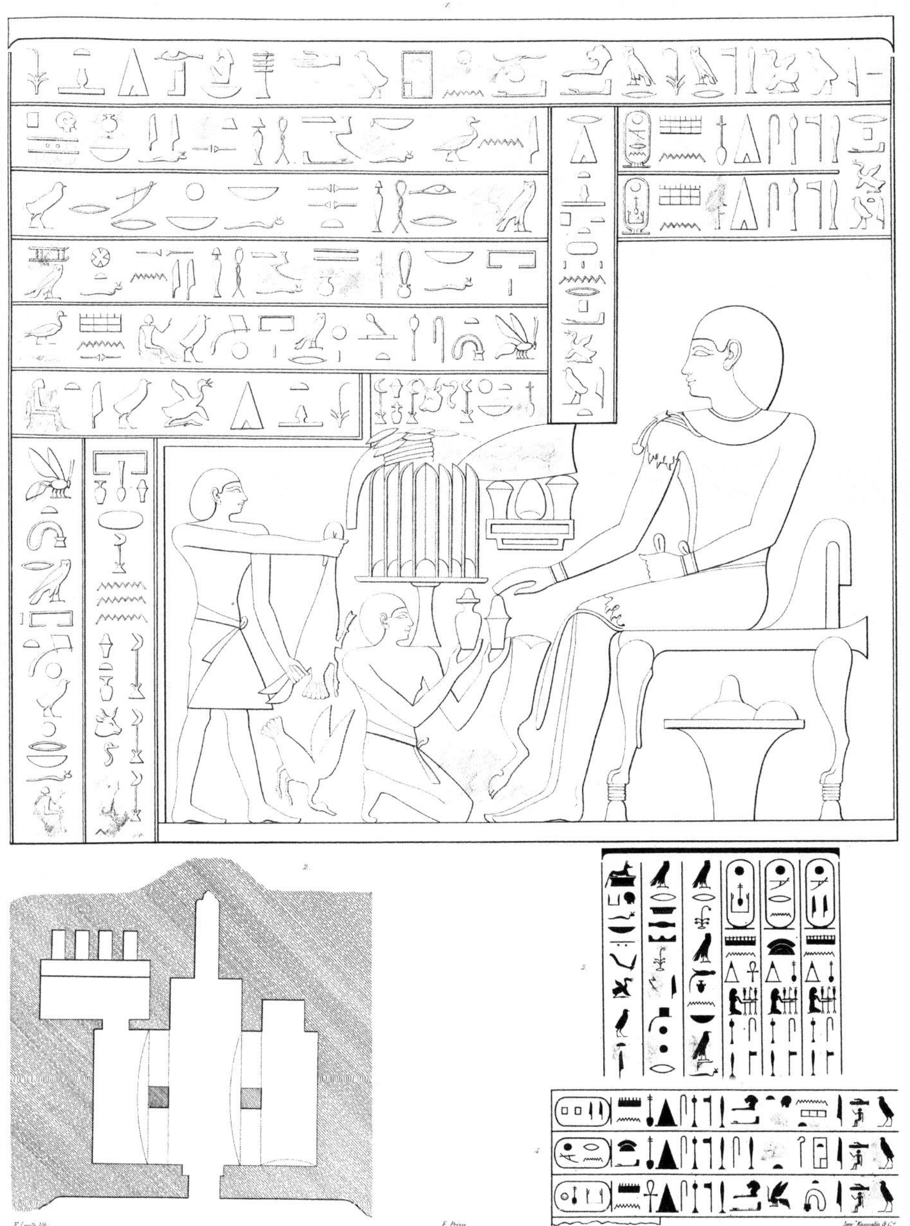

1, PROSCYNÈME GRAVÉ A L'ENTRÉE DE L'HYPOGÉE PRINCIPAL. 2, PLAN DE CET HYPOGÉE. 3 & 4 INSCRIPTIONS.

VALLEY OF QUSAIR

Inscriptions engraved on the rocks at Wadi Hammamat

No. 1. Bas-relief dedicated to Amun-Ra. No. 2. Fragment of a large inscription. This vertical legend contains the banner and the titles of a pharaoh whose cartouche was not finished. No. 3. Inscription of the 27th day of Epiphi, year 18 of the reign of Meryre. No. 4. Inscription with the complete titulary of Pepi I Meryre, whose two cartouches, which are almost always separate, are here joined together in a way which leaves no doubt as to their association. No. 5. Act of worship by Pet-Osiris before the great Horus, son of Isis. No. 6. Worship of Hor-Amun. No. 7. Worship scene of a pharaoh whose prenomen can be found in the table from the chamber of the ancestors, number 17 in the series on the right. No. 8. The first cartouche of this inscription contains characters which are so worn that their reading is uncertain. No. 9. Another worship scene of Mentuhotep, the beloved of Soba.

TAL VON QUSAIR

In die Felsen von Wadi Hammamat eingravierte Inschriften

Nr. 1. Ein dem Amun-Re geweihtes Flachrelief. Nr. 2. Bruchstück einer großen Inschrift. Diese vertikale Hieroglypheninschrift enthält Namen und Titulatur eines Pharaos, dessen Kartusche unveröffentlicht war. Nr. 3. Inschrift vom 27. Tag des [Monats] Epiphi im 18. Jahr der Herrschaft von Merire. Nr. 4. Inschrift mit den vollständigen Hieroglyphen von Pepi I. Merire, dessen zwei – nahezu immer einzeln vorkommende – Kartuschen hier gemeinsam vertreten sind, sodass an ihrer Zusammengehörigkeit kein Zweifel besteht. Nr. 5. Anbetungshandlung des Petosiris vor Horus dem Großen, Sohn der Isis. Nr. 6. Proskynema an Hor-Amun. Nr. 7. Proskynema eines Pharaos, dessen Vorname sich auch auf dem Bild vom Saal der Ahnen findet, unter Nr. 17 der rechten Reihe. Nr. 8. Die erste Kartusche dieser Inschrift enthält sehr stark verwitterte Schriftzeichen, die nicht sicher zu entziffern sind. Nr. 9. Weiteres Proskynema des von Soba geliebten Mentuhotep.

VALLÉE DE QOSSEYR

Inscriptions gravées sur les rochers d'el-Hamamat

N° 1. Bas-relief consacré à Amon-Ra. N° 2. Fragment d'une grande inscription. Cette légende verticale contient la bannière et les titres d'un pharaon dont le cartouche était inédit. N° 3. Inscription du 27e jour d'Épêp [Epiphi], l'an 18 du règne de [Pépi I] Maïré [Méryrê]. N° 4. Inscription qui porte la légende complète de [Pépi I] Maïré-Papi, dont les deux cartouches, presque toujours isolés, se trouvent ici réunis de façon à ne laisser aucun doute sur leur liaison. N° 5. Acte d'adoration de Pet-Osiris au grand Horus, fils d'Isis. N° 6. Proscynème à Horammon. N° 7. Proscynème d'un pharaon dont le prénom se retrouve sur le tableau de la chambre des ancêtres, N° 17 de la série droite. N° 8. Le premier cartouche de cette inscription contient des caractères tellement frustes, que sa lecture est douteuse. N° 9. Autre proscynème de Mentouôpht [Mentouhotep], l'aimé de Soba.

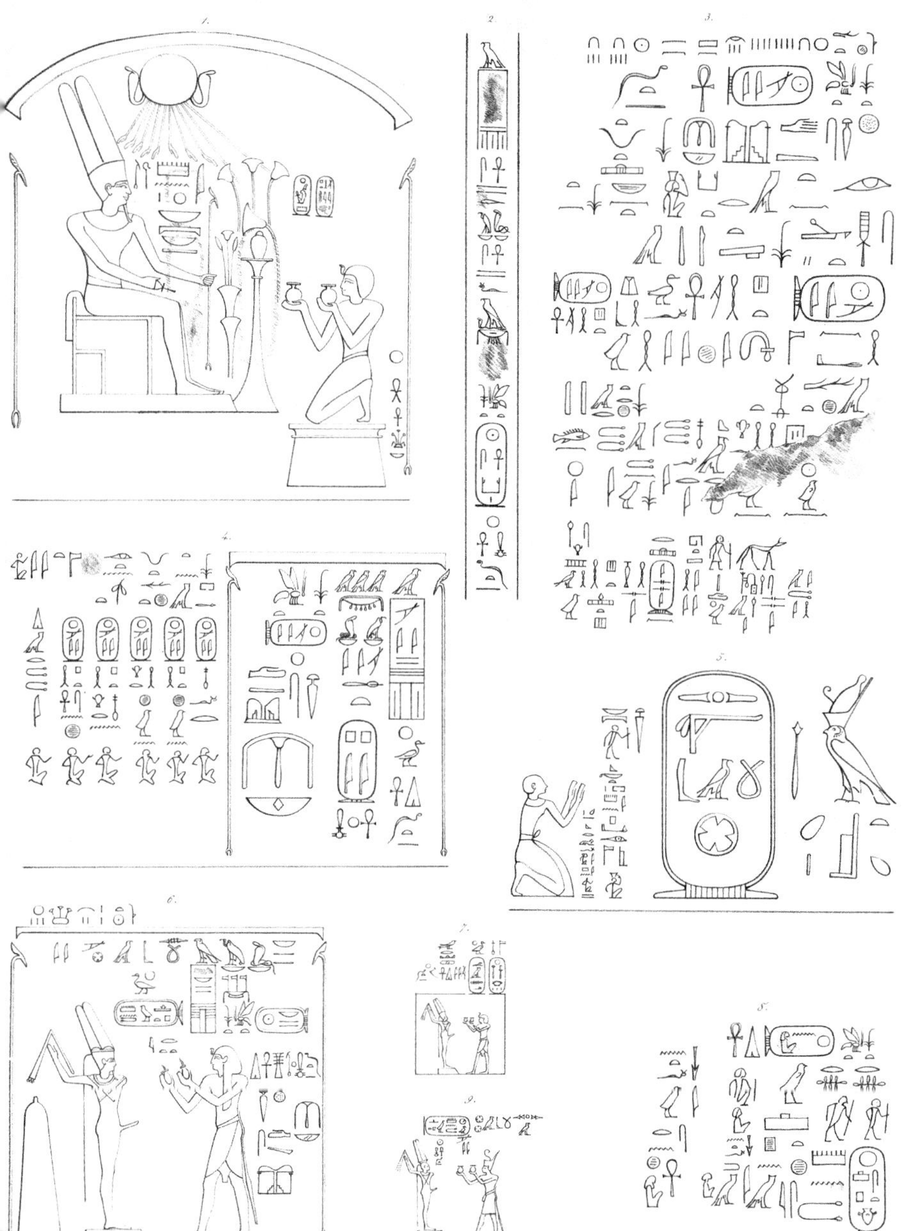

INSCRIPTIONS GRAVÉES SUR LES ROCHERS D'EL-HAMAMAT.

EGYPTIAN MONUMENTS

Stele from the reign of Mentuhotep

Funerary stele from Abydos. This stele in fine-grained limestone is divided into three sections: the first bears an inscription whose first line contains the royal titles and the cartouche name of Mentuhotep. Beneath the inscription is a bas-relief whose left section is occupied by two standing figures, Irtysen and his wife Hapu. The lower part of this stele is occupied by a small bas-relief set within a recess carved in the form of a naos; here Irtysen and his wife can be seen sitting on the same seat before a platter laden with offerings.

ÄGYPTISCHE DENKMÄLER

Stele aus der Regierungszeit von Mentuhotep

Aus Abydos stammende Grabstele. Diese Stele aus feinkörnigem Kalkstein ist in drei Felder unterteilt: Das erste ist mit einer Inschrift ausgefüllt, deren erste Zeile die königliche Titulatur und die Namenskartusche von Mentuhotep enthält. Unterhalb der Inschrift befindet sich ein Flachrelief, dessen linken Teil zwei stehende Personen einnehmen: Irtysen und seine Gemahlin Hapu. Im unteren Teil der Stele ist ein kleines Flachrelief in eine als Naos ausgearbeitete Vertiefung eingelassen; dort sind Irtysen und seine Gemahlin, auf ein und demselben Stuhl sitzend, vor einem mit Opfergaben beladenen Tablett zu sehen.

MONUMEN[T]S ÉGYPTIENS

Stèle du règne de Mentouôph

Stèle funéraire provenant d'Abydos. Cette stèle en pierre calcaire d'un grain fin, est divisée en trois compartiments : le premier est chargé d'une inscription dont la première ligne renferme les titres royaux et le cartouche-nom de Mentouôph [Mentouhotep]. Au-dessous de l'inscription est un bas-relief dont la partie gauche est occupée par deux personnages debout, Aaçen ou Niriçen et sa femme Hapevé ou Hapefé. La partie inférieure de cette stèle est occupée par un petit bas-relief ménagé dans un enfoncement taillé en forme de naos ; on y voit Niriçen et son épouse assis sur un même siège, et devant un plateau chargé d'offrandes.

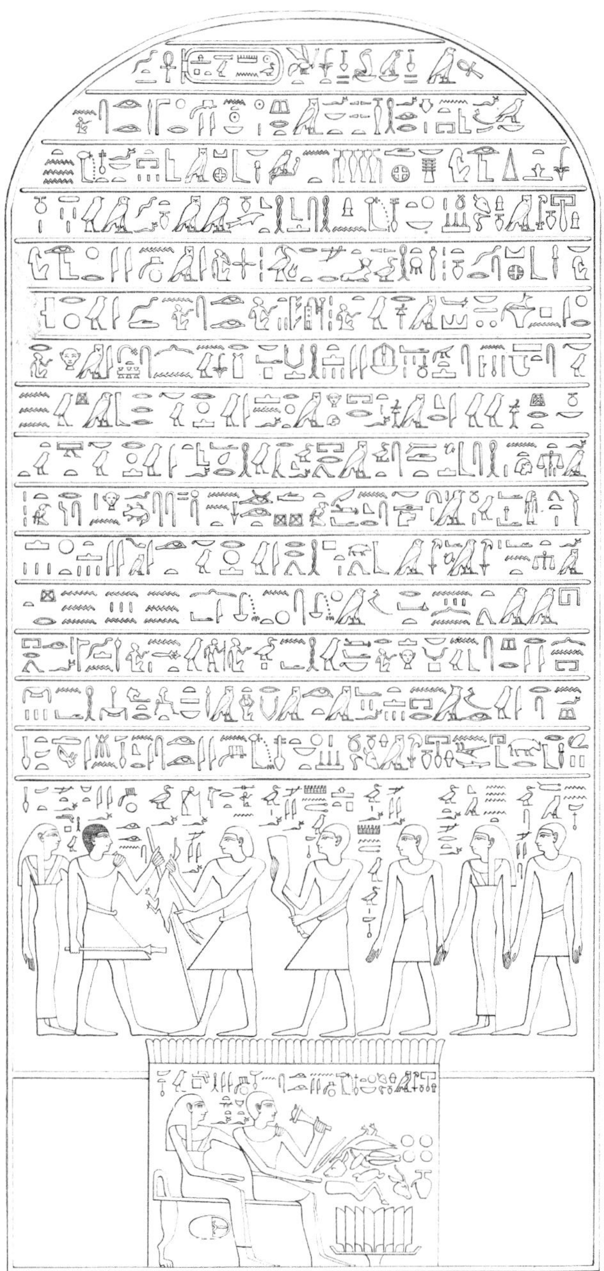

G. Barry, lith. E. Prisse. Imp. Kaeppelin & C.

STÈLE DU RÈGNE DE MENTOUÔPH.

EGYPTIAN MONUMENTS

Worship scene of the daughters of Sebekhotep

To date, this is the only monument known to bear the complete titulary of this pharaoh, the name of his two daughters and of their mother. [...] A similar description of this particular pharaoh features on a glazed ceramic scarab which I bought in Thebes: his titulary is composed of a cartouche containing both his prenomen and the name of Sebekhotep, followed by an inscription which is most interesting but whose real meaning seems to me to be rather difficult to determine.

ÄGYPTISCHE DENKMÄLER

Proskynema der Töchter Sobekhoteps

Dies ist das einzige bis heute bekannte Denkmal, das die vollständigen Hieroglypheninschriften dieses Pharaos sowie die Namen seiner beiden Töchter und ihrer Mutter trägt. [...] Dieser spezielle Pharao wird in ähnlicher Weise auf einem Skarabäus aus emailliertem Ton, den ich in Theben erwarb, bezeichnet: Seine Hieroglypheninschrift setzt sich aus einer Kartusche, die sowohl den Vornamen Sobekhoteps als auch seinen Namen enthält, und einer äußerst seltsamen Inschrift zusammen, deren tatsächliche Bedeutung mir recht schwer zu bestimmen scheint.

MONUMEN[T]S ÉGYPTIENS

Proscynème des filles de Sevekôtph

C'est le seul monument connu jusqu'à ce jour qui porte les légendes complètes de ce pharaon, le nom de ses deux filles et de leur mère. [...] Le pharaon qui nous occupe est qualifié d'une manière analogue sur un scarabée de terre émaillée que j'ai acheté à Thèbes : sa légende se compose d'un cartouche contenant à la fois le prénom et le nom de Sevekôtph [Sobekhotep], suivi d'une inscription fort curieuse, mais dont il me paraît assez difficile de déterminer le véritable sens.

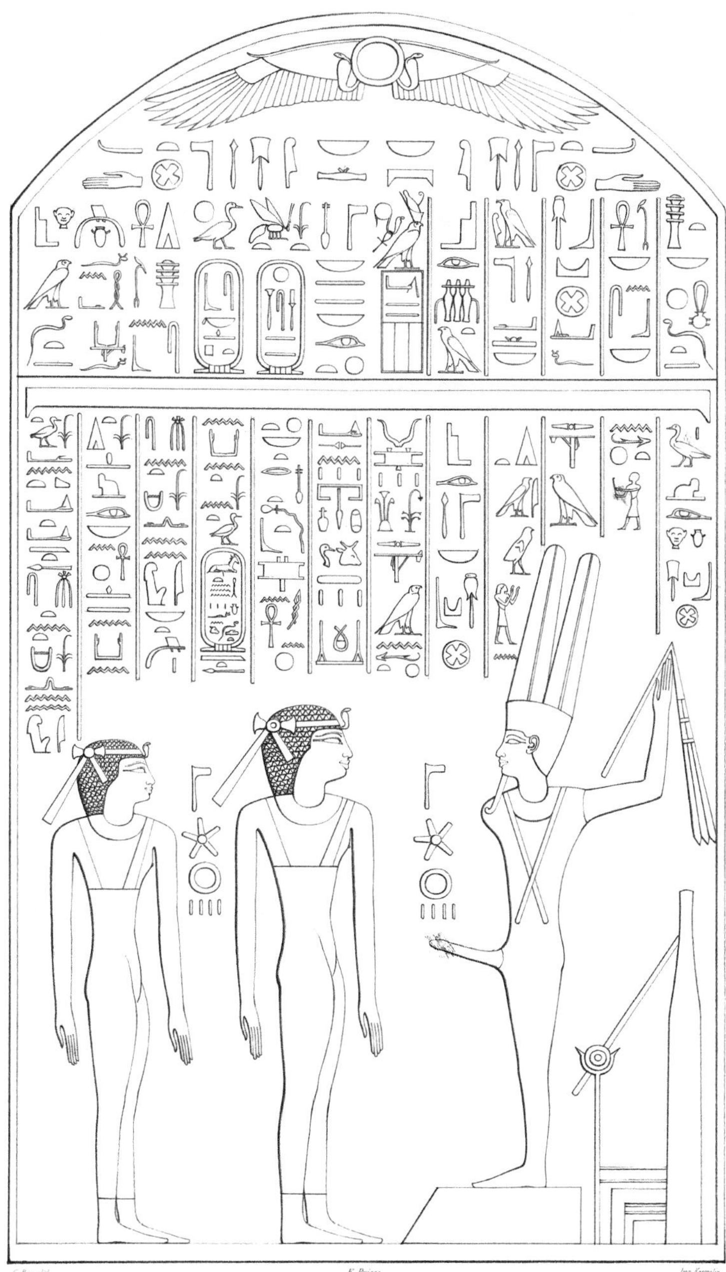

G. Barry lith. E. Prisse. Imp. Kaeppelin.

PROSCYNÈME DES FILLES DE SEVEKÔTPH.

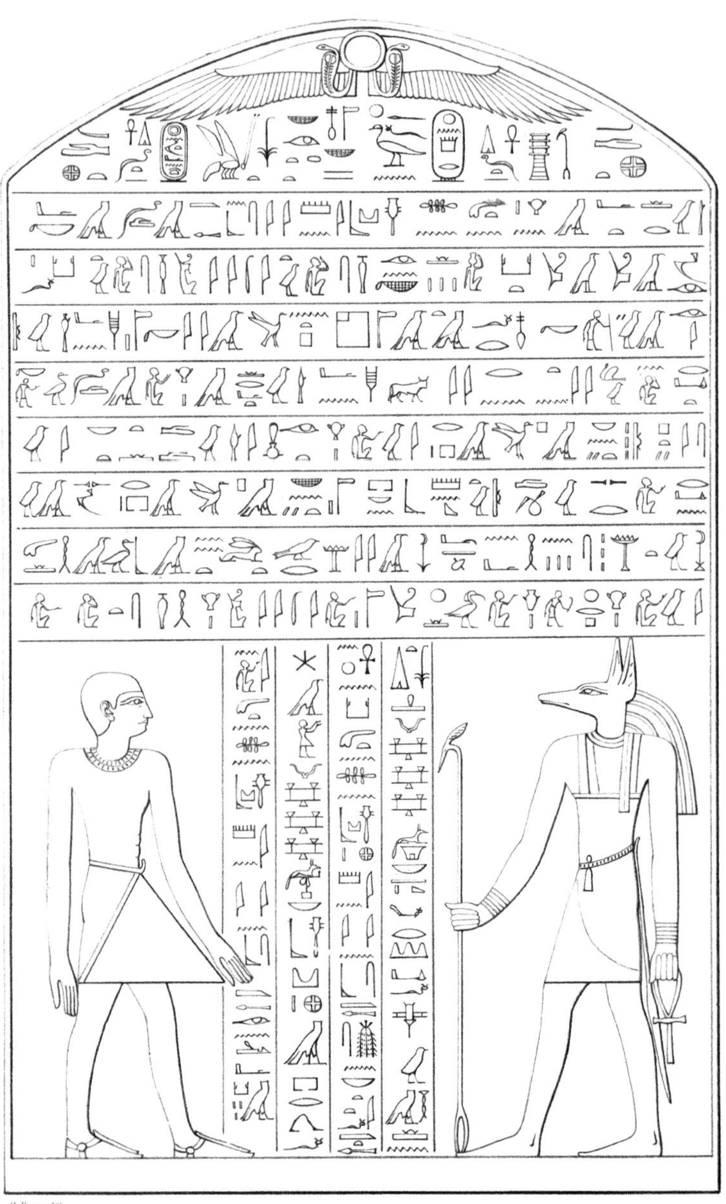

G. Barry, lith.

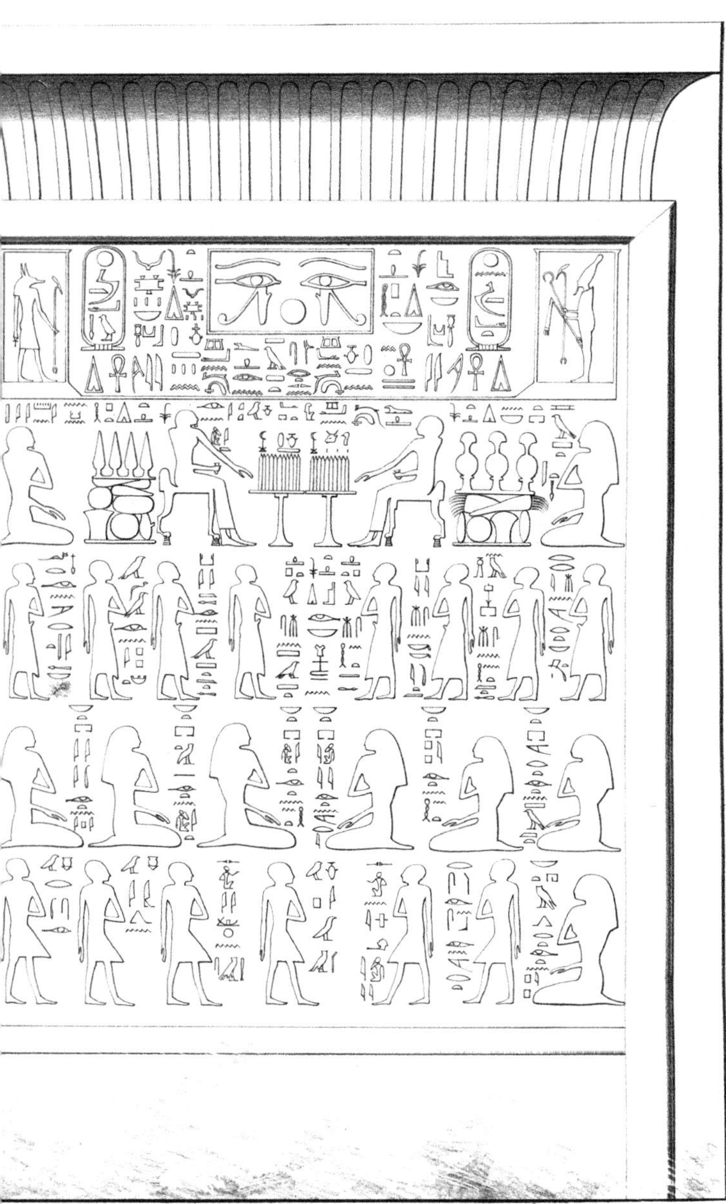

Imp Kaeppelin & Cie

DE SON SUCCESSEUR.

(Pages/Seite 86/87)

EGYPTIAN MONUMENTS

Stelae from the reign of Amenemhat III and his successor

No. 1. Worship scene of a high-ranking functionary from Abydos whose name was Ameniseneb, who lived during the reign of Khendjer, a pharaoh whose prenomen is very similar to those of the last of the Amenemhats but which must belong to a more recent king, probably to one of the early kings of the 13th Dynasty, since the 12th Dynasty is complete and firmly established by the monuments. This assertion is based in part on another worship scene about which M[onsieur] de Rougé has informed me. This worship scene, which dates from the same period and was probably taken from the same hypogeum, also bears the name and titles of Ameniseneb and quotes the improvements carried out under Sesostris I; this fact is important as it tells us more or less what position this pharaoh occupies in the royal lists. No. 2. Stele from the reign of Amenemhat III and of his successor, or rather of a pharaoh who reigned jointly with him.

ÄGYPTISCHE DENKMÄLER

Stelen aus der Regierungszeit von Amenemhet III. und seinem Nachfolger

Nr. 1. Proskynema eines hohen Beamten namens Ameniseneb aus Abydos, der unter der Herrschaft des Pharaos Chendjer lebte – dessen Vorname dem der letzten Amenemhets sehr ähnlich ist, aber einem jüngeren König zugehören muss; da die 12. Dynastie vollständig und gut durch die Denkmäler dokumentiert ist, dürfte es sich dabei um einen der ersten der 13. Dynastie handeln. Diese Behauptung stützt sich teilweise auf ein anderes Proskynema, über das M[onsieur] de Rougé mich in Kenntnis gesetzt hat. Dieses Proskynema – das aus derselben Zeit stammt und wahrscheinlich demselben Hypogäum entnommen ist – gibt ebenfalls Namen und Titulatur des Ameniseneb wieder und berichtet über die unter Sesostris I. ausgeführten Verschönerungen; dieser wichtige Beleg gibt uns annähernd die Stelle an, die dieser Pharao in den Königslisten einnehmen muss. Nr. 2. Stele aus der Regierungszeit von Amenemhet III. und seinem Nachfolger – oder eher eines Pharaos, der gemeinsam mit ihm regiert hat.

MONUMEN[T]S ÉGYPTIENS

Stèles du règne d'Aménemhé III et de son successeur

N° 1. Proscynème d'un haut fonctionnaire d'Abydos, nommé Amoumaïsenh, qui vivait sous le règne de Rentor [Khendjer], pharaon dont le prénom ressemble beaucoup à ceux des derniers Aménemhé [Amménémès], mais doit appartenir à un roi plus récent, probablement à un des premiers de la XIIIe dynastie, puisque la XIIe est complète et bien fixée par les monuments. Cette assertion est fondée en partie sur un autre proscynème que m'a communiqué M[onsieur] de Rougé. Ce proscynème, qui date de la même époque, et fut probablement tiré du même hypogée, rapporte aussi le nom et les titres de Amoumaïsenh, et cite des embellissements exécutés sous Osortasen [Sésostris] Ier; fait important qui nous donne à peu près la place que doit occuper ce pharaon dans les listes royales. N° 2. Stèle du règne d'Aménemhé III et de son successeur, ou plutôt d'un pharaon qui régna conjointement avec lui.

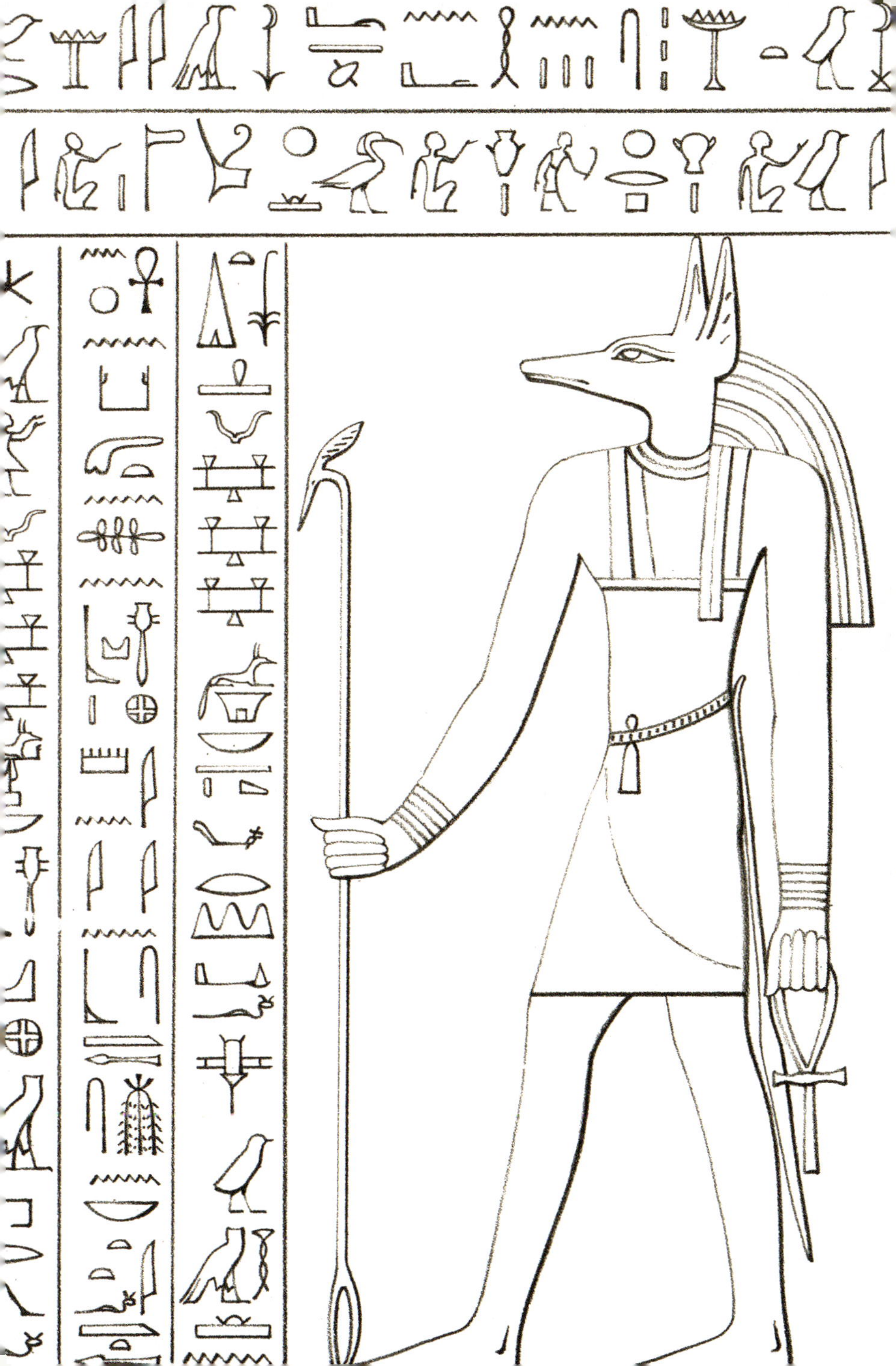

THEBES – KARNAK

Ancient stones used in the construction of the southern propylaea

Bas-reliefs from monuments destroyed by the last kings of the 18th Dynasty and used in the construction of the southern propylaea at Karnak. No. 1. Bas-relief representing the double image of the pharaoh Bakh- or Baskh-en-Aten-Ra (the splendour of Aten-Ra [Akhenaten]), burning incense to Aten-Ra, the sun god, who is depicted in the form of a disc from which there radiate many sunbeams ending in hands which stroke the king or which present him with the insignia of power and immortality and with panegyrics. No. 2. Baskh-en-Aten [Akhenaten], in the emblematic form of a sphinx, presents a small image of justice to the god of the dynasty, whose two large cartouches can be seen in front of those of the king.

THEBEN – KARNAK

Steine aus älteren Bauten, die man bei der Errichtung der südlichen Propyläen wiederverwendet hat

Flachreliefs aus den Denkmälern, die durch die letzten Könige der 18. Dynastie zerstört wurden und in Karnak für den Bau der südlichen Propyläen Verwendung fanden. Nr. 1. Flachrelief mit einer doppelten Abbildung des Pharaos Bach- oder Basch-en-Aten-Ra (der Glanz des Aton-Re [Echnaton]), der für den Sonnengott Aton Weihrauch verbrennt; dargestellt ist Aton als Sonnenscheibe mit zahlreichen in Hände auslaufenden Strahlen, die den König liebkosen oder ihm Zeichen der Macht und der Unsterblichkeit sowie Lobreden darbieten. Nr. 2. Basch-en-Aten [Echnaton], hier in der sinnbildlichen Form einer Sphinx dargestellt, bietet dem Gott der Dynastie, dessen zwei große Kartuschen vor denen des Königs zu sehen sind, ein kleines Bild der Justiz dar.

THÈBES – KARNAC

Anciennes pierres employées dans les constructions des propylées du sud

Bas-reliefs provenant des monuments détruits par les derniers rois de la XVIIIe dynastie, et employés à la construction des propylées du sud, à Karnac. N° 1. Bas-relief représentant la double image du pharaon Bakh ou Basch-n-Aten-ré (la splendeur d'Aten-ré [Akhénaton]), brûlant de l'encens à Aten-ré, le dieu-soleil, sous la forme d'un disque d'où partent de nombreux rayons terminés par des mains qui caressent le roi, ou lui présentent les signes de la puissance, de l'immortalité et des panégyries. N° 2. Basch-n-Aten [Akhénaton], sous la forme emblématique d'un sphinx, présente une petite image de la justice au dieu dynaste, dont on voit les deux larges cartouches en avant de ceux du roi.

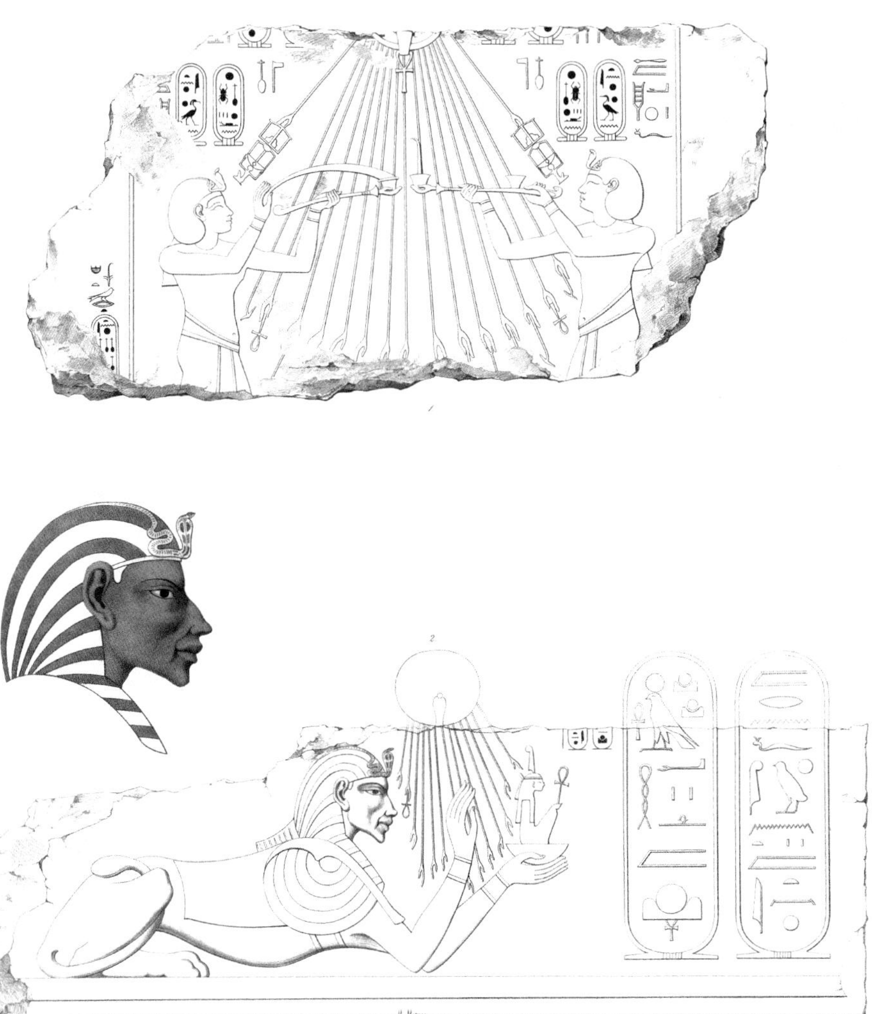

ANCIENNES PIERRES EMPLOYÉES DANS LES CONSTRUCTIONS DES PROPYLÉES DU SUD.

THEBES – KARNAK

Bas-reliefs sculpted on stones used in the construction work

No. 1. Fragment of a military bas-relief of Amuntuankh or Ankhamun [Tutankhamun], pharaoh of the 18th Dynasty. No. 2. Portrait of Baskh-en-Aten [Akhenaten], from a stone in the pylon of Horus. This portrait bears no resemblance to the other representations of this pharaoh which survive. With the exception of the bas-relief which we are discussing here and which appears to me to have been embellished through flattery typical of the priesthood, he is always shown with a flat nose, thick lips, skinny neck, prominent nipples and protruding belly, a feminine shape which is most unattractive. No. 3. This bas-relief represents an act of worship by Baskh-en-Aten [Akhenaten], accompanied by his wife and his two daughters. No. 4. An interesting fragment of a sculpture of Amenophis III, removed from the pylon of the hypostyle hall.

THEBEN – KARNAK

Flachreliefs, die in für Bauten verwendete Steine eingearbeitet sind

Nr. 1. Fragment eines militärischen Flachreliefs von Tutanchamun, einem Pharao der 18. Dynastie. Nr. 2. Porträt des Basch-en-Aten [Echnaton], nach einem Stein aus dem Horus-Pylon. Dieses Porträt ähnelt in keiner Weise den sonstigen Darstellungen, die uns von diesem Pharao überliefert sind. Mit Ausnahme des uns hier beschäftigenden Flachreliefs, das mir durch eine ganz und gar priesterliche Schmeichelei geschönt zu sein scheint, ist diese Persönlichkeit immer mit einer Stumpfnase, dicken Lippen, dürrem Hals, hervortretenden Brüsten, vorspringendem Bauch und femininen, unattraktiven Körperformen dargestellt. Nr. 3. Dieses Flachrelief stellt eine Anbetungshandlung des Basch-en-Aten [Echnaton] in Begleitung seiner Gemahlin und seiner beiden Töchter dar. Nr. 4. Eigenartiges Bruchstück einer Skulptur Amenophis' III., aus dem Pylon des Hypostyls entnommen.

THÈBES – KARNAC

Bas-reliefs sculptés sur des pierres employées dans les constructions

N° 1. Fragment d'un bas-relief militaire d'Amentouonkh ou Onkhamoun [Toutânkhamon], pharaon de la XVIIIe dynastie. N° 2. Portrait de Basch-n-Aten [Akhénaton], d'après une pierre du pylône d'Horus. Ce portrait ne ressemble nullement aux autres représentations qui nous restent de ce pharaon. Excepté sur le bas-relief qui nous occupe, et qui me paraît avoir été embelli par une flatterie toute sacerdotale, ce personnage est toujours représenté avec le nez épaté, les lèvres épaisses, le cou grêle, les mamelles saillantes, le ventre proéminent, des formes féminines, et fort peu attrayantes. N° 3. Ce bas-relief représente un acte d'adoration de Basch-n-Aten [Akhénaton], accompagné de sa femme et de ses deux filles. N° 4. Curieux fragment d'une sculpture d'Amounôph [Aménophis] III, extrait du pylône de la salle hypostyle.

THÈBES-KARNAC.

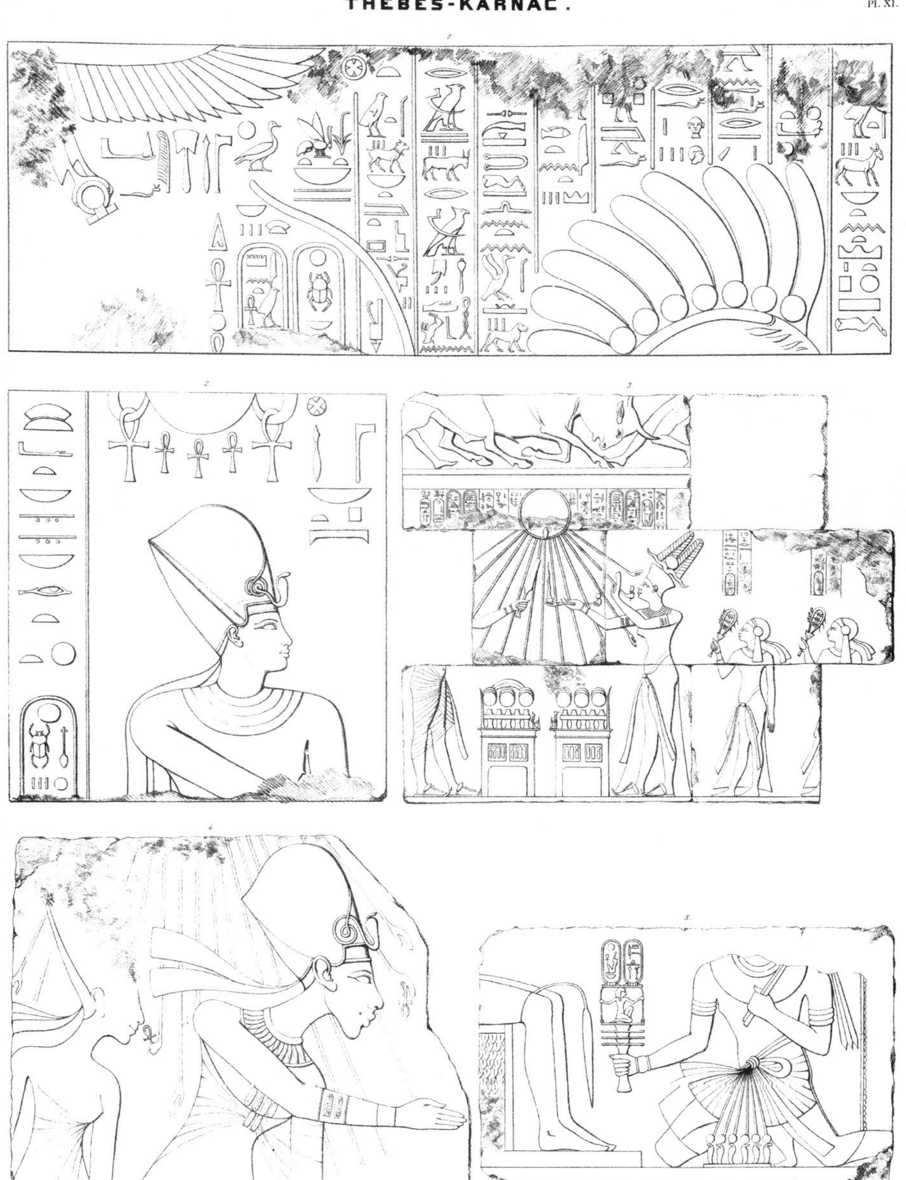

BAS-RELIEFS SCULPTÉS SUR DES PIERRES EMPLOYÉES DANS LES CONSTRUCTIONS.

TELL EL-AMARNA. PSINAULA

Worship scene engraved on a rock

On the side of a mountain in a ravine choked with fallen stones which separates the hypogea of Tell el-Amarna from those of el Hagg Qandil can be seen a colossal stele, nine metres high, which contains 24 lines of hieroglyphs. In the upper part it is decorated with a bas-relief depicting Baskh-en-Aten [Akhenaten], his wife Nefertiti and his two daughters, Meritaten and Meketaten, presenting an offering to the radiating disc of the sun. I must myself point out that my copies of the worship scenes at Tell el-Amarna and at Tuna [el-Gebel] are not accurate, but the elevated position of these stelae and their damaged condition make an exact copy impossible without using ladders or scaffolding, which I was unable to obtain in this area.

TELL EL-AMARNA. PSINAULA

In einen Felsen eingearbeitetes Proskynema

In einer durch herabgefallene Felsen versperrten Schlucht zwischen den Hypogäen von Tell el-Amarna und Hadji Qandil ist an einer Bergwand eine 9 m hohe Kolossalstatue zu sehen, die 24 Zeilen Hieroglyphen trägt. Ihr oberer Teil ist mit einem Flachrelief verziert, das Basch-en-Aten [Echnaton], seine Gemahlin Nofretete und ihre beiden Töchter, Meritaton und Maketaton, bei der Opferung an die strahlende Sonnenscheibe darstellt. Ich muss selbst darauf hinweisen, dass meine Kopien der Proskynema von Tell el-Amarna und Tuna [el-Gebel] fehlerhaft sind: Aufgrund des schlechten Erhaltungszustandes und der Höhe, in der sich diese Stelen befinden, ist es jedoch ohne Leitern oder Gerüste – die ich mir an diesem Ort nicht beschaffen konnte – nicht möglich, sie genau abzuzeichnen.

TELL EL-AMARNA. PSINAULA

Proscynème sculpté sur un rocher

Dans un ravin tout encombré de roches éboulées qui sépare les hypogées de Tell el-Amarna de ceux d'Hadji-Qandyl, on voit sur la paroi de la montagne une stèle colossale de neuf mètres de hauteur, contenant vingt-quatre lignes d'hiéroglyphes. Elle est ornée, dans sa partie supérieure, d'un bas-relief représentant Basch-n-Aten [Akhénaton], sa femme Nofre-Ati [Néfertiti], et ses deux filles, Mai, ou Meri-Aten [Mérytaton], et Mak-Aten [Mâkhétaton], faisant offrande au disque rayonnant du soleil. Je dois faire observer, moi-même, que mes copies des proscynèmes de Tell el-Amarna et de Touneh [el-Gebel] sont fautives : mais la situation élevée de ces stèles et leur état de dégradation empêchent de les copier exactement sans échelles ou échafaudages, qu'il me fut impossible de me procurer dans ces localités.

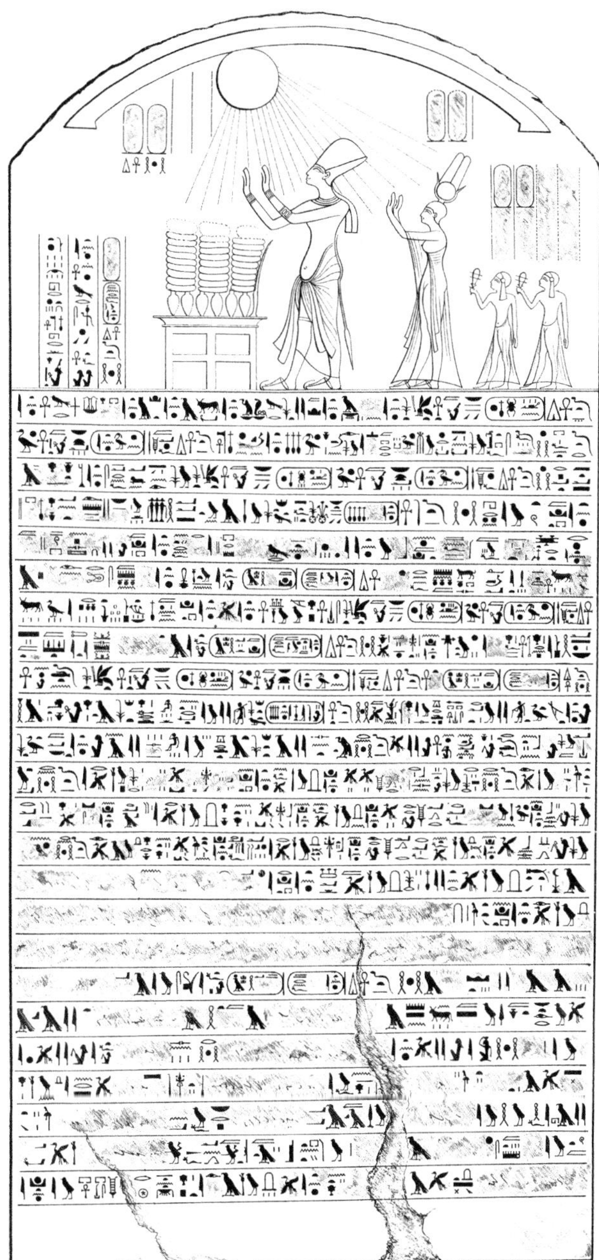

G. Barry, lith. E. Prisse. Imp. Kaeppelin & Cie.

PROSCYNÈME SCULPTÉ SUR UN ROCHER.

TELL EL-AMARNA. PSINAULA

Worship scene sculpted on a rock

Stele sculpted on the rocks of Tell el-Amarna. The copy of this inscription appears to me to contain some errors; however, as it has not been published before, I thought I ought to publish it in this collection. This worship scene, which dates from the 13th day of Pharmouthi, year 6 or 8 in the reign of Baskh-en-Aten [Akhenaten], recalls all the royal titles of this pharaoh and the names of his two daughters, Meritaten and Meketaten. It contains the commemoration of a great panegyric to Aten-Ra, in which it is told how the king was crowned in his chariot of gold, like the disc which lights up the gates of the sun, and how he filled the world with his love.

TELL EL-AMARNA. PSINAULA

In einen Felsen eingearbeitetes Proskynema

In die Felsen von Tell el-Amarna eingearbeitete Stele. Die Wiedergabe dieser Inschrift scheint mir einige Fehler zu enthalten: Da sie jedoch unveröffentlicht ist, meinte ich sie in dieser Sammlung herausgeben zu müssen. Dieses Proskynema, das vom 13. Tag des [Monats] Pharmuti im 6. oder 8. Regierungsjahr des Basch-en-Aten [Echnaton] datiert, listet alle königlichen Titel dieses Pharaos und die Namen seiner beiden Töchter, Meritaton und Maketaton, auf. Es enthält das Gedenken an eine große Lobrede auf Aton-Re. Der König sei auf seinem goldenen Wagen gekrönt worden und habe – so wie die Scheibe die Türen der Sonne erleuchte – die Welt mit seiner Liebe angefüllt.

TELL EL-AMARNA. PSINAULA

Proscynème sculpté sur un rocher

Stèle sculptée sur les rochers de Tell el-Amarna. La copie de cette inscription me paraît contenir quelques erreurs : mais comme elle est inédite, j'ai cru devoir la publier dans ce recueil. Ce proscynème, qui date du 13e jour de Parmouté [Pharmouthi], l'an 6 ou 8 du règne de Basch-n-Aten [Akhénaton], rappelle tous les titres royaux de ce pharaon, et le nom de ses deux filles Meri-Aten [Mérytaton] et Mak-Aten [Mâkhétaton]. Il contient la commémoration d'une grande panégyrie d'Aten-Ra. Le roi est dit avoir été couronné sur son chariot d'or, comme le disque qui illumine les portes du soleil, et remplit le monde de son amour.

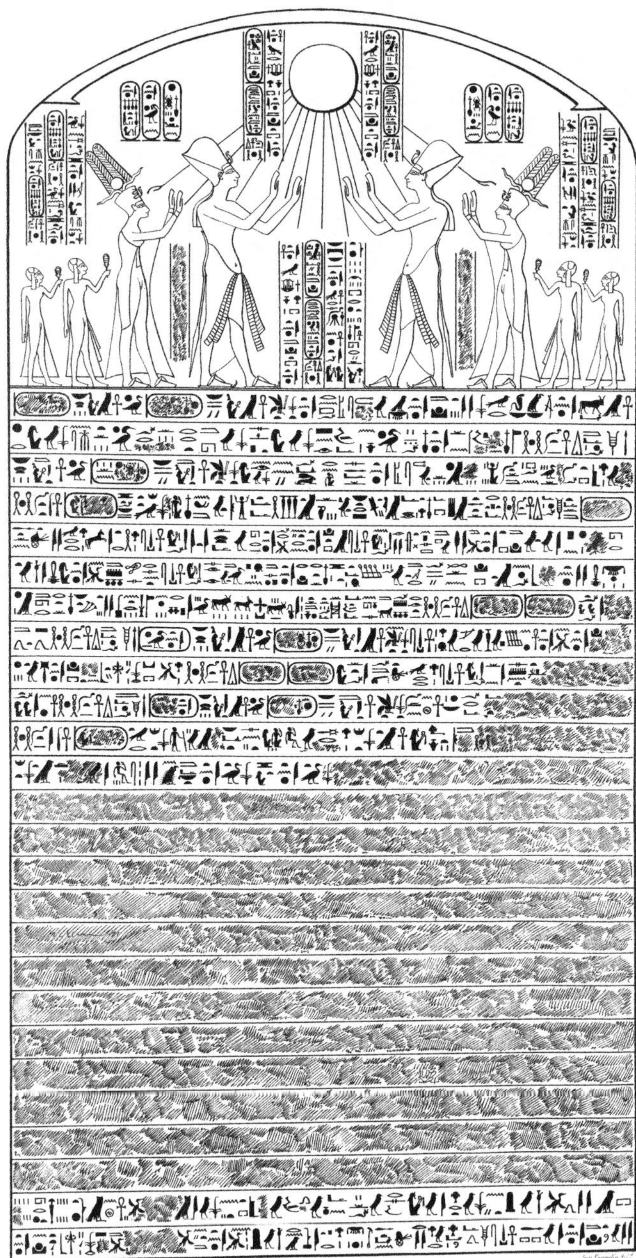

G. Berry, Sc. G. Lloyd. Imp. Kaeppelin & Cie

PROSCYNÈME SCULPTÉ SUR UN ROCHER.

TUNA EL-GEBEL. TANIS SUPERIOR

Worship scene sculpted on a rock

Stele sculpted on the rock at Gebel Tuna, the ancient Thynis, also known by the name of Tanis Superior, to distinguish it from the Tanis in the delta. The monument reproduced in our plate is carved on the face of a rock of nummulitic limestone, some distance from the village of Tuna and separated from it by a sandy plain. This colossal stele, between five and six metres in height, dates from the 13th day of Mesore, year 6 of the reign of Baskh-en-Aten-Ra [Akhenaten]; it depicts a scene of worship similar to those shown on the monuments of Tell el-Amarna, and the text of the inscription, which is unfortunately severely damaged, also relates to panegyrics to the sun.

TUNA EL-GEBEL. TANIS SUPERIOR

In einen Felsen eingearbeitetes Proskynema

Die Stele ist in den Felsen von Gebel Tuna eingearbeitet, das alte Thynis, das auch als Tanis Superior bezeichnet wird, um es von dem im Nildelta gelegenen Ort Tanis zu unterscheiden. Das auf unserer Tafel wiedergegebene Denkmal ist in der Nähe des Dorfes Tuna – von dem es durch eine sandige Ebene getrennt ist – in die Oberfläche des Nummulitenkalkstein Felsens gehauen. Diese Kolossalstele von 5 bis 6 m Höhe datiert vom 13. Tag des [Monats] Mesori im 6. Regierungsjahr des Basch-en-Aten-Ra [Echnaton]; die dargestellte Anbetungsszene ähnelt der, die von den Denkmälern in Tell el-Amarna bekannt ist, und der – leider stark beschädigte – Text der Inschrift bezieht sich ebenfalls auf das Lob der Sonne.

TOÛNEH EL-GEBEL. TANIS SUPERIOR

Proscynème sculpté sur un rocher

Stèle sculptée sur le rocher de Djébel Touneh, l'ancienne Thôni, désignée aussi sous le nom de Tanis Superior, pour la distinguer de la Tanis du Delta. Le monument reproduit sur notre planche est taillé sur la face du rocher de calcaire numismal, à quelque distance du village de Touneh, dont il est séparé par une plaine sablonneuse. Cette stèle colossale, de cinq à six mètres de hauteur, date du 13e jour de Mesôré, l'an 6 du règne de Basch-n-Aten-Ré [Akhénaton] ; elle représente une scène d'adoration semblable à celle des monuments de Tell el-Amarna, et le texte de l'inscription, malheureusement fort endommagé, est aussi relatif aux panégyries du soleil.

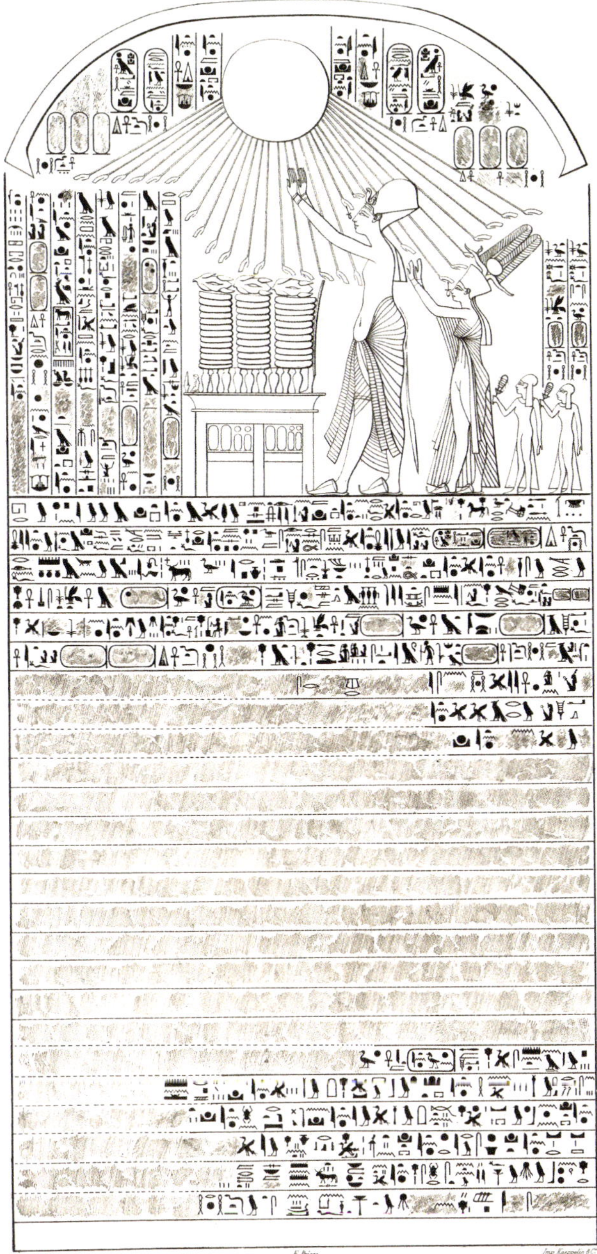

F. Lepelle lith. E. Prisse. Imp. Kaeppelin & Cie.

PROSCYNÈME SCULPTÉ SUR UN ROCHER.

1.

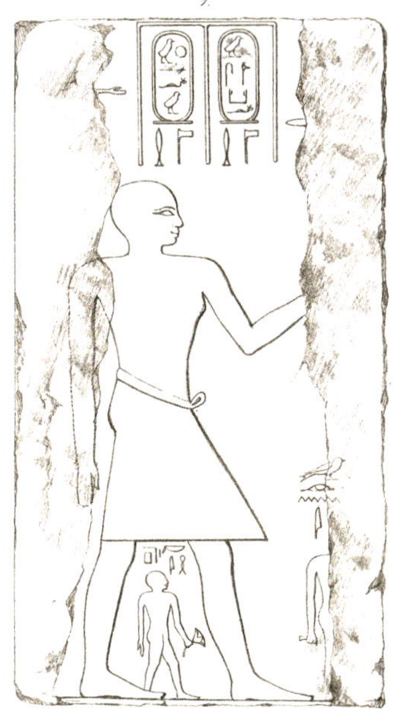

2.

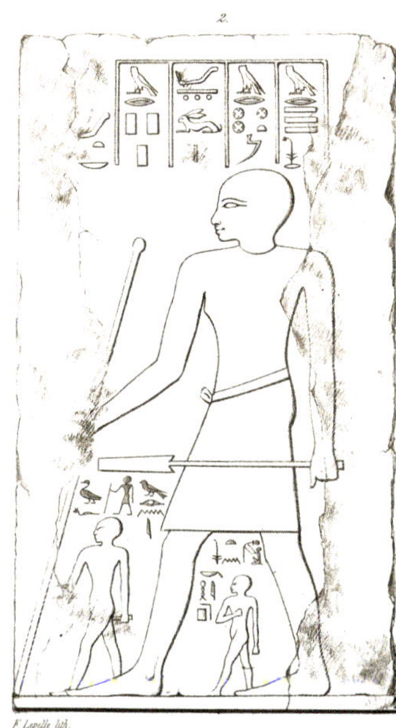

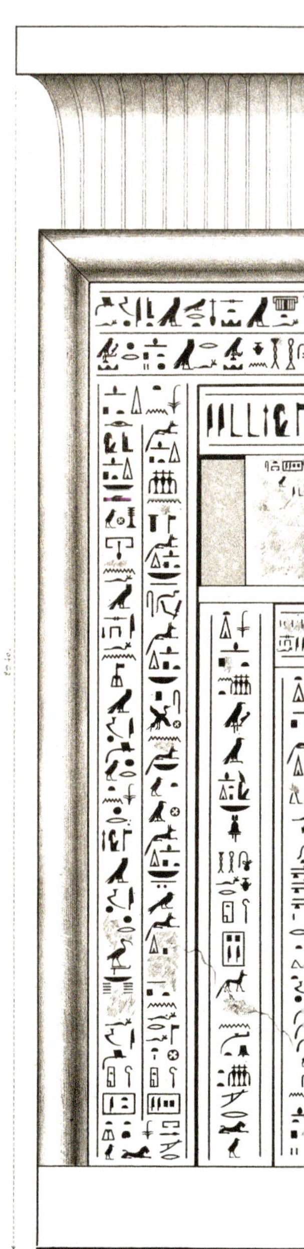

F. Lapelle lith.

3.

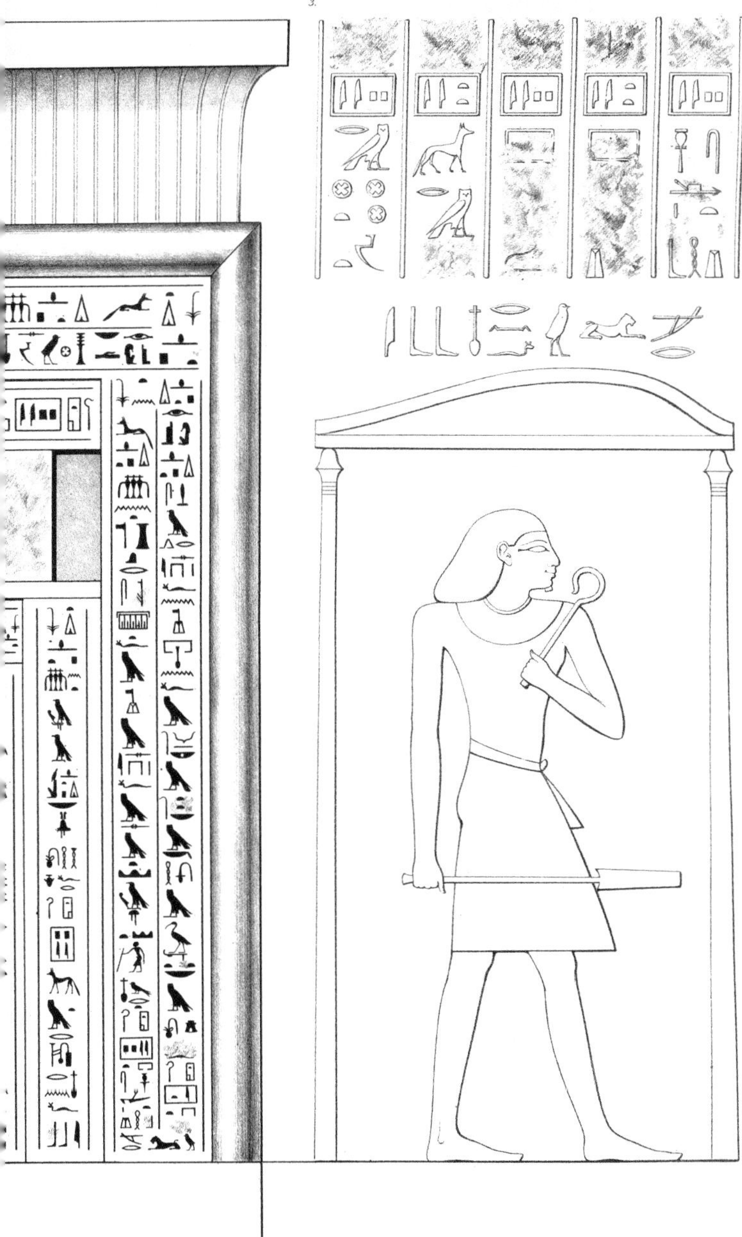

Imp. Kaeppelin & Cie

TIRÉS DES HYPOGÉES.

(Pages/Seite 100/101)

DEIR EL-BERSHA AND EL-SHEIKH SAID

Bas-reliefs and worship scene taken from hypogea

Bas-relief and worship scene, taken from hypogea at Deir el-Bersha and at El-Sheikh Said. Nos. 1 and 2. Figures engraved on the inside of a door frame of a very ancient hypogeum at Sheikh Said, to the north of Tell el-Amarna. These two representations are of the same person: Userkaf, founder of the 5th Dynasty. The man buried in this hypogeum was a member of the priestly caste, responsible for the administration of the estates. No. 3. Worship scene and bas-relief taken from a hypogeum at Deir el-Bersha. They confirm the discovery of the cartouche of Teti or Atet (see plate XVb) which I made at Kom el-Ahmar and which fixes his chronological position.

DEIR EL-BERSCHE UND SCHEICH SAID

Den Hypogäen entnommene Flachreliefs und Proskynema

Den Hypogäen von Deir el-Bersche und Scheich Said entnommene Flachreliefs und Proskynema. Nr. 1 und 2. In das Innere der Türzarge eines sehr alten Hypogäums in Scheich Said – nördlich von Tell el-Amarna – eingearbeitete Gestalten. Diese beiden Darstellungen beziehen sich auf ein und dieselbe Persönlichkeit: Userkaf, den Begründer der 5. Dynastie. Die in diesem Hypogäum bestattete Persönlichkeit war ein mit der Verwaltung der Ländereien beauftragtes Mitglied der Priesterkaste. Nr. 3. Den Hypogäen von Deir el-Bersche entnommene Proskynema und Flachreliefs. Sie bestätigen die von mir in Kom el-Ahmar entdeckte Kartusche von Teti (siehe Tafel XVb) und erlauben die Bestimmung seiner chronologischen Stellung.

BERCHEH ET CHEIKH-SAYD

Bas-reliefs et proscynème tirés des hypogées

Bas-relief et proscynème, tirés des hypogées de Bercheh et de Cheikh-Sayd. N°s 1 et 2. Figures sculptées à l'intérieur d'un chambranle de porte d'un hypogée fort ancien de Cheikh-Sayd, au nord de Tell el-Amarna. Ces deux représentations appartiennent à un même personnage : Ouserchéres [Ouserkaf], chef de la Ve dynastie. Le personnage enseveli dans cet hypogée était un membre de la caste sacerdotale, chargé de l'administration des terres. N° 3. Proscynème et bas-relief tirés d'un hypogée de Bercheh. Ils confirment la découverte que j'ai faite à Koum el-Ahmar du cartouche de Toti [Téti] ou Atet (voir planche XVbis), et fixent son ordre chronologique.

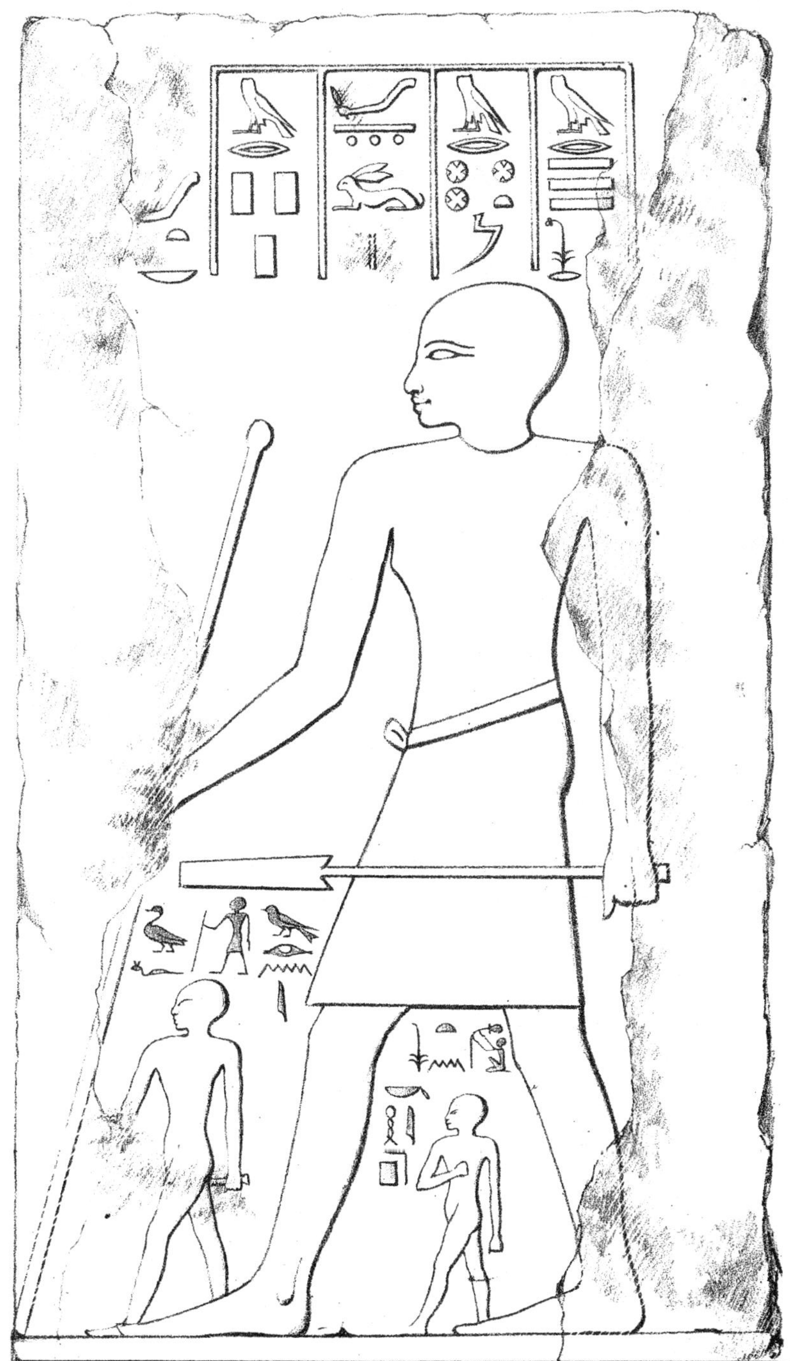

F. Lepelle lith:

HEPTANOMIS [THE SEVENTH NOME]

Bas-reliefs taken from hypogea at Zawyet el-Maiyitin and Tell el-Amarna

No. 1. Choir of musicians and singers whose shaved heads indicate that they are members of the priestly caste. The style of these figures is quite exceptional; those who are clapping their hands to keep time are particularly remarkable. Never have the Egyptians represented the features of the human face with such accuracy and such clarity. No. 2. Bas-relief carved at the entry of an unfinished tomb from Kom el-Ahmar at Zawyet el-Maiyitin, which according to some writers is the site of the ancient Alabastron. Nos. 3 and 4. Bas-reliefs taken from different hypogea in the same locality. No. 5. Offering of various fruits of the earth.

HEPTANOMIA [DER SIEBTE GAU]

Den Hypogäen von Saujet el-Meitin und Tell el-Amarna entnommene Flachreliefs

Nr. 1. Chor von Musikern und Sängern, deren kahle Köpfe darauf hindeuten, dass sie Angehörige der Priesterkaste sind. Der Typus dieser Darstellungen ist äußerst bemerkenswert; vor allem diejenigen, die durch Händeklatschen den Takt angeben, sind gut zu erkennen. Nie stellten die Ägypter die Züge des menschlichen Antlitzes so echt und genau dar. Nr. 2. In den Eingang des unvollendeten Grabes von Kom el-Ahmar in Saujet el-Meitin – wo einige Schriftsteller das antike Alabastron ansiedeln – eingearbeitetes Flachrelief. Nr. 3 und 4. Aus verschiedenen Hypogäen derselben Ortschaft entnommene Flachreliefs. Nr. 5. Opfergabe verschiedener Agrarprodukte.

HEPTANOMIDE [LE SEPTIÈME NOME]

Bas-reliefs tirés des hypogées de Zawyet el-Mayetin et de Tell el-Amarna

N° 1. Chœur de musiciens et chanteurs, dont les têtes rases indiquent des personnages de la caste sacerdotale. Le type de ces figures est fort remarquable ; on distingue surtout celles qui marquent la mesure en battant des mains. Jamais les Égyptiens n'ont représenté avec autant de vérité et d'exactitude les traits de la face humaine. N° 2. Bas-relief sculpté à l'entrée d'un tombeau inachevé de Koum el-Ahmar, à Zawyet el-Mayetin [Zaouiet el-Meïtin], où quelques écrivains ont placé l'ancienne Alabastron. N°s 3 et 4. Bas-reliefs tirés de différents hypogées de la même localité. N° 5. Offrande des divers produits du sol.

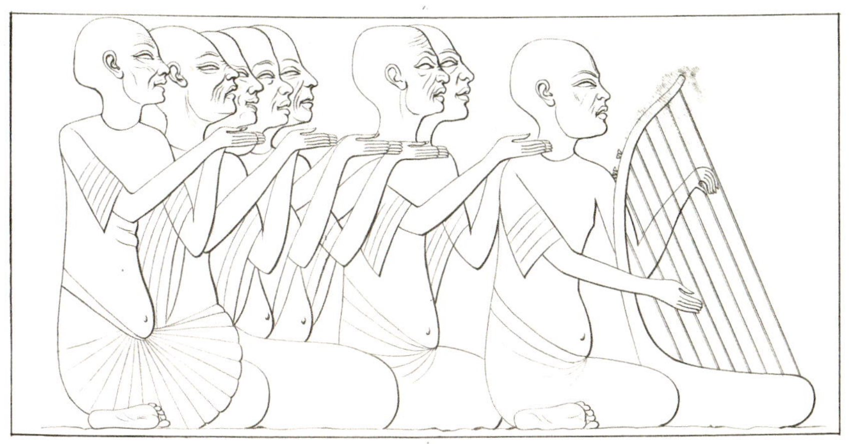

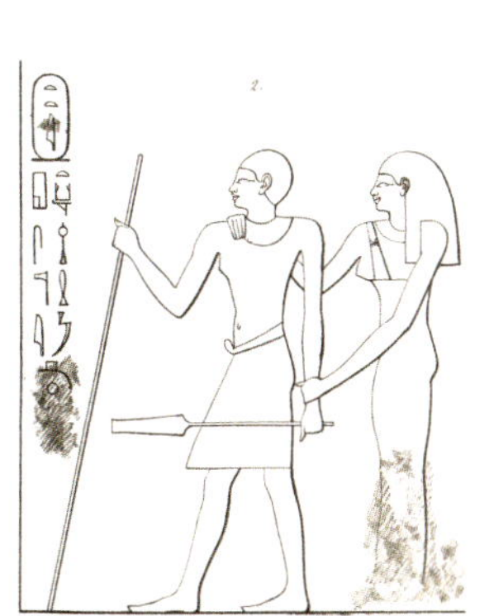

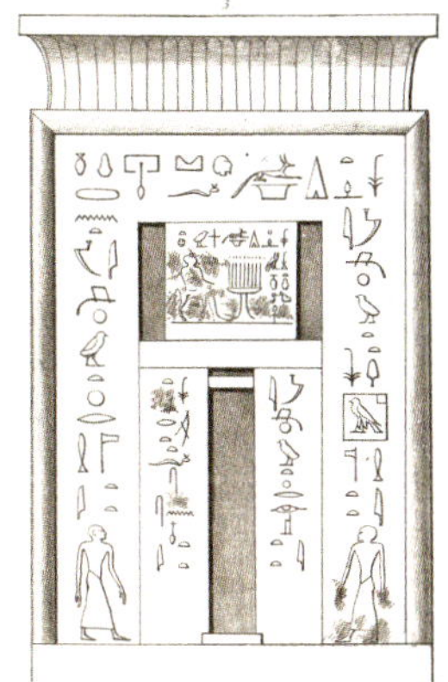

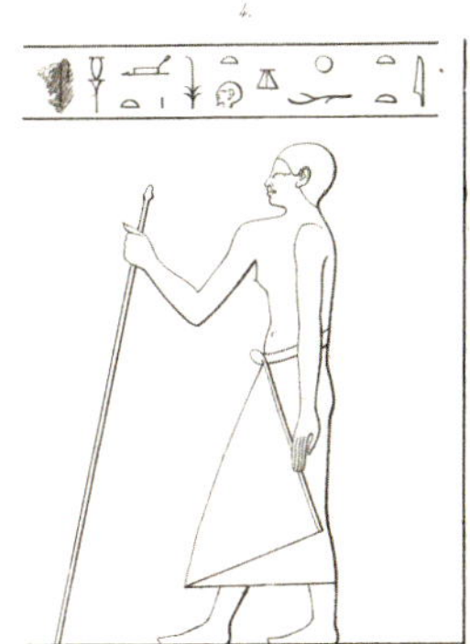

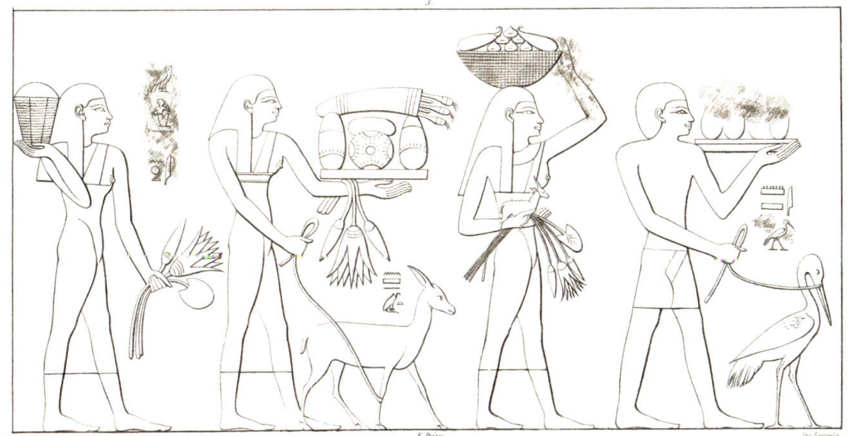

BAS-RELIEFS TIRÉS DES HYPOGÉES DE ZAWYET EL-MAYETIN ET DE TELL-AMARNA.

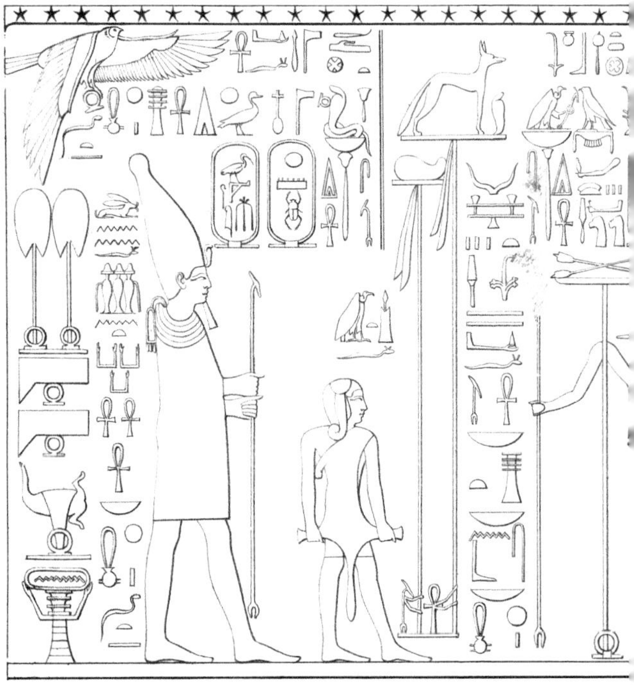

2.

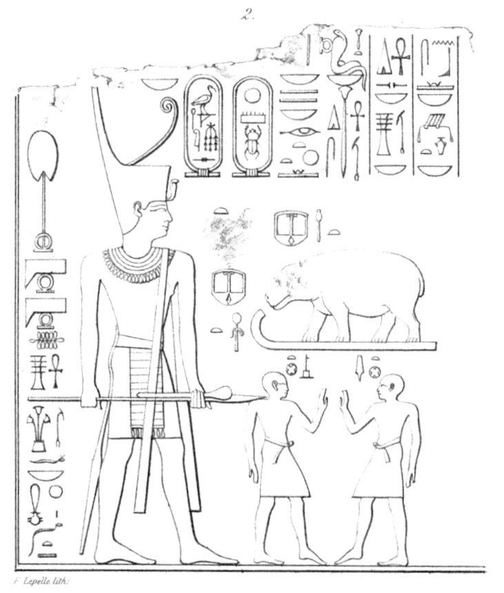

F. Lepelle lith:

1, 2, 3 BAS-I

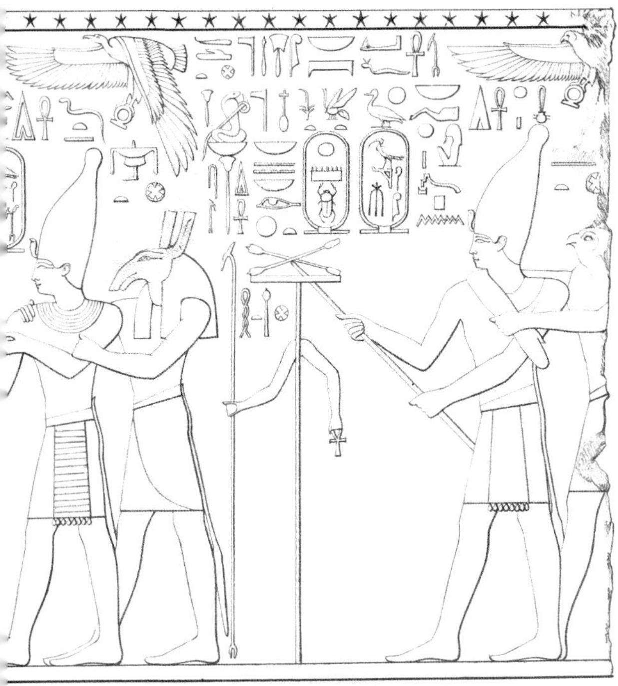

3.

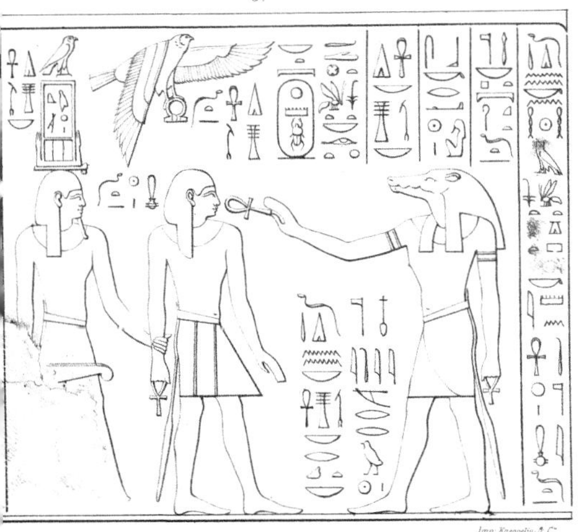

Imp. Kaeppelin & Cie

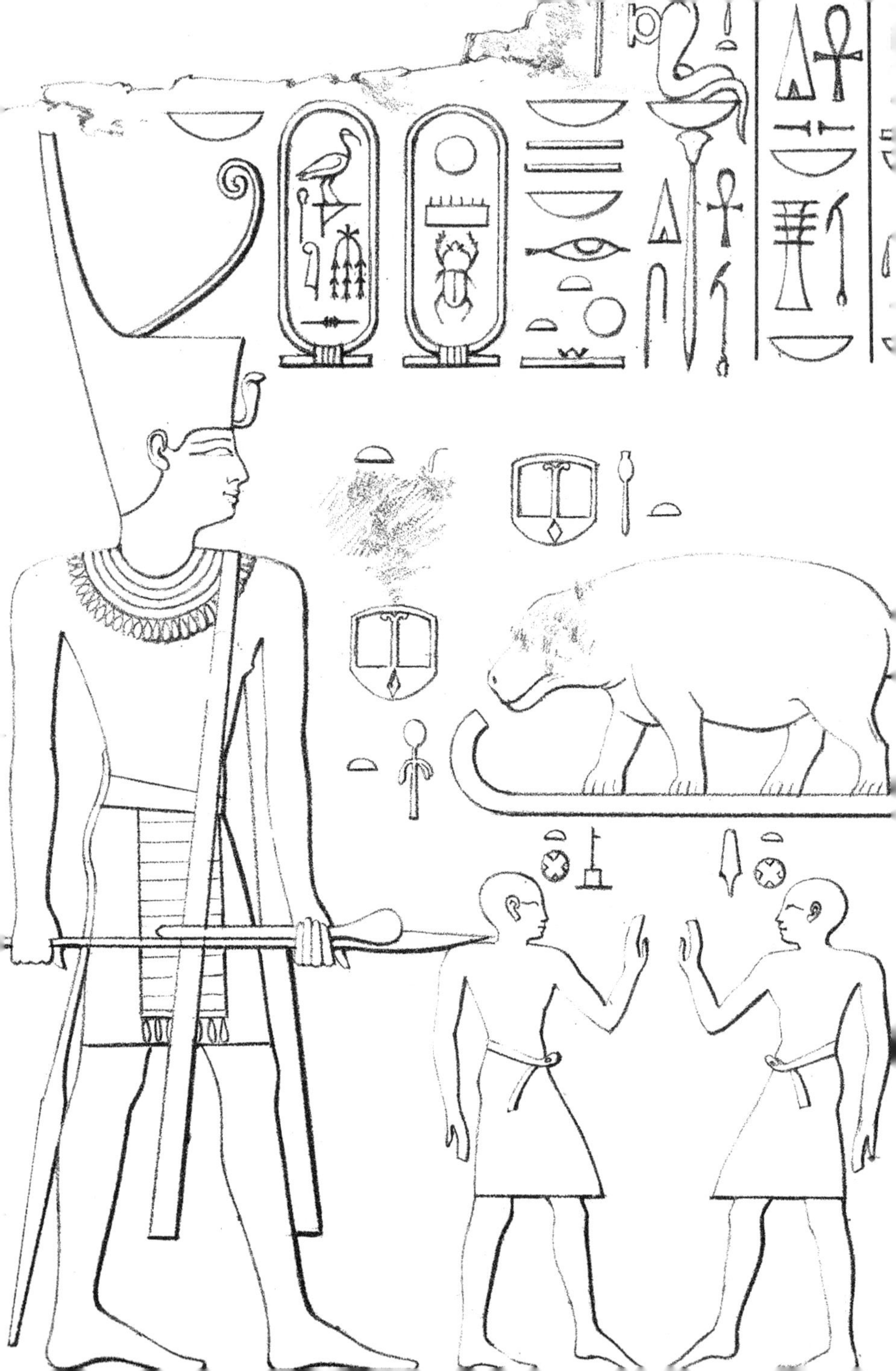

(Pages/Seite 106/107)

PALACE OF KARNAK

1, 2, 3. Bas-reliefs from the Thutmoseum

No. 1. The mystical education of Thutmosis III under the direction of the gods Anubis and Phre. The divinity on this bas-relief whose head has been mutilated appears to have borne different names: with a human head Anubis; Seth as the northern divinity of [the place of worship] Shot; in the form of a griffon he bears the name Bore or Patchi-Nub. No. 2. Fragment of a bas-relief depicting a religious ceremony and featuring the image of a hippopotamus; this is the only example of this genre which I have ever encountered on the Egyptian monuments. No. 3. Thutmosis, accompanied by a standard-bearer, his genie or his *Avatar*, receives divine life from Sobek-Ra.

PALAST VON KARNAK

1, 2, 3. Flachreliefs aus der Festhalle von Thutmosis III.

Nr. 1. Mystische Unterweisung Thutmosis' III. unter Anleitung der Götter Anubis und Phre. Die Gottheit, deren Kopf auf diesem Flachrelief verstümmelt ist, scheint verschiedene Namen getragen zu haben: Anubis mit einem menschlichen Kopf; Seth als nördliche Gottheit von [der Anbetungsstätte] Shot; in der Darstellung als Greif trägt er die Namen Bore und Patchi-Noub. Nr. 2. Bruchstück eines Flachreliefs, auf dem eine religiöse Zeremonie mitsamt dem Bild eines Flusspferdes dargestellt ist; es handelt sich um die einzige derartige Szene, die ich jemals auf den ägyptischen Denkmälern gefunden habe. Nr. 3. Sobek verleiht dem in Begleitung seines Bannerträgers – seines Genius oder Avatars – abgebildeten Thutmosis das göttliche Leben.

PALAIS DE KARNAC

1, 2, 3. Bas-reliefs du Thoutmoséïu

N° 1. Éducation mystique de Thoutmès [Thoutmôsis] III, sous la direction des dieux Noub [Anubis] et Phré. La divinité dont la tête a été mutilée sur ce bas-relief paraît avoir porté différents noms : avec une tête humaine Noub ou Noubi [Anubis] ; Seth comme divinité septentrionale du [lieu de culte] Shot ; sous la forme d'un griffon, elle porte le nom de Boré et de Patchi-Noub. N° 2. Fragment d'un bas-relief représentant une cérémonie religieuse où figure l'image d'un hippopotame ; c'est la seule de ce genre que j'aie jamais rencontrée sur les monuments égyptiens. N° 3. Thoutmès, accompagné d'un porte-bannière, son génie ou Avatar, reçoit la vie divine de Sevek[Sobek]-Ra.

EGYPTIAN MONUMENTS

Stele from the reign of Ay, 18th Dynasty

Stele [of Nakhtmin] from the reign of Sekeray or Acherai [Ay], pharaoh of the 18th Dynasty. The prenomen of this pharaoh can still be seen in a reasonable state of preservation at the bottom of the inscription. This stele, which unfortunately carries no date, depicts an act of piety by Nakht-Hor-Amun, chief of all the priests of Opet, high priest of Hor-Amun and of Isis, in charge of the offerings made in the royal dwelling of Ay, guardian of building works for the eternal throne.

ÄGYPTISCHE DENKMÄLER

Stele aus der Regierungszeit des Eje, 18. Dynastie

Stele [des Nachtmin] aus der Regierungszeit des Scherai oder Acherai [Eje oder Aja], Pharao der 18. Dynastie. Der Name dieses Pharaos befindet sich im unteren Teil der Inschrift, wo er recht gut erhalten ist. Die Stele trägt leider kein Datum mehr und stellt einen Akt der Frömmigkeit von Nacht-hor-Ammon dar, dem Vorsteher aller Opet-Priester, dem ersten Pontifex des Hor-Amun und der Isis, dem Beauftragten für die Opfergaben am königlichen Wohnsitz Ejes und dem Bewahrer der Bauten des ewigen Throns.

MONUMEN[T]S ÉGYPTIENS

Stèle du règne de Ay, XVIIIe dynastie

Stèle [de Nakhtmin] du règne de Schéraï ou Achéraï [Ay], pharaon de la XVIIIe dynastie. Le prénom de ce pharaon se retrouve encore assez bien conservé au bas de l'inscription. Cette stèle, qui ne porte malheureusement plus de date, est un acte de la piété de Nacht-hor-Ammon, chef de tous les prêtres de Opet, premier pontife de Hor-Ammon et d'Isis, chargé des offrandes dans la demeure royale de Schéraï, conservateur des constructions du trône éternel.

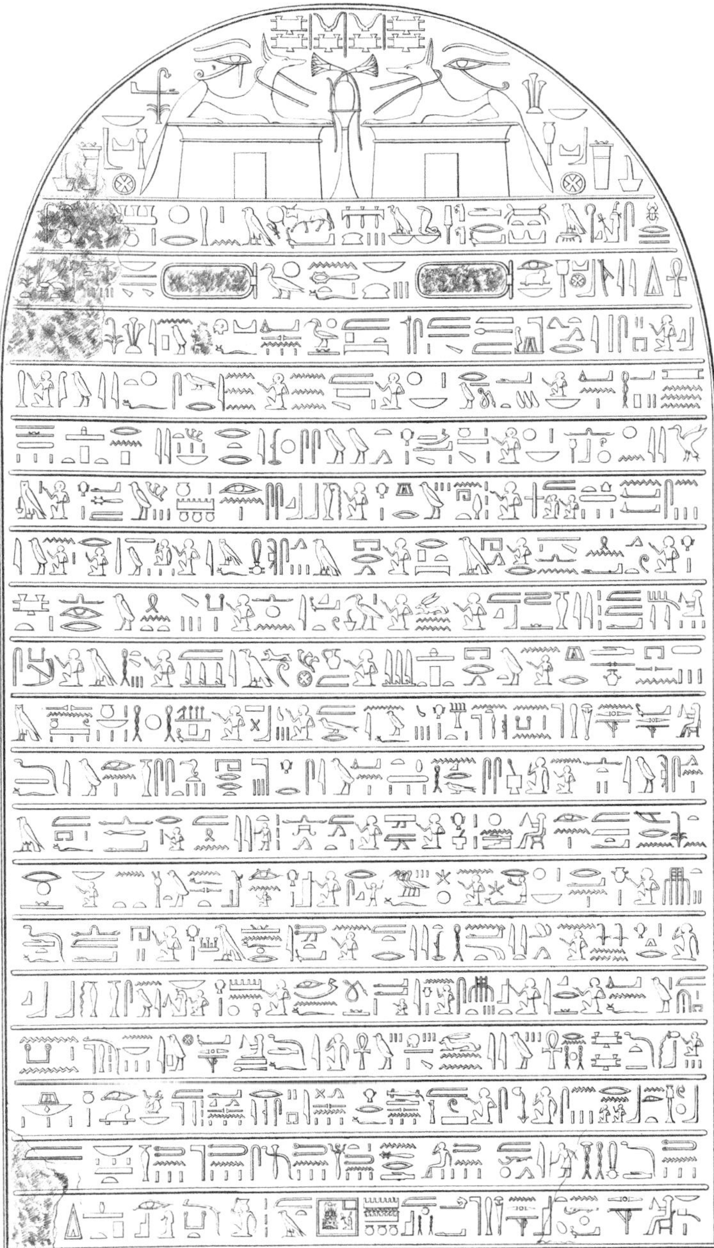

Lepelle lith. F. Prisse. Imp. Kaeppelin & Cie

STÈLE DU RÈGNE DE SCHERAI, XVIIIe DYNASTIE.

PALACE OF KARNAK

Horizontal inscription from the great obelisk

Supplement to plates CCCXIV and CCCXV in volume IV of *Monuments de l'Égypte et de la Nubie* by Jean-François Champollion. Horizontal inscription from the great obelisk of the palace of Karnak. On the plinth which supports this handsome monolith is another inscription which is so badly damaged that it is impossible to gain any information from it.

PALAST VON KARNAK

Horizontale Inschrift auf dem großen Obelisken

Ergänzung der Tafeln CCCXIV und CCCXV, Band IV der *Monuments de l'Égypte et de la Nubie* von Jean-François Champollion. Horizontale Inschrift auf dem großen Obelisken im Palast von Karnak. Die Basis, die diesen schönen Monolithen trägt, weist eine weitere, sehr stark beschädigte Inschrift auf, der keine Informationen mehr zu entnehmen sind.

PALAIS DE KARNAC

Inscription horizontale du grand obélisque

Complément des planches CCCXIV et CCCXV, tome IV des *Monuments de l'Égypte et de la Nubie* de Jean-François Champollion. Inscription horizontale du grand obélisque du palais de Karnac. La base qui porte ce beau monolithe présente une autre inscription tellement endommagée qu'il est impossible d'en tirer aucun renseignement.

PALAIS DE KARNAC.

Sud.

Ouest.

Nord.

Est.

F. Lepelle, lith. E. Prisse. Imp. Kaeppelin.

INSCRIPTION HORIZONTALE DU GRAND OBÉLISQUE.

LOWER EGYPT

1, 2, 3. Monolith from Tell Abu Seifa. 4, 5. Monolith from Tell el-Maskhuta

Nos. 1, 2 and 3. Monolith from Tell Abu Seifa, Lower Egypt. This is of ferruginous sandstone and is covered with skilfully cut hieroglyphs giving the names of three pharaohs of the 19th Dynasty: Ramesses I, his son Merneptah [*sic*] and his grandson Ramesses II. Nos. 4 and 5. Monolith from Tell el-Maskhuta. This depicts Ramesses the Great sitting between the mythical double figure of Phre and Atum, who were very closely linked in relation to functions and emblems. They were images of the appearance and of the disappearance of the sun: Phre represented the sun in the east, the upper and constantly luminous hemisphere, while Atum represented the sun in the west, or lower hemisphere, inhabited by those subject to mortality.

UNTERÄGYPTEN

1, 2, 3. Monolith aus Tell Abu-Sefeh. 4, 5. Monolith aus Tell el-Maschuta.

Nr. 1, 2 und 3. Monolith aus Tell Abu-Sefeh, Unterägypten. Er besteht aus eisenhaltigem Sandstein und ist von gut geschnittenen Hieroglyphen bedeckt, die die Namen dreier Pharaonen der 19. Dynastie wiedergeben: Ramses I., dessen Sohn Merenptah [*sic*] und dessen Enkelsohn Ramses II. Nr. 4 und 5. Monolith aus Tell el-Maschuta. Er stellt Ramses den Großen zwischen einer mythologischen Doppelpersönlichkeit sitzend dar; diese ist aus den Gottheiten Phre und Atum zusammengesetzt, die unter dem Gesichtspunkt ihrer Kennzeichen und Zuständigkeitsbereiche eng miteinander verbunden waren,. Es handelte sich um die Bilder vom Aufgang und Untergang der Sonne: Phre verkörperte das Tagesgestirn im Osten – die stets erleuchtete obere Hemisphäre – und Atum die Sonne im Westen – oder die untere, von sterblichen Lebewesen bewohnte Hemisphäre.

BASSE-ÉGYPTE

1, 2, 3. Monolithe d'Abou-Seyfeh. 4, 5. Monolithe d'Abou-Keycheyd

N°s 1, 2 et 3. Monolithe d'Abou-Seyfeh [Tell Abou Seifa], Basse-Égypte. Il est de grès ferrugineux et couvert d'hiéroglyphes bien taillés, qui retracent les noms de trois pharaons de la XIXe dynastie : Ramsès Ier, Menephtha [Mérenptah] son fils, et Ramsès II son petit-fils. N°s 4 et 5. Monolithe d'Abou-Keycheyd [Tell el-Maskhouta]. Il représente Ramsès le Grand assis entre un double personnage mythique, Phré et Atmou [Atoum], qui avaient une liaison fort intime sous les rapports des attributions et des emblèmes. C'étaient les images de l'apparition et de la disparition du soleil : Phré représentait l'astre du jour à l'orient, l'hémisphère supérieur toujours lumineux, et Atmou, le soleil à l'occident, ou l'hémisphère inférieur, habité par des êtres soumis à une vie mortelle.

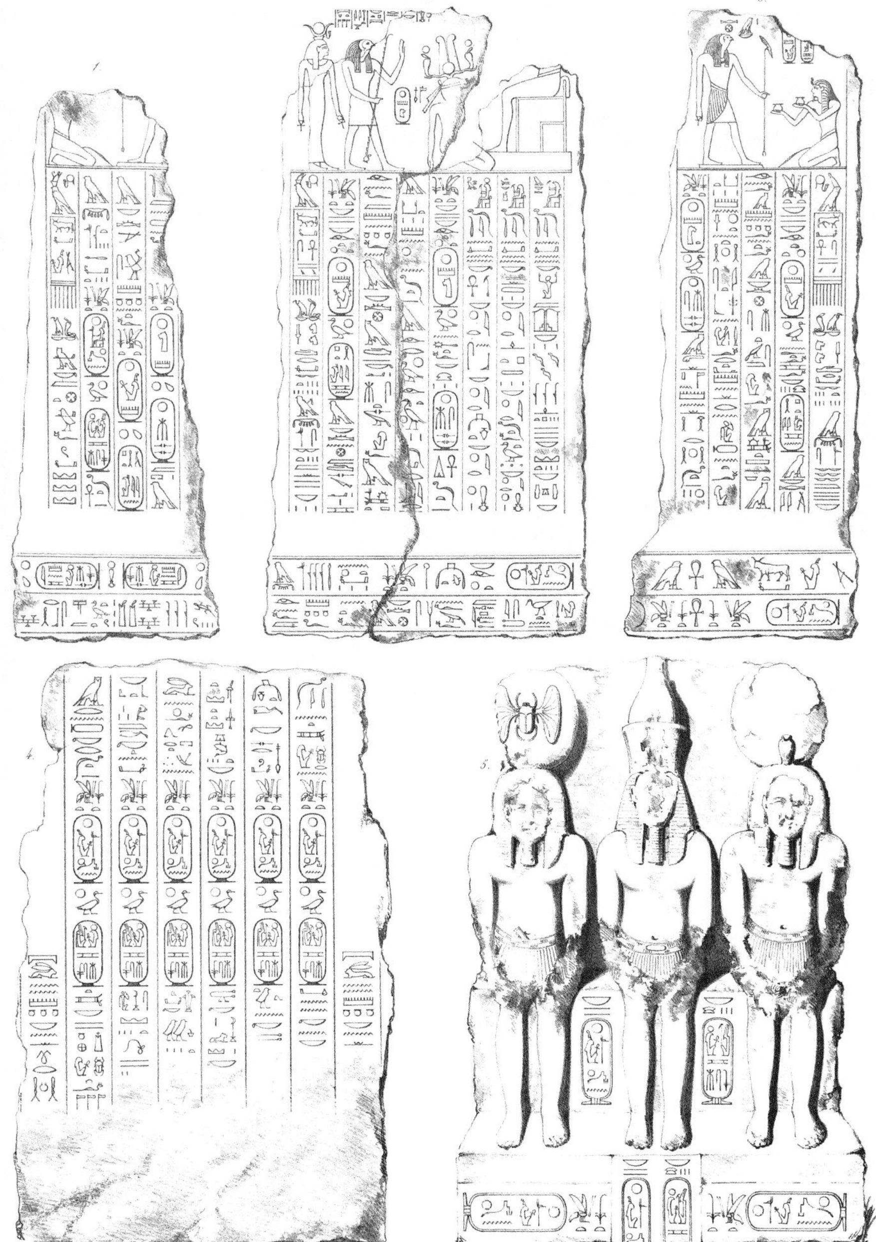

1, 2, 3, MONOLITHE D'ABOU-SEYFEH. ___ 4, 5, MONOLITHE D'ABOU-KEYCHEYD.

EGYPTIAN MONUMENTS

1–5. Statuettes of a son of Ramesses II. 6. Colossus of Ramesses II at Wadi es-Sebua

Nos. 1 to 5. Statuettes of a son of Ramesses II and of his queen Isetnefret. Inscription no. 2 forms part of the first figurine and nos. 4 and 5 are from the second. This dearly-loved son of Ramesses the Great had been involved with the empire to the detriment of his older brothers [and] all the inscriptions recall his pre-eminence. No. 6. Colossus from Wadi es-Sebua in Nubia. This statue represents Ramesses the Great who carries, resting against his arm, sacred insignia decorated with the ram's head symbol of Amun. The face of the king is mutilated; his head-dress consists of a wig plaited in Nubian fashion, circled with a diadem, the whole surmounted by a Pschent [Double Crown]. His body is almost naked; he wears nothing but a short kilt clasped with a richly ornamented belt bearing the royal titulary and into which is stuck a dagger decorated with the head of a falcon. The king, one leg thrust forward, is shown in the act of walking; the little figure of a woman, probably one of his wives, appears to be encouraging and directing his steps.

ÄGYPTISCHE DENKMÄLER

1–5. Statuetten eines Sohnes von Ramses II. 6. Koloss von Ramses II. in Wadi es-Sebua

Nr. 1 bis 5. Statuetten eines Sohnes von Ramses II. und Königin Isisnofret. Die Inschrift Nr. 2 gehört zum ersten Figürchen, die Nr. 4 und 5 zum zweiten. Dieser von Ramses dem Großen geliebte Sohn war auf Kosten seiner älteren Brüder am Imperium beteiligt worden, [und] alle Inschriften erinnern an seine Vorrangstellung. Nr. 6. Koloss aus Wadi es-Sebua in Nubien. Diese Statue zeigt Ramses den Großen, der, auf seinen Arm gestützt, ein heiliges, mit einem Widderkopf – dem Sinnbild des Amun – verziertes Banner trägt. Das Gesicht des Königs ist verstümmelt, sein Kopfputz besteht aus einer auf nubische Art geflochtenen Perücke, die von einem Diadem umfasst und von einem Pschent [Doppelkrone] überragt wird. Der Körper ist fast nackt; einziges Kleidungsstück ist ein kurzer Schurz mit einem reich verzierten Gürtel, in dem ein mit einem Sperberkopf verzierter Dolch steckt und der die königliche Hieroglypheninschrift trägt. Der König ist, mit einem vorgestellten Bein, gehend dargestellt; eine kleine Frauenfigur, bei der es sich wahrscheinlich um eine seiner Gemahlinnen handelt, scheint seine Schritte zu lenken und anzutreiben.

MONUMEN[T]S ÉGYPTIENS

1–5. Statuettes d'un fils de Ramsès II. 6. Colosse de Ramsès II à Wady Esseboua

N°s 1 à 5. Statuettes d'un fils de Ramsès II et de la reine Isinofré [Isis-Nofret]. L'inscription N° 2 fait partie de la première figurine ; les N°s 4 et 5, de la seconde. Ce fils chéri de Ramsès le Grand avait été associé à l'empire au détriment de ses frères aînés [et] toutes les inscriptions rappellent sa prééminence. N° 6. Colosse de Wady Esseboua, en Nubie. Cette statue représente Ramsès le Grand, portant, appuyée contre son bras, une enseigne sacrée, décorée d'une tête de bélier, symbole d'Amon. La figure du roi est mutilée, sa coiffure se composait d'une perruque nattée à la nubienne, ceinte d'un diadème et surmontée d'un pschent [la double couronne] sur le tout. Le corps est presque nu ; il a pour tout vêtement une courte schantéi [un pagne], dont la ceinture richement ornée porte la légende royale, et retient un poignard décoré d'une tête d'épervier. Le roi, une jambe en avant, est représenté dans l'action de marcher ; une petite figure de femme, probablement une de ses épouses, semble exciter et diriger ses pas.

1. 2. 3. 4. 5. 6.

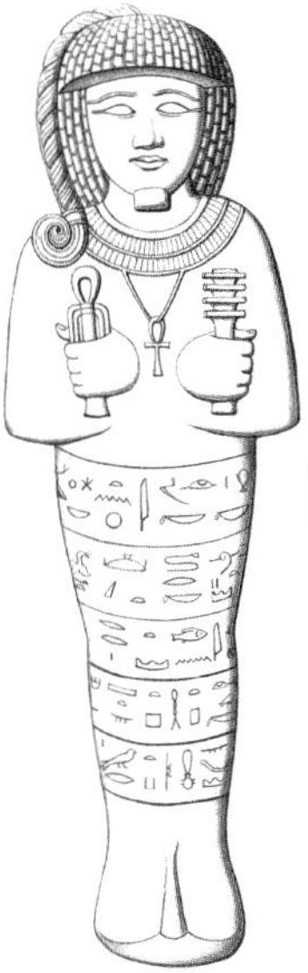

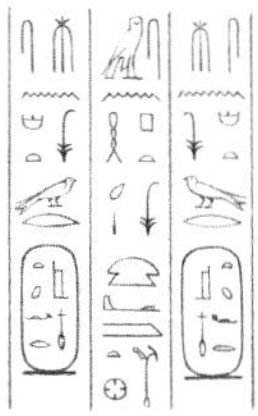

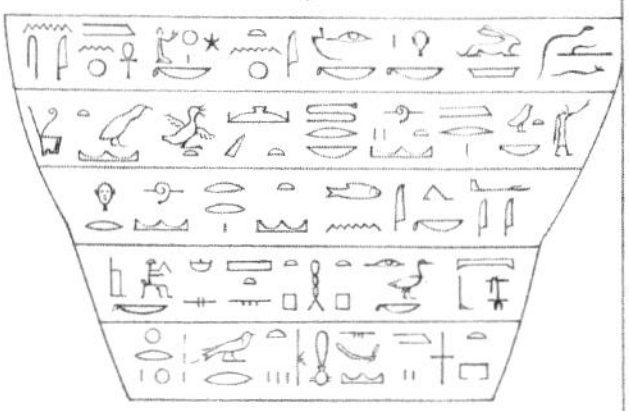

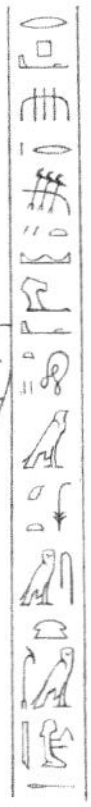

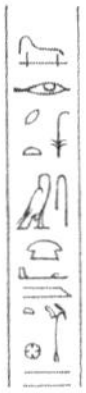

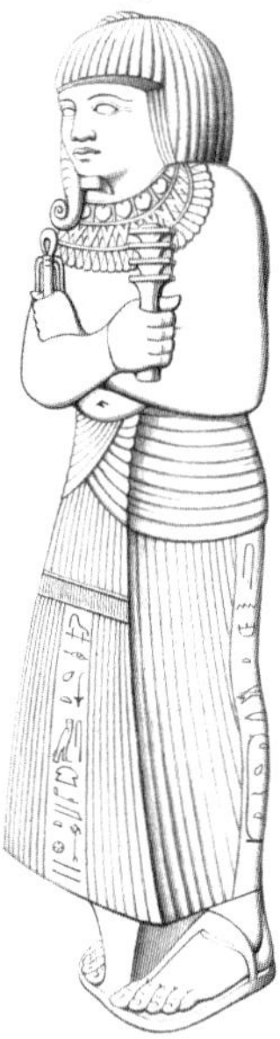

G. BARRY 1848

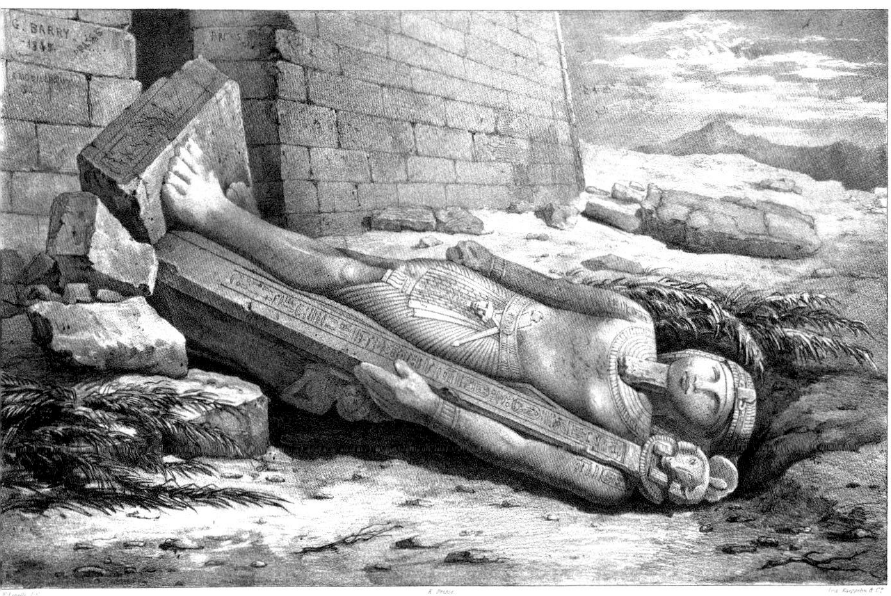

1—5. STATUETTES D'UN FILS DE RAMSÈS II. 6. COLOSSE DE RAMSÈS II A WADY ESSEBOUA.

KUBBAN. CONTRA-PSELCHIS

Worship scene of Ramesses II

Stele of Ramesses II, taken from the ruins of Kubban which are near Dakka in Nubia. This area, which has not yet been thoroughly explored, must be Contra-Pselchis, or rather Tachompso, according to Ptolemy. This granite stele is of fairly mediocre workmanship; its lower part has been broken into a number of pieces and all that remains of it is one part which I have shown in the middle of the plate, since I have no idea of its real position. In spite of its mutilated state, this monument is of considerable interest for the history of Ramesses II, who according to this inscription was already famed for the military victories he had achieved as early as the third year of his reign.

KUBAN. CONTRA-PSELCHIS

Proskynema von Ramses II.

Stele von Ramses II. aus den baulichen Überresten von Kuban, die gegenüber von Ad-Dakka in Nubien liegen. Bei diesem noch nicht genauer untersuchten Ort muss es sich um Contra-Pselchis oder eher das von Ptolemäus erwähnte Tachompso handeln. Diese Granitstele ist teilweise recht mangelhaft ausgeführt; ihr unterer Teil ist in mehrere Teile zerbrochen; es ist davon nur ein Bruchstück übrig, das ich in der Mitte der Tafel abgebildet habe – ohne zu wissen, wo es tatsächlich hingehörte. Im Hinblick auf die Geschichte Ramses' II. ist dieses Denkmal trotz seines verstümmelten Zustandes von großem Interesse, da er nach Aussage der Inschrift durch seine Siege schon von seinem dritten Regierungsjahr an Berühmtheit erlangt hatte.

KOÛBÁN. CONTRA-PSELCIS

Proscynème de Ramsès II

Stèle de Ramsès II, tirée des ruines de Koûbán [Qouban], situées vis-à-vis de Dakkeh en Nubie. Cette localité, qui n'a pas encore été bien examinée, doit être Contra-Pselcis, ou plutôt Tachompso, selon Ptolémée. Cette stèle de granite est d'un travail assez médiocre ; sa partie inférieure a été brisée en plusieurs pièces ; il n'en reste qu'un morceau que j'ai figuré au milieu de la planche, dans l'ignorance où j'étais de sa véritable place. Malgré ses mutilations, ce monument est fort intéressant pour l'histoire de Ramsès II, qui, au dire de cette inscription, s'était déjà rendu illustre par ses victoires dès la troisième année de son règne.

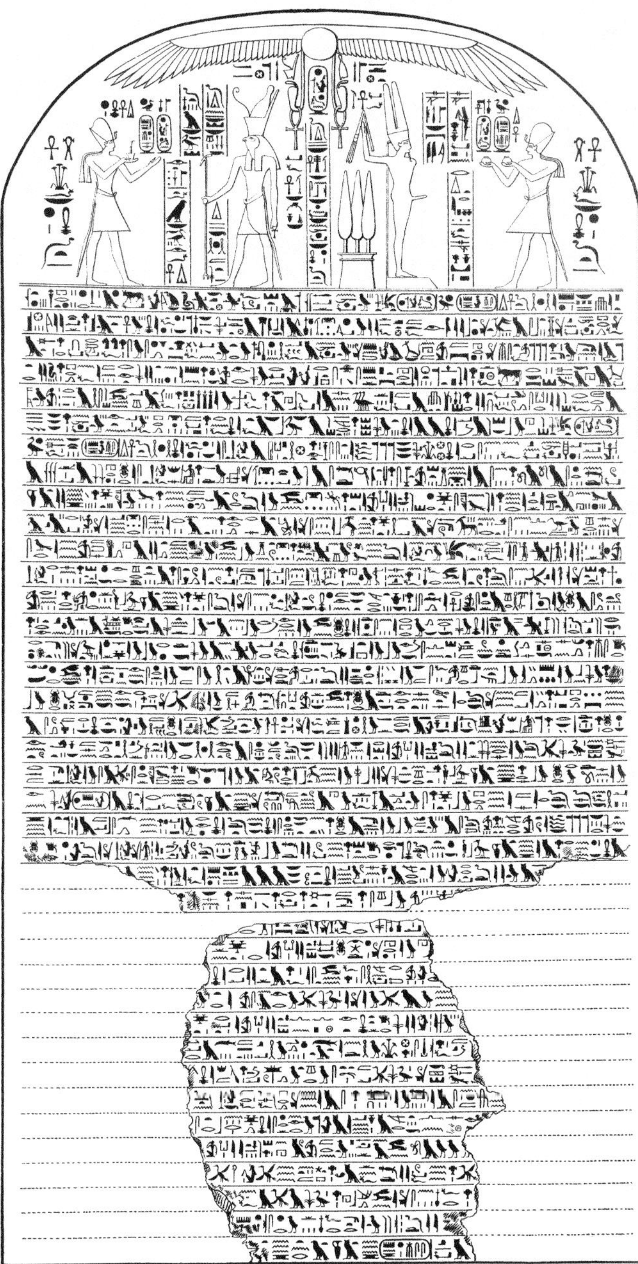

E. Prisse

PROSCYNÈME DE RAMSÈS II.

TEMPLE OF KHONSU. THEBES

1. Bas-relief depicting the entrance to the palace. 2. List of the sons of Amun-se-Pehor [Herihor]

Bas-relief and inscription from the temple of Khonsu, commonly known as the great temple of the south at Karnak. No. 1. Bas-relief depicting the façade of a temple or palace, probably that of Karnak, the only one to be decorated with eight triumphal masts. The Egyptians varied the number of these masts [which were only dressed on certain sacred days] according to the importance of the building: some, probably the least important, had none at all, while others had two, as at Philae, four as at Edfu, or eight as at the grand palace of Karnak. It is certainly the latter, which was the only building whose façade was ever crowned with so many points, which was meant to feature in these bas-reliefs. No. 2. List of the sons of Amun-se-Pehor [Herihor].

CHONS-TEMPEL. THEBEN

1. Den Palasteingang darstellendes Flachrelief. 2. Liste der Söhne von Amensi-Pehor [Herihor]

Flachrelief und Inschrift aus dem Chons-Tempel, der für gewöhnlich als großer Südtempel von Karnak bezeichnet wird. Nr. 1. Flachrelief, das eine Tempel- oder Palastfassade darstellt – vermutlich die von Karnak, die als einzige mit vier Triumphmasten geschmückt ist. Die Anzahl dieser Masten [die nur zu bestimmten Feiertagen aufgestellt wurden] richtete sich bei den Ägyptern nach der Bedeutung dieser Gebäude. Während die einen – wahrscheinlich die unbedeutendsten – keine aufwiesen, waren andere mit zweien, wie in Philæ, mit vieren, wie in Edfu, oder gar mit acht Masten ausgestattet – so wie der große Palast von Karnak; und zweifellos wollte man den letztgenannten – den einzigen, über dessen Fassade jemals so viele Spitzen aufragten – auf diesen Flachreliefs abbilden. Nr. 2. Liste der Söhne von Amensi-Pehor [Herihor].

TEMPLE DE KHONS. THÈBES

1. Bas-relief représentant l'entrée du palais. 2. Liste des fils d'Amon-Se-Pehôr [Hérihor]

Bas-relief et inscription du temple de Khons [Khonsou], appelé communément le grand temple du sud de Karnac. N° 1. Bas-relief représentant la façade d'un temple ou palais, probablement celui de Karnac, le seul qui soit orné de huit mâts triomphaux. Les Égyptiens variaient le nombre de ces mâts [qui n'étaient dressés qu'à certains jours de fête], en raison de l'importance des édifices : les uns, et probablement les moins importants, en étaient privés, tandis que les autres en avaient deux comme à Philæ, quatre comme à Edfou, huit comme au grand palais de Karnac, et c'est sans doute ce dernier, le seul dont la façade ait jamais été surmontée d'autant d'aiguilles, qu'on a voulu figurer dans les bas-reliefs. N° 2. Liste des fils d'Amon-Se-Pehôr [Hérihor].

TEMPLE DE KHONS. (THÈBES.)

Pl. XXII.

1

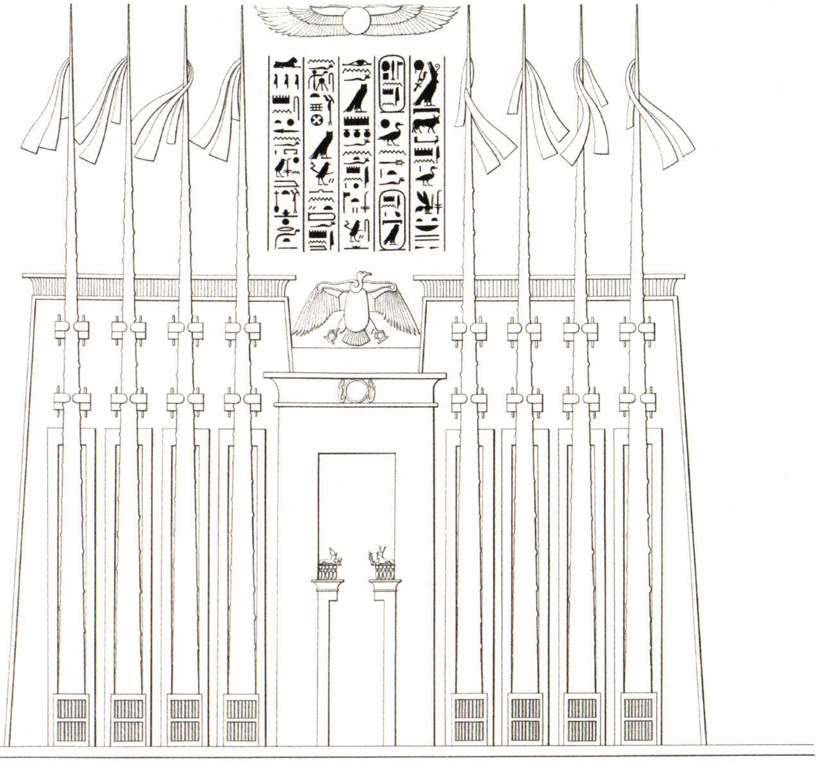

2.

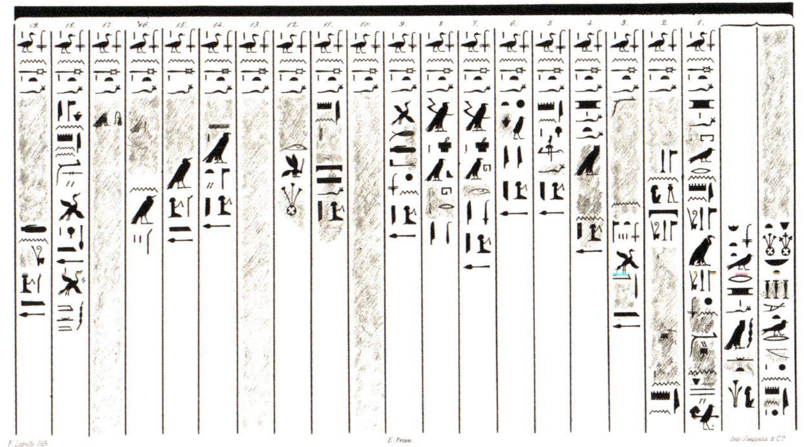

F. Lepelle lith. — E. Prisse. — Imp. Kaeppelin & Cie.

1, BAS-RELIEF REPRÉSENTANT L'ENTRÉE DU PALAIS. 2, LISTE DES FILS D'AMON-SE PEHÔR.

HEPTANOMIS AND THEBAID

Names stamped on bricks

Names stamped on bricks found in the Heptanomis and the Thebaid. Unbaked bricks, that is to say bricks dried in the open air and hardened in the sun, go back to the earliest times in Egypt. Very simply made from sticky mud kneaded and mixed with chopped straw, they are in this climate almost as durable as baked bricks. [...] Many of them carry on the side laid on the inside of the building-work a quite prominent hieroglyphic imprint which appears to have been made with a stone or bronze stamp. These inscriptions contain a religious dedication, the cartouches of the reigning king or the name of the functionary who was in charge of the manufacture of the building materials.

HEPTANOMIA UND THEBAIS

Hieroglyphenstempel auf Ziegeln

In der Heptanomia und der Thebais gefundene, auf Ziegel gestempelte Hieroglypheninschriften. In Ägypten kommen die ungebrannten, d. h. die luftgetrockneten, in der Sonne ausgehärteten Lehmziegel seit sehr alter Zeit vor. Unter diesen klimatischen Bedingungen sind diese Ziegel, die einfach aus durchgearbeitetem und mit gehacktem Stroh gemischtem Lehm geformt sind, fast genauso haltbar wie gebrannte Ziegel. [...] Auf der Seite zum Gebäude-Inneren weisen viele dieser Lehmziegel einen relativ hervorstechenden Hieroglyphenabdruck auf, der anscheinend mittels eines steinernen oder bronzenen Stempels erzeugt wurde. Diese Inschriften enthalten eine religiöse Widmung, die Kartusche des herrschenden Königs oder den Namen des Beamten, der die Herstellung dieser Baumaterialien beaufsichtigt hat.

HEPTANOMIDE ET THÉBAÏDE

Légendes estampées sur des briques

Légendes estampées sur des briques trouvées dans l'Heptanomide et la Thébaïde. Les briques crues, c'est-à-dire séchées à l'air et durcies au soleil, remontent en Égypte à une haute antiquité. Façonnées tout simplement avec de la terre grasse, pétrie et mêlée de paille hachée, elles sont sous ce climat presque aussi durables que les briques cuites. [...] Beaucoup d'entre elles portent sur la partie placée dans l'intérieur de la construction une empreinte hiéroglyphe assez saillante, et qui paraît avoir été faite avec une estampille de pierre ou de bronze. Ces inscriptions contiennent une consécration religieuse, les cartouches du roi régnant ou le nom du fonctionnaire qui présidait à la fabrication de ces matériaux.

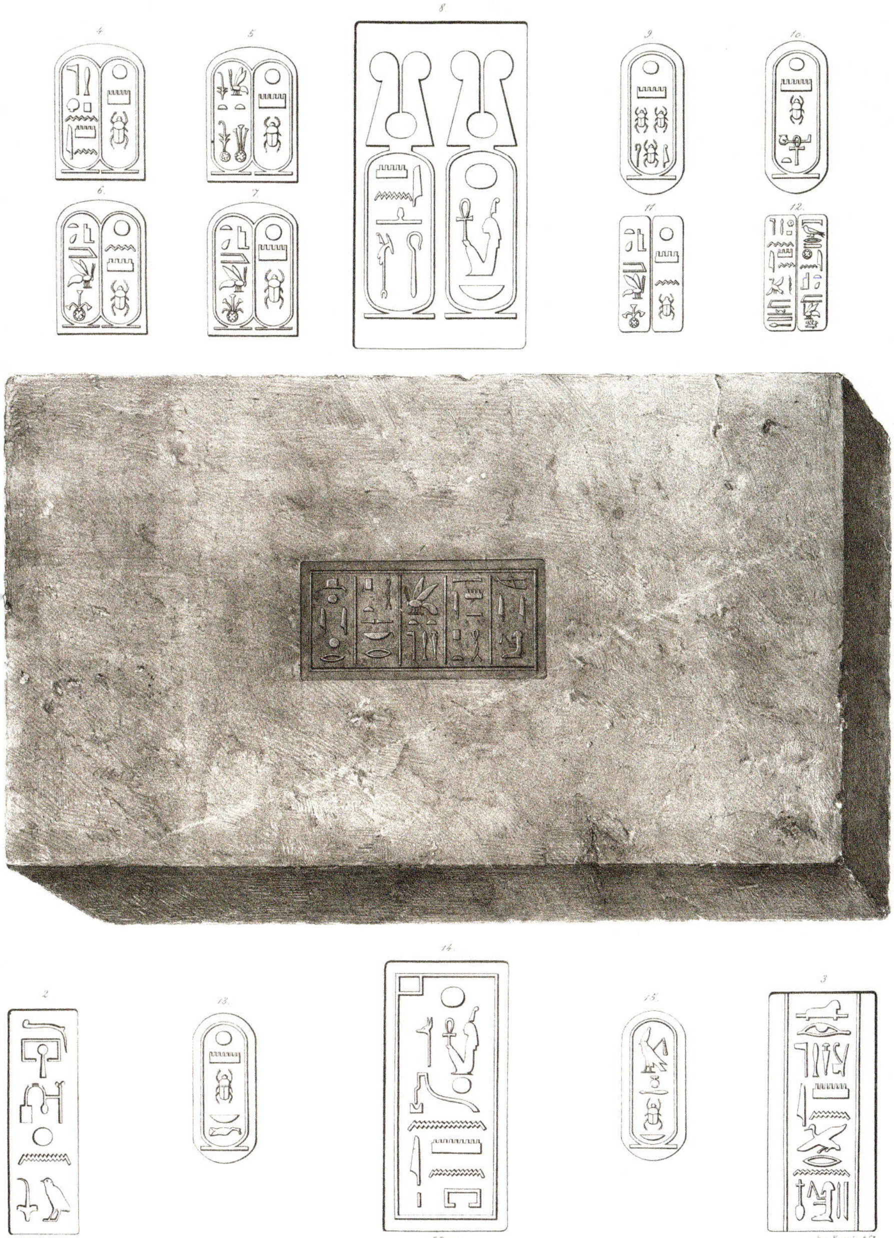

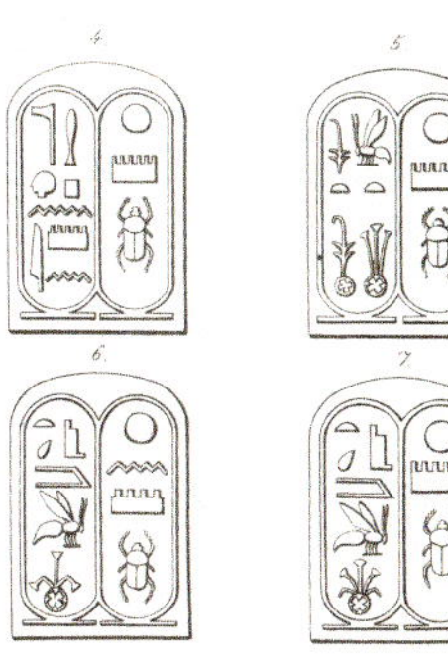

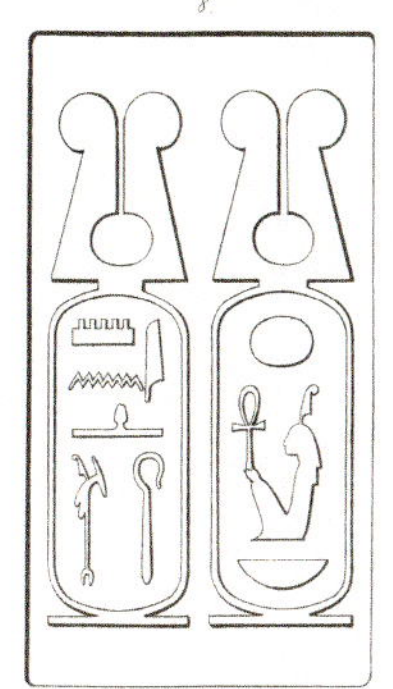

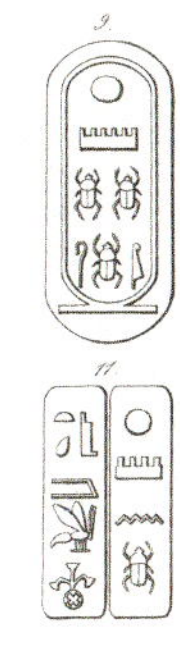

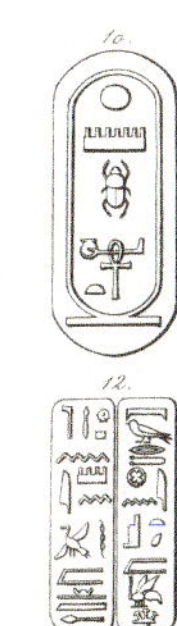

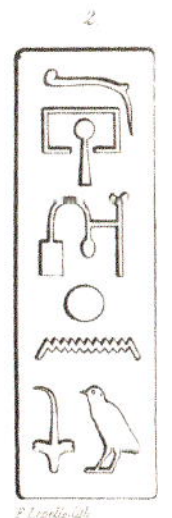

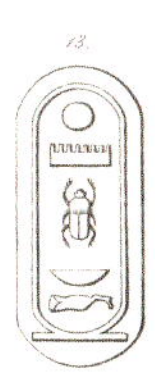

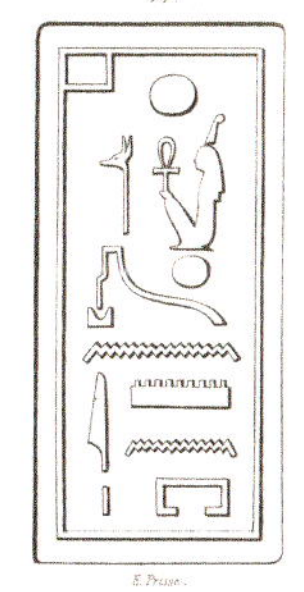

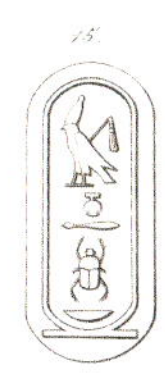

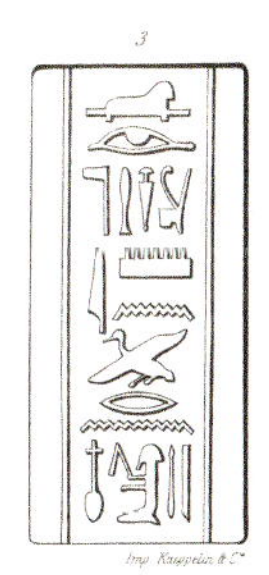

P. Lepelle lith. E. Prisse. Imp. Kaeppelin & Cie

LÉGENDES ESTAMPÉES SUR DES BRIQUES.

THEBES – KARNAK

Stele of Ramesses XV [sic, II]

Stele of Ramesses XV [II] taken from the ruins of a small temple to the east of the palace of Karnak. From this monument we learn that in the 23rd year of his reign he made an expedition into the country of Naharina (Mesopotamia), and that the inhabitants begged him to accept tribute in the form of porcelain or enamel, brass or wood, which they carried to him on their backs. The ruler of the country of Bakhten came with his eldest daughter to implore the king's mercy. She was tall and beautiful and stole the king's heart and so she became his royal wife and was given, on her arrival in Egypt, the name of Neferu-Ra or sun of goodness. The following year the ruler of Bakhten made the journey to the Nile valley to visit his daughter and brought her sister to her: their visit was celebrated with magnificent feasts. [...] This stele, which is of the greatest interest to the history of Egypt, was copied by Champollion, who quoted a number of passages from it in his *Grammaire*.

THEBEN – KARNAK

Stele von Ramses XV. [sic, II.]

Stele von Ramses XV. [II.] aus den baulichen Überresten eines kleinen im Osten des Palastes von Karnak gelegenen Tempels. Dieses Denkmal lehrt uns, dass dieser in seinem 23. Regierungsjahr einen Feldzug in das Land Naharina (Mesopotamien) durchführte und dass die Einwohner ihn flehentlich baten, einen Tribut aus Porzellan oder Emaille, aus Kupfer und aus Holz anzunehmen, den sie auf ihrem Rücken überbrachten. Das Oberhaupt des Landes Bechten kam mit seiner ältesten Tochter, um die Gnade des Königs zu erflehen. Da sie groß und schön war und eine starke Wirkung auf das Herz Ihrer Majestät hatte, wurde sie seine königliche Gemahlin und erhielt bei ihrer Ankunft in Ägypten den Namen Neferu-Ra. Im darauf folgenden Jahr unternahm das Oberhaupt des Landes Bechten eine Reise ins Niltal, um seine Tochter zu besuchen, und brachte ihr ihre Schwester: Ihnen zu Ehren wurden prachtvolle Feste gefeiert. [...] Diese Stele, die für die ägyptische Geschichte von größtem Interesse ist, wurde von Champollion abgezeichnet, der einige Passagen daraus in seiner *Grammaire* zitiert hat.

THÈBES – KARNAC

Stèle de Ramsès XV [sic, II]

Stèle de Ramsès XV [II] tirée des ruines d'un petit temple à l'est du palais de Karnac. Ce monument nous apprend qu'il fit une expédition, l'an 23 de son règne, dans le pays de Naharina (la Mésopotamie), et que les habitants le supplièrent d'accepter un tribut en porcelaine ou émail, en cuivre et en bois, qu'ils apportèrent sur leur dos. Le chef du pays de Bischtan vint avec sa fille aînée implorer la clémence du roi. Étant belle, grande et puissante sur le cœur de Sa Majesté, elle devint sa royale épouse, et reçut à son arrivée en Égypte le nom de Raninofré ou soleil des biens. Le chef de Bischtan [Bekhten], l'année suivante, entreprit un voyage dans la vallée du Nil pour visiter sa fille et lui amena sa sœur : on fit à leur occasion des fêtes magnifiques. [...] Cette stèle, du plus grand intérêt pour l'histoire égyptienne, avait été copiée par Champollion, qui en a cité divers passages dans sa *Grammaire*.

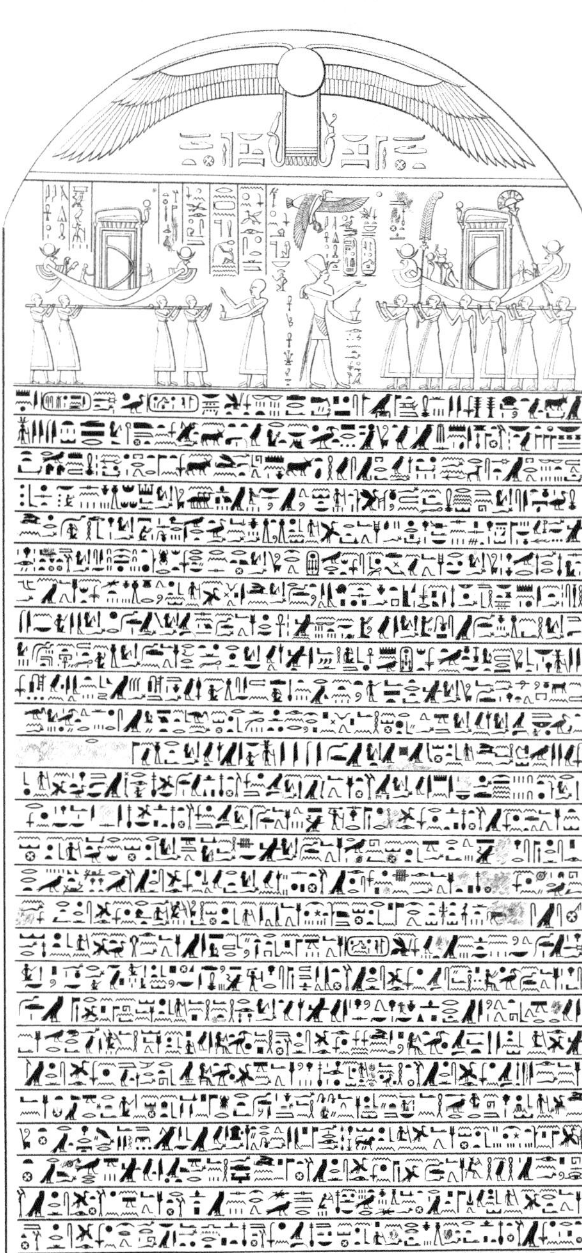

F. Lepelle lith. E. Prisse. Imp. Kaeppelin & Cie

STÈLE DE RAMSÈS (XV?)

THEBES – PALACE OF KARNAK

1. Engraving on the third pylon of the south avenue. 2. Architrave from the Thutmoseum. 3. Temple of Thoth

Various subjects taken from the ruins of Karnak. No. 1. Worship scene of the great triad of Thebes: Amun, Mut and Khonsu their son, followed by the goddess Taweret, by the queen Ahmose Nefertari and by Amenophis, probably the first of that name. This little worship scene is engraved in the stairway of the third pylon of the southern propylaea. No. 2. Inscription carved on an architrave of the gallery of Thutmosis III. It dates from year 2 of the reign of Takelot I and mentions one of his sons, who was high priest of Amun and chief of the archers. No. 3. One of the kings called Ptolemy, certainly Euergetes II, in the form of a sphinx, making an offering of a figure of Maat (truth and justice) to the ibis-headed god Thoth (another Hermes), who dwelt in the land of Hocer. This bas-relief was found in a small temple of Thoth.

THEBEN – PALAST VON KARNAK

1. In den 3. Pylon der südlichen Allee eingraviert. 2. Architrav der Festhalle von Thutmosis III. 3. Thot-Tempel

Verschiedene Motive aus den baulichen Überresten von Karnak. Nr. 1. Proskynema der großen Triade von Theben – Amun, Mut und ihr gemeinsamer Sohn Chons, gefolgt von der Göttin Taweret, der Königin Ahmose Nefertari und von Amenophis, vermutlich dem ersten dieses Namens. Dieses kleine Proskynema ist beim dritten Pylon der südlichen Propyläen in die Treppe eingraviert. Nr. 2. In einen Architrav im Wandelgang von Thutmosis III. eingearbeitete Inschrift. Sie datiert aus dem Jahr 2 der Herrschaft von Takelot I. und nennt einen seiner Söhne, der Hohepriester des Amun und Oberhaupt der Bogenschützen war. Nr. 3. Einer der Ptolemäerkönige, bei dem es sich zweifellos um den – hier als Sphinx dargestellten – Euergetes II. handelt, opfert dem ibisköpfigen Thot (dem zweiten Hermes), der im Land des Hocer wohnt, eine Maat-Figur (Verkörperung von Wahrheit und Gerechtigkeit). Dieses Flachrelief befindet sich in einem kleinen Thot-Tempel.

THÈBES – PALAIS DE KARNAC

1. Gravé sur le IIIe pylône de l'avenue du sud. 2. Architrave du Thoutmoseium. 3. Temple de Thoth

Sujets divers tirés des ruines de Karnac. N° 1. Proscynème à la grande triade de Thèbes, Amon, Mauth [Mout] et Khons [Khonsou], leur fils, suivis de la déesse Taoueri, de la reine Amès-Nofré-Atari [Ahmès-Néfertari] et d'Amounôph [Aménophis], probablement le premier du nom. Ce petit proscynème est gravé dans l'escalier du troisième pylône des propylées du sud. N° 2. Inscription sculptée sur une architrave du promenoir de Thoutmès [Thoutmôsis] III. Elle est datée de l'an 2 du règne de Takelothe Ier, et fait mention d'un de ses fils, qui était grand prêtre d'Amon, et chef des archers. N° 3. Un des rois Ptolémées, sans doute Évergète II, sous la forme d'un sphinx, fait offrande d'une figure de Tmei ([Maât], la vérité et la justice) au dieu Thoth ibiocéphale (le second Hermès), résidant dans la terre de Hocer. Ce bas-relief se trouve dans un petit temple de Thoth.

1.

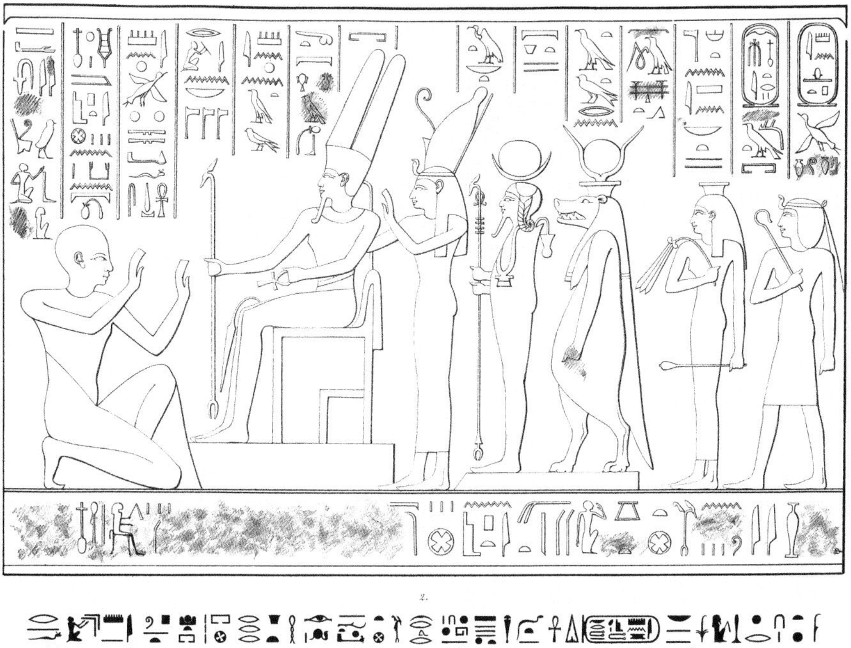

2.

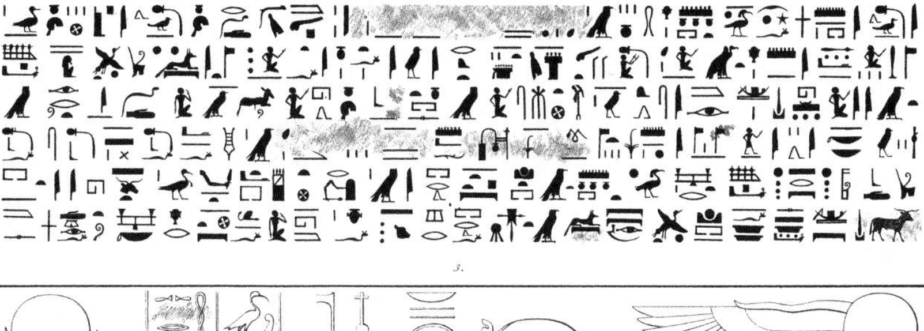

3.

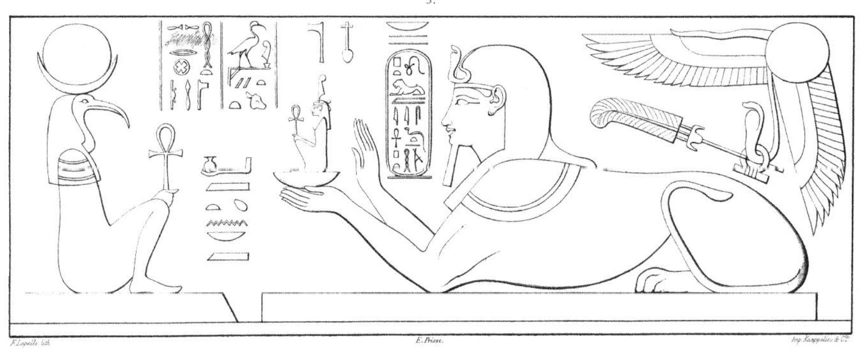

F. Lepelle lith. E. Prisse. Imp. Kaeppelin & Cie.

1, GRAVÉ SUR LE III? PYLÔNE DE L'AVENUE DU SUD. 2, ARCHITRAVE DU THOUTMOSEIUM. 3, TEMPLE DE THOTH.

MEMPHIS

Funerary stele of the high priest Pasherienptah

Funerary stele found at Memphis. This fine stele recalls the principal events of the life of a high-ranking person, a high priest of Memphis whose name was Pasherienptah, son of a high priest who carried out a number of very important functions; today it is no longer possible to determine their names or character. The following gives an approximate idea of the information furnished by [the text]: "Pasherienptah was born on the 21st day of Phaophi, in year 25 of the reign of Ptolemy Soter II or Lathyros (the year 91 BC). When he reached the age of 13, his father died. In the tenth year of the reign of Ptolemy he was promoted to the priestly office which his father had held, on the day when the king came to Memphis, probably to be inaugurated there according to the custom of the country. [...] Finally Pasherienptah died, at the age of 49, on the 10th day of Epiphi in the 11th year of Cleopatra and of her son Caesar."

MEMPHIS

Grabstele des Hohepriesters Psenptah

In Memphis gefundene Grabstele. Diese schöne Stele vergegenwärtigt die wichtigsten Ereignisse aus dem Leben einer hochstehenden Persönlichkeit, eines aus Memphis stammenden Hohepriesters namens Psenptah; der Sohn eines Hohepriesters übte zahlreiche wichtige Ämter aus, deren Art und Bezeichnung sich heute kaum noch bestimmen lässt. Dies sind annäherungsweise die Informationen, die [der Text] liefert: „Psenptah wurde im 25. Regierungsjahr des Ptolemaios Soter II. oder Latyros (im Jahr 91 nach christlicher Zeitrechnung), am 21. Tag des [Monats] Phaophi geboren. Als er das Alter von 13 Jahren erreichte, verstarb sein Vater. Im zehnten Regierungsjahr des Ptolemaios wurde er an dem Tag, an dem der König nach Memphis kam – vermutlich um dort der Landessitte entsprechend gekrönt zu werden – in das priesterliche Amt erhoben, das sein Vater innegehabt hatte. [...] Psenptah III. starb schließlich im Alter von 49 Jahren, am 10. Tag des [Monats] Epiphi, im 11. Regierungsjahr der Kleopatra und ihres Sohnes Caesarion."

MEMPHIS

Stèle funéraire du grand prêtre Pischarenptah

Stèle funéraire trouvée à Memphis. Cette belle stèle rappelle les principaux événements de l'existence d'un haut personnage, un grand prêtre de Memphis, nommé *Pischarenptah*, fils d'un grand prêtre qui remplissait d'importantes et nombreuses fonctions, dont il n'est guère possible aujourd'hui de déterminer les noms et la nature. Voici à peu près les renseignements qu'il [le texte] fournit : « Pischarenptah naquit le 21e jour de paôphi, l'an 25 du règne de Ptolémée Sôter II ou Lathyre (l'an 91 avant l'ère chrétienne). Quand il atteignit l'âge de treize ans, son père mourut. La dixième année du règne de Ptolémée il fut promu au poste sacerdotal que son père avait occupé, le jour de la venue du roi à Memphis, probablement pour y être inauguré selon l'usage du pays. [...] Enfin Pischarenptah mourut, âgé de quarante-neuf ans, le 10e jour d'épiphi de la onzième année de Cléopâtre et de son fils César. »

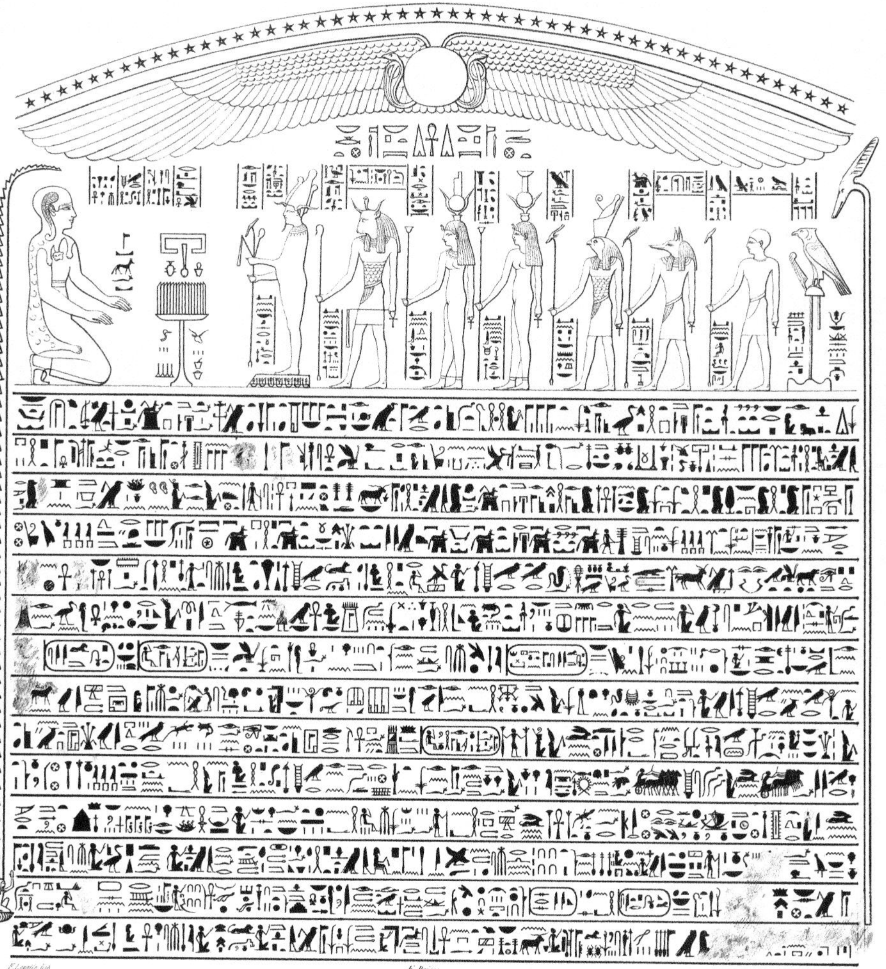

F. Lepoitte lith. E. Prisse. Imp. Kaeppelin

STÈLE FUNÉRAIRE DU GRAND PRÊTRE PISCHARENPTAH.

Tiré de la collection de Mr. A. C. Harris, à Alexandrie.

MEMPHIS

Funerary stele of the priestess Nefertemhotep

Funerary stele of the priestess Nefertemhotep, sister and wife of the high priest Pasherienptah, with whom she seems to have shared the principal priestly functions in the temples of Memphis. There can be no doubt that this stele was found in the same tomb as the preceding one, whose text it completes and corroborates.

MEMPHIS

Grabstele der Priesterin Nefertemhotep

Grabstele der Priesterin Nefertemhotep, Schwester und Gemahlin des Hohepriesters Psenptah, mit dem sie anscheinend die bedeutendsten priesterlichen Ämter der Tempel von Memphis teilte. Diese Stele, die den Text der vorhergehenden vervollständigt, wurde zweifellos in demselben Grab gefunden.

MEMPHIS

Stèle funéraire de la prêtresse Timôpt

Stèle funéraire de la prêtresse *Timôpt* ou *Teimôtph*, sœur et femme du grand prêtre Pischarenptah, avec lequel elle paraît avoir partagé les principales fonctions sacerdotales des temples de Memphis. Cette stèle a été trouvée sans aucun doute dans le même tombeau que la précédente, dont elle complète et corrobore le texte.

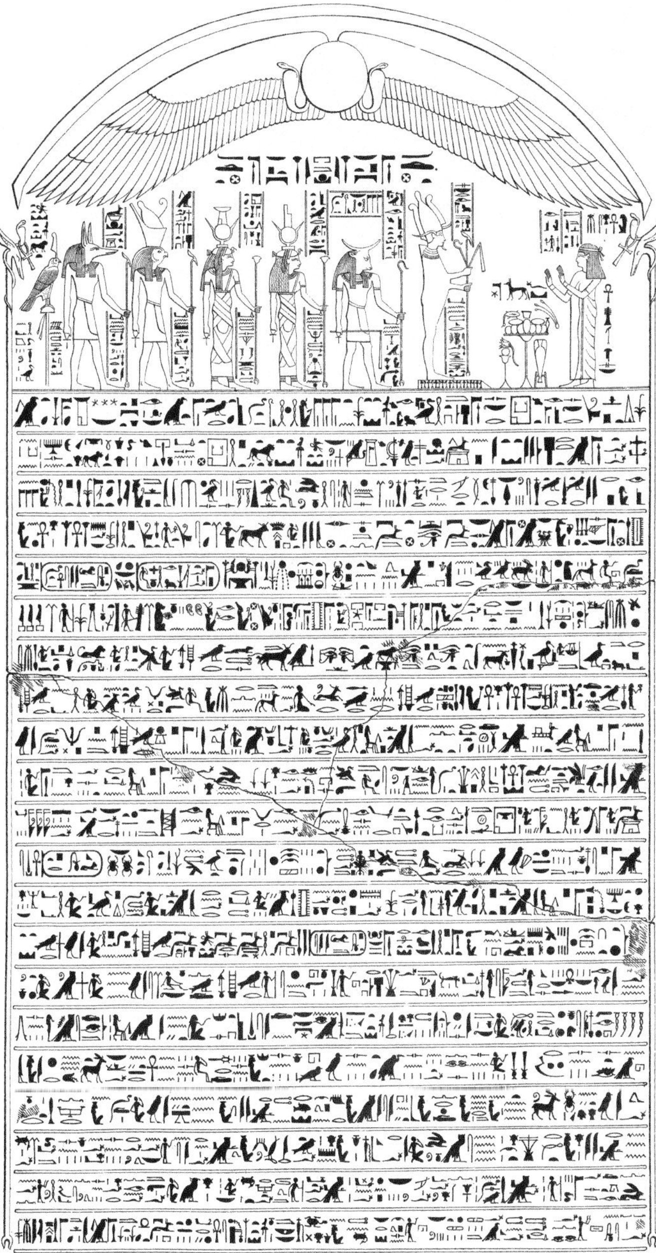

Maurice lith. E. Prisse. Imp. Kaeppelin & Cie

STÈLE FUNÉRAIRE DE LA PRÊTRESSE TIMÔPT,

(Musée Britannique.)

NECROPOLIS OF THEBES

Funerary cones

I am inclined to think that these cones served, like tesserae, as admission tokens to take part in certain distributions or as a means to summon people to attend the funerary ceremonies which were performed in the tombs; this would explain why so many of these baked-clay objects are found buried near the hypogea. Whatever the case may be, these cones, which are generally considered of little account, often feature very important documents, together with titles of public functions which are found nowhere else at all; a complete table of these, which is yet to be produced, could give us an idea of the social organisation of the Egyptians.

NEKROPOLE VON THEBEN

Grabkegel

Ich wäre versucht zu glauben, dass diese Kegel – wie die *Tesserae* – als Erkennungszeichen dienten, um an bestimmten Versorgungsmaßnahmen teilzuhaben, oder dazu aufforderten, an Begräbniszeremonien teilzunehmen, die in den Gräbern gefeiert wurden; die Folge ist, dass man diese Tonwaren in großer Zahl in der Nähe der Hypogäen vergraben findet. Wie dem auch sei – diese Kegel, von denen im Allgemeinen wenig Aufhebens gemacht wird, enthalten häufig wichtige Dokumente und Bezeichnungen öffentlicher Ämter, die nirgendwo sonst zu finden wären und deren – noch zu erstellende – vollständige Übersicht uns einen Eindruck von der Sozialstruktur der Ägypter verschaffen würde.

NÉCROPOLE DE THÈBES

Cônes funéraires

Je serais tenté de croire que ces cônes servaient, comme les tessères, de signes de reconnaissance pour avoir part à certaines distributions, ou de moyen de convocation pour assister à des cérémonies funéraires qui se célébraient dans les tombeaux, ce qui fait qu'on trouve un grand nombre de ces terres cuites enfouies près des hypogées. Quoi qu'il en soit, ces cônes, dont on fait généralement peu de cas, contiennent souvent des documents fort importants et des titres de fonctions publiques qu'on ne trouverait nulle part ailleurs, et dont le tableau complet, encore à faire, nous donnerait une idée de l'organisation sociale des Égyptiens.

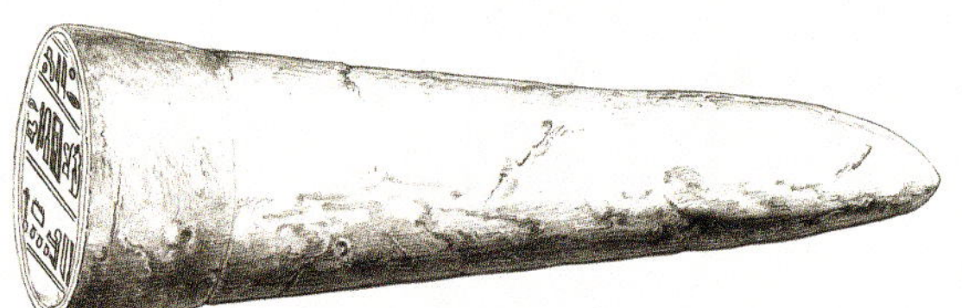

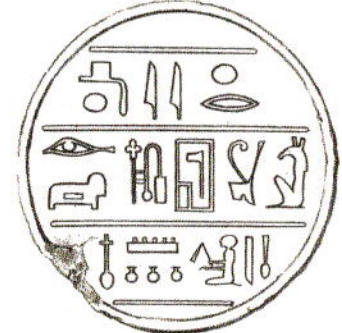

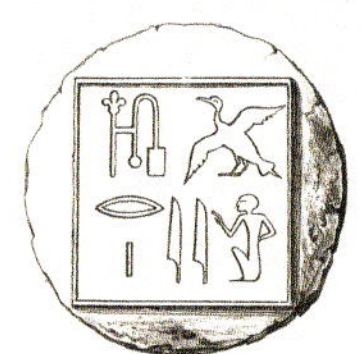

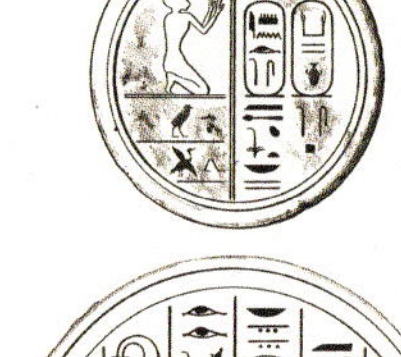

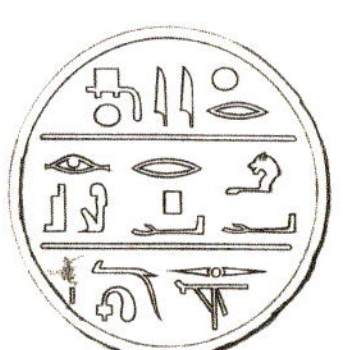

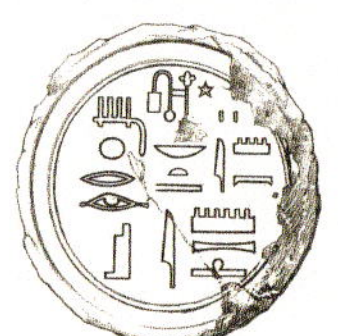

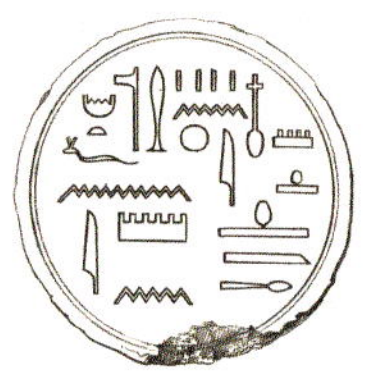

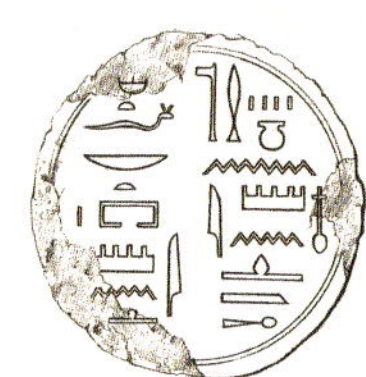

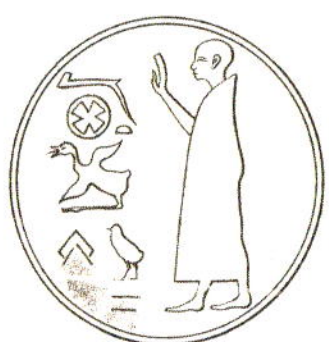

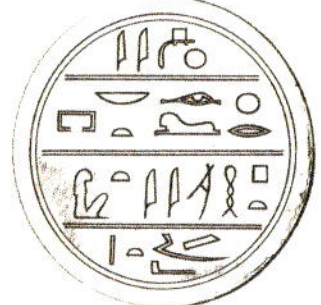

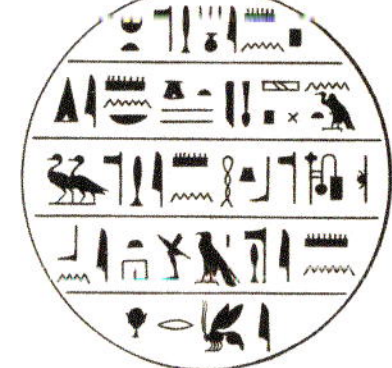

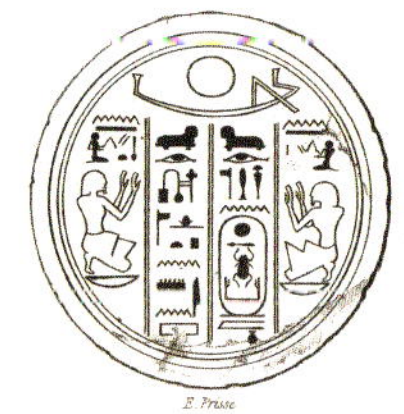

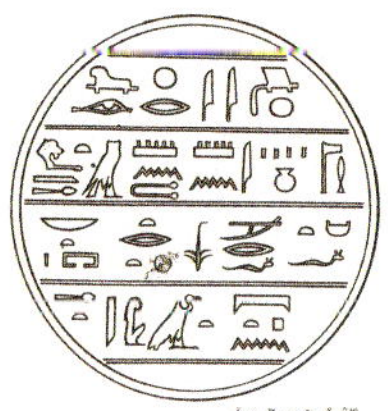

F. Lapelle lith. E. Prisse Imp. Kaeppelin & Cie

CÔNES FUNÉRAIRES.

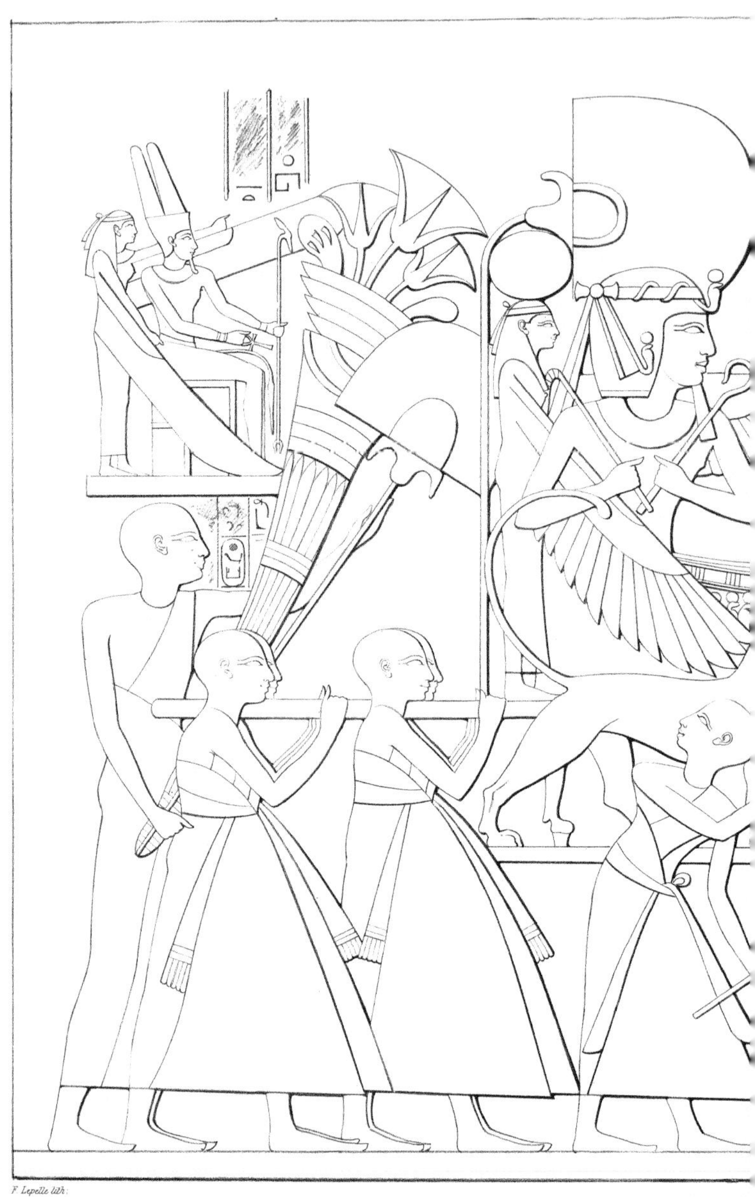

F. Lepelle lith:

AMOUNOPH IER

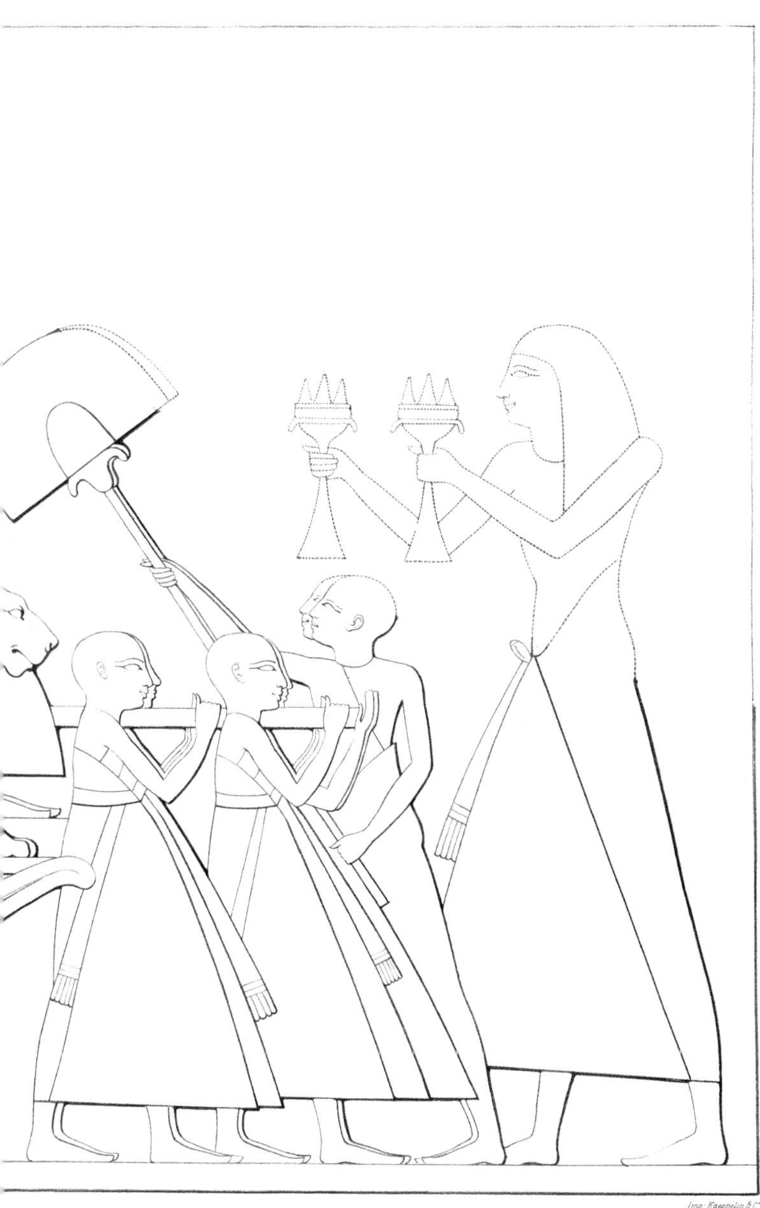

Imp. Kaeppelin & Cie

ON PALANQUIN .

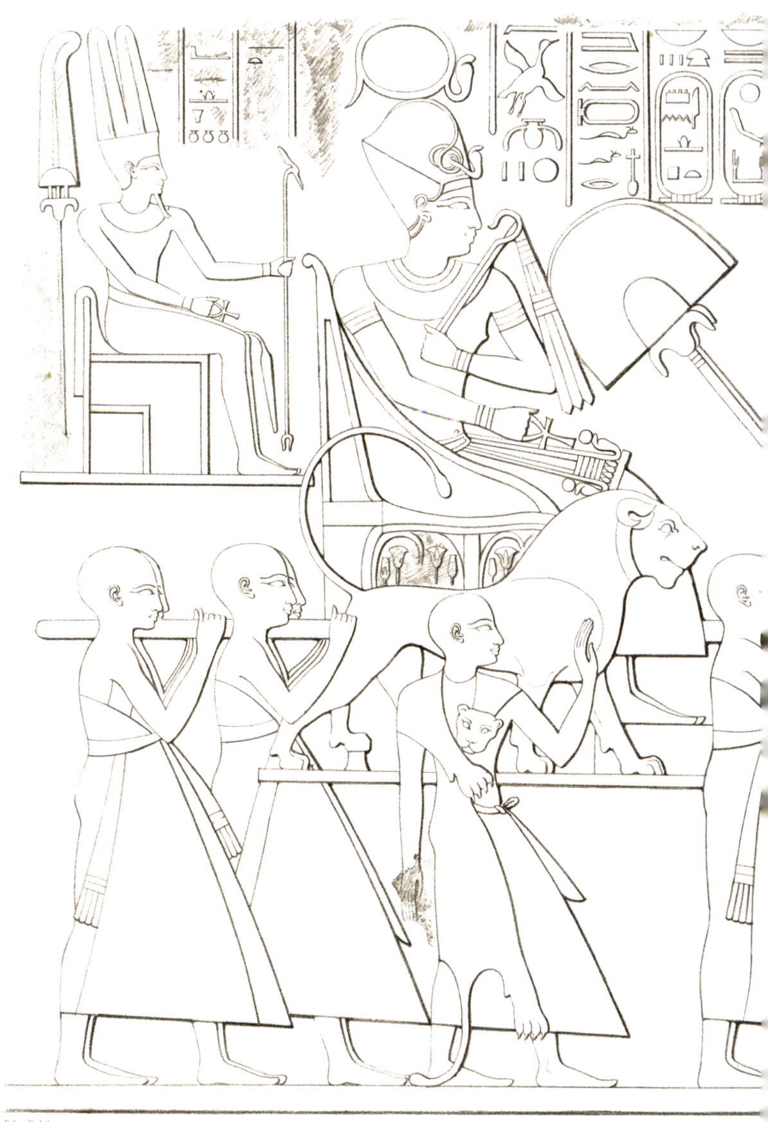

F. Lapelle, lith.

AMOUNOPH 1ER P

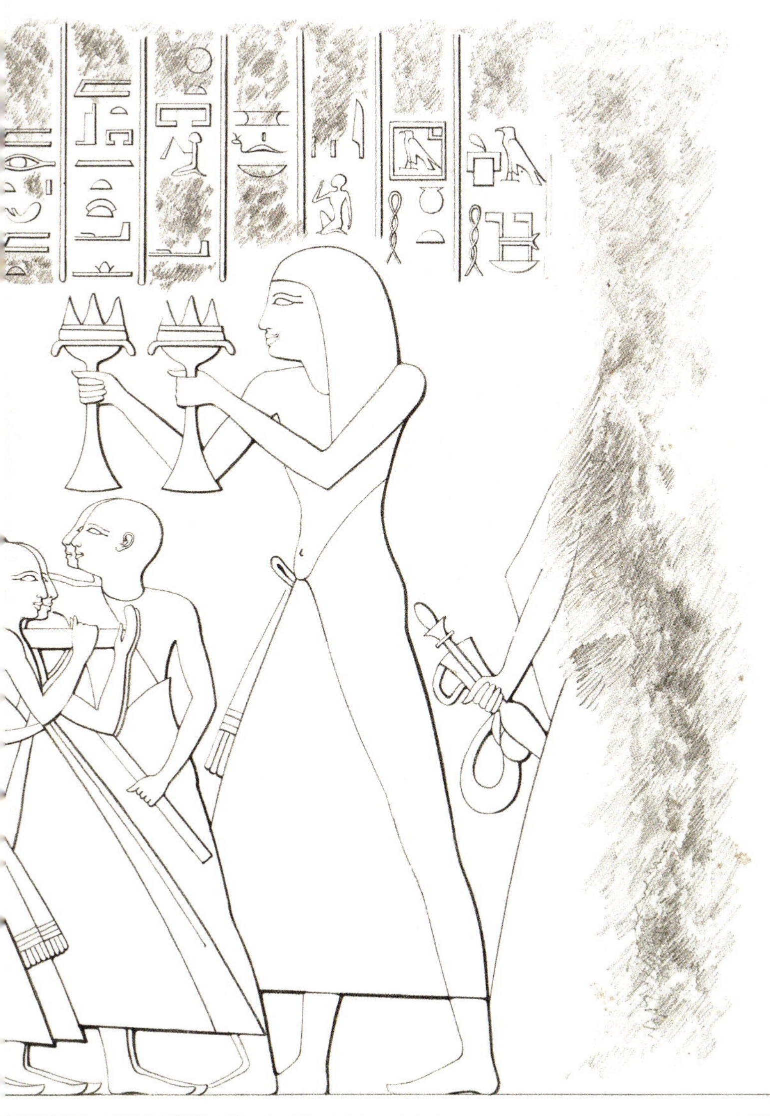

Imp. Kaeppelin & Cie

PALANQUIN .

(Pages/Seite 134/135)

NECROPOLIS OF THEBES

Amenophis I carried in his palanquin

These two plates [XXVIII and XXIX] depict two bas-reliefs taken from the tomb of Khabekhnet, the legal auditor of the throne-room in the time of Amenophis I, founder of the 18th Dynasty. In plate XXVIII, the king is represented in civil costume, holding in his hands the crook and the flail. Sitting on a throne adorned with a lion, shaded by a large "flabellum" and protected by the goddess Maat, he is borne solemnly by eight priests, who can be identified by their shaven heads and long robes. Two slaves bearing fans freshen the air around the pharaoh, while behind him another priest, attached to the personal service of Amenophis, carries a large bunch of flowers.

NEKROPOLE VON THEBEN

Amenophis I. wird in seiner Sänfte getragen

Diese beiden Tafeln [XXVIII und XXIX] zeigen zwei Flachreliefs aus dem Grab von Khabekhnet – Rechtsvorsteher des Thronsaals unter Amenophis I., dem Begründer der 18. Dynastie. Auf der Tafel XXVIII ist der König in Zivilkleidung dargestellt und hält Krummstab und Wedel in den Händen. Auf seinem mit einem Löwen verzierten und durch einen breiten Fächer beschatteten Thron sitzend und von der Göttin Maat beschützt, wird er feierlich von acht an ihrem kahlen Kopf und ihrem langen Gewand zu erkennenden Priestern getragen. Zwei Fächerträger erfrischen die Luft in der Umgebung des Pharaos, und hinter ihm trägt ein weiterer, ausdrücklich im Dienst des Amenophis stehender Priester einen großen Blumenstrauß.

NÉCROPOLE DE THÈBES

Amounôph Ier porté dans son palanquin

Ces deux planches [XXVIII et XXIX] représentent deux bas-reliefs tirés du tombeau de Sonhem [Khâbekhnet], auditeur de justice dans la salle du trône sous Amounôph [Aménophis] Ier, chef de la XVIIIe dynastie. Sur la planche XXVIII, le roi est représenté en costume civil, tenant dans ses mains l'aspersoir et le pedum. Assis sur un trône décoré d'un lion, ombragé d'un large *flabellum*, et protégé par la déesse Tmei [Maât], il est porté solennellement par huit prêtres, qu'on reconnaît à leur tête rase et à leur long costume. Deux flabellifères rafraîchissent l'air autour du pharaon, et derrière lui un autre prêtre, attaché expressément au service d'Amounôph, porte un large bouquet de fleurs.

(Pages/Seite 136/137)

NECROPOLIS OF THEBES

Amenophis I carried in his palanquin

The subject of [this] plate is more or less the same [as that of plate XXVIII], and these two bas-reliefs, which should have been reduced in size and placed together on the same sheet, were lithographed on separate stones, either inadvertently or possibly through guesswork on the part of the artist. The pharaoh in military costume is borne in procession in a type of palanquin by priests, with two slaves bearing fans, and is accompanied by a sotem [sem-priest], clad in a panther skin.

NEKROPOLE VON THEBEN

Amenophis I. wird in seiner Sänfte getragen

Das Thema [dieser] Tafel ist annähernd dasselbe [wie auf Tafel XXVIII], und die beiden Flachreliefs, die in verkleinerter Form auf demselben Blatt erscheinen sollten, sind – durch ein Versehen oder eher durch die Spekulation des Künstlers – auf getrennten Steinen lithografiert worden. In einer Prozession wird der militärisch gekleidete Pharao von zwei Priestern in Begleitung zweier Wedelträger – und eines mit einem Pantherfell bekleideten Setem [Sem-Priesters] – in einer Art Sänfte getragen.

NÉCROPOLE DE THÈBES

Amounôph Ier porté dans son palanquin

Le sujet de [cette] planche est à peu près le même [que sur la planche XXVIII], et ces deux bas-reliefs qui devaient être réduits et réunis sur la même feuille, ont été lithographiés sur des pierres séparées, par inadvertance ou plutôt par spéculation d'artiste. Le pharaon en costume militaire est porté processionnellement sur une espèce de palanquin par des prêtres de deux flabellifères, et accompagnés d'un Sothem [prêtre de Sem], vêtu d'une dépouille de panthère.

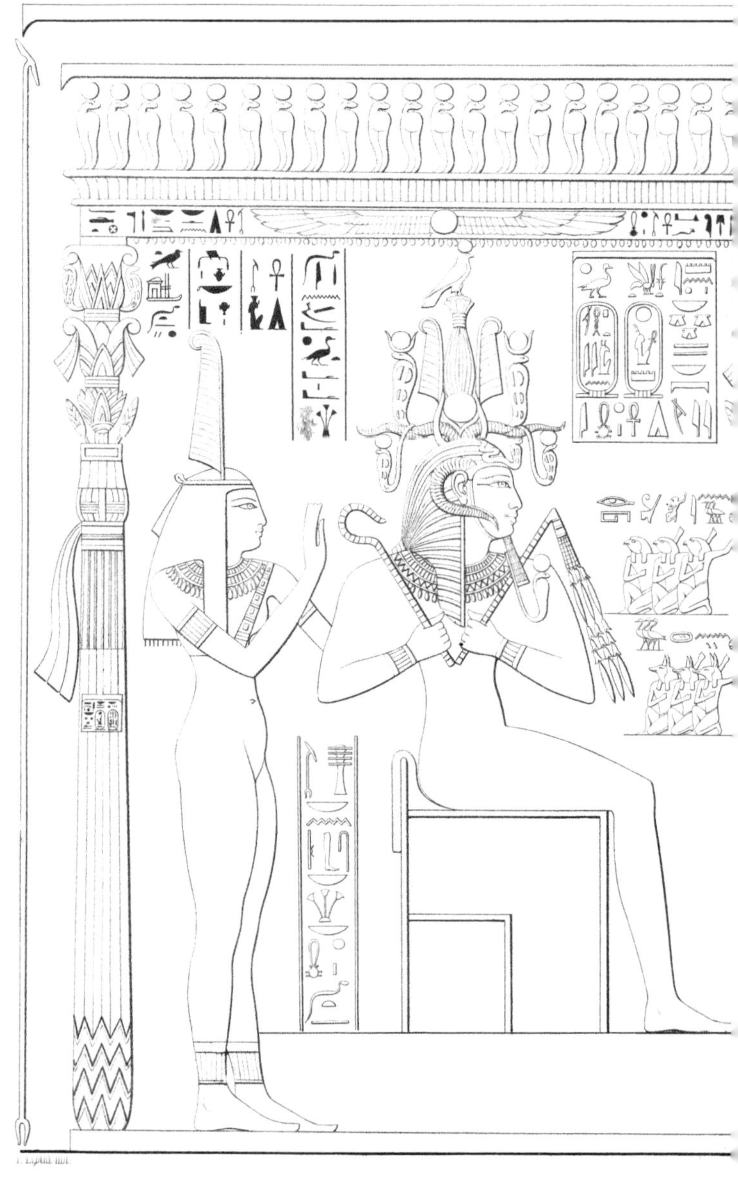

HYPOGÉE DE POÉRI, ADMINISTRATEUR D

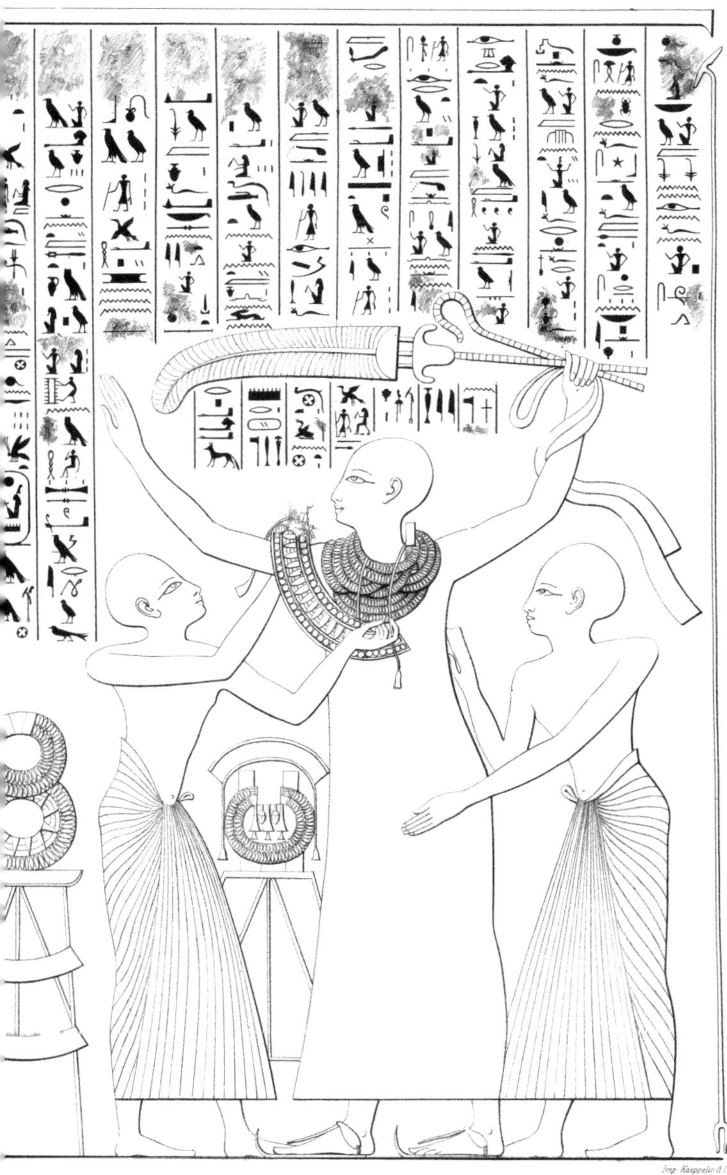

Imp. Kaeppelin & Cie.

:RRITORIAUX SOUS MENEPHTHAH 1ER.

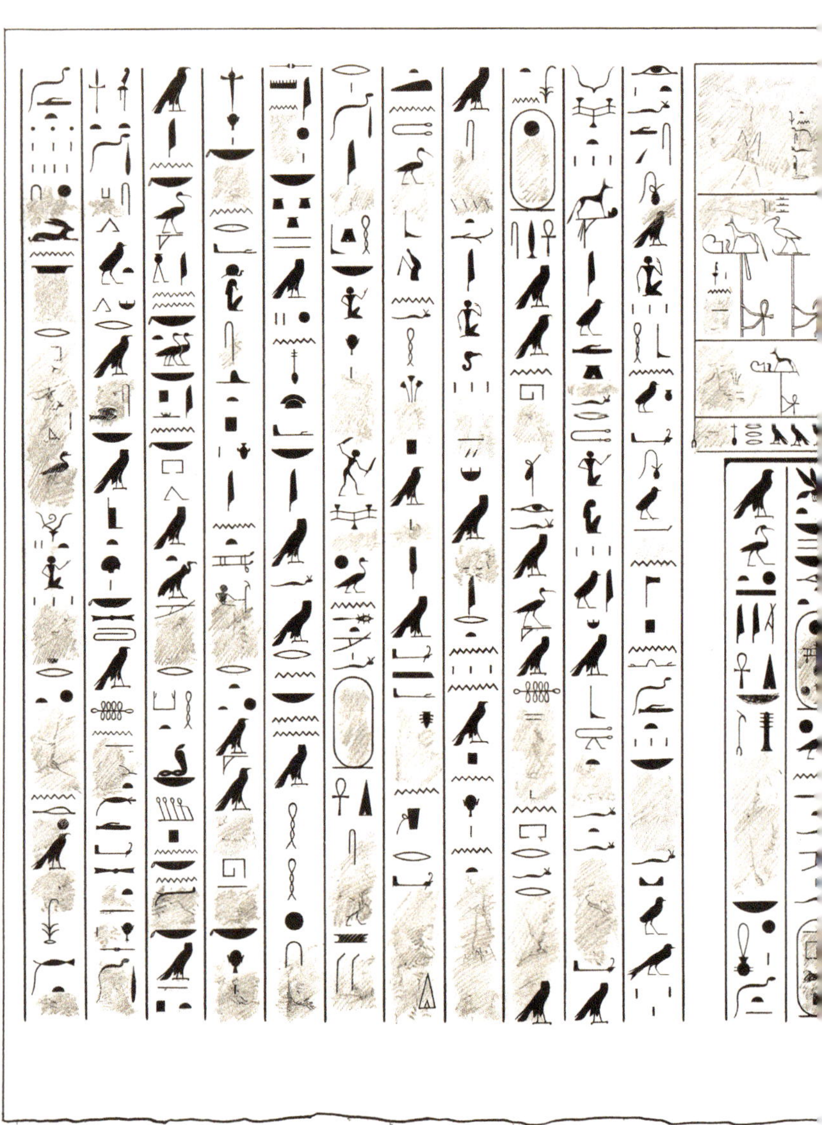

F. Lenelle lith.

1, PLAN D'UN PETIT EDIFICE DE TAHR

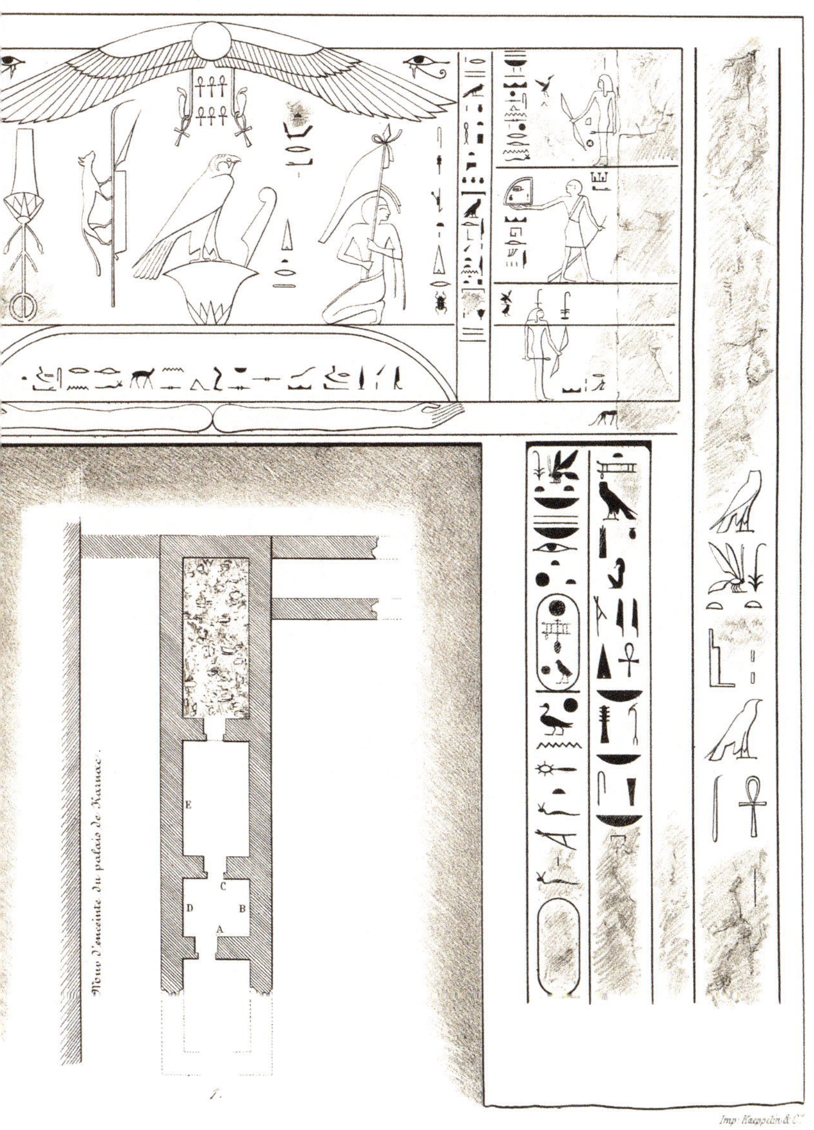

Impr. Kaeppelin & Cie

-RELIEF DE LA PAROI *A* DU PLAN .

(Pages/Seite 140/141)

NECROPOLIS OF THEBES

Hypogeum of Paser. Administrator of land revenues under Merneptah [Seti] I

Merneptah-Seti [Seti I] wearing the head-dress of Sokar, sitting on a throne which is surmounted by a rich naos, holds in his hands the insignia of royal power; in the presence of the goddess Maat, he is decorating a member of the priesthood with a magnificent enamel collar. This high priest, whose name was Paser, was administrator of the land revenues of Egypt; it appears that he is being invested here with the functions of the Athlophore at the king's left hand. With favours heaped upon him, the high priest raises his arms and waves above his head, rejoicing, the insignia of the high honours to which the king has just raised him.

NEKROPOLE VON THEBEN

Hypogäum von Paser. Verwalter der Einkünfte aus den Provinzen unter Meneptah [Sethos] I.

Meneptah-Sethi [Sethos I.] ist mit dem Kopfputz des Sokar geschmückt, sitzt auf einem von einem prächtigen Naos überragten Thron, hält die Insignien der Königswürde in den Händen und lässt mit Unterstützung der Göttin Maat eine der Priesterkaste angehörende Persönlichkeit mit einem prachtvollen emaillierten Halsband auszeichnen. Dieser Hohepriester namens Paser war Verwalter der Einkünfte aus den ägyptischen Provinzen und scheint hier in das Amt des Athlophoros zur Linken des Königs eingesetzt zu werden. Zum Zeichen seiner Freude erhebt der mit Gunstbeweisen überhäufte Pontifex die Arme und schwenkt die Zeichen der hohen Amtswürden, in die der König ihn soeben eingesetzt hat, über dem Kopf.

NÉCROPOLE DE THÈBES

Hypogée de Poëri. Administrateur des revenus territoriaux sous Menephtha [Séthi] Ier

Menephtha-Sethéi [Séthi Ier] coiffé en Socharis [Sokar], assis sur un trône surmonté d'un riche naos, tient en main les insignes du pouvoir royal, et, assisté de la déesse Tmei [Maât], fait décorer d'un magnifique collier émaillé un personnage de la caste sacerdotale. Ce grand prêtre, nommé Poëri [Paser], était administrateur des revenus territoriaux de l'Égypte, et paraît recevoir ici l'investiture des fonctions d'Athlophore à la gauche du roi. Comblé de faveurs, le pontife élève les bras, et agite au-dessus de sa tête, en signe de joie, les marques des hautes dignités auxquelles le roi vient de l'élever.

(Pages/Seite 142/143)

THEBES – KARNAK

1. Plan of a small building of Taharqa. 2. Bas-relief from wall A of the plan

Bas-reliefs from a small building of Taharqa, situated outside the wall surrounding the palace of Karnak, close to the hypostyle hall. The excavations made in the last room, which is choked with debris, have only allowed us to see walls whose stones had still not been roughly hewn. The door leading into it was shown by mistake; I do not know its real position but I am sure, from my own excavations, that there could not have been a door in this partition wall.

THEBEN – KARNAK

1. Grundriss eines kleinen Gebäudes von Taharqa. 2. Flachrelief von der Wand A der Grundrisszeichnung

Flachreliefs aus einem kleinen Gebäude von Taharqa, das sich außerhalb der Umfassungsmauer des Palasts von Karnak in der Nähe des Hypostyls befindet. Die im letzten, völlig verschütteten Raum durchgeführten Ausgrabungen haben nur Mauern zutage gefördert, deren Steine noch unbearbeitet waren. Die Tür, die dort hinführt, ist falsch angegeben; ihre tatsächliche Lage ist mir unbekannt – nach den von mir durchgeführten Ausgrabungen bin ich jedoch sicher, dass es in dieser Trennwand keine Tür gegeben haben kann.

THÈBES – KARNAC

1. Plan d'un petit édifice de Tahraka. 2. Bas-relief de la paroi A du plan

Bas-reliefs d'un petit édifice de Tahraka [Taharqa], situé à l'extérieur du mur d'enceinte du palais de Karnac, près de la salle hypostyle. Les fouilles faites dans la dernière pièce, qui est entièrement encombrée, n'ont laissé voir que des murs dont les pierres n'avaient pas encore été dégrossies. La porte qui y conduit a été indiquée par erreur ; j'ignore son véritable emplacement, mais je suis certain, d'après mes fouilles, qu'il ne devait point y en avoir dans ce mur de séparation.

THEBES – KARNAK

1. Bas-relief from wall B of the small building of Taharqa. 2. Wall D

This little monument, whose royal legends have been carefully hammered off, does, however, still retain quite distinctly a cartouche of the Ethiopian king Taharqa, whose face has not suffered any damage. Plates XXXI to XXXIII depict all of the decoration on four walls of a small chamber, the only one to remain intact. Among the remains of the sculptures which can still be seen in the first room, we note Taharqa making an offering, followed by worshipping baboons. There is also in this chamber a royal cartouche which is different from that of the Ethiopian but which is completely illegible.

THEBEN – KARNAK

1. Flachrelief von der Wand B im kleinen Gebäude von Taharqa. 2. Wand D

In diesem kleinen Denkmal, in dem die Königsnamen durch sorgfältiges Behämmern zerstört sind, ist gleichwohl eine gut sichtbare Kartusche des äthiopischen Königs Taharqa erhalten, dessen Antlitz keinerlei Schmähung erlitten hat. Die Tafeln XXXI bis XXXIII zeigen die gesamte Ausschmückung der vier Wände eines kleinen Raumes, der als einziger unversehrt überliefert ist. Unter den im ersten Raum noch sichtbaren Skulpturenresten erkennt man den Opfergaben darbringenden Taharqa, dem Kynokephale in Anbetungshaltung folgen. Auch gibt es in diesem Raum eine vollkommen unleserliche Königskartusche, die sich von der des Äthiopiers unterscheidet.

THÈBES – KARNAC

1. Bas-relief de la paroi B du petit édifice de Tahraka. 2. Paroi D

Ce petit monument, dont les légendes royales ont été martelées avec soin, conserve pourtant encore fort distinct un cartouche du roi éthiopien Tahraka [Taharqa], dont la figure n'a subi aucun outrage. Les planches XXXI à XXXIII représentent l'ensemble de la décoration des quatre parois d'une petite salle, la seule qui subsiste intacte. Parmi les restes de sculptures qu'on aperçoit encore dans la première pièce, on remarque Tahraka faisant une offrande, suivi de cynocéphales en adoration. Il y a aussi dans cette salle un cartouche royal différent de celui de l'éthiopien, mais tout à fait illisible.

1.

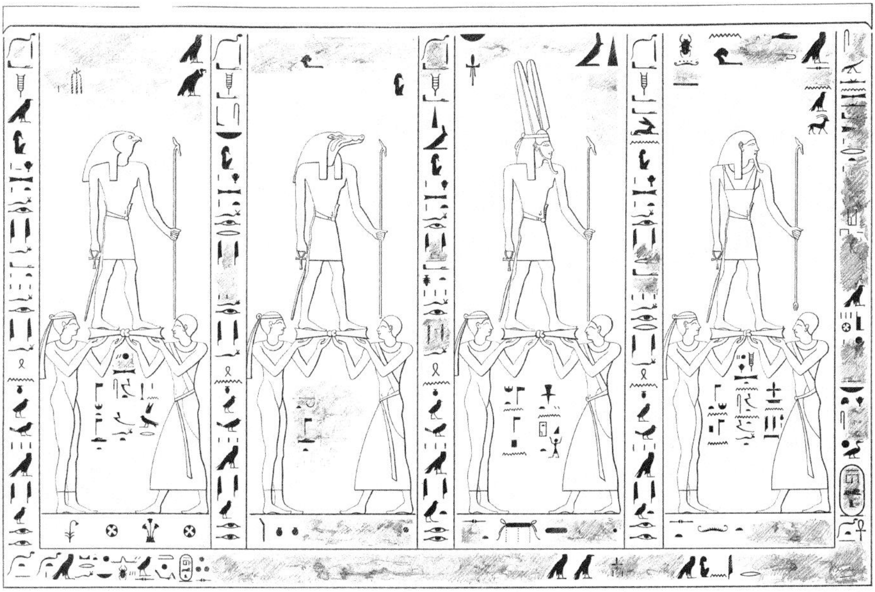

2.

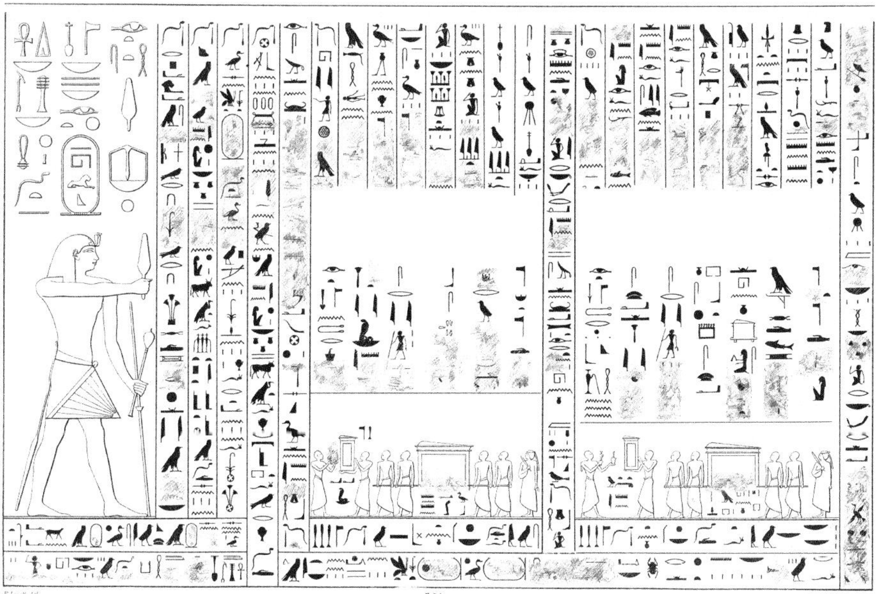

F. Lepelle, lith. E. Prisse. Imp. Kaeppelin & Cie

1, BAS-RELIEF DE LA PAROI *B* DU PETIT ÉDIFICE DE TAHRAKA. 2 PAROI *D*.

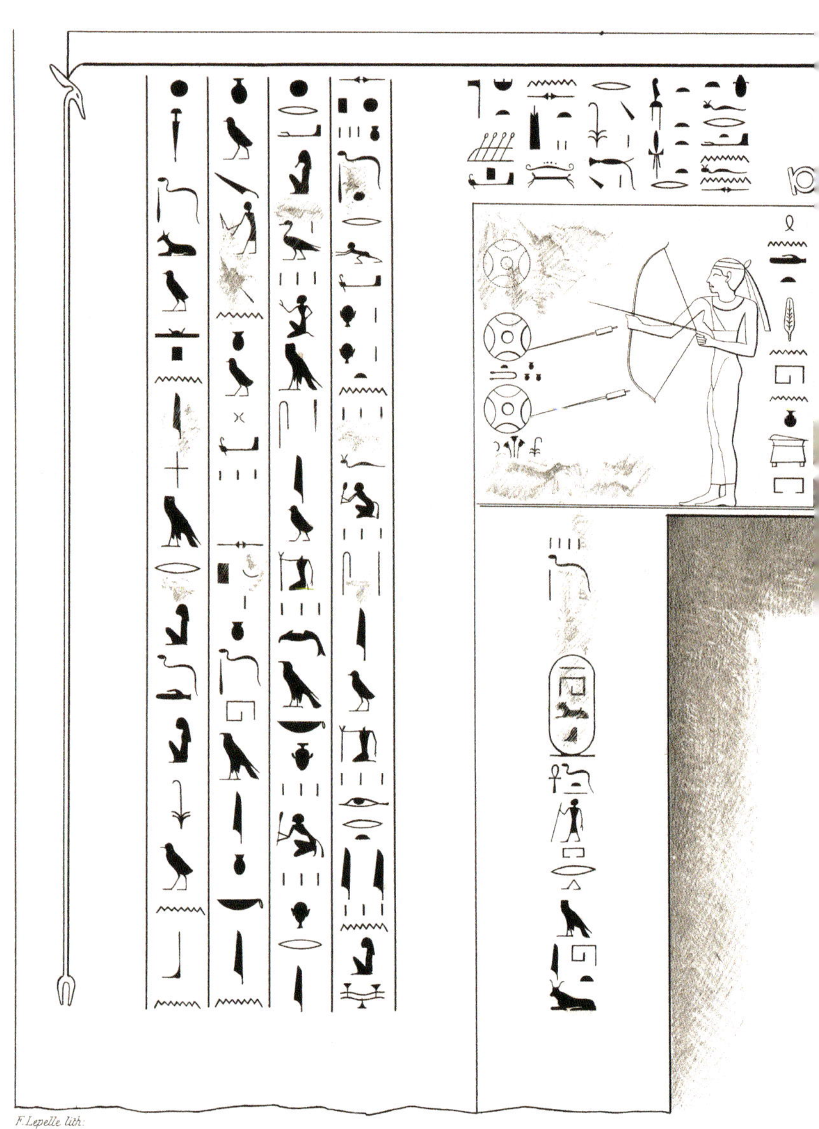

F. Lepelle lith.

ÉDIFICE DE TAHRAKA, BA

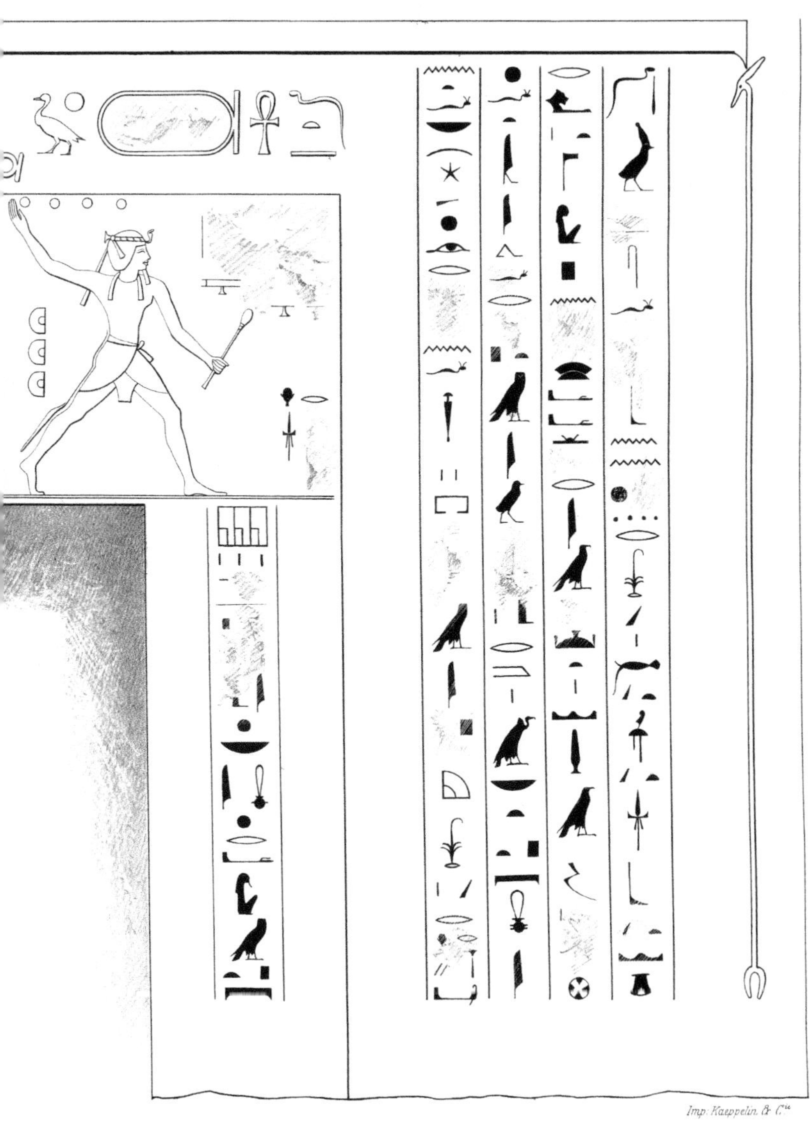

Imp: Kaeppelin & Cie

E LA PAROI *C* DU PLAN.

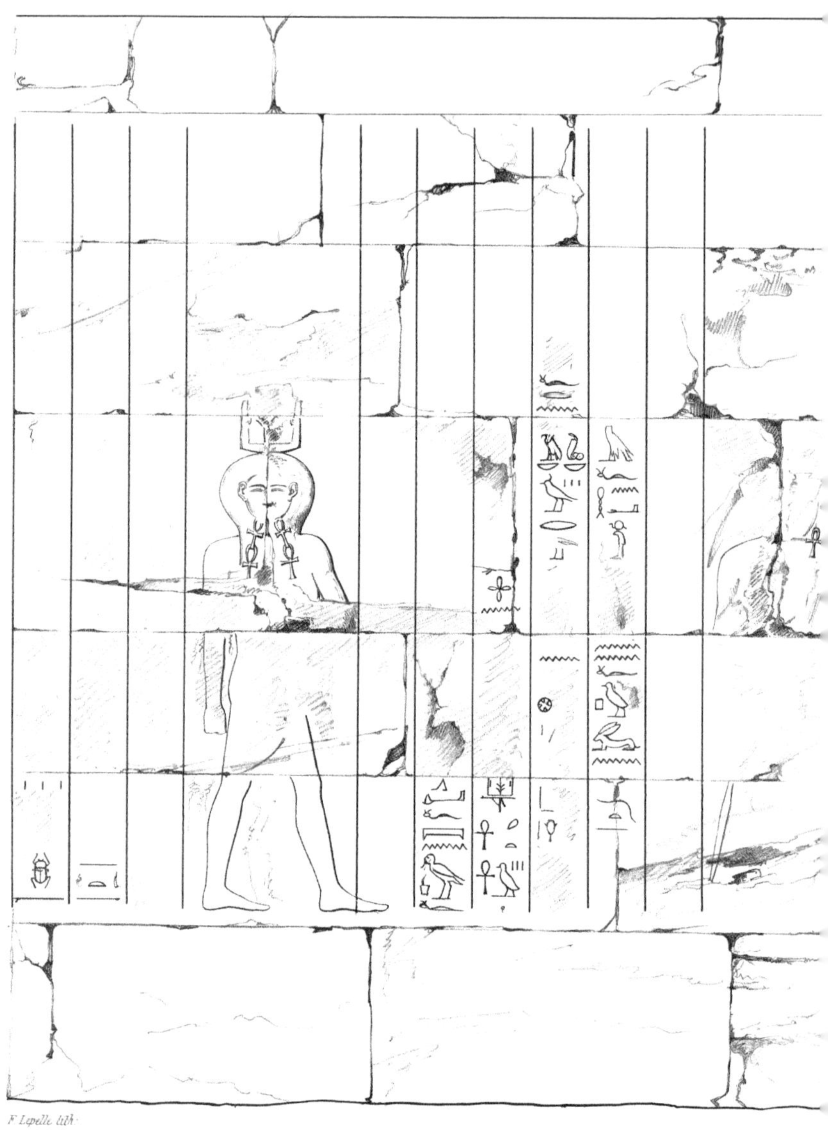

F. Lepelle lith.

EDIFICE DE TAHRAKA

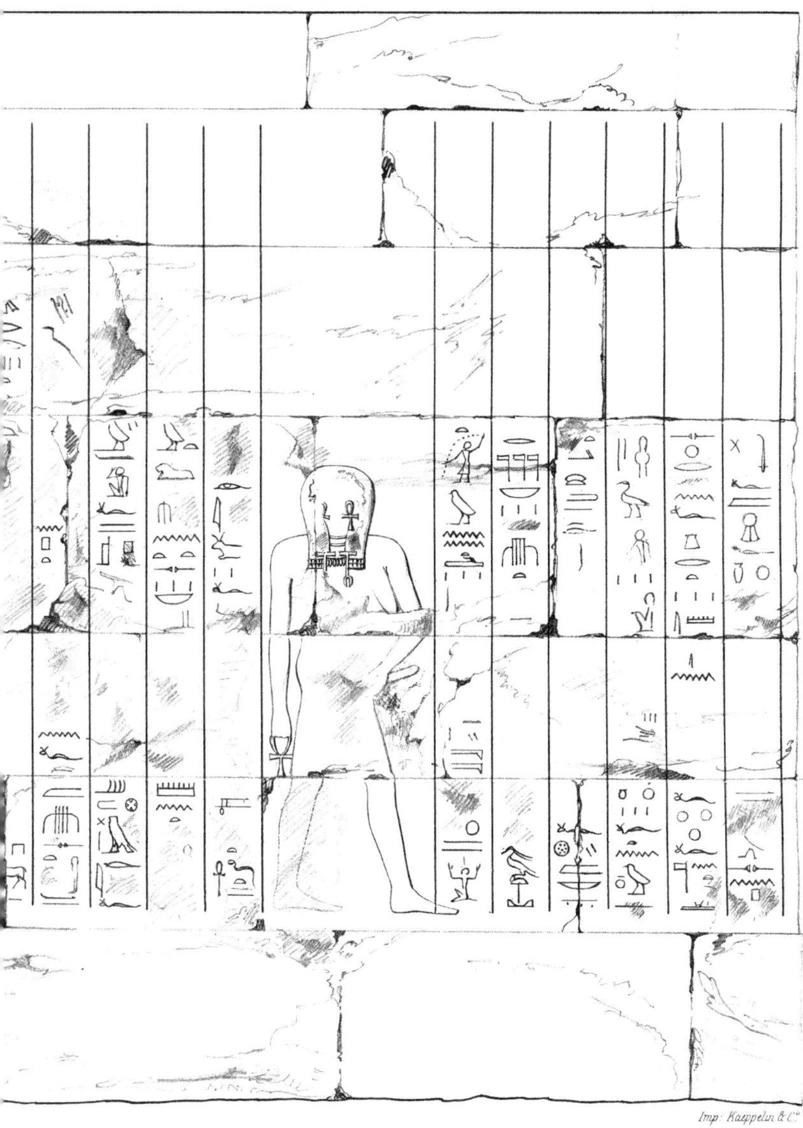

Imp: Kaeppelin & Cie

F DE LA PAROI *E* .

(Pages/Seite 148/149)

THEBES – KARNAK

Building of Taharqa. Bas-relief from wall C of the plan

The internal walls of this small building, which I understand has been completely cleared since Champollion's expedition, are covered with bas-reliefs which are quite different from the usual representations.

THEBEN – KARNAK

Gebäude von Taharqa. Flachrelief von der Wand C der Grundrisszeichnung

Die Innenwände dieses kleinen Gebäudes, das – glaube ich – nach der Expedition Champollions freigelegt wurde, sind mit Flachreliefs bedeckt, die sich vollständig von den gebräuchlichen Darstellungen unterscheiden.

THÈBES – KARNAC

Édifice de Tahraka [Taharqa]. Bas-relief de la paroi C du plan

Les murs intérieurs de ce petit édifice, déblayé, je crois, depuis l'expédition de Champollion, sont couverts de bas-reliefs tout à fait différents des représentations usuelles.

(Pages/Seite 150/151)

THEBES – KARNAK

Building of Taharqa. Bas-relief from wall E

In one of the rooms (the third), which is unfortunately very damaged because of the friable nature of the stone and also through the action of saltpetre, there can be seen a number of very worn figures of new divinities, whose strange forms are in some ways reminiscent of the sculptures of the temples of Naga, the ancient Meroë. This building seems to have been dedicated to funerary rites, although the gods represented here are not met with, so far as I know, in the Ritual of the Dead. These unusual androgynous divinities, with faces like Typhon but with pendulous breasts like the Nile god, must have held in their hands their fully erect phallus, like Neith and Mut.

THEBEN – KARNAK

Gebäude von Taharqa. Flachrelief von der Wand E

In einem der Räume (dem dritten), der leider – sowohl aufgrund der Brüchigkeit des Gesteins als auch durch die Einwirkung des Salpeters – stark beschädigt ist, sind mehrere eher grobe Darstellungen neuer Gottheiten zu erkennen, die in ihren heterogenen Formen ein wenig an die Skulpturen in den Tempeln von Naqa, dem früheren Meroe, erinnern. Dieses Gebäude scheint Begräbnisriten gewidmet gewesen zu sein – obgleich die dargestellten Götter meines Wissens im Totenritual nicht vorkommen. Diese seltsamen, androgynen Gottheiten, die wie Typhon in Vorderansicht dargestellt sind und wie der Nilgott Hängebrüste aufweisen, dürften – wie Neith und Mut – ihren voll erigierten Phallus in der Hand gehalten haben.

THÈBES – KARNAC

Édifice de Tahraka [Taharqa]. Bas-relief de la paroi E

Dans l'une des salles (la 3e), malheureusement fort endommagée tant à cause de la nature friable de la pierre que par l'action du salpêtre, on voit plusieurs figures bien frustes de divinités nouvelles dont les formes hétéroclites rappellent quelque chose des sculptures des temples de Naga, l'ancienne Méroé. Cet édifice paraît avoir été consacré à des rites funéraires, bien que les dieux qu'il représente ne se rencontrent pas, que je sache, sur le Rituel des morts. Ces singulières divinités androgynes, figurées de face comme Typhon, et les mamelles pendantes comme le dieu Nil, devaient tenir à la main leur phallus dans toute son intumescence, comme Neith et Mauth [Mout].

TEMPLE OF KHONSU. THEBES

1, 2. Bas-reliefs carved on stones used in the construction of the temple.
2, 3. [sic: 3, 4.] Inscriptions engraved on the terrace

Temple of Khonsu at Karnak. Nos. 1 and 2. Bas-reliefs carved on stones used in the construction of the temple. The first forms part of a military scene, probably relating to the campaigns of Amenophis III. The second bas-relief depicts an Egyptian cottage with all the household utensils of a farming family. Nos. 3 and 4. Inscriptions engraved on the terrace of the temple of Khonsu. Judging by the large number of hieroglyphic, hieratic and demotic inscriptions engraved on the terrace in association with representations of feet or of sandals, this temple must at some period have been the object of a very specific cult.

CHONS-TEMPEL. THEBEN.

1, 2. Flachreliefs in Steinen, die für den Bau verwendet wurden.
2, 3. [sic: 3, 4.] In die Terrasse eingravierte Inschriften

Chons-Tempel in Karnak. Nr. 1 und 2. Flachreliefs in Steinen, die man für den Bau des Tempels verwendet hat. Das erste war Bestandteil einer militärischen Szene, die sich wahrscheinlich auf die Feldzüge von Amenophis III. bezog. Das zweite Flachrelief stellt eine einfache ägyptische Hütte mit allen Haushaltsgegenständen einer Bauernfamilie dar. Nr. 3 und 4. In die Terrasse des Chons-Tempels eingravierte Inschriften. Nach den zahlreichen Inschriften zu urteilen, die – neben Darstellungen von Füßen oder Sandalen – in Hieroglyphen sowie hieratischen und demotischen Schriftzeichen in die Terrasse eingraviert sind, dürfte dieser Tempel zu einer bestimmten Zeit Gegenstand einer ganz besonderen Verehrung gewesen sein.

TEMPLE DE KHONS. THÈBES

1, 2. Bas-reliefs sculptés sur des pierres employées dans la construction.
2, 3. [sic: 3, 4.] Inscriptions gravées sur la terrasse

Temple de Khons [Khonsou], à Karnac. N°s 1 et 2. Bas-reliefs sculptés sur des pierres employées dans les constructions du temple. Le premier faisait partie d'une scène militaire, relative probablement aux campagnes d'Amounôph [Aménophis] III. Le second bas-relief représente une chaumière égyptienne, et tous les ustensiles de ménage d'une famille de cultivateurs. N°s 3 et 4. Inscriptions gravées sur la terrasse du temple de Khons. A en juger par les nombreuses inscriptions hiéroglyphiques, hiératiques et démotiques, gravées sur la terrasse et accompagnées de représentations de pieds ou de sandales, ce temple a dû être à une certaine époque l'objet d'une dévotion toute particulière.

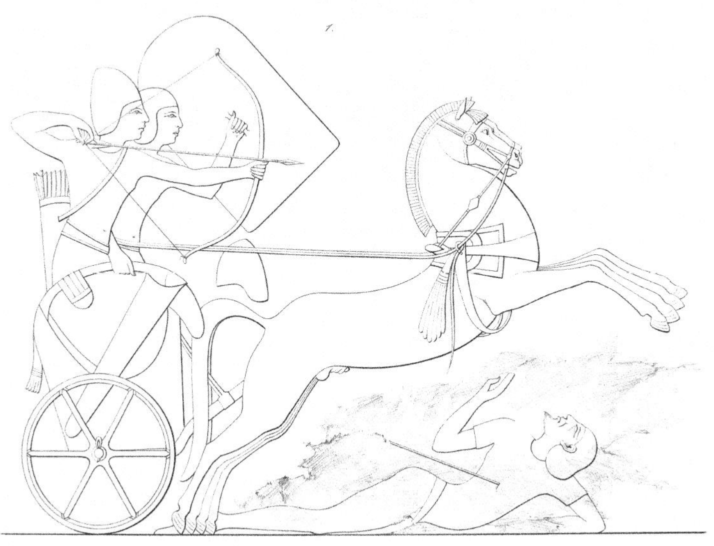

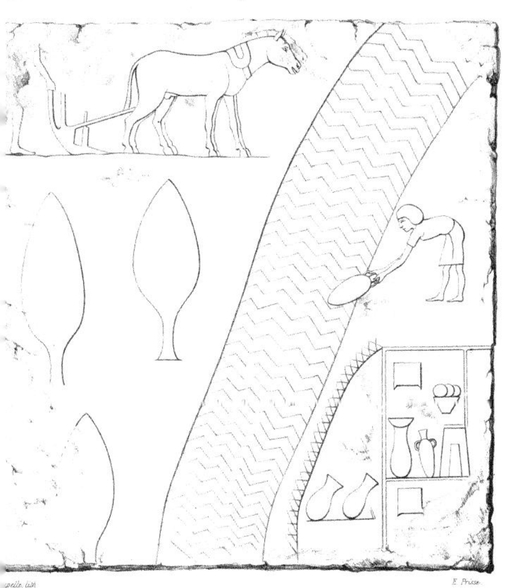

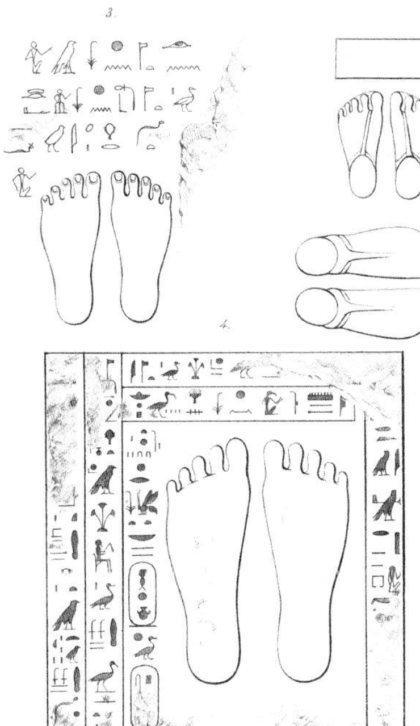

...pelle, lith. E. Prisse. Imp. Kaeppelin & Cie.

1, 2. BAS-RELIEFS SCULPTÉS SUR DES PIERRES EMPLOYÉES DANS LA CONSTRUCTION. 2, 3. INSCRIPTIONS GRAVÉES SUR LA TERRASSE.

THEBES – KARNAK

1. Bas-relief from the temple of Khonsu.
2. Drawing of the three walls of the sanctuary niche in the temple of Opet

No. 1. Bas-relief taken from the temple of Khonsu at Karnak. It depicts Ramesses-Meryamun [Ramesses II] offering libations and incense to Amun, the progenitor, and to Khonsu. No. 2. Drawing made from the three walls of the sanctuary niche in the temple of Opet, at Karnak. The bas-reliefs which decorate this part of the sekos date from the time of Ptolemy VIII Euergetes II and represent three forms of a goddess whom Champollion considered to be the symbol of humid and passive nature. This divinity, who presided over one of the months of the zodiac, is one of the forms of Neith, whose titles she often uses: here she is called Opet, the great progenitrix of the gods, lady of heaven, regent of the world.

THEBEN – KARNAK

1. Flachrelief aus dem Chons-Tempel.
2. Rekonstruktionszeichnung der drei Nischenwände im Heiligtum des Ipet-Tempels

Nr. 1. Flachrelief aus dem Chons-Tempel in Karnak. Es stellt Ramses Meriamun [Ramses II.] dar, der dem Amun – als Erzeuger des Chons – Trank- und Weihrauchopfer darbringt. Nr. 2. Rekonstruktionszeichnung der drei Nischenwande im Heiligtum des Ipet-Tempels in Karnak. Die diesen Teil des Sekos zierenden Flachreliefs datieren aus der Zeit von Ptolemaios VIII. Euergetes II. und stellen drei Varianten einer Göttin dar, die Champollion als Sinnbild der feuchten und passiven Natur ansah. Diese Gottheit, die einem Monat des Zodiaks vorstand, ist eine Art Neith, deren Titel sie häufig entlehnt: Hier heißt sie Opet, die große Erschafferin der Götter, die Herrin des Himmels, Herrscherin der Welt.

THÈBES – KARNAC

1. Bas-relief du temple de Khons.
2. Développement des 3 parois de la niche du sanctuaire du temple de Opet

N° 1. Bas-relief tiré du temple de Khons [Khonsou] à Karnac. Il représente Ramsès-Meiamoun [Ramsès II], libant et encensant Amon générateur et Khons. N° 2. Développement des trois parois de la niche du sanctuaire du temple de Opet, à Karnac. Les bas-reliefs qui décorent cette partie du sékos datent de Ptolémée Évergète II, et représentent trois formes d'une déesse que Champollion considérait comme le symbole de la nature humide et passive. Cette divinité, qui présidait à un des mois du zodiaque, est une des formes de Netpé [Neith], dont elle emprunte souvent les titres : elle est appelée ici Opet, la grande génératrice des dieux, dame du ciel, régente du monde.

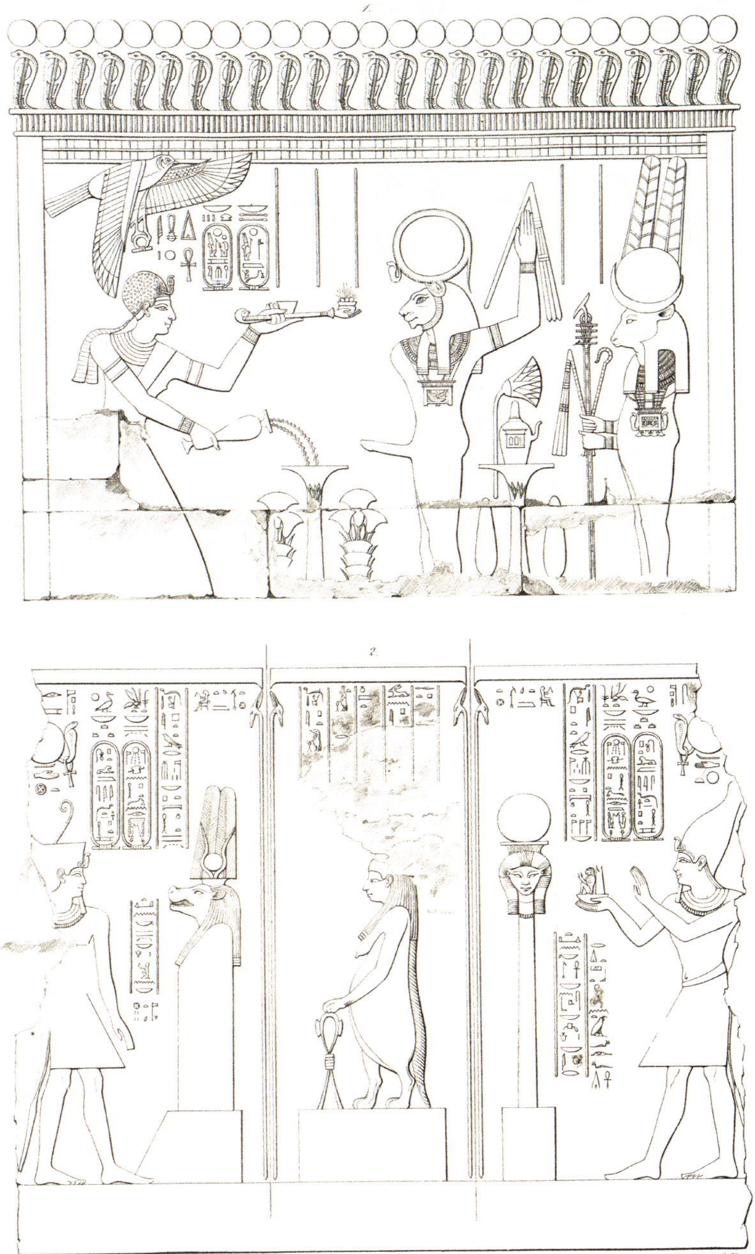

F. Lepelle lith. E. Prisse. Imp. Kaeppelin & Cie

1. BAS-RELIEF DU TEMPLE DE KHONS. 2 DÉVELOPPEMENT DES 3 PAROIS DU SANCTUAIRE DU TEMPLE DE ÔPT.

EGYPTIAN MONUMENTS

Stele from the British Museum

This small limestone stele is of the greatest interest with regard to mythology. The upper register is occupied by a bas-relief depicting a goddess seen full-face; her hair is dressed in the style of Hathor and she stands on a lion *passant* which is sculpted, like the divinity herself, in almost full relief. [...] The legend above the goddess, which translates as Ken or Kun, "queen of heaven", appears to indicate that this divinity represents the female principle of nature. The goddess portrayed in the lower register is Anat or Tanata, primeval origin of the Greek word for "death", and which carries the same meaning in the Semitic languages.

ÄGYPTISCHE DENKMÄLER

Stele aus dem Britischen Museum

Diese kleine Kalksteinstele ist unter mythologischen Gesichtspunkten von größtem Interesse. Das Flachrelief, das das obere Register einnimmt, stellt eine Göttin mit einem nach Art einer Hathor in Vorderansicht gestalteten Kopfschmuck dar; die Gottheit steht auf einem vorbeilaufenden Löwen und ist – ebenso wie das sie tragende Tier – nahezu freistehend gearbeitet. [...] Die Inschrift dieser Göttin – die in der Übersetzung Ken oder Kun, „Königin des Himmels" bedeutet – scheint darauf hinzudeuten, dass diese Gottheit ein weibliches Naturgesetz darstellt. Bei der im unteren Register abgebildeten Göttin handelt es sich um Anat oder Tanata, wovon sich ursprünglich das griechische Wort für „Tod" ableitete, das in den semitischen Sprachen dieselbe Bedeutung hat.

MONUMEN[T]S ÉGYPTIENS

Stèle du Musée Britannique

Cette petite stèle en pierre calcaire est du plus haut intérêt sous le rapport de la mythologie. Le registre supérieur est occupé par un bas-relief représentant une déesse coiffée à la manière d'Hathor vue de face, et placée debout sur un lion passant, sculpté, comme la divinité qu'il porte, presqu'en ronde bosse. [...] La légende de la déesse, qui se traduit Ken ou Koun, « reine du ciel », semble indiquer que cette divinité représente le principe femelle de la nature. La déesse représentée dans le registre inférieur est Anta ou Tanata, l'origine primordiale du grec « la mort », et qui a la même signification dans les langues sémitiques.

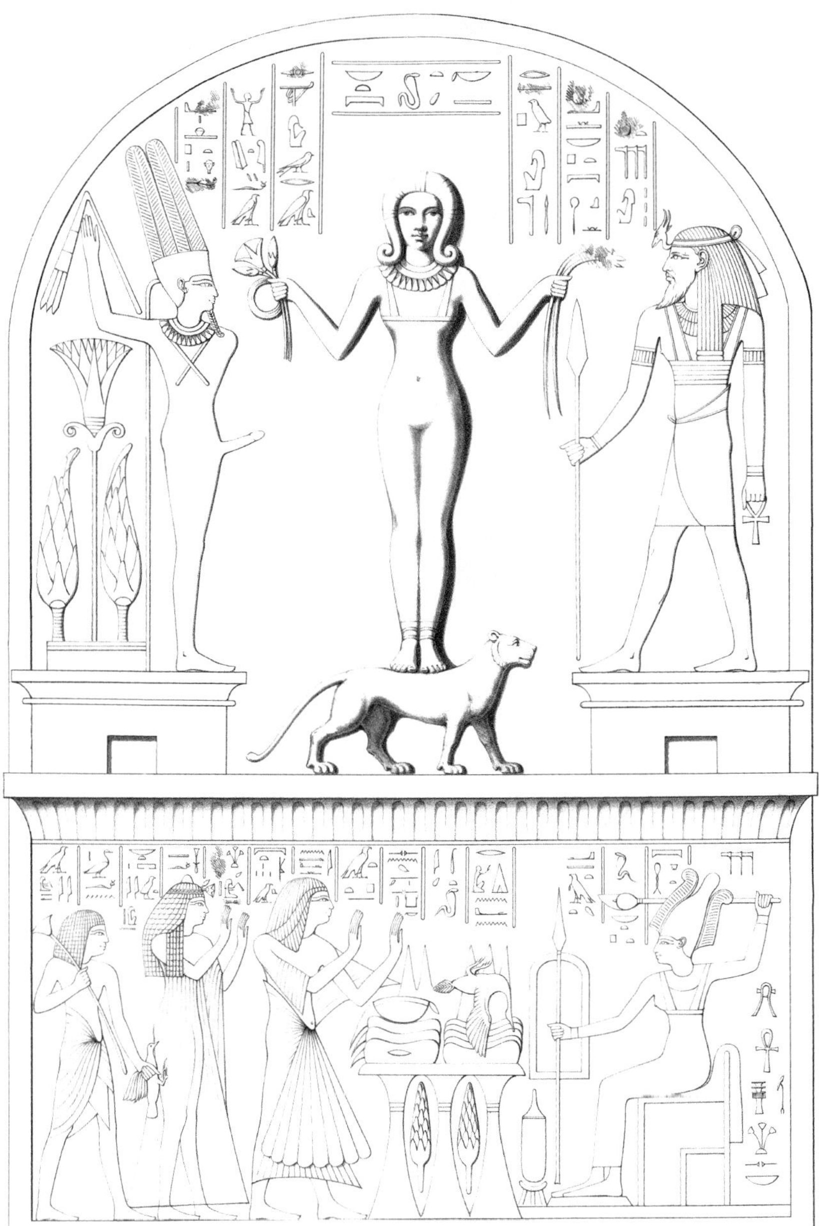

G. Barry lith. E. Prisse Imp. Kaeppelin & Cie

STÈLE DU MUSÉE BRITANNIQUE.

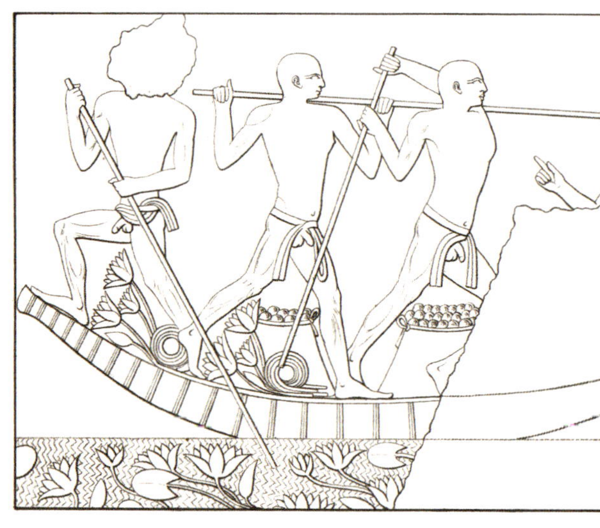

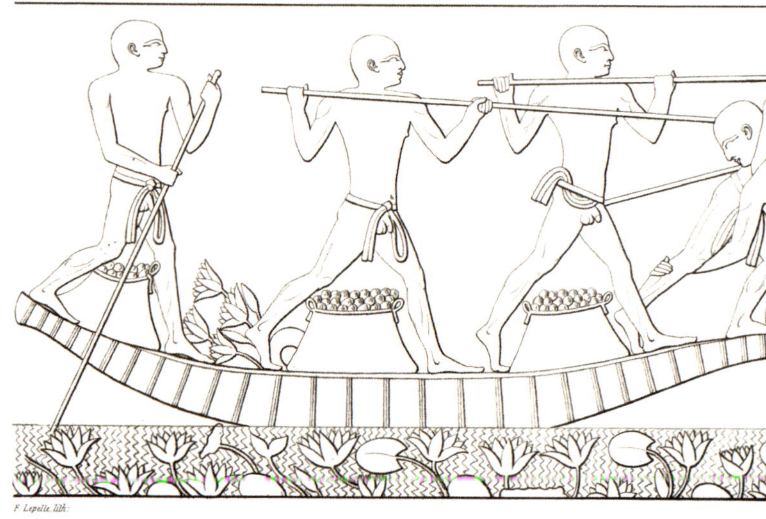

F. Lepelle, lith:

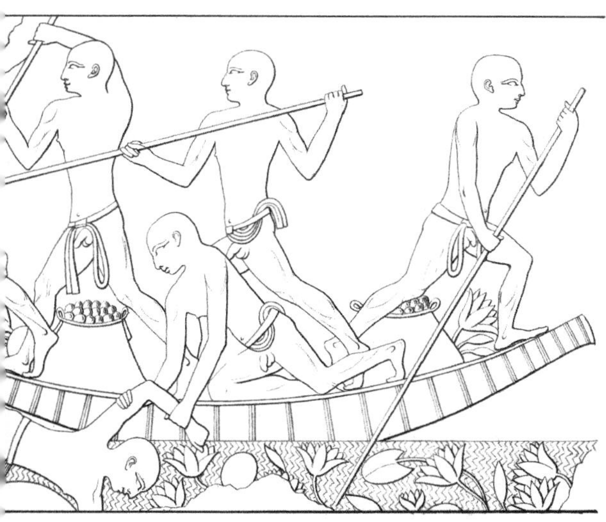

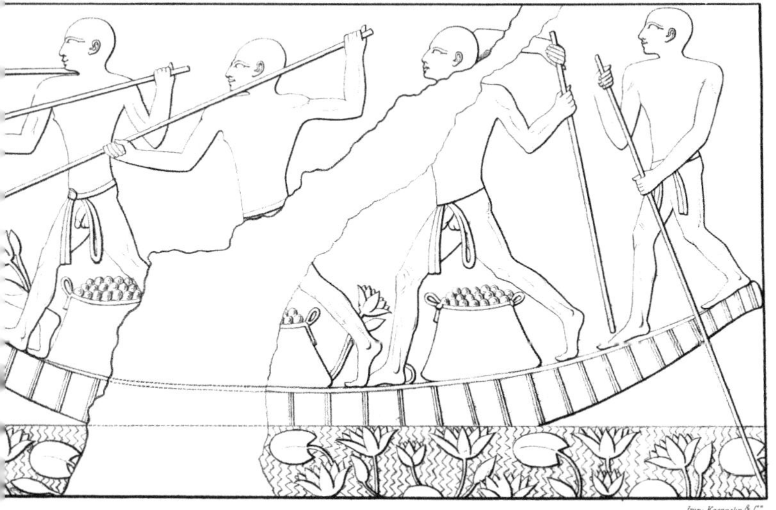

Imp: Kaeppelin & C.ie

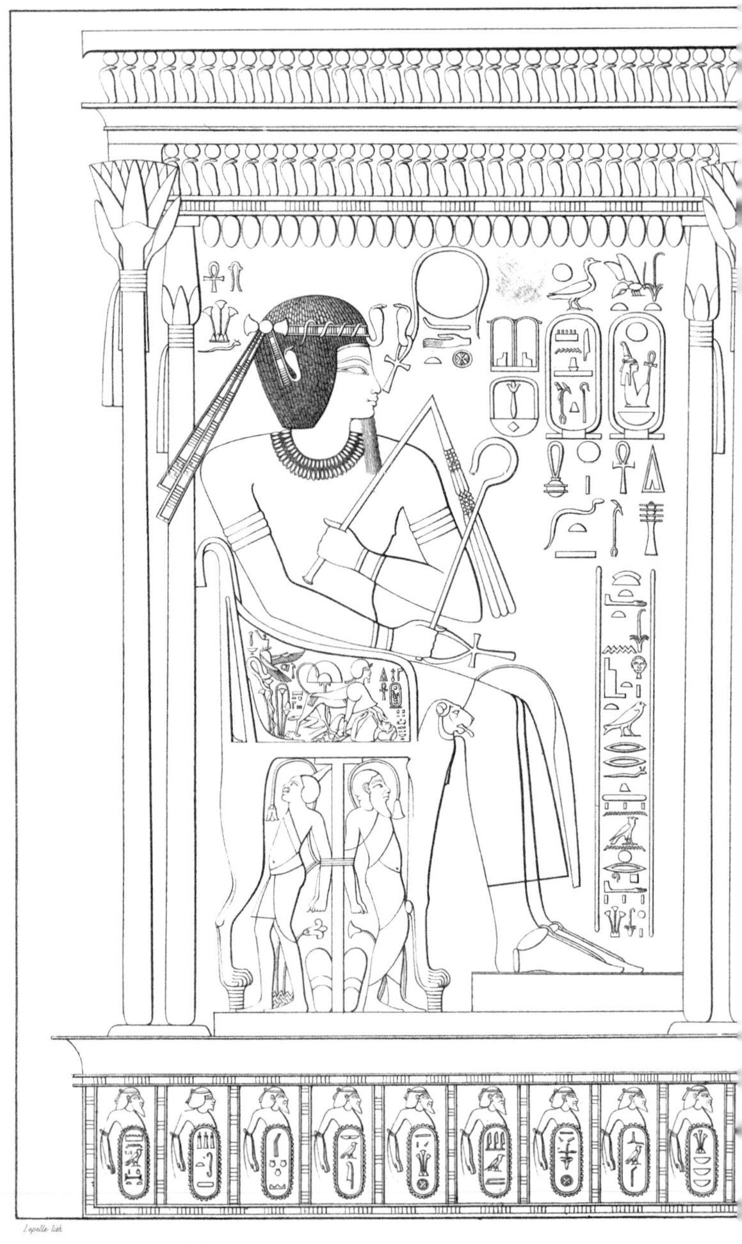

Lepelle lith.

AMOUNÔPH III RECEVANT LES H

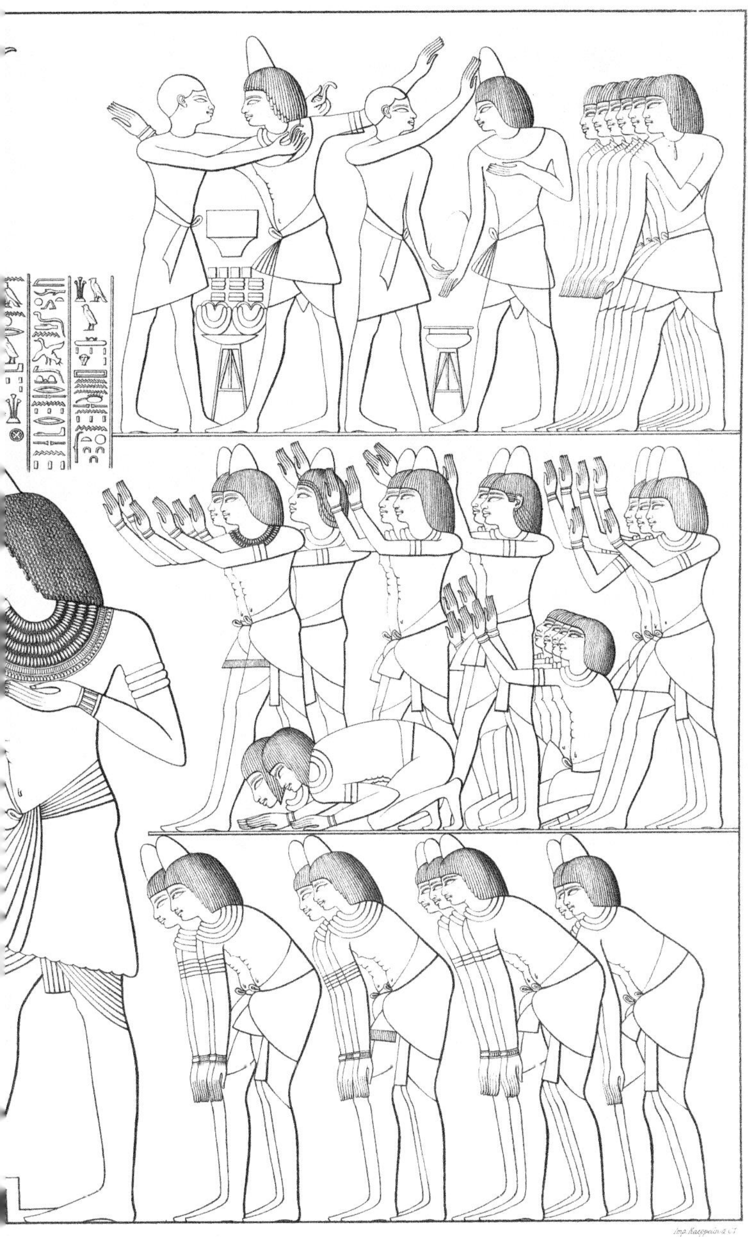

Imp. Kaeppelin & C.ie

MTHÉ ET DES PRINCIPAUX CHEFS.

(Pages/Seite 160/161)

KOM EL-AHMAR

Sailors fighting

Battle on the water in barques made of papyrus, laden with flowers and fruits. This bas-relief, taken from the hypogea of Kom el-Ahmar, at Zawyet el-Maiyitin, is in a very unusual archaic style: the figures are more pronounced and the muscles in much higher relief than elsewhere. This scene of sailors fighting and raining blows on each other with oars and boat-hooks, in their light barques made from papyrus stems, is a masterpiece of Egyptian art. Nowhere else in Egypt, even in the finest military scenes of pharaohs of the 18th and 19th Dynasties, have I seen such realism and animation.

KOM EL-AHMAR

Schifferstechen

Kampf auf dem Wasser, in mit Blumen und Früchten beladenen Papyrusbooten. Dieses den Hypogäen von Kom el-Ahmar in Saujet el-Meitin entnommene Flachrelief weist einen äußerst bemerkenswerten archaischen Stil auf: Die Formen der Figuren sind markanter und die Muskeln deutlicher dargestellt als anderswo. Diese Szene, in der Flussschiffer auf leichten, aus Papyrusstängeln gefertigten Booten mit Rudern und Bootshaken gegeneinander kämpfen, ist ein Meisterwerk der ägyptischen Kunst. In Ägypten habe ich nirgendwo sonst – nicht einmal unter den schönsten militärischen Szenen mit den Pharaonen der 18. und der 19. Dynastie – so viel Lebhaftigkeit und Lebensechtheit gesehen.

KOUM EL-AHMAR

Combat de mariniers

Lutte sur l'eau dans des barques de papyrus portant des fleurs et des fruits. Ce bas-relief, tiré des hypogées de Koum el-Ahmar, à Zawyet-el-Mayetin [Zaouiet el-Meïtin], est d'un style archaïque fort remarquable : les formes sont plus prononcées, les muscles plus accusés qu'ailleurs. Cette scène de mariniers qui se battent à coup de gaffes et d'avirons sur des barques légères, formées de tiges de papyrus, est un chef-d'œuvre de l'art égyptien. Je n'ai vu nulle part en Égypte, même dans les plus belles scènes militaires des pharaons de la XVIIIe et de la XIXe dynastie, autant de vérité et d'animation.

(Pages/Seite 162/163)

NECROPOLIS OF THEBES

Amenophis III receiving the homage of Khaemhat and the principal chiefs

Subjects taken from the tomb of Khaemhat, royal scribe and overseer of harvests under Amenophis III. Plate XXXIX shows Amenophis III receiving homage from Khaemhat and the principal chiefs of Upper and Lower Egypt. The pharaoh, holding the crook, the flail and the Tau [the ankh], is seated on a richly adorned throne, surmounted by a double naos. The arm-rests of the royal seat represent the pharaoh in the form of a sphinx trampling on African and Asiatic captives, who are also to be seen on the supports of the throne, where they feature bound around a symbol of power and command. The base of the rich naos beneath which Amenophis rests is decorated with nine figures of subjugated nations or tribes, represented by Asiatic or African captives with their hands tied behind their backs.

NEKROPOLE VON THEBEN

Amenophis III. empfängt die Huldigungen Chaemhats und der wichtigsten Vorsteher

Motive aus dem Grab von Chaemhat, königlicher Schreiber und Oberverwalter der Ernte unter Amenophis III. Die Tafel XXXIX stellt Amenophis III. beim Empfang der Huldigungen Chaemhats und der wichtigsten Vorsteher Ober- und Unterägyptens dar. Der Pharao, der Krummstab, Wedel und Taukreuz [Anch-Kreuz] hält, sitzt auf einem reich verzierten, von einem Doppel-Naos überragten Thron. Die Armlehnen des königlichen Sessels stellen den Pharao als Sphinx dar, der die afrikanischen und asiatischen Gefangenen in den Staub tritt; diese tauchen auch an den Stützen des Thrones auf, wo sie an ein Sinnbild der Macht und Herrschaft gefesselt sind. Die Basis des prächtigen Naos, unter dem Amenophis ruht, ist mit neun Verkörperungen der unterworfenen Stämme oder Völker verziert, die durch asiatische oder afrikanische Gefangene mit auf dem Rücken gefesselten Händen dargestellt sind.

NÉCROPOLE DE THÈBES

Amounôph III recevant les hommages de Schamthé et des principaux chefs

Sujets tirés du tombeau de Schamthé [Khâemhat], scribe royal, intendant général des récoltes sous Amounôph[Aménophis] III. La planche XXXIX représente Amounôph III recevant les hommages de Schamthé et des principaux chefs de la Haute- et de la Basse-Égypte. Le pharaon, tenant l'aspersoir, le crochet et le Tau [l'ânkh], est assis sur un trône richement orné, et surmonté d'un double naos. Les accotoirs du siège royal représentent le pharaon sous la forme d'un sphinx foulant des captifs africains et asiatiques, personnifiés aussi au montant du trône, où ils figurent liés autour d'un symbole de la puissance et du commandement. La base du riche naos, sous lequel Amounôph repose, est ornée de neuf figures des nations ou des tribus soumises, représentées par des captifs asiatiques ou africains, les mains liées derrière le dos.

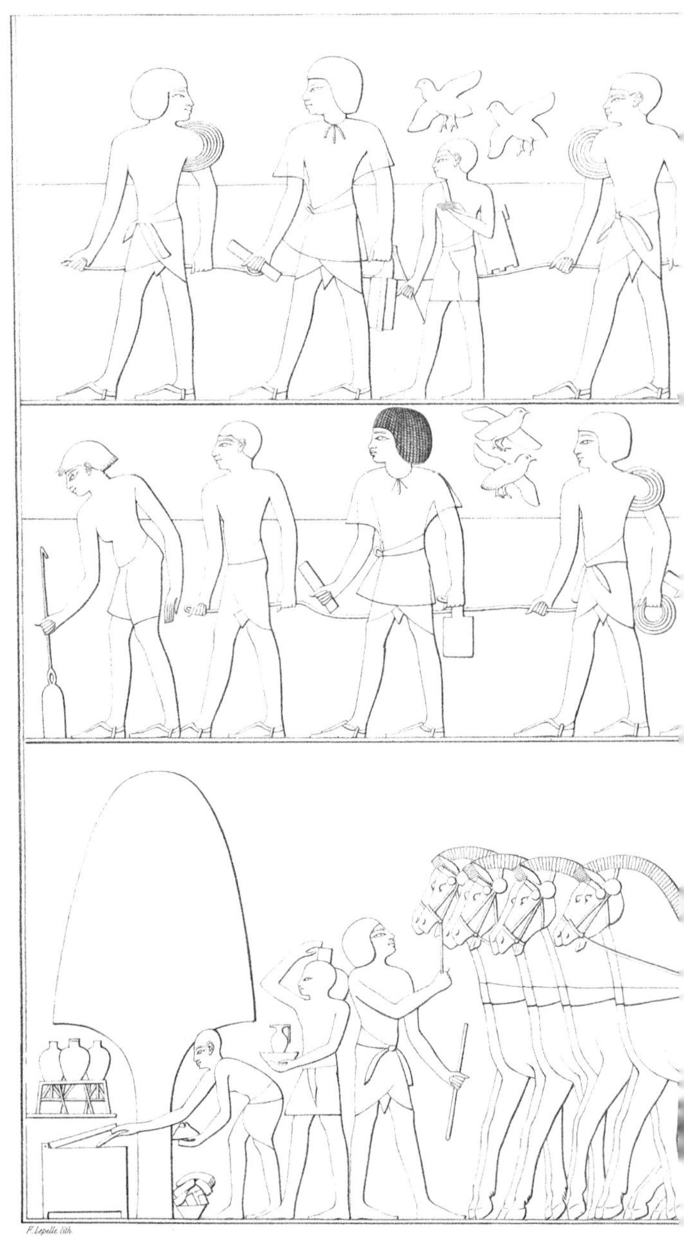

SCHAMTHÉ, SCRIBE ROYAL CHARGÉ D

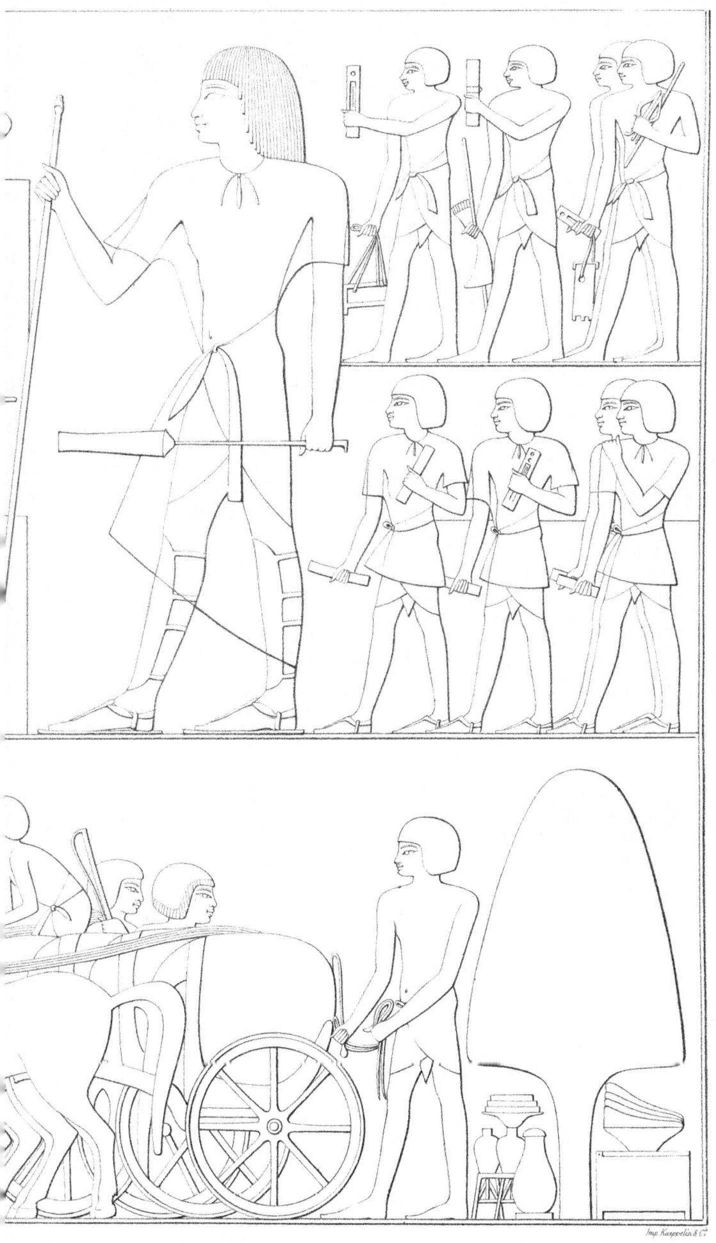

Imp. Kaeppelin & Cie.

PRÉSIDANT A L'ARPENTAGE DES TERRES.

NÉCROPO

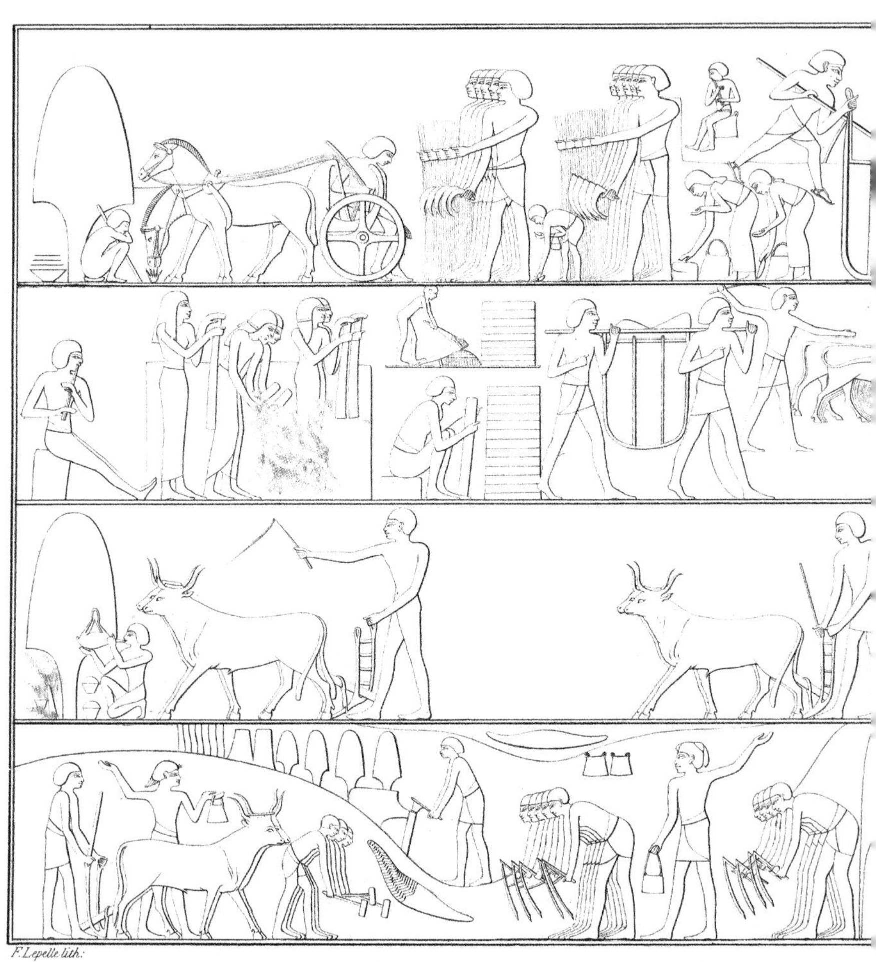

F. Lepelle lith:

SCHAMTHÉ, SCRIBE ROYAL CHARGÉ DES

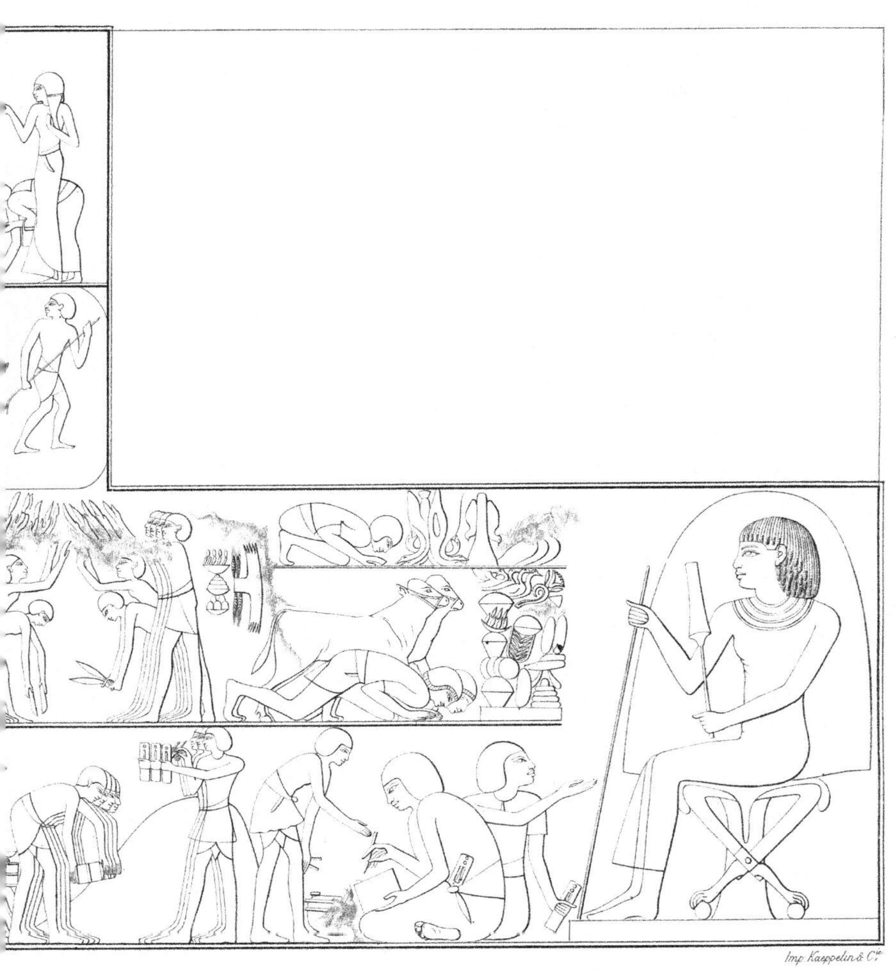
Imp. Kaeppelin & Cie.

PRÉSIDANT AUX TRAVAUX DES CHAMPS.

(Pages/Seite 166/167)

NECROPOLIS OF THEBES

Khaemhat. The royal scribe in charge of harvests presiding over the survey of the lands

In [this] plate we see Khaemhat, followed by many servants, presiding over the survey of the lands subject to his jurisdiction. The survey is carried out using cords and pegs; a scribe writes down the results. The lower register represents the retinue of this high-ranking official, with carts and all the necessary preparations for a meal in the open air.

NEKROPOLE VON THEBEN

Chaemhat. Königlicher Schreiber und Vorsteher der Kornspeicher, beim Überwachen der Landvermessung

Auf [dieser] Tafel ist Chaemhat zu sehen, der – mit zahlreichen Dienern im Gefolge – die Vermessung der seiner Rechtssprechung unterstehenden Ländereien überwacht. Die Vermessung wird mithilfe von Schnüren und Messlatten durchgeführt; ein Schreiber notiert die Ergebnisse. Das untere Register stellt das Gefolge dieser hochstehenden Persönlichkeiten dar, auch die Wagen und alle Vorbereitungen, die für eine ländliche Mahlzeit getroffen werden.

NÉCROPOLE DE THÈBES

Schamthé. Scribe royal chargé des récoltes, présidant à l'arpentage des terres

Dans [cette] planche, on voit Schamthé [Khâemhat], suivi de nombreux serviteurs, présidant à l'arpentage des terres soumises à sa juridiction. L'arpentage se fait au moyen de cordeaux et de jalons ; un scribe en écrit le résultat. Le registre inférieur représente la suite de ce haut personnage, les chars et tous les préparatifs d'un repas champêtre.

(Pages/Seite 168/169)

NECROPOLIS OF THEBES

Khaembat. The royal scribe in charge of harvests presiding over work on the lands

Plate XLI represents different agricultural tasks, over which the Overseer of Harvests once again presides. As he looks on, the field-workers proceed to clear the land, then to plough and sow, to reap the ears of corn and carry them to be trodden out by the oxen. The grain is cleaned and measured and tied up in sacks. Scribes make notes of the number of measures. In the background, men are working at the harvesting and stripping of flax. Finally the peasants come to pay homage and to offer many presents to the overseer of lands who, sitting in the shade of a sycamore fig, cane in one hand and aba sceptre in the other, observes the different tasks.

NEKROPOLE VON THEBEN

Chaembat. Königlicher Schreiber und Vorsteher der Kornspeicher, beim Überwachen der Feldarbeiten

Die Tafel XLI stellt die verschiedenen Feldarbeiten dar, die der Vorsteher der Kornspeicher auch überwacht. Unter seinen Augen nehmen die Bauern die Urbarmachung des Landes, das Pflügen, das Säen, das Mähen des Weizens, den Abtransport der Ähren und das Dreschen mittels Rindern vor. Das gereinigte und abgemessene Korn wird in Säcke verpackt. Die Schreiber protokollieren die Anzahl der abgemessenen Einheiten. Etwas weiter entfernt werden die Ernte und das Brechen des Flachses durchgeführt. Schließlich kommen die Bauern, um dem Verwalter der Ländereien – der mit dem Stock in der einen und dem Aba-Zepter in der anderen Hand unter einer Sykomore sitzt und den verschiedenen Arbeiten beiwohnt – zu huldigen und ihm zahlreiche Geschenke darzubieten.

NÉCROPOLE DE THÈBES

Schamthé [Khâembat]. Scribe royal chargé des récoltes, présidant aux travaux des champs

La planche XLI représente les divers travaux des champs auxquels préside encore l'intendant des récoltes. Les cultivateurs procèdent sous ses yeux au défrichement des terres, au labourage, aux semailles, au fauchage des blés, au transport des épis, et au foulage par les bœufs. Le grain nettoyé et mesuré est renfermé dans des sacs. Des scribes tiennent note du nombre des mesures. Plus loin, on procède à la récolte et au tillage du lin. Enfin, des paysans viennent rendre hommage et offrir de nombreux présents à l'intendant des terres, qui, assis à l'ombre d'un sycomore, la canne d'une main, le pat de l'autre, assiste à ces divers travaux.

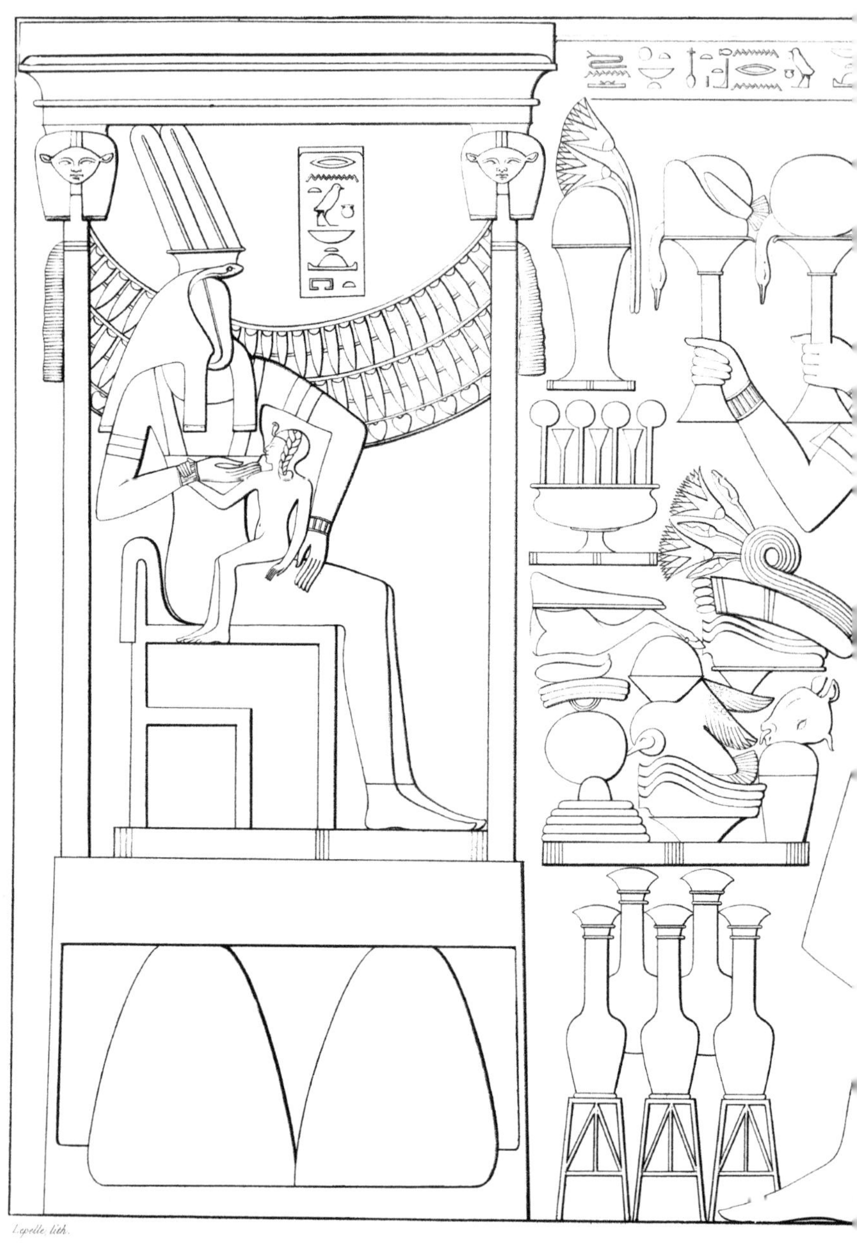

Lepelle lith.

OFFRANDE A LA DÉES

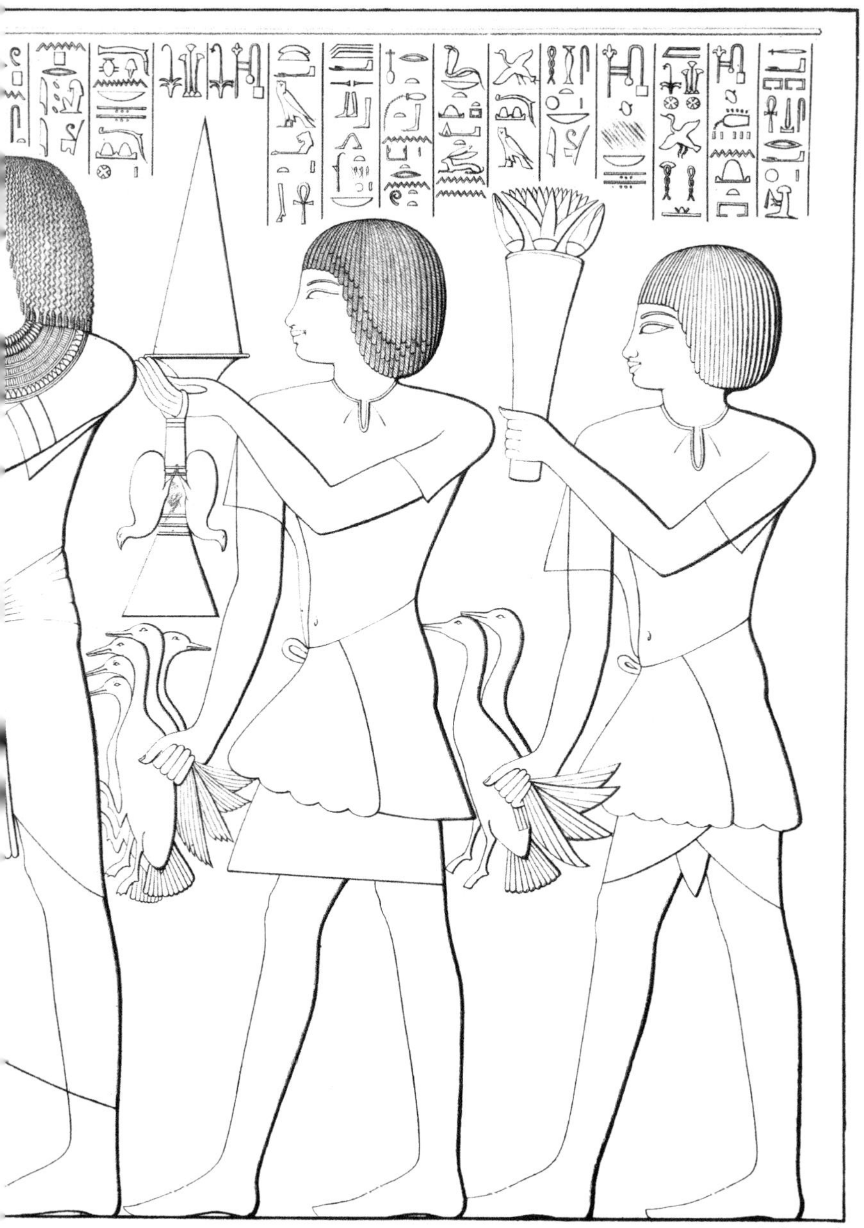

Imp. Kaeppelin & Cie

AME DES RÉCOLTES.

1.

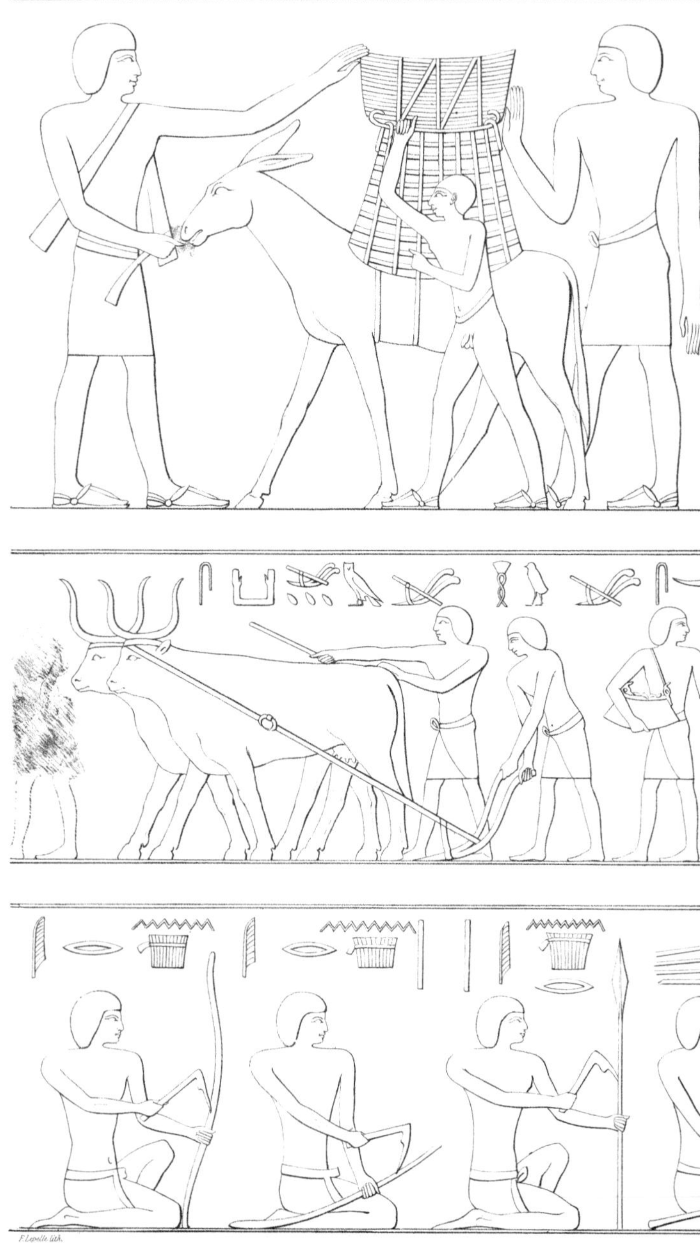

F. Lepelle lith.

2.

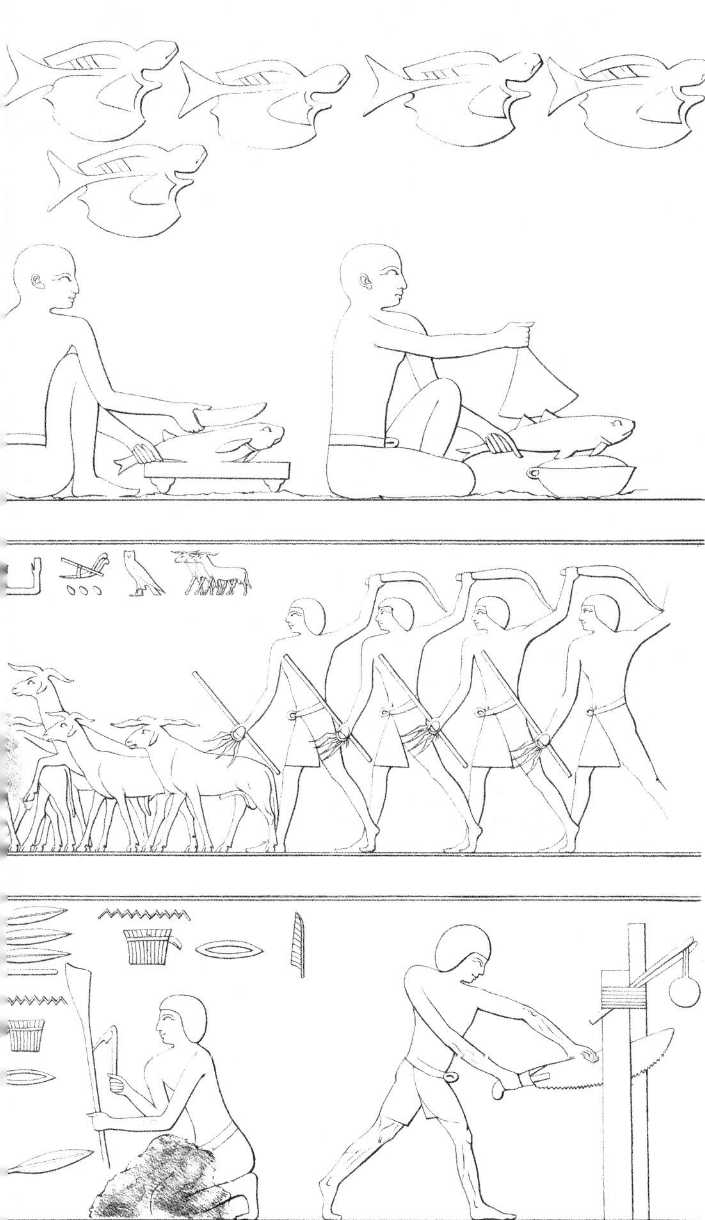

POGEES.

(Pages/Seite 172/173)

NECROPOLIS OF THEBES

Offering to Renenutet, lady of the harvests

The subject of this plate is also taken from the hypogeum of Khaemhat. It depicts an offering to Renenutet, lady of the harvests. The uraeus-headed goddess, seated beneath an elegant naos decorated with garlands of leaves and supported by two small columns carved with the head of Hathor, all resting on two piles of corn, is shown suckling the young Amenophis III. If we compare this scene to the beautiful painting which serves as vignette to the frontispiece of my work [see p. 2], we can see the two forms which Renenutet most commonly assumed.

NEKROPOLE VON THEBEN

Opfergabe an die Göttin Renenutet, Herrin der Ernte

Der Gegenstand dieser Tafel ist ebenfalls dem Hypogäum von Chaemhat entnommen. Wiedergegeben ist eine Opfergabe an die Göttin Renenutet, die Herrin der Ernte. Die uräusköpfige Göttin, die unter einem eleganten, mit Blättergirlanden verzierten, durch zwei Hathorsäulen gestützten und von zwei Weizenhaufen getragenen Naos sitzt, nährt in dieser Darstellung den jungen Amenophis III. mit ihrer Milch. Vergleicht man diese Szene mit der schönen Malerei, die als Zierbild auf dem Titelblatt meines Werkes [siehe S. 2] erscheint, so zeigen uns die beiden Bilder die beiden Gestalten, die die Göttin Renenutet am häufigsten annimmt.

NÉCROPOLE DE THÈBES

Offrande à la déesse Rannou, dame des récoltes

Le sujet de cette planche est aussi tiré de l'hypogée de Schamthé [Khâemhat]. Il représente une offrande à Rannou, dame des récoltes. La déesse uréocéphale, assise sous un élégant naos décoré de guirlandes de feuilles, soutenu par deux colonnettes à tête d'Hathor et porté par deux monceaux de blé, est représentée nourrissant de son lait le jeune Amounôph [Aménophis] III. En rapprochant cette scène de la belle peinture qui sert de vignette au frontispice de mon ouvrage [voir p. 2], les deux tableaux nous offrent les deux formes que Rannou affecte le plus ordinairement.

(Pages/Seite 174/175)

DEIR EL-BERSHA AND EL-SHEIKH SAID

Bas-reliefs taken from hypogea

Bas-reliefs taken from hypogea at Deir el-Bersha and el-Sheikh Said, which relate to the skills and crafts of the ancient Egyptians. No. 1. Transporting fruit to market. The donkey is loaded with a type of pannier woven from date branches, a skill which is still in daily use today. No. 2. A method of preparing fish, which the Egyptians used a great deal: they salted it and dried it in the sun, a method which is still in current use. No. 3. Ploughing the land and sowing the seed. [...] No. 4. Various stages in the production of bows and spears. This bas-relief finishes with a man sawing tree trunks, using a lever to hold the cut planks together.

DEIR EL-BERSCHE UND SCHEICH SAID

Den Hypogäen entnommene Flachreliefs

Den Hypogäen von Deir el-Bersche und Scheich Said entnommene Flachreliefs, die sich auf das Handwerk der alten Ägypter beziehen. Nr. 1. Transport der Früchte zum Markt. Der Esel ist mit einer Art Korb aus Dattelpalmzweigen beladen, wie es auch heute noch täglich vorkommt. Nr. 2. Zubereitung der Fische, die die Ägypter häufig verwendeten: Sie wurden eingesalzen und in der Sonne getrocknet – eine Sitte, die sich bis auf den heutigen Tag gehalten hat. Nr. 3. Pflügen und Einsäen. [...] Nr. 4. Verschiedene Arbeitsgänge der Herstellung von Bögen und Spießen. Der am Schluss dieses Flachreliefs abgebildete Sägende mit der Langsäge verwendet einen Hebel, um die von ihm abgesägten Bretter zusammenzuhalten.

BERCHEH ET CHEIKH-SAYD

Bas-reliefs tirés des hypogées

Bas-reliefs tirés des hypogées de Bercheh et Cheikh-Sayd, et relatifs aux arts et métiers des anciens Égyptiens. N° 1. Transport des fruits au marché. L'âne est chargé d'une espèce de panier fait de branches de dattier, comme cela se pratique encore journellement. N° 2. Préparation des poissons dont les Égyptiens faisaient un grand usage : ils les salaient et les séchaient au soleil, coutume qui s'est conservée jusqu'à nos jours. N° 3. Labourage et ensemencement des terres. [...] N° 4. Diverses opérations de la fabrication des arcs et des piques. Le scieur de long qui termine ce bas-relief emploie un levier pour retenir assemblées les planches qu'il débite.

NECROPOLIS OF THEBES

Games and dances

No. 1. Depiction of a type of dance which was performed to the noise of rhythmical hand-clapping and the sound of an instrument which was shaken, possibly like castanets or cymbals. No. 2. Musicians and dancers. This subject is taken from a small mud-brick pyramid in the necropolis of the temple of Maat and Hathor, behind Medinet Habu. From the nudity of the figures, which are barely covered by a fine, transparent, gauze material, one would be more inclined to take this scene for a lascivious dance than for a religious ceremony; however, the name of Amun, which is mentioned in the legend, leaves no doubt as to its character.

NEKROPOLE VON THEBEN

Spiel und Tanz

Nr. 1. Die Darstellung zeigt eine Art Tanz, der zum rhythmischen Klatschen der Hände und zum Klang eines Instruments, das man vielleicht wie Kastagnetten oder Klappern handhabte, ausgeführt wurde. Nr. 2. Musiker und Tänzerinnen. Dieses Motiv stammt aus einer kleinen Pyramide aus luftgetrockneten Lehmziegeln; sie steht in der Nekropole des Tempels der Maat und der Hathor hinter Medinet Habu. In Anbetracht der Nacktheit der – von feinen, transparenten Stoffen kaum verhüllten – Figuren könnte man diese Szene eher für einen sinnlichen Tanz als für eine religiöse Zeremonie halten; der Name des Amun, an den in der Inschrift erinnert wird, lässt jedoch keinen Zweifel an ihrer Wesensart aufkommen.

NÉCROPOLE DE THÈBES

Jeux et danses

N° 1. Représentation d'une espèce de danse qui s'exécutait au bruit des mains frappant en cadence et au son d'un instrument qu'on agitait peut-être comme des castagnettes ou des crotales.
N° 2. Musiciens et danseuses. Ce sujet est tiré d'une petite pyramide de briques crues de la nécropole du temple de Tmei [Maât] et Hathor, derrière Medineh-Tabou [Médinet Habou]. À voir la nudité des figures, à peine gazées de fines et transparentes étoffes, on prendrait plutôt cette scène pour une danse lascive que pour une cérémonie religieuse; mais le nom d'Amon, rappelé dans la légende, ne laisse aucun doute sur leur caractère.

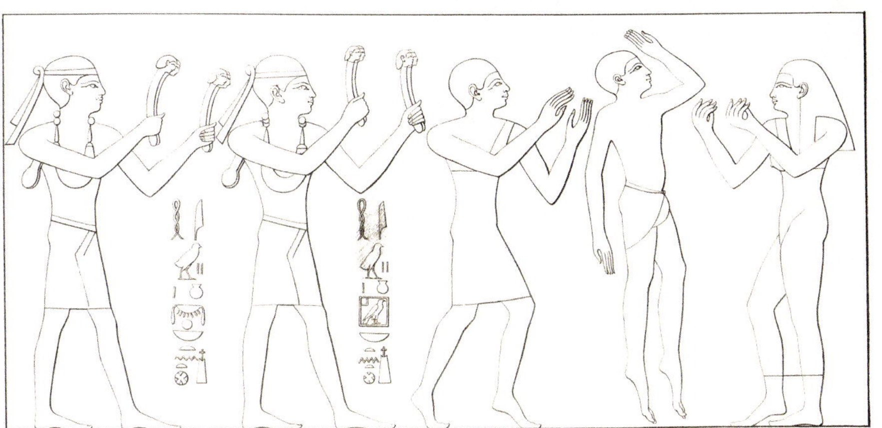

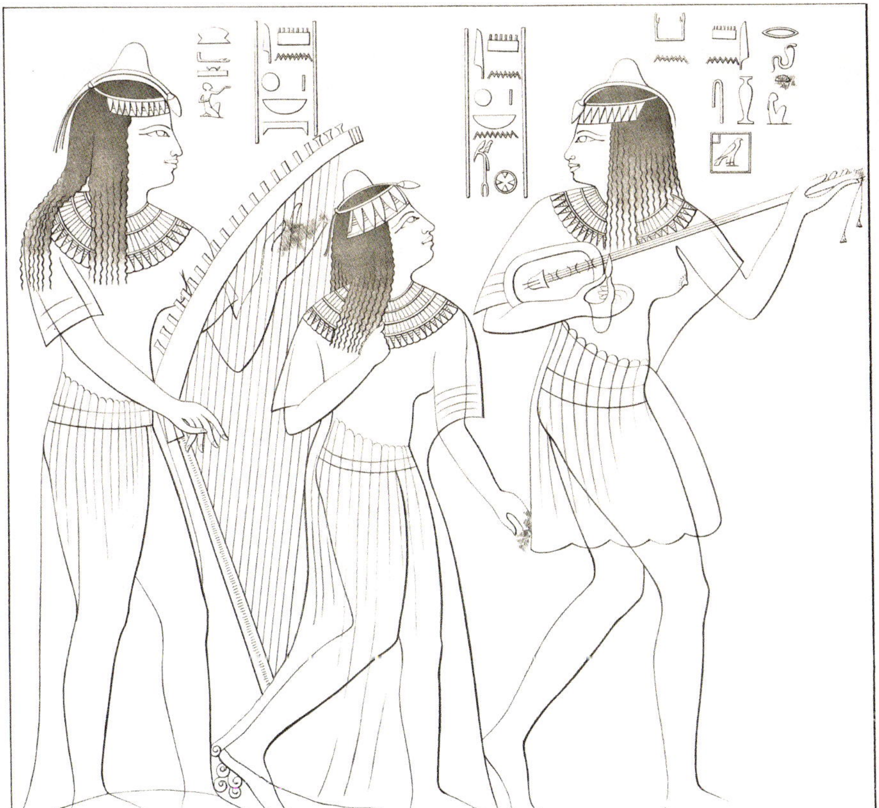

P. Lepelle lith. E. Prisse Imp. Kaeppelin

JEUX ET DANSES.

NECROPOLIS OF THEBES

Painting copied in a hypogeum

Domestic scenes taken from a hypogeum at Thebes. The upper register is of a gathering of women waited upon by young girls who, like Venus, are clad in nothing but a belt. The lower register represents the toilet of an Egyptian lady. A chamber-maid invites her to inhale the scent of a lotus bud, while other waiting-women pour perfumes on her hair or attend to the details of her jewellery. This charming scene, which falls somewhat outside the mainstream of ritual portrayals hallowed by long-established practice, is full of expression and the bodies of the young girls are drawn with delicacy.

NEKROPOLE VON THEBEN

Aus einem Hypogäum abgezeichnete Malerei

Vertraute, aus einem Hypogäum in Theben entnommene Szenen. Das obere Register zeigt eine Versammlung von Frauen, die von jungen Mädchen bedient werden und – wie Venus – als einziges Kleidungsstück nur einen Gürtel tragen. Das zweite Register stellt die Toilette einer ägyptischen Dame dar. Eine Kammerfrau lässt sie den Geruch einer Lotusknospe einatmen, während andere Frauen ihr die Haare parfümieren oder auf die Einzelheiten ihres Geschmeides achten. Diese reizende Szene, die sich ein wenig von den feierlichen, durch starre Gebräuche festgeschriebenen abhebt, ist voller Ausdruck; der Körper der jungen Mädchen ist anmutig wiedergegeben.

NÉCROPOLE DE THÈBES

Peinture copiée dans un hypogée

Scènes familières tirées d'un hypogée de Thèbes. Le registre supérieur d'une réunion de femmes servies par des jeunes filles n'ayant, comme Vénus, qu'une ceinture pour tout vêtement. Le second registre représente la toilette d'une dame égyptienne. Une camériste lui fait respirer l'odeur d'un bouton de lotus, pendant que les autres femmes versent des parfums sur ses cheveux ou président aux détails de sa parure. Cette charmante scène, qui sort un peu des représentations hiératiques consacrées par d'immuables usages, est pleine d'expression ; le corps des jeunes filles est dessiné avec grâce.

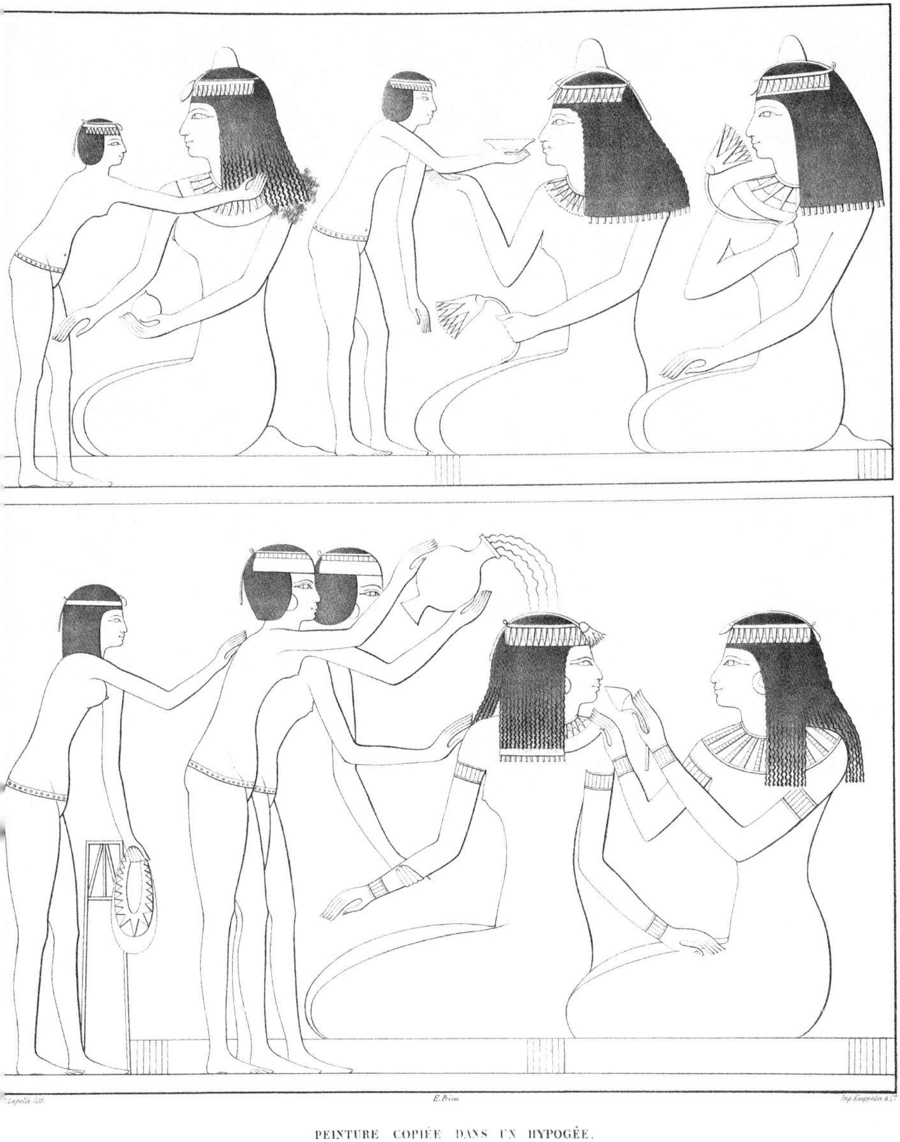

NÉCROPOLE DE THÈBES.

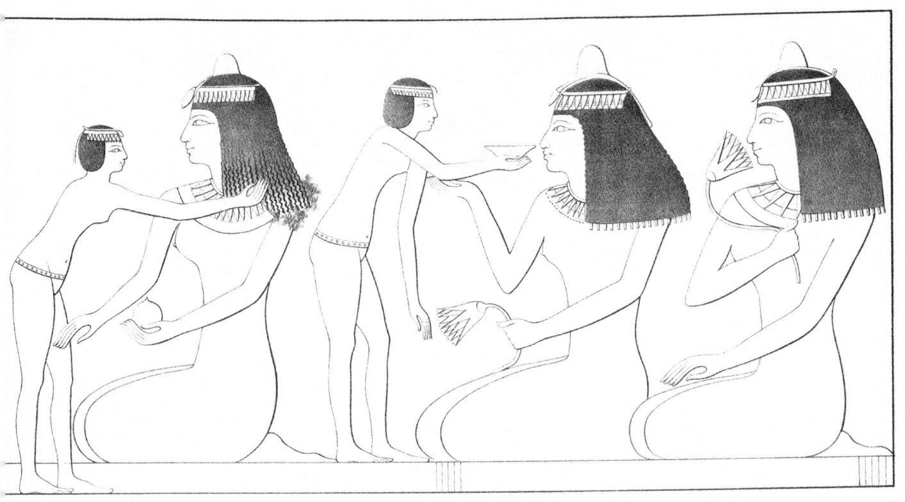

Lepelle lith. E. Prisse Imp. Kaeppelin & C.ie

PEINTURE COPIÉE DANS UN HYPOGÉE.

EGYPTIAN MONUMENTS

Weapons

Offensive and defensive weapons. No. 1. Bow similar to those carried by light-armed soldiers. No. 2. Arrow made from a reed, with a sharp, flint point. No. 3. Fragment of a cuirass made from bronze scales laid over and sewn on to a "sagum" or tight leather jerkin. Nos. 4 and 5. Battle-axes similar to those carried by military leaders and which often figure in miniature in hieroglyphs to designate a god. No. 6. A blunt instrument, a club in curved acacia wood. No. 7. Dagger whose blade is perfectly grooved, in the style of eastern Damascus blades. Nos. 8 and 9. Canes of hardwood, bearing hieroglyphic legends. Nos. 10, 11, 12, 13 and 14. Arrow-heads, in bronze and in iron.

ÄGYPTISCHE DENKMÄLER

Waffen

Angriffs- und Verteidigungswaffen. Nr. 1. Bogen von der Art, wie sie die leicht bewaffneten Soldaten trugen. Nr. 2. Mit einem scharfen Silex bewehrter Binsenpfeil. Nr. 3. Bruchstück eines Panzers, der aus übereinander angeordneten und auf ein „Sagum" oder Lederwams aufgenähten Bronzeplättchen gebildet ist. Nr. 4 und 5. Streitäxte von der Art, wie sie die Militärführer trugen und wie sie häufig verkleinert unter den Hieroglyphen vorkommen, um eine Gottheit zu bezeichnen. Nr. 6. Stumpfe Waffe, Keule aus gekrümmtem Akazienholz.. Nr. 7. Dolch, dessen Klinge in der Art der orientalischen Damaszenerklingen gerillt ist. Nr. 8 und 9. Hartholzstöcke, die Hieroglypheninschriften tragen. Nr. 10, 11, 12, 13 und 14. Pfeilspitzen aus Bronze und Eisen.

MONUMENTS ÉGYPTIENS

Armes

Armes offensives et défensives. N° 1. Arc semblable à ceux que portaient les soldats armés à la légère. N° 2. Flèche de jonc armée d'un silex aigu. N° 3. Fragment d'une cuirasse formée d'écailles de bronze superposées et cousues sur un « sagum » ou justaucorps de cuir. N°s 4 et 5. Haches d'armes semblables à celles que portent les chefs militaires, et qui sont souvent figurées en petit dans les hiéroglyphes pour désigner un dieu. N° 6. Arme contondante, casse-tête en bois d'acacia courbé. N° 7. Poignard dont la lame est parfaitement cannelée, dans le genre des damas d'Orient. N°s 8 et 9. Cannes en bois dur, portant des légendes hiéroglyphiques. N°s 10, 11, 12, 13 et 14. Armatures de flèches, en bronze et en fer.

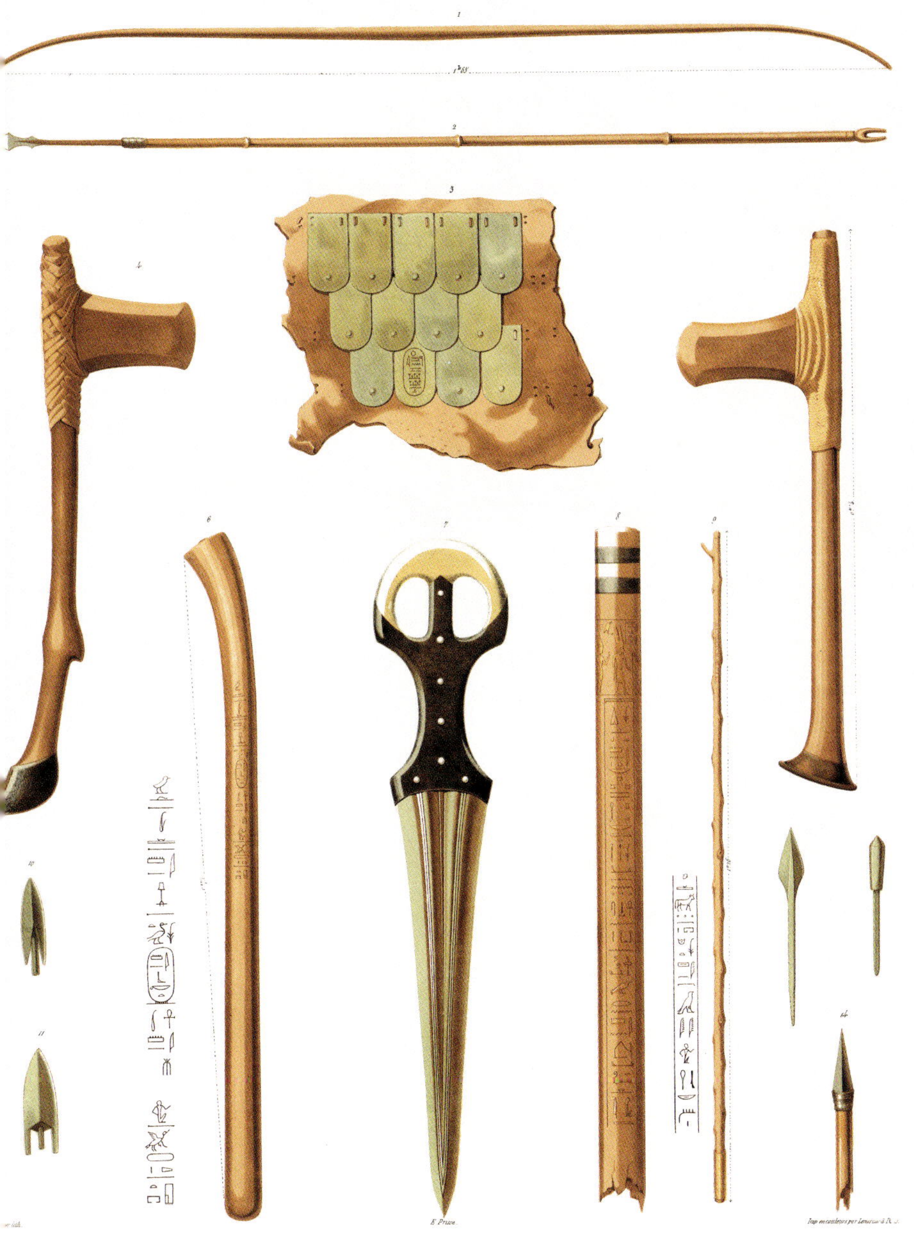

ARMES.

EGYPTIAN MONUMENTS

Jewellery and furnishings

Nos. 1 and 2. Gold ear-rings and collar, bearing the name of Menai, identical to that of Menes, the earliest king of Egypt. No. 3. Gold ring bearing the prenomen of Amenophis II, described as son of Amun-Ra. No. 4. Gold ring, decorated with a hieroglyphic legend, containing the cartouche of Cheops, second king of the 4th Dynasty. No. 5. Collar in pearls and plates of gold, decorated with various symbols. No. 6. Bronze ring. Nos. 7 and 9. Drop ear-rings in gold. No. 8. Ring with a setting in lapis lazuli and coral. No. 10. Bronze ring, bearing the name of Tutankhamun, pharaoh of the 18th Dynasty. No. 11. Figurine in bloodstone, representing one of the types of Horus. No. 12. Gold figurine of Amun. Nos. 13, 14, 15 and 16. Rings. Nos. 17 and 18. Statuette used to hold black antimony, powdered or in any other preparation and similar to the "surma" [kohl] of the Orientals. Nos. 19 and 20 represent collars in lapis lazuli and gold. Nos. 21 and 22. Mirrors in polished metal. No. 23. A head-rest, called an "ouol".

ÄGYPTISCHE DENKMÄLER

Geschmeide und Möbel

Nr. 1 und 2. Ohrgehänge und Halskette aus Gold, auf denen der Name Meni steht – der mit Menes, dem ältesten ägyptischen König, identisch ist. Nr. 3. Goldring mit dem Namen von Amenophis II., der als Sohn des Amun-Re bezeichnet wird. Nr. 4. Mit einer Hieroglypheninschrift verzierter Goldring, in der die Kartusche von Cheops, dem zweiten König der vierten Dynastie, erscheint. Nr. 5. Halskette aus Perlen und aus mit verschiedenen Sinnbildern verzierten Goldplättchen. Nr. 6. Bronzering. Nr. 7 und 9. Goldene Ohrgehänge. Nr. 8. Mit einer Fassung aus Lapislazuli und Koralle verzierter Ring. Nr. 10. Bronzering mit dem Namen von Tutanchamun, einem Pharao der 18. Dynastie. Nr. 11. Figürchen aus Hämatit, das einen Horus darstellt. Nr. 12. Goldenes Amun-Figürchen. Nr. 13, 14, 15 und 16. Ringe. Nr. 17 und 18. Statuetten, die zur Aufbewahrung von Stibium, Antimonpulver oder jedweder anderen, dem orientalischen „Surma" [Kohlkajal] entsprechenden Substanz dienten. Nr. 19 und 20. stellen Halsketten aus Gold und Lapislazuli dar. Nr. 21 und 22. Spiegel aus poliertem Metall. Nr. 23. Kopfstütze, die „Ouol" genannt wird.

MONUMENTS ÉGYPTIENS

Parures et meubles

N°s 1 et 2. Pendants d'oreilles et collier en or, portant le nom de Menaï, identique à celui de Ménès, le plus ancien roi d'Égypte. N° 3. Bague en or portant le prénom d'Amounôph [Aménophis] II, qualifié de fils d'Amon-Ra. N° 4. Bague en or, ornée d'une légende hiéroglyphique, contenant le cartouche de Schoufou [Khéops], second roi de la IVe dynastie. N° 5. Collier formé de perles et de plaques d'or ornées de divers symboles. N° 6. Bague en bronze. N°s 7 et 9. Pendants d'oreilles en or. N° 8. Bague ornée d'un chaton de pierre lazuli et de corail. N° 10. Bague en bronze portant le nom d'Amentouonkh [Toutânkhamon], pharaon de la XVIIIe dynastie. N° 11. Figurine en sanguine, représentant un des Horus. N° 12. Figurine d'Amon, en or. N°s 13, 14, 15 et 16. Bagues. N°s 17 et 18. Statuette servant à contenir le stibium, l'antimoine en poudre ou toute autre préparation analogue au « surmé » [kôhl] des Orientaux. Les n°s 19 et 20 représentent des colliers en lapis-lazuli et en or. N°s 21 et 22. Miroirs en métal poli. N° 23. Chevet appelé « ouol ».

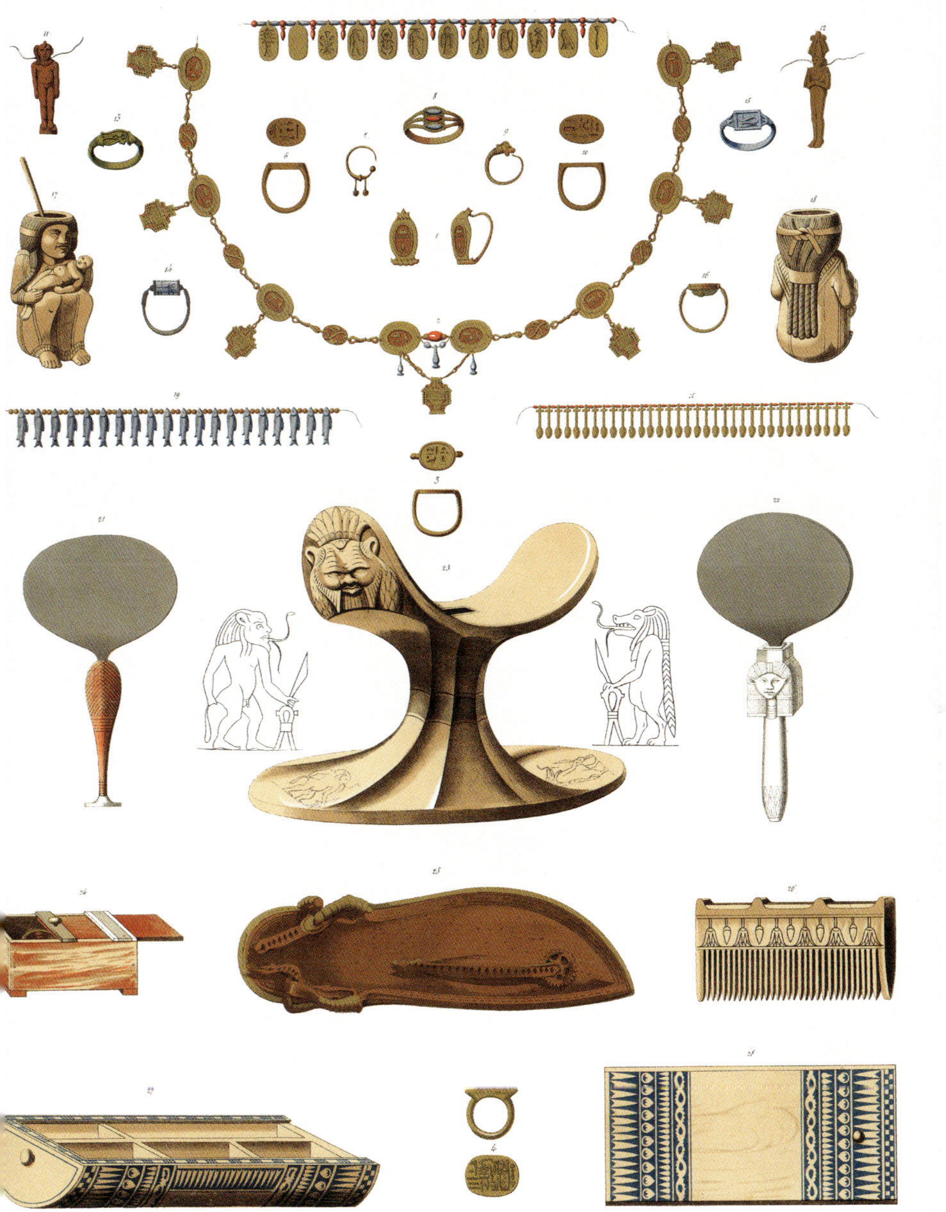

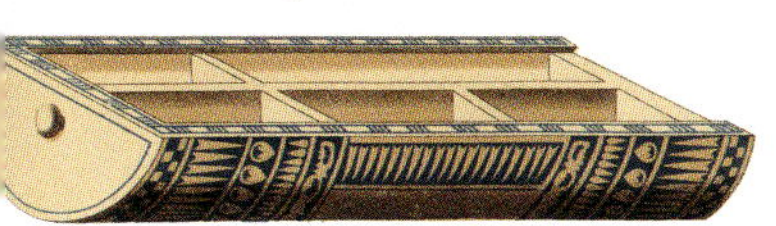

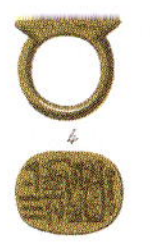

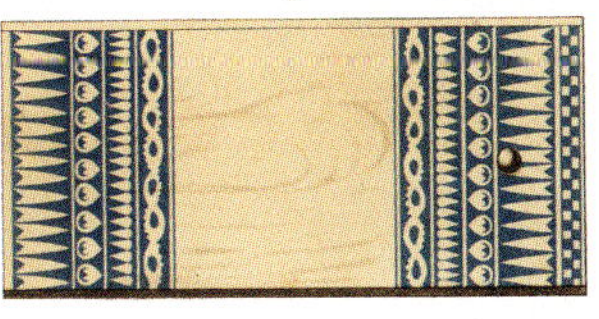

E. Prisse

PARURES ET MEUBLES.

EGYPTIAN MONUMENTS

Boxes and offertories

No. 1. Offertory or perfume spoon in alabaster. No. 2. Toilet box depicting a woman carrying a bag and a vase. No. 3. Offertory in ebony, a masterpiece of taste and elegance. It represents an Ethiopian woman with hair dressed in the same way as her modern counterpart, her body completely naked, adorned only with a gilded collar and belt. Our statuette is elongated; she stretches out her arms and holds a little vase in the shape of a fish, which was doubtless used to hold some sort of cosmetic for an elegant lady of the era of Baskh-en-Aten [Akhenaten]. No. 4. Perfume box. No. 5. Offertory in the shape of a cartouche. No. 6. Fragment of a perfume box. No. 7. Offertory in alabaster.

ÄGYPTISCHE DENKMÄLER

Dosen und Opfergefäße

Nr. 1. Opfergefäß oder Parfümlöffel aus Alabaster. Nr. 2. Gefäß für die Toilette in Gestalt einer Frau, die einen Beutel und eine Vase trägt. Nr. 3. Opfergefäß aus Ebenholz – ein Meisterwerk an Geschmack und Anmut. Es stellt eine wie die Frauen von heute frisierte Äthiopierin dar, deren vollkommen nackter Körper lediglich mit einem vergoldeten Halsband und Gürtel geschmückt ist. Unsere Statuette hat einen ausgestreckten Körper und trägt auf ihren ausgestreckten Armen eine kleine fischförmige Vase, die zweifellos dazu diente, irgendeine Kosmetik für eine Dame aus der Zeit des Basch-en-Aten [Echnaton] aufzunehmen. Nr. 4. Parfümdose. Nr. 5. Opfergefäß in Form einer Kartusche. Nr. 6. Bruchstück einer Parfümdose. Nr. 7. Opfergefäß aus Alabaster.

MONUMENTS ÉGYPTIENS

Boîtes et offertoirs

N° 1. Offertoir ou cuiller à parfums en albâtre. N° 2. Boîte de toilette représentant une femme portant un sac et un vase. N° 3. Offertoir en ébène, chef-d'œuvre de goût et d'élégance. Il représente une Éthiopienne coiffée comme les femmes d'aujourd'hui, le corps entièrement nu, et orné simplement d'un collier et d'une ceinture qui ont été dorés. Notre statuette a le corps allongé, et soutient sur ses bras étendus un petit vase en forme de poisson, qui servait sans doute à renfermer quelque cosmétique à l'usage d'une élégante de l'époque de Basch-n-Aten [Akhénaton]. N° 4. Boîte à parfums. N° 5. Offertoir ayant la forme d'un cartouche. N° 6. Fragment de boîte à parfums. N° 7. Offertoir en albâtre.

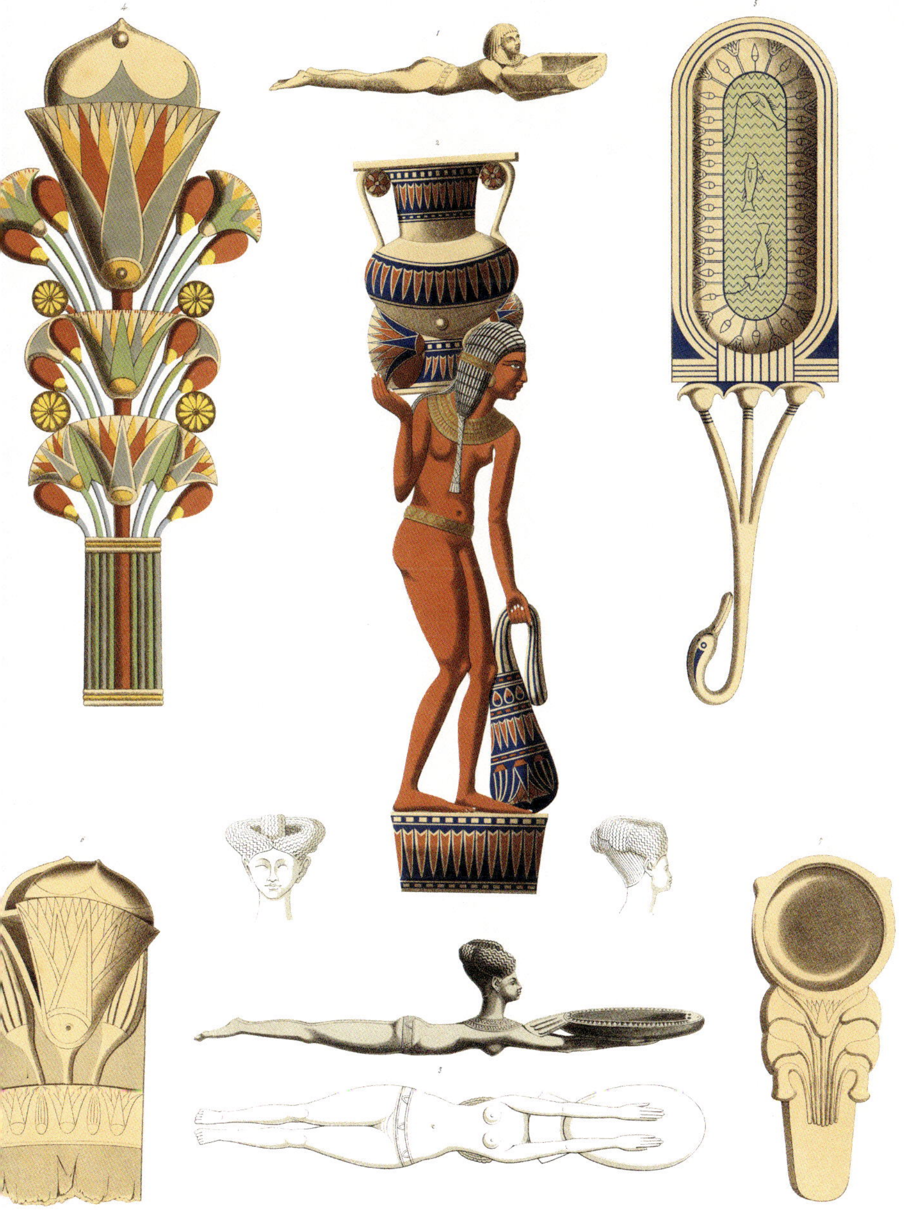

BOÎTES ET OFFERTOIRS.

EGYPTIAN MONUMENTS

Vases and games

No. 1. Faience cup with a lid of sky-blue enamel, decorated with bunches of lotus and fish. No. 2. Terracotta vase with a lid of green enamel. Nos. 3 and 4. Box with a drawer at both ends for games similar to draughts or chess. Next to them are depicted some "latrunculi" or little cones in enamelled clay which seem to have been used as pawns or playing pieces. No. 5. Alabaster vase bearing the standard and cartouche of Neferkare. No. 6. Alabaster vase decorated with the standard and cartouche of Unas, the last pharaoh of the 5th Dynasty. No. 7. Alabaster vase bearing the royal titles of Pepi, son of Isis, lady of Punt. Nos. 8, 9, 10, 11, 12, 13 and 14. Vases of various shapes and materials.

ÄGYPTISCHE DENKMÄLER

Vasen und Spiele

Nr. 1. Fayence-Schale mit einer Glasur aus himmelblauer Emaille, die mit Lotussträußen und Fischen verziert ist. Nr. 2. Terrakotta-Vase mit einer Glasur aus grüner Emaille. Nr. 3 und 4. Kasten, der auf den beiden gegenüberliegenden Seiten Fächer mit Spielen aufweist, die unserem Dame- oder Schachspiel entsprechen. Daneben sind „Latrunculi" oder kleine Kegel aus emailliertem Ton abgebildet, die anscheinend als Spielfiguren oder Spielsteine dienten. Nr. 5. Alabastervase mit dem Zeichen und der Kartusche von Neferkare. Nr. 6. Alabastervase mit dem Zeichen und der Kartusche von Unas, dem letzten Pharao der 5. Dynastie. Nr. 7. Alabastervase mit der königlichen Hieroglypheninschrift von Pepi, Sohn der Isis, Herrin von Punt. Nr. 8, 9, 10, 11, 12, 13 und 14. Unterschiedlich geformte Vasen aus verschiedenen Materialien.

MONUMENTS ÉGYPTIENS

Vases et jeux

N° 1. Coupe en faïence avec une couverte d'émail bleu céleste, ornée de bouquets de lotus et de poissons benni ou latus. N° 2. Vase en terre cuite avec une couverte d'émail vert. N°s 3 et 4. Boîte portant sur les deux faces opposées des casiers de jeux analogues aux dames ou aux échecs. On a représenté à côté des « latrunculi » ou petits cônes en terre émaillée qui paraissent avoir servi de pions et de pièces pour jouer. N° 5. Vase d'albâtre portant la bannière et le cartouche de Nofrekaré [Néferkarê]. N° 6. Vase d'albâtre orné de la bannière et du cartouche de Ounas, dernier pharaon de la Ve dynastie. N° 7. Vase d'albâtre portant la légende royale de Papi [Pépi], fils d'Isis, dame de Pouné. N°s 8, 9, 10, 11, 12, 13 et 14. Vases de formes et de matières diverses.

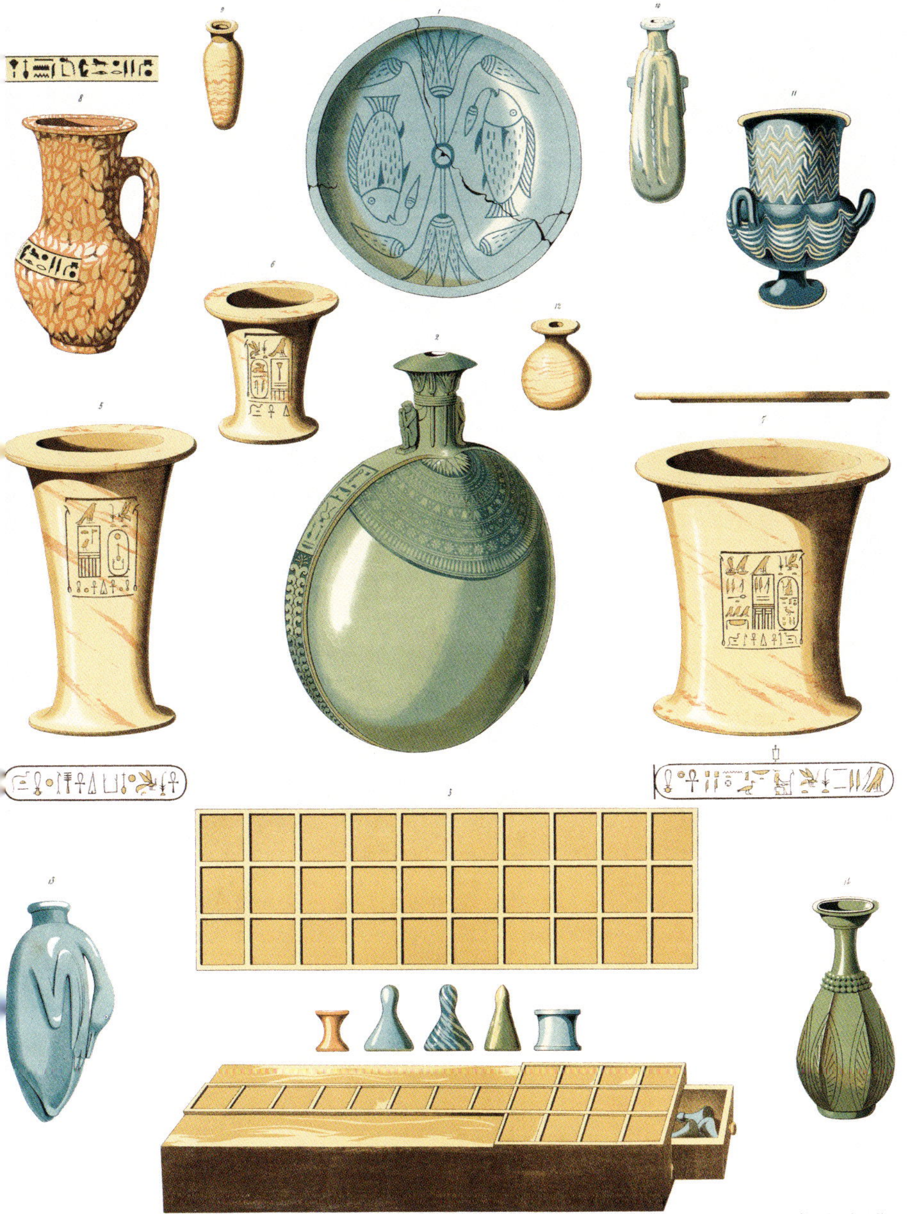

Bisager lith. E. Prisse Imp. en couleurs par Lemercier à Paris.

VASES ET JEUX.

EGYPTIAN MONUMENTS

Vases and utensils

Nos. 1 and 5. Vases intended to hold black antimony or powdered kohl, with which women painted their eye-lids. No. 3. Plaster lid which was used to stopper an amphora: it carries the seal of the dwelling of Merneptah I. No. 4. Horn cupping-glass. Nos. 2, 6, 7, 8, 11, 12, 13 and 14. Household and ointment vases of various shapes. No. 9. A carved box in the shape of an antelope. No. 10. Bronze vase, a winnowing basket or a great handled pail designed for carrying water from the Nile in religious ceremonies.

ÄGYPTISCHE DENKMÄLER

Vasen und Utensilien

Nr. 1 und 5. Vasen, die dazu bestimmt waren, das Stibium und die Kohlkajalpaste aufzunehmen, mit der sich die Frauen die Augenlider schminkten. Nr. 3. Gipsdeckel, der zum Verschluss einer Amphore gedient hat: Er trägt das Siegel vom Domizil Merenptahs I. Nr. 4. Saugnapf aus Horn. Nr. 2, 6, 7, 8, 11, 12, 13 und 14. Haushalts- und Salbgefäße unterschiedlicher Form. Nr. 9. Geschnitzte Dose in Form einer Antilope. Nr. 10. Bronzevase, geweihte Kornwanne oder großer Henkeleimer, der bei religiösen Zeremonien das Nilwasser aufnehmen konnte.

MONUMENTS ÉGYPTIENS

Vases et ustensiles

N°s 1 et 5. Vases destinés à contenir le stibium ou collyre sec, dont les femmes se peignaient les paupières. N° 3. Couvercle en plâtre ayant servi à boucher une amphore : il porte le sceau de la demeure de Menephta Ier. N° 4. Ventouse en corne. N°s 2, 6, 7, 8, 11, 12, 13 et 14. Vases domestiques et onguentaires de formes variées. N° 9. Boite sculptée en forme d'antilope. N° 10. Vase de bronze, van sacré ou grand seau ansé destiné à porter l'eau du Nil dans les cérémonies religieuses.

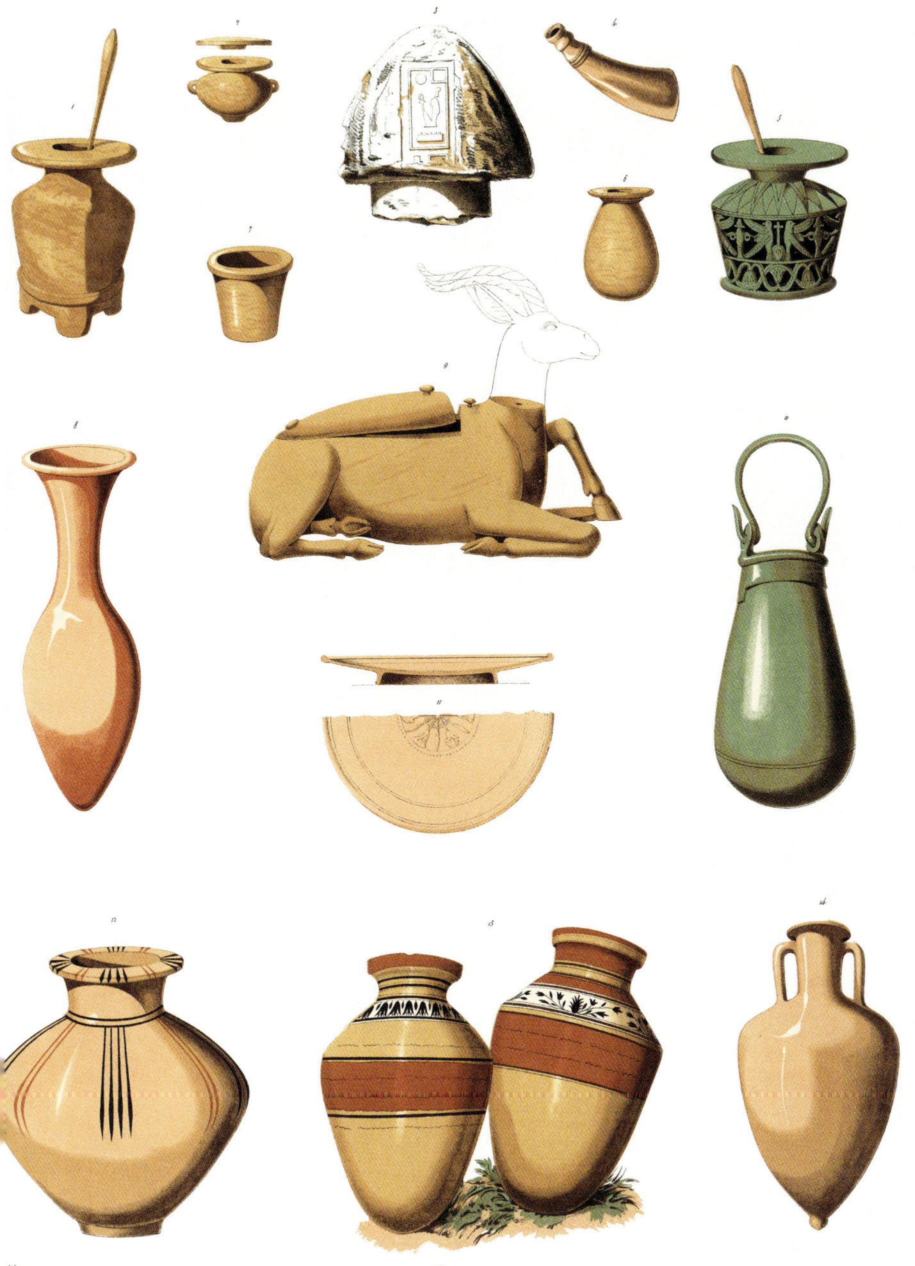

Lith. E. Prisse. Imp. en couleurs par Lemercier à Paris.

VASES ET USTENSILES.

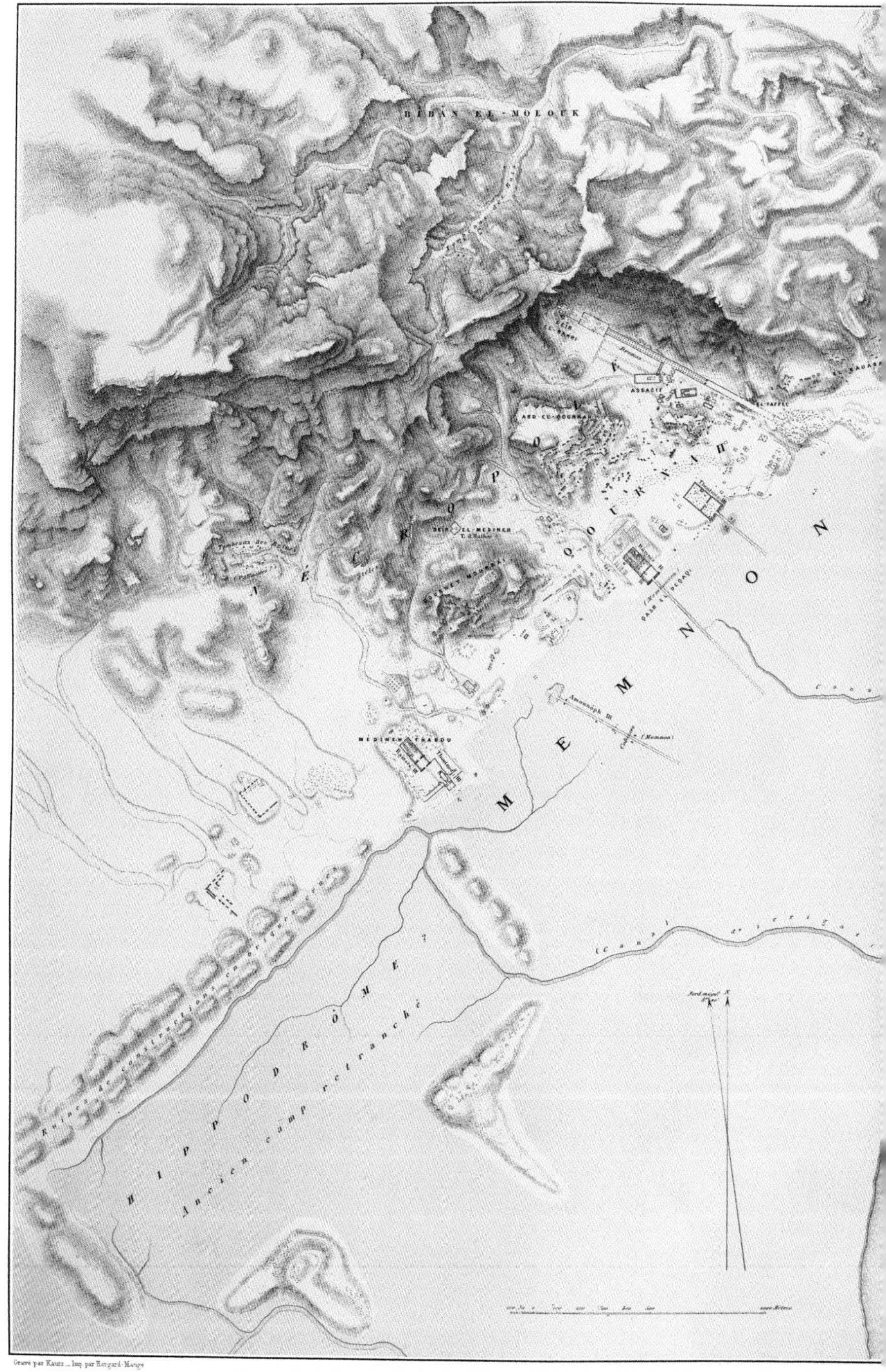
BIBAN EL-MOLOUK
DEIR EL-BAHRI
ASSACIF
EL-TAFFEL
ABD-EL-GOURNAH
N É C R O P O L E
Q O U R N A H
DEIR EL-MEDINEH
T. d'Hathor
Tombeaux des Reines
Stèles
GOURNET MOURRAI
QASR EL-ROUBAYQ
MÉDINET-HABOU
Amenoph III
Colosses
(Memnon)
M E M N O N
H I P P O D R Ô M E ?
Ancien camp retranché
Ruines de constructions en briques crues
(Canal d'irrigation
Nord magnét
Mètres
Gravé par Kautz — Imp. par Hengard-Mange

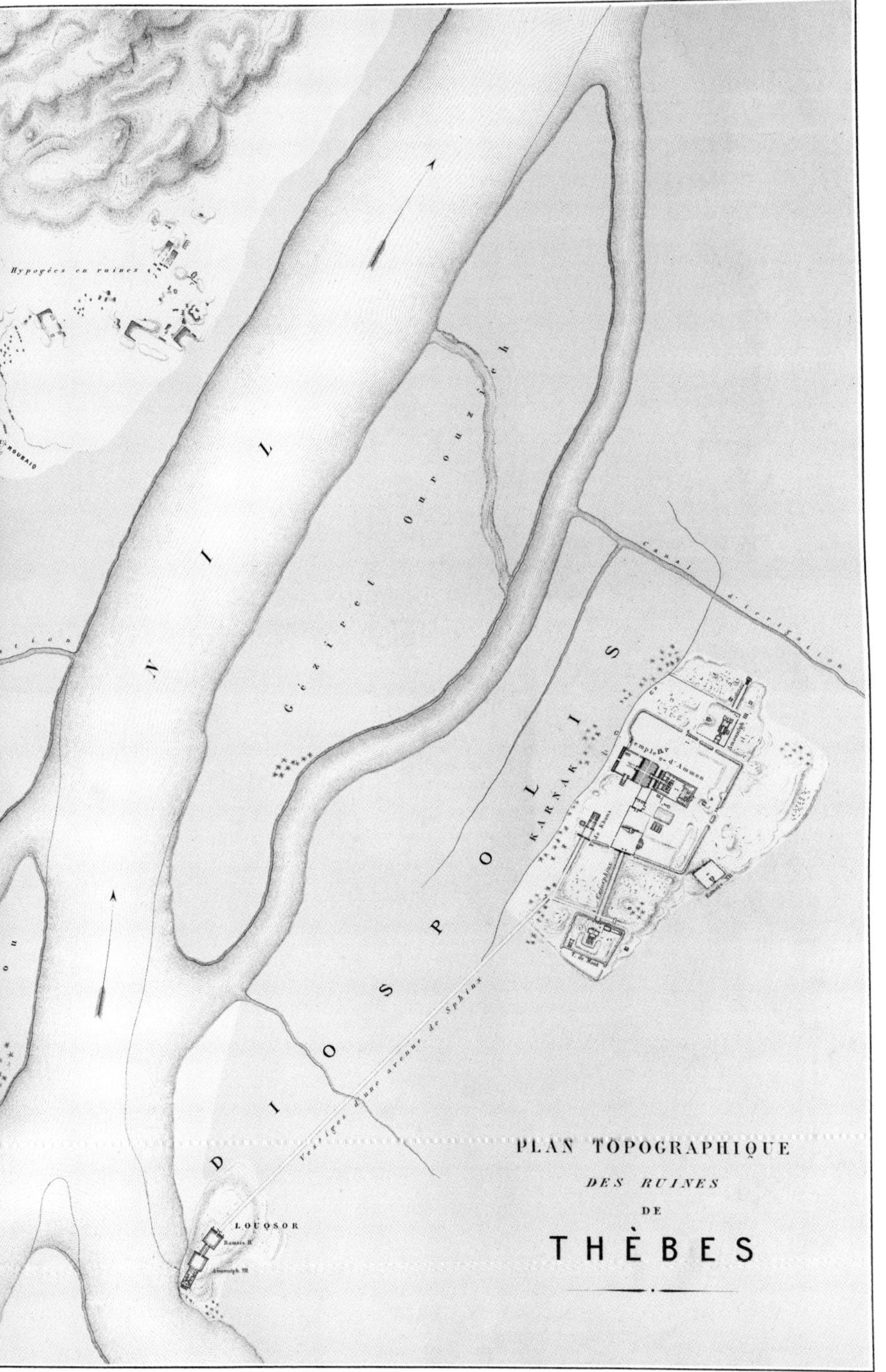

Publié par Arthus-Bertrand, Editeur

Architecture / Architektur / Architecture

(Pages/Seite 192/193)

TOPOGRAPHICAL PLAN OF THE RUINS OF THEBES

Thebes was at various times the seat of government of the pharaohs, and they took pleasure in embellishing the city by the addition of splendid contemporary works of art of every conceivable type. The temples and palaces of Thebes are spread out along both banks of the Nile and occupy a very substantial area. The river divides the city into two large sections. In the Greek papyri about Thebes the section on the Libyan side of the river is frequently referred to by the Greeks as Memnonia, as opposed to the section known as Diospolis, to specify that part of Thebes which was situated on the further bank [the left bank]. All of this portion is covered by imposing temples, luxurious palaces, and a vast hippodrome. However, it is only that part of Thebes which is situated on the right bank which was worthy of the name "City of Cities", capital of the old civilisation. The temple of Luxor and the houses which surrounded it constituted the main approach to Thebes . The great temple of Karnak, the Ammonium, grew to become the largest temple in the world.

TOPOGRAFISCHE KARTE DER RUINEN VON THEBEN

Theben war zu verschiedenen Zeiten Regierungssitz der Pharaonen, denen es Freude bereitete, die Stadt mit den herrlichsten Schöpfungen der zeitgenössischen Künste zu verschönern. Die verstreut zu beiden Seiten des Nils liegenden Tempel und Paläste Thebens nehmen eine Fläche von erheblicher Ausdehnung ein. Der Fluss teilte die Stadt in zwei große Bezirke. In den griechischen Papyri Thebens ist häufig vom libyschen Teil die Rede, den die Griechen Memnonia nannten; anscheinend verwendeten sie diesen Begriff als Gegensatz zu Diospolis, um den am anderen Ufer [dem linken Ufer] gelegenen Bezirk Thebens zu bezeichnen. In diesem gesamten Gebiet standen dicht gedrängt eindrucksvolle Tempel, prunkvolle Paläste und ein weitläufiges Hippodrom. Jedoch verdiente allein der am rechten Ufer gelegene Teil Thebens den Namen „Stadt der Städte", Hauptstadt der alten Kultur. Der Tempel von Luxor bildete mit den ihn umgebenden Wohnstätten den wichtigsten Anlaufpunkt Thebens. Der große Tempel von Karnak, der Amun-Tempel, wurde zum größten Tempel der Welt.

PLAN TOPOGRAPHIQUE DES RUINES DE THÈBES

Thèbes fut, à diverses époques, le siège du gouvernement des pharaons, qui se plurent à l'embellir de toutes les merveilleuses créations des arts contemporains. Les temples et les palais de Thèbes, disséminés sur l'une et l'autre rive du Nil, occupent une étendue assez considérable. Le fleuve partageait la ville en deux grandes divisions. Il est souvent question dans les papyrus grecs de Thèbes, de la portion libyque appelée par les Grecs Memnonia, nom qui semble avoir été employé en opposition avec celui de Diospolis, pour désigner spécialement la partie de Thèbes située sur l'autre rive [la rive gauche]. Toute cette partie se couvrit de temples imposants, de luxueux palais et d'un vaste hippodrome. Mais c'est la partie de Thèbes située sur la rive droite qui mérita seule le nom de « Ville des Villes », de capitale de la vieille civilisation. Le temple de Louksor formait, avec les habitations qui l'entouraient, le principal abordage de Thèbes. Le grand temple de Karnac, l'Ammonium, devint le plus vaste temple du monde.

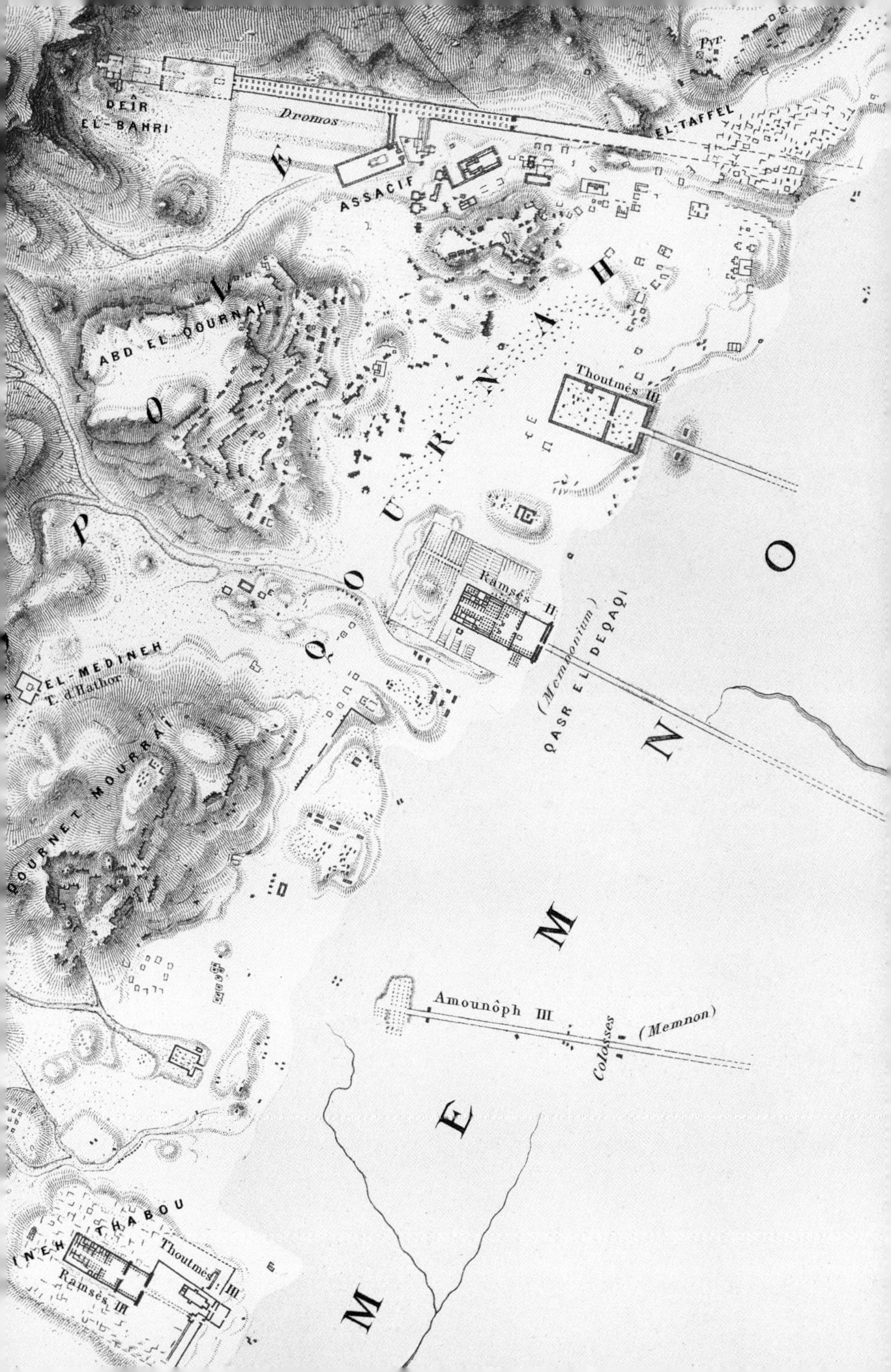

DEIR EL-BAHRI
Dromos
ASSACIF
EL-TAFFEL
Pyr.
ABD EL QOURNAH
QOURNAH
Thoutmès III
Ramsès II
(Memnonium)
QASR EL DEQAQI
EL-MEDINEH
T. d'Hathor
QOURNET MOURRAÏ
Amounôph III
Colosses
(Memnon)
Thoutmès III
Ramsès III

THE ISLAND OF PHILAE

General plan of the ruins

The island of Philae or Philes is situated at the outer edges of Egypt and Nubia; in Egyptian it is called Maulak or Pilak, in other words, "the boundary". It rears up at the extreme end of a group of islands. Formed by a build-up of sediment around a few granite rocks, this island is no more than 400 metres long by 140 metres wide. As one can see from the plan, a quay runs all the way round it. The great temple of Philae, dedicated to Isis, together with its many chapels, annexes and avenues, occupies almost half the island. The most ancient parts date from the period of the last pharaoh, Nectanebo, while the most recent are from the period of Caracalla. After climbing up to the temple by the dilapidated small staircase which can be seen to the east, the visitor finds himself in a type of dromos formed by two colonnades. Opposite the double pylon which serves as main entrance to the great temple there were formerly two small granite obelisks 27 metres high and two crouching lions.

DIE INSEL PHILAE

Übersichtskarte der Ruinen

Die Insel Philae oder Philes, die im Grenzbereich zwischen Ägypten und Nubien liegt, hieß auf Ägyptisch Maulak oder Pilak, das heißt „die Grenze". Sie befindet sich am äußersten Ende eines Archipels. Diese Insel besteht aus Schwemmböden, die sich an einigen Granitfelsen abgelagert haben, und ist höchstens 400 m lang und 140 m breit. Sie ist, wie man auf der Karte sieht, durch eine Kaimauer eingefasst. Der große Tempel von Philae, der der Isis geweiht ist, nimmt mit seinen zahlreichen Bethäusern, Nebengebäuden und Prachtstraßen fast die Hälfte der Insel ein. Die ältesten Teile datieren aus der Zeit des Nektanebos, des letzten Pharaos, die jüngsten aus der Zeit des Kaisers Caracalla. Steigt man über die kleine verfallene Treppe, die man im Osten sieht, zum Tempel hinauf, befindet man sich inmitten einer Art Dromos, der durch zwei Säulengänge gebildet wird. Gegenüber den beiden Pylonen, die als Haupteingang zum großen Tempel dienen, standen früher zwei 27 m hohe Obelisken aus Granit und zwei kniende Löwen.

ÎLE DE PHILÆ

Plan général des ruines

L'île de Philæ ou Philes, située aux confins de l'Égypte et de la Nubie, se nommait en égyptien Maulak ou Pilak, c'est-à-dire la limite. Elle s'élève à l'extrémité d'un archipel. Créée par des atterrissements accumulés autour de quelques rochers de granit, cette île n'a pas plus de 400 mètres de longueur sur 140 de large. Elle est entourée, comme on le voit sur le plan, par un quai. Le grand temple de Philæ, consacré à Isis, occupe avec ses nombreuses chapelles, ses annexes et ses avenues près de la moitié de l'île. Les plus anciennes parties datent de Nectanèbe, le dernier pharaon, les plus récentes [parties], de l'empereur Caracalla. En montant au temple par le petit escalier délabré qui se voit à l'est, on se trouve au milieu d'une espèce de dromos, formé par deux colonnades. En face du double pylône qui sert d'entrée principale au grand temple s'élevaient, autrefois, deux petits obélisques de granit de 27 mètres de hauteur et deux lions accroupis.

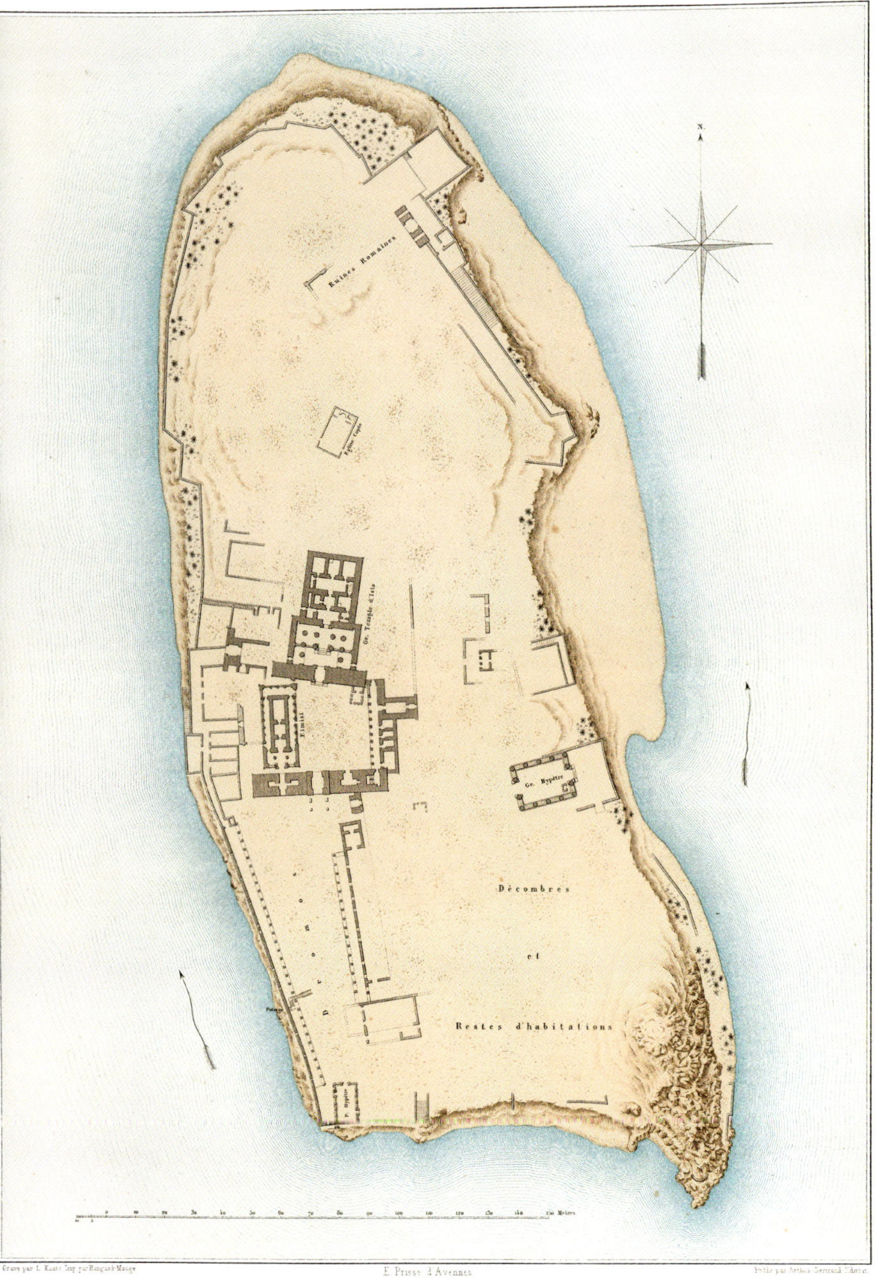

ILE DE PHILÆ

(PLAN GÉNÉRAL DES RUINES)

CROSS-SECTIONS AND DETAILS FROM THE GREAT PYRAMID OF GIZA (4th Dynasty)

Cheops or Khufu

From the moment a king was ceremonially invested with power, consideration was given to his tomb, his final, and for the ancient Egyptians, most important dwelling-place, to which they gave the name "eternal dwelling". The pyramids which can be seen next to Cairo, on the plateau which dominates the plain of Giza, are the oldest buildings in Egypt. The three most important are those of Cheops [Khufu], Chephren [Khafre] and Mykerinos [Menkaure]. The biggest and most famous is that of King Cheops, the Khufu of hieroglyphic inscriptions. It takes the form of a step pyramid, with vast foundation stones of irregular limestone blocks bonded with a mortar composed of quicklime, earth and clay. No inscription is to be seen in the chambers of the pyramid. However, inscriptions have been found, on the rough surfaces of stones used in parts of the building work, traced in red and used as quarry marks. There are several examples here of the cartouche of the second pharaoh of the 4th Dynasty, Khufu. These coarsely incised lines leave no doubt as to the identity of the person buried in the Great Pyramid.

SCHNITT- UND DETAILZEICHNUNGEN DER GROSSEN PYRAMIDE VON GIZEH (4. Dynastie)

Cheops oder Chufu

Sobald ein König feierlich in sein Amt eingesetzt war, kümmerte man sich um sein Grabmal – jene letzte Ruhestätte, die die alten Ägypter für die wichtigste hielten und als „ewige Wohnung" bezeichneten. Die Pyramiden, die Kairo gegenüber auf dem Plateau zu sehen sind, das die Ebene von Gizeh beherrscht, sind die ältesten Bauwerke Ägyptens. Die drei Hauptpyramiden tragen die Namen von Cheops [Chufu], Chephren [Chafre] und Mykerinos [Menkare]. Die größte und bekannteste [ist] die des Königs Cheops, des aus den Hieroglypheninschriften bekannten Chufu. Sie weist eine stufenförmige Struktur auf, mit Lagen aus riesigen Kalksteinen uneinheitlicher Größe, die durch einen Mörtel aus Kalk, Erde und Lehm zusammengehalten werden. In den Räumen der Pyramide findet sich keinerlei Inschrift. Jedoch hat man auf der rauen Oberfläche der in Teilen der Bauwerke verwendeten Steine Inschriften in roter Farbe gefunden, die in den Steinbrüchen als Markierung dienten. Mehrfach ist dort die Kartusche des Chufu, des zweiten Pharaos der 4. Dynastie, zu sehen. Diese grob ausgeführten Zeilen lassen keinen Zweifel zu, welche bedeutende Persönlichkeit in der großen Pyramide begraben ist.

COUPES ET DÉTAILS DE LA GRANDE PYRAMIDE DE GIZEH (IVe dynastie)

Chéops ou Choufou

Dès qu'un roi était solennellement investi du pouvoir, on s'occupait de son tombeau, cette dernière habitation, que les anciens Égyptiens considéraient comme la plus importante et appelaient « la demeure éternelle ». Les pyramides qu'on voit en face du Kaire, sur le plateau qui domine la plaine de Gizeh, sont les plus anciennes constructions qu'il y ait en Égypte. Les trois principales portent les noms de Chéops [Khoufou], Chéphren [Khafrê] et Mycérinus [Menkaourê]. La plus grande et la plus célèbre [est] cette du roi Chéops, le Choufou [Khoufou] des légendes hiéroglyphiques. Elle présente une pyramide à degrés, dont les énormes assises sont formées de pierres calcaires inégales, maçonnées avec un mortier composé de chaux, de terre et d'argile. Les salles de la pyramide n'offrent aucune inscription. Mais on a trouvé, sur les faces dégrossies des pierres employées aux cavités de décharge, des inscriptions tracées en rouge et ayant servi de marque dans les carrières. On y voit à plusieurs reprises le cartouche du deuxième pharaon de la IVe dynastie, Choufou. Ces lignes grossières ne laissent aucun doute sur le personnage enseveli dans la grande pyramide.

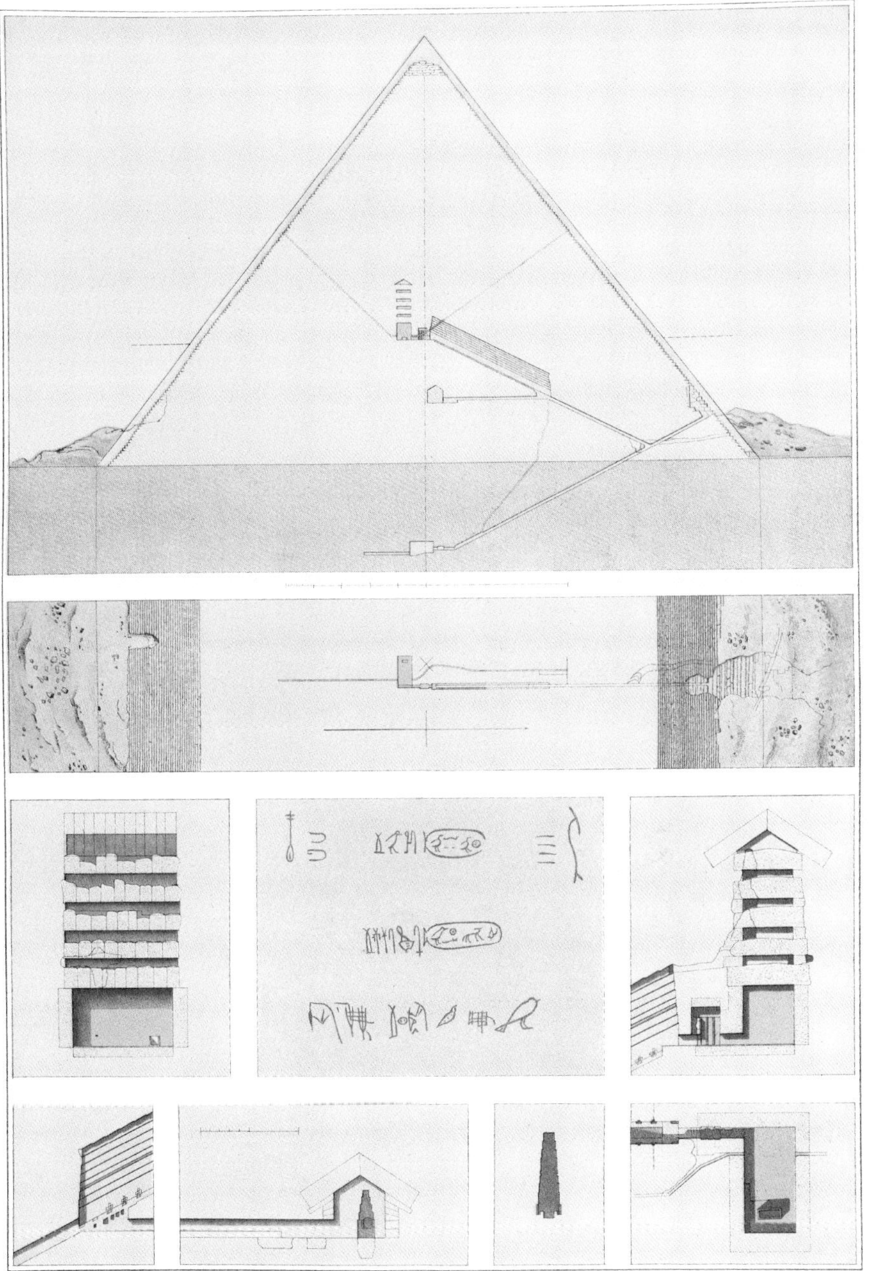

Lith par Levié Imp. par Hangard Maugé. E. Prisse d'Avennes. Publié par Arthus Bertrand, Editeur.

COUPES ET DÉTAILS DE LA GRANDE PYRAMIDE DE GIZEH.

(CHÉOPS OU CHOUFON, IVe DYNASTIE.)

PLANS, CROSS-SECTIONS AND ELEVATIONS OF THE PYRAMIDS OF MEROË (Ptolemaic Period)

The pyramids of Memphis served the cult of the deified king after his death. However, it is now only in Ethiopia that there is any hope of finding intact examples of these religious edifices, which completed the funerary monument by placing, beside the tomb, which was closed for ever, the sanctuary (chapel) where the special office of the dead would be celebrated every month. The pyramids of Meroë, the ancient Meru or Merua of the Ethiopians, are not built on the colossal scale of the pyramids of Egypt; however, the entrances to the small temples which are annexed to them are usually turned towards the east, following Egyptian doctrine. The chapels backing on to the pyramids contain no more than one or two chambers, often decorated with bas-reliefs and inscriptions. [...] But the subjects from mythology are definitely Egyptian, with their deities given local attributes and titles taken from the cities of the Thebaid or of the Delta which had been dedicated to them.

GRUNDRISS-, ANSICHTS- UND SCHNITTZEICHNUNGEN DER PYRAMIDEN VON MEROE (Ptolemäerzeit)

Die Pyramiden von Memphis dienten der Verehrung des nach seinem Tode zum Gott erhobenen Königs. Nur noch in Äthiopien kann man auf Beispiele von Kultanlagen hoffen, bei denen zum Grabmal ein Heiligtum hinzukam, das neben der – für immer verschlossenen – Gruft stand und in dem man monatlich eine besondere Totenmesse feierte. Die Pyramiden von Meroe, des alten Meru oder Merua der Äthiopier, sind keine riesenhaften Bauten wie die Pyramiden Ägyptens; der Eingang der kleinen Tempel, die ihnen beigefügt sind, ist jedoch meistens – der ägyptischen Lehre folgend – nach Osten orientiert. Die an die Pyramiden angebauten Bethäuser weisen kaum mehr als ein oder zwei häufig mit Flachreliefs und Inschriften geschmückte Räume auf. [...] Dabei sind die mythologischen Themen jedoch ägyptisch – den Gottheiten sind örtliche Beinamen und Ehrennamen aus den einst ihnen geweihten Städten der Thebais oder des Deltas beigefügt.

PLANS, COUPES ET ÉLÉVATIONS DES PYRAMIDES DE MÉROÉ (époque des Ptolémées)

Les pyramides de Memphis servaient au culte du roi déifié après sa mort. Aussi n'est-ce plus qu'en Éthiopie qu'on peut espérer retrouver intacts les spécimens de ces édifices religieux, qui complétaient le monument funéraire en plaçant à côté du tombeau, fermé à jamais, le sanctuaire où se célébrait mensuellement l'office spécial des morts. Les pyramides de Méroé, l'ancienne Merou ou Meroua des Éthiopiens, n'ont pas la structure colossale des pyramides d'Égypte ; mais l'entrée des petits temples qui leur sont annexés est généralement tournée vers l'est, suivant les doctrines égyptiennes. Les chapelles adossées aux pyramides ne présentent guère qu'une ou deux salles souvent ornées de bas-reliefs et d'inscriptions. [...] Cependant, les sujets mythologiques sont bien égyptiens, les divinités y sont accompagnées des épithètes locales et de titres pris des villes de la Thébaïde ou du Delta, qui leur avaient été consacrées.

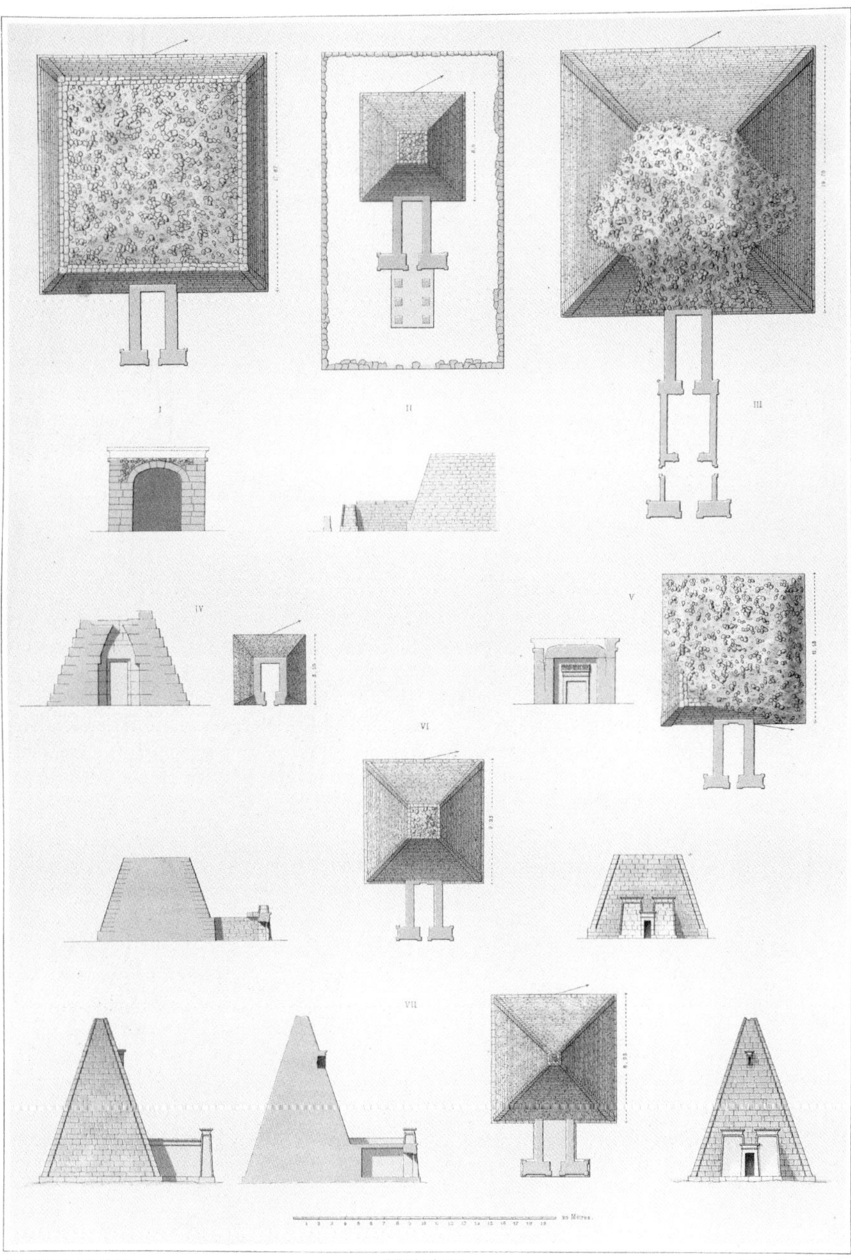

Lith. par C. Walter. Imp. par Hangard-Maugé. Cailliaud & Lepsius. Publié par Arthus-Bertrand, Éditeur.

PLANS, COUPES & ÉLÉVATIONS DES PYRAMIDES DE MÉROÉ .

(ÉPOQUE DES PTOLÉMÉES.)

NECROPOLIS OF MEMPHIS (4th Dynasty)

Tombs situated to the east of the Great Pyramid

With the exception of certain hypogea which are cut into the rock, the tombs are usually built of limestone and brick. The name of the deceased is written on a small semi-cylindrical beam which serves as soffit to the door at the entrance. [...] Most of these tombs take the form of a large pyramid truncated at around 6 or 8 metres from the base, with doors piercing its façade and decorative panels encircling it. The main pillars are coloured to imitate granite and the pilasters are adorned with green hieroglyphs framed in blue. The Egyptian preference for monoliths and colossal blocks is already apparent in these structures: the pillars and the architraves which occupy an entire façade are each made from one single stone.

NEKROPOLE VON MEMPHIS (4. Dynastie)

Östlich der großen Pyramide gelegene Grabmale

Die Grabmale sind, mit Ausnahme einiger in den Fels geschlagener Hypogäen, zumeist aus Kalkstein und Ziegeln errichtet. Ein kleiner, halbzylindrischer Balken, der der Eingangstür als Soffitte dient, trägt den Namen des Verstorbenen. [...] Die Grabdenkmäler sehen zum größten Teil aus wie eine breite, in 6 oder 8 m Höhe über der Basis verstümmelte Pyramide, die mit Tafeln verkleidet und deren Fassade mit Türen durchbrochen ist. Die Bemalung der Hauptpfeiler ist der Farbe des Granits nachempfunden, und die Wandpfeiler sind mit grünen, blau eingerahmten Hieroglyphen verziert. An diesen Bauten ist bereits die Vorliebe der Ägypter für Monolithen und riesige Steinblöcke zu erkennen: Die Architrave und Pfeiler, die eine ganze Fassade einnehmen, sind aus einem einzigen Stein hergestellt.

NÉCROPOLE DE MEMPHIS (IVe dynastie)

Tombeaux situés à l'est de la grande pyramide

À l'exception de quelques hypogées, taillés dans le roc, les tombeaux sont généralement bâtis en calcaire et en briques. Le nom du défunt est écrit sur une poutrelle demi-cylindrique, qui sert de soffite à la porte d'entrée. [...] La plupart des tombeaux présentent l'aspect d'une large pyramide tronquée à 6 ou 8 mètres de la base, percée sur sa façade de portes et entourée d'une décoration à panneaux. Les piliers principaux sont coloriés de façon à imiter le granit, et les pilastres sont ornés d'hiéroglyphes verts encadrés de bleu. On remarque déjà dans ces constructions le goût des Égyptiens pour les monolithes et les blocs colossaux ; les piliers et les architraves, qui occupent toute une façade, sont faits d'une seule pierre.

ARCHITECTURE

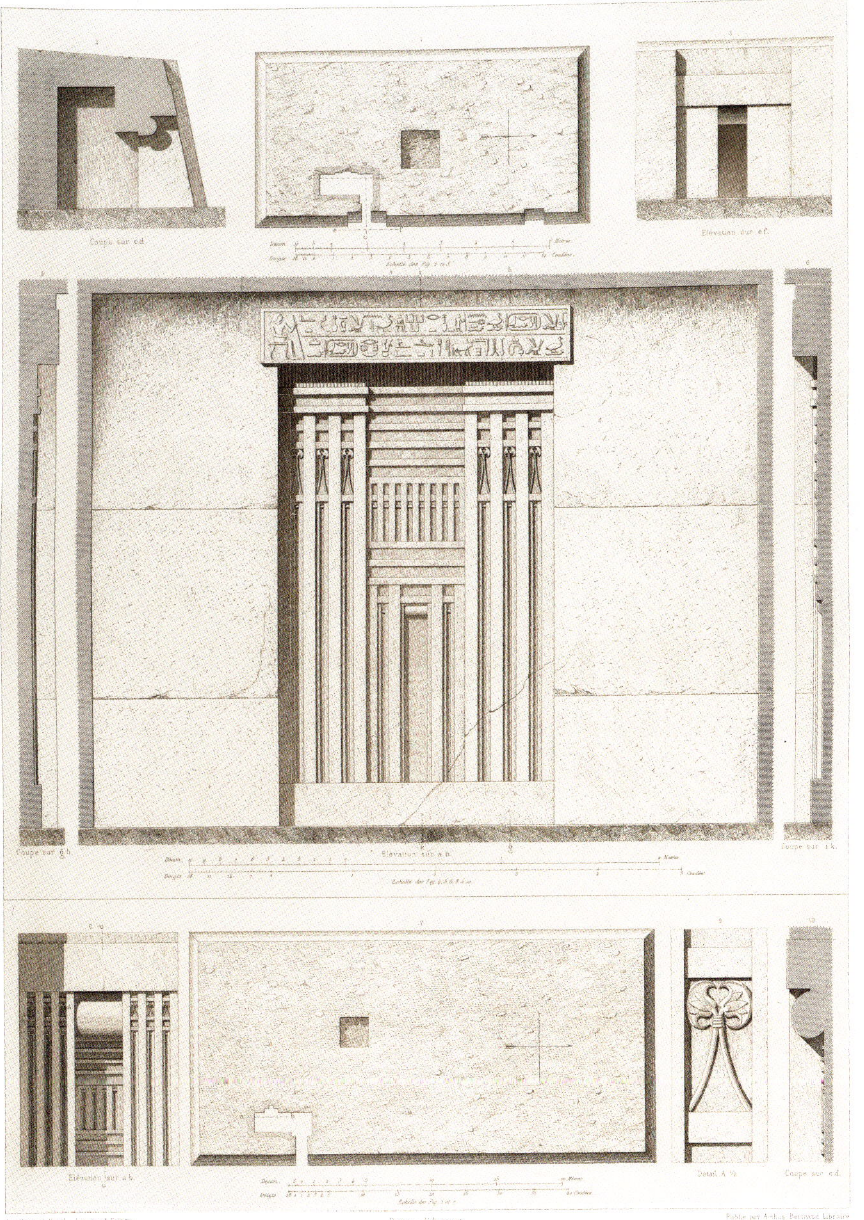

Gravé par J. Petot. Imp. par A. Salmon.

Prisse d'Avennes

Publié par Arthus Bertrand Libraire

NÉCROPOLE DE MEMPHIS

TOMBEAUX SITUÉS A L'EST DE LA GRANDE PYRAMIDE

(IVe DYNASTIE)

SARCOPHAGI OF MENKAURE AND OF AY (4th and 18th Dynasties)

The sarcophagus represented at the top of this plate comes from the third pyramid of Giza and is that of the pharaoh Menkaure or Mykerinos of the 4th Dynasty. The arrangement of the decoration, with its simple intersecting vertical and horizontal mouldings, is particularly effective, with two lotus flowers head-to-head providing the only touch of animation in an otherwise severe composition. The second sarcophagus, at the bottom of the plate, contained the mummy of the pharaoh Ay, a usurper who reigned towards the end of the 18th Dynasty. This rose granite sarcophagus is of unusual elegance. It has suffered damage and the crack shows that the superb monolith was not even 10 centimetres thick. Four winged goddesses, Neith, Selket, Nephthys and probably Isis, stand at the four corners, their arms extended, protecting with their long wings the four sides of the sarcophagus which are covered with hieroglyphic inscriptions. The symbolic winged globe features on both façades.

DIE SARKOPHAGE DES MENKARE UND DES EJE (4. und 18. Dynastie)

Der im oberen Teil dieser Tafel abgebildete Sarkophag stammt aus der dritten Pyramide von Gizeh und gehört dem Pharao Menkare oder Mykerinos (4. Dynastie). Er ist mit einfachen, waagerechten und senkrechten Zierleisten geschmückt, die sich kreuzen – eine Anordnung, die eine vortreffliche Wirkung erzielt. Nur zwei einander gegenüberstehende Lotusblüten beleben diese strenge Verzierung. Der zweite Sarkophag auf dem unteren Teil der Tafel enthielt die Mumie des Pharaos Eje, eines Usurpators, der gegen Ende der 18. Dynastie regierte. Dieser Sarkophag aus rosa Granit ist von bemerkenswerter Eleganz. Er ist entzweigebrochen, und die Bruchstelle zeigt, dass dieser prächtige Monolith nicht einmal einen Dezimeter stark war. Vier geflügelte Göttinnen – Neith, Selket, Nephthys und wahrscheinlich Isis – stehen mit ausgestreckten Armen an den vier Ecken und schützen mit ihren langen Flügeln die vier mit Hieroglypheninschriften bedeckten Seiten des Sarkophages. Vorder- und Rückseite tragen das Sinnbild der geflügelten Kugel.

SARCOPHAGES DE MENKARÉ ET DE AÏ (IVe et XVIIIe dynasties)

Le sarcophage représenté en tête de cette planche provient de la troisième pyramide de Gizeh et appartient au pharaon Menkaré ou Mycérinus de la IVe dynastie. Il est décoré de simples moulures verticales coupées par d'autres horizontales dont l'arrangement produit un excellent effet. Deux fleurs de lotus affrontées animent seules cette sévère ornementation. Le second sarcophage, celui du bas de la planche, a contenu la momie du pharaon Aï [Ay], usurpateur qui régna vers la fin de la XVIIIe dynastie. Ce sarcophage, de granit rose, est d'une élégance remarquable. Il a été brisé, et cette fracture montre que ce superbe monolithe n'avait pas un décimètre d'épaisseur. Quatre déesses ptérophores, Neith, Selk [Selket], Nepthys et probablement Isis, debout aux quatre angles, les bras étendus, protègent de leurs longues ailes les quatre parois du sarcophage qui sont couvertes de légendes hiéroglyphiques. Les deux façades portent le globe ailé symbolique.

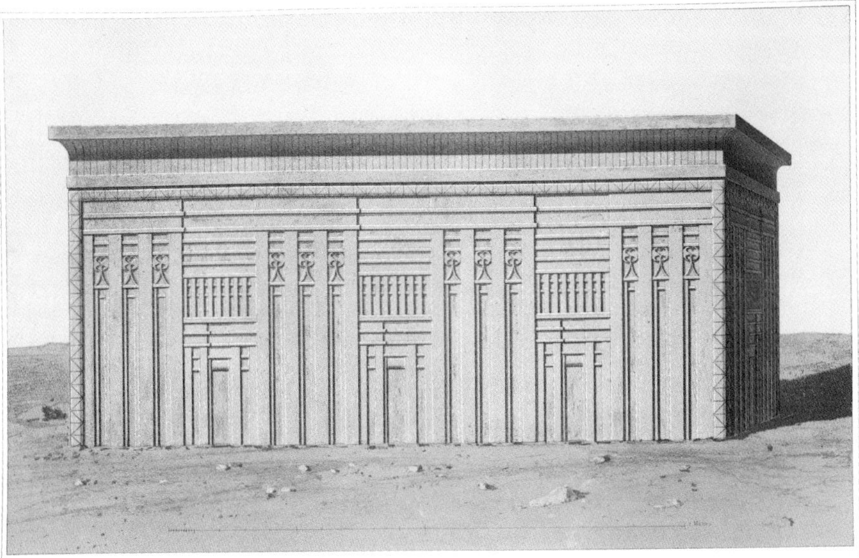

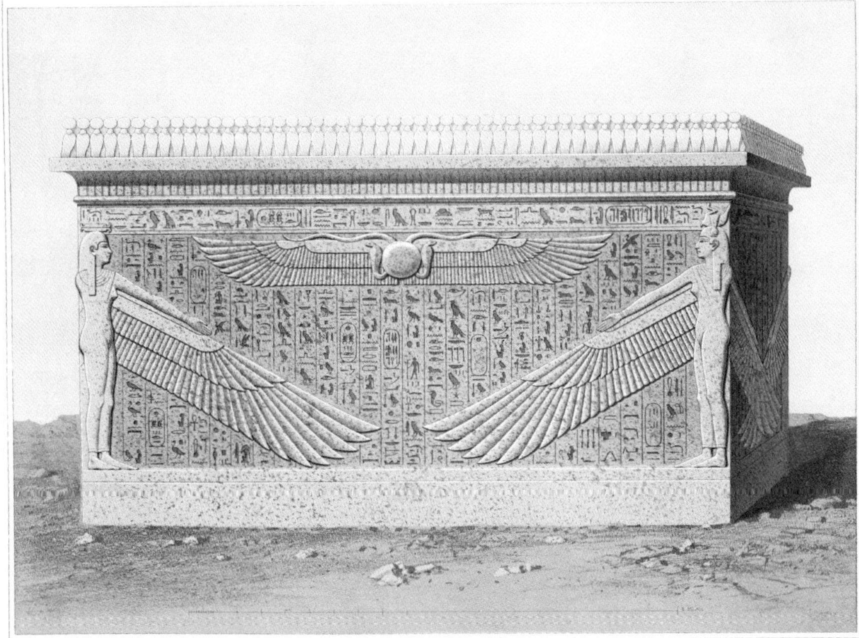

T6

E. Prisse d'Avennes

SARCOPHAGES DE MENKARE & DE AI.

(IVe ET XVIIIe DYNASTIES.)

TOMBS OF THE NECROPOLIS OF MEMPHIS (5th Dynasty)

Cemetery of Saqqara

The plan of the tomb of Rashepses is simple and beautiful: six monolithic pillars arranged in two rows adorn the main chamber. The three small rooms at the end seem to have been devoted to the cult of the dead: this is exactly the layout to be found in the temples of the [1]8th Dynasty and if it were not for the pictures decorating the walls, the inscriptions carved on the pillars, the architrave and the door frames, one could imagine oneself in a small temple of Thutmosis III. Prince Rashepses lived in the time of Djedkare [Isesi] and performed a number of high-ranking functions, among them those of superintendent of all royal buildings and constructor of the great enclosure. Near the tomb of Rashepses can be seen the tomb of Bu, or Sabu. All that remains of it is one small chamber; at the back there is a small architectural decoration in panels while there are superb bas-reliefs on the façade.

GRABMALE DER NEKROPOLE VON MEMPHIS (5. Dynastie)

Friedhof von Sakkara

Der Grundriss des Grabmals des Raschepses ist einfach und schön; sechs in zwei Reihen aufgestellte monolithische Pfeiler schmücken den Hauptraum. Drei hintere, kleine Räume scheinen dem Totenkult geweiht gewesen zu sein: Genau diese Anordnung findet man in den kleinen Tempeln der [1]8. Dynastie – und wären da nicht die mit Malereien geschmückten Wände, die in die Pfeiler eingemeißelten Inschriften, der Architrav und die Zargen, dann wähnte man sich in einem kleinen Tempel von Thutmosis III. Der Prinz Raschepses lebte unter Djedkare [Isesi]: Er übte mehrere hohe Ämter aus, unter anderem als Oberverwalter aller königlichen Bauvorhaben, als Baumeister der großen Umfassungsmauer. In der Nähe des Grabmals des Raschepses erblickte man das Grabmal des Sabu. Es ist davon nur ein kleiner, hinten mit einer kleinen architektonischen Tafelverzierung geschmückter Raum erhalten, dessen Fassade prachtvolle Flachreliefs zieren.

TOMBEAUX DE LA NÉCROPOLE DE MEMPHIS (V[e] dynastie)

Cimetière de Sakkara

Le plan du tombeau de Raasès [Rachepsès] en est simple et beau ; six piliers monolithes, disposés par deux rangs, ornent la principale salle. Au fond, trois petites pièces semblent avoir été consacrées au culte des morts : c'est tout à fait la disposition qu'on retrouve dans les petits temples de la [X]VIIIe dynastie, et si ce n'étaient les peintures qui décorent les murs, les légendes sculptées sur les piliers, l'architrave et les chambranles des portes, on se croirait dans un petit temple de Thoutmès [Thoutmôsis] III. Le prince Raasès vivait sous Takare [Djedkarê/Isési] : il exerçait plusieurs hautes fonctions, entre autres celles de surintendant de toutes les constructions royales, constructeur de la grande enceinte. Près du tombeau de Raasès, on voyait le tombeau de Bou, ou Sabou. Il n'en reste qu'une petite salle, ornée au fond d'une petite décoration architecturale de panneaux et sur sa façade de superbes bas-reliefs.

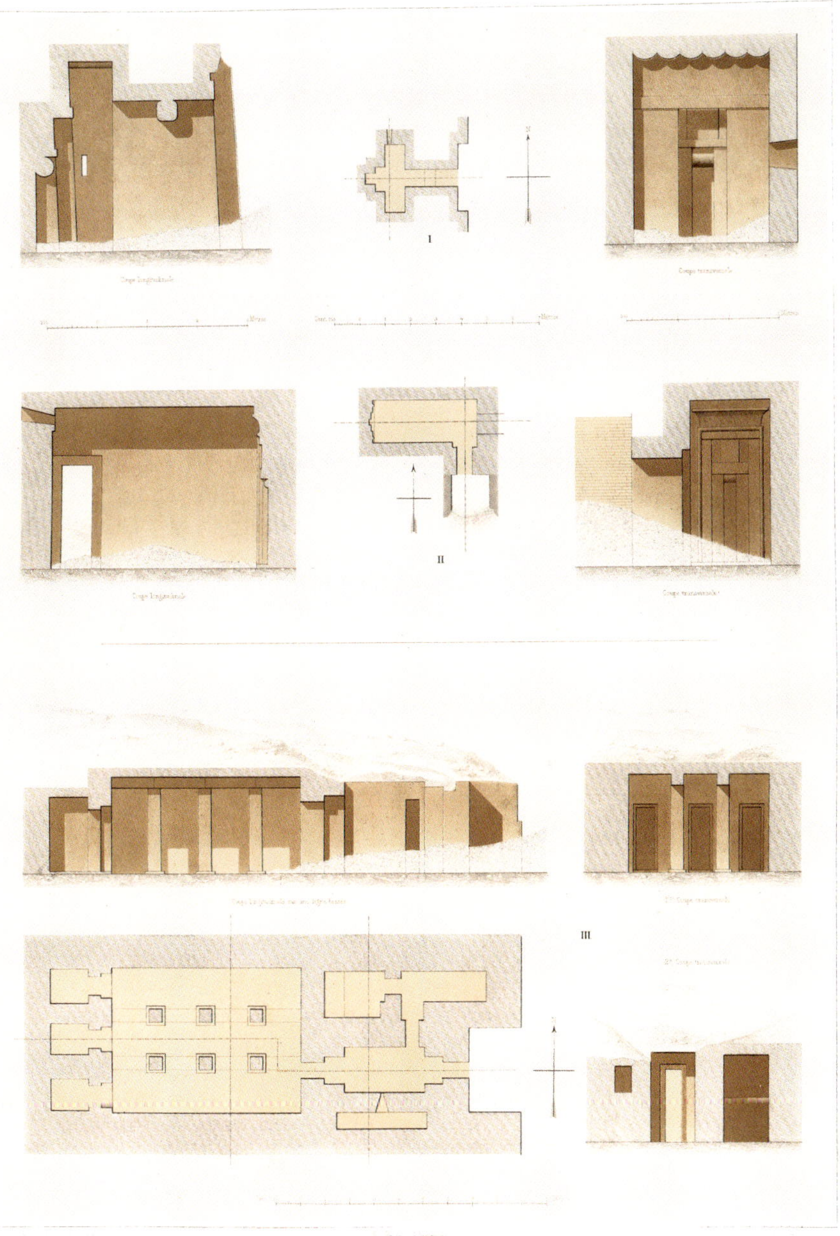

TOMBEAUX DE LA NÉCROPOLE DE MEMPHIS

NECROPOLIS OF THEBES (18th and 19th Dynasties)

Biban el-Muluk. Royal hypogea

The hypogea of Biban el-Muluk, where the pharaohs deployed a truly regal magnificence to embellish their final dwelling-place, adopt a more or less uniform plan. A fairly narrow door serves as entrance to a long gallery or corridor which leads towards the centre of the mountain on a variably inclined angle to the horizon. The tomb of Ramesses II is distinguished from all the others by its entrance, decorated with two cows' heads, symbol of Hathor, the rectorial goddess of Amenti, the Egyptian hell. [...] Some of these tombs occupy a huge area, their length varying from 16 to as much as 120 metres. The architecture of the royal hypogea is extremely simple: there are no mouldings, cornices or architraves, the great walls are without profile, the pilasters are plain squares and the ceilings are flat or barrel-shaped. The richness of the decoration increases progressively until one reaches the golden chamber, where the royal mummy was laid.

NEKROPOLE VON THEBEN (18. und 19. Dynastie)

Biban el-Muluk. Königliche Hypogäen

Die Hypogäen im Biban el-Muluk, in denen die Pharaonen bei der Verschönerung ihrer letzten Ruhestätte eine wahrhaft königliche Pracht entfalteten, sind in gewisser Hinsicht nahezu einheitlich. Eine recht enge Tür bildet den Eingang zu einem langen Gang oder Flur, der mit mehr oder weniger starkem Gefälle in die Mitte des Berges führt. Das Grab von Ramses II. unterscheidet sich von allen anderen durch seinen Eingangsbereich mit zwei Pilastern, die mit Kuhköpfen geschmückt sind, dem Sinnbild der Hathor, der über den Amenti oder die ägyptische Hölle herrschenden Gottheit. [...] Einige dieser Gräber sind von enormer Ausdehnung, und ihre Länge variiert zwischen 16 und bis zu 120 m. Die Architektur der königlichen Hypogäen ist von äußerster Einfachheit: weder Zierleisten an den Gesimsen noch Architrave, konturlose Mauern, quadratische Pilaster und flache oder gewölbte Decken. Der Reichtum der Innenausstattung steigert sich bis hin zu dem vergoldeten Raum, in dem die königliche Mumie ruhte.

NÉCROPOLE DE THÈBES (XVIIIe et XIXe dynasties)

Biban el-Molouk. Hypogées royaux

Les hypogées de Biban el-Molouk, où les pharaons ont déployé une magnificence vraiment royale à l'embellissement de leur dernière demeure, sont sur un plan à peu près uniforme. Une porte assez étroite sert d'entrée à une longue galerie ou couloir qui se dirige vers le centre de la montagne, suivant un angle plus ou moins incliné à l'horizon. Le tombeau de Ramsès II se distingue de tous les autres par son entrée, ornée de deux pilastres à tête de vache, symbole d'Hathor, déesse rectrice de l'Amenti ou enfer égyptien. [...] Quelques-uns de ces tombeaux sont d'une étendue immense, et leur longueur varie depuis 16 jusqu'à 120 mètres. L'architecture des hypogées royaux est extrêmement simple : point de moulures et de corniches, ni d'architraves, des murailles sans profil, des pilastres carrés et des plafonds plats ou taillés en berceau. La richesse des décorations va croissant jusqu'à la salle dorée, où reposait la momie royale.

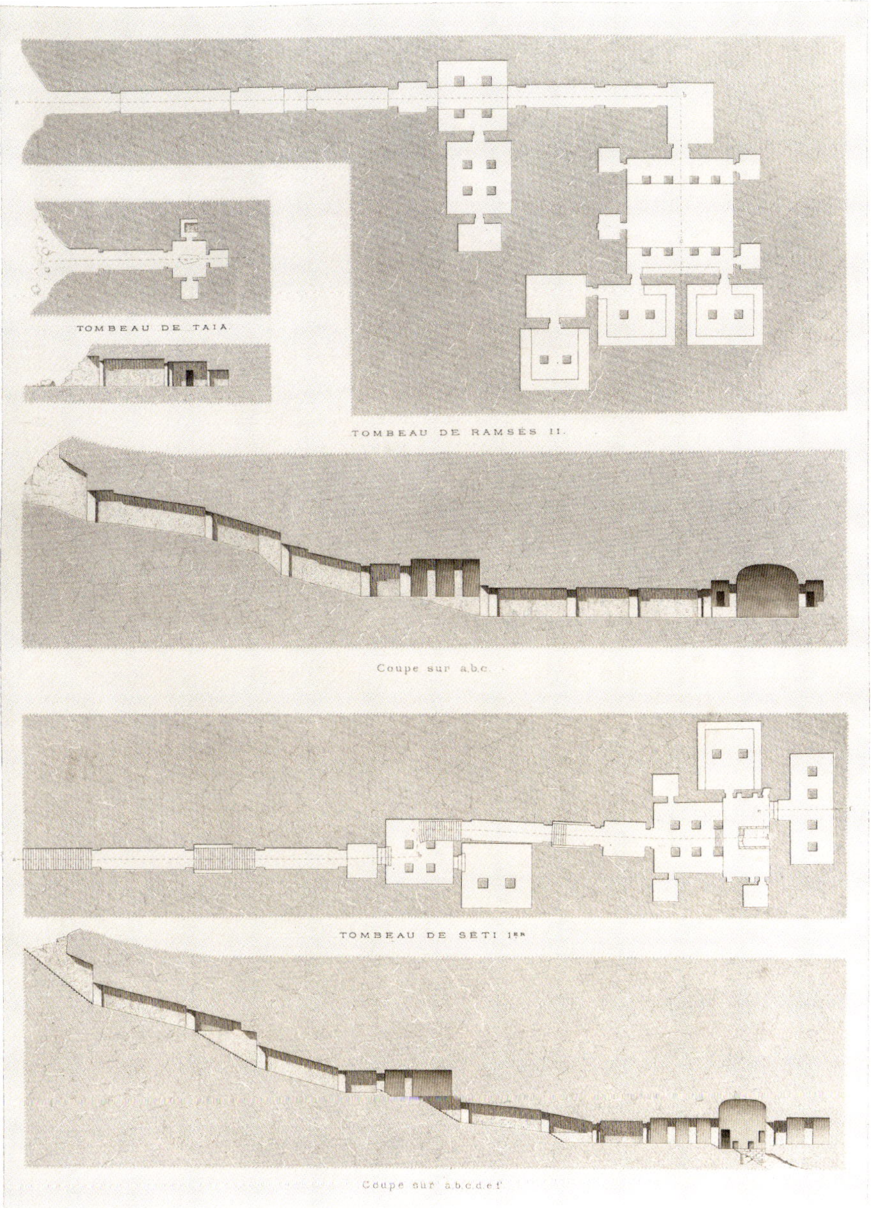

Gravé par J. Pouel. Imp. par Ch. et A. Chardon. Publié par Arthus Bertrand.

NÉCROPOLE DE THÈBES

BÎBÂN EL-MOLOUK —— HYPOGÉES ROYAUX

(XVIIIe ET XIXe DYNASTIES)

NECROPOLIS OF THEBES (18th Dynasty)

Plan and cross-sections of the hypogeum of the high priest Petamenophis

The most remarkable of the priestly hypogea is that of the Prophet or Basilicogrammate Petamenophis, the extent of which is greater even than that of the largest of the hypogea of the kings. This tomb is situated near the valley of el-Assasif. One enters through an archway into a vestibule which is also open to the sky. All of the other 28 rooms are underground. To properly understand the layout and huge extent of this vast and mysterious underground complex on three floors, it is necessary to look at the plan; without this, it is impossible to appreciate and to form an idea of this funerary labyrinth. Apart from the well and the channels, all the walls of the hypogeum are completely covered with carefully executed hieroglyphs. This hypogeum is testament to the power and the wealth of the priestly caste. The high priest Petamenophis lived in the reign of Horemheb, a pharaoh of the 18th Dynasty, and fulfilled the highest state functions for him: he was the royal scribe and officer of the seal, the eyes and ears of the pharaoh.

NEKROPOLE VON THEBEN (18. Dynastie)

Grundriss und Schnittzeichnungen vom Hypogäum des Hohepriesters Petamenophis

Das bemerkenswerteste unter den priesterlichen Hypogäen ist das des Propheten oder Basilikogrammaten Petamenophis, das in seiner Ausdehnung selbst die größten der königlichen Hypogäen übertrifft. Dieses Grab befindet sich in der Nähe des Tales von El-Assasif. Durch einen Bogen gelangt man in ein Vestibül, das sich unter freiem Himmel befindet. Alle übrigen Räume, es sind 28 an der Zahl, liegen unter der Erde. Um die enorme Ausdehnung und die Aufteilung dieser geheimnisvollen unterirdischen Anlage richtig zu verstehen, muss man den Bauplan vor Augen haben; ohne Zeichnung ist es unmöglich, sich eine Vorstellung von diesem Grablabyrinth zu machen und sich über seine Eigenarten klar zu werden. Außer in Brunnen und Kanälen sind alle Wände dieses Hypogäums vollständig mit sorgfältig ausgeführten Hieroglyphen bedeckt. Dieses Hypogäum zeugt von Macht und Reichtum der Priesterkaste. Der Hohepriester Petamenophis lebte während der Regierungszeit von Haremhab, eines Pharaos der 18. Dynastie, und bekleidete unter diesem Herrscher wichtigste Staatsämter: Er war königlicher Schreiber, Siegelbewahrer, Wahrsager und Vertrauter des Königs.

NÉCROPOLE DE THÈBES (XVIIIe dynastie)

Plan et coupes de l'hypogée du grand prêtre Pétamounôph

Le plus remarquable des hypogées sacerdotaux est celui du Prophète ou Basilicogrammate Pétamounôph [Padiamenopé], dont l'étendue surpasse même le plus grand hypogée des rois. Ce tombeau est situé près de la vallée d'El-Assacif. D'un arc, on pénètre dans un vestibule qui est aussi à ciel ouvert. Toutes les autres pièces, au nombre de vingt-huit, sont souterraines. Pour bien comprendre la distribution et l'immense étendue de ce vaste et mystérieux souterrain à trois étages, il faut en avoir le plan sous les yeux ; sans dessin, il est impossible de se rendre compte et de se faire une idée de ce labyrinthe funéraire. À l'exception du puits et des canaux, toutes les parois de cet hypogée sont entièrement couvertes d'hiéroglyphes exécutés avec soin. Cet hypogée témoigne du pouvoir et des richesses de la caste sacerdotale. Le grand prêtre Pétamounôph vivait sous le règne de Horemheb, pharaon de la XVIIIe dynastie, et occupait près de ce souverain les plus importantes fonctions de l'État : il était scribe royal, chargé du sceau, le voyant et l'écouteur royal.

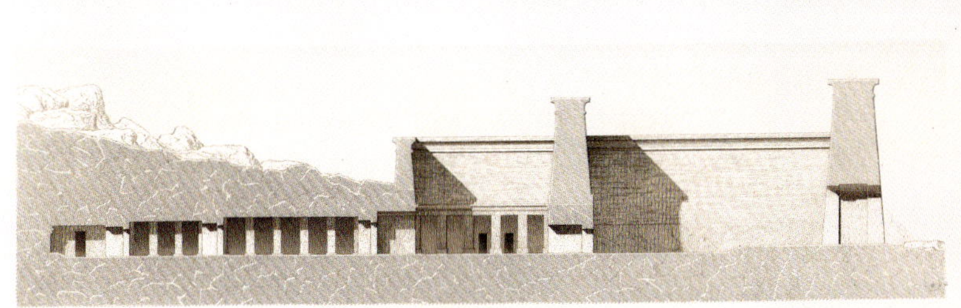

Coupe sur a b.

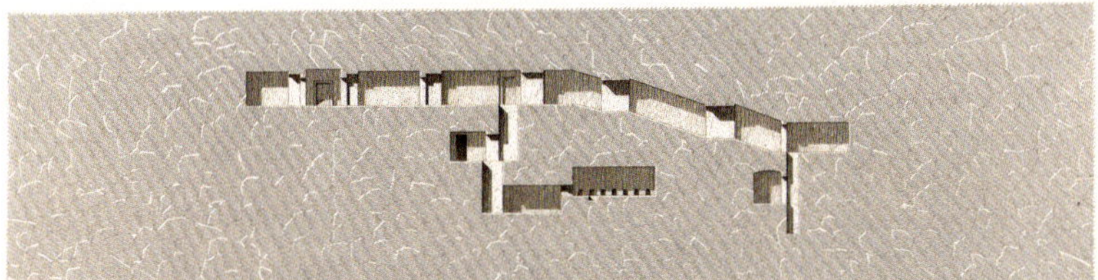

Coupe sur e f.

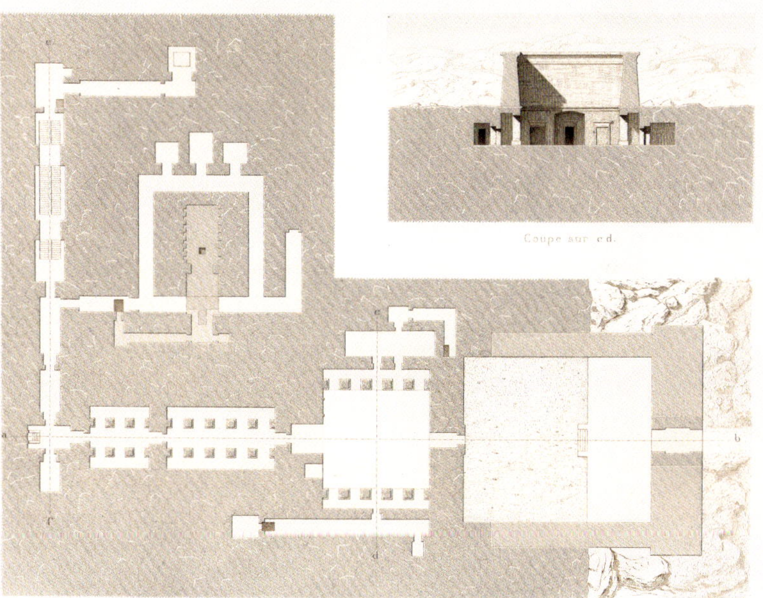

Coupe sur c d.

Prisse d'Avennes

Publié par Arthus Bertrand, Libraire

NÉCROPOLE DE THÈBES.

PLAN ET COUPES DE L'HYPOGÉE DU GRAND PRÊTRE PETAMOUNOPH.

(XVIIIE DYNASTIE)

TEMPLE OF DENDUR (reign of Augustus)

Plan, longitudinal cross-section and side door

I have grouped together on this plate plans and drawings necessary to form an exact idea of one of the small temples built under Roman supremacy. This one, constructed in the time of Augustus, in Nubia, is one of the most unusual of the period. The first two diagrams give the plan of the temple in cross-section; it is composed solely of a portico with two columns, a naos and a sekos, at the back of which is a small representation of Isis in bas-relief. The architect used the slope of the land to develop the elegance of the building to its full potential. No trace of a stairway can be found: it seems that one gained entry to the sacred enclosure through side doorways. The frame of this door [on the south side] is decorated with a winged globe and scarab, two decorated stems of lotus flowers and two mitred uraei, symbols of Upper and Lower Egypt.

TEMPEL VON DENDUR (Regierungszeit von Augustus)

Grundriss, Längsschnitt und Seitentür

Auf dieser Tafel habe ich alle Abbildungen zusammengestellt, die erforderlich sind, um sich eine genaue Vorstellung von einem der kleinen unter römischer Herrschaft erbauten Tempel zu machen. Dieser – in augusteischer Zeit in Nubien erbaut – ist einer der ungewöhnlichsten aus dieser Zeit. Die beiden ersten Darstellungen zeigen den Grundriss und den Längsschnitt dieses Tempels: Er setzt sich lediglich aus einem Portikus mit zwei Säulen, einem Naos und einem Sekos zusammen, in dem sich hinten ein kleines Flachrelief mit einer Isisdarstellung befindet. Der Architekt hat sich die Neigung des Untergrundes zunutze gemacht, um die Anmut des Gebäudes zu vervollkommnen. Man findet keine Spur einer Treppe: Wie es scheint, gelangte man durch Seitentüren in den heiligen Bezirk. Die Zarge dieser Tür [südliche Seitentür] ist mit einer geflügelten Kugel und einem geflügelten Skarabäus, zwei mit Lotusblüten geschmückten Stängeln sowie zwei bekrönten Uräusschlangen – Sinnbildern Ober- und Unterägyptens – verziert.

TEMPLE DE DANDOUR (règne d'Auguste)

Plan, coupe longitudinale et porte latérale

J'ai réuni, sur cette planche, les représentations nécessaires pour se former une idée exacte d'un des petits temples bâtis sous la domination romaine. Celui-ci, construit du temps d'Auguste, en Nubie, est un des plus curieux de cette époque. Les deux premières figures donnent le plan de la coupe de ce temple : il se compose seulement d'un portique à deux colonnes, d'un naos et d'un sékos au fond duquel se trouve un petit bas-relief représentant Isis. L'architecte a profité de la déclivité du terrain pour rendre plus complète l'élégance de l'édifice. On ne trouve aucune trace d'escalier : il paraît qu'on pénétrait dans l'enceinte sacrée par des portes latérales. Le chambranle de cette porte [latérale du sud] est décoré par un globe et un scarabée ailés, deux tiges ornées de fleurs de lotus et deux uréus mitrés, symboles de la Haute- et de la Basse-Égypte.

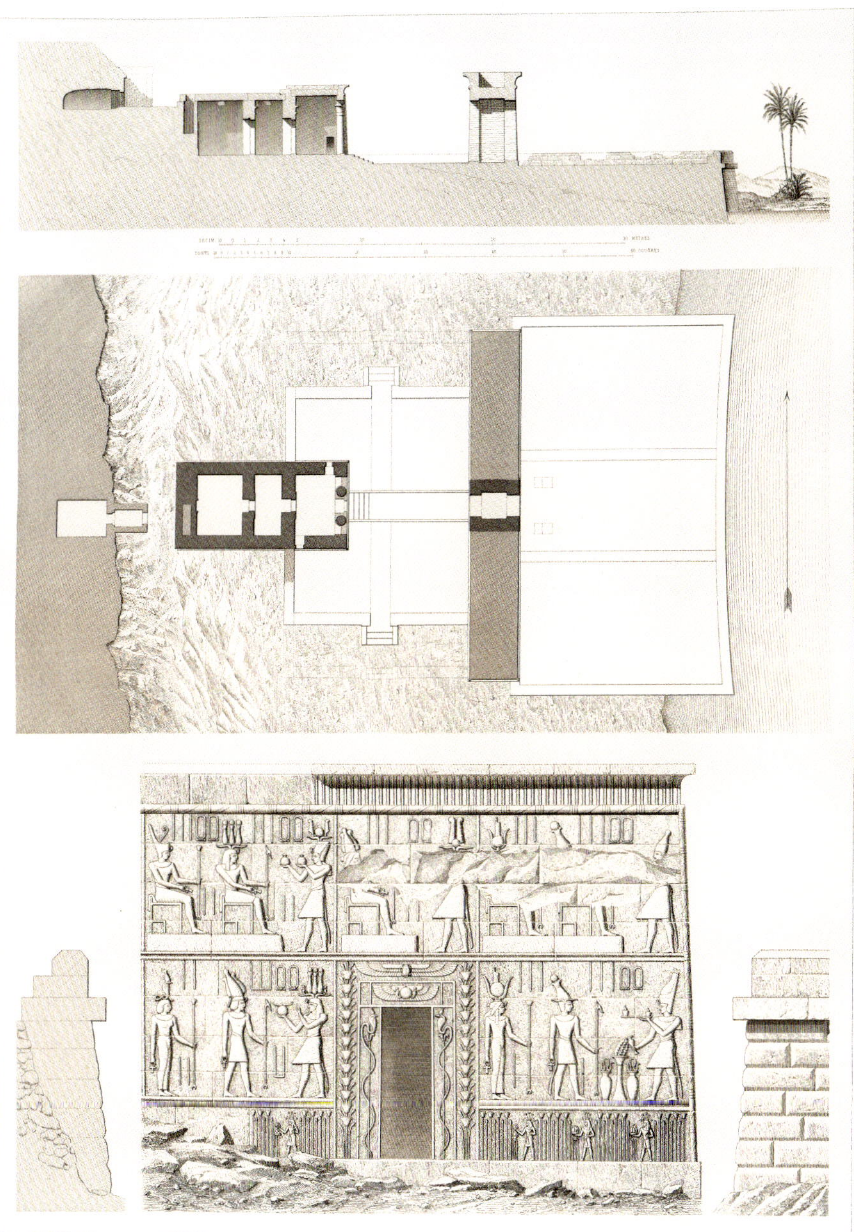

Gravé par J. Féraud . Imp. par Eudes. Prisse d'Avennes Arthus Bertrand, Editeur.

TEMPLE DE DANDOUR

PLAN, COUPE LONGITUDINALE, PORTE LATERALE

[RÈGNE D'AUGUSTE]

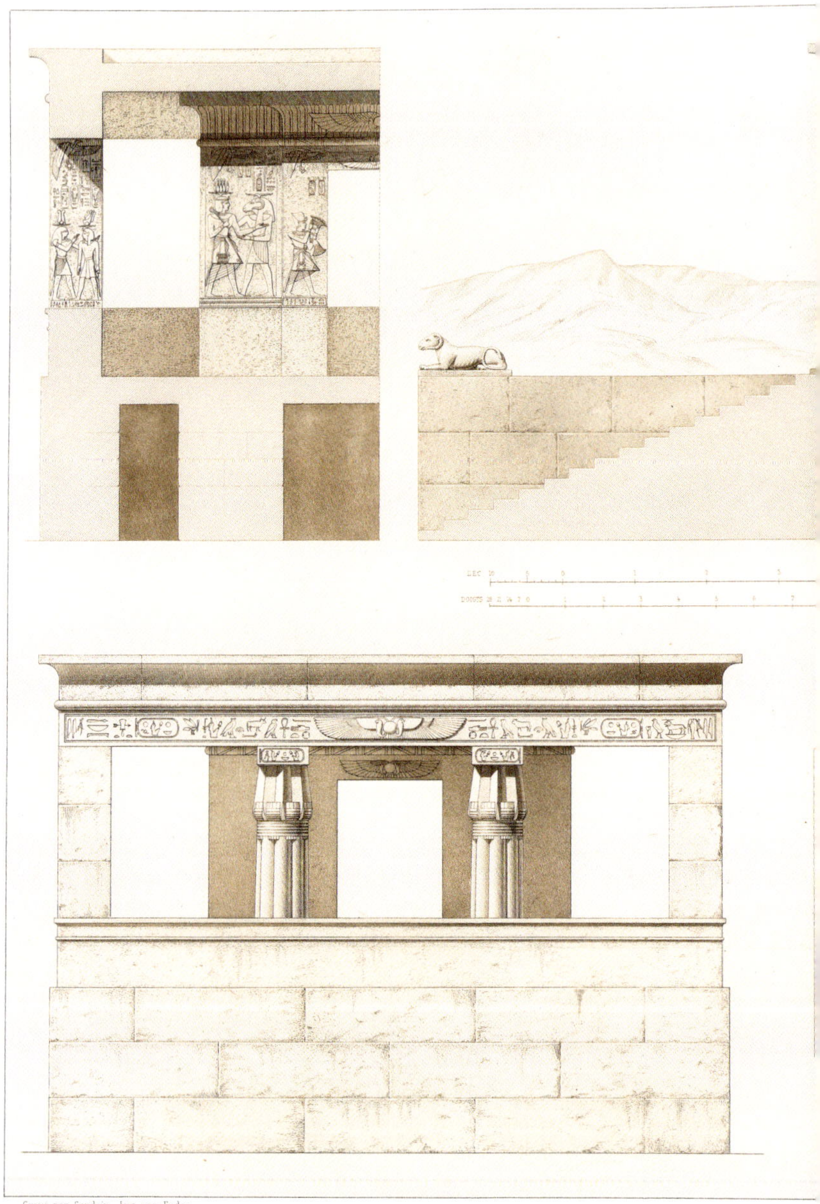

Gravé par Soudain. Imp par Eudes.

TEMPLE PÉRIPTÈRE D

RE.

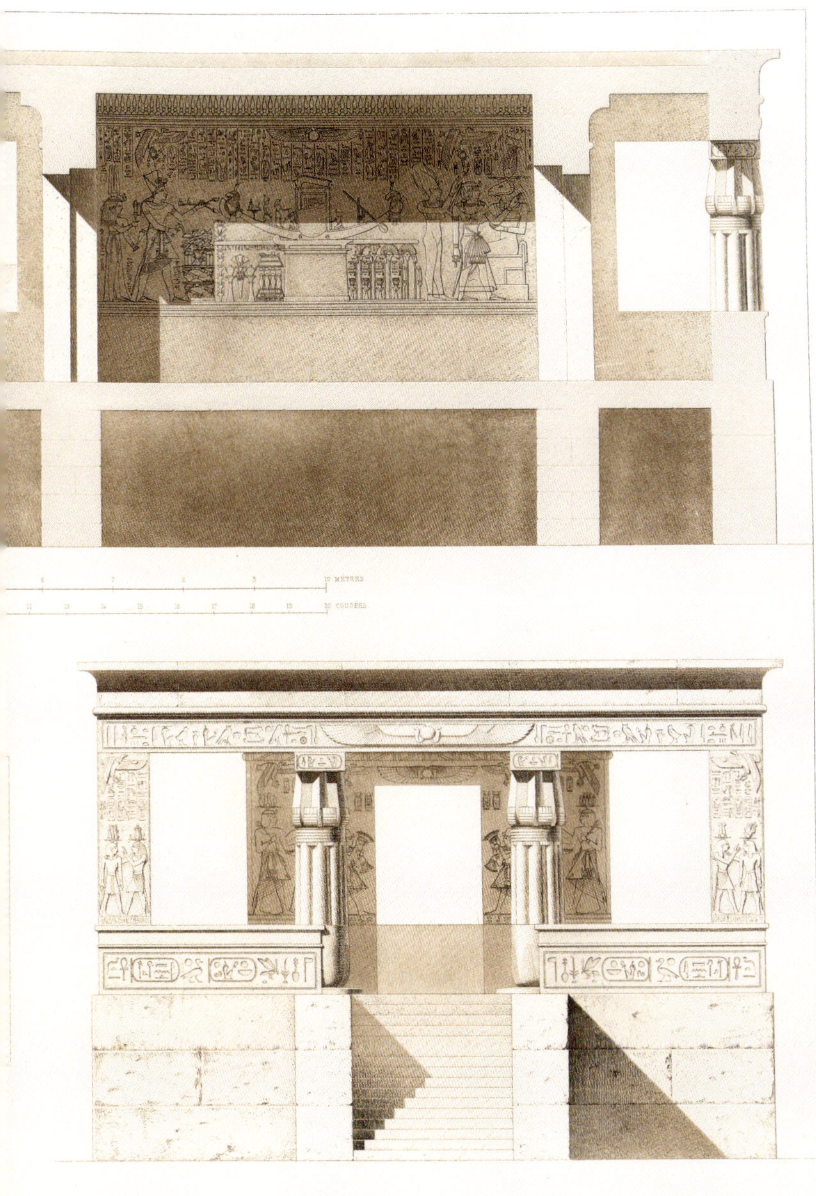

IS III A ÉLÉPHANTINE

(Pages/Seite 214/215)

PERIPTERAL TEMPLE OF AMENOPHIS III AT ELEPHANTINE (18th Dynasty)

The temple of Elephantine was dedicated to Khnum or Khnubis, who presided over the inundation and whose principal place of worship was at the cataracts. The temple was built on the orders of Amenophis III, who is shown there with his queen making offerings to Khnum, in his barque. In the upper part of the picture the pharaoh is received by this god and by the goddess Satis. The layout of this small building is a model of simplicity and purity, conforming to that known to the ancients as peripteral. Vitruvius applies this term to a square or rectangular temple surrounded by columns which form a continuous gallery right round the building. The elevation of this small temple is composed of very simple and apparently artless lines, which satisfy the eye through the harmony which reigns between the different architectural components.

PERIPTERALTEMPEL VON AMENOPHIS III. IN ELEPHANTINE (18. Dynastie)

Der Tempel von Elephantine war Knuphis oder Chnum geweiht, der die Nilschwemme lenkte und hauptsächlich an den Katarakten verehrt wurde. Errichten ließ ihn Amenophis III., der dort gemeinsam mit der Königin in seiner Barke abgebildet war, während er Chnum Opfergaben darbrachte. Im oberen Teil dieses Gemäldes empfingen diese Gottheit und die Göttin Satis den Pharao. Die Gliederung dieser kleinen Anlage ist ein Muster an Einfachheit und Klarheit – [sie] entspricht derjenigen, die die Alten Peripteros nannten. Vitruv verwendet diese Bezeichnung für einen quadratischen oder rechteckigen Tempel, der von einem durch einen Säulenkranz begrenzten Umgang eingefasst ist. Die Ansicht dieses kleinen Tempels, der sich aus so einfachen und scheinbar anspruchslosen Strichen zusammensetzt, befriedigt das Auge durch die zwischen den architektonischen Bestandteilen herrschende Harmonie.

TEMPLE PÉRIPTÈRE D'AMÉNOPHIS III À ÉLÉPHANTINE (XVIIIe dynastie)

Le temple d'Éléphantine était dédié à Kneph ou Chnoubis [Khnoum], qui présidait à l'inondation, et était principalement adoré aux cataractes. Il fut élevé par ordre d'Aménophis III, qui y était représenté avec la reine faisant des offrandes à Kneph, dans sa bari. Dans la partie supérieure de ce tableau, le pharaon était reçu par cette divinité et la déesse Saté [Satis]. La disposition de ce petit édifice est un modèle de simplicité et de pureté, [elle] est conforme à celle que l'on appelait périptère chez les anciens. Vitruve donne ce nom à un temple carré ou rectangulaire environné de colonnes formant tout autour une galerie continue. L'élévation de ce petit temple, composée de lignes si simples et en apparence sans art, satisfait l'œil par l'harmonie qui règne entre les membres de l'architecture.

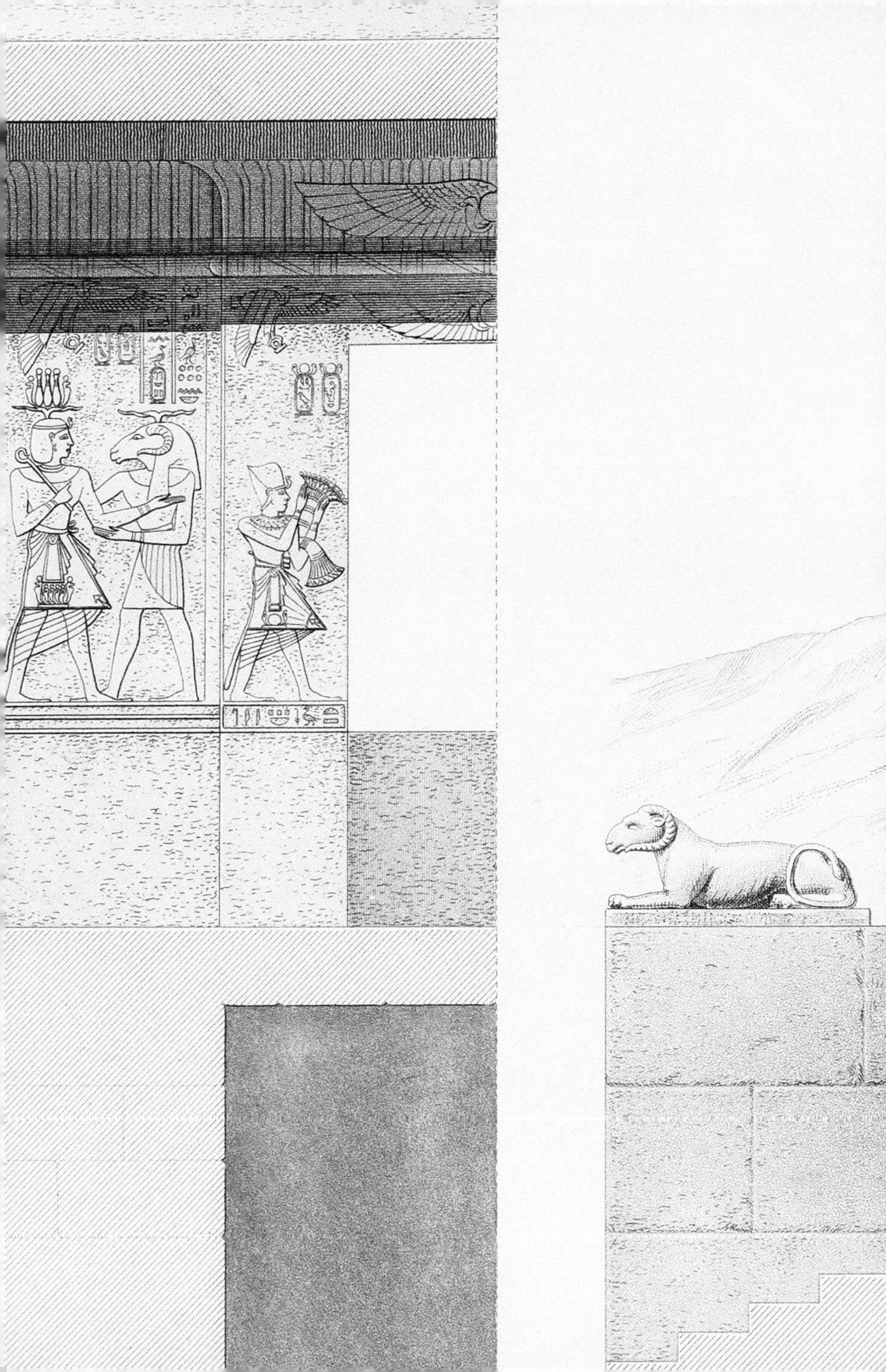

DECORATIVE PANELS ABOVE INTERIOR DOORS (18th Dynasty)

Thebes and Sedeinga

In the monuments of the early dynasties of the New Kingdom, particularly in the tombs, decorative panels over the doors and false doors are frequent features. The first example on this plate can be seen at Thebes in the hypogeum of the foster father of Amenophis II (18th Dynasty). It is strangely reminiscent of a bygone decorative style, that of the full-blown lotus flowers or rather the linked papyrus umbels that adorn the sarcophagi and the naoi of tombs of the time of the pyramids. Two crouching lions decorate the segments of the angles and above, in the corner angles on both sides, have been sculpted symbolic eyes. The second example shows the decoration of a door in the temple of Sedeinga in Nubia. Here one can see two sphinxes symbolising Queen Tiye, wife of Amenophis III, uraei and characteristic symbols of Hathor, the goddess to whom the building was apparently dedicated.

BEKRÖNUNG VON INNENTÜREN (18. Dynastie)

Theben und Sedeinga

In den Denkmälern der ersten Dynastien des Neuen Reiches, insbesondere in den Gräbern, findet man häufig Türbekrönungen oder falsche Türen. Die erste Türbekrönung auf dieser Tafel befindet sich in Theben, im Hypogäum des Pflegevaters von Amenophis II. (18. Dynastie). Sie weist eigenartige Anklänge an ältere Verzierungen auf – namentlich die des erblühten Lotus oder eher die der Papyrusdolden-Bündel –, die die Sarkophage und Naos der Gräber aus der Pyramidenzeit schmücken. Zwei kniende Löwen zieren die Winkelsegmente, und in den darüber liegenden Ecksteinen sind auf beiden Seiten Augensymbole ausgemeißelt. Die Nr. 2 stellt die Verzierung einer Tempeltür in Sedeinga in Nubien dar. Es sind darauf zwei die Königin Teje – die Gemahlin des Amenophis III. – versinnbildlichende Sphingen, Uräusschlangen und Zeichen der Göttin Hathor, der die Anlage anscheinend geweiht war, zu sehen.

COURONNEMENTS DE PORTES INTÉRIEURES (XVIIIe dynastie)

Thèbes et Sedeinga

Dans les monuments des premières dynasties du nouvel Empire, et en particulier dans les tombeaux, on trouve souvent des dessus de portes ou des fausses portes. Le premier dessus de porte de cette planche se voit à Thèbes dans l'hypogée du père nourricier d'Aménophis II (XVIIIe dynastie). Il offre une curieuse réminiscence des plus anciennes décorations, celle des fleurs de lotus épanouies ou plutôt d'ombelles de papyrus réunies qui ornent les sarcophages et les naos des tombeaux contemporains des pyramides. Deux lions accroupis décorent les segments des angles, et au-dessus, dans les écoinçons de chaque côté, on a sculpté les yeux symboliques. Le n° 2 représente la décoration d'une porte du temple de Sedeinga, en Nubie. On y voit deux sphinx symbolisant la reine Taïa [Tiyi], épouse d'Aménophis III, des uréus et des marques d'Hathor, déesse à laquelle l'édifice paraît avoir été consacré.

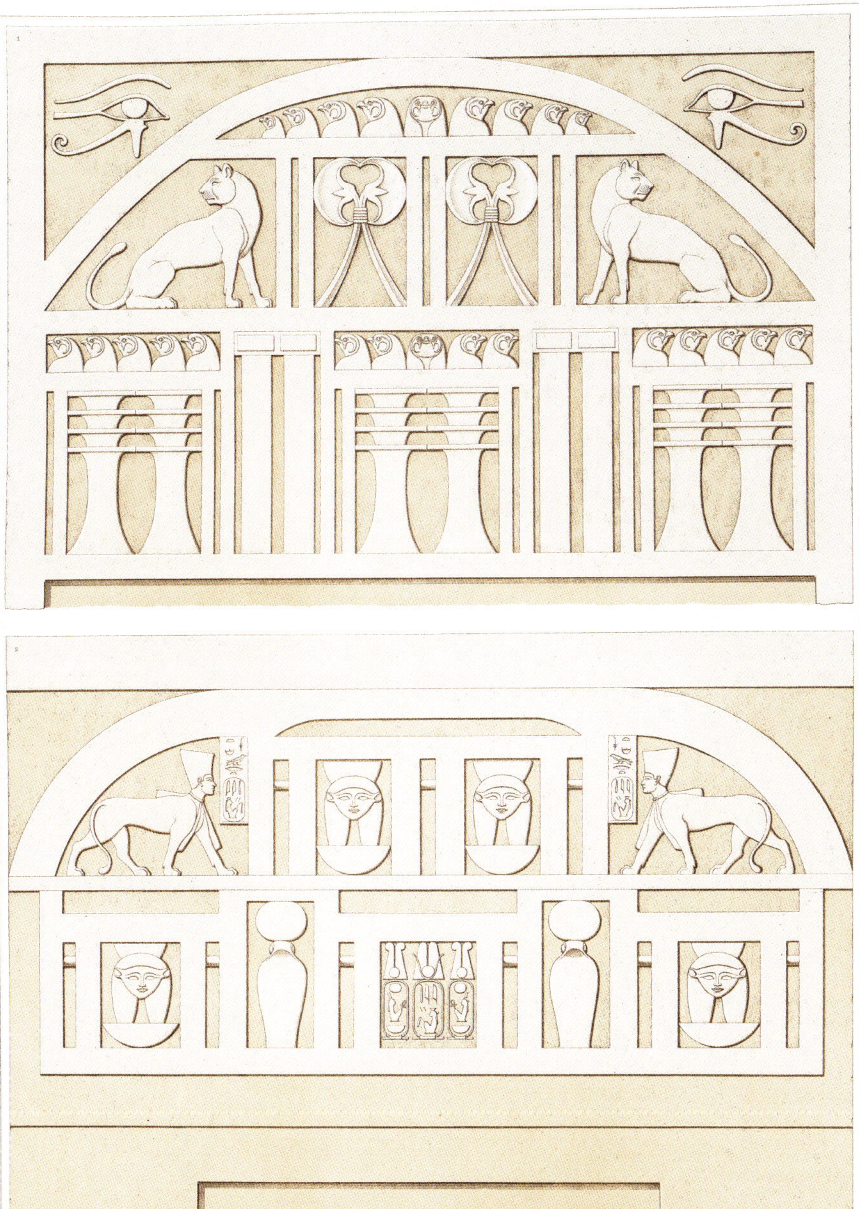

Lith par Ch. Walter. _ Imp. par Hangard-Maugé. E. Prisse d'Avennes. Publié par Arthus-Bertrand, Éditeur.

COURONNEMENTS DE PORTES INTÉRIEURES .

(1 THÈBES _ 2 SEDEINGA _ XVIIIe DYNASTIE.)

DECORATIVE PANELS AND FRIEZES WITH FLEURONS

(18th and 20th Dynasties)

Necropolis of Thebes

This plate completes the preceding one and offers, as does that, various decorative motifs taken in the main from hypogea. Nos. 1 and 2 display lanciform friezes, used as balusters in the preceding plate. This unusual ornamentation, known as "kheker" frieze in Egyptian, is the hieroglyph which is the symbol for embellishment or adornment. No. 3 is a decorative panel composed of heads of Isis or Hathor, crowned by a small naos. Below the dedicatory border hang rosettes, flowers and buds which form a frieze above the main scene. Nos. 4 to 11 show various arrangements of lotus flowers or papyrus umbels with rosettes, fruits etc.; they give some idea of the variety of decoration which is to be found in all the tombs, thanks to the skill of the Egyptian artists. The borders or friezes of nos. 12 and 13 are also copied from hypogea and are models of elegance and taste.

BEKRÖNUNGEN UND BLUMENFRIESE

(18. und 20. Dynastie)

Nekropole von Theben

Diese Tafel vervollständigt die vorhergehende und zeigt ebenfalls verschiedene Schmuckmotive, die hauptsächlich Hypogäen entnommen sind. Nr. 1 und 2 stellen lanzettförmige Bekrönungen dar, die man wie die Docken der vorherigen Tafel verwendete. Dieses eigenartige Ornament, Cheker-Fries genannt, ist die Hieroglyphe, die Verschönerung oder Schmuck versinnbildlicht. Die Nr. 3 ist eine Bekrönung aus Isis- oder Hathor-Köpfen, die ein kleiner Naos überragt. Unter der üblichen Einfassung hängen Rosetten, Blumen und Knospen herab, die oberhalb des Gemäldes einen Fries bilden. Die Nr. 4 bis 11 zeigen verschiedenartige Zusammenstellungen von Lotusblüten oder Papyrusdolden mit Rosetten, Früchten usw.; sie vermitteln einen Eindruck vom Abwechslungsreichtum, den die ägyptischen Künstler diesem Zierwerk zu verleihen wussten, das sich in allen Grabmalen findet. Die Zierleisten oder Friese Nr. 12 und 13 – ebenfalls in Hypogäen abgezeichnet – sind ein Muster an Gefälligkeit und Schönheitssinn.

COURONNEMENTS ET FRISES FLEURONNÉES

(XVIIIe et XXe dynasties)

Nécropole de Thèbes

Cette planche, qui complète la précédente, offre, comme elle, différents motifs d'ornementation tirés principalement d'hypogées. Les n°s 1 et 2 représentent des couronnements, lanciformes, employés comme les balustres de la planche précédente. Ce singulier ornement, appelé en égyptien « Khakerou » [Kheker], est l'hiéroglyphe, symbole d'embellissement ou de parure. Le n° 3 est un couronnement composé de têtes d'Isis ou d'Hathor, surmontées d'un petit naos. Au-dessous de la bordure consacrée pendent des rosaces, des fleurs et des boutons, qui forment une frise au-dessus du tableau. Les n°s 4 à 11 présentent divers agencements de fleurs de lotus ou d'ombelles de papyrus avec des rosaces, des fruits, etc. ; ils donnent une idée de la variété que les artistes égyptiens savaient apporter dans ces décorations qu'on retrouve dans tous les tombeaux. Les bordures ou frises n°s 12 et 13, copiées également dans les hypogées, sont des modèles d'élégance et de goût.

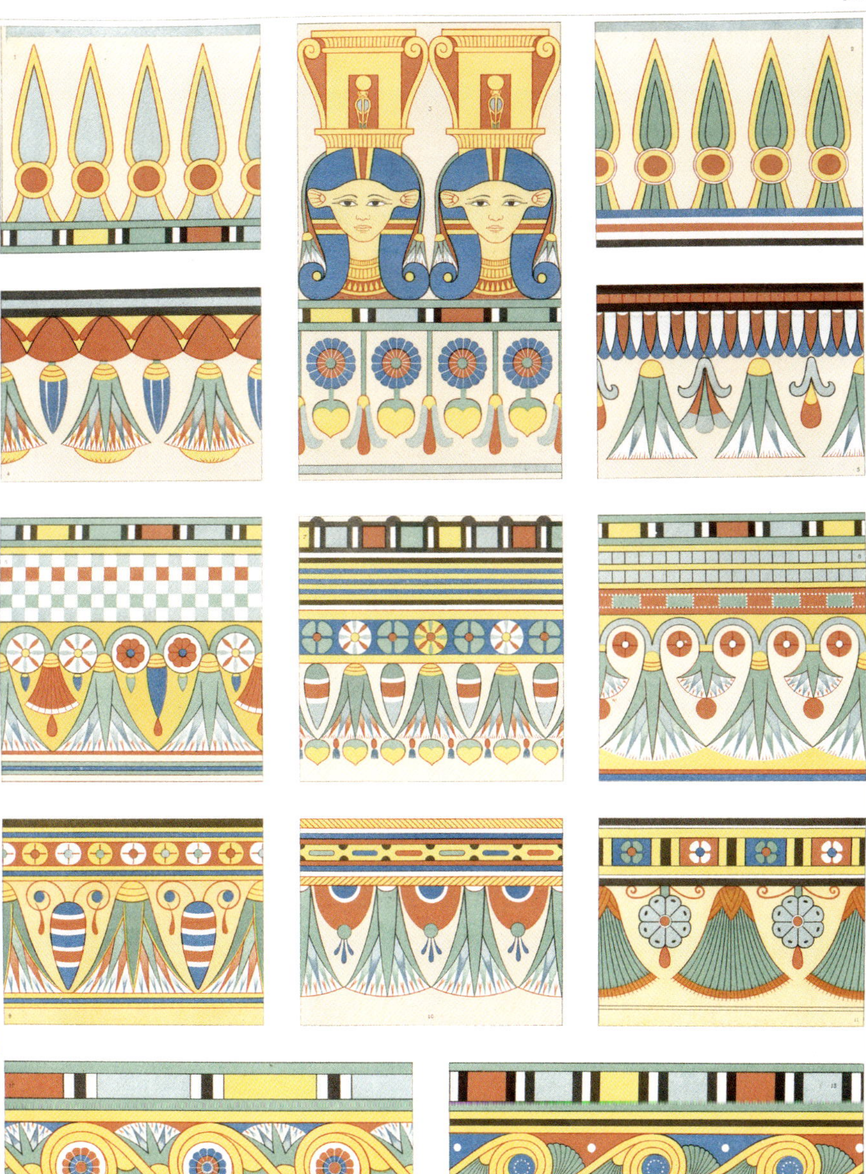

Lith. par Monin. Imp. Fraipont-Marge.

E. Prisse d'Avennes

Publié par Arthus-Bertrand Éditeur

COURONNEMENTS & FRISES FLEURONNÉES.

(NÉCROPOLE DE THÈBES _ XVIIIe-XXe DYNASTIES.)

PILLARS OF THUTMOSIS III AT KARNAK (18th Dynasty)

These two pillars are each decorated with three lotus and papyrus stems which are slightly different: the front and back faces are decorated with a sunken bas-relief executed with great delicacy. [...] Only the decorated parts were coloured, and they stood out against the background of granite which, before age had tarnished its brilliant sheen, was a vivid red spotted with black, lending prominence to the reliefs. The height of these elegant pillars [9 metres], together with the way in which they are positioned at the entrance to the granite sanctuary, would seem to indicate that they never had any architrave; however, they would certainly once have had some royal emblem as entablature, possibly cartouches or splendid hawks in enamel cloisonné.

PFEILER VON THUTMOSIS III. IN KARNAK (18. Dynastie)

Die beiden Pfeiler sind mit drei Lotus- und Papyrusstängeln verziert, die sich ein wenig voneinander unterscheiden: Die Vorder- und Rückseiten sind durch versenkte, mit sehr viel Sorgfalt ausgemeißelte Flachreliefs geschmückt. [...] Lediglich die dekorativen Teile waren ausgemalt und hoben sich vom Untergrund aus Granit ab, dessen kräftiges, mit schwarzen Sprenkeln durchsetztes Rot die Reliefs hervortreten ließ, als die Zeit den Glanz der Politur noch nicht getrübt hatte. Die Höhe dieser anmutigen Pfeiler [9 m] und die Art, wie sie am Eingang des granitenen Heiligtums platziert sind, scheinen darauf hinzudeuten, dass sie niemals einen Architrav getragen haben; sicher waren sie jedoch einst durch irgendein königliches Emblem aus Cloisonné bekrönt, wahrscheinlich durch schimmernde Kartuschen oder funkelnde Sperber.

PILIERS DE THOUTMÈS III, À KARNAC (XVIIIe dynastie)

Ces deux piliers sont décorés de trois tiges de lotus et de papyrus qui diffèrent un peu : les faces antérieures et postérieures sont ornées de bas-reliefs dans le creux, sculptés avec beaucoup de finesse. [...] Les parties décoratives étaient seules coloriées et se détachaient sur le fond de granit qui, lorsque le temps n'avait pas encore terni l'éclat du poli, était d'un rouge vif moucheté de noir qui faisait saillir les reliefs. La hauteur de ces élégants piliers [9 mètres] ainsi que la façon dont ils sont placés à l'entrée du sanctuaire de granit sembleraient indiquer qu'ils n'ont jamais porté d'architrave ; cependant, ils étaient certainement autrefois couronnés de quelque emblème royal, probablement de cartouches ou d'éperviers resplendissants, d'émaux cloisonnés.

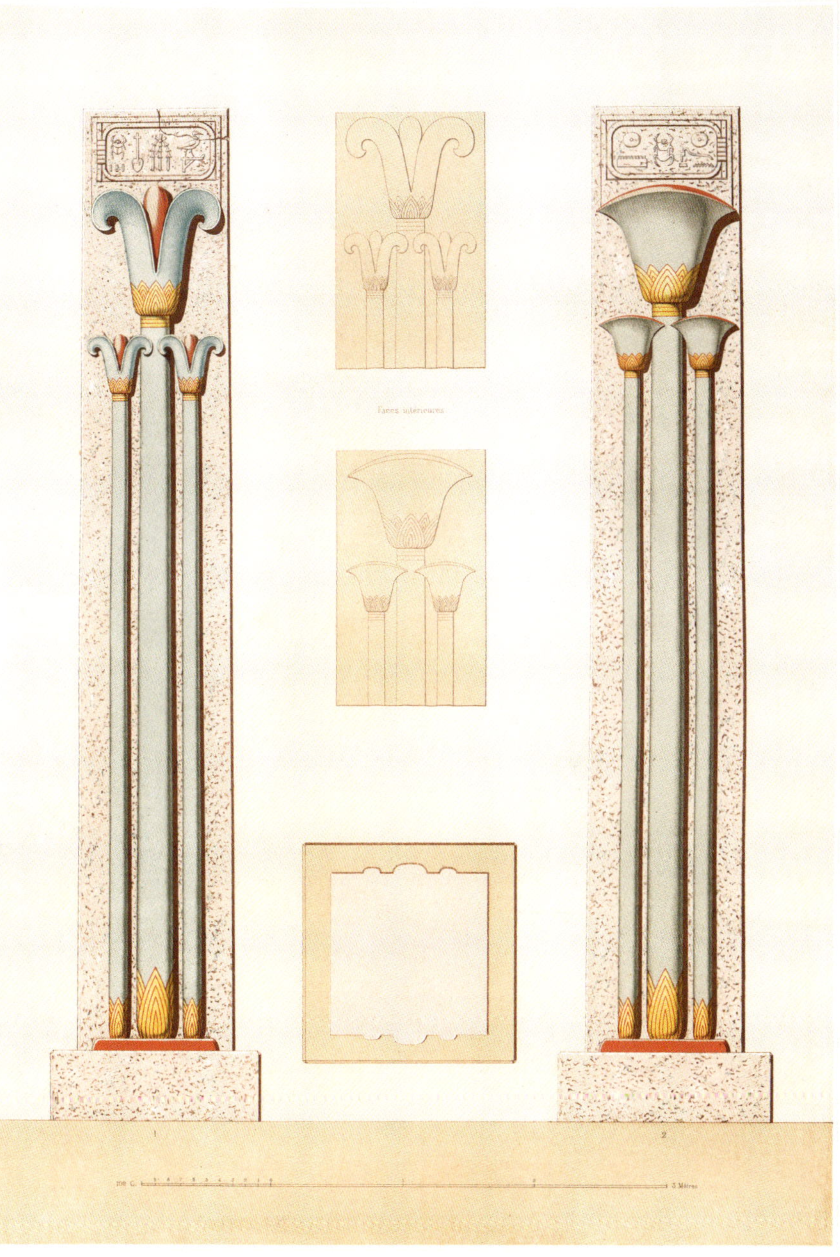

Lith par Rivard. Imp par Hangard Maugé. E. Prisse d'Avennes. Publié par Arthus Bertrand Éditeur

PILIERS DE THOUTMÈS III À KARNAC.

(XVIIIe DYNASTIE.)

PILLARS OF HYPOGEA AT ZAWYET EL-MAIYITIN (18th Dynasty)

Zawyet el-Maiyitin, which means "Oratory of the dead", is the name of a small village in Upper Egypt where the inhabitants of Minya and the surrounding area go to bury their dead. These tombs are carved from limestone with a high shell content, and unfortunately little of the detail of their decoration has been preserved. Two of these hypogea, which belonged to high-ranking officials, are particularly remarkable. They have retaining pillars whose two principal faces are decorated with small columns with full-blown lotus flowers carved in bas-relief. [...] All that is now left of the first tomb is one room supported by four pillars whose opposite faces are decorated with the form of a small column in relief. The second hypogeum, which consists of two rooms and a small sanctuary, now has only a single column whose capital and architrave retain some traces of colour.

PFEILER DER HYPOGÄEN VON SAUJET EL-MEITIN (18. Dynastie)

Saujet el-Meitin bedeutet „Oratorium der Toten" und ist der Name eines kleinen oberägyptischen Dorfes, in dem die Einwohner von Al-Minya und Umgebung ihre Toten begraben. In diesen Gräbern, die in einen sehr groben Muschelkalk gehauen sind, haben sich leider nur wenige Einzelheiten der Ausstattung erhalten. Unter diesen Hypogäen sind vor allem zwei, die hohen Beamten gehörten, bemerkenswert. Sie weisen Stützpfeiler auf, deren beide Hauptseiten mit Flachreliefs kleiner Lotussäulen mit Blütenkapitell geschmückt sind. [...] Vom ersten Grab ist lediglich ein Raum erhalten, der auf vier Pfeilern ruht; diese sind an den einander gegenüberliegenden Seiten jeweils mit einer plastisch herausgearbeiteten kleinen Säule geschmückt. Im zweiten Hypogäum, das aus zwei Räumen und einem kleinen Heiligtum besteht, hat nur eine einzige Säule überdauert, an deren Kapitell und Architrav einige Farbspuren erhalten sind.

PILIERS DES HYPOGÉES DE ZAWIET EL-MAYETIN (XVIIIe dynastie)

Zawiet el-Mayetin [Zaouit el-Meïtin], qui signifie l'« Oratoire des morts », est le nom d'un petit village de la Haute-Égypte où les habitants de Myniah et des environs vont enterrer leurs morts. Ces tombeaux, taillés dans un calcaire coquillier très grossier, ont malheureusement conservé peu de détails de leur décoration. Deux de ces hypogées, qui ont appartenu à de hauts fonctionnaires, sont surtout remarquables. Ils présentent des piliers de soutènement dont les deux faces principales sont ornées de colonnettes à fleur de lotus épanouie sculptée en bas-relief. [...] Le premier tombeau ne présente plus qu'une seule pièce soutenue par quatre piliers dont les faces opposées sont ornées d'une colonnette en relief. Le second hypogée, composé de deux pièces et d'un petit sanctuaire, ne présente plus qu'une seule colonne dont le chapiteau et l'architrave ont gardé quelques traces de couleurs.

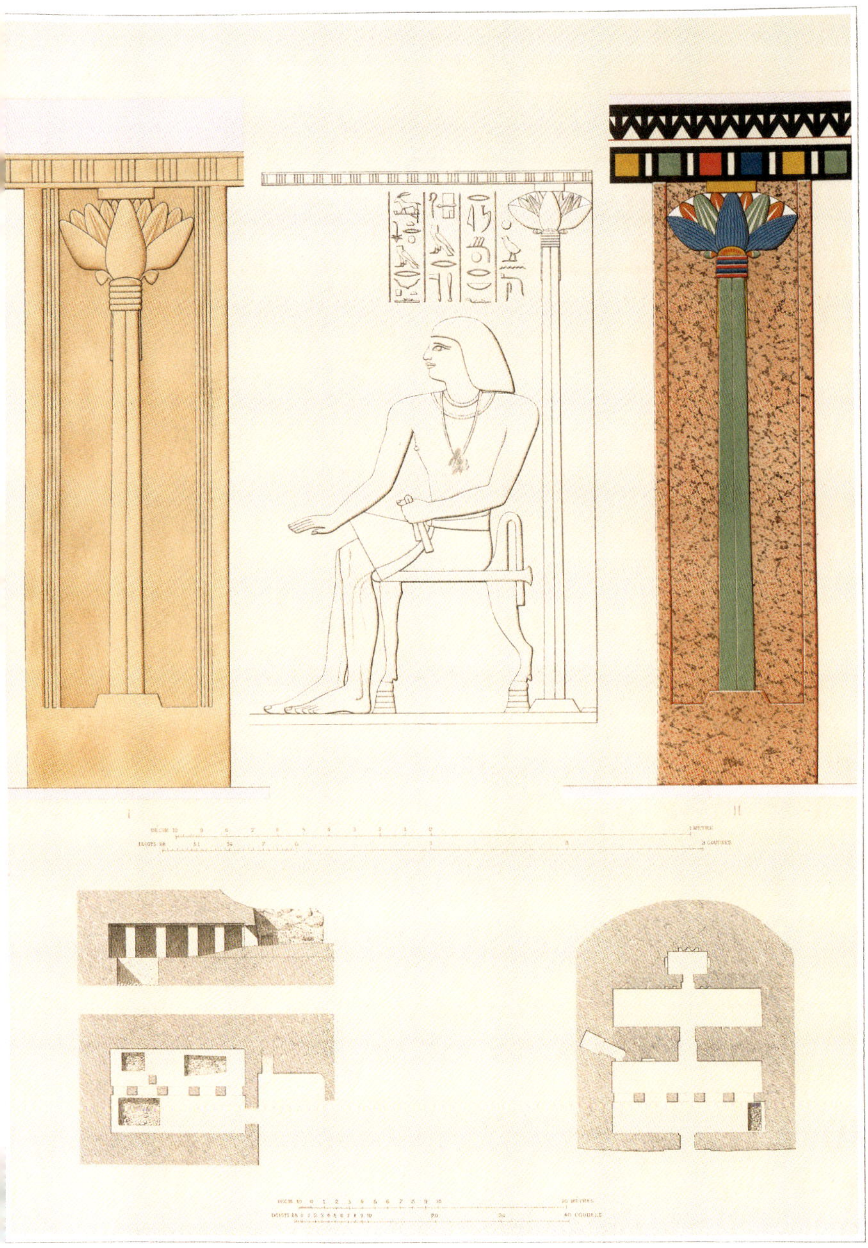

Exécuté par Levie Imp. Lemercier & Cie Paris — Prisse d'Avennes — Publié par Arthus Bertrand, Éditeur

PILIERS DES HYPOGÉES DE ZAWIET EL-MAYETIN

(XVIIIE DYNASTIE)

PILASTERS OR SQUARE COLUMNS (18th Dynasty)

Thebes

Egyptian architecture often makes use of simple or decorated pillars, which offer almost as much variety as true columns. Isolated pilasters are rare in ancient Greek or Roman architecture, but they occur very frequently in ancient Egyptian architecture. I have reproduced in this plate the finest examples known of pillars crowned with a cornice or capital. These are at Thebes; they both date from the same dynasty and yet, in spite of this, show great variation in their proportions. One is elegant and slender, the other massive and squat. [...] The first pilaster is 5.33 metres high and is taken from a small building of Amenophis II. The second is 4 metres high and is part of a small building of Amenophis III whose ruins can be seen close to the temple of Mut. The pharaoh is shown making an offering to the goddess Hathor.

PILASTER ODER QUADRATISCHE SÄULEN (18. Dynastie)

Theben

In der ägyptischen Architektur werden häufig einfache oder verzierte Pfeiler verwendet, die eine nahezu ebenso große Vielfalt aufweisen wie die eigentlichen Säulen. In der Architektur der griechischen oder römischen Antike sind frei stehende Pilaster selten, in der ägyptischen Architektur kommen sie sehr häufig vor. Auf dieser Tafel habe ich die schönsten bekannten Exemplare der mit einem Kranzgesims oder einem Kapitell bekrönten Säulen abgebildet. Sie befinden sich in Theben, datieren alle beide aus derselben Dynastie und weisen dennoch hinsichtlich ihrer Proportionen himmelweite Unterschiede auf. Die eine ist hoch und schlank; die andere ist wuchtig und gedrungen. [...] Der erste Pilaster ist 5,33 m hoch und einer kleinen Anlage von Amenophis II. entnommen. Der zweite Pilaster war 4 m hoch. Er gehörte zu einer kleinen Anlage von Amenophis III., deren Ruinen sich in der Nähe des Mut-Tempels befinden. Die Darstellung zeigt den Pharao, während er der Göttin Hathor Opfergaben darbringt.

PILASTRES OU COLONNES QUADRANGULAIRES (XVIIIe dynastie)

Thèbes

L'architecture égyptienne fait un fréquent usage de piliers simples ou ornés, et ils offrent presque autant de variétés que les colonnes proprement dites. Les pilastres isolés sont rares dans l'architecture antique, grecque ou romaine, mais très fréquents dans l'architecture égyptienne. J'ai reproduit, dans cette planche, les plus beaux spécimens connus de piliers couronnés d'une corniche ou chapiteau. Ils se trouvent à Thèbes, datent tous deux de la même dynastie et présentent, malgré cela, dans leurs proportions, d'énormes différences. L'un est svelte, élancé ; l'autre est massif, trapu. [...] Le premier pilastre, qui a 5,33 mètres de hauteur, est tiré d'un petit édifice d'Amounôph [Aménophis] II. Le second pilastre avait 4 mètres de hauteur. Il faisait partie d'un petit édifice de Amounôph III dont les ruines se trouvent près du temple de Mauth. Le pharaon est représenté faisant offrande à la déesse Hathor.

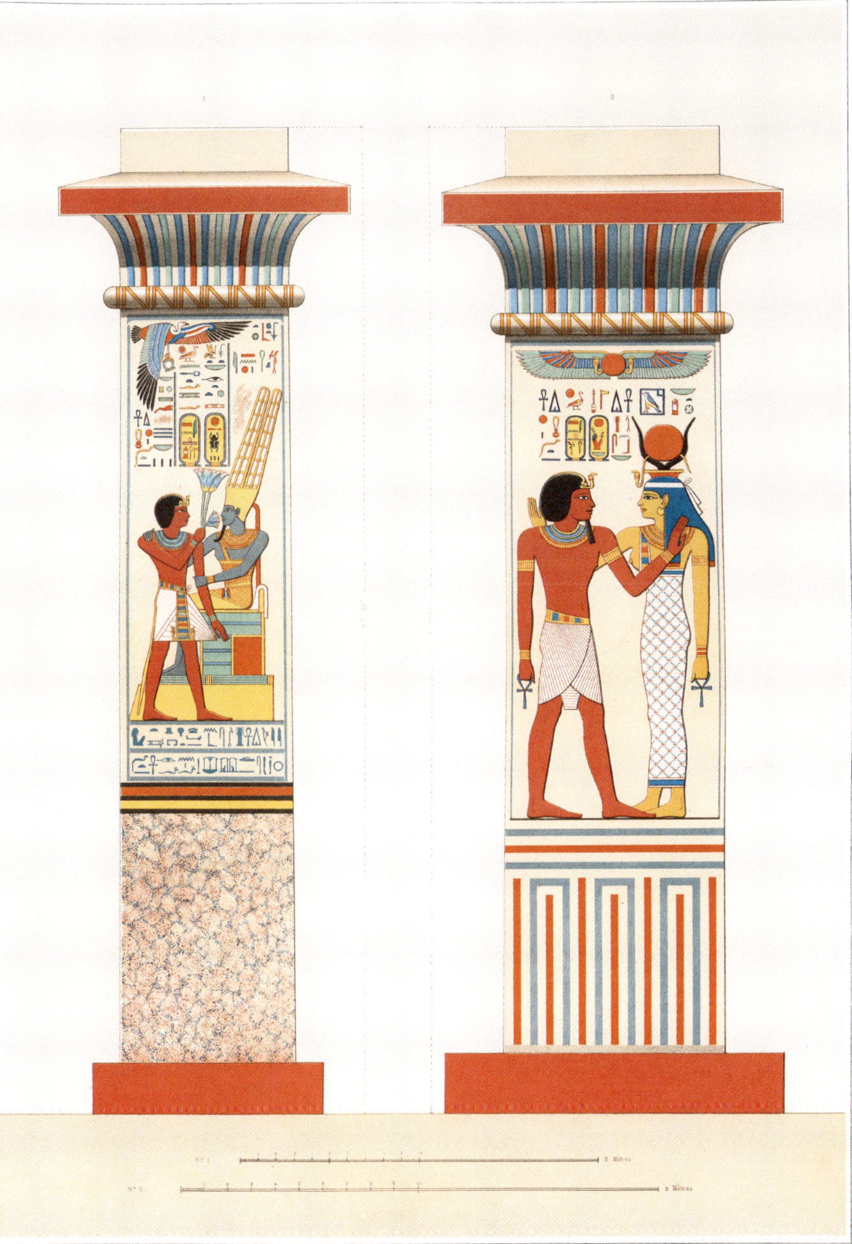

Lith. par Moulin. Imp. par Hangard-Maugé.

E. Prisse d'Avennes.

Publié par Arthus-Bertrand, Éditeur.

PILASTRES OU COLONNES QUADRANGULAIRES.

(THÈBES _ XVIIIe DYNASTIE)

WOODEN BUILDINGS. SMALL COLUMNS FROM KIOSKS

(4th [sic; 5th] and 18th Dynasties)

These small columns were comparatively simple in the early stages of this type of architecture, but they became more elegant and even graceful, like a bouquet of flowers, as art and civilisation developed during the 18th Dynasty. No. 1 is a small column reproduced, at Saqqara, in the tomb of Ti, a high-ranking official who lived during the 5th Dynasty. It portrays a half-open lotus bud flanked by two smaller buds. No. 2 is a small column reproduced from a hypogeum of the 18th Dynasty at Zawyet el-Maiyitin. Here the flower is open and is even more evocative of the plant whose type it represents. No. 3 is another column, this one from a kiosk of the temple of Semna, rebuilt by Thutmosis III. No. 4 depicts a small column sculpted in a hypogeum at Thebes from the 18th Dynasty. No. 5 is another small column of the same period, reproduced from the tomb of a royal scribe called Nefersekheru who was the palace steward.

HOLZBAUTEN. KLEINE SÄULEN DER ÄDIKULÄ

(4. [sic; 5.] und 18. Dynastie)

Diese anfänglich recht einfachen kleinen Säulen wurden im Verlauf der 18. Dynastie – mit der Entwicklung von Kunst und Kultur – immer eleganter und quasi so anmutig wie ein Strauß Blumen. Die Nr. 1 ist eine in Sakkara im Grabmal des Ti – eines hohen Beamten, der während der 5. Dynastie lebte – abgezeichnete kleine Säule. Sie stellt eine halb geöffnete, von zwei kleineren Knospen flankiere Lotusblüte dar. Die Nr. 2 ist eine in einem Hypogäum in Saujet el-Meitin kopierte kleine Säule aus der 18. Dynastie. Hier ist die Blüte geöffnet und gibt das Urbild, nach dem sie geschaffen wurde, noch besser wieder. Die Nr. 3 ist eine weitere kleine Säule aus einer Ädikula in dem von Thutmosis III. wiederaufgebauten Tempel von Semna. Die Nr. 4 stellt eine in Stein gehauene kleine Säule aus einem Hypogäum der 18. Dynastie in Theben dar. Die Nr. 5 ist eine weitere kleine Säule der gleichen Zeitstellung, die im Grabmal eines königlichen Schreibers und Palastverwalters namens Nefersecheru abgezeichnet wurde.

CONSTRUCTIONS EN BOIS. COLONNETTES DES ÉDICULES

(IVe [sic ; V^e^] et XVIIIe dynasties)

Ces colonnettes, assez simples au début de l'architecture, devinrent plus élégantes, et même gracieuses comme des bouquets, avec le développement de l'art et de la civilisation, sous la XVIIIe dynastie. Le n° 1 est une colonnette copiée, à Sakkara, dans le tombeau de Teï, haut fonctionnaire, qui vivait sous la Ve dynastie. Elle représente un bouton de lotus entr'ouvert, flanqué de deux boutons plus petits. Le n° 2 est une colonnette copiée dans un hypogée de Zawyet el-Mayetin [Zaouiet el-Meïtin] de la XVIIIe dynastie. Ici, la fleur est ouverte et rappelle encore mieux la plante dont elle a pris le type. Le n° 3 est encore une colonnette d'un édicule du temple de Semneh, reconstruit par Thoutmès [Thoutmôsis] III. Le n° 4 représente une colonnette sculptée dans un hypogée de Thèbes de la XVIIIe dynastie. Le n° 5 est une autre colonnette de la même époque copiée dans le tombeau d'un scribe royal, intendant du palais nommé Nofré-Sekhorou.

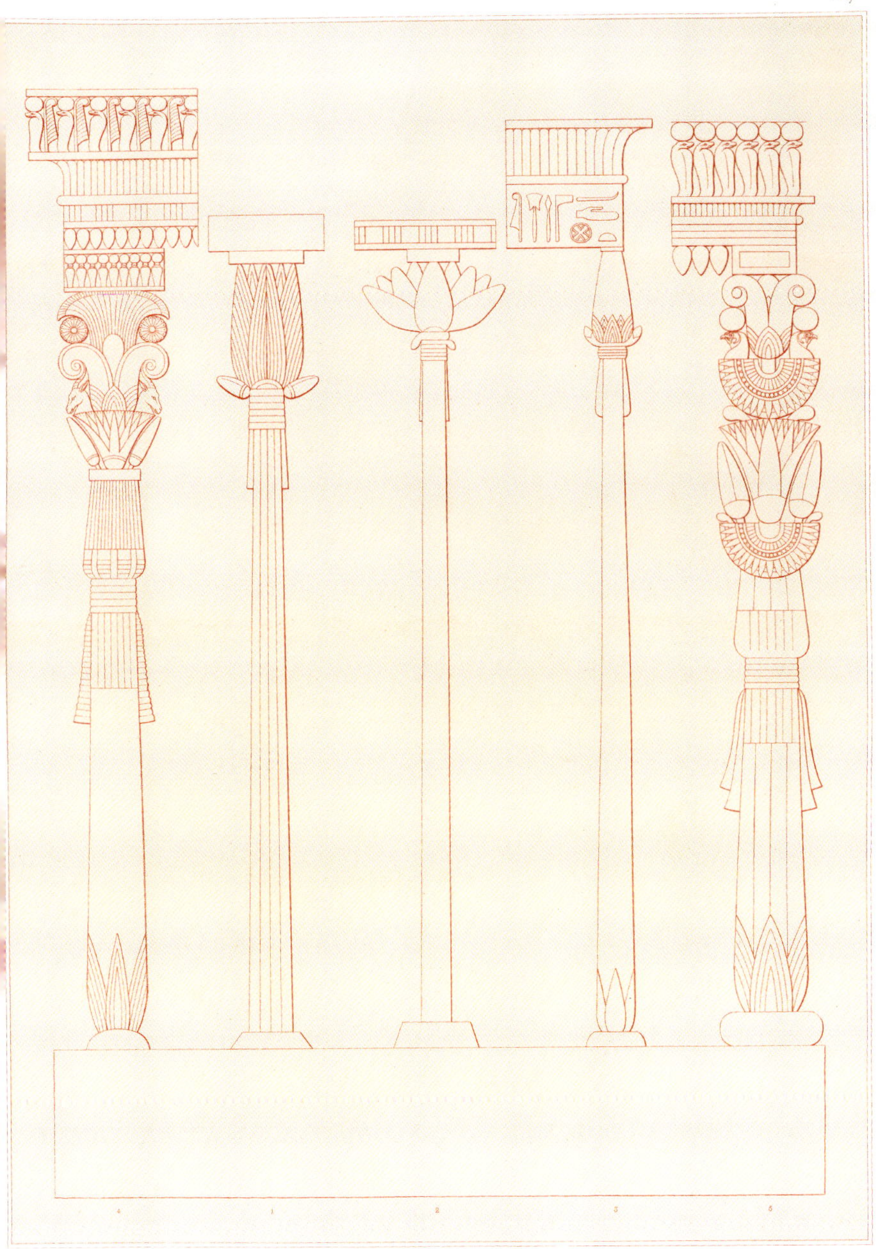

Gravé par Mathet. Imp. par Hangard Maugé. E. Prisse d'Avennes. Publié par Arthus-Bertrand, Éditeur

CONSTRUCTIONS EN BOIS. — COLONNETTES DES ÉDICULES.

(IVe ET XVIIIe DYNASTIES.)

WOODEN BUILDINGS. SMALL COLUMNS FROM KIOSKS

(18th and 19th Dynasties)

No. 1 is an elegant example of the type of small column commonly found at Tell el-Amarna under Akhenaten, the pharaoh who introduced into Egypt the exclusive worship of the sun. The capital consists of a bouquet of lotus flowers adorned with a double collar from which there hangs a group of geese, then wreaths of foliage. Nos. 2 and 5, taken from the necropolis of Thebes, date from the same period, that is from the reign of Amenophis III (18th Dynasty), and are reminiscent of the primitive columns. No. 3 is taken from a tomb in Thebes from the reign of Seti I (19th Dynasty). No. 4 comes from a pavilion of the goddess Hathor, whose symbolic head serves as capital to the column.

HOLZBAUTEN. KLEINE SÄULEN DER ÄDIKULÄ

(18. und 19. Dynastie)

Die Nr. 1 stellt ein anmutiges Exemplar jener kleinen Säulen dar, wie sie in Tell el-Amarna unter dem Pharao Echnaton gebräuchlich waren, der in Ägypten einen allein auf die Sonne ausgerichteten Kult einführte. Das Kapitell besteht aus einem mit einem Doppelring geschmückten Lotusstrauß, darunter hängt eine Gruppe Gänse, dann folgen Blattverzierungen. Die Nr. 2 und 5 sind der Nekropole von Theben entnommen, datieren aus derselben Zeit – das heißt, aus der Regierungszeit von Amenophis III. (18. Dynastie) – und erinnern an die ursprünglichen einfachen Säulchen. Die Nr. 3 ist einem Grab aus der Regierungszeit von Sethos I. (19. Dynastie) in Theben entnommen. Die Nr. 4 stammt aus einer Ädikula der Göttin Hathor, deren symbolischer Kopf der Säule als Kapitell dient.

CONSTRUCTIONS EN BOIS. COLONNETTES DES ÉDICULES

(XVIIIe et XIXe dynasties)

Le n° 1 offre un élégant spécimen des colonnettes usitées à Tell el-Amarna, sous Khouenaten [Akhénaton], pharaon qui introduisit en Égypte le culte exclusif du soleil. Le chapiteau est formé d'un bouquet de lotus garni d'un double collier au-dessous duquel pend un groupe d'oies, puis des garnitures de feuilles. Les n°s 2 et 5, tirés de la nécropole de Thèbes, datent de la même époque, c'est-à-dire du règne d'Aménophis III (XVIIIe dynastie), ils rappellent les colonnettes primitives. Le n° 3 [est] tiré d'un tombeau de Thèbes du règne de Séti Ier (XIXe dynastie). Le n° 4 provient d'un édicule de la déesse Hathor, dont la tête symbolique sert de chapiteau à la colonne.

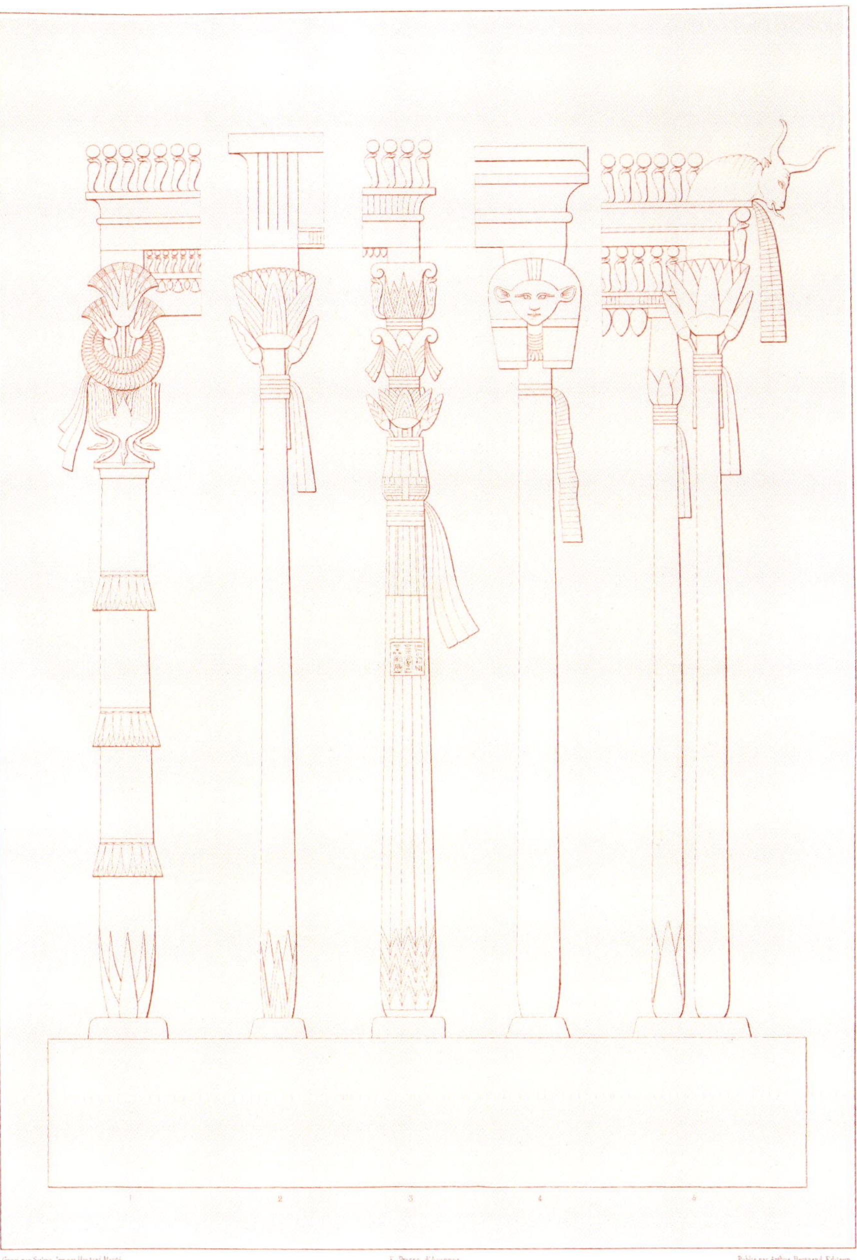

Gravé par Sulpis. Imp. par Hangard Maugé. E. Prisse d'Avennes. Publié par Arthus Bertrand, Éditeur.

CONSTRUCTIONS EN BOIS. — COLONNETTES DES ÉDICULES.

(XVIIIe ET XIXe DYNASTIES.)

SMALL WOODEN COLUMNS (18th and 20th Dynasties)

Thebes

The two fragments, which flank the small column, date from the 18th Dynasty. No. 2 comes from a tomb in Thebes whose inscriptions have been effaced. No. 3 comes from another hypogeum in the same necropolis, which was dug for a royal scribe whose name was Horemheb, who lived under Thutmosis IV: the design of the triple capital which decorates the shaft shows great taste. The small column in the centre is part of a splendid naos of Ramesses IX, which is painted in the hypogeum of Imiseba, the high priest in charge of the altar and scriptures of the temple of Amun at Thebes. This is the finest example from the 20th Dynasty.

KLEINE HOLZSÄULEN (18. und 20. Dynastie)

Theben

Die beiden Bruchstücke, die die kleine Säule flankieren, datieren aus der 18. Dynastie. Die Nr. 2 entstammt einem Grabmal in Theben, dessen Inschriften verloren gegangen sind. Die Nr. 3 ist einem weiteren Hypogäum aus derselben Nekropole entnommen, das für einen königlichen Schreiber namens Haremhab ausgehoben wurde, der unter der Herrschaft von Thutmosis IV. lebte: Das den Schaft zierende dreifache Kapitell ist mit viel Geschmack gestaltet. Die kleine Mittelsäule gehört zu einem wunderschön gemalten Naos von Ramses IX. im Hypogäum von Imiseba, dem für den Altar und die Schriften des Amun-Tempels in Theben zuständigen Hohepriester. Es handelt sich um das schönste Exemplar der 20. Dynastie.

COLONNETTES EN BOIS (XVIIIe et XXe dynasties)

Thèbes

Les deux fragments, qui flanquent les colonnettes, datent de la XVIIIe dynastie. Le n° 2 provient d'un tombeau de Thèbes dont les légendes sont effacées. Le n° 3 est tiré d'un autre hypogée de la même nécropole creusé pour un scribe royal nommé Horemheb, qui vivait sous Thoutmès [Thoutmôsis] IV : le triple chapiteau qui décore le fût est agencé avec beaucoup de goût. La colonnette médiale appartient à un splendide naos de Ramsès IX, peint dans l'hypogée d'Aïchesi [Imiseba], grand-prêtre chargé de l'autel et des écritures du temple d'Amon, à Thèbes. C'est le plus beau spécimen de la XXe dynastie.

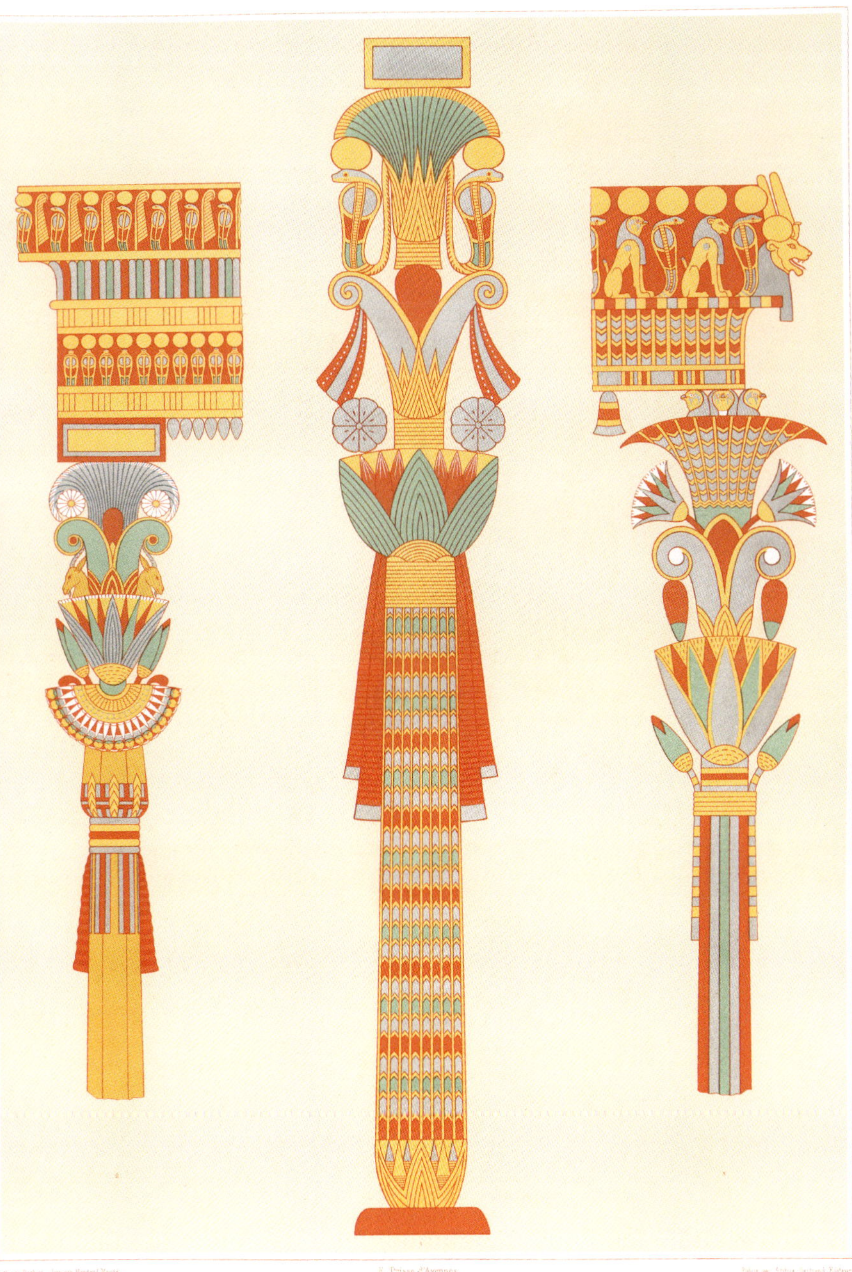

Lith. par Barbier. Imp. par Hangard-Maugé. E. Prisse d'Avennes. Publié par Arthus Bertrand, Éditeur.

COLONNETTES EN BOIS.

(THÈBES ... XVIIIe & XXe DYNASTIES.)

DETAILS OF SMALL WOODEN COLUMNS

Taken from various hypogea

No. 1, taken from hypogea at Zawyet el-Maiyitin, displays in all its richness the palette of shades of the lotus. No. 2 dates from the 12th Dynasty and comes from Deir el-Bersha. As decoration, the architrave carried a hieroglyphic inscription which has been half worn away. No. 3 comes from the same period and can be seen in a tomb at Beni Hassan. Nos. 4, 5 and 6 are fragments of small columns and come from the tomb of the foster father of Amenophis II, at Thebes. The inscriptions painted on the architraves relate to the god Hor-Hat [Hathor]: the two small columns crowned with lions' heads, together with the capitals decorated with the heads of antelopes and hawks which can be seen in nos. 2 and 3 of the preceding plate, recall the capitals of Assyria and India. The height of the columns, always in proportion to the height of the human personages represented, is no more than a bare 3 metres.

DETAILZEICHNUNGEN KLEINER HOLZSÄULEN

Verschiedenen Hypogäen entnommen

Die Nr. 1 ist den Hypogäen von Saujet el-Meitin entnommen und zeigt die ganze Vielfalt der Farbtöne, die die Lotuspflanze aufweist. Die Nr. 2 datiert aus der 12. Dynastie und stammt aus Deir el-Bersche. Der Architrav trug eine halb verloren gegangene Hieroglypheninschrift als Verzierung. Die Nr. 3 datiert aus derselben Zeit und ist in einem Grabmal in Beni Hassan zu sehen. Die Nr. 4, 5, und 6 sind Bruchstücke kleiner Säulen: Sie stammen vom Pflegevater des Amenophis II. in Theben. Die auf die Architrave aufgemalten Inschriften gehören zur Gottheit Hor-Hat [Hathor]: Die beiden kleinen, von Löwenköpfen gekrönten Säulen und die mit Antilopen- und Sperberköpfen verzierten Kapitelle, die man auf den Nr. 2 und 3 der vorhergehenden Tafel sieht, erinnern an die Kapitelle in Assyrien und Indien. Die Höhe der kleinen Säulen wahrt immer die Relation zur Größe der menschlichen Darstellungen: Sie übersteigt fast nie 3 m.

DÉTAILS DE COLONNETTES EN BOIS

Tirés de divers hypogées

Le n° 1, tiré des hypogées de Zawyet el-Mayetin [Zaouiet el-Meïtin], déploie toute la richesse de ton que présentent les lotus. Le n° 2 date de la XIIe dynastie, et provient de Bercheh. L'architrave portait, comme ornement, une inscription hiéroglyphique à demi effacée. Le n° 3 date de la même époque, et se voit dans un tombeau de Beni-Haçen. Les n°s 4, 5 et 6 sont de fragments de colonnettes : ils proviennent du père nourricier d'Aménophis II, à Thèbes. Les légendes peintes sur les architraves appartiennent au dieu Hor-Hat [Hathor] : les deux colonnettes surmontées de têtes de lion, ainsi que les chapiteaux, ornés de têtes d'antilope et d'épervier, qu'on voit sur les n°s 2 et 3 de la planche précédente, rappellent les chapiteaux de l'Assyrie et de l'Inde. La hauteur de ces colonnettes est toujours en rapport avec la hauteur des représentations humaines : elle ne dépasse guère 3 mètres.

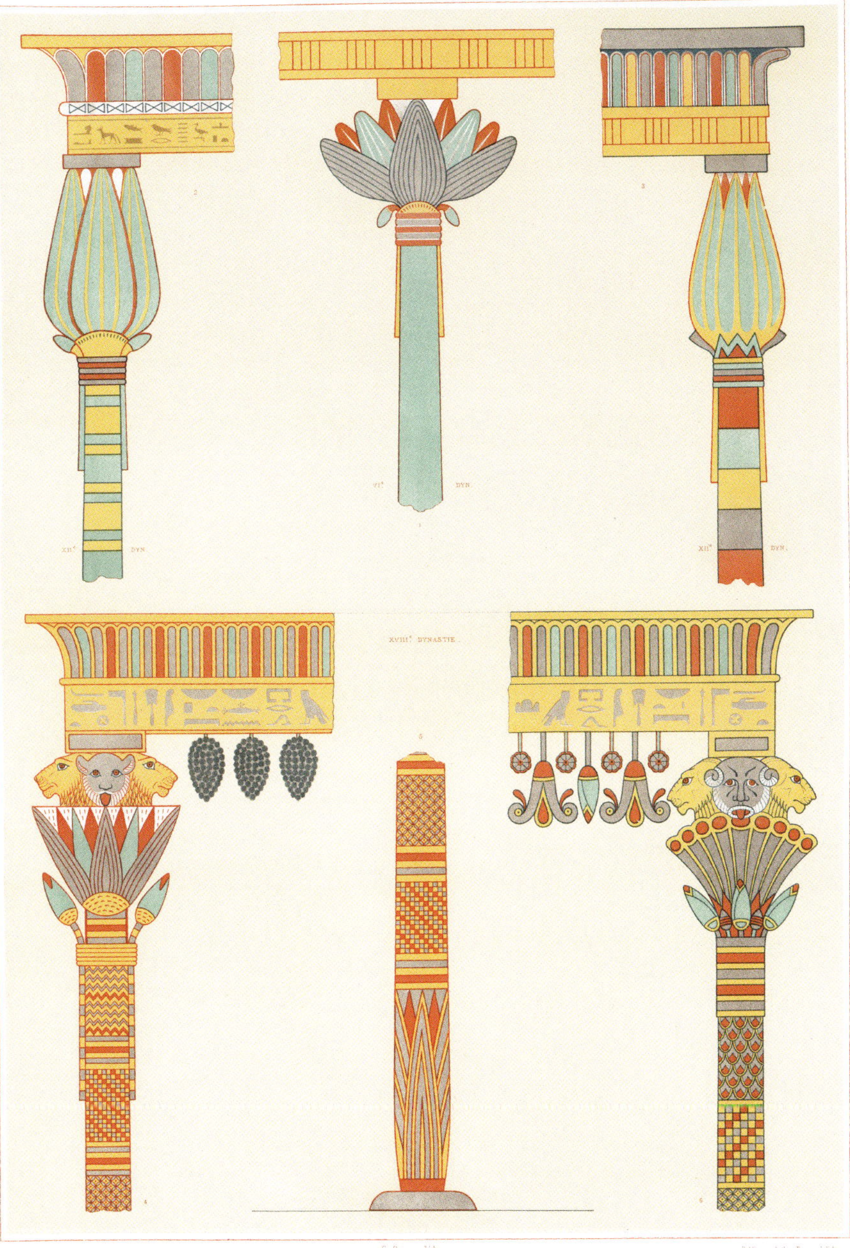

Lith par Barbier ... Imp. par Haugard-Maugé

E. Prisse d'Avennes.

Publié par Arthus-Bertrand Editeur.

DÉTAILS DE COLONNETTES EN BOIS

TIRÉS DE DIVERS HYPOGÉES.

(Pages 237–239)

PAPYRIFORM COLUMNS (18th Dynasty)

Papyriform columns of Thutmosis III, at Karnak
Papyriform columns of Amenophis III, at Thebes

The origin of these columns, which I have designated by the term bundle columns, goes back to at least the 5th Dynasty. Similar columns are to be found on the bas-reliefs of the tomb of Ti at Saqqara. These columns are composed of lotus [papyrus] stems which are drawn together into a bundle decorated with bands: the capital, instead of opening out into the shape of a bellflower, swells out and then narrows again like a flower in bud. The base, which tapers to take the shape of a half-sphere like the stem of the lotus, has a continuously recurring decoration of stipules. The bundle columns which feature in the first plate [see p. 237] are to be found to the east of the covered walkway of Thutmosis III at Karnak.

The second plate [see p. 239] shows two bundle columns from the reign of Amenophis III. The one in rose granite is a monolith, originally from Memphis, from where it was transported to Cairo. The decoration alone was coloured, and so stands out against the marbled background of the syenite.

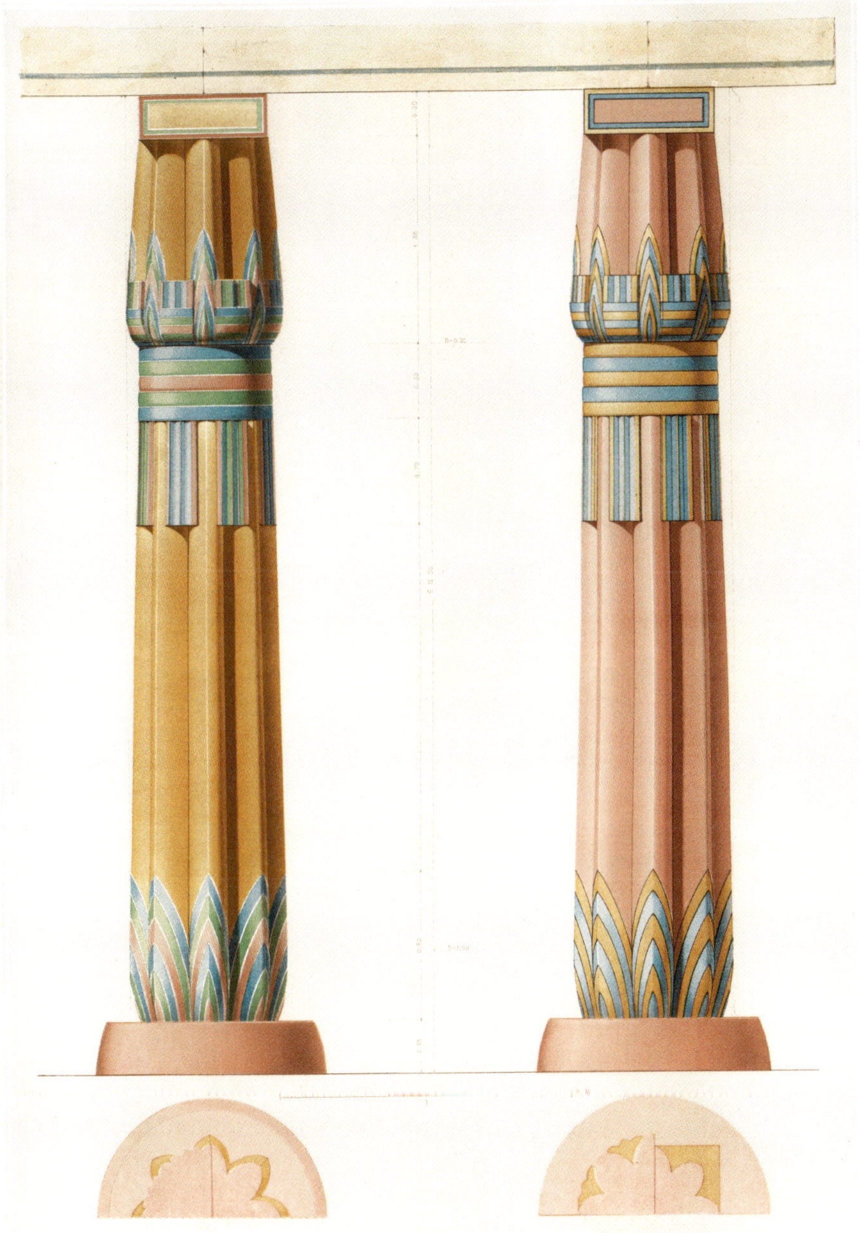

COLONNES À FAISCEAU DE THOUTMÈS III, À KARNAC.

(XVIIIE DYNASTIE.)

(Pages/Seite 237–239)

BÜNDELSÄULEN (18. Dynastie)

Bündelsäulen von Thutmosis III., in Karnak. Bündelsäulen von Amenophis III., in Theben

Der Ursprung der von mir als Bündelsäulen bezeichneten Säulen geht mindestens auf die 5. Dynastie zurück. Man findet sie auf den Flachreliefs im Grabmal des Ti in Sakkara. Diese Säulen setzen sich aus zu Bündeln zusammengeschnürten und mit Bändern verzierten Lotus-[Papyrus-]Stängeln zusammen: Anstatt sich glockenförmig zu erweitern, schwillt das Kapitell wie eine Blüte in der Knospe an und verengt sich dann wieder. Der Sockel, der sich wie ein Lotusstängel zu einer Halbkugelform verjüngt, ist ebenmäßig mit Nebenblättern verziert. Die auf der ersten Tafel [siehe S. 237] dargestellten Bündelsäulen befinden sich östlich vom Wandelgang des Thutmosis III. in Karnak. Die zweite Tafel [siehe S. 239] stellt zwei Bündelsäulen aus der Regierungszeit von Amenophis III. dar. Die Säule aus rosa Granit ist ein aus Memphis stammender Monolith, der von dort aus nach Kairo transportiert wurde. Lediglich die Verzierung war farbig und hob sich vom marmorierten Untergrund aus Syenit ab.

COLONNES À FAISCEAU (XVIIIe dynastie)

Colonnes à faisceau de Thoutmès III, à Karnac. Colonnes à faisceau d'Aménophis III, à Thèbes

L'origine des colonnes, que j'ai désignées sous le nom de colonnes à faisceau, remonte au moins à la Ve dynastie. On en trouve sur les bas-reliefs du tombeau de Teï à Sakkara. Ces colonnes se composent de tiges de lotus [papyrus], réunies en un faisceau garni de liens : le chapiteau, au lieu de s'évaser, pour prendre une forme campanulée, se gonfle, puis se resserre comme la fleur dans son bourgeon.
La base, qui se rétrécit pour prendre une forme demi-globuleuse, comme la tige du lotus, est constamment ornée de stipules. Les colonnes à faisceau, représentées dans la première planche [voir p. 237], se trouvent à l'est du promenoir de Thoutmès [Thoutmôsis] III à Karnac. La seconde planche [voir p. 239] représente deux colonnes à faisceau du règne d'Aménophis III. Celle en granit rose est monolithe, et provient de Memphis d'où elle a été transportée au Kaire. La décoration seule était coloriée et se détachait sur le fond jaspé du syénite.

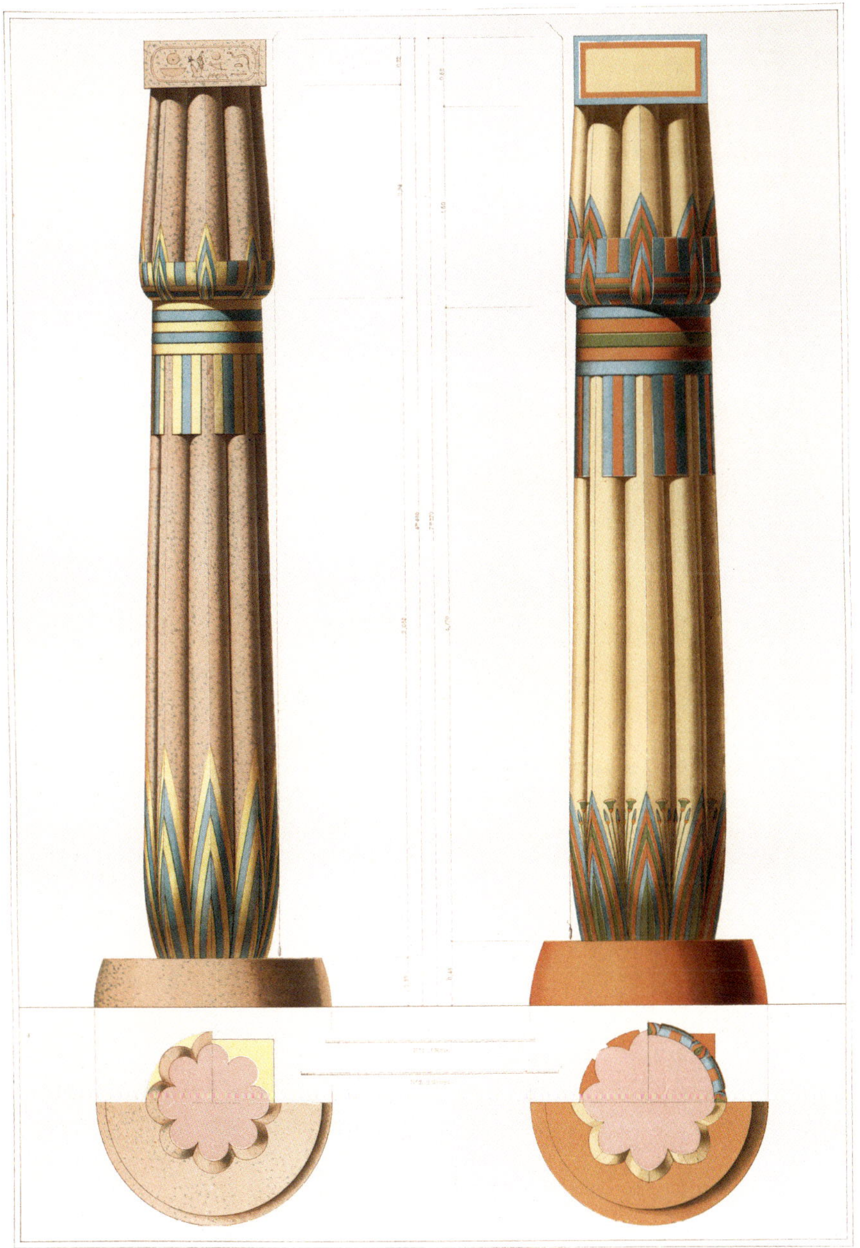

COLONNES A FAISCEAU D'AMENOPHIS III, A THÈBES

(XVIIIE DYNASTIE.)

COLUMN FROM THE RAMESSEUM (18th [sic, 19th] Dynasty)

Thebes

Architects claim to have identified the origin of columns in tree trunks planted in the soil: on this hypothesis, the base and the capital would be the imitation of the bands of green wood and of iron which were later fastened round the tops of the trees to prevent them from splitting. It does in fact seem that the Egyptian builders retained the memory of this original form in a number of their columns, where the shaft is incised and covered with scales and the capital decorated with palms and fruits. The bell-shaped capital with the flower or the bud of the lotus or papyrus was commonly used, as also was the dactyliform column. Finally, a capital with a bunch of flax or any other kind of flowers often features in the most ancient paintings.

SÄULE AUS DEM RAMESSEUM (18. [sic, 19.] Dynastie)

Theben

Die Architekten behaupten, in dem am Boden aufgestellten Baumstamm den Ursprung der Säule erkennen zu können: Sockel und Kapitell ahmten die Bänder aus grünem Holz und später aus Eisen nach, die man an der Spitze anbrachte, damit sich der Baum nicht spalten konnte. Tatsächlich scheinen die ägyptischen Baumeister die Erinnerung an diesen Ursprung in einigen ihrer Säulen bewahrt zu haben, deren ziselierter Schaft mit Schuppen bedeckt und deren Kapitell mit Palmzweigen und Früchten verziert ist. Das glockenförmige Kapitell mit der Lotus- oder Papyrus-Knospe oder -Blüte und auch die Palmsäule waren gebräuchlich. Die ältesten Malereien stellen schließlich auch ein Kapitell mit Flachsbüscheln oder irgendeiner anderen Blume dar.

COLONNE DU RAMESSEUM (XVIIIe [sic, XIXe] dynastie)

Thèbes

Les architectes prétendent reconnaître l'origine des colonnes dans les troncs d'arbres plantés en terre : la base et le chapiteau seraient l'imitation des liens de bois vert et du fer que, plus tard, on mit au sommet des arbres pour les empêcher de se fendre. Les constructeurs égyptiens semblent en effet avoir conservé le souvenir de cette origine dans plusieurs de leurs colonnes dont le fût est ciselé et couvert d'écailles, et dont le chapiteau est orné de palmes et de fruits. Le chapiteau à campane avec la fleur ou le bouton de lotus ou de papyrus, et aussi la colonne dactyliforme, furent usités. Enfin, un chapiteau à touffe de lin ou toute autre fleur est aussi représenté dans les plus anciennes peintures.

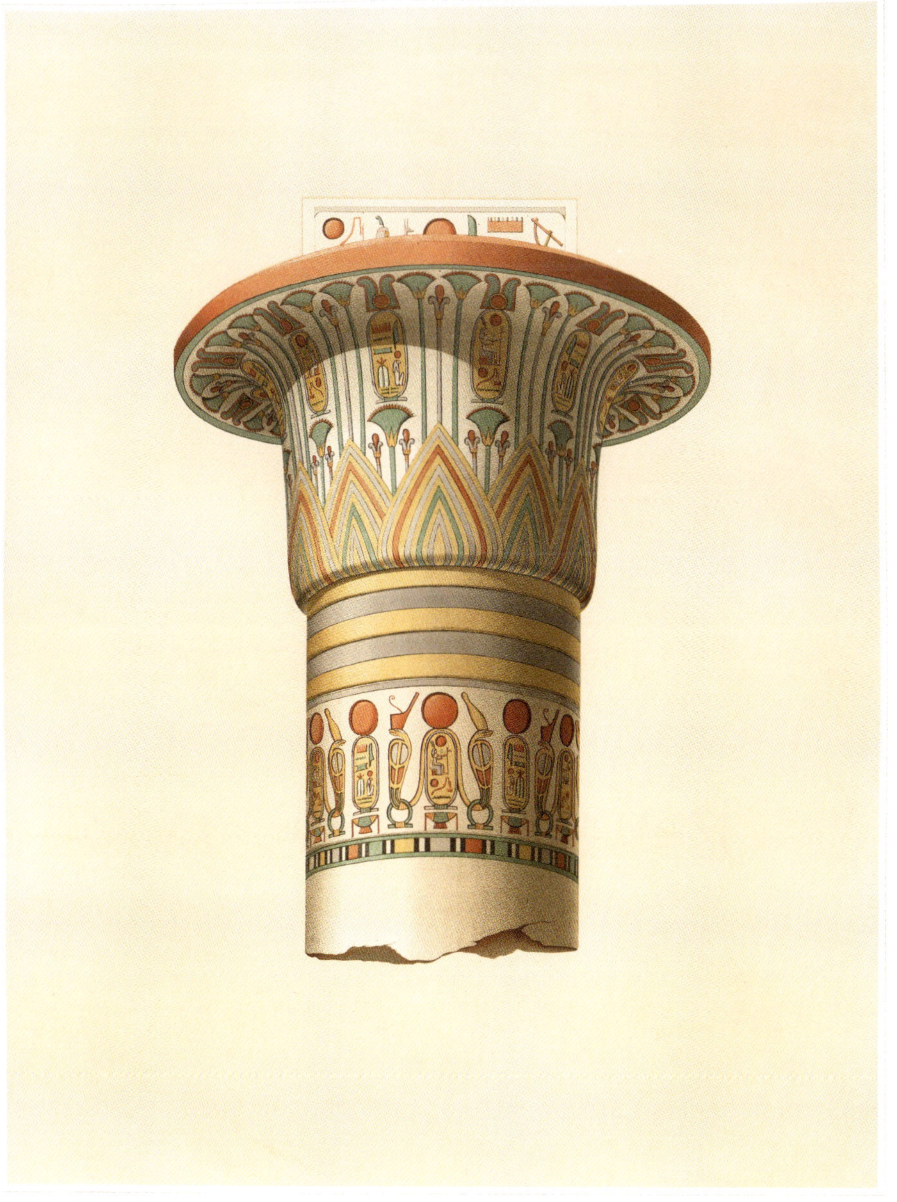

COLONNE DU RAMESSEUM.

(THÈBES)

CAPITALS FROM THE TEMPLES AT EDFU AND PHILAE (18th Dynasty)

Considering the variety of capitals which decorate the temples of Esna, Edfu, Kom Ombo and Philae, most of which combine purity of contour with a quite remarkable richness and choice of ornamentation, it is astonishing that it was once thought that just three architectural orders alone constituted the true beauty of that art and that, beyond these, nothing was in good taste and nothing was correct. The Greeks invented stories to disguise their plagiarism of Egyptian forms, but the Egyptians had no need of similar fabrications: they copied nature and in her found inspiration to produce their most beautiful works of art. The calyx of the lotus flower poised on its clustering stem furnished the shape of the column, its base and its capital, while the palm tree provided a second model and the rushes yet another, of great originality, amongst forms which were as graceful as they were varied.

KAPITELLE DER TEMPEL VON EDFU UND PHILAE (18. Dynastie)

Betrachtet man den Abwechslungsreichtum der Kapitelle, die die Tempel von Esna, Edfu, Kom Ombo und Philae zieren und bei denen sich klare Konturen zumeist mit einer bemerkenswerten Vielfalt in der Ornamentwahl paaren, so verwundert, wie man glauben konnte, dass drei [Säulen-]Ordnungen die alleinige Schönheit der Kunst ausmachten und es darüber hinaus nichts Besseres, Geschmackvolleres gäbe. Die Griechen erfanden Geschichten, um ihre kleinen Diebereien zu verbergen. Die Ägypter haben solche Fabeln nicht nötig: Sie haben in der Natur die schönsten Hervorbringungen der Kunst gefunden und diese nachgeahmt. Der Kelch der Lotusblume über dem Büschel ihrer Stängel hat der Säule mit Sockel und Kapitell die Form verliehen. Das zweite Vorbild war die Palme. Die Binse hat zu den ebenso anmutigen wie abwechslungsreichen Formen eine weitere, sehr bemerkenswerte beigesteuert.

CHAPITEAUX DES TEMPLES D'EDFOU ET DE PHILÆ (XVIIIe dynastie)

Lorsqu'on considère cette variété de chapiteaux qui ornent les temples d'Esné [Esna], d'Edfou, d'Ombos [Kôm Ombo] et de Philæ, et qui pour la plupart joignent à la pureté des contours une richesse et un choix d'ornements remarquables, on est tout étonné d'avoir cru que trois ordres étaient les seules beautés de l'art, que, hors de là, point de goût, point de correction. Les Grecs, pour pallier leurs larcins, ont inventé des histoires. Les Égyptiens n'ont pas besoin de fables pareilles : ils ont copié la nature et ont trouvé chez elle les plus belles productions de l'art. Le calice de la fleur de lotus, au-dessus du faisceau de sa tige, a fourni la forme de la colonne, de sa base et de son chapiteau. Le palmier a été le second modèle. Les joncs en ont fourni un autre très remarquable parmi les formes aussi gracieuses que variées.

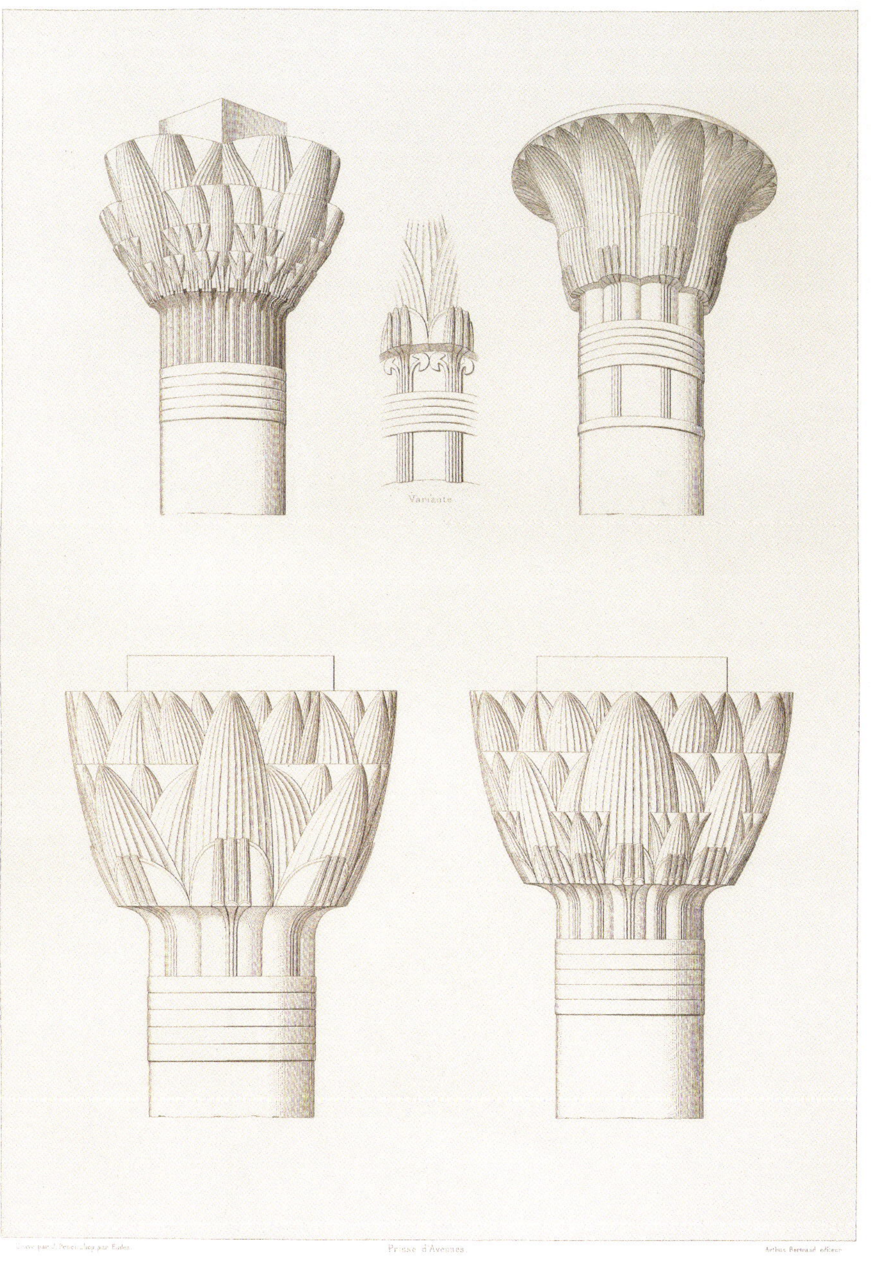

Gravé par J. Penel, imp. par Eudes. Prisse d'Avennes. Arthus Bertrand éditeur

CHAPITEAUX DES TEMPLES D'EDFOU ET DE PHILÆ.

(XVIIIE DYNASTIE)

COMPOSITE CAPITALS (18th Dynasty)

Temple of Philae

This capital, decorated with caulicole leaves with pendant drops and palm fronds with curved supports, has been painted at least twice; the most ancient colour scheme features blue leaves with green fronds, while the colours of the most recent scheme are as seen in the plate. The volutes, which are always found at the edges of scrolled leaves, are of the same colour.

BLATTKAPITELL (18. Dynastie)

Tempel von Philae

Dieses durch gestielte Blätter mit herabhängenden Tropfen und Palmetten mit gewölbtem Boden verzierte Kapitell wurde mindestens zweimal bemalt. Die ältere Bemalung zeigte blaue Blätter mit grüner Äderung; die jüngere ist wie auf der Tafel gefärbt. Die Voluten, bei denen es sich stets um die aufgerollten Blattspitzen handelt, sind von derselben Farbe.

CHAPITEAU À CAULICOLES (XVIIIe dynastie)

Temple de Philæ

Ce chapiteau, orné de feuilles à caulicoles avec gouttes pendantes et de palmettes à culot bombé, a été colorié au moins deux fois. La plus ancienne coloration présentait des feuilles bleues avec des aigrettes vertes ; la plus récente est coloriée comme sur la planche. Les volutes, qui sont toujours les extrémités des feuilles enroulées, sont de la même couleur.

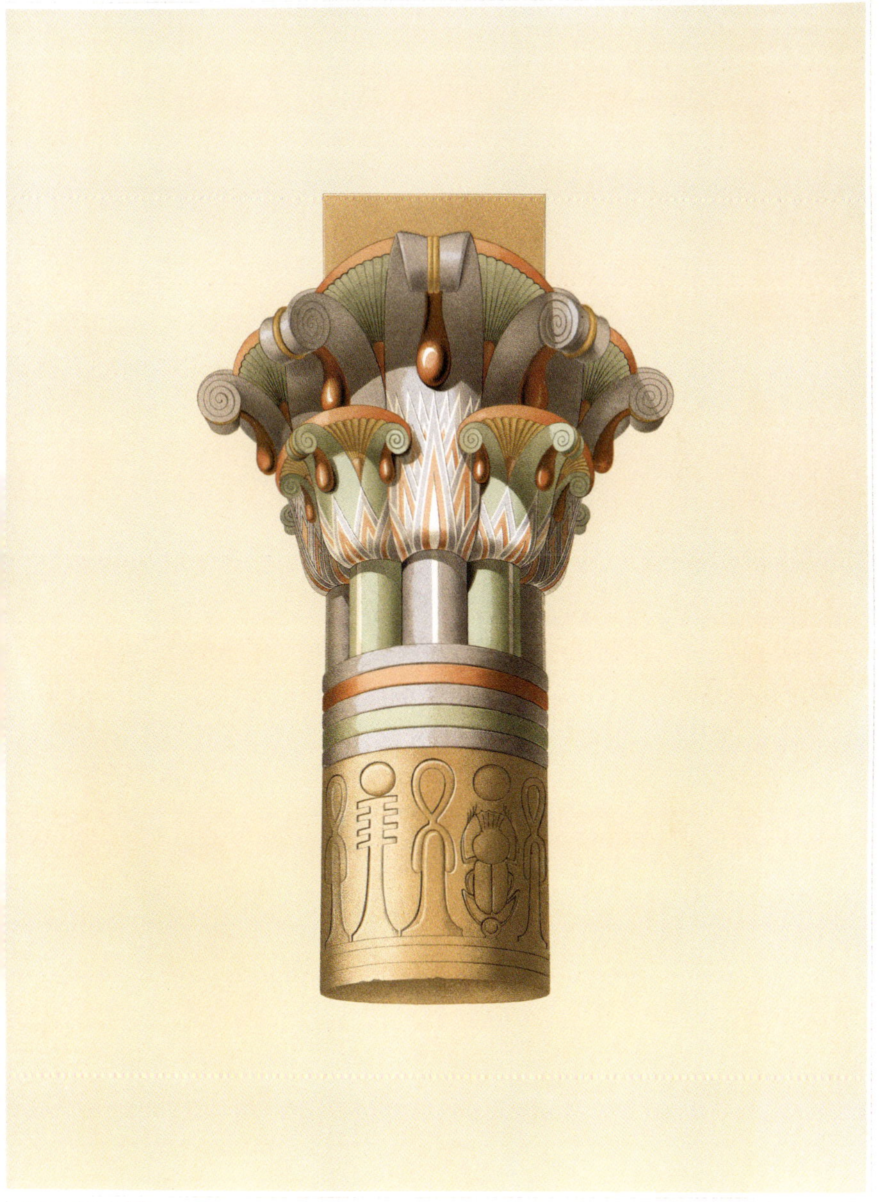

Publié par Arthus Bertrand Éditeur

CHAPITEAU À CAULICOLES

(TEMPLE DE PHILÆ. XVIIIe DYNASTIE)

CRATERIFORM CAPITAL (18th Dynasty)

This capital shaped like a cup or a vase whose form, like that of all the others, was taken from nature, presents a picture of the "ciborium" or lotus fruit described by Herodotus, Athenaeus and Theophrastus. There can be no doubt of this in view of the fact that Athenaeus compares the "ciborium" to a honeycomb. Yet further proof that this capital is indeed imitated from the capsule of the lotus is that it is clearly covered with folia, alternately thin and sharp or oval and irregular, and these correspond exactly with the appearance of the fruits of the *Nymphæa* lotus and of the *Nymphæa curulea*. It is called crateriform after the name of the vase which the people of antiquity used for the lotus capsules.

KRATERFÖRMIGES KAPITELL (18. Dynastie)

Dieses Kapitell in Form einer Schale oder Vase, dessen Gestalt wie die aller anderen der Natur nachempfunden ist, ist ein Abbild der von Herodot, Athenaios und Theophrastos beschriebenen Lotusfrucht *(„ciborium")*. Bedenkt man, dass Athenaios das *„ciborium"* mit den Honigwaben der Biene vergleicht, ist daran kein Zweifel möglich. Dass dieses Kapitell tatsächlich ein nachempfundenes Samengehäuse der Lotuspflanze darstellt, zeigt sich auch daran, dass es bald mit schmalen und spitzen, bald mit ungleichmäßigen eiförmigen Blättchen bedeckt ist; diese beiden Merkmale kennzeichnen nun aber die Früchte der *Nymphæa lotus* und der *Nymphæa curulea*. Nach dem Vasennamen, den die Alten der Lotusblüte gaben, bezeichnete man es als kraterförmig.

CHAPITEAU CRATÉRIFORME (XVIIIe dynastie)

Ce chapiteau en forme de coupe ou de vase, dont la forme, comme celle de tous les autres, est puisée dans la nature, représente l'image du « ciborium » ou fruit du lotus décrit par Hérodote, Athénée et Théophraste. Il est impossible d'en douter quand on voit qu'Athénée compare le « ciborium » aux rayons du miel des abeilles. Ce qui prouve encore que ce chapiteau est bien l'imitation de la capsule du lotus, c'est qu'on le voit recouvert tantôt de folioles étroites et aiguës, tantôt de folioles ovoïdes et inégales ; or, ces deux caractères appartiennent exactement aux fruits du *nymphæa lotus* et au *nymphæa curulea*. [On] l'a appelé cratériforme, d'après le nom de vase que les anciens ont donné à la capsule du lotus.

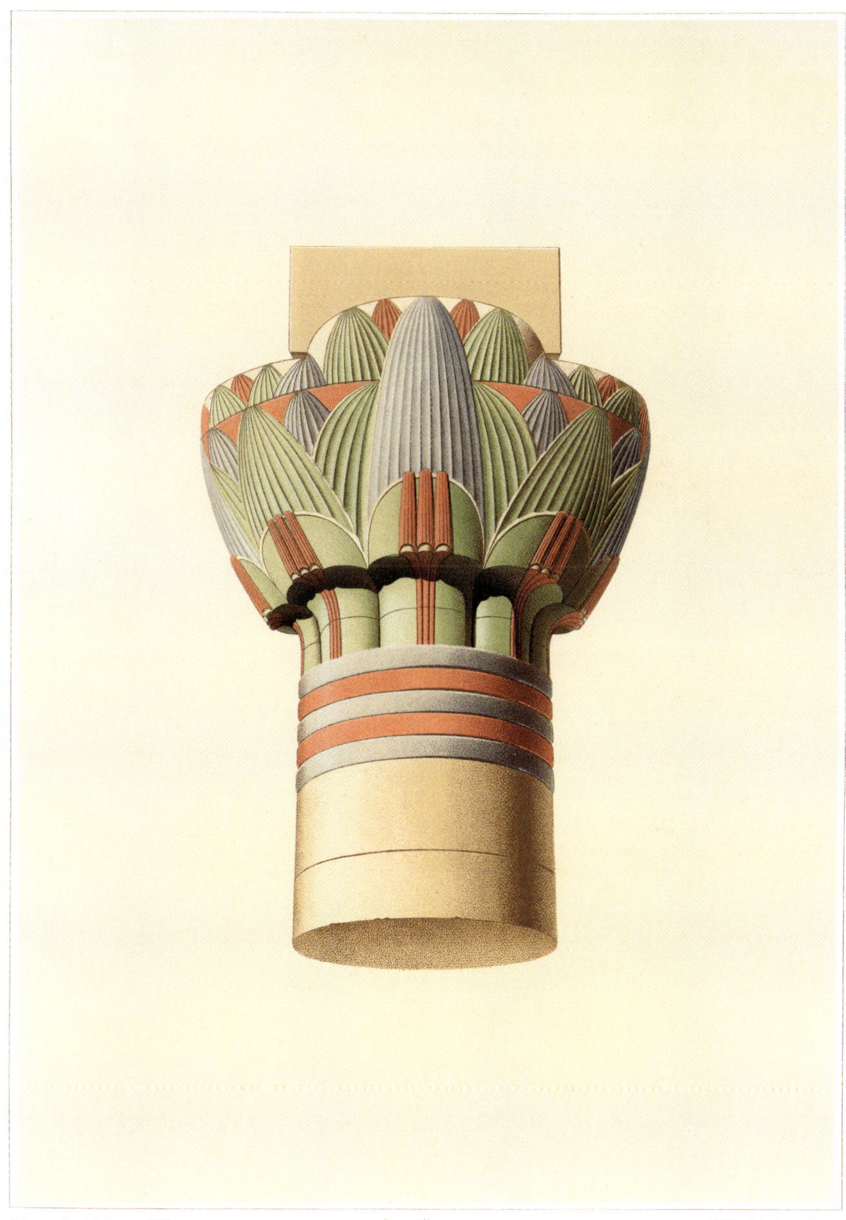

Exécuté par Levil . Imp. Lemercier & Cie Paris — Prisse d'Avennes — Publié par Arthus Bertrand, Éditeur

CHAPITEAU CRATÉRIFORME

(XVIIIe DYNASTIE)

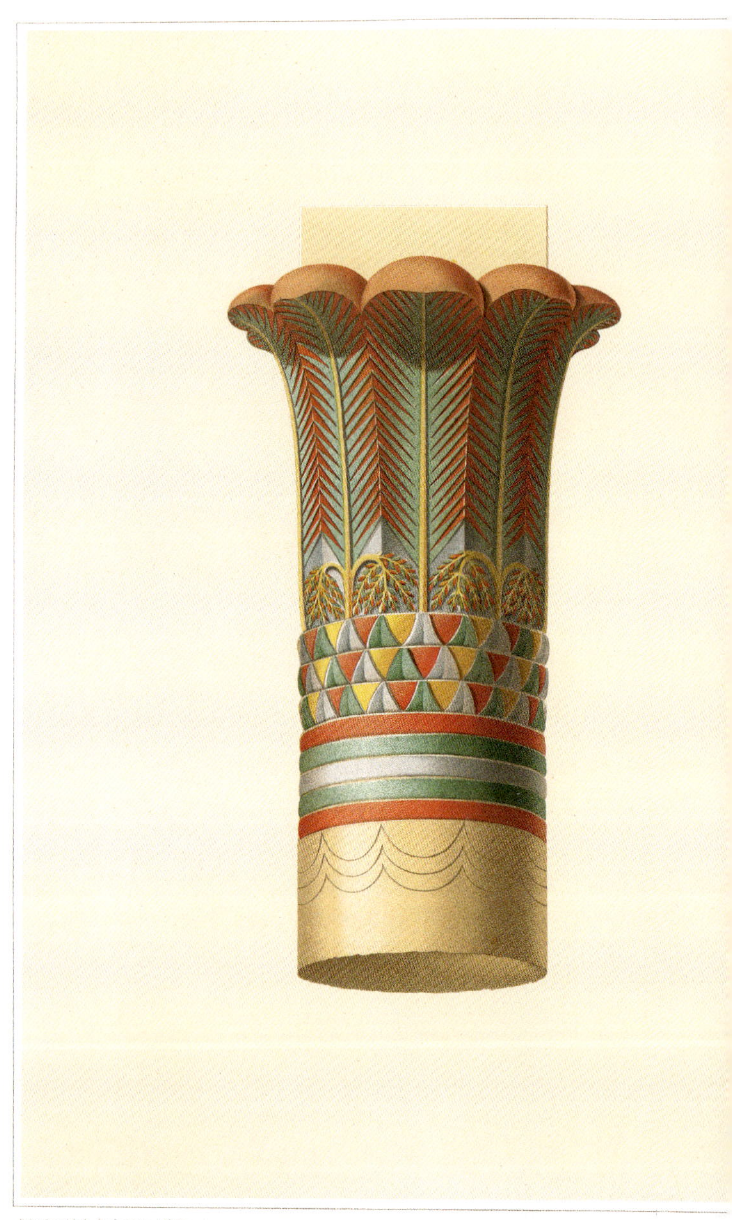

Exécuté par Lévié Imp. Lemercier & Cie Paris

CHAPITE

I 58

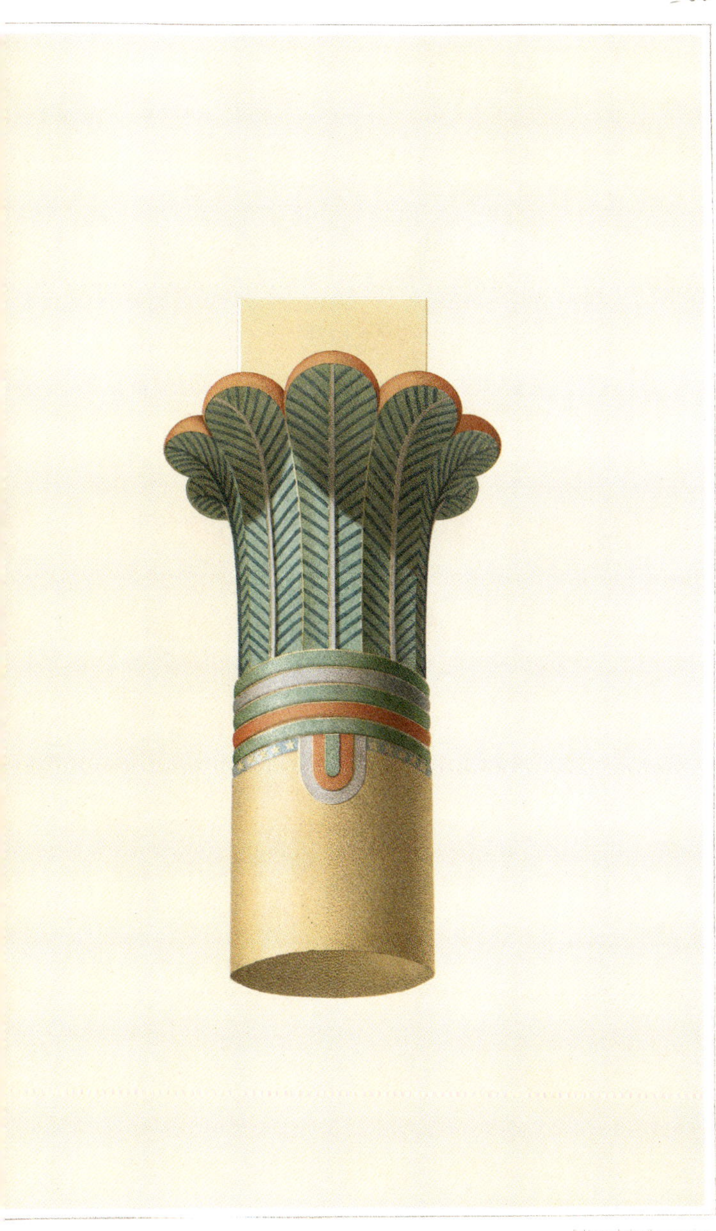

Publié par Arthus Bertrand, éditeur

IFORMES

(Pages/Seite 248/249)

DACTYLIFORM CAPITALS (18th Dynasty)

Philae

In the buildings at Philae there are five dactyliform capitals, each of which presents very different features. This plate shows two of these capitals: the first, which is part of the west gallery, is much more regular than the other. It is decorated with scales above the collars and with bunches of dates immediately above the scales, but the whole is fairly crudely carved. The second is not decorated with fruits and the collars are placed directly against the bottom of the palm fronds, while the base is decorated with chevrons similar to those of the other columns in this gallery.

PALMWEDEL-KAPITELLE (18. Dynastie)

Philae

In den Bauwerken von Philae finden sich fünf Palmwedel-Kapitelle, die alle deutliche Unterschiede aufweisen. Auf dieser Tafel sind zwei dieser Kapitelle abgebildet: Das erste stammt aus dem westlichen Wandelgang und ist viel harmonischer gestaltet als das andere; es ist oberhalb der Manschetten mit Schuppen und unmittelbar oberhalb der Schuppen mit Dattelbüscheln verziert; das Ganze ist jedoch recht grob gearbeitet. Was das zweite betrifft, so ist es nicht mit Früchten verziert, und die Manschetten beginnen unterhalb der Palmwedel, wobei der Sockel mit einem Fischgrätmuster geschmückt ist, das dem der anderen Säulen in diesem Wandelgang ähnelt.

CHAPITEAUX DACTYLIFORMES (XVIIIe dynastie)

Philæ

Il y a dans les édifices de Philæ cinq chapiteaux dactyliformes qui présentent tous des différences notables. Cette planche représente deux de ces chapiteaux : le premier, qui fait partie de la galerie de l'ouest, est beaucoup plus régulier que l'autre ; il est orné d'écailles au-dessus des viroles, et de grappes de dattes immédiatement au-dessus des écailles ; mais le tout est assez grossièrement sculpté. Quant au second, il n'est pas orné de fruits, et les viroles commencent en bas des palmes, tandis que la base est décorée de chevrons semblables à ceux des autres colonnes de cette galerie.

CEILING PATTERNS: EARLY FORMS
(12th to 22nd Dynasties)

The taste displayed in these free-style compositions definitely did not come from the printed fabrics originating in India. It was born in Egypt, where its appearance occurs well before the inhabitants made their first conquests in Asia. As early as the period of the pyramids, ceilings and in particular hangings or backgrounds of rush-work are to be found which reveal considerable taste and which clearly constitute the origins of a decorative style which developed as advances were made in the art. The squares composed of lozenges, zigzags or chevrons, the spirals and of course the free-style designs which are typical of the earliest attempts at decoration were adornments which were born of themselves under the hand of the craftsman producing the rush-work.

DECKENVERZIERUNGEN: URSPRÜNGLICHE FORMEN
(12. bis 22. Dynastie)

Die Vorliebe für diese eigenwilligen Arrangements kam keineswegs mit den bedruckten Stoffen aus Indien. Sie entstand in Ägypten, lange bevor dieses Volk seine Eroberungen in Asien machte. Bereits von der Pyramidenzeit an fallen die Decken und vor allem die Wandbehänge oder auch die Böden in Flechtwerk auf, die viel Schönheitssinn erkennen lassen und offensichtlich den Ursprung einer Ornamentik bilden, die sich mit der Entfaltung der Künste entwickelt hat. Die aus Rauten zusammengesetzten Quadrate, die Zickzack- oder Fischgrätmuster, die Spiralen, schließlich die Launen, die die ersten Verzierungsproben kennzeichnen, sind Muster, die ganz von selbst unter der Hand des Korb- und Mattenflechters entstehen.

ORNEMENTATION DES PLAFONDS : FORMES PRIMITIVES
(XIIe à XXIIe dynastie)

Le goût de ces compositions capricieuses n'est point venu de l'Inde par ses toiles imprimées. Il est né en Égypte, où on le voit paraître bien avant les conquêtes de ce peuple en Asie. Dès l'époque des pyramides, on remarque déjà des plafonds et surtout des tentures ou fonds de sparterie, qui décèlent beaucoup de goût, et ont été, visiblement, l'origine d'une ornementation qui s'est développée avec les progrès de l'art. Les carrés composés de losanges, les zigzags ou chevrons, les spirales, les caprices, enfin, qui marquent les premiers essais de décoration, sont des ornements qui naissent d'eux-mêmes sous la main du faiseur de sparterie.

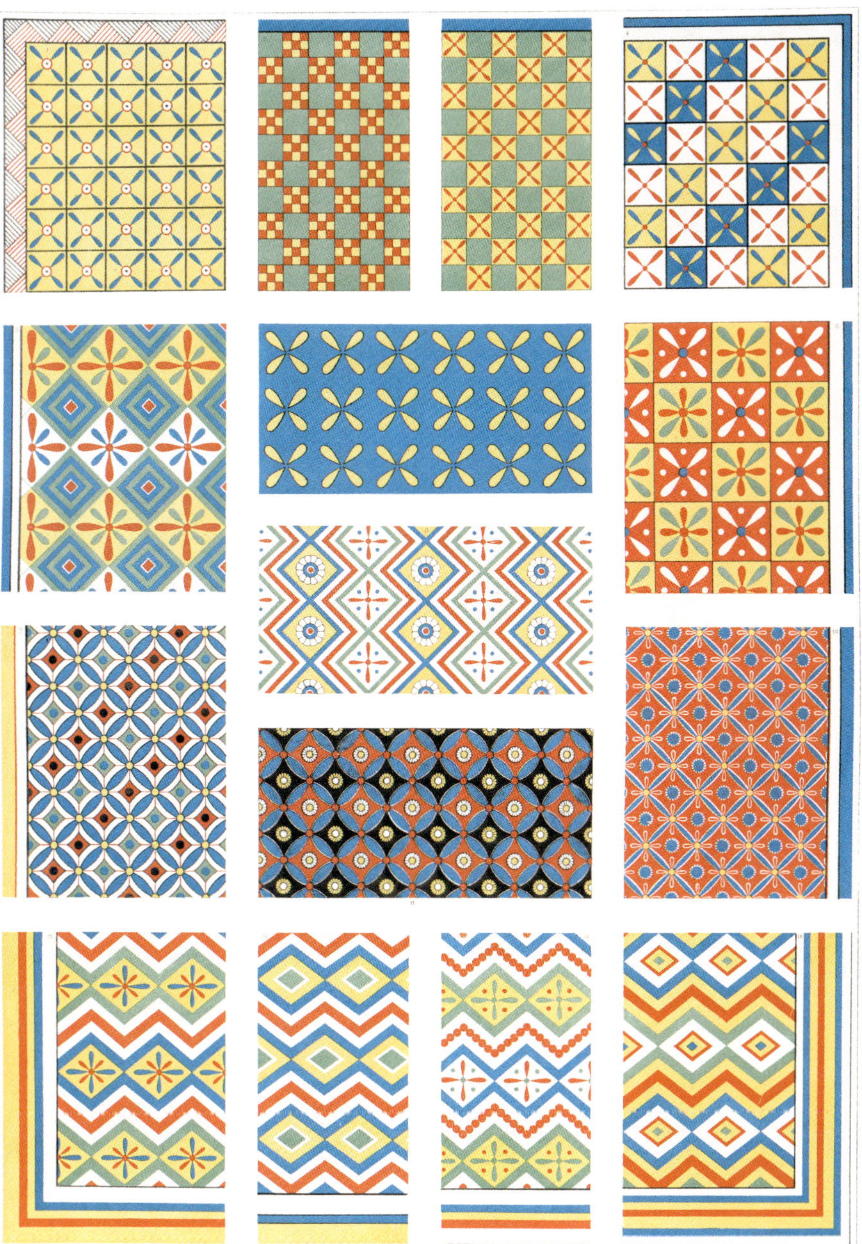

Lith. par Saladin. Imp. par Hangard Maugé.   E. Prisse d'Avennes.   Publié par Arthus Bertrand, Editeur.

ORNEMENTATION DES PLAFONDS : FORMES PRIMITIVES

DE LA XIIe A LA XXIIe DYNASTIE.

CEILING PATTERNS: GUILLOCHES AND MEANDERS (17th to 20th Dynasties)

Necropolis of Thebes

Widely differing types of decoration have often been confused under the same name by including them in the general category of Greek-style ornamentation, whereas they actually belong in the Egyptian artistic tradition. The "guilloche", which is incorrectly confused with the meander, is a decoration consisting of two lines running in parallel, but they must always create a right angle. The name meander should be reserved for the scrolls which are also known as posts, whose twisting and turning can only represent the sinuous curves of a river. [...] On examining the three sections at the top of the plate, all three being taken from the same tomb, it can be seen that the two outer ones are created from a medial guilloche and that it is basically only in their colouring that the sections differ. In the middle row, the scrolls spring from the preceding guilloches, although at first sight the three designs all appear very different.

DECKENVERZIERUNGEN: GUILLOCHEN UND MÄANDER (17. bis 20. Dynastie)

Nekropole von Theben

Häufig vermengte man sehr unterschiedliche Muster unter demselben Namen, indem man sie unter der allgemeinen Bezeichnung „griechisches Ornament" zusammenfasste, obwohl sie zur ägyptischen Kunst gehören. Die Guilloche, die man zu Unrecht mit dem Mäander verwechselt, ist ein Ornament, das sich aus zwei parallel verlaufenden Linien zusammensetzt, die jedoch immer einen rechten Winkel bilden müssen. Die Bezeichnung Mäander sollte den auch Wellenband genannten Schneckenlinien vorbehalten bleiben, die allein durch ihren Wechsel die Windungen eines Flusses abbilden können. [...] Bei Betrachtung der drei oberen Felder der Tafel – die alle demselben Grab entnommen sind – sieht man, dass die beiden äußeren sich aus der mittleren Guilloche entwickelt haben und dass diese Felder sich im Wesentlichen nur durch die Farbgebung unterscheiden. Im mittleren Register entstehen die Spiralen – trotz des großen Unterschiedes, den sie auf den ersten Blick aufweisen – aus den ihnen vorhergehenden Guillochen.

ORNEMENTATION DES PLAFONDS : GUILLOCHIS ET MÉANDRES (XVIIe à XXe dynastie)

Nécropole de Thèbes

On a souvent confondu, sous le même nom, des ornements fort divers, en les comprenant sous la dénomination générale d'ornements à la grecque, bien qu'ils appartinssent à l'art égyptien. Le guillochis, que l'on confond à tort avec le méandre, est un ornement composé de deux lignes qui marchent parallèlement ensemble, cependant elles doivent toujours faire l'angle droit. Le nom de méandres doit être réservé aux enroulements appelés aussi postes, qui peuvent seuls représenter par leurs retours les sinuosités d'un fleuve. [...] Si l'on examine les trois compartiments supérieurs de la planche, tous trois tirés d'un même tombeau, on verra que les deux extrêmes s'engendrent du guillochis médial et que ces compartiments ne diffèrent essentiellement que par les couleurs. Dans le registre intermédiaire, les enroulements naissent du guillochis qui les précède, malgré la grande différence qu'ils présentent au premier coup d'œil.

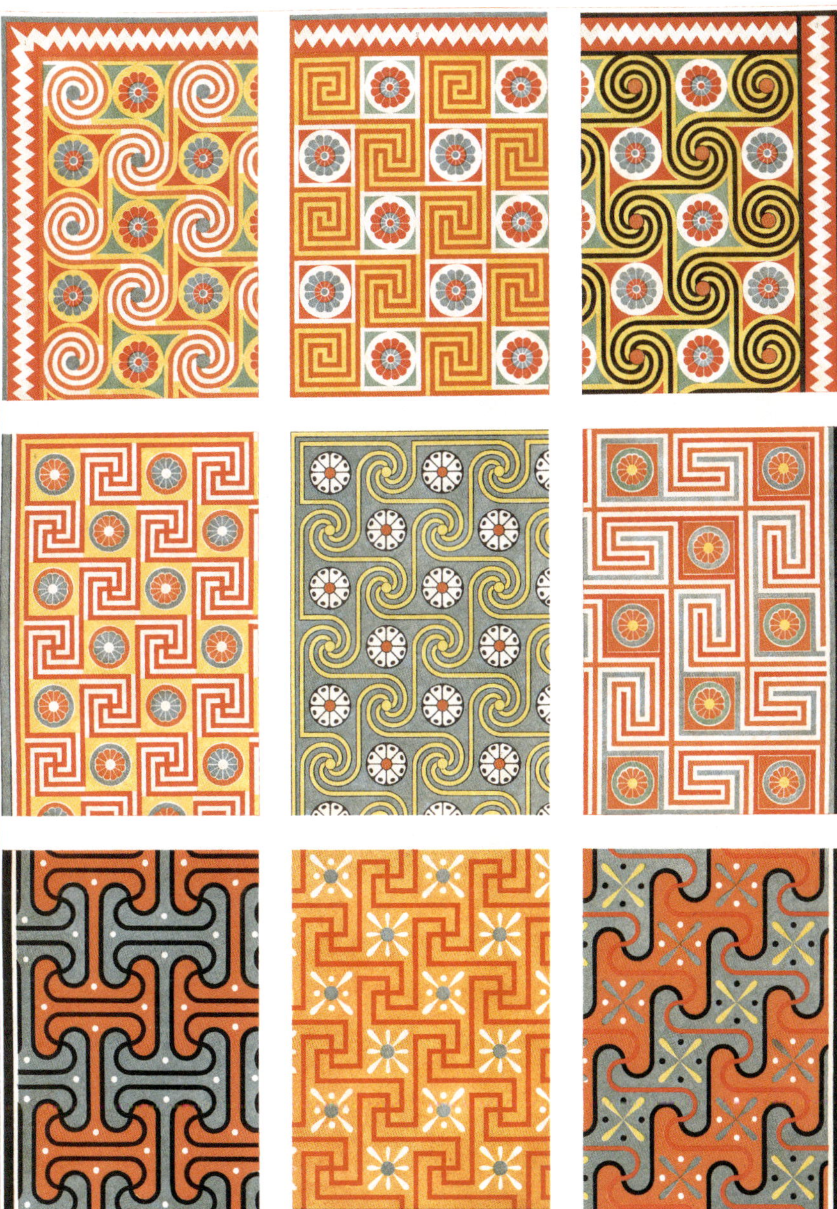

Lith. par Saladini. Imp. par Hangar! Maugé. E. Prisse d'Avennes. Publié par Arthus-Bertrand, Editeur.

ORNEMENTATION DES PLAFONDS : GUILLOCHIS & MÉANDRES.

(NÉCROPOLE DE THÈBES. — XVIIe à XXe DYN.)

CEILING PATTERNS: INSCRIPTIONS AND SYMBOLS (18th Dynasty)

Necropolis of Thebes

The scrolls and lotus flowers which framed the bucrania are shown here as being almost the same; they are grouped around rosaces alternating with hieroglyphic inscriptions or winged scarabs. The ceiling at the top of the plate is taken from the hypogeum of the "Divine Father Neferhotep", whose repeated name and titles are worked into the decoration. [...] The ceiling beneath was copied from an alcove in the tomb of Ramose, located a hundred paces south of the hypogeum of Neferhotep. The scarab with spread wings supporting the globe of the sun and rolling another sphere between its hind legs is the symbol of rebirth into life eternal for humanity. According to Egyptian belief, the scarab was always male; this is why they made it the symbol of paternal and, in a mystical sense, divine procreation. Hence, in the Ptolemaic and Roman Periods, the scarab became the symbol of the world.

DECKENVERZIERUNGEN: INSCHRIFTEN UND SYMBOLE (18. Dynastie)

Nekropole von Theben

Die Spiralen und die Lotusblüten, die die Bukranien einrahmten, stellen sich hier annähernd gleich dar, obwohl sie als Einfassung für Rosetten dienen, die alternierend mit Hieroglypheninschriften oder geflügelten Skarabäen versehen waren. Die obere Decke ist dem Hypogäum des „Göttlichen Vaters Neferhotep“ entnommen, wobei die Wiederholungen seines Namens und seiner Titel zur Verzierung beitragen. [...] Die untere Decke wurde in einer Nische im Grab des Ramose abgezeichnet, das sich hundert Schritte südlich des Hypogäums von Neferhotep befindet. Der Skarabäus, der mit ausgebreiteten Flügeln die Sonnenkugel trägt und mit seinen Hinterbeinen eine weitere Kugel rollt, ist das Sinnbild der menschlichen Wiedergeburt zum ewigen Leben. Im Glauben der Ägypter waren alle Skarabäen männlichen Geschlechts; deshalb machten sie daraus das Sinnbild der männlichen und – in einem mystischen Sinn – der göttlichen Fortpflanzung. Daher wurde der Skarabäus in ptolemäischer und römischer Zeit zum Weltsymbol.

ORNEMENTATION DES PLAFONDS : LÉGENDES ET SYMBOLES (XVIIIe dynastie)

Nécropole de Thèbes

Les enroulements et les fleurs de lotus qui encadraient les bucrânes se représentent ici à peu près les mêmes, quoique servant d'entourage à des rosaces, alternées de légendes hiéroglyphiques ou de scarabées ailés. Le plafond supérieur est tiré de l'hypogée du « Père divin Nofrehotep » [Néferhotep], dont le nom et les titres répétés concourent à l'ornementation. [...] Le plafond intérieur a été copié dans une niche du tombeau de Ramés, situé à cent pas au sud de l'hypogée de Nofrehotep. Le scarabée aux ailes déployées soutenant le globe du soleil, roulant entre ses pattes inférieures une autre boule, est le symbole de la renaissance du genre humain pour une vie éternelle. Dans la croyance des Égyptiens, les scarabées étaient tous mâles ; c'est pourquoi ils en avaient fait le symbole de la génération paternelle et, dans un sens mystique, de la génération divine. C'est de là qu'aux époques ptolémaïques et romaines le scarabée est devenu le symbole du monde.

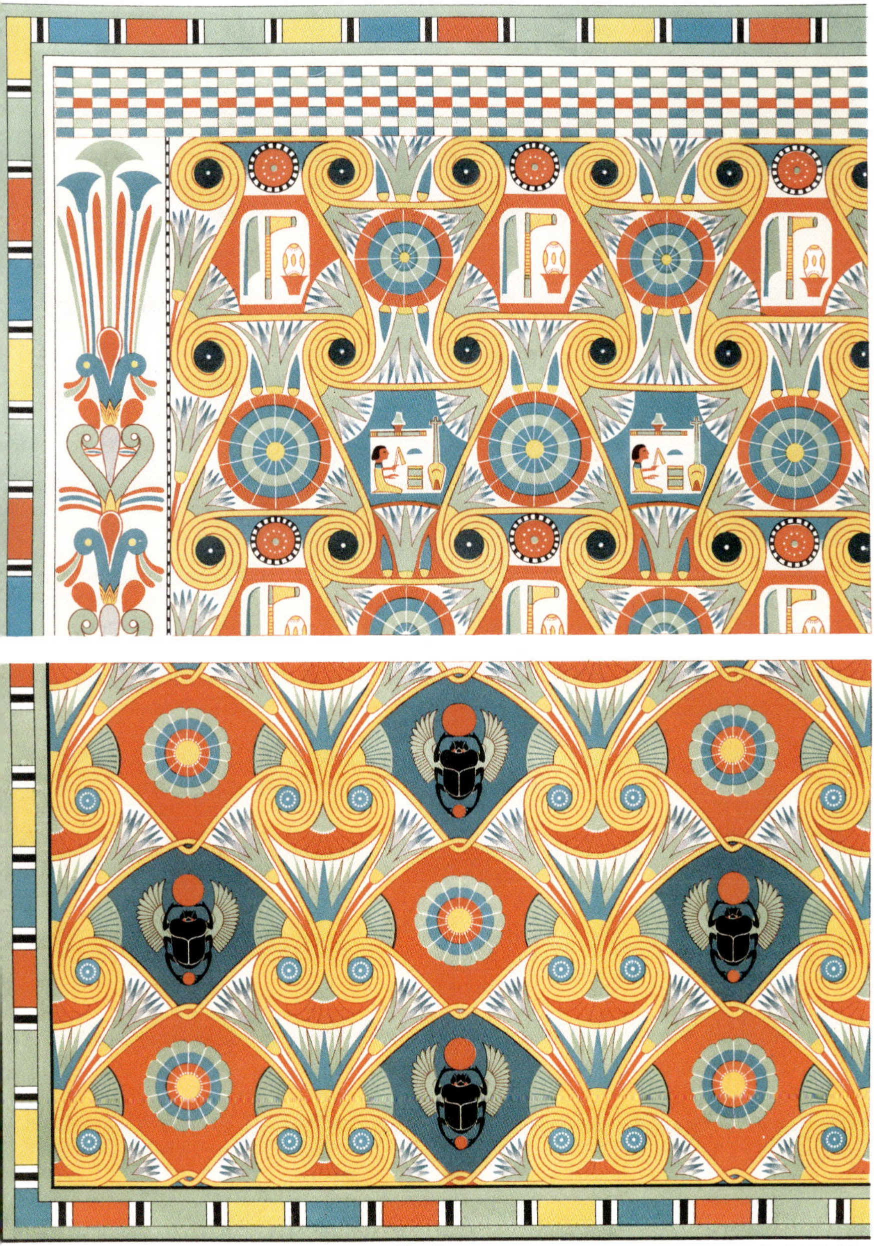

Lith par Saladin. _ Imp par Hangard-Maugé.

E. Prisse d'Avennes.

Publié par Arthus Bertrand, Éditeur.

ORNEMENTATION DES PLAFONDS : LÉGENDES ET SYMBOLES.

(NÉCROPOLE DE THÈBES : XVIIIe DYNASTIE.)

CEILING PATTERNS: POSTS WITH FLEURONS (18th to 19th Dynasties)

Necropolis of Thebes

This plate features nine examples of decorations which all stem from the same principle, namely that of rippling lines formed of ropes scrolled into volutes or unrolling into spirals, types of posts which cross or confront each other, enclosing in the spaces which they define lotus flowers, rosettes, fleurons or simple squares. Nos. 1, 2 and 3 display the same combination, varied only by a few details of form or colour. No. 3 comes from the beautiful hypogeum of Imiseba. No. 4, drawn from the hypogeum of Neferhotep, and no. 6 display an identical layout. No. 5 also comes from the same tomb of Imiseba. No. 8 comes from a hypogeum which retains almost nothing apart from this piece of decoration. And finally nos. 7 and 9 constitute the two adjoining sections of the ceiling of a small tomb situated near the temple of Hathor in the valley of el-Assasif.

DECKENVERZIERUNGEN: WELLENBÄNDER MIT BLUMENZIERRAT (18. und 19. Dynastie)

Nekropole von Theben

Auf dieser Tafel befinden sich neun Ornamentbeispiele, die alle demselben Prinzip entspringen, nämlich dem der durch Seile gebildeten, wellenförmigen Linien, die sich zu Voluten zusammen- oder in Spiralen entrollen – eine Art von Wellenbändern, die sich verschränken oder kreuzen und in den durch sie begrenzten Räumen Lotus, Rosetten, stilisierte Blumen und Blätter oder einfache Quadrate umschließen. Die Nr. 1, 2 und 3 weisen dieselbe Zusammenstellung auf, mit Abweichungen in einigen farblichen oder formalen Einzelheiten. Die Nr. 3 stammt aus dem schönen Hypogäum des Imiseba. Die Nr. 4, die dem Hypogäum des Neferhotep entnommen ist, und die Nr. 6 zeigen genau dieselbe Anordnung. Die Nr. 5 stammt ebenfalls aus dem Grab des Imiseba. Die Nr. 8 stammt aus einem Hypogäum, von dem kaum mehr als dieser Teil seiner Innenausstattung erhalten ist. Die Nr. 7 und 9 schließlich bilden zwei benachbarte Deckenfelder in einem kleinen Grab, das sich in der Nähe des Hathor-Tempels im Tal von El-Assasif befindet.

ORNEMENTATION DES PLAFONDS : POSTES FLEURONNÉES (XVIIIe à XIXe dynastie)

Nécropole de Thèbes

Cette planche contient neuf spécimens d'ornements qui découlent tous du même principe, celui de lignes ondoyantes formées par des cordes s'enroulant en volutes ou se déroulant en spirales, espèces de postes qui se croisent ou se contrarient et renferment dans les espaces qu'elles limitent des lotus, des rosaces, des fleurons ou de simples carrés. Les n°s 1, 2, 3 présentent la même combinaison variée, seulement par quelques détails de formes ou de couleurs. Le n° 3 provient d'un bel hypogée d'Aïchési [Imiseba]. Le n° 4, tiré de l'hypogée de Nofrehotep [Néferhotep], et le n° 6 offrent, exactement, la même disposition. Le n° 5 provient aussi de ce tombeau d'Aïchesi. Le n° 8 provient d'un hypogée qui n'a guère conservé que cette partie de sa décoration. Enfin, les n°s 7 et 9 forment les deux compartiments contigus du plafond d'un petit tombeau situé prés du temple d'Hathor, dans la vallée d'El-Assacif.

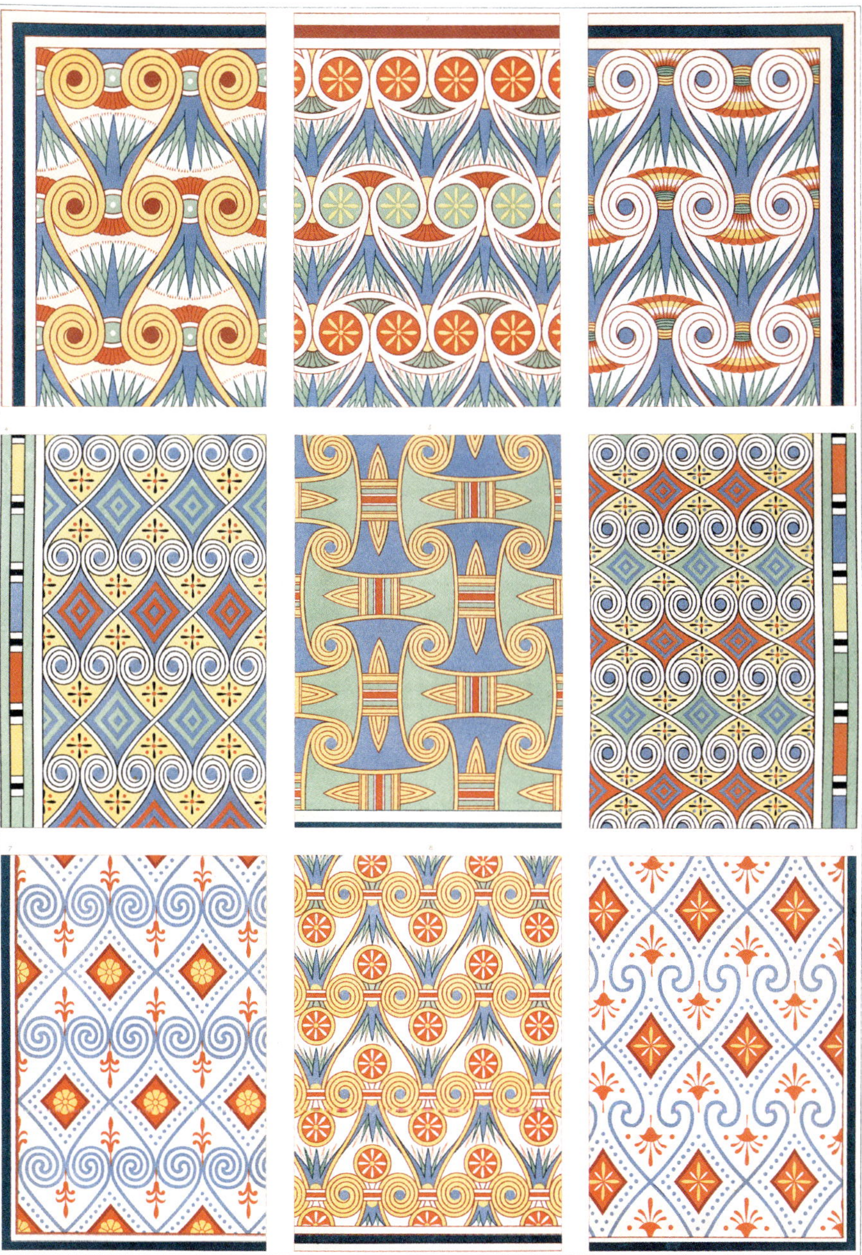

Lith. par G. Walter. Imp. par Hangard Maugé — E. Prisse d'Avennes. — Publié par Arthus-Bertrand, Éditeur

ORNEMENTATION DES PLAFONDS : POSTES FLEURONNÉES.

(NÉCROPOLE DE THÈBES. XVIIIᵉ à XIXᵉ DYN.)

CEILING PATTERNS:
POSTS AND FLOWERS (18th to 20th Dynasties)

Necropolis of Thebes

Most of the examples in this plate fall somewhat outside the forms commonly met with, in that here flowers play the principal role. Nos. 1, 2, 4 and 5 are taken from the tomb of Imiseba, high priest in charge of the altar and scriptures of the temple of Amun under Ramesses IX, a pharaoh of the 20th Dynasty. Nos. 1 and 4 decorate the main body of the ceiling. Others, like nos. 2 and 5, adorn the underside of the architraves, a very specific feature which is hardly ever met with except in this tomb, since everywhere else the underside of the architraves is monochrome or decorated with hieroglyphic inscriptions. No. 3 comes from the hypogeum of Neferhotep. No. 6 presents a variant of the ornamentation of no. 4. Nos. 7 and 9 are two charming examples of the decoration of the small ceilings to the windows of the gynaeceum of Ramesses III. Unfortunately all that is now visible of the background is a deep greyish tone, although I believe that it must originally have been indigo.

DECKENVERZIERUNGEN:
WELLENBÄNDER UND BLUMEN (18. bis 20. Dynastie)

Nekropole von Theben

Da hier die Blumen die Hauptrolle spielen, fällt der größte Teil der auf dieser Tafel zusammengestellten Beispiele ein wenig aus dem Rahmen der allgemein gebräuchlichen Formen. Die Nr. 1, 2, 4 und 5 sind dem Grab des Imiseba entnommen – des unter Ramses IX., einem Pharao der 20. Dynastie, im Amun-Tempel für Altar und Schriften verantwortlichen Hohepriesters. Die Nr. 1 und 4 zieren die eigentliche Decke; die übrigen, wie die Nr. 2 und 5, schmücken die Unterseite der Architrave – eine Besonderheit, die eigentlich nur in diesem Grab zu finden ist, denn sonst ist die Unterseite der Architrave überall einfarbig oder mit Hieroglypheninschriften verziert. Die Nr. 3 stammt aus dem Hypogäum des Neferhotep. Die Nr. 6 ist eine Variante des Ornaments Nr. 4. Die Nr. 7 und 9 zeigen zwei bezaubernde Exemplare der Verzierungen an den kleinen Decken der Fenster im Gynaeceum von Ramses III. Leider ist auf dem Feld nur noch ein dunkelgrauer Farbton zu erkennen; ich glaube jedoch, dass es sich um Indigoblau handelte.

ORNEMENTATION DES PLAFONDS :
POSTES ET FLEURS (XVIIIe à XXe dynastie)

Nécropole de Thèbes

La majeure partie des spécimens réunis sur cette planche sortent un peu des formes généralement usitées parce que les fleurs y jouent le principal rôle. Les n°s 1, 2, 4, 5 sont tirés du tombeau d'Aïchesi [Imiseba], grand prêtre chargé de l'autel et des écritures du temple d'Amon, sous Ramsès IX, pharaon de la XXe dynastie. Les n°s 1 et 4 décorent le plafond proprement dit ; d'autres, comme les n°s 2 et 5, ornent le dessous des architraves, particularité que l'on ne rencontre guère que dans ce tombeau ; car, partout ailleurs, la face inférieure des architraves est monochrome ou décorée de légendes hiéroglyphiques. Le n° 3 provient de l'hypogée de Nofrehotep [Néferhotep]. Le n° 6 est une variante de l'ornement n° 4. Les n°s 7 et 9 offrent deux charmants spécimens de la décoration des petits plafonds des fenêtres du gynécée de Ramsès III. On ne voit plus sur le champ, malheureusement, qu'un ton grisâtre foncé ; mais je crois qu'il a dû être indigo.

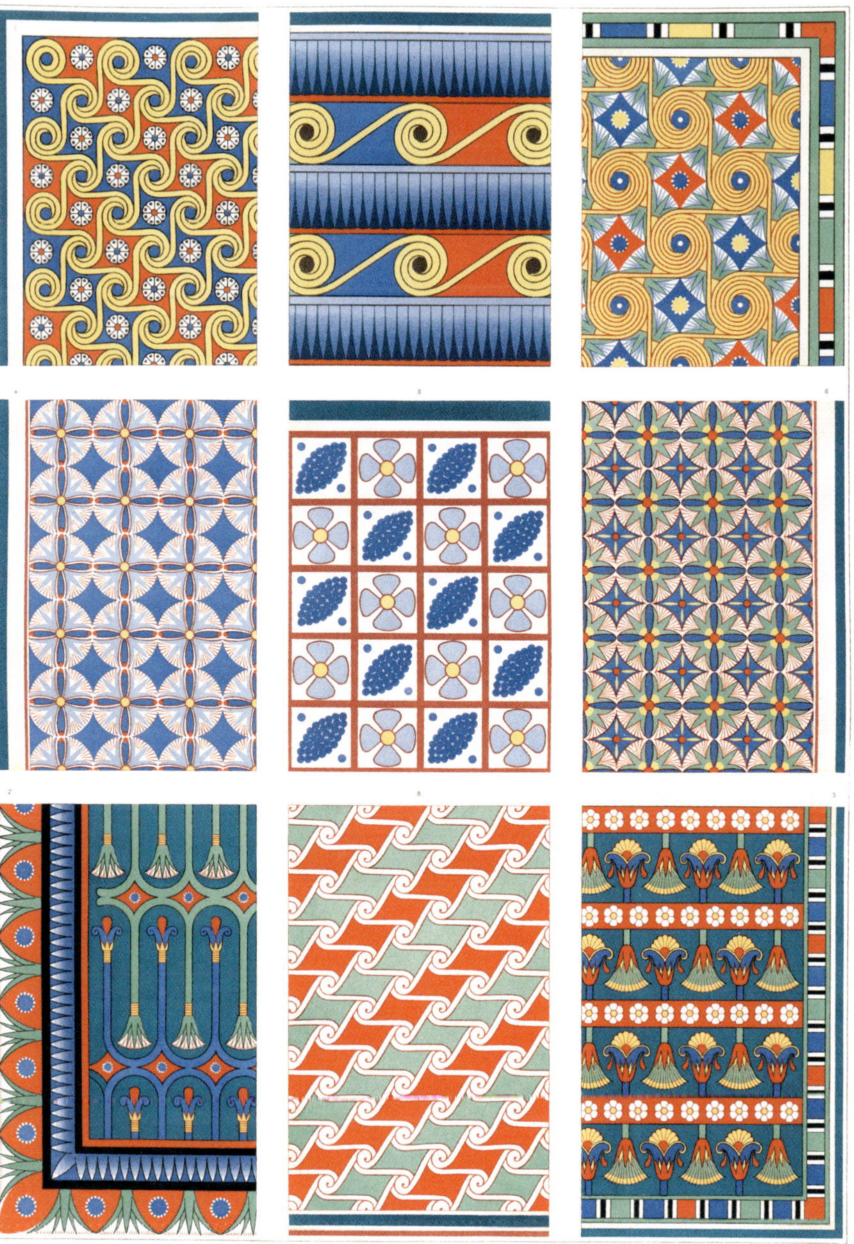

Lith. par C. Walter. Imp. par Hangard-Maugé.

E. Prisse d'Avennes

Publié par Arthus Bertrand, Éditeur

ORNEMENTATION DES PLAFONDS : POSTES & FLEURS.

(NÉCROPOLE DE THÈBES, XVIIIe À XXe DYN.)

CEILING PATTERNS: BUCRANIA (18th and 20th Dynasties)

Necropolis of Thebes

These two ceilings, composed of scrolls, lotus flowers and skeletal bulls' heads crowned with a patera or rosette, are amazingly evocative of Classical Antiquity. The two ceilings featured on this plate derive their particular interest from a passage in Herodotus where he reports how, in the course of sacrifices, a curse was put on the animals' heads. No Egyptian would eat them and the priests would throw them in the river, unless there was some market close by where they could sell them to Greek merchants who did not share their scruples. Herodotus was wrong; two [animals' heads] are to be seen amongst the victuals offered by Ramesses VII to the barque of Amun, in the beautiful hypogeum from which ceiling no. 2 is taken: and this custom appears to have been in force at all periods, even in the time of Herodotus. Is it not strange to see how a plate of decorations can refute a passage in the works of the Father of History?

DECKENVERZIERUNGEN: BUKRANIEN (18. und 20. Dynastie)

Nekropole von Theben

Es ist erstaunlich, dass diese beiden Decken – die sich aus Spiralen, Lotusblüten und entfleischten, mit einer Rosette oder einem Patera-Ornament bekrönten Rinderköpfen zusammensetzen – aussehen, als datierten sie aus der klassischen Antike. Die beiden auf dieser Tafel abgebildeten Decken sind laut einer Textstelle bei Herodot von ganz besonderer Bedeutung; dieser berichtet, dass die Tierköpfe während der Opferung mit Verwünschungen aufgeladen wurden. Kein Ägypter wollte davon essen, sodass die Priester sie in den Fluss warfen – wenn ihnen nicht irgendein Markt zur Verfügung stand, auf dem sie diese an griechische Händler ohne solche Bedenken verkaufen konnten. Herodot hat sich geirrt; unter den Lebensmitteln, die Ramses VII. in dem schönen Hypogäum, dem die Decke Nr. 2 entnommen ist, an der Barke des Amun opfert, fallen zwei [Tierköpfe] auf: Und diese Sitte scheint zu allen Zeiten bestanden zu haben, selbst im Zeitalter Herodots. Ist es nicht sonderbar, eine Ornamenttafel zu sehen, die eine Textstelle des Vaters der Geschichtsschreibung widerlegt?

ORNEMENTATION DES PLAFONDS : BUCRÂNES (XVIIIe et XXe dynasties)

Nécropole de Thèbes

Ces deux plafonds, composés d'enroulements, de fleurs de lotus et de têtes décharnées de bœuf couronnées d'une patère ou d'une rosace, ont un air étonnant d'antiquité classique. Les deux plafonds qui forment cette planche tirent leur intérêt tout particulier d'un passage d'Hérodote ; celui-ci rapporte que, dans les sacrifices, la tête des animaux était chargée d'imprécations. Aucun Égyptien ne voulait en manger, et les prêtres la jetaient dans le fleuve s'ils n'avaient à leur portée quelque marché où ils puissent la vendre à des marchands grecs qui ne partageaient pas le même scrupule. Hérodote s'est trompé ; on en remarque deux [têtes d'animaux] parmi les victuailles offertes par Ramsès VII à la bari d'Amon, dans le bel hypogée d'où est tiré le plafond n° 2 : et cet usage paraît avoir été en vigueur à toutes les époques, même au temps d'Hérodote. N'est-il pas curieux de voir une planche d'ornements réfuter un passage du père de l'histoire ?

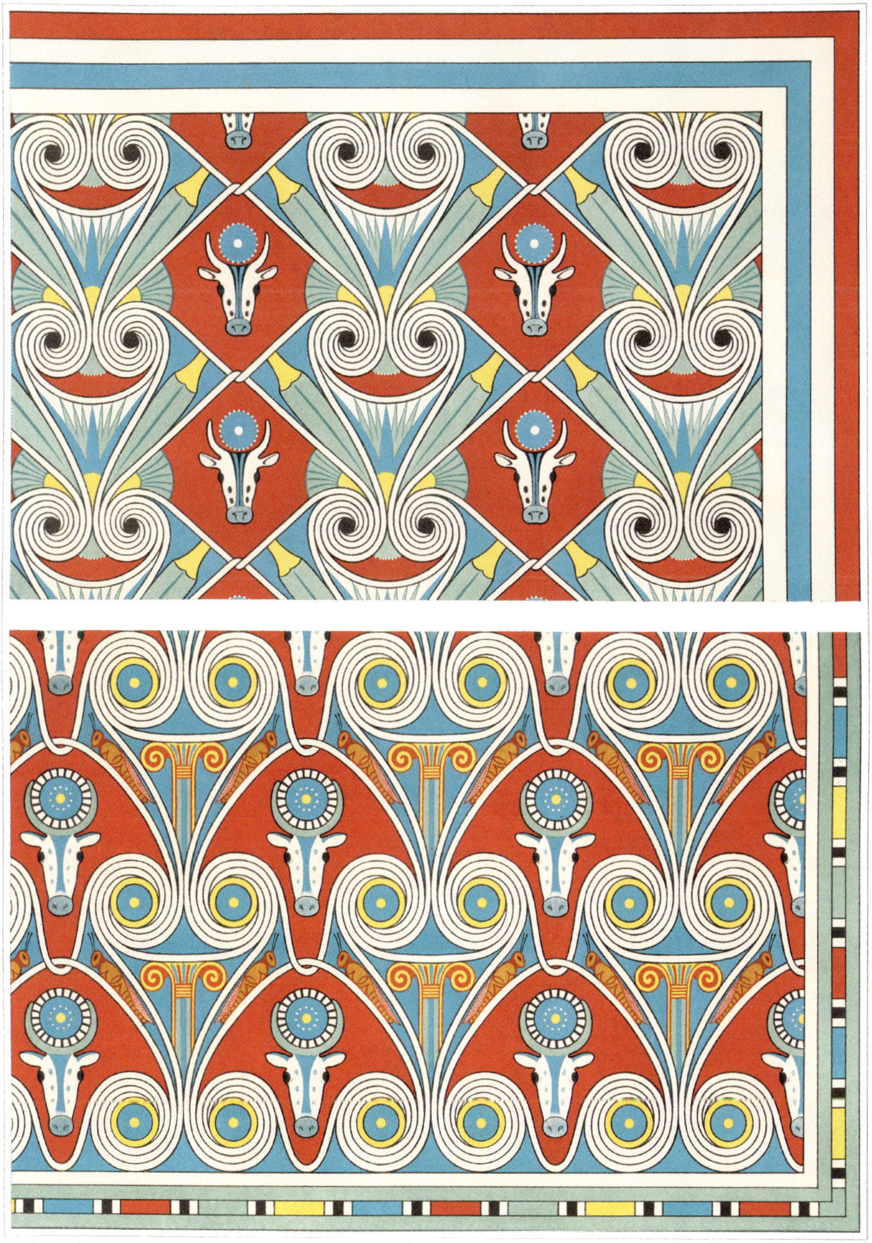

Lith par Levé . Imp par Hangard-Maugé

E. Prisse d'Avennes

Publié par Arthus-Bertrand, Editeur.

ORNEMENTATION DES PLAFONDS : BUCRÂNES.

(NÉCROPOLE DE THÈBES.__ XVIIIe et XXe DYNASTIES.)

DECORATION OF CEILINGS (26th Dynasty)

Thebes and Memphis

Here a number of ceilings from the same period, that of the Saite rulers, are grouped together. After the 26th Dynasty, sepulchral monuments become rare, and almost no decoration as such is found. Both nos. 1 and 2 decorate half of a surbased vault carved at the entrance of the tomb of a high priest called Petamenophis who was buried in the valley of el-Assasif at Thebes. No. 1 is extremely elegant and is found in different colours in other tombs of the same period. No. 3, which shows another meander, alternating with rosettes, can be seen on the ceiling of another tomb of the same period which was dug in the necropolis of Thebes. Nos. 4, 5, 6 and 7 show different sections of the ceiling in the great chamber of the superb hypogeum of Bakenrenef at Saqqara.

DECKENVERZIERUNGEN (26. Dynastie)

Theben und Memphis

Zusammenstellung von Decken derselben Periode, d. h. der Saïten-Dynastie. Nach der 26. Dynastie werden Grabdenkmäler selten, und man findet kaum noch Ausschmückungen im eigentlichen Sinne. Die Nr. 1 und 2 verzieren jeweils die Hälfte eines Flachbogens, der am Eingang zum Grab des Hohepriesters *Petamenophis* im Tal von El-Assasif in Theben ausgehauen ist. Die Nr. 1 ist sehr geschmackvoll und findet sich mit anderer Farbgebung in weiteren Gräbern derselben Zeit. Die Nr. 3 ist ein weiterer, mit Rosetten alternierender Mäander, der auch an der Decke eines anderen in der Nekropole von Theben ausgehobenen Grabes derselben Zeit zu sehen ist. Die Nr. 4, 5, 6 und 7 zeigen verschiedene Deckenfelder aus dem großen Saal des prachtvollen Hypogäums des Bakenranef in Sakkara.

ORNEMENTATION DES PLAFONDS (XXVIe dynastie)

Thèbes et Memphis

Réunion de plafonds d'une même époque, c'est-à-dire du règne des Saïtes. Après la XXVIe dynastie, les monuments sépulcraux deviennent rares, et l'on ne trouve plus guère d'ornements proprement dits. Les n°s 1 et 2 décorent chacun la moitié d'une voûte surbaissée taillée à l'entrée du tombeau d'un grand prêtre nommé Pétamounôph [Padiamenopé] enseveli dans la vallée d'El-Assacif, à Thèbes. Le n° 1 est fort élégant et se trouve colorié différemment dans d'autres tombeaux de la même époque. Le n° 3 est un autre méandre alterné de rosaces qui se voit au plafond d'un autre tombeau de la même époque, creusé dans la nécropole de Thèbes. Les n°s 4, 5, 6 et 7 offrent divers compartiments du plafond dans la grande salle du superbe hypogée de Bekenranef [Bokenrenef] à Sakkara.

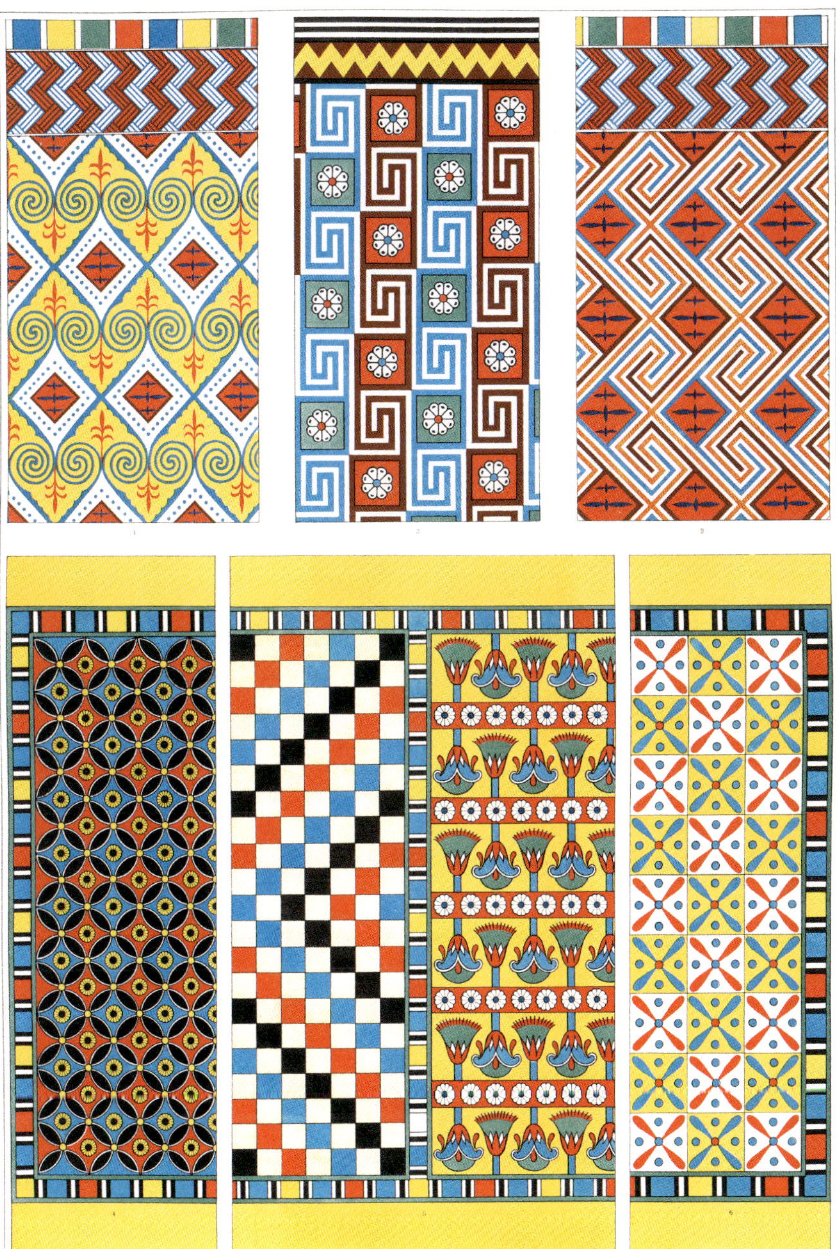

W. de Famars Testas

Publié par Arthus Bertrand Éditeur

ORNEMENTATION DES PLAFONDS.

(THÈBES & MEMPHIS — XXVIE DYNASTIE.)

CEILING PATTERNS (18th to 30th Dynasties)

Memphis and Thebes

No. 1 is a medial ceiling from the huge tomb of Bakenrenef at Saqqara. The vultures have a wingspan of 1.53 metres and stand out against a greyish background decorated with a blue sky studded with stars. Vultures with spread wings holding feathers in their talons, symbols of victory, are widely used as decoration on ceilings and the soffits of temple doors, but are very rarely found on tomb ceilings. They display a great variety of colouring. The first of the two vultures shown at the bottom of the plate is from the Ptolemaic Period and decorates the ceiling or the soffit of the door of the great temple of Philae. The second comes from the same site and decorates the propylaeum of Nectanebo. The ceiling in the middle shows geese wheeling around their nests and is taken from the tomb of Imiseba (20th Dynasty).

DECKENVERZIERUNGEN (18. bis 30. Dynastie)

Memphis und Theben

Die Nr. 1 ist eine Mitteldecke aus dem weitläufigen Grab des Bakenranef in Sakkara. Die Geier haben eine Spannweite von 1,53 m und heben sich vom ins Graue spielenden Untergrund ab, der mit einem blauen, mit Sternen übersäten Himmel geschmückt ist. Geier mit ausgebreiteten Flügeln, die Federn als Sinnbild des Sieges in ihren Fängen tragen, zieren im Allgemeinen die Decken und die Soffitten der Tempeltüren, aber nur selten die Decken von Gräbern. Ihre Farbgebung weist eine große Vielfalt auf. Der erste der beiden unten auf der Tafel dargestellten Geier ist aus ptolemäischer Zeit: Er ziert die Decke oder die Soffitte der Tür des großen Tempels von Philae. Der zweite, der vom selben Ort stammt, ziert den Propylon des Nektanebos. Die dazwischen befindliche Decke, auf der über ihrem Nest hin und her fliegende Gänse abgebildet sind, ist dem Grab des Imiseba (20. Dynastie) entnommen.

ORNEMENTATION DES PLAFONDS (XVIIIe à XXXe dynastie)

Memphis et Thèbes

Le n° 1 est un plafond médial du vaste tombeau de Bekenranef [Bokenrenef] à Sakkara. Les vautours ont 1,53 m d'envergure et s'y détachent sur un fond grisâtre, orné d'un ciel bleu constellé d'étoiles. Les vautours aux ailes déployées et tenant dans leurs serres des plumes, symboles de la victoire, ornent généralement les plafonds et les soffites des portes de temples, mais bien rarement les plafonds des tombeaux. Ils offrent une grande variété dans leur coloration. Le premier des deux vautours représentés au bas de la planche est de l'époque ptolémaïque : il orne le plafond ou soffite de la porte du grand temple de Philæ. Le second, qui provient de la même localité, décore le propylon de Nectanèbe. Le plafond intermédiaire, représentant des oies voltigeant autour de leur nid, est tiré du tombeau d'Aïchesi ([Imiseba] XXe dynastie).

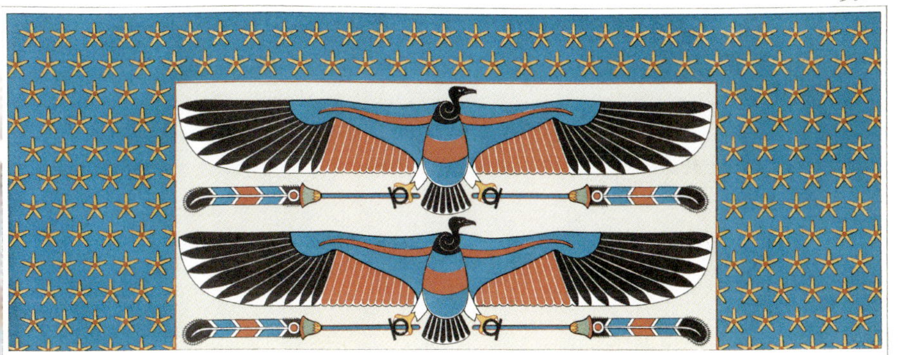

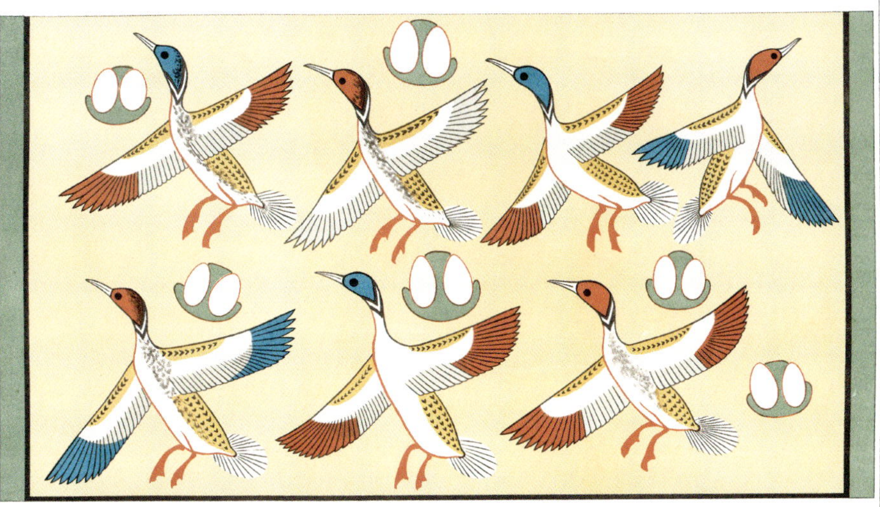

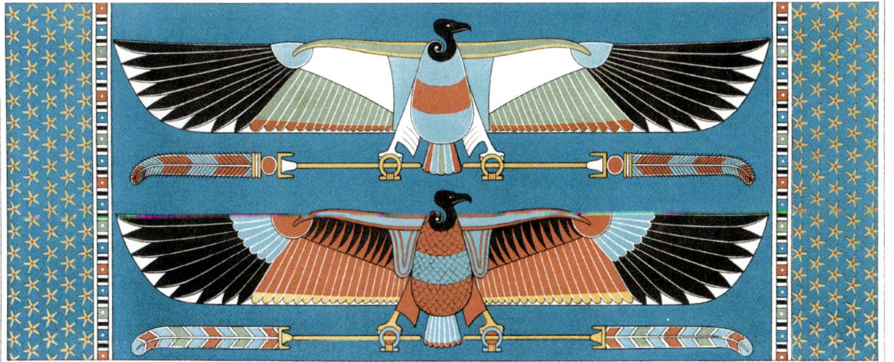

Lith. par Levié. _ Imp. par Hangard-Maugé. W. de Famars-Testas. Publié par Arthus Bertrand, Éditeur.

ORNEMENTATION DES PLAFONDS.

(MEMPHIS & THÈBES. _ XVIIIe à XXXe DYNASTIES.)

TEMPLE OF DEIR EL-MEDINA (18th Dynasty)

Plan, cross-sections and details

There is now little left of this temple of Pharaonic architecture although it appears that it was previously of considerable size. It is built on an artificial mound which extends 30 metres from the building on both the north and south sides. The geographical situation of the Memnonium of Thebes is known to be midway between Qurna or el-Qurna and Medinet Habu. One reaches the temple through a door situated on the west and facing the Nile. The south part of the building is the best preserved, but the corridor is in complete darkness: three rooms open on to it which are longer than they are wide and which are all covered with carvings.

TEMPEL VON DEIR EL-MEDINA (18. Dynastie)

Grundriss, Detail- und Schnittzeichnungen

Es handelt sich um einen Tempel pharaonischer Bauart, der heute zwar nicht mehr besonders ansehnlich ist, einst aber sehr stattlich gewesen zu sein scheint. Er ist auf einem künstlichen Hügel errichtet, der sich 30 m nördlich und südlich des Gebäudes erstreckt. Es ist bekannt, dass das Memnonium von Theben eine geografische Mittellage zwischen Scheich Abd el-Qurna oder al-Qurna und Medinet Habu einnimmt. Zum Tempel gelangt man durch eine im Westen, dem Nil gegenüber gelegene Tür. Der Südteil des Gebäudes ist am besten erhalten; der Flur liegt jedoch in tiefer Dunkelheit: Er dient drei Räumen als Ausgang, die länger als breit und alle mit Skulpturen geschmückt sind.

TEMPLE DE DEYR EL-MEDINEH (XVIIIe dynastie)

Plan, coupes et détails

C'est un temple d'architecture pharaonique, maintenant peu considérable, mais qui paraît l'avoir été beaucoup autrefois. Il est construit sur une butte factice qui s'étend à 30 mètres de l'édifice du côté du nord, comme du côté du sud. On sait que le Memnonium de Thèbes est une situation géographique intermédiaire entre Gournah ou el-Gournah et Medineh-Tabou [Médinet Habou]. On arrive au temple par une porte située à l'ouest et en face du Nil. La partie sud de l'édifice est la mieux conservée ; mais le couloir est dans une obscurité profonde : il sert d'issue à trois pièces plus longues que larges et toutes ornées de sculptures.

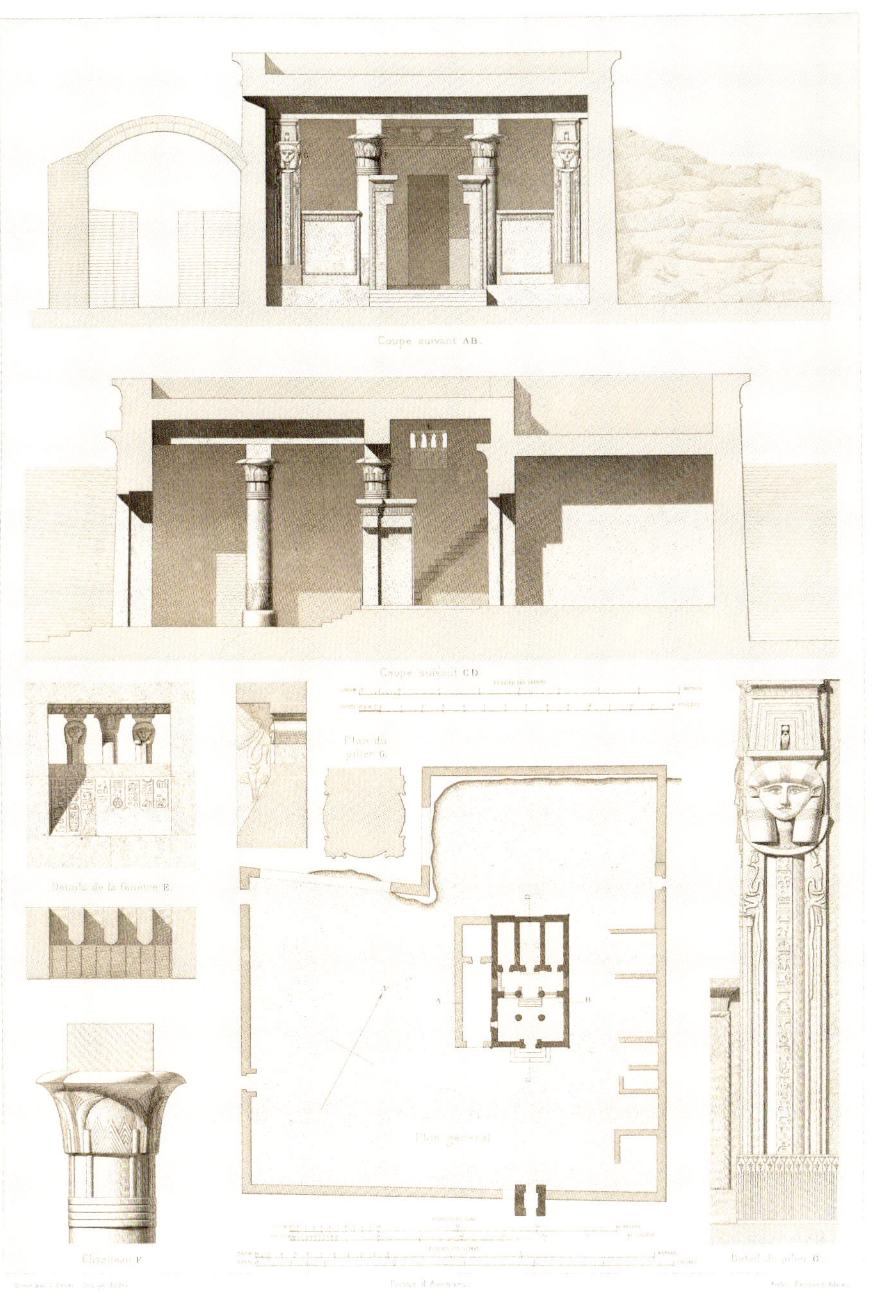

TEMPLE DE DEYR EL-MEDINEH.

PLAN, COUPES ET DÉTAILS.

ISIS [HATHOR] PILLARS (18th Dynasty)

Caryatid pillars, frequently used during the 18th and 19th Dynasties, cannot be categorised with columns; neither can the pillar with a head of Hathor nor the pilaster with the head of a cow. All the figures supported against pillars are statues of pharaohs in the form of Osiris, which is why they are called Osirid pillars; they are never load-bearing parts of the building but are purely decorative. In fact the Egyptians never used caryatids as such and the only figures of which they ever made use to support some part of the building were always representations of captives.

ISIS- [HATHOR-] PFEILER (18. Dynastie)

Was die Karyatiden und Atlanten anbelangt, die während der 18. und 19. Dynastie sehr gebräuchlich waren, so können sie nicht den Säulen zugerechnet werden, ebenso wenig wie der Hathor-Pfeiler und der Kalbskopf-Pilaster. Alle mit dem Rücken an die Pfeiler angelehnten Figuren sind Pharaonenstatuen in der Gestalt des Osiris, daher werden sie Osiris-Pfeiler genannt; ihre Funktion ist rein dekorativ, und sie tragen niemals irgendeinen Teil eines Gebäudes: Tatsächlich haben die Ägypter keine Karyatiden im eigentlichen Sinne verwendet; vielmehr waren die einzigen Figuren, die dazu dienten, einige Teile der Denkmäler zu tragen, immer Darstellungen von Gefangenen.

PILIERS [D'HATHOR] ISIAQUES (XVIIIe dynastie)

Quant au pilier caryatide atlante, fréquemment usité sous les XVIIIe et XIXe dynasties, il ne peut être classé avec les colonnes ; non plus que le pilier à tête d'Hathor, ni le pilastre à tête de génisse. Toutes les figures adossées aux piliers sont des statues des pharaons, sous la forme d'Osiris, ce qui leur a fait donner le nom de piliers osiriaques ; qu'elles ne supportent jamais aucune partie de l'édifice, e t sont purement décoratives : les Égyptiens n'ont pas employé, en effet, les caryatides proprement dites ; les seules figures qu'ils aient fait servir à supporter quelque partie des monuments ayant toujours été des représentations de captifs.

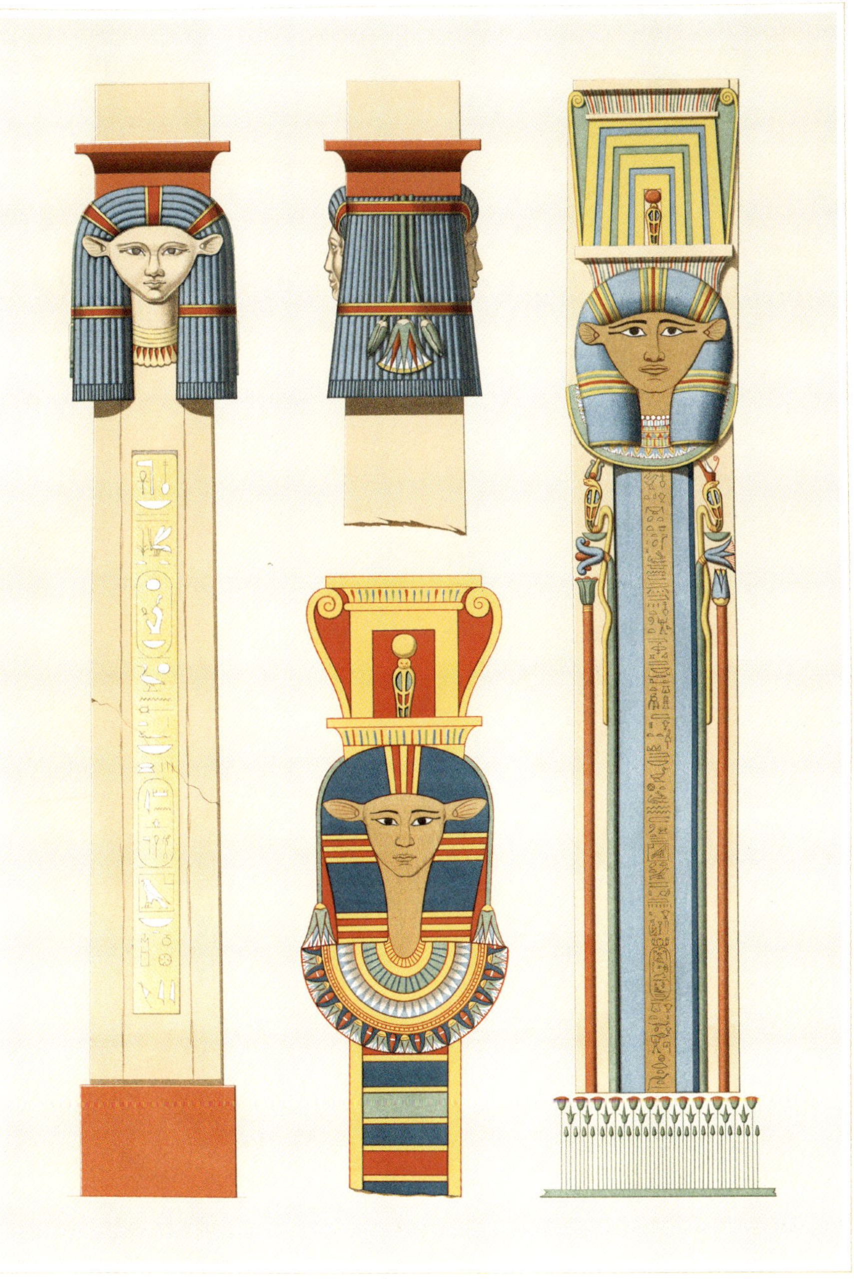

Prisse d'Avennes. Publié chez Arthus Bertrand, Libraire

PILIERS ISIAQUES.

PLAN OF THE RUINS OF TELL EL-AMARNA (18th Dynasty)

This city, which was believed to represent the ancient Psinaula, was one of the largest after Thebes and Memphis. It was situated in the Seventh Nome, on the right bank of the Nile, in a sandy plain. The city was divided from north to south by a broad longitudinal avenue. The most important quarter was in the north and enclosed temples and various other buildings, one of which is particularly noteworthy for its large number of brick pillars; this was probably a palace. [...] A number of dwellings built of sun-baked bricks have not been destroyed and have escaped the hand of man and the ravages of time. In this capital, which was constructed very rapidly in order to provide a centre for the new cult of the Sun, the builders had to use those materials which were the easiest to obtain. In the main street, towering over the rubble, can be seen the two massive supports of a pylon whose colossal door, opening to 11 metres wide, must have been crowned by a vault with a number of concentric arches.

ÜBERSICHTSKARTE DER BAULICHEN ÜBERRESTE VON TELL EL-AMARNA (18. Dynastie)

Diese Stadt, von der man annahm, dass sie das alte Psinaula darstelle, war nach Theben und Memphis eine der größten. Sie befand sich in einer sandigen Ebene am rechten Nilufer, im siebten Gau. Eine breite Straße teilte die Stadt der Länge nach von Norden nach Süden. Das im Norden gelegene Hauptviertel umfasste Tempel und verschiedene Gebäude, unter denen eines durch seine zahlreichen Ziegelpfeiler besonders auffällt; vermutlich war es ein Palast. [...] Mehrere Wohngebäude aus luftgetrockneten Ziegeln haben die Eingriffe der Menschen und die Verheerungen des Alters überdauert. In dieser schnell errichteten Hauptstadt, die dem neuen Sonnenkult ein Zentrum bieten sollte, musste man sich der Baustoffe bedienen, die am einfachsten zu beschaffen waren. In der Hauptstraße sieht man die beiden massiven Sockel eines Pylonen, dessen riesenhaftes Tor mit einer Öffnung von 11 m Durchmesser durch ein Gewölbe mit mehreren konzentrischen Bögen bekrönt gewesen sein muss.

PLAN DES RUINES DE TELL EL-AMARNA (XVIIIe dynastie)

Cette ville, qu'on croyait représenter l'ancienne Psinaula, était une des plus grandes après Thèbes et Memphis. Elle était située dans l'Heptanomide [la septième nome], sur la rive droite du Nil, dans une plaine sablonneuse. La ville était partagée du nord au sud par une large voie longitudinale. Le quartier principal, situé au nord, renfermait des temples et divers édifices, dont l'un surtout est fort remarquable par de nombreux piliers en briques ; c'était, probablement, un palais. [...] Plusieurs habitations en briques crues n'ont pas été détruites et ont échappé à la main des hommes et aux ravages du temps. Dans cette capitale, élevée rapidement pour offrir un centre au nouveau culte du Soleil, on a dû faire usage des matériaux les plus faciles à se procurer. On voit, dans la rue principale, s'élever au-dessus des décombres les deux massifs d'un pylône dont la porte colossale, de 11 mètres d'ouverture, n'a pu être couronnée que par une voûte à plusieurs cintres concentriques.

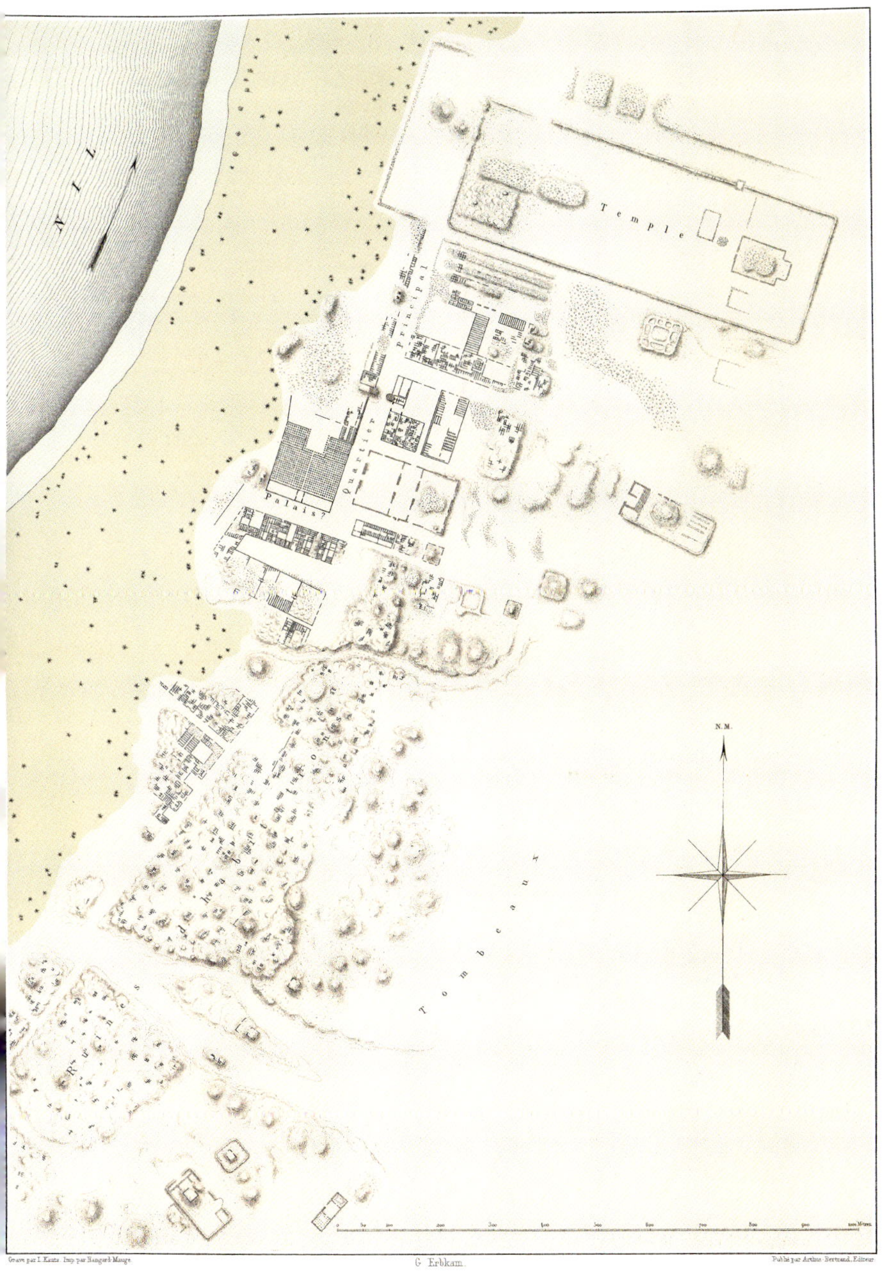

Gravé par L. Kautz. Imp. par Hangard-Maugé. G. Erbkam. Publié par Arthus-Bertrand, Editeur

PLAN DES RUINES DE TELL EL-AMARNA

(XVIIIe DYNASTIE)

BIRD'S-EYE VIEWS OF BUILDINGS IN TELL EL-AMARNA (18th Dynasty)

Bas-reliefs in the hypogea

The top plan appears to represent the most secluded part of a temple, which must be that of the Sun, the only deity worshipped in Tell el-Amarna. On the right, in the temple, a great door opens on to a vast courtyard where a monumental stele, or hermetic column, can be seen. Between the columns in a type of pronaos are royal statues crowned alternately with tiaras symbolising Upper and Lower Egypt. [...] The second plan is much more complicated, filled with tables of offerings and apparently also belonging to a temple of the Sun; here the deity was worshipped in the form of a globe shooting out rays which terminated in hands, as can be seen on the upper part of the pylon. Ten masts are shown, flying tricoloured pennants: these masts broke the monotony of the horizontal lines of the building and the sinuous curves of the banners floating with the wind breathed life into the straight, rigid lines of the architecture.

PERSPEKTIVISCHE ÜBERSICHTSZEICHNUNGEN DER BAUWERKE VON TELL EL-AMARNA (18. Dynastie)

Flachreliefs aus den Hypogäen

Die obere Karte scheint den entlegensten Winkel eines Tempels darzustellen, bei dem es sich nur um den Tempel der Sonne, der einzigen in Tell el-Amarna verehrten Gottheit, handeln kann. Rechts im Tempel geht eine große Tür auf einen weiten Hof hinaus, auf dem eine gewaltige Stele oder ein Hermenpfeiler zu sehen ist. Zwischen den Säulen in einer Art Pronaos befinden sich Königsstatuen, die abwechselnd eine ober- und eine unterägyptische Krone tragen. [...] Der wesentlich schwieriger zu deutende, vollständig mit Tischen voller Opfergaben ausgefüllte Hintergrund scheint ebenfalls zu einem Sonnentempel zu gehören; in ihm wird die Sonne in Gestalt einer Strahlenkugel verehrt, bei der Hände den Abschluss der Strahlen bilden, wie im oberen Teil des Pylonen zu erkennen ist. Man sieht dort zehn mit dreifarbigen Verklickern verzierte Masten: Diese Masten brachen die Eintönigkeit der horizontalen Linien des Gebäudes, wobei die im Wind flatternden Wimpel mit ihren wogenden Windungen die Starre der geraden Linien des Gebäudes belebten.

PLANS CAVALIERS DES ÉDIFICES DE TELL EL-AMARNA (XVIIIe dynastie)

Bas-reliefs des hypogées

Le plan supérieur paraît représenter la partie la plus reculée d'un temple, qui ne peut être que celui du Soleil, seule divinité adorée à Tell el-Amarna. À droite, dans le temple, une grande porte débouche sur une vaste cour où l'on voit une stèle monumentale, ou colonne hermétique. Entre les colonnes d'une espèce de pronaos, sont des statues royales coiffées alternativement d'une tiare, symbole de la Haute-Égypte, et d'une autre qui exprime la basse. [...] Beaucoup plus compliqué, le second plan, tout chargé de tables d'offrandes, semble appartenir aussi à un temple du Soleil, où celui-ci était adoré sous la forme d'un globe lançant des rayons qui se terminent par des mains, comme on le voit dans la partie supérieure du pylône. On y voit dix mâts, ornés de penons tricolores : ces mâts rompaient la monotonie des lignes horizontales de l'édifice, et les banderoles, flottant au gré du vent, animaient de leurs courbes ondoyantes la rigidité des lignes droites de l'architecture.

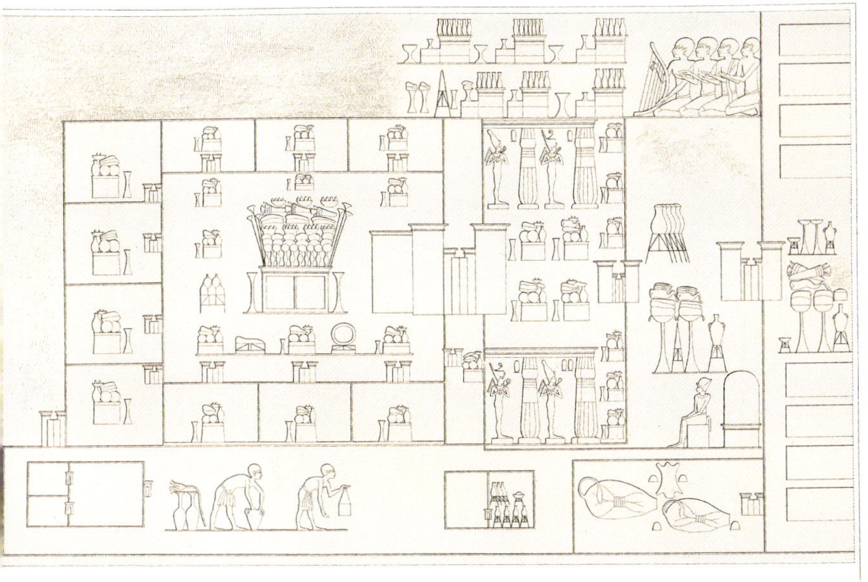

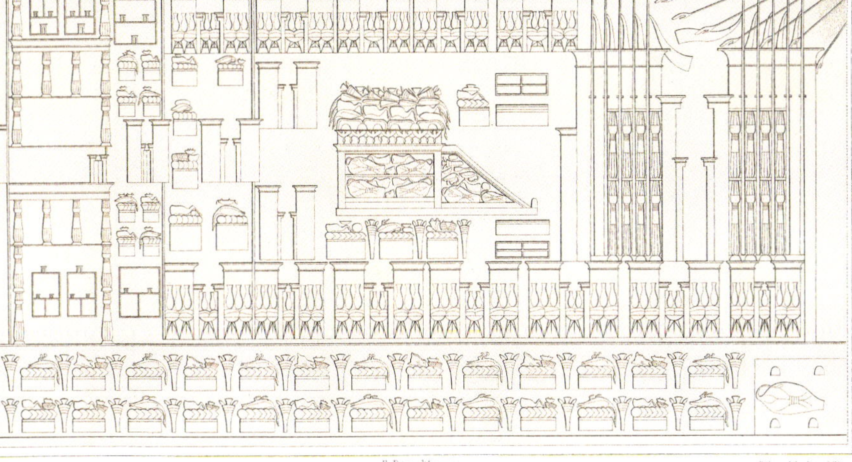

Gravé par [illegible] _ Imp. par Hangard-Maugé

E. Prisse d'Avennes.

Publié par Arthus Bertrand Éditeur

PLANS CAVALIERS DES ÉDIFICES DE TELL EL-AMARNA.

(BAS-RELIEFS DES HYPOGÉES _ XVIIIe DYNASTIE.)

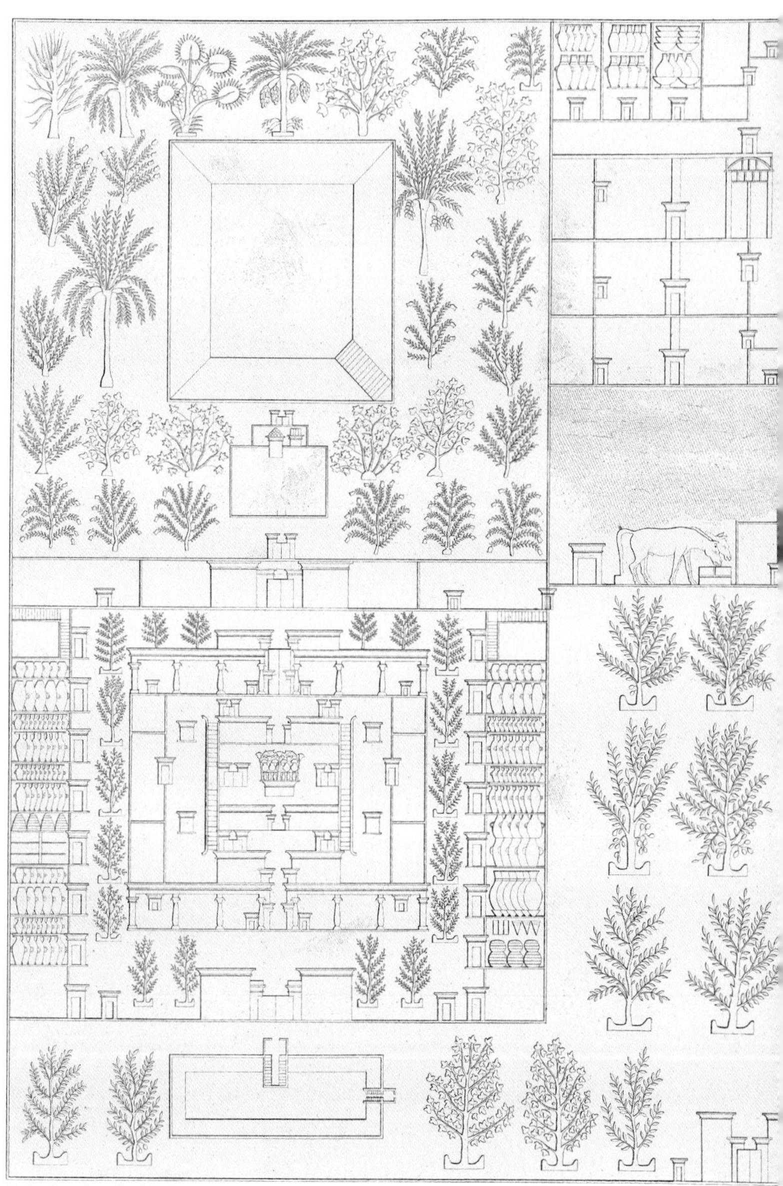

Gravé par Kautz.__ Imp. par Hangard-Maugé.

PLAN CAVAL

(BAS-RELIEF D'UN HYPOC

E.

I 37

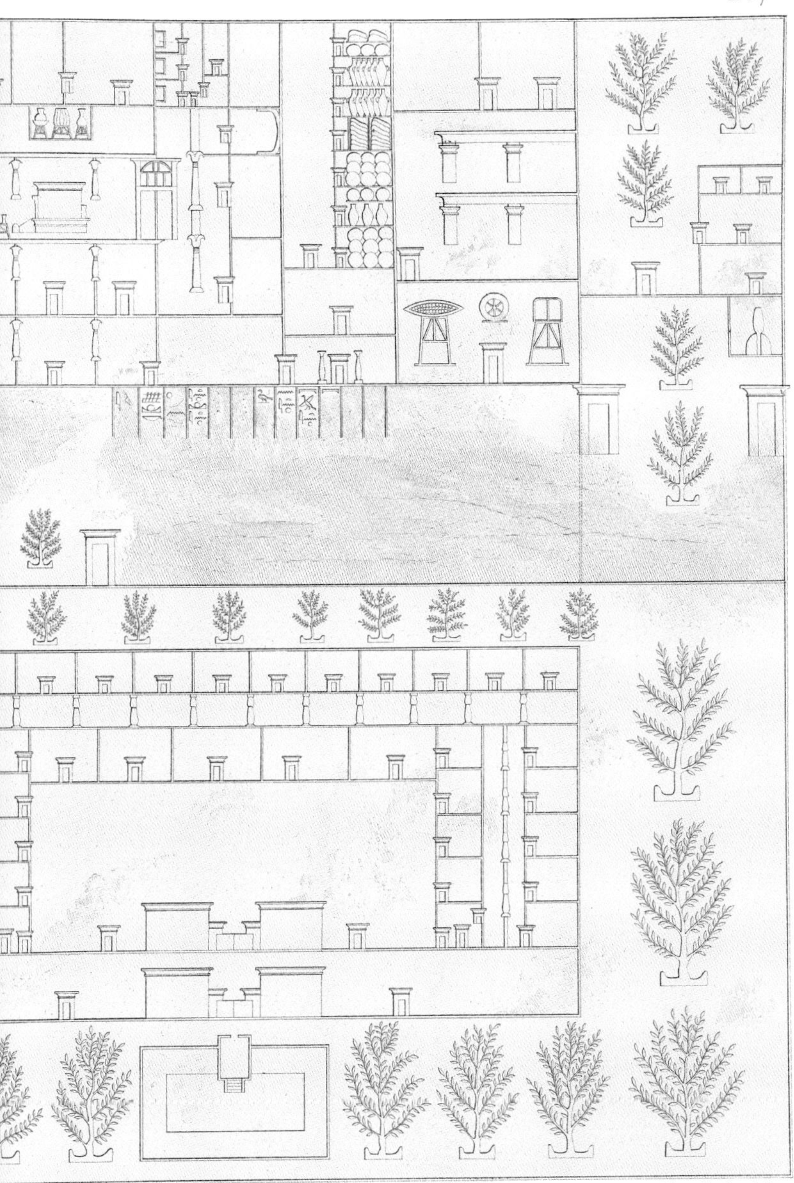

Publié par Arthus Bertrand Editeur

VILLA ROYALE.

- AMARNA. — XVIIIᵉ DYNASTIE)

(Pages/Seite 276/277)

BIRD'S-EYE VIEW OF A ROYAL VILLA (18th Dynasty)

Bas-relief from a hypogeum at Tell el-Amarna

Country life held a very special charm for the Egyptians. The varied paintings which decorate their spacious tombs always feature agricultural work and gardening, as well as the sports and amusements which took place in the fields, such as hunting and fishing. The hypogea which contain architectural plans, such as those at Tell el-Amarna, give a reasonably exact idea of the beauty and layout of the Egyptian villas. However, the villa which is represented in this plate is of specific interest in that it appears to have formed part of the royal estate. It is carved in the tomb of a high-ranking official called Ram-Eri. Towards the middle of the great circumvallate wall can be seen a pylon or principal door flanked by two smaller doors. The transverse avenue led to two separate buildings in front of which were dug two large ponds adorned with staircases.

PERSPEKTIVISCHE ÜBERSICHTSZEICHNUNG EINER KÖNIGLICHEN VILLA (18. Dynastie)

Flachrelief aus einem Hypogäum in Tell el-Amarna

Das Landleben hatte für die alten Ägypter einen ganz besonderen Reiz. Die verschiedenen Malereien, die ihre geräumigen Gräber ausschmücken, zeigen stets Ackerbau- und Gartenarbeiten sowie die Übungen und Vergnügungen, mit denen man sich auf dem Lande die Zeit vertreiben kann, wie z. B. Jagd und Fischfang. Die Hypogäen, in denen wie in Tell el-Amarna Baupläne dargestellt sind, geben uns eine recht genaue Vorstellung von der Aufteilung und Schönheit der ägyptischen Villen. Die auf dieser Tafel abgebildete Villa ist deshalb von besonderem Interesse, weil sie anscheinend zum königlichen Besitz gehörte. Es handelt sich um eine Bildhauerarbeit aus dem Grab eines hohen Beamten namens Ram-Eri. Etwa in der Mitte der Umfassungsmauer fällt ein Pylon oder ein von zwei kleineren Türen flankiertes Haupttor auf. Die quer verlaufende Prachtstraße führte zu zwei Gebäudetrakten, vor denen zwei mit Treppen versehene Wasserbecken angelegt waren.

PLAN CAVALIER D'UNE VILLA ROYALE (XVIIIe dynastie)

Bas-relief d'un hypogée de Tell el-Amarna

La vie de la campagne avait pour les anciens Égyptiens un charme tout particulier. Les diverses peintures qui ornent leurs spacieux tombeaux représentent toujours des travaux de l'agriculture et de jardinage, ainsi que les exercices et les amusements qu'on peut prendre aux champs, tels que la chasse et la pêche. Les hypogées qui offrent des plans d'architecture, tels que ceux de Tell el-Amarna, nous donnent une idée assez exacte de la beauté et de la distribution des villas égyptiennes. Mais la villa qui se trouve représentée dans cette planche offre cet intérêt particulier qu'elle paraît avoir fait partie du domaine royal. Elle est sculptée dans le tombeau d'un haut fonctionnaire nommé Ram-Eri. Vers le milieu de la muraille de circonvallation, on remarque un pylône ou porte principale flanquée de deux portes plus petites. L'avenue transversale menait à deux corps de bâtiment au devant desquels étaient creusées de grandes pièces d'eau, garnies d'escaliers.

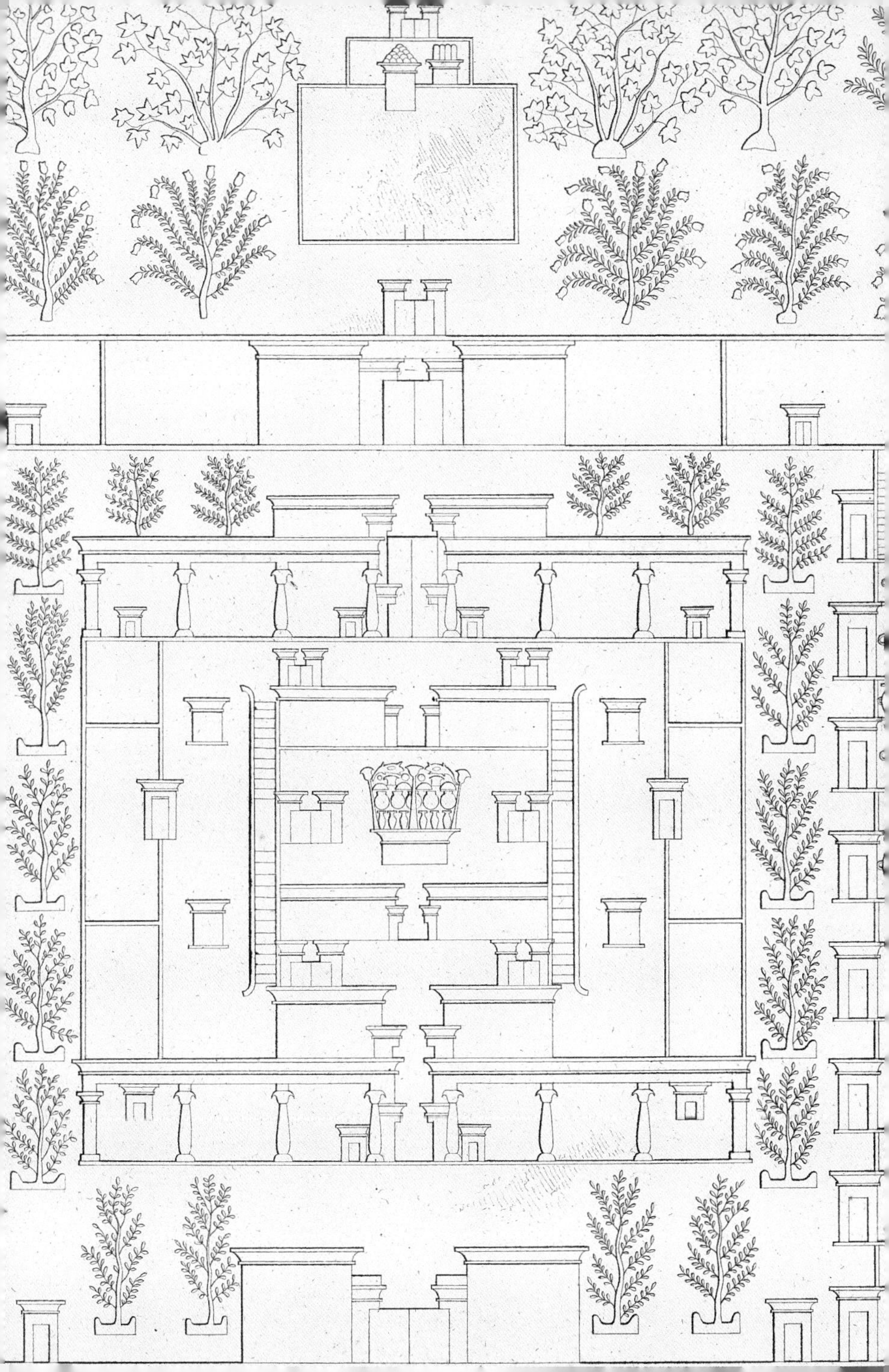

BIRD'S-EYE VIEWS OF THE BUILDINGS OF TELL EL-AMARNA (18th Dynasty)

Sculpted in the hypogea

Above the plan of the royal villa I have placed a fragment of another plan of a palace, taken from the first of the rock-cut tombs situated to the south of this area. Although it is not rich in architectural details it is, nevertheless, extremely interesting from the point of view of customs and costumes. Indeed, to the right can be seen a dining-room beside which is a bedroom with a bed adorned with small columns and a canopy. In a service area, which is separated from the royal apartment by a corridor, servants can be seen preparing fine food; further on there are huge rooms for the specific use of the palace staff, amongst whom can be distinguished musicians and singers. Near them can be seen harps, lyres and lutes, as well as the furnishings and utensils in everyday use amongst them.

PERSPEKTIVISCHE ÜBERSICHTSZEICHNUNGEN DER BAUWERKE VON TELL EL-AMARNA (18. Dynastie)

Bildhauerarbeiten aus den Hypogäen

Ich habe das Bruchstück einer anderen Palastkarte über den Plan der königlichen Villa gesetzt; es entstammt dem ersten Grab der südlich des Ortes gelegenen Hypogäen. Obgleich nicht viele bauliche Einzelheiten abgebildet sind, ist sie unter dem Gesichtspunkt der Sitten und Gebräuche doch sehr interessant. Auf der rechten Seite fällt in der Tat ein Speiseraum auf, neben dem sich ein Schlafzimmer mit einem Bett befindet, das mit kleinen Säulen und einem Baldachin ausgestattet ist. In einem von der königlichen Wohnung durch einen Korridor getrennten Anrichtezimmer sieht man die mit der Zubereitung der Speisen beschäftigten Diener: Weiter hinten sind dem Dienstpersonal des Palastes – darunter Musiker und Sängerinnen – geräumige Zimmer vorbehalten; und neben diesem sind Harfen, Lyren, Lauten und schließlich die bei ihm gebräuchlichen Möbel und Gerätschaften zu sehen.

PLANS CAVALIERS DES ÉDIFICES DE TELL EL-AMARNA (XVIIIe dynastie)

Sculptés dans les hypogées

J'ai placé, au-dessus du plan de la villa royale, le fragment d'un autre plan de palais : tiré du premier tombeau des hypogées situés au sud de la localité. S'il n'offre pas beaucoup de détails d'architecture, il est, néanmoins, fort intéressant au point de vue des mœurs et des coutumes. À droite, en effet, on remarque une salle à manger à côté de laquelle se trouve une chambre à coucher avec un lit orné de colonnettes et d'un baldaquin. Dans un office, séparé de l'appartement royal par un corridor, on voit les serviteurs occupés à préparer les mets : plus loin, de vastes pièces sont consacrées au personnel du palais dans le nombre duquel se rencontrent des musiciens et des chanteuses ; et l'on voit à côté de ceux-ci les harpes, les lyres, les mandores, enfin les meubles et les ustensiles qui étaient en usage parmi eux.

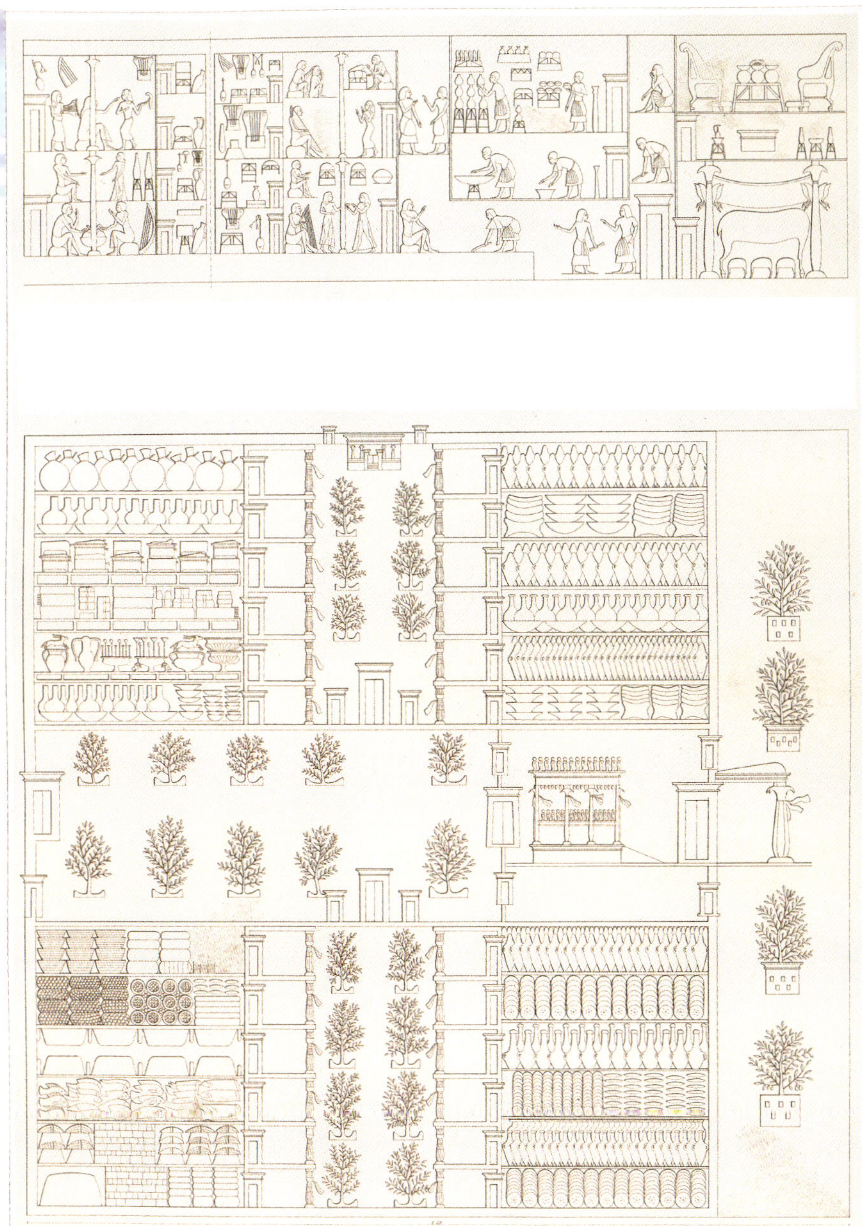

E. Prisse d'Avennes

PLANS CAVALIERS DES ÉDIFICES DE TELL EL-AMARNA

SCULPTÉS DANS LES HYPOGÉES

SPEOS OF KALABSHA. TALMIS (Ramesses II, 19th Dynasty)

Plan, cross-sections, and details

The speos of Kalabsha, the ancient Talmis, which was dug during the reign of Ramesses II, is reached by way of a vestibule whose two longitudinal walls are covered with exceptionally interesting bas-reliefs. Those on the right depict episodes in a campaign against an Asiatic race, the Khari. The bas-reliefs on the left show the scene of a battle and of tribute imposed after victory on an African race, the Kushites [...]. The pharaoh sits on his throne, which is depicted beneath a rich naos, and receives gifts sent by the Ethiopians, who are led in by their conqueror, the prince of Kush Amenemopet; a young priest is placing a golden collar around his neck, as a token of respect and reward. In the next scene Ramesses II can be seen mounted in his war chariot followed by his two young sons, who are also standing in chariots driven by charioteers who are urging the horses on at top speed.

SPEOS VON KALABSCHA. TALMIS (Ramses II., 19. Dynastie)

Grundriss, Detail- und Schnittzeichnungen

Der unter Ramses II. ausgehobene Speos von Kalabscha – dem antiken Talmis – ist über ein Vestibül zugänglich, dessen beide Längswände mit äußerst interessanten Flachreliefs bedeckt sind. Auf der rechten Seite sind Begebenheiten aus einem Feldzug gegen das asiatisches Volk der Khari dargestellt. Die Flachreliefs links zeigen ein Schlachtengemälde sowie den Tribut, der den afrikanischen Völkern, d. h. hier den Kuschiten, durch den Sieg auferlegt wurde [...]. Der Pharao, der auf seinem unter einem reich ausgestatteten Naos platzierten Thron sitzt, empfängt die von den Äthiopiern gesandten Geschenke, denen ihr Bezwinger – der kuschitische Prinz Amenemapet – vorangeht; ein junger Priester legt ihm als Ehrenauszeichnung ein goldenes Collier um den Hals. Auf dem folgenden Bild ist Ramses II. auf seinem Streitwagen zu sehen, gefolgt von seinen Söhnen, die ebenfalls auf Wagen stehen, geführt von Lenkern, die die Pferde zum Eiltempo antreiben.

SPÉOS DE KALABCHÉ. TALMIS (Ramsès II, XIXe dynastie)

Plan, coupes et détails

Le Spéos de Kalabché [Kalabsha], l'ancienne Talmis, creusé sous Ramsès II, est précédé d'un vestibule dont les deux parois longitudinales sont couvertes de bas-reliefs très intéressants. Ceux de droite représentent les épisodes d'une campagne contre un peuple asiatique, les Châri. Les bas-reliefs de gauche offrent le tableau d'une bataille et d'un tribut imposé par la victoire à des peuples africains, les Kouchiets [...]. Le pharaon, assis sur son trône placé sous une riche naos, reçoit les présents envoyés par les Éthiopiens, précédés par le prince de Kousch Aménemapet, leur vainqueur, auquel, en signe de récompense honorifique, un jeune prêtre passe au cou un collier d'or. Dans le tableau suivant on voit Ramsès II monté sur son char de bataille, suivi de ses deux jeunes fils, debout aussi sur des chariots guidés par des conducteurs qui poussent les chevaux à toute vitesse.

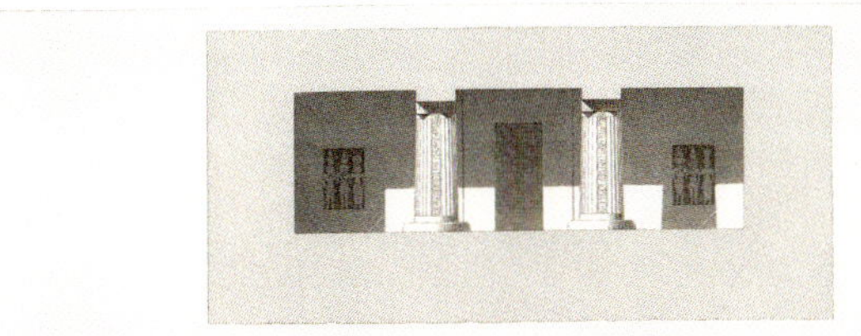

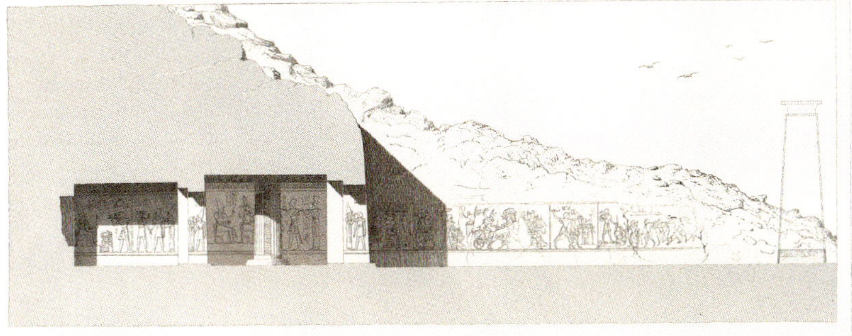

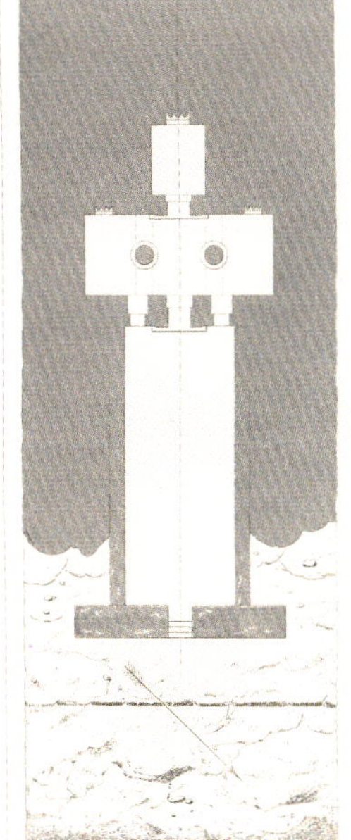

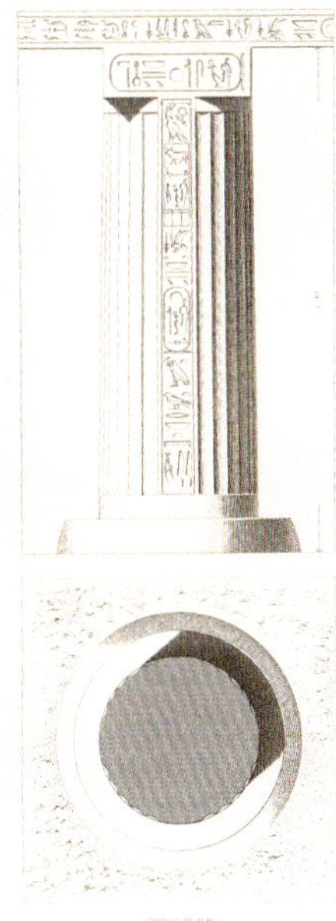

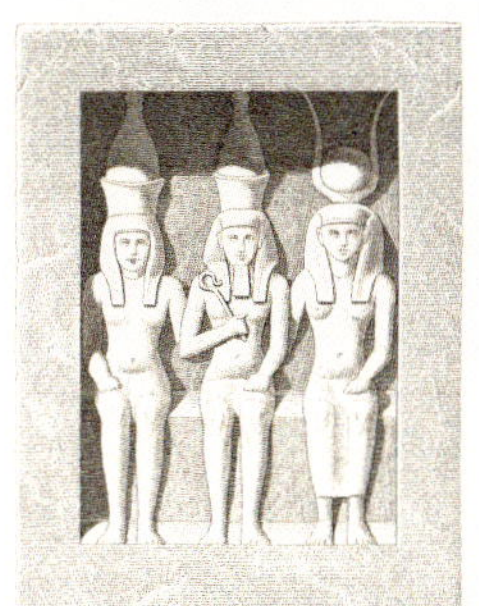

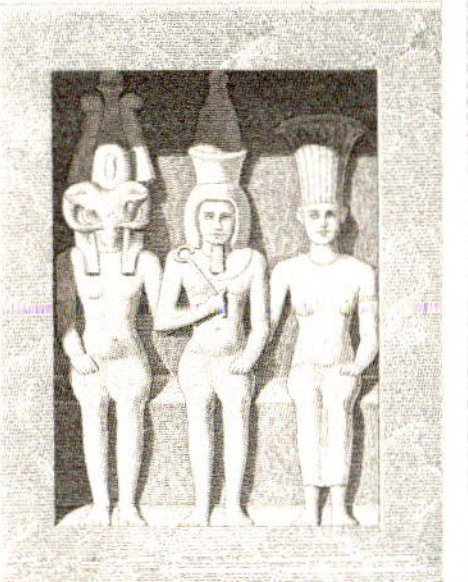

Gravé par Sulpis. Imp. par Eudes. Publié par Arthus Bertrand, Libraire.

SPÉOS DE KALABCHÉ (*TALMIS*)

PLAN, COUPES ET DÉTAILS.

(RAMSES II, XIXe DYNASTIE)

COLUMN FROM THE HYPOSTYLE HALL AT KARNAK (19th Dynasty)

Thebes

This splendid bell-shaped capital, like the umbel of the papyrus, is 3 metres tall by 6.7 metres in diameter at the top. Eight stipules decorated with chevrons in four colours, arranged so that they overlap like the appendages attached to the petiole of the lotus, decorate the base of the capital; they cover the nodes from which emerge the many stalks grouped in threes which terminate in the papyrus umbels. [...] The cartouches contain the prenomen and the nomen of Ramesses II, upon whose orders the decoration of the hypostyle hall was executed. These same cartouches, flanked on either side by uraei, symbols of royalty, form the border beneath the collars of the shaft. Although these details are based entirely on the hieroglyphics, this splendid capital, seen from the base of the columns, resembles a basket of flowers hanging from a candelabrum.

SÄULE AUS DEM HYPOSTYL VON KARNAK (19. Dynastie)

Theben

Dieses prachtvolle glockenförmige Kapitell – einer Papyrusdolde gleich – ist 3 m hoch und hat einen oberen Durchmesser von 6,70 m. Acht mit einem vierfarbigen Fischgrätmuster verzierte Nebenblätter, die in derselben Weise dachziegelartig angeordnet sind wie die am Blattstiel der Lotuspflanze befestigten Blattansätze, schmücken den unteren Teil des Kapitells; sie bedecken den Ansatz zahlreicher in Dreiergruppen zusammengefasster Stängel, die in Papyrusdolden auslaufen. [...] Diese Kartuschen enthalten den Namen und den Vornamen von Ramses II., der die Ausschmückung des Hypostyls vollenden ließ. Die gleichen, abwechselnd von Uräusschlangen – als Sinnbild der Königswürde – flankierten Kartuschen bilden unterhalb der Manschetten eine Einfassung am Schaft. Trotz dieser gänzlich hieroglyphischen Details ähnelt dieses prächtige Kapitell, vom Säulensockel aus gesehen, einem auf einen großen Armleuchter gesetzten Blumenkorb.

COLONNE DE LA SALLE HYPOSTYLE DE KARNAC (XIXe dynastie)

Thèbes

Ce splendide chapiteau campanuliforme, comme l'ombelle du papyrus, a 3 mètres de hauteur sur 6,70 m de diamètre supérieur. Huit stipules, décorés de chevrons quadricolores et disposés ou imbriqués de la même manière que les appendices attachés sur le pétiole du lotus, ornent le bas du chapiteau ; ils recouvrent la naissance de nombreuses tiges, groupées trois par trois et terminées par des ombelles de papyrus. [...] Ces cartouches contiennent le prénom et le nom de Ramsès II qui fit achever la décoration de la salle hypostyle. Ces mêmes cartouches, alternativement flanqués d'uréus, symboles de la royauté, forment bordure au-dessous des viroles du fût. Malgré ces détails tout hiéroglyphiques, ce splendide chapiteau, vu du bas des colonnes, ressemble à une corbeille de fleurs portée sur un candélabre.

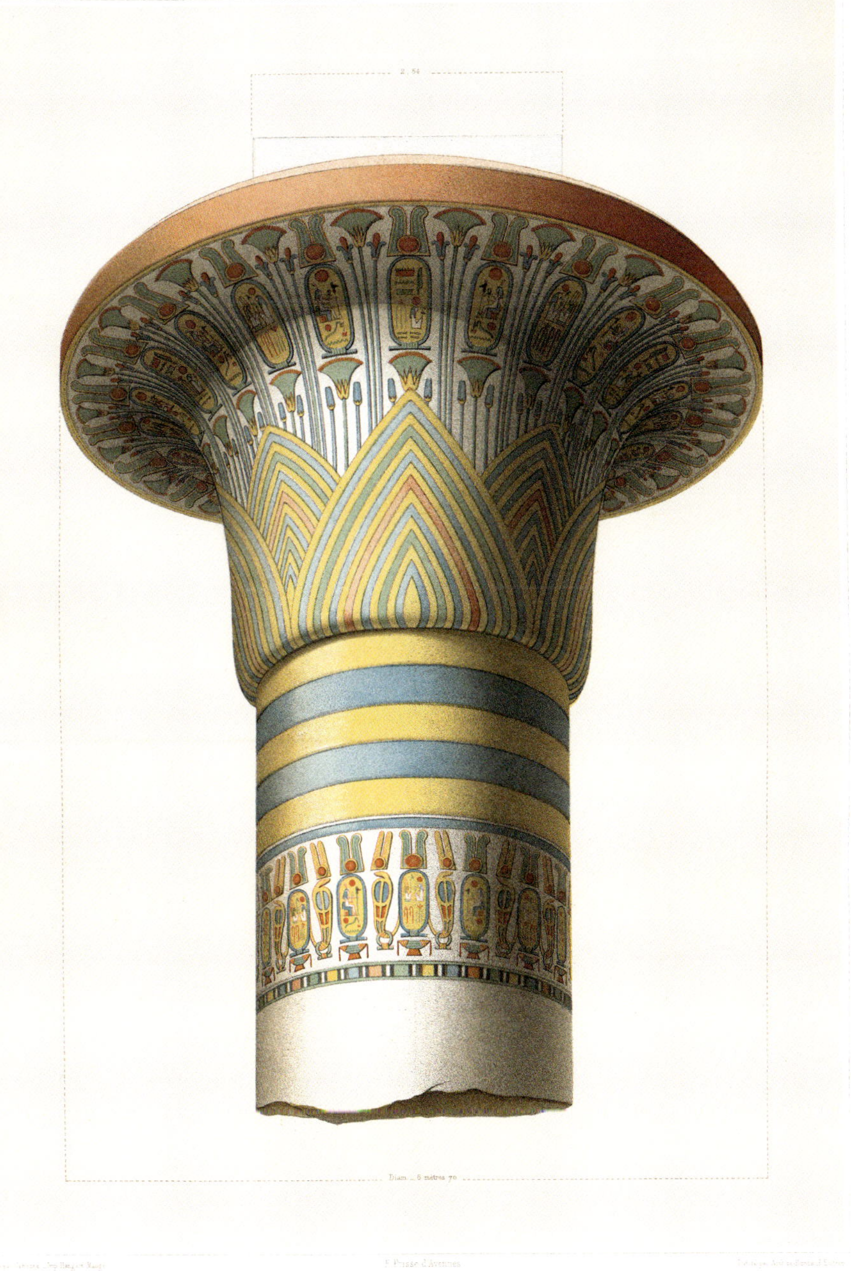

E. Prisse d'Avennes

COLONNE DE LA SALLE HYPOSTYLE DE KARNAC.

(THÈBES _ XIXe DYNASTIE.)

CARYATID PILLARS FROM THE TEMPLE OF RAMESSES III (20th Dynasty)

Medinet Habu

The first courtyard of the great temple of Medinet Habu is closed to the north-east by a gallery composed of seven caryatid pillars approximately 7.5 metres high. These colossi show the image of Ramesses III in Osirid form. The heavy headdress covering the head and falling on to the shoulders supports all those attributes to be found in the cartouche indicating the king's prenomen: these were thus used like an anaglyph to identify him. The Egyptians often had recourse to this method of indicating names by means of hieroglyphic decoration arranged symmetrically. The figures all have their arms crossed on their breast and hold in their hands the crook and the flail. A dagger is tucked into their belt and a small ornamental band decorated with uraei hangs from their rich shendit [kilt]. To left and right of the pharaoh are shown, almost sculpted in the round, two of his children, a son and a daughter, whose names are not engraved; on his head the pharaoh wears the Atef crown.

KARYATIDEN-PFEILER AUS DEM TEMPEL VON RAMSES III. (20. Dynastie)

Medinet Habu

Ein aus sieben Karyatidenpfeilern von etwa 7,50 m Höhe bestehender Wandelgang schließt den ersten Hof des großen Tempels von Medinet Habu im Nordosten ab. Diese Kolosse sind das Abbild von Ramses III. in der Gestalt des Osiris. Die schwere, auf Kopf und Schultern lastende Kopfbedeckung umfasst alle in der Kartusche – die den Vornamen des Königs angibt – genannten Attribute: Diese dienten also dazu, ihn auf anaglyphische Weise zu benennen. Die Ägypter haben sich häufig dieser Form bedient, Namen mithilfe symmetrisch verteilter Hieroglyphen-Ornamente auszudrücken. Alle [Kolosse] weisen auf der Brust gekreuzte Arme auf und halten Krummstab und Wedel in den Händen. Im Gürtel steckt ein Dolch, und am prächtigen Schendit hängt eine mit Uräusschlangen verzierte Binde. Zur Rechten und zur Linken des Pharaos hat man zwei seiner Kinder – einen Sohn und eine Tochter, deren Namen nicht eingraviert sind – fast freistehend dargestellt: Auf dem Kopf trägt der Pharao die Atef-Krone.

PILIERS CARIATIDES DU TEMPLE DE RAMSÈS III (XXe dynastie)

Medineh-Thabou

La première cour du grand temple de Medineh-Thabou est fermée au nord-est par une galerie composée de sept piliers cariatides d'environ 7,50 m de hauteur. Ces colosses offrent l'image de Ramsès III sous la forme osiriaque. La lourde coiffure qui couvre leur tête et descend sur leurs épaules renferme tous les attributs qui se trouvent dans le cartouche qui indique le prénom du roi : ceux-ci servaient ainsi à le désigner d'une façon anaglyphique. Les Égyptiens ont fait un fréquent usage de cette manière d'exprimer des noms à l'aide d'ornements hiéroglyphiques, distribués symétriquement. Tous ont les bras croisés sur la poitrine, et tiennent en main le fouet et le crochet. Un poignard est passé dans leur ceinture, et sur leur riche schantie [shendyt] pend une bandelette ornée d'uréus. À droite et à gauche du pharaon, on a représenté, presque de ronde-bosse, deux de ses enfants, un fils et une fille, dont les noms ne sont pas gravés : la tête du pharaon est coiffée du claft [la couronne Atef].

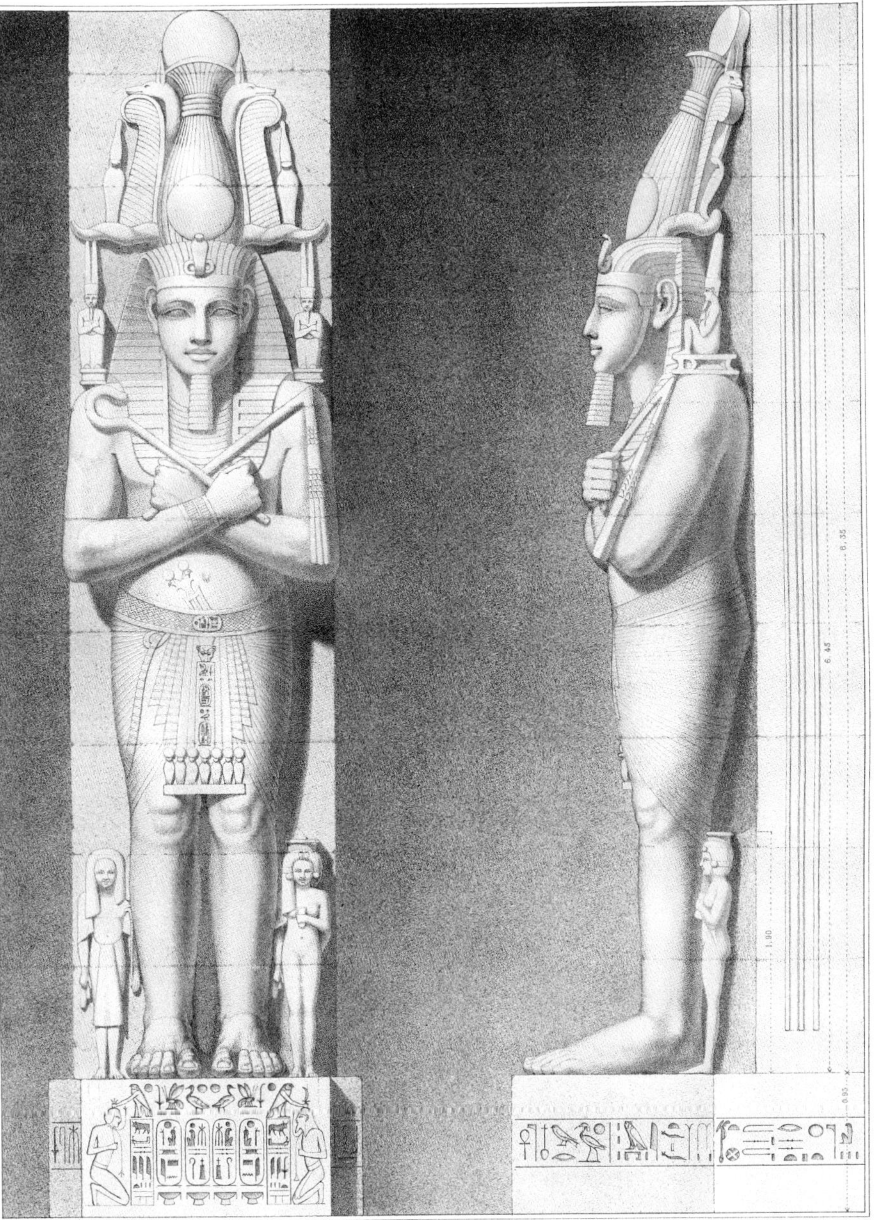

Lith par Jehenne. Imp. par Hangard-Maugé
E. Prisse d'Avennes
Publié par Arthus Bertrand Editeur

PILIERS CARYATIDES DU TEMPLE DE RAMSÈS III

(MEDINEH THABOU _ XX.e DYNASTIE)

INTERIOR DECORATIONS FROM THE GYNAECEUM OF RAMESSES III (20th Dynasty)

Medinet Habu

The exterior bas-reliefs of this small palace show only religious scenes or records of the conquests of the pharaoh who had it built, whereas the interior bas-reliefs feature only scenes from his private life. No. 1 shows the decoration of the west wall of a small chamber. On one side the pharaoh can be seen with one of his ladies, taking pleasure in playing a game similar to our game of draughts; on the other side, he is accepting and encouraging the caresses of a half-naked young girl who offers him a piece of fruit. No. 2 shows scenes of the same type. Because the headdress of these young girls is like that of princesses and queens, it has long been thought that here Ramesses was playing with his children. But apart from the fact that these figures are not named, they are naked and could hardly have been portrayed wearing nothing but a flimsy gauze.

INNENAUSSTATTUNG DES GYNAECEUMS VON RAMSES III. (20. Dynastie)

Medinet Habu

Die äußeren Flachreliefs dieses kleinen Palastes zeigen lediglich religiöse Szenen oder erinnern an die Eroberungen des Pharaos, der sie errichten ließ; die inneren Flachreliefs bilden hingegen nur Szenen aus seinem Privatleben ab. Die Nr. 1 stellt die Ausschmückung der Westwand eines kleinen Raumes dar. Auf der einen Seite ist der Pharao zu sehen, der sich mit einer seiner Frauen bei einem Spiel die Zeit vertreibt, das unserem Damespiel entspricht: Auf der anderen Seite entfacht und empfängt er die Liebkosung eines halbnackten jungen Mädchens, das ihm eine Frucht anbietet. Die Nr. 2 zeigt Szenen der gleichen Art. Der Kopfputz dieser jungen Mädchen ist der von Prinzessen und Königinnen; auch hat man lange geglaubt, Ramses spiele mit seinen Kindern. Abgesehen davon, dass keine dieser Figuren einen Namen trägt, sind jedoch alle nackt und können kaum mit mehr als einer leichten Gaze bekleidet dargestellt gewesen sein.

DÉCORATIONS INTÉRIEURES DU GYNÉCÉE DE RAMSÈS III (XXe dynastie)

Medineh-Thabou

Les bas-reliefs extérieurs de ce petit palais ne présentent que des scènes religieuses, ou des souvenirs des conquêtes du pharaon qui le fit élever ; les bas-reliefs intérieurs, au contraire, n'offrent que des scènes de sa vie privée. Le n° 1 représente la décoration du mur occidental d'une petite salle. On voit, d'un côté, le pharaon s'amusant avec une de ses femmes, à un jeu analogue à notre jeu de dames : de l'autre côté, il reçoit et provoque les caresses d'une jeune fille demi-nue qui lui présente un fruit. Le n° 2 offre des scènes du même genre. La coiffure que portent ces jeunes filles est celle des princesses et des reines ; aussi a-t-on cru longtemps que Ramsès jouait avec ses enfants. Mais outre qu'aucune de ces figures ne porte de nom, elles sont nues et ne pourraient guère avoir été représentées vêtues que d'une gaze légère.

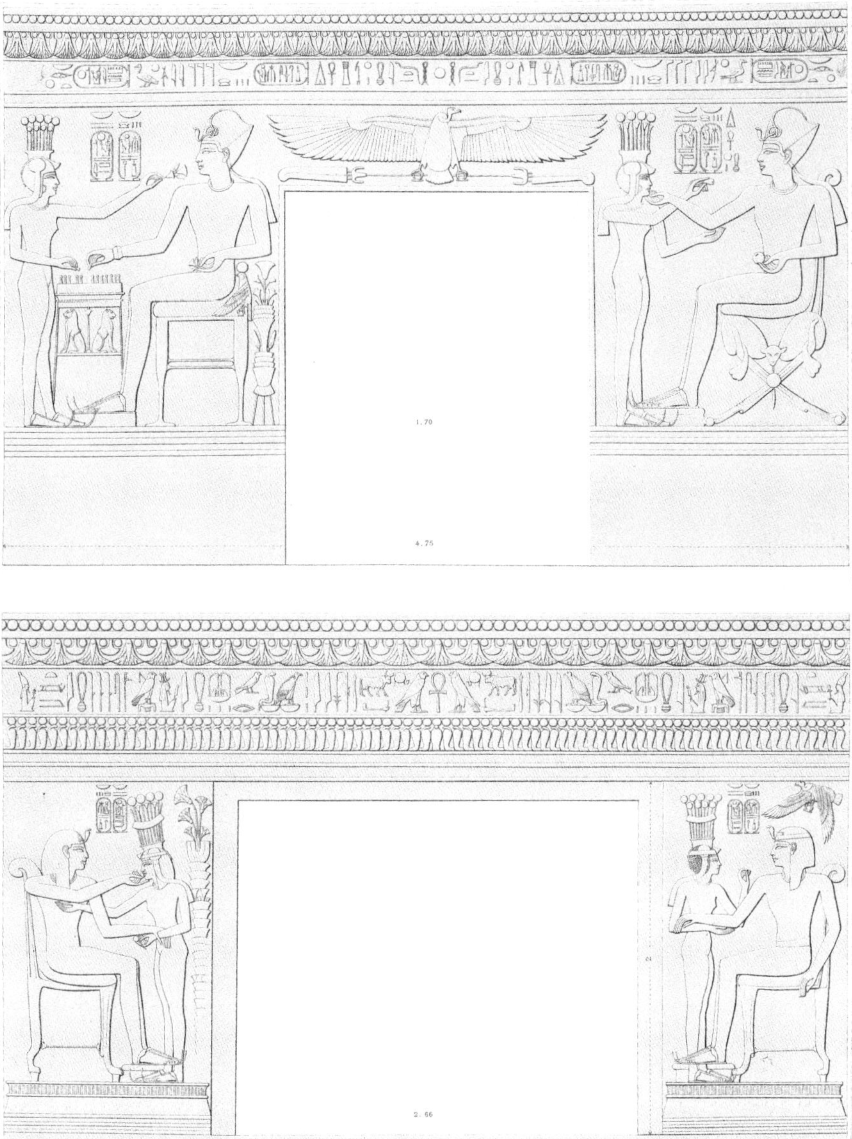

1.70

4.75

2.66

4.96

Lith par Daumont. Imp par Haugard-Maugé

W. de Famars-Testas.

Publié par Arthus-Bertrand Éditeur.

DÉCORATIONS INTÉRIEURES DU GYNECÉE DE RAMSÈS III.

(MEDINEH-THABOU._ XXe DYNASTIE.)

NECROPOLIS OF THEBES (26th Dynasty)

Tombs from the valley of el-Assasif

This [pyramidal] tomb is built of brick directly on the ground: two layers of brick are placed flat, side by side, on top of the vault. The conical shape is constructed by placing bricks in horizontal courses and corbelling them. The vertical course, already published in reproduction in the plate drawn by Lepsius, is the only one to remain; this would appear to indicate that the vault was open to the sky. The two doors inserted into the pylons were covered by a full arch constructed from a number of courses of bricks stacked on top of each other. A number of these pyramids can be seen in Thebes; they are built of sun-baked bricks and contain small chambers beneath barrel vaulting. A particularly interesting feature of the huge enclosure of el-Assasif, whose plan is reproduced in our drawing together with sketches of those fragments still standing, is that hollows have been gouged out of the sun-baked-brick walls; Victor Moreau believes that the corpses were placed here and that awnings were fixed over them to protect the embalmers from the fierce heat of the sun.

NEKROPOLE VON THEBEN (26. Dynastie)

Gräber aus dem Tal von El-Assasif

Dieses [pyramidenförmige] Grabmal ist aus hochkant verbauten Ziegeln errichtet; zwei Ziegellagen wurden dabei miteinander flach auf das Gewölbe gelegt. Den Konus errichtete man aus auskragend gesetzten und in horizontalen Lagen angeordneten Ziegeln. Die vertikale – bereits auf einer von Lepsius gezeichneten Tafel wiedergegebene – Lage ist die letzte erhaltene Schicht; sie hätte darauf hindeuten müssen, dass das Gewölbe offen ist. Die beiden in den Pylonen angelegten Tore waren mit Rundbogen aus mehreren übereinanderliegenden Ziegelreihen überwölbt. Diese Pyramiden, von denen in Theben mehrere vorkommen, sind aus luftgetrockneten Ziegeln erbaut und bergen mehrere kleine, mit Tonnengewölben überwölbte Räume. Die weitläufige Einfriedung von El-Assasif – von der auf unserer Zeichnung der Grundriss und die noch stehenden Überreste abgebildet sind – fiel durch die Aussparungen auf, die in den Mauern aus luftgetrockneten Ziegeln angelegt waren; Victor Moreau meint, dass diese dazu bestimmt waren, die Toten aufzunehmen, und dass an ihnen Schutzzelte befestigt waren, die die Einbalsamierer vor der Sonnenglut schützen sollten.

NÉCROPOLE DE THÈBES (XXVIe dynastie)

Tombeaux de la vallée d'El-Assacif

Ce tombeau [pyramidal] est construit en briques sur champ ; deux lits de briques, ensemble, placées à plat sur la voûte. Le cône est construit au moyen de briques disposées en assises horizontales et posées en encorbellement. L'assise verticale, déjà reproduite par la planche dessinée par Lepsius, est la dernière assise qui reste ; elle aurait dû indiquer que la voûte est à ciel ouvert. Les deux portes ménagées dans les pylônes étaient voûtées à plein cintre par plusieurs rangs de briques superposés. Ces pyramides, dont on voit plusieurs à Thèbes, sont construites en briques crues et recèlent des petites salles voûtées en berceau. Le vaste enclos d'El-Assacif, dont notre dessin reproduit le plan et les vestiges encore debout, était remarquable par les évidements ménagés dans ses murs de brique crue, Victor Moreau pense qu'ils étaient destinés à recevoir les morts auxquels étaient fixées les bannes qui protégeaient les embaumeurs contre les ardeurs du soleil.

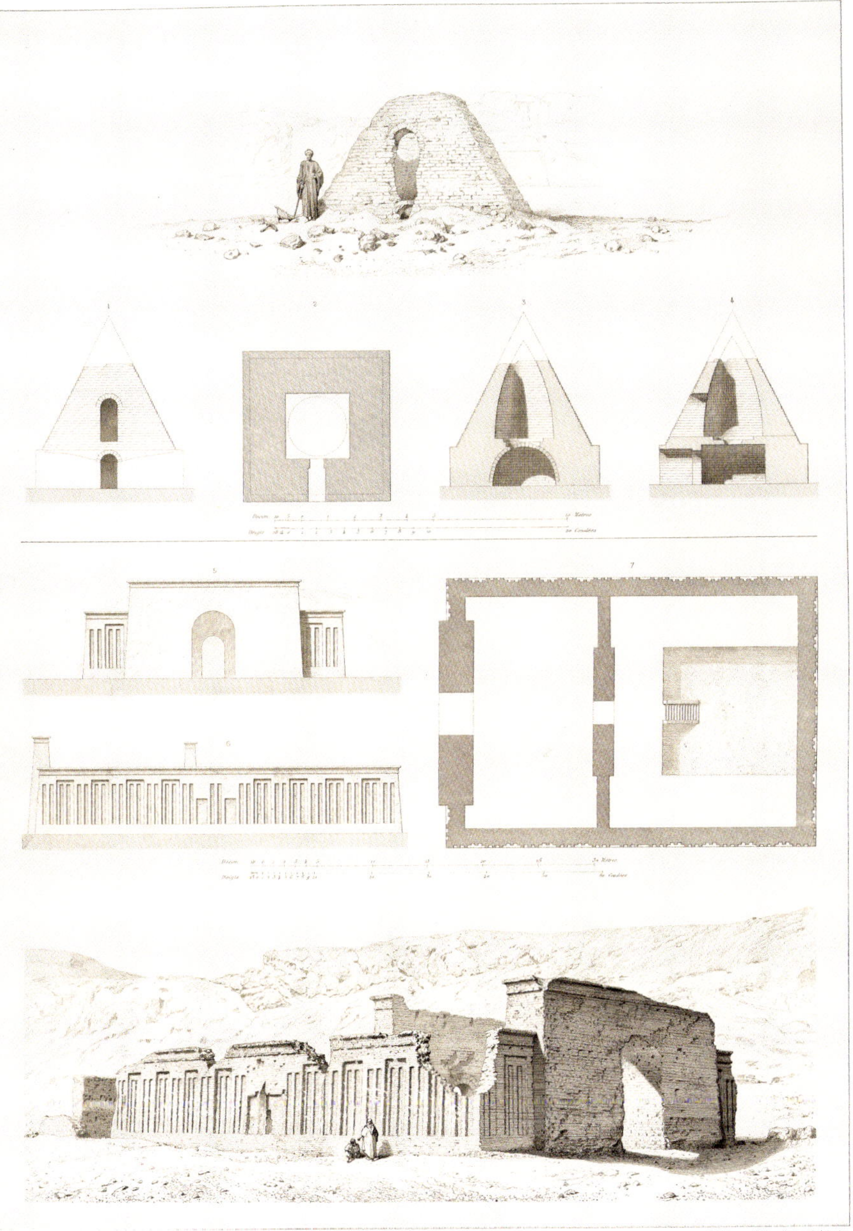

Gravé par A. Guillaumot. Imp. par Salmon.   Prisse d'Avennes   Publié par Arthus Bertrand Libraire

NÉCROPOLE DE THÈBES

TOMBEAUX DE LA VALLÉE D'EL-ASSACIF.

(XXVIe DYNASTIE)

COLUMNS FROM THE TEMPLE OF NECTANEBO, AT PHILAE (30th Dynasty)

In the buildings at Philae there are five dactyliform capitals which all display noticeable differences. Two of these capitals are shown in this plate: the first, which forms part of the west gallery, is much more regular than the other; it is decorated with scales above the collars, and with bunches of dates immediately above the scales. The second column has no fruit ornamentation and the collars begin beneath the palm fronds, while the base is decorated with chevrons similar to those on the other columns in this gallery.

SÄULEN DES NEKTANEBOS-TEMPELS, AUF PHILAE (30. Dynastie)

In den Bauwerken von Philae finden sich fünf Palmwedel-Kapitelle, die alle deutliche Unterschiede aufweisen. Auf dieser Tafel sind zwei dieser Kapitelle abgebildet: Das erste stammt aus dem westlichen Wandelgang und ist viel harmonischer gestaltet als das andere; es ist oberhalb der Manschetten mit Schuppen und unmittelbar oberhalb der Schuppen mit Dattelbüscheln verziert. Was das zweite betrifft, so ist es nicht mit Früchten verziert, und die Manschetten beginnen unterhalb der Palmwedel, wobei der Sockel mit einem Fischgrätmuster geschmückt ist, das dem der anderen Säulen in diesem Wandelgang ähnelt.

COLONNES DU TEMPLE DE NECTANÈBE, À PHILÆ (XXXe dynastie)

Il y a dans les édifices de Philæ cinq chapiteaux dactyliformes qui présentent tous des différences notables. Cette planche représente deux de ces chapiteaux : le premier, qui fait partie de la galerie de l'ouest, est beaucoup plus régulier que l'autre ; il est orné d'écailles au-dessus des viroles, et de grappes de dattes immédiatement au-dessus des écailles. Quant au second, il n'est pas orné de fruits, et les viroles commencent en bas des palmes, tandis que la base est décorée de chevrons semblables à ceux des autres colonnes de cette galerie.

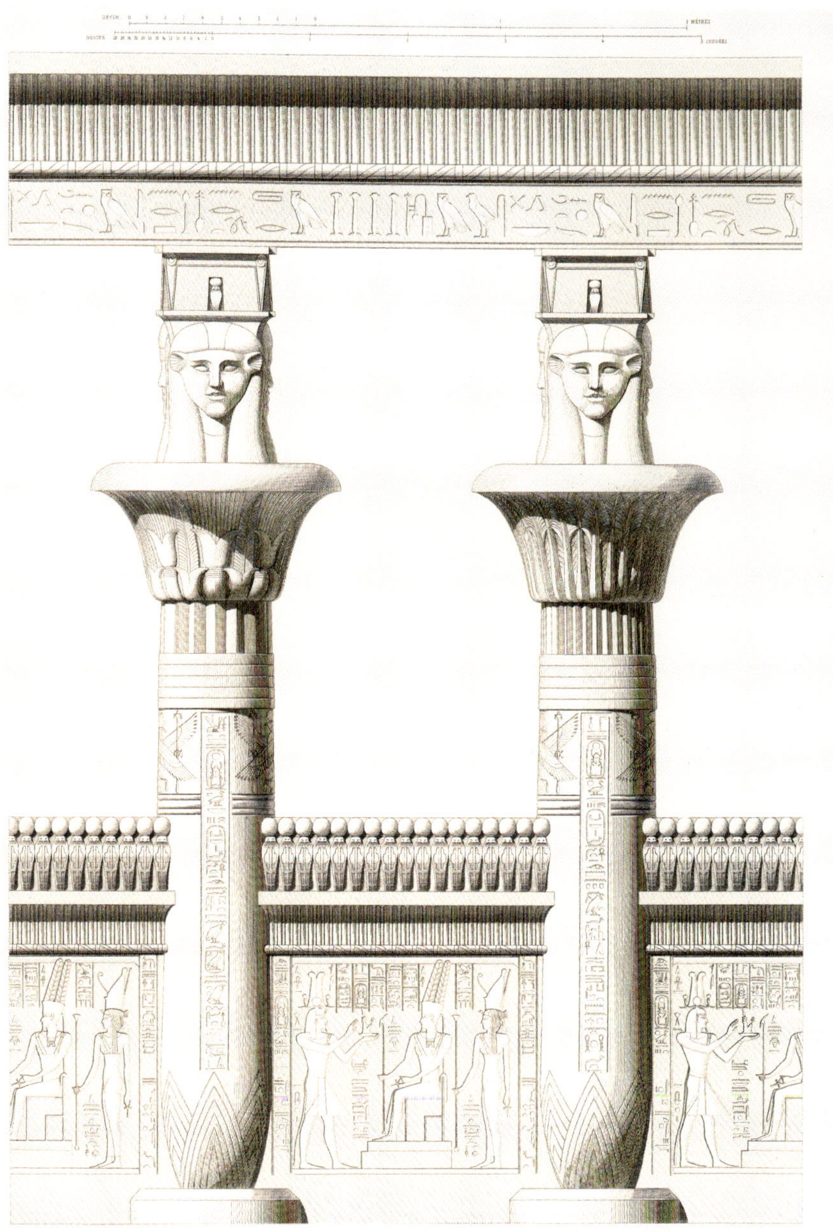

Prisse d'Avennes

Arthus Bertrand Editeur

COLONNES DU TEMPLE DE NECTANÈBE

(PHILAE_XXXᴱ DYNASTIE)

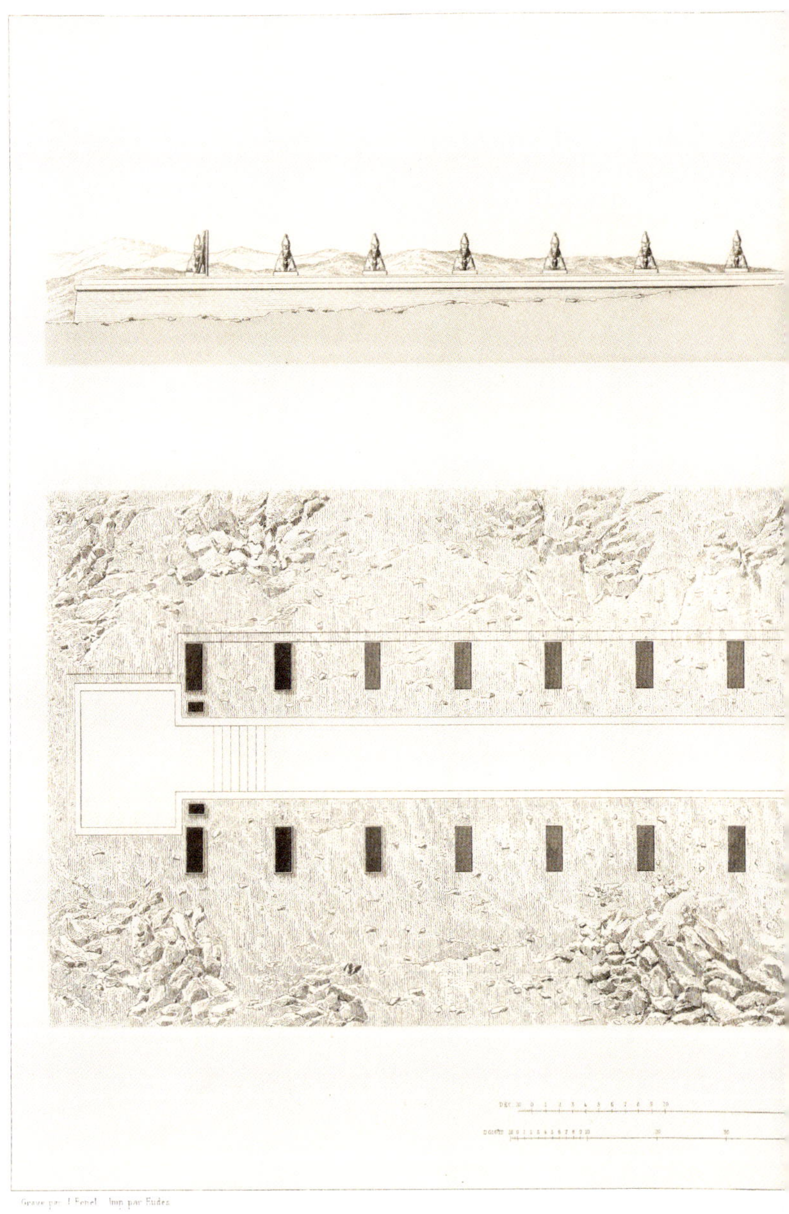

Gravé par J. Fenel · Imp. par Eudes

HEMI-S

1

RE

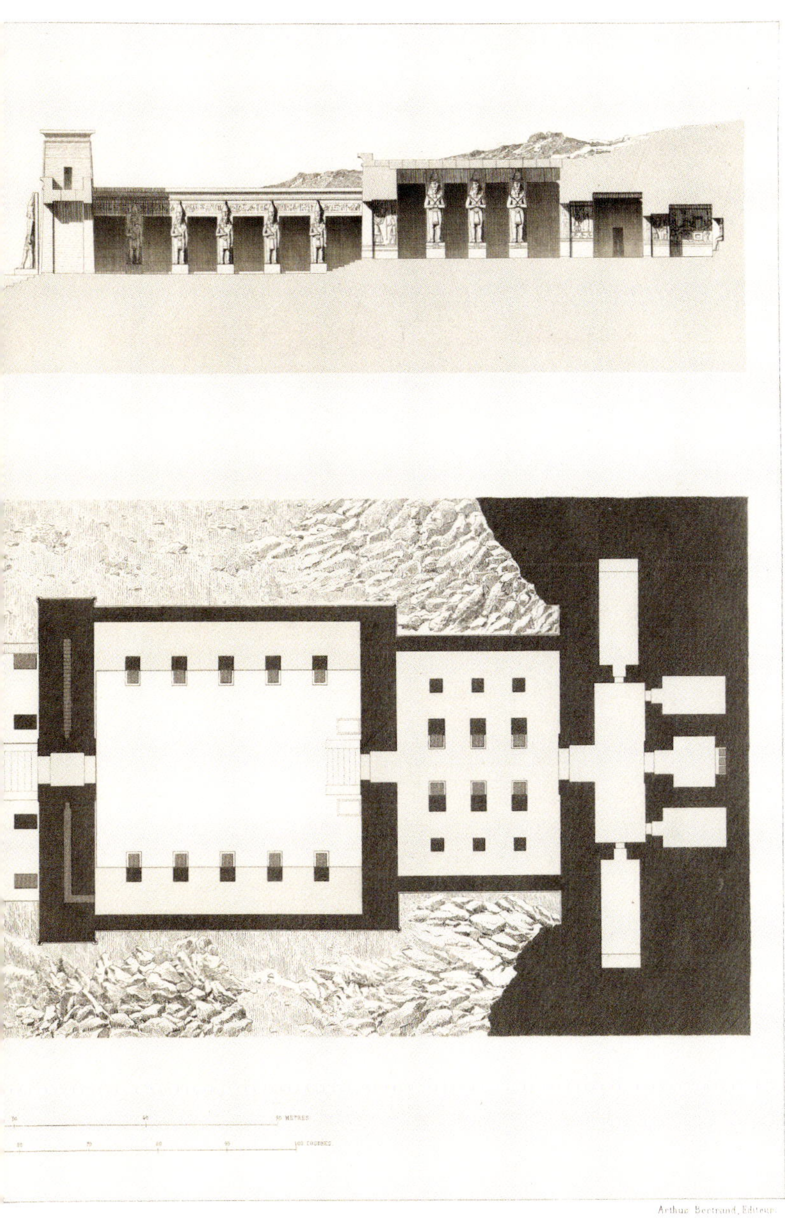

Arthus Bertrand, Éditeur

UIRCHÉ

E

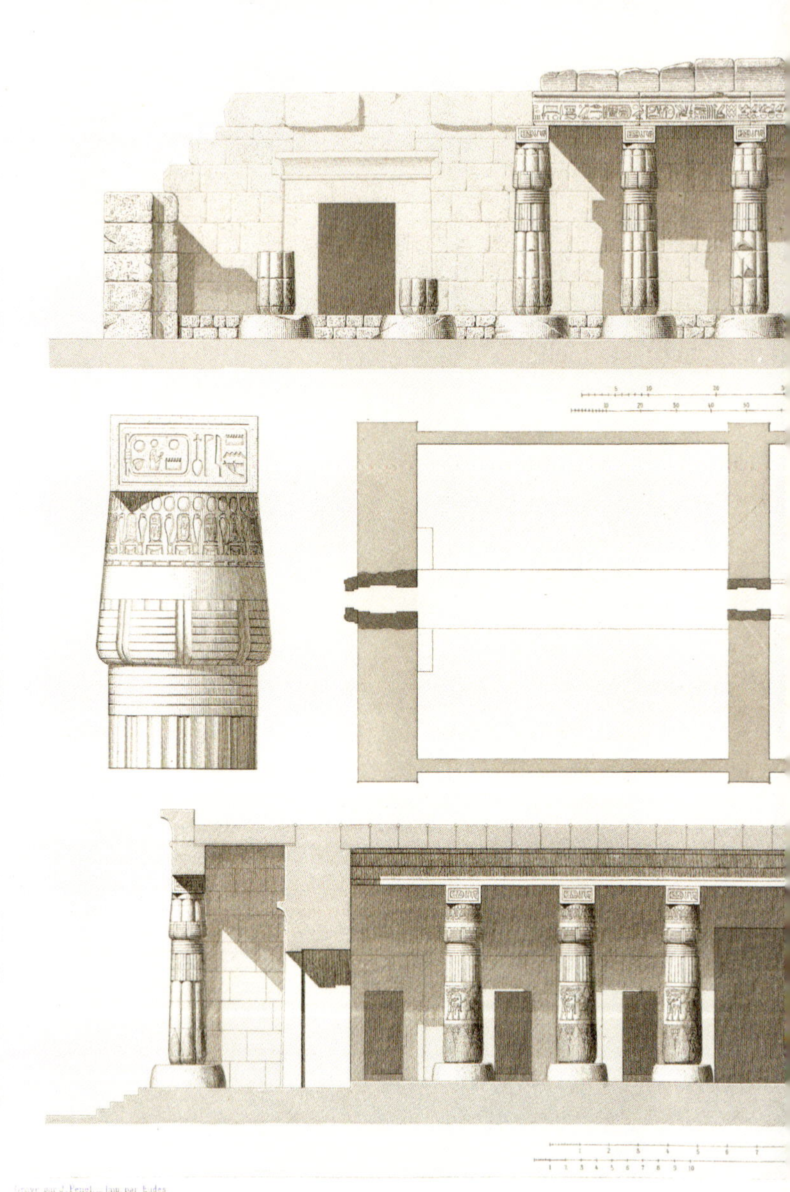

Gravé par J. Penel... Imp. par Eudes

TEMPLE

PLAN,

RE

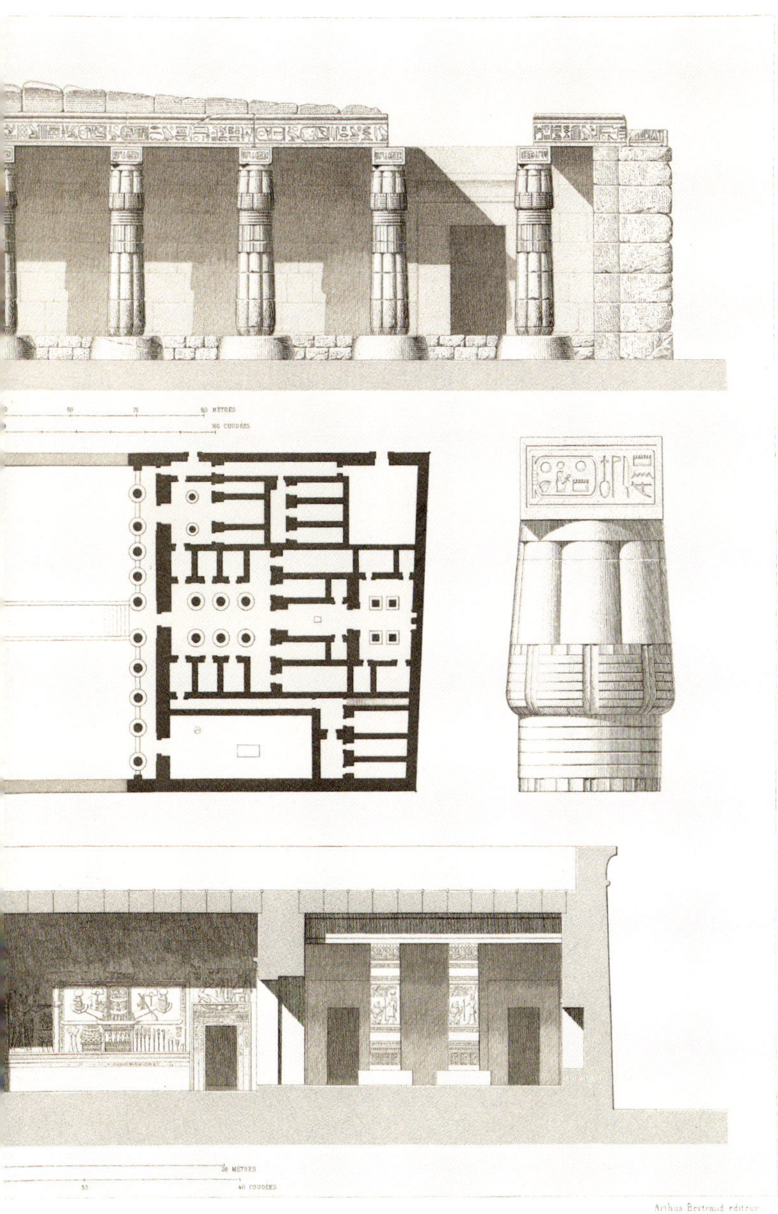

Arthus Bertrand éditeur

HTEHUM

TION]

(Pages/Seite 294/295)

HEMI-SPEOS OF GERF HUSSEIN: PLAN AND CROSS-SECTION

Nubia

Gersha or Gerf Hussein is a small village situated on the left bank of the Nile, in Lower Nubia. This area was formerly known by the same name as Memphis: it was called Ptaheï or Typtah, "the dwelling of Ptah". The temple of Gerf Hussein was a hemi-speos, whose most ancient part was carved into the rock, while the more recent part was built of sandstone. At the foot of the mountain, separated from the Nile by a sandy plain, can be seen mutilated statues and the debris of sphinxes: these sphinxes appear to have adorned a staircase or dromos. The four pillars that joined the colonnade to the speos on each side were adorned with colossal statues with the mitre called the Pschent on their heads; they wore a simple kilt and in their hands, crossed on their breast, they carried the crook and the flail, the usual emblems of Osiris. He is here represented with the features of a Ramesses, possibly the Great.

HEMISPEOS VON GERF HUSSEIN: GRUNDRISS UND SCHNITTZEICHNUNG

Nubien

Gerscha oder Gerf Hussein ist ein kleines Dorf am linken Nilufer, in Unternubien. Dieser Ort trug einst denselben Namen wie Memphis; er hieß Ptahei oder Typtah, „die Wohnung des Ptah". Der Tempel von Gerf Hussein war ein Hemispeos, dessen älterer Teil aus dem Felsen geschlagen und dessen jüngerer Teil aus Sandstein erbaut war. Am Fuß des Gebirges, vom Nil durch eine sandige Ebene getrennt, fallen verstümmelte Statuen und Bruchstücke von Sphingen auf: Diese Sphingen zierten anscheinend eine Treppe oder einen Dromos. Die vier Pfeiler, die diese Kolonnade auf jeder Seite mit dem Speos verbanden, sind mit Kolossalstatuen geschmückt, die auf dem Kopf die altägyptische Doppelkrone (Pschent) tragen, mit einem einfachen Schurz bekleidet sind und in den auf der Brust gekreuzten Händen Krummstab und Wedel – die üblichen Attribute des Osiris – halten. Dieser [Osiris] weist die Züge eines Ramses auf, bei dem es sich vielleicht um Ramses den Großen handelt.

HEMI-SPÉOS DE GUIRCHÉ : PLAN ET COUPE

Nubie

Guirché ou Gerf-Hussein est un petit village situé sur la rive gauche du Nil, dans la Basse-Nubie. Cette localité portait jadis le même nom que Memphis ; elle s'appelait Ptaheï ou Typtah, « la demeure de Ptah ». Le temple de Guirché était un hémi-spéos, dont la partie la plus ancienne était taillée dans la roche, et la partie la plus récente était bâtie en grès. Au pied de la montagne, séparée du Nil par une plaine sablonneuse, on remarque des statues mutilées et des débris de sphinx : ces sphinx paraissent avoir décoré un escalier ou dromos. Les quatre piliers, qui joignaient, de chaque côté, cette colonnade au spéos, sont ornés de statues colossales, coiffées de la mitre appelée pschent, vêtues d'un simple giron, et portant, dans leurs mains croisées sur la poitrine, l'aspersoir et la crosse, emblèmes ordinaires d'Osiris. Celui-ci est représenté sous les traits d'un Ramsès, peut-être le Grand.

(Pages/Seite 296/297)

TEMPLE OF MERNEPTEUM

Plan, cross-section and elevation

When the traveller disembarks at the Sycamore in el-Qurna the first monument to catch his eye is an old palace which is known locally as Qasr el-Kubayg. The debris of a propylon shows that the overall enclosure of this palace extended on that side to more than 100 metres from the portico in front of the building. This sandstone propylon bears the inscriptions of Merneptah I and of Ramesses II and its interior façade was once adorned with two colossal sphinxes. [...] The plan of this building bears no resemblance to those of other Egyptian monuments: the layout, elevation and extent of the chambers all seem to indicate that the architect's intention here was to build a dwelling which was perhaps not particularly spacious but which was at least well adapted to normal everyday needs. Although it is in fact the dwelling-place of a sovereign, Merneptah or Seti according to the inscriptions, it is also a temple dedicated to Amun, so intimately was the cult linked to royalty and so firmly attached to an obligatory ritual was the private life of the king.

TEMPEL DES MERENPTEUM

Grundriss, Detail- und Schnittzeichnung

Das erste Denkmal, das bei der Ankunft an der Sykomore von el-Qurna den Blick des Reisenden auf sich zieht, ist ein alter Palast, der in der Gegend Gasr el-Koubayg genannt wird. Die Trümmer eines Propylons deuten darauf hin, dass die Umfassungsmauer des Palastes sich auf dieser Seite mehr als 100 m über den diesem vorgelagerten Portikus hinaus erstreckte. Die Innenfassade dieses Propylons aus Sandstein, der die Inschriften von Merenptah I. und Ramses II. trägt, war einst mit zwei riesenhaften Sphingen geschmückt. [...] In nichts ähnelt der Grundriss dieses Gebäudes dem der anderen ägyptischen Denkmäler: Die Verteilung, die Größe und die Erhabenheit der Räume – alles weist darauf hin, dass der Architekt hier damit befasst war, eine wenn auch nicht praktische, so doch den ganz gewöhnlichen Bedürfnissen des Lebens angemessene Behausung zu errichten. Tatsächlich ist dies die Wohnung eines Herrschers – nach Aussage der Inschriften die von Merenptah oder Sethos; dies ist aber auch ein dem Amun geweihter Tempel – solchermaßen waren Kult und Königswürde miteinander verknüpft und das Privatleben der Könige an ein verpflichtendes Ritual gebunden.

TEMPLE DE MÉNEPHTEHUM

Plan, coupe et élévation

En débarquant au Sycomore de Gournah, le premier monument qui attire l'œil des voyageurs est un vieux palais, appelé dans le pays Gasr el-Koubayg. Les débris d'un propylon annoncent que l'enceinte générale de ce palais s'étendait de ce côté à plus de 100 mètres du portique qui le précède. Ce propylon de grès, qui porte les légendes de Menephthah [Mérenptah] Ier et de Ramsès II, avait jadis sa façade intérieure ornée de deux sphinx colossaux. [...] Le plan de cet édifice ne ressemble en rien à ceux des autres monuments égyptiens : la distribution, l'élévation et l'étendue des salles, tout semble annoncer que l'architecte s'est occupé ici de construire une habitation sinon commode, du moins appropriée aux besoins les plus habituels de la vie. C'est en effet la demeure d'un souverain, de Menephthah ou Séti, ainsi que le disent les légendes ; mais c'est aussi un temple dédié à Amon, tant le culte était lié à la royauté, tant la vie privée des rois se rattachait à un rituel obligé.

TOPOGRAPHICAL PLAN OF PART OF THE NECROPOLIS OF MEMPHIS

Pyramids of Giza

To the south-east of the Great Sphinx can be seen an enormous building which on the plan we have simply identified by the word "Tomb" and which was formerly taken, wrongly, to be a temple; there can in fact be no doubt that it is a tomb. This huge granite construction is surrounded by a limestone wall which rises to a greater height than the building, inside which was found a beautiful statue of Chephren [Khafre], and it is therefore possible that it was the burial place of this pharaoh: it was built of colossal blocks of alabaster and granite. It seems likely that entry into this building was through a door situated in the north-east angle, which gave on to a corridor 18 metres long; half-way along another door gave access to another gallery of the same length, as well as a huge chamber adorned with ten pillars. This chamber appears to have been laid out like this in order to contain the sarcophagi of the family of the dead man; however, his sarcophagus has disappeared, along with all the others.

TOPOGRAFISCHE ÜBERSICHTSKARTE EINES TEILS DER NEKROPOLE VON MEMPHIS

Pyramiden von Gizeh

Südöstlich der großen Sphinx ist ein unermesslich großes Bauwerk zu sehen, das auf der Karte lediglich mit dem Wort „Grab" verzeichnet ist und das man zu Unrecht für einen Tempel hielt: Ganz offensichtlich handelt es sich um ein Grabmal. Dieser unmessbar große Granitbau, umgeben von einer höheren Kalksteinmauer, in der sich eine schöne Statue des Chephren [Chafre] fand, war vielleicht ein Pharaonengrab: Er war aus riesigen Alabaster- und Granitblöcken errichtet. In das Bauwerk gelangte man wahrscheinlich durch eine in der Nordostecke gelegene Tür, die auf einen 18 m langen Korridor führt; in dessen Mitte stellt eine weitere Tür die Verbindung zu einem weiteren Gang derselben Länge sowie zu einem geräumigen, mit zehn Pfeilern ausgeschmückten Saal her. Diese Halle scheint uns so angelegt zu sein, um die Sarkophage der Familie des Verstorbenen aufnehmen zu können; wie alle übrigen ist jedoch auch sein Sarkophag verschwunden.

PLAN TOPOGRAPHIQUE D'UNE PARTIE DE LA NÉCROPOLE DE MEMPHIS

Pyramides de Gizeh

On voit, au sud-est du grand Sphinx, une immense construction que sur le plan nous avons désignée simplement par le mot « Tombe », et qu'on a prise, à tort, pour un temple : c'est, incontestablement, un tombeau. Cette immense construction de granit, entourée d'un mur de calcaire qui s'élevait plus haut, et dans laquelle on a trouvé une belle statue de Schafré [Khafrê], était, peut-être, la sépulture de ce pharaon : elle était construite en blocs colossaux d'albâtre et de granit. On pénétrait, probablement, dans cette construction par une porte, située à l'angle nord-est, et qui aboutit dans un corridor de 18 mètres de longueur, au milieu duquel une autre porte met en communication une autre galerie de la même longueur, ainsi qu'une vaste salle ornée de dix piliers. Cette salle nous paraît avoir été distribuée ainsi pour contenir les sarcophages de la famille du défunt ; mais son sarcophage a disparu comme les autres.

I 46

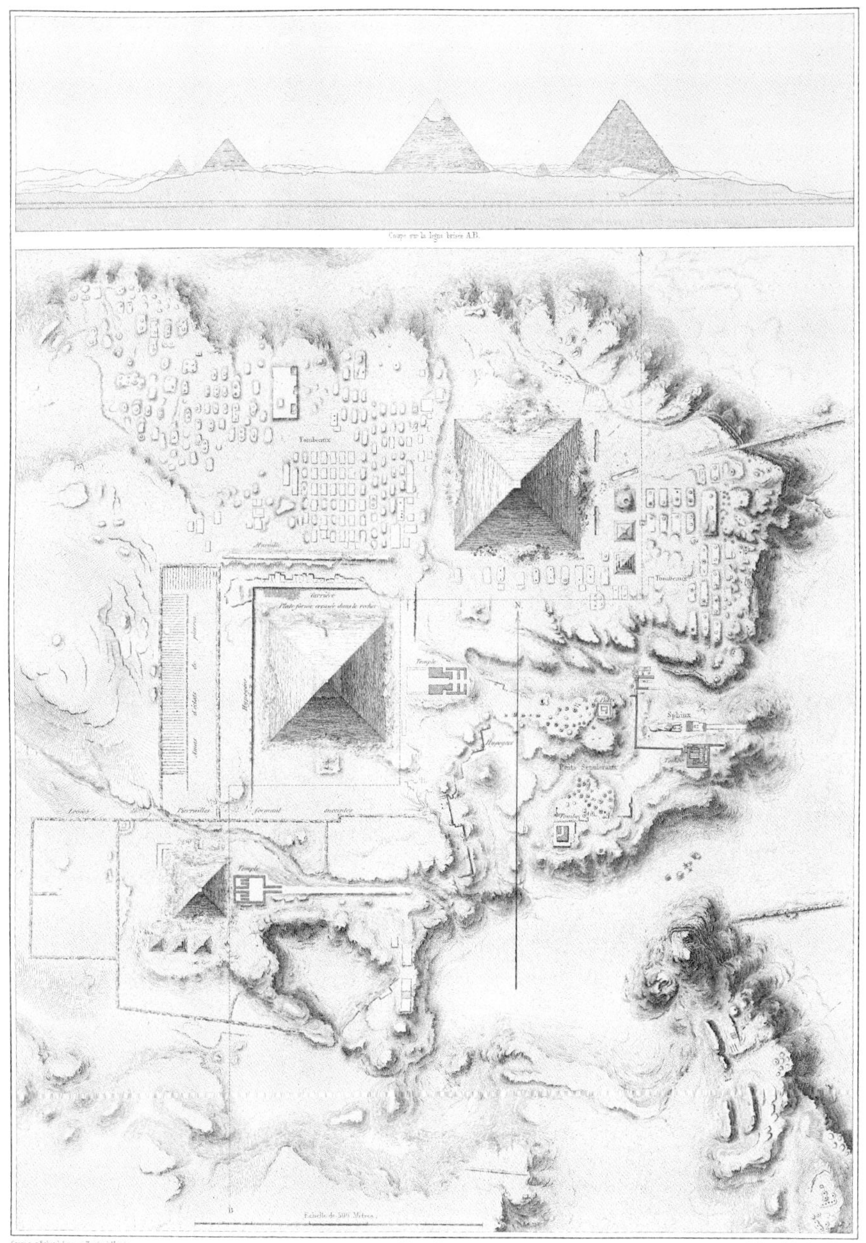

Gravé par Erhard Imp. par Hanfer Lemercier

E. Prisse d'Avennes

Publié par Arthus Bertrand Editeur

PLAN TOPOGRAPHIQUE D'UNE PARTIE DE LA NÉCROPOLE DE MEMPHIS.

(PYRAMIDES DE GIZEH.)

TEMPLE OF DAKKA. PSELCHIS (Ptolemaic and Roman Period)

Plan, cross-section and view in perspective

This plate shows a representation of an ancient temple of Mercury, which is fairly well preserved. It is therefore possible to demonstrate that all Egyptian temples, not only the large ones but the smallest ones as well, incorporated every element demanded by the cult and that the architects were obliged, both in the overall execution of their work and in every detail of their building, to conform to the absolute priestly rules which applied to large temples. Dakka, the ancient Pselchis, is situated 80 kilometres north-north-east of Deir el-Medina.

TEMPEL VON AD-DAKKA. PSELCHIS (Ptolemäer- und Römerzeit)

Grundriss, Schnittzeichnung und perspektivische Ansicht

Diese Tafel zeigt die Darstellung eines alten Merkur-Tempels, der sich in einem recht guten Erhaltungszustand befindet; an diesem Beispiel lässt sich zeigen, dass selbst die kleinsten ägyptischen Tempel – ebenso wie die großen – über alle für die Ausübung des Kultes erforderlichen Bestandteile verfügten und dass die Architekten bei ihrer gesamten Arbeit und in Bezug auf alle Baudetails gehalten waren, sich wie auch bei den letztgenannten an zwingende religiöse Vorgaben zu halten. Ad-Dakka, das frühere Pselchis, liegt 80 km im Nordnordosten von Deir el-Medina.

TEMPLE DE DAKKEH. PSELCIS (époque ptolémaïque et romaine)

Plan, coupe et vue perspective

Cette planche offre la représentation d'un ancien temple de Mercure, qui se trouve être assez bien conservé ; il permet de démontrer que les temples égyptiens, même les plus petits, possédaient, aussi bien que les grands, toutes les parties exigées par le culte ; et que les architectes étaient tenus, dans l'ensemble de leur travail et dans tous les détails de leur édification, de se soumettre comme pour ces derniers à des règles hiératiques absolues. Dakkeh ou Dakkah, l'ancienne Pselcis, est située à 80 kilomètres nord-nord-est de Deyr el-Medineh.

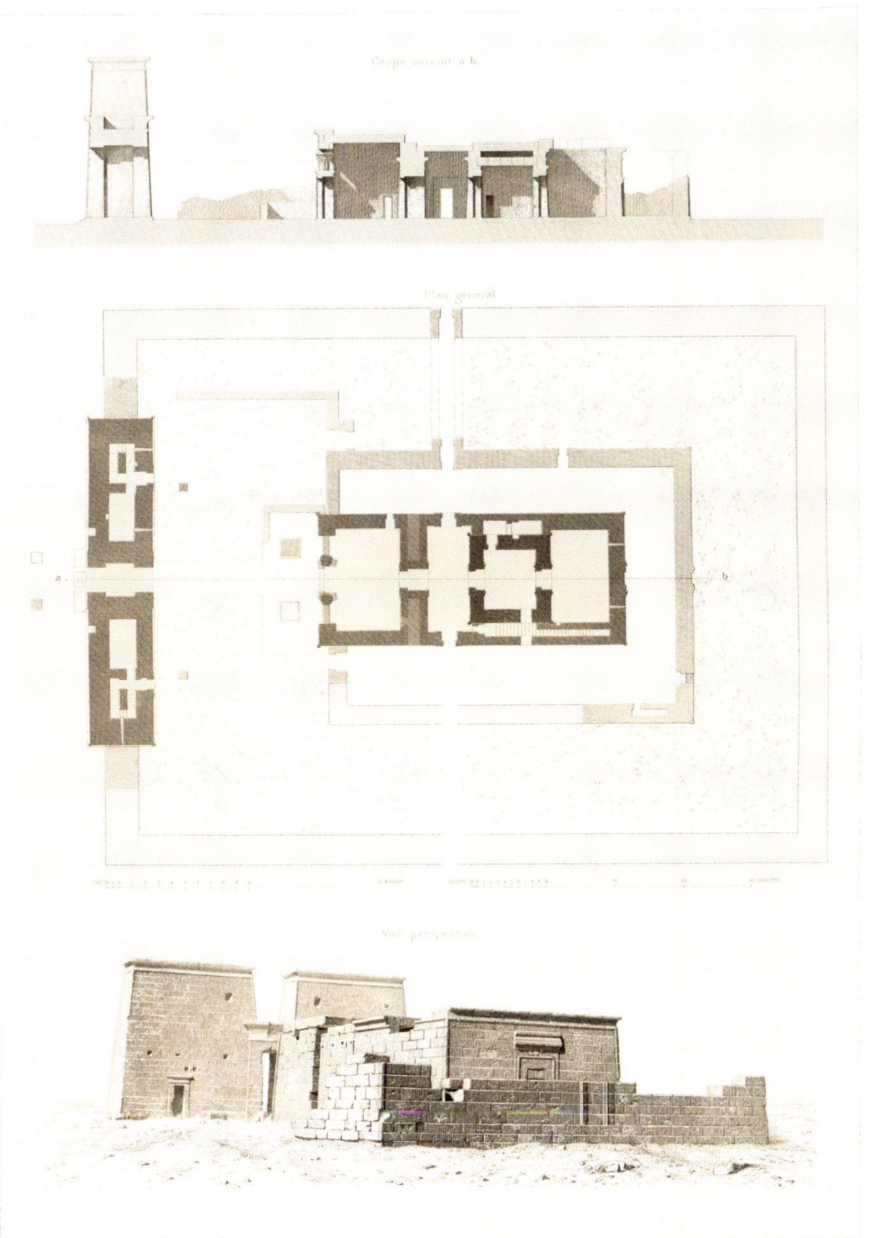

Prisse d'Avennes

Publié par Arthus Bertrand, éditeur

TEMPLE DE DAKKEH. (*PSELCIS*)

PLAN, COUPE ET VUE PERSPECTIVE

(ÉPOQUES PTOLÉMAÏQUE ET ROMAINE)

ELEVATION OF A PYLON AND PLAN OF A DWELLING

From bas-reliefs

The upper part of the plate represents the façade of a temple, probably that of Karnak, which was embellished with eight decorative masts on days of solemn ritual. These masts were sometimes gilded. The Egyptians varied the number of masts in relation to the importance of the building: some had two, as at Philae, some four, like Edfu, or some eight, as at the great palace of Karnak. It is assumed that the blue, red and green banners which flew from the masts represented the three main divisions of the country, Upper, Middle and Lower Egypt. The plan of the dwelling, which is featured beneath the pylon, gives detailed information on the house of a dead man, where it appears that Anubis has just come to tell him that he must prepare to leave his temporary home for the eternal dwelling-place. In the garden can be seen an ornamental lake surrounded by date palms, a square plot with irrigation channels, two tall trees and two obelisks opposite the house.

AUFRISS EINES PYLONS UND GRUNDRISS EINES WOHNGEBÄUDES

Nach den Flachreliefs

Der obere Teil der Tafel stellt eine Tempelfassade dar – wahrscheinlich die des Tempels von Karnak –, die an Feiertagen mit acht Ziermasten geschmückt war. Diese Masten waren manchmal vergoldet. Je nach Bedeutung des Gebäudes veränderten die Ägypter die Anzahl der Masten: Einige hatten zwei, wie in Philae, andere vier, wie in Edfu, oder acht, wie im großen Palast von Karnak. Es ist anzunehmen, dass die blauen, roten und grünen Wimpel, mit denen diese Masten beflaggt waren, die drei wichtigsten Unterteilungen des Landes verkörperten – nämlich Ober-, Mittel- und Unterägypten. Der Grundriss eines Wohnhauses, der unter dem Pylon abgebildet ist, zeigt die Einzelheiten des Hauses eines Verstorbenen – dem Anubis anzukündigen scheint, dass nun die Zeit gekommen ist, um die vergängliche Wohnung zu verlassen und die ewige Ruhestätte aufzusuchen. Im Garten sind ein mit Dattelpalmen umgebenes Wasserbecken, eine durch Gräben bewässerte Ackerfläche, zwei große Bäume und zwei dem Haus gegenüberstehende Obelisken zu sehen.

ÉLÉVATION D'UN PYLONE ET PLAN D'UNE HABITATION

D'après les bas-reliefs

La partie supérieure de la planche représente la façade d'un temple, probablement celui de Karnac, qui était orné de huit mâts décoratifs dans les jours de solennité. Ces mâts étaient quelquefois dorés. Les Égyptiens variaient le nombre de ces mâts, à raison de l'importance des édifices : les uns en avaient deux, comme à Philæ, les autres quatre comme à Edfou, huit comme au grand palais de Karnac. On suppose que les banderoles bleues, rouges et vertes qui pavoisaient ces mâts, représentaient les trois divisions principales de ce pays, la Haute-, la Moyenne- et la Basse-Égypte. Le plan d'habitation, représenté au-dessous du pylône, nous fait connaître en détail la maison d'un défunt auquel Anubis semble venir annoncer qu'il faut se décider à quitter l'habitation passagère pour la demeure éternelle. On voit, dans le jardin, un bassin entouré de dattiers, un carré arrosé par des rigoles, deux grands arbres et deux obélisques en face de la maison.

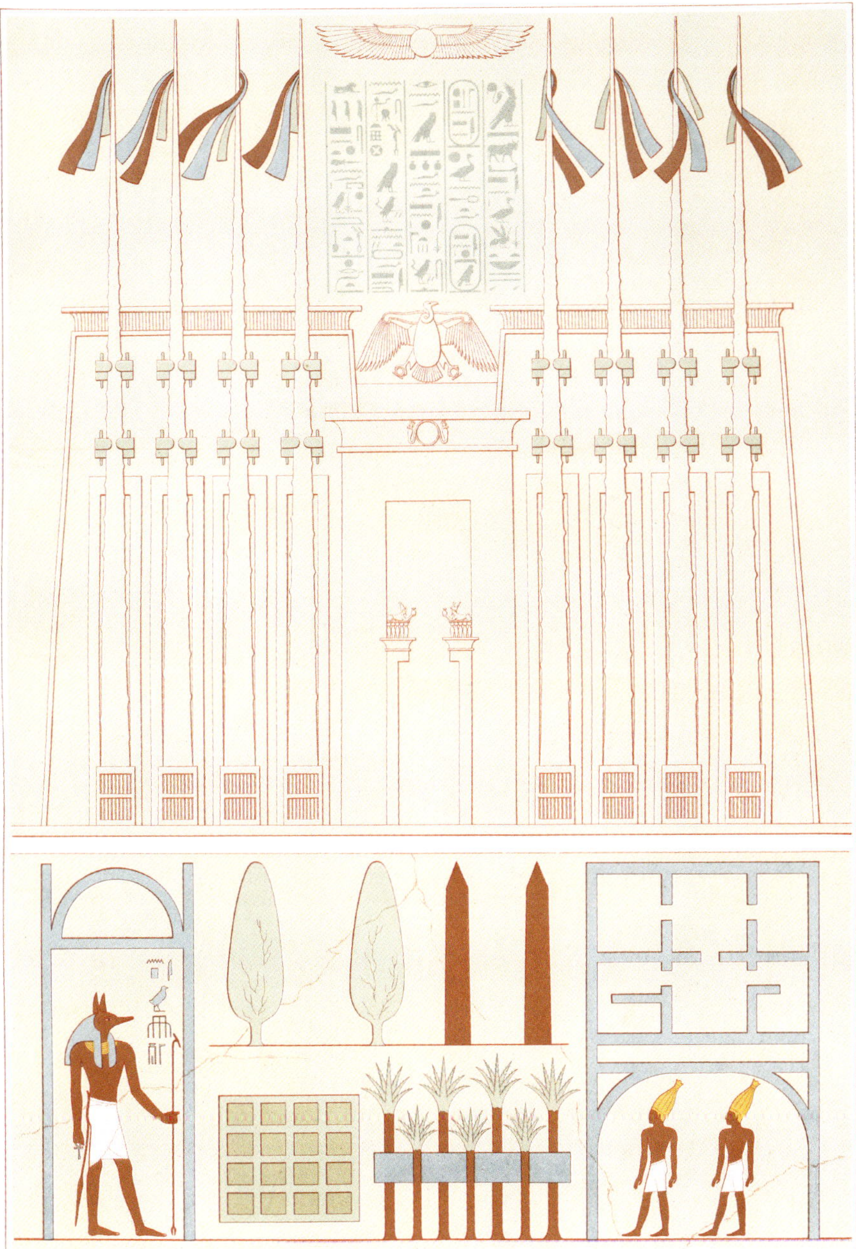

Lith. par Barbier, Imp. par Hangard-Maugé

E. Prisse d'Avennes

Publié par Arthus Bertrand, Éditeur

ÉLÉVATION D'UN PYLONE ET PLAN D'UNE HABITATION.

D'APRÈS LES BAS-RELIEFS.

DECORATION OF THE NICHE OF THE MAMMISI, AT DENDERA

(reign of Trajan)

The niche which adorns the far end of the mammisi of the temple of Dendera is formed of two small columns which project from a plain wall and which support a cornice and a row of uraei crowned with the solar disc. This first surround frames another rather simpler door whose cornice, like the outer one, again bears a winged globe [...]. On each side and outside the small columns, a crowned uraeus coils around a stem of lotus or papyrus, recognised as the symbols of Upper and Lower Egypt. Finally, the embrasure shown, which is not very deep and which still bears the scratches of the mason's tool, was never covered with carvings or hieroglyphs; it was obviously intended to contain and screen a type of small naos or tabernacle, probably of granite.

AUSSCHMÜCKUNG DER NISCHE DES MAMMISI, IN DENDERA

(Regierungszeit von Trajan)

Die den hintersten Teil des Mammisi im Tempel von Dendera zierende Nische besteht aus zwei kleinen, aus der nackten Mauer hervorspringenden Säulen, die ein Gesims und eine Reihe mit der Sonnenscheibe bekrönter Uräusschlangen tragen. Diese erste Zarge rahmt eine weitere, recht einfache Tür ein, deren Gesims – wie bei der, die sie überragt – mit einer geflügelten Kugel beschwert ist [...]. An der Außenseite der kleinen Säulen schlingt sich – als bekanntes Sinnbild Ober- und Unterägyptens – auf beiden Seiten eine bekrönte Uräusschlange um einen Lotus- oder Papyrusstängel. Die falsche Wandöffnung schließlich, die nur wenig eingetieft ist und noch Werkzeugspuren aufweist, war niemals von Skulpturen oder Hieroglyphen bedeckt; sie muss eine Art kleinen, in sie eingepassten, wahrscheinlich aus Granit gefertigten Naos oder ein Tabernakel aufgenommen haben.

DÉCORATION DE LA NICHE DE L'EIMISI, À DENDERAH

(règne de Trajan)

La niche qui décore le fond de l'Eimisi [Mammisi] du temple de Denderah est formée de deux colonnettes en saillie sur le nu du mur, qui soutiennent une corniche et une rangée d'uréus couronnés du disque solaire. Ce premier chambranle encadre une autre porte un peu plus simple dont la corniche est, comme celle qui la surmonte, chargée d'un globe ailé [...]. De chaque côté, en dehors des colonnettes, un uréus mitré s'enroule autour d'une tige de lotus ou de papyrus, symboles connus de la Basse- et de la Haute-Égypte. Enfin, la baie figurée, dont le fond est peu creusé et porte encore les striures de l'outil, n'a jamais été couverte de sculptures ou d'hiéroglyphes ; elle a dû recevoir et encastrer une espèce de petit naos ou tabernacle probablement en granit.

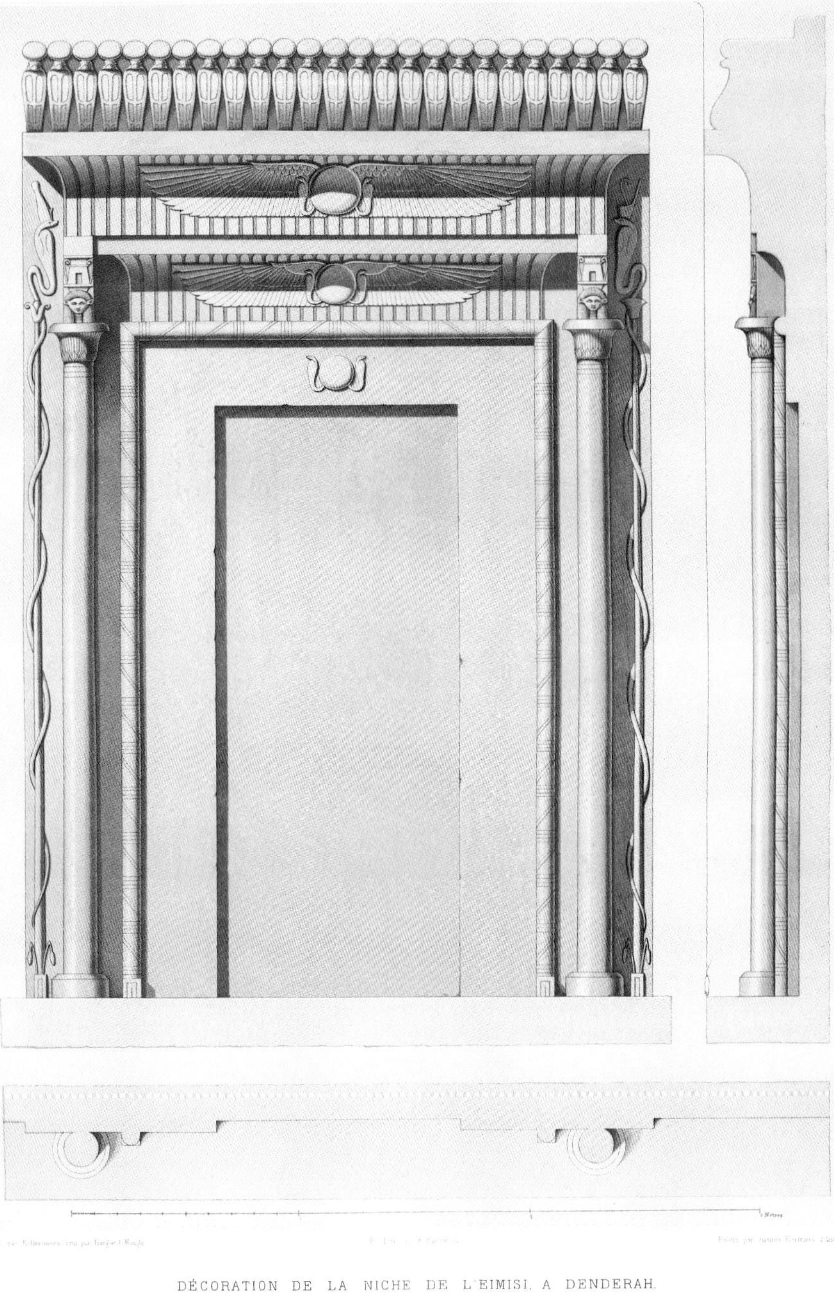

DÉCORATION DE LA NICHE DE L'EIMISI, A DENDERAH.

(RÈGNE DE TRAJAN)

FRIEZES WITH FLEURONS

Painted in the tombs

These friezes with fleurons are rarely met with outside the hypogea; the only other monuments on which they were employed were those kiosks which served as naos of the gods and the pharaohs, where they are found as embellishments to the architraves, beneath which they hang like garlands of flowers. They have also been noted as part of the interior decoration of the gynaeceum of Ramesses III. It is also likely that this usage was quite widespread in palaces and dwellings, because a frieze of this type in mosaic of enamelled clay has been found in the ruins of a palace built of sun-dried bricks. These [friezes] which I have depicted in this plate all come from hypogea in the necropolis of Thebes.

BLUMENFRIESE

Malereien aus Gräbern

Diese Blumenfriese kommen nur selten außerhalb der Hypogäen vor; in den Denkmälern fanden sie nur in den Ädikulä sowie in den Naos der Götter und der Pharaonen Verwendung, wo sie unten an den Architraven – an denen diese Verzierungen wie Blumengirlanden hängen – als Beifügung zu finden sind. Sie waren auch im Gynaecaeum von Ramses III. zu beobachten. Es ist ebenfalls möglich, dass sie in Wohnungen und Palästen verbreitet Verwendung fanden, da man in den Überresten eines aus luftgetrockneten Ziegeln errichteten Palastes ein derartiges Fries als Mosaik aus emailliertem Ton gefunden hat. Die auf dieser Tafel abgebildeten [Friese] stammen alle aus den Hypogäen der Nekropole von Theben.

FRISES FLEURONNÉES

Peintes dans les tombeaux

Ces frises fleuronnées se rencontrent rarement hors des hypogées ; on ne les employait sur les monuments que dans les édicules, les naos des dieux et des pharaons, où on les rencontre placés comme appendices des architraves, au bas desquelles ces ornements pendent comme des guirlandes de fleurs. On a pu les remarquer aussi dans les décorations intérieures du gynécée de Ramsès III. Il est également probable que l'usage en était assez répandu dans les palais et les habitations, puisqu'on a retrouvé dans les ruines d'un palais en briques crues, une frise de ce genre en mosaïque de terre émaillée. Celles [les frises] que j'ai représentées dans cette planche proviennent toutes des hypogées de la nécropole de Thèbes.

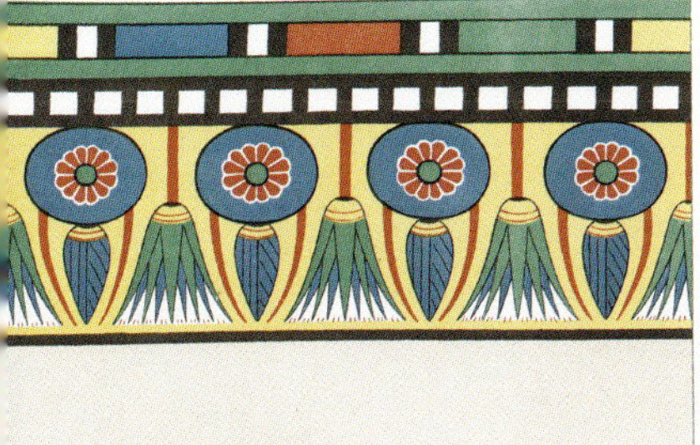

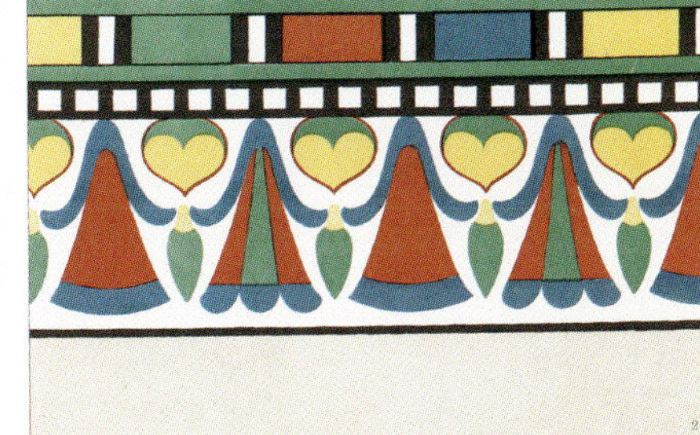

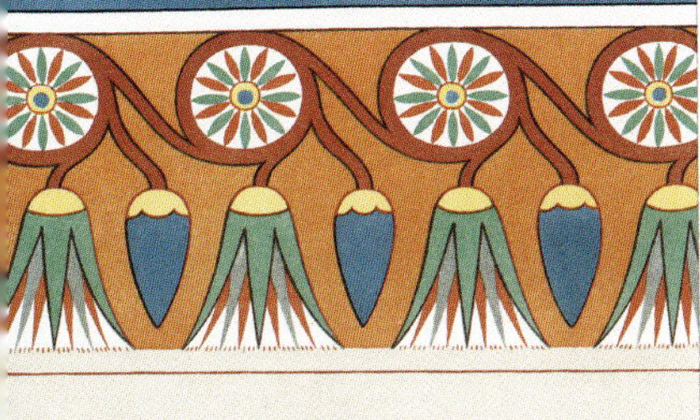

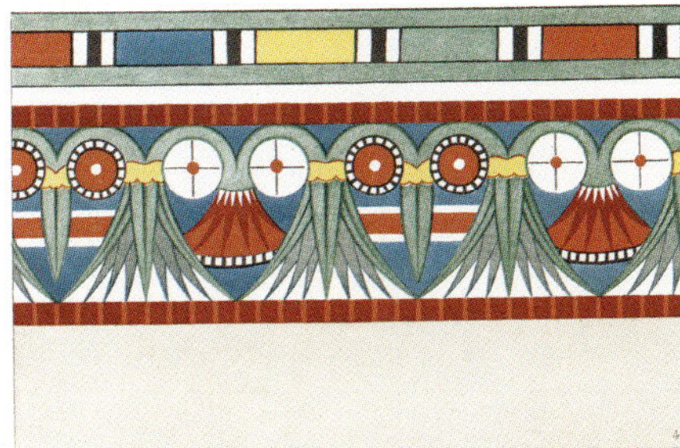

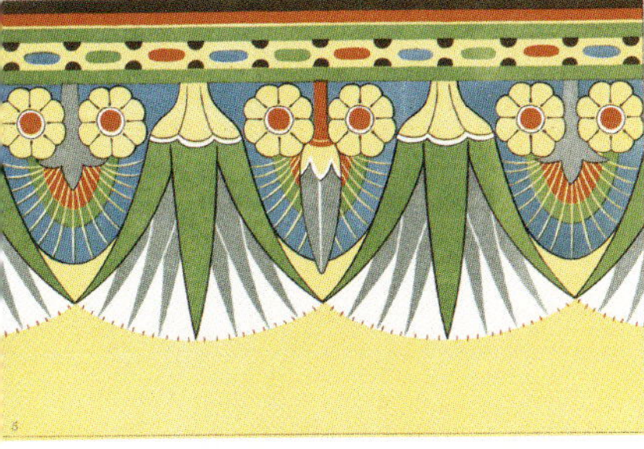

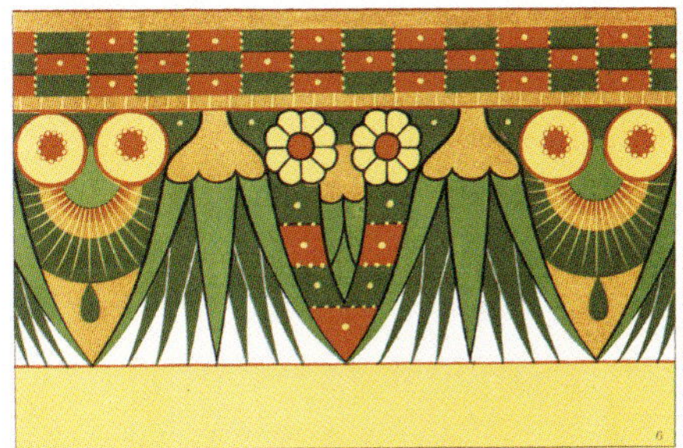

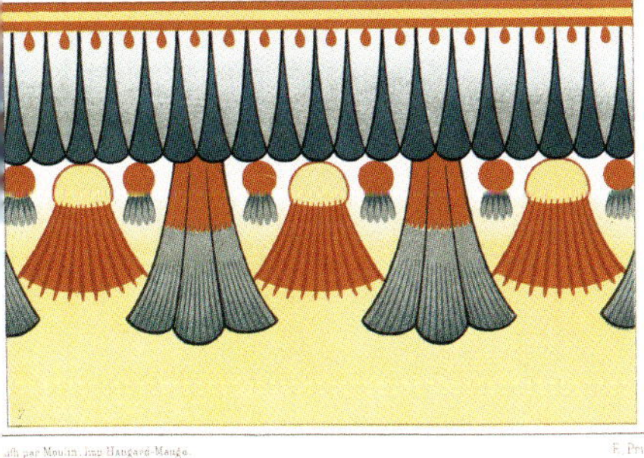

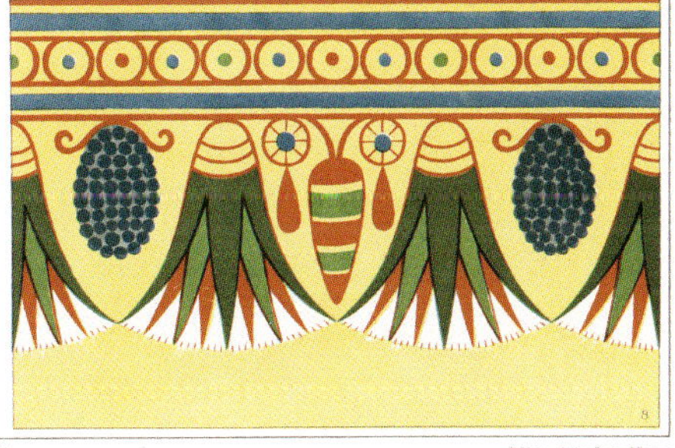

Lith par Moulin. Imp Hangard-Maugé. E. Prisse d'Avennes. Publié par Arthus Bertrand Editeur.

FRISES FLEURONNÉES.

PEINTES DANS LES TOMBEAUX.

DECORATION OF CORNICES (from various periods)

Throughout the whole duration of the monarchy, the only variations in the cornice were in the degree of skill of the execution of its curve, in its proportions and in its decorative accessories. During the early dynasties, the sole decoration consisted of tricoloured bands and of scrolled ribbons on the torus. It was in the period of the 12th Dynasty that the winged globe, symbol of Hat, the lord of heaven and the good god, appeared. [...] The uraei which flank it often wear the crowns of Upper and Lower Egypt. A little later, during the 19th Dynasty, the bands trace on the concave moulding a type of triglyph whose metopes contain one or two cartouches, also sometimes flanked with uraei. It was also at around this time that the cornices were crowned with a series of uraei bearing the solar globe on their head. Finally, in the reign of Nectanebo (30th Dynasty), a series of hawks is sometimes found crowning the cornice instead of the customary uraei.

GESIMSVERZIERUNGEN (aus verschiedenen Dynastien)

Während der gesamten Dauer der Monarchie wurde sie [die Verdachung] nur hinsichtlich ihrer mehr oder weniger kunstvollen Krümmung, ihrer Proportionen und des schmückenden Beiwerks abgewandelt. Unter den frühen Dynastien war sie einfach mit dreifarbigen Streifen und um den Torus gewickelten Bändern verziert. In der Zeit der 12. Dynastie erscheint die geflügelte Kugel, Sinnbild des guten Gottes Hat – des Herrn des Himmels. [...] Die Uräusschlangen, die diese flankieren, tragen häufig die Kronen Ober- und Unterägyptens. Ein wenig später, unter der 19. Dynastie, werden die Streifen auf der Hohlleiste ähnlich wie Triglyphe angeordnet, deren Metopen mit ein oder zwei – mitunter ebenfalls von Uräusschlangen flankierten – Kartuschen gefüllt sind. In dieser Zeit werden auch die Gesimse mit einer Reihe von Uräusschlangen bekrönt, die auf ihrem Kopf die Sonnenkugel tragen. In der Regierungszeit von Nektanebos (30. Dynastie) schließlich findet sich mitunter – anstatt der üblichen Uräusschlangen – eine Reihe von Sperbern als Gesimsbekrönung.

DÉCORATION DES CORNICHES (à diverses époques)

Elle [la corniche] n'a varié, durant toute la durée de la monarchie, que dans sa courbe plus ou moins savante, dans ses proportions et dans les accessoires de sa décoration. Sous les premières dynasties, elle était, simplement, ornée de bandes tricolores et de rubans enroulés sur le tore. À l'époque de la XIIe dynastie apparaît le globe ailé, symbole de Hat le seigneur du ciel, le dieu bon. [...] Les uréus, qui le flanquent, portent souvent les couronnes de la Haute- et de la Basse-Égypte. Un peu plus tard, sous la XIXe dynastie, les bandes dessinent sur le cavet des espèces de triglyphes dont les métopes sont remplies par un ou deux cartouches, flanqués aussi quelquefois d'uréus. C'est aussi vers cette époque que les corniches se couronnent d'une suite d'uréus portant sur leur tête le globe du soleil. Enfin, on rencontre quelquefois sous le règne de Nectanèbe (XXXe dynastie) une suite d'éperviers qui couronnent la corniche au lieu des uréus habituels.

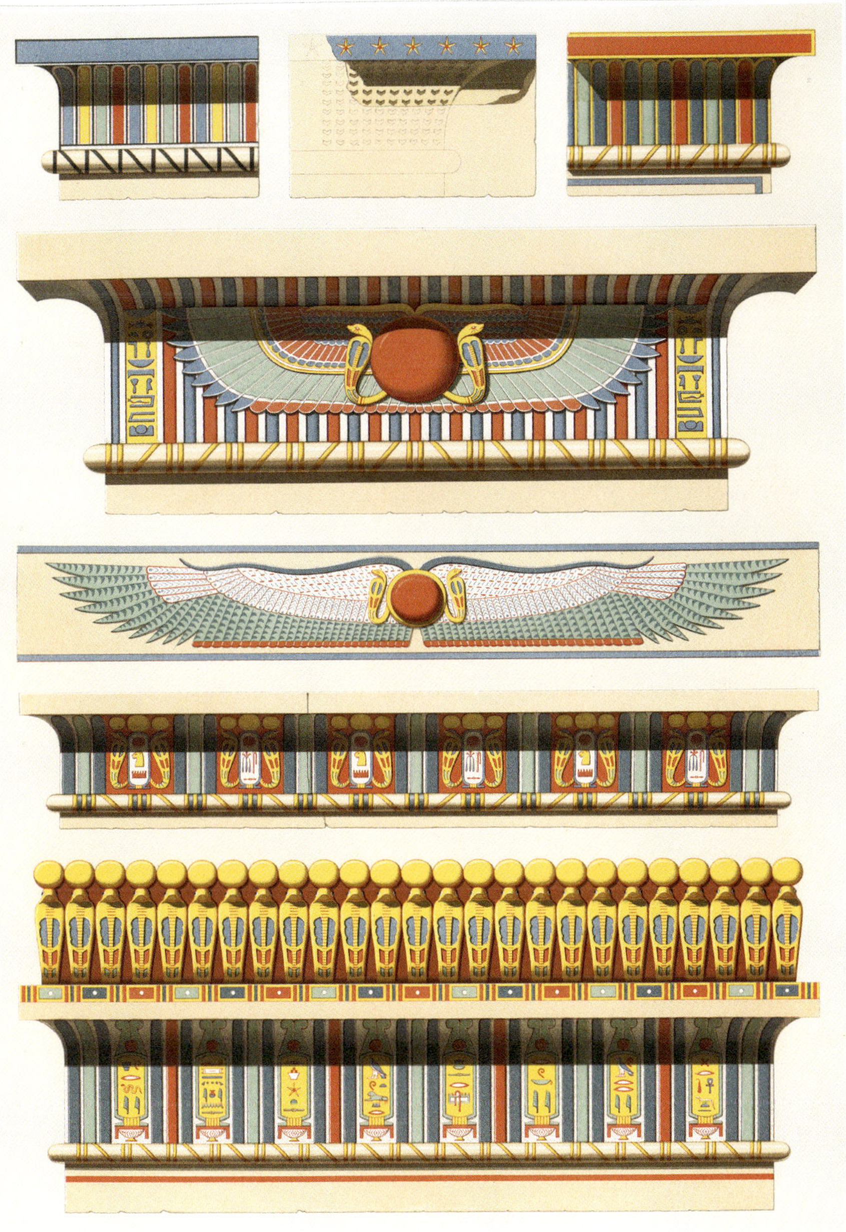

E. Prisse d'Avennes

Publié par Arthus-Bertrand Éditeur

DÉCORATION DES CORNICHES.

À DIVERSES ÉPOQUES.

ENTABLATURES, BORDERS AND DADOS (from various periods)

In this plate I have grouped together the principal ornaments which serve as entablatures, borders and lower sections to the scenes which were painted or carved on all the Egyptian edifices. All of the subjects or motifs which are represented here can be seen on monuments from the 18th Dynasty onwards up to the fall of the Roman Empire. No. 1 is taken from the tomb of Djehutihotep at Deir el-Bersha. No. 2 was copied in the sanctuary of a hypogeum at Beni Hassan; both date from the 12th Dynasty. No. 3, which is extremely elegant, comes from a hypogeum in the necropolis of Thebes from the 18th Dynasty. Nos. 4 to 8 show ornaments which were used in the lower sections. They are for the most part composed of interwoven lotus and papyrus in the three stages of development of these two plants. No. 9 shows the lower section of the sanctuary in the tomb of Queen Tiye, the wife of Amenophis III; this decoration occurs quite frequently during the 18th Dynasty.

BEKRÖNUNGEN, ZIERLEISTEN UND SOCKEL (aus verschiedenen Zeiten)

Auf dieser Tafel habe ich die wichtigsten Ornamente zusammengestellt, die in allen ägyptischen Bauwerken den Bildern als Bekrönungen, Zierleisten oder Sockel dienten. Alle hier dargestellten Themen oder Motive sind von der 18. Dynastie an bis zum Fall des Römischen Reiches an den Denkmälern zu sehen. Die Nr. 1 ist dem Grab des Djehutihotep in Deir el-Bersche entnommen. Die Nr. 2 wurde in Beni Hassan im Heiligtum eines Hypogäums abgezeichnet. Beide datieren aus der 12. Dynastie. Die sehr anmutige Nr. 3 stammt aus der Nekropole von Theben, aus einem Hypogäum der 18. Dynastie. Die Nr. 4 bis 8 zeigen an Sockeln verwendete Ornamente. Sie setzen sich im Allgemeinen aus Lotus- und Papyrusgeweben in den drei Entwicklungsstufen dieser beiden Pflanzen zusammen. Die Nr. 9 stellt den Sockel des Heiligtums im Grab von Königin Teje – der Gemahlin von Amenophis III. – dar; in der 18. Dynastie kommt diese Verzierung recht häufig vor.

COURONNEMENTS, BORDURES ET SOUBASSEMENTS (de diverses époques)

J'ai groupé, sur cette planche, les principaux ornements qui servent de couronnements, de bordures et de soubassements aux tableaux peints ou sculptés sur tous les édifices égyptiens. Tous les sujets ou motifs, représentés ici, se voient sur les monuments à partir de la XVIIIe dynastie jusqu'à la chute de l'Empire romain. Le no 1 est tiré du tombeau de Thouthotep [Djéhoutihotep] à Bercheh. Le no 2 a été copié dans le sanctuaire d'un hypogée de Beni-Haçen. Tous deux datent de la XIIe dynastie. Le no 3, qui est fort élégant, provient d'un hypogée de la nécropole de Thèbes de la XVIIIe dynastie. Les nos 4 à 8 offrent des ornements employés en soubassements. Ils sont composés généralement des tissus du lotus et du papyrus dans les trois états de développement de ces deux plantes. Le no 9 représente le soubassement du sanctuaire, dans le tombeau de la reine Taïa [Tiyi], épouse d'Aménophis III ; cette décoration est assez fréquente sous la XVIIIe dynastie.

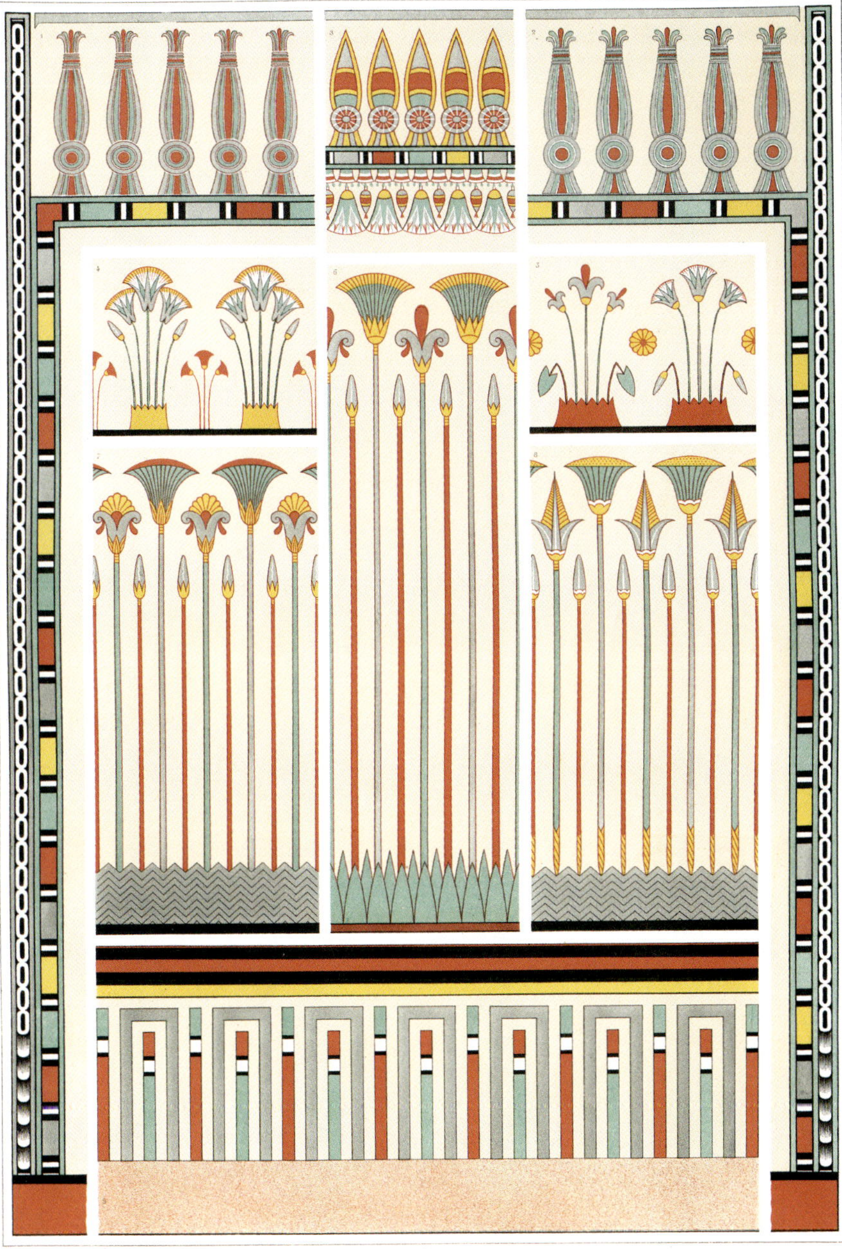

Lith par Barbier . Imp par Hangard-Maugé

E. Prisse d'Avennes.

Publié par Arthus Bertrand, Editeur.

COURONNEMENTS, BORDURES & SOUBASSEMENTS

DE DIVERSES ÉPOQUES.

BASES AND DADOS (Ptolemaic and Roman Periods)

Nos. 1 and 2 represent a series of lotus plants which act as base to the registers of the bas-reliefs which decorate the walls of the buildings. The first is taken from the temple of Dendur in Nubia, the second from the great temple of Dendera, which was built at the command of the famous Cleopatra. No. 3, formed from two groups of alternating plants, symbols of the north and the south, can be seen on the columns of the pronaos of Dendera. No. 4 shows a type of dado. No. 5 is carved in the second sanctuary of the temple in the same location (Dendera). Five lotus stalks alternate with another bouquet supporting a basket crowned with a bird. No. 6 is a copy of lower sections which were in vogue under the pharaohs. Nos. 7 and 8 represent flowers which fill in the spaces between consecutive stipules or chevrons. Nos. 9 and 10, which are drawings inspired by the columns of the pronaos of Esna, display the most beautiful example of the decorations which were used at the base of the shafts in the buildings of the Roman domination.

BASIS UND SOCKEL (ptolemäische und römische Zeit)

Die Nr. 1 und 2 stellen eine Folge von Lotuspflanzen dar, die den Registern der die Gebäudewände zierenden Flachreliefs als Basis dienen. Die erste ist dem Tempel von Dendur in Nubien entnommen, die zweite dem großen, auf Geheiß der berühmten Kleopatra errichteten Tempel von Dendera. Die Nr. 3, die aus zwei alternierenden Pflanzengruppen gebildet ist, die den Norden und den Süden versinnbildlichen, ist an den Säulen des Pronaos von Dendera zu sehen. Die Nr. 4 zeigt eine Art Lambris. Die Nr. 5 ist eine Bildhauerarbeit aus dem zweiten Heiligtum des Tempels derselben Ortschaft (Dendera). Fünf Lotusstängel wechseln sich mit einem weiteren Gebinde ab, das einen mit einem Vogel bekrönten Korb trägt. Die Nr. 6 ist die Kopie eines Sockels, der unter den Pharaonen in Mode war. Die Nr. 7 und 8 stellen Blumen dar, die den Zwischenraum zwischen den aufeinander folgenden Nebenblättern oder Fischgrätmustern füllen. Die nach den Säulen des Pronaos von Esna gezeichneten Nr. 9 und 10 zeigen das schönste Exemplar der während der römischen Herrschaft am unteren Säulenschaft verwendeten Ornamente.

BASES ET SOUBASSEMENTS (époque ptolémaïque et romaine)

Les n°s 1 et 2 représentent une suite de lotus servant de base aux registres des bas-reliefs qui décorent les parois des édifices. La première est tirée du temple de Dendour en Nubie, la seconde, du grand temple de Denderah, bâti par ordre de la célèbre Cléopâtre. Le n° 3, formé de deux groupes de plantes alternées, symboles du nord et du sud, se voit sur les colonnes du pronaos de Denderah. Le n° 4 présente une espèce de lambris. Le n° 5 est sculpté dans le second sanctuaire du temple de la même localité (Denderah). Cinq tiges de lotus y alternent avec un autre bouquet supportant une corbeille couronnée d'un oiseau. Le n° 6 est la copie des soubassements en vogue sous les pharaons. Les n°s 7 et 8 représentent des fleurs qui remplissent l'intervalle des stipules ou chevrons consécutifs. Les n°s 9 et 10, dessinés d'après les colonnes du pronaos d'Esné [Esna], présentent le plus beau spécimen des ornements employés au bas du fût dans les édifices de la domination romaine.

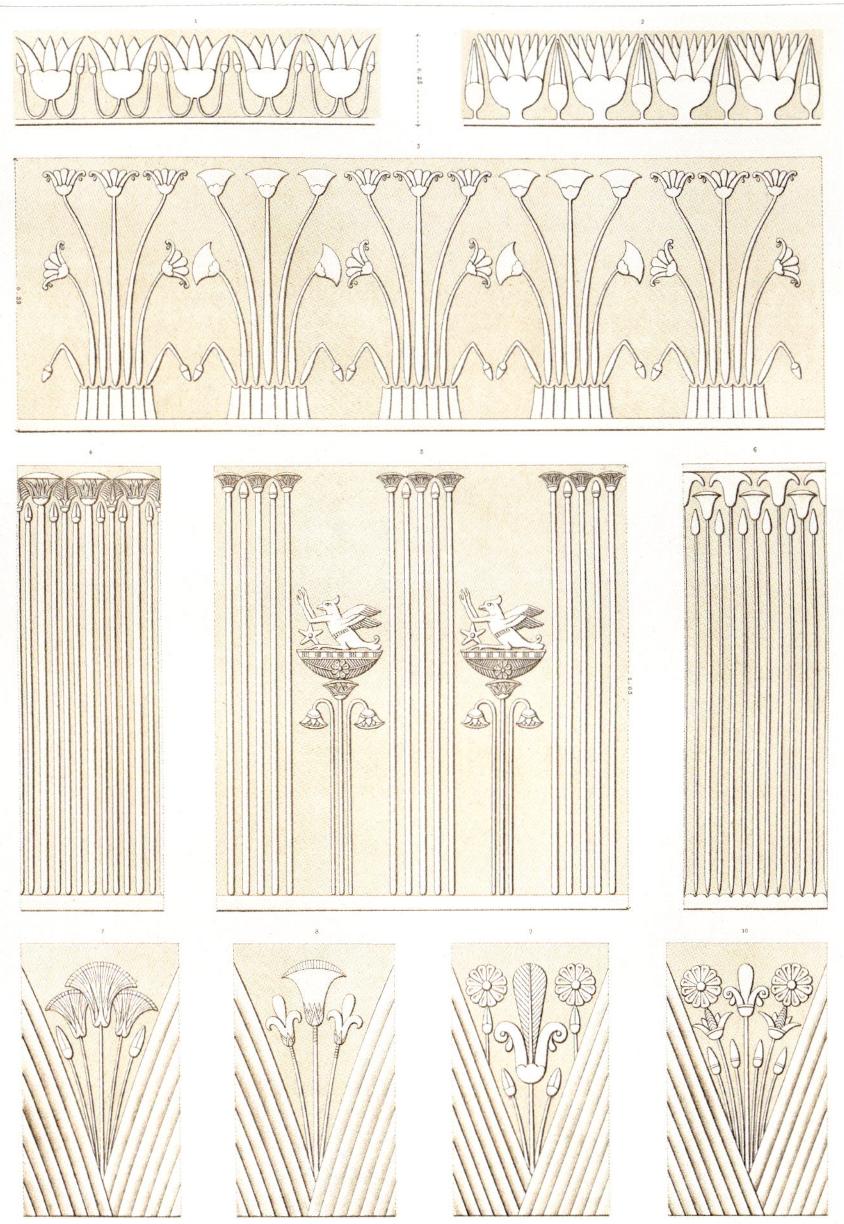

Lith. par Walter. Imp. par Hangard-Maugé
E. Prisse d'Avennes
Publié par Arthus-Bertrand Éditeur

BASES ET SOUBASSEMENTS.

(ÉPOQUE PTOLÉMAÏQUE ET ROMAINE.)

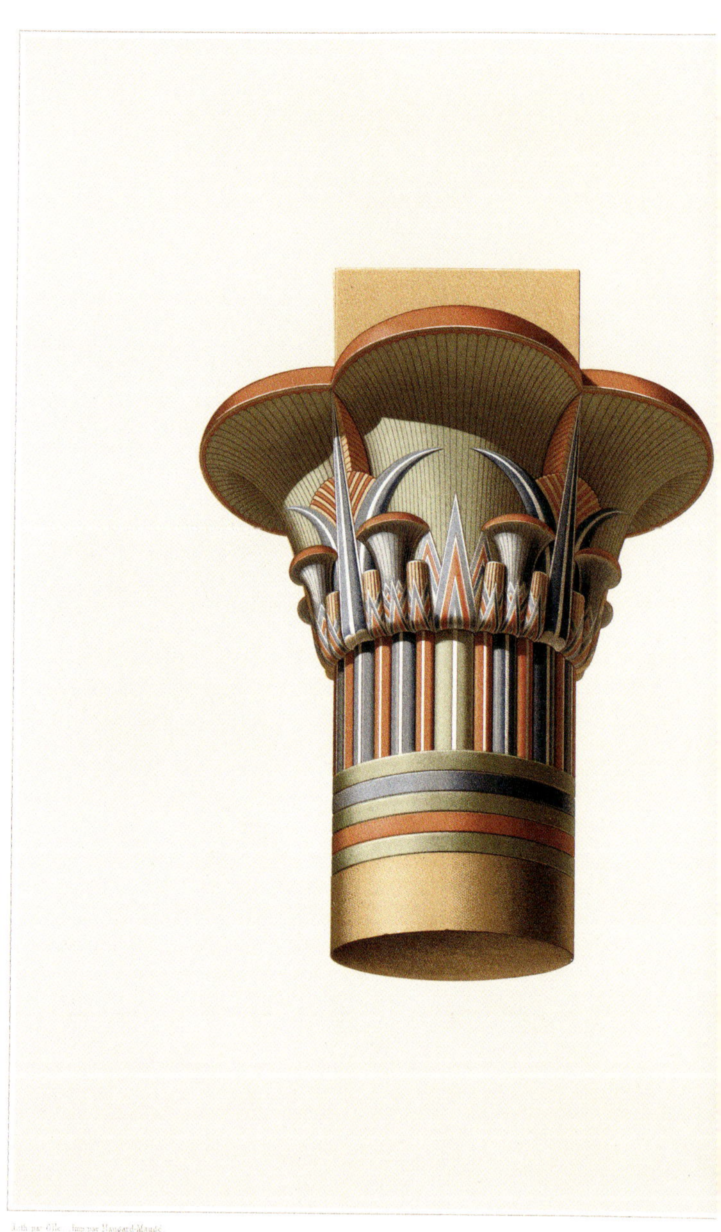

Lith par Gille. Imp par Hangard-Maugé.

CHAPITEAUX DU C

(RÈGNE

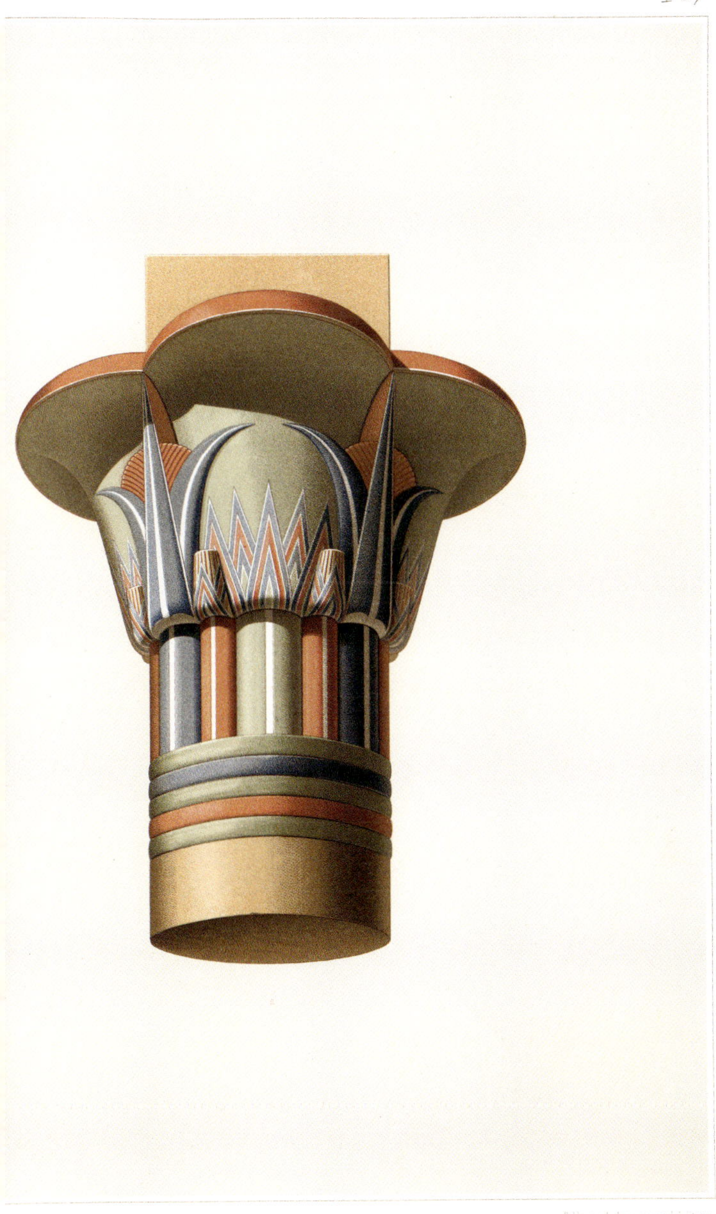

Publié par [illegible] Éditeur.

E D'ISIS, A PHILÆ.

STE II.)

(Pages/Seite 316/317)

CAPITALS FROM THE GREAT TEMPLE OF ISIS AT PHILAE

(reign of Ptolemy VIII Euergetes II)

The two pylons [of the great temple of Isis] are decorated with sunken bas-reliefs. The courtyard which separates the first pylon from the second is flanked to the right by a gallery. This courtyard is closed in on the other side by a small temple which has a private entrance pierced through the first pylon. This was a building to commemorate the childbirth of Isis and was dedicated to Horus, commissioned by Ptolemy V Epiphanes and his son Euergetes II. The second pylon, which is smaller and more dilapidated than the first, was built on a rock of rose granite [...]. This pylon, which forms the true façade of the temple, is part of a whole which was built in one single operation under Euergetes II. The pronaos is formed of ten columns more than 7.5 metres high; they are crowned with a variety of capitals whose colours, perfectly preserved, provide a splendid example of polychrome architecture.

KAPITELLE AUS DEM GROSSEN ISIS-TEMPEL, AUF PHILAE

(Regierungszeit von Ptolemaios VIII. Euergetes II.)

Die beiden Pylone [des großen Isis-Tempels] sind mit versenkten Flachreliefs verziert. Auf der rechten Seite flankiert ein Gang den Hof, der den ersten Pylon vom zweiten trennt. Ein kleiner Tempel, dessen gesonderter Eingang aus dem ersten Pylon herausgebrochen ist, schließt diesen Hof auf der anderen Seite ab. Zum Gedenken an die Niederkunft der Isis widmeten Ptolemaios V. Epiphanes und sein Sohn Euergetes II. dieses Gebäude dem Horus. Der zweite, kleinere und stärker als der erste verfallene Pylon war auf einem Felsen aus rosa Granit erbaut worden [...]. Dieser Pylon bildet die eigentliche Tempelfassade und ist Teil eines unter Euergetes II. in einem Zug errichten Ganzen. Den Pronaos bilden zehn Säulen von mehr als 7,50 m Höhe; sie sind von unterschiedlichen Kapitellen bekrönt, deren vollkommen erhaltene Farben ein wunderbares Beispiel mehrfarbiger Architektur bieten.

CHAPITEAUX DU GRAND TEMPLE D'ISIS, À PHILÆ

(règne de Ptolémée [VIII] Évergète II)

Les deux pylônes [du grand temple d'Isis] sont décorés de bas-reliefs dans le creux. La cour, qui sépare le premier pylône du second, est flanquée à droite par une galerie. Cette cour est fermée, de l'autre côté, par un petit temple qui a son entrée particulière percée dans le premier pylône. C'était un édifice commémoratif de l'accouchement d'Isis, dédié à Horus, par les soins de Ptolémée [V] Épiphanes et de son fils Évergète II. Le second pylône, plus petit, plus délabré que le premier, était bâti sur un roc de granit rose [...]. Ce pylône, qui forme la véritable façade du temple, fait partie d'un tout bâti d'un seul jet sous Évergète II. Le pronaos est formé par dix colonnes de plus de 7,50 m de hauteur, couronnées de chapiteaux variés et dont les couleurs, parfaitement conservées, offrent un spécimen admirable d'architecture polychrôme.

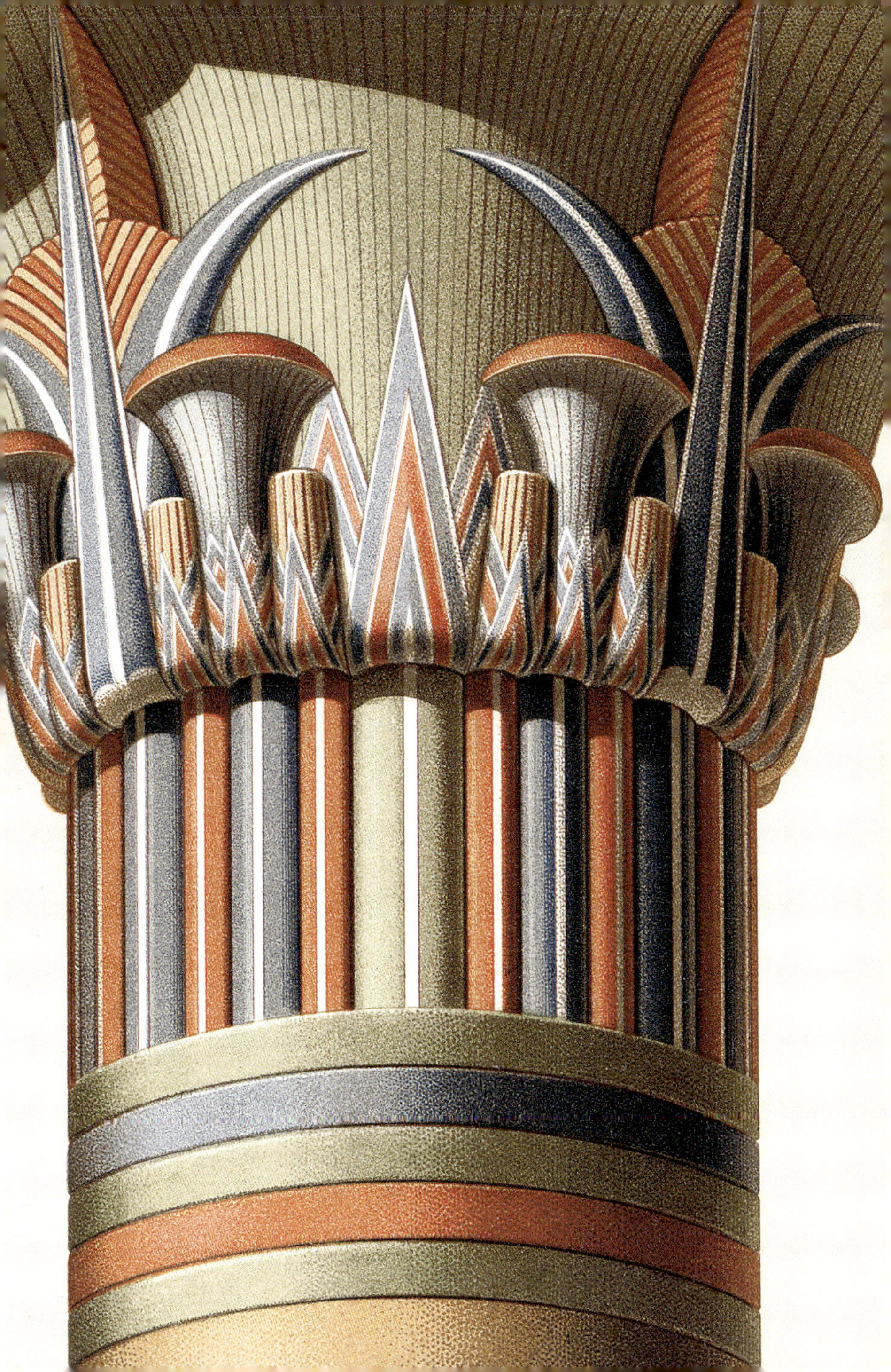

CAPITALS FROM THE GALLERY OF THE DROMOS AT PHILAE (reign of Augustus)

These magnificent capitals originate from Philae itself, in the small hypaethral temple of Nectanebo built at the entrance to this dromos. No. 1, elegant in its uniformity, represents a clump of aquatic plants set round the core of the capital like a bouquet, whose stems would have appeared beneath the capital and would then have disappeared beneath the collars of the shaft. No. 2 is more complicated: the core of its capital is decorated, on the central sections which correspond with the four faces of the abacus, with tall aloes bearing the startling aigrette characteristic of certain plants of this family. The spaces between are filled with bigger but less brilliant aigrettes, which terminate in chevroned stipules [...].This charming ornamentation was in fact quite commonly found in the decoration of capitals in the Ptolemaic and Roman Periods.

KAPITELLE AUS DEM GANG DES DROMOS, AUF PHILAE (Regierungszeit von Augustus)

Der Ursprung dieser herrlichen Kapitelle ist auf Philae selbst in dem kleinen, am Eingang dieses Dromos errichteten, dachlosen Tempel von Nektanebos zu finden. Die Nr. 1, die von anmutiger Ebenmäßigkeit ist, stellt ein Büschel Wasserpflanzen dar, das um eine Glocke herum angelegt ist – wie ein Bukett, dessen Stängel unterhalb des Kapitells auftauchen und sich unter den Manschetten des Schaftes verlieren. Die Nr. 2 ist komplizierter. Sie zeigt eine Glocke, die jeweils in der – den vier Seiten der Kapitelldeckplatten entsprechenden – Mitte durch große Aloen mit strahlenden Aigretten, wie sie bei einigen Vertretern dieser Pflanzenfamilie vorkommen, verziert ist. Die Zwischenräume sind offensichtlich mit breiteren Aigretten von schlichterer Färbung gefüllt, die in Nebenblätter mit Fischgrätmuster auslaufen [...]. Diese reizende Ornamentierung war tatsächlich in ptolemäischer und römischer Zeit für die Verzierung von Kapitellen sehr gebräuchlich.

CHAPITEAUX DE LA GALERIE DU DROMOS, À PHILÆ (règne d'Auguste)

L'origine de ces magnifiques chapiteaux se retrouve à Philæ même, dans le petit hypètre de Nectanèbe élevé à l'entrée de ce dromos. Le n° 1, d'une élégante uniformité, représente une touffe de plantes aquatiques appliquées autour d'une campane comme un bouquet dont les tiges apparaîtraient au-dessous du chapiteau, et iraient se perdre sous les viroles du fût. Le n° 2 est plus compliqué. Il présente une campane décorée, sur les milieux correspondant aux quatre faces du tailloir, de grandes plantes d'aloès portant une éclatante aigrette comme certaines plantes de cette famille. On peut voir que les intervalles sont remplis par des aigrettes plus larges et plus sobres de couleurs, terminées par des stipules chevronnés [...]. Ainsi, cette charmante ornementation était fort usitée dans la décoration des chapiteaux des époques ptolémaïque et romaine.

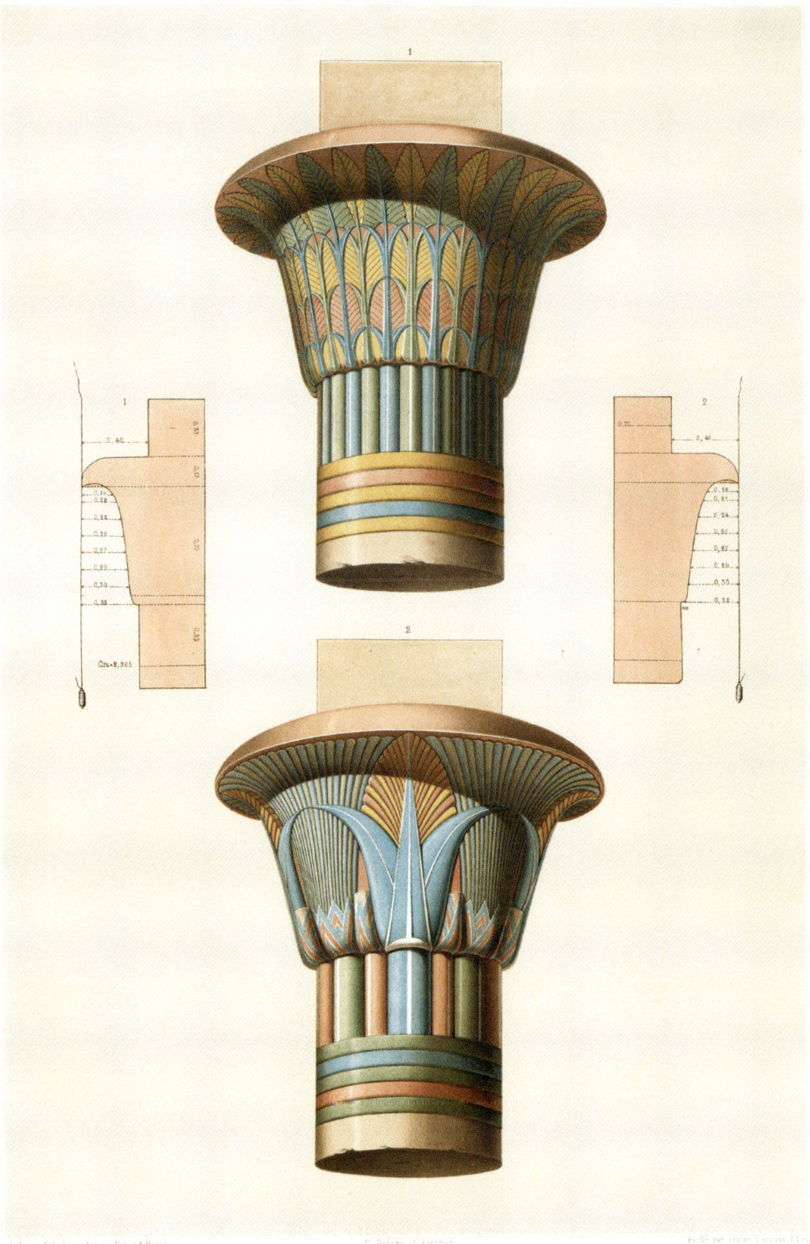

Lith. par Kellerhoven. Imp. par Hangard Maugé — E. Prisse d'Avennes — Publié par Arthus Bertrand, Éditeur

CHAPITEAUX DE LA GALERIE DU DROMOS, A PHILÆ.

(RÈGNE D'AUGUSTE)

CAPITALS OF THE COLONNADE OF THE DROMOS AT PHILAE

(reigns of Augustus, Tiberius and Claudius)

Here, all the ornamentation stems from an artistry which aimed to confer a quite specific style on the columns of this long dromos, by decorating their heads in a different fashion. However, one should not believe that these elegant constructions are owing to foreign initiative, neither the Roman artists nor the emperors offered any inspiration to Egypt.

KAPITELLE AUS DEM GANG DES DROMOS, AUF PHILAE

(Regierungszeit von Augustus, Tiberius und Claudius)

Die gesamte Ornamentierung ist hier der Kunst zu verdanken, durch die ungewöhnliche Verzierung des Kopfes den Säulen dieses langen Dromos einen besonderen Charakter zu verleihen. Man sollte jedoch nicht meinen, dass diese anmutigen Werke auf die Erfindungsgabe von Fremden zurückgehen. Ägypten hat weder den römischen Künstlern noch den römischen Kaisern irgendetwas zu verdanken.

CHAPITEAUX DE LA COLONNADE DU DROMOS, À PHILÆ

(règnes d'Auguste, de Tibère et de Claude)

Ici, toute l'ornementation est due à l'art qui a voulu imprimer aux colonnes de ce long dromos un type particulier en ornant leur tête d'une façon différente. Cependant, il ne faudrait pas s'imaginer que ces élégantes productions sont dues à l'initiative des étrangers. Les artistes romains, non plus que les Empereurs, n'ont rien donné à l'Égypte.

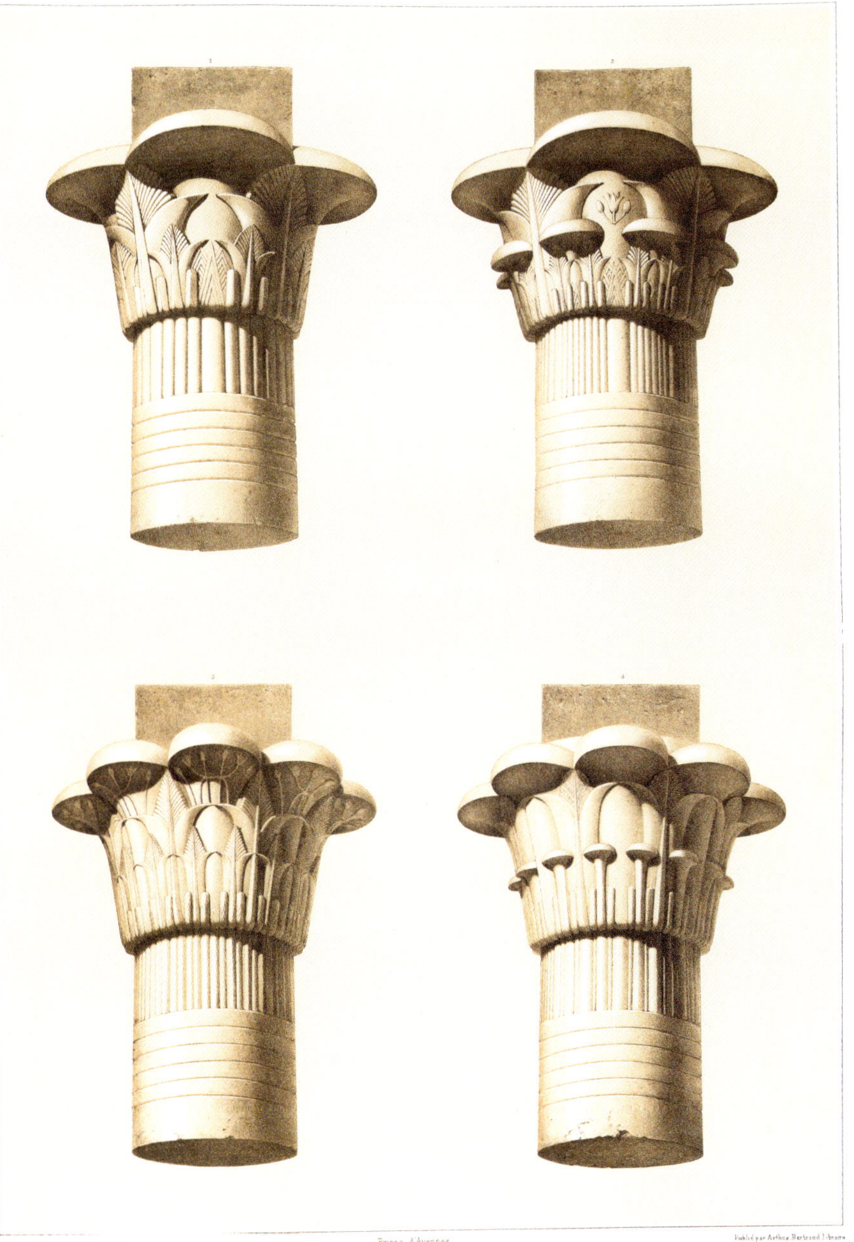

Lith par Hoffbauer _ Imp par Haugard-Maugé

Prisse d'Avennes

Publié par Arthus Bertrand Libraire

CHAPITEAUX DE LA COLONNADE DU DROMOS, A PHILÆ.

(RÈGNES D'AUGUSTE, DE TIBÈRE & DE CLAUDE.)

CAPITALS IN VARIOUS FORMS

In order to draw a parallel between the finest periods of Pharaonic and Roman art, I have reproduced in the final plates here a series of capitals which show that, although the Romans may have demanded from the Egyptian artists a finer finish to their work, they did not seek a genuine transformation in those forms made sacrosanct by religion or long usage.

KAPITELLE UNTERSCHIEDLICHER FORM

Zum Vergleich zwischen den schönen Epochen der pharaonischen und der römischen Kunst habe ich auf den letzten Tafeln dieser Serie eine Reihe von Kapitellen abgebildet, die vor Augen führen, dass die Römer zwar eine sorgfältigere Ausführung ihrer Arbeit von den ägyptischen Künstlern verlangten, nicht aber eine echte Umgestaltung der entweder durch Religion oder Brauch festgeschriebenen Formen.

CHAPITEAUX DE DIVERSES FORMES

Dans les dernières planches de cette série, j'ai reproduit, à titre de parallèles entre les belles époques de l'art pharaonique et l'époque romaine, une suite de chapiteaux qui nous démontrent que, si les Romains ont exigé des artistes égyptiens un plus grand fini dans leur travail, ils n'exigèrent pas une transformation véritable des formes consacrées soit par la religion, soit par l'usage.

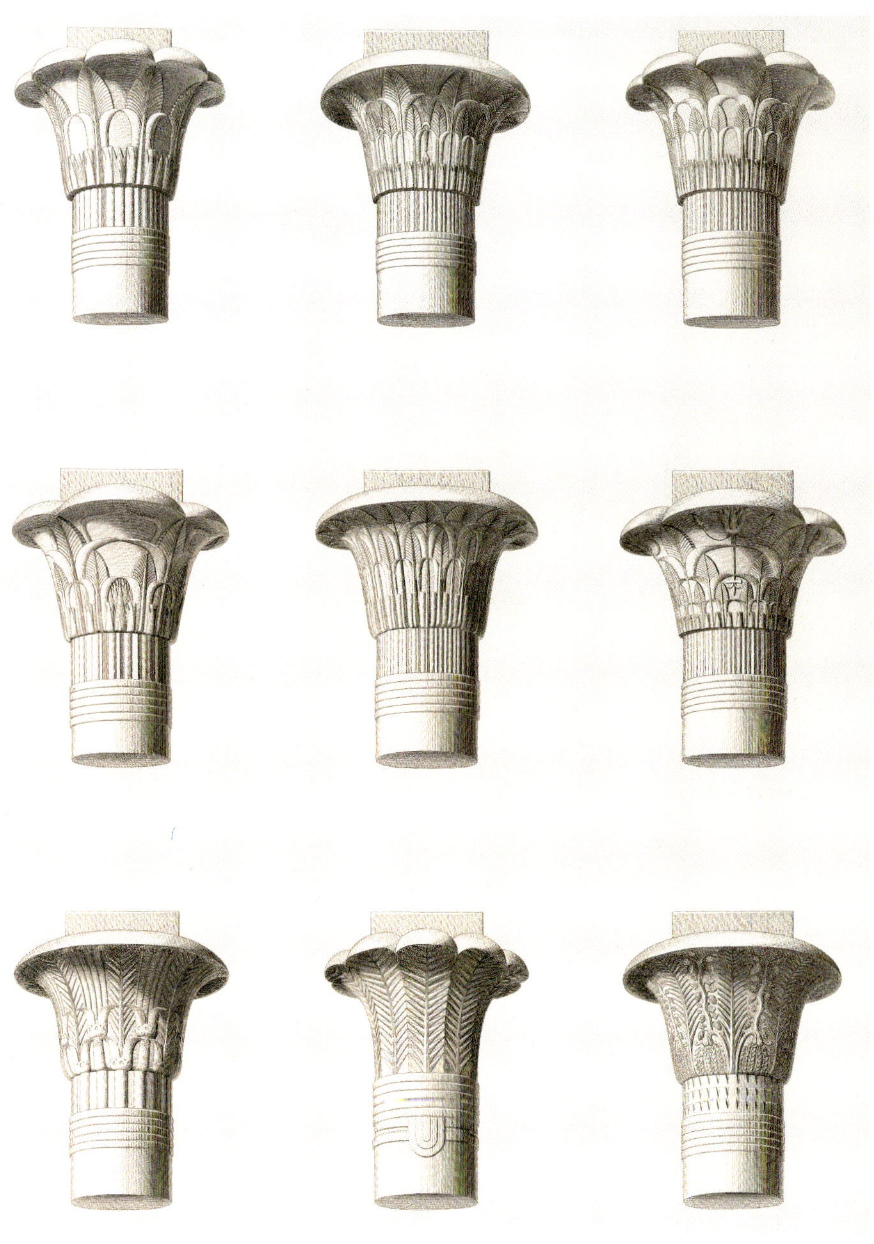

Prisse d'Avennes

Arthus Bertrand Éditeur

CHAPITEAUX DE DIVEPSES FORMES.

OBELISK OF RAMESSES [II] MERYAMUN

Taken from Luxor to Paris

This obelisk, which stands today on the Place de la Concorde in Paris, could formerly be seen in front of the pylon at Luxor, on a symbolic base of which a few fragments remain which are kept in the museum of the Louvre. To north and south this base was flanked by four baboons sculpted in high relief, while on the other two sides were bas-reliefs representing three figures of the Nile god bearing offerings. It was long maintained that it would be impossible to carry out the project [of transporting the obelisk to Paris]. The removal of the obelisk from Luxor attracted many more tourists than usual to Egypt, waiting for the day when this superb monolith would be lowered. The operation began amidst a general silence: displaced from its centre of gravity, the obelisk tilted slowly towards the track which had been specially prepared so that it could be dragged on board the barge which was to transport it from the banks of the Nile to the banks of the Seine.

OBELISK VON RAMSES [II.] MERIAMUN

Von Luxor nach Paris verbracht

Dieser Obelisk, der heute auf der Place de la Concorde in Paris zu sehen ist, stand einst auf einem symbolischen Sockel – von dem einige erhaltene Überreste im Louvre aufbewahrt werden – vor dem Pylon von Luxor. Im Norden und Süden flankierten vier freistehend gearbeitete Kynokephale dieses Fundament; auf den beiden anderen Seiten war es mit Flachreliefs verziert, die drei Opfergaben darbringende Nilgottheiten abbildeten. Man behauptete seit Langem, dass dieses Vorhaben [die Beförderung des Obelisken nach Paris] unmöglich durchzuführen sei. In Ägypten hatte der Abtransport des Obelisken aus Luxor mehr Touristen als üblich angezogen, die den Abrisstag des prächtigen Monolithen erwarteten. Die Unternehmung begann dennoch inmitten allgemeinen Schweigens: Der aus seinem Schwerpunkt verlagerte Obelisk neigte sich langsam dem für ihn vorbereiteten Transportweg zu, auf dem er an Bord des Lastkahns gebracht wurde, der ihn von den Ufern des Nils an die Ufer der Seine befördern sollte.

OBÉLISQUE DE RAMSÈS-MEÏAMOUN [RAMSÈS II]

Transporté de Louksor à Paris

Cet obélisque, élevé aujourd'hui sur la place de la Concorde à Paris, se voyait, autrefois, en avant du pylône de Louksor, sur une base symbolique dont il est resté des fragments qu'on conserve au musée du Louvre. Cette base était flanquée, au sud et au nord, de quatre cynocéphales sculptés en ronde bosse ; elle était ornée, sur les deux autres faces, de bas-reliefs représentant trois figures du dieu Nil portant des offrandes. Depuis longtemps, on prétendait qu'il serait impossible de réaliser ce projet [le transport de l'obélisque à Paris]. L'enlèvement de l'obélisque de Louksor avait-il attiré, en Égypte, plus de touristes que de coutume, attendant le jour de l'abattage de ce superbe monolithe. L'opération commença au milieu du silence général : l'obélisque déplacé de son centre de gravité s'inclinait lentement vers la voie qu'on lui avait préparée pour le traîner à bord de l'allège qui devait le transporter des rives du Nil aux rives de la Seine.

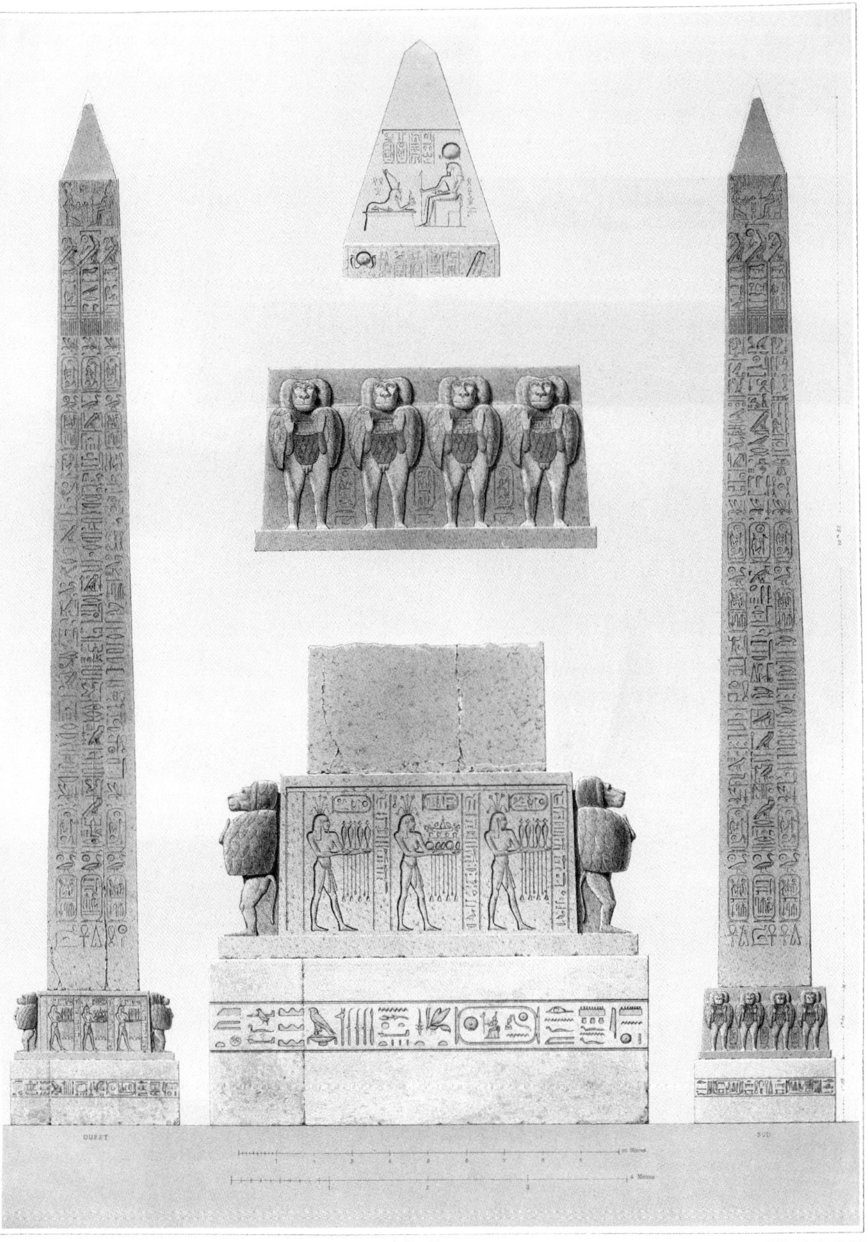

E. Prisse d'Avennes

Publié par Arthus Bertrand, Éditeur

OBÉLISQUE DE RAMSÈS – MEÏAMOUN.

TRANSPORTÉ DE LOUKSOR À PARIS

Drawing/Zeichnung/Dessin

ANCIENT CANON OF PROPORTIONS OF THE HUMAN BODY

(in common use from the 5th up to the 26th Dynasty)

From the most remote times, Egyptian artists had adopted a scale of rules for the proportions of the human body. In the unfinished parts of the oldest monuments, tombs contemporary with the pyramids of Memphis, can be seen rough sketches where perfectly straight lines traced in red chalk or red ochre mark out squares of proportion. The oldest canon of proportions was divided into 19 parts, from the sole of the foot right up to the top of the head. The height and the divisions are the same for both sexes. In this first plate I give five examples of the ancient canon taken from various periods, from the building of the pyramids up to the artistic renaissance under Psammetichus I and his successors, a period when the Egyptian artists modified the ancient canon.

ALTER KANON DER PROPORTIONEN DES MENSCHLICHEN KÖRPERS

(von der 5. bis zur 26. Dynastie gebräuchlich)

Seit ältester Zeit hatten die ägyptischen Künstler einen kanonischen Maßstab für die Proportionen des menschlichen Körpers angewandt. Die ältesten Denkmäler – die Gräber aus der Zeit der Pyramiden von Memphis – weisen in ihren unvollendeten Bereichen Skizzen auf, an denen schnurgerade, mit Rötel oder rotem Ocker gezeichnete Netzraster für die Proportionen auffallen. Der älteste Proportionenkanon untergliederte [den menschlichen Körper] vom Scheitel bis zur Sohle in 19 Teile. Die Höhe und die Unterteilungen sind für beide Geschlechter gleich. Auf dieser ersten Tafel zeige ich fünf Beispiele des alten Kanons, die von Denkmälern unterschiedlicher Zeitstellung stammen – von der Errichtung der Pyramiden bis zur Kunstrenaissance unter der Saïten-Dynastie, während der die ägyptischen Künstler den alten Kanon abwandelten.

ANCIEN CANON DES PROPORTIONS DU CORPS HUMAIN

(usité depuis la Ve jusqu'à la XXVIe dynastie)

Dès les temps les plus reculés, les artistes égyptiens avaient adopté une échelle au canon pour les proportions du corps humain. Les monuments les plus anciens, les tombeaux contemporains des pyramides de Memphis présentent, dans leurs parties inachevées, des ébauches où l'on remarque des carreaux de proportion tracés au cordeau avec de la sanguine ou de l'ocre rouge. Le plus ancien canon de proportions était divisé en dix-neuf parties depuis la plante des pieds jusqu'au sommet de la tête. La hauteur et les divisions sont les mêmes pour les deux sexes. J'ai donné dans cette première planche cinq spécimens de l'ancien canon pris sur des monuments de diverses époques, depuis l'érection des pyramides jusqu'à la renaissance de l'art sous les Psammétiques, époque où les artistes égyptiens modifièrent l'ancien canon.

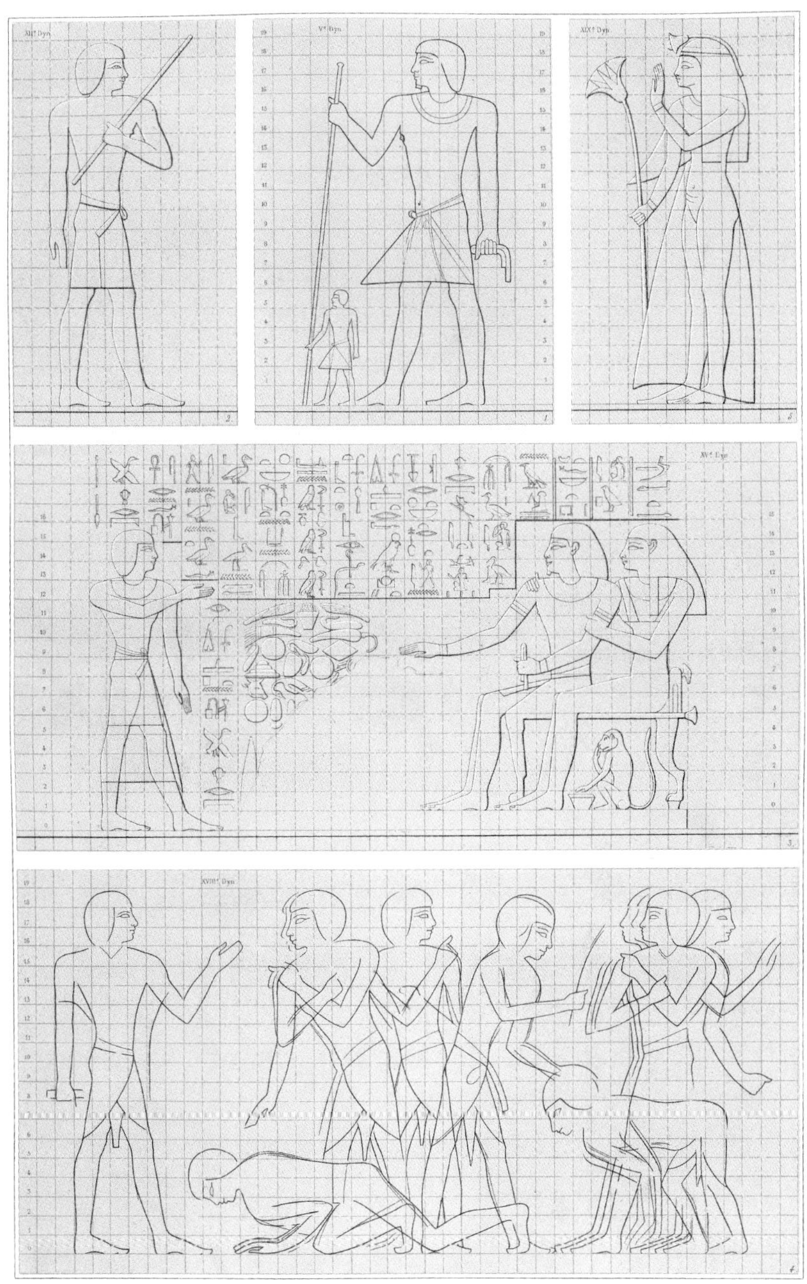

Lith. par Daumont _ Imp. par Hangard Maugé

E. Prisse d'Avennes.

Publié par Arthus Bertrand Editeur.

ANCIEN CANON DES PROPORTIONS DU CORPS HUMAIN

USITÉ DEPUIS LA Vᵉ JUSQU'À LA XXVIᵉ DYNASTIE.

NEW CANON OF PROPORTIONS OF THE HUMAN BODY

(in use from the time of Psammetichus I up to Caracalla)

From the 26th Dynasty onwards, that is from the artistic renaissance, Egyptian artists adopted a new canon divided into 23 parts. This survived the Egyptian monarchy and in fact, in the Nile valley, lasted right up until the total extinction of the cult of Osiris. In this second plate of the canon of proportions of the human body I give four examples from the new canon. The first is taken from a hypogeum at el-Assasif in Thebes, which was dug out and decorated for an official of the time of Psammetichus I. No. 2 is a figure copied from the ruins of an unfinished building of the reign of Nectanebo. No. 3 is taken from a group drawn in the temple of Thoth the ibis-headed, near Medinet Habu; it represents Ptolemy VIII Euergetes II and his wife, Cleopatra. No. 4 dates from the Roman Period, from the reign of Caracalla.

NEUER KANON DER MENSCHLICHEN PROPORTIONEN

(von Psammetich I. bis Caracalla gebräuchlich)

Von der Renaissance der Künste in der 26. Dynastie an übernahmen die ägyptischen Künstler einen neuen, in 23 Teile untergliederten Kanon. Er überlebte die ägyptische Monarchie, und schließlich überdauerte er im Niltal bis zum vollständigen Aussterben des Osiris-Kultes. Auf dieser zweiten den Kanon der menschlichen Proportionen betreffenden Tafel zeige ich vier Beispiele des neuen Kanons. Die Nr. 1 ist einem Hypogäum entnommen, das im Tal von El-Assasif in Theben für einen Beamten aus der Zeit des Psammetich I. ausgehoben und ausgeschmückt wurde. Die Nr. 2 ist eine in den Ruinen eines unvollendeten Gebäudes aus der Regierungszeit von Nektanebos kopierte Darstellung. Die Nr. 3 entstammt einer im Tempel des ibisköpfigen Thot bei Medinet Habu gezeichneten Gruppe: Sie stellt Ptolemaios VIII. Euergetes II. und seine Gemahlin Kleopatra dar. Die Nr. 4 stammt aus römischer Zeit, d. h. hier aus der Regierungszeit von Caracalla.

NOUVEAU CANON DES PROPORTIONS DU CORPS HUMAIN

(en usage depuis Psammetik Ier jusqu'à Caracalla)

À partir de la XXVIe dynastie, c'est-à-dire de la renaissance des arts, les artiste égyptiens adoptèrent un nouveau canon divisé en vingt-trois parties. Il survécut à la monarchie égyptienne et dura, enfin, dans la vallée du Nil, jusqu'à l'extinction totale du culte d'Osiris. J'ai donné dans cette seconde planche du canon des proportions du corps humain quatre spécimens du nouveau canon. Le n° 1 est tiré d'un hypogée de l'Assacif, à Thèbes, qui fut creusé et décoré pour un fonctionnaire du temps de Psammetik Ier. Le n° 2 est une figure copiée sur les ruines d'un édifice inachevé du règne de Nectanèbe. Le n° 3 est tiré d'un groupe dessiné dans le temple de Thoth Ibiocéphale, près de Medineh-Thabou : il représente Ptolémée [VIII] Évergète II et Cléopâtre, sa femme. Le n° 4 date de l'époque romaine, du règne de Caracalla.

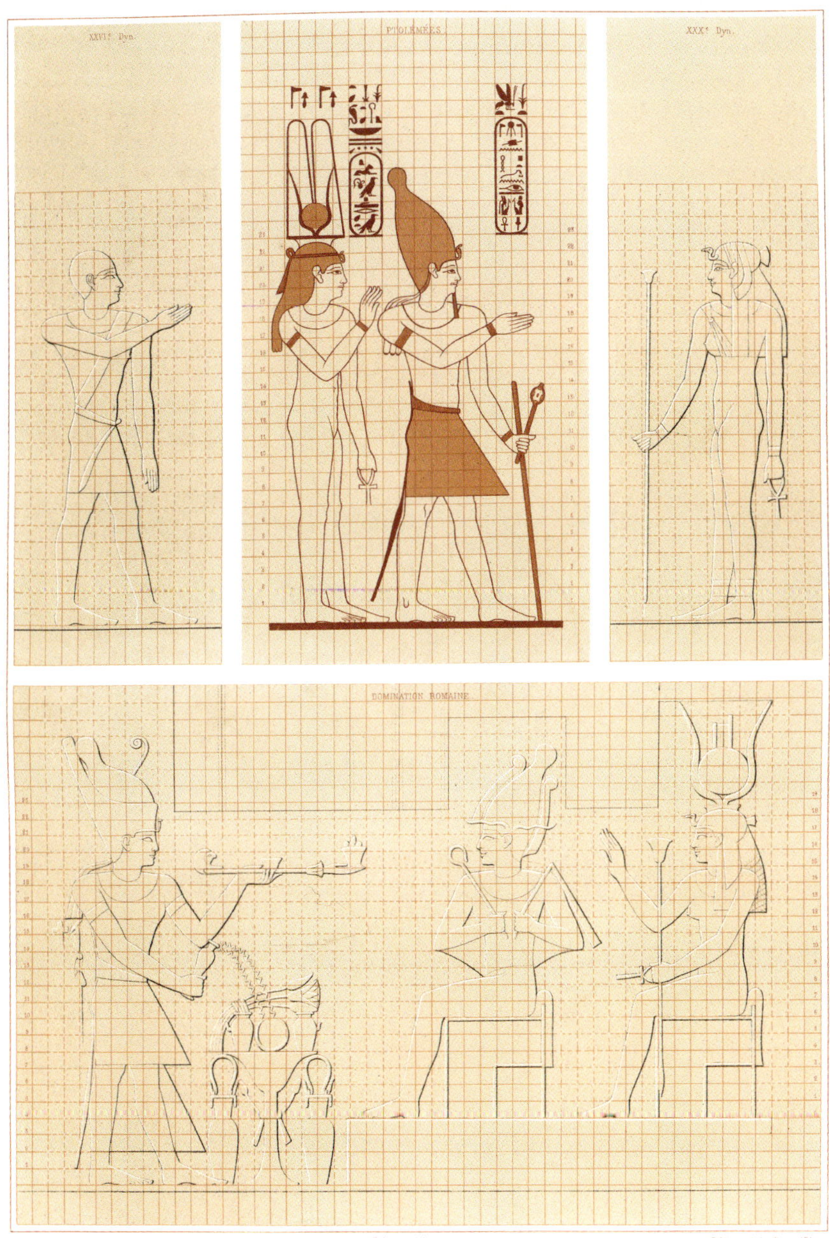

Lith par Dumont. Imp par Hangard-Maugé. E. Prisse d'Avennes. Publié par Arthus Bertrand Éditeur.

NOUVEAU CANON DES PROPORTIONS DU CORPS HUMAIN

EN USAGE DEPUIS PSAMMETIK Iᵉʳ JUSQU'À CARACALLA.

FACSIMILE OF A SKETCH (18th Dynasty)

Necropolis of Thebes

This group is also taken from a series of Asiatic and African captives, drawn in black, and of a remarkable purity, on one of the walls of the tomb of Ramose, a high-ranking official who lived during the early years of the reign of Akhenaten. All the types of head are skilfully captured, and it is possible to recognise the chiefs of those races with whom the Egyptians were constantly at war. Of the two Asiatics with light eyes, the first has features which are very well characterised: he is bearded and moustached and appears to me to represent a Syrian; as for the second Asiatic, whose sharp, cunning profile stands out in front of the others, with hair falling over his forehead and the nape of his neck, he must be intended as the image of a Rebu, the most formidable enemy whom the Egyptians encountered in Asia [Libya]. They were at war with this race from at least the beginning of the reign of Akhenaten into the reign of Ramesses III.

FAKSIMILE EINER SKIZZE (18. Dynastie)

Nekropole von Theben

Diese Gruppe ist ebenfalls einer Reihe asiatischer und afrikanischer, mit bemerkenswerter Klarheit in Schwarz gezeichneter Gefangener entnommen und stammt von einer der Wände aus dem Grab von Ramose – einem hohen Beamten, der während der ersten Jahre der Herrschaft Echnatons lebte. Alle Kopf-Typen sind geschickt erfasst; die Anführer der Völker, mit denen sich die Ägypter ständig im Krieg befanden, sind zu erkennen. Der erste der beiden Asiaten mit hellen Augen scheint mir – mit seinen charakteristischen Gesichtszügen, dem Bart und dem Schnurrbart – einen Syrer darzustellen: Was den zweiten Asiaten anbetrifft, dessen Haar auf Stirn und Schultern fällt und dessen schmales, schlaues Profil sich vor die anderen schiebt, so dürfte es sich um das Bild eines Rebu handeln – des furchtbarsten Gegners, auf den die Ägypter in Asien [Libyen] trafen. Sie waren mit ihm mindestens von der Regierungszeit Echnatons an bis zu der von Ramses III. im Krieg.

FAC-SIMILÉ D'UNE ESQUISSE (XVIIIe dynastie)

Nécropole de Thèbes

Ce groupe est tiré d'une série de captifs asiatiques et africains, tracés en noir, de cette grandeur et avec une pureté remarquable, sur une des parois du tombeau de Ramés [Ramosé], haut fonctionnaire qui vivait dans les premières années du règne de Khouenaten [Akhénaton]. Tous les types de têtes y sont habilement saisis ; on peut y reconnaître les chefs des peuples avec lesquels les Égyptiens étaient constamment en guerre. Des deux Asiatiques aux yeux clairs, le premier à la physionomie bien caractérisée, et portant barbe et moustache, me paraît représenter un Syrien : quant au second Asiatique, celui dont le profil effilé et rusé se projette sur les autres, avec les cheveux tombant sur le front et la nuque, il doit offrir l'image d'un Robou, qui fut le plus formidable ennemi que les Égyptiens rencontrèrent en Asie [Libye]. Ils furent en guerre avec lui, au moins depuis le règne de Khouenaten jusque sous Ramsès III.

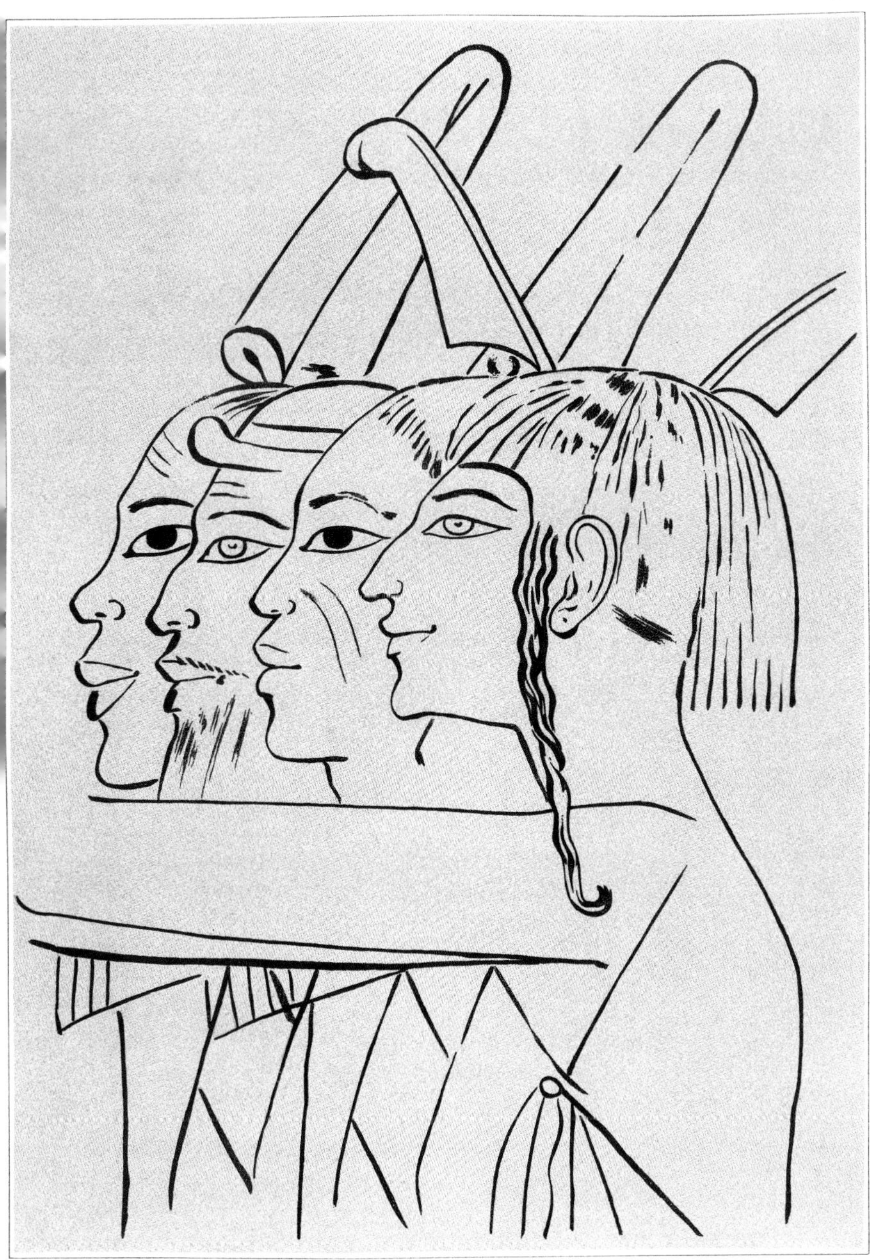

Lith par Saladini . Imp. par Hangard Maugé.

F. Prisse d'Avennes.

Publié par Arthus Bertrand, Éditeur.

FAC-SIMILE D'UNE ESQUISSE.

(NÉCROPOLE DE THÈBES... XVIIIe DYNASTIE)

FACSIMILE OF A WORKING SKETCH (18th Dynasty)

Necropolis of Thebes

By including the handsome group which is the subject of this plate, I wished to show a complete example of this type of sketch, including its pentimenti and its hesitations. This is a portrayal of a group of captives in varying attitudes. An [African] stands, clad in a panther skin and with two feathers, the symbol of authority, as head decoration, stretching out his arms to implore clemency from the pharaoh who rests impassive; two kneeling Asiatics, recognisable from their features and their beards, appear to be entreating his mercy even more passionately; finally, a fourth captive prostrates himself yet more humbly than his companions and seems to be kissing the earth.

FAKSIMILE EINER BEREINIGTEN SKIZZE (18. Dynastie)

Nekropole von Theben

Mit der schönen Gruppe, die den Gegenstand dieser Tafel bildet, wollte ich ein vollständiges Beispiel derartiger Skizzen – mit den Irrtümern und tastenden Versuchen – zeigen. Es stellt eine Gruppe Gefangener in unterschiedlichen Haltungen dar. Ein stehender, mit einem Pantherfell bekleideter [Afrikaner], dessen Kopf zwei seine Würde versinnbildlichende Federn schmücken, erfleht mit ausgebreiteten Armen die Gnade des unbewegten Pharaos; zwei kniende, an ihren Zügen ebenso wie an ihrem Bart erkennbare Asiaten scheinen diesen noch inbrünstiger um Erbarmen zu bitten; ein vierter Gefangener wirft sich ihm noch demütiger als seine Gefährten zu Füßen und scheint den Boden zu küssen.

FAC-SIMILÉ D'UNE ESQUISSE ÉPURÉE (XVIIIe dynastie)

Nécropole de Thèbes

J'ai voulu, en donnant le beau groupe qui fait le sujet de cette planche, présenter un complet spécimen de ce genre d'esquisse, avec ses repentirs et ses tâtonnements. Celle-ci représente également un groupe de captifs dans des attitudes variées. Un [Africain] debout, vêtu d'une peau de panthère et la tête ornée de deux plumes, symbole d'autorité, implore, les bras étendus, la clémence du pharaon qui reste impassible ; deux Asiatiques agenouillés et reconnaissables à leurs traits, comme à leur barbe, paraissent lui demander grâce avec plus d'ardeur ; enfin, un quatrième captif se prosterne avec plus d'humilité encore que ses compagnons et semble baiser la terre.

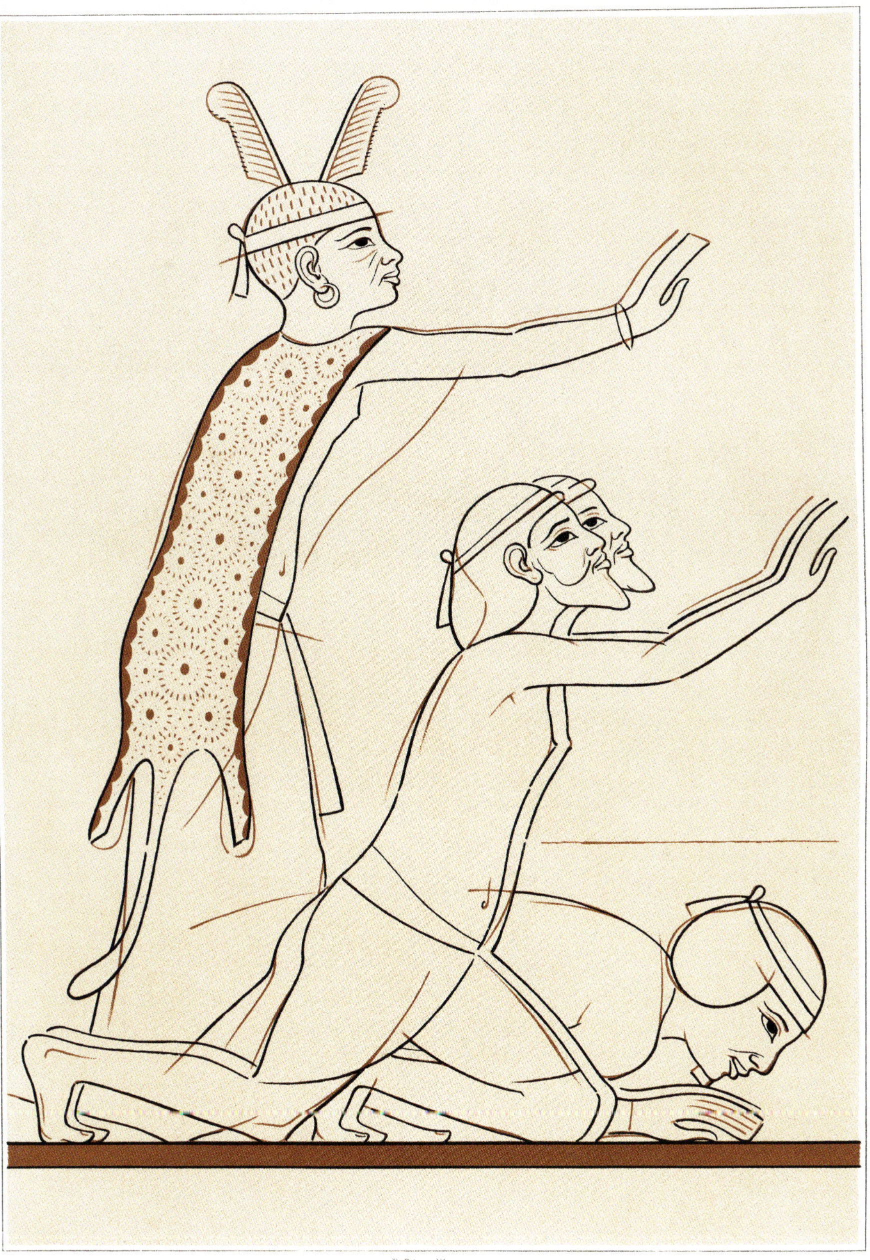

Lith. par Bodin _ Imp. Hangard Maugé. E. Prisse d'Avennes. Publié par Arthus Bertrand Éditeur.

FAC-SIMILE D'UNE ESQUISSE ÉPURÉE.

(NÉCROPOLE DE THÈBES _ XVIII.e DYNASTIE.)

REDUCED COPY OF A SKETCH REPRESENTING SETI I (19th Dynasty)

Necropolis of Thebes

The Egyptian artists were accustomed to drawing without looking at a live model and were also constrained by the rules of an inflexible procedural method. It was therefore inevitable that their work fell far short of presenting any true, natural image and so they wielded their reed pen or their chisel every day to produce the same well-worn and repeated forms. The art on the monuments of the Old Kingdom developed in a remarkable manner: its designs are of a surprising confidence, purity, and one could almost say nobility. However, it must be admitted that the Egyptian artists had no knowledge of how to group their figures together, or of combining and arranging them in the same scene. The human figure, animals, various objects, all seem to have been composed in the same way.

VERKLEINERUNG EINER SETHOS I. DARSTELLENDEN SKIZZE (19. Dynastie)

Nekropole von Theben

Da die ägyptischen Künstler daran gewöhnt waren, ohne lebendes Modell vor Augen zu zeichnen, und sich zudem den Gesetzen einer unerbittlichen Routine beugen mussten, waren Abweichungen von der natürlichen Wirklichkeit unvermeidlich. Auch erzeugten sie Tag für Tag mit Pinsel und Schreibrohr dieselben Formen, dasselbe Klischee. An den Denkmälern des Alten Reiches haben sich die Künste wunderbar entwickelt: Die Zeichnungen sind von erstaunlicher Kraft und Klarheit, man könnte sogar sagen Erhabenheit. Jedoch kommt man nicht umhin festzustellen, dass die ägyptischen Künstler die Fertigkeit, einzelne Figuren zusammenzustellen oder verschiedene Gestalten in einer szenischen Darstellung anzuordnen und zu untergliedern, nicht beherrschten. Die menschliche Gestalt, die Tiere, die unterschiedlichen Gegenstände scheinen alle auf ein und dieselbe Weise komponiert zu sein.

RÉDUCTION D'UNE ESQUISSE REPRÉSENTANT SÉTI Ier (XIXe dynastie)

Nécropole de Thèbes

Habitués à dessiner sans avoir un modèle vivant sous leurs yeux, courbés, en outre, sous les lois d'une routine inflexible, les artistes égyptiens devaient s'écarter, inévitablement, de la vérité naturelle : aussi les mêmes formes, le même poncif se produisaient-ils, chaque jour, sous leur calam ou sous leur ciseau. L'art s'est développé sur les monuments de l'ancien Empire d'une manière admirable : le dessin en est d'une fermeté, d'une pureté, et on peut même dire, d'une noblesse surprenante. Il est, cependant, impossible de ne pas reconnaître que les artistes égyptiens ignoraient l'art de grouper leurs figures, ou de combiner et d'agencer les divers personnages d'une même scène. La figure humaine, les animaux, les objets divers semblent avoir été composés de la même manière.

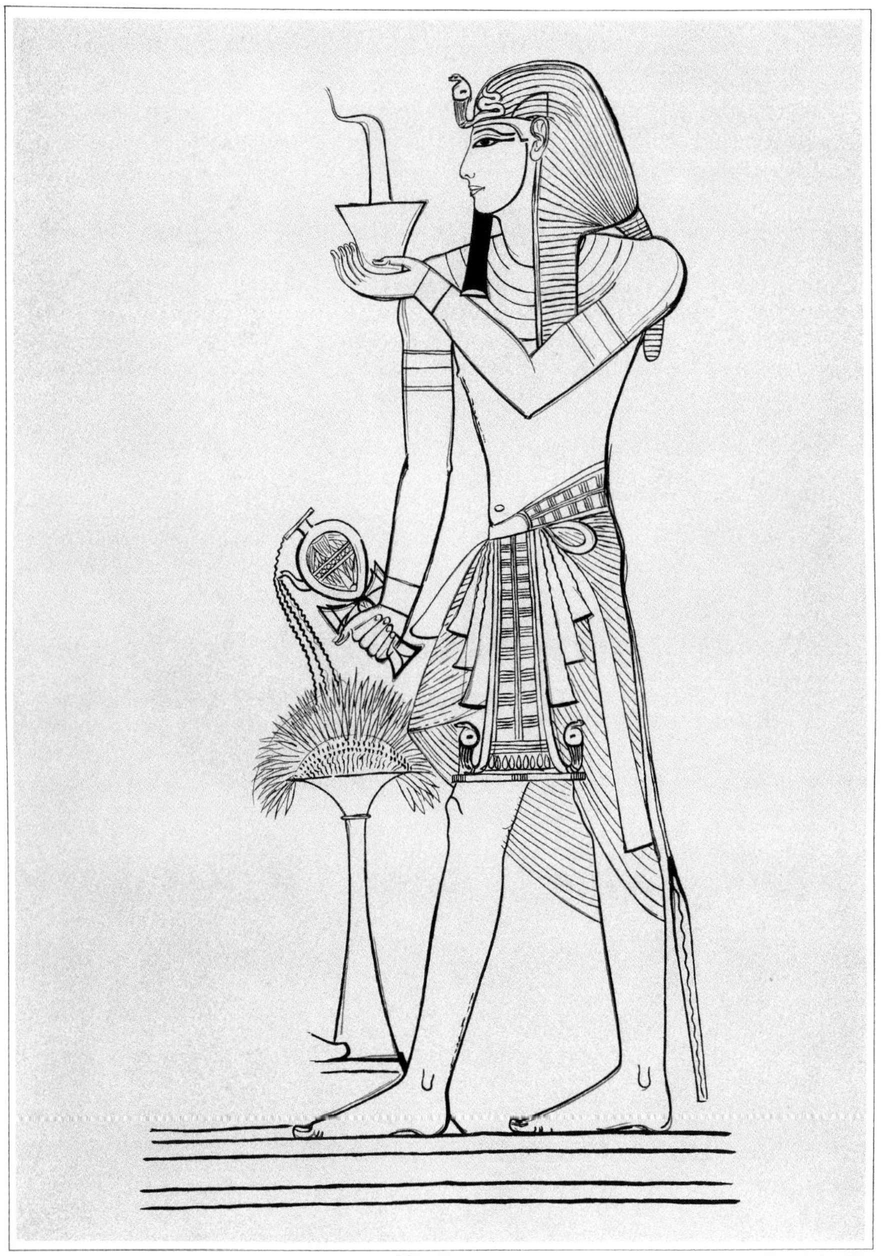

Heliog. par Durand. _ Imp. par Hangard-Maugé

E. Prisse d'Avennes.

Publié par Arthus-Bertrand, Éditeur

RÉDUCTION D'UNE ESQUISSE REPRÉSENTANT SÉTI 1ER

(NÉCROPOLE DE THÈBES. _ XIXe DYN.)

HUNTING IN THE MARSHES (17th and 18th Dynasties)

In most of the tombs which contain varied scenes relating to the arts, occupations, customs and costumes of the Egyptians, a scene of hunting or fishing, favourite pastimes of high-ranking officials, always features as the principal illustration. A vast clump of papyrus and reeds, in which birds of a variety of species perch or nest, rises from the middle of a lagoon and usually separates the subject into two parts. Standing in a light boat made of papyrus, the deceased is shown at the two sides of the picture. On one side he is seen engaged in spearing huge fish [here a hippopotamus] with a type of harpoon; on the other, he is hunting different types of aquatic bird with flat, curved sticks, tipped with a bronze head. I owe these two sketches to the kindness of a French artist, M[onsieur] Dupuy, who died in Cairo; he had drawn them most meticulously in 1827 or 1828; all I have done is to reduce very slightly these two scenes, which should properly carry his name rather than mine.

JAGDSZENEN AUS DEN SÜMPFEN (17. und 18. Dynastie)

In den meisten Grabmalen, die abwechslungsreiche Szenen zu Kunst und Gewerbe sowie Sitten und Gebräuchen der Ägypter enthalten, bildet stets eine Szene über die Jagd oder den Fischfang, den bevorzugten Zeitvertreib der hohen Beamten, das wichtigste Bild. Inmitten einer Lagune erhebt sich ein riesiger Papyrus- und Binsenbüschel – auf dem Vögel vieler verschiedener Arten sitzen oder brüten – und teilt das Sujet für gewöhnlich in zwei Teile auf. Der Verstorbene ist, auf einem leichten Papyrusboot stehend, an den beiden Außenseiten des Bildes dargestellt. Auf der einen Seite ist er damit beschäftigt, riesengroße Fische [hier: ein Flusspferd] mit einer zweizackigen Harpune aufzuspießen; auf der anderen jagt er Wasservögel mittels flacher, krummer, mit einem bronzenen Kopf bewehrter Stecken. Ich verdanke diese beiden Skizzen der Freundschaft des in Kairo verstorbenen französischen Künstlers M[onsieur] Dupuy; er hatte sie im Jahre 1827 oder 1828 mit aller möglichen Sorgfalt angefertigt; ich habe die beiden Szenen lediglich ein ganz kleines bisschen verkleinert: Statt meines Namens müssten sie seinen tragen.

CHASSES AU MARAIS (XVIIe et XVIIIe dynasties)

Dans la plupart des tombeaux, qui contiennent des scènes variées relatives aux arts et métiers, aux mœurs et coutumes des Égyptiens, une scène de chasse ou de pêche, amusements favoris des hauts fonctionnaires, forme toujours le principal tableau. Une énorme touffe de papyrus et de joncs, sur lesquels sont posés ou nichés des oiseaux d'espèces très variées, s'élève au milieu d'une lagune et sépare d'ordinaire le sujet en deux parties. Debout, sur une barque légère de papyrus, le défunt est représenté aux deux extrémités du tableau. D'un côté, on le voit occupé à percer d'énormes poissons avec une espèce de « bident » [un harpon]; de l'autre, à chasser divers oiseaux aquatiques avec des bâtons plats, courbés, armés d'une tête de bronze. Je dois ces deux esquisses à l'amitié d'un artiste français, M[onsieur] Dupuy, mort au Caire ; il les avait dessinées en 1827 ou 1828 avec tout le soin dont il était capable ; je n'ai fait que réduire un tant soit peu les deux scènes : elles devraient porter son nom au lieu du mien.

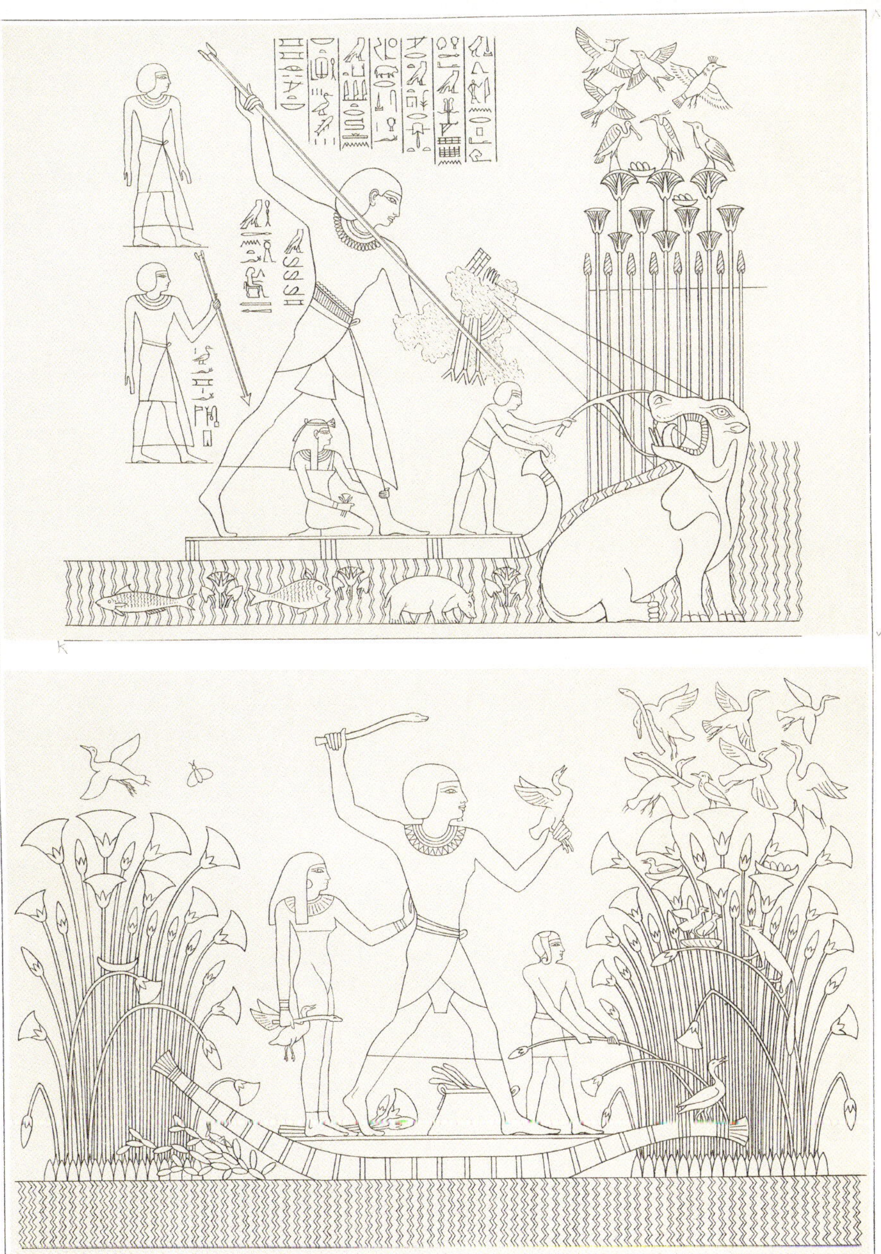

Aut. par Moulin. – Imp. par Hangard-Maugé. E. Prisse d'Avennes. Publié par Arthus-Bertrand, Editeur.

CHASSES AU MARAIS.

(XVIIe & XVIIIe DYN.)

FEMALE MUSICIANS AND DANCERS (18th Dynasty)

Necropolis of Thebes

It is from the 18th Dynasty onwards in particular that this type of depiction acquires great significance because of the beauty of its drawing, the voluptuous attitude of its figures and the elegance of the instruments in use at that period. The first register is noteworthy for a female lute-player, seen from behind, and two female dancers who, with bent head, seem to be following with their eyes the movement of their feet. All three are clothed in transparent dresses and wear decorative bands around their hips. The second register, whose drawing is less pure and elegant than the first, is sculpted in bas-relief in a hypogeum [...]. The female musicians carry a harp, a double flute, a lyre which seems to have served as a model for the Greeks and a tympanum made from a wooden frame with the skin of an onager stretched over it.

MUSIKERINNEN UND TÄNZERINNEN (18. Dynastie)

Nekropole von Theben

Durch die Schönheit der Zeichnungen, die sinnenfreudige Haltung der Figuren und die Anmut der in dieser Zeit gebräuchlichen Instrumente erlangen derartige Darstellungen vor allem von der 18. Dynastie an große Bedeutung. Das erste Register fällt durch eine in Rückansicht abgebildete Lautenspielerin und zwei Tänzerinnen mit geneigtem Kopf auf, die mit den Augen der Bewegung ihrer Füße zu folgen scheinen. Alle drei sind mit durchscheinenden Gewändern bekleidet; ihre Hüften sind mit einer Kette geschmückt. Das zweite Register mit einer weniger klaren und anmutigen Zeichnung als das erste, ist als Flachrelief in einem Hypogäum ausgemeißelt [...]. Die Musikerinnen teilen sich hier eine Harfe, eine gedoppelte Rohrpfeife, eine Lyra – die den Griechen als Vorbild gedient haben mag – und ein Tympanon, das aus einem Holzrahmen mit einer darübergespannten Onager-Haut geformt ist.

MUSICIENNES ET DANSEUSES (XVIIIe dynastie)

Nécropole de Thèbes

C'est surtout à partir de la XVIIIe dynastie que ce genre de représentations acquiert une grande importance par la beauté du dessin, l'attitude voluptueuse des figures et l'élégance des instruments en usage à cette époque. Le premier registre est remarquable par une joueuse de mandore, vue de derrière, et deux danseuses qui, la tête penchée, semblent suivre de l'œil le mouvement de leurs pieds. Toutes trois sont vêtues de robes transparentes ; elles ont les hanches garnies du cercle lombaire. Le second registre, d'un dessin moins pur et moins élégant que le premier, est sculpté en bas-relief dans un hypogée [...]. Les musiciennes s'y répartissent une harpe, une flûte double, une lyre qui semble avoir servi de modèle aux Grecs et un tympanon formé d'un cadre de bois tendu d'une peau d'onagre.

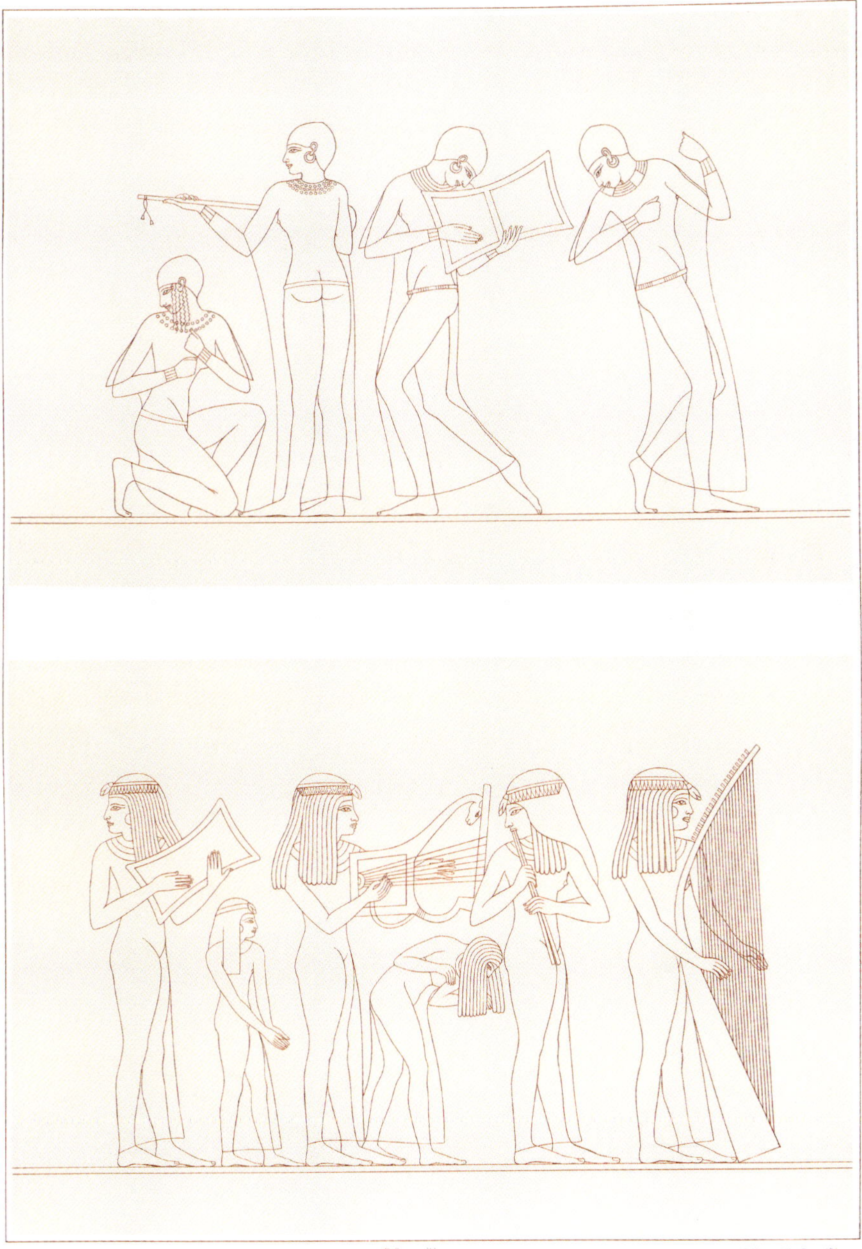

Lith par Werner . Imp par Hangard-Maugé

E. Prisse d'Avennes

Publié par Arthus-Bertrand Éditeur

MUSICIENNES & DANSEUSES.

(NÉCROPOLE DE THÈBES ... XVIIIe DYNASTIE.)

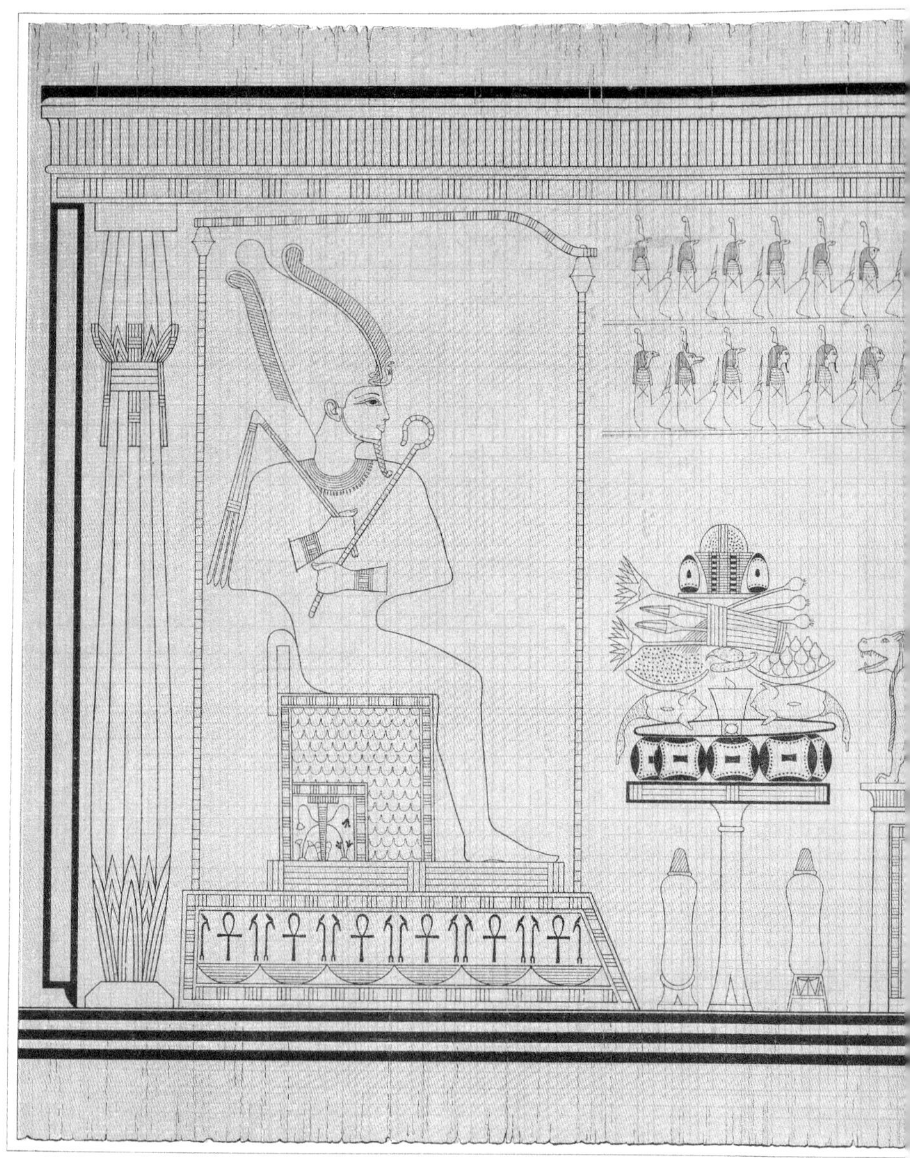

Autog. par Melisson   Imp. par Hangard-Maugé

PESÉE & JUGEMENT

(RITUEL FU

II 8

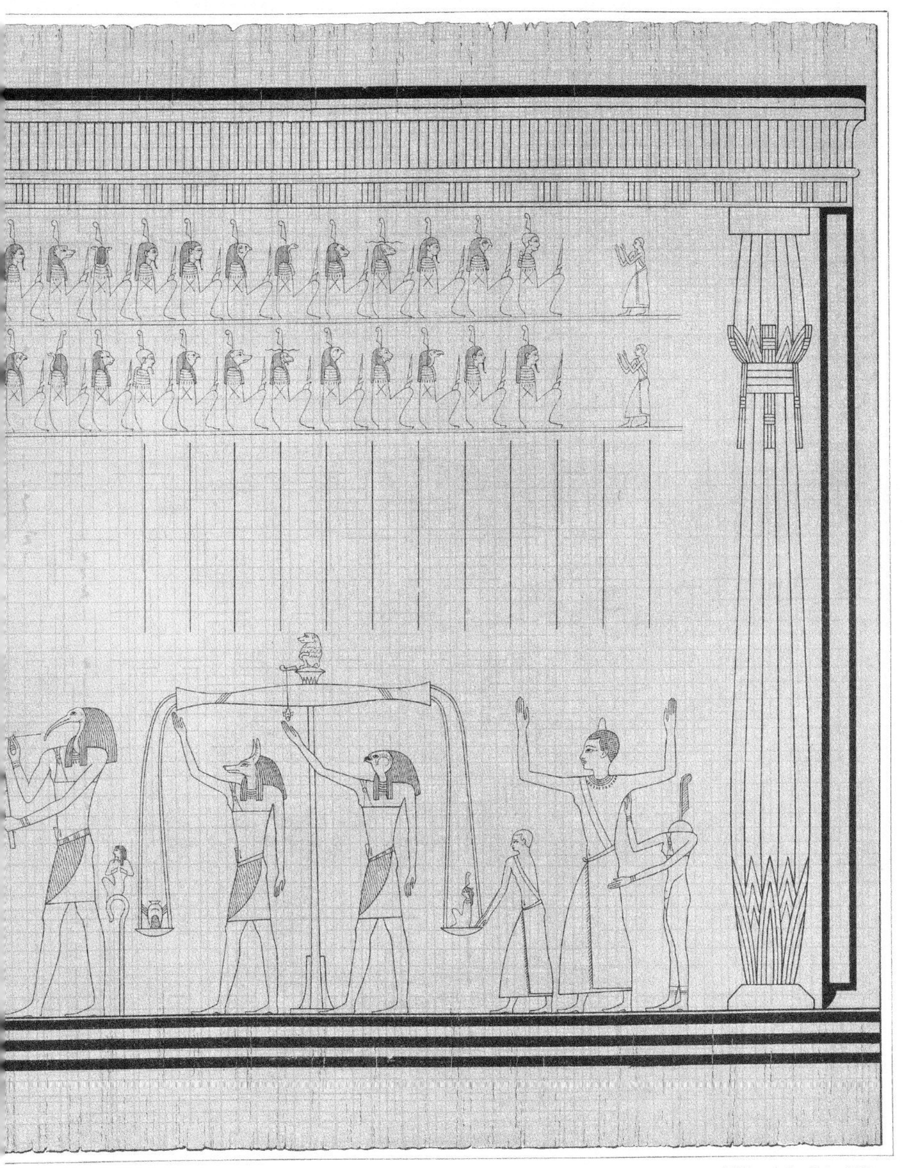

Publié par Arthus Bertrand, Éditeur.

AU TRIBUNAL D'OSIRIS.

DYNASTIE.)

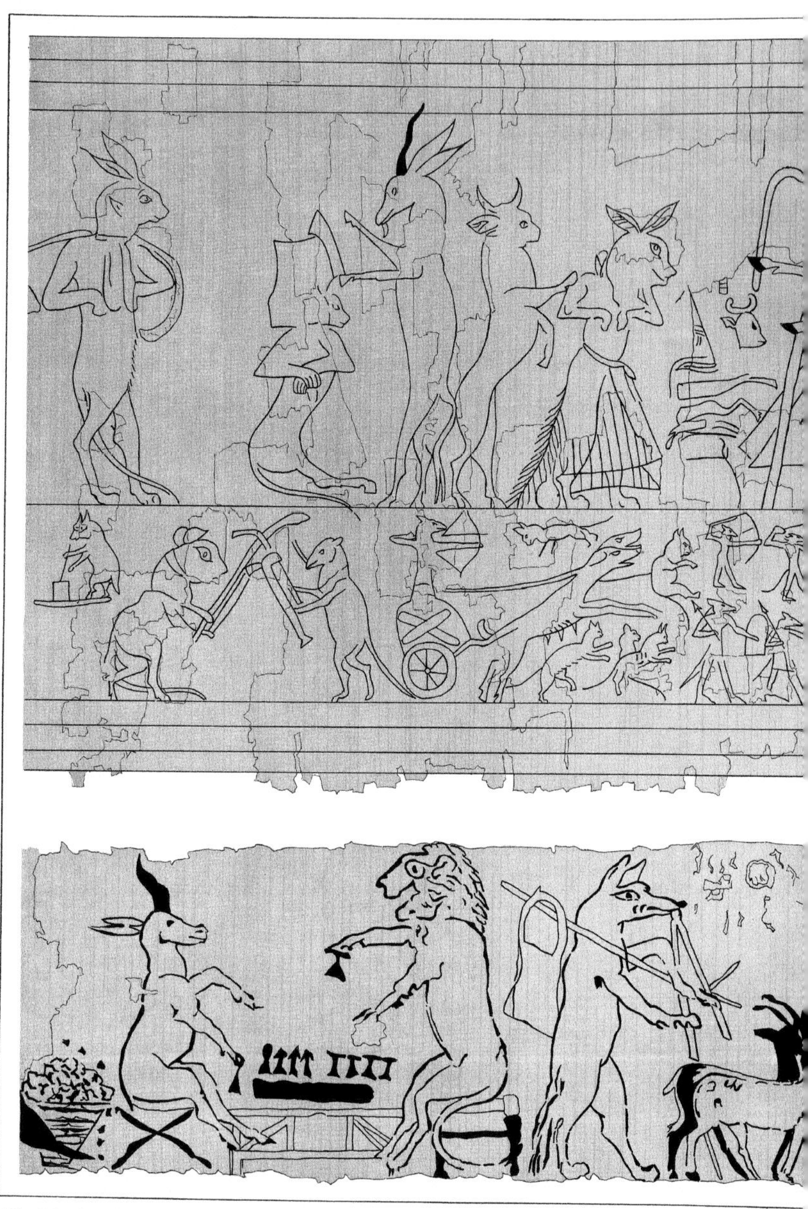

Lith. par Hédouin Imp. par Hangard-Maugé.

FRAGMENTS D

(MUSÉE DE

#9

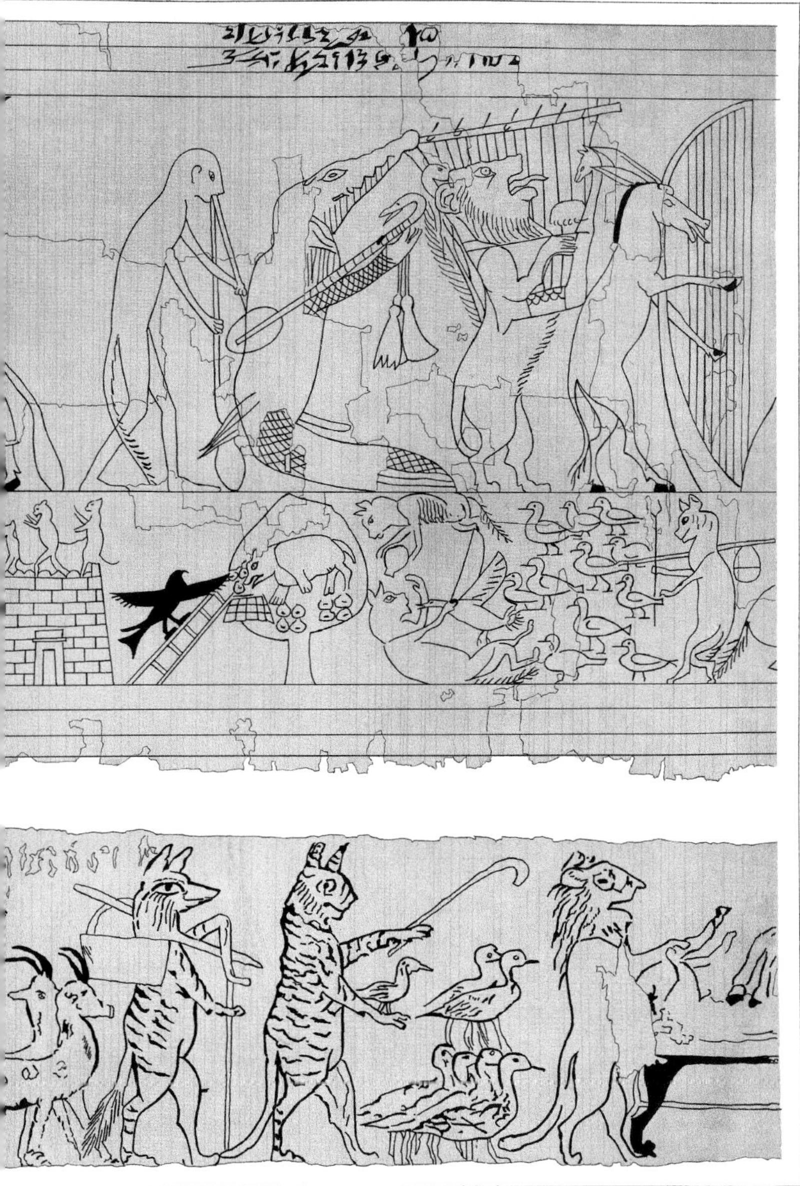

Publié par Arthus-Bertrand, Éditeur.

SATIRIQUES

E LONDRES.)

(Pages/Seite 342/343)

WEIGHING AND JUDGEMENT OF THE SOUL BEFORE THE TRIBUNAL OF OSIRIS (18th Dynasty)

Funerary ritual

The god [Osiris], seated on his throne with the Atef crown on his head and holding in one hand the crook and the other the flail, presides over the ceremony. On an altar laden with food and flowers are spread the offerings of the deceased; behind the altar can be seen the great guardian creature of hell – the typical Cerberus with gaping jaws. Further on there is a great balance with a baboon sitting on it; in one of the scales is placed the heart of the deceased while in the other, as counterweight, is an image of justice. The two brothers Anubis and Horus are witnesses of the weighing of the good and evil deeds of the dead man; Thoth, the sacred scribe, writes down the result, with the sceptre of Osiris with a small human figure on top at his side. Supported by justice, who is not here represented as blind but has no head, the deceased, arms raised in supplication, stands at the back of the judgement hall awaiting the decision of the sovereign judge. At the top of the scene in two rows are lined up the ranks of the 42 assessors of Osiris.

TOTENGERICHT DES OSIRIS, WIEGEN DER SEELE UND URTEILSSPRUCH (18. Dynastie)

Begräbnisritual

Der Gott [Osiris] sitzt auf seinem Thron, trägt die Atef-Krone auf dem Kopf, hält in einer Hand den Krummstab, in der anderen den Wedel und überwacht die Zeremonie. Die Opfergaben des Verstorbenen sind auf einem mit Blumen und Esswaren beladenen Altar ausgebreitet: Und hinter dem Altar erscheint die große Vorsteherin der Hölle; das Urbild des Höllenhundes, mit weit aufgerissenem Maul. Weiter hinten erhebt sich eine große, von einem Kynokephalen überragte Waage; das Herz des Verstorbenen hat man in die eine Waagschale gelegt; ein Bild der Justitia als Gegengewicht in die andere. Die beiden Brüder Anubis und Horus wohnen dem Wiegen der guten und schlechten Taten des Toten bei; Thot, der heilige Schreiber, mit dem von einer kleinen menschlichen Figur überragten Osiris-Szepter an seiner Seite, notiert das Ergebnis. Hinten im Gerichtssaal erwartet der Verstorbene, mit erhobenen Armen – und mit Unterstützung der zwar nicht blind, aber ohne Kopf dargestellten Justitia – flehentlich bittend, das Urteil des richtenden Herrschers. Oberhalb dieser Szene sind – in zwei Reihen aufgereiht – die 42 Beisitzer des Osiris zu sehen.

PESÉE ET JUGEMENT DE L'ÂME AU TRIBUNAL D'OSIRIS (XVIIIe dynastie)

Rituel funéraire

Le dieu [Osiris], assis sur son trône, coiffé du claft [la couronne Atef], tenant d'une main le fouet, et, de l'autre le pedum, préside à la cérémonie. Sur un autel, chargé de victuailles et de fleurs, s'étalent les offrandes du défunt : et derrière l'autel apparaît la grande directrice de l'enfer ; le type du cerbère, la gueule béante. Plus loin s'élève une grande balance surmontée d'un cynocéphale ; dans l'un des plateaux on a placé le cœur du défunt ; dans l'autre, pour contrepoids, une image de la justice. Les deux frères Anubis et Horus assistent au pèsement des bonnes et des mauvaises actions du mort ; Thoth, l'écrivain sacré, inscrit le résultat, ayant à ses côtés le sceptre d'Osiris surmonté d'une petite figure humaine. Le défunt, les bras élevés en suppliant et soutenu par la justice représentée, sinon aveugle, du moins sans tête, attend au fond du prétoire la décision du souverain juge. Au-dessus de la scène, on voit rangés sur deux lignes les quarante-deux assesseurs d'Osiris.

(Pages/Seite 344/345)

FRAGMENTS FROM SATIRICAL PAPYRI

Some papyri have been preserved on which contemporary artists amused themselves by drawing grotesque, satirical scenes. The upper register belongs to a fragment of a long papyrus. In the first group four animals, a donkey, a lion, a crocodile and a monkey, form a quartet with their instruments. Next to them, a boastful donkey, dressed and equipped like a pharaoh, majestically receives the offerings which a splendidly decked-out cat has just presented to him. Next to them, an oryx appears to be threatening with his harp another cat who is kneeling. The next group again shows a cat. The lowest register shows a similar type of composition. Here there is a flock of geese led by a cat, and a herd of goats led by two wolves carrying crooks and sacks of bread slung over their shoulders, one of them playing the double flute. At the other end a lion can be seen playing a game of draughts with an antelope.

FRAGMENTE SATIRISCHER PAPYRI

Es sind Papyri erhalten, auf denen sich die zeitgenössischen Künstler die Zeit damit vertrieben haben, groteske oder satirische Szenen zu skizzieren. Das obere Register gehört zum Fragment eines langen Papyrus. In einer ersten Gruppe bilden vier Tiere – ein Esel, ein Löwe, ein Krokodil und ein Affe – mit Musikinstrumenten ein Quartett. Ein Stück weiter empfängt ein wichtigtuender, wie ein Pharao bewaffneter und gekleideter Esel würdevoll die Opfergaben, die ihm soeben eine Katze von hoher Geburt dargeboten hat. Daneben scheint eine Oryxantilope mit ihrer Harfe eine weitere, kniende Katze zu bedrohen. Die folgende Gruppe zeigt noch eine Katze. Das untere Register stellt eine Komposition derselben Art dar. Darauf sind eine Katze zu beobachten, die eine Gruppe Gänse hütet, und eine Ziegenherde in Begleitung zweier mit Brotbeutel und Hirtenstab ausgestatteter Wölfe, von denen einer auf der gedoppelten Rohrpfeife spielt. Am anderen Ende ist schließlich ein Löwe zu sehen, der mit einer Antilope eine Partie Dame spielt.

FRAGMENTS DE PAPYRUS SATIRIQUES

On conserve des papyrus sur lesquels les artistes du temps se sont amusés à tracer des scènes grotesques et satiriques. Le registre supérieur appartient à un fragment d'un long papyrus. Dans un premier groupe, quatre animaux, un âne, un lion, un crocodile et un singe, forment un quatuor avec les instruments. Plus loin, un âne fanfaron, vêtu et armé comme un pharaon, reçoit majestueusement les offrandes que vient de lui offrir un chat de haut parage. À côté, un oryx semble menacer de sa harpe un autre chat qui est à ses genoux. Le groupe suivant montre encore un chat. Le registre inférieur représente une composition du même genre. On y remarque un troupeau d'oies, conduit par un chat, et un troupeau de chèvres, mené par deux loups portant panetière et houlette, dont l'un joue de la flûte double. Puis à l'autre extrémité, on voit un lion faisant une partie de dames avec une antilope.

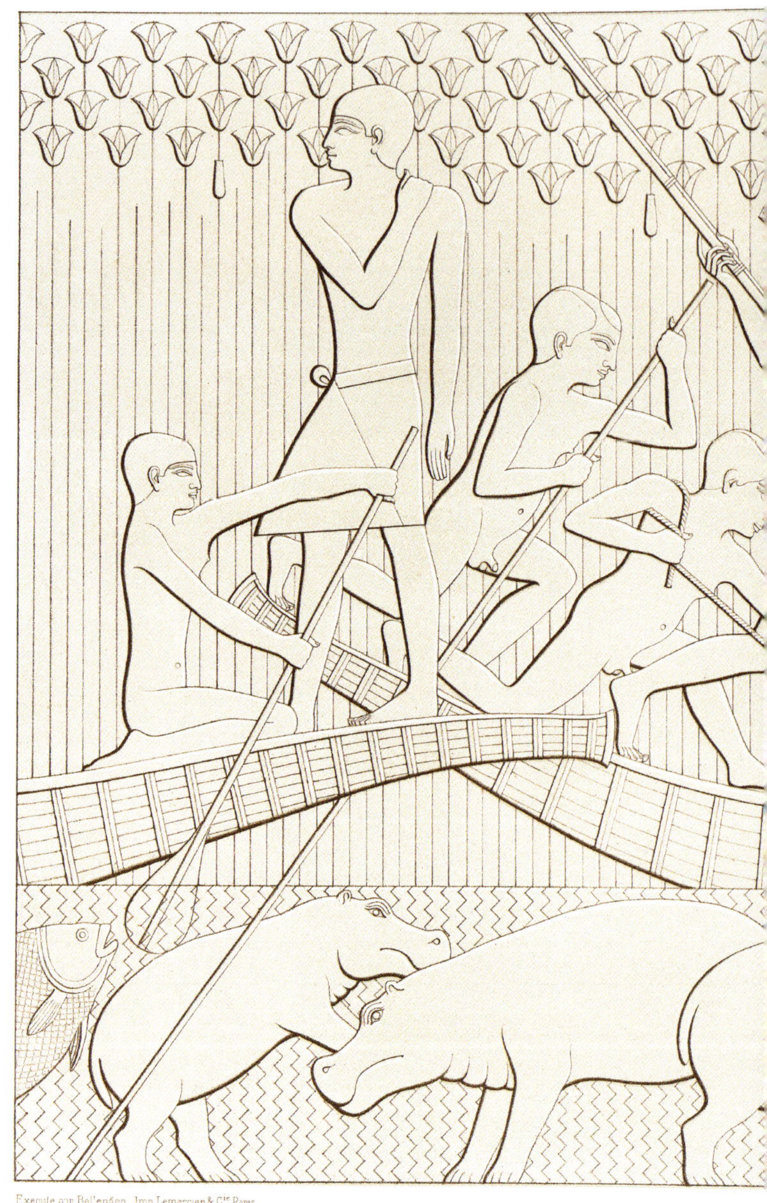

Executé par Bellenger Imp. Lemercier & Cie, Paris

CHASSE A L'HIPPOP

(MEM

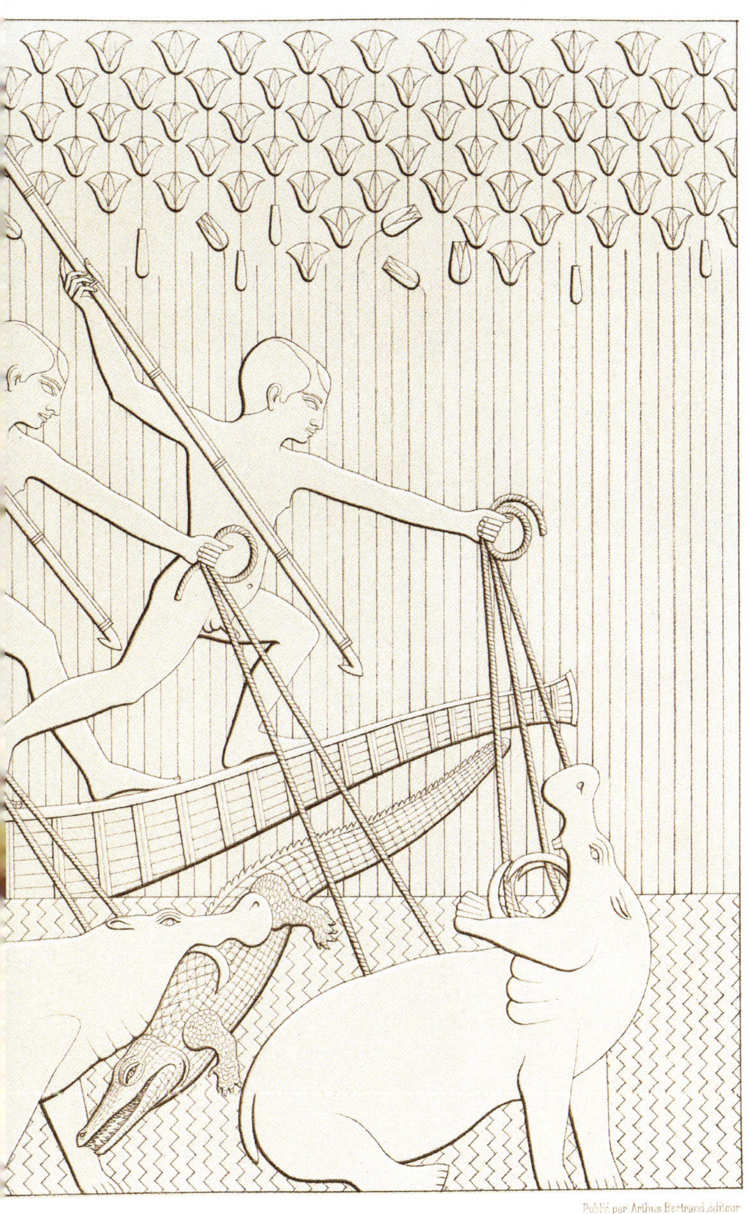

Publié par Arthus Bertrand, éditeur

DANS LES MARAIS.

STIE]

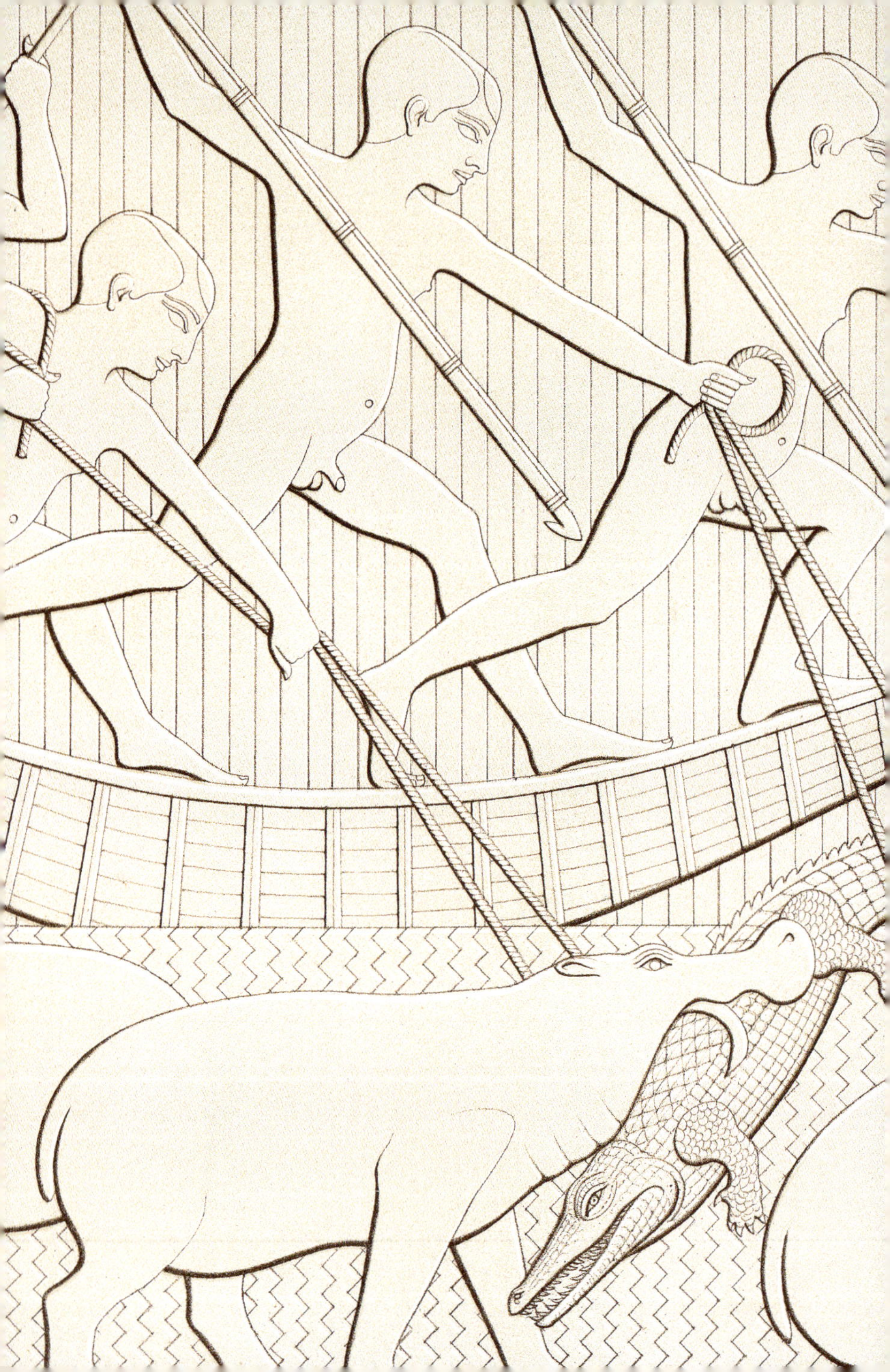

Sculpture/Skulptur/Sculpture

(Pages/Seite 348/349)

HUNTING HIPPOPOTAMUS IN THE MARSHES (6th Dynasty)

Memphis

Huntsmen armed with harpoons and borne by light boats of papyrus which allow them easy passage, even through the tall clumps of lotus, are pursuing a herd of hippopotami which are in the marsh in great numbers. The person who appears to be in command of the expedition is the only one wearing clothes; all the rest are completely nude, which reveals that they have been circumcised. A crocodile is shown in the grip of the terrible jaws of one of the hippopotami, which shows that this huge reptile often met with a formidable enemy in the waters of the Nile, or rather in its floodwaters. These scenes are often to be seen in the tombs of various necropoleis, showing us that hippopotami and crocodiles were found in abundance at certain times in all the lagoons of Upper and Lower Egypt.

FLUSSPFERDJAGD IN DEN SÜMPFEN (6. Dynastie)

Memphis

Mit Harpunen bewaffnete Jäger verfolgen auf leichten Plattbodenschiffen aus Papyrus – mit denen sie mühelos selbst hohe Lotusbüschel durchqueren können – eine Schar Flusspferde, die sich im Sumpf tummelt. Die Person, die den Jagdzug anzuführen scheint, ist als einzige bekleidet – die vollständige Nacktheit aller übrigen lässt erkennen, dass sie beschnitten sind. Das auf dem Bild von den furchtbaren Kiefern eines der Flusspferde erfasste Krokodil verdeutlicht, dass dieses riesige Reptil in den Wassern des Nils oder eher der Nilschwemme häufig einen fürchterlichen Gegner vorfand. Auch bezeugen diese Szenen, die sich recht oft in den Gräbern der unterschiedlichen Nekropolen finden, dass Flusspferde und Krokodile zu bestimmten Zeiten in allen Lagunen Ober- und Unterägyptens reichlich vorhanden waren.

CHASSE À L'HIPPOPOTAME DANS LES MARAIS (VIe dynastie)

Memphis

Des chasseurs armés de harpons et montés sur de légers batelets de papyrus qui leur permettent de passer facilement, même à travers les hautes touffes de lotus, poursuivent une bande d'hippopotames qui grouillent dans le marais. Le personnage qui paraît commander l'expédition est seul vêtu, la complète nudité de tous les autres fait reconnaître qu'ils sont circoncis. Le crocodile représenté enlevé par les terribles mâchoires d'un des hippopotames nous fait voir que cet énorme reptile rencontrait souvent un formidable ennemi dans les eaux du Nil, ou plutôt de l'inondation. Ces scènes, qu'on retrouve assez fréquemment, dans les tombeaux des diverses nécropoles, nous démontrent que les hippopotames et les crocodiles abondaient à certaines époques dans toutes les lagunes de la Haute- et de la Basse-Égypte.

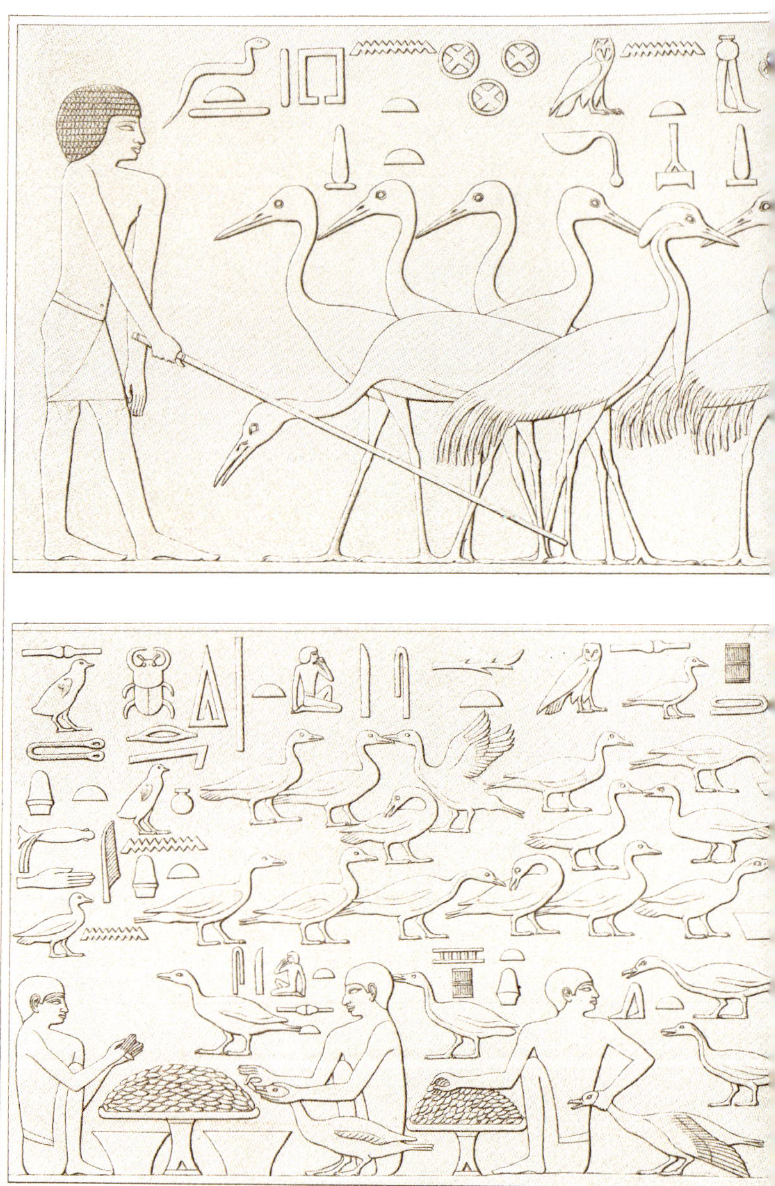

Lith. par Graille _ Imp. par Hangard Maugé.

TROUPEAU DE GRUES &

(NÉCROPOLE

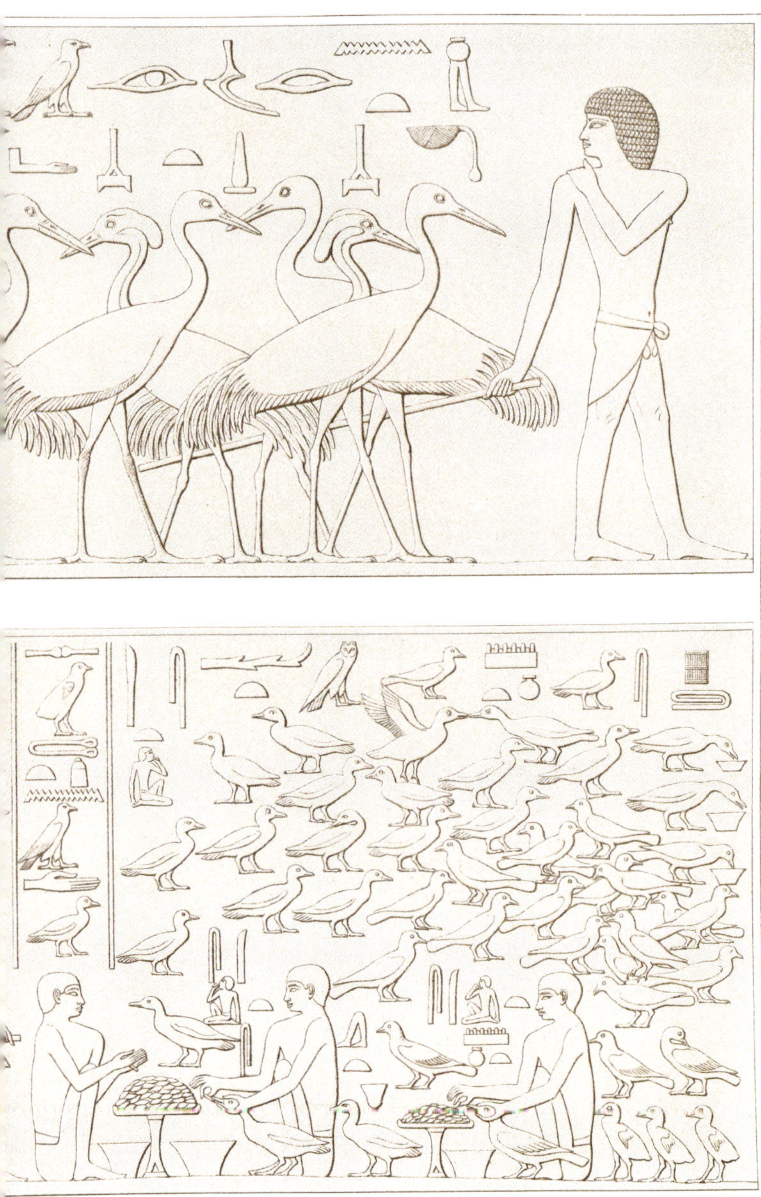

Publié par Arthus-Bertrand, Editeur.

DES DOMAINES DE TEÏ .

NASTIE .)

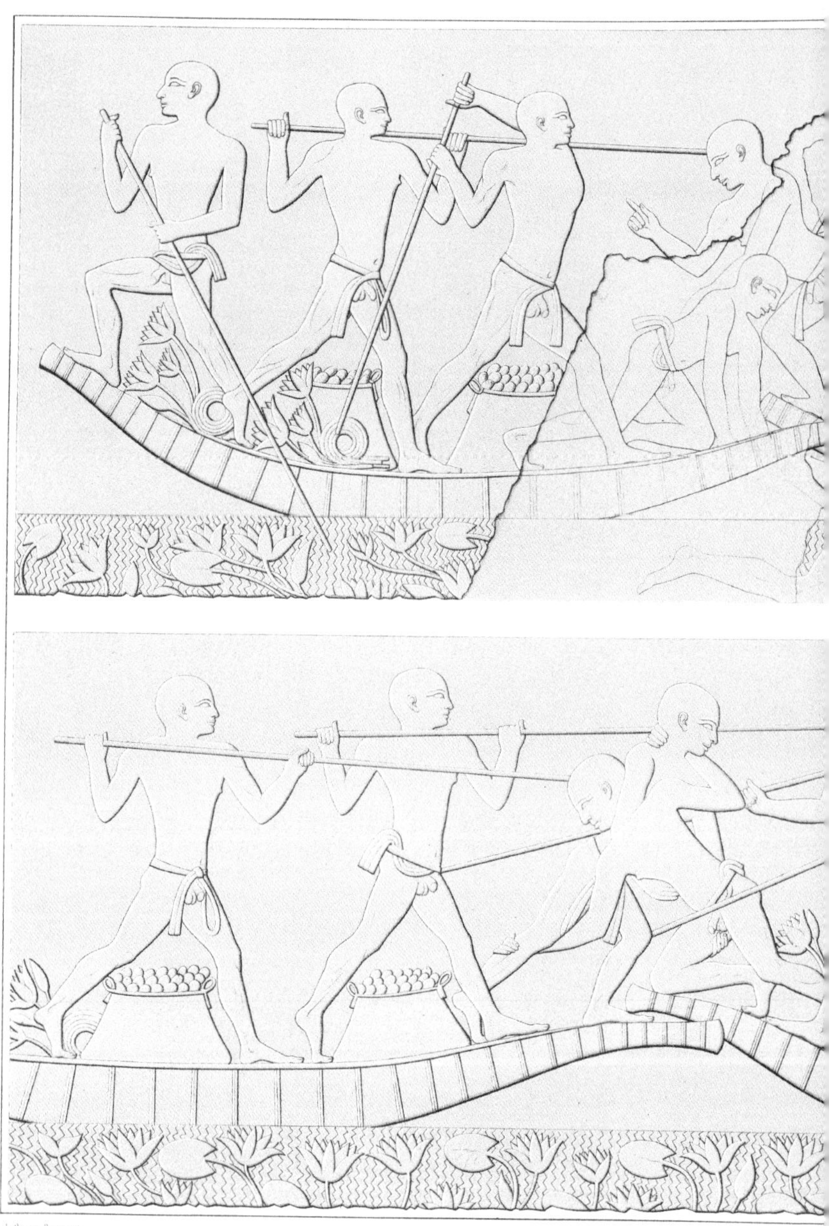

Lith. par Daumont

JOÛT

(KOU

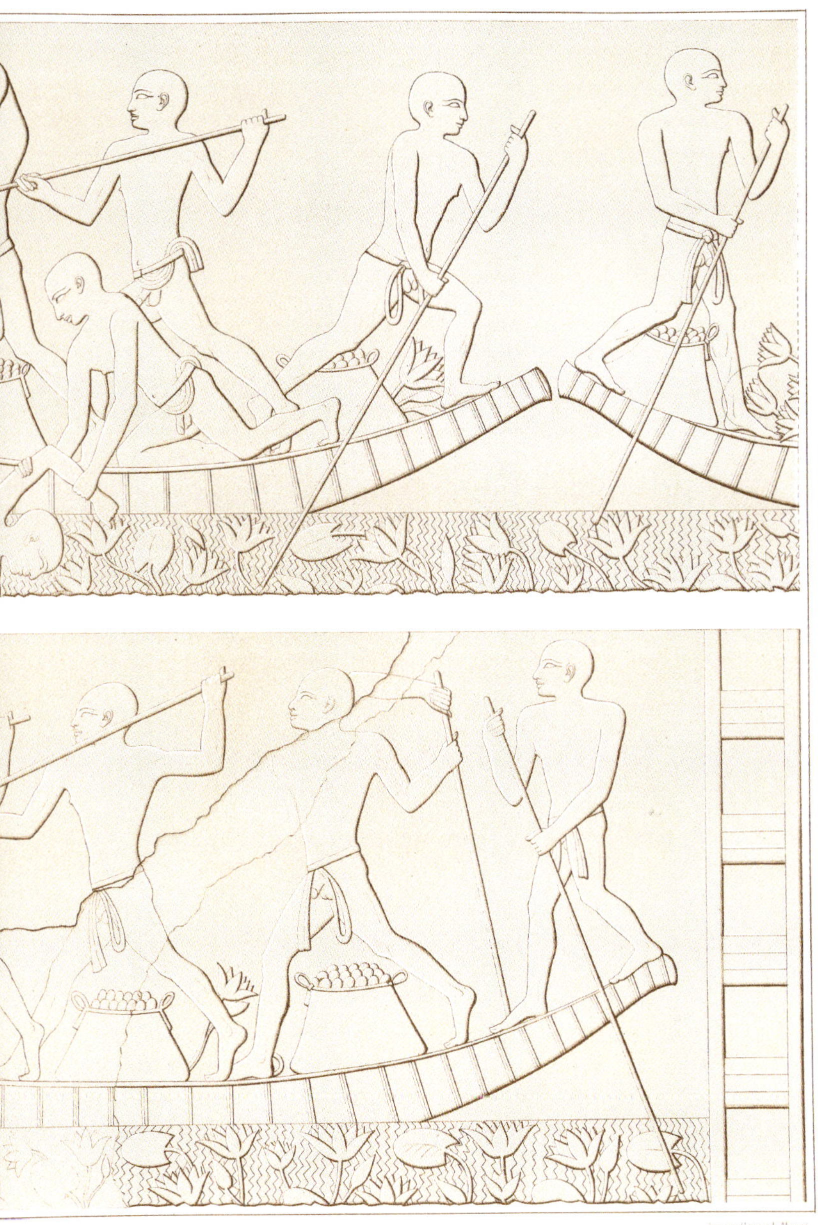

Imp. par Hangard-Maugé

NIERS.

ASTIE.)

(Pages/Seite 352/353)

FLOCK OF CRANES AND FARMYARD FOWL FROM THE LANDS OF TI (5th Dynasty)

Necropolis of Memphis

These two scenes form part of a collection of pictures of the same type which fill an entire chamber of the vast tomb of the high-ranking official named Ti. The first register shows a flock of cranes tended by two servants, equipped with long sticks. We can recognise here the common crane, with its light grey plumage which is very similar to that of the crane known in Europe; there is also another wading bird belonging to a species called "maid of Numidia", which can be identified by the two crests formed from the slender, elongated feathers which cover the ear. The second register shows a farm-yard whose further section, which is shown on another plate, was adorned with small columns. In both parts various types of fowl can be seen, being looked after by servants under the eye of a scribe. Some are preparing the dough, rolling it into little balls in their hands and placing it on small tables; others are stuffing the birds with it.

KRANICHSCHAR UND GEFLÜGELHOF DER LÄNDEREIEN DES TI (5. Dynastie)

Nekropole von Memphis

Die beiden Szenen sind Bestandteil einer Gruppe gleichartiger Bilder, die im weitläufigen Grab eines hohen Beamten namens Ti einen ganzen Raum einnimmt. Das erste Register stellt eine Kranichschar dar, die von zwei für das Federvieh zuständigen, mit langen Stecken bewaffneten Dienern gehütet werden. Man erkennt den gemeinen Kranich, dessen aschgraues Gefieder kaum von dem des europäischen Vertreters dieser Art abweicht, und einen anderen Stelzvogel, der zu der „Jungfernkranich" genannten Art gehört; er ist an den beiden Federbüscheln auszumachen, die durch die Verlängerung der schmalen, die Ohren bedeckenden Federn gebildet werden. Das zweite Register stellt einen Geflügelhof dar, dessen vorderer, auf einer anderen Tafel abgebildeter Teil mit kleinen Säulen geschmückt war. In den beiden Feldern ist unterschiedliches Geflügel zu sehen, um das sich die Diener unter Aufsicht eines Schreibers kümmern. Die einen bereiten den Teig, formen ihn mit ihren Händen zu Kügelchen und legen diese auf kleinen Tischen ab; die anderen stopfen die Vögel damit.

TROUPEAU DE GRUES ET BASSE-COUR DES DOMAINES DE TEÏ (V[e] dynastie)

Nécropole de Memphis

Ces deux scènes font partie d'un ensemble de tableaux du même genre qui occupe toute une salle du vaste tombeau du haut fonctionnaire nommé Teï. Le premier registre représente un troupeau de grues conduit par deux serviteurs gallinaires, armés de longs bâtons. On y distingue la grue commune, dont le plumage cendré diffère peu de celle connue en Europe ; et un autre échassier appartenant à l'espèce appelée « demoiselle de Numidie », reconnaissable aux deux aigrettes formées par le prolongement des plumes effilées qui couvrent l'oreille. Le second registre représente une basse-cour dont la partie antérieure, reportée sur une autre planche, était ornée de colonnettes. Dans les deux compartiments, on voit divers volatiles auxquels des serviteurs donnent leurs soins sous l'inspection d'un scribe. Les uns préparent la pâte, la roulent en boulettes dans leurs mains et la déposent sur de petites tables ; les autres en gavent les oiseaux.

(Pages/Seite 354/355)

BOATMEN JOUSTING (6th Dynasty)

Kom el-Ahmar

This plate shows a bas-relief copied in the tomb at Zawyet el-Maiyitin which belonged to a person called Souten-Zokh [Khunes] who lived during the 6th Dynasty. This picture, which is remarkable for art of this period, was reproduced by Lepsius, but a large number of details were omitted: in fact, in this very defective reproduction, the lotus which stud the water appear to be flowers and leaves detached from their stems, whereas in the original they are all connected together. In the second boat a man is depicted pulling in a type of net while he drags a corpse from the water; this can be easily verified on the cast which I have presented to the museum of the Louvre. Finally, it is no longer possible to understand what the two fighting men who can be seen at the end of the two last boats were doing; all of them have shaven heads.

SCHIFFERSTECHEN (6. Dynastie)

Kom el-Ahmar

Das auf dieser Tafel dargestellte Flachrelief wurde im Grab von Saujet el-Meitin abgezeichnet, das einem unter der 6. Dynastie lebenden Souten-Zokh [Chunes] gehörte. Lepsius hat das für die Kunst dieser Zeit so bemerkenswerte Bild reproduziert; zahlreiche Einzelheiten wurden jedoch darauf vergessen: Auf dieser – genauer gesagt – allzu fehlerhaften Abbildung erscheinen die auf dem Wasser verstreuten Lotuspflanzen als von ihren Stängeln getrennte Blüten und Blätter, wohingegen im Original alle Teile beieinander sind. Auch ist in der zweiten Barke ein Mann abgebildet, der eine Art Netz einholt, wohingegen er einen Kadaver aus dem Wasser zieht, wie sich an dem von mir im Louvre hinterlegten Gipsabdruck problemlos überprüfen lässt; darüber hinaus weisen die beiden Ringer, die am Ende der beiden letzten Barken zu sehen sind, keine nachvollziehbaren Bewegungen mehr auf; alle haben kahl geschorene Köpfe.

JOÛTE DE[S] MARINIERS (VIe dynastie)

Koum el-Ahmar

Cette planche représente un bas-relief copié dans le tombeau de Zawyet el-Mayetin [Zaouiet el-Meïtin], appartenant à un Souten-Zokh [Khunes] qui vivait sous la VIe dynastie. Ce tableau si remarquable pour l'art de cette époque a été reproduit par Lepsius ; mais il y a été oublié maints détails : dans cette reproduction par trop fautive, en effet, les lotus qui parsèment l'eau, semblent des fleurs et des feuilles détachées de leurs tiges, tandis que tout se groupe, au contraire, dans l'original. Il est figuré, dans la seconde barque, un homme tirant une espèce de filet, tandis qu'il tire un cadavre de l'eau, comme on peut le vérifier, facilement, sur le plâtre que j'ai donné au musée du Louvre ; en outre, les deux lutteurs qu'on voit à l'extrémité des deux dernières barques n'ont plus de mouvement compréhensible ; ils ont tous la tête rase.

ANIMALS. FELINE SPECIES (17th and 18th Dynasties)

Thebes

No. 1 represents two cheetahs, which were commonly employed for various types of hunting. They wear a collar showing that they are tame. These two animals feature on the walls of the temple of el-Assasif. No. 2 is a panther taken from the same monument. This panther can easily be distinguished from other big cats of a similar type: its gait is less noble than that of the lion, with which it forms an admirable contrast. These animals are drawn with far greater realism than is the human figure, which is always treated in a more or less stereotyped fashion. They are full of life, lithe, softly rounded and true to nature. No. 3 features a lion carved in hollow outline and in relief; this is a symbolic lion that decorates the base of the throne of Thutmosis III at Karnak. Here, therefore, instead of copying from nature, the artist wished to idealise the lion and to represent the strength and the majesty which characterise the beautiful animal which he was using as a symbol.

TIERE. KATZENARTIGE (17. und 18. Dynastie)

Theben

Die Nr. 1 stellt zwei Geparden dar, die man im Allgemeinen für die Jagd verwendete. Das Halsband, das sie tragen, kündet von ihrer Gefangenschaft. Diese beiden Tiere sind auf den Wänden des Tempels von El-Assasif abgebildet. Die Nr. 2 ist ein demselben Denkmal entnommener Panther. Dieser Panther ist gut von anderen Raubkatzen derselben Gattung zu unterscheiden: Sein Gang ist weniger edel als der des Löwen, zu dem er einen wunderbaren Kontrast bildet. Diese Tierzeichnungen sind denen der menschlichen Gestalten, die stets auf mehr oder weniger konventionelle Weise behandelt werden, weit überlegen. Sie sind voller Leben und weisen die Üppigkeit und Geschmeidigkeit der Natur auf. Die Nr. 3 zeigt einen als Tiefrelief ausgearbeiteten Löwen; er zierte den Thronsockel von Thutmosis III. in Karnak; es handelt sich um einen sinnbildlichen Löwen. Anstatt die Natur nachzubilden, war der Künstler hier also um Idealisierung bemüht – um die Kraft und Erhabenheit wiederzugeben, die das schöne, von ihm als Sinnbild verwendete Tier kennzeichnen.

ANIMAUX. RACE FÉLINE (XVIIe et XVIIIe dynasties)

Thèbes

Le n° 1 représente deux guépards employés, ordinairement, à différentes sortes de chasse. Le collier qu'ils portent témoigne de leur domesticité. Ces deux animaux figurent sur les murailles du temple d'El-Assacif. Le n° 2 est une panthère tirée du même monument. Cette panthère se distingue bien des autres félins du même genre : sa démarche est moins noble que celle du lion avec lequel elle contraste admirablement. Ces animaux sont dessinés d'une manière bien supérieure à la figure humaine, qui est toujours traitée plus ou moins conventionnellement. Ils sont pleins de vie et ont la souplesse et le moelleux de la nature. Le n° 3 offre un lion sculpté en creux et en relief ; il ornait la base du trône de Thoutmès [Thoutmôsis] III à Karnac ; c'est un lion symbolique. Ici, l'artiste, au lieu de copier la nature, a donc cherché à l'idéaliser, à rendre la force et la majesté qui caractérisent le bel animal qu'il employait comme symbole.

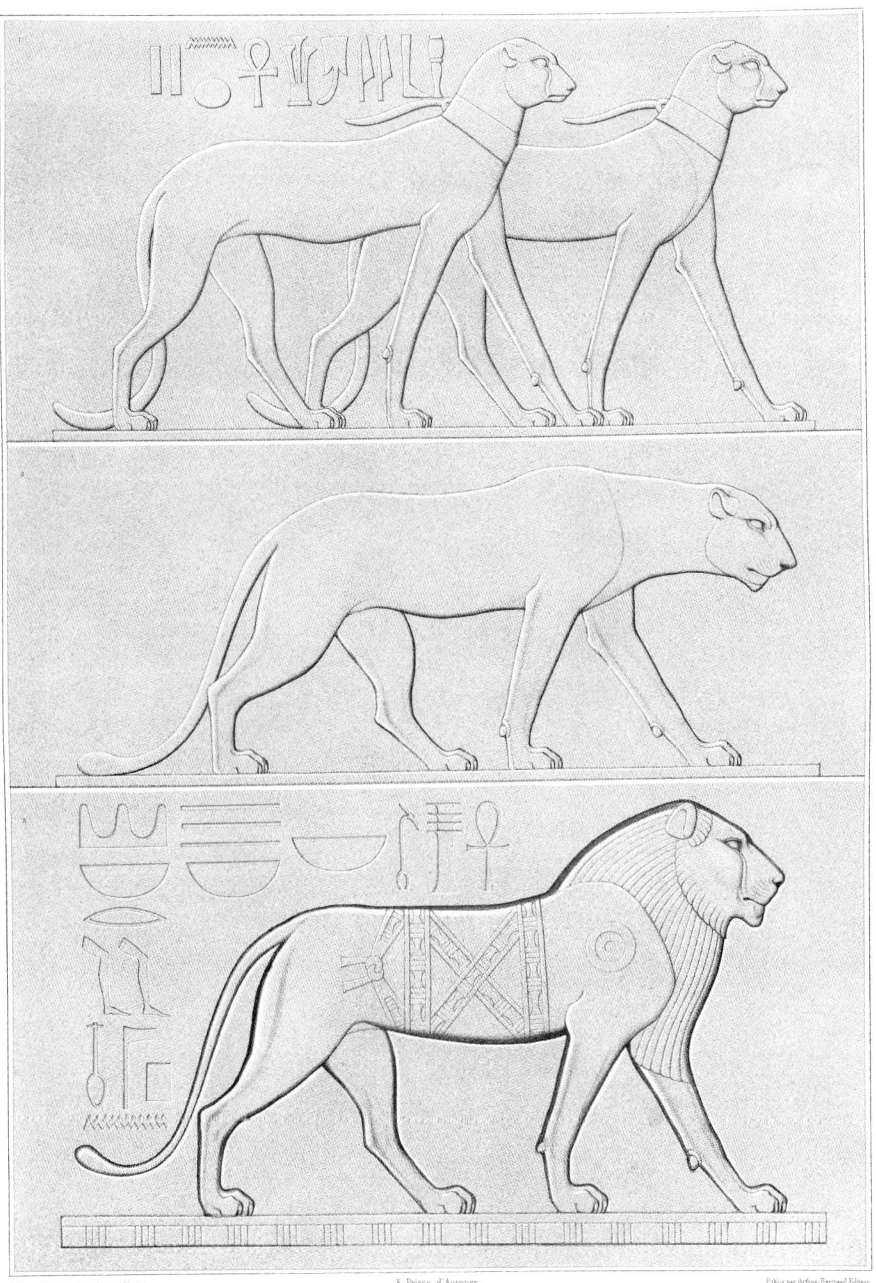

Lith. par Jehenne. _ Imp. par Hangard-Maugé. E. Prisse d'Avennes. Publié par Arthus-Bertrand, Éditeur

ANIMAUX. _ RACE FÉLINE.

(THÈBES _ XVIIᵉ et XVIIIᵉ DYNASTIES.)

TYPES AND PORTRAITS (18th Dynasty)

Necropolis of Thebes

The exceptional impetus given to all forms of art under the restoration of the Egyptian empire led to a great advance in sculpture in bas-relief which, under the 17th and 18th Dynasties, achieved the highest perfection of which it was capable. The bas-reliefs executed under the Setis, the Thutmosoids and the Amenophises are the masterpieces of this genre. A small hypogeum in Thebes, the tomb of Khaemhat, steward of estates under Amenophis III, contains bas-reliefs of an admirable purity and finish. The heads are beautifully drawn and full of expression. In another hypogeum can be seen the figure of a young woman; the head is ravishingly beautiful and the profile could not be more perfect, with one eye seen from the front. All the bas-reliefs from this period present heads with a beautiful profile, where the artist has taken pains to create a genuine likeness. It is also possible to see that in certain scenes the same individual retains the same face and that this is evidently a portrait.

TYPEN UND PORTRÄTS (18. Dynastie)

Nekropole von Theben

Der ungeheure, allen Künsten durch die Restauration des ägyptischen Reiches verliehene Schwung brachte große Fortschritte auf dem Gebiet der Skulptur und des Flachreliefs mit sich; und hier wurde im Verlauf der 17. und 18. Dynastie die denkbar größte Perfektion erreicht. Die unter den Sethos, den Thutmosiden und den Amenophiden gearbeiteten Flachreliefs sind Meisterwerke ihrer Gattung. In Theben weist ein kleines Hypogäum – das Grab von Chaemhat, dem Verwalter der Ländereien unter Amenophis III. – Flachreliefs von bewundernswert klarer Ausarbeitung auf. Die gut gezeichneten Köpfe sind sehr ausdrucksvoll. Ein weiteres Hypogäum zeigt das Gesicht einer jungen Frau, deren Kopf bezaubernd und deren Profil so vollkommen ist, wie es mit einem in Vorderansicht abgebildeten Auge nur sein kann. Alle Flachreliefs dieser Zeit zeigen Köpfe mit schönem Profil, bei denen der Künstler bestrebt war, ihnen Ähnlichkeit [mit dem Vorbild] zu verleihen. Auch ist in einigen Szenen zu beobachten, dass dieselbe Person dasselbe Gesicht behält, bei dem es sich natürlich um ein Porträt handelt.

TYPES ET PORTRAITS (XVIIIe dynastie)

Nécropole de Thèbes

L'élan prodigieux donné à tous les arts avec la restauration de l'Empire égyptien amena un grand progrès dans la sculpture en bas-relief ; et sous les XVIIe et XVIIIe dynasties, elle atteignit toute la perfection dont elle était susceptible. Les bas-reliefs exécutés sous les Séti, les Thoutmès [Thoutmôsis] et les Aménophis sont les chefs-d'œuvre de ce genre. Un petit hypogée de Thèbes, le tombeau de Chamhati [Khâemhat], intendant des domaines sous Aménophis III, présente des bas-reliefs d'une pureté et d'un fini admirables. Les têtes sont bien dessinées et pleines d'expression. Un autre hypogée présente la figure d'une jeune femme dont la tête est ravissante et le profil aussi parfait qu'il peut l'être avec un œil de face. Les bas-reliefs de cette époque offrent tous des têtes d'un beau profil et auxquelles l'artiste s'est attaché à donner de la ressemblance. On voit aussi, dans quelques scènes, le même individu conserver la même figure, qui est évidemment un portrait.

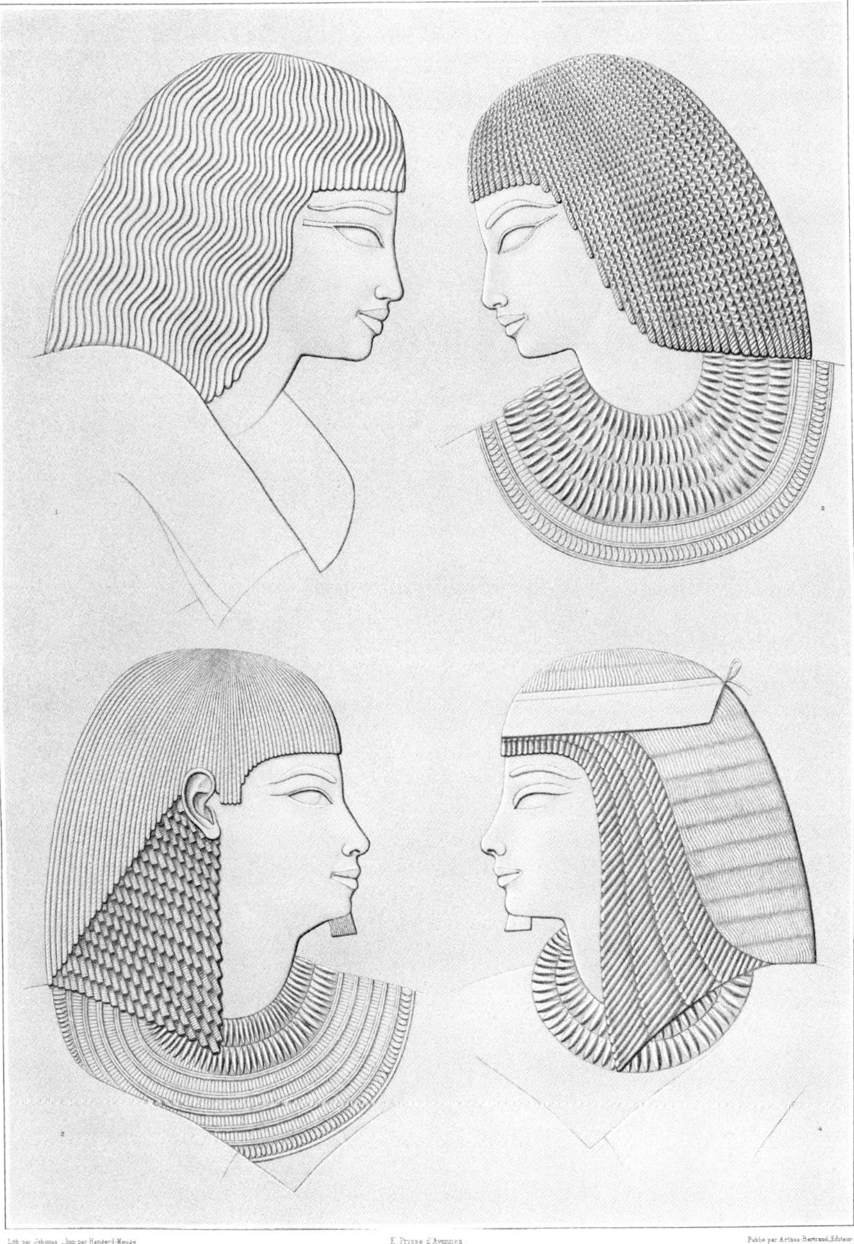

Lith. par Jehenne. _ Imp. par Hangard-Maugé. E. Prisse d'Avennes. Publié par Arthus-Bertrand, Éditeur.

TYPES & PORTRAITS.

(NÉCROPOLE DE THÈBES. __ XVIIIᵉ DYNASTIE.)

SCRIBE AND PRIESTESS OF AMUN (18th Dynasty)

Necropolis of Thebes

This flat bas-relief with a cameo-like finish is carved in the border cut into the entrance to the tomb of Neferhotep [Néferhotep], the principal scribe of the temple of Amun at Thebes. It is noteworthy for the slender elegance of the shape the artist was moved to ascribe to the sister of Neferhotep, who was without doubt a priestess, a pallacide of Amun to judge from the sistrum which she holds in her hand. [...] The toes were not engraved with the chisel; they must no doubt have been painted in, together with the details of the collar, the headband and the bracelets. Neferhotep and his sister wear on their heads a cone, which is a funerary emblem. The young girl, called Ra-Maat [his wife Meryetre], bears the title of divine consort of Amun and must have been attached to the temple or dedicated to that god.

SCHREIBER UND AMUN-PRIESTERIN (18. Dynastie)

Nekropole von Theben

Dieses – wie eine Kamee ausgearbeitete – Plattrelief ist am Eingang zum Grab von Neferhotep, dem Hauptschreiber des Amun-Tempels in Theben, in die Einfassung einziseliert. Bemerkenswert ist es durch die schlanken Formen, die der Künstler der Schwester Neferhoteps – die, nach dem Sistrum in ihrer Hand zu urteilen, mit Sicherheit eine Priesterin, eine Gottesgemahlin des Amun war – freudig verliehen hat. [...] Die Zehen sind nicht mit dem Meißel ausgearbeitet; ebenso wie die Einzelheiten der Halskette sowie der Haar- und Armbänder müssen sie zweifellos aufgemalt gewesen sein. Auf dem Kopf tragen Neferhotep und seine Schwester einen Kegel, bei dem es sich um ein Begräbnisattribut handelt. Das junge Mädchen namens Ramait [seine Frau Meryetre] trägt den Titel der göttlichen Gemahlin des Amun und muss dem Tempel verbunden oder diesem Gott geweiht gewesen sein.

SCRIBE ET PRÊTRESSE D'AMON (XVIIIe dynastie)

Nécropole de Thèbes

Ce bas-relief méplat, d'un fini de camée, est ciselé dans le contour creusé à l'entrée du tombeau de Nofrehotep [Néferhotep], scribe principal du temple d'Amon, à Thèbes. Il est remarquable par la sveltesse des formes que l'artiste s'est plu à donner à la sœur de Nofrehotep, qui était, incontestablement, une prêtresse, une pallacide d'Amon, à en juger par le sistre qu'elle tient en main. [...] Les orteils ne sont pas indiqués au ciseau ; ils devaient, sans doute, être peints, ainsi que les détails du collier, des bandeaux et des bracelets. Nofrehotep et sa sœur portent sur la tête un cône, c'est un emblème funéraire. La jeune fille nommée Ramait [son épouse Meryetre] porte le titre de divine épouse d'Amon, et devait être attachée au temple ou consacrée à ce dieu.

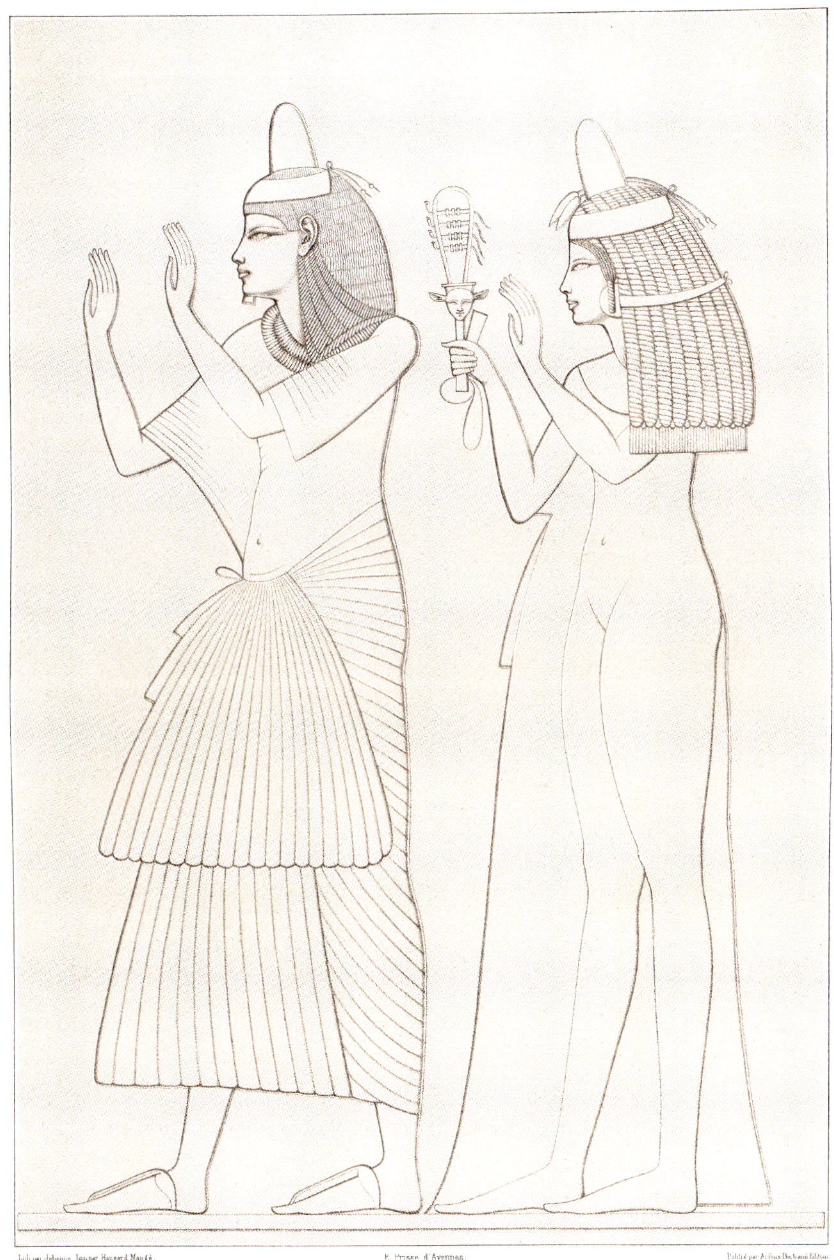

Lith. par Jehenne. Imp. par Hangard Maugé. E. Prisse d'Avennes. Publié par Arthus-Bertrand Editeur.

SCRIBE ET PRÊTRESSE D'AMMON.

(NÉCROPOLE DE THÈBES _ XVIIIe DYNASTIE.)

PHARAOH AKHENATEN SERVED BY THE QUEEN (18th Dynasty)

Tell el-Amarna

This plate is one of the rare examples which tell of the emotional transformation in the sovereigns of Pharaonic Egypt which took place at a certain period, under the influence of a type of religious renewal. There is therefore no reason to be surprised that such scenes of family life have not been reproduced previously. From this particular period onwards everything changed completely: speaking specifically of the two personages who are the subject of this plate, they appear together on all occasions and are frequently represented with their children. It is therefore some consolation to be able to say that the absence of such scenes of affection, which was sadly a feature of paintings of the life of man during the preceding periods, is amply compensated for in the representations of Psinaula [Tell el-Amarna].

DER PHARAO ECHNATON WIRD VON DER KÖNIGIN BEDIENT (18. Dynastie)

Tell el-Amarna

Als ein seltenes Beispiel kündet die auf dieser Tafel gezeigte Szene von dem Gefühlswandel, der sich unter dem Einfluss einer gewissen religiösen Erneuerung bei den Herrschern im pharaonischen Ägypten zu einer bestimmten Zeit ereignete. Es besteht also kein Anlass zur Verwunderung darüber, dass zuvor keine Wiedergaben solcher ungezwungenen Szenen zu finden sind. Von dieser Zeit an kommt das Gegenteil vor – und um nur die beiden Persönlichkeiten anzuführen, die Gegenstand dieser Tafel sind, sie erscheinen zu allen Gelegenheiten gemeinsam und sind häufig mit ihren Kindern dargestellt. Zum Trost ist auch zu sagen, dass die Darstellungen von Psinaula [Tell el-Amarna] den Mangel an gefühlsbetonten Szenen, ein trauriges Kennzeichen der Malereien über das Leben der Menschen in allen anderen Zeiten, reichlich wettmachen.

LE PHARAON KHOUENATEN SERVI PAR LA REINE (XVIIIe dynastie)

Tell el-Amarna

Cette planche est un des rares spécimens qui font connaître la transformation sentimentale qui s'opéra à une certaine époque, chez les souverains de l'Égypte pharaonique, sous l'influence d'une sorte de rénovation religieuse. Il n'y a donc pas lieu de s'étonner si l'on ne trouve pas, reproduites auparavant, de ces scènes familières. À partir de cette époque, le contraire existe, et pour ne parler que des deux personnages qui font l'objet de cette planche, ils apparaissent, ensemble, dans toutes les occasions, et sont fréquemment représentés avec leurs enfants. Aussi peut-on dire, avec consolation, que l'absence des scènes d'affection, qui caractérisent si tristement les peintures de la vie de l'homme, dans les autres époques, se trouve grandement compensée dans les représentations de Psinaula.

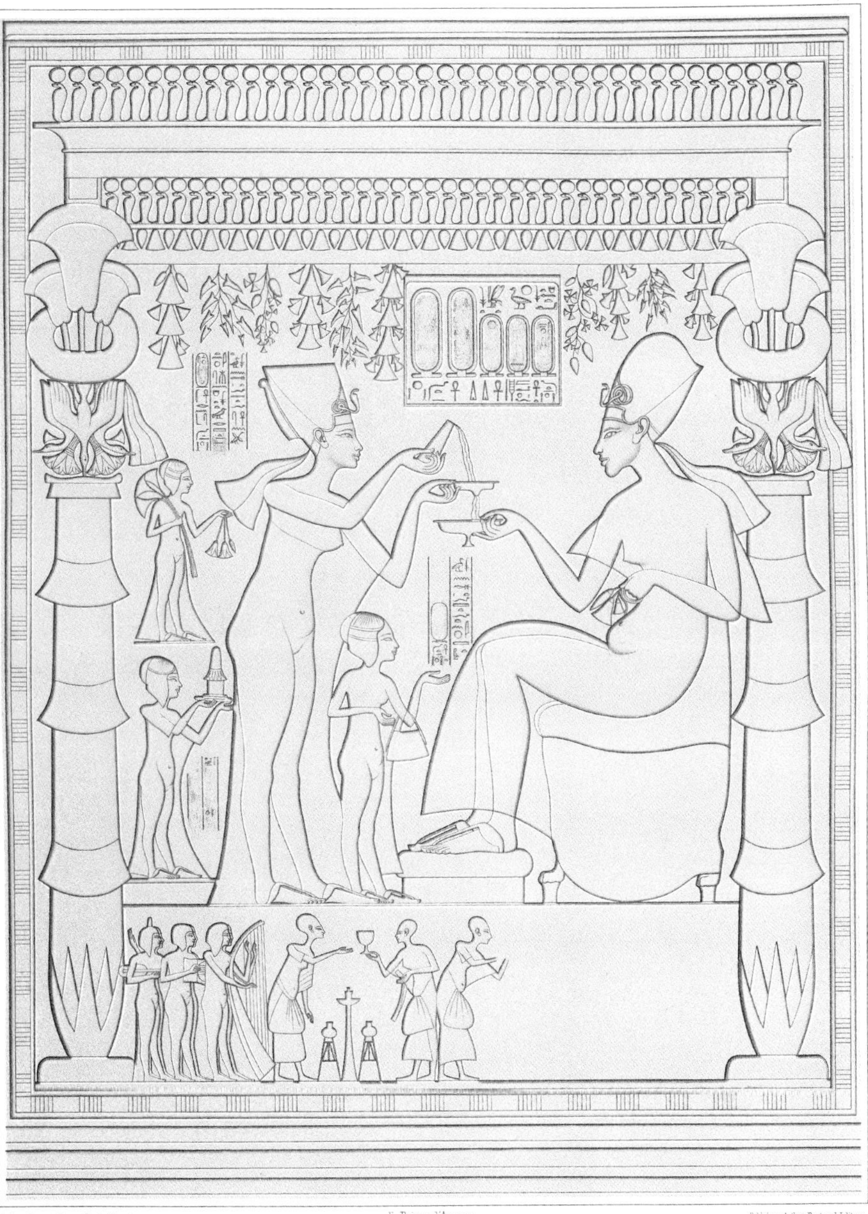

Lith. par Dumont. Imp. par Hangard-Maugé. E. Prisse d'Avennes. Publié par Arthus-Bertrand, Editeur.

LE PHARAON KHOUENATEN SERVI PAR LA REINE.

(TELL EL-AMARNA _ XVIIIe DYNASTIE.)

S

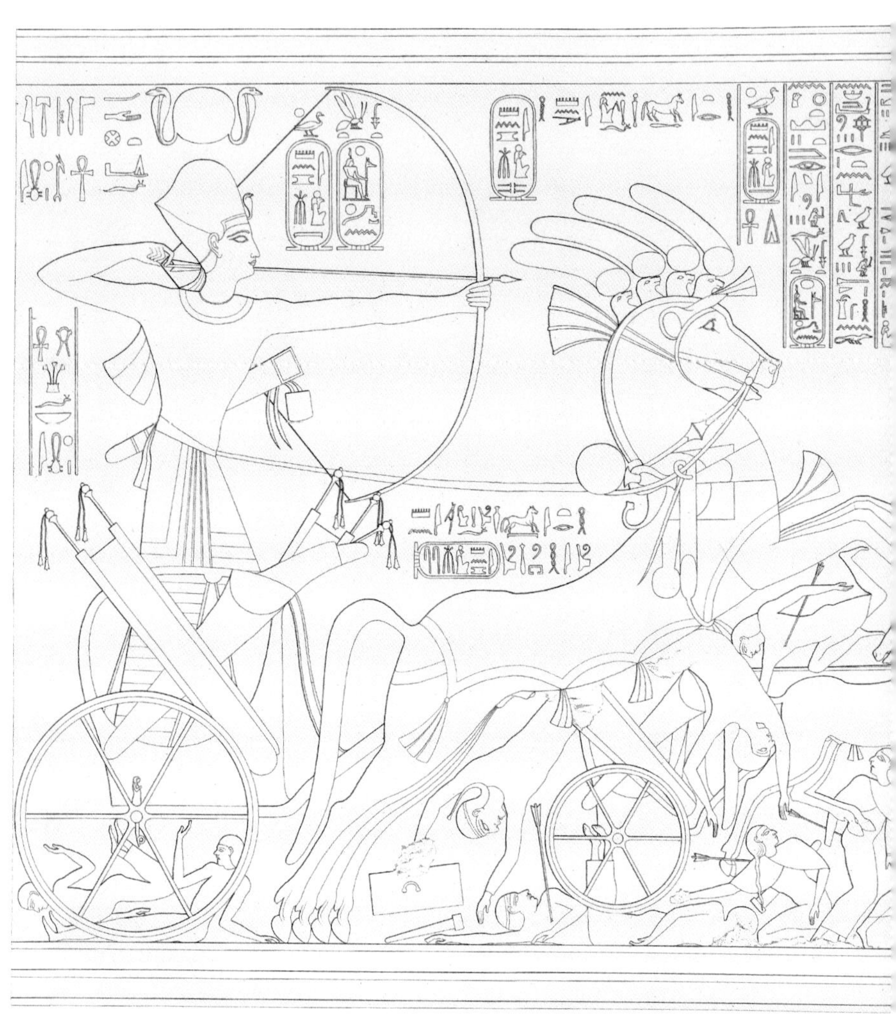

Gravé par J. Penel... imp. par Eudes

PPISE D'UNE F

(THÈBES RA

E

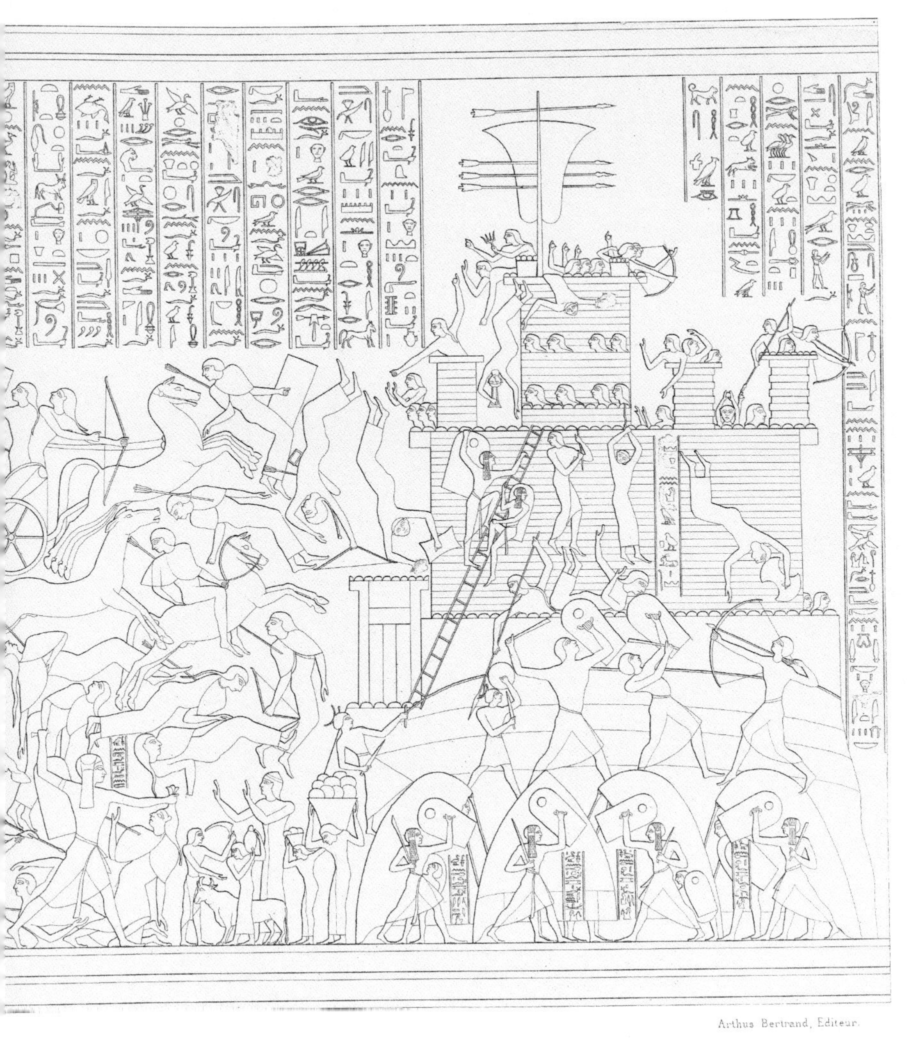

Arthus Bertrand, Editeur.

SE PAP RAMSÈS II

VIIIE DYNASTIE]

(Pages/Seite 366/367)

CAPTURE OF A FORTRESS BY RAMESSES II (18th [19th] Dynasty)

Thebes. Ramesseum

In the two plates [see pp. 420–423] I have already given an interesting insight into the military capability at that period. But I felt it necessary to complete this story in pictures by a representation which would make very clear the resources which the Egyptian pharaohs had at their disposal to repulse, wage war on and even conquer the neighbouring countries. The Egyptian artist, as usual, has accorded to the pharaoh a disproportionately prominent position by comparison to the other parts of his picture, to signify that genuine power and the ability to protect his troops was only to be found in their chief.

EINNAHME EINER FESTUNG DURCH RAMSES II. (18. [19.] Dynastie)

Theben. Ramesseum

Auf den beiden Tafeln [siehe S. 420–423] habe ich [dem Leser] bereits einen aufschlussreichen Einblick in den Zustand des zeitgenössischen Militärwesens verschafft. Ich hielt es jedoch für nötig, diese bebilderte Erzählung durch eine Darstellung zu ergänzen, an der gut zu erkennen ist, über welche Möglichkeiten die ägyptischen Pharaonen verfügten, um benachbarte Staaten zurückzuschlagen, zu bekämpfen und sogar zu erobern. Wie üblich hat der ägyptische Künstler – um kundzutun, dass die wirkliche Stärke und der Schutz der Soldaten nur auf ihrem Anführer beruhen – dem Pharao eine Stellung eingeräumt, die in keinem Verhältnis zu den übrigen Teilen seiner Zeichnung steht.

PRISE D'UNE FORTERESSE PAR RAMSÈS II (XVIIIe [XIXe] dynastie)

Thèbes. Ramesseum

J'ai donné dans les deux planches [voir pp. 420–423] une idée déjà intéressante de l'état militaire à cette époque. Mais il m'a paru nécessaire de compléter cette narration en images par une représentation qui fît bien comprendre les ressources que possédaient les pharaons égyptiens, pour repousser, combattre et même conquérir les nations voisines. L'artiste égyptien, comme d'ordinaire, a donné au pharaon une situation hors de proportion avec les autres parties de son dessin, pour signifier que la puissance réelle et la protection des soldats ne résidaient bien que dans leur chef.

(Pages/Seite 370-377)

TOMB OF KHAEMHAT, STEWARD OF THE ROYAL ESTATES (18th Dynasty)

Homage to Amenophis III. Surveying the estates, with Khaemhat overseeing
Agricultural work. Counting the oxen

The tomb of Khaemhat, the administrator of the royal lands under Amenophis III, is one of the most remarkable in the necropolis of Thebes. The vestibule is decorated in its entirety with scenes relating to the life of the deceased, depicted on bas-reliefs of an exceptionally pure style and fine finish. The first [plate] shows Khaemhat paying homage to the pharaoh and bringing him the accounts of his management. The pharaoh, under a rich naos, sits on a throne supported by two captives [African and Asiatic]. In the second plate, whose subject is the surveying of the lands, the pharaoh's steward can be seen standing overseeing the various types of work which are demanded. In the third plate Khaemhat sits under a tree watching the different agricultural tasks and, by his presence, makes the labourers work harder. The subject of the fourth plate follows on from the first and shows Khaemhat presenting the finest animals from his herds.

GRAB VON CHAEMHAT, VERWALTER DER LÄNDEREIEN (18. Dynastie)

Huldigung an Amenophis III.. Landvermessung unter Leitung von Chaemhat
Landwirtschaftliche Arbeiten. Zählung der Rinder

Eines des bemerkenswertesten Gräber in der Nekropole von Theben ist das Grab von Chaemhat, der unter Amenophis III. Verwalter der königlichen Ländereien war. Das Vestibül ist vollständig mit in sehr klarem Stil gehaltenen und kunstvoll ausgearbeiteten Flachreliefs geschmückt, die Szenen aus dem Leben des Verstorbenen darstellen. Die erste [Tafel] stellt den dem Pharao huldigenden Chaemhat dar, der diesem die Abrechnung über seine Verwaltungsführung überbringt. Der unter einem prächtigen Naos platzierte Pharao sitzt auf einem von zwei [afrikanischen und asiatischen] Gefangenen getragenen Thron. Auf der zweiten Tafel, die die Landvermessung zum Gegenstand hat, ist der Verwalter des Pharaos zu sehen, der stehend die erforderlichen Arbeiten überwacht. Auf der dritten Tafel wohnt der unter einem Baum sitzende Chaemhat verschiedenen Arbeiten auf den Feldern bei und zwingt die Arbeiter durch seine Anwesenheit zu größerer Betriebsamkeit. Die vierte Tafel bildet thematisch das Pendant zur ersten; sie zeigt, wie Chaemhat die schönsten Erzeugnisse seiner Herden darbietet.

TOMBEAU DE CHAMHATI, INTENDANT DES DOMAINES (XVIIIe dynastie)

Hommage à Aménophis III. Arpentage des terres, sous la présidence de Chamhati
Travaux agricoles. Dénombrement des bœufs

Le tombeau de Chamhati [Khâemhat], l'administrateur des terres royales sous Aménophis III, est un des plus remarquables de la nécropole de Thèbes. Le vestibule est entièrement décoré de scènes relatives à la vie du défunt, représentées sur bas-reliefs d'un style très pur et d'un fini précieux. La première [planche] représente Chamhati rendant hommage au pharaon, et lui apportant les comptes de sa gestion. Le pharaon, placé sous un riche naos, est assis sur un trône que soutiennent deux captifs [africains et asiatiques]. Dans la seconde planche, dont le sujet est l'arpentage des terres, on voit l'intendant du pharaon debout, présidant aux différents travaux exigés. Dans la troisième planche, Chamhati, assis sous un arbre, assiste aux divers travaux des champs et force, par sa présence, les travailleurs à une plus grande dépense d'activité. Le sujet de la quatrième planche faisait pendant à celui de la première ; il montre Chamhati présentant les plus beaux produits de ses troupeaux.

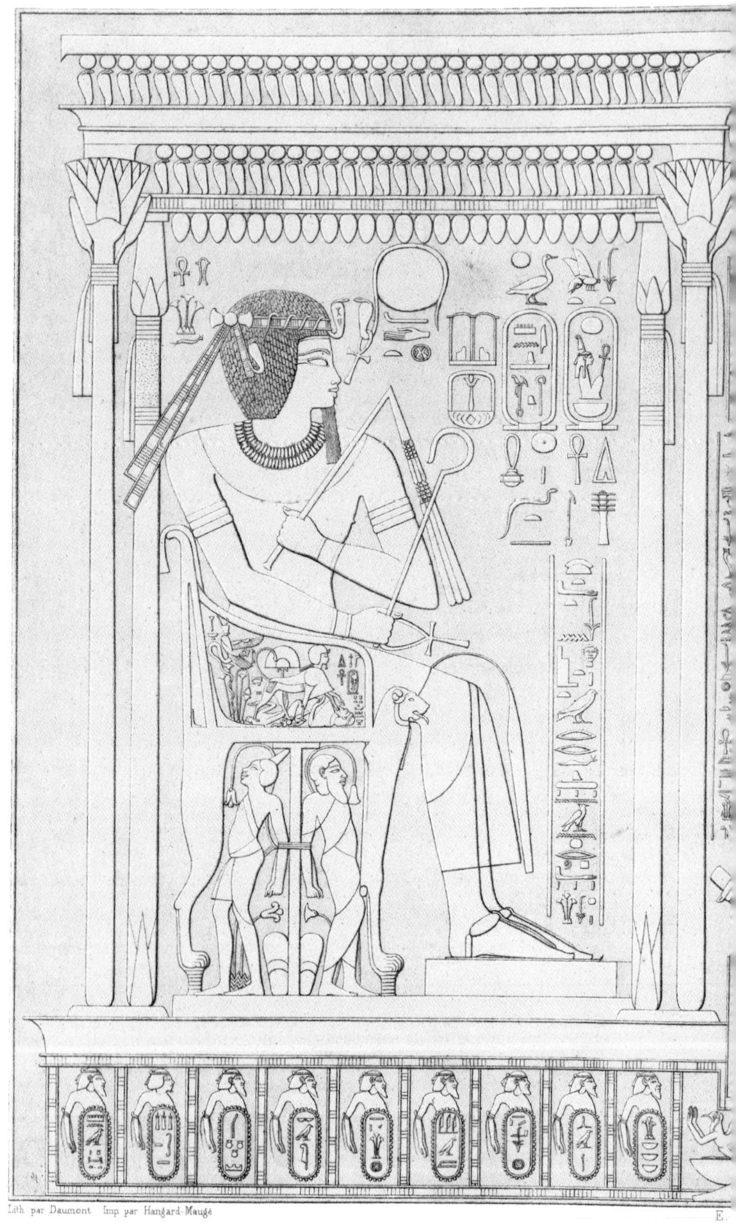

Lith. par Daumont Imp. par Hangard-Maugé

E.

HOMMAGE

TOMBEAU DE CHAMHATI INTE

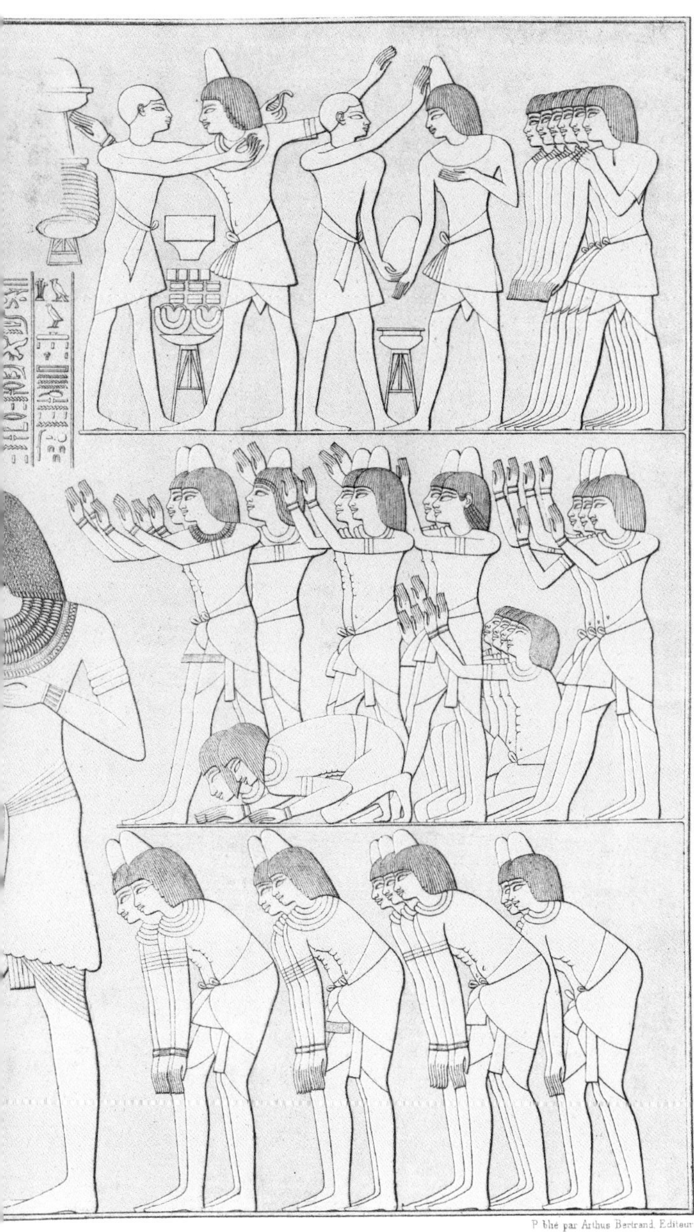

P blié par Arthus Bertrand, Editeur

HIS III

DOMAINES. XVIIIe DYNASTIE

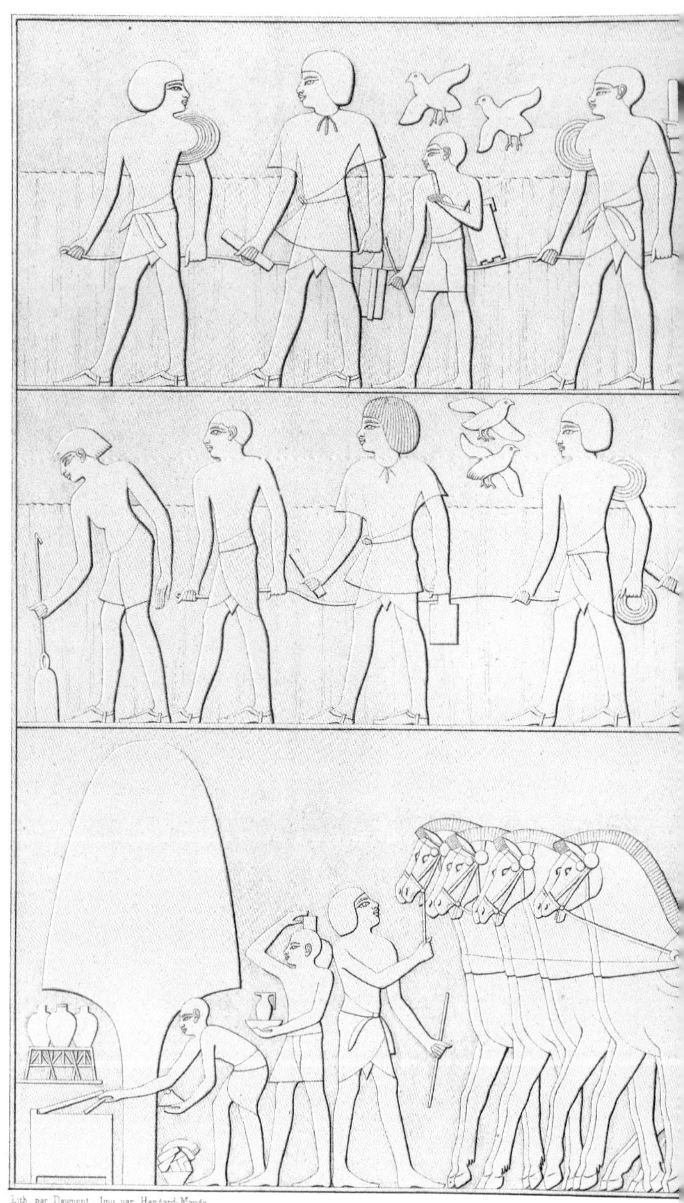

Lith. par Daumont _ Imp. par Hangard-Maugé.

ARPENT

SOUS LA PRESIDENCE DE CHAMHA

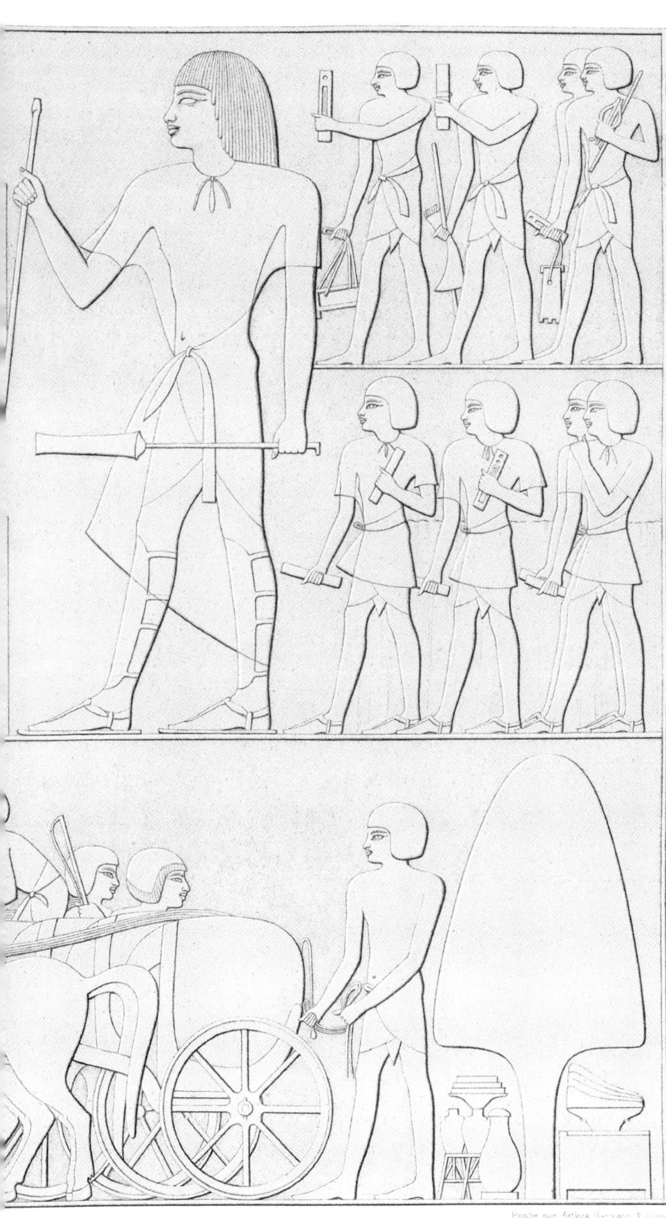

Publié par Arthus Bertrand Éditeur

TERRES

T DES DOMAINES. — XVIIIᵉ DYNASTIE.

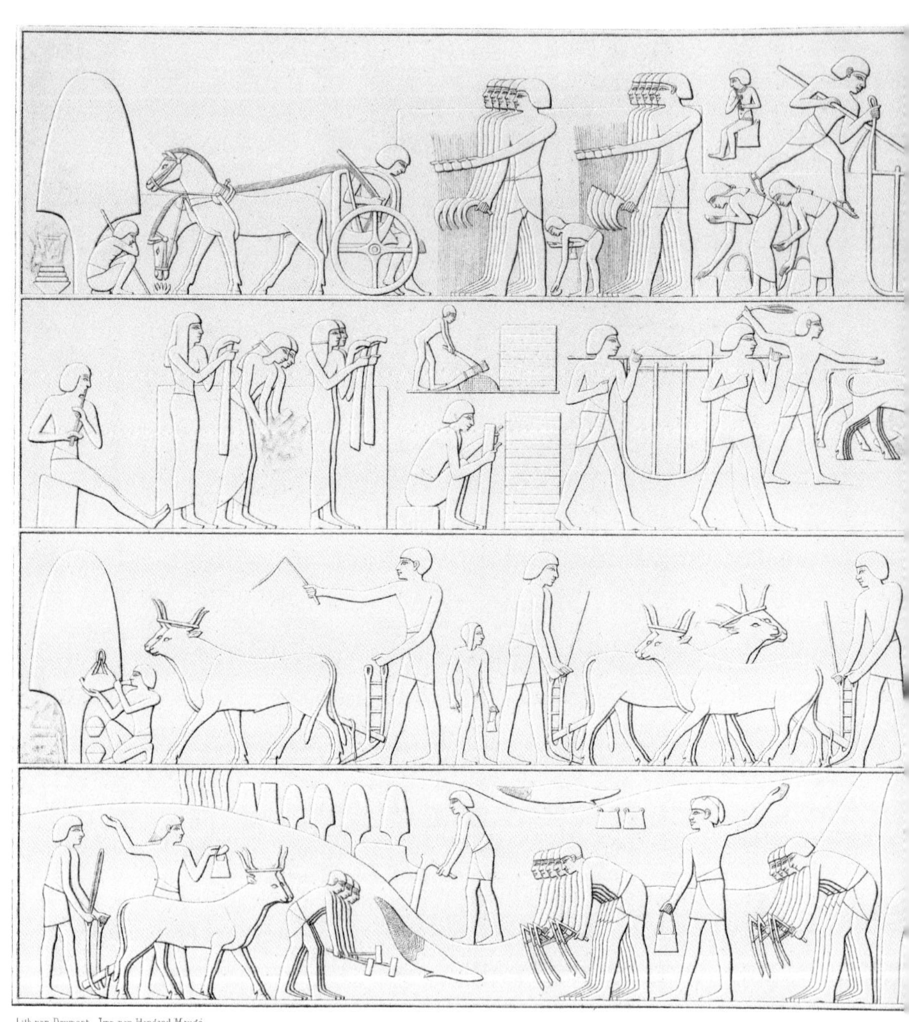

Lith par Daumont. _Imp. par Hangard-Maugé.

TRAV

TOMBEAU DE CHAMHATI, INT

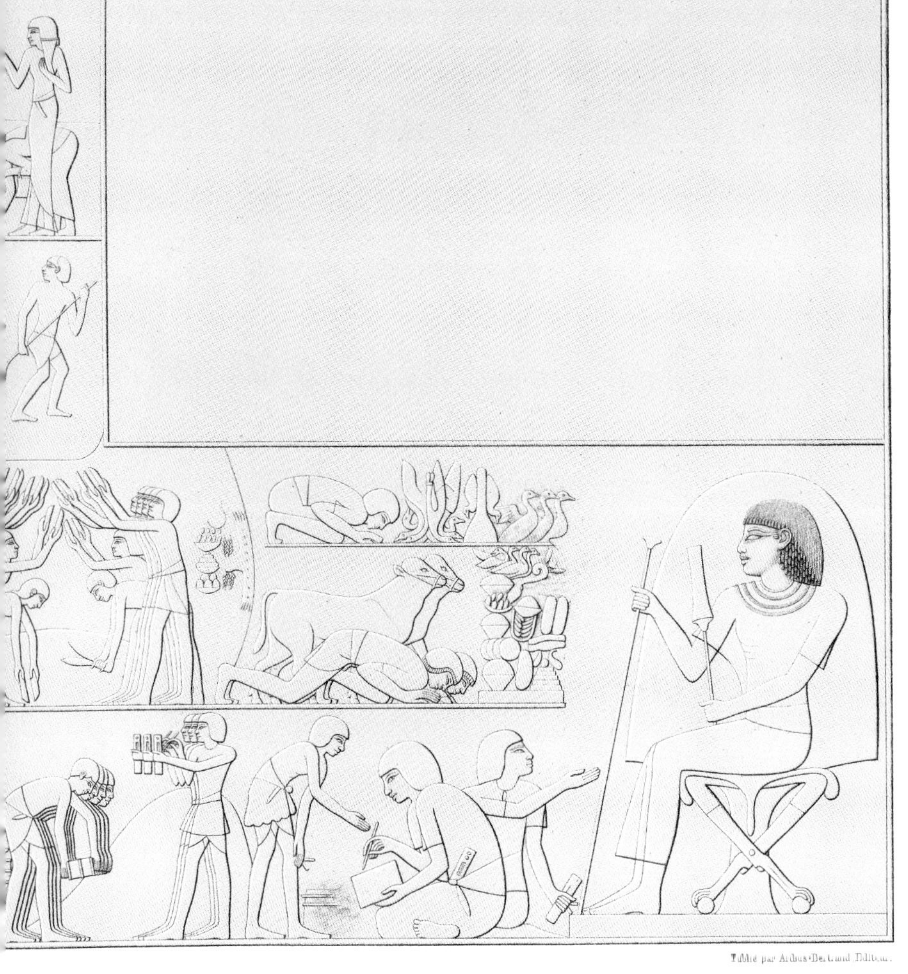

Publié par Arthus-Bertrand Éditeur.

OLES .

DOMAINES. — XVIIIᵉ DYNASTIE .

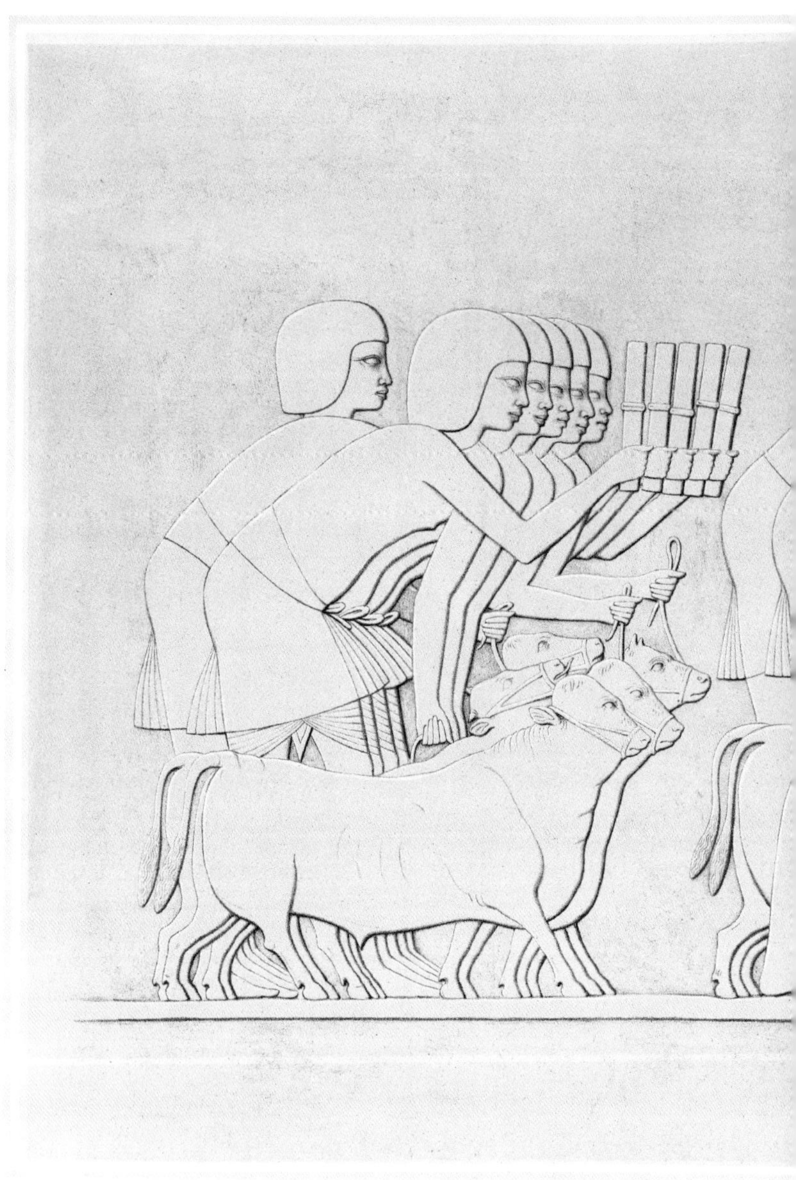

Lith. par Greillo _ Imp. par Hangard-Maugé

DÉNOMBR

TOMBEAU DE CHAMHATI, IN

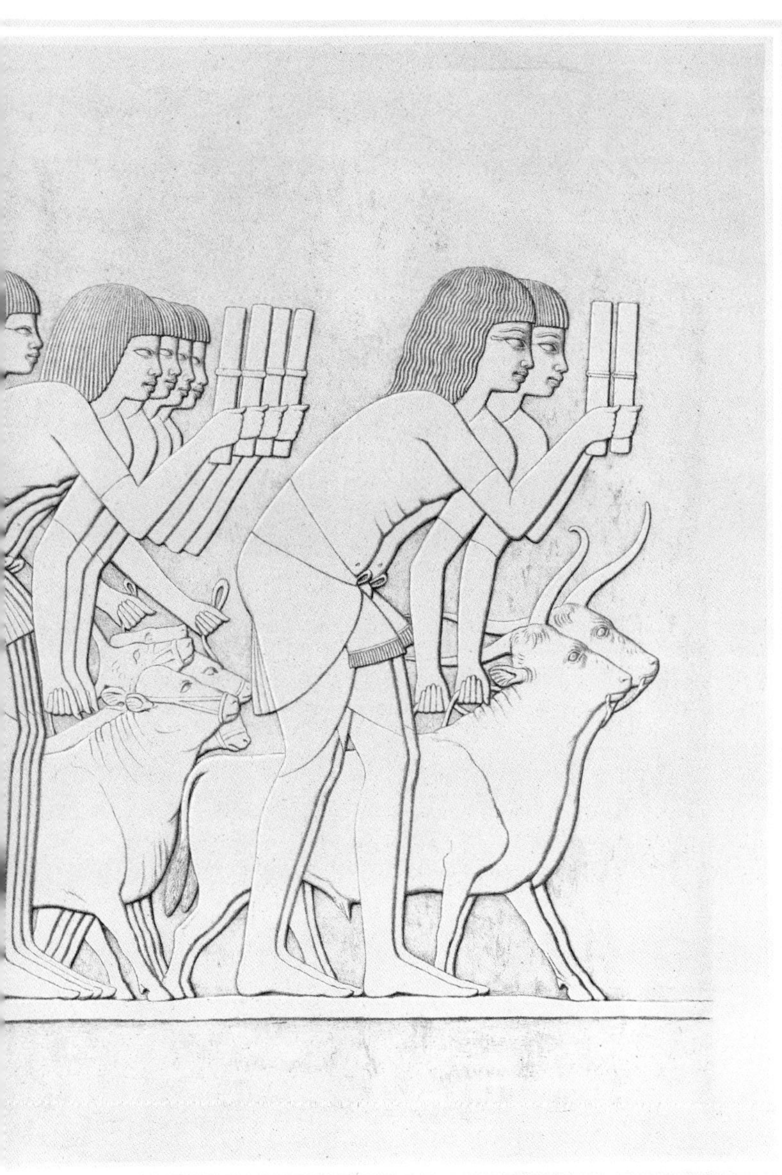

Publié par Arthus Bertrand Editeur

S BŒUFS

DOMAINES. — XVIIIE DYNASTIE.

(Pages/Seite 380/381)

PRINCELY CHARIOT (18th Dynasty)

Tell el-Amarna

In presenting this study of painted horses, I wished at the same time to show the harness and the chariot which, at this period, combined simplicity with great elegance. The chariot, bare of any ornamentation and furnished with a large case for the bow, is simply painted in the Egyptians' favourite colours: inscriptions of the time do mention chariots embellished with gold, silver and agates which came from the lands of Retjenu and Naharin. As for the harness, this is much simpler than that which is usually portrayed and is covered with braids which are arranged with restraint and taste. Everything here goes well together, even the saddle, compared to the saddles which are more generally depicted

FÜRSTLICHER WAGEN (18. Dynastie)

Tell el-Amarna

Der hier gezeigten farbigen Pferde-Studie wollte ich auch die Darstellung von Geschirr und Wagen beifügen, die in dieser Zeit bestechende Schlichtheit und wunderbare Anmut miteinander verbanden. Der mit einem breiten Köcher für den Bogen ausgestattete Wagen ist – ohne Ornamente – bescheiden in den Lieblingsfarben der Ägypter bemalt: In den Inschriften dieser Zeit ist von Wagen die Rede, die mit Gold, Silber und Agaten angereichert seien und aus den Ländern Retjenu und Naharina stammten. Was die Geschirre anbetrifft, so sind sie – wesentlich einfacher, als man sie im Allgemeinen sieht – mit ebenso nüchtern wie anmutig angeordneten Stickereien geschmückt. Alles ist hier leicht zu erfassen – sogar der Sattel, im Vergleich zu denen, die für gewöhnlich abgebildet sind.

CHAR PRINCIER (XVIIIe dynastie)

Tell el-Amarna

Tout en donnant cette étude de chevaux coloriés, j'ai voulu aussi représenter des harnais et un char, ceux-ci, à cette époque, joignant l'alliance de la simplicité à une élégance admirable. Le char dénué d'ornement, muni d'un large étui pour renfermer l'arc, est modestement peint des couleurs favorites des Égyptiens : il est fait mention dans les inscriptions de cette époque de chars enrichis d'or, d'argent et d'agates, qui venaient du pays de Routen [Rétjénou] et de Naharina. Quant aux harnais, beaucoup plus simples qu'on ne les voit généralement, ils sont couverts de broderies disposées avec autant de sobriété que de goût. Tout ici se comprend bien, même la selle, comparée à celles qu'on trouve ordinairement représentées.

(Pages/Seite 382/383)

HUNTING WITH THE BOW AND RUNNING DOGS (18th Dynasty)

Necropolis of Thebes

Hunting had originally been a vital skill for all the inhabitants of the Nile valley. However, as happened everywhere with the progress of civilisation, it became the sport *par excellence* and the noblest form of relaxation, in short the favourite exercise of people of high rank. In addition, the owner of every great estate had huntsmen whose task was to provide different species of game for the table. The bas-relief reproduced in this plate represents a high-ranking official abandoning himself to the pleasure of hunting with the bow, with a pack of hounds; the hunting area is enclosed with nets, into which the beaters have driven different types of game and even some carnivores. Behind the hero of this scene are several valets carrying a hyena, an antelope and a hare.

BOGENJAGD MIT HUNDEMEUTE (18. Dynastie)

Nekropole von Theben

Die Jagd, die anfänglich eine für alle Einwohner des Niltales lebensnotwendige Kunst war, hatte sich – wie überall – mit dem Fortschritt der Zivilisation zur körperlichen Ertüchtigung schlechthin, zur edelsten Form der Entspannung entwickelt; sie war, mit einem Wort, der bevorzugte Zeitvertreib hochgestellter Persönlichkeiten. Jeder Großgrundbesitzer hatte darüber hinaus Jäger eigens dafür angestellt, seinen Tisch mit unterschiedlichen Arten von Jagdwild zu versorgen. Das auf dieser Tafel abgebildete Flachrelief stellt einen hohen Beamten dar, der sich dem Vergnügen einer Bogenjagd mit Hundemeute hingibt; dazu haben die Treiber unterschiedliches Jagdwild und sogar fleischfressende Tiere in einer von Netzen umgebenen Einfriedung versammelt. Hinter dem Helden dieser Szene sind mehrere Bediente zu sehen, die damit beschäftigt sind, eine Hyäne, eine Antilope und einen Hasen fortzutragen.

CHASSE À TIR AVEC CHIENS COURANTS (XVIIIe dynastie)

Nécropole de Thèbes

La chasse, après avoir été un art de première nécessité pour tous les habitants de la vallée du Nil, était devenue comme partout, avec les progrès de la civilisation, l'exercice par excellence, le plus noble délassement ; en un mot, l'amusement favori des hauts personnages. Chaque grand propriétaire avait, en outre, des chasseurs employés à approvisionner leur table de gibier de différentes espèces. Le bas-relief reproduit sur cette planche représente un haut fonctionnaire se livrant au plaisir d'une chasse à tir, aux chiens courants, dans une enceinte entourée de filets, où des rabatteurs ont réuni différents gibiers et même des bêtes carnassières. Derrière le héros de cette scène, on voit plusieurs valets employés à porter une hyène, un antilope, un lièvre.

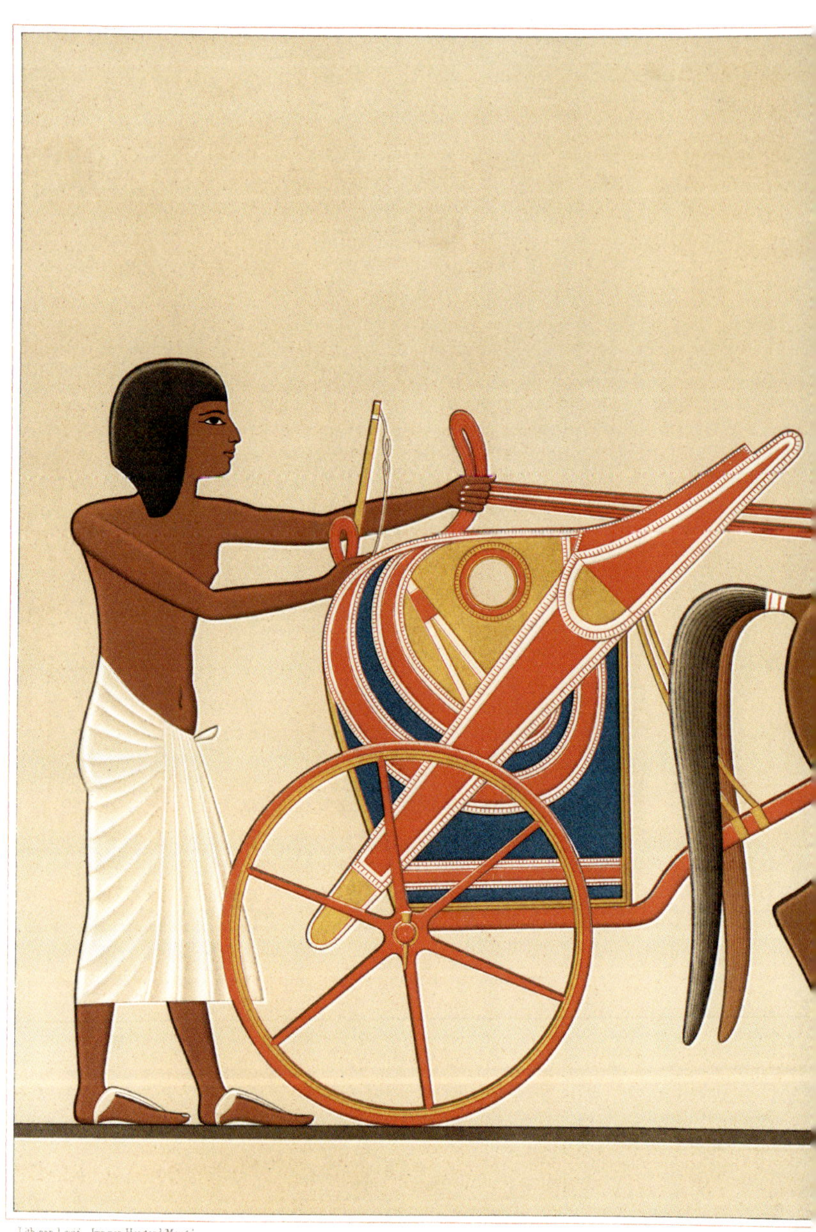

Lith. par Levié. _ Imp. par Hangard-Maugé.

CH

(TELL EL

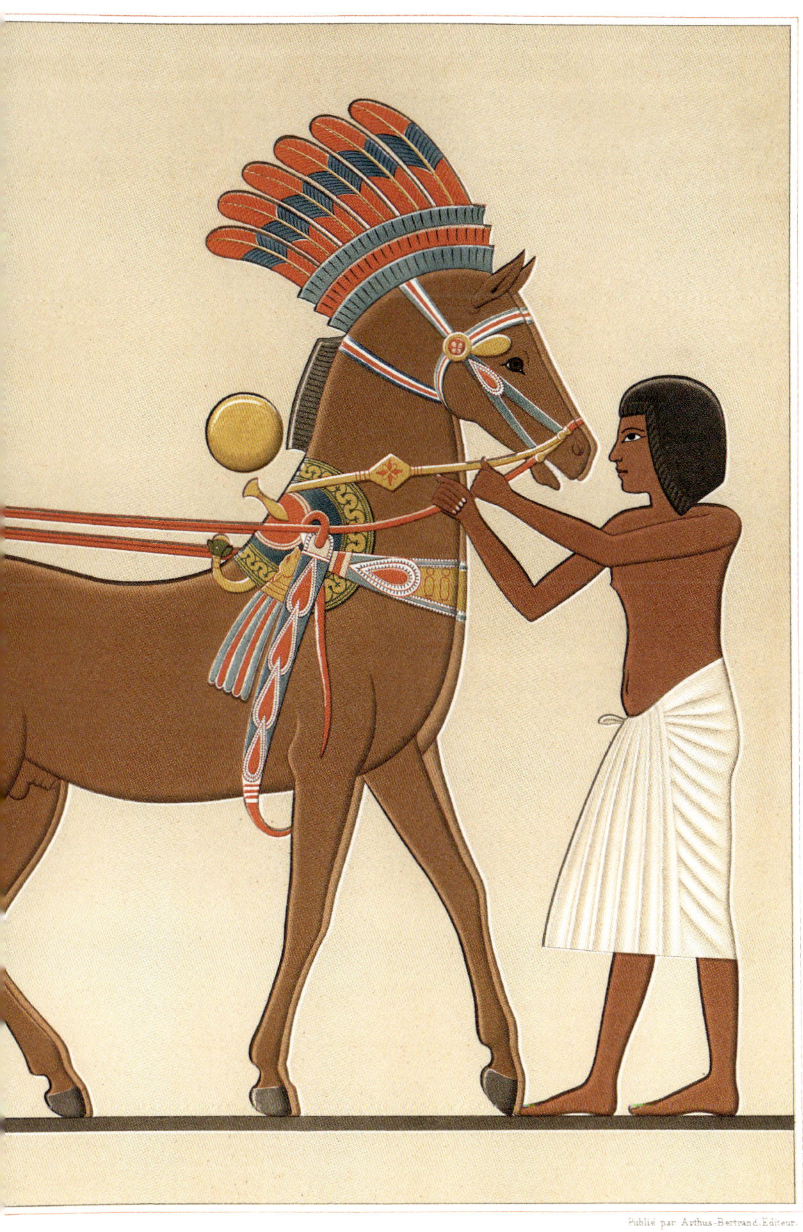

Publié par Arthus-Bertrand, Éditeur.

ER .

DYNASTIE.)

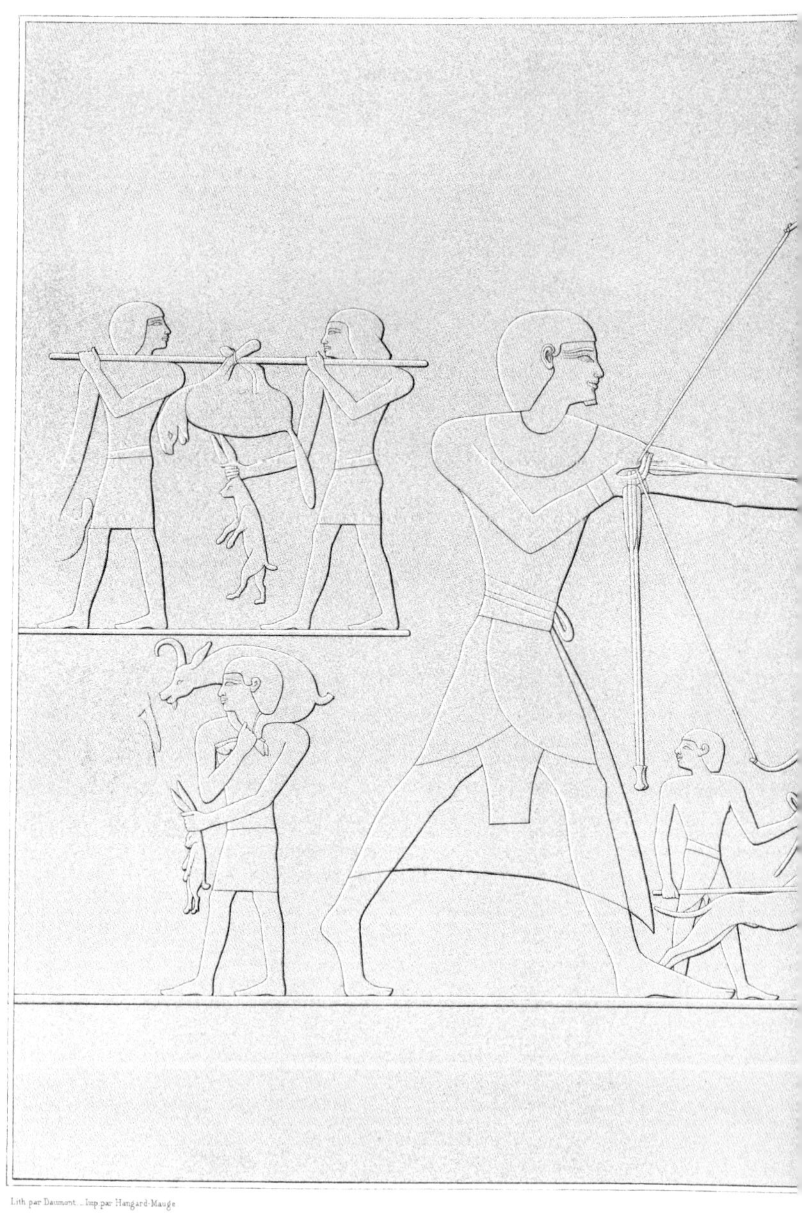

Lith. par Daumont. – Imp. par Hangard-Maugé

CHASSE A T

(NÉCROPO

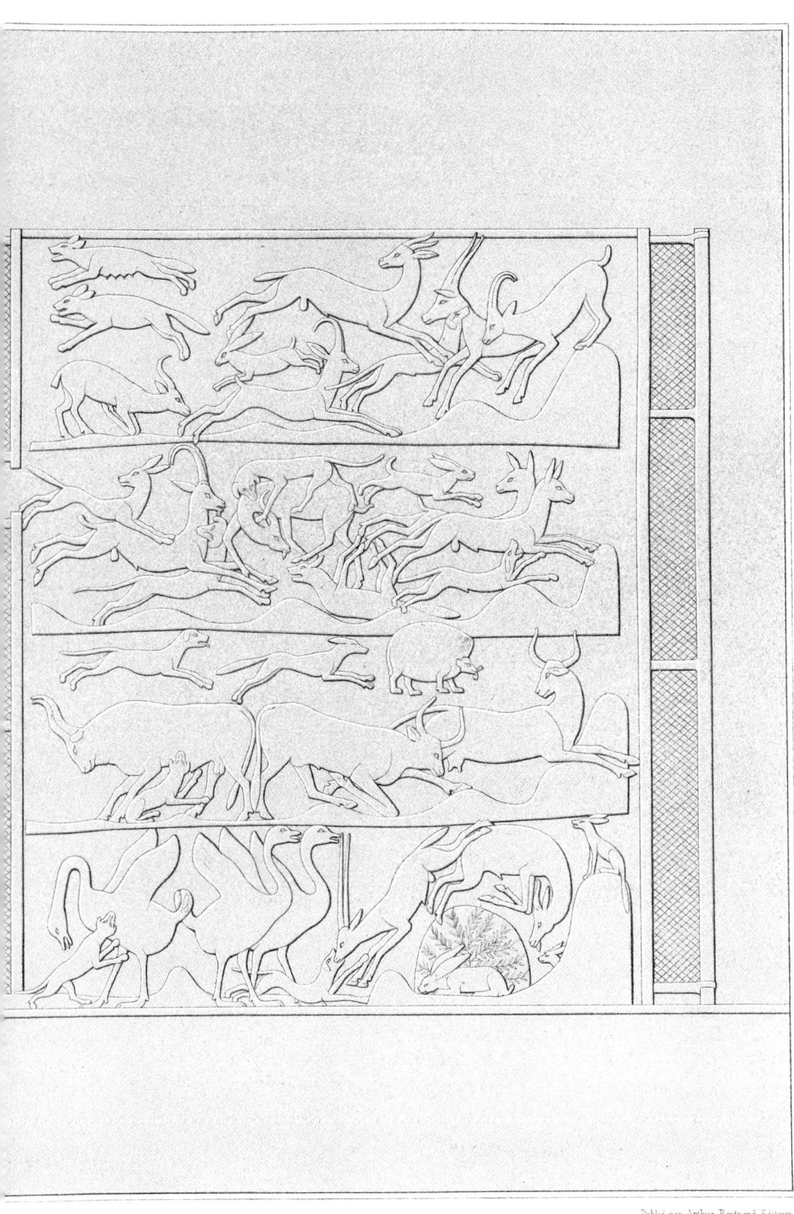

Publié par Arthus-Bertrand, Editeur.

NS COURANTS.

DYNASTIE.)

FRAGMENTS FROM BAS-RELIEFS: TEAMS OF HORSES (18th Dynasty)

Thebes

The Egyptians were never practised in the skill of horse-riding as such and never mounted a horse; they only used this handsome animal in harness for carts used in the town or the countryside. For this reason the horse is practically never represented on monuments except when drawing some sort of wheeled vehicle. [...] The cart in general use in the town had just one man up who drove himself. The war chariot, as was the case amongst the Assyrians, Persians and Homeric Greeks, had a warrior up as well as a driver, who also had the task of protecting his master or companion with a huge shield during the height of the battle. The upper bas-relief portrays a young prince accompanied by his squire. It appears to date from the reign of Amenophis III, 18th Dynasty. To the period of the same pharaoh belongs the small cart harnessed to two colts, with their manes hogged and their tails flowing free, which is shown in the lower register.

BRUCHSTÜCKE VON FLACHRELIEFS: GESPANNE (18. Dynastie)

Theben

Die Ägypter, die nie eine Reitkunst im eigentlichen Sinne gekannt haben, ritten nicht auf Pferden; sie bedienten sich dieses schönen Tieres lediglich, um es auf dem Lande oder in der Stadt vor den Wagen zu spannen. In den Denkmälern findet man es im Grunde genommen fast nie ohne das von ihm gezogene Fahrzeug abgebildet. [...] Auf dem in der Stadt gebräuchlichen Wagen fuhr ein einzelner Mann, der ihn selbst lenkte. Wenn ein Krieger den Streitwagen bestieg, wurde dieser – wie bei den Assyrern, den Persern und den homerischen Griechen – von einem Führer gelenkt, der in der Hitze des Gefechts auch damit befasst war, seinen Herrn oder Gefährten mit einem großen Schild zu schützen. Das obere Flachrelief zeigt einen jungen Prinzen, dem sein Knappe hilfreich zu Seite steht. Es scheint aus der Regierungszeit von Amenophis III. in der 18. Dynastie zu datieren. Der im unteren Register dargestellte kleine Wagen, vor den zwei Fohlen mit bürstenartig geschnittener Mähne und schmucklosem Schweif gespannt sind, steht mit der Zeit desselben Pharaos in Zusammenhang.

FRAGMENTS DE BAS-RELIEFS : ATTELAGES (XVIIIe dynastie)

Thèbes

Les Égyptiens n'ayant jamais connu l'équitation proprement dite, ne montaient pas à cheval ; ils ne se servaient de ce bel animal que pour l'atteler aux chars des villes ou de la campagne. Aussi, on ne le trouve presque jamais représenté sur les monuments sans le véhicule qu'il traîne. [...] Le char usité dans les villes était monté par un seul homme qui conduisait lui-même. Le char de guerre était, comme celui des Assyriens, des Perses et des Grecs homériques, monté par un guerrier et conduit par un guide qui, au fort du combat, était occupé aussi à protéger son maître ou son compagnon par un vaste bouclier. Le bas-relief supérieur représente un jeune prince assisté de son écuyer. Il paraît dater du règne d'Aménophis III, XVIIIe dynastie. C'est à l'époque du même pharaon que se rapporte aussi le petit char attelé de deux poulains, la crinière taillée en brosse et la queue dégarnie, que j'ai représenté dans le registre inférieur.

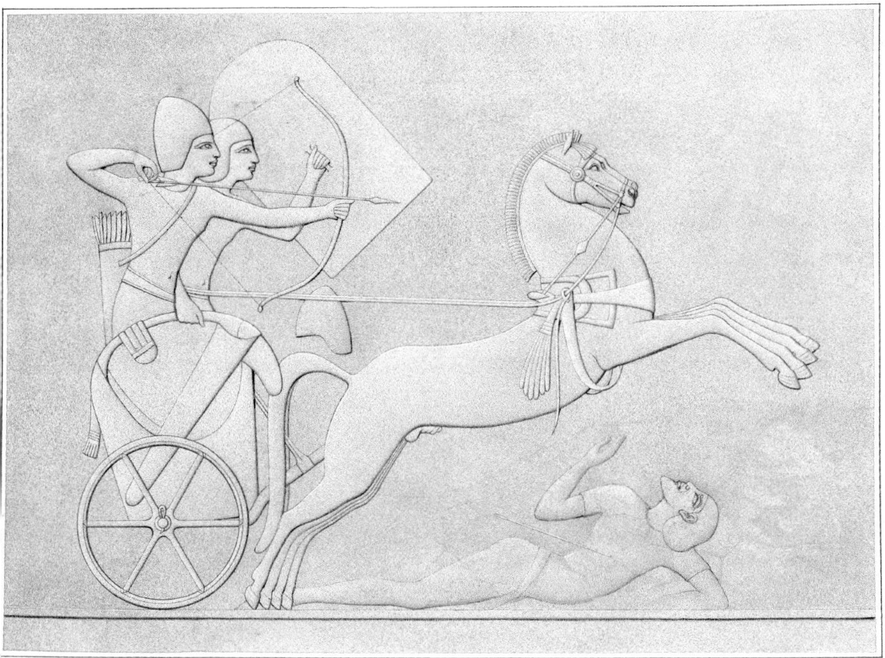

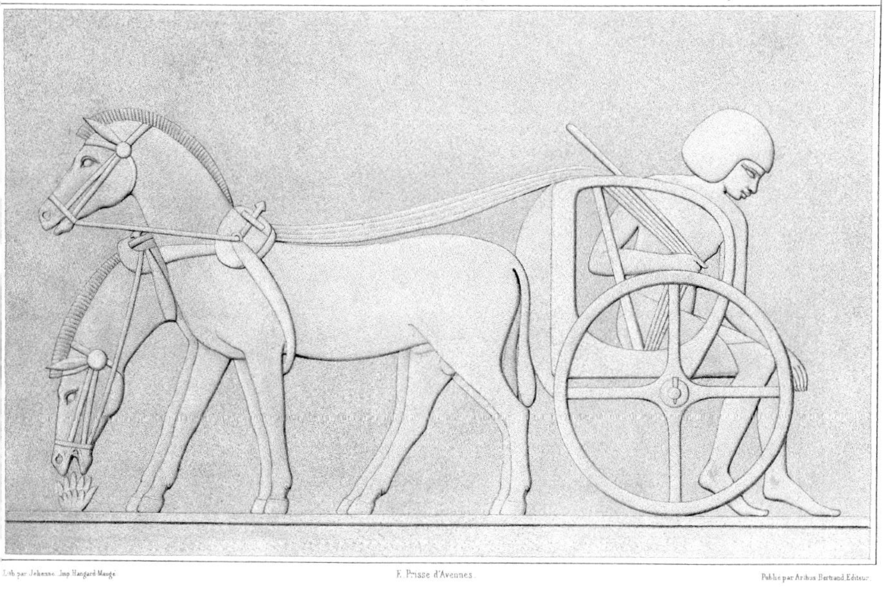

Lith par Jehenne. Imp. Hangard-Maugé.

E. Prisse d'Avennes.

Publié par Arthus Bertrand, Éditeur.

FRAGMENTS DE BAS-RELIEFS : ATTELAGES.

(THÈBES._ XVIIIe DYNASTIE.)

RAMS (18th Dynasty)

Temple of Mut and Khonsu

This plate portrays one of the rams from the avenue of the temple of Khonsu at Karnak, where this animal was worshipped as an emblem of Amun, the eponymous deity of Thebes [called the "City of Amun"]. Most of these rams have been mutilated, their heads are broken, and the globe adorned with the uraeus, with which they were crowned, lies buried beneath the sand or debris. The figurine leaning against their chest and serving as bracket to support their beard is an image of Amenophis III, who had them carved in the fine sandstone quarries of Silsila. The principal places where this sacred animal was worshipped were Thebes, Hypsela, Sais and the Libyan part of Egypt.

WIDDER (18. Dynastie)

Tempel der Mut und des Chons

Diese Tafel stellt einen der Widder aus der Prachtstraße des Chons-Tempels in Karnak dar, wo dieses Tier als Sinnbild des Amun, der namengebenden Gottheit von Theben [„Die Stadt von Amun" genannt], verehrt wurde. Die meisten dieser Widder wurden verstümmelt, ihre Köpfe sind zerbrochen, und die mit einer Uräusschlange geschmückte Kugel, die sie bekrönte, liegt unter dem Sand oder den Trümmern begraben. Bei dem kleinen Hermenpfeiler, der [den Widdern] den Bart stützt und an ihre Brust angelehnt ist, handelt es sich um ein Bildnis Amenophis' III., der sie in den schönen Sandstein-Steinbrüchen von Dschabal as-Silsila behauen ließ. Dieses heilige Tier wurde hauptsächlich in den Städten Theben, Hypselis, Sais und im libyschen Teil Ägyptens verehrt.

BÉLIERS (XVIIIe dynastie)

Temple de Mauth et Khons

Cette planche représente un des béliers de l'avenue du temple de Khons [Khonsou], à Karnac, où cet animal était vénéré comme un emblème d'Amon, divinité éponyme de Thèbes [appelée « la Ville d'Amon »]. La plupart de ces béliers ont été mutilés, leurs têtes sont brisées, et le globe orné d'uréus qui les couronnait gît enfoui sous les sables ou les débris. La figurine en gaine, qui soutient leur barbe et s'appuie contre leur poitrail, est une image d'Aménophis III, qui les fit tailler dans les belles carrières de grès de Silsilis [Gebel el-Silsileh]. Cet animal sacré était principalement adoré dans les villes de Thèbes, Hypselis, Saïs, ainsi que dans la partie libyque de l'Égypte.

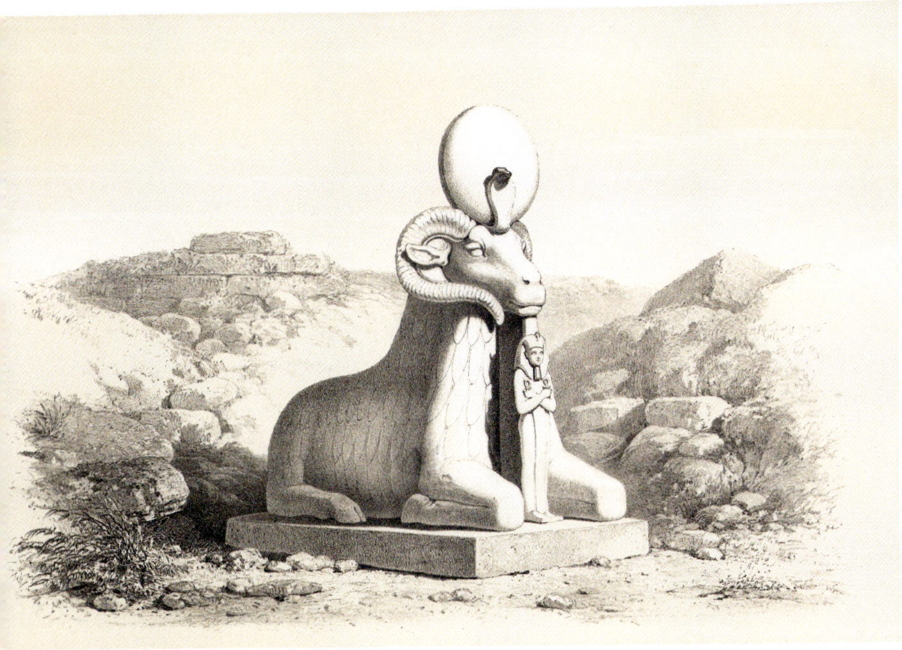

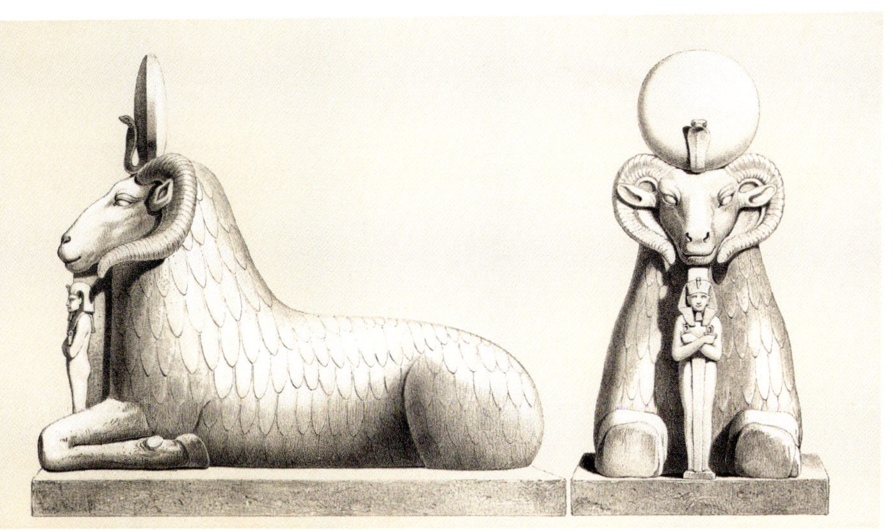

Exécuté par Mouilleron _ Imp. Lemercier & C.ie Paris. Prisse d'Avennes Publié par Arthus Bertrand Éditeur

BÉLIERS.

(TEMPLE DE MAUTH ET KHONS _ XVIIIE DYNASTIE.)

ANDROSPHINX AND CRIOSPHINX (Amenophis III, 18th Dynasty)

The androcephalic sphinxes or androsphinxes are quite often found in buildings built by pharaohs from the 18th to the 21st Dynasties. The head of these sphinxes is always a portrait of the king who had them carved. The one reproduced in the upper register of this plate has a head carved in the likeness of Amenophis III. This superb pink granite monolith, of the finest craftsmanship, was found in 1825. The androsphinxes generally wore the state head-dress of the "nemes", striped and adorned with a uraeus, the emblem of royalty, over which was placed a full Pschent, symbol of domination over Upper and Lower Egypt. The criocephalic sphinxes, with the head of a ram, animal sacred to the god Amun, are fairly common in this capital. The one shown here is one of the criosphinxes from the avenue of the great temple of Karnak. Its overall length is around 5 metres while its head is more than a metre long.

ANDROSPHINX UND CRIOSPHINX (Amenophis III., 18. Dynastie)

In den durch die Pharaonen der 18. bis 21. Dynastie errichteten Gebäuden kommen Androsphingen oder Sphingen mit menschlichem Gesicht recht häufig vor. Der Kopf dieser Sphingen ist immer ein Porträt des Königs, der sie anfertigen ließ. Die im oberen Register dieser Tafel Abgebildete trägt einen nach dem Vorbild von Amenophis III. geformten Kopf. Dieser herrliche Monolith aus rosa Granit, der im Jahre 1825 gefunden wurde, ist erstklassig gearbeitet. Im Allgemeinen trugen die Androsphingen als standesgemäßen Kopfputz das gestreifte und mit einer Uräusschlange – dem Sinnbild der Königswürde – geschmückte Nemes-Kopftuch, auf das man die vollständige altägyptische Doppelkrone (Pschent) als Symbol der Herrschaft über Ober- und Unterägypten setzte. Die Criosphingen, d. h. diejenigen, die den Kopf eines Widders – eines dem Gott Amun geweihten Tieres – tragen, sind in dieser Hauptstadt recht verbreitet. Die auf dieser Tafel dargestellte Criosphinx stammt von der Prachtstraße des großen Tempels in Karnak. Ihre Gesamtlänge beträgt etwa 5 m und die Länge des Kopfes mehr als 1 m.

ANDROSPHINX ET CRIOSPHINX (Aménophis III, XVIIIe dynastie)

Les sphinx androcéphales ou androsphinx se rencontrent, assez fréquemment, dans les édifices élevés par les pharaons de la XVIIIe à la XXIe dynastie. La tête de ces sphinx est toujours un portrait du roi qui les fit tailler. Celui que reproduit le registre supérieur de cette planche porte une tête sculptée à la ressemblance d'Aménophis III. Ce superbe monolithe de granit rose, du plus beau travail, a été trouvé en 1825. Les androsphinx portaient, ordinairement, le « némès », coiffure civile, striée et ornée d'un uréus, emblème de la royauté, au-dessus duquel on mettait le pschent entier, symbole de la domination sur la Haute- et la Basse-Égypte. Les sphinx criocéphales, c'est-à-dire à tête de bélier, animal consacré au dieu Amon, sont assez communs dans cette capitale. Celui représenté dans cette planche est un des criosphinx de l'avenue du grand temple à Karnac. Sa longueur totale est d'environ 5 mètres et la longueur de la tête de plus d'un mètre.

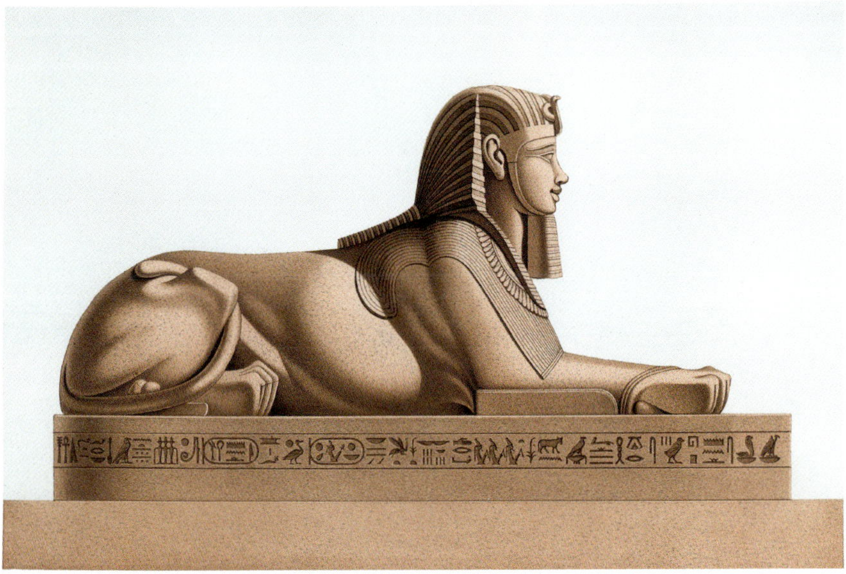

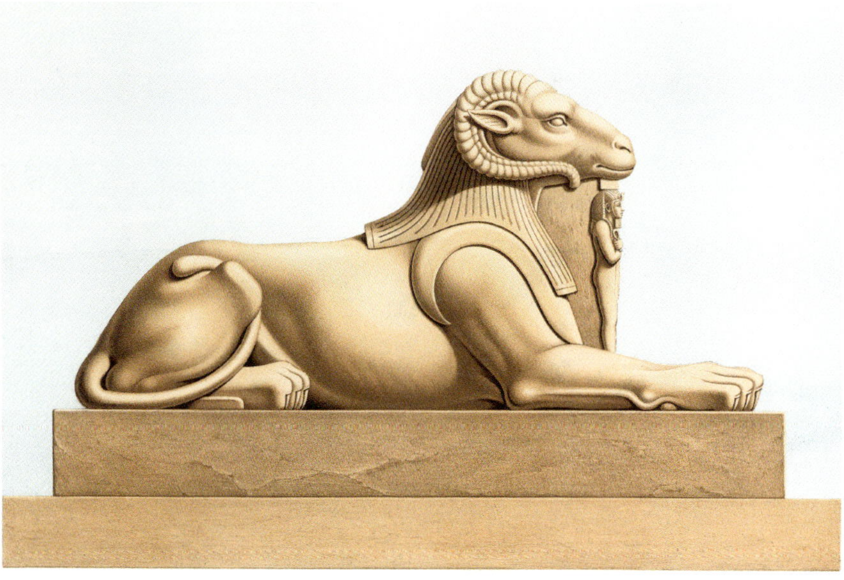

Lith par Kellerhoven. Imp. par Hangard Maugé.

E. Prisse d'Avennes.

Publié par Arthus Bertrand, Éditeur.

ANDROSPHINX & CRIOSPHINX.

(AMENOPHIS III. _ XVIIIe DYNASTIE.)

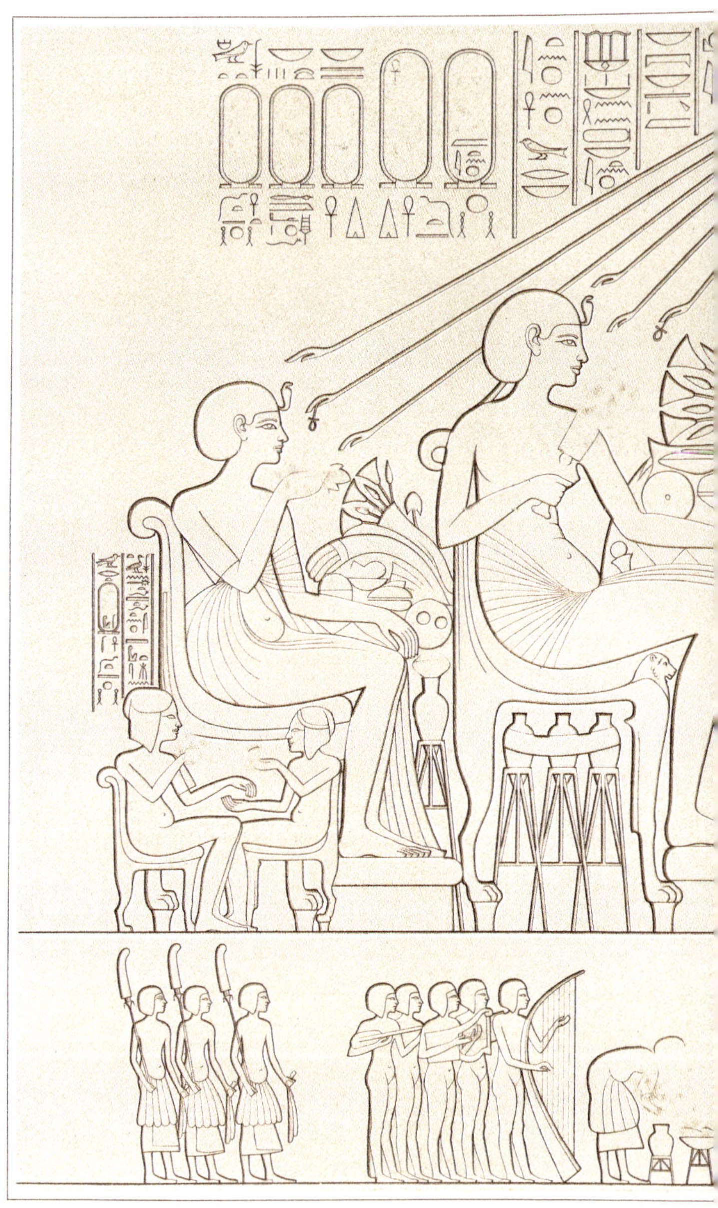

Lith. par Daumont _ Imp. par Hangard-Maugé.

OFFRA

(HYPOGÉES DE

III 17

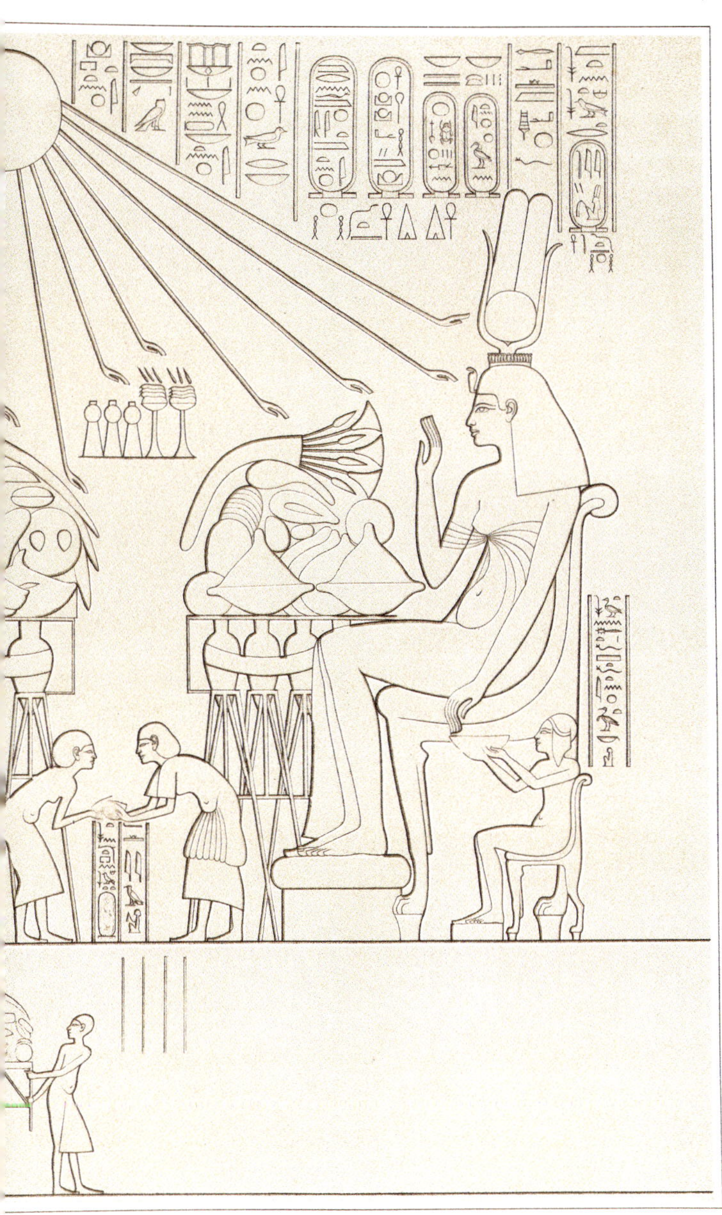

Pulhé par Arthus Bertrand, Editeur

OLEIL.

.XVIIIe DYNASTIE.)

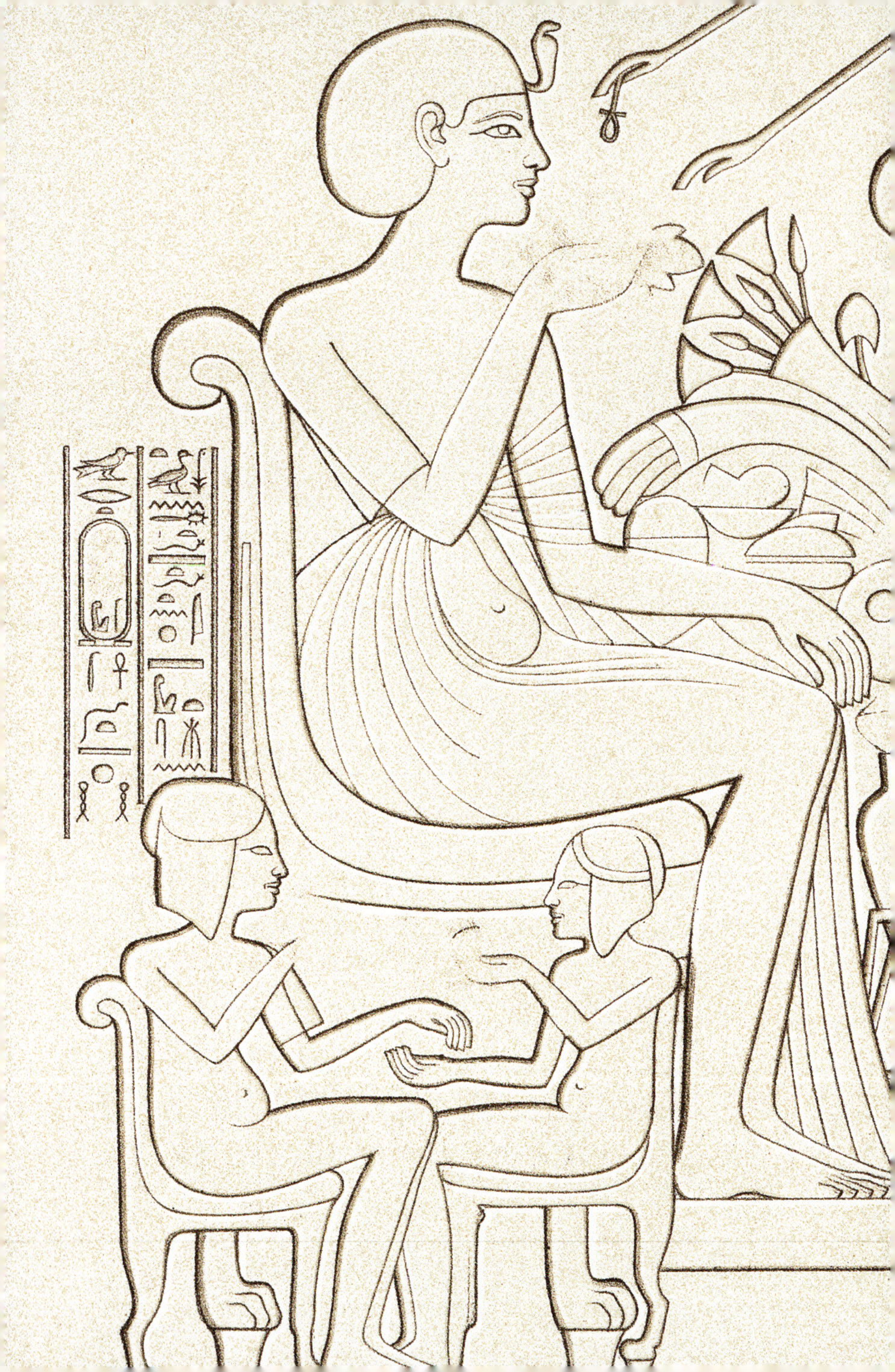

(Pages/Seite 390/391)

OFFERINGS TO THE SUN (18th Dynasty)

Hypogea from Tell el-Amarna

Three altars laden with food and flowers divide the scene into two main parts. On the left, the pharaoh Akhenaten and his wife, both holding in their hands emblems which have been effaced, take part in a religious ceremony in honour of Aten-Ra, the radiant sun, who at that period, thanks to the particular favour and devotion of the pharaoh portrayed here, represented the one exclusive god of Egypt. Behind the queen, two young princesses, her daughters, appear to be taking part in the ceremony. On the right the queen mother, Tiye, is portrayed with one of her grand-daughters at her side; this is the princess Atenbek, who seems to be offering a basket to her. The lower register is half filled with a series of minor characters. These are officials of the king, musicians and servants who are busy preparing the offerings. The picture was never completed, possibly as a result of the premature death of the personage for whom this hypogeum had been prepared.

OPFERGABEN AN DIE SONNE (18. Dynastie)

Hypogäen von Tell el-Amarna

Drei mit Blumen und Esswaren beladene Altäre teilen die Szene in zwei Hauptteile. Auf der linken Seite wohnen der Pharao Echnaton und seine Gemahlin, die beide ausgelöschte Embleme in den Händen halten, einer religiösen Zeremonie zu Ehren von Aton-Ra bei – der strahlenden Sonnenscheibe, die dank der besonderen Ergebenheit des hier abgebildeten Pharaos in dieser Zeit die einzige und ausschließliche Gottheit Ägyptens darstellte. Hinter der Königin scheinen zwei junge Prinzessinnen – ihre Töchter – der Zeremonie zuzusehen. Auf der rechten Seite ist die Königsmutter Teje an der Seite einer ihrer Enkeltöchter, der Prinzessin Atenbek, dargestellt, die ihr anscheinend einen Korb anbietet. Das untere Register ist zur Hälfte mit untergeordneten Figuren angefüllt. Es handelt sich um die königlichen Offiziere, die Musikerinnen und die mit der Vorbereitung der Opfergaben beschäftigten Diener. Das Bild blieb unvollendet – vielleicht infolge des vorzeitigen Ablebens der Persönlichkeit, für die man dieses Hypogäum hergerichtet hatte.

OFFRANDES AU SOLEIL (XVIIIe dynastie)

Hypogées de Tell el-Amarna

Trois autels, chargés de victuailles et de fleurs, divisent la scène en deux parties principales. À gauche, le pharaon Khouenaten [Akhénaton] et sa femme, tenant tous deux en mains des emblèmes effacés, assistent à une cérémonie religieuse en l'honneur d'Aten-ré, le soleil rayonnant, qui à cette époque, et grâce à la dévotion toute spéciale du pharaon qu'on voit ici, représentait le dieu unique, exclusif de l'Égypte. Derrière la reine, deux jeunes princesses, ses filles, semblent assister à la cérémonie. À droite, la reine mère, Tii [Tiyi], est représentée ayant à ses côtés une de ses petites-filles, la princesse Atenbek, qui paraît lui offrir une corbeille. Le registre inférieur est à demi rempli par une série de personnages secondaires. Ce sont les officiers du roi, des musiciennes et des serviteurs occupés à préparer des offrandes. Le tableau n'a jamais été terminé, peut-être par suite de la mort prématurée du personnage pour lequel on avait préparé cet hypogée.

TYPES AND PORTRAITS

Ladies from various periods

These ladies are all wives and daughters of high-ranking officials from different periods; they are therefore members of the aristocracy of the country. No. 1, from the 6th Dynasty, is a figure taken from a ruined tomb at Saqqara: the hair of great ladies was always dressed in this elegant style, which remained in vogue until the 12th Dynasty. The daughter of Djehutihotep, portrayed at the entrance to the tomb of her father at Deir el-Bersha, has a similar hairstyle. No. 2 is from the 12th Dynasty: this head is carved on a fragment of a funerary stele from Abydos from the reign of Amenemhat II. No. 3, from the 18th Dynasty, represents the wife or daughter of a priest buried in that part of the necropolis of Thebes now called Abd el-Qurna. Finally, no. 4 is from the 19th Dynasty and portrays the wife of a "sotem" who lived under Seti I; it is taken from the necropolis of Thebes.

TYPEN UND PORTRÄTS

Damen aus verschiedenen Zeiten

Alle diese Damen sind Töchter und Gemahlinnen hoher Beamter aus verschiedenen Zeiten; sie gehören also zur Aristokratie des Landes. Die Nr. 1, aus der 6. Dynastie, ist ein aus einem zerstörten Grab in Sakkara entnommenes Antlitz: Ihre anmutige Frisur wurde stets von großen Damen getragen; sie blieb bis in die 12. Dynastie hinein gebräuchlich. Die am Eingang zum Grab ihres Vaters in Deir el-Bersche dargestellte Tochter von Djehutihotep trägt eine ähnliche Frisur. Die Nr. 2 datiert aus der 12. Dynastie: Dieser Kopf ist in das Bruchstück einer Begräbnisstele aus Abydos eingearbeitet, die aus der Regierungszeit von Amenemhet II. datiert. Die Nr. 3, aus der 18. Dynastie, stellt die Gemahlin oder die Tochter eines Priesters dar, der in dem heute Scheich Abd el-Qurna genannten Teil der Nekropole von Theben begraben wurde. Die Nr. 4 datiert schließlich aus der 19. Dynastie: Sie stellt die Gemahlin eines „Setem" dar, der unter Sethos I. lebte. Auch sie entstammt der Nekropole von Theben.

TYPES ET PORTRAITS

Dames de diverses époques

Ces dames sont toutes filles et femmes de hauts fonctionnaires de diverses époques ; elles appartiennent donc à l'aristocratie du pays. Le n° 1, de la VIe dynastie, est une figure tirée d'un tombeau ruiné à Sakkara : sa coiffure, élégante, était toujours portée par de grandes dames ; elle resta en usage jusque sous la XIIe dynastie. La fille de Thouthotep [Djéhoutihotep], représentée à l'entrée du tombeau de son père à Bercheh, porte une coiffure semblable. Le n° 2 est de la XIIe dynastie : cette tête est sculptée sur un fragment de stèle funéraire d'Abydos, appartenant au règne d'Amenemhé [Amménémès] II. Le n° 3, de la XVIIIe dynastie, représente la femme ou la fille d'un prêtre enseveli dans la partie de la nécropole de Thèbes, appelée aujourd'hui Abd el-Gournah. Enfin, le n° 4 est de la XIXe dynastie : il représente la femme d'un « sotem » qui vivait sous Séti Ier. Il est tiré de la nécropole de Thèbes.

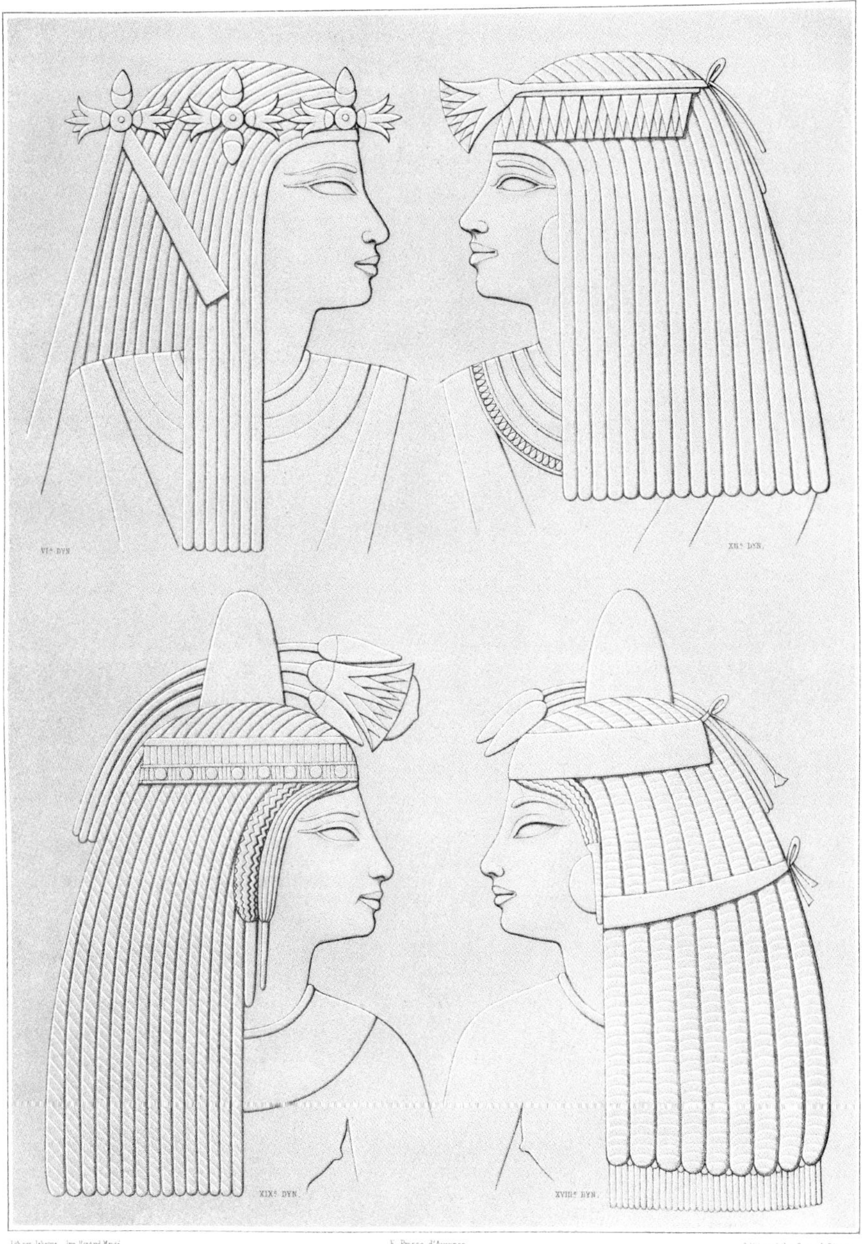

Lith par Jobenne. – Imp Hangard Maugé

E. Prisse d'Avennes.

Publié par Arthus Bertrand, Editeur.

TYPES & PORTRAITS.

(DAMES DE DIVERSES ÉPOQUES.)

TYPES AND PORTRAITS

High-ranking officials from various periods

No.1 is a portrait of Ti, reproduced in a group, from a painted bas-relief on one of the walls of his tomb in the necropolis of Memphis near Saqqara. No. 2 represents Rekhmire. This name means "Learned as the sun" and was that of an official who was governor to Thutmosis III (18th Dynasty) and who had a huge hypogeum excavated and decorated. No. 3 is the portrait of Djehutihotep, carved at the back of the niche in his tomb at Deir el-Bersha. This figure is more youthful than those drawn in other parts of the hypogeum where there were pictures of this high-ranking official of Sesostris. No. 4 represents Petamenophis, the high priest who seems to have lived in the Saite period and to have exercised supreme authority in Thebes.

TYPEN UND PORTRÄTS

Hohe Beamte aus verschiedenen Zeiten

Die Nr. 1 ist das Abbild von Ti, das hier in einer Gruppe wiedergegeben ist; Vorbild ist ein bemaltes Flachrelief von einer Wand seines Grabes, das in der Nekropole von Memphis bei Sakkara erbaut wurde. Die Nr. 2 stellt Rechmire dar. Dieser Name bedeutet: „Gelehrt wie die Sonne". Ein Beamter – ein Verwalter von Thutmosis III. (18. Dynastie) –, der ein weitläufiges Hypogäum ausheben und ausschmücken ließ, trug ihn. Die Nr. 3 ist das Porträt von Djehutihotep, das hinten in die Nische seines Grabes in Deir el-Bersche eingearbeitet ist. Dieses Gesicht ist jugendlicher als die zeichnerischen Darstellungen in den anderen Teilen des Hypogäums, in denen man diesen hohen Beamten des Sesostris vergegenwärtigt hat. Die Nr. 4 stellt den Hohepriester Petamenophis dar, der anscheinend in der Saïtenzeit lebte und in Theben herrschaftliche Gewalt ausübte.

TYPES ET PORTRAITS

Hauts fonctionnaires de diverses époques

Le n° 1 est celui de Teï, reproduit dans un groupe d'après un bas-relief peint sur une des parois de son tombeau bâti dans la nécropole de Memphis près de Sakkara. Le n° 2 représente Rekhmara. Ce nom signifie : « Savant comme le soleil ». Il a été porté par un fonctionnaire, intendant de Thoutmès [Thoutmôsis] III (XVIIIe dynastie), qui a fait creuser et décorer un vaste hypogée. Le n° 3 est le portrait de Thouthotep [Djéhoutihotep], sculpté, au fond de la niche de son tombeau, à Bercheh. Cette figure est plus juvénile que celles retracées dans les autres parties de l'hypogée où l'on a représenté ce haut fonctionnaire d'Osortasen [Sésostris Ier]. Le n° 4 représente Pétamounôph [Padiamenopé], grand prêtre qui paraît avoir vécu à l'époque des Saïtes et exercé une autorité souveraine à Thèbes.

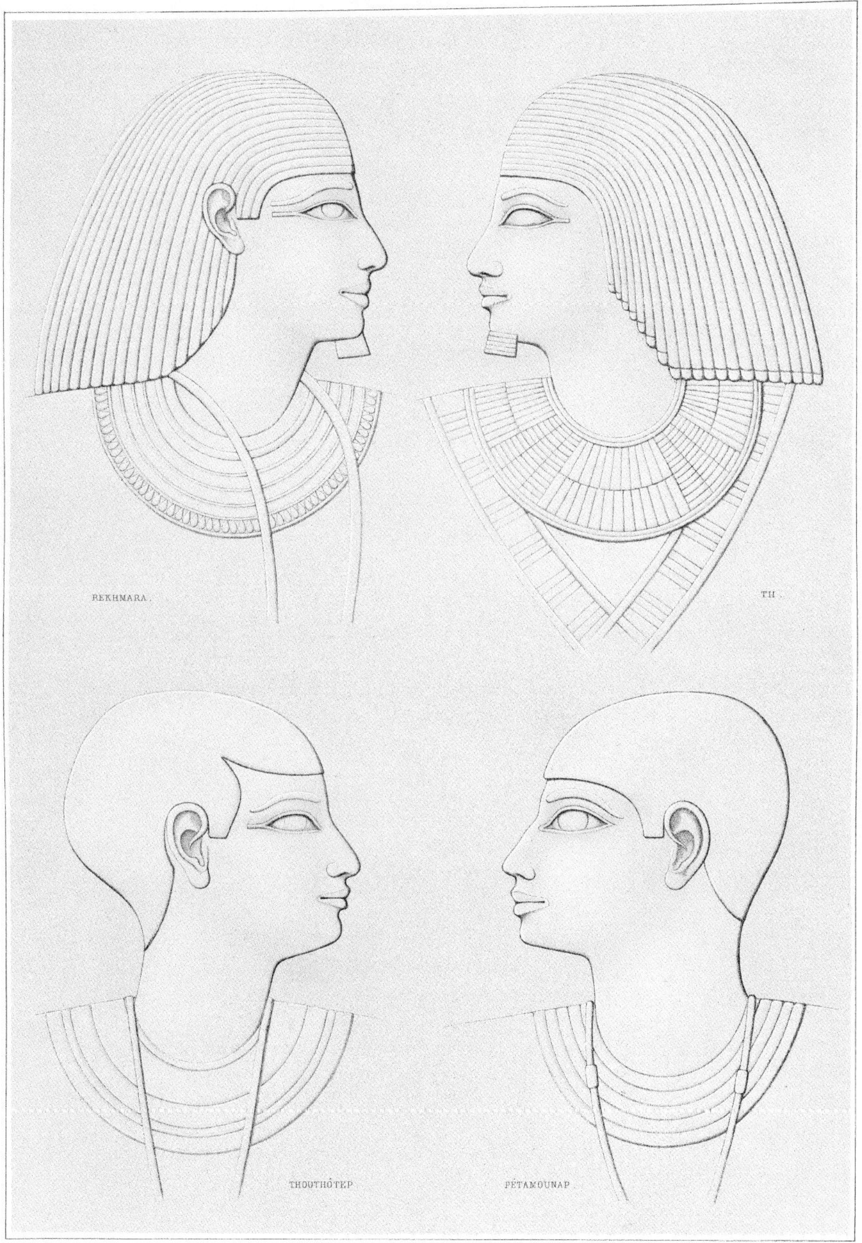

Lith. par Jehenne. Imp. par Bangard-Maugé. E. Prisse d'Avennes. Publié par Arthus Bertrand, Éditeur.

TYPES & PORTRAITS

(HAUTS-FONCTIONNAIRES DE DIVERSES ÉPOQUES.)

STATUE OF QUEEN AMENIRDIS

Cairo Museum

This magnificent statue was found buried under the ruins of a small temple situated at the north of the great enclosure of Karnak. It is in oriental alabaster or aragonite. Its height from the soles of the feet to the top of the head is 1.47 metres. The inscription carved on the base of the statue gives two cartouches containing the official prenomen ("the divine consort", Mut-kha-neferu) and the nomen ("the divine hand", Amenirdis or Amunartis), as if this were a ruling monarch. This exceptional circumstance leads one to suppose that she reigned in her own name. Amenirdis was the daughter of Kashta, who claimed descent from Bocchoris or Bakenrenef, the only king of the first Saite Dynasty (24th in the lists). She married Piankhi [Piye], who seems to have been one of the last offspring of the sovereign pontiffs of the 21st Dynasty, and their daughter had as husband Psammetichus I.

STATUE DER KÖNIGIN AMENIRDIS

Museum von Kairo

Diese herrliche Statue wurde verschüttet unter den Trümmern eines kleinen Tempels nördlich der großen Umfassungsmauer von Karnak gefunden. Sie besteht aus orientalischem Alabaster oder Aragonit. Ihre Höhe beträgt vom Scheitel bis zur Sohle 1,47 m. Die in den Sockel der Statue eingravierte Inschrift setzt sich aus zwei Kartuschen zusammen, die den offiziellen Vornamen („Gottesgemahlin", Maut-cha-neferu) und den Eigennamen („die göttliche Hand", Amenirtis oder Amonartis) enthalten, als ob es sich um eine Herrscherin handelte. Dieser außergewöhnliche Umstand lässt vermuten, dass diese selbst regiert hat. Amenirdis war die Tochter des Kaschta – von dem man behauptet, er stamme von Bocchoris oder Bakenranef, dem einzigen König der ersten Saïten-Dynastie (der 24. der Listen), ab. Sie heiratete Pianchi [Pije], der einer der letzten Abkömmlinge der hohen Herrscher der 21. Dynastie gewesen zu sein scheint, und ihre Tochter hatte Psammetich I. zum Gemahl.

STATUE DE LA REINE AMÉNÉRITÈS

Musée du Kaire

Cette magnifique statue a été trouvée ensevelie sous les ruines d'un petit temple situé au nord de la grande enceinte de Karnac. Elle est en albâtre oriental ou arragonite. Sa hauteur, de la plante des pieds au sommet de la tête, est de 1,47 m. L'inscription gravée sur la base de la statue offre deux cartouches contenant le prénom officiel (« la divine épouse », Maut-cha-neferou) et le nom propre (« la divine main », Aménérités ou Amnartaïs [Aménardis]), comme s'il s'agissait d'une souveraine. Cette circonstance exceptionnelle fait supposer qu'elle a régné elle-même. Aménérités était fille de Kachto [Kachta], que l'on prétend descendre de Bocchoris ou Bekenranef [Bokenrenef], unique roi de la première dynastie saïte (la XXIVe des listes). Elle épousa Piankhi [Piye], qui paraît avoir été un des derniers rejetons des souverains pontifes de la XXIe dynastie, et leur fille eut pour époux Psammétik Ier.

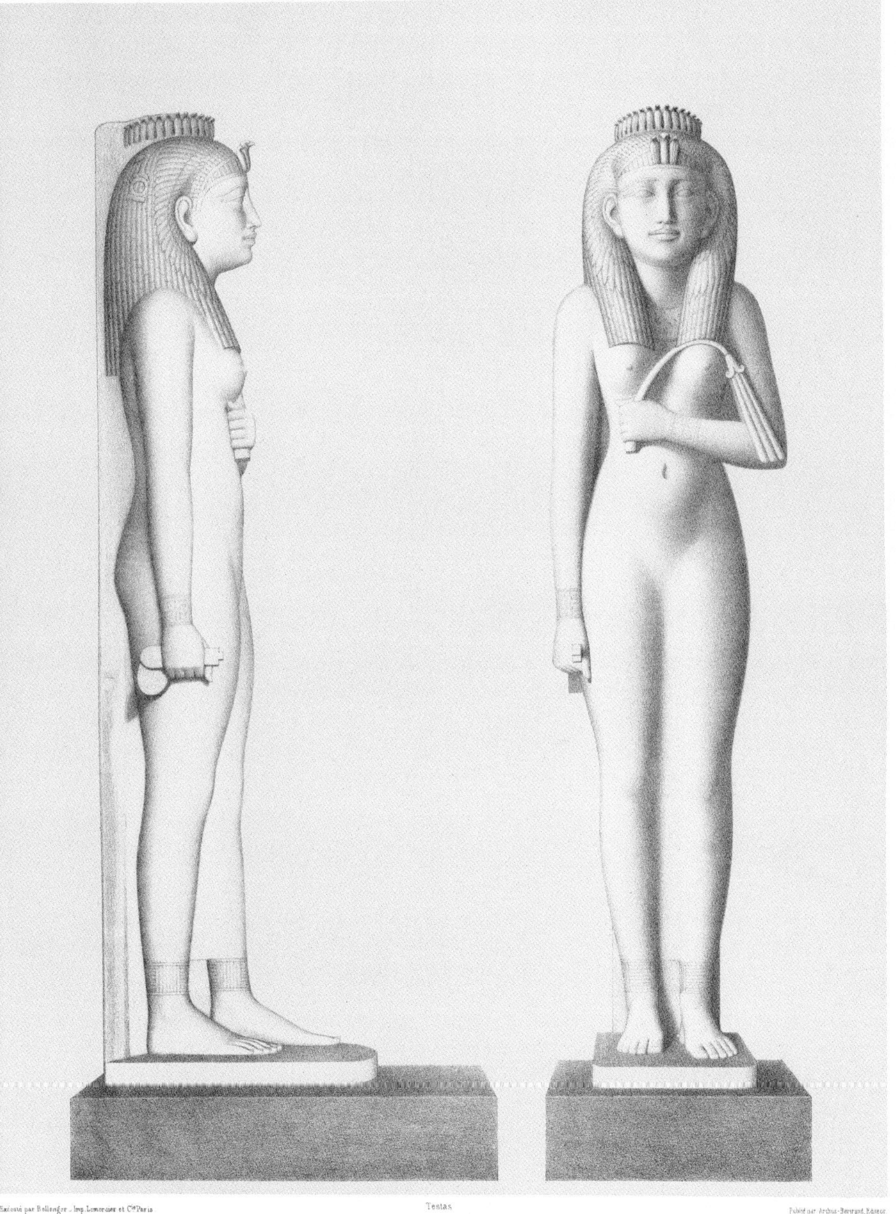

Exécuté par Bellenger. Imp. Lemercier et Cie Paris — Testas — Publié par Arthus-Bertrand, Éditeur

STATUE DE LA REINE AMÉNÉRITÈS

(MUSÉE DU KAIRE)

STUDIES OF HEADS BASED ON THE CANON OF PROPORTION

Workshops of Memphis and Thebes

This plate shows a collection of small busts in soft white limestone. Apart from the finished heads featured at nos. 5 and 6, all were for the most part rough-hewn following a canon of proportion, and traces of the drawn outline are still to be seen on the most prominent parts. All are of the same dimensions and present a similar type, with a round face and an open, smiling expression; they represent the different stages in the execution of a figure from the first rough-hewn carving right through to the finished model. The sculptors were more numerous than any other artists and in their profession they were also subjected to a more rigorous training than other artists. In the great cities they were possibly bound to spend a long period of apprenticeship copying models, particularly of the head of the reigning pharaoh, before they were permitted to work on public buildings.

KOPFSTUDIEN, NACH DEM PROPORTIONENKANON

Werkstätten von Memphis und Theben

Diese Tafel stellt eine Sammlung kleiner Büsten aus weichem, weißem Kalkstein dar. Mit Ausnahme der vollendeten Köpfe, die hier unter Nr. 5 und 6 erscheinen, sind alle mithilfe eines Proportionenkanons noch reichlich grob gearbeitet, wobei auf den hervorstehendsten Bereichen noch Spuren der Vorzeichnung zu erkennen sind; alle weisen dieselben Abmessungen auf und zeigen einen ähnlichen Typus, ein rundes Gesicht und eine offene, heitere Physiognomie; sie stellen die verschiedenen Stadien der Ausführung eines Gesichts dar – von dem grob behauenen Rohentwurf bis zum vollendeten Modell. Die Bildhauer, deren Arbeit die meisten Studien erforderte, bildete die größte Künstlergruppe. Vielleicht waren sie in den Städten genötigt, über lange Zeit Modelle und vor allem das Antlitz des herrschenden Pharaos zu kopieren, bevor sie zur Arbeit an den öffentlichen Gebäuden zugelassen wurden.

ÉTUDES DE TÊTES D'APRÈS LE CANON DE PROPORTION

Ateliers de Memphis et de Thèbes

Cette planche représente une collection de petits bustes en calcaire blanc et tendre. À l'exception des têtes terminées, qui figurent sous les n°s 5 et 6, toutes ont été largement ébauchées à l'aide d'un canon de proportion, et l'on voit encore les restes du tracé sur les parties les plus saillantes ; toutes, de mêmes dimensions, offrent un type pareil, un visage rond, une physionomie ouverte et souriante ; elles représentent les divers degrés d'exécution d'une figure depuis l'ébauche dégrossie jusqu'au modèle parfait. Les sculpteurs étaient les artistes les plus nombreux, et ceux dont la profession exigeait le plus d'études. Ils étaient peut-être astreints dans les grandes villes à copier longtemps des modèles et surtout la tête du pharaon régnant, avant d'être admis à travailler dans les édifices publics.

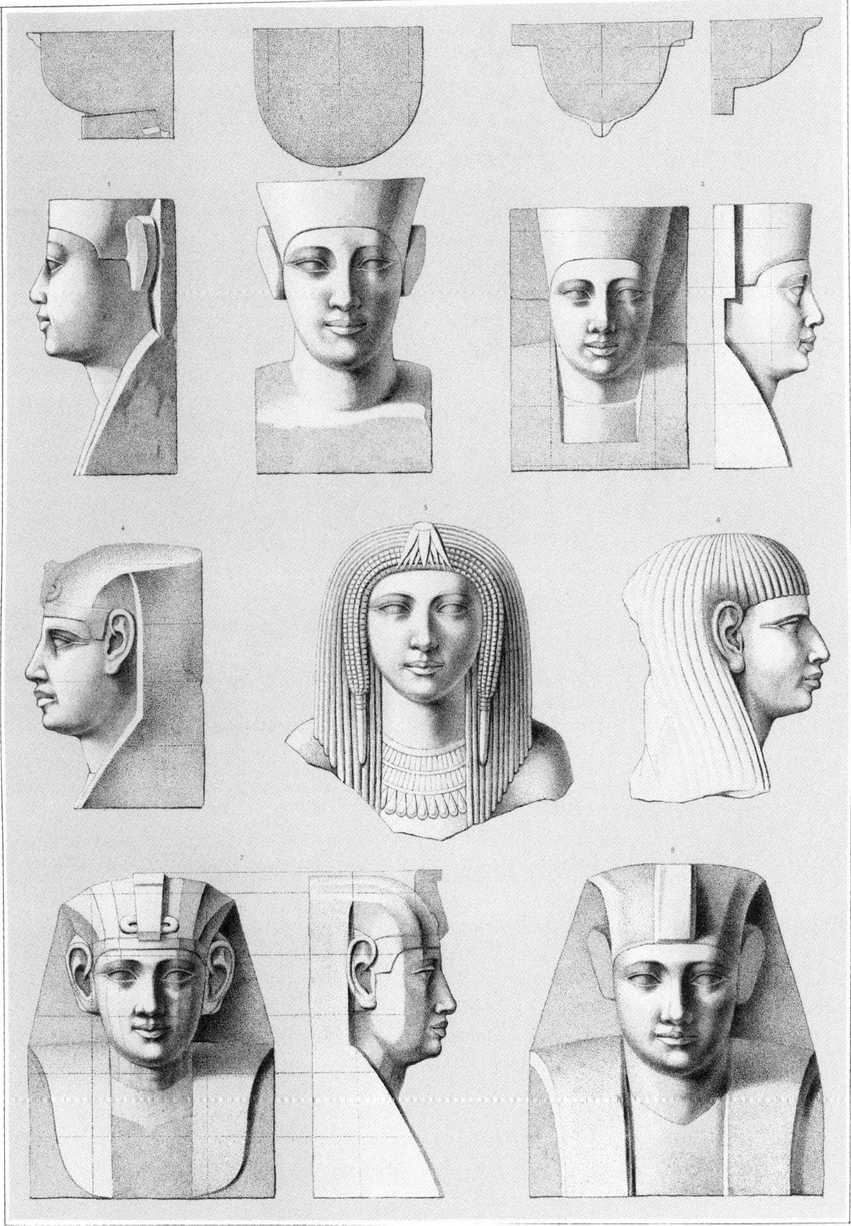

Lith. par Jehenne _ Imp. par Baugard-Maugé. E. Prisse d'Avennes. Publié par Arthus-Bertrand, Éditeur.

ÉTUDES DE TÊTES D'APRÈS LE CANON DE PROPORTION.

(ATELIERS DE MEMPHIS & DE THÈBES.)

CHAFRE [RANOFER], SCRIBE

Red-painted limestone

This statue of white, painted limestone, which is of remarkable craftsmanship, seemed to me an example well worth reproducing. Its height from the heel-bone to the top of the head is 1.7 metres. The skin was [probably] first tinted in deep yellow ochre or even thinly gilded with gold, like many other statues of the same period. The pupils are coloured reddish-brown and impart a striking quality to the gaze; the lips are delicate, the contours of the eyes are absolutely life-like and the mouth is well formed. In addition, this plate has been executed in such a way that my description is easy to understand. It is [however] annoying that the Egyptian artist, who no doubt had his reasons, should have been prompted to make the head proportionately too small for the rest of the body, particularly in comparison to the torso, which is exceptionally broad at shoulder height.

CHAFRE [RANEFER], SCHREIBER

Rot bemalter Kalkstein

Diese in bemerkenswerter Weise ausgeführte Statue aus weißem, bemaltem Kalkstein schien mir ein wirklich reproduktionswürdiges Exemplar zu sein. Ihre Höhe beträgt vom Scheitel bis zum Fersenbein 1,70 m. Das Inkarnat wurde wahrscheinlich wie bei vielen anderen Statuen derselben Zeit zunächst mit dunkelgelbem Ocker gefärbt oder sogar mit Feingold vergoldet. Die rotbraun gefärbten Pupillen lassen den Blick durchdringend wirken; die Lippen sind fein, die Augenumrisse von vollkommener Natürlichkeit, und der Mund ist schön gezeichnet. Im Übrigen ist diese Tafel so ausgeführt, dass sich meine Beschreibung gut nachvollziehen lässt. Es ist misslich, dass der ägyptische Künstler – zweifellos aus besonderen Gründen – veranlasst war, den Kopf im Verhältnis zum restlichen Körper und vor allem in Beziehung zu dem auf der Höhe der Schultern sehr breiten Torso zu klein zu gestalten.

CHAFRÉ [RANEFER], ÉCRIVAIN

Calcaire peint en rouge

Cette statue, en calcaire blanc colorié, d'une exécution remarquable, m'a paru être un spécimen vraiment digne d'être reproduit. Sa hauteur, du calcanéum au sommet de la tête, est de 1,70 m. [Probablement] la carnation fut d'abord teintée en ocre jaune foncé ou même dorée en or fin, comme beaucoup d'autres statues de la même époque. Les pupilles, qui sont colorées en brun rouge, donnent un aspect saisissant au regard ; les lèvres sont fines, les contours des yeux d'un naturel parfait et la bouche bien faite. Cette planche est, du reste, exécutée de façon à bien faire saisir ma description. Il est fâcheux que l'artiste égyptien, pour des motifs particuliers sans doute, ait été conduit à faire la tête, proportionnellement, trop petite pour le reste du corps, surtout par rapport au torse, qui est très large à la hauteur des épaules.

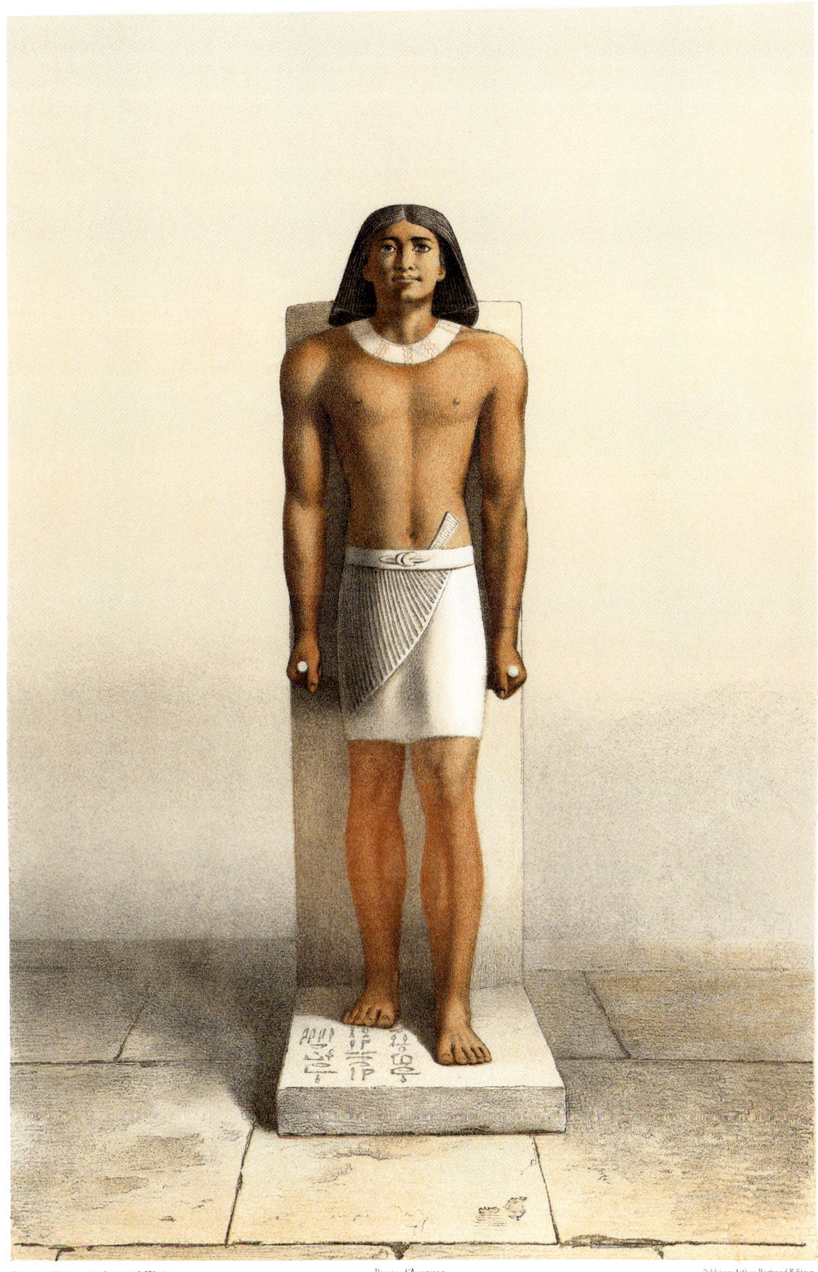

Exécuté par J. Laurens _ Imp. Lemercier & Cie Paris

Prisse d'Avennes

Publié par Arthus Bertrand, Editeur

CHAFRÉ, ÉCRIVAIN.

(CALCAIRE PEINT EN ROUGE)

FRAGMENTS FROM ICONIC STATUES (from different periods)

No. 1, an exceptionally beautiful head in white quartz, is incontestably a portrait; we owe it to an outstanding artist of one of the early Dynasties, probably the 4th.The principal feature is its remarkably good-humoured expression which is combined with the flaccidity of old age. It does not represent an Egyptian but rather one of the foreigners who, according to Herodotus, lived in a particular quarter of Memphis. [The head] was found in 1854 under buildings of Ramesses II, in a deep excavation made at Mit Rahina (Memphis) on the site of the famous temple of Ptah. No. 2 presents the head of a queen [...]. It appears to date from the Middle Kingdom and represents the pure type. No. 3 seems to me to represent perfectly the coarse type of the scholar as in no. 1, a true fellah.

BRUCHSTÜCKE IKONISCHER STATUEN (aus verschiedenen Zeiten)

Die Nr. 1, ein sehr schöner Kopf aus weißem Quartz, ist mit Sicherheit ein Porträt; sie ist einem ausgezeichneten Künstler der ersten Dynastien – wahrscheinlich der 4. – zu verdanken. Der bemerkenswert gutmütige Ausdruck ist, in Verbindung mit der Schlaffheit des Alters, ihr wichtigster Wesenszug. Sie dürfte keinen Ägypter darstellen, sondern eher einen dieser Fremden, die nach Aussage Herodots in Memphis ein bestimmtes Viertel bewohnten. Im Jahre 1854 wurde [der Kopf] in Mit Rahina (Memphis) bei einer tiefen Ausgrabung am Standort des berühmten Ptah-Tempels unter Bauwerken von Ramses II. gefunden. Die Nr. 2 zeigt den Kopf einer Königin [...]. Sie scheint aus dem Mittleren Reich zu datieren und stellt den zierlichen Typus dar. Die Nr. 3 scheint mir genau den derben Typus desselben Gelehrten darzustellen, einen echten Fellachen.

FRAGMENTS DE STATUES ICONIQUES (de différentes époques)

Le n° 1 est une fort belle tête en quartz blanc, et incontestablement, un portrait ; elle est due à un artiste distingué des premières dynasties, probablement de la IVe. Son expression remarquable de bonhomie, unie à la flaccidité du vieil âge, en fait le principal caractère. Elle ne doit pas représenter un Égyptien, mais plutôt un de ces étrangers qui occupaient à Memphis, au dire d'Hérodote, un quartier particulier. [La tête] a été trouvée, en 1854, sous des constructions de Ramsès II, dans une profonde excavation faite à Metrahenneh (Memphis) sur l'emplacement du célèbre temple de Ptah. Le n° 2 offre une tête de reine [...]. Elle paraît dater du Moyen Empire et représente le type fin. Le n° 3 me paraît représenter exactement le type grossier du même savant, un véritable fellah.

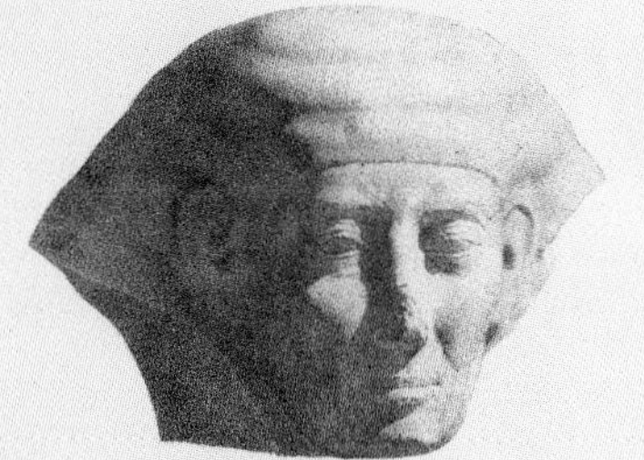

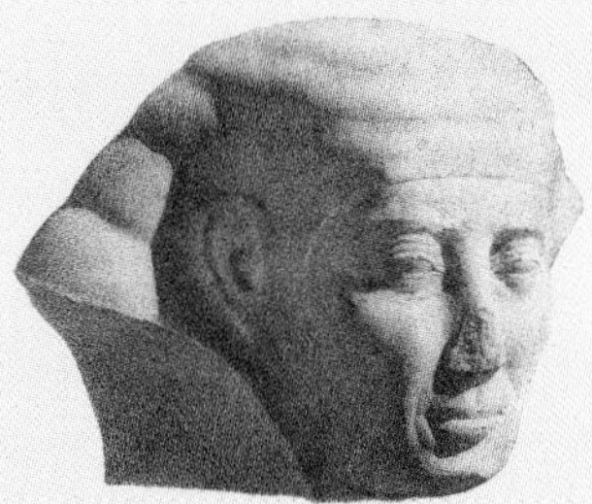

1

2

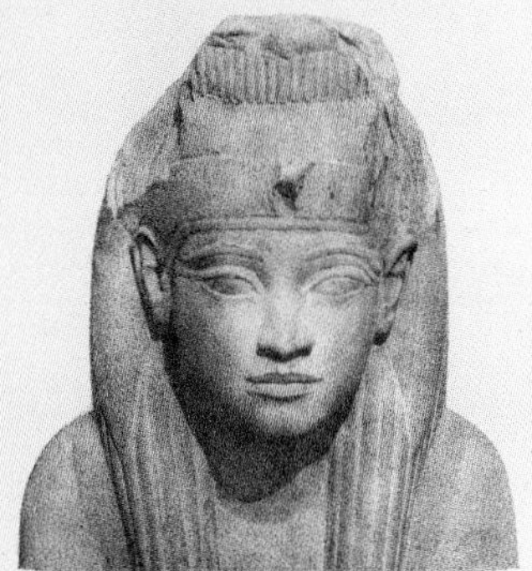

3

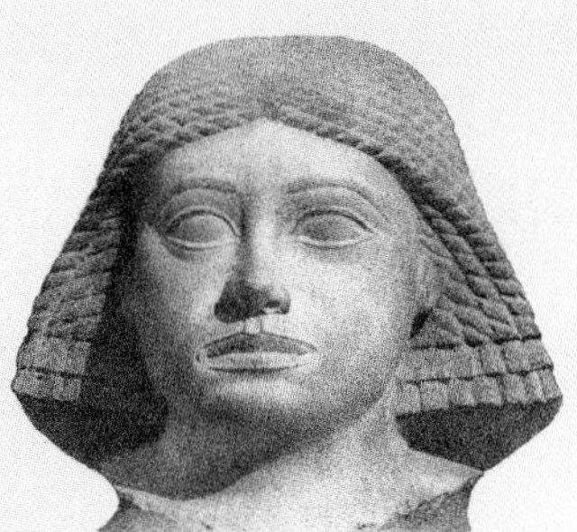

Lith par Bellenger Imp par Lemercier &Cie

Prisse d'Avennes

Publié chez Arthus-Bertrand Libraire

FRAGMENTS DE STATUES ICONIQUES

DE DIFFÉRENTES ÉPOQUES

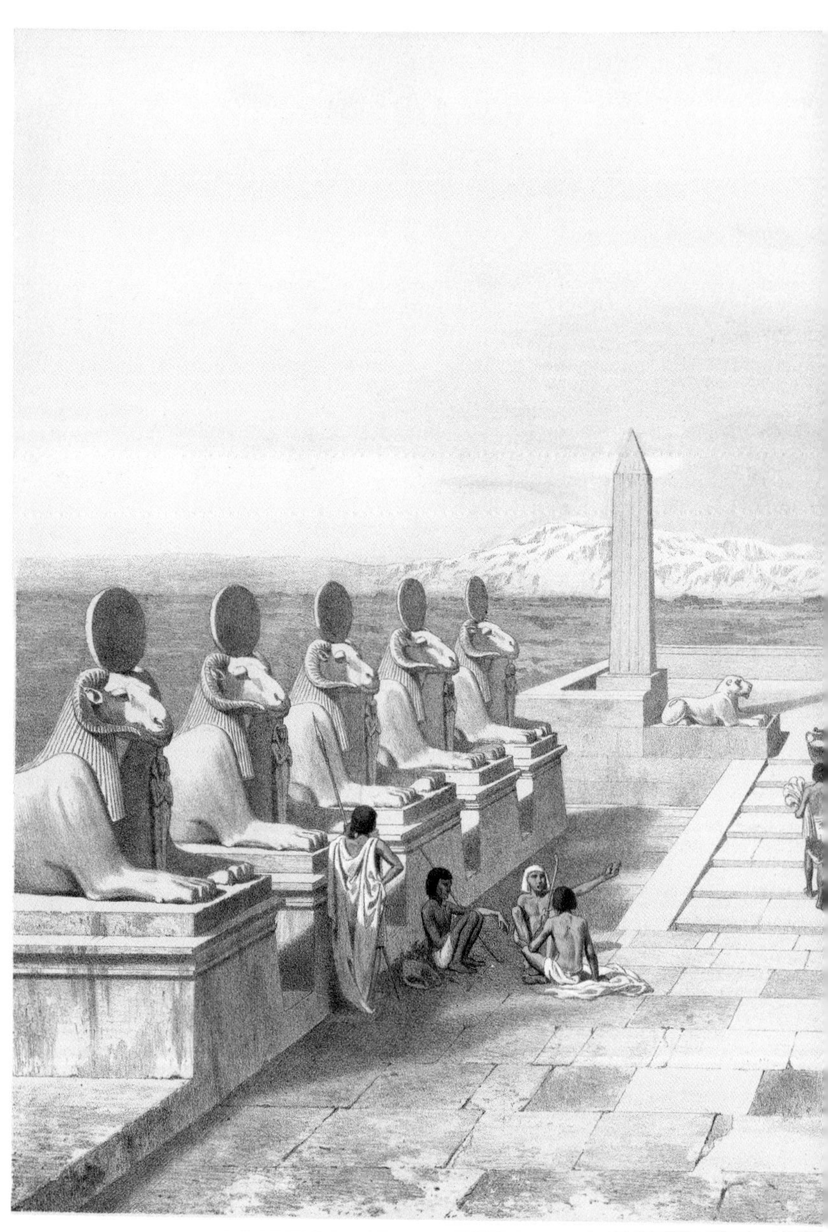

Exécuté par Didier — Imp. Lemercier et Cie Paris.

DROMOS DU G

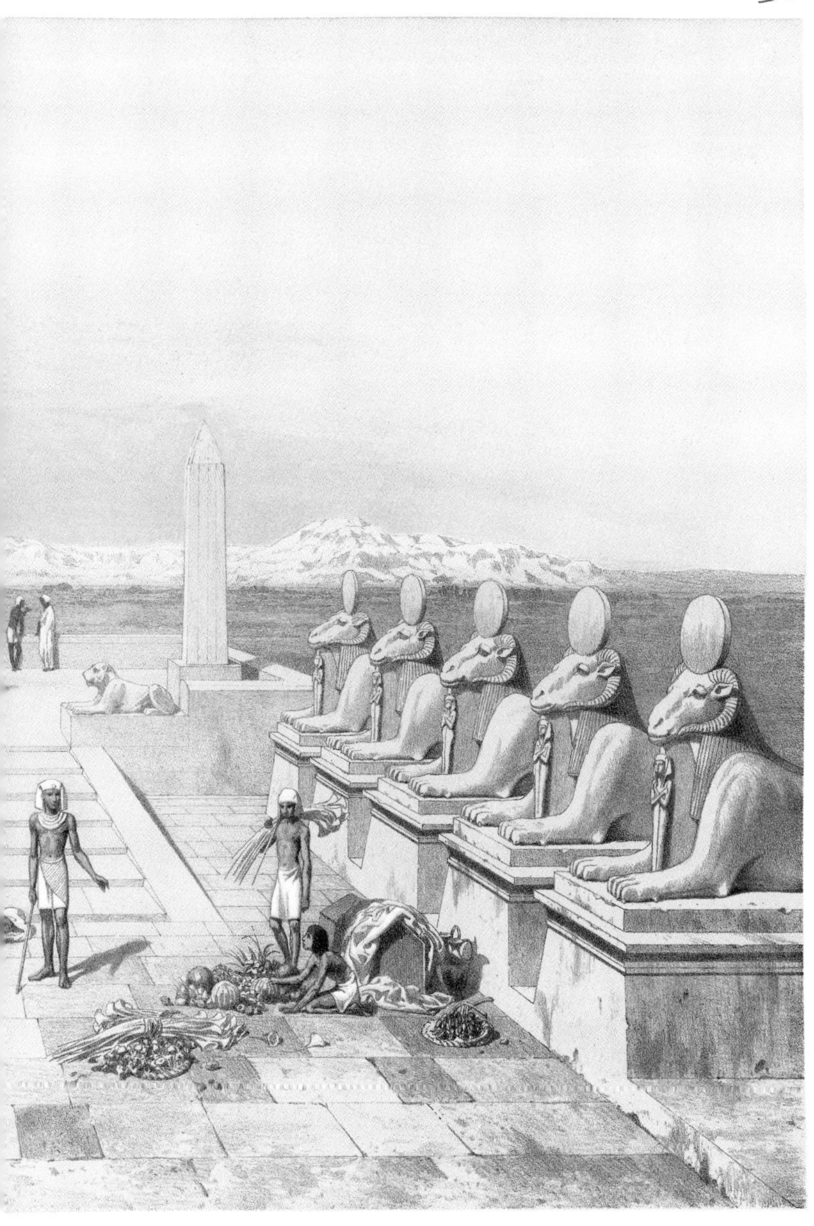

Publié par Arthus Bertrand éditeur

PLE A KARNAC.

(Pages/Seite 406/407)

DROMOS OF THE GREAT TEMPLE AT KARNAK

After the construction of all the additional buildings which made the great temples so magnificent, the principal sanctuaries were adorned with dromoi bordered with sphinxes or criosphinxes. The medial avenues were blocked 100 cubits in from the entrance by an altar raised on a platform, which in all probability was used for the presentation of public offerings and for sacrifices. [...] It is still possible to see, at the far end of the dromos of the great temple situated to the north of the Ammonium of Karnak, a stepped platform which must once have served as an altar *sub dio*. It can be seen, therefore, that this dromos was never used as an entrance, even for kings. In my opinion, this was a divine avenue leading from the sanctuary of the initiated to the altar of the people. The royal entrance to the great temples was the wonderful avenue which can be seen to the south, which is decorated with a long series of propylaea adorned with statues and masts.

DROMOS DES GROSSEN TEMPELS IN KARNAK

Als an den großen Tempeln alle Erweiterungen vorgenommen worden waren, die sie so prachtvoll werden ließen, schmückte man die wichtigsten Heiligtümer mit Dromoi, die von Sphingen oder Criosphingen gesäumt waren. Ein auf der Plattform errichteter Altar – der aller Wahrscheinlichkeit nach für Opferungen bestimmt war und öffentlich die Opfergaben aufnehmen sollte – begrenzte in etwa hundert Ellen Entfernung vom Eingang die Mittelgänge. [...] Am Ende des nördlich vom Tempel des Amun-Re [Ammonium] in Karnak gelegenen Dromos ist noch eine über Stufen zugängliche Plattform zu sehen, die einst als Altar *sub dio* gedient haben muss. Offensichtlich hat dieser Dromos also niemals als Eingang gedient, nicht einmal für die Könige. Meines Erachtens handelt es sich um eine göttliche Prachtstraße, die vom Heiligtum der Eingeweihten zum Altar des einfachen Volkes führte. Der den Königen zugedachte Eingang zu den großen Tempeln war derjenige, der im Süden zu bewundern ist und den eine lange Reihe mit Statuen und Masten geschmückter Propyläen ziert.

DROMOS DU GRAND TEMPLE À KARNAC

Quand les grands temples eurent reçu tous les accroissements qui les rendent si splendides, les principaux sanctuaires furent ornés de dromos bordés de sphinx ou de criosphinx. Les allées médiales étaient bornées à une centaine de coudées de l'entrée, par un autel, élevé sur la plate-forme, et destiné, suivant toute probabilité, à recevoir publiquement des offrandes et à servir aux sacrifices. [...] On voit encore, à l'extrémité du dromos du grand temple situé au nord de l'Ammonium de Karnac, une plate-forme précédée de gradins, qui a dû servir autrefois d'autel *sub dio*. Ce dromos, comme on le voit, n'a donc jamais servi d'entrée, même aux rois. Selon moi, c'était une avenue divine allant du sanctuaire des initiés à l'autel populaire. L'entrée royale des grands temples était celle qu'on admire au sud, et que décore une longue suite de propylées ornés de statues et de mâts.

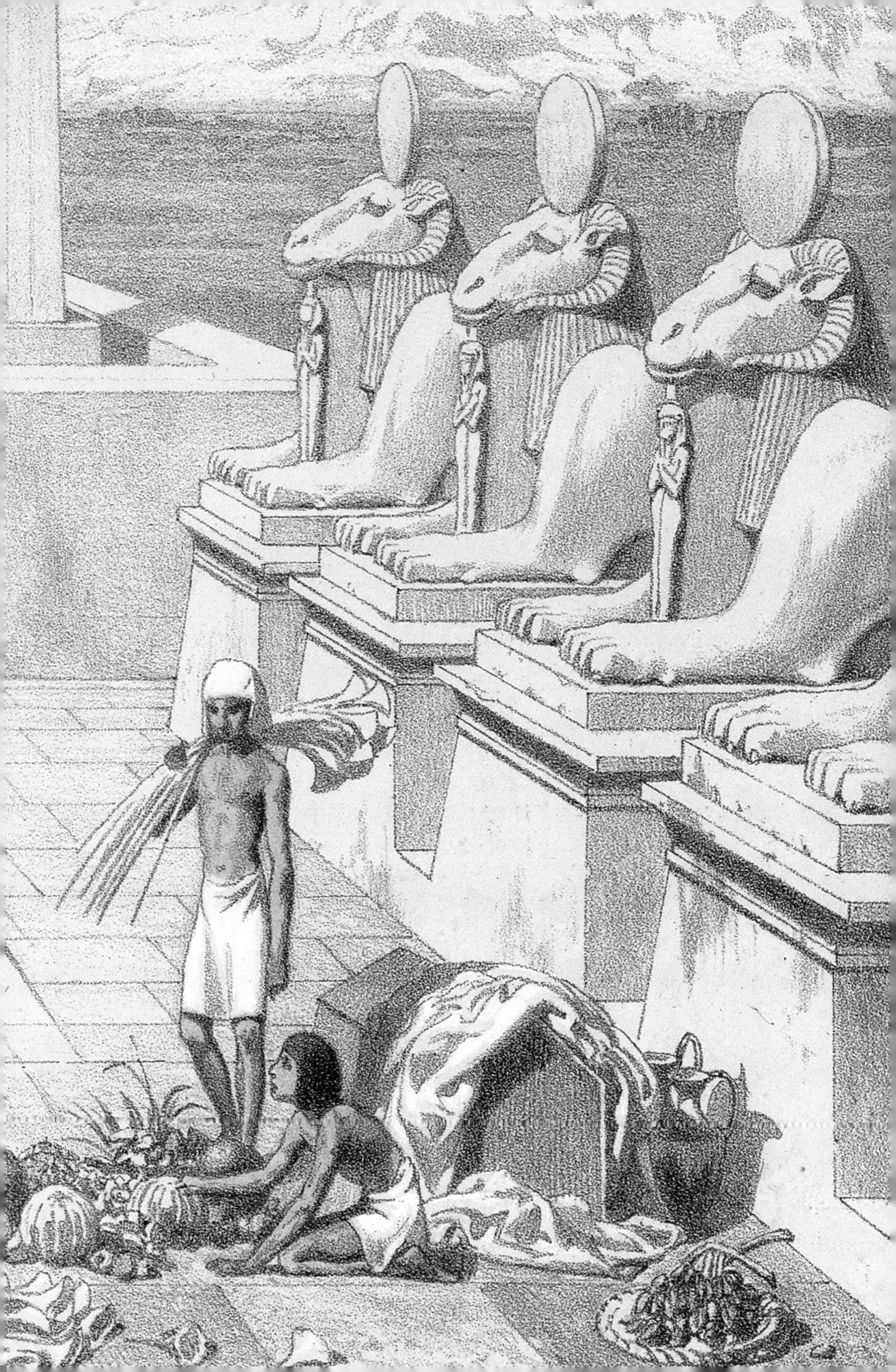

TYPES OF SPHINX

Taken from various monuments

The sphinxes represented in the bas-reliefs are of a much greater variety than those sculpted in the round. I have attempted to bring together examples of the main types in the accompanying plate. No. 1 shows a sphinx squatting on its haunches, copied from a bas-relief from the ruins of Armant. Nos. 2 and 3 are hieracosphinxes carved under Amenophis II at Karnak. No. 2 can be seen in the pronaos of the temple of Kom Ombo: on its head it wears the Pschent adorned with the uraeus and it bears the inscription of Haroeris, lord of Kom Ombo, the great god. He was the brother of Osiris and Isis. No. 4 is a handsome winged sphinx which represents the famous queen Hatshepsut. No. 5 is a winged sphinx carved on a vase in the gynaeceum of Ramesses III at Medinet Habu. No. 6 represents Amenophis III in the form of a standing sphinx, trampling beneath his feet African and Asiatic prisoners. No. 8 is a bas-relief which represents Psammetichus I or perhaps Apries, depending on whether the cartouche is a prenomen or a nomen. No. 9 is a divine sphinx, carved on a block which was subsequently used for hovels in the town of Esna. It represents the god Heka who was worshipped in that area.

SPHINX-TYPEN

Verschiedenen Denkmälern entnommen

Die als Flachrelief dargestellten Sphingen bieten weit mehr Abwechslung als die freistehend gearbeiteten. Auf der hier beigefügten Tafel habe ich versucht, die wichtigsten Typen [der Sphingen aus den Flachreliefs] zusammenzustellen. Die Nr. 1, die von einem Flachrelief aus den Überresten von Armant abgezeichnet ist, zeigt eine hockende Sphinx. Die Nr. 2 und 3 sind unter Amenophis II. in Karnak geschaffene Hierakosphingen. Die Nr. 2 ist in den Pronaos des Tempels von Kom Ombo zu sehen: Ihren Kopf ziert ein mit einem Uräus geschmückter Pschent, und sie trägt die Inschrift des Haroeris – des Herrn von Kom Ombo, des großen Gottes. Er war der Bruder der Isis und des Osiris. Die Nr. 4 ist eine hübsche geflügelte Sphinx, die die berühmte Königin Hatschepsut darstellt. Die Nr. 5 ist eine geflügelte, auf einer Vase im Gynaeceum von Ramses III. in Medinet Habu abgebildete Sphinx. Die Nr. 6 stellt Amenophis III. als stehende Sphinx dar, die mit ihren Tatzen die afrikanischen und asiatischen Gefangenen in den Staub tritt. Die Nr. 8 ist – in Abhängigkeit davon, ob es sich bei der Kartusche um einen Namen oder einen Vornamen handelt – ein Psammetich I. oder Apries darstellendes Flachrelief. Die Nr. 9 ist eine göttliche Sphinx, eingearbeitet in einen Block, der seither in den baufälligen Häusern der Stadt Esna verwendet wurde. Sie stellt den in dieser Ortschaft verehrten Gott Heka dar.

TYPES DE SPHINX

Tirés de divers monuments

Les sphinx représentés dans les bas-reliefs offrent beaucoup plus de variétés que ceux sculptés en ronde bosse. J'ai essayé d'en réunir les principaux types, dans la planche ci-jointe. Le n° 1 offre un sphinx accroupi, copié sur un bas-relief des ruines d'Erment. Les n°s 2 et 3 sont des hiéracosphinx sculptés sous Aménophis II à Karnac. Le n° 2 se voit dans les pronaos du temple d'Ombos [Kôm Ombo] : il est coiffé du pschent orné de l'uréus, et porte la légende de Haroëri [Haroéris], seigneur d'Ombos, le dieu grand. Il était frère d'Osiris et d'Isis. Le n° 4 est un joli sphinx ailé qui représente la fameuse reine Hatasou [Hatchepsout]. Le n° 5 est un sphinx ailé, sculpté sur un vase du gynécée de Ramsès III à Medineh-Tabou. Le n° 6 représente Aménophis III sous la forme d'un sphinx debout, et foulant sous ses pattes des prisonniers africains et asiatiques. Le n° 8 est un bas-relief qui représente Psammétik Ier ou peut-être Apriès, suivant que le cartouche est un prénom ou un nom. Le n° 9 est un sphinx divin, sculpté sur un bloc utilisé depuis dans les masures de la ville d'Esné. Il représente le dieu Hake [Héka] adoré dans cette localité.

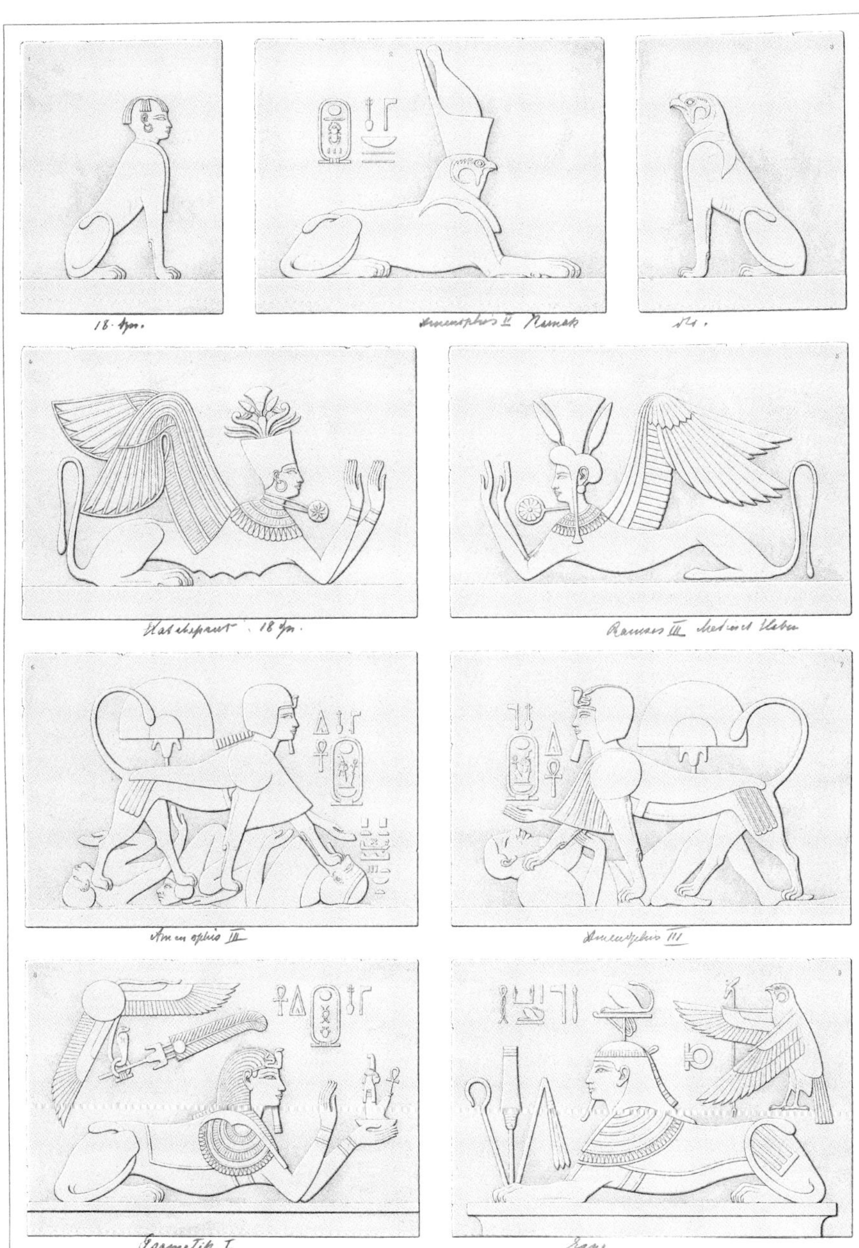

Lith. par Ollé. Imp. par Hangard-Maugé

E. Prisse d'Avennes

Publié par Arthus Bertrand, Éditeur

TYPES DE SPHINX

TIRÉS DE DIVERS MONUMENTS

ANIMALS. BREEDS OF CATTLE AND SHEEP

Cairo Museum

The talent of the Egyptian artist is at its height in the reproduction of every species of animal. It has often been said that the animals sculpted by the Egyptians were in general of far higher quality than the human figures, and that this was because the artists were allowed greater freedom in their interpretation. The works of art of the sculptors do indeed bear out the fact that they had an especial preference for the study of animal forms: the figure of the quadrupeds in particular is more vital and its essence conveyed with greater depth than that of the human figure; the pose is natural and the likeness perfect. The animals which feature most frequently on the monuments are rams, lions, oxen, horses, jackals, monkeys, hawks, ibis, vultures, crocodiles and scarabs.

TIERE. SCHAF- UND RINDERARTEN

Museum von Kairo

Die ägyptischen Künstler schulten ihre Begabung vor allem an der Wiedergabe von Tieren aller Art. Es wurde schon häufig darauf hingewiesen, dass die von den Ägyptern in Stein gehauenen Tiere im Allgemeinen wesentlich besser gelungen sind als die menschlichen Figuren und dass dies an der größeren Freiheit liegt, die die Künstler diesbezüglich genossen. Tatsächlich bezeugen die Werke der Bildhauer, dass sie die tierische Gestalt mit besonderer Vorliebe studierten: Vor allem die Gestalt der Vierbeiner wird besser erfasst und lebendiger wiedergegeben als die der Menschen; ihre Haltung ist natürlich, und die Nachahmung ist perfekt. Die am häufigsten in den Denkmälern abgebildeten Tiere sind: die Widder, die Löwen, die Rinder, die Pferde, die Schakale, die Affen, die Sperber, die Ibisse, die Geier, die Krokodile und die Skarabäen.

ANIMAUX. RACES OVINE ET BOVINE

Musée du Kaire

Le talent des artistes égyptiens s'exerça, surtout, sur les reproductions de toutes espèces d'animaux. On a remarqué souvent que les animaux sculptés par les Égyptiens avaient, en général, beaucoup plus de mérite que les figures humaines, et que cela provenait d'une plus grande liberté laissée à l'artiste. Les œuvres des sculpteurs témoignent, en effet, qu'ils étudiaient les formes animales avec une prédilection particulière : la figure des quadrupèdes surtout est rendue avec plus de vie et saisie avec plus de profondeur que la figure humaine ; la pose en est naturelle et l'imitation parfaite. Les animaux le plus souvent figurés sur les monuments sont : les béliers, les lions, les bœufs, les chevaux, les chacals, les singes, les éperviers, les ibis, les vautours, les crocodiles et les scarabées.

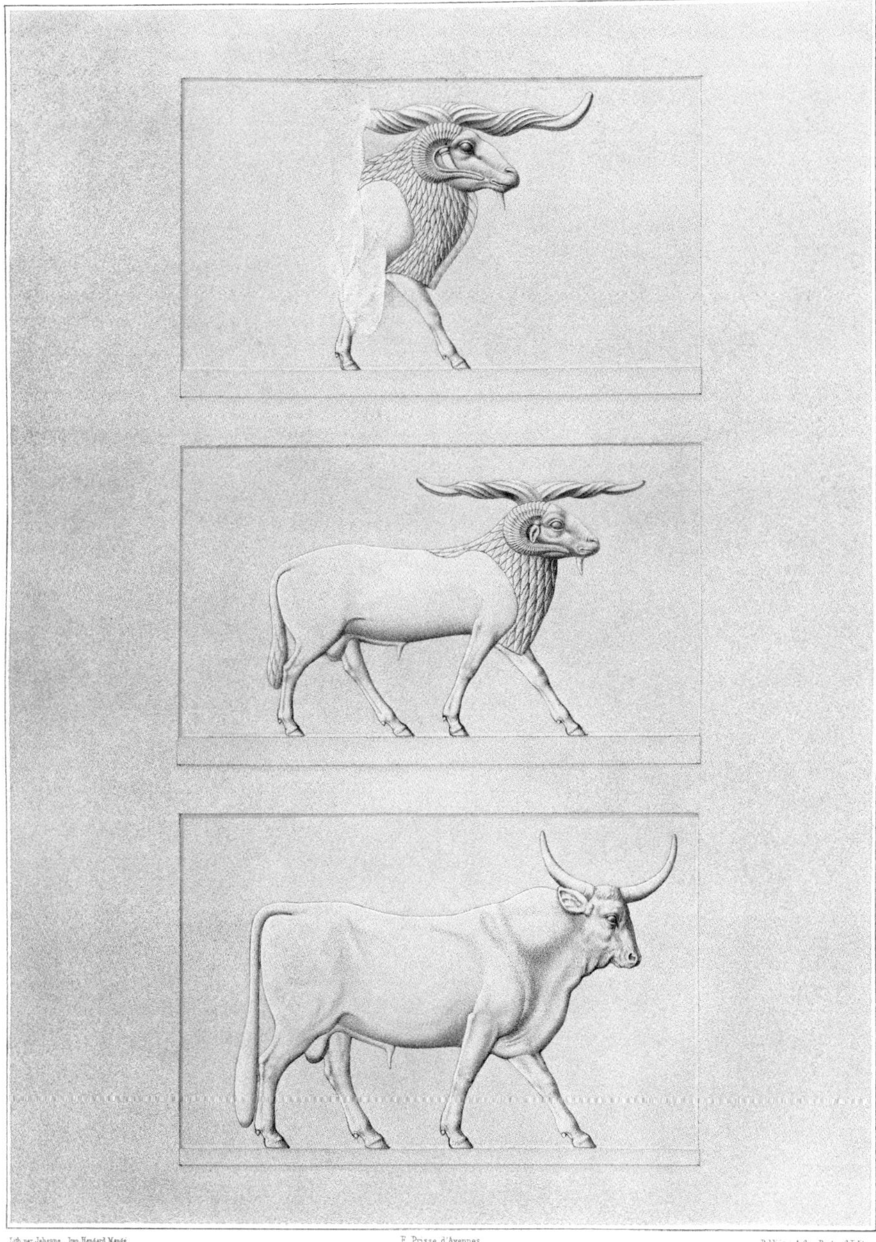

Lith. par Jehenne. Imp. Hangard Maugé. E. Prisse d'Avennes. Publié par Arthus Bertrand, Editeur.

ANIMAUX _ RACES OVINE & BOVINE.

(MUSÉE DU KAIRE. _ GRANDEUR D'EXÉCUTION.)

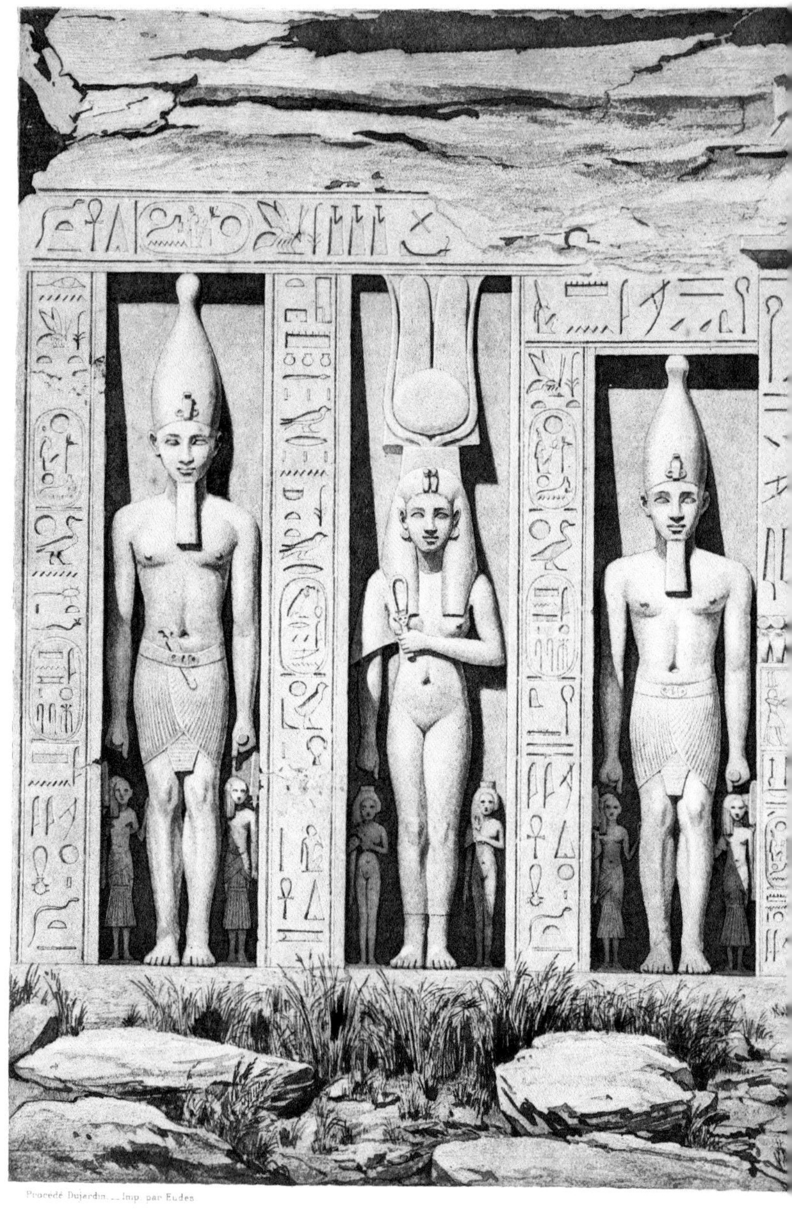

Procédé Dujardin. — Imp. par Eudes

GRAND S

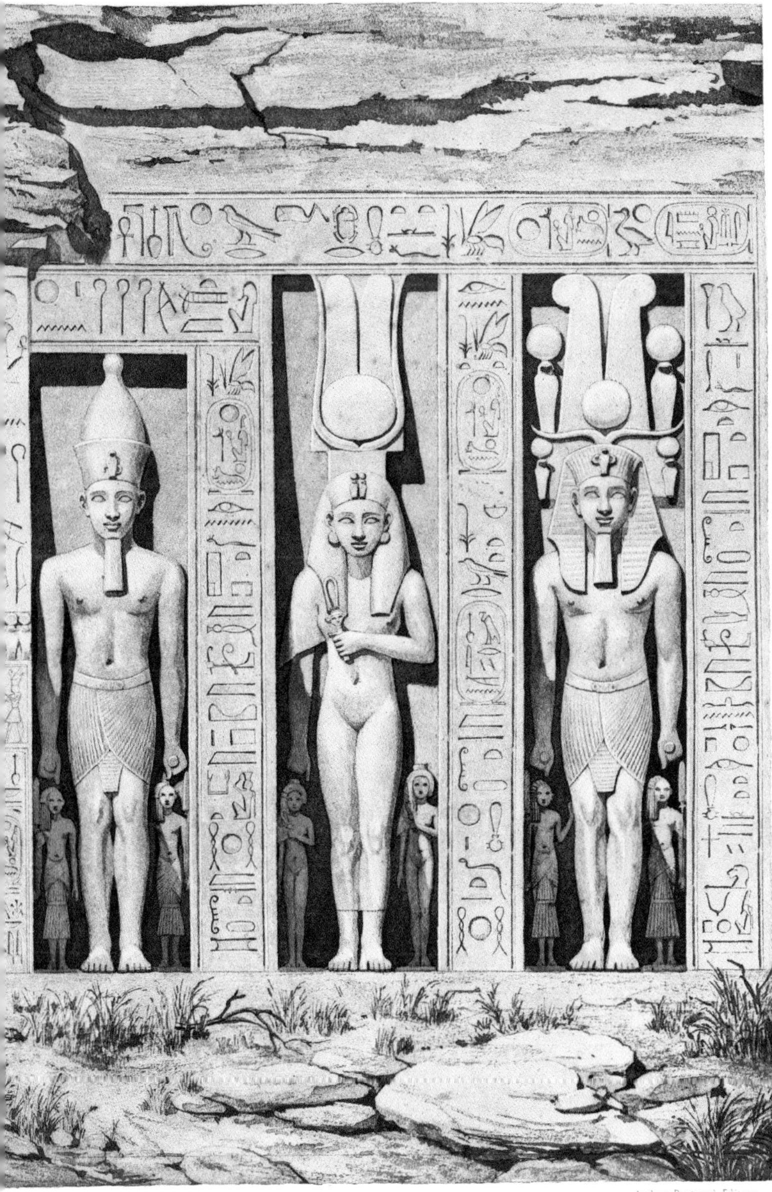
Arthus Bertrand, Editeur.

BOCHEK.

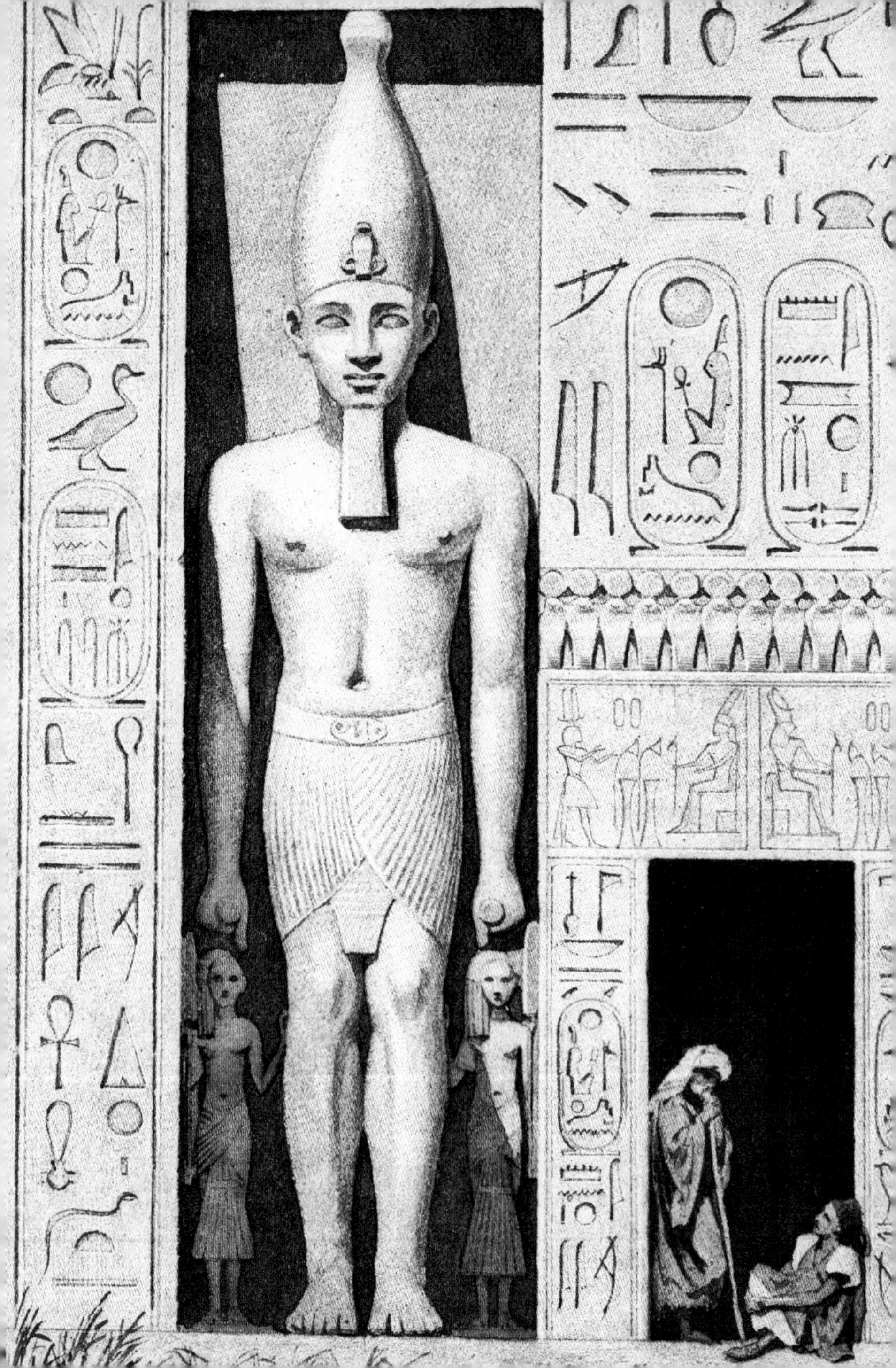

(Pages/Seite 414/415)

THE GREAT SPEOS OF ABSHEK

Nubia

I brought back from my last assignment in Egypt this very successful photographic proof of one of the rock temples of Abshek (also known as Ipsambul or Abu Simbel). Of the two rock temples which were completely hewn out of the rock here, this is the one which is normally identified by the name of Temple of Hathor; this speos is believed to have been erected by that Ramesses to whom the Greeks gave the surname Sesostris the Great in memory of his favourite wife. [...] The sculptural picture presented by this arrangement of a large number of people, superb in both its ensemble and its detail, was believed to be the façade of the underground building, doubtless because of the gigantic size of the colossi, none of which are less than 12 metres tall; however, in my opinion, it was in fact the decoration of the vestibule of the sekos, or sanctuary, which was brought to light by the destruction caused by the tomb robbers.

GROSSER SPEOS VON ABOCHEK

Nubien

Ich habe von meiner letzten Forschungsreise nach Ägypten diesen wunderbar gelungenen fotografischen Abzug eines der Felsentempel in Abochek (mit anderen Worten Ipsambul oder Abu Simbel) mitgebracht. Es handelt sich um denjenigen der beiden Felsentempel, die hier vollständig aus dem Felsen ausgehoben sind, der üblicherweise als Hathor-Tempel bezeichnet wird und von dem man annimmt, dass er von demjenigen unter den Ramessiden zum Gedenken an seine Lieblingsgemahlin errichtet wurde, dem die Griechen den Beinamen Sesostris der Große gaben. [...] Ich bin der Auffassung, dass das in seiner Gesamtheit und in seinen Einzelheiten so wunderbare bildhauerische Werk, das die Zusammenstellung all dieser Figuren bietet und das man als Fassade der unterirdischen Anlage betrachtet hat (dies sicher aufgrund der gewaltigen Größe der Kolosse, die nicht weniger als 12 m hoch sind), nichts anderes als die Ausschmückung des Vestibüls des Heiligtums oder Sekos war; freigelegt wurde das Vestibül durch die Zerstörungen, die Plünderer anrichteten.

GRAND SPÉOS D'ABOCHEK

Nubie

J'ai rapporté, lors de ma dernière mission en Égypte, cette épreuve photographique, admirablement venue d'un des spéos d'Abochek (autrement dit Ibsambout ou Abousambil [Abou Simbel]). C'est celui des deux spéos, ou temples complètement creusés à cet endroit dans le roc, qu'on a coutume de désigner par le nom de Temple d'Hathor, spéos que l'on suppose avoir été édifié par celui des Ramsès, que les Grecs ont surnommé Sésostris le Grand, à la mémoire de son épouse favorite. [...] Je pense que le tableau sculptural, si merveilleux dans son ensemble et dans ses détails, qu'offre le groupement de tous ces personnages, et qu'on a considéré comme la façade de l'édifice souterrain (sans doute en raison de la taille gigantesque des colosses qui n'ont pas moins de 12 mètres de hauteur), n'était autre chose que la décoration du vestibule du sékos, ou sanctuaire, que les dévastations des déprédateurs auront mis à découvert.

ROYAL PORTRAITS (18th, 19th and 25th Dynasties)

Thebes

All the figures of kings sculpted on the monuments are so clearly portraits that the different pharaohs have quite distinct features, and their likeness is retained throughout the different stages of life. No. 1 is the portrait of Horemheb, the pharaoh who is generally considered to be the last of the 18th Dynasty; he is sculpted on the pylon of the southern propylae at Karnak. No. 2 is the portrait of queen Tausret, of the 19th Dynasty, which is sculpted in her tomb at Thebes. No. 3 represents that queen Amenirdis who played an important role at the end of the Ethiopian occupation. She was the daughter of Kashta, sister of Shabaka and wife of Piankhi [Piye]. No. 4 presents the portrait of Taharqa, the Ethiopian conqueror, who reigned over Egypt for a quarter of a century. This sovereign belonged to the same family as the preceding queen and there is, besides, a strong resemblance between them. His portrait appears several times sculpted on the columns to the east of the great temple of Karnak.

KÖNIGLICHE PORTRÄTS (18., 19. und 25. Dynastie)

Theben

Die in den Denkmälern ausgehauenen Gesichter der Könige sind alle insoweit als Porträts anzusehen, als sich das Aussehen der verschiedenen Pharaonen deutlich voneinander unterscheidet und die Ähnlichkeit über die verschiedenen Lebensalter hinweg erhalten bleibt. Die Nr. 1 ist das Porträt des Haremhab, der als letzter Pharao der 18. Dynastie gilt; es ist im Pylon des südlichen Propyläums von Karnak ausgemeißelt. Die Nr. 2 ist das Porträt der Königin Tausret aus der 19. Dynastie; es ist in ihrem Grabmal in Theben ausgemeißelt. Die Nr. 3 stellt die Königin Amenirdis dar, die am Ende der äthiopischen Besetzung eine wichtige Rolle spielte. Sie war die Tochter des Kaschta, die Schwester des Schabaka und die Gemahlin des Pianchi [Pije]. Die Nr. 4 zeigt das Porträt des Taharqa, eines äthiopischen Eroberers, der Ägypten ein Vierteljahrhundert lang regierte. Dieser Herrscher gehört zu derselben Familie wie die zuvor erwähnte Königin, mit der er im Übrigen viel Ähnlichkeit hat. Sein Porträt erscheint mehrfach auf den Säulen im Osten des großen Tempels von Karnak.

PORTRAITS ROYAUX (XVIIIe, XIXe et XXVe dynasties)

Thèbes

Toutes les figures de rois sculptées sur les monuments sont si bien des portraits, que les différents pharaons ont des figures fort distinctes, et que leur ressemblance est conservée dans les différents âges de la vie. Le n° 1 est le portrait de Horemheb, le pharaon qui passe pour clore la XVIIIe dynastie ; il est sculpté sur le pylône des propylées du sud à Karnac. Le n° 2 est le portrait de la reine Taousert, de la XIXe dynastie ; il est sculpté dans son tombeau à Thèbes. Le n° 3 représente cette reine Aménérités [Aménardis], qui a joué un rôle important à la fin de l'occupation éthiopienne. Elle était fille de Kaschta, sœur de Sabacon [Chabaka] et épouse de Piankhi [Piye]. Le n° 4 offre le portrait de Tahraka [Taharqa], conquérant éthiopien, qui pendant un quart de siècle a régné en Égypte. Ce souverain appartient à la même famille que la reine précédente, avec laquelle il a beaucoup de ressemblance. Son portrait est sculpté, plusieurs fois, sur les colonnes à l'est du grand temple de Karnac.

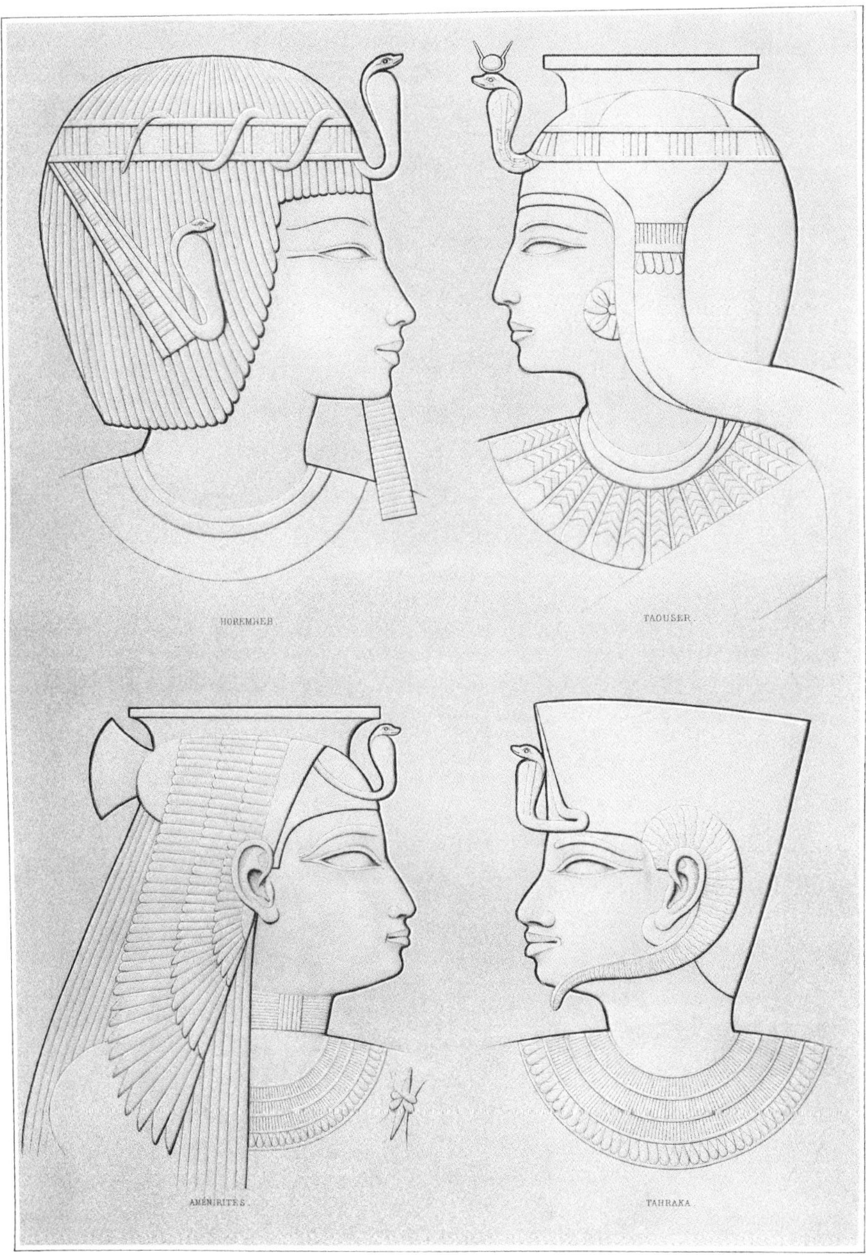

Lith. par Jehenne. Imp. Hangard-Maugé.

E. Prisse d'Avennes

Publié par Arthus Bertrand, Editeur

PORTRAITS ROYAUX.

(THÈBES. _ XVIIIe. XIXe. & XXVe. DYNASTIES.)

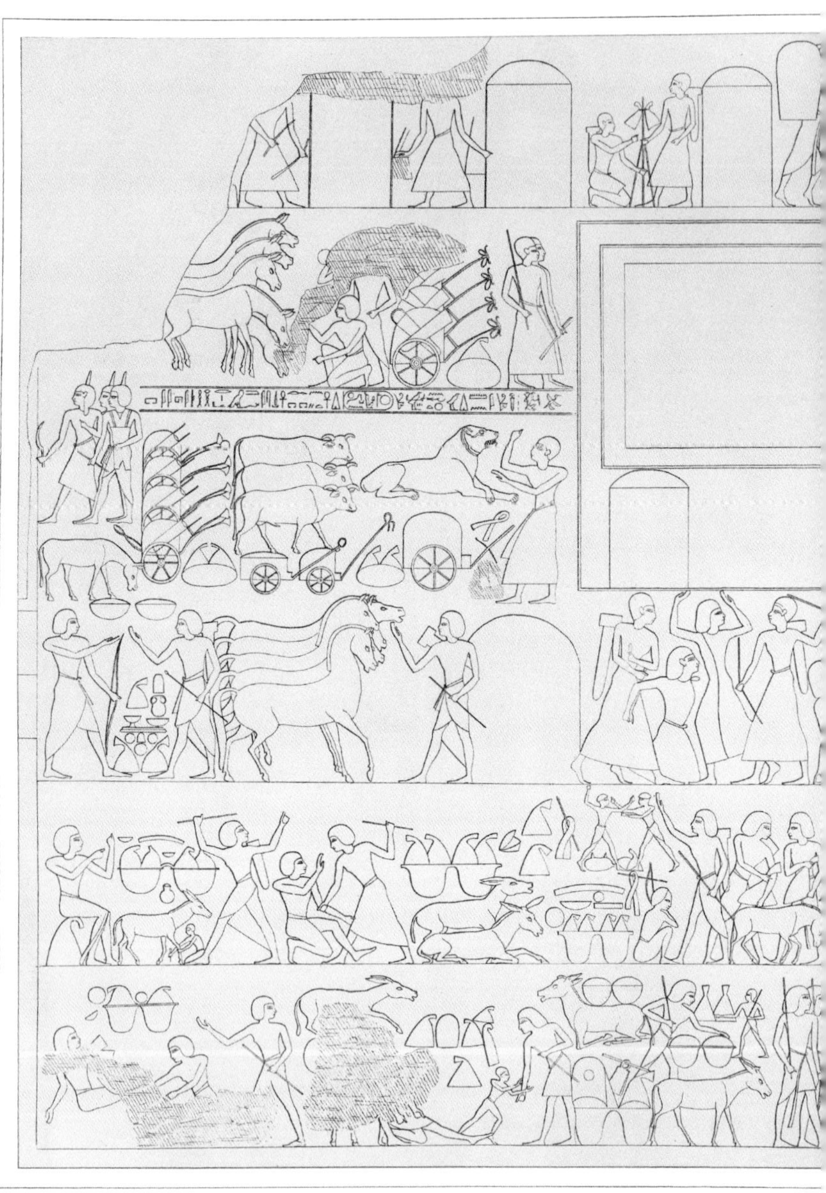

Lith. par Durand. Imp. Hangard-Maugé.

CAMP DE RAMSÈS-MEÏAMOUN I

(THÈBES._RA

E

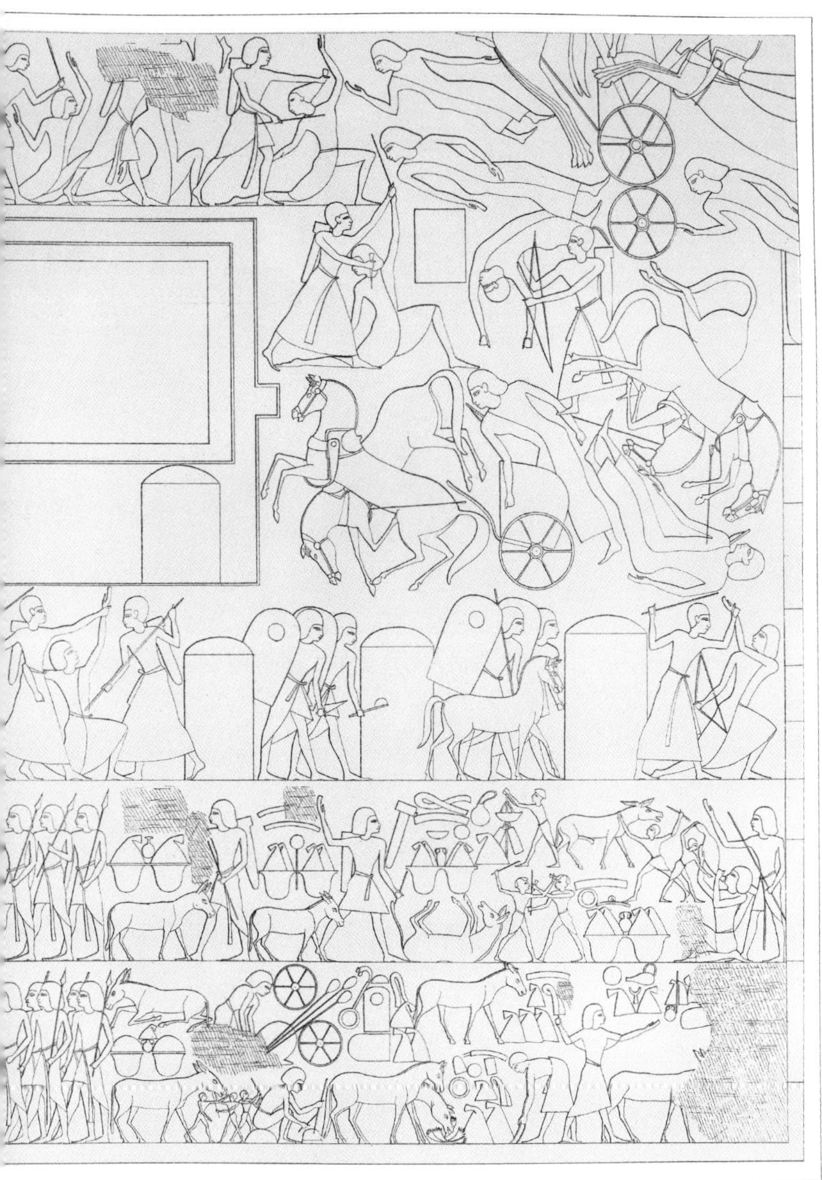

Pl. 27

Publié par Arthus-Bertrand, Éditeur

AMPAGNE CONTRE LES KHÉTAS.

DYNASTIE.)

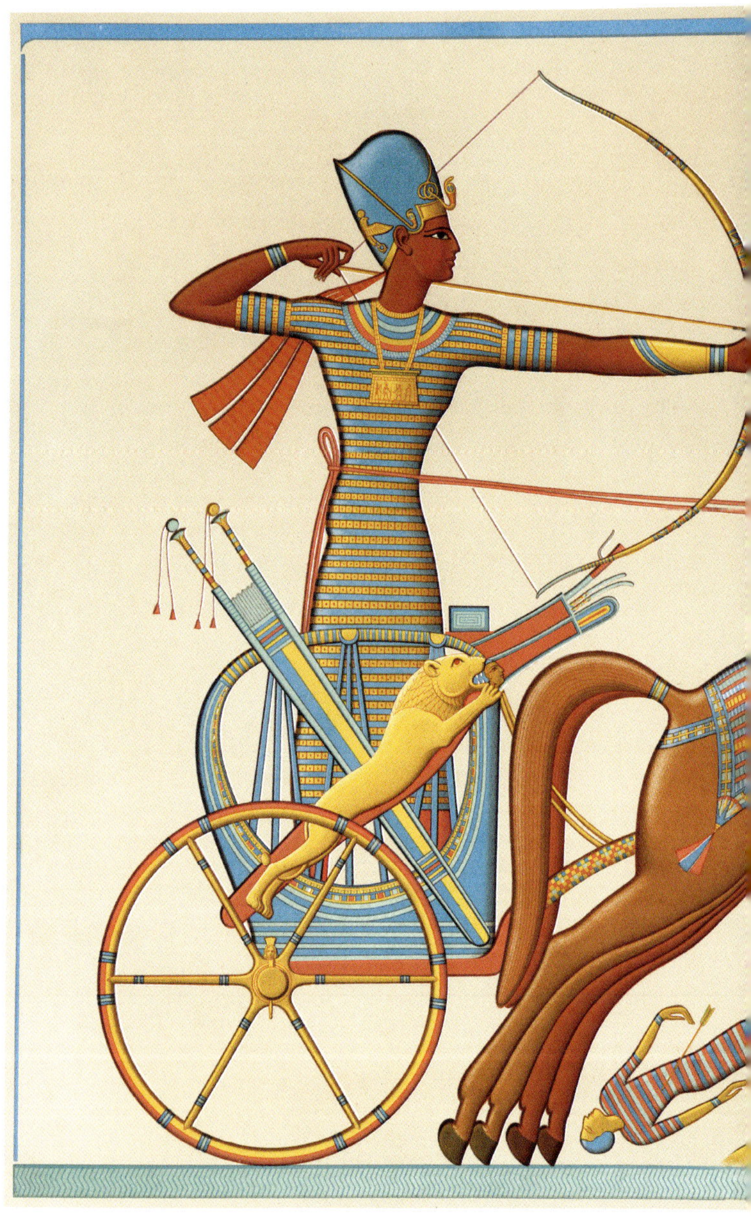

Lith par Moulin _ Imp par Hangard-Maugé

COMBAT DE RAMSÈS-MEÏAMOUN CONT

(THEBES. _ I

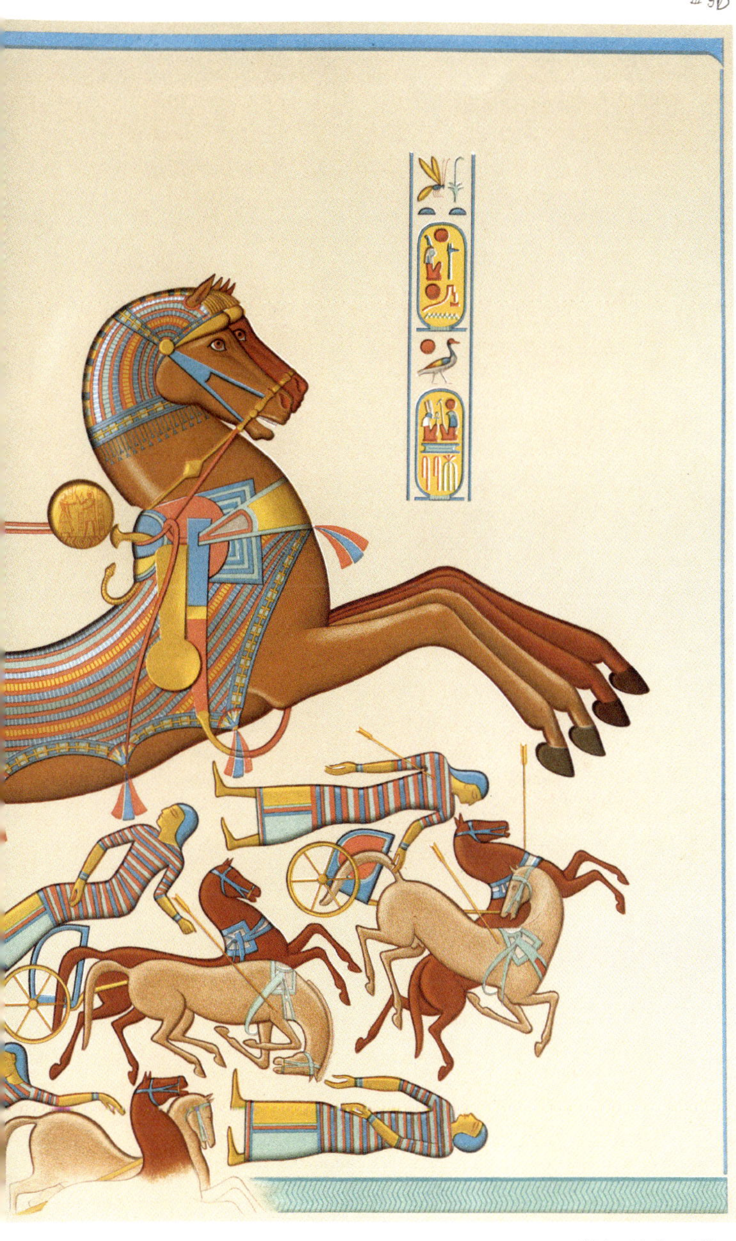

Publié par Arthus-Bertrand, Éditeur.

IÉTAS SUR LES BORDS DE L'ORONTE.

(e DYNASTIE.)

(Pages 420–423)

RAMESSES [II] MERYAMUN FIGHTING THE HITTITES (19th Dynasty)

Camp of Ramesses [II] Meryamun during his campaign against the Hittites
Battle of Ramesses [II] Meryamun against the Hittites on the banks of the Orontes
Thebes. Ramesseum

The Hittites were an ancient race of western Asia. They were often either in contact or in conflict with the Egyptians. The Hittites had extended their conquests into Syria and had chosen as their seat of power there a fortified town called Kadesh ("The Holy"). Seti I fought a long war with them. Some years later, after this Asiatic people had shaken off the Egyptian yoke and regained their independence, when Ramesses II, son of Seti I, came to the throne, he had to begin his father's campaign again in order to claim and maintain his rights. A bloody battle took place beneath the walls of Kadesh, in the valley of the Orontes, in which Ramesses was separated from his men and fought alone, performing prodigious feats of valour. This is one of the episodes forming the subject of the plate. This campaign was not destined to put an end to the war between the Egyptians and the Hittites, since it was not until the 21st year of the reign of Ramesses that a lasting truce was achieved, when a treaty of peace and alliance was signed between the two kings. The first plate represents the camp at the moment when the Egyptians were surprised by the enemy and shows the disarray caused amongst the pharaoh's troops. In the second plate Ramesses [II] Meryamun can be seen in single combat with his enemies.

(Seite/Pages 420–423)

RAMSES [II.] MERIAMUN GEGEN DIE HETHITER (19. Dynastie)

Lager Ramses' [II.] Meriamun bei seinem Feldzug gegen die Hethiter
Schlacht Ramses' [II.] Meriamun gegen die Hethiter, am Ufer des Orontes
Theben. Ramesseum

Die Hethiter waren alte Völker Westasiens. Sie hatten Auseinandersetzungen oder standen in Kontakt mit den Ägyptern. Die Hethiter hatten ihre Eroberungen bis nach Syrien ausgedehnt und als Machtzentrum eine befestigte Stadt namens Kadesch („die Heilige") auserkoren. Sethos I. führte lange Krieg gegen sie. Nachdem diese Asiaten einige Jahre später – zu der Zeit, als Ramses II. als Sohn von Sethos I. den Thron bestieg – das Joch Ägyptens abgeschüttelt und ihre Unabhängigkeit wiedererlangt hatten, war dieser Pharao gezwungen, den Feldzug seines Vaters von vorne zu beginnen, um seine Rechte einzufordern und zu wahren. Im Tal des Orontes fand unter den Mauern von Kadesch eine blutige Schlacht statt, in der Ramses – von den Seinen getrennt – tapfer allein kämpfte und dabei wahre Wunder vollbrachte. Die Tafel hat eine dieser Episoden zum Gegenstand. Da es vor dem 21. Regierungsjahr des Ramses – als ein Friedens- und Bündnispakt zwischen den beiden Herrschern unterzeichnet wurde – keinen dauerhaften Waffenstillstand gab, sollte dieser Feldzug den Krieg zwischen Ägyptern und Hethitern jedoch noch nicht beenden. Die erste Tafel stellt das Lager im Moment des überraschenden feindlichen Überfalls und die dadurch unter den Truppen des Pharaos verursachte Verwirrung dar. Auf der zweiten sieht man Ramses [II.] Meriamun allein im Kampf gegen seine Feinde.

RAMSÈS-MEÏAMOUN [RAMSÈS II] CONTRE LES KHÉTAS (XIXe dynastie)

Camp de Ramsès-Meïamoun [Ramsès II] dans sa campagne contre les Khétas
Combat de Ramsès-Meïamoun [Ramsès II] contre les Khétas sur les bords de l'Oronte
Thèbes. Ramesseum

Les Khétas étaient d'anciens peuples de l'Asie occidentale. Ils furent souvent en rapport ou aux prises avec les Égyptiens. Les Khétas [les Hittites] avaient étendu leurs conquêtes jusqu'en Syrie et choisi, pour siège de leur puissance, une ville fortifiée appelée Qodesh (« la Sainte »). Séti Ier leur fit une longue guerre. Quelques années après, ces Asiatiques ayant secoué le joug de l'Égypte et recouvré leur indépendance, à l'époque où Ramsès II, fils de Seti Ier, parvenait au trône, ce pharaon fut obligé de recommencer la campagne de son père pour revendiquer et maintenir ses droits. Une bataille sanglante eut lieu sous les murs de Qodesh [Kadesh], dans la vallée de l'Oronte, dans laquelle Ramsès, séparé des siens, combattit seul et fit des prodiges de valeur. C'est un des épisodes qui forme le sujet de la planche. Cette campagne ne devait pas mettre fin à la guerre entre les Égyptiens et les Khétas, puisqu'elle n'eut point de trêve durable avant la 21e année du règne de Ramsès, époque à laquelle fut signé un traité de paix et d'alliance entre les deux souverains. La première planche représente le camp au moment de la surprise de l'ennemi, et le désarroi qu'elle causa parmi les troupes du pharaon. Dans la seconde, on voit Ramsès-Meïamoun [Ramsès II], combattant seul ses ennemis.

COMBAT OF SETI I AGAINST THE CHIEFS OF THE TJEHENU (19th Dynasty)

Thebes. Karnak

This magnificent picture forms part of the historic bas-reliefs carved on the surrounding walls of the hypostyle hall of the great temple of Karnak. The Egyptian hero has got down from his chariot and is fighting hand to hand with the enemy chiefs. One of them has already fallen, struck down by the pharaoh's javelins; the pharaoh tramples him underfoot so that he can grasp the arm of the other chief, who has been felled to the ground, wounded and can offer no further resistance to the blow which threatens him. The inscriptions, which are unfortunately very worn, identify these two princes as chiefs of the Tjehenu or Libyans and sons of kings; they have long hair with feathers in it and wear floating robes.

SCHLACHT SETHOS' I. GEGEN DIE ANFÜHRER DER TEHENU (19. Dynastie)

Theben. Karnak

Dieses prachtvolle Bild gehört zu den historischen Flachreliefs, die in die Umfassungsmauer des Hypostyls im großen Tempel von Karnak eingearbeitet sind. Der von seinem Wagen herabgestiegene ägyptische Held kämpft Mann gegen Mann gegen die feindlichen Anführer. Einer von ihnen ist bereits unter den Speeren des Pharaos gefallen und wird in den Staub getreten, um den anderen Anführer – der verletzt und erschöpft dem bedrohlichen Schlag keinen Widerstand mehr entgegensetzt – am Arm packen zu können. Die beiden Prinzen, die die leider sehr knappen Inschriften als Anführer der Tehenu oder Libyer und Königssöhne bezeichnen, tragen lange, von Federn überragte Zöpfe und ein fließendes Gewand.

COMBAT DE SÉTI Ier CONTRE LES CHEFS DES TÉHENNOU (XIXe dynastie)

Thèbes. Karnac

Ce magnifique tableau fait partie des bas-reliefs historiques sculptés sur les murs d'enceinte de la salle hypostyle du grand temple de Karnac. Descendu de son char, le héros égyptien combat corps à corps avec les chefs ennemis. Un d'eux, déjà tombé sous les javelots du pharaon, est foulé aux pieds pour saisir par le bras l'autre chef qui, blessé et terrassé, n'offre plus de résistance au coup qui le menace. Ces deux princes, que les inscriptions, malheureusement très frustes, désignent comme chefs des Téhennou ou Libyens et comme fils de roi, portent de longues tresses surmontées de plumes et une robe flottante.

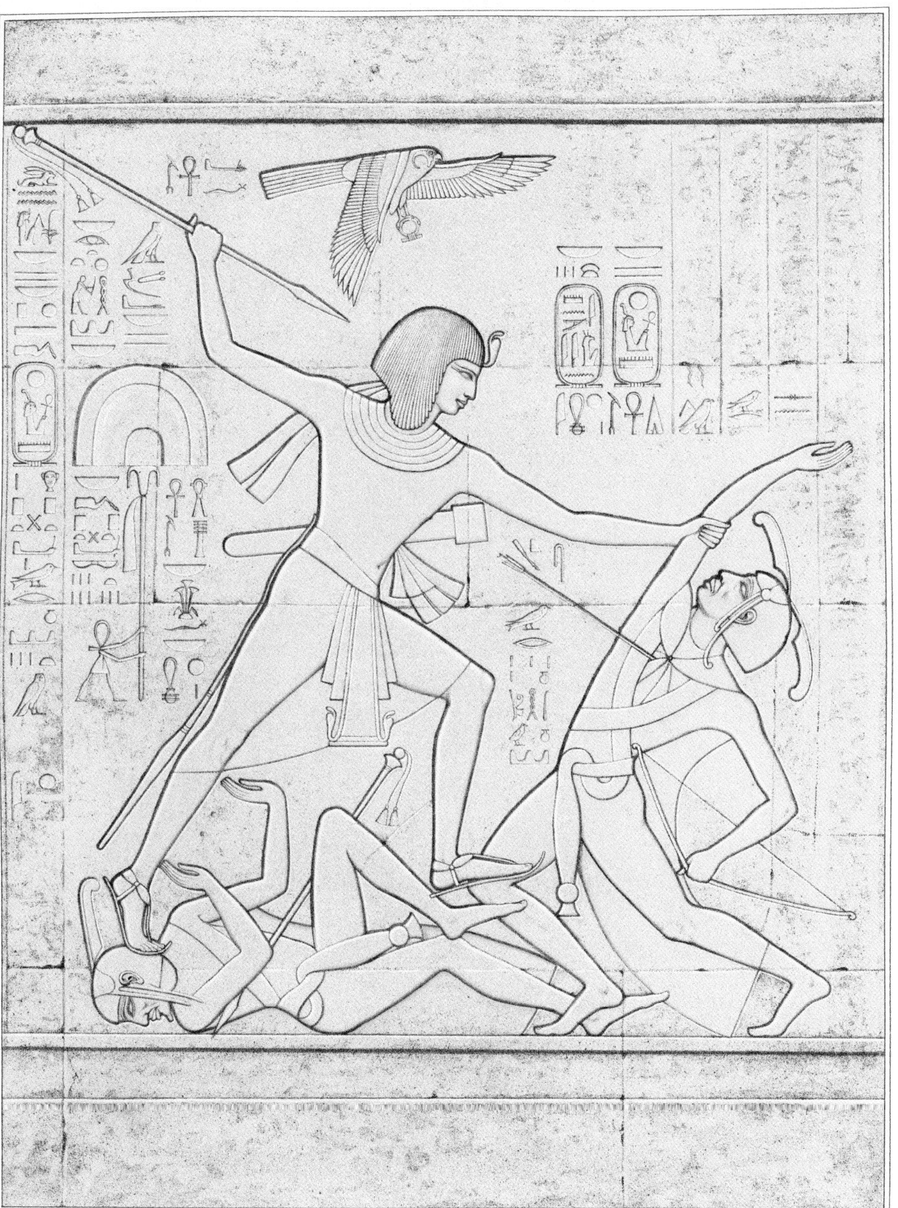

Lith. par Jeheune _ Imp. par Hangard-Maugé. E. Prisse d'Avennes. Publié par Arthus Bertrand Éditeur

COMBAT DE SÉTI 1ER CONTRE LES CHEFS DES TÉHENNOU.

(THÈBES-KARNAC. _ XIXe DYNASTIE.)

THE GODDESS ANUKIS AND RAMESSES II (19th Dynasty)

Talmis

This painting on a bas-relief illustrates the manner in which the Egyptian artists, at four different periods, represented goddesses suckling. [This] subject appears most frequently from the New Kingdom onwards, where a goddess is suckling the third person of the triad or, by assimilation, the son of the king, since in the triads the god son always plays a role which makes him more nearly akin to humanity. In the same way that Anukis (who in my opinion was the inspiration for the goddess Ananke of the Greeks) is seen at Silsila feeding Ramesses II, so Isis also appears suckling Horus at Philae and Hathor giving the breast to Seti I at Karnak.

DIE GÖTTIN ANUKIS UND RAMSES II. (19. Dynastie)

Talmis

Dieses bemalte Flachrelief soll zeigen, auf welche Weise die ägyptischen Künstler zu vier verschiedenen Zeiten die Nährmutter-Gottheiten darstellten. Vom Neuen Reich an erscheint [das] Thema einer Göttin am häufigsten, die der dritten Figur der Trias oder dem mit dieser gleichgesetzten Königssohn die Brust gibt – der Gottessohn spielt in den Triaden immer eine Rolle, die ihn der Menschheit annähert. Geradeso, wie Anukis – die uns die Vorläuferin der griechischen Göttin Ananke zu sein scheint – [den Pharao] Ramses II. in Dschabal as-Silsila nährt, so stillt auch Isis auf Philae Horus, und Hathor gibt in Karnak dem Pharao Sethos I. die Brust.

LA DÉESSE ANOUKÉ ET RAMSÈS II (XIXe dynastie)

Talmis

Cette peinture sur bas-relief est une reproduction pour faire connaître de quelle façon, à quatre époques différentes, les artistes égyptiens avaient représenté les déesses nourricières. [Ce] sujet se présente le plus fréquemment à partir du nouvel Empire, celui d'une déesse allaitant le troisième personnage de la triade ou sous son assimilation le fils du roi, parce que, dans les triades, le dieu fils joue toujours un rôle qui le rapproche de l'humanité. De même que l'on voit Anouké, qui nous paraît être l'idée mère de l'Anankè des Grecs, nourrissant Ramsès II à Silsilis [Gebel el-Silsileh], on voit encore Isis allaitant Horus à Philæ, et Hathor donnant le sein à Séti Ier à Karnac.

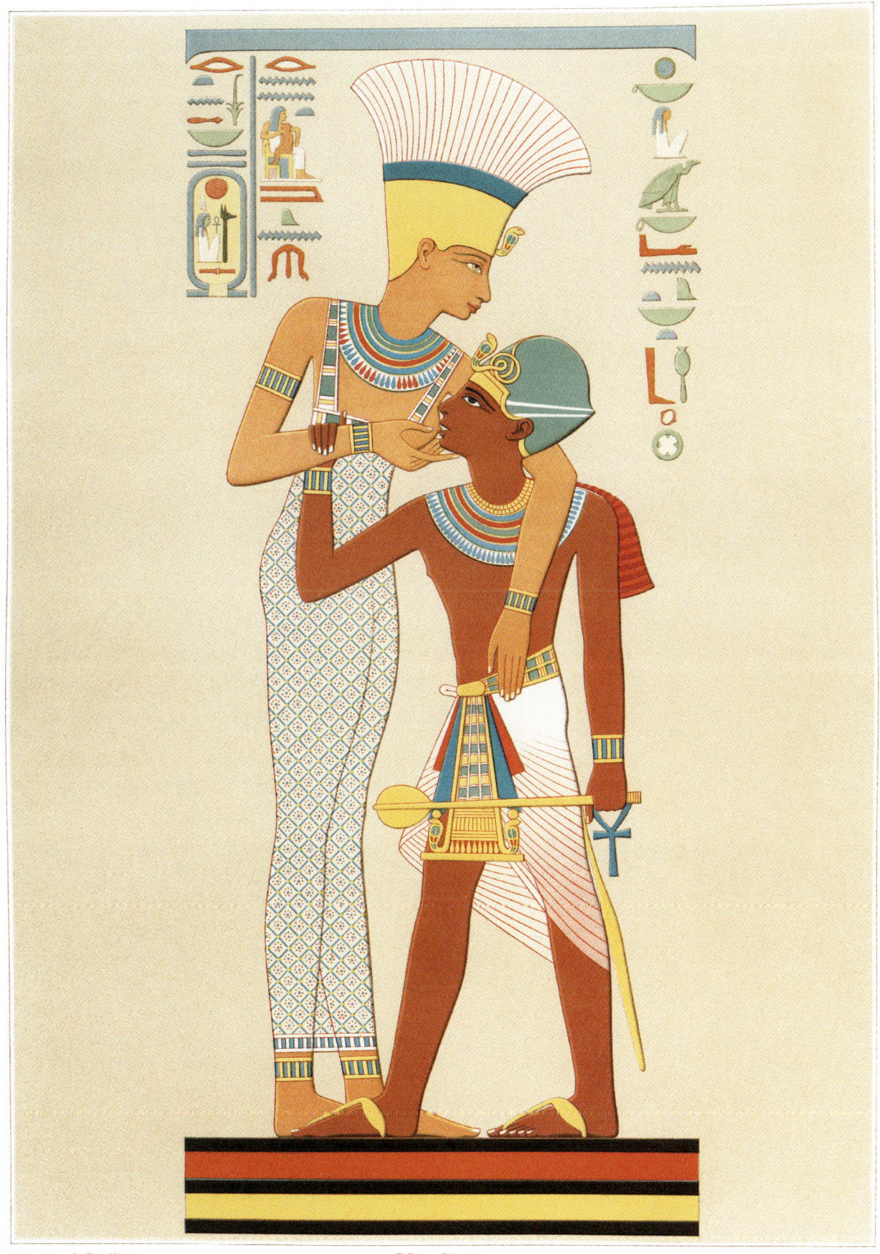

Lith par Jehenne. Imp. Hangard-Maugé — E. Prisse d'Avennes — Publié par Arthus-Bertrand, Éditeur

LA DÉESSE ANOUKÉ & RAMSÈS II.

(TALMIS. — XIXe DYNASTIE.)

COLOSSUS OF RAMESSES II (19th Dynasty)

Memphis

Colossi invariably represent pharaohs and not gods. The colossus which is the subject of this plate represents one of the most famous pharaohs of the New Kingdom. This statue, which is equally remarkable for its size and for the beauty of its shape and nobility of its style, was found buried at Memphis. It is much damaged: the Pschent which crowned the head is half broken, the feet are broken off and the supporting pillar at the back of the statue is completely fragmented. It is one of the finest portraits of Ramesses II, whose name is engraved in hieroglyphic characters on the belt and on the roll of papyrus held in the left hand. On that side, on the mount which supported the leg, can be seen the remains of a figure in bas-relief and a hieroglyphic inscription which relate to a princess, probably Bintanath, who appears to be guiding the steps of her father. When it [the colossus] was complete, it must have measured around 14 metres from the top of the Pschent to the pedestal.

KOLOSS VON RAMSES II. (19. Dynastie)

Memphis

Die Kolosse stellen stets Pharaonen, aber keine Götter dar. Der Koloss, der Gegenstand dieser Tafel ist, stellt einen der berühmtesten Pharaonen des Neuen Reiches dar. Diese Statue, die nicht weniger durch die Schönheit der Formen und die Erhabenheit des Stils als durch ihre Größe bemerkenswert ist, wurde auf dem Boden von Memphis gefunden. Sie ist stark verstümmelt: Die Doppelkrone [Pschent], die auf dem Kopf saß, ist halb zerbrochen, die Füße sind abgebrochen, und der Rückenpfeiler, der die Statue stützte, ist vollständig verwittert. Es ist eines der schönsten Porträts von Ramses II., dessen Name in Hieroglyphenschrift auf dem Gürtel und auf der Rolle, die er in der linken Hand hält, eingeschnitten ist. Auf dieser Seite sind auf dem Pfosten, der das Bein stützte, die Reste einer als Flachrelief gearbeiteten Figur und einer Hieroglypheninschrift zu erkennen; diese bezog sich auf eine Prinzessin – wahrscheinlich Bintanat –, die die Schritte ihres Vaters zu lenken scheint. Als er [dieser Koloss] vollständig war, muss er von der Kronenspitze bis zum Postament etwa 14 m gemessen haben.

COLOSSE DE RAMSÈS II (XIXe dynastie)

Memphis

Les colosses représentent, invariablement, des pharaons, et non des dieux. Le colosse qui fait l'objet de cette planche représente un des plus célèbres pharaons du nouvel Empire. Cette statue, remarquable par sa grandeur non moins que par la beauté des formes et la noblesse du style, a été retrouvée sur le sol de Memphis. Elle est fort mutilée : le pschent qui couronnait la tête est à demi brisé, les pieds sont rompus et le pilier dorsal qui soutenait la statue est entièrement délité. C'est un des plus beaux portraits de Ramsès II, dont le nom est gravé, en caractères hiéroglyphiques, sur la ceinture et sur le rouleau que tient la main gauche. On aperçoit de ce côté, sur le montant qui soutenait la jambe, les restes d'une figure en bas-relief et d'une légende hiéroglyphique qui se rapportent à une princesse, probablement Batianti [Bentanat], qui semble guider les pas de son père. Quand il [ce colosse] était dans son entier, il devait avoir, du sommet du pschent au piédestal, environ 14 mètres.

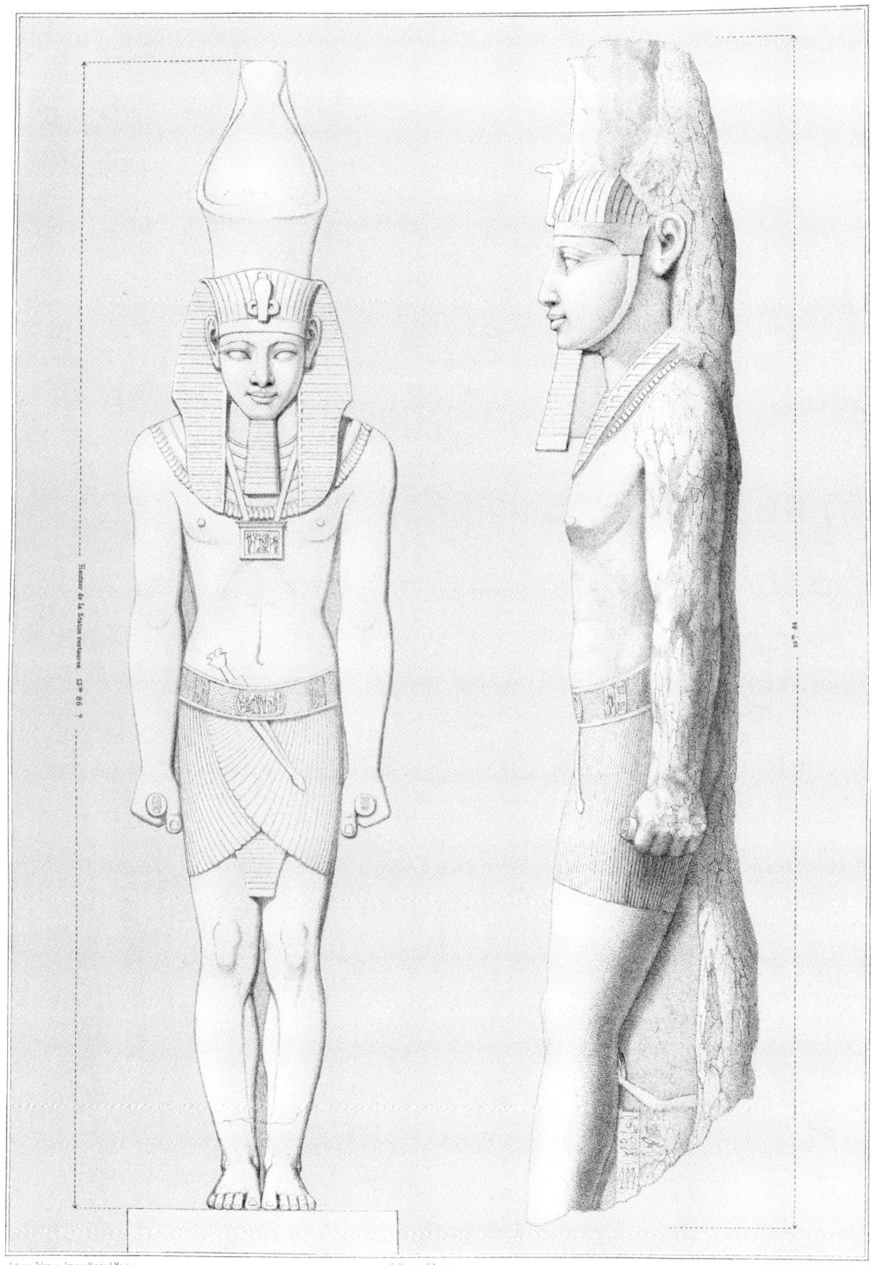

Lith par Jobarne . Imp par Hangard-Maugé. E. Prisse d'Avennes. Publié par Arthus Bertrand, Éditeur

COLOSSE DE RAMSÈS II.

(MEMPHIS _ XIXe DYNASTIE.)

FRAGMENTS FROM MILITARY BAS-RELIEFS (19th Dynasty)

Abshek and Thebes

On this plate I have included two bas-reliefs showing war chariots, in order to present two groups of horses. The first one forms part of the huge composition [in the] great speos of Abu Simbel, the ancient Abshek, where we find represented the camp of Ramesses II during his famous campaign against the confederation of the Hittites in Asia. It is the king's chariot that is seen here, crowned by a type of standard or parasol; it was surrounded by the soldiers of his guard. [...] The second picture is taken from the campaigns of the father of Ramesses II, Seti I, who can be seen sculpted on the wall of the great temple of Karnak. Mounted on his war chariot and still holding in his hand his axe and his bow, the pharaoh returns triumphant from an expedition against the Hittites; some of their heads can be seen poking out of the chariot, to which four of the wretched captives are attached. The horses have plumes on their heads, and their bodies are covered with a light harness and a long cover. In the inscription above them they are called: "His majesty's finest horses".

BRUCHSTÜCKE VON FLACHRELIEFS MIT MILITÄRISCHEN DARSTELLUNGEN (19. Dynastie)

Abochek und Theben

Auf dieser Tafel habe ich zwei Flachreliefs mit Streitwagen zusammengestellt, um zwei Pferdegruppen zu zeigen. Das erste ist [im] großen Speos von Abu Simbel, dem früheren Abochek, Bestandteil einer riesigen Komposition, in der das Lager Ramses' II. während seines berühmten Asien-Feldzuges gegen die hethitische Konföderation dargestellt ist. Der hier gezeigte Wagen ist der des Königs, den eine Art Standarte oder Sonnenschirm überragt; er war von den Soldaten seiner Garde umgeben. [...] Das zweite Bild bezieht sich auf die Feldzüge Sethos' I., des Vaters von Ramses II., die auf der Mauer des großen Tempels von Karnak zu sehen sind. Der Pharao, der in den Händen noch Krummschwert und Bogen hält, kehrt auf seinem Streitwagen siegreich von einem Feldzug gegen die Hethiter zurück; aus dem Wagen, in dem vier der Unglücklichen angebunden sind, schauen die Köpfe heraus. Den Kopf der Pferde ziert ein Federbusch, ihr Körper ist mit einem leichten Geschirr und einer langen Schutzhülle bedeckt. In der Inschrift darüber heißt es: „Die besten Pferde seiner Majestät".

FRAGMENTS DE BAS-RELIEFS MILITAIRES (XIXe dynastie)

Abochek et Thèbes

J'ai réuni sur cette planche deux bas-reliefs où l'on voit des chars de guerre, afin de présenter deux groupes de chevaux. Le premier fait partie de l'immense composition [dans le] grand spéos d'Abousambil [Abou Simbel], l'ancienne Abochek, où se trouve représenté le camp de Ramsès II dans sa fameuse campagne contre la confédération des Khétas [Hittites], en Asie. Le char qu'on voit ici est celui du roi surmonté d'une espèce d'étendard ou de parasol ; il était entouré des soldats de sa garde. [...] Le second tableau est tiré des campagnes de Seti Ier, père de Ramsès II, qu'on voit sculptées sur le mur du grand temple de Karnac. Monté sur son char de bataille et tenant encore en main sa harpe et son arc, le pharaon revient triomphant d'une expédition contre les Khétas dont on voit quelques têtes saillir du char, où quatre de ces malheureux sont attachés. Les chevaux ont la tête empanachée, le corps couvert d'un léger harnais et d'une longue housse. Dans l'inscription qui les surmonte ils sont appelés : « Le premiers chevaux de sa Majesté ».

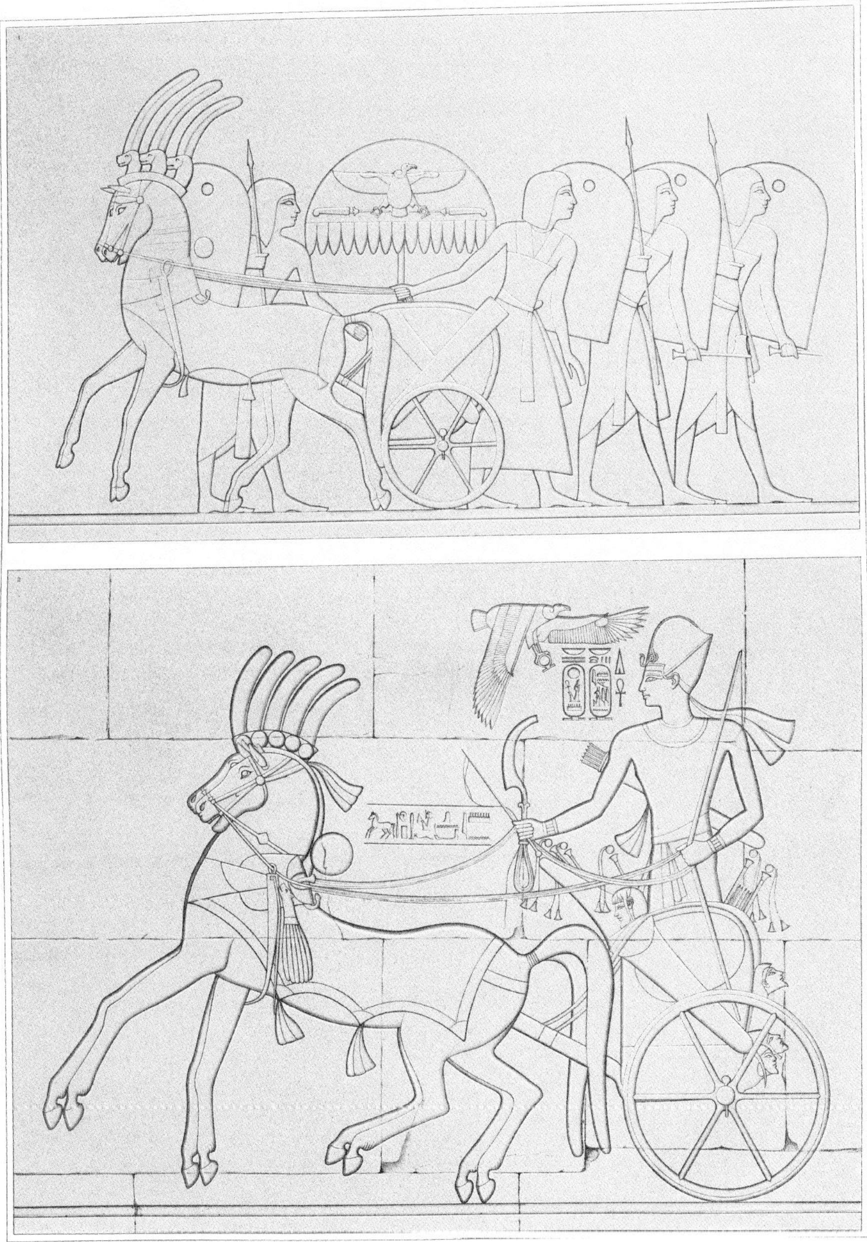

Lith. par Daumont. Imp. par Hangard-Maugé. E. Prisse d'Avennes. Publié par Arthus Bertrand, Éditeur.

FRAGMENTS DE BAS-RELIEFS MILITAIRES.

(ABOCHEK & THÈBES. — XIXe DYNASTIE.)

FRAGMENTS FROM FUNERARY BAS-RELIEFS (19th Dynasty)

Necropolis of Thebes

The scene in no. 1, taken from a long funerary procession, shows a grief-stricken family, hands placed on their heads and saying their final farewells to a mummy which they are about to place in the tomb. The coffin, in the form of a herm crowned with the funerary cone, is supported against a stele opposite which can be seen the symbol of the West (the land of the dead), the Imenty personified, with her two long arms which have already grasped the corpse and will never give it back. Behind this whole grieving family, two priests wearing leopard skins burn incense or pour libations before the mummy, thus completing the funeral ceremony. No. 2 represents a funeral dance performed to the sound of the tambourine and probably accompanied by laudatory chanting. Two young naked girls with long hair appear to be controlling the measure of the dance to the sound of an instrument similar to castanets. Two men with outstretched hands impose silence on a turbulent, noisy crowd.

BRUCHSTÜCKE VON BEGRÄBNIS-FLACHRELIEFS (19. Dynastie)

Nekropole von Theben

In der Nr. 1 zeigt die – einer langen Begräbnisprozession entnommene – Szene eine trauernde Familie, die im Begriff ist, eine Mumie ins Grab zu legen, und mit auf den Kopf gelegten Händen von ihr Abschied nimmt. Der wie eine Herme gestaltete, mit einem Grabkegel bekrönte Sarg ist an eine Stele gelehnt, vor der als Sinnbild des Westens (des Totenreiches) die personifizierte Amentet zu sehen ist, deren lange Arme bereits von der Leiche Besitz ergriffen haben und sie nicht mehr hergeben werden. Hinter der ganzen jammernden Familie verbrennen zwei mit einer Leopardenhaut bekleidete Priester Weihrauch oder bringen vor der Mumie Trankopfer dar – und beenden auf diese Weise die Begräbniszeremonie. Die Nr. 2 stellt einen zum Klang des Tamburins ausgeführten und wahrscheinlich von apologetischen Gesängen begleiteten Totentanz dar. Zwei nackte junge Mädchen, deren Kopf mit langen Zöpfen geschmückt ist, scheinen mit einer Art Klapper den Takt anzugeben. Zwei Männer bringen die laute, bewegte Menge mit ausgestreckten Händen zum Schweigen.

FRAGMENTS DE BAS-RELIEFS FUNÉRAIRES (XIXe dynastie)

Nécropole de Thèbes

Dans le n° 1, la scène, tirée d'une longue procession funèbre, représente une famille éplorée, les mains placées sur la tête et adressant ses derniers adieux à une momie qu'on va déposer au tombeau. Le cercueil, en forme d'hermès couronné du cône funéraire, est adossé à une stèle contre laquelle on voit le symbole de l'Occident (la terre des morts), l'Amenthès personnifiée, armée de deux longs bras qui se sont déjà emparés du cadavre et ne le rendront plus. Derrière toute cette famille qui se dolente, deux prêtres, revêtus d'une peau de léopard, brûlent de l'encens ou font des libations devant la momie, achevant ainsi la cérémonie des funérailles. Le n° 2 représente une danse funèbre exécutée au son du tambourin et probablement accompagnée de chants apologétiques. Deux jeunes filles nues, la tête ornée de longues tresses, semblent régler la danse au son d'une espèce de crotale. Deux hommes, les mains étendues, imposent silence à une foule tumultueuse et bruyante.

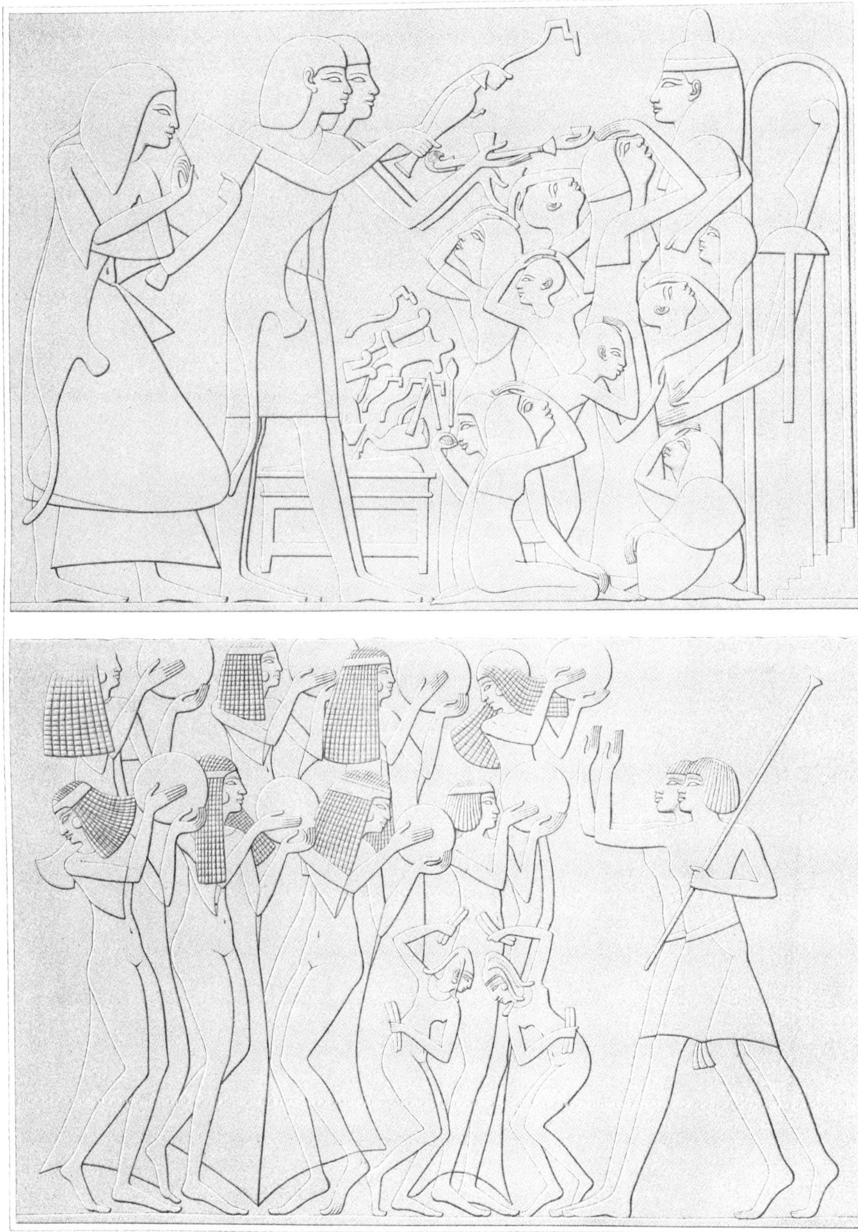

Lith. par Daumont. Imp. par Hangard-Maugé. E. Prisse d'Avennes. Publié par Arthus-Bertrand Éditeur.

FRAGMENTS DE BAS-RELIEFS FUNÉRAIRES.

(NÉCROPOLE DE THÈBES. — XIXe DYNASTIE.)

Painting / Malerei / Peinture

ICONIC GROUP OF TI AND HIS WIFE (5th Dynasty)

Necropolis of Memphis

What first catches the eye in this plate is the background of rush-work against which the group of Ti and his wife stands out. This is in fact the most remarkable part of the design, since it demonstrates what the origin was of the ornaments which decorate the walls and ceilings of the tombs: the squares, the lozenges and the chevrons shown on these plaited mats were the earliest decorative motifs apart from the symbolism which was commonly used in the temples. [...] The noticeable difference in size between the two figures is the result of the subordinate status to which, at that remote time, the wife was still relegated, and yet this lady, whose name was Neferhetepes, priestess of Hathor and relative of the king, was well loved and respected by her husband. These two personages are on an uneven bas-relief which is barely raised above the background on which the plaited mats are painted.

IKONISCHE GRUPPE MIT TI UND SEINER GEMAHLIN (5. Dynastie)

Nekropole von Memphis

Das auf den ersten Blick Reizvolle an dieser Tafel ist der Hintergrund aus Flechtwerk, vor dem sich die Gruppe mit Ti und seiner Gemahlin abhebt. Dies ist nämlich der bemerkenswerteste Teil, weil er uns den Ursprung der Ornamente zeigt, die Wände und Decken der Gräber zieren: Abgesehen von der allgemein in den Tempeln gebräuchlichen Symbolik waren die Quadrate, Rauten und Fischgrätmuster, die diese Matten aufweisen, die ersten Schmuckmotive. [...] Der auffällige Größenunterschied zwischen den beiden Personen hat seinen Grund in dem untergeordneten Rang, auf den die Frau in dieser fernen Zeit noch beschränkt war; und dabei wurde diese, die Nofrehotepes hieß, mit dem König verwandt und Hathor-Priesterin war, von ihrem Gemahl halbwegs geliebt und geachtet. Diese beiden Personen bilden ein Plattrelief, das sich kaum von dem Hintergrund hervorhebt, auf den die Matte aufgemalt ist.

GROUPE ICONIQUE DE TEÏ ET DE SA FEMME (V[e] dynastie)

Nécropole de Memphis

Ce qui attire la vue tout d'abord dans cette planche, c'est le fond de sparterie sur lequel se détache le groupe de Teï et de sa femme. C'est en effet la partie la plus remarquable, parce qu'elle nous montre quelle fut l'origine des ornements qui décorent les murs et les plafonds des tombeaux : les carrés, les losanges et les chevrons que présentent ces nattes ont été les premiers motifs de décoration en dehors de la symbolique usitée généralement dans les temples. [...] La différence de proportion, qui se remarque entre les deux personnages, a pour cause l'état de subalternité auquel la femme était encore réduite à cette époque reculée ; et cependant celle-ci, nommée Nofrehotepes, prêtresse d'Hathor et parente du roi, était assez aimée et considérée de son mari. Ces deux personnages sont d'un bas-relief méplat qui se distingue à peine du fond sur lequel est peinte la natte.

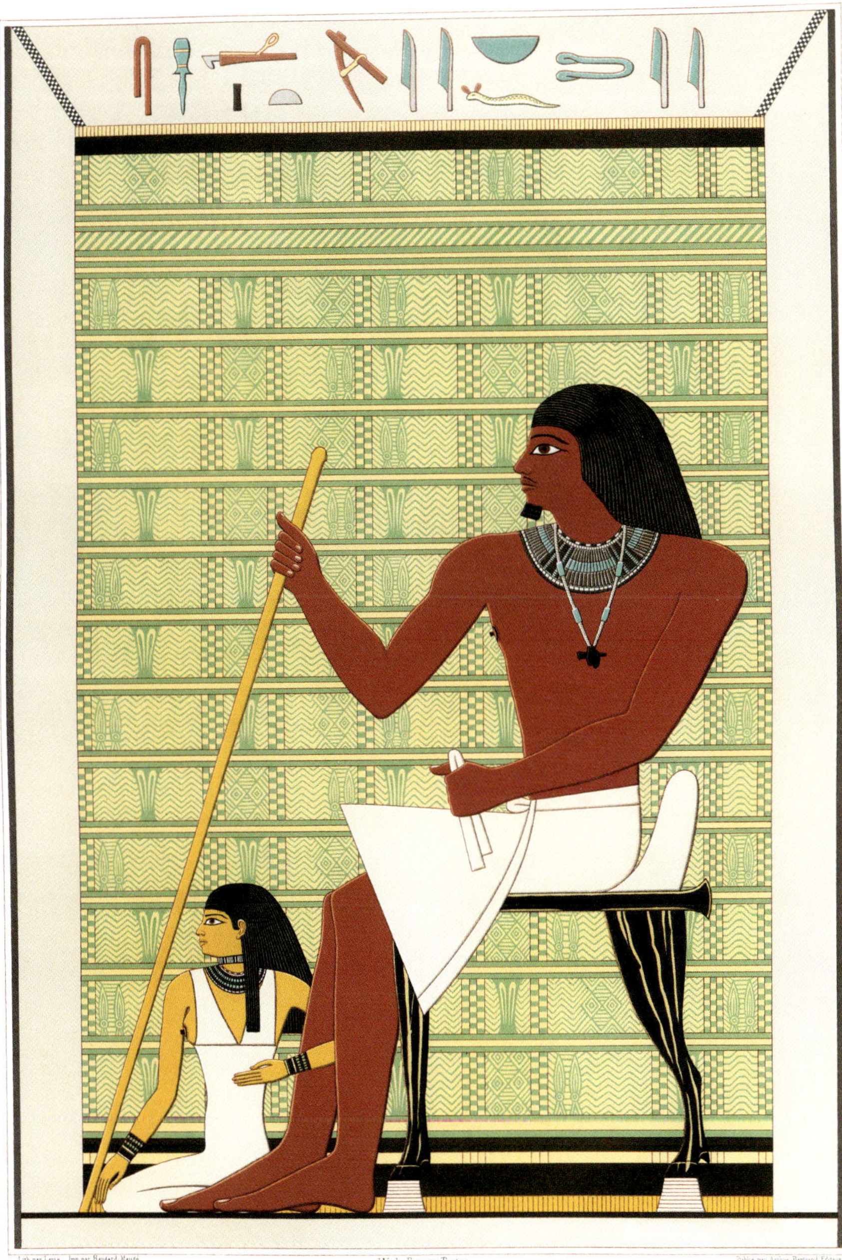

Lith par Levié _ Imp par Hangard-Maugé

W. de Famars-Testas

Publié par Arthus-Bertrand, Éditeur

GROUPE ICONIQUE DE TEÏ & DE SA FEMME.

(NÉCROPOLE DE MEMPHIS. _ Ve DYNASTIE.)

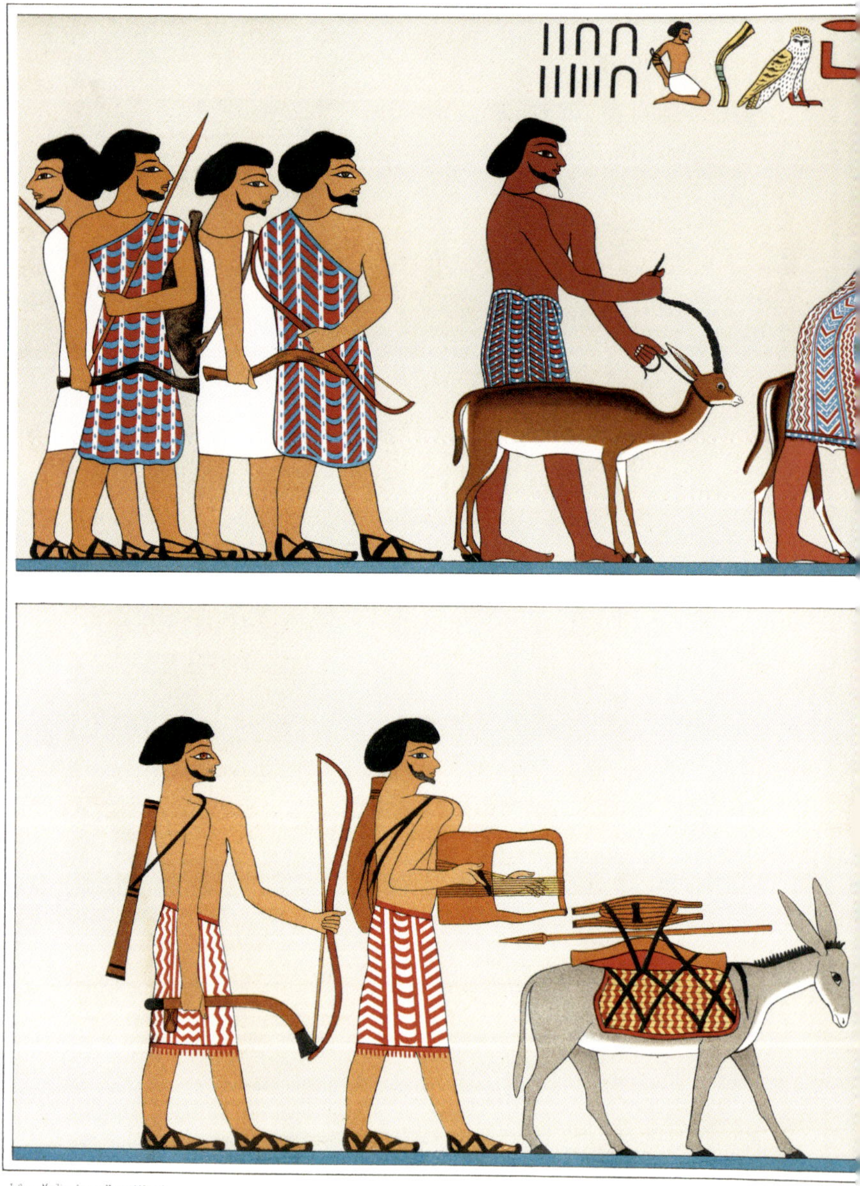

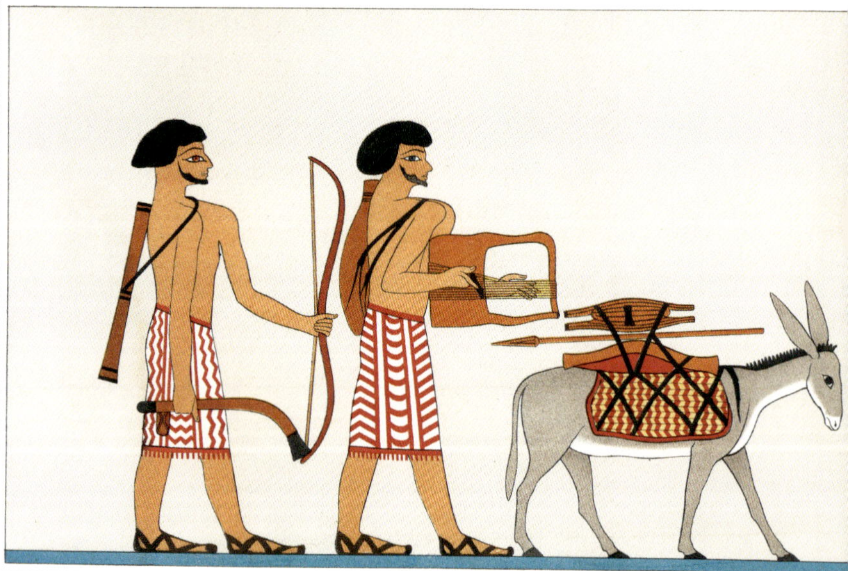

Lith. par Moulin. Imp. par Hangard-Maugé.

ARRIVÉE D'UNE FAM

(BENI

V 2

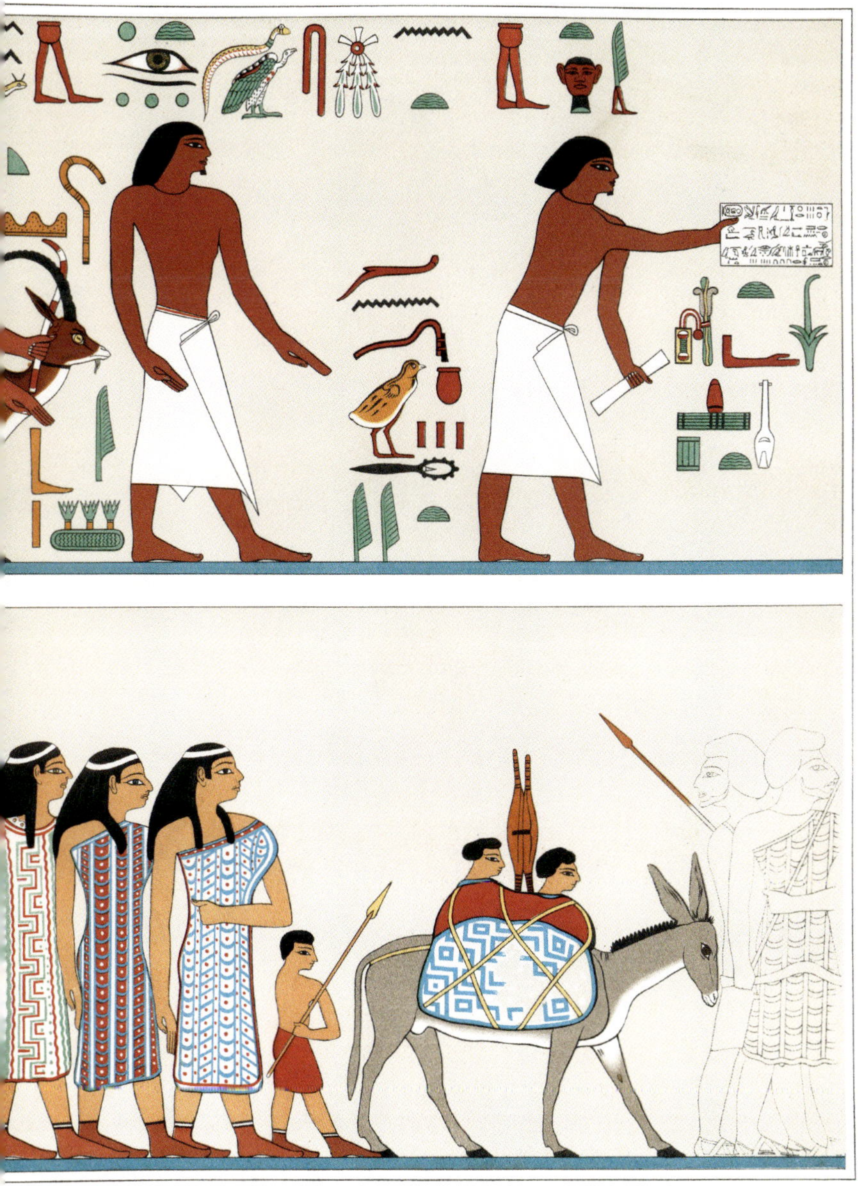

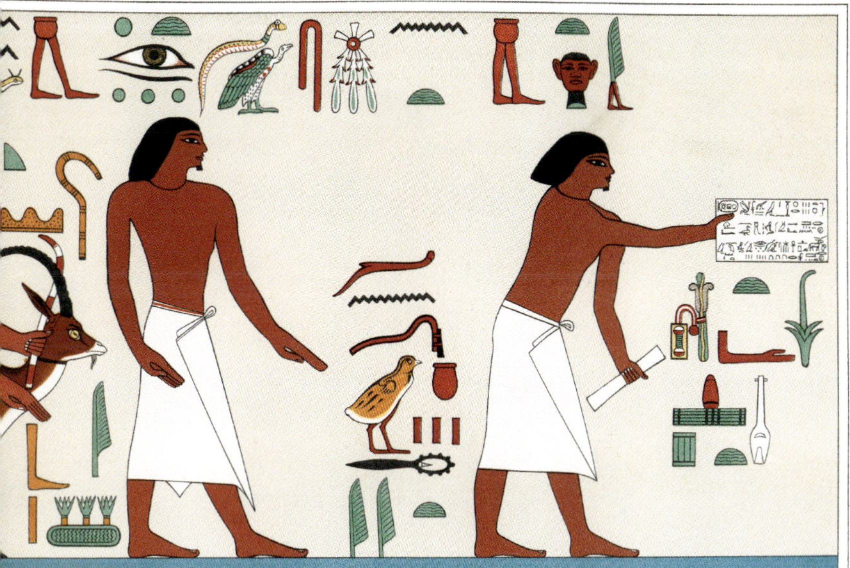

Publié par Arthus-Bertrand, Editeur.

TIQUE EN ÉGYPTE .

STIE .)

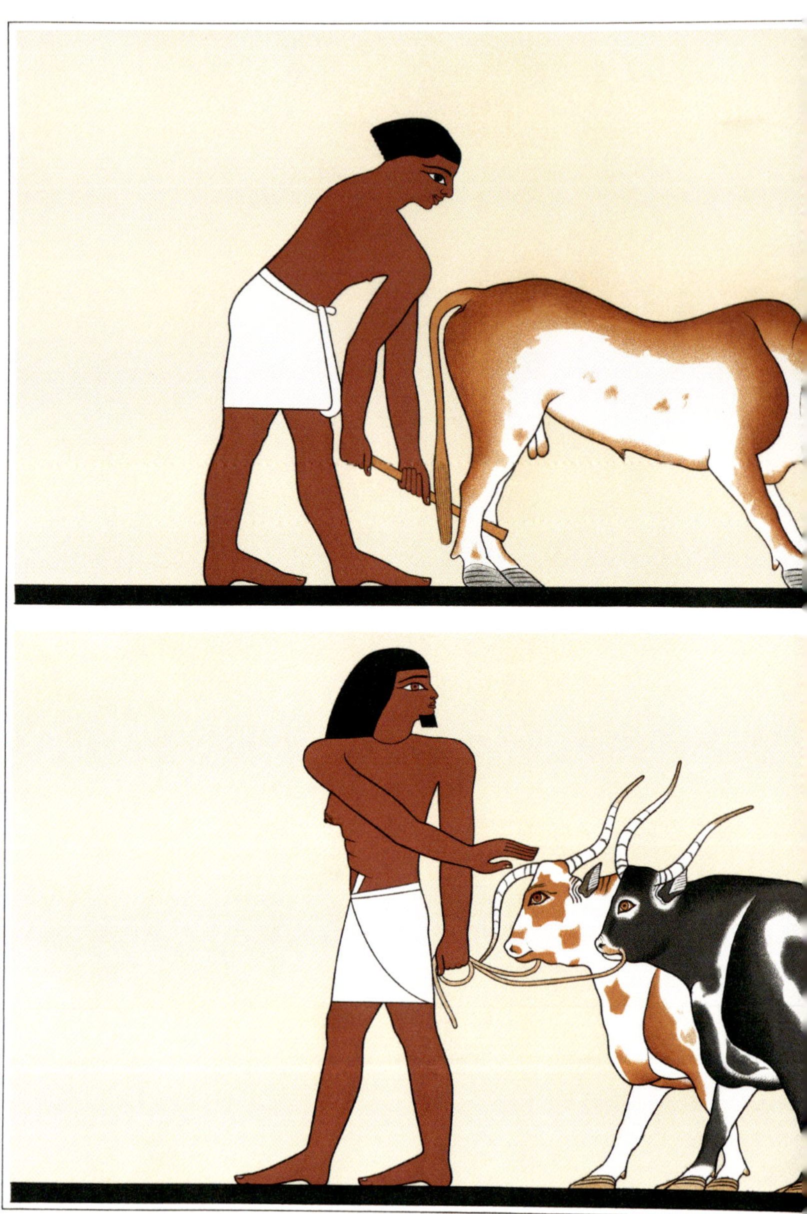

Lith. par Daumont. _ Imp. par Hangard-Maugé.

SCÈNES

(HYPOGÉES

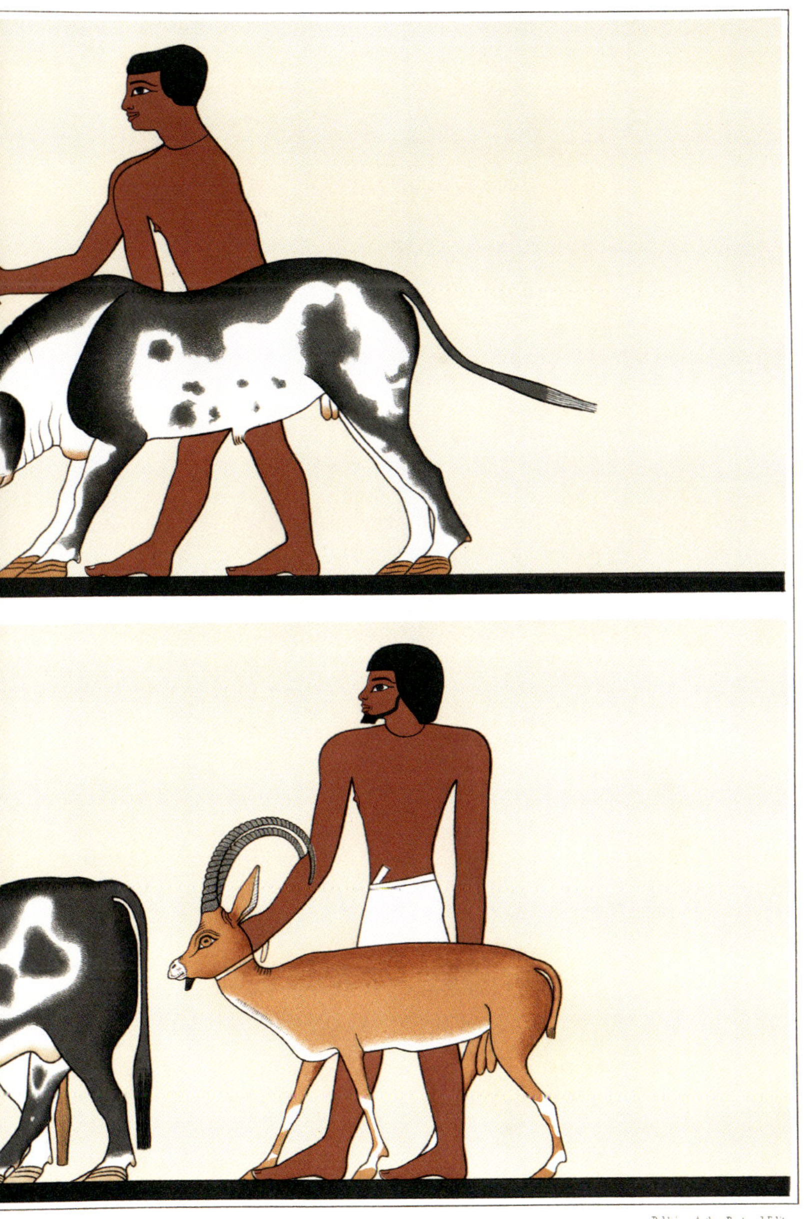

Publié par Arthus-Bertrand Editeur

; RURALE .

(IIe DYNASTIE.)

(Pages/Seite 438/439)

ARRIVAL OF AN ASIATIC FAMILY IN EGYPT (12th Dynasty)

Beni Hassan

The artist has painted a series of foreigners being presented to Khumhotep by two Egyptian officials, the first of whom is a royal scribe holding in his hand a tablet covered with hieroglyphs. These foreigners have a striking appearance, with aquiline nose and clear skin, apart from the chiefs: they wear clothes of very rich fabric. In front are two chiefs leading antelopes; one is called "Ibsha", the other is noteworthy for the pearl attached to the end of his beard. Four warriors follow, armed with spears, bows and clubs, then four women wearing multi-coloured tunics preceded by a young man driving a donkey with two children on its back. At the end comes a donkey laden with utensils looked after by a man playing a lyre who is followed by a warrior armed with a bow and a club.

ANKUNFT EINER ASIATISCHEN FAMILIE IN ÄGYPTEN (12. Dynastie)

Beni Hassan

Der Künstler hat eine Reihe Fremder gemalt, die Chnumhotep durch zwei ägyptische Beamte vorgestellt werden; einer von ihnen ist ein königlicher Schreiber, der eine mit Hieroglyphen bedeckte Tafel in der Hand hält. Mit Ausnahme der Anführer weisen diese Fremden mit ihrer Adlernase und ihrer hellen Gesichtsfarbe eine besondere Physiognomie auf. Es handelt sich zunächst um zwei Anführer, die Antilopen mit sich führen; der eine heißt Abscha, der andere hat eine auffällige, an der Spitze seines Bartes befestigte Perle. Danach folgen vier mit Lanzen, Bogen und Keulen bewaffnete Krieger. Anschließend vier in bunte Tuniken gekleidete Frauen, vor denen ein junger Mann hergeht; er treibt einen Esel vor sich her, auf dem zwei Kinder sitzen; schließlich wandert ein mit Gerätschaften beladener Esel unter Führung eines jungen, die Lyra spielenden Mannes dahin, dem ein mit Bogen und Keule bewaffneter Krieger folgt.

ARRIVÉE D'UNE FAMILLE ASIATIQUE EN ÉGYPTE (XIIe dynastie)

Beni-Haçen

L'artiste a peint une suite d'étrangers présentés à Noumhotep [Khnoumhotep] par deux fonctionnaires égyptiens, dont le premier est un scribe royal qui tient à la main une tablette couverte d'hiéroglyphes. Ces étrangers ont une physionomie particulière, le nez aquilin, le teint clair à l'exception des chefs ; ils sont vêtus d'étoffes très riches. Ce sont d'abord deux chefs conduisant des antilopes ; l'un est nommé Abscha, l'autre est remarquable par une perle attachée à l'extrémité de la barbe. Viennent après quatre guerriers armés de lances, d'arcs et de casse-tête. Puis quatre femmes couvertes de tuniques bariolées, précédées d'un jeune homme poussant devant lui un âne qui porte deux enfants ; enfin, un âne chargé d'ustensiles chemine sous la conduite d'un homme jouant de la lyre et suivi d'un guerrier armé d'un arc et d'un casse-tête.

(Pages/Seite 440/441)

SCENES FROM RURAL LIFE (12th Dynasty)

Hypogea of Beni Hassan

Subjects without number are represented on the walls of the tombs: the civil, public or private life of the Egyptians as well as their religious ceremonies can all be found there and it can therefore be said that those details of their habits and customs which we do know, we owe to the paintings in the dwellings of the dead. [...] Above all, it is the animals which have been depicted with astonishing realism. Not only are their outlines exceptionally pure, but the detail is executed in a most remarkable way: bearing in mind the meagre resources of the Egyptian palette, there is every reason to marvel at the manner in which the quadrupeds are shown in their natural colouring, as cattle, antelopes and dogs are often shown faithfully represented. This [plate] helps us to understand what standard of agriculture Egypt had reached and how the rural inhabitants cared for their animals.

SZENEN AUS DEM LANDLEBEN (12. Dynastie)

Hypogäen von Beni Hassan

Auf den Wänden der Gräber sind zahllose Themen dargestellt: Es finden sich dort Abbildungen des öffentlichen und privaten bürgerlichen Lebens der Ägypter sowie [Darstellungen] religiöser Zeremonien: Ebenso lässt sich feststellen, dass es den Malereien in den Wohnungen der Toten zu verdanken ist, wenn wir bereits bestimmte Einzelheiten ihrer Sitten und Gebräuche kennen. [...] Vor allem die Tiere sind erstaunlich naturgetreu dargestellt. Nicht nur die Umrisse sind sehr klar, sondern auch die Einzelheiten sind äußerst bemerkenswert: In Anbetracht der geringen Möglichkeiten der ägyptischen Farbpalette ist es erstaunlich, dass die Vierbeiner in ihren natürlichen Farben dargestellt sind; denn gute Abbildungen von Rindern, Antilopen und Hunden sind häufig zu sehen. Anhand der [Tafel] ist es möglich, sich darüber klar zu werden, welche Kulturstufe die Landwirtschaft in diesem Land erreicht hatte; welche Aufmerksamkeit die Landbewohner ihren Tieren angedeihen ließen.

SCÈNES DE LA VIE RURALE (XIIe dynastie)

Hypogées de Beni-Haçen

Les sujets représentés sur les parois des tombeaux sont innombrables : la vie civile publique ou privée des Égyptiens ainsi que les cérémonies religieuses s'y trouvent représentées : aussi peut-on affirmer que, si nous connaissons déjà certains détails de leurs mœurs et coutumes, c'est aux peintures des demeures des morts que nous en sommes redevables. [...] Ce sont les animaux qui ont été, surtout, représentés avec une vérité étonnante. Non seulement les contours en sont très purs, mais les détails en sont fort remarquables : il y a lieu de s'étonner que les quadrupèdes soient représentés avec leurs couleurs naturelles, lorsqu'on sait le peu de ressources de la palette égyptienne ; car on voit souvent des bœufs, des antilopes et des chiens bien figurés. Par la [planche], il est permis de se rendre compte à quel degré de civilisation était arrivée l'agriculture dans ce pays ; quels soins les habitants de la campagne prenaient de leurs animaux.

RETURN OF THE HUNTER IN HIS BOAT (12th Dynasty)

Beni Hassan

The hieroglyphic title translates as: "The hunter in his boat." This is probably one of those peasants who were employed on the rural estates of rich people and who were responsible for furnishing their master's table with all sorts of fowl. When these bird-catchers were not tending their nets in the marshes, they were chasing ducks and wild geese, standing in small light boats made of papyrus and making use of a small curved stick. The hunter is holding one goose in his hand and carries the rest of his game on a yoke across his shoulders. to one end is attached a crudely made cage with three ducks inside while from the other, suspended on the end of a cord, hang two ash-grey cranes with their necks strapped up.

RÜCKKEHR DES JÄGERS AUF DER BARKE (12. Dynastie)

Beni Hassan

Der hieroglyphische Titel lautet übersetzt: „Der Jäger auf der Barke". Vermutlich war dies einer jener – auf den Landgütern wohlhabender Persönlichkeiten angestellter – Bauern, deren Aufgabe darin bestand, den Tisch ihres Herrn mit Geflügel aller Art zu versorgen. Wenn diese Vogelfänger ihre Netze nicht in den Sümpfen auslegten, dann jagten sie auf leichten Plattbodenschiffen aus Papyrus mithilfe eines kleinen, krummen Steckens wilde Enten und Gänse. Der Jäger hält eine Gans in der Hand und trägt das restliche Wild mittels eines über die Schulter gelegten Jochs: Auf der einen Seite ist ein grob ausgeführter Käfig befestigt, der drei Enten enthält; auf der anderen Seite hängen am Ende des Stricks zwei mit einem Riemen stramm gefesselte Graukraniche.

RETOUR DU CHASSEUR EN BARQUE (XIIe dynastie)

Beni-Haçen

Le titre hiéroglyphique se traduit : « Le chasseur en barque. » C'était, probablement, un de ces paysans employés dans les domaines ruraux des riches personnages, qui avait pour charge de fournir la table du maître de toutes sortes de volatiles. Quand ces oiseleurs ne tendaient pas leurs filets dans les marécages, ils chassaient les canards et les oies sauvages, montés sur de légers batelets en papyrus et à l'aide d'un petit bâton courbé. Le chasseur tient une oie à la main et porte le reste de son gibier au moyen d'un joug posé sur l'épaule : d'un côté est attachée une cage grossière renfermant trois canards ; de l'autre, pendent, au bout de la corde, deux grues cendrées, étroitement garrottées dans une courroie.

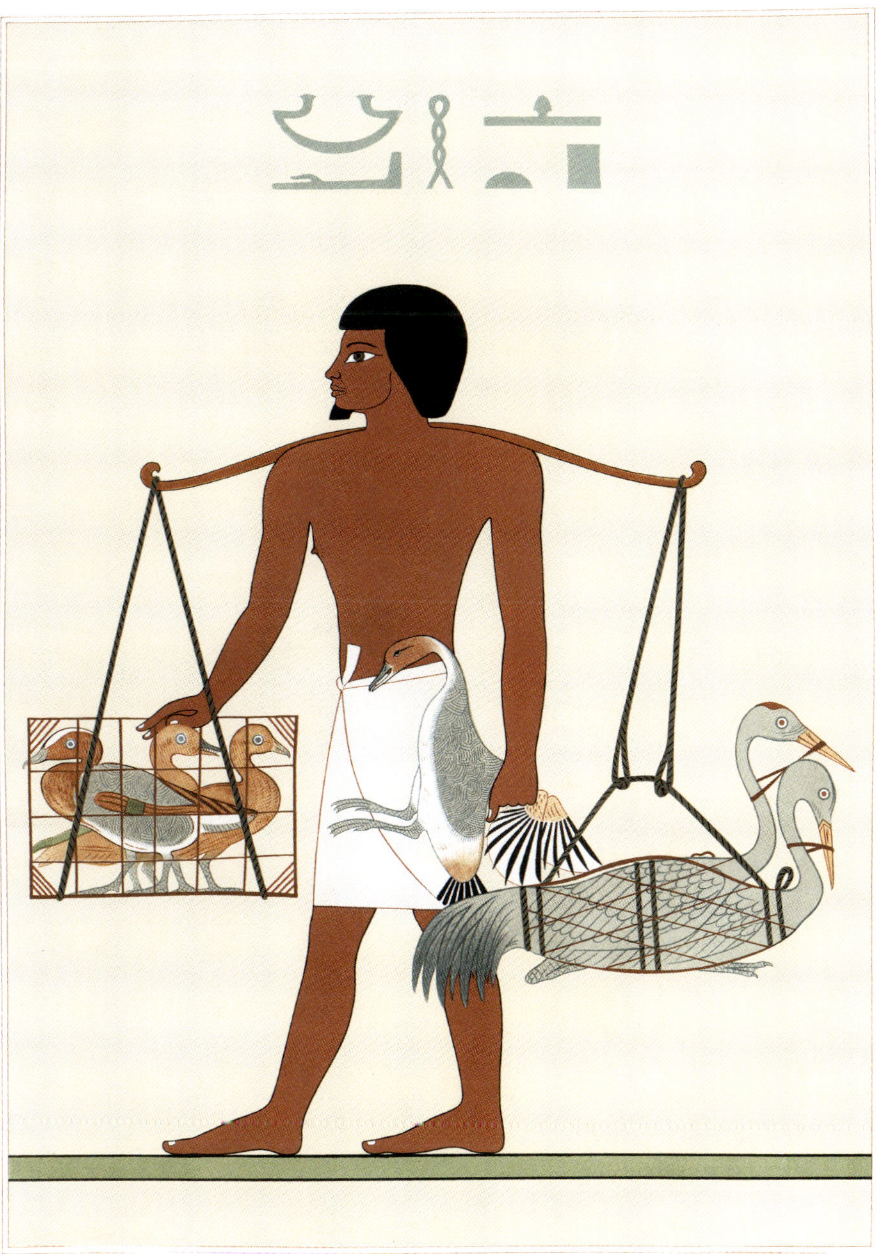

Lith. par Levié. Imp. par Hangard-Maugé.

E. Prisse d'Avennes.

Publié par Arthus-Bertrand, Éditeur

RETOUR DU CHASSEUR EN BARQUE.

(BENI-HAÇEN _ XIIe DYNASTIE.)

NATIVE OF THE LAND OF PUNT (17th Dynasty)

Thebes. El-Assasif

Dressed in a simple loin-cloth and armed with a stick, an Asiatic with male features, a native of the land of Punt, which is believed to be Arabia Felix, is driving a donkey laden with full panniers. Behind the animal is a tree in full leaf from which a startled bird takes flight; the whole scene stands out against a yellowish background which looks like an Eastern sky during the season of the simoom. This attractive genre picture was sculpted and painted on the external wall of the temple at el-Assasif, under the reign of the last king of the 17th Dynasty. It forms part of a large scene representing the bringing of the tribute imposed by the pharaoh on the chief of the land of Punt.

EINGEBORENER AUS DEM LANDE PUNT (17. Dynastie)

Theben. El-Assasif

Ein Asiat mit männlichen Zügen – ein Eingeborener dieses Landes Punt, das man mit dem glücklichen Arabien gleichsetzt –, der mit einem einfachen Lendenschurz bekleidet und mit einem Stock bewaffnet ist, treibt einen mit vollen, strohgeflochtenen Tragetaschen beladenen Esel vor sich her: Hinter dem Tier erhebt sich ein Laubbaum, dem ein aufgeschreckter Vogel entfliegt; die gesamte Szene zeichnet sich gegen den gelblichen Hintergrund ab, der dem orientalischen Himmel bei einem Samum ähnelt. Dieses hübsche Genrebild wurde in der Regierungszeit des letzten Königs der 17. Dynastie in die Außenmauer des Tempels von El-Assasif gemeißelt und bemalt. Es gehört zu einer großen Szene, die die Lieferung des Tributs darstellt, den der Pharao dem Anführer des Landes Punt auferlegt hat.

INDIGÈNE DU PAYS DE POUNT (XVIIe dynastie)

Thèbes. El-Assacif

Un Asiatique, aux traits mâles, indigène de ce pays de Pount, qu'on assimile à l'Arabie Heureuse, vêtu d'un simple pagne et armé d'un bâton, pousse devant lui un âne chargé de couffes remplies : derrière l'animal s'élève un arbre feuillu duquel s'échappe un oiseau effrayé ; toute la scène se détache sur un fond jaunâtre assez semblable au ciel d'Orient par un temps de simoon. Ce joli tableau de genre a été sculpté et peint, sur la muraille extérieure du temple d'El-Assacif, sous le règne du dernier roi de la XVIIe dynastie. Il fait partie d'une grande scène qui représente l'apport du tribut imposé par le pharaon au chef du pays de Pount.

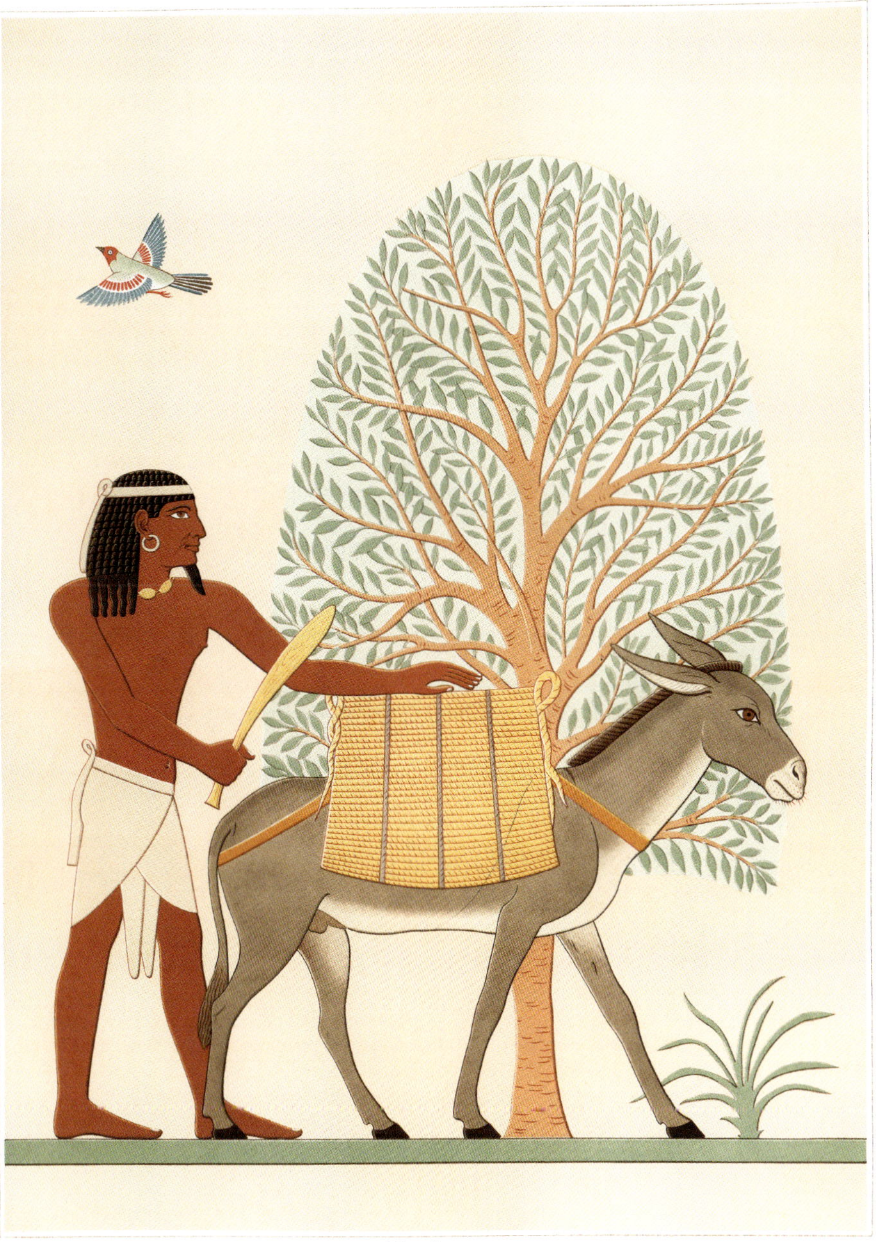

Lith. par Levie _ Imp. par Hangard-Maugé.

E. Prisse d'Avennes

Publié par Arthus Bertrand, Éditeur

INDIGÈNE DU PAYS DE POUNT.

(THÈBES . EL-ASSACIF _ XVIIe DYNASTIE)

RETURNING FROM THE HUNT (17th Dynasty)

Necropolis of Thebes

This group, painted or sculpted, is often seen in the tombs, occasionally with variations; however, almost everywhere it has been damaged or destroyed because of the beauty of the ensemble and its composition, which means that it is a type of small genre picture which is particularly prized by collectors. The net result is that very often all that the tourists, and sometimes even the Arabs, have succeeded in doing as they attempt to detach the paintings is to crack the surface to which the paint is applied and so to destroy these delightful examples of Egyptian art. This is why, on my second journey along the banks of the Nile, I could no longer find the subject of this plate, which I had copied in one of the hypogea of Thebes nearly 30 years earlier.

RÜCKKEHR VON DER JAGD (17. Dynastie)

Nekropole von Theben

Diese gemalte oder ausgemeißelte Gruppe findet sich häufig, mitunter mit Abweichungen, in den Gräbern; wegen der Schönheit des Gesamteindruckes und der Komposition – die sie in gewisser Weise zu einem kleinen, für Liebhaber kostbaren Genrebild macht – ist sie jedoch überall beschädigt oder zerstört. Dies liegt vor allem an Folgendem: Die Touristen und manchmal sogar die Araber haben bei ihren Versuchen, die Malereien abzulösen, zumeist lediglich den Putz zerbrechen können, auf dem sie aufgetragen waren, und in der Folge diese reizenden Exemplare der ägyptischen Kunst zerstört. Während meiner zweiten Reise an die Ufer des Nils habe ich den Gegenstand dieser Tafel, den ich fast dreißig Jahre zuvor in einem der Hypogäen von Theben abgezeichnet hatte, ebenfalls nicht wiederfinden können.

RETOUR DE LA CHASSE (XVIIe dynastie)

Nécropole de Thèbes

Ce groupe, peint ou sculpté, se rencontrait fréquemment dans les tombeaux, quelquefois avec des variantes ; mais il a été presque partout endommagé ou détruit à cause de sa beauté d'ensemble, et sa composition, qui en fait en quelque sorte un petit tableau de genre fort précieux pour les amateurs. Cela tient surtout à ceci : que les touristes et même quelquefois les Arabes, en essayant de détacher ces peintures, n'ont réussi le plus souvent qu'à briser l'enduit qui les portait et, par suite, à détruire ces charmants spécimens de l'art égyptien. Aussi, à mon second voyage sur les rives du Nil, n'ai-je plus retrouvé le sujet de cette planche que j'avais copiée dans un des hypogées de Thèbes, près de trente ans auparavant.

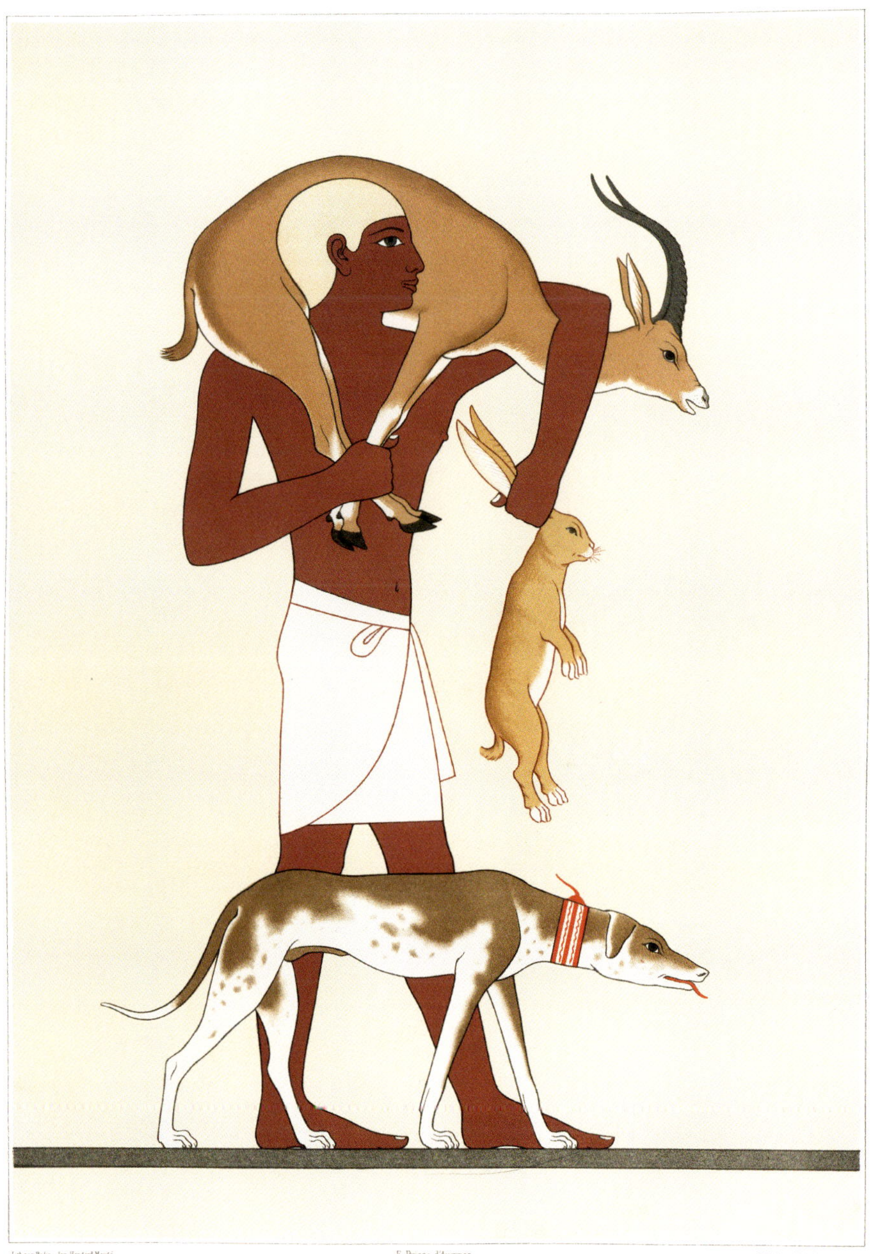

Lith par Bodin. Imp Hangard-Maugé. E. Prisse d'Avennes. Publié par Arthus-Bertrand Editeur.

RETOUR DE LA CHASSE.

(NÉCROPOLE DE THÈBES. XVIIIe DYNASTIE.)

PORTRAIT OF QUEEN TIYE (18th Dynasty)

Consort of Amenophis III

This delightful portrait is taken from the last corridor in the queen's tomb. It is carved in a very low bas-relief which only just outlines and models the contour and which is coloured very meticulously. The skin colouring, which is lighter and pinker than in my drawing, would seem to indicate a foreigner, probably an Asiatic woman. It is the only portrait I know where the skin colouring is so delicate and so true to life. The flesh shows through the striped muslin of the dress and lends a stamp of undeniable authenticity to the whole. The queen wears a cap representing a vulture, which grasps in its talons a type of ring, emblem of a period of many centuries; this cap is crowned with a bonnet also bearing a crowned vulture, the symbol of maternity, fronted by two uraei.

PORTRÄT DER KÖNIGIN TEJE (18. Dynastie)

Gemahlin von Amenophis III.

Dieses reizende Porträt ist dem letzten Korridor im Grab der Königin entnommen. Es ist in einem sehr flachen Relief ausgearbeitet, das kaum die Konturen nachzeichnet und modelliert, und es ist sorgfältig koloriert. Das Inkarnat, das noch heller und rosiger als meine Zeichnung ist, scheint auf eine Fremde, wahrscheinlich eine Asiatin hinzudeuten. Es ist nach meiner Kenntnis das einzige Porträt mit einem so zarten und naturgetreuen Inkarnat. Die Haut, die durch den gestreiften Musselin des Kleides durchscheint, gibt ihm ein unbestreitbar natürliches Gepräge. Die Königin trägt ein Scheitelkäppchen mit der Darstellung eines Geiers, der in seinen Fängen eine Art Ring – Sinnbild eines Jahrhunderte währenden Zeitalters – hält, und darüber einen Modius, der einen bekrönten, zwei Uräusschlangen folgenden Geier – Sinnbild der Mutterschaft – trägt.

PORTRAIT DE LA REINE TAÏA (XVIIIe dynastie)

Épouse d'Aménophis III

Ce charmant portrait est tiré du dernier couloir du tombeau de la reine [Tiyi]. Il est sculpté, d'un relief très bas, qui dessine et modèle à peine le contour et est colorié avec soin. La carnation, plus claire encore et plus rosée que mon dessin, semble indiquer une étrangère, probablement une femme asiatique. C'est le seul portrait que je connaisse d'une carnation aussi délicate et aussi vraie. La chair, qui transparaît à travers la mousseline rayée dont la robe est faite, lui donne un cachet de vérité incontestable. La reine est coiffée d'une calotte représentant un vautour, tenant dans ses serres une espèce d'anneau, emblème d'une longue période de siècles, et qui est surmontée d'un modius portant aussi un vautour mitré, symbole de la maternité, et que précèdent deux uréus.

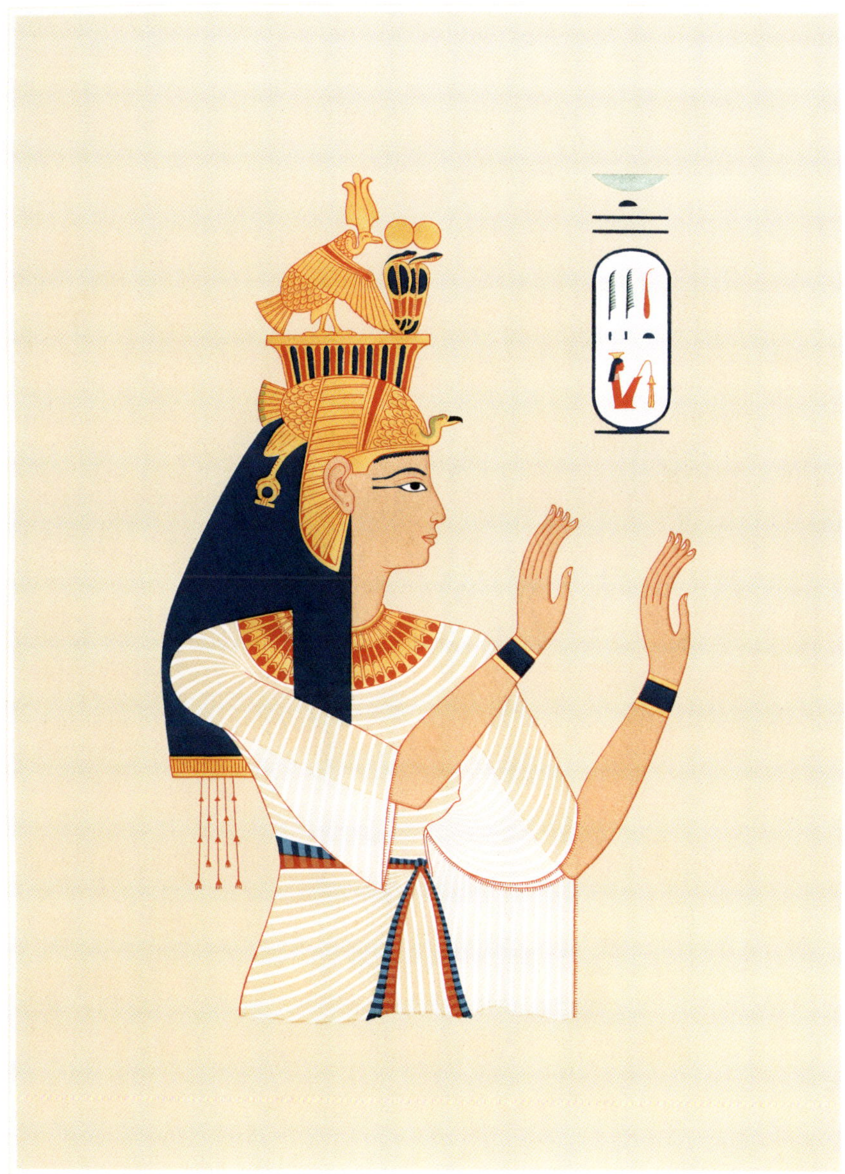

Lith. p. Moulin — Imp. par Hangard-Maugé. E. Prisse d'Avennes. Publié par Arthus Bertrand, Éditeur.

PORTRAIT DE LA REINE TAÏA,

ÉPOUSE D'AMÉNOPHIS III.

(XVIIIe DYNASTIE)

AMENOPHIS II AND HIS GOVERNESS (18th Dynasty)

Necropolis of Thebes

This painting can be seen in a hypogeum in Abd el-Qurna (Thebes). The young pharaoh is shown in the lap of his governess, or some say his wet-nurse; in order to accustom him to the concept of rigid rulership, he is being made to hold the ropes which bind together the heads of a number of captives whom he is trampling beneath his feet. In the original painting the governess was shown accompanied by her women singing and playing the lute; unfortunately this delightful scene has been almost entirely destroyed.

AMENOPHIS II. UND SEINE GOUVERNANTE (18. Dynastie)

Nekropole von Theben

Dieses Gemälde ist in einem Hypogäum in Scheich Abd el-Qurna (Theben) zu sehen. Der junge Pharao ist auf den Knien seiner Gouvernante – andere behaupten, seiner Amme – dargestellt; um ihn an eine unnachgiebige Machtausübung zu gewöhnen, lässt man ihn in den Händen Bänder halten, an die die Köpfe mehrerer Gefangener gefesselt sind, die er mit Füßen tritt. Die Gouvernante war im Originalgemälde in Begleitung ihrer singenden und Laute spielenden Begleiterinnen dargestellt; diese reizende Szene ist leider fast vollständig zerstört.

AMOUNÔPH II ET SA GOUVERNANTE (XVIIIe dynastie)

Nécropole de Thèbes

Cette peinture se voit dans un hypogée d'Abd el Gournah (Thèbes). Le jeune pharaon est représenté sur les genoux de sa gouvernante, d'autres prétendent sa nourrice ; on lui fait tenir dans ses mains, pour l'habituer à une domination inflexible, des liens qui retiennent ensemble plusieurs têtes de captifs qu'il foule sous ses pieds. Dans la peinture originale, la gouvernante était représentée accompagnée de ses femmes chantant et jouant de la mandore ; malheureusement cette scène charmante est presque entièrement détruite.

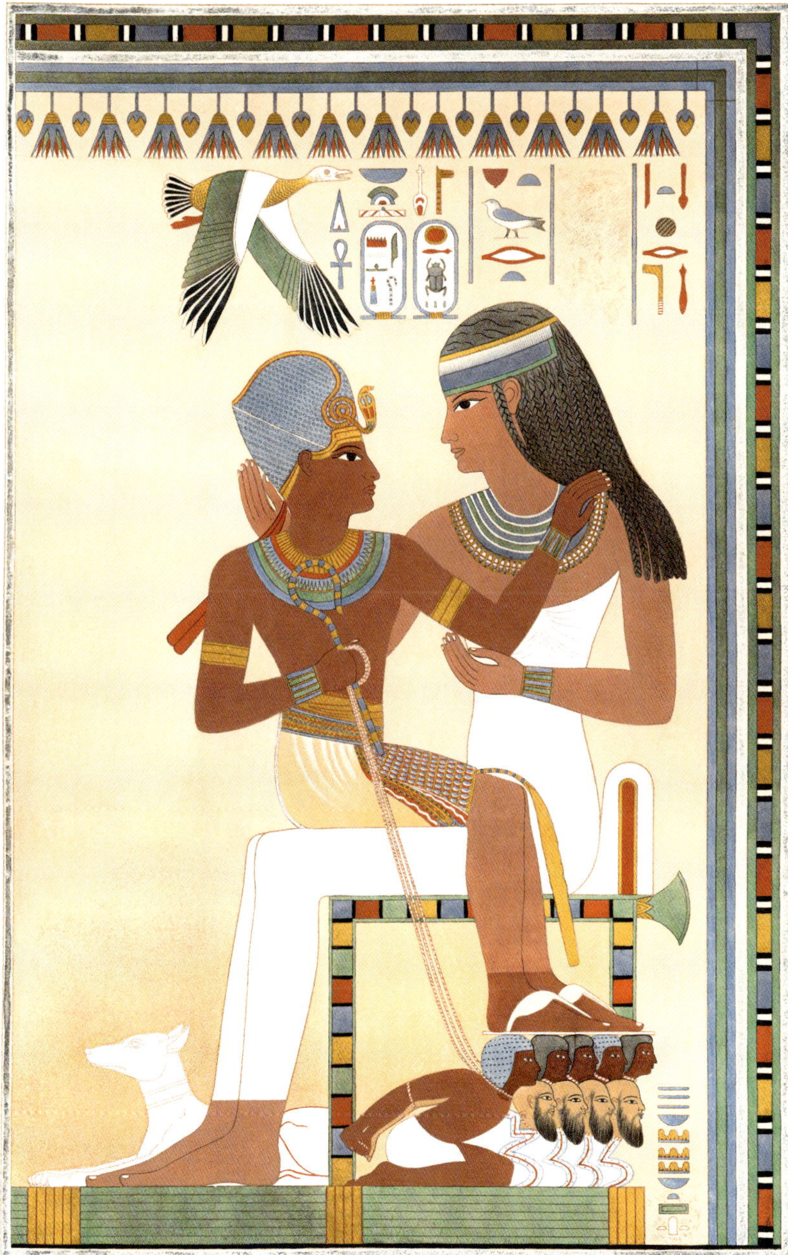

Lith. par Denny. — Imp. par Lemercier et Cie. Prisse d'Avennes Publié chez Arthus Bertrand, Libraire

AMOUNÔPH II ET SA GOUVERNANTE

NÉCROPOLE DE THÈBES

(XVIIIe DYNASTIE)

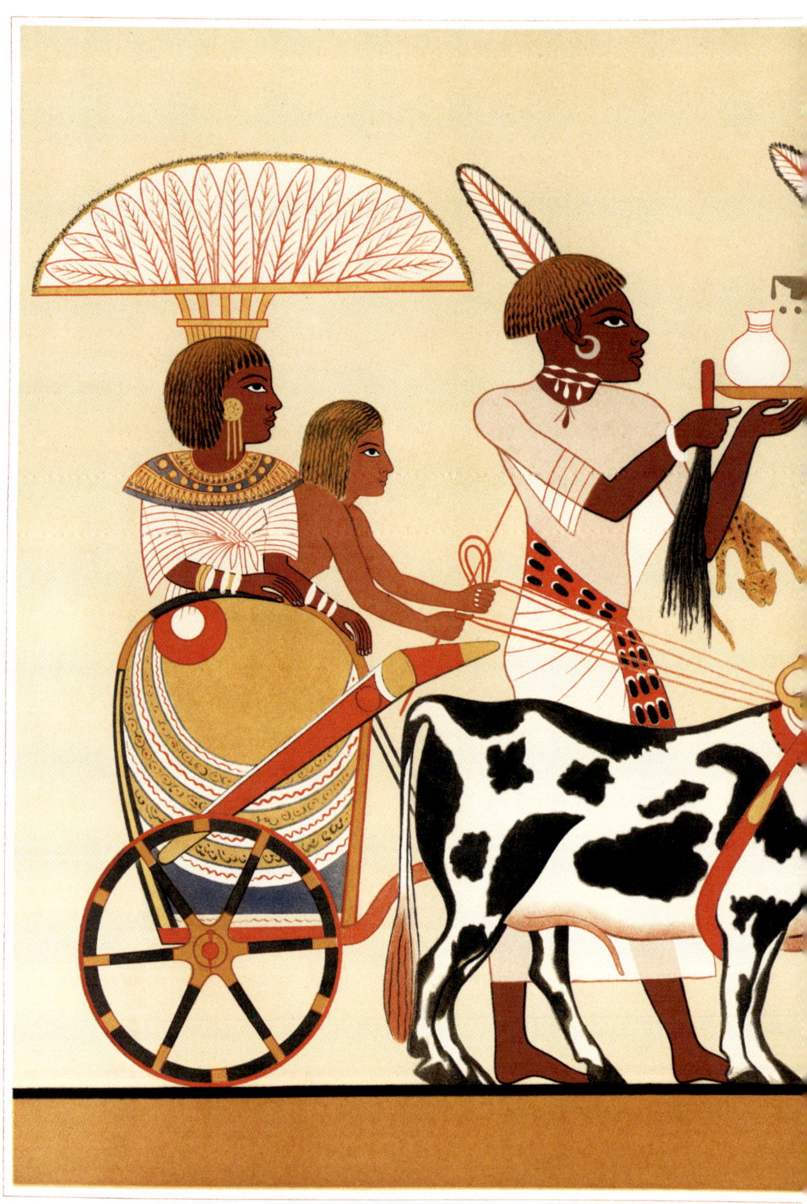

Lith par Levié _ Imp par Hangard-Maugé.

ARRIVÉE À THÈBES

SOUS LE RÈGNE

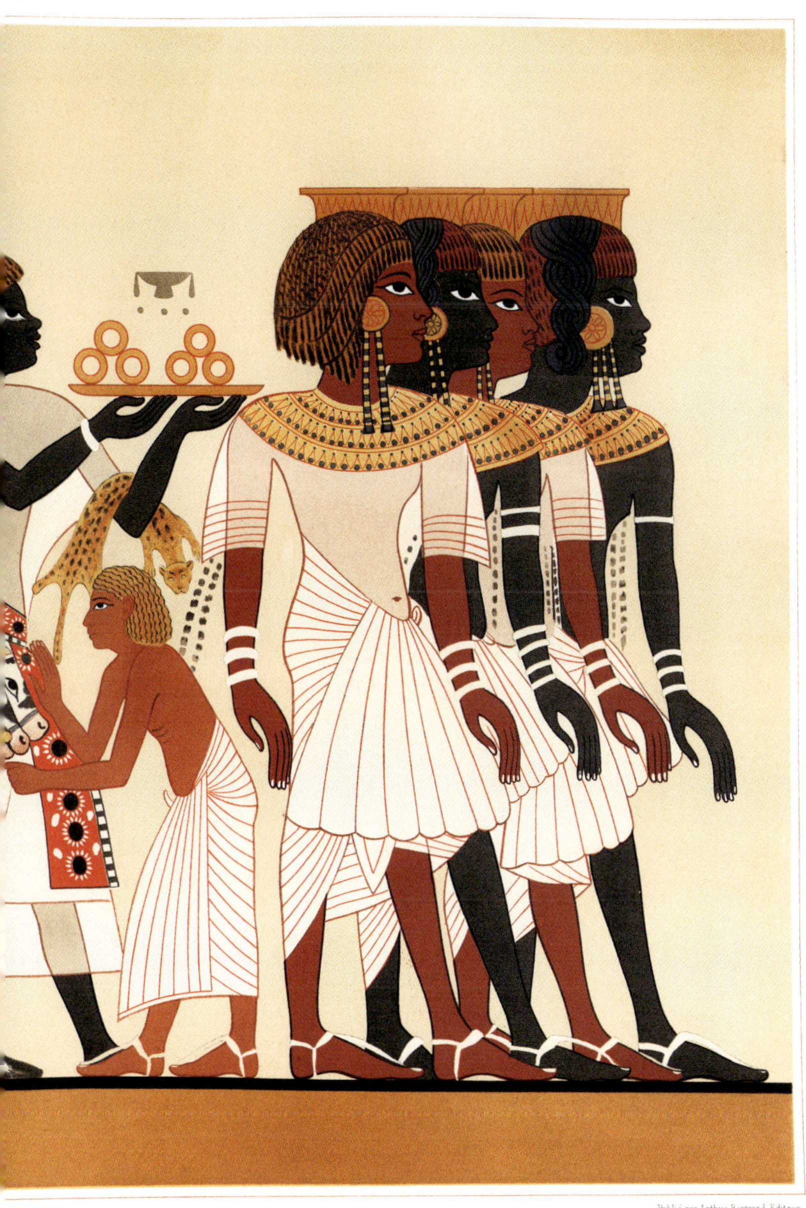

Publié par Arthus-Bertrand, Editeur.

CESSE ÉTHIOPIENNE.

, XVIIIe DYNASTIE.

(Pages/Seite 454/455)

ARRIVAL OF AN ETHIOPIAN PRINCESS IN THEBES (18th Dynasty)

During the reign of Tutankhamun

This scene is taken from a large picture painted in the hypogeum of a governor of Ethiopia called Huy. According to the inscription itself, the picture would have represented the arrival in Thebes of the tribute from Ethiopia during the reign of Tutankhamun. The princess who is a member of the deputation presents herself before the pharaoh, accompanied by her principal chiefs and seated in an ox-drawn chariot led by Egyptians. Her head is covered by an umbrella of ostrich feathers; she wears large ivory bracelets, as also do the other black- or brown-skinned characters. The representatives are bearing their country's tribute of shekels and of powdered gold, shields, furnishings, a chariot and a variety of finely worked articles in gold and silver. It is apparent from this tribute that Ethiopian art had attained a very high standard during the period of Egyptian dominion. My drawing was carefully traced and then reduced in size by means of a pantograph, thus retaining its character in full.

ANKUNFT EINER ÄTHIOPISCHEN PRINZESSIN IN THEBEN (18. Dynastie)

Unter der Herrschaft des Tutanchamun

Diese Szene ist einem großen Gemälde im Hypogäum eines Gouverneurs von Äthiopien namens Huy entnommen. Das Bild soll nach Aussage der Inschrift die Ankunft der äthiopischen Tribute in Theben unter der Herrschaft Tutanchamuns zeigen. Die zur Abordnung gehörige Prinzessin stellt sich in Begleitung der wichtigsten Anführer auf ihrem von Rindern gezogenen und von Ägyptern geführten Wagen dem Pharao vor. Ein Sonnenschirm aus Straußenfedern überragt ihren Kopf: Ihre Haut ist, wie bei den anderen Figuren, schwarz oder braun, und sie trägt breite Armbänder aus Elfenbein. Die Abgeordneten überbringen Schekel und Goldstaub, Schilde, Möbel, einen Wagen und verschiedene Goldschmiedearbeiten aus ihrem Land. An diesem Tribut ist zu erkennen, dass die Künste unter der ägyptischen Herrschaft in Äthiopien eine gewisse Vollendung erreicht hatten. Meine sorgfältig gepauste Zeichnung wurde mittels eines Pantografen verkleinert, wodurch ihre Eigenart gänzlich erhalten blieb.

ARRIVÉE À THÈBES D'UNE PRINCESSE ÉTHIOPIENNE (XVIIIe dynastie)

Sous le règne d'Amentouonkh [Toutânkhamon]

Cette scène est tirée d'un grand tableau peint dans l'hypogée d'un gouverneur d'Éthiopie nommé Haï. Le tableau représenterait, au dire de l'inscription elle-même, l'arrivée à Thèbes des tributs de l'Éthiopie, sous le règne d'Amentouonkh [Toutânkhamon]. La princesse qui fait partie de la députation se présente devant le pharaon, accompagnée des principaux chefs et montée sur un char traîné par des bœufs que conduisent des Égyptiens. Sa tête est surmontée d'une ombrelle en plumes d'autruche : elle porte, ainsi que les autres personnages à peau noire ou brune, de larges bracelets d'ivoire. Les députés apportent de leur pays des sicles et de la poudre d'or, des boucliers, des meubles, un chariot et diverses pièces d'orfèvrerie. On voit par ce tribut que, sous la domination égyptienne, l'art avait atteint en Éthiopie une certaine perfection. Mon dessin, calqué soigneusement, a été réduit au pantographe, ce qui lui a conservé tout son caractère.

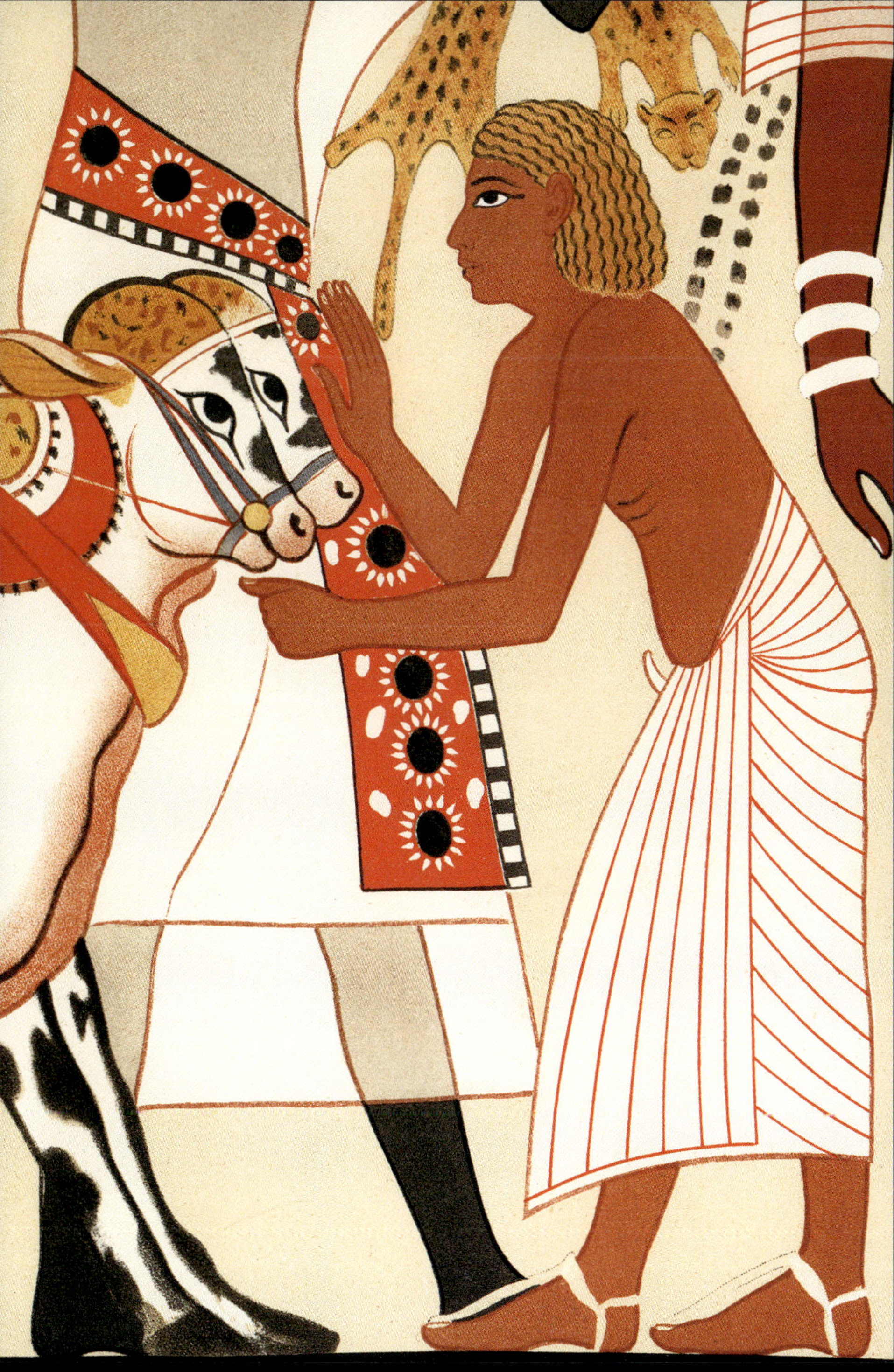

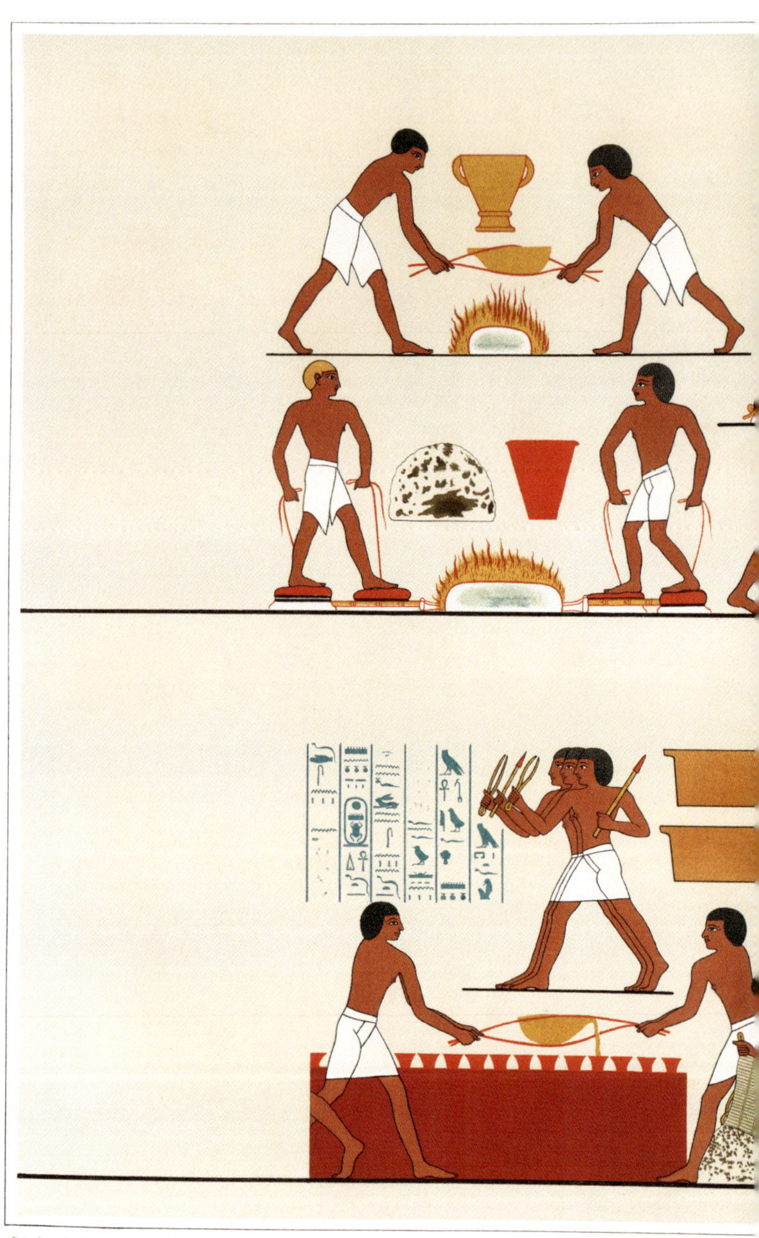

Exécuté par Levié _ Imp. Lemercier & Cie Paris.

ATELIER DES FONDEU

(TEMPLE DE K

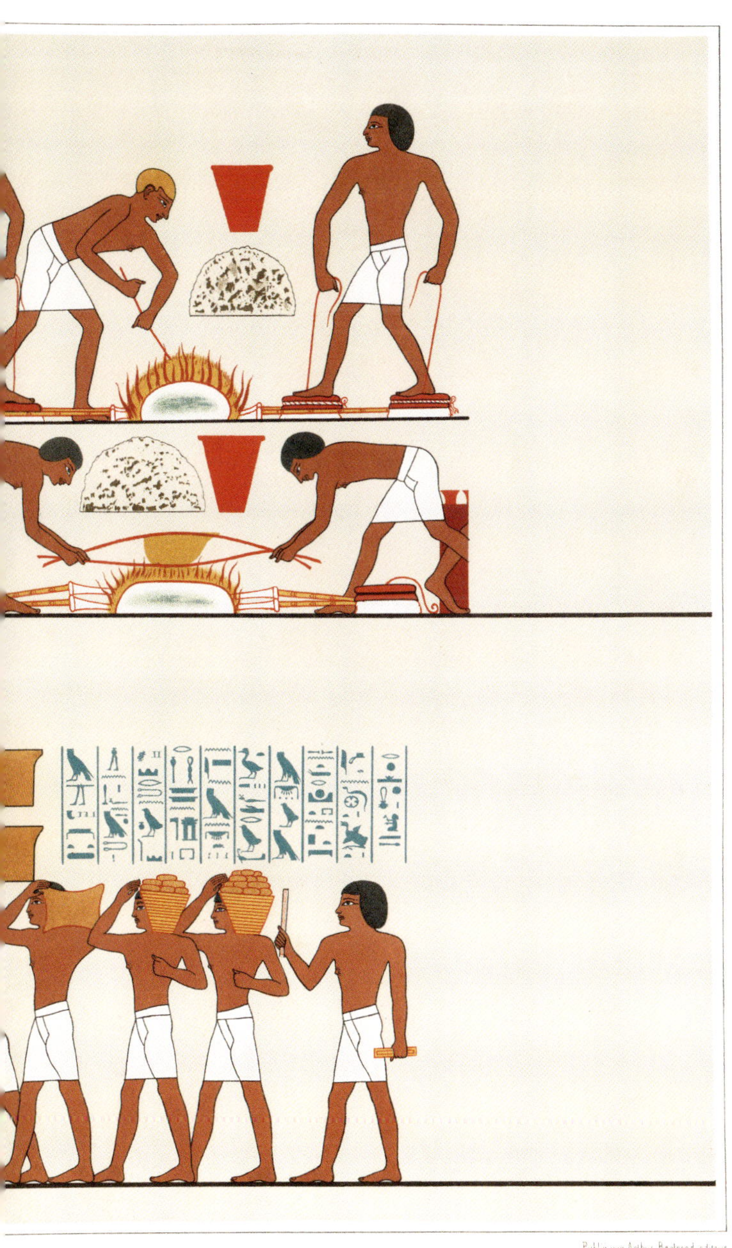

Publié par Arthus Bertrand éditeur

OR DES ROTHENNOU

E DYNASTIE)

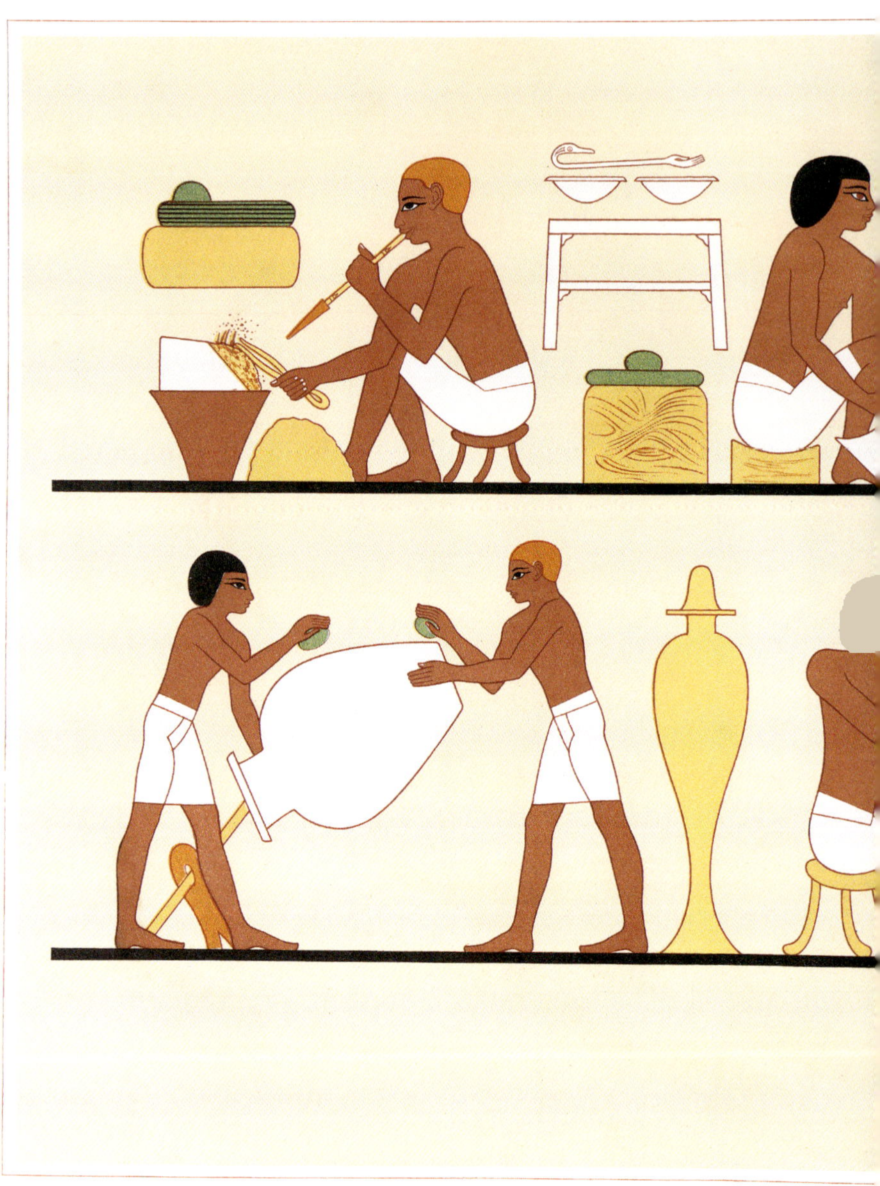

Lith par Leichum. _ Imp. Hangard-Maugé.

FABRICATION D

(NÉCROPOLE

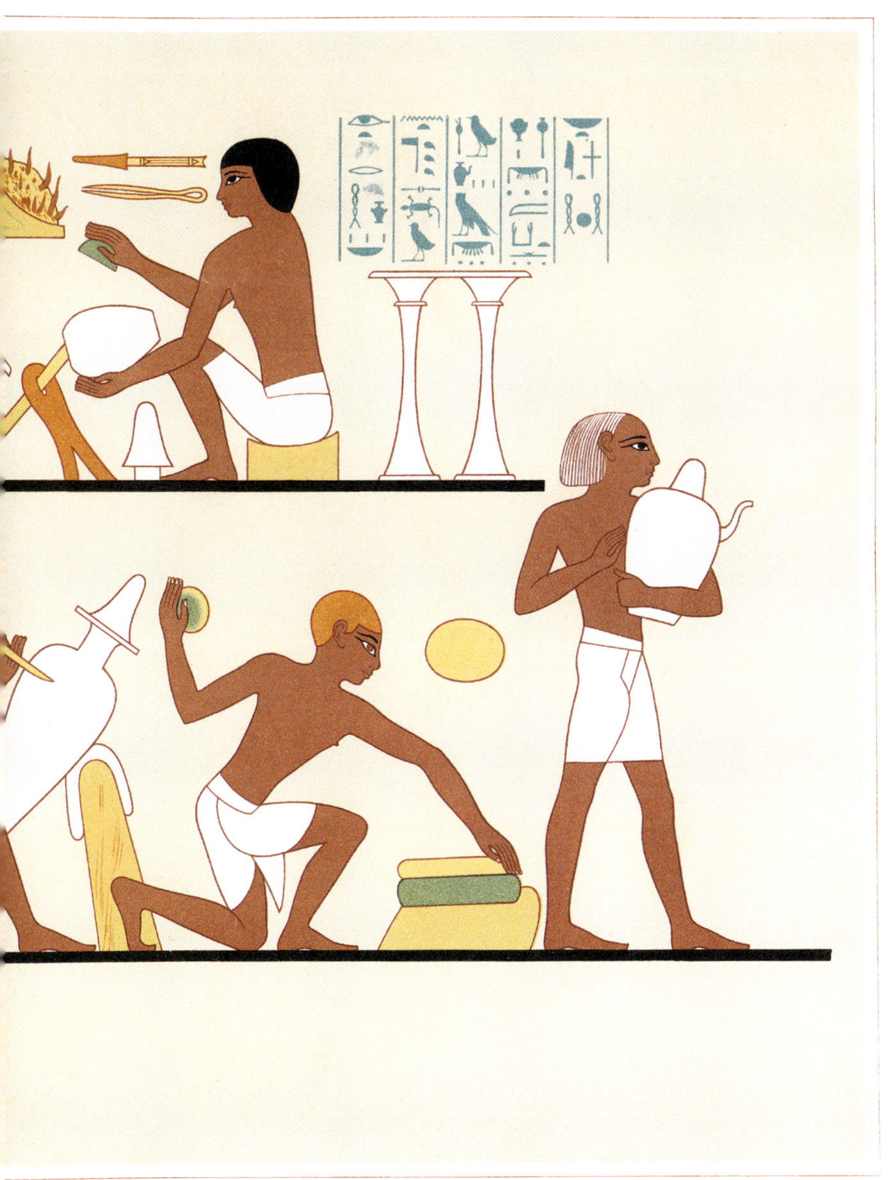

es .

Publié par Arthus-Bertrand, Éditeur

D'OR & D'ARGENT .

XVIIIe DYNASTIE .)

(Pages/Seite 458/459)

GOLDSMITHS' WORKSHOP OF RETJENU (18th Dynasty)

Temple of Karnak

Thanks to their scientific knowledge of metallurgy, the early Egyptians painstakingly exploited all the minerals to be found in their soils. When Pharaonic civilisation was at its apogee, the natural abundance of precious stones and metals channelled the national taste towards work crafted from these materials, to the detriment of terracotta and enamelled faience-work. However, once the races they had conquered had been reduced to slavery, preference seems to have been given to gold from Retjenu, an Asiatic land whose people had been enslaved and forced to work for their conquerors. The metal that was identified by the description 'gold of Retjenu' was highly prized for its brilliance and appears to have been a gold alloy of superb effect, which was equal in value to, or even surpassed the gold which was normally used for artistic work; the secret of its mixture seems to have been lost.

GOLDGIESSERWERKSTATT IN RETJENU (18. Dynastie)

Tempel von Karnak

Dank ihrer wissenschaftlichen Kenntnisse auf dem Gebiet der Metallurgie nutzten die frühen Ägypter sorgfältig alle Mineralien, die sich in ihrem Boden befanden. Auf dem Höhepunkt der pharaonischen Kultur lenkte die Fülle an Halbedelsteinen und wertvollen Metallen den Volksgeschmack – auf Kosten von Keramik und emailliertem Steingut – auf Werke hin, die aus diesen Materialien gefertigt waren; mit der Versklavung der eroberten Völker scheint man jedoch den Erzeugnissen den Vorzug gegeben zu haben, die aus dem Gold aus Retjenu hergestellt waren – von einem versklavten asiatischen Volk, das für die Eroberer zu arbeiten gezwungen war. Das für seinen Glanz so geschätzte Gold, das wegen dieser Eigenschaft als Gold aus Retjenu bekannt war, scheint eine Goldlegierung von wunderbarer Wirkung gewesen zu sein, deren Wert dem des üblicherweise für Kunstwerke verwendeten Goldes gleichkam oder dieses übertraf; ihr Geheimnis soll verloren gegangen sein.

ATELIER DES FONDEURS DE L'OR DES ROTHENNOU (XVIIIe dynastie)

Temple de Karnac

Les premiers Égyptiens, grâce à ces connaissances scientifiques en métallurgie, exploitèrent avec soin tous les minerais que pouvait renfermer leur sol. À l'apogée de la civilisation pharaonique, l'abondance des pierres fines et des métaux précieux dirigea le goût national vers les ouvrages façonnés avec ces matières, au détriment des terres cuites et des faïences émaillées ; mais, à partir de la réduction en esclavage des peuples conquis, la préférence paraît avoir été accordée aux produits provenant de l'or des Rothennou [Rétjénou], peuple asiatique réduit en esclavage et forcé de travailler pour ses conquérants. Le métal, si prisé pour son éclat, qui était désigné par cette qualification d'or des Rothennou, paraît avoir été un alliage d'or d'un merveilleux effet, qui égalait en valeur, s'il ne le surpassait, l'or employé dans les travaux d'art ; le secret en aurait été perdu.

(Pages/Seite 460/461)

MANUFACTURE OF GOLD AND SILVER VASES (18th Dynasty)

Necropolis of Thebes

The importance which was attached to the crafting of the great set-pieces of the goldsmith's art can be understood when one considers the four funerary vases [canopic jars] in which it was customary to seal the entrails of the dead, vases which the wealthiest people demanded should be made of the most precious materials. They were placed at the four corners of the coffin of the mummy, from which they borrowed something of its form in its final shroud. All four vases were identical in shape but were crowned with different symbolic heads.

HERSTELLUNG VON VASEN AUS GOLD UND SILBER (18. Dynastie)

Nekropole von Theben

Dass man der Ausführung großer Goldschmiedearbeiten solche Bedeutung zumaß, erklärt sich, sobald man an die vier Begräbnisvasen denkt, in denen üblicherweise die Eingeweide der Toten aufbewahrt wurden und für die die wohlhabendsten Persönlichkeiten die kostbarsten Materialien verlangten. Man stellte sie an den vier Ecken des Sarges mit der Mumie auf, deren Form im Leichentuch sie ein wenig übernahmen. Alle vier hatten dieselbe Form; sie waren jedoch mit unterschiedlichen Sinnbildern bekrönt.

FABRICATION DE VASES D'OR ET D'ARGENT (XVIIIe dynastie)

Nécropole de Thèbes

L'importance qu'on attachait à l'exécution des grandes pièces d'orfèvrerie s'explique, lorsqu'on pense aux quatre vases funéraires dans lesquels il était d'usage d'enfermer les entrailles des morts, vases que les personnes les plus riches exigeaient être des matières les plus précieuses. On les plaçait aux quatre coins du cercueil de la momie, à laquelle ils empruntaient quelque chose de sa forme dans son dernier linceul. Ils étaient tous quatre de forme identique ; mais couronnés de têtes symboliques différentes.

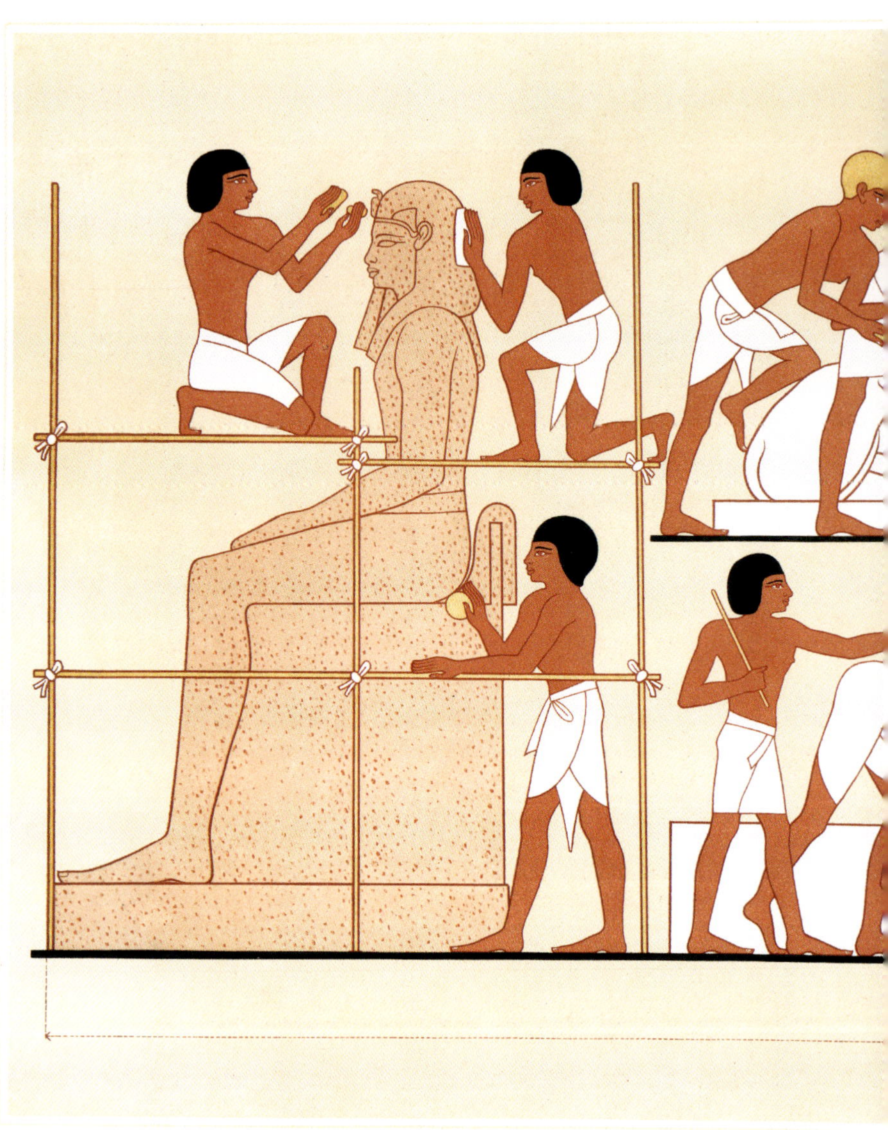

Lith par Daumont. Imp par Hangard-Maugé

ATELIE

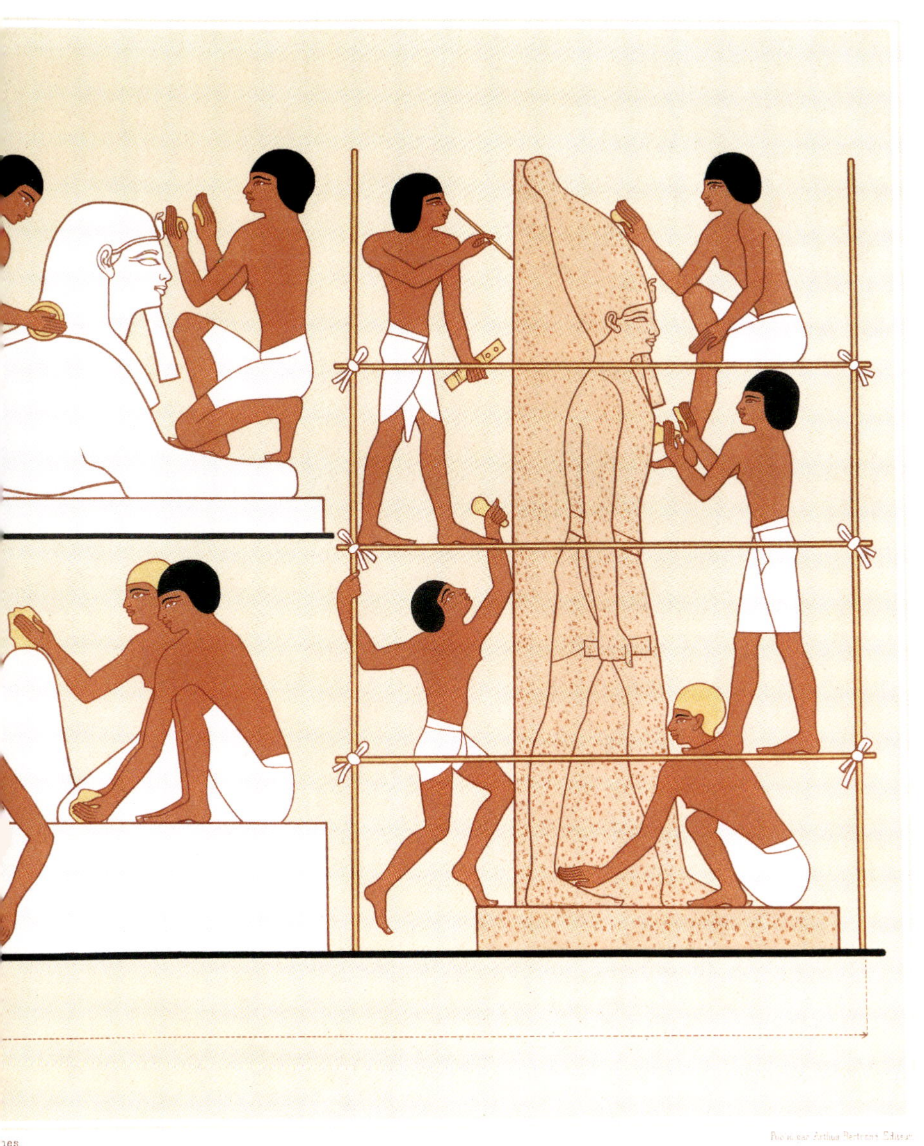

nes

Publié par Arthus Bertrand, Éditeur

JLPTEURS.

IE.)

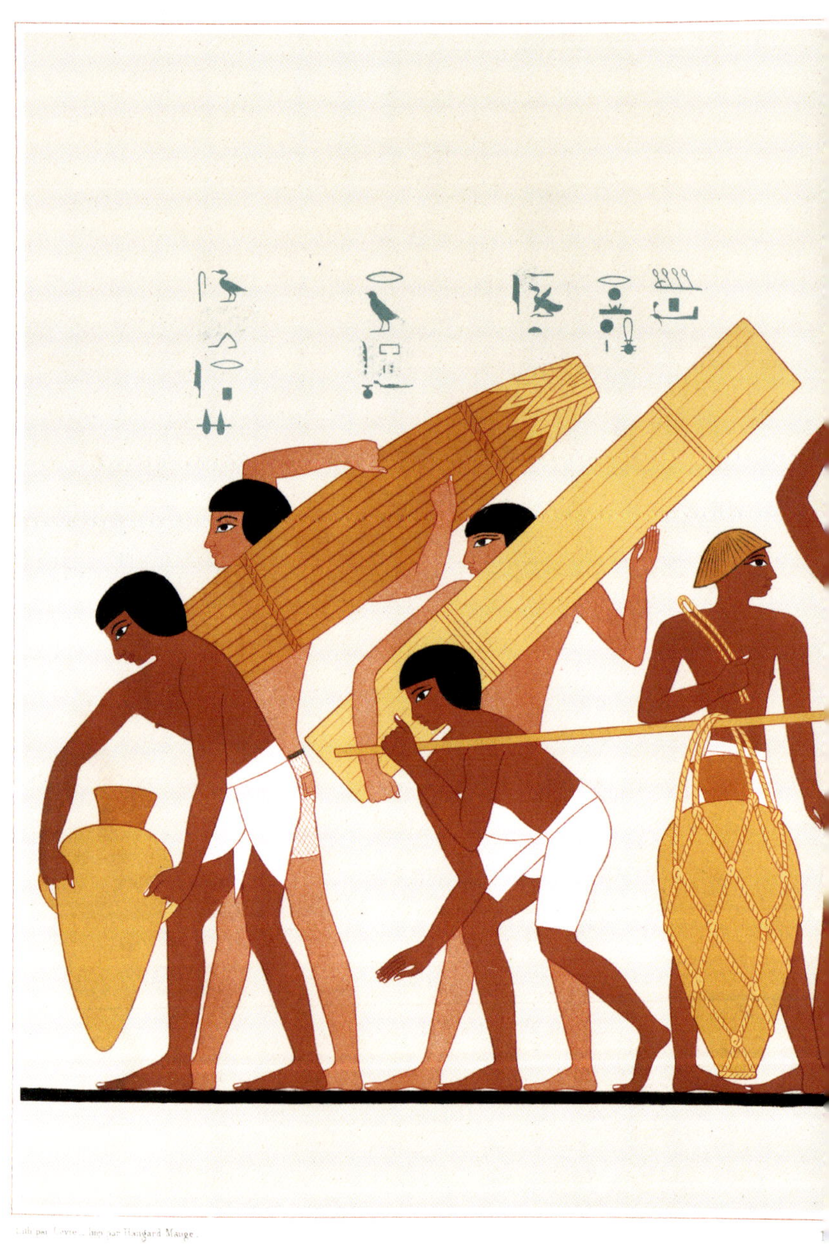

Lith par Levret. Imp par Hangard Maugé.

TRANSPORT D'USTE

(NÉCROPOLE

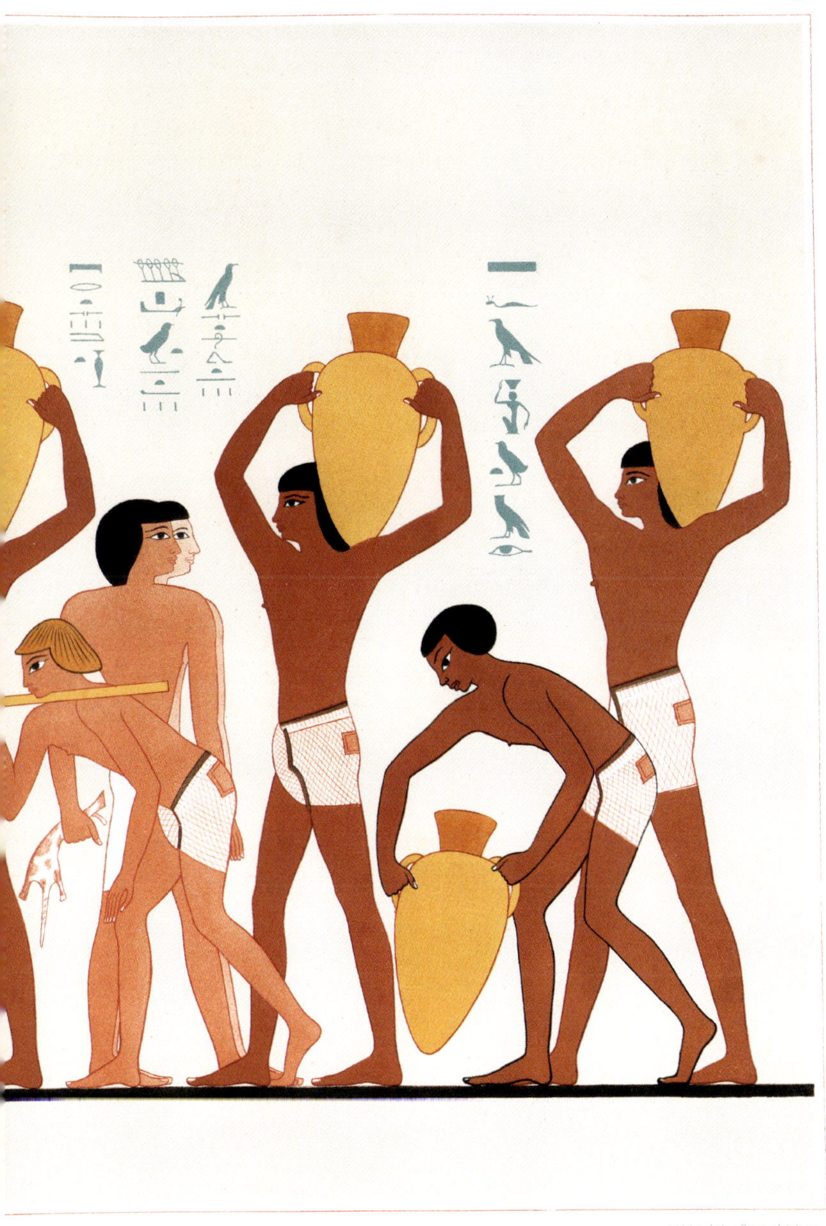

Publié par Arthus-Bertrand, éditeur

ET DE PROVISIONS.

1? DYNASTIE.)

(Pages/Seite 464/465)

SCULPTORS' WORKSHOP (18th Dynasty)

This painting was copied in the tomb of Rekhmire, vizier of Thutmosis III and governor of a city, probably Thebes, who wished to adorn his final resting-place with particularly interesting pictures. These enable us to understand the state of the arts at that period, the most brilliant of the 18th Dynasty; they prove that the techniques of the Egyptians were still at a very early stage, for the tools then were even more primitive than the scaffolding. This makes the grandeur and the finish of the works quite astonishing in comparison to the simplicity of the means.

BILDHAUERWERKSTATT (18. Dynastie)

Dieses Gemälde wurde im Grab von Rechmire kopiert, der Verwalter von Thutmosis III. und Gouverneur einer Stadt – wahrscheinlichen Thebens – war; es beliebte ihm, seine letzte Ruhestätte mit höchst interessanten Darstellungen zu verschönern, anhand derer sich der Stand der Künste in dieser Zeit – der Glanzzeit der 18. Dynastie – feststellen lässt. Sie beweisen, dass die Ägypter mit ihren Techniken in den Kinderschuhen stecken geblieben waren; denn die Werkzeuge sind hier noch einfacher als die Gerüste. Auch ist man im Verhältnis zur Einfachheit der Mittel stets über die Größe und sorgfältige Ausführung der Werke verblüfft.

ATELIER DE SCULPTEURS (XVIIIe dynastie)

Cette peinture a été copiée dans le tombeau de Rekhmara, intendant de Thoutmès [Thoutmôsis] III et gouverneur d'une ville, probablement Thèbes, qui s'est plu à faire embellir sa dernière demeure de représentations fort intéressantes, et qui permettent de se rendre compte de l'état des arts à cette époque, la plus brillante de la XVIIIe dynastie : elles prouvent que les procédés des Égyptiens s'étaient maintenus dans l'enfance ; car les outils y sont plus primitifs encore que les échafaudages. Aussi est-on toujours étonné de la grandeur et du fini des œuvres, comparés à la simplicité des moyens.

(Pages/Seite 466/467)

TRANSPORT OF UTENSILS AND PROVISIONS (18th Dynasty)

Necropolis of Thebes

In this scene, which is fairly crudely painted on the walls of the tomb of Rekhmire, vizier of Thutmosis III, there is more movement and more vitality than is normally met with in the subjects represented on the walls of temples. There is no doubt that here the artist had more freedom, and although he did not depart from the typical style which was sanctioned, he knew how to make use of this to create a greater variety in attitude and a more natural pose on the part of the characters. The Egyptians employed in this work were mixed with captive foreigners who can be recognised by their skin colouring and their cross-hatched "sabu" [loin-cloths] rather than their features, which fall within the conventional type common to all.

TRANSPORT VON GERÄTSCHAFTEN UND VORRÄTEN (18. Dynastie)

Nekropole von Theben

Diese recht grob auf die Wände des Grabes von Rechmire – dem Verwalter Thutmosis' III. – gemalte Szene ist bewegter und lebendiger, als es die gewöhnlich auf den Tempelmauern dargestellten Themen sind. Zweifellos hatte der Künstler hier mehr Freiheit; und ohne sich von den üblich gewordenen Mustern zu entfernen, hat er sich dies zunutze gemacht, um dem Verhalten der Figuren mehr Abwechslung und ihrer Körperhaltung mehr Natürlichkeit zu verleihen. Unter die mit dieser Arbeit beschäftigten Ägypter mischen sich fremde Gefangene, die eher an ihrem Teint und an ihrem gitternetzartigen Schurz („sabu") als an ihren Gesichtszügen zu erkennen sind, entsprechen diese doch dem allen gemeinsamen herkömmlichen Typus.

TRANSPORT D'USTENSILES ET DE PROVISIONS (XVIIIe dynastie)

Nécropole de Thèbes

Il y a dans cette scène, peinte assez grossièrement sur les parois du tombeau de Rekhmara, intendant de Thoutmès [Thoutmôsis] III, plus de mouvement et de vie qu'on n'en rencontre, habituellement, dans les sujets représentés sur les murs des temples. L'artiste, sans doute, avait ici plus de liberté ; et sans s'écarter des types consacrés, il en aura su profiter pour mettre plus de variété dans les attitudes et plus de naturel dans la pose des personnages. Aux Égyptiens employés à ces travaux se mêlent des captifs étrangers, reconnaissables à leur teint et à leur « sabou » réticulaire plutôt qu'à leurs traits, qui rentrent dans le type conventionnel commun à tous.

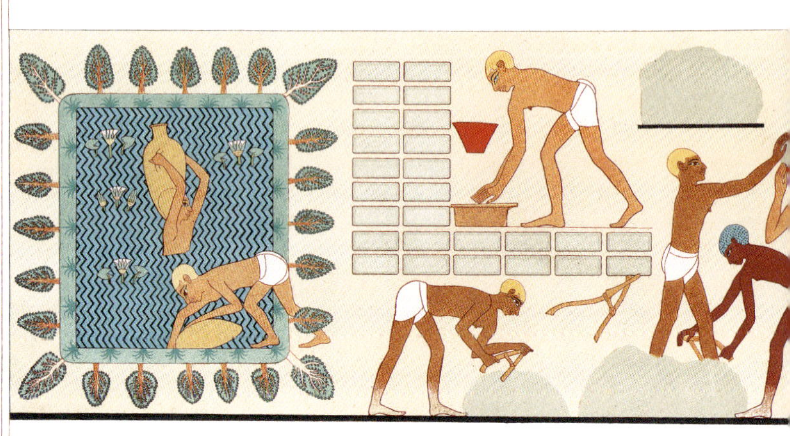

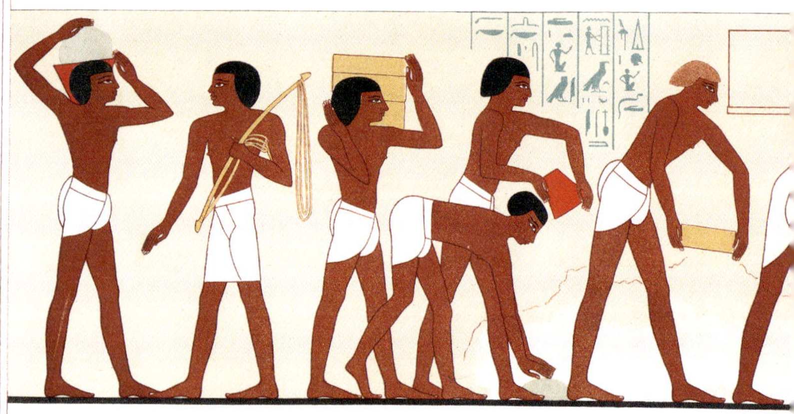

Lith. par Levié. Imp. par Hangard Maugé.

CAPTIFS EMPLOYÉS A

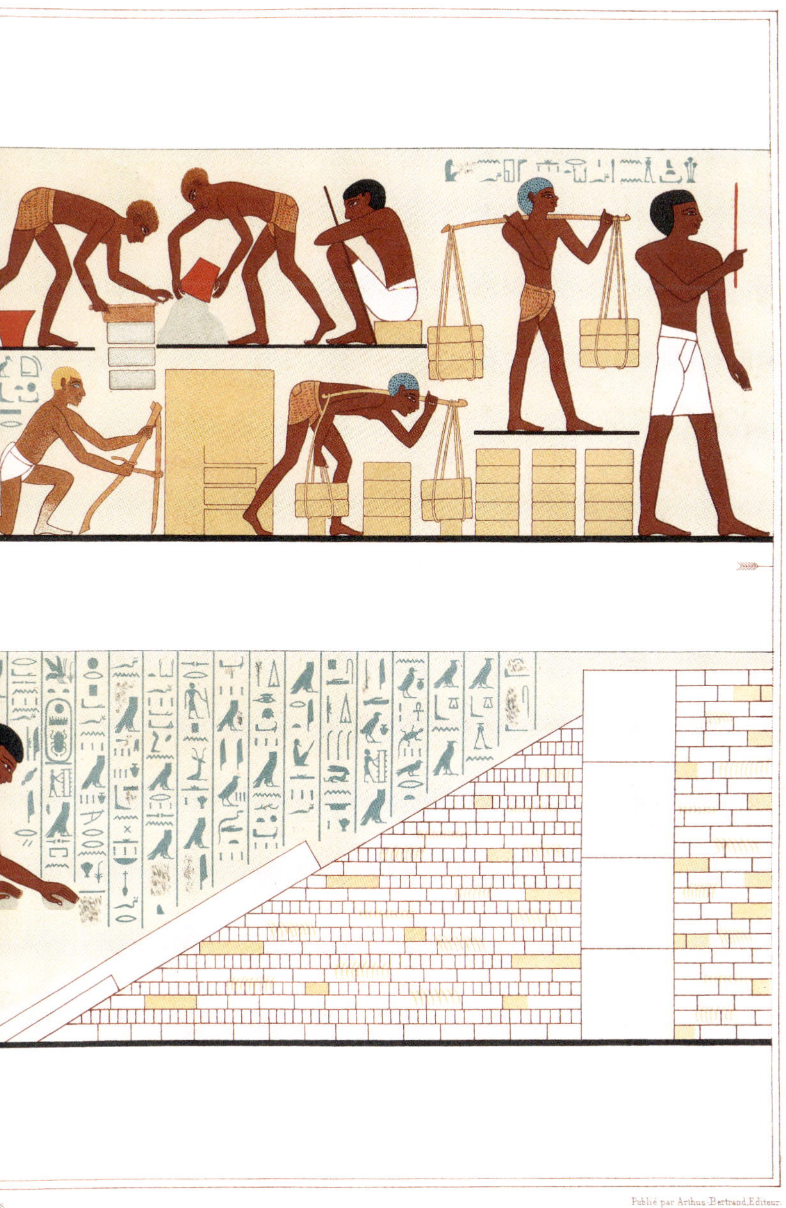

es.

Publié par Arthus-Bertrand, Editeur.

'EMPLE D'AMON, A THÈBES.

E.)

(Pages/Seite 470/471)

CAPTIVES EMPLOYED IN BUILDING A TEMPLE OF AMUN, IN THEBES (18th Dynasty)

The various expeditions of Thutmosis III in Asia led to a large number of conquered people or slaves being dispersed to different places and used by the king in the construction of temples of Amun. They were probably also used as unpaid labour for public benefit, particularly for work on the construction of canals and irrigation networks. [This plate] of the splendid tomb of Rekhmire shows us these prisoners busy drawing water, putting mud into moulds, making bricks out of it, transporting them and finally constructing the walls of a temple of Amun. Those workers employed on the more skilful areas of the work are Egyptians, as are other workmen employed as foremen. they are armed with sticks and are overseeing the work of the foreigners, who are easily recognisable by their light skin and their characteristic physiognomy.

GEFANGENE BAUEN EINEN AMUN-TEMPEL, IN THEBEN (18. Dynastie)

Die verschiedenen Asien-Feldzüge Thutmosis' III. erbrachten eine große Zahl Besiegter oder Sklaven, die auf unterschiedliche Stellen verteilt und vom König zum Bau der Amun-Tempel angestellt wurden. Wahrscheinlich stellte man sie auch zu Diensten von öffentlichem Nutzen an, insbesondere zu Kanalisations- und Bewässerungsarbeiten. [Diese Tafel] aus dem prächtigen Grab Rechmires zeigt uns Gefangene, die damit beschäftigt sind, Wasser zu schöpfen, Ton zu kneten, Ziegel daraus zu formen, diese zu befördern und schließlich die Mauern eines Amun-Tempels zu errichten. Die mit dem schwierigsten Teil des Werkes befassten Arbeiter sind Ägypter, ebenso wie andere, die als Führer angestellt sind: Mit Knüppeln bewaffnet, überwachen sie die Arbeit der Fremden, die im Übrigen an ihrem hellen Teint und ihrer besonderen Physiognomie gut zu erkennen sind.

CAPTIFS EMPLOYÉS À BÂTIR UN TEMPLE D'AMON, À THÈBES (XVIIIe dynastie)

Les diverses expéditions de Thoutmès [Thoutmôsis] III en Asie amenèrent un grand nombre de vaincus ou d'esclaves qui furent disséminés sur différents points et employés par le roi à la construction des temples d'Amon. Ils furent probablement aussi employés à des corvées d'utilité publique, et en particulier aux travaux de canalisation et d'irrigation. [Cette planche] du splendide tombeau de Rekhmara nous montre ces prisonniers occupés à puiser l'eau, à pétrir la terre, à en former des briques, à les transporter et finalement à construire les murs d'un temple d'Amon. Les ouvriers occupés de la partie la plus difficile de l'œuvre sont égyptiens, ainsi que d'autres employés comme conducteurs : armés de bâtons, ils surveillent le travail des étrangers, fort reconnaissables d'ailleurs à leur teint clair et à leur physionomie particulière.

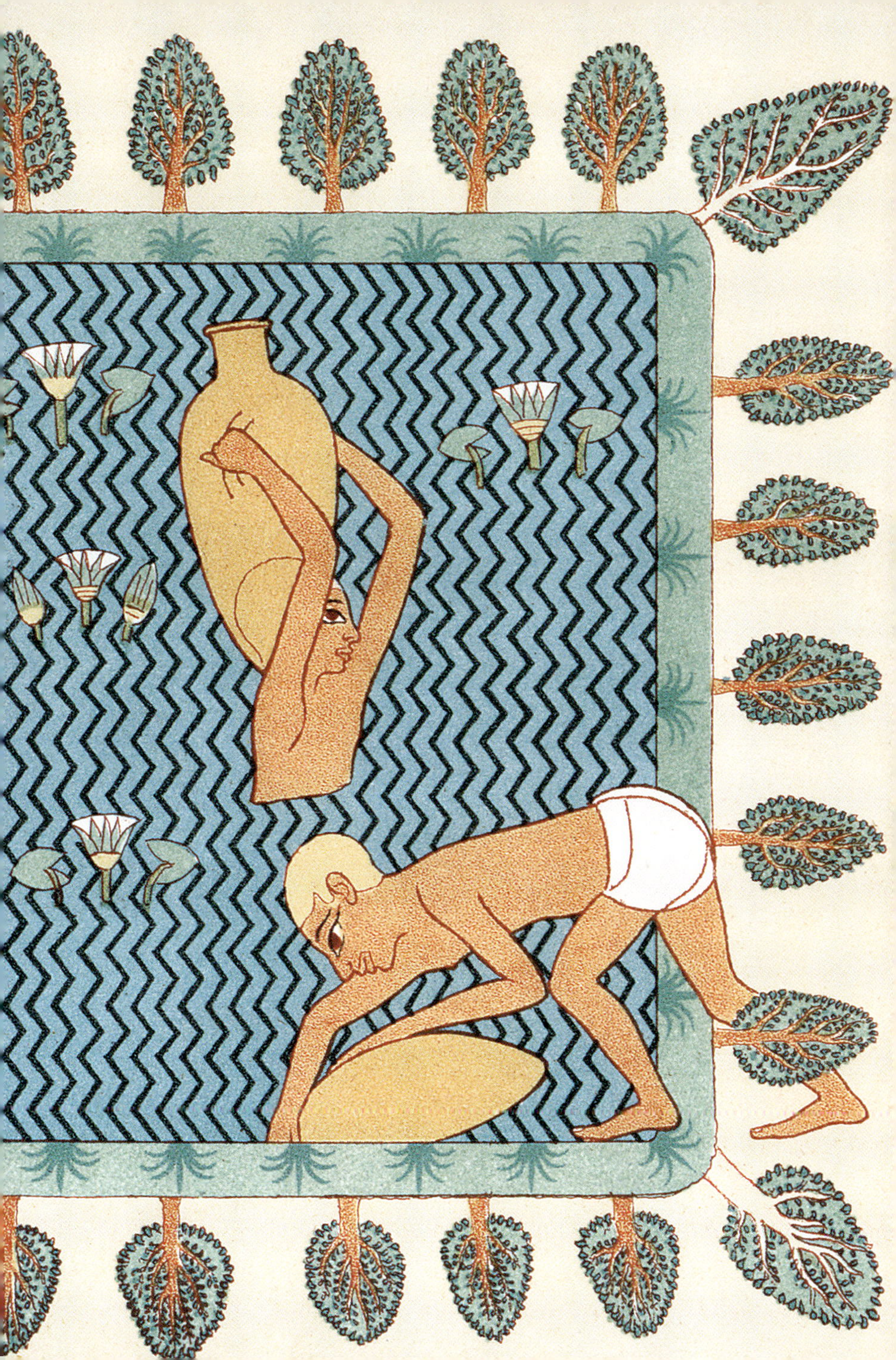

WOMAN PLAYING A LUTE (18th Dynasty)

Necropolis of Thebes

This young woman is playing the "mandora" (or lute with an extended finger-board). This charming bust presents us with a picture of one of the servants of the wet-nurse of Amenophis II. It is preserved in the same kiosk as that of its mistress, who is shown holding the young pharaoh on her lap [see p. 453]. There is a more natural quality to the figure, the contours are more supple, and the pose is more graceful than is normally found in Egyptian painting. The two nipples are clearly indicated, something which I have never encountered elsewhere. The same can be said of the hair, which again I have never seen so accurately depicted anywhere else.

LAUTENSPIELERIN (18. Dynastie)

Nekropole von Theben

Ein junges, Laute (oder Mandoline) spielendes Mädchen. Dieses reizende Brustbild zeigt uns das Porträt einer der Begleiterinnen der Amme Amenophis' II. Es ist unter derselben Ädikula erhalten wie das ihrer Herrin, die mit dem jungen Pharao auf den Knien dargestellt ist [siehe S. 453]. Das Gesicht ist natürlicher, die Umrisse sind geschmeidiger und die Haltung ist anmutiger, als man es für gewöhnlich in der ägyptischen Malerei findet. Eine Besonderheit, auf die ich sonst nirgendwo gestoßen bin, sind die beiden deutlich markierten Brustwarzen. Diese Bemerkung trifft ebenfalls auf die Haare zu, die man nirgends so gut dargestellt findet.

JOUEUSE DE MANDORE (XVIIIe dynastie)

Nécropole de Thèbes

Jeune fille jouant de la mandore (ou mandole à long manche). Ce buste charmant nous offre le portrait d'une des suivantes de la nourrice d'Aménophis II. On le trouve conservé sous le même édicule que celui de sa maîtresse, qui est représentée portant, sur ses genoux, le jeune pharaon [voir p. 453]. Il y a plus de naturel dans la figure, plus de souplesse dans les contours et plus de grâce dans la pose qu'on n'en trouve ordinairement dans les peintures égyptiennes. Les deux mamelons sont bien indiqués, particularité que je n'ai jamais rencontrée ailleurs. Cette remarque s'applique, également, aux cheveux qu'on ne trouve jamais aussi bien représentés.

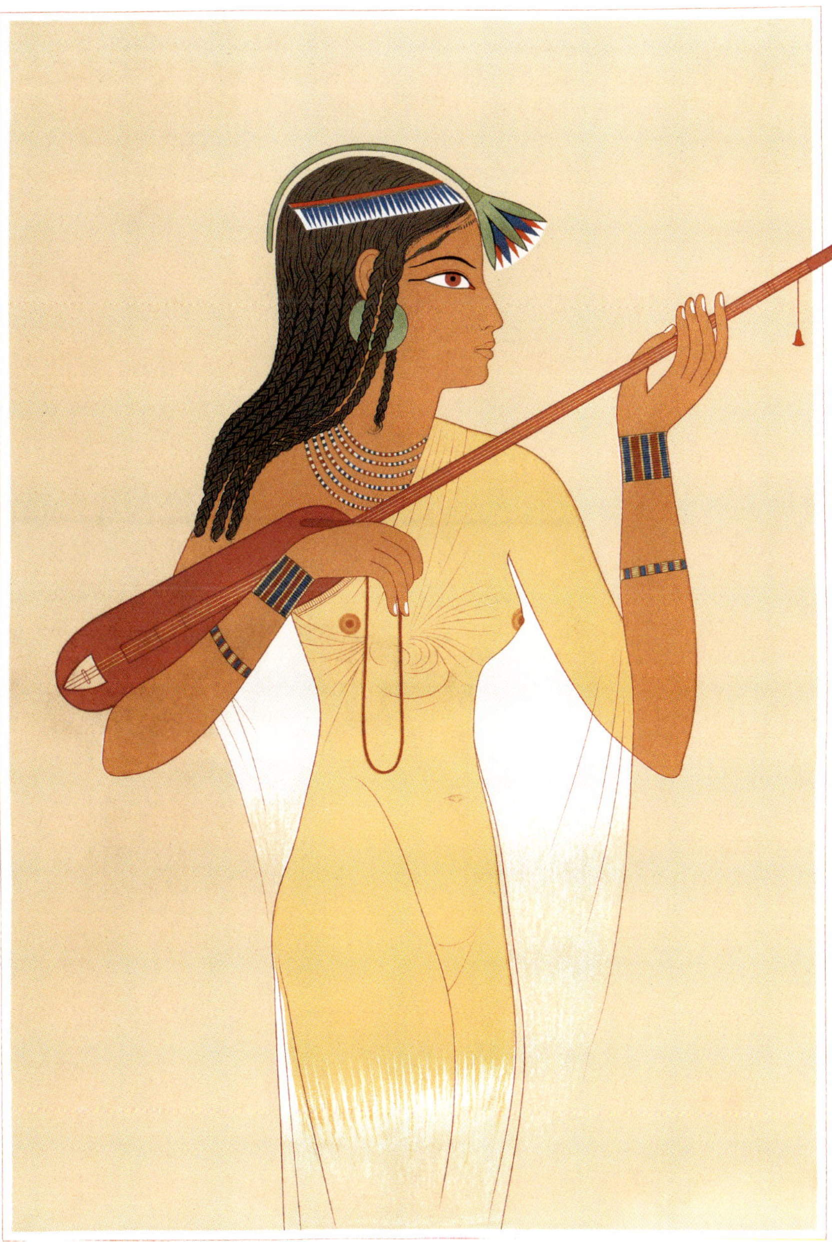

Lith par Levié. Imp par Hangard-Maugé. E. Prisse d'Avennes. Publié par Arthus Bertrand Éditeur.

JOUEUSE DE MANDORE.

(NÉCROPOLE DE THÈBES.— XVIIIe DYNASTIE.)

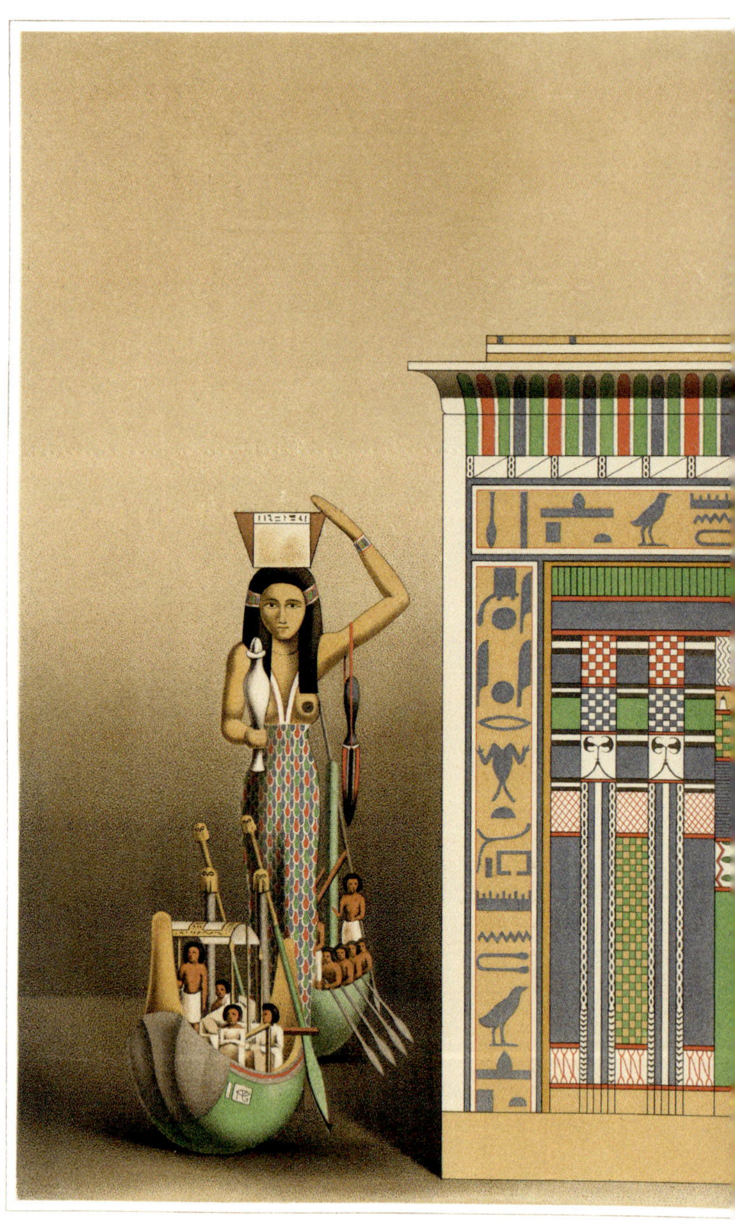

Executé par Levié. Imp. Lemercier & Cie, Paris

TOMBEAU DÉCOUVERT

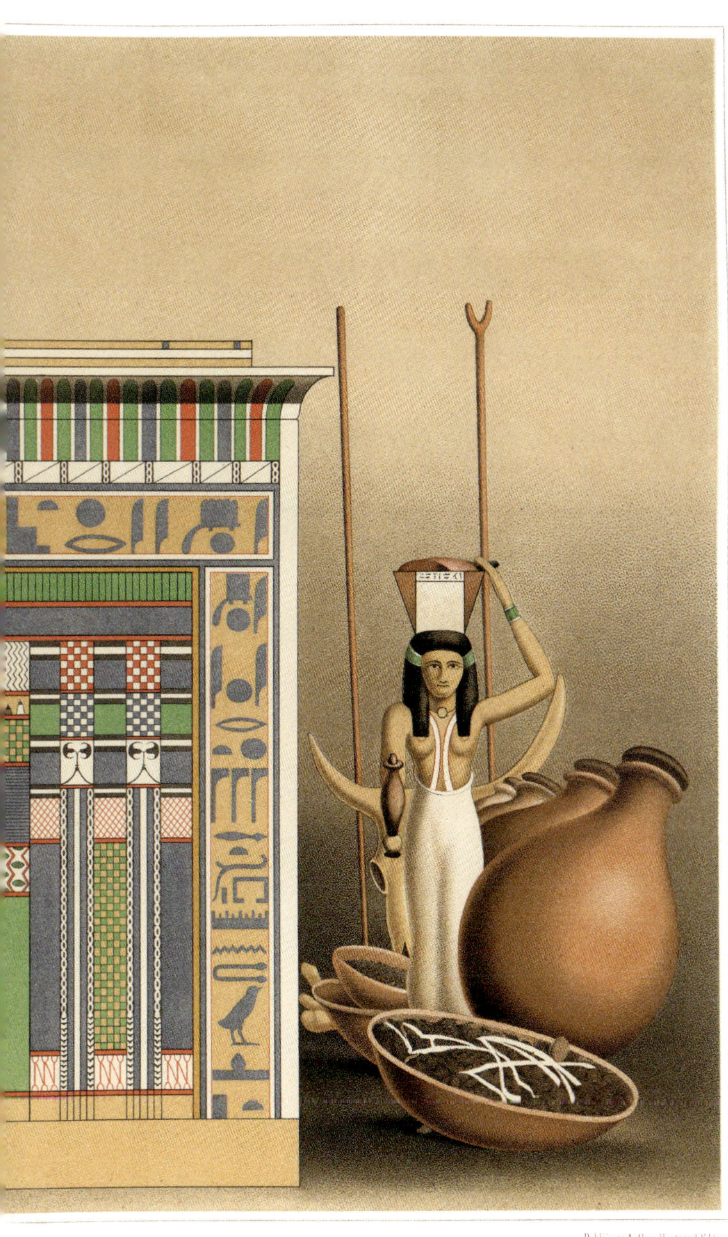

Publié par Arthus Bertrand, Éditeur

VALLÉE D'EL-ASSACIF.

(Pages/Seite 476/477)

TOMB DISCOVERED IN THE VALLEY OF EL-ASSASIF

Thebes

A painted reconstruction of a tomb from this valley which has such a wealth of funerary monuments. I have included this beautiful plate to demonstrate yet again the importance of the painted representations in the hypogea with regard to customs and costumes. This is above all because the durability of Egyptian customs throughout the ages meant that they never ceased to surround the dead in their hypogea with those beings or objects which had been dear to them during their life.

IM TAL VON EL-ASSASIF ENTDECKTES GRAB

Theben

Gemalte Darstellung eines Grabes aus diesem an Grabdenkmälern so reichen Tal. Ich habe diese schöne Tafel hinzugefügt, um ein weiteres Mal die Bedeutung aufzuzeigen, die den Malereien in den Hypogäen unter dem Gesichtspunkt der Sitten und Gebräuche zukommt. Und dies vor allem deshalb, weil die Beständigkeit der ägyptischen Gebräuche es ihnen zu keiner Zeit erlaubte, die Toten in ihren Hypogäen nicht mehr mit den Wesen oder den Gegenständen zu umgeben, die ihnen im Leben etwas wert waren.

TOMBEAU DÉCOUVERT DANS LA VALLÉE D'EL-ASSACIF

Thèbes

Représentation peinte d'un tombeau de cette vallée si riche en monuments funéraires. J'ai donné cette belle planche pour démontrer une fois de plus l'importance qu'offre au point de vue des mœurs et des coutumes les représentations peintes des hypogées. Et cela surtout parce que la stabilité des usages égyptiens, à toute époque, ne leur permit pas de cesser d'entourer les morts, dans leurs hypogées, soit des êtres, soit des objets qui leur avaient été chers pendant leur vie.

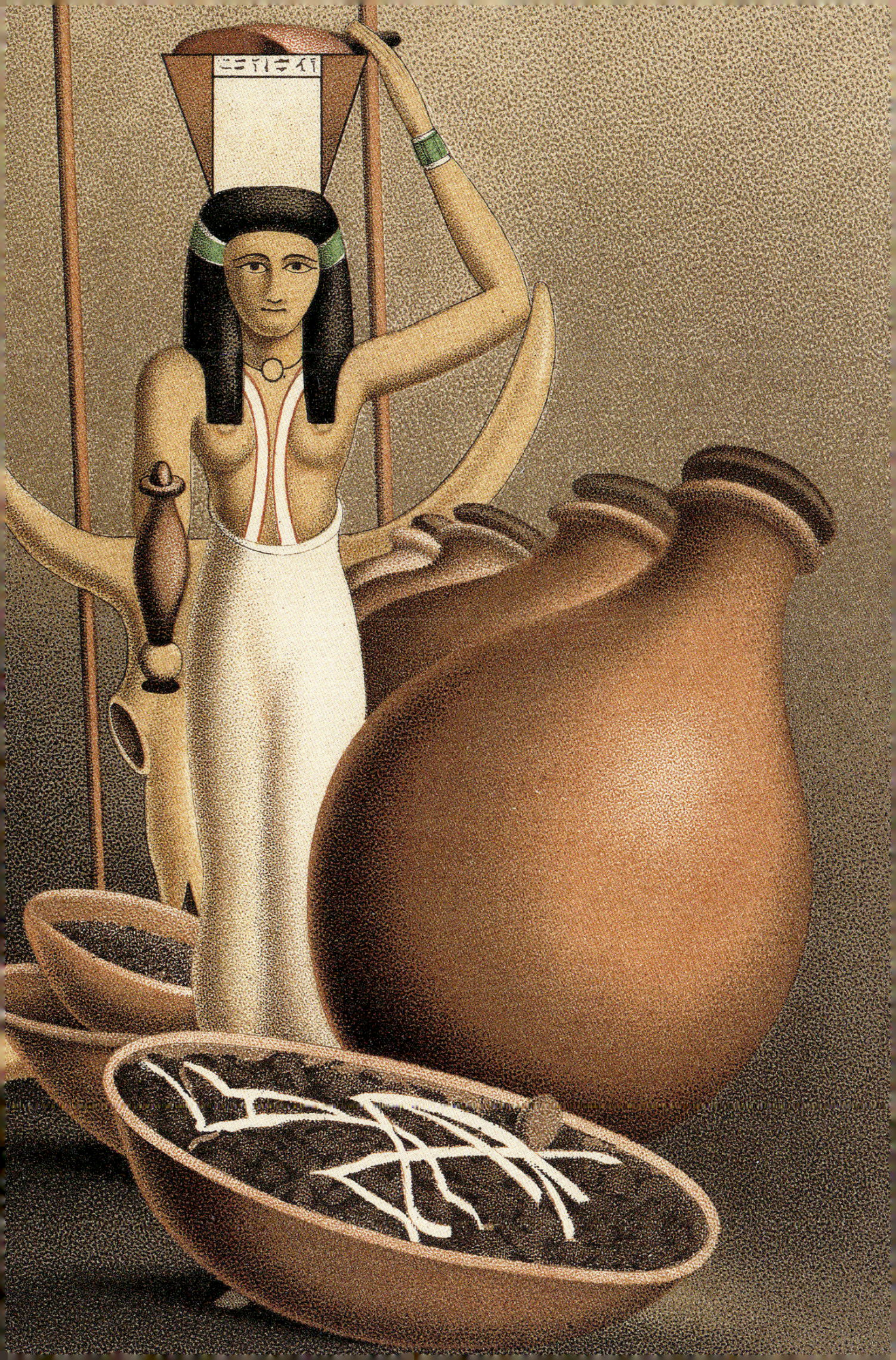

PLANTS AND FLOWERS

Taken from various monuments

No. 1 represents the umbel of a papyrus-type plant which is painted in a hypogeum at el-Bawaba in Thebes. The most remarkable thing about it is the slug which is shown arching on its stalk. This animal, which represents the sound F in the hieroglyphic alphabet, was initially considered by all Egyptologists to be an Egyptian viper. No. 2 represents a papyrus umbel painted in a hypogeum in the necropolis of Thebes. This is the sole plant to be depicted with the stamp of absolute authenticity. In no. 3 I wished to show the papyrus umbels which can be seen painted in the space between two toothed leaves on the bases of the great columns at Karnak. Nos. 4 and 5 are flowers painted in hypogea. Nos. 6, 7 and 8 show plants painted in the tomb of Ramesses III [and] in a small hypogeum of the same period situated in the Valley of the Queens.

PFLANZEN UND BLUMEN

Verschiedenen Denkmälern entnommen

Die Nr. 1 stellt die gemalte Dolde einer papyrusförmigen Pflanze aus einem Hypogäum in el-Bawaba in Theben dar. Das Bemerkenswerteste daran ist eine Art Nacktschnecke, die über ihren Stängel kriecht. Auf den ersten Blick hatten alle Ägyptologen dieses Tier, das im Hieroglyphenalphabet den Ton F darstellt, für eine ägyptische Hornviper gehalten. Die Nr. 2 stellt eine gemalte Papyrusdolde aus einem Hypogäum in der Nekropole von Theben dar. Es ist die einzige Pflanze, die ein unwiderlegbar lebensechtes Gepräge aufweist. Mit der Nr. 3 wollte ich die Papyrusdolden darstellen, die an der Basis der großen Säulen in Karnak in die Zwischenräume zwischen zwei Blättern mit Fischgrätmuster gemalt sind. Die Nr. 4 und 5 sind in Hypogäen gemalte Blumen. Die Nr. 6, 7 und 8 zeigen im Grab von Ramses III. [und] in einem kleinen Hypogäum aus derselben Zeit, das sich im Tal der Königinnen befindet, gemalte Pflanzen.

PLANTES ET FLEURS

Tirées de divers monuments

Le n° 1 représente une ombelle de plante papyriforme peinte dans un hypogée d'El-Bauaba à Thèbes. Ce qu'elle offre de plus remarquable, c'est une espèce de limace rampant sur sa tige. Cet animal, qui représente dans l'alphabet hiéroglyphique le son F, avait été considéré par tous les égyptologues, au premier abord, comme un céraste. Le n° 2 représente une ombelle de papyrus peinte dans un hypogée de la nécropole de Thèbes. C'est la seule plante qui se présente avec un cachet de vérité irrécusable. Dans le n° 3 j'ai voulu représenter les ombelles de papyrus qu'on voit peintes dans l'intervalle de deux feuilles chevronnées sur les bases des grandes colonnes de Karnac. Les n°s 4 et 5 sont des fleurs peintes dans les hypogées. Les n°s 6, 7 et 8 offrent des plantes peintes dans le tombeau de Ramsès III [et] dans un petit hypogée de la même époque situé dans la vallée des Reines.

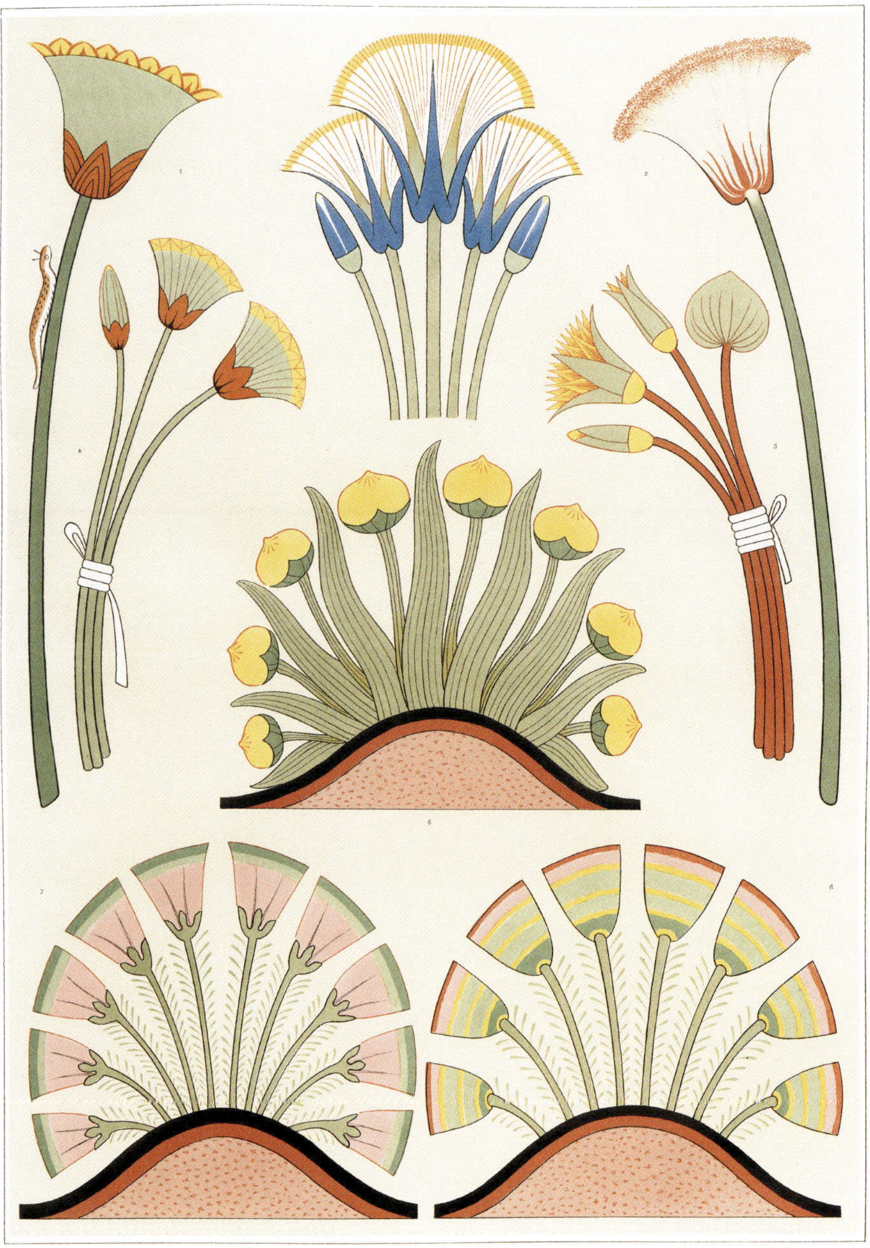

Lith. par Bodin. Imp. par Haugard-Maugé. E. Prisse d'Avennes. Publié par Arthus Bertrand, Éditeur.

PLANTES & FLEURS

TIRÉES DE DIVERS MONUMENTS.

PORTRAIT OF PRINCE MONTUHERKHEPESHEF (19th Dynasty)

Son of Ramesses [II] Meryamun

This painting is remarkable for the delicacy of the profile and the sweetness and regularity of the features; it represents the fifth son of Ramesses the Great, known as Montuherkhepeshef, which means: Mont has grasped his double-edged sword. The prince's tomb is situated at the end of the valley of Biban el-Muluk and in it he is shown on various occasions, almost always in the same costume, making offerings to the principal deities. In all these depictions the head is extremely handsome, the nose slightly curved, the lips finely delineated and the smile serene; briefly, the sweet but proud expression lends a particular charm to this beautiful portrait.

PORTRÄT DES PRINZEN MONTHHERCHEPESCHEF (19. Dynastie)

Sohn von Ramses [II.] Meriamun

Dieses Gemälde, das durch die Feinheit des Profils sowie die Zartheit und Ebenmäßigkeit der Züge bemerkenswert ist, stellt den fünften Sohn Ramses' des Großen namens Monthherchepeschef dar, was bedeutet: Mont ist auf seinem Schwert. Im Grab dieses Prinzen, das sich hinten im Tal der Könige, dem Biban el-Muluk, befindet, ist er mehrfach und fast immer in demselben Gewand dabei dargestellt, wie der den wichtigsten Göttern opfert. Der Kopf ist überall sehr schön; die leicht gebogene Nase, die kunstvoll geformten Lippen und das stille Lächeln, in einem Wort, ein sanfter und stolzer Ausdruck verleiht diesem schönen Porträt einen besonderen Reiz.

PORTRAIT DU PRINCE MANTOUHICHOPCHF (XIXe dynastie)

Fils de Ramsès [II] Meïamoun

Cette peinture, remarquable par la délicatesse du profil, la douceur et la régularité des traits, représente le cinquième fils de Ramsès le Grand, nommé Mantouhichopchf ou Monthixopeshef, c'est-à-dire : Mont est sur son glaive. Dans le tombeau de ce prince, situé au fond de la vallée de Biban el-Molouk, on l'a représenté, à diverses reprises, faisant des offrandes aux principales divinités et presque toujours sous le même costume. Partout, la tête est fort belle, le nez légèrement courbé, les lèvres découpées et le sourire calme ; en un mot, une expression douce et fière donne un charme particulier à ce beau portrait.

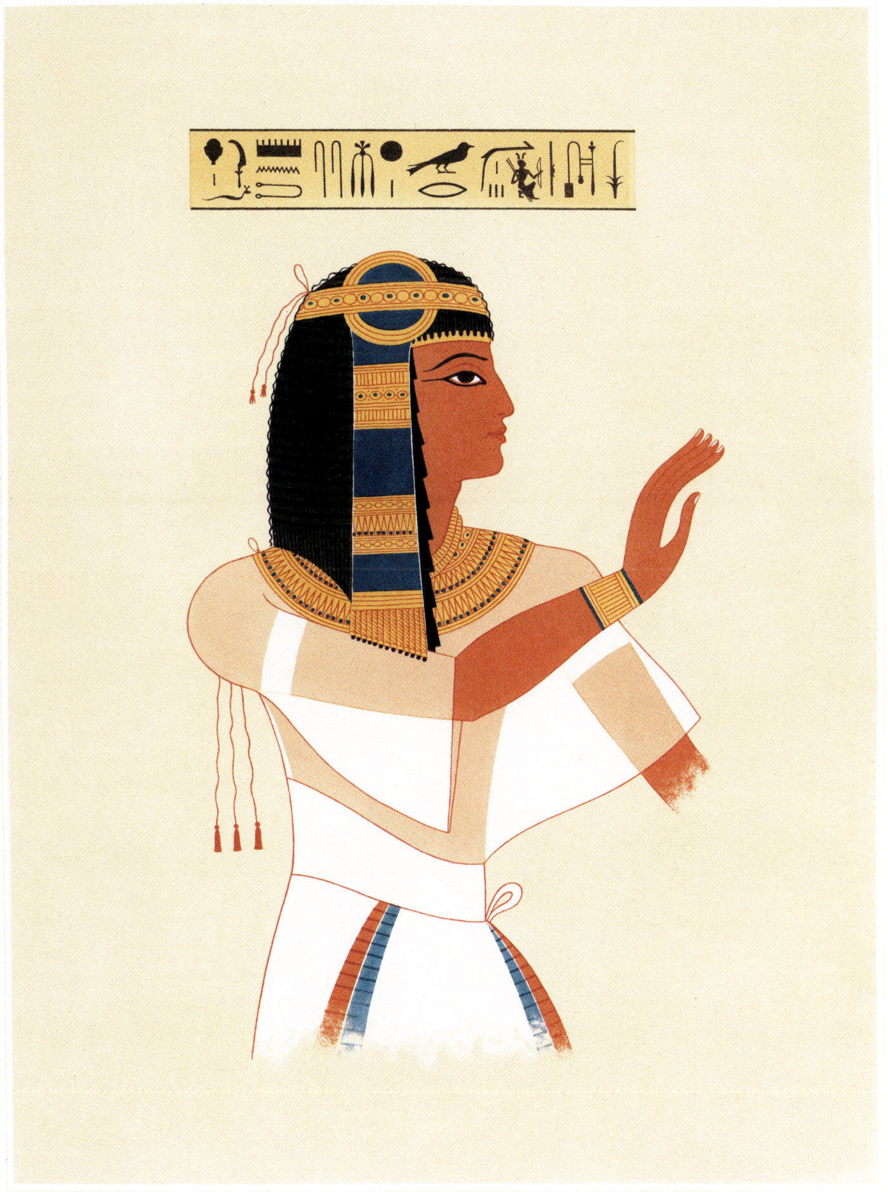

Lith. par Moulin. _ Imp. par Hangard-Maugé. E. Prisse d'Avennes. Publié par Arthus Bertrand Editeur.

PORTRAIT DU PRINCE MANTOUHICHOPCHF,

FILS DE RAMSÈS-MEÏAMOUN.

(XIXe DYNASTIE.)

PORTRAIT OF RAMESSES [II] MERYAMUN (19th Dynasty)

This beautiful portrait of Ramesses the Great was copied in 1843 in a small hypogeum situated behind the Ramesseum, which has now completely disappeared thanks to the pickaxes of the fellahs who used it to feed the lime-kilns of Qena; fortunately an identical portrait still exists on the internal face of the southern wall of the hypostyle hall at Karnak. The king is shown with his hanging side-lock finishing in the fat curl which is known to have been the emblem of adolescence at that time; he wears the panther skin which was the distinguishing sign of a certain order of priests. The head painted in the hypogeum appears to have been made from the same stencil as that sculpted in the royal hall.

PORTRÄT VON RAMSES [II.] MERIAMUN (19. Dynastie)

Dieses schöne Porträt von Ramses dem Großen wurde im Jahre 1843 in einem kleinen – heute vollständig zur Belieferung der Kalköfen von Qina unter der Spitzhacke der Fellachen verschwundenen – Hypogäum kopiert, das sich hinter dem Ramesseum befand; glücklicherweise gibt es auf der Innenwand der südlichen Mauer des Hypostyls von Karnak noch ein ganz ähnliches Porträt. Der König ist mit einem Pantherfell, dem Erkennungszeichen eines bestimmten Priesterordens, bekleidet und mit einem herabhängenden Zopf dargestellt, der in einer großen Locke endet – von der man weiß, dass sie damals das Attribut des Jugendalters war. Der im Hypogäum gemalte scheint ebenso wie der in der Säulenhalle ausgemeißelte Kopf mit derselben Schablone hergestellt zu sein.

PORTRAIT DE RAMSÈS [II] MEÏAMOUN (XIXe dynastie)

Ce beau portrait de Ramsès le Grand a été copié, en 1843, dans un petit hypogée qui se trouvait situé derrière le Ramesseum, et qui a entièrement disparu aujourd'hui sous le pic des fellahs pour alimenter les fours à chaux de Kéné [Qena] heureusement, il se trouve encore un portrait absolument semblable sur la paroi intérieure du mur méridional de la salle hypostyle de Karnac. Le roi est représenté avec la tresse pendante, dont l'extrémité se termine par une grosse boucle qu'on sait avoir été alors l'emblème de l'adolescence, et vêtu de la peau de panthère, signe distinctif d'un certain ordre des prêtres. La tête peinte dans l'hypogée de même que celle sculptée dans la salle royale semblaient faites sur le même poncif.

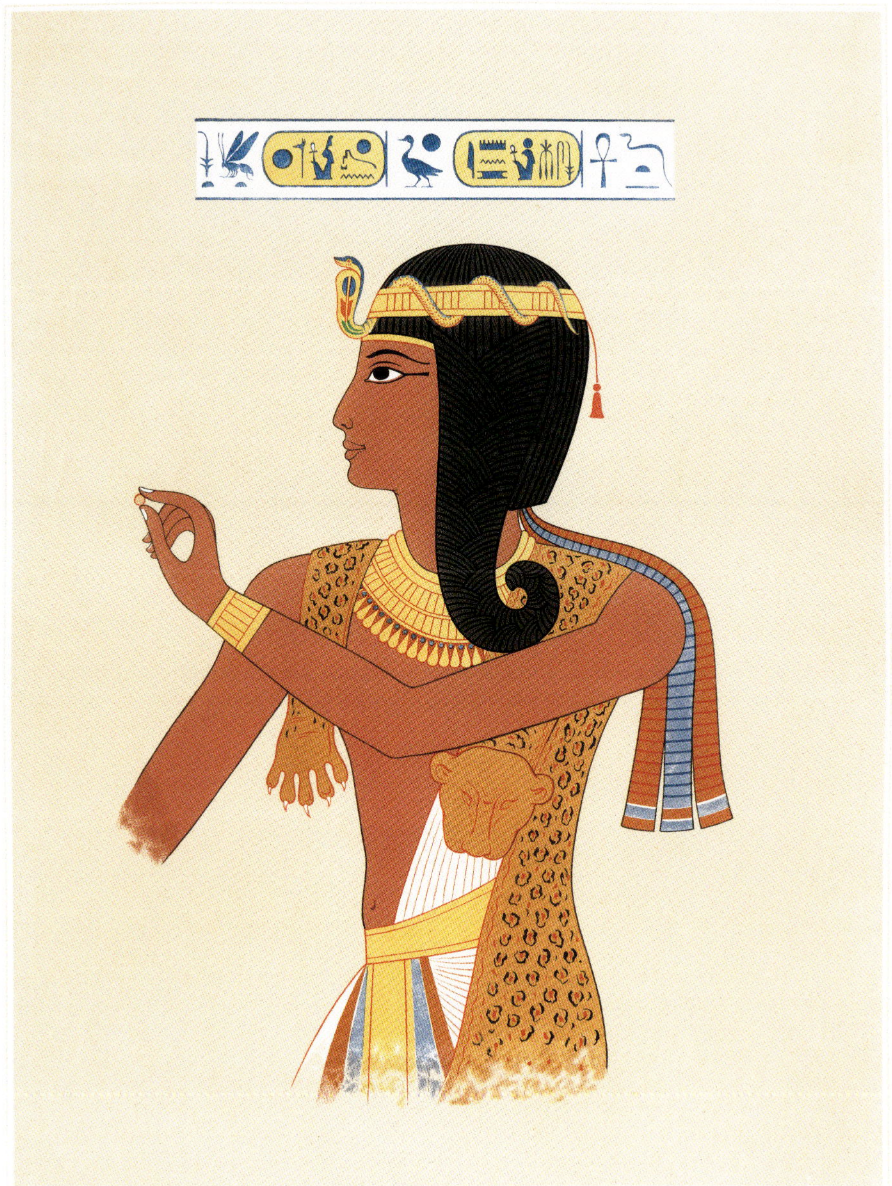

Lith. par Moulin. _ Imp. par Hangard-Maugé. E. Prisse d'Avennes. Publié par Arthur Bertrand, Editeur.

PORTRAIT DE RAMSÈS-MEÏAMOUN.

(RAMSÈS II - XIXe DYNASTIE.)

PORTRAIT OF PHARAOH MERNEPTAH HETEPHERMAAT

(19th Dynasty)

Necropolis of Thebes

The sovereign whose portrait I give here was a shepherd king: there is a legend about these kings who oppressed Egypt and who have gone down in history as absolute iconoclasts. Not only did the shepherd kings have their names carved in hieroglyphs on the statues of other pharaohs, they also had statues carved in their own image, contrary to accepted practice up to that time. The sphinxes found at Tanis, which are obviously portraits of Apophis, were carved by Egyptian artists who imparted to these kings who had come from abroad a tough, vigorous character; and instead of the usual hairstyle, they covered their head with a lion's mane, which they drew falling on to the breast and back in imitation of the Egyptian "nemes". These figures are not mutilated; they were even decorated, later on, with the titulary of Merneptah Hetephermaat which proves that the name of this shepherd king was not abominated as has been presumed.

PORTRÄT DES PHARAOS MERENPTAH HETEPHERMAAT

(19. Dynastie)

Nekropole von Theben

Der Herrscher, dessen Porträt ich hier vorstelle, war ein Hirtenkönig: Über die Könige, die Ägypten unterjochten und in der Geschichte als Bilderstürmer bekannt sind, gibt es eine Legende. Die Hirtenkönige ließen nicht nur ihren Namen in Hieroglyphen in die Statuen der anderen Pharaonen eingravieren, sondern sie ließen – im Gegensatz zu dem, was bis dahin statthaft war – auch Statuen nach ihrem Bilde anfertigen. Bei den in Tanis gefundenen Sphingen handelt es sich natürlich um von ägyptischen Künstlern angefertigte Porträts des Apopi – die diesen aus der Fremde stammenden Königen ein derbes und kräftiges Gepräge verliehen haben; und statt der üblichen Haartracht fassten sie ihren Kopf mit einer Löwenmähne ein, die sie in Nachahmung des Nemes-Kopftuches auf Brust und Rücken malten. Diese Statuen wurden nicht verstümmelt; sie wurden sogar – im Nachhinein – mit der Inschrift des Merenptah Hetephermaat geschmückt, was beweist, dass der Name dieses Hirtenkönigs nicht so verabscheut wurde, wie man angenommen hatte.

PORTRAIT DU PHARAON MIENPTAH [MÉRENPTAH]-HOTÉPHIMAT

(XIXe dynastie)

Nécropole de Thèbes

Le souverain, dont je donne ici le portrait, était un roi pasteur : il existe, à l'égard de ces rois qui opprimaient l'Égypte et sont réputés dans l'histoire comme de véritables iconoclastes, une légende. Non seulement les rois pasteurs firent graver leurs noms en hiéroglyphes sur les statues des autres pharaons, mais ils firent encore sculpter des statues à leur image, contrairement à ce qui avait été admis jusqu'à ce jour. Les sphinx trouvés à Tanis, et qui sont évidemment des portraits d'Apapi [Apophis], ont été sculptés par des artistes égyptiens qui ont donné à ces rois, venus de l'étranger, le caractère rude et vigoureux ; et au lieu de la coiffure ordinaire, ils ont entouré leur tête d'une crinière de lion, qu'ils ont dessinée sur la poitrine et sur le dos, à l'imitation du claft égyptien. Ces figures ne sont pas mutilées ; elles furent même ornées, plus tard, de la légende de Mienptah [Mérenptah] Hotéphimat ce qui prouve que le nom de ce roi-pasteur n'était pas en abomination comme on l'a prétendu.

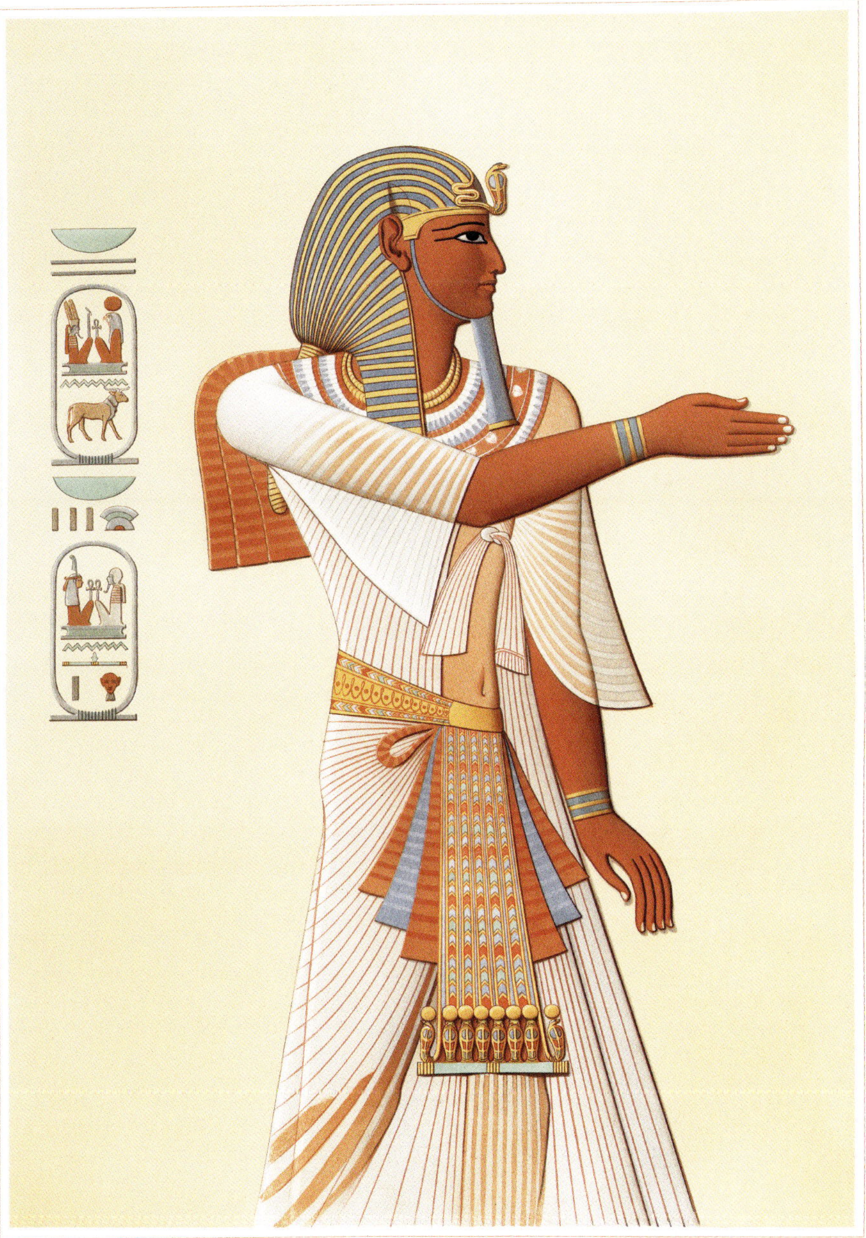

Lith. par J. Jury — E. Prisse d'Avennes. — Imp. par Hangard-Maugé

PORTRAIT DU PHARAON MIENPTAH-HOTÉPHIMAT.

(NÉCROPOLE DE THÈBES. _ XIXe DYNASTIE.)

PORTRAIT OF QUEEN NEBETTAWY (19th Dynasty)

Daughter of Ramesses [II] Meryamun

This portrait, which was copied in Thebes in a hypogeum in the Valley of the Queens, where they were buried, has now been almost entirely destroyed. This queen wears on her head a cap representing a vulture, made in cloisonné enamel like certain of the Egyptian jewels which we admire in our museums. This strange, rich head-dress, composed of brilliant feathers probably obtained from the skin of one of these birds, has long since disappeared from the valley of the Nile.

PORTRÄT DER KÖNIGIN NEBETTAUI (19. Dynastie)

Tochter von Ramses [II.] Meriamun

Dieses in Theben in einem Hypogäum im Tal der Königinnen abgezeichnete Porträt ist heute fast vollständig zerstört. Diese Königin trägt – nach dem Vorbild gewisser ägyptischer Schmuckstücke, die wir in unseren Museen bewundern – ein wahrscheinlich aus dem Balg eines dieser Vögel in Cloisonné gefertigtes Scheitelkäppchen, das einen Geier darstellt. Dieser sonderbar prächtige, aus schimmernden Federn gestaltete Kopfputz ist seit langer Zeit aus dem Niltal verschwunden.

PORTRAIT DE LA REINE NEBTO (XIXe dynastie)

Fille de Ramsès [II] Meïamoun

Ce portrait, qui a été copié à Thèbes, dans un hypogée de la vallée sépulcrale des Reines, est aujourd'hui presque entièrement détruit. Cette reine est coiffée d'une calotte représentant un vautour, provenant probablement de la dépouille d'un de ces oiseaux, et fabriquée en émaux cloisonnés, à l'imitation des quelques bijoux égyptiens qu'on admire dans nos musées. Cette étrange et riche coiffure, formée de plumes brillantes, a disparu depuis longtemps de la vallée du Nil.

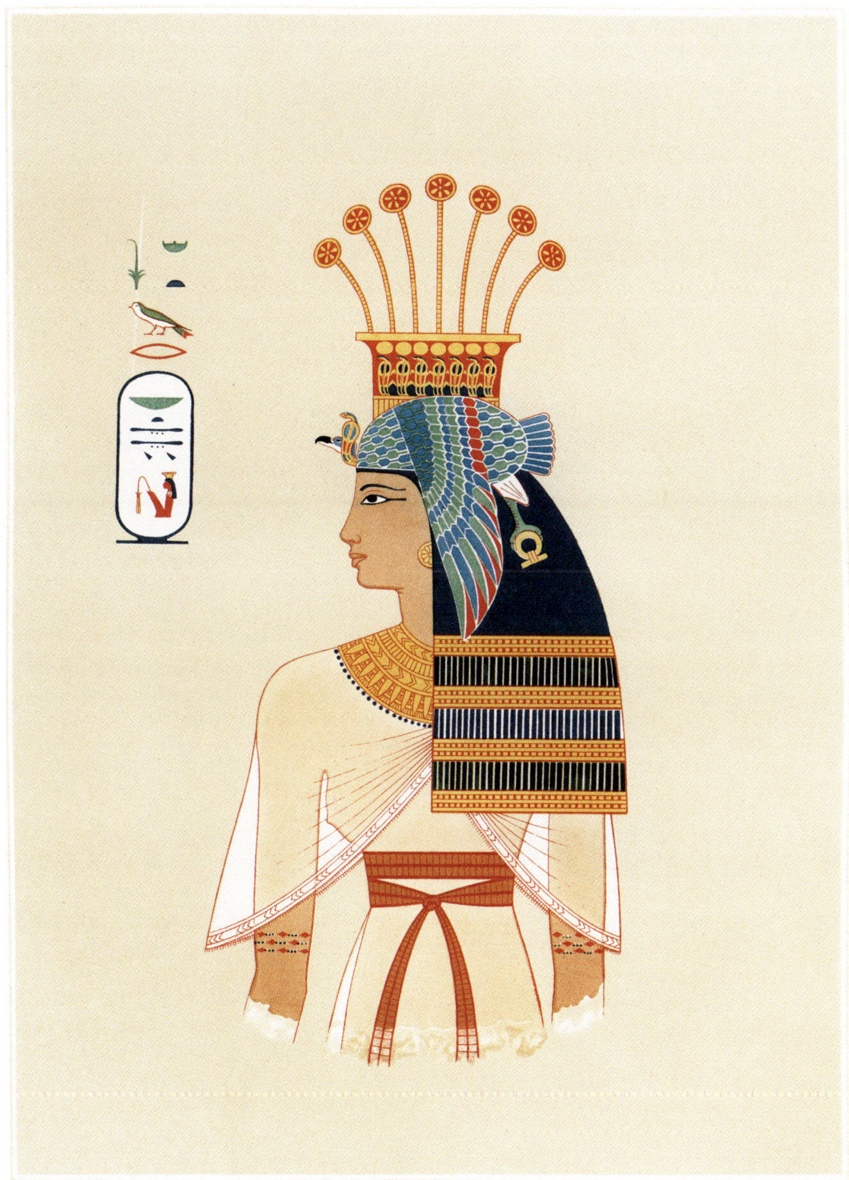

Lith. par Moulin. _ Imp. par Hangard-Maugé   E. Prisse d'Avennes   Publié par Arthus Bertrand Editeur

PORTRAIT DE LA REINE NEBTO,

FILLE DE RAMSÈS-MEÏAMOUN.

(XIX.e DYNASTIE.)

OFFERING OF FLOWERS AND FRUITS (19th Dynasty)

Necropolis of Thebes

I offer one further example to show how the activities of civil and domestic life were always represented in the tombs of individuals. It is known that the lotus was a symbolic plant and that its meaning, as a sign of life and of immortality, was recognised through evidence from Classical times, which can be confirmed by the use to which the plant is put on Greek and Etruscan monuments.

OPFERGABE VON BLUMEN UND FRÜCHTEN (19. Dynastie)

Nekropole von Theben

Ich habe ein weiteres Beispiel dafür hinzugefügt, dass in den Privatgräbern stets Darstellungen von Handlungen des bürgerlichen und häuslichen Lebens zu finden waren. Der Lotus ist bekanntermaßen eine sinnbildliche Pflanze; seine Bedeutung als Zeichen des Lebens und der Unsterblichkeit ist in den klassischen Zeugnissen belegt und findet sich durch seine Verwendung in den griechischen und etruskischen Denkmälern bestätigt.

OFFRANDE DE FLEURS ET DE FRUITS (XIXe dynastie)

Nécropole de Thèbes

J'ai ajouté un exemple de plus, que les actes de la vie civile et domestique se trouvaient toujours représentés dans les tombeaux des particuliers. On sait que le lotus est une plante symbolique et que sa signification, comme signe de vie et d'immortalité, est connue par des témoignages classiques qui se trouvent justifiés par l'emploi qu'on en a fait sur des monuments grecs et étrusques.

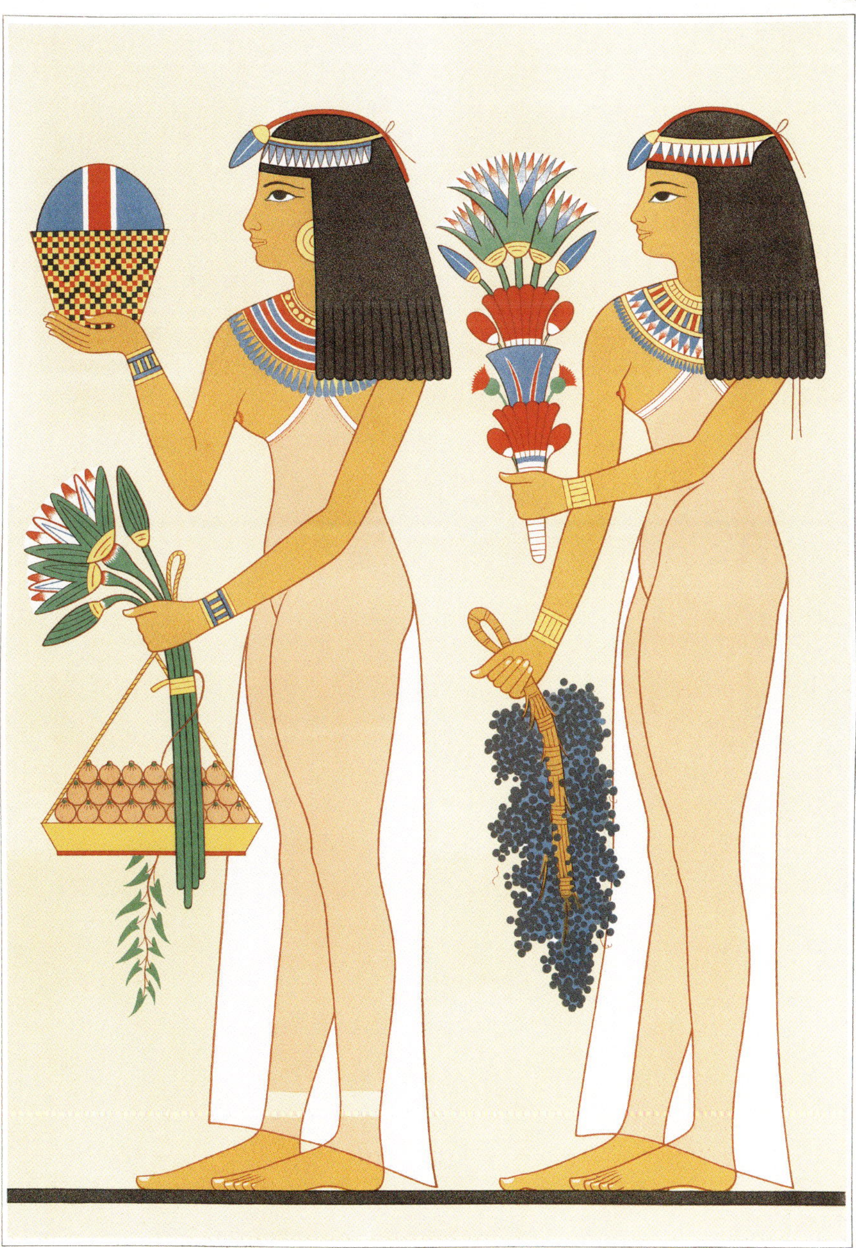

Lith. par Leichum _ Imp. Hangard-Mangé

E. Prisse d'Avennes.

Publié par Arthus-Bertrand, Éditeur.

OFFRANDE DE FLEURS & DE FRUITS.

(NÉCROPOLE DE THÈBES _ XIXe DYNASTIE.)

Grandeur d'exécution.

BOUQUETS PAINTED IN HYPOGEA (19th and 20th Dynasties)

The bouquets depicted in this plate are the most beautiful I have ever seen. The two large ones, which are enormous when compared to the individuals who are bearing them in their hands, are painted in a hypogeum of the 19th Dynasty situated behind the Memnonium. The intention of the artists who painted these bouquets was evidently to represent natural flowers, worked according to the style of their age: however, it is very difficult to recognise any of the varieties with the exception of the papyrus and the lotus. It is the papyrus umbel which crowns the first two bouquets and which is in general everywhere dominant, as if in homage to a plant which served to transmit the signs of thought. [...] One can also identify poppies, but as for the species of grain or fruit which features so prominently in all these compositions, this is some unknown fruit, which has been taken to be the grain of *Mimosa elengi*.

GEMALTE STRÄUSSE AUS DEN HYPOGÄEN (19. und 20. Dynastie)

Die auf dieser Tafel dargestellten Sträuße sind die schönsten, die mir unter die Augen gekommen sind. Bei den beiden großen, die – im Vergleich zu den Einzelpersonen, die sie mit beiden Händen tragen – riesig sind, handelt es sich um Malereien aus einem Hypogäum der 19. Dynastie, das sich hinter dem Memnonium befindet. Die Künstler, die diese Buketts gemalt haben, hatten selbstverständlich die Absicht, echte, nach der zeitgenössischen Mode zusammengestellte Blumen abzubilden: Mit Ausnahme von Papyrus und Lotus ist es gleichwohl sehr schwierig, die abgebildeten Arten zu bestimmen. Es ist die Papyrusdolde, die die beiden ersten Blumensträuße krönt und die auch allgemein überall vorherrschte – als Huldigung an die Pflanze, die der Aufzeichnung und Übermittlung von Gedanken diente. [...] Auch der Klatschmohn ist zu erkennen; was die Beere oder Frucht anbetrifft, die in allen diesen Arrangements eine große Rolle spielt, so handelt es sich um eine unbekannte Frucht, die man für das Samenkorn der *Mimosa elengi* hielt.

BOUQUETS PEINTS DANS LES HYPOGÉES (XIXe et XXe dynasties)

Les bouquets représentés dans cette planche sont des plus beaux que j'aie vus. Les deux grands qui sont énormes, comparés aux individus qui les portent à deux mains, sont peints dans un hypogée de la XIXe dynastie, situé derrière le Memnonium. L'intention des artistes qui ont peint ces bouquets a été évidemment de représenter des fleurs naturelles agencées à la mode de leur temps : néanmoins, il est fort difficile d'en reconnaître les espèces, à l'exception des papyrus et des lotus. C'est l'ombelle de papyrus qui couronne les deux premiers bouquets, et qui, généralement, dominait partout, comme un hommage rendu à la plante qui servait à transmettre les signes de la pensée. [...] On y reconnaît aussi les coquelicots ; quant à l'espèce de graine ou de fruit qui joue un grand rôle dans toutes ces compositions, c'est un fruit inconnu que l'on a pris pour des grains de *mimosa elengi*.

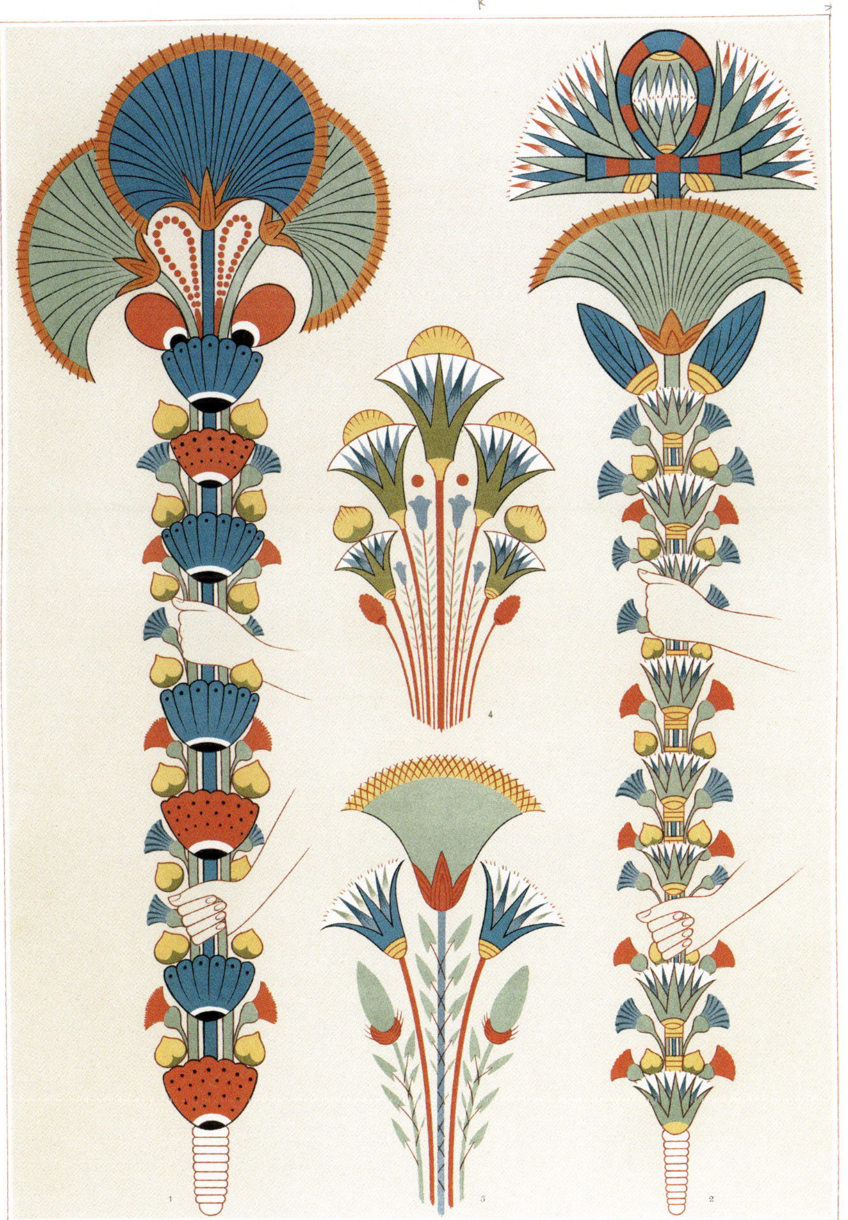

Lith par Levié. Imp par Haugard-Maugé. E. Prisse d'Avennes. Publié par Arthus Bertrand Editeur.

BOUQUETS PEINTS DANS LES HYPOGÉES.

(XIX.e & XX.e DYNASTIES.)

FULL-LENGTH PORTRAIT OF RAMESSES III (20th Dynasty)

Necropolis of Thebes

It is always at the entrance to the royal hypogea and generally on the left-hand wall that one sees the finest portrait of the pharaoh, who is here represented full-figure performing his devotions to the hawk-headed god Phre. Set back and carved in relief, this figure of Ramesses III is executed and coloured with exceptional care. It is hard to imagine that the detail could be more meticulous or that the finish could be more perfect. The head is extremely handsome, the nose is slightly curved and the lips are strongly delineated; all told, a gentle and gracious expression lends a particular charm to this handsome physiognomy. This profile is of remarkable character: it is always the same on all the walls of the hypogeum, which constitutes sufficient proof that this is a portrait.

GANZFIGURIGES PORTRÄT VON RAMSES III. (20. Dynastie)

Nekropole von Theben

Immer am Eingang – in der Regel an der linken Wand – der königlichen Hypogäen befindet sich das schönste Porträt des Pharaos, der ganzfigurig bei der Ausübung seiner religiösen Pflichten gegenüber dem Gott Phre mit dem Sperberkopf dargestellt ist. Diese als versenktes Relief gearbeitete Abbildung von Ramses III. ist mit bemerkenswerter Sorgfalt ausgeführt und koloriert. Mehr Eleganz in allen Einzelheiten und mehr Sorgfalt in der Ausführung sind kaum vorstellbar. Der Kopf ist sehr schön, die leicht gebogene Nase, die kunstvoll geformten Lippen; ein sanfter und freundlicher Gesichtsausdruck verleiht dieser schönen Physiognomie schließlich einen besonderen Reiz. Auf allen Wänden des Hypogäums findet sich immer wieder dasselbe Profil mit seinem bemerkenswerten Gepräge – womit hinreichend bewiesen ist, dass es sich bei dieser Figur um ein Porträt handelt.

PORTRAIT EN PIED DE RAMSÈS III (XXe dynastie)

Nécropole de Thèbes

C'est toujours à l'entrée des hypogées royaux, généralement sur la paroi de gauche, qu'on voit le plus beau portrait du pharaon, qui est représenté en pied faisant ses dévotions au dieu Phré à tête d'épervier. Sculptée en relief dans le creux, cette figure de Ramsès III est exécutée et coloriée avec un soin remarquable. On ne saurait imaginer plus de recherche dans les détails et plus de fini dans l'exécution. La tête est fort belle ; le nez légèrement recourbé, les lèvres largement découpées ; enfin, une expression douce et gracieuse donne un charme particulier à cette belle physionomie. Ce profil, d'un caractère remarquable, se retrouve toujours le même sur toutes les parois de l'hypogée et prouve assez que cette figure est un portrait.

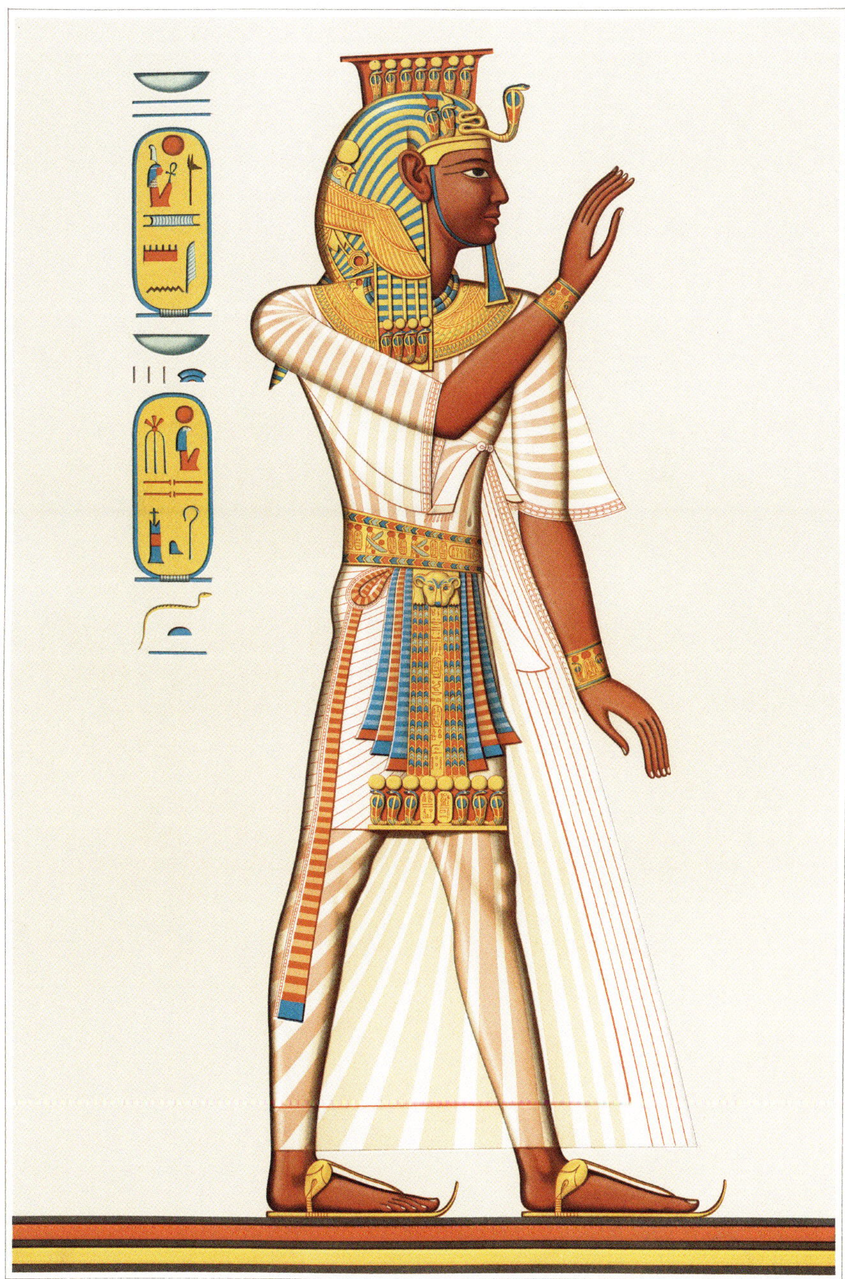

Lith. par Moulin. _ Imp. par Hangard-Maugé. E. Prisse d'Avennes. Publié par Arthus-Bertrand, Éditeur.

PORTRAIT EN PIED DE RAMSÈS III.

(NÉCROPOLE DE THÈBES._XXᵉ DYNASTIE.)

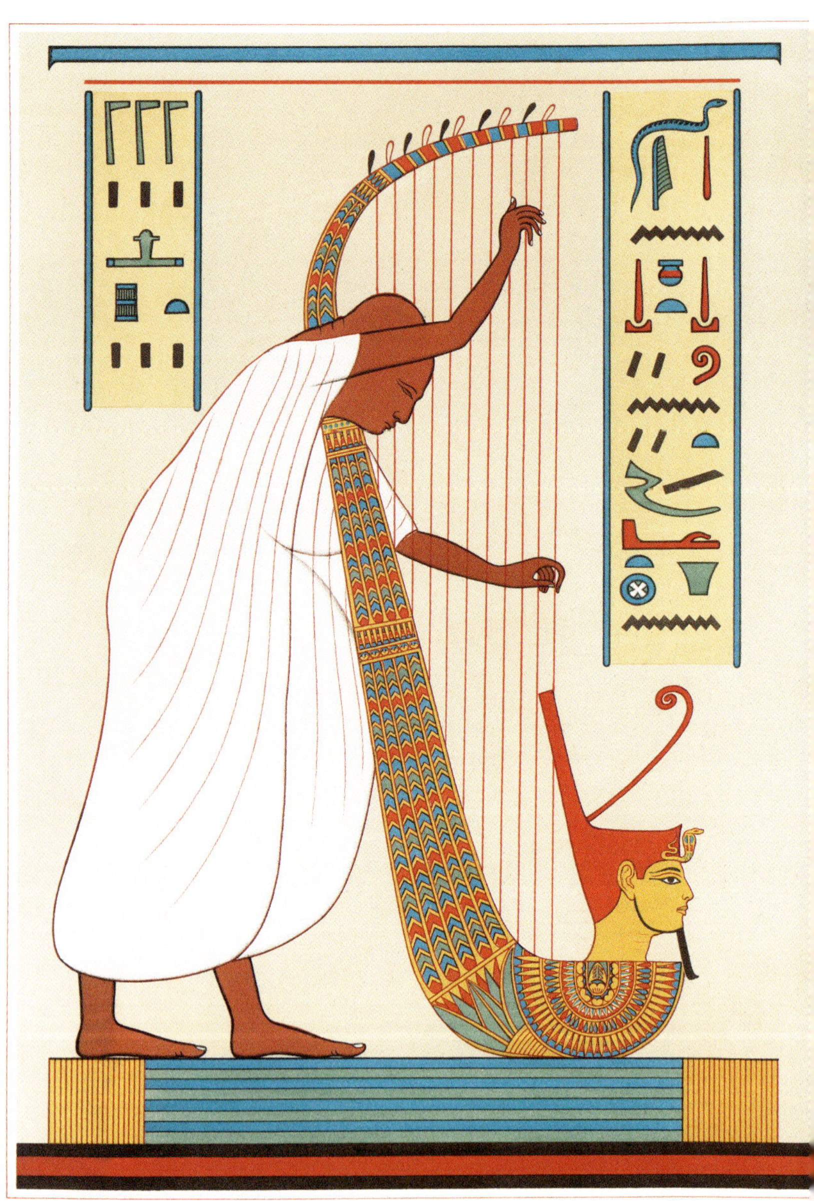

Lith par Levié — Imp par Hangard-Maugé.

BARDES

(THÈB

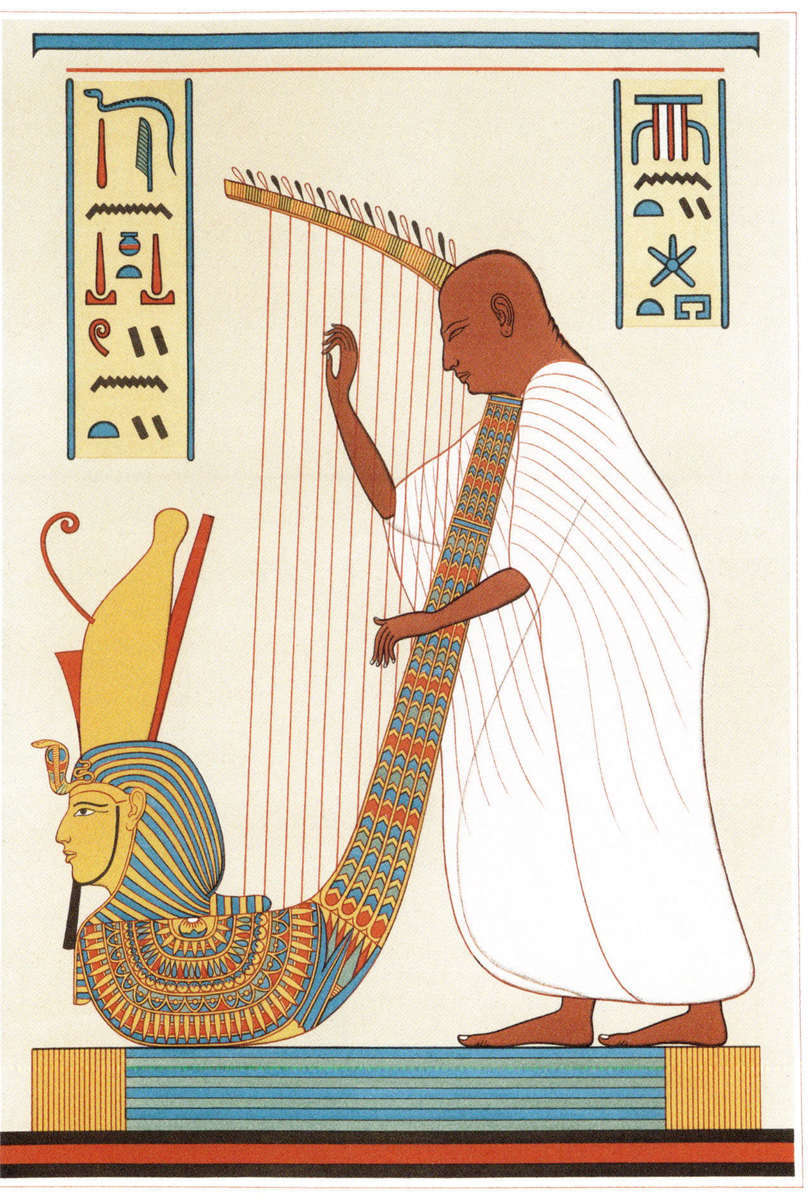

Publié par Arthus-Bertrand, Editeur.

:SÈS III.

STIE.)

(Pages/Seite 496/497)

HARPERS OF RAMESSES III (20th Dynasty)

Thebes

The harp can be seen on the very earliest Egyptian monuments, in the hands of priests, in the temple sanctuaries and in the hands of ordinary people during the festivities of private life. The harps shown on the buildings of the Old Kingdom are quite simple, but from the 18th Dynasty onwards they assume an extremely elegant form and are richly decorated; sometimes they were quite extraordinarily luxurious. Their shaven heads and long robes make it clear that these two harpists belong to the priestly caste, since in ancient Egypt music was considered to be a branch of sacred knowledge. One is playing an eleven-stringed harp while the other plucks a thirteen-stringed instrument. One of the heads which decorate the bases of the two harps is covered by the symbolic head-dress of the upper region and the other by the head-dress emblematic of the lower region. They [the two harpists] are blind, like all those whom one sees in Egyptian paintings.

BARDEN RAMSES' III. (20. Dynastie)

Theben

In den Tempelheiligtümern der ältesten ägyptischen Denkmäler ist die Harfe in den Händen der Priester zu sehen, auf privaten Festen aber in den Händen des Volkes. Die in den Gebäuden des Alten Reiches dargestellten Harfen sind recht einfach; von der 18. Dynastie an erhalten sie jedoch eine sehr anmutige Form und sind reich verziert; mitunter waren sie von außerordentlicher Pracht. An den kahlen Köpfen und den langen Gewändern ist zu erkennen, dass die beiden Harfenisten zum priesterlichen Orden gehören; in Ägypten zählte die Musik zu den heiligen Wissenschaften. Der eine spielt eine Harfe mit 11 Saiten; der andere zupft eine Harfe mit 13 Saiten. Die Köpfe, die die Füße der beiden Harfen zieren, tragen zum einen den symbolischen Kopfputz des oberen und zum anderen den emblematischen Kopfputz des unteren Gebiets. Sie [die beiden Harfenisten] sind blind – wie alle, die in den ägyptischen Malereien zu sehen sind.

BARDES DE RAMSÈS III (XXe dynastie)

Thèbes

On voit la harpe sur les monuments égyptiens de la plus haute antiquité, entre les mains des prêtres, dans le sanctuaire des temples, et entre les mains du peuple, dans les fêtes de la vie privée. Les harpes représentées sur les édifices de l'ancien Empire sont assez simples ; mais à partir de la XVIIIe dynastie, elles acquièrent une forme très élégante et richement ornée ; elles étaient quelquefois d'un luxe extraordinaire. À leurs têtes rases, à leurs longs vêtements, on reconnaît que ces deux harpistes appartiennent à l'ordre sacerdotal ; la musique étant mise, en Égypte, au nombre des sciences sacrées. L'un joue d'une harpe à 11 cordes ; l'autre pince une harpe à 13 cordes. Les têtes qui ornent la base de ces deux harpes sont couvertes, l'une de la coiffure symbolique de la région supérieure, l'autre de la coiffure emblématique de la région inférieure. Ils [les deux harpistes] sont aveugles comme tous ceux qu'on voit dans les peintures égyptiennes.

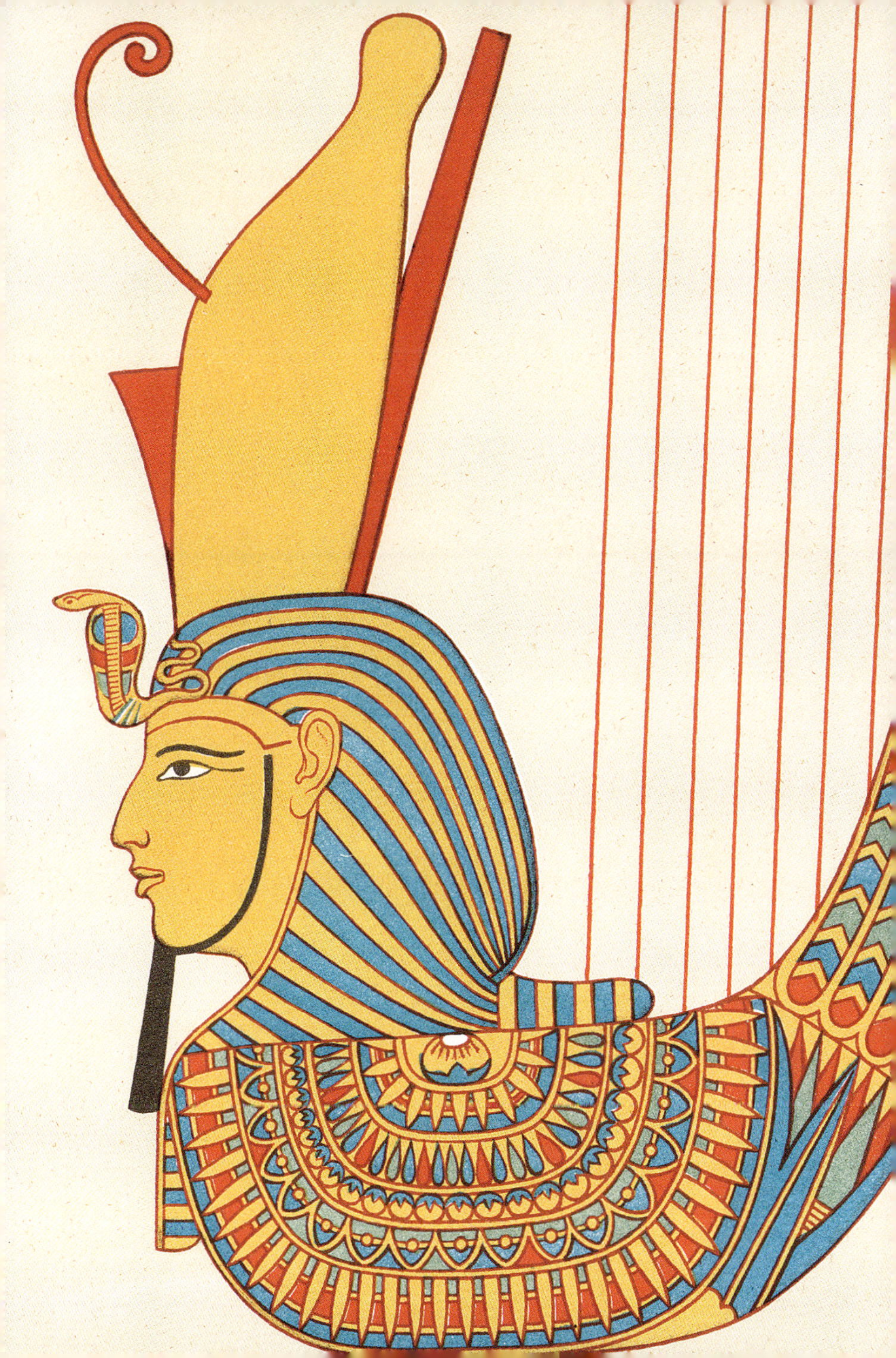

OFFERING TO OSIRIS (20th Dynasty)

Stele painted on the coffin of a mummy. Necropolis of Thebes

It is believed that the beautiful mummy-cases covered with a yellowish lacquer and painted with pictures in many colours were used above all in Thebes during the 20th Dynasty. The example which I brought back from Egypt shows quite clearly that during this period the profusion of ornamentation was taken to great lengths and that the vignettes used were authorised according to the rules of the priests, just like the hieroglyphic inscriptions for all that pertained to the ritual of the dead. The inside of the coffin was equally rich in ornamentation, with the central subject always consisting of the most important figures of deities and mythological characters painted in vibrant colours. It was during this period that the art of embalming attained its peak of perfection in Thebes.

OPFERGABEN AN OSIRIS (20. Dynastie)

Auf einen Mumiensarg gemalte Stele. Nekropole von Theben

Man glaubt, dass die schönen, gelblich lackierten Mumienkästen, auf die farbenfrohe Darstellungen aufgemalt waren, vor allem in Theben während der 20. Dynastie gebräuchlich waren. Das von mir aus Ägypten mitgebrachte Exemplar führt recht klar vor Augen, dass die verschwenderische Fülle der Verzierungen in diesen Zeiten ein hohes Maß erreicht hatte und dass die feierlichen Vorschriften zum Totenritual sowohl Zierleisten als auch Hieroglypheninschriften erlaubten. Das Sarginnere war nicht weniger reich geschmückt, wobei die in leuchtenden Farben gemalten Bilder der wichtigsten Götter und Genien stets das zentrale Thema bildeten: In Theben erreichte die Kunst des Einbalsamierens in dieser Zeit echte Perfektion.

OFFRANDE À OSIRIS (XXe dynastie)

Stèle peinte sur un cercueil de momie. Nécropole de Thèbes

On croit que les belles caisses de momies, couvertes d'un vernis jaunâtre, et sur lesquelles étaient peintes des représentations en toutes couleurs, étaient surtout en usage à Thèbes, sous la XXe dynastie. Le spécimen que j'ai rapporté d'Égypte démontre assez clairement que la profusion des ornements était portée à un haut degré à ces époques et que les vignettes étaient autorisées, par les règles hiératiques, aussi bien que les légendes hiéroglyphiques pour ce qui avait rapport au rituel des morts. L'intérieur du cercueil n'était pas moins riche d'ornements, les principales figures de divinités et de génies, peintes en couleurs vives, en formaient toujours le sujet central : c'est à cette époque que l'art de l'embaumement atteignit, à Thèbes, sa véritable perfection.

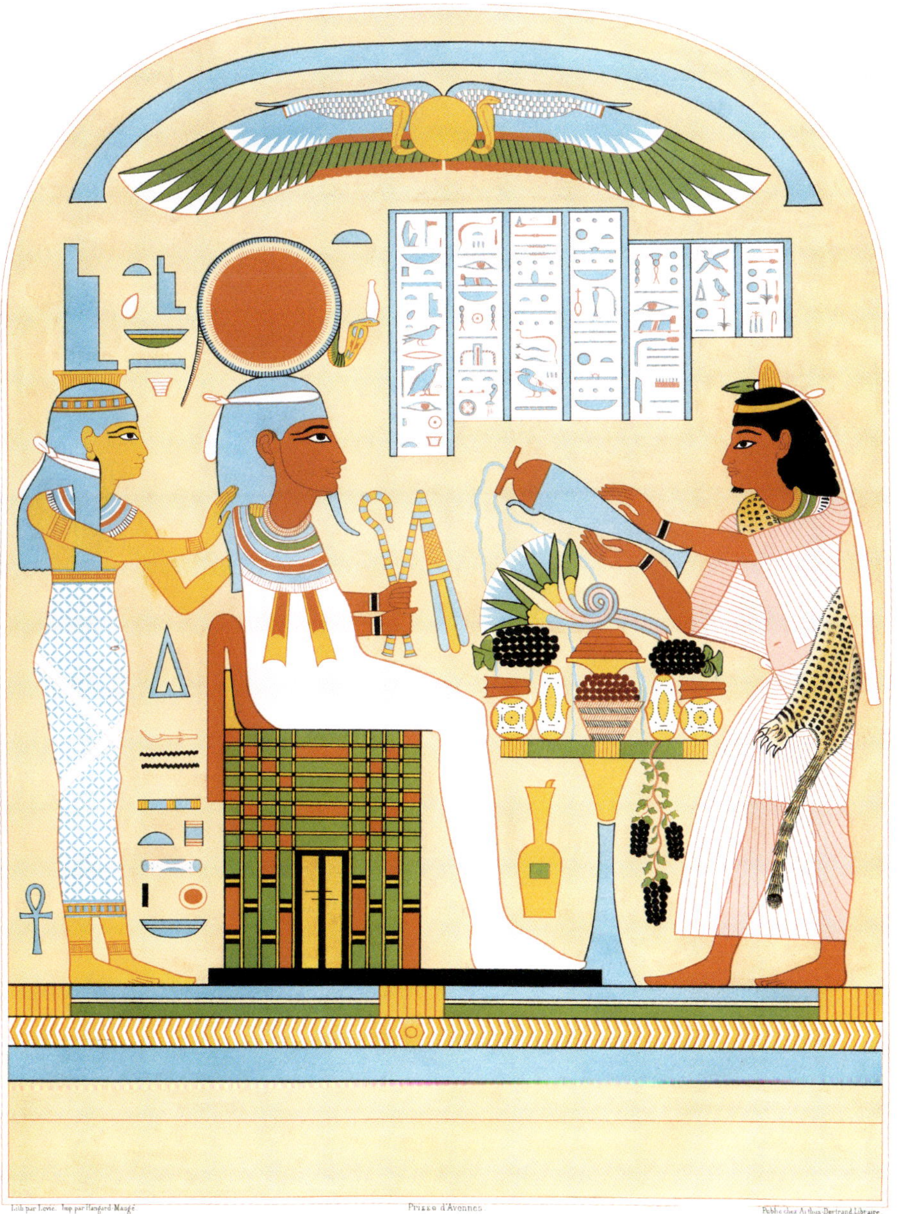

Lith par Levié. Imp par Hangard-Maugé. Prisse d'Avennes Publié chez A. Morel-Bertrand, Libraire.

OFFRANDE À OSIRIS

STÈLE PEINTE SUR UN CERCUEIL DE MOMIE

(NÉCROPOLE DE THÈBES—XXe DYNASTIE)

Decorative Arts / Kunstgewerbe / Art industriel

SELECTION OF VASES CONTEMPORARY WITH THE PYRAMIDS (4th and 5th Dynasties)

Necropolis of Memphis

Judging from the colours that are still preserved on a number of these vases, Egyptian ceramics were already an accomplished form at this period. Most of these vases are painted in red and yellow, with some parts still showing decoration in green and blue, or applied to imitate crazing. From the originals which were found in the excavations, it seems likely that these ancient vases were all in soft paste, unglazed, and decorated with colours fixed by mordants without passing through the kiln. All these vases were copied in tombs round the pyramids at Saqqara; similar vases have been found in tombs either excavated or built near the pyramids of Giza. Nos. 1, 2, 6, 7, 10, 19, 20 and 21 are taken from the tomb [mastaba] of Ptahshepses at Saqqara; nos. 3, 4 and 5 are from the tomb [mastaba] of Rashepses. All the others come from the tomb [mastaba] of Ti; one of these, no. 9, must be in brass.

AUSWAHL VON VASEN AUS DER PYRAMIDENZEIT (4. und 5. Dynastie)

Nekropole von Memphis

Die ägyptische Keramik war, nach den auf mehreren dieser Vasen erhaltenen Farben zu urteilen, bereits äußerst bemerkenswert. Sie sind zumeist rot oder gelb bemalt und weisen einige blaue und grüne oder mit Krakelüren-Imitationen verzierte Bereiche auf. Nach den bei Ausgrabungen gefundenen Originalen ist es wahrscheinlich, dass diese alten Vasen sämtlich unglasiert waren, aus kaolinfreiem Ton bestanden und dass die farbige Verzierung – ohne Feuereinwirkung – mithilfe von Beizen fixiert wurde. Alle diese Vasen wurden in Gräbern in der Umgebung der Pyramiden von Sakkara abgezeichnet; ähnliche sind in den Gräbern zu finden, die bei denen von Gizeh ausgehoben oder errichtet wurden. Die Nr. 1, 2, 6, 7, 10, 19, 20 und 21 sind dem Grab [Mastaba] von Ptahschepses in Sakkara entnommen; die Nr. 3, 4 und 5 dem Grab [Mastaba] von Raschepses; alle übrigen Vasen stammen aus dem Grab [Mastaba] von Ti. Eine der letzteren, die Nr. 9, muss aus Kupfer sein.

CHOIX DE VASES CONTEMPORAINS DES PYRAMIDES (IVe et V^e^ dynasties)

Nécropole de Memphis

À en juger par les couleurs que conservent encore plusieurs de ces vases, la céramique égyptienne était déjà fort remarquable. La plupart peints en rouge, en jaune, présentent certaines parties décorées en bleu et en vert, ou de façon à imiter le craquelé. Il est probable, d'après les originaux qui ont été trouvés dans les fouilles, que ces anciens vases étaient tous en pâte tendre, sans glaçure, et décorées de couleurs fixées par des mordants sans l'intermédiaire du feu. Tous ces vases ont été copiés dans les tombeaux autour des pyramides de Sakkara ; on en retrouve de semblables dans les tombeaux creusés ou bâtis près de celles de Gizeh. Les n°s 1, 2, 6, 7, 10, 19, 20 et 21 sont tirés du tombeau [mastaba] de Ptahasès [Ptahchepsès] à Sakkara ; les n°s 3, 4 et 5 du tombeau [mastaba] de Raasès [Rachepsès] ; tous les autres vases proviennent du tombeau [mastaba] de Teï. L'un de ces derniers, le n° 9, doit être en cuivre.

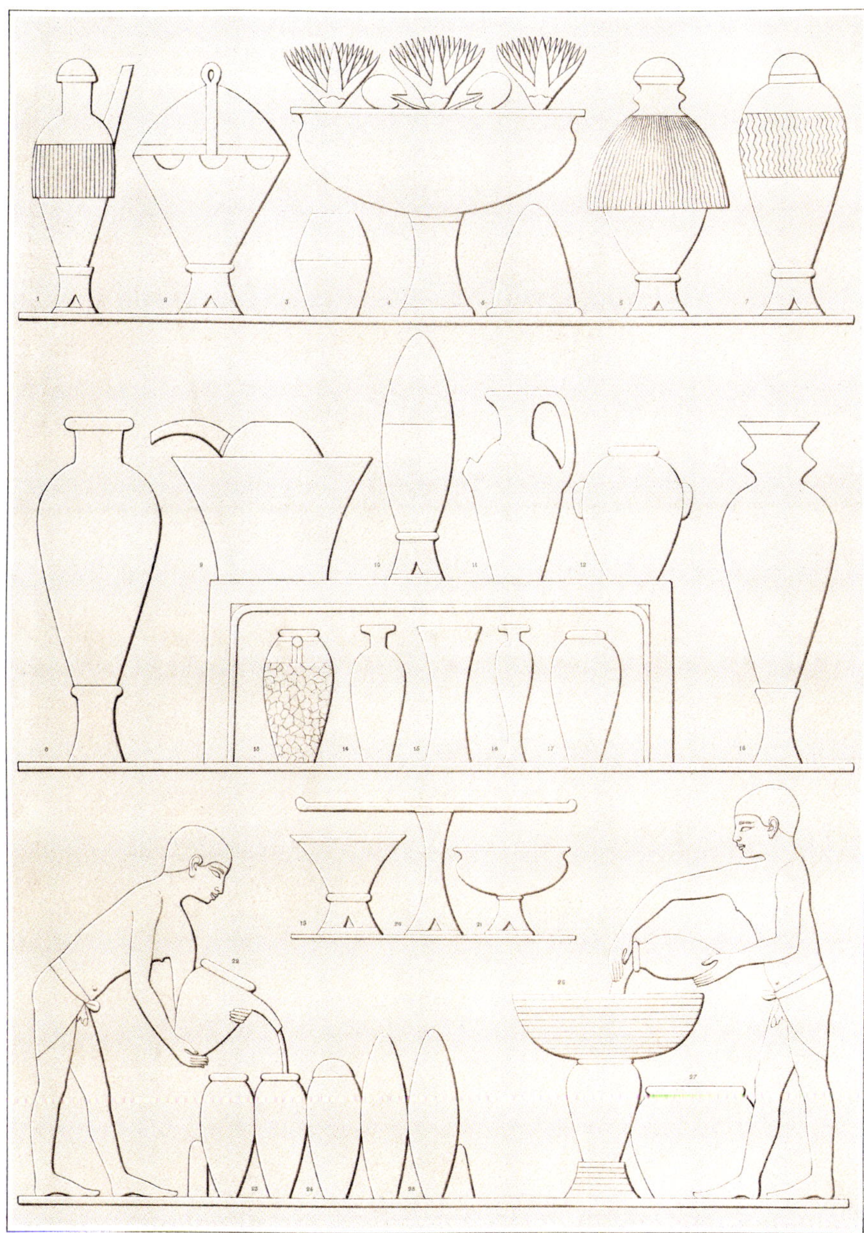

Lith. par Dhartingue. _ Imp. par Hangard-Maugé.

E. Prisse d'Avennes.

Publié par Arthus-Bertrand, Editeur.

CHOIX DE VASES CONTEMPORAINS DES PYRAMIDES.

(NÉCROPOLE DE MEMPHIS. _ IVe et Ve DYNASTIES.)

VASES FROM THE REIGN OF THUTMOSIS III (18th Dynasty)

Thebes and Hermonthis

All the vases shown on this plate are from the same period but from different locations. Nos. 1, 5 and 6 come from an ancient temple at Hermonthis [Armant], which was restored or rebuilt by queen Hatshepsut, the sister of Thutmosis III; it was already ruinous in the time of the Romans, who re-used most of this fine material in the foundations of the new temple. The only reason I have included the table of offering, no. 1, is to show the bouquets of lotus flowers, which here attain a greater degree of realism than anywhere else. Nos. 2, 3 and 4 were copied from bas-reliefs in the sanctuary of the great temple at Karnak.

VASEN AUS DER REGIERUNGSZEIT VON THUTMOSIS III. (18. Dynastie)

Theben und Hermonthis

Diese Tafel stellt Vasen derselben Zeitstellung dar, die aber von unterschiedlichen Orten stammen. Die Nr. 1, 5 und 6 stammen aus einem alten Tempel in Hermonthis [Armant], den Königin Hatschepsut – die Schwester von Thutmosis III. – restauriert oder wiedererrichtet hatte, der aber schon in römischer Zeit zerstört war, da die Römer den größten Teil der schönen Baumaterialien für die Fundamente des neuen Tempels verwendeten. Den Opfertisch Nr. 1 gebe ich lediglich deshalb wieder, um die Lotussträuße zu zeigen, die hier lebensechter als überall sonst sind. Die Nr. 2, 3 und 4 wurden von den Flachreliefs im Heiligtum des großen Tempels von Karnak abgezeichnet.

VASES DU RÈGNE DE THOUTMÈS III (XVIIIe dynastie)

Thèbes et Hermonthis

Cette planche représente des vases d'une même époque, mais de localités différentes. Les nos 1, 5 et 6 proviennent d'un ancien temple d'Hermonthis [Ermant], restauré ou rebâti par la reine Hatasou [Hatchepsout], sœur de Thoutmès [Thoutmôsis] III, et déjà ruiné du temps des Romains, qui ont employé la plupart de ces beaux matériaux dans les fondations du nouveau temple. Je n'ai reproduit la table d'offrandes no 1 que pour montrer les bouquets de lotus qui présentent, ici, plus de vérité que partout ailleurs. Les nos 2, 3 et 4 ont été copiés sur les bas-reliefs du sanctuaire du grand temple de Karnac.

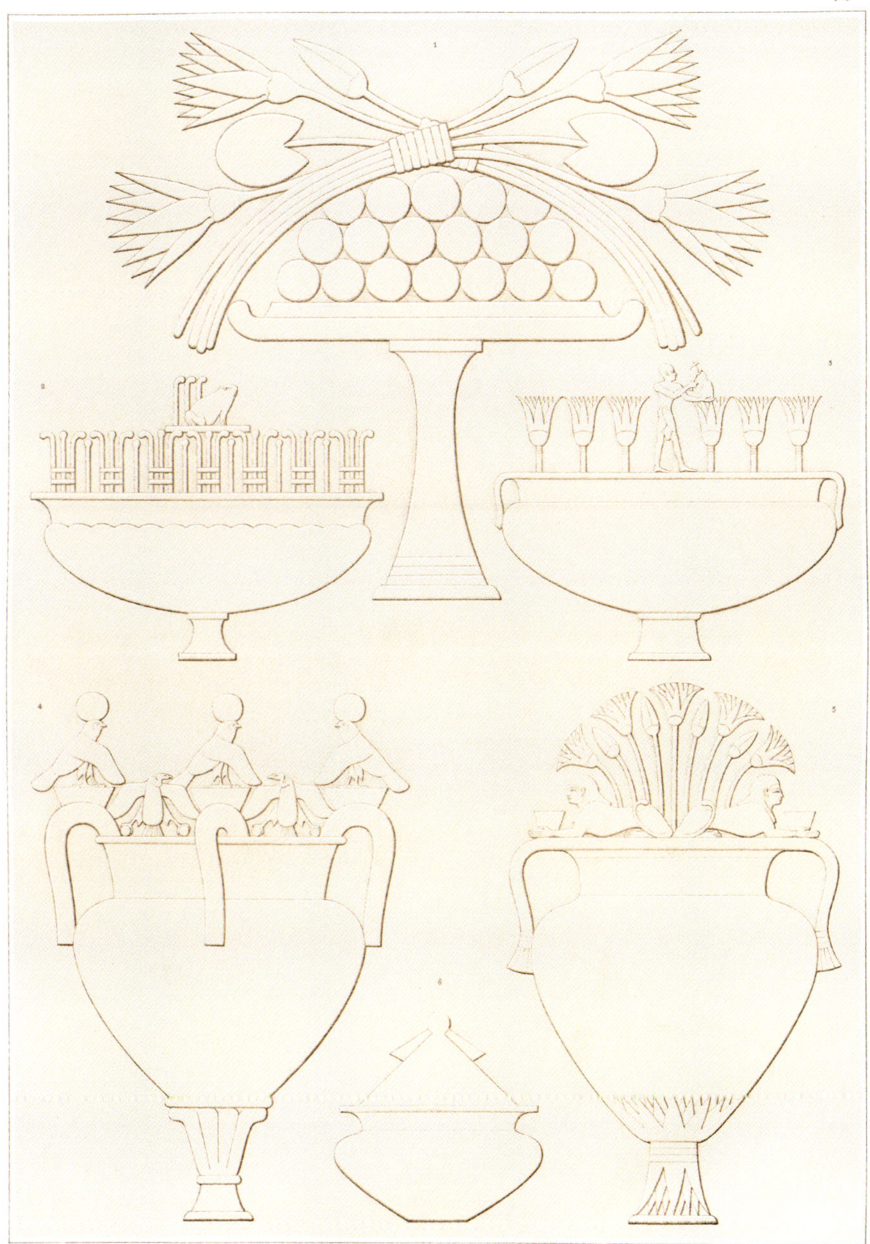

Lith. par Lefèvre . Imp. par Hangard Maugé

E. Prisse d'Avennes.

Publié par Arthus Bertrand, Éditeur

VASES DU RÈGNE DE THOUTMÈS III.

(THÈBES & HERMONTHIS _ XVIIIe DYN.)

SELECTION OF VASES
FROM THE REIGN OF THUTMOSIS III (18th Dynasty)

Thebes

The varied, elegant and pure shapes of these vases bear witness to the fact that in this reign the arts of design had attained a degree of perfection which was never to be surpassed and which can be recognised in all the works of art produced in the time of Thutmosis III, one of the most splendid in Egypt's history. Most of them were copied from a bas-relief adjacent to the sanctuary of the great temple at Karnak; according to the inscription, they are in gold or silver and form part of the offerings made by this pharaoh on return from his campaigns in Asia. The others come from different halls in the same temple, decorated on the orders of the pharaoh. Side by side with the most commonplace vases, the cooking pot, the jug, the amphora or the drinking vessel, one can marvel at much richer and more distinctive vases, such as kraters, ciboria, chalices, calathi and lamps, whose pure contours rival those of Greek works of art.

AUSWAHL VON VASEN
AUS DER REGIERUNGSZEIT VON THUTMOSIS III. (18. Dynastie)

Theben

Diese Vasen bezeugen durch ihre abwechslungsreichen, anmutigen und reinen Formen, dass die Zeichenkünste unter der Herrschaft Thutmosis' III. einen nie übertroffenen Grad der Perfektion erreicht hatten, der sich in allen Erzeugnissen aus seiner Zeit – einer der glorreichsten Ägyptens – wiederfindet. Die meisten wurden von einem Flachrelief abgezeichnet, das an das Heiligtum des großen Tempels von Karnak angrenzte; nach Aussage der Inschrift sind sie aus Gold oder Silber und gehören zu den Opfergaben, die dieser Pharao bei seiner Rückkehr von den Asien-Feldzügen überbrachte. Die anderen stammen aus verschiedenen, nach Anordnung des Pharaos geschmückten Räumen desselben Tempels. Neben den gebräuchlichsten und einfachsten Gefäßen – dem Kessel, dem Krug, der Amphore oder dem Pokal – sind auch prächtigere und vornehmere Gefäße zu bewundern, wie die Kratere, die Ziborien, die Kelche, die Kalathoi und die Lampen, die es in der Klarheit der Umrisse mit den Werken der Griechen aufnehmen.

CHOIX DE VASES
DU RÈGNE DE THOUTMÈS III (XVIIIe dynastie)

Thèbes

Par leurs formes variées, élégantes et pures, ces vases attestent que les arts du dessin étaient arrivés, sous ce règne, à un degré de perfection qui ne fut jamais surpassé, et qui est reconnaissable dans toutes les productions de l'époque de Thoutmès [Thoutmôsis] III, une des plus glorieuses pour l'Égypte. La plupart ont été copiés d'après un bas-relief attenant au sanctuaire du grand temple de Karnac ; ils sont en or ou en argent, au dire de l'inscription, et font partie des offrandes faites par ce pharaon, au retour de ses campagnes en Asie. Les autres proviennent des différentes salles du même temple, décorées par ordre du pharaon. À côté des vases les plus usuels et les plus humbles, la marmite, la cruche, l'amphore ou le hanap, on admire des vases plus riches et plus distingués, tels que des cratères, des ciboires, des calices, des calathi et des lampes dont la pureté des contours rivalise avec les œuvres des Grecs.

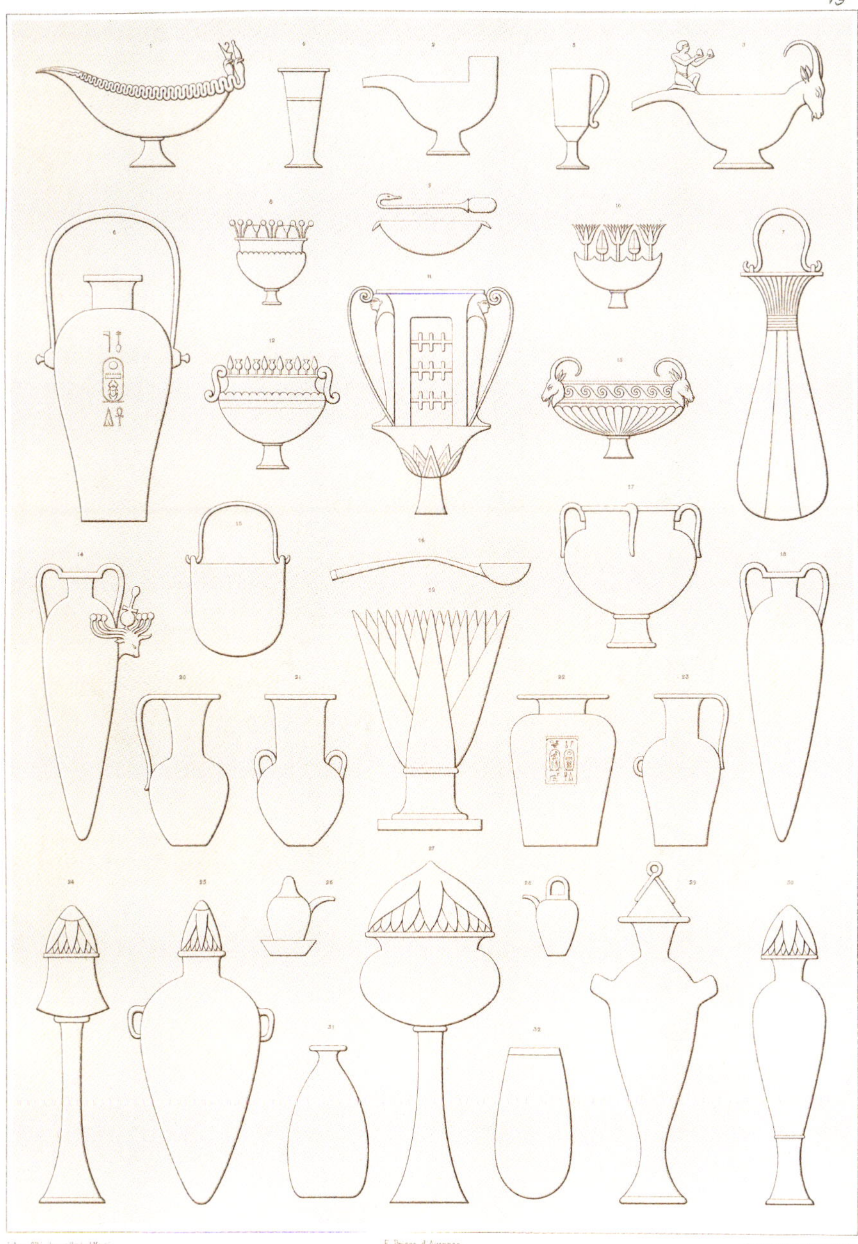

Lith. par Gillé . Imp. par Hangard Maugé

E. Prisse d'Avennes.

Publié par Arthus Bertrand, Éditeur

CHOIX DE VASES DU RÈGNE DE THOUTMÈS III.

(THÈBES — XVIIIᵉ DYNASTIE.)

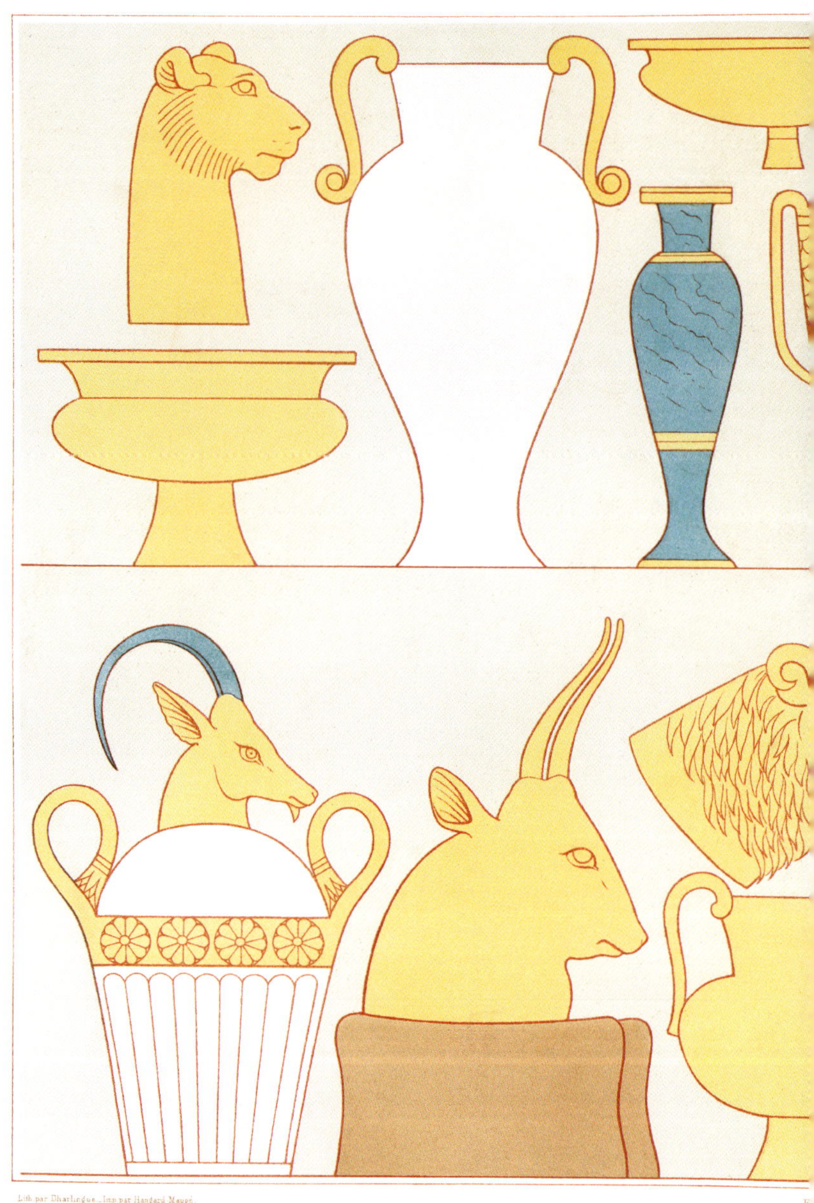

Lith. par Dharlingue. Imp. par Hangard Maugé.

E

VASES DU PAYS DE KA

(NÉCROPOLE D

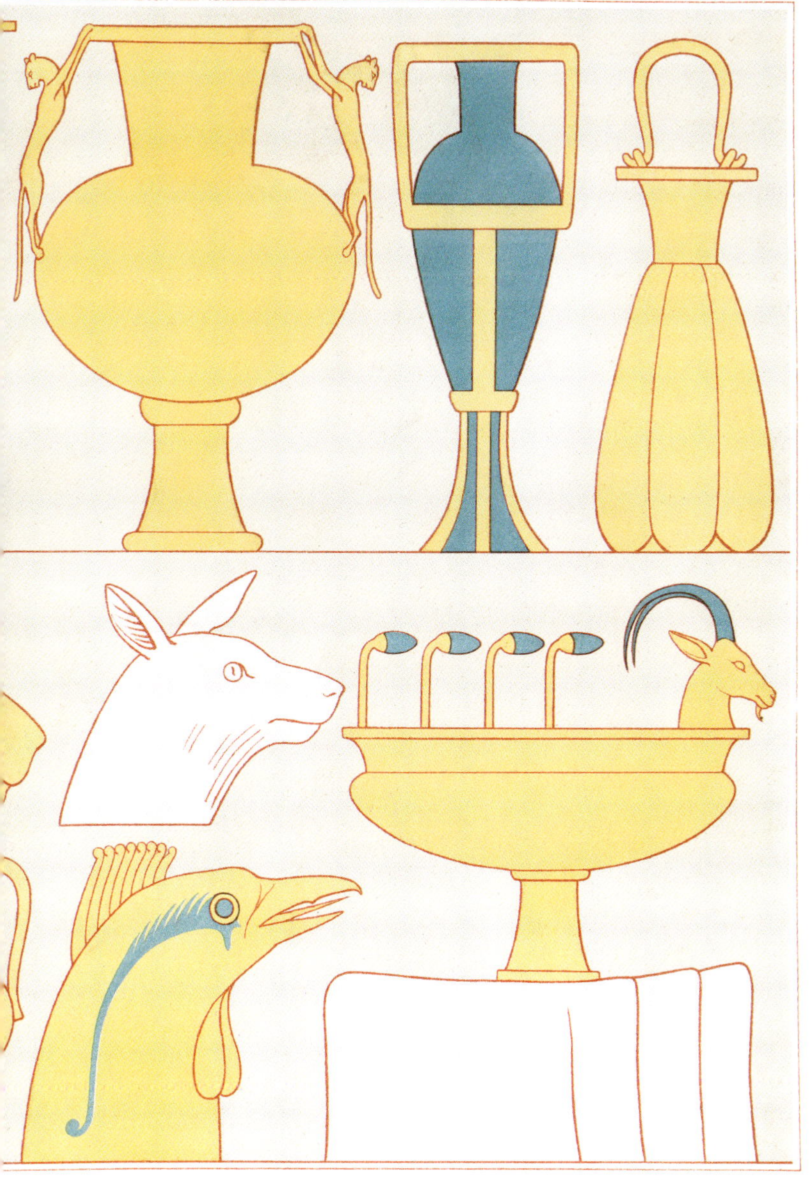

Publié par Arthus-Bertrand, Éditeur

RE DE THOUTMÈS III .

(DYNASTIE .)

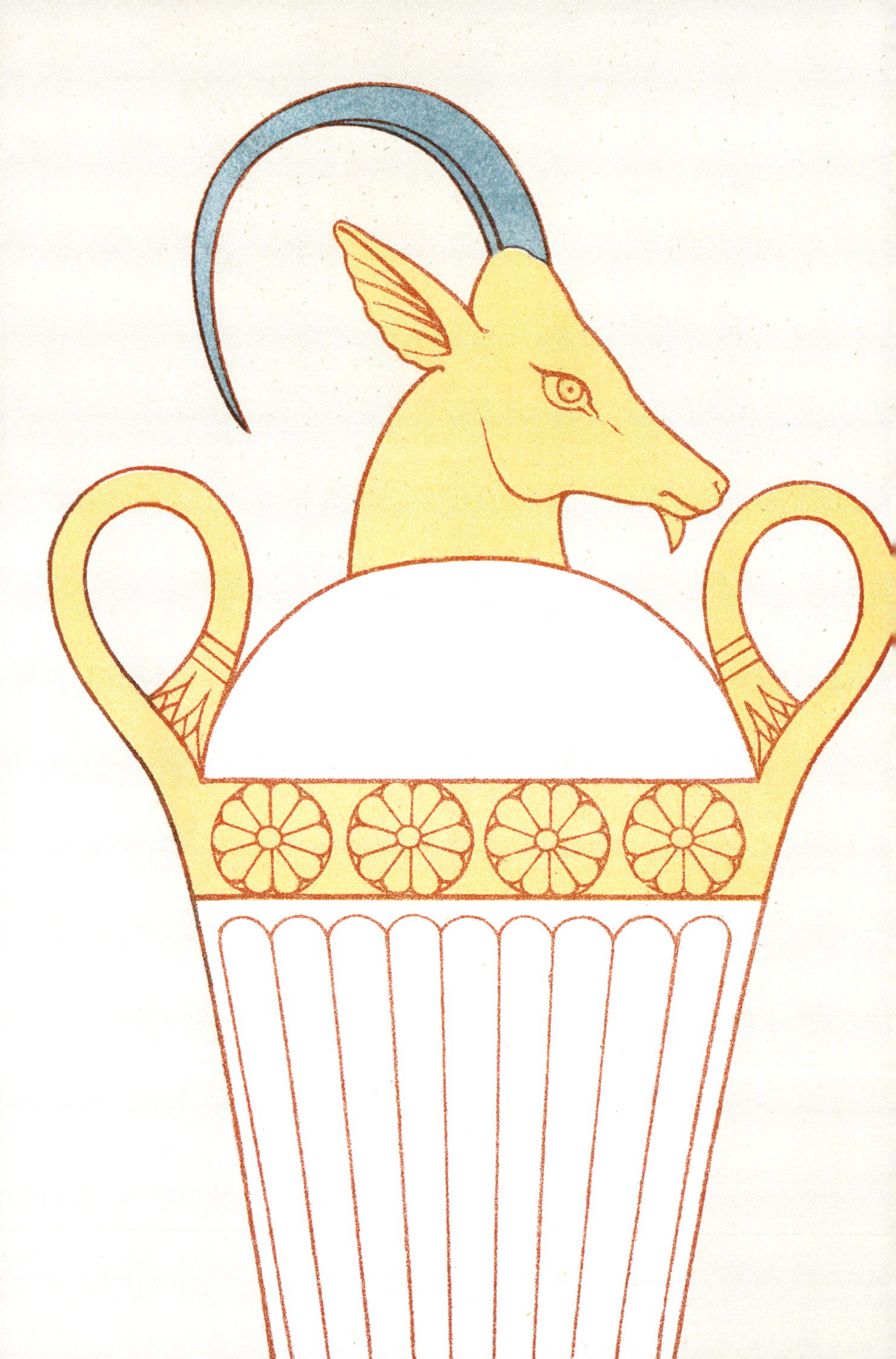

(Pages/Seite 508/509)

VASES FROM THE LAND OF KEFTIU, TRIBUTARY OF THUTMOSIS III (18th Dynasty)

Necropolis of Thebes

This group of vases, faithfully modelled on the original painting, is part of the tribute presented by the legates from the land of Keftiu to Thutmosis III, or rather to his vizier Rekhmire, who had this scene painted in his tomb. It is not known for certain which was the land of Keftiu; according to the hieroglyphic text, it consisted of an island or islands in the middle of the great sea, the Northern sea. The people of Keftiu, well known for their industrial production, could well be identified with the natives of Cyprus or Crete. The vases which they bring as tribute are not markedly different from Egyptian articles, with the exception of three or four cups in the shape of rhytons and two other vases in opaque iridescent glass.

VASEN AUS DEM LAND DER KAFA, TRIBUTPFLICHTIGE THUTMOSIS' III. (18. Dynastie)

Nekropole von Theben

Diese originalgetreu von der Malerei abgepauste Vasengruppe gehört zu dem Tribut, den die Gesandten des Landes der Kafa Thutmosis III. oder eher seinem Verwalter Rechmire überreichten, der diese Szene in sein Grab malen ließ. Man weiß nicht wirklich, was das Land der Kafa oder Kefa war, bei dem es sich nach Aussage der Hieroglyphentexte um eine oder mehrere Inseln inmitten des großen Meeres – des Nordmeeres – handelt. Diese für ihre kunstgewerblichen Produkte berühmten Kafa ließen sich gut mit den Eingeborenen Zyperns oder Kretas gleichsetzen. Mit Ausnahme von drei oder vier Gefäßen in Form eines Rhytons und zwei weiteren Vasen aus opakem, in den Regenbogenfarben schillerndem Glas unterscheiden sich die von ihnen überbrachten Vasen nur wenig von den ägyptischen Erzeugnissen.

VASES DU PAYS DE KAFA, TRIBUTAIRE DE THOUTMÈS III (XVIIIe dynastie)

Nécropole de Thèbes

Ce groupe de vases, calqué fidèlement sur la peinture originale, fait partie du tribut présenté par les députés du pays de Kafa [Keftiou] à Thoutmès [Thoutmôsis] III, ou plutôt à son intendant Rekhmara, qui a fait peindre cette scène dans son tombeau. On ne sait pas positivement quel était ce pays des Kafa ou Kéfa, qui, au dire du texte hiéroglyphique, formait une île ou des îles au milieu de la grande mer, la mer du Nord. Ces Kafa, distingués par leurs productions industrielles, pourraient bien être identifiés avec les aborigènes de Chypre ou de Crète. Les vases qu'ils apportent ne se distinguent pas beaucoup des produits égyptiens, à l'exception de trois ou quatre coupes en forme de rithons et de deux autres vases en verre opaque irisé.

VASES FROM THE TRIBUTARIES OF KEFTIU (18th Dynasty)

Necropolis of Thebes

It is worth remembering that the Keftiu, a subject people from the 18th Dynasty onwards, are always portrayed wearing luxurious clothes and bearing as tribute the rich products of an already highly developed industry, consisting principally of vases of remarkable taste. These articles must necessarily have had an influence on the industrial art of the Egyptians, who would have been inspired by them. The contours and the decoration of vases nos. 2, 6 and 9, taken from the same group of tribute bearers, are certainly within the repertoire of the skilful Egyptian ceramists. Nos. 4, 5, 7 and 10, which were in use at the same time amongst the Keftiu, were found in the tomb of Rekhmire, differently coloured and with no indication of location. Everything therefore leads me to believe that these shapes and ornaments were already familiar to the Egyptians, since at the date of this painting there is a contemporaneous [Egyptian] ceiling that is decorated with bulls' heads crowned with rosettes.

VASEN DER TRIBUTPFLICHTIGEN AUS KAFA (18. Dynastie)

Nekropole von Theben

Es ist nicht zu vergessen, dass dieses von der 18. Dynastie an unterworfene Volk [der Kafas] immer prächtig gekleidet dargestellt ist und kostbare Erzeugnisse eines bereits gut entwickelten Gewerbes überbringt, hauptsächlich bemerkenswert geschmackvolle Vasen. Diese Tribute müssen sich zwangsläufig auf das Kunstgewerbe der Ägypter ausgewirkt haben, die sich davon anregen lassen konnten. Die anmutig geschwungene Form und die Verzierung der derselben Trägergruppe entnommenen Vasen Nr. 2, 6 und 9 sind den geschickten ägyptischen Keramikern zuzuordnen. Die auch bei den Kafas gebräuchlichen Nr. 4, 5, 7 und 10 finden sich, anders gefärbt und ohne Herkunftsbezeichnung, im Grab Rechmires. Für mich legt also alles die Vermutung nahe, dass diese Formen und Ornamente den Ägyptern bereits vertraut waren – da zum Zeitpunkt dieser Darstellung die von Rosetten überragten Bukranien eine zeitgenössische Decke zieren.

VASES DES TRIBUTAIRES DE KAFA (XVIIIe dynastie)

Nécropole de Thèbes

N'oublions pas que ce peuple [de Kafa], soumis dès la XVIIIe dynastie, est toujours représenté vêtu avec luxe, et apportant les riches produits d'une industrie déjà fort développée, qui consistent principalement en vases d'un goût remarquable. Ces tributs ont dû nécessairement influer sur l'art industriel des Égyptiens qui ont pu s'en inspirer. Les galbes et les décorations des vases n°s 2, 6 et 9, tirés du même groupe de porteurs, appartiennent bien aux habiles céramistes égyptiens. Les n°s 4, 5, 7 et 10, en usage à la fois chez les Kafa [Keftiou], se retrouvent dans le tombeau Rekhmara, coloriés différemment et sans désignation de localité. Tout me porte donc à croire que ces formes et ornements étaient déjà familiers aux Égyptiens, puisqu'à la date de cette représentation les bucrânes surmontés de rosaces décorent un plafond de la même époque.

V5

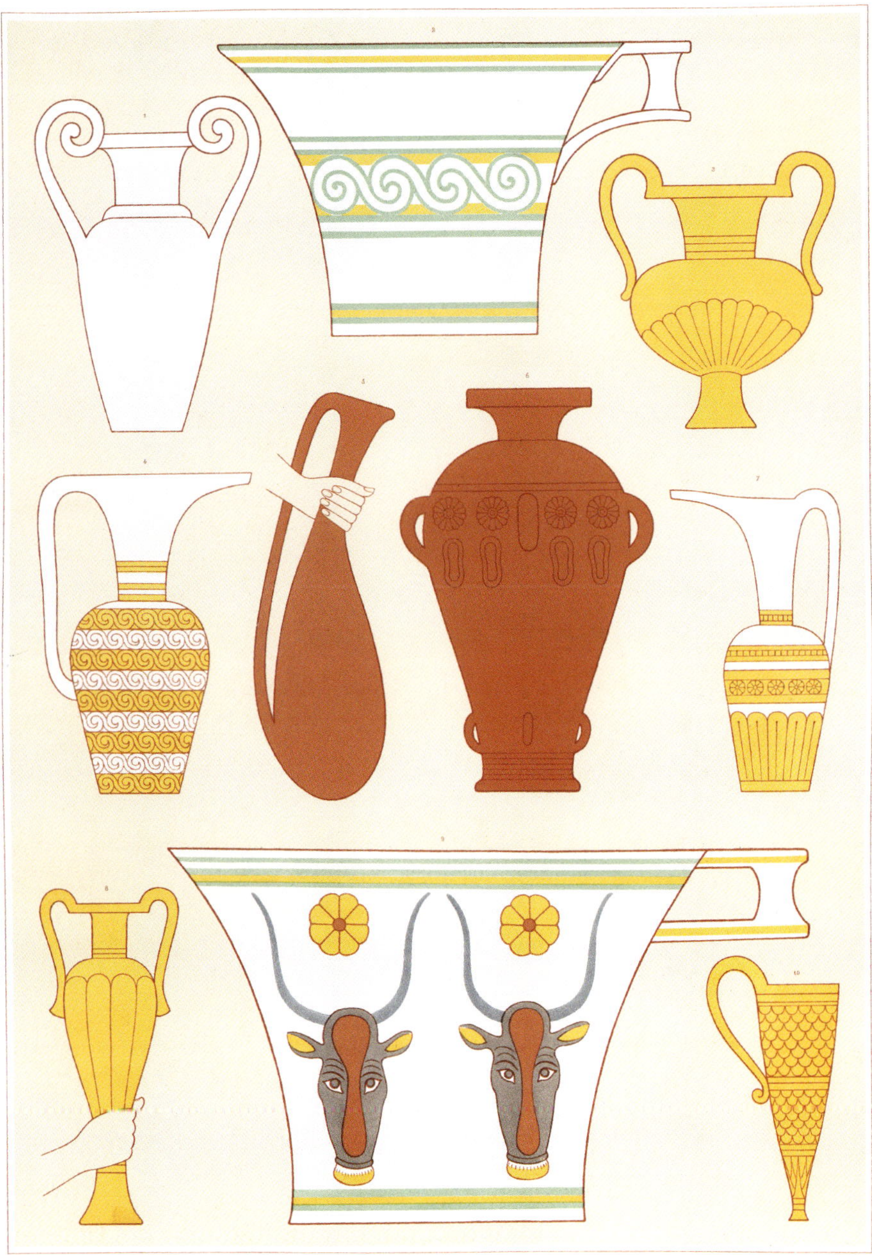

Lith. par Bedat. Imp. par Haugard-Maugé

E. Prisse d'Avennes.

Publié par Arthus Bertrand, Éditeur.

VASES DES TRIBUTAIRES DE KAFA.

(NÉCROPOLE DE THÈBES. XVIIIe DYNASTIE.)

VASES FROM ASIATIC TRIBUTARIES (18th Dynasty)

Necropolis of Thebes

These vases are portrayed in the tomb of a high-ranking functionary who lived at the court of the pharaohs Amenophis II and Thutmosis IV; they are carried by Asiatic tribute-bearers. All of these beautiful vases must have been in gold and silver, decorated with cloisonné enamel. No. 4, which has a lid shaped like a bull's head of which only the horns can now be seen, has been restored from another vase that is painted in the same hypogeum. With the exception of the great bowl-shaped vase that dominates the top half of the plate, all the other vases have shapes which are to be found in the lekythos, the Bacchic amphora and certain amphorae from Nola, several centuries later than the tomb where the paintings copied on this plate were found.

VASEN DER ASIATISCHEN TRIBUTPFLICHTIGEN (18. Dynastie)

Nekropole von Theben

Diese Vasen sind im Grab eines hohen Beamten dargestellt, der am Hof der Pharaonen Amenophis II. und Thutmosis IV. lebte. Sie werden von asiatischen Tributpflichtigen getragen. Diese schönen Vasen müssen alle aus Gold und Silber gefertigt und in Cloisonné verziert gewesen sein. Die Nr. 4, die als Deckel einen Rinderkopf trug, von dem nur noch die Hörner zu erkennen waren, wurde nach dem Vorbild einer anderen gemalten Vase aus demselben Hypogäum restauriert. Mit Ausnahme des Kraters, der den oberen Teil der Tafel beherrscht, weisen alle übrigen Vasen Formen auf, die man auch beim Lekythos, bei der Bacchusamphore und bestimmten nolanischen Amphoren findet – und diese sind mehrere Jahrhunderte jünger als das Grab, in dem sich die auf dieser Tafel abgebildeten Darstellungen befanden.

VASES DES TRIBUTAIRES ASIATIQUES (XVIIIe dynastie)

Nécropole de Thèbes

Ces vases sont représentés dans le tombeau d'un haut fonctionnaire qui vivait à la cour des pharaons Aménophis II et Thoutmès [Thoutmôsis] IV. Ils sont portés par des tributaires asiatiques. Tous ces beaux vases devaient être en or et en argent, et décorés d'émaux cloisonnés. Le n° 4, qui porte pour couvercle une tête de bœuf dont on ne voyait plus que les cornes, a été restauré d'après un autre vase peint dans le même hypogée. À l'exception du cratère qui domine au sommet de la planche, tous les autres vases ont des formes qu'on retrouve dans le lekythos [lécythe], l'amphore bachique et certaines amphores de Nola, postérieures de plusieurs siècles au tombeau où se trouvaient les représentations retracées sur cette planche.

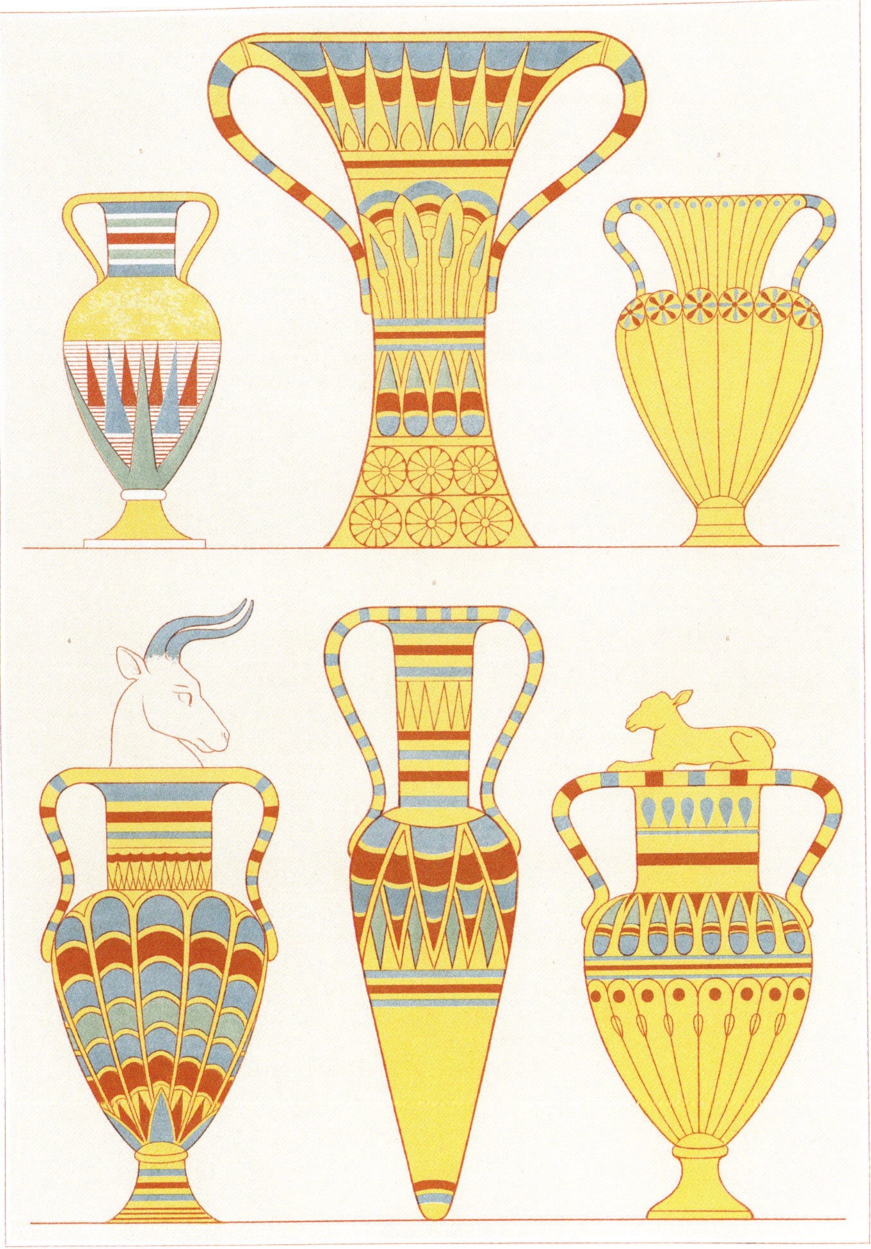

Lith par Saladin. — Imp par Hangard-Maugé

E. Prisse d'Avennes

Publié par Arthus-Bertrand Éditeur

VASES DE TRIBUTAIRES ASIATIQUES.

(NÉCROPOLE DE THÈBES. — XVIIIe DYNASTIE.)

VASES OF VARIOUS MATERIALS (18th and 20th Dynasties)

Necropolis of Thebes

No. 1 is a vase in opaque glass, mounted in gold, whose decorations on the base are half destroyed. It comes from the tomb of the foster father of Amenophis II; other vases in opaque glass, to be described later, come from the same tomb. Nos. 2 and 3 were copied in a hypogeum in the vicinity. Nos. 4 and 5 come from the tomb of Ramaitha [Mery]. All these four appear to be of gold covered with cloisonné enamel. Nos. 6, 7 and 8 were copied in a pyramidal tomb, which can be seen between the temple of Deir el-Medina and the ruins of Medinet Habu; it goes back to the 20th Dynasty. These three vases appear to me to be of enamelled clay, mounted in gold.

VASEN AUS UNTERSCHIEDLICHEN MATERIALIEN (18. und 20. Dynastie)

Nekropole von Theben

Die Nr. 1 ist eine Vase aus opakem, mit Gold besetztem Glas, dessen Verzierungen am Fuß halb zerstört sind. Sie stammt aus dem Grab des Pflegevaters von Amenophis II., dem auch die nachstehend beschriebenen Vasen aus opakem Glas entnommen sind. Die Nr. 2 und 3 wurden in einem benachbarten Hypogäum abgezeichnet. Die Nr. 4 und 5 stammen aus dem Grab von Ramaitha [Meri]. Alle vier scheinen mit Gold und Cloisonné bedeckt gewesen zu sein. Die Nr. 6, 7 und 8 wurden in einem Pyramidengrab abgezeichnet, das zwischen dem Tempel von Deir el-Medina und den Ruinen von Medinet Habu zu sehen ist. Es datiert aus der Zeit der 20. Dynastie. Diese drei Vasen scheinen mir aus emailliertem, mit Gold besetztem Ton gefertigt zu sein.

VASES DE DIVERSES MATIÈRES (XVIIIe et XXe dynasties)

Nécropole de Thèbes

Le n° 1 est un vase en verre opaque, monté en or, et dont les ornements, à la base, sont à demi détruits. Il provient du tombeau du père nourricier d'Aménophis II, d'où ont aussi été tirés ceux de verre opaque décrits ci-après. Les n°s 2 et 3 ont été copiés dans un hypogée du voisinage. Les n°s 4 et 5 proviennent du tombeau de Ramaitha [Méry]. Tous quatre paraissent être d'or couvert d'émaux cloisonnés. Les n°s 6, 7 et 8 ont été copiés dans un tombeau pyramidal, qui se voit entre le temple de Deyr el-Medineh et les ruines de Medineh-Tabou [Médinet Habou]. Il remonte à l'époque de la XXe dynastie. Ces trois vases me paraissent être de terre émaillée, montée en or.

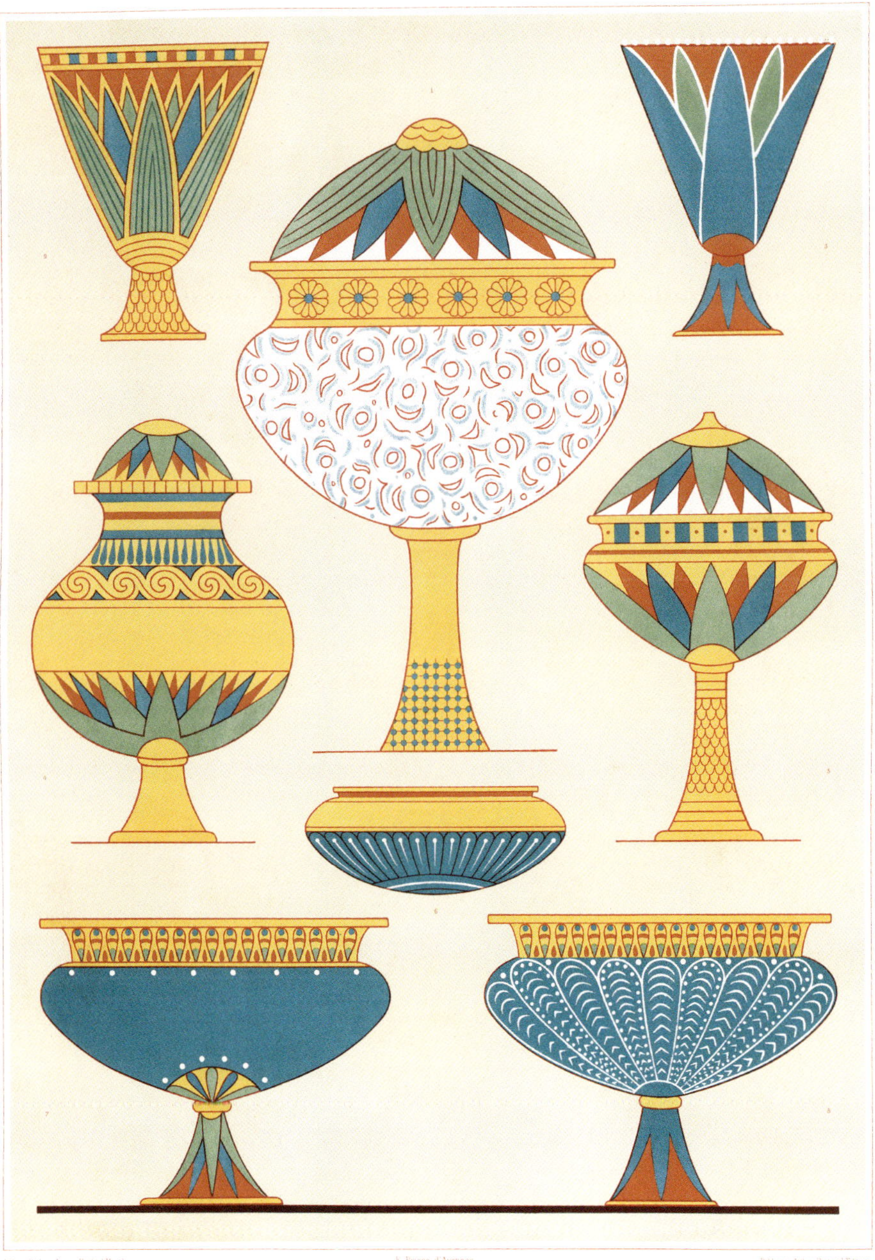

Lith par Stelzer . Imp par Hangard-Maugé — E. Prisse d'Avennes — Publié par Arthus-Bertrand Éditeur.

VASES DE DIVERSES MATIÈRES .

(NÉCROPOLE DE THÈBES _ XVIII.e & XX.e DYNASTIES.)

BOWL-SHAPED VASES (18th and 20th Dynasties)

Necropolis of Thebes

We have seen that the Egyptians excelled in the use to which they put terracotta. Egyptian terracotta, which has a 92% silica content, is so close-grained and so singularly adapted to hold the finest relief and the most delicate impression that it has long been given the name of "Egyptian porcelain". To make it possible to appreciate the exceptional interest of the innumerable series of Egyptian vases we owe to the skill of the ceramists, the most remarkable of which are portrayed in these plates, we shall list the names of the most popular forms. The name "ciborium" [or crateriform] is normally given to the vase which narrows at the base in the category of ciboria known as Egyptian bean; there are some grounds for thinking that it is because of this imitation that the Egyptian vases have a base which is barely able to support the body.

KRATERFÖRMIGE VASEN (18. und 20. Dynastie)

Nekropole von Theben

Wie man sehen konnte, leisteten die Ägypter Hervorragendes bei der Verwendung von Terrakotta. Die ägyptischen Terrakotten, die zu 92 % aus Siliziumdioxid bestehen, sind so dicht und so gut geeignet, die feinsten Reliefs und die zartesten Abdrücke aufzunehmen, dass man sie lange Zeit als „ägyptisches Porzellan" bezeichnete. Damit der Leser anhand der Darstellung der bemerkenswertesten Modelle auf unseren Tafeln die unübersehbare Folge ägyptischer Vasen gebührend würdigen kann, die der Begabung der Keramiker zu verdanken ist, werden wir ein Verzeichnis der bevorzugten Formen erstellen. Man bezeichnete für gewöhnlich als „Ziborium" [oder kraterförmig] eine unten am Fuß verengte Vase in der Art der Ziborien, bekannt als ägyptische Bohne, der Frucht der Lotusblüte; es besteht Anlass zu der Vermutung, dass die ägyptischen Vasen aufgrund dieser Nachahmung einen Sockel aufweisen, der ihren Körper kaum tragen kann.

VASES CRATÉRIFORMES (XVIIIe et XXe dynasties)

Nécropole de Thèbes

On a vu que les Égyptiens excellèrent dans les applications de la terre cuite. Les terres cuites égyptiennes, composées de 92 pour 100 de silice, sont si serrées, sont tellement aptes à conserver les plus fins reliefs et les empreintes les plus délicates, qu'on les a longtemps désignées sous l'appellation de « porcelaines d'Égypte ». Maintenant qu'il est permis d'apprécier combien était intéressante l'innombrable série des vases égyptiens dus au talent des céramistes par la représentation, dans nos planches, des modèles les plus remarquables, nous allons établir la nomenclature des formes préférées. On désigne ordinairement par le nom de « Ciborion » [ou cratériforme], le vase rétréci par le bas dans le genre des ciboires de la fève d'Égypte ; il y a lieu de penser que c'est en raison de cette imitation que les vases égyptiens présentent une base qui peut à peine soutenir le corps.

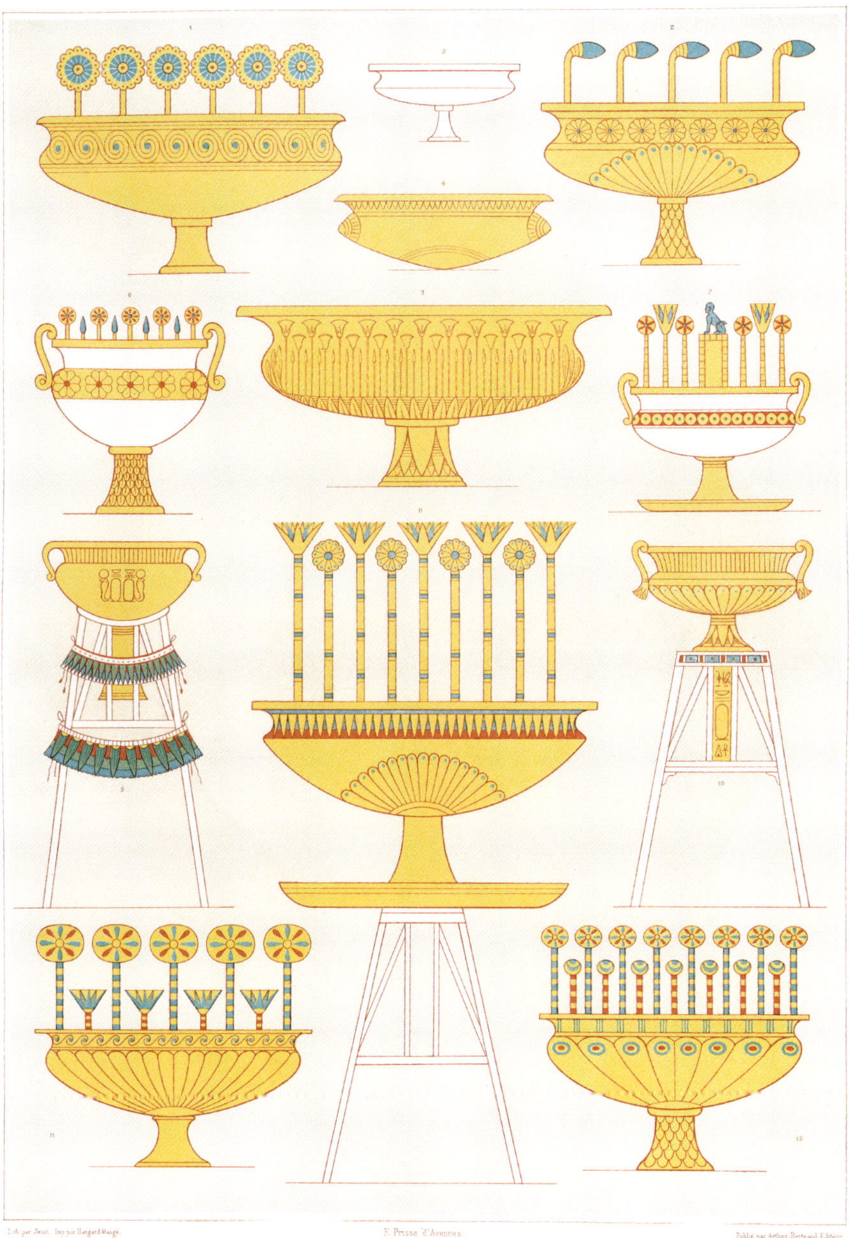

Lith. par Jenot. Imp. par Hangard-Maugé. E. Prisse d'Avennes. Publié par Arthus-Bertrand, Éditeur.

VASES CRATÉRIFORMES.

(NÉCROPOLE DE THÈBES. _ XVIIIe._XX^e. DYNASTIES.)

VASES IN OPAQUE GLASS (18th Dynasty)

Thebes

A representation of glass makers is to be seen in the hypogea of Beni Hassan, which date from the 12th Dynasty, but strictly speaking, the most ancient example of glass that is known in collections goes back no further than the 18th Dynasty, in other words the period of the vases which are the subject of this plate. [...] These vases were particularly noteworthy, as much for the intrinsic beauty of the material as for their iridescence and the different-coloured meanders which are either incorporated into the main body or scattered across them as decoration. Quite often one comes upon different examples of this beautiful [glass-making] industry in excavations in Egypt, but these vases are usually small with an undulating surface, iridescent, dappled or grained like the large vases that are grouped together in this plate. These different vases were copied from paintings in the same tomb, that of the foster father of Amenophis II.

VASEN AUS OPAKEM GLAS (18. Dynastie)

Theben

In den Hypogäen von Beni Hassan, die aus der 12. Dynastie datieren, ist eine Glasmacher-Darstellung zu sehen; die ältesten Glasstücke, die in den Sammlungen vorliegen, stammen jedoch nicht aus der Zeit vor der 18. Dynastie – d. h. aus der Epoche von Vasen, die den Gegenstand dieser Tafel bilden. [...] Diese Vasen waren höchst bemerkenswert, wegen der Schönheit des Materials, des Schillerns in den Regenbogenfarben und der verschiedenfarbigen, der Masse beigemengten oder als Ornament verteilten Mäander. In Ägypten werden nicht selten unterschiedliche Beispiele dieser schönen [Glas-] Produktion bei Ausgrabungen gefunden, im Allgemeinen handelt es sich jedoch um kleine Vasen, die – wie die auf dieser Tafel zusammengestellten großen Vasen – wellenförmig irisieren, bunt schillern oder gekörnt sind. Diese verschiedenen Vasen wurden von den Malereien in ein und demselben Grab abgezeichnet – dem des Pflegevaters von Amenophis II.

VASES EN VERRE OPAQUE (XVIIIe dynastie)

Thèbes

On voit dans les hypogées de Beni-Haçen, qui datent de la XIIe dynastie, une représentation de verriers ; mais le plus ancien échantillon de verre, proprement dit, que l'on possède dans les collections, ne remonte pas au delà de la XVIIIe dynastie, c'est-à-dire de l'époque des vases qui font le sujet de cette planche. [...] Ces vases étaient fort remarquables, tant par la beauté de la matière que par leurs irisations et leurs méandres de différentes couleurs, incorporés dans la masse ou distribués en ornements. Il n'est pas rare de rencontrer dans les fouilles en Égypte différents spécimens de cette belle industrie [de verre], mais, généralement, ce sont des petits vases ondulés irisés, diaprés ou granités comme les grands vases réunis dans cette planche. Ces divers vases ont été copiés sur les peintures, dans un même tombeau, celui du père nourricier d'Aménophis II.

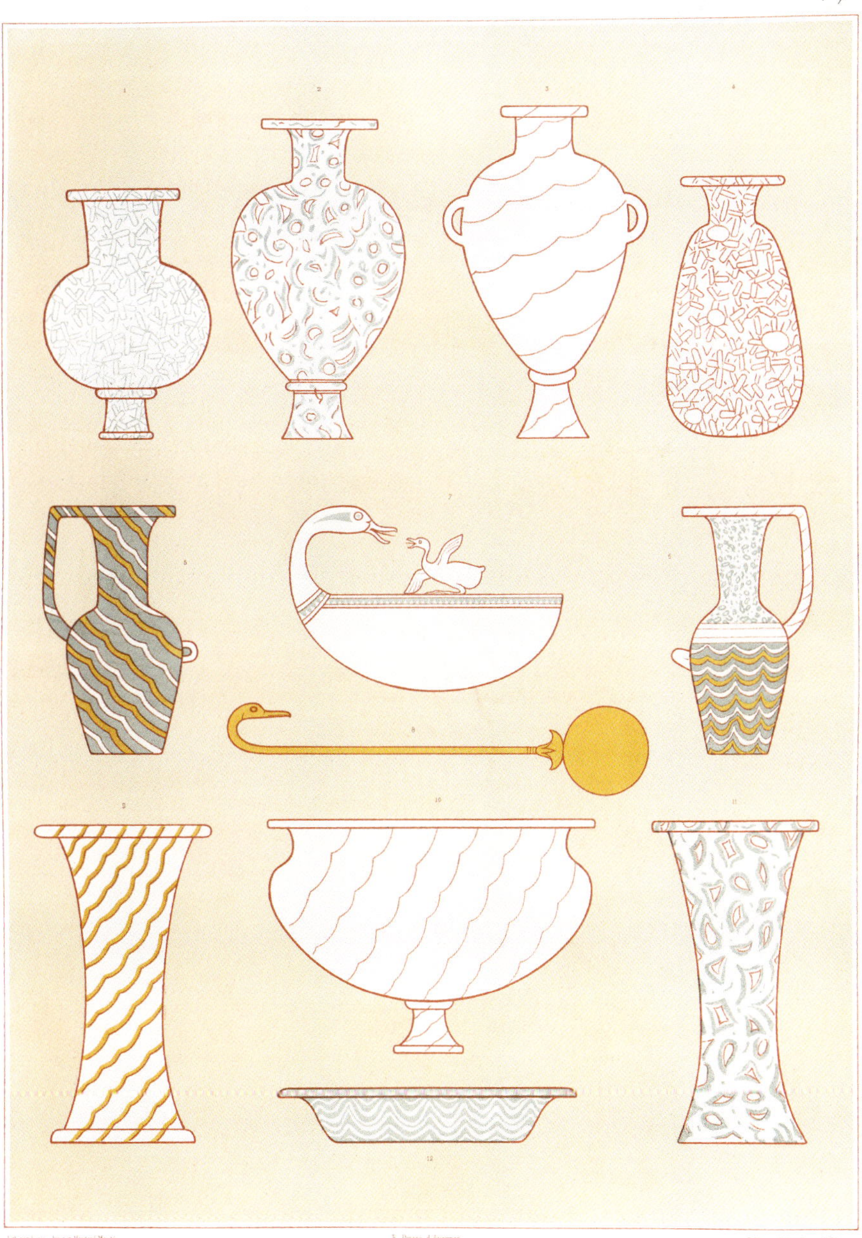

Lith par Levie. Imp par Hangard-Maugé — E. Prisse d'Avennes — Publié par Arthus Bertrand, Éditeur

VASES EN VERRE OPAQUE.

(THEBES. — XVIIIe DYNASTIE.)

AMPHORAE, JARS AND OTHER VASES (18th and 19th Dynasties)

Thebes

The [amphora] decorated with two calves gambolling in the fields shows a delightful freedom of line and recalls the vases known as Phoenician-style found in Greece. The other is more restrained in its form and decoration and features an attractive flower motif. No. 3, taken from the same hypogeum, has as sole decoration a garland of lotus flowers. All three vases grouped under no. 7 have the distinction of bearing an inscription indicating their function: the vase on the left has three undulating lines, the symbol of water, while the other two, which were intended to hold different wines, have the names of the wines inscribed on them. The other four vases, nos. 4, 5 and 6, were in hard pottery or enamelled clay.

AMPHOREN, GROSSE TONKRÜGE UND ANDERE VASEN (18. und 19. Dynastie)

Theben

Die mit zwei inmitten der Felder herumtollenden Kälbern geschmückte [Amphore] ist von bezaubernder Ungezwungenheit und erinnert an die in Griechenland gefundenen Vasen im sogenannten phönizischen Stil. Die andere, in Form und Verzierung strengere [Vase] zeigt ein hübsches Blumenmotiv. Die Nr. 3 stammt aus demselben Hypogäum und trägt als einzigen Schmuck eine Girlande aus Lotusblättern. Die mit der Nr. 7 bezeichnete Vasengruppe zeichnet sich durch die Besonderheit aus, dass alle drei eine Inschrift tragen, die ihren Zweck angibt: Die linke Vase weist drei Wellenlinien, ein Sinnbild des Wassers, auf; die beiden anderen, die verschiedene Weine aufnehmen sollten, tragen deren Namen. Die vier anderen Vasen, Nr. 4, 5 und 6, bestanden aus harter oder glasierter Keramik.

AMPHORES, JARRES ET AUTRES VASES (XVIIIe et XIXe dynasties)

Thèbes

Celle [amphore]qui est décorée de deux veaux qui prennent leurs ébats au milieu des champs est d'une liberté charmante et rappelle les vases, dits de style phénicien, trouvés en Grèce. L'autre, plus sevère dans sa forme et son ornementation, offre un joli motif de fleurs. Le n° 3, tiré du même hypogée, porte pour unique décoration une guirlande de feuilles de lotus. Le groupe de vases désigné par le n° 7 offre cette particularité qu'ils portent, tous trois, une inscription qui indique leur destination : le vase de gauche présente trois lignes ondulées, symbole de l'eau ; les deux autres, destinés à contenir des vins différents, en portent les noms. Les quatre autres vases, n°s 4, 5 et 6, étaient en poterie dure ou terre émaillée.

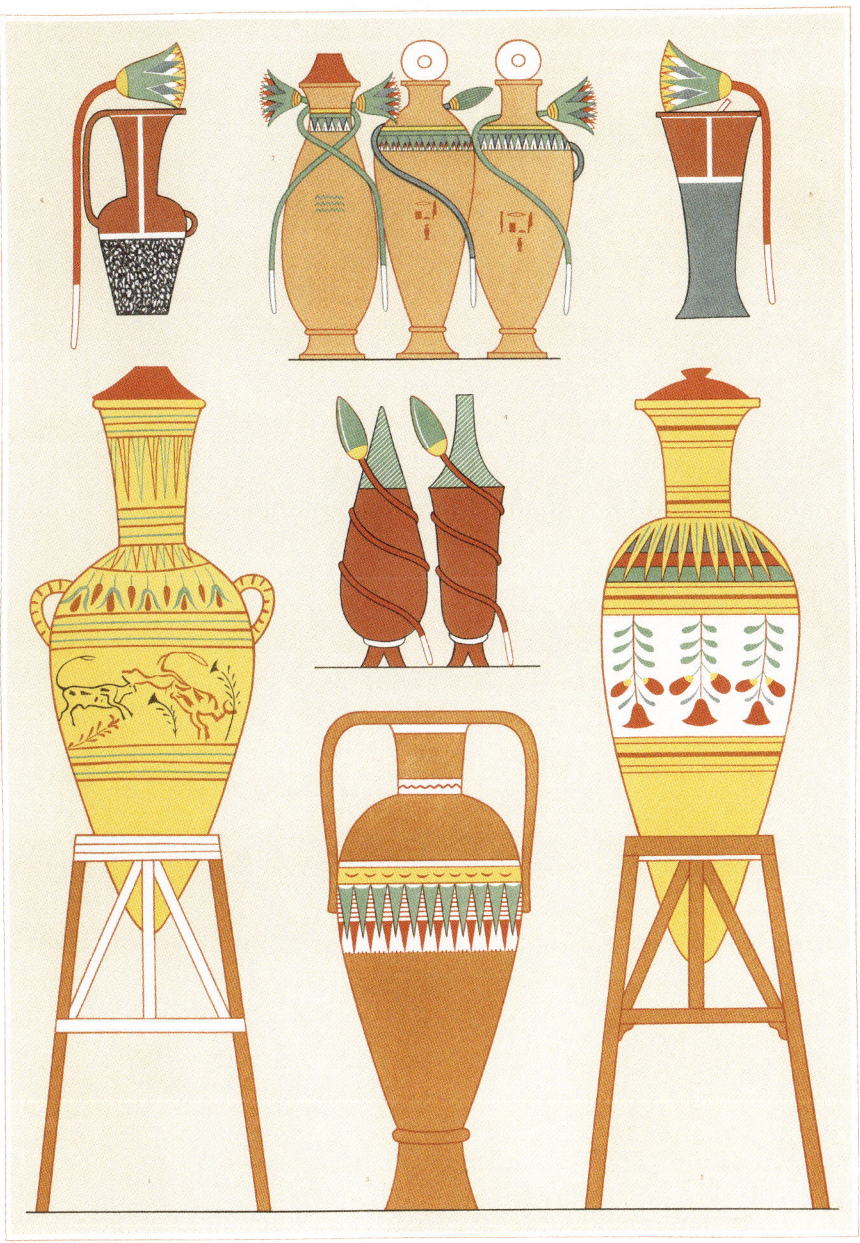

Lith. par Barbier. Imp. par Hangard-Maugé.   E. Prisse d'Avennes.   Publié par Arthus-Bertrand, Éditeur.

AMPHORES, JARRES ET AUTRES VASES.

(THÈBES — XVIIIe & XIXe DYNASTIES.)

JARS AND AMPHORAE (18th Dynasty)

Necropolis of Thebes

The upper register portrays terracotta pots for keeping water cool and other vases, set out like this in a painting from a hypogeum excavated for a functionary called Suemnut who lived in the reign of Amenophis II. A young man equipped with a brick or a sandy pottery shard is employed in buffing one of these vases. The first three vases in the second register all come from the same picture painted in a hypogeum in Abd el-Qurna, from the reign of Thutmosis III. I have included nos. 5 and 2 on the same plate in order to draw a parallel between two vases decorated with bunches of grapes and obviously intended to contain wine. No. 8 was found in another painting of the same period, where this vase is suspended from a yoke carried by two men. As for nos. 6 and 7, the two vases with the same bulbous shape and adorned with a type of collar with lotus flowers, there is nothing to indicate their function

GROSSE TONKRÜGE UND AMPHOREN (18. Dynastie)

Nekropole von Theben

Das obere Register zeigt poröse Gefäße zum Kühlen des Wassers und weitere ebenso aufgestellte Vasen aus einem Hypogäum für einen Beamten namens Soumka, der unter der Herrschaft von Amenophis II. lebte. Ein mit einem Ziegel oder einer Scherbe sandiger Keramik ausgerüsteter junger Mann ist damit beschäftigt, eine der Vasen abzureiben. Die beiden ersten Vasen des zweiten Registers gehören zu ein und demselben Bild, das in der Regierungszeit von Thutmosis III. in ein Hypogäum in Scheich Abd el-Qurna gemalt wurde. Die Nr. 5 und 2 habe ich auf derselben Tafel vereinigt, um zwei mit Weinreben verzierte Vasen, die natürlich Wein aufnehmen sollten, nebeneinanderzustellen. Die Nr. 8 stammt von einem anderen Gemälde aus derselben Zeit, bei dem diese Vase an einem von zwei Männern getragenen Kummetbügel hängt. Was die beiden Vasen mit derselben anmutig geschwungenen Form betrifft, die mit Lotusblüten-Manschetten geschmückt und als Nr. 6 und 7 markiert sind, so deutet nichts auf ihre Funktion hin.

JARRES ET AMPHORES (XVIIIe dynastie)

Nécropole de Thèbes

Le registre supérieur représente des hydrocérames à rafraîchir l'eau et d'autres vases disposés ainsi dans une peinture d'un hypogée creusé pour un fonctionnaire nommé Soumka qui vivait sous Aménophis II. Un jeune homme, armé d'une brique ou d'un tesson de poterie sableuse, est occupé à frotter un de ces vases. Les trois premiers vases du second registre appartiennent à un même tableau peint dans un hypogée d'Abd el-Gournah, sous le règne de Thoutmès [Thoutmôsis] III. J'ai réuni les n°s 5 et 2 sur la même planche pour mettre en parallèle deux vases ornés de pampres de raisins, et destinés, évidemment, à contenir du vin. Le n° 8 se trouve dans une autre peinture de la même époque, où ce vase est suspendu à une attelle portée par deux hommes. Quant aux deux vases de même galbe, ornés de collerins à fleurs de lotus et marqués 6 et 7, rien n'indique leur destination.

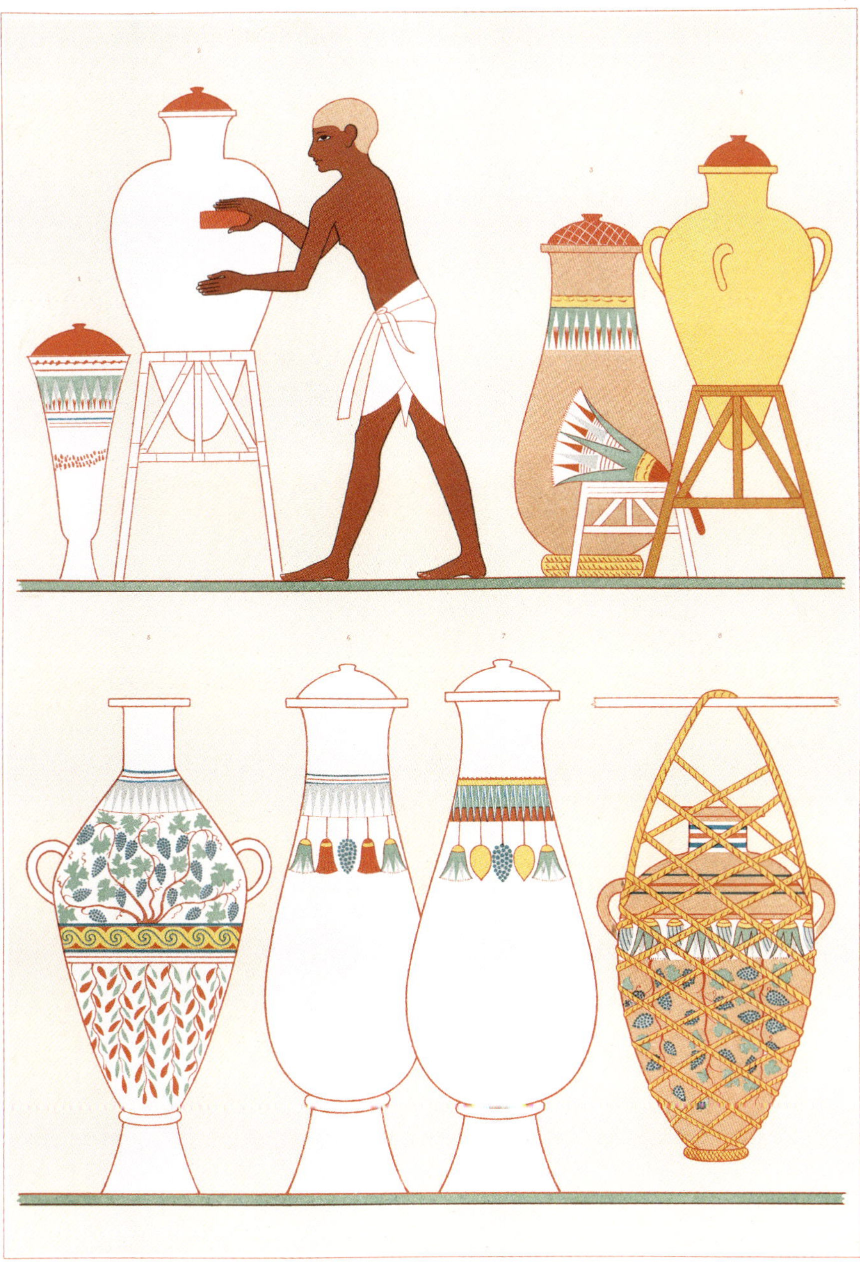

Lith. par Saladini. Imp. par Hangard-Maugé.

E. Prisse d'Avennes.

Publié par Arthus-Bertrand, Éditeur.

JARRES & AMPHORES.

(NÉCROPOLE DE THÈBES _ XVIIIe DYNASTIE.)

COLLECTION OF VASES FROM THE REIGN OF RAMESSES III (20th Dynasty)

Karnak and Medinet Habu

This plate is the reproduction of two bas-reliefs where these two groups of vases, arranged in this way on the walls of the memorial temple of Medinet Habu, form part of the rich offerings that Ramesses III presented to the gods of Egypt. According to the dedicatory inscription they were made of silver, gold, lapis, brass and precious stones. Since the colours of these two bas-reliefs have been worn away by time, it is no longer possible to identify all the details of the decoration; only the principal outlines remain, but these are sufficient to give some idea of the elegance of these products of Egyptian artistry during the 20th Dynasty.

VASENSAMMLUNG AUS DER REGIERUNGSZEIT VON RAMSES III. (20. Dynastie)

Karnak und Medinet Habu

Diese Tafel gibt Flachreliefs von zwei Vasengruppen wieder, die so an den Wänden des Gedächtnis-Tempels von Medinet Habu aufgestellt waren; hier gehören sie zu den prächtigen Opfergaben, die Ramses III. den ägyptischen Göttern präsentierte. Nach Aussage der Weihe-Inschrift waren sie aus Silber, Gold, Lasurstein, Kupfer und Edelsteinen gefertigt. Da die Farben der beiden Flachreliefs mit der Zeit verwittert sind, ist es unmöglich, sämtliche Einzelheiten der Verzierung festzustellen; es sind lediglich die wichtigsten Umrisslinien erhalten – die jedoch genügen, um sich eine Vorstellung von der Anmut der ägyptischen Kunsterzeugnisse unter der 20. Dynastie zu machen.

COLLECTION DE VASES DU RÈGNE DE RAMSÈS III (XXe dynastie)

Karnac et Medineh-Tabou

Cette planche est la reproduction de deux bas-reliefs où ces deux groupes de vases, disposés ainsi sur les murs du temple commémoratif de Medineh-Tabou [Médinet Habou], font partie des riches offrandes que Ramsès III présenta aux dieux de l'Égypte. Au dire de l'inscription dédicatoire, ils étaient faits d'argent, d'or, de lapis, de cuivre et de pierres précieuses. Les couleurs de ces deux bas-reliefs ayant été effacées par le temps, il est impossible de se rendre compte de tous les mêmes détails de l'ornementation ; il n'en reste plus que les contours principaux, mais ils suffisent pour donner une idée de l'élégance de ces produits de l'art égyptien sous la XXe dynastie.

V 12

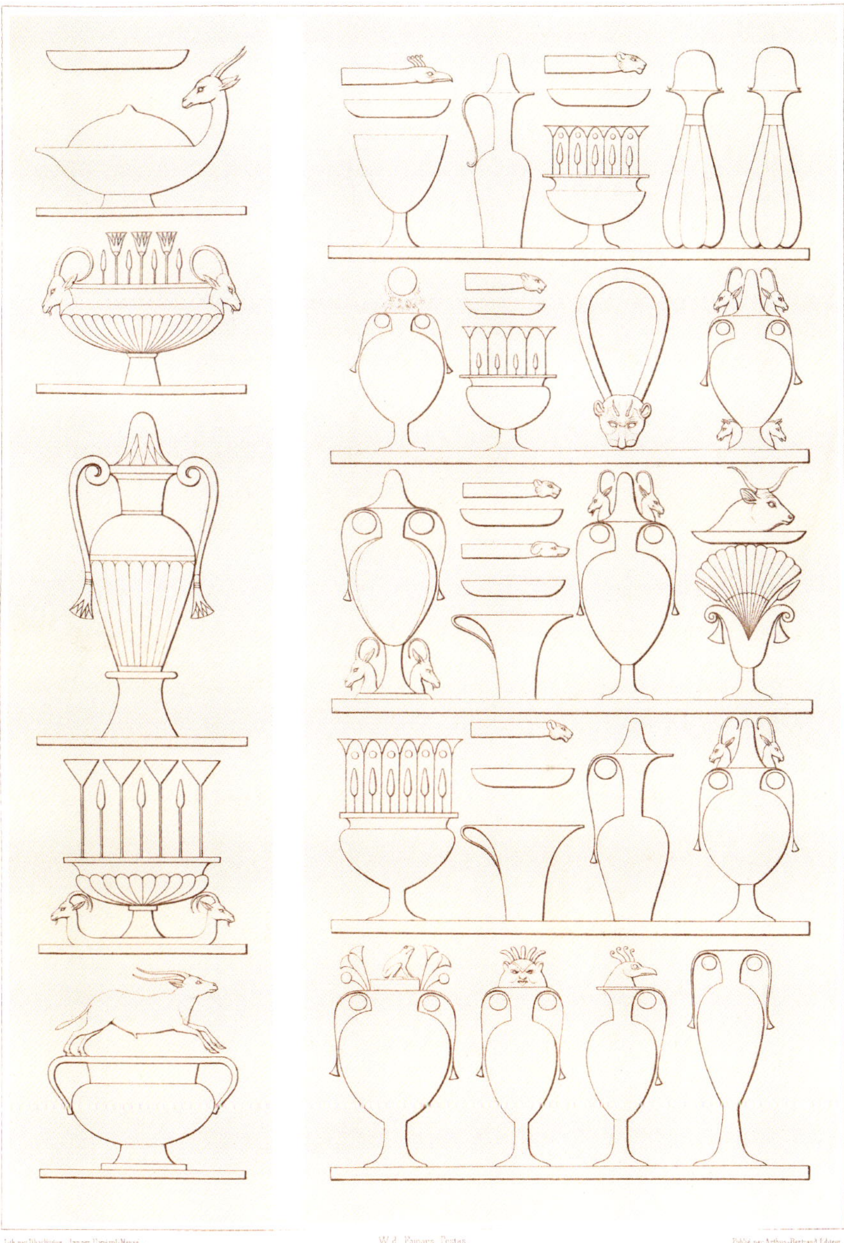

Lith. par Dhorlingue. Imp. par Hangard-Maugé.

W. d. Prisse d'Avennes, Pestas.

Publié par Arthus-Bertrand Éditeur.

COLLECTION DE VASES DU RÈGNE DE RAMSÈS III.

(KARNAC & MEDINEH-THABOU. XXe DYNASTIE.)

VASES FROM THE TOMB OF RAMESSES III (20th Dynasty)

Thebes

This one [this plate] shows more commonplace vases, probably those which were used on a daily basis in the palace. With the exception of the ewer and its basin and the three types of basket reproduced at the bottom of the plate, the other vases are either bronze cooking utensils or basic items of pottery such as jars, amphorae, water pots. These types of vases are found in many tombs, as their design was so well adapted to the needs of life in a hot climate. With regard to the two baskets at the bottom of the plate, they present an unusual example of the type of decoration commonly found on certain terracotta or wooden vessels. It recalls the Assyrian "nisr" which decorates the pharaoh's shield painted in this tomb, but could the griffon drawn with a flowing brush-line be a figure borrowed from Asia?

VASEN AUS DEM GRAB RAMSES' III. (20. Dynastie)

Theben

Diese [Tafel] stellt gewöhnlichere Vasen dar, wahrscheinlich solche, die im Palast täglich in Gebrauch waren. Mit Ausnahme der unten auf der Tafel abgebildeten Wasserkanne, dem dazugehörigen Becken und der drei unten auf der Tafel wiedergegebenen korbähnlichen Gebilde sind alle anderen Vasen bronzenes Küchengerät oder einfache Töpferwaren – wie große Tonkrüge, Amphoren, poröse Gefäße zum Kühlen des Wassers. Derartige Vasen finden sich in zahlreichen Gräbern; ihre Form war den Bedürfnissen des Lebens in heißem Klima bestens angepasst. Was die beiden unten auf der Tafel abgebildeten Körbe betrifft, so zeigen sie ein sonderbares Beispiel der für bestimmte Vasen aus Ton oder Holz gebräuchlichen Verzierung. Handelt es sich bei dem mit dem Pinsel umrissenen Greif um eine aus Asien entlehnte Figur, obgleich er an den assyrischen „Nisr" erinnert, der auch den Schild des in diesem Grab dargestellten Pharaos zierte?

VASES DU TOMBEAU DE RAMSÈS III (XXe dynastie)

Thèbes

Celle-ci [cette planche] représente des vases plus communs ; probablement ceux qui étaient employés, journellement, dans le palais. À l'exception de l'aiguière, de son bassin et des trois espèces de corbeilles reproduites au bas de la planche, les autres vases sont des ustensiles culinaires en bronze ou de simples poteries, telles que jarres, amphores, hydrocérames. On retrouve de ces vases dans beaucoup de tombeaux ; leur forme était bien appropriée aux besoins de la vie dans les climats chauds. Quant aux deux corbeilles du bas de la planche, elles offrent un curieux spécimen de la décoration usitée pour certains vases en terre ou en bois. Le griffon tracé au courant du pinceau est-il une figure empruntée à l'Asie, quoiqu'il rappelle le « nisr » assyrien qui ornait aussi le bouclier du pharaon représenté dans ce tombeau ?

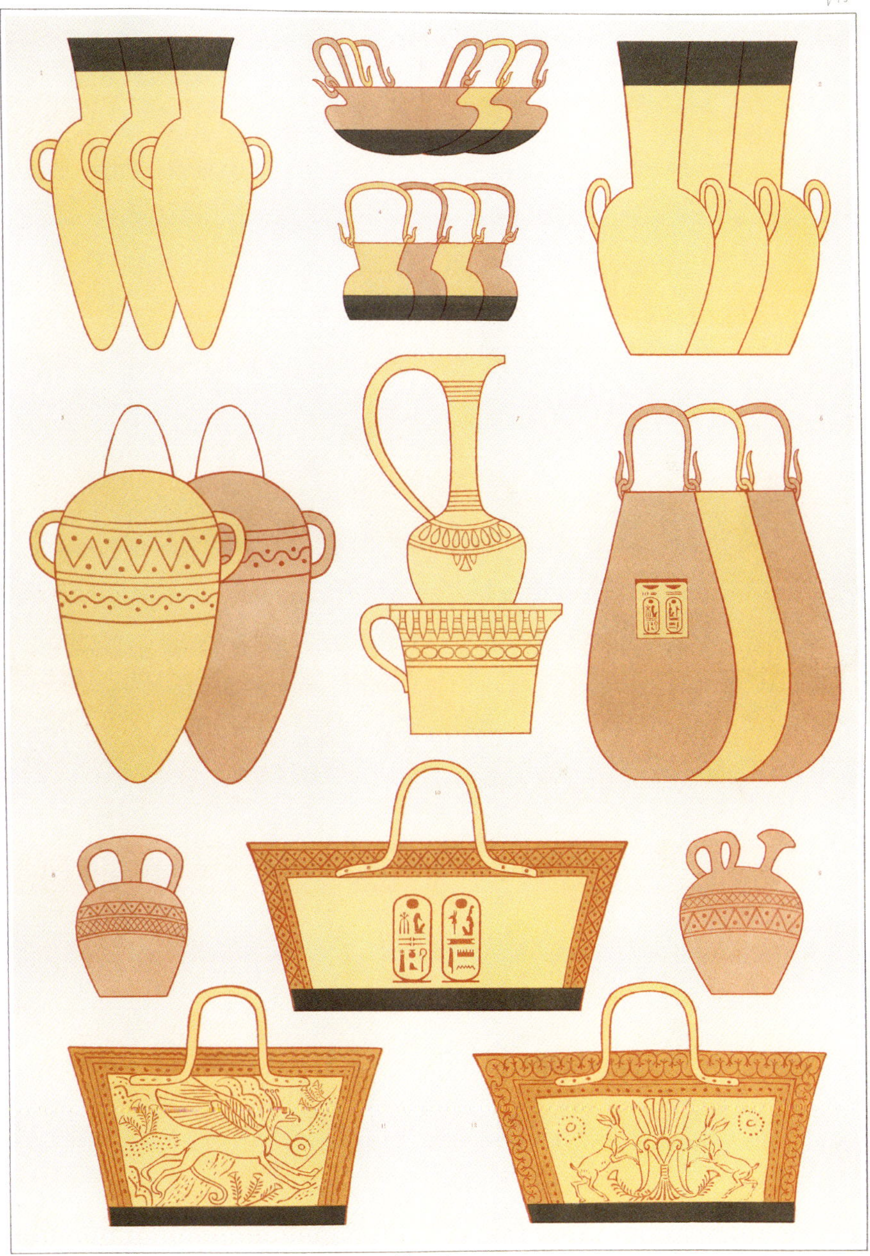

Lith par Bodin. Imp par Hangard-Maugé — E. Prisse d'Avennes. — Publié par Arthus Bertrand, Éditeur.

VASES DU TOMBEAU DE RAMSÈS III.

(THÈBES. — XXe DYNASTIE.)

ENAMELLED GOLD OR CLOISONNÉ VASES (20th Dynasty)

Thebes

The beautiful vases in enamelled gold, which take many different forms, bear no inscription to indicate their provenance, but they are all exactly the same as those shown in portrayals of Asiatic tribes. The vases contained in this plate are taken from the tomb of Imiseba. No. 1, decorated with the inscription of Ramesses IX, is heavy and squat in shape and is hardly redeemed by the lotus blossoms which crown it and encircle the upper part, whose details have unfortunately been effaced. No. 2 shows two vases that are more or less the same, linked by the same handle and with their bases in a large basin. This entire composition is dominated by the monstrous head of Bes, the god of the dance and of wine. Nos. 3, 4, 5 and 6 are like the fusiform vases that occur so frequently on monuments from the 18th Dynasty onwards.

VASEN AUS EMAILLIERTEM GOLD ODER CLOISONNÉ (20. Dynastie)

Theben

Die schönen Vasen aus emailliertem Gold, die so abwechslungsreiche Formen aufweisen und bei denen keine Inschrift die Herkunft angibt, gleichen alle denen, die unter den Stämmen der Asiaten dargestellt sind. Die Vasen, die diese Tafel einschließt, sind alle dem Grab Imisebas entnommen. Die mit der Inschrift Ramses' IX. verzierte Nr. 1 ist von schwerfälliger und gedrungener Gestalt, was durch die Lotusblüten kaum ausgeglichen wird, die daraus herausragen und den oberen, im Detail leider verwitterten Teil umgeben. Die Nr. 2 zeigt zwei einander sehr ähnliche Vasen, die durch gemeinsame Henkel miteinander verbunden sind und mit den Füßen in einem breiten Becken stehen. Der monströse Kopf des Bes, der Gottheit des Tanzes und des Weines, beherrscht die gesamte Komposition. Die Nr. 3, 4, 5 und 6 ähneln den spindelförmigen Vasen, die von der 18. Dynastie an auf den Denkmälern so häufig zu finden sind.

VASES EN OR ÉMAILLÉ OU CLOISONNÉ (XXe dynastie)

Thèbes

Les beaux vases d'or émaillé, si variés de formes, dont aucune inscription n'indique la provenance, sont tout pareils à ceux représentés parmi les tribus des Asiatiques. Les vases que renferme cette planche sont tirés du tombeau d'Aïchesi [Imiseba]. Le n° 1, orné de la légende de Ramsès IX, est d'une forme lourde et trapue que rachètent à peine les lotus qui les surmontent et qui entourent la partie supérieure dont les détails sont malheureusement effacés. Le n° 2 présente deux vases à peu près semblables, reliés par des anses communes et baignant leurs pieds dans un large bassin. La tête monstrueuse de Bès, le dieu de la danse et du vin, domine l'ensemble de cette composition. Les n°s 3, 4, 5 et 6 ressemblent aux vases fusiformes si fréquents sur les monuments à partir de la XVIIIe dynastie.

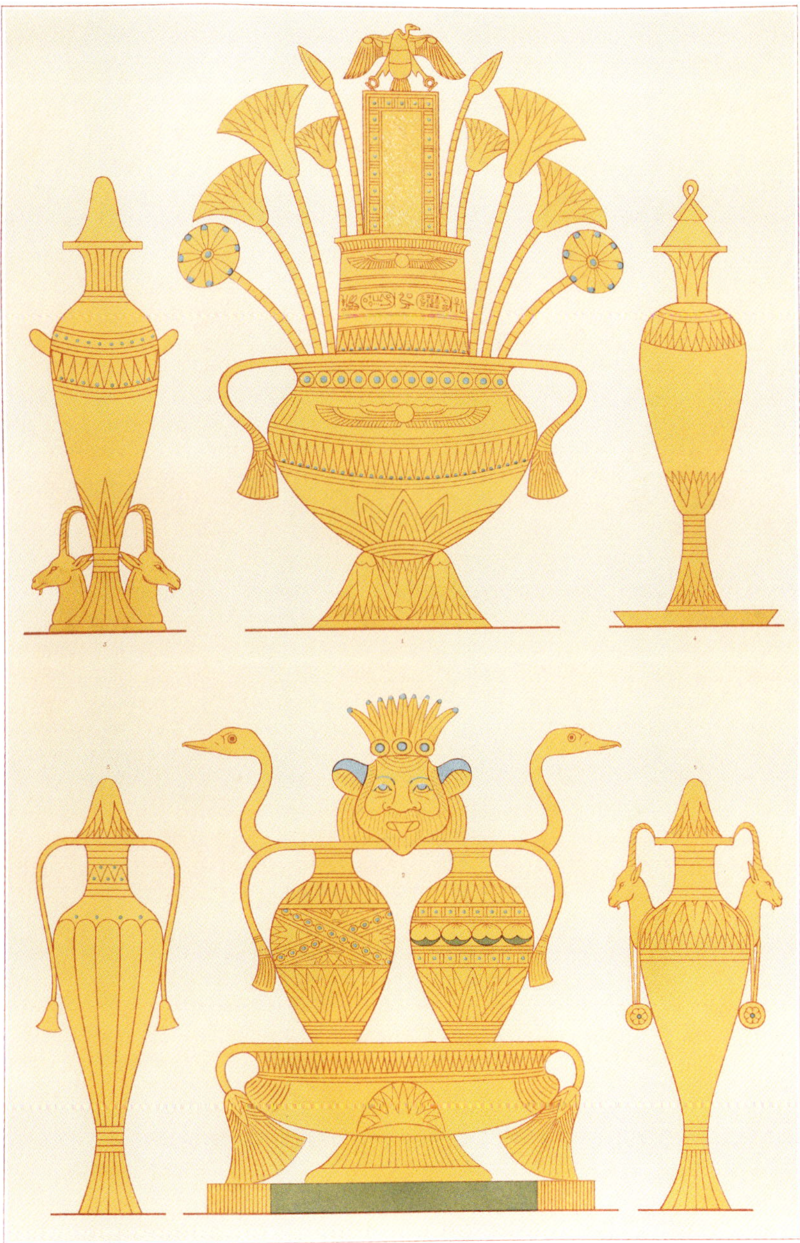

Lith par Delang. Imp par Hangard Maugé. E. Prisse d'Avennes. Publié par Arthus Bertrand Éditeur

VASES EN OR ÉMAILLÉ OU CLOISONNÉ.

(THÈBES XXe DYNASTIE.)

RHYTONS AND OTHER VASES (20th Dynasty)

Thebes

It appears to me that in many countries animal horn, which furnished the material, was the origin of drinking vases. The two rhytons that are shown on this plate at nos. 2 and 3 bear out my assertion. One is adorned with the bearded head of the god Bes, a deity borrowed from Asia; the other shows a head whose hair is dressed like that of certain Asiatic captives who are portrayed at Medinet Habu. The vase shown between the two rhytons has an unusual shape. No. 4 [is] decorated with two plumed horses' heads. The two vases (nos. 5 and 6) are pails whose function was to carry holy or purified water; they are often represented in temples from the 18th Dynasty onwards. All of these vases, which were probably made of chased gold with lapis lazuli inlay, are taken from the tomb of Imiseba.

RHYTA UND ANDERE VASEN (20. Dynastie)

Theben

Das Tierhorn scheint mir in mehreren Ländern sowohl Material als auch Ursprung der Trinkgefäße gewesen zu sein. Die beiden auf dieser Tafel unter den Nr. 2 und 3 dargestellten Rhyta bestätigen meine Behauptung. Das eine ist mit dem bärtigen Kopf des Gottes Bes, einer aus Asien entlehnten Gottheit, verziert; das andere zeigt einen Kopf, dessen Kopfputz dem bestimmter asiatischer Gefangener ähnelt, die in Medinet Habu zu sehen sind. Die zwischen den beiden Rhyta dargestellte Vase hat eine ungebräuchliche Form. Die Nr. 4 [ist] mit zwei Pferdeköpfen verziert, die mit Federbüschen geschmückt sind. Die beiden Vasen mit der Nr. 5 und 6 sind für Weihwasser bestimmte Gefäße, die von der 18. Dynastie an häufig in Tempeln dargestellt sind. Alle diese wahrscheinlich aus ziseliertem Gold gefertigten und mit Lapislazuli emaillierten Vasen sind dem Grab Imisebas entnommen.

RITHONS ET AUTRES VASES (XXe dynastie)

Thèbes

La corne des animaux me paraît avoir été, dans plusieurs pays, la matière et l'origine des vases à boire. Les deux rithons, représentés dans cette planche sous les n°s 2 et 3, confirment mon assertion. L'un est orné de la tête barbue du dieu Bès, divinité empruntée à l'Asie ; l'autre offre une tête coiffée comme celles de certains captifs asiatiques, qu'on voit à Medineh-Tabou [Médinet Habou]. Le vase représenté entre les deux rithons a une forme inusitée. Le n° 4 [est] orné de deux têtes de chevaux empanachées. Les deux vases n°s 5 et 6 sont des seaux destinés à l'eau lustrale et fréquemment représentés dans les temples à partir de la XVIIIe dynastie. Tous ces vases, faits probablement d'or ciselé et cloisonné de lapis-lazuli, sont tirés du tombeau d'Aïchesi [Imiseba].

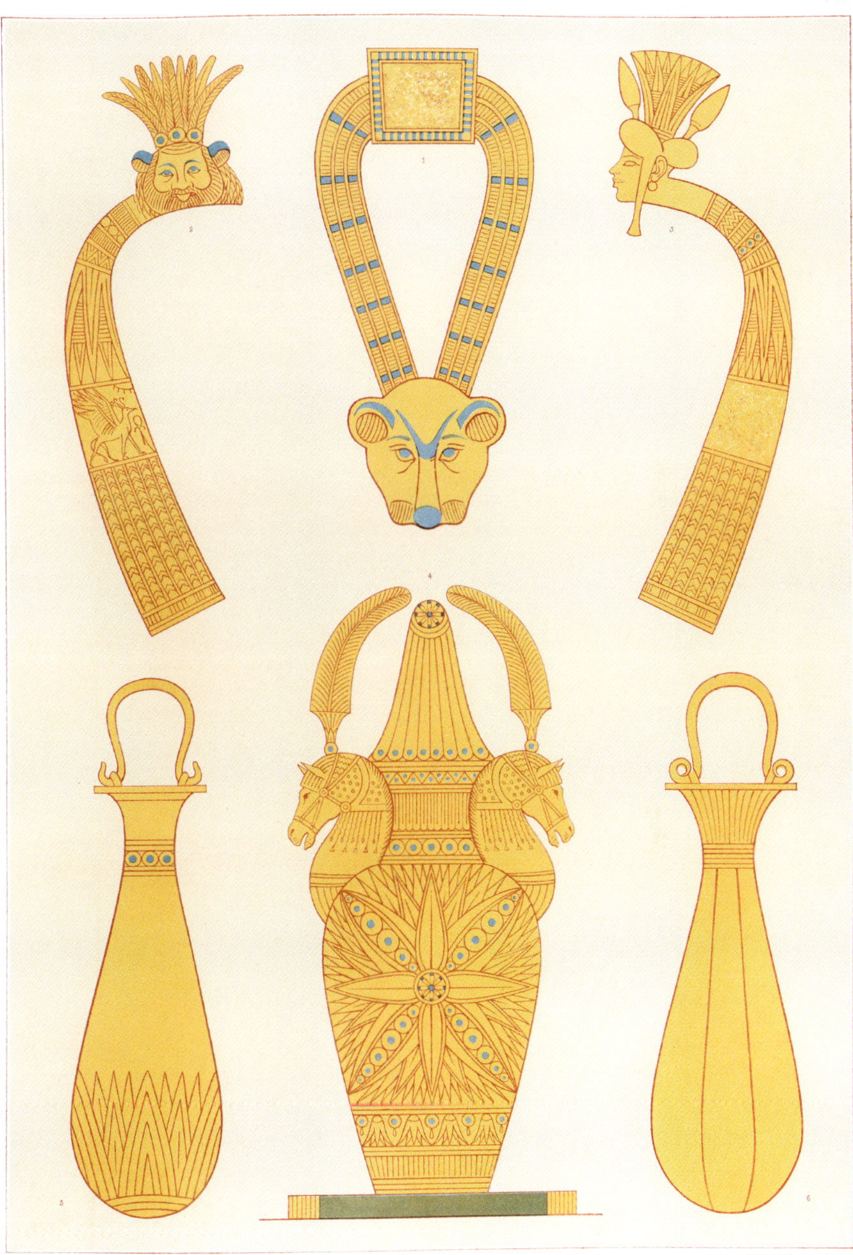

Lith. par Dufeug. Imp. par Hangard-Maugé.

E. Prisse d'Avennes.

Publié par Arthus Bertrand, Éditeur.

RITHONS ET AUTRES VASES.

(THÈBES — XXe DYNASTIE.)

THRONES FROM THE FURNITURE OF RAMESSES III (20th Dynasty)

Necropolis of Thebes

The chairs, thrones and footstools shown on these plates [see pp. 535 and 541] are taken from a small chamber in the tomb of Ramesses III. The throne, which was supposed to have been an article of furniture from the West, is in fact of extremely ancient origin in the East and in Egypt in particular, where the custom of sitting crouching or cross-legged only applied to subordinates. The honour of the throne belonged to princes of the blood: it was thus a mark of distinction for those of the highest rank. No. 1 shows a seat supported by the symbol of power and decorated with flower-bearing stalks. No. 2 is adorned with lions' heads and the king's cartouches are flanked by a hawk holding in its talons the ring symbolising a period of many centuries. No. 3 presents the form of a folding chair covered in animal skin and decorated with two kneeling captives, an African and an Asiatic. No. 4 is decorated with lions as arm-rests and with figures of captives chained by the neck around the symbol of power.

SESSEL AUS DEM INVENTAR VON RAMSES III. (20. Dynastie)

Nekropole von Theben

Die auf diesen Tafeln [siehe S. 535 und 541] dargestellten Stühle, Sessel und Schemel sind einem kleinen Raum im Grab Ramses' III. entnommen. Der Sessel, ein vorgeblich westliches Möbelstück, ist im Orient und vor allem in Ägypten schon sehr alt – wo die Sitte, hockend und mit gekreuzten Beinen zu sitzen, nur für Untergebene gebräuchlich war. Die Ehre des Sessels war den Prinzen von Geblüt vorbehalten: Er war somit ein Erkennungszeichen hoher Persönlichkeiten. Die Nr. 1 zeigt einen vom Sinnbild der Macht getragenen und mit Stängeln voller Blumen versehenen Sitz. Die Nr. 2 ist mit Löwenköpfen verziert, auch mit Königskartuschen, die von einem Sperber flankiert sind, der in seinen Fängen einen Ring – Sinnbild eines Jahrhunderte währenden Zeitalters – hält. Die Nr. 3 zeigt die Form eines Klappstuhls, der mit einer Tierhaut bedeckt und mit zwei knienden Gefangenen – einem Afrikaner und einem Asiaten – verziert ist. Die Nr. 4 weist Löwen als Armlehnen auf und ist mit Figuren gefesselter Gefangener verziert, die das Sinnbild der Macht umgeben.

FAUTEUILS DU MOBILIER DE RAMSÈS III (XXe dynastie)

Nécropole de Thèbes

Les chaises, les fauteuils et les tabourets représentés sur ces planches [voir pp. 535 et 541] sont tirés d'une petite salle du tombeau de Ramsès III. Le fauteuil que l'on a prétendu être le meuble de l'Occident, est très ancien en Orient et surtout en Égypte, où la coutume de s'asseoir accroupi et les jambes croisées n'était en usage que pour les subalternes. L'honneur du fauteuil appartenait aux princes du sang : il était donc une marque de distinction pour les grands personnages. Le nº 1 présente un siège soutenu par le symbole de la puissance et garni de tiges fleuronnées. Le nº 2 est orné de têtes de lion, des cartouches du roi flanqués d'un épervier tenant, dans ses serres, l'anneau symbole d'une longue période de siècles. Le nº 3 offre la forme d'un pliant couvert d'une peau d'animal et orné de deux captifs agenouillés, un nègre et un Asiatique. Le nº 4 est orné de lions pour accottoirs et de figures de captifs garrottés autour du symbole de la puissance.

V 16

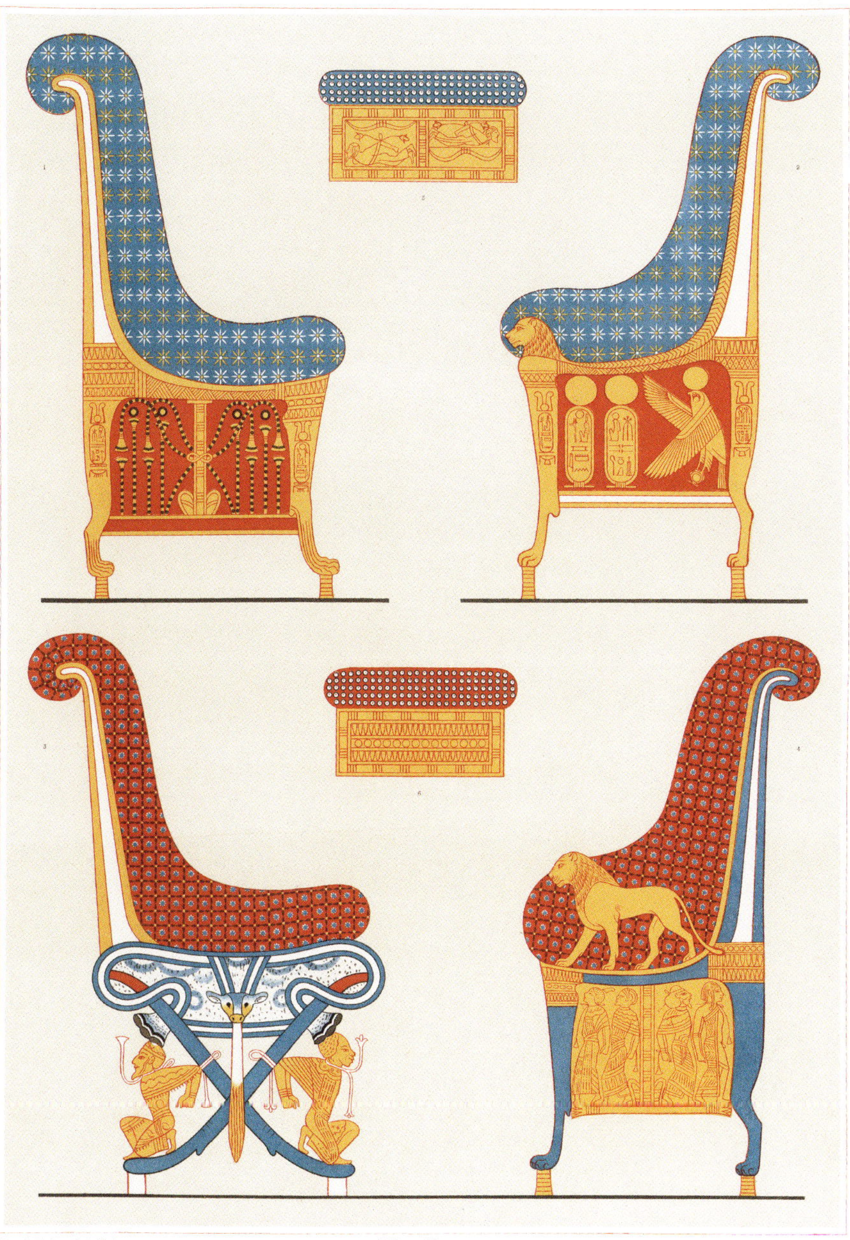

Lith par Lemé. Imp par Hangard-Maugé

E. Prisse d'Avennes.

Publié par Arthus-Bertrand, Editeur.

FAUTEUILS DU MOBILIER DE RAMSÈS III.

(NÉCROPOLE DE THÈBES _ XXe DYNASTIE.)

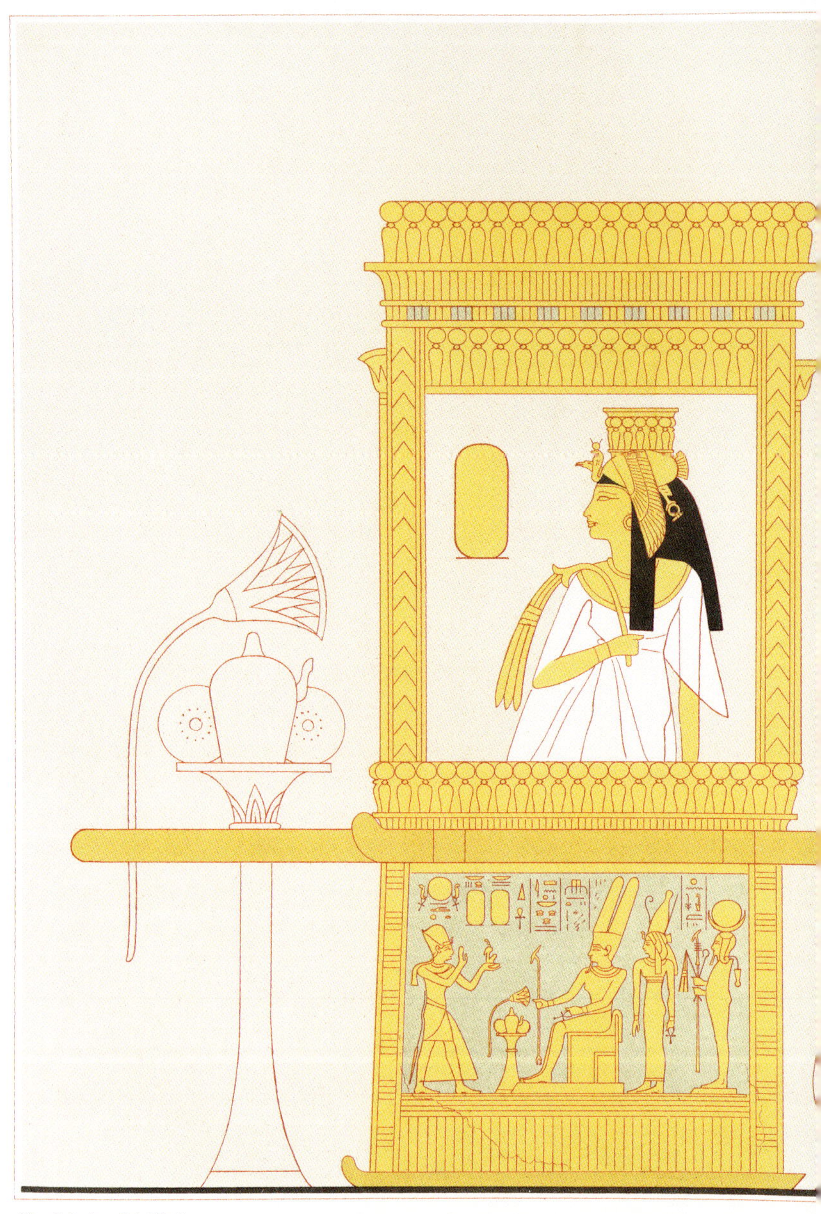

Lith. par Bodin — Imp. par Hangard-Maugé.

P.

(NÉCROPOLE

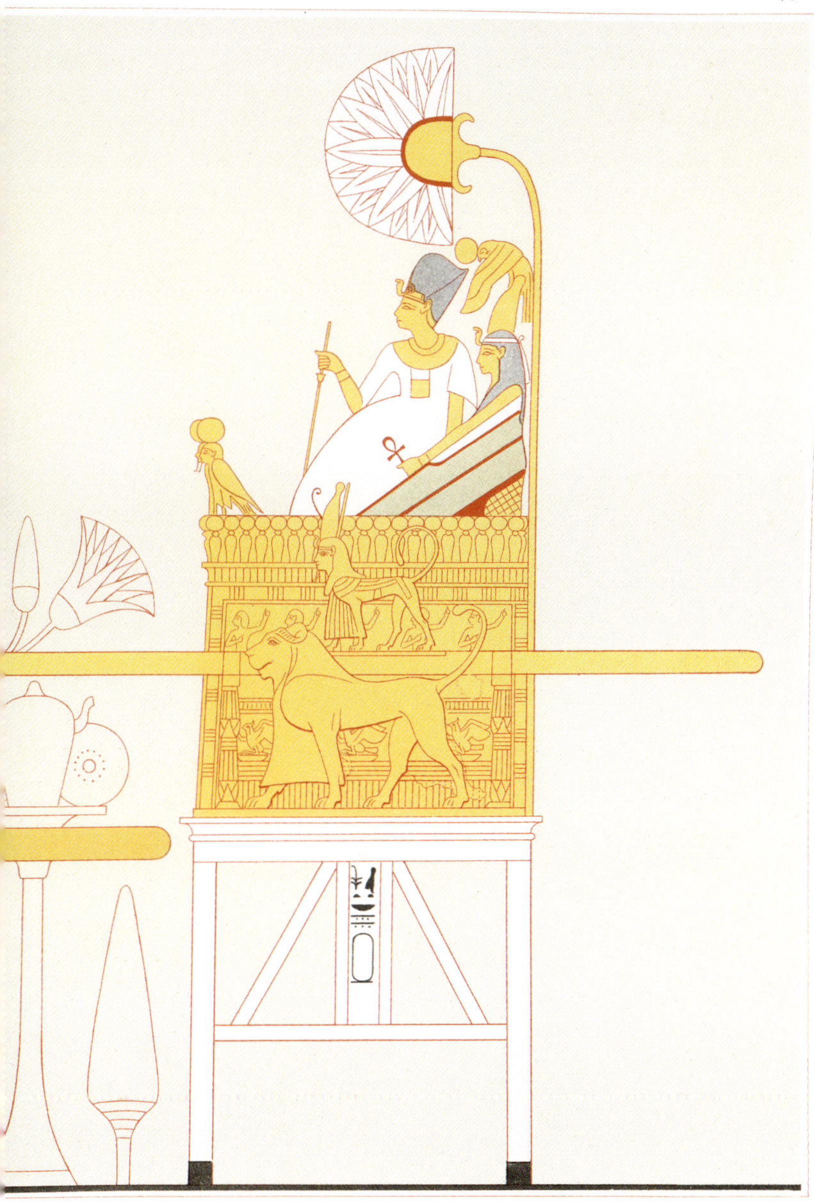

Publié par Arthus-Bertrand Éditeur

NS .

(DYNASTIE .)

(Pages/Seite 536/537)

PALANQUINS (20th Dynasty)

Necropolis of Thebes

These two palanquins are taken from paintings that decorate the tomb of Imiseba, high priest in charge of scriptures in the temple of Amun in the reign of Ramesses IX. The names of those portrayed here have been effaced; they do not appear to me to have been those of the pharaoh who was then reigning and of his wife, but rather those of Amenophis I and of Ahmose Nefertari, from whom Ramesses IX claimed descent. The litter-palanquin of the queen contains a most lifelike figure shown from the waist upwards. As for the two hawks with human heads seen in the upper angle of the second palanquin, they are very badly damaged in the original.

SÄNFTEN (20. Dynastie)

Nekropole von Theben

Diese beiden Sänften sind den Malereien entnommen, die das Grab von Imiseba, dem unter der Herrschaft von Ramses IX. für die Schriften im Amun-Tempel verantwortlichen Hohepriester, zieren. Die Namen der hier dargestellten Persönlichkeiten sind verwittert; mir scheint, dass es nicht die des in dieser Zeit herrschenden Pharaos und seiner Gemahlin waren, sondern eher die von Amenophis I. und Ahmose Nefertari, von denen Ramses IX. abzustammen vorgab. Die Tragsessel-Sänfte der Königin enthielt in der Tat eine stehende Gestalt, deren Körper zur Hälfte zu sehen war. Was die beiden in der oberen Ecke des zweiten Tragsessels erkennbaren Sperber mit Menschenkopf betrifft, so sind sie im Original stark beschädigt.

PALANQUINS (XXe dynastie)

Nécropole de Thèbes

Ces deux palanquins sont tirés des peintures qui décorent le tombeau d'Aïchesi [Imiseba], grand prêtre chargé des écritures du temple d'Amon, sous le règne de Ramsès IX. Les noms des personnages représentés ici sont effacés ; ils ne me paraissent pas avoir été ceux du pharaon régnant alors et de son épouse, mais plutôt ceux d'Aménophis Ier et d'Ahmès-Nofreari [Ahmès-Néfertari], dont Ramsès IX prétendait descendre. Le palanquin-litière de la reine contenait bien réellement une figure debout, vue à mi-corps. Quant aux deux éperviers à tête humaine qu'on voit à l'angle supérieur du second palanquin, ils sont fort détériorés sur l'original.

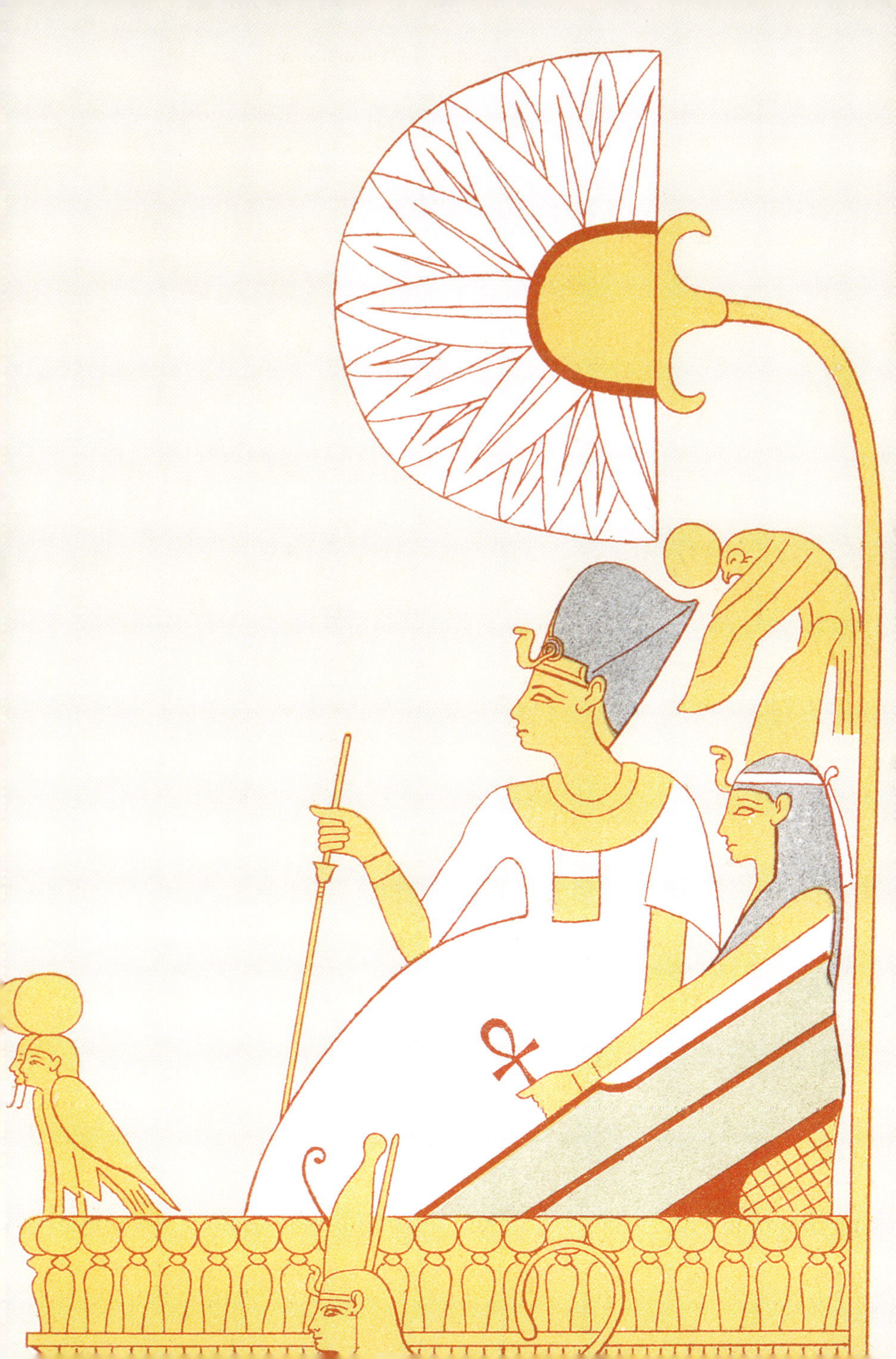

SEATS (18th and 20th Dynasties)

Necropolis of Thebes

Seats complied with the requirements of their function, but also followed the caprices of fashion. Thus the massive, square seats portrayed in the monuments of the early dynasties were gradually succeeded by more elegant and comfortable articles of furniture. I have selected the most elegant models [taken from the tomb of Ramesses III], those whose shape gives a very exact idea of the taste and luxury of this period, even when Egyptian artistry was no longer at its most brilliant. These seats were extremely high and necessitated footstools for the feet, which makes it likely that they served as thrones. The top and sides of these footstools or steps often appear with a decoration of a group of captives who have been thrown down and chained at the throat.

SESSEL (18. und 20. Dynastie)

Nekropole von Theben

Die Sitzmöbel richteten sich nach den wechselnden Anforderungen der Bedürfnisse und den Launen der Mode. Den in den Denkmälern der frühen Dynastien dargestellten eckigen und wuchtigen Sesseln folgten nach und nach elegantere und behaglichere Möbel. Ich habe die elegantesten [dem Grab Ramses' III. entnommenen] Modelle ausgewählt, deren Form einen präzisen Eindruck vom Geschmack und vom Luxus in dieser Zeit geben kann, als die Künste schon nicht mehr in vollem Glanz erstrahlten. Diese Sessel sind sehr hoch, sodass die Füße auf Schemel gestellt werden mussten; dies lässt vermuten, dass sie als Thron dienten. Oben und an den Seiten sind diese Schemel oder Trittleitern häufig mit einer Gruppe gefesselter, am Boden liegender Gefangener verziert.

SIÈGES (XVIIIe et XXe dynasties)

Nécropole de Thèbes

Les sièges ont suivi les exigences du besoin et les caprices de la mode. Aux sièges carrés et massifs représentés dans les monuments des premières dynasties ont succédé peu à peu des meubles plus élégants et plus confortables. J'ai choisi les modèles les plus élégants [tirés du tombeau de Ramsès III], ceux dont la forme peut donner une idée exacte du goût et du luxe de cette époque où l'art ne brillait déjà plus de tout son éclat. Ces fauteuils sont très élevés et des tabourets étaient nécessaires pour poser les pieds ; ce qui ferait supposer qu'ils servaient de trônes. Ces tabourets ou marchepieds se voient souvent ornés, sur la partie supérieure et sur les côtés, d'un groupe de captifs renversés et garrottés.

V 17

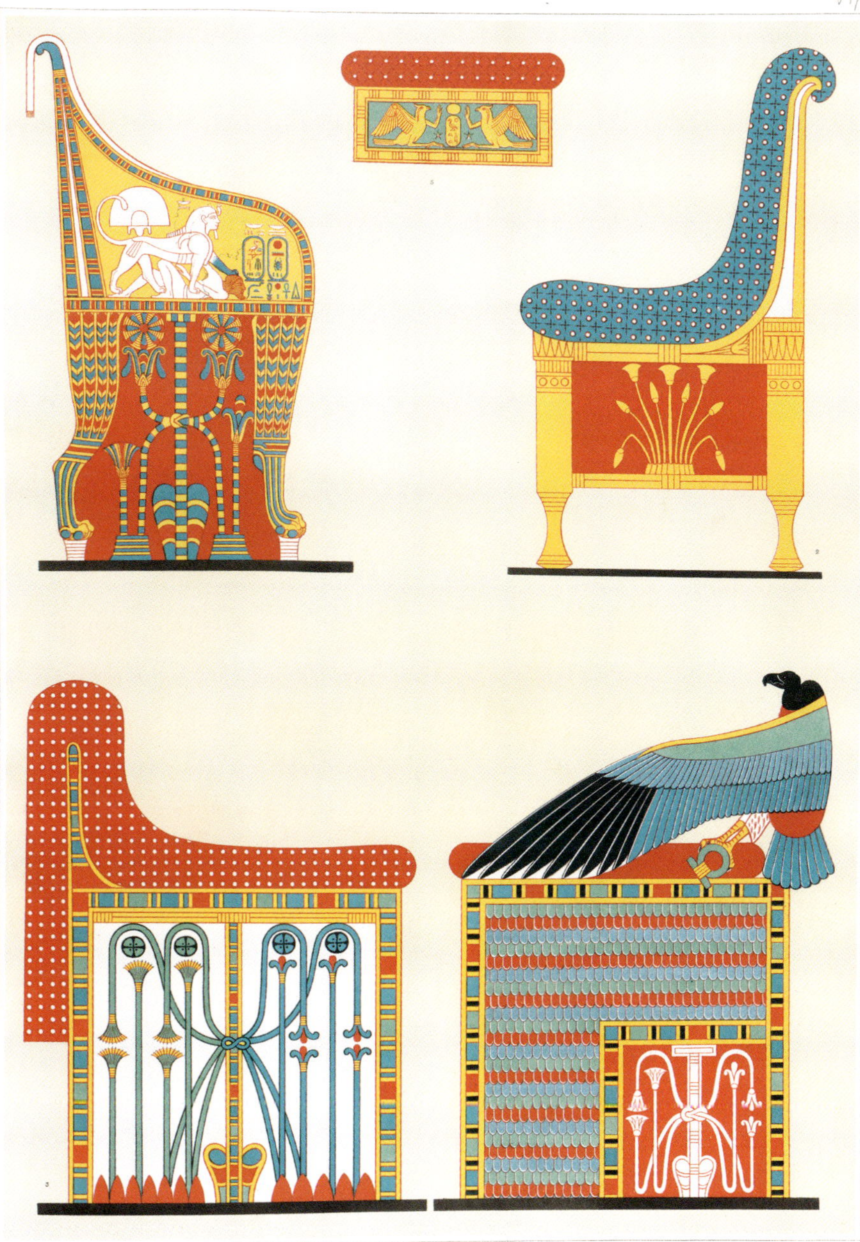

Lith par Bauer. Imp. Hangard-Maugé

E. Prisse d'Avennes.

Publié par Arthus-Bertrand, Editeur.

SIÉGES.

(NÉCROPOLE DE THÈBES. — XVIIIe & XXe DYN.)

TEXTILES AND EMBROIDERIES

Not all of these textiles are Egyptian: the only ones that are genuinely Egyptian are the two pieces of blue cloth which must have been sewn on to the tunics of foreign soldiers in the pharaoh's service. They certainly show all the features of Egyptian textiles, which are always smooth or ribbed and whose only decoration is a little embroidery. [...] It seems to me more likely that the pieces of cloth with a squared design, cut into a strip to decorate the two tunics, come from a hanging fabric similar to that covering the elegant thrones of Ramesses III. As for the other pieces of cloth, they have an unmistakable Asiatic stamp.

GEWEBE UND STICKEREIEN

Es stammen nicht alle Stoffe aus Ägypten: Echt ägyptisch sind lediglich die beiden blauen Stoffstücke, die von Tuniken fremder, im Dienst des Pharaos stehender Soldaten stammen müssen und auf diese aufgenäht waren. Sie zeigen deutlich alle Eigenarten der ägyptischen Stoffe, die stets glatt oder gerippt und – von einer leichten Stickerei abgesehen – unverziert sind. [...] Die karierten, zum Schmuck der beiden Tuniken in Streifen geschnittenen Stoffstücke scheinen mir eher von einem Gewebe zu stammen, das eine ähnliche Färbung aufweist wie die eleganten Sessel Ramses' III.. Was die anderen Stücke anbetrifft, so haben sie ein unbestreitbar asiatisches Gepräge.

TISSUS ET BRODERIES

Toutes ces étoffes ne sont pas égyptiennes : il n'y a réellement d'égyptien que les deux morceaux d'étoffe bleue qui ont dû provenir de tuniques ayant appartenu à des soldats étrangers au service des pharaons, et sur lesquelles ils étaient cousus. Ils offrent bien tous les caractères des étoffes égyptiennes, qui sont toujours lisses ou à côtes et sans autre ornement qu'une légère broderie. [...] Les morceaux d'étoffe quadrillés, coupés en bande pour orner les deux tuniques, me paraissant plutôt provenir d'une étoffe de tenture semblable à celle qui recouvre les élégants fauteuils de Ramsès III, j'ai fait doubler ce fragment pour lui restituer sa forme première. Quant aux autres morceaux, ils portent un cachet asiatique incontestable.

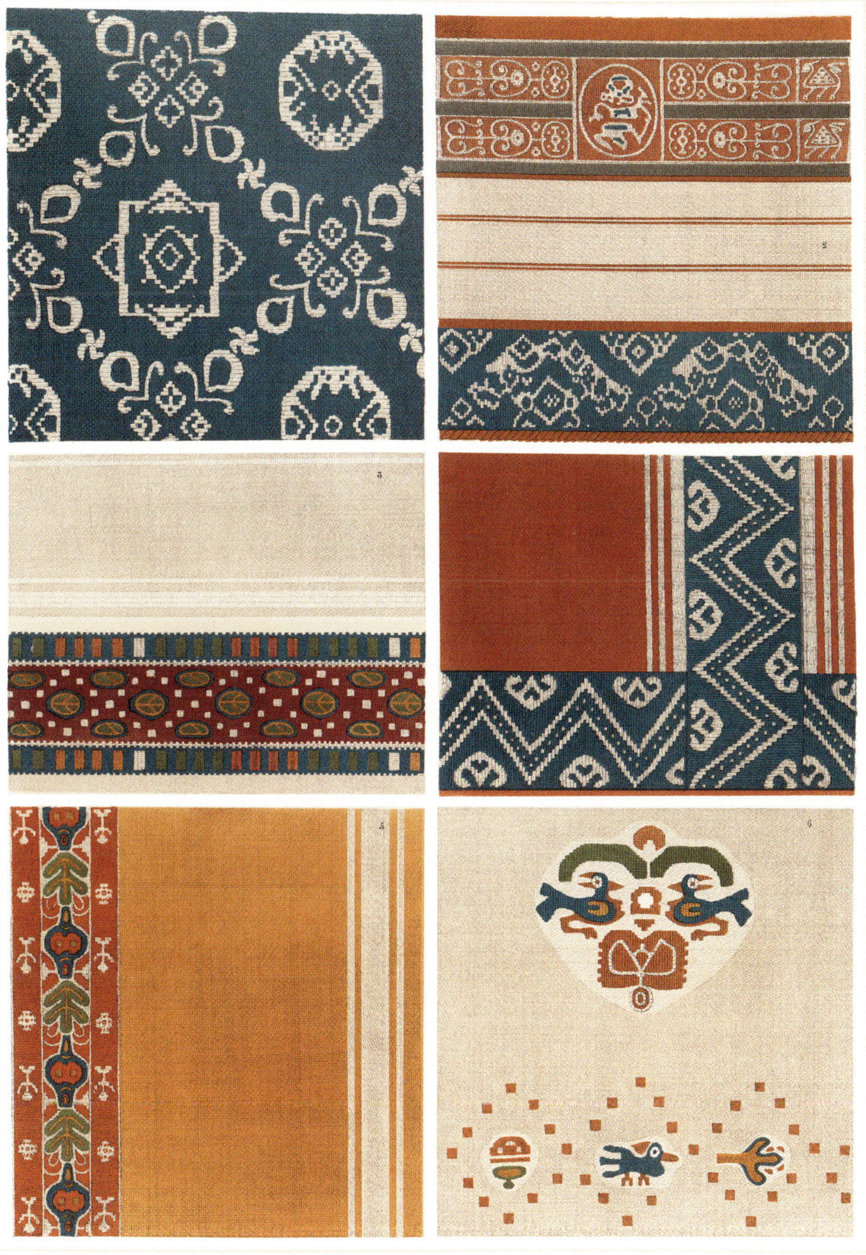

Lith. par Kellerhoven. Imp. par Haugard Maugé — E. Prisse d'Avennes — Publié par Arthus Bertrand, Éditeur

TISSUS ET BRODERIES.

(GRANDEUR D'EXÉCUTION.)

SELECTION OF JEWELLERY (from various periods)

Egypt and Ethiopia

It has not been possible for me to show here the magnificent jewels from the museum of Cairo, as I was not given permission to see them; however, I decided to reproduce in this plate the most beautiful examples that I could portray. *Frontals or Pectorals* (nos. 1, 2, 3, 4, 5, 6, 16): no. 6 is a hawk with a ram's head, symbol of Amun, in gold with enamel cloisonné. *Earrings – gold necklaces* (nos. 7, 12, 13, 22, 23, 24, 25, 26, 27, 28): no. 13 is an uncut emerald, regular in shape, enclosed in a golden mesh. *Chain*: No. 19 is a chain composed of three flies, set in solid gold. *Various rings* (nos. 8, 9, 10, 11, 18, 20, 21, 29, 30): no. 8 shows an exceptionally solid ring which was used only as a seal. no. 29 shows a ring decorated with insets of lapis lazuli and coral. *Bracelets* (nos. 14, 15, 17, 31, 32, 33): no. 14 is half of a gold bracelet with cloisonné of precious stone; it represents two griffons facing each other, separated by a flower stem.

AUSWAHL VON SCHMUCKSTÜCKEN (aus unterschiedlichen Epochen)

Ägypten und Äthiopien

Da es mir unmöglich ist, die prachtvollen Schmuckgegenstände des Museums von Kairo zu zeigen, das mir zu sehen nicht freistand, habe ich mich bemüht, auf dieser Tafel die schönsten Stücke wiederzugeben, die ich zeichnen konnte. *Stirnschmuck oder Brustschmuck* (Nr. 1, 2, 3, 4, 5, 6, 16): Die Nr. 6 ist ein Sperber mit Widderkopf, dem Sinnbild des Amun, aus in Cloisonné verziertem Gold. *Ohrgehänge – goldene Halsketten* (Nr. 7, 12, 13, 22, 23, 24, 25, 26, 27, 28): Die Nr. 13 ist ein roher, in ein Goldnetz eingeschlossener Smaragd. *Kette:* Die Nr. 19 ist eine aus drei Fliegen aus massivem Gold zusammengesetzte Kette. *Verschiedene Ringe* (Nr. 8, 9, 10, 11, 18, 20, 21, 29, 30): Die Nr. 8 stellt einen sehr wuchtigen Ring dar, der ausschließlich als Siegel diente. Die Nr. 29 stellt einen mit Fassungen aus Lapislazuli und Koralle verzierten Ring dar. *Armbänder* (Nr. 14, 15, 17, 31, 32, 33): Die Nr. 14 ist die Hälfte eines goldenen, mit Halbedelsteinen in Cloisonné verzierten Armbandes, das zwei einander gegenüberstehende, durch einen Blumenstiel getrennte Greife zeigt.

CHOIX DE BIJOUX (de diverses époques)

Égypte et Éthiopie

Dans l'impossibilité de représenter les magnifiques bijoux du musée du Kaire, qu'il ne m'a pas été loisible de voir, je me suis attaché, dans cette planche, à reproduire les plus beaux spécimens que j'ai pu dessiner. *Frontels ou Pectoraux* (n°s 1, 2, 3, 4, 5, 6, 16) : le n° 6 est un épervier à tête de bélier, symbole d'Amon, en or cloisonné d'émaux. *Pendants d'oreilles – Colliers en or* (n°s 7, 12, 13, 22, 23, 24, 25, 26, 27, 28) : le n° 13 est une émeraude brute, uniforme, renfermée dans une résille d'or. *Chaîne* : le n° 19 est une chaîne composée de trois mouches, en or massif. *Bagues diverses* (n°s 8, 9, 10, 11, 18, 20, 21, 29, 30) : le n° 8 représente une bague très massive et qui servait uniquement de cachet. Le n° 29 représente une bague ornée de chatons de pierre lazuli et de corail. *Bracelets* (n°s 14, 15, 17, 31, 32, 33) : le n° 14 est la moitié d'un bracelet en or cloisonné de pierres fines représentant deux griffons affrontés et séparés par une tige de fleurs.

V20

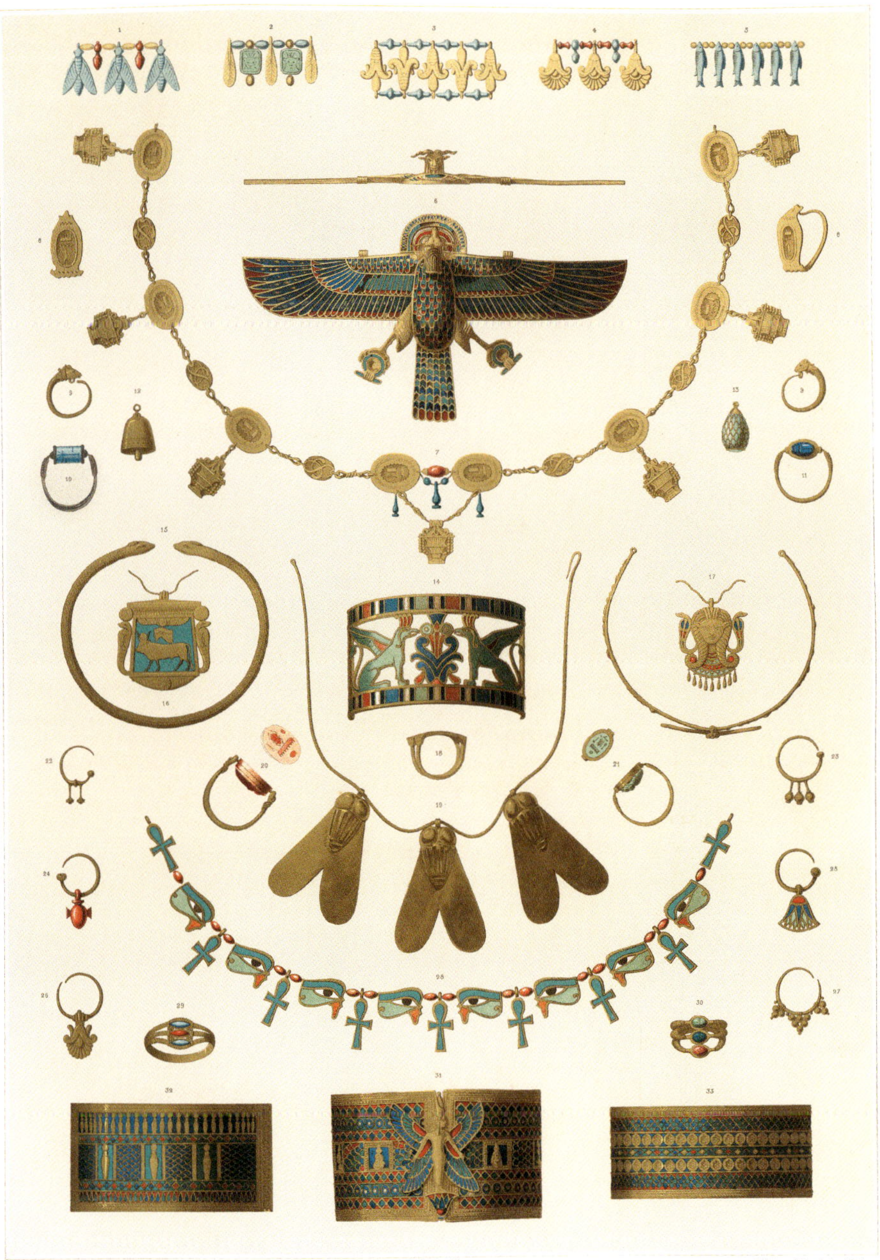

Lith par Laine. Imp par Hangard Maugé. E. Prisse d'Avennes. Publié par Arthus-Bertrand, Editeur

CHOIX DE BIJOUX DE DIVERSES ÉPOQUES.

(ÉGYPTE & ETHIOPIE.)

COSMETIC BOXES AND UTENSILS [WITH HUMAN FORMS]

These small objects carved from inlaid acacia wood and meant to contain cosmetic pastes of various colours are crafted with both elegance and taste. They show how profoundly art had already penetrated the private life of the Egyptians. The most beautiful objects usually represent slaves or women bearing vases; the upper part of the vase pivots so as to create boxes convenient for holding perfumes or small toilet articles. Others show a small oval or rectangular basin. No. 5 presents the image of an Asiatic captive. No. 6 is particularly noteworthy for the gracefulness of the composition.

GEFÄSSE UND UTENSILIEN FÜR DIE TOILETTE [MENSCHLICHE FORMEN]

Diese kleinen, aus Akazienholz geschnitzten und mit Einlegearbeiten verzierten Objekte, die dazu bestimmt waren, verschiedenfarbige Pasten aufzunehmen, sind ebenso geschmackvoll wie anmutig. Sie zeugen davon, dass die Künste bereits weit in das Privatleben der Ägypter vorgedrungen waren. Die schönsten stellen im Allgemeinen Sklaven oder Frauen dar; bei den Vasen, die sie tragen, dreht sich das Oberteil auf einem Zapfen, sodass sie ein verschließbares Gefäß für Parfüm oder kleine Toiletteartikel bilden. Andere weisen ein kleines ovales oder rechteckiges Becken auf. Die Nr. 5 zeigt das Bild eines asiatischen Gefangenen. Die Nr. 6 ist durch den Liebreiz der Komposition besonders bemerkenswert.

BOÎTES ET USTENSILES DE TOILETTE [FORMES HUMAINES]

Ces petits meubles sculptés en bois d'acacia incrusté, et destinés à recevoir des pâtes de diverses couleurs, sont faits avec autant d'élégance que de goût. Ils témoignent que l'art avait déjà pénétré profondément dans la vie privée des Égyptiens. Les plus beaux représentent, généralement, des esclaves ou des femmes portant des vases dont la partie supérieure tournait sur un pivot, mais de façon à former des boîtes propres à renfermer des parfums ou des menus objets de toilette. D'autres offrent un petit bassin ovoïde ou rectangulaire. Le n° 5 offre l'image d'un captif asiatique. Le n° 6 est particulièrement remarquable par la grâce de la composition.

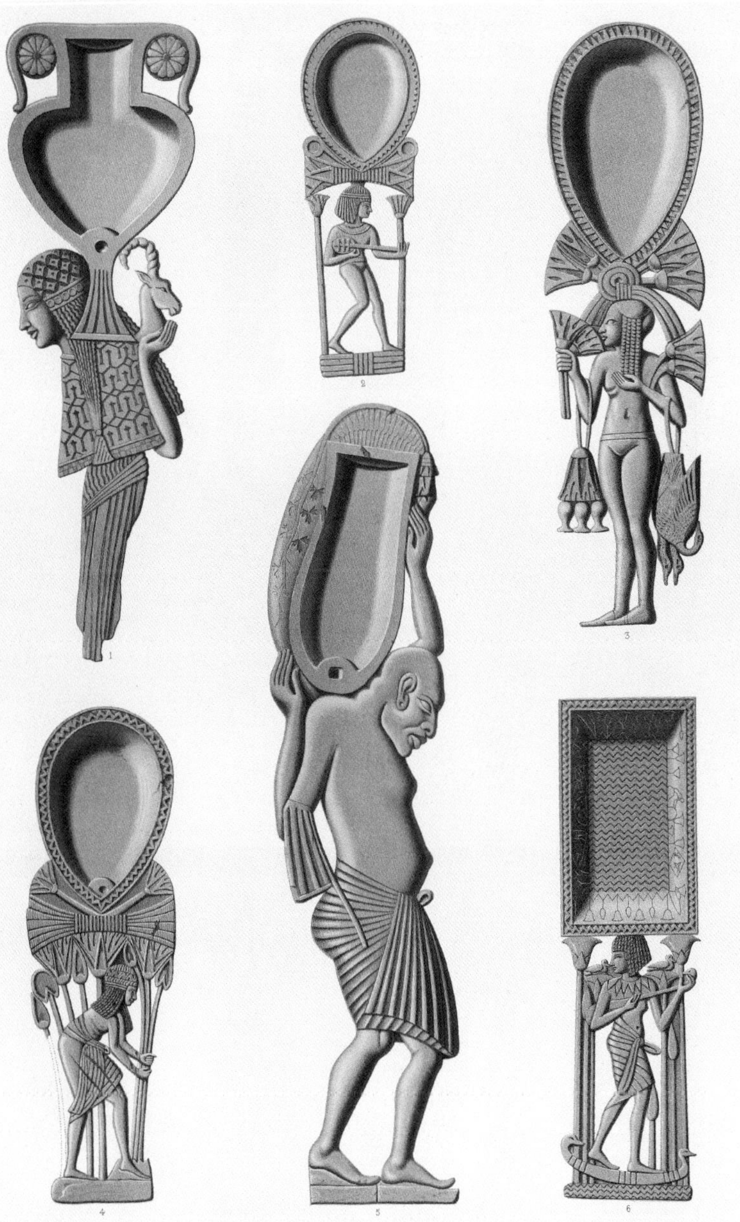

Lith. par Kellerhoven. Imp. par Hangard-Maugé. E. Prisse d'Avennes. Publié par Arthus Bertrand, Éditeur

BOITES ET USTENSILES DE TOILETTE.

(GRANDEUR D'EXÉCUTION)

COSMETIC BOXES AND UTENSILS [WITH VEGETAL FORMS]

Nos. 1 and 3 are in the form of a cartouche whose inside is hollowed out like a basin and decorated with fish and lotus. Nos. 2 and 5 represent bouquets; the main flowers open on a pivot to reveal tiny boxes probably intended to hold perfumes.

GEFÄSSE UND UTENSILIEN FÜR DIE TOILETTE [PFLANZLICHE FORMEN]

Die Nr. 1 und 3 weisen die Form einer Kartusche auf, deren wie ein Becken ausgehobener Boden mit Fischen und Lotuspflanzen verziert ist. Die Nr. 2 und 5 stellen Blumensträuße dar, deren größte Blumen sich durch Drehen am Zapfen öffnen lassen und kleine Gefäße aufweisen, die wahrscheinlich zur Aufnahme von Parfüm bestimmt waren.

BOÎTES ET USTENSILES DE TOILETTE [FORMES VÉGÉTALES]

Les n°s 1 et 3 offrent la forme d'un cartouche dont le fond, creusé comme un bassin, est orné de poissons et de lotus. Les n°s 2 et 5 représentent des bouquets dont les principales fleurs s'ouvrent en tournant sur pivot, et présentent des boîtelettes destinées probablement à contenir des parfums.

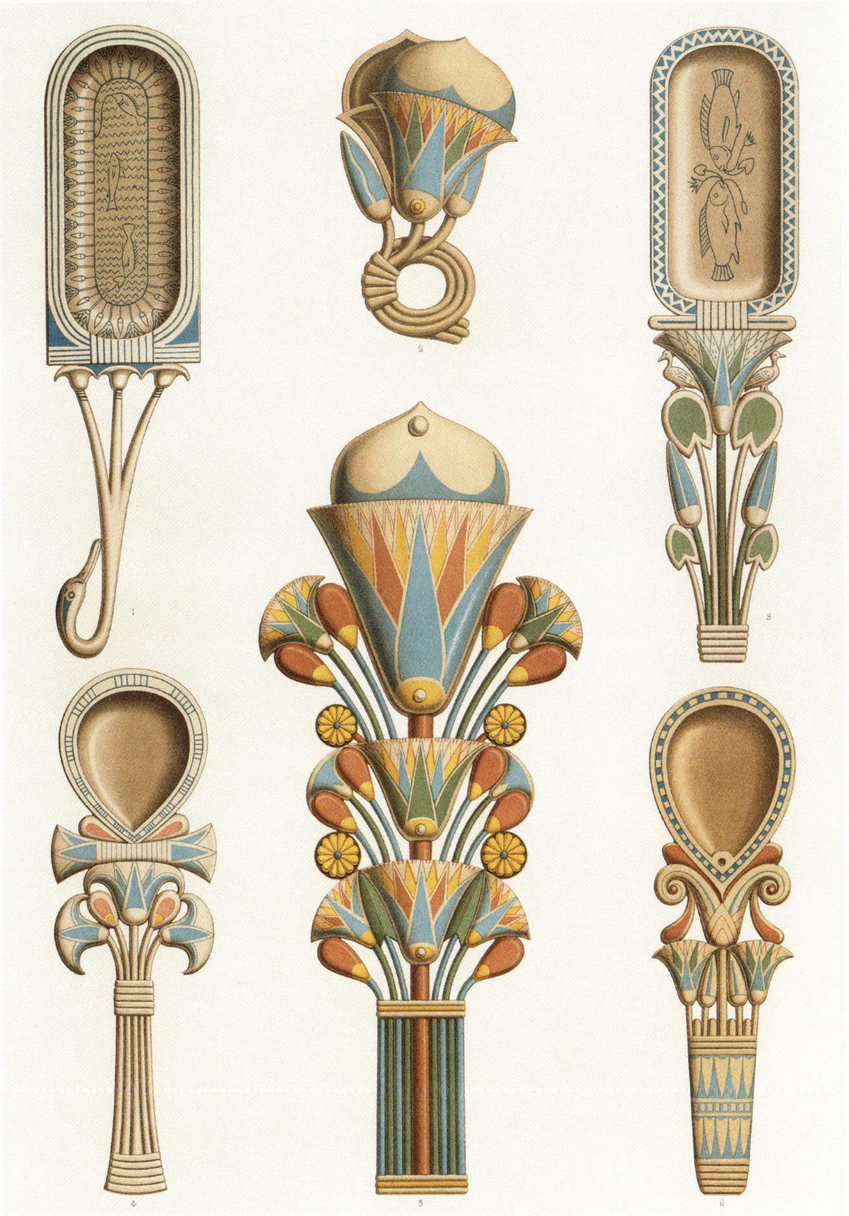

Lith. par Moulin. — Imp. par Hangard-Maugé. E. Prisse d'Avennes. Publié par Arthus Bertrand, Éditeur

BOITES ET USTENSILES DE TOILETTE.

(GRANDEUR D'EXECUTION.)

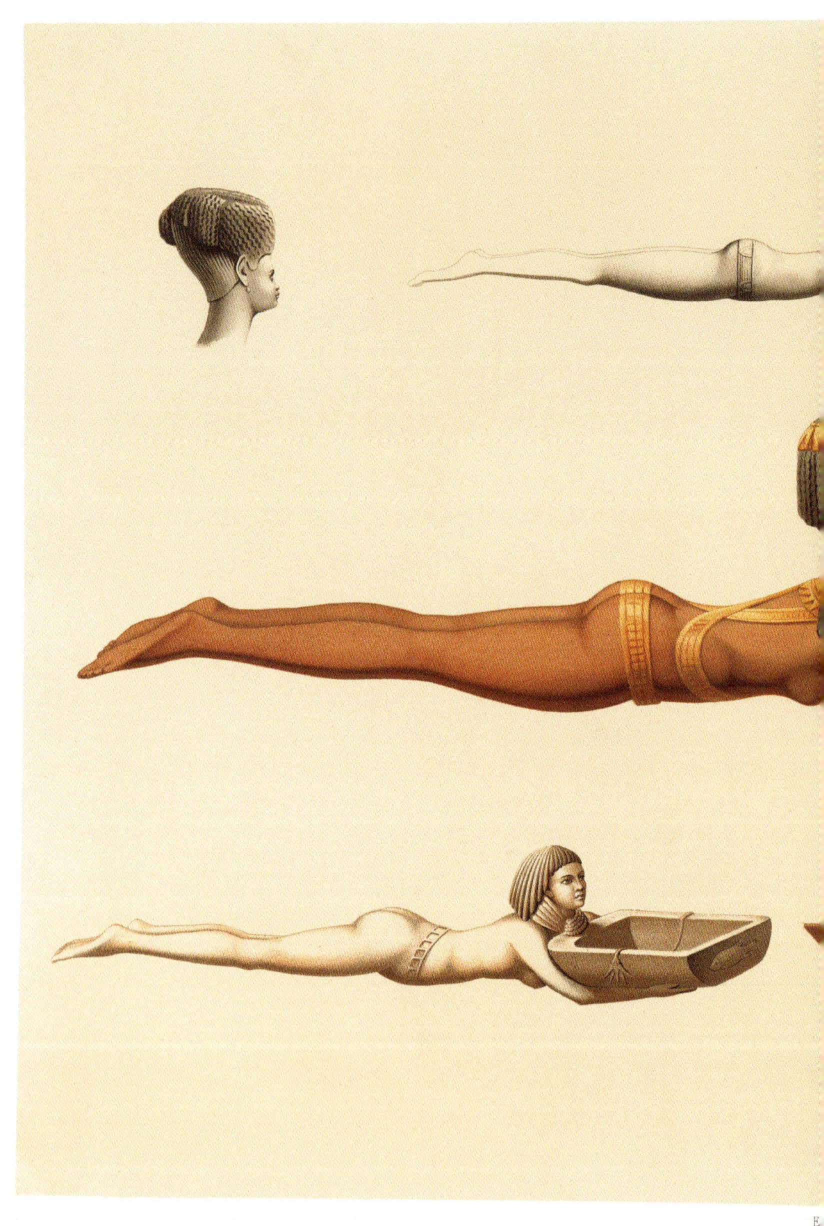

E

CUILLERS

USTEN

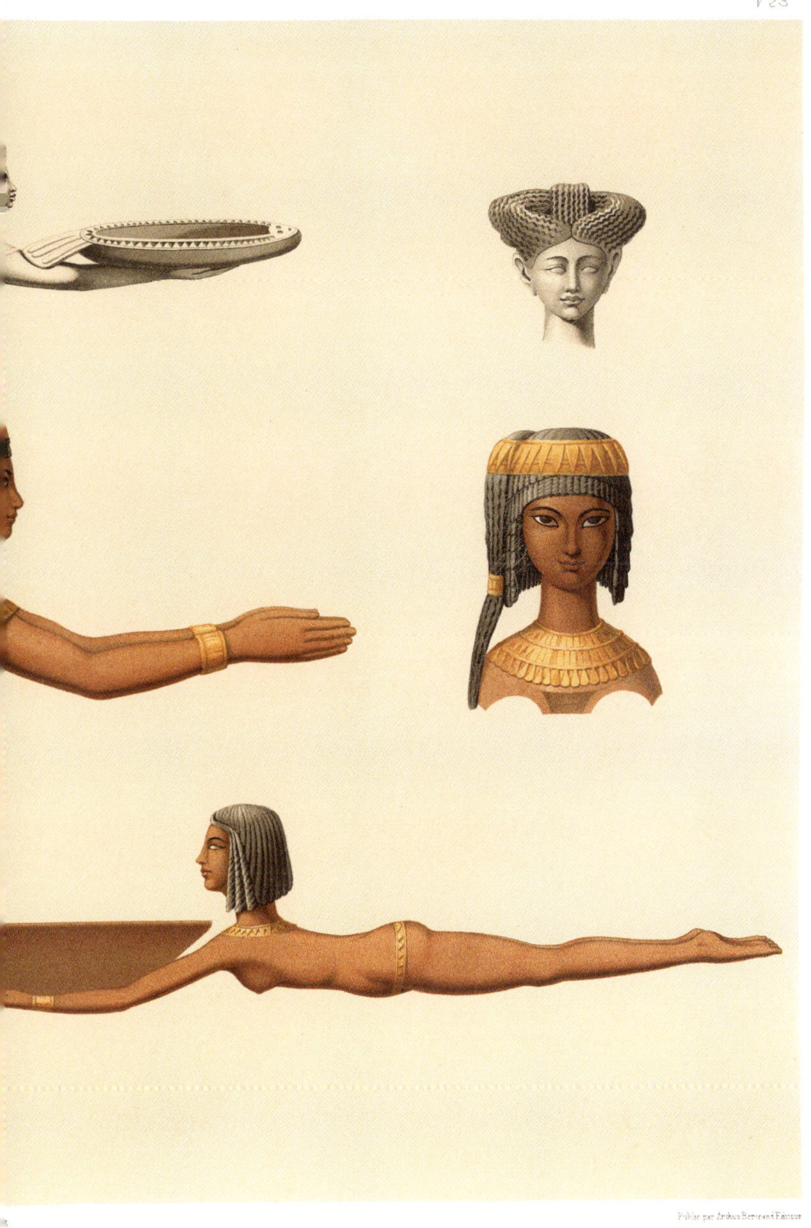

Publié par Arthus Bertrand Éditeur

IS PEINT

UMS.

(Pages/Seite 550/551)

PAINTED WOODEN SPOONS

Utensils for perfumes

This plate shows perfume spatulas in ebony or acacia wood; several of them are carved in the likeness of a naked young girl, stretched out as if swimming and apparently trying to keep her cosmetic dish afloat in the water. Many similar images from various periods can be seen: they sometimes differ according to the hairstyle, the shape of the cosmetic dish or the detail of the circlet worn around the lower back like a belt, sometimes according to the material itself.

LÖFFEL AUS BEMALTEM HOLZ

Parfümgerätschaften

Diese Tafel zeigt Parfümspatel aus Akazien- oder Ebenholz; mehrere sind in der Form eines nackten jungen Mädchens geschnitzt, das in Schwimmhaltung ausgestreckt ist und den Anschein erweckt, ihr Gefäß für Duftessenzen mitten im Wasser hochhalten zu wollen. Es gibt viele ähnliche Bilder aus unterschiedlichen Zeiten: Sie unterscheiden sich mitunter durch die Haartracht, die Form des Duftbehältnisses und die Einzelheiten des Hüftringes, den sie anstelle des Gürtels tragen, oder schließlich durch das Material selbst.

CUILLERS DE BOIS PEINT

Ustensiles à parfums

Cette planche représente des spatules à parfums, en bois d'ébène ou d'acacia ; plusieurs sont sculptées à l'image d'une jeune fille nue et allongée dans une pose de natation et qui semblent vouloir soutenir leur cassolette au milieu de l'eau. On rencontre beaucoup d'images semblables, appartenant à diverses époques : elles diffèrent quelquefois par la coiffure, la forme de la cassolette et les détails du cercle lombaire qu'elles portent en guise de ceinture, ou enfin par la matière elle-même.

(Page/Seite 554)

VASES IN ENAMELLED GOLD (19th and 20th Dynasties)

Nos. 1 and 2 are taken from the magnificent tomb of Imiseba. The vase decorated with two captive Africans has been completely erased, while the vase that is supported by two Asiatics retains only a part of its original detail.

VASEN AUS EMAILLIERTEM GOLD (19. und 20. Dynastie)

Die Nr. 1 und 2 sind dem prächtigen Grab Imisebas entnommen. Die mit vier gefangenen Afrikanern verzierte Vase ist vollständig verwittert, was die von zwei Asiaten getragene betrifft, so sind die Details nur zum Teil erhalten.

VASES EN OR ÉMAILLÉ (XIXe et XXe dynasties)

Les n°s 1 et 2 sont tirés du magnifique tombeau d'Aïchesi [Imiseba]. Le vase orné de deux captifs nègres est entièrement effacé, quant à celui qui est supporté par deux Asiatiques, il ne conserve plus qu'une partie des détails.

(Page/Seite 555)

VASES IN ENAMELLED GOLD (19th and 20th Dynasties)

Nos. 1 and 3 are taken from a hypogeum at Thebes, decorated in the reign of Ramesses III. The other vases were also copied at Thebes, on the walls of the tomb of Imiseba. Nos. 2 and 6 are today completely effaced.

VASEN AUS EMAILLIERTEM GOLD (19. und 20. Dynastie)

Die Nr. 1 und 3 sind einem unter der Herrschaft Ramses' III. in Theben ausgeschmückten Hypogäum entnommen. Die anderen Vasen wurden ebenfalls in Theben von den Wänden im Grab Imisebas abgezeichnet. Die Nr. 2 und 6 sind heute vollständig verwittert.

VASES EN OR ÉMAILLÉ (XIXe et XXe dynasties)

Les n°s 1 et 3 sont tirés d'un hypogée de Thèbes, décoré sous le règne de Ramsès III. Les autres vases ont été copiés également à Thèbes, sur les parois du tombeau d'Aïchesi [Imiseba] Les n°s 2 et 6 sont aujourd'hui entièrement effacés.

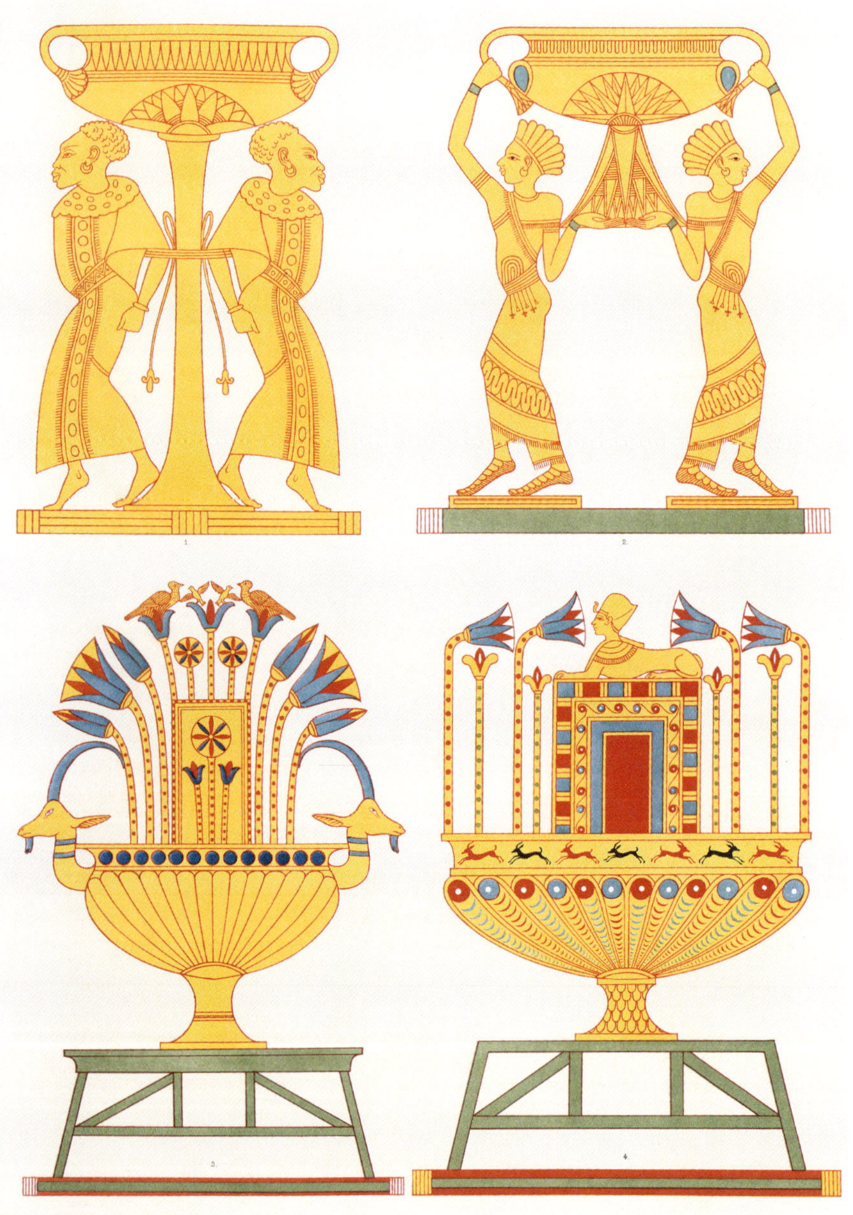

Lith. par Moulin _ Imp. par Hangard-Maugé · E. Prisse d'Avennes · Publié par Arthus Bertrand, Éditeur.

VASES EN OR ÉMAILLÉ.

(XIXe et XXe DYNASTIES.)

V 25

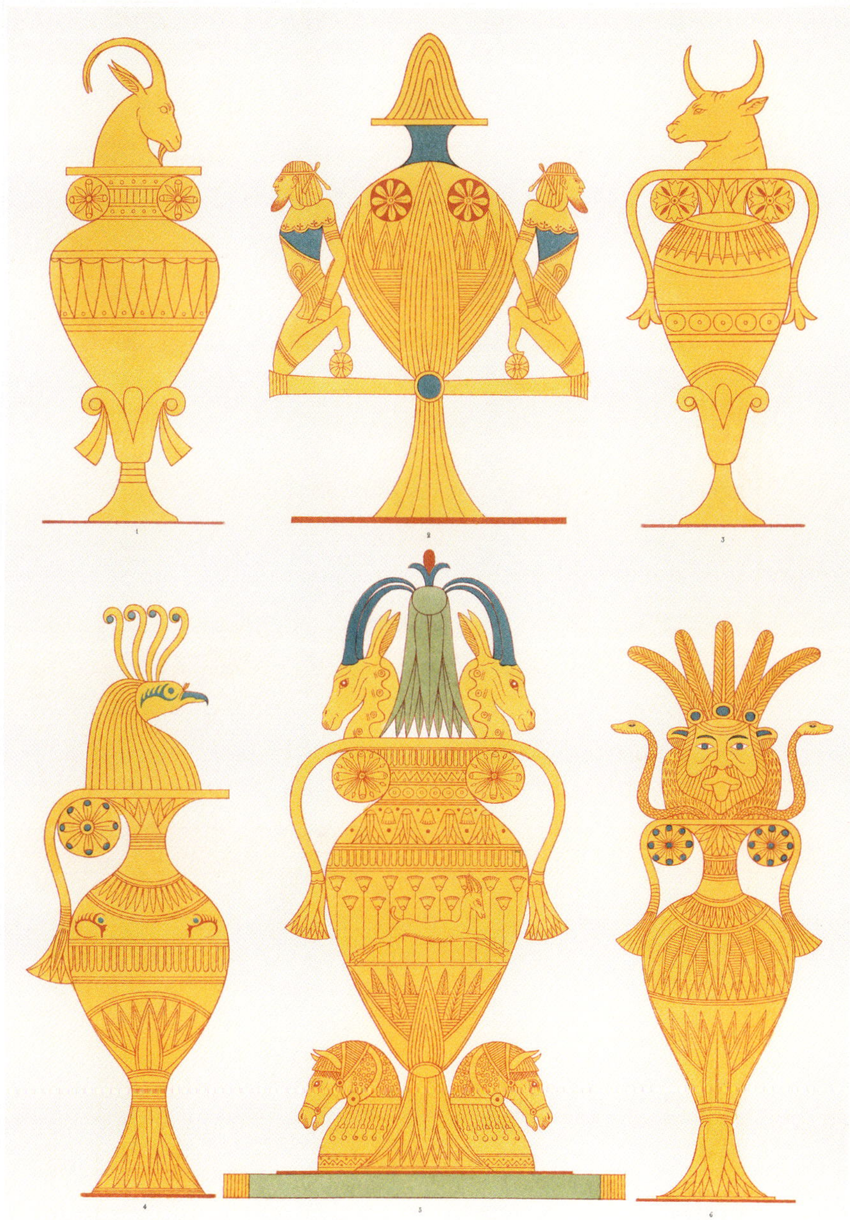

Lith. par Moulin. — Imp. par Haugard-Maugé — E. Prisse d'Avennes — Publié par Arthus Bertrand, Éditeur

VASES EN OR ÉMAILLÉ.

(XIXe et XXe DYNASTIES.)

OFFERINGS OF SETI I AND OF RAMESSES II (19th Dynasty)

Thebes

This plate shows a collection of vases copied separately, particularly from the offerings featured in the great temple of Amun at Karnak. Nos. 1, 2, 3, 4, 5, 8, 9, 10 and 11 belong to the reign of Seti I, nos. 6 and 7 to that of his son, Ramesses II. Although these vases are generally attributed to conquered peoples, there is no real proof that they were either the rich spoils of war or the craftsmanship of foreign artists. In addition, it is my belief that they were produced by Egyptian artists. In fact, Thutmosis III, who had made so many foreign conquests, never offered the gods a single vase seized from defeated peoples when he returned home victorious. And on the vases that concern us here, we see prisoners begging the pharaohs and the gods for mercy. The vanquished would certainly not portray themselves in the attitude of suppliants. These vases are not, therefore, rich spoils; they are definitely part of Egyptian art, where the artist sought to dispense with the traditional curves and decorations in order to make quite clear what was the origin of the offerings presented to the kings of the gods.

OPFERGABEN VON SETHOS I. UND RAMSES II. (19. Dynastie)

Theben

Diese Tafel stellt eine Sammlung einzeln abgezeichneter Vasen dar, insbesondere von den im großen Amun-Tempel in Karnak dargestellten Opfergaben. Die Nr. 1, 2, 3, 4, 5, 8, 9, 10, 11 datieren aus der Regierungszeit von Sethos I.; die Nr. 6 und 7 aus der seines Sohnes Ramses II. Im Allgemeinen schreibt man diese Vasen den besiegten Völkern zu; es gibt jedoch keinen Beweis dafür, dass es sich wirklich um reiche Beute oder um Werke fremder Künstler handelt. Im Übrigen glaube ich, dass ägyptische Künstler sie hergestellt haben. Nach der Rückkehr von seinen Eroberungen hat nämlich Thutmosis III., der so viele Völker besiegte, niemals eine in der Fremde eroberte Vase den Göttern geopfert. Sind auf den Vasen, die uns beschäftigen, nicht Gefangene dargestellt, die die Gnade des Pharaos oder der Götter erflehen? Die Besiegten haben sich sicherlich nicht selbst in die Haltung der Flehenden versetzt. Diese Vasen sind demnach keine reiche Beute; sie sind vielmehr der ägyptischen Kunst zuzurechnen, die von den üblichen Verzierungen und anmutig geschwungenen Formen abzuweichen suchte, um die Herkunft der den Herrschern der Götter präsentierten Opfergaben zu verdeutlichen.

OFFRANDES DE SÉTI Ier ET DE RAMSÈS II (XIXe dynastie)

Thèbes

Cette planche représente une collection de vases copiés isolément, particulièrement parmi les offrandes figurées dans le grand temple d'Amon, à Karnac. Les n°s 1, 2, 3, 4, 5, 8, 9, 10, 11 appartiennent au règne de Seti Ier ; les n°s 6 et 7 à celui de son fils, Ramsès II. On attribue, généralement, ces vases aux peuples vaincus ; rien ne prouve cependant que ce soient réellement des dépouilles opimes, ni des œuvres d'artistes étrangers. Je crois en outre qu'ils ont été fabriqués par des artistes égyptiens. En effet, Thoutmès [Thoutmôsis] III, qui avait vaincu tant de peuples, n'offrit jamais aux dieux aucun des vases conquis sur l'étranger au retour de ses conquêtes. Ne voit-on pas, sur les vases qui nous occupent, des prisonniers implorant la clémence des pharaons ou des dieux ? Ce ne sont certes pas les vaincus qui se sont placés eux-mêmes dans l'attitude de suppliants. Ces vases ne sont donc pas des dépouilles opimes ; ils appartiennent bien à l'art égyptien, qui a cherché à s'écarter des galbes et des ornements habituels, pour préciser l'origine des offrandes présentées aux souverains des dieux.

V26

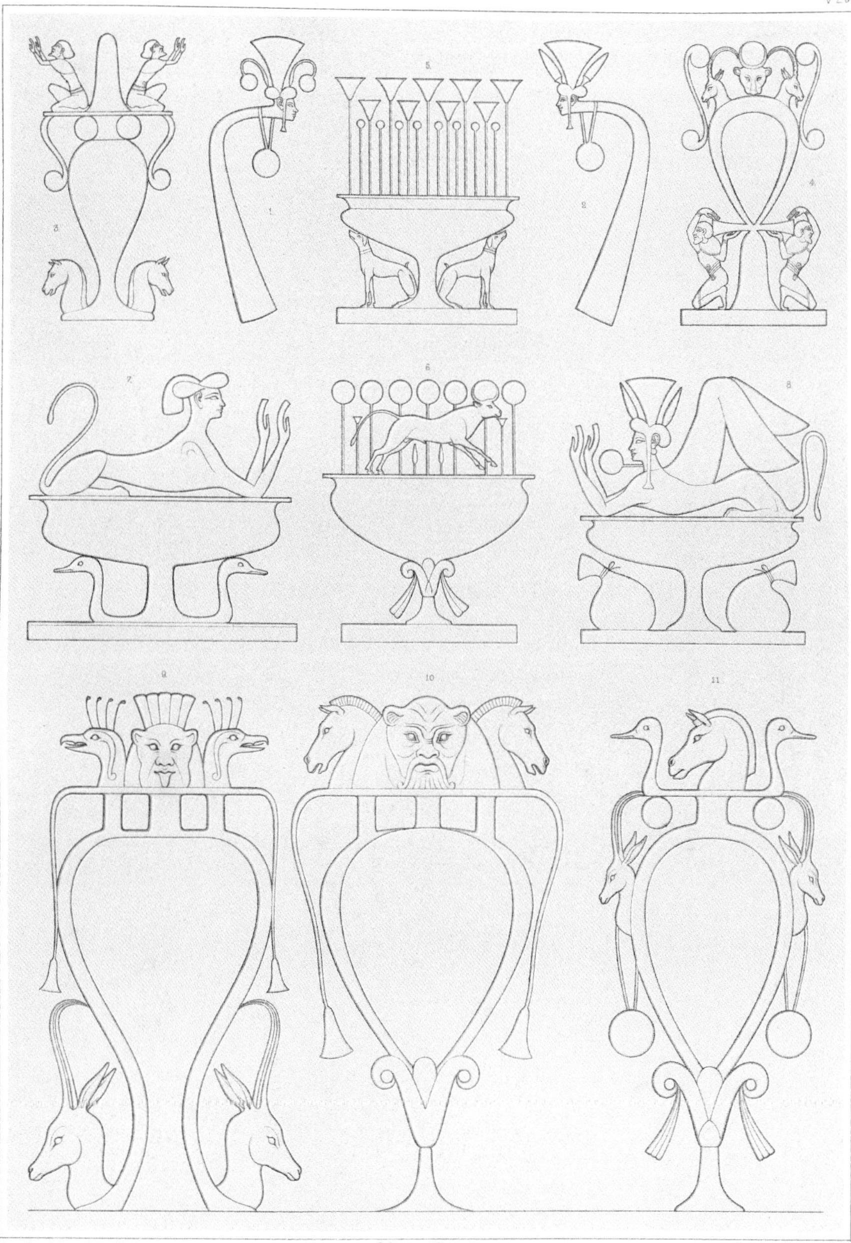

Lith. par Dassout. Imp. par Bagard Monge. E. Prisse d'Avennes. Publié par Arthus-Bertrand Editeur.

OFFRANDES DE SÉTI Ier ET DE RAMSÈS II.

(THÈBES — XIXe DYNASTIE)

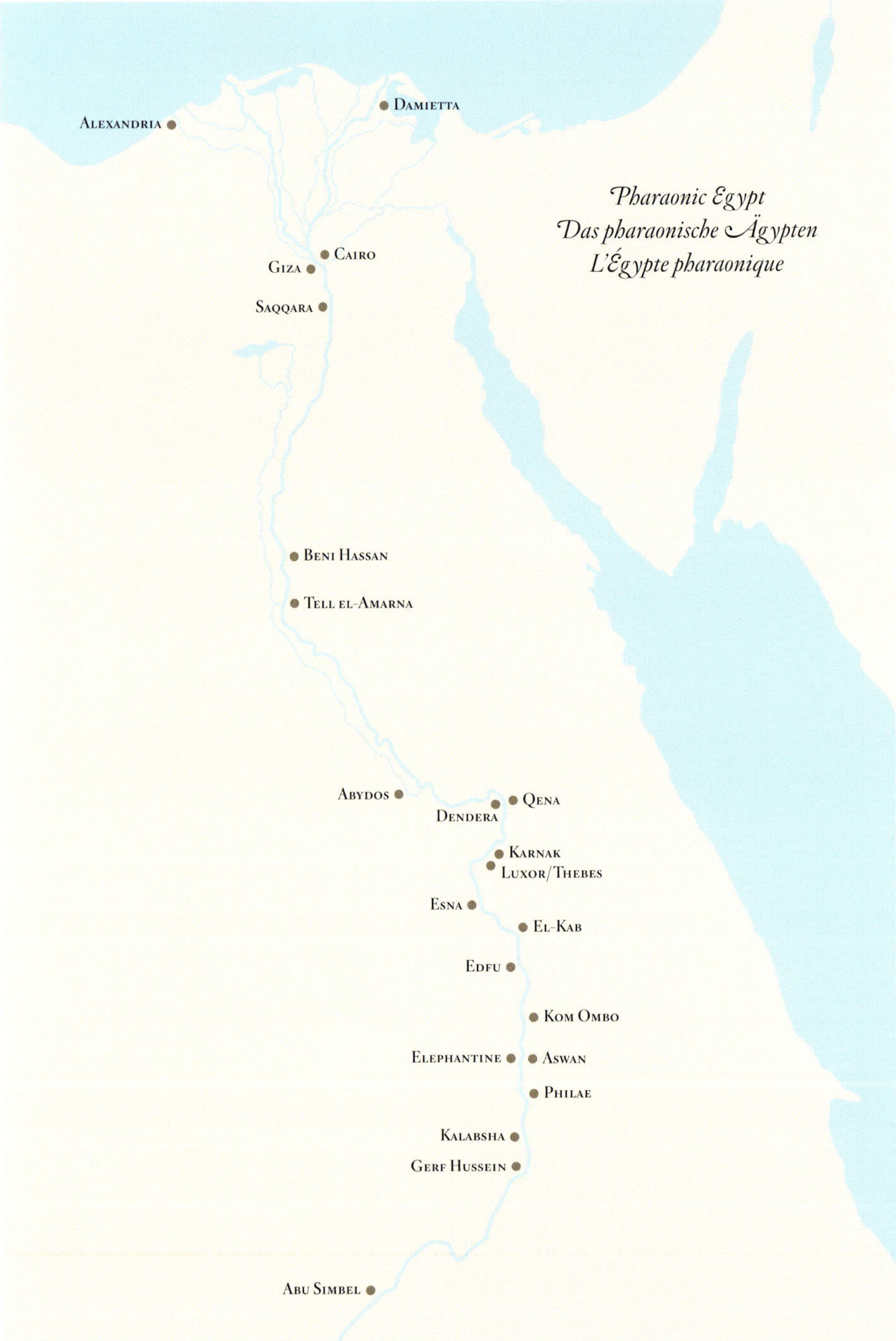

Pharaonic Egypt
Das pharaonische Ägypten
L'Égypte pharaonique

Damietta
Alexandria
Cairo
Giza
Saqqara
Beni Hassan
Tell el-Amarna
Abydos
Qena
Dendera
Karnak
Luxor/Thebes
Esna
El-Kab
Edfu
Kom Ombo
Elephantine
Aswan
Philae
Kalabsha
Gerf Hussein
Abu Simbel

Bibliography / Bibliografie / Bibliographie

– Carré, Jean-Marie, *Voyageurs et écrivains français en Égypte*, 2 vols., Cairo, 1932 (facsimile reprod. 1990).

– Curl, James Stevens, *Egyptomania. The Egyptian Revival: A Recurring Theme in the History of Taste*, Manchester, 1994.

– Dewachter, Michel, *Champollion: un scribe pour l'Égypte*, Paris, 1990.

– Dewachter, Michel, *Un Avesnois: l'égyptologue Prisse d'Avennes (1807–1879)*, Société archéologique et historique de l'arrondissement d'Avesnes (Mémoires, 30), Avesnes sur-Helpe, 1988.

– Dewachter, Michel, "Nouvelles informations relatives à l'exploitation de la nécropole royale de Drah Aboul Neggah", in: *Revue d'Égyptologie*, 36, 1985, pp. 43–66.

– Dewachter, Michel, "À propos du temple de Thot à Karnak Nord", in: *Revue d'Égyptologie*, 36, 1985, pp. 175–177.

– Dewachter, Michel, "Exploitation des manuscrits d'un égyptologue du XIXe siècle: Prisse d'Avennes", in: *Bulletin de la Société française d'égyptologie*, 101, 1984, pp. 49–71.

– M***, E., *Notice biographique sur Émile Prisse d'Avennes*, Paris, 1896.

– Manniche, Lise, *The Tombs of the Nobles at Luxor*, Cairo, 1987.

– *Le Mirage égyptien: contribution des Bourguignons au rêve oriental de Bonaparte*, exhibition catalogue, ed. Françoise Duvernier, Marie Michaut and Alain Cattagni, Auxerre, 1998.

– Norton, Mary, "Prisse d'Avennes", in: *Aramco World*, 41.6, 1990, pp. 39–46.

– Peltrisot, C.-N., *Biographie de Prisse d'Avennes rédigée par C.-N. Peltrisot, membre de la société archéologique et historique de l'arrondissement d'Avennes*, [no place], 1934.

– Prévost, Marie-Laure (et al.), *Visions d'Égypte, Émile Prisse d'Avennes (1807–1879)*, Paris, 2011.

– Raven, Maarten J., "Prisse d'Avennes: between Facts and Fiction", in: *Prisse d'Avennes: Atlas of Egyptian Art by Prisse d'Avennes*, Cairo, 2007.

– Robins, Gay, *Proportion and Style in Ancient Egyptian Art*, Austin, 1994.

–Volait, Mercedes (ed.), *Émile Prisse d'Avennes. Un artiste-antiquaire en Égypte au XIXe siècle*, Cairo, 2013.

Chronology

1807 Birth of Achille Constant Théodore Émile Prisse at Avesnes-sur-Helpe, on 27 January, to Ignace Eugène Constant Prisse and Claire Constance Thérèse Victoire Pillot

1809–1828 Publication of *Description de l'Égypte*

1814 Death of Prisse's father on 2 January

1822 Prisse enters the École d'Arts et Métiers at Châlons-sur-Marne

1825–1826 Prisse joins the Greek War of Independence, then travels to the Near East, and finally Egypt

1826 Prisse is awarded the title of Knight of the Sepulchre in Jerusalem

1826–1836 Prisse works for Muhammad Ali Pasha in various capacities, including that of civil and hydraulic engineer, and tutor to his grandsons

1833–1836 Prisse works as professor of fortification at the Infantry School of Damietta

1836–1839 Prisse travels through Egypt and the Near East, excavating and recording monuments

1839–1843 Prisse lives mainly in Luxor with George Lloyd, the botanist

1842–1845 Karl Richard Lepsius's expedition to Egypt

1843 Death of George Lloyd

1844 Prisse returns to France and gives the Prisse Papyrus to the Bibliothèque nationale (pBN 183–194) and the Chamber of the Ancestors to the Louvre

1845 Prisse is awarded the Legion of Honour despite refusing to swear fealty to King Louis-Philippe

1847 Publication of the *Monuments égyptiens, bas-reliefs, peintures, inscriptions* (Paris, Didot Frères)

1849 Death of Muhammad Ali Pasha.
Marriage of Prisse to Marie-Euphémie Joséphine Bisiaux (1828–1916)

1858 Establishment of the Egyptian Antiquities Service under the direction of Auguste Mariette

1858–1860 Prisse's second expedition to Egypt, sponsored by Napoleon III, accompanied by Willem de Famars Testas (Dutch artist) and Édouard Jarrot (French photographer)

1859 Publication of Richard Lepsius's 12-volume *Denkmaeler aus Aegypten und Aethiopien*.
Prisse and his group move south, joined by Edwin Smith.

1860 Jarrot leaves early because of stress brought on from being overworked.
Prisse and the rest of the expedition depart Egypt later, in June

1867 Prisse works on the lakes of Lower Egypt for Ismail Pasha, and the World Exposition

1869–1877 Publication of the three atlas volumes of *L'Art arabe d'après les monuments du Kaire* (Paris, V. A. Morel)

1878 Publication of the plates of the *Histoire de l'art égyptien* (Paris, A. Bertrand)

1879 Death of Prisse in Paris on 16 February.
Publication of the text of the *Histoire de l'art égyptien* by P. Marchandon de la Faye, based on Prisse's notes

1889 Prisse's remains are moved to Montparnasse cemetery

1897 A street in the 14th *arrondissement* is named after Prisse (rue Prisse d'Avennes)

Zeittafel

1807 Achille Constant Théodore Émile Prisse wird am 27. Januar in Avesnes-sur-Helpe als Sohn von Ignace Eugène Constant Prisse und Claire Constance Thérèse Victoire Pillot geboren

1809–1828 Veröffentlichung der *Description de l'Égypte*

1814 Tod von Prisse' Vater am 2. Januar

1822 Eintritt in die École d'Arts et Métiers in Châlons-sur-Marne

1825–1826 Teilnahme am griechischen Unabhängigkeitskrieg, gefolgt von Reisen in den Nahen Osten bis schließlich nach Ägypten

1826 Ernennung zum Ritter vom Heiligen Grab zu Jerusalem

1826–1836 Prisse steht in den Diensten von Muhammad Ali Pascha in diversen Funktionen, u. a. als Bau- und Hydraulikingenieur und als Privatlehrer von dessen Enkeln

1833–1836 Tätigkeit als Dozent für Befestigungsanlagen an der Infanterieschule von Damiette

1836–1839 Reisen durch Ägypten und den Nahen Osten; Ausgrabungen und Dokumentation von Monumenten

1839–1843 Prisse lebt vornehmlich in Luxor, in Begleitung des Botanikers George Lloyd

1842–1845 Karl Richard Lepsius' Ägypten-Expedition

1843 Tod von George Lloyd

1844 Prisse kehrt nach Frankreich zurück und übereignet der französischen Nationalbibliothek den Papyrus Prisse (pBN 183–194) sowie dem Louvre die Königsliste von Karnak

1845 Auszeichnung der Ehrenlegion, obwohl Prisse König Louis-Philippe den Treueeid verweigert

1847 Veröffentlichung der *Monuments égyptiens, bas-reliefs, peintures, inscriptions* (Paris: Didot Frères)

1849 Tod von Muhammad Ali Pascha. Prisse heiratet Marie-Euphémie Joséphine Bisiaux (1828–1916)

1858 Gründung des Ägyptischen Antikendienstes unter Leitung von Auguste Mariette

1858–1860 Prisse' zweite Expedition nach Ägypten, die zum Teil von Napoleon III. finanziert wird. Prisse reist in Begleitung des niederländischen Künstlers Willem de Famars Testas und des französischen Fotografen Édouard Jarrot

1859 Veröffentlichung von Lepsius' zwölfbändigem Werk *Denkmaeler aus Aegypten und Aethiopien*. Prisse und seine Begleiter reisen Richtung Süden, Edwin Smith schließt sich der Gruppe an

1860 Jarrot reist wegen Überarbeitung vorzeitig ab. Prisse und die übrigen Expeditionsteilnehmer verlassen Ägypten etwas später, im Juni

1867 Prisse arbeitet für Ismail Pascha in der Seenregion Unterägyptens und ist für die Weltausstellung tätig

1869–1877 Veröffentlichung der drei Atlas-Bände von *L'Art arabe d'après les monuments du Kaire* (Paris: V. A. Morel)

1878 Veröffentlichung der Tafelbände der *Histoire de l'art égyptien* (Paris: A. Bertrand)

1879 Prisse verstirbt am 16. Februar in Paris. Veröffentlichung des Textbandes der *Histoire de l'art égyptien* von P. Marchandon de la Faye, beruhend auf Prisse' Aufzeichnungen

1889 Überführung seiner sterblichen Überreste auf den Friedhof von Montparnasse

1897 Eine Straße im 14. Pariser Arrondissement wird nach Prisse benannt (rue Prisse d'Avennes)

Chronologie

1807 Naissance d'Achille Constant Théodore Émile Prisse, le 27 janvier à Avesnes-sur-Helpe. Il est le fils d'Ignace Eugène Constant Prisse et de Claire Constance Thérèse Victoire Pillot

1809–1828 Publication de la *Description de l'Égypte*

1814 Décès du père de Prisse le 2 janvier

1822 Entre à l'École d'Arts et Métiers de Châlons-sur-Marne

1825–1826 S'engage dans la guerre d'indépendance grecque, puis voyage à travers le Proche-Orient et l'Égypte

1826 Est fait chevalier de l'ordre du Saint-Sépulcre de Jérusalem

1826–1836 Prisse entre au service de Méhémet Ali Pacha pour lequel il exerce diverses fonctions, parmi lesquelles celles d'ingénieur dans le génie civil et l'hydraulique et de précepteur de ses petits-fils

1833–1836 Professeur de fortification à l'École d'infanterie de Damiette

1836–1839 Parcourt l'Égypte et le Proche-Orient, effectue des fouilles et recense des monuments

1839–1843 Séjourne principalement à Louxor, en compagnie du botaniste George Lloyd

1842–1845 Expédition de Karl Richard Lepsius en Égypte

1843 Décès de George Lloyd

1844 Retour de Prisse en France où celui-ci offre le Papyrus Prisse à la Bibliothèque nationale (pBN 183–194) et la Chambre des Ancêtres au Louvre

1845 Décoré de la Légion d'honneur, bien qu'il ait refusé de faire allégeance au roi Louis-Philippe

1847 Publication des *Monuments égyptiens, bas-reliefs, peintures, inscriptions* (Paris : Didot Frères)

1849 Décès de Méhémet Ali Pacha

Épouse Marie-Euphémie Joséphine Bisiaux (1828–1916)

1858 Création du Service des Antiquités Égyptiennes sous la direction d'Auguste Mariette

1858–1860 Deuxième expédition de Prisse en Égypte, sous l'égide de Napoléon III. Il est accompagné de Willem de Famars Testas, artiste hollandais, et d'Édouard Jarrot, photographe français

1859 Publication du *Denkmaeler aus Aegypten und Aethiopien* en douze volumes de Lepsius

Prisse et ses hommes se rendent au sud de l'Égypte, rejoints par Edwin Smith

1860 Surmené, Jarrot quitte prématurément l'expédition. Prisse et les autres hommes quittent l'Égypte plus tard, en juin

1867 Travaille sur les lacs de Basse-Égypte pour Ismaïl Pacha et pour l'Exposition universelle

1869–1877 Publication des trois volumes de l'atlas de *L'Art arabe d'après les monuments du Kaire* (Paris : V. A. Morel)

1878 Publication des planches de l'*Histoire de l'art égyptien* (Paris : A. Bertrand)

1879 Décès de Prisse à Paris le 16 février

Publication du texte de l'*Histoire de l'art égyptien*, par P. Marchandon de la Faye, d'après les notes de Prisse

1889 Ses cendres sont transférées au cimetière du Montparnasse

1897 Le nom de Prisse est donné à une rue du 14e arrondissement de Paris (rue Prisse d'Avennes)

Glossary

Aba sceptre: Insignia of royalty and/or divine power.
Abu Simbel: Site of two rock-cut temples in Nubia, southern Egypt, built by Ramesses II.
Abydos: Ancient city and important necropolis on the west bank of the Nile in Upper Egypt. Reputed to have been the burial place of the god Osiris, ruler of the Afterworld.
Acherai: Ay, successor to Tutankhamun, a pharaoh of the 18th Dynasty (New Kingdom).
Adytum: Enclosed room, inaccessible from outside the temple, in the rear wall of the cella, the largest room in a temple.
Ahmose I: Pharaoh, founder of the 18th Dynasty (New Kingdom) in ancient Egypt.
Ahmose Nefertari: Queen, sister and Great Wife of Ahmose I and mother of Amenophis I, 18th Dynasty (New Kingdom).
Akhenaten: Amenophis IV, later Akhenaten, pharaoh of the 18th Dynasty (New Kingdom). He raised the deity Aten, who was worshipped as the sun disc, to the status of chief and almost sole god of ancient Egypt.
Alabastron: Ancient city in Upper Egypt.
Amenemhat I: Pharaoh of the 12th Dynasty (Middle Kingdom).
Amenemhat II: Pharaoh of the 12th Dynasty (Middle Kingdom).
Amenemhat III: Pharaoh of the 12th Dynasty (Middle Kingdom).
Amenirdis: Kushite name popular with princesses and holders of the title "God's Wife of Amun", particularly during the 25th Dynasty (Third Intermediate Period).
Amenophis I: Ancient Egyptian Amenhotep I, pharaoh of the 18th Dynasty (New Kingdom).
Amenophis II: Ancient Egyptian Amenhotep II, pharaoh of the 18th Dynasty (New Kingdom).
Amenophis III: Ancient Egyptian Amenhotep III, pharaoh of the 18th Dynasty (New Kingdom).
Amenti: "The West", the ancient Egyptian underworld.
Amphora: Large long-necked jar used in antiquity for storing and transporting liquids.
Amun, Amun-Ra: Chief state god of the Middle and New Kingdoms whose principal residence was located at Thebes, modern Luxor.
Amun-se-Pehor: See Herihor.
Anubis: Canine-headed deity who presided over funerary rites, particularly mummification.
Anukis: Also Anuket, goddess of the Nile who, in early periods of Egyptian history, was associated with the Nile flood as well as hunting.
Apophis, Apopi: Pharaoh of the 15th Dynasty (Second Intermediate Period), that is, the Hyksos Period.
Apries: Pharaoh of the 26th Dynasty (Late Period).
Armant: Ancient Greek "Hermonthis", town on the west bank of the Nile in Upper Egypt.
Assyrians: People of ancient Mesopotamia.
Atef crown: A crown worn by Osiris and by the pharaoh consisting of a long central hat flanked by feathers and sometimes surmounting a pair of horns.
Athlophore: From ancient Greek, "victorious" (horses, men).
Atum: The first Egyptian god, creator of the other gods and a solar deity.
Augustus: First Roman emperor (63 BC–AD 14), born Gaius Octavius (Octavian), who ruled in Rome after the death of Julius Caesar (founded the Julio-Claudian dynasty).
Ay: See Acherai.
Bakenrenef, Bocchoris: Pharaoh of the 24th Dynasty (Third Intermediate Period).
Bakhten: A mythical distant kingdom, possibly in Asia, mentioned in Ramesside texts and most no-

tably in the sandstone tablet taken from the Karnak temple complex to France by Prisse in 1846.

Basilicogrammate: Ancient Egyptian official, royal secretary or court scribe.

Baskh-en-Aten: See Akhenaten.

Beni Hassan: Cemetery of rock-cut tombs, near Minya in Middle Egypt.

Bes: Deity overseeing birth, protector of women in labour, guardian of sleeping people.

Biban el-Muluk: Ancient Egyptian necropolis on the west bank of the Nile opposite Thebes/Luxor, known as the "Valley of the Kings".

Bintanath: Daughter of Ramesses II and his wife Isetnefret, 19th Dynasty (New Kingdom).

Bucranium: Decorative motif representing an ox skull.

Bundle column: See Lotus bundle column.

Calathos: Basket (here used as an ancient cooling vessel or cooler), woven of various materials.

Canopic jar: Vessels used for preserving internal organs removed for the mummification of corpses and buried separately.

Caracalla: Marcus Aurelius Antoninus, called Caracalla (AD 188–217), Roman emperor of the Severan dynasty.

Cartouche: Elongated oval framing for a king's name, symbol of infinity, used in inscriptions and in the ancient Egyptian hieroglyphic script.

Cataract: White-water rapids in the Nile, especially in Upper Egypt.

Champollion: Jean-François Champollion (1790–1832), French Orientalist and Egyptologist who was the first to decipher Egyptian hieroglyphs correctly.

Chenoboskion: Ancient city on the west bank of the Nile in Upper Egypt, now Nag Hammadi.

Cheops: Ancient Egyptian Khufu, pharaoh of the 4th Dynasty (Old Kingdom).

Chephren: Ancient Egyptian Khafre, pharaoh of the 4th Dynasty (Old Kingdom).

Ciborium: Vessel, covered drinking cup.

Claudius: Tiberius Claudius Nero Germanicus (10 BC–AD 54), Roman emperor (Julio-Claudian dynasty).

Cleopatra: Specifically Cleopatra VII (69–30 BC), female pharaoh and last Ptolemaic queen of Egypt.

Cloisonné: Enamelling technique that separates colours by wire or strips of metal.

Crook: Together with the flail, part of the insignia of the ancient Egyptian pharaoh, symbolising the care-giving aspect of the king.

Dactyliform capital: Capital consisting of palm fronds represented bending outwards.

Dado: Lower part of interior wall between skirting-board and chair (dado) rail.

Dakka: Site in Lower Nubia, south of Aswan.

Deir el-Bersha: A village on the east bank of the Nile in Middle Egypt, site of the ancient necropolis of Hermopolis Magna.

Deir el-Medina: Ruins of an artisans' settlement and cemetery in ancient Thebes (Luxor's west bank).

Dendera: Town on the west bank of the Nile in Upper Egypt, site of a temple to the goddess Hathor.

Dendur: Once a town on the west bank of the Nile in Lower Nubia, now covered by the waters of Lake Nasser.

Djedkare, Isesi: Greek Tanchares, pharaoh of the 5th Dynasty (Old Kingdom).

Djehutihotep: Nomarch (regional governor) in Upper Egypt and High Priest in the 12th Dynasty (Middle Kingdom).

Dromos: Passageway, entrance passage to a building, tomb.

Edfu: City on the Nile's west bank in Upper Egypt, site of a temple dedicated to the god Horus.

El-Assasif: Necropolis on the west bank at Thebes.

El-Sheikh Said: Site in Middle Egypt near Deir el-Bersha of another ancient necropolis associated with Hermopolis Magna.

Elephantine: Island in the Nile at Aswan, inhabited since the Predynastic era until modern times.

Epiphi: Third month of the season of Shemu in the ancient Egyptian calendar, which corresponds to the period from May to June in the Gregorian calendar.

Esna: City on the west bank of the Nile in Upper Egypt.

Fellah: Arabic term for peasant farmer or member of a settled rural population.

Flail: Together with the crook, part of the insignia of the ancient Egyptian pharaoh. Flails were used to thresh grain and were thus a symbol of the aspect of the king that punished wrongdoers and maintained civic order.

Gebel el-Silsila: Ancient Egyptian sandstone quarry site in Upper Egypt.

Gerf Hussein: The site of a temple of Ramesses II south of Aswan in Nubia; portions were moved during the Nubian Salvage Campaign to save the temple from the rising waters of Lake Nasser.

Giza: City near Cairo, site of the Great Pyramids.

Guilloche: A running pattern formed of interlacing bands giving a braided appearance.

Gynaeceum: The part of an ancient Greek house reserved for women.

Haroeris: Horus the Elder, a form of the god Horus.

Hathor: Goddess of love and beauty as well as Mistress of the West, who welcomed the dead to the underworld.

Hatshepsut: Female pharaoh, half-sister and wife of pharaoh Thutmosis II, 18th Dynasty (New Kingdom).

Heka: God of magic, creative power.

Hemispeos: Temple, partly free-standing and partly rock-cut.

Heptanomis: Meaning seven nomes (administrative subdivisions of ancient Egypt), political entity in Middle Egypt; Prisse's text on Tell el-Amarna refers to the seventh nome.

Herihor: A general who lived at Thebes during the transition from the 20th to the 21st Dynasty (New Kingdom) and seized power over part of the country at this time.

Hermonthis: See Armant.

Hermopolis Magna: Ancient city on the west bank of the Nile in Middle Egypt, modern Ashmunein and its cemetery at Tuna el-Gebel.

Hor-Amun: Fusion of the child-god Horus with Amun (Hellenistic Greek Harpocrates).

Horemheb: Last pharaoh of the 18th Dynasty (New Kingdom), who started his career as a general and became pharaoh at the end of the Amarna period.

Horus: Sky god, god of kingship.

Hypogeum: Rock-cut chamber tomb, often for multiple burials.

Hypostyle: Hall of an Egyptian temple, full of columns.

Hypsela: Ancient site in Upper Egypt, now Qus.

Imiseba: Chief of the Altar of Amun, Scribe of the Royal Accounts, 20th Dynasty (New Kingdom), took over the tomb of Nebamun, Tomb No. TT 65.

Isetnefret: A Great Royal Wife of Ramesses II.

Isis: Goddess of magic, motherhood, wife of Osiris and mother of Horus.

Kadesh: Ancient city on the Orontes, now in Syria, site of battles between the Egyptians and various Near Eastern kingdoms. The most famous battle here was fought by Ramesses II.

Kalabsha: Site south of Aswan now submerged beneath Lake Nasser, surviving remains relocated to near the Aswan High Dam.

Karnak: Site of the largest temple to Amun, located north of Luxor on the east bank of the Nile in Upper Egypt; Prisse removed the King List that is now in the Louvre from here.

Kashta: Kushite pharaoh of the 25th Dynasty (Third Intermediate Period).

Keftiu: Egyptian name for Minoans.

Khaemhat: Also called Mahu, Royal Scribe and Overseer of Royal Granaries of Upper and Lower Egypt, 18th Dynasty (New Kingdom), buried in Tomb No. TT 57.

Khafre: See Chephren.

Kheker frieze: Motif of stylised knotted plants running along the top of ancient Egyptian walls.

Khendjer: Throne name of Userkare, pharaoh of the 13th Dynasty (Second Intermediate Period).

Khnum: Deity originally associated with the flooding of the Nile; later the temple of Elephantine was dedicated to him.

Khonsu: God associated with the new moon, son of Amun and Mut.
Khufu: See Cheops.
Kiosk: Small shrine or sacred area framed by two or more columns.
Kom el-Ahmar: Hierakonpolis, a capital of Predynastic Upper Egypt. The name Kom el-Ahmar, "the mound of red", is often applied to a number of sites throughout Egypt as it denotes the piles of red pottery sherds to be found there.
Kom Ombo: Site of an extensive ancient Egyptian necropolis and the Temple of Kom Ombo in Upper Egypt.
Krater: An ancient Greek vase form containing wine mixed with water.
Kubban: Contra-Pselchis, ancient site near Dakka, Lower Nubia.
Lekythos: Ancient Greek oil jug.
Lepsius: Karl Richard Lepsius (1810–1884), German archaeologist and Egyptologist.
Lotus bundle column: Ancient Egyptian column with a convex fluted shaft representing bundled lotus stalks and a capital in the form of a lotus bud.
Luxor: Modern city in Upper Egypt on the east bank of the Nile; site of the religious capital of Egypt from the Middle Kingdom onward.
Lyre: Ancient Greek hand-held instrument that was plucked, resembling a harp.
Maat: Goddess of cosmic order and justice.
Mammisi: Small chapel located near the front of an Egyptian temple, also known as a birth house as this was where the birth of the young god, generally Horus and the king as Horus, was celebrated.
Mastaba: Ancient Egyptian tomb shaped like a mud-brick bench found in vernacular architecture.
Medinet Habu: Site of the Memorial Temple of Ramesses III and other rulers of Thebes.
Meketaten: Ancient Egyptian princess, daughter of Akhenaten.
Memnonium: See Ramesseum.
Memphis: Capital of the first nome (administrative district) of Lower Egypt and Egypt's administrative capital throughout much of its history.
Menes: According to tradition, the pharaoh who founded the 1st Dynasty of ancient Egypt (Early Dynastic Period).
Menkaure: See Mykerinos.
Menkheperre: Throne name of Thutmosis III.
Mentuhotep II: Pharaoh of the 11th Dynasty (Middle Kingdom).
Mercury: Roman god, messenger of the gods and deity of tradesmen and thieves.
Merenptah/Merneptah: Pharaoh of the 19th Dynasty (New Kingdom).
Merenre: Also called Merenre II or Nyemtemsaf II, son of Pepi II, pharaoh of the 6th Dynasty (Old Kingdom).
Meritaten: Ancient Egyptian princess, daughter of pharaoh Akhenaten.
Meroë: Capital of the Kingdom of Kush (*c.* 400 BC–AD 300), now in Sudan.
Meryre: Throne name of Pepi I, pharaoh of the 6th Dynasty (Old Kingdom).
Mesore: According to the ancient Egyptian calendar, the fourth month of the season of Shemu, which corresponds to the period from June to July in the Gregorian calendar.
Metope: Square space between two frieze triglyphs in the Doric order (see Triglyph).
Minya: Governorate capital on the west bank of the Nile in Middle Egypt.
Montuherkhepeshef: Ancient Egyptian prince, son of Ramesses II, and also the name of a son of Ramesses III.
Mut: Mother goddess, symbolic mother of the pharaohs.
Mykerinos: Ancient Egyptian Menkaure, pharaoh of the 4th Dynasty (Old Kingdom).
Naga: Site of ruins of an ancient Kushitic city, now in Sudan, part of the Kingdom of Meroë.
Naharina: Ancient Egyptian name for northern Syria.
Nakht-Hor-Amun: High Priest during the reign of the pharaoh Ay.
Naos: The sanctuary in a temple.
Necho II: Pharaoh of the 26th Dynasty (Late Period).

Nectanebo II: Pharaoh of the 30th Dynasty (Late Period).
Neferkare: Throne name of Pepi II, pharaoh of the 6th Dynasty (Old Kingdom).
Nefertiti: Great Royal Wife (chief consort) of Akhenaten, pharaoh of the 18th Dynasty (New Kingdom).
Neith: One of the four goddesses who protected the Four Sons of Horus.
Nemes: The striped head-cloth worn by ancient Egyptian pharaohs.
Nephthys: One of the four goddesses who protected the Four Sons of Horus.
Nile god: Hapy, deification of the yearly flooding of the Nile.
Obelisk: A tall, tapering single block of stone forming an extremely attenuated pyramid with a square base: a commemorative monument in ancient Egypt.
Onager: Wild ass *(Equus hemionus)* native to the Near and Middle East.
Opet: Also called Ipet, goddess of fertility, procreation and protection celebrated in the annual Opet festival.
Orontes: River flowing through Lebanon, Syria and Turkey.
Osiris: Ancient Egyptian god of the afterlife, the underworld and the dead.
Paser: Vizier of the 19th Dynasty, in the reigns of Seti I and Ramesses II (New Kingdom).
Pepi I: Pharaoh of the 6th Dynasty (Old Kingdom).
Pepi II: Pharaoh of the 6th Dynasty (Old Kingdom).
Peripteral temple: Surrounded by a single line of columns.
Petosiris: Ancient Egyptian High Priest of Thoth, buried at Tuna el-Gebel.
Phaophi: According to the ancient Egyptian calendar, the second month of the season of Akhet, which corresponds to the period from July to October in the Gregorian calendar.
Pharaoh: Ancient Egyptian word for king, literally meaning "Great House", with the implication being that the king was the one who resided in the Great House. The term started to be used during the New Kingdom.
Pharmouthi: According to the ancient Egyptian calendar, the fourth month of the season of Peret, which corresponds to the period from November to February in the Gregorian calendar.
Phre: Meaning "the sun", sun-god.
Piye: Also Piankhi, Kushite pharaoh of the 25th Dynasty (Third Intermediate Period).
Pronaos: The room through which the sanctuary (the naos) was reached.
Propylon: (Free-standing) gateway, usually as the entrance to temple precincts.
Psammetichus I, Psamtik I: Pharaoh who founded the 26th Dynasty (Late Period).
Pschent: Double crown of ancient Egypt.
Psinaula: See Tell el-Amarna.
Ptahshepses: Vizier and High Priest of Ptah, 5th Dynasty (Old Kingdom), buried in a mastaba at Abusir, near Saqqara.
Ptolemy: Claudius Ptolemaeus (*c.* AD 100–*c.* 168 or 178), Greek mathematician and astronomer. The Ptolemy World Map was named after him.
Ptolemy V Epiphanes: Pharaoh of the Ptolemaic Dynasty.
Ptolemy VIII Euergetes II: Pharaoh of the Ptolemaic Dynasty.
Ptolemy IX Soter II Lathyros: Pharaoh of the Ptolemaic Dynasty.
Punt, land of: A region from where the ancient Egyptians imported precious raw materials like gold, ebony and ivory. Its precise location is still disputed.
Pylon: Rectangular tower-like structure usually flanking ancient Egyptian temple gateways.
Qena: Governorate capital on the east bank of the Nile in Upper Egypt, called Kaine in the Graeco-Roman period.
Qurna: See Sheikh Abd el-Qurna.
Qusair: Al-Qusair, Ptolemaic Myos Hormos, ancient city on the Red Sea coast.
Ramesses I: Pharaoh who founded the 19th Dynasty (New Kingdom).
Ramesses II: Pharaoh of the 19th Dynasty (New Kingdom).

Ramesses III: Pharaoh of the 20th Dynasty (New Kingdom).
Ramesses VII: Pharaoh of the 20th Dynasty (New Kingdom).
Ramesses IX: Pharaoh of the 20th Dynasty (New Kingdom).
Ramesseum: Mortuary temple of Ramesses II at Thebes/Luxor on the west bank of the Nile.
Retjenu: Ancient Egyptian name for the region between the Negev Desert and the Orontes River.
Rhyton: Single-handled Greek vessel used for pouring libations.
Sagum: Roman military garment, a square of woollen cloth, worn over armour.
Sais: Ancient Egyptian city in the western Nile delta, capital of the 26th Dynasty.
Saqqara: Ancient Egyptian necropolis south of Cairo on the west bank of the Nile.
Satet, Satis: Goddess worshipped at Elephantine and giver of the "cool waters that come from Elephantine".
Scarab: The sacred scarab (*Scarabaeus sacer*), or dung beetle, which in ancient Egypt was associated with the sun god who similarly rolled the solar disc across the sky; often used as amulets or name seals made from stone or ceramic.
Sebbakhin: Local farmers, who dug up and destroyed archeological sites in their quest for fertiliser.
Sebekhotep: Pharaoh of the 13th Dynasty (Second Intermediate Period).
Sedeinga: Site of temple probably dedicated to Queen Tiye in Nubia, now Sudan.
Sekenenra: Seqenenre Tao, also Sekenenra Taa, ruler of Thebes and environs during the 17th Dynasty (Second Intermediate Period).
Sekos: A sacred enclosure, sanctuary of a temple.
Selket: Goddess who protected against scorpion bites; one of the four protectors of the Four Sons of Horus.
Semna: Fortified town (12th Dynasty) in Nubia, now Sudan.
Sesostris I, Senusert I: Pharaoh of the 12th Dynasty (Middle Kingdom), son of Amenemhat I.
Seth: God of deserts, storms and chaos.
Seti I: Pharaoh of the 19th Dynasty (New Kingdom).
Seti II: Pharaoh of the 19th Dynasty (New Kingdom).
Shabaka: Pharaoh of the Kushite 25th Dynasty (Third Intermediate Period).
Sheikh Abd el-Qurna: Also el-Qurna, site of a major New Kingdom necropolis on the west bank of the Nile across from Luxor.
Shendit, Shendyt: A kilt worn exclusively by the king until the First Intermediate Period when this mode of dress was adopted by the elite.
Simoom: A dust storm with dry, hot desert wind carrying clouds of sand.
Sistrum: Rattle used in the rites of Isis.
Sobek: Solar god taking the form of the Nile crocodile.
Sokar: Falcon god, linked to death and the underworld.
Sotem: Word for a high priest.
Speos: Rock-cut temple.
Sphinx: Statue with a lion's body and the head of a man (androsphinx), woman (gynosphinx), ram (criosphinx), falcon or sparrowhawk (hieracosphinx).
Surma: Indian word for kohl (sulphide of antimony), used in ancient Egypt to outline the eyes in black.
Sycamore fig: Fig-mulberry (*Ficus sycomorus*), cultivated in ancient Egypt as the "tree of life" and associated with the goddess Hathor.
Taharqa: Pharaoh of the Kushite 25th Dynasty (Third Intermediate Period).
Takelot I: Pharaoh of the 22nd Dynasty (Third Intermediate Period).
Talmis: Ancient Egyptian site, now New Kalabsha.
Tanis: Ancient Egyptian town in the north-eastern Nile delta, royal capital and cemetery of the 21st Dynasty.
Tausret: Also Tawosret, Great Royal Wife of Seti II, last pharaoh of the 19th Dynasty (New Kingdom).
Taweret: Goddess of childbirth and fertility, protector of pregnant women, often depicted as a hippopotamus.

Tell Abu Seifa: Ancient Egyptian Tjaru, or Silu (Greek Sile); site in the eastern Nile delta of an ancient Egyptian fortress.

Tell el-Amarna: Site on the east bank of the Nile in Middle Egypt of the ruins of the capital city of Akhetaten founded by the pharaoh Akhenaten.

Tell el-Maskhuta: Site of Per-Temu Tjeku, founded by pharaoh Necho II in the eastern Nile delta.

Teti: Pharaoh, founder of the 6th Dynasty (Old Kingdom).

Thebaid: Region near ancient Thebes, comprising the southern nomes (administrative districts) of Upper Egypt.

Thebes: City on the Upper Nile, at various times the capital and more consistently, religious capital, of Egypt.

Thoth: God of wisdom and writing, often depicted with the head of an ibis or a baboon.

Thutmosis II: Pharaoh of the 18th Dynasty (New Kingdom).

Thutmosis III: Pharaoh of the 18th Dynasty (New Kingdom).

Thutmosis IV: Pharaoh of the 18th Dynasty (New Kingdom).

Tiberius: Tiberius Julius Caesar Augustus (42 BC–AD 37), Roman emperor of the Julio-Claudian dynasty.

Tiye: Ancient Egyptian queen, Great Royal Wife of Amenophis III, 18th Dynasty (New Kingdom).

Triglyph: Block with vertical grooves and half grooves separating metopes (see entry above) in a frieze of the Doric order.

Tuna el-Gebel: Site of the ancient necropolis of Hermopolis Magna on the west bank of the Nile in Middle Egypt.

Tutankhamun: Pharaoh of the 18th Dynasty (New Kingdom).

Tympanum: Ancient tambourine-like handheld instrument.

Typhon: Ancient Greek deity and monster, half-man, half-animal, sometimes equated with the ancient Egyptian god Seth.

Unas: Last pharaoh of the 5th Dynasty (Old Kingdom).

Userkaf: Pharaoh who founded the 5th Dynasty (Old Kingdom).

Vitruvius: Marcus Vitruvius Pollio (1st century BC), Roman architect and engineer who wrote *De architectura libri decem* (The Ten Books on Architecture).

Wadi es-Sebua: Valley of the Lions, named after the sphinxes that lined the approach to the temple located here on the west bank of the Nile in Lower Nubia.

Wadi Hammamat: Dry riverbed in the Eastern Desert of Egypt, ancient Egyptian quarrying area for gold and one of the most important routes linking the Nile and the Red Sea. Also a source of greywacke, a special stone.

Zawyet el-Maiyitin: Village near the site of the Middle Egyptian city of Minya.

Glossar

Aba-Zepter: Herrschaftsinsignium und/oder Machtsymbol des Königs.

Abu Simbel: Stätte zweier von König Ramses II. in Nubien, Südägypten, erbauter Felsentempel.

Abydos: Antike Stadt und bedeutende Nekropole westlich des Nils in Oberägypten. Angebliche Grablege des Gottes Osiris, Herrscher des Jenseits.

Acherai: Eje II., als Nachfolger von Tutanchamun Pharao der altägyptischen 18. Dynastie (Neues Reich).

Ad-Dakka: Ort in Unternubien, südlich von Assuan

Ädikula: Hier: Kleines Bauwerk oder Heiligtum, von zwei oder mehr Säulen gerahmt.

Adyton: Abgeschlossener Raum an der Rückwand des inneren Hauptraumes eines Tempels, von außerhalb des Tempels nicht zugänglich.

Ahmose I.: Pharao, Begründer der altägyptischen 18. Dynastie (Neues Reich).

Ahmose Nefertari: Altägyptische Königin, Schwestergemahlin von Ahmose I. und Mutter von Amenophis I., 18. Dynastie (Neues Reich).

Al-Minya: Provinzhauptstadt westlich des Nils in Mittelägypten.

Alabastron: Alabastronopolis, antike Stadt nahe Tell el-Amarna. Auch ein kleines, schmal geformtes Gefäß, das ursprünglich im Alten Ägypten aus Alabaster gefertigt wurde.

Amenemhet I.: Pharao der altägyptischen 12. Dynastie (Mittleres Reich).

Amenemhet II.: Pharao der altägyptischen 12. Dynastie (Mittleres Reich).

Amenemhet III.: Pharao der altägyptischen 12. Dynastie (Mittleres Reich).

Amenirdis: Kuschitischer Name, beliebt für Prinzessinnen und Trägerinnen des Titels „Gottesgemahlin des Amun", insbesondere während der 25. Dynastie (Dritte Zwischenzeit).

Amenophis I.: Amenhotep I., Pharao der altägyptischen 18. Dynastie (Neues Reich).

Amenophis II.: Amenhotep II., Pharao der altägyptischen 18. Dynastie (Neues Reich).

Amenophis III.: Amenhotep III., Pharao der altägyptischen 18. Dynastie (Neues Reich).

Amensi-Pehor: Siehe Herihor.

Amenti: „Der Westliche", die altägyptische Unterwelt.

Amphore: Großer, langhalsiger Krug, der in der Antike als Speicher- und Transportgefäß diente.

Amun, Amun-Re: Allumfassender Reichsgott des Mittleren und Neuen Reiches, dessen Hauptresidenz in Theben, heute Luxor, lag.

Anubis: Gott mit Hunde- oder Schakalkopf, der die Totenriten, insbesondere die Mumifizierung, überwachte.

Anukis: Auch Anuket, Göttin des Nils, die in der Frühzeit der ägyptischen Geschichte mit der Nilschwemme und der Jagd in Verbindung gebracht wurde.

Apophis, Apopi: Pharao der altägyptischen 15. Dynastie (Zweite Zwischenzeit), also der Hyksos-Zeit.

Apries: Pharao der altägyptischen 26. Dynastie (Spätzeit).

Armant: Altgriechisch „Hermonthis", Ort westlich des Nils in Oberägypten.

Assyrer: Antikes Volk aus Mesopotamien (Zweistromland).

Atef-Krone: Von Osiris und dem Pharao getragene Krone, bestehend aus einem langen Hut in der Mitte und Federn an den Seiten, gelegentlich durch ein Hörnerpaar ergänzt.

Athlophoros: Altgriechisch für „der/die Siegreiche" (Menschen, Pferde).

Atum: Große Urgottheit der Ägypter, Schöpfer- und Himmelsgott.

Augustus: Erster römischer Kaiser (63 v. Chr. – 14 n. Chr.), auch Oktavian genannt, der nach dem Tode Julius Cäsars die Herrschaft übernahm (Begründer der julisch-claudischen Dynastie).
Bakenranef, Bocchoris: Pharao der altägyptischen 24. Dynastie (Dritte Zwischenzeit).
Basch-en-Aten: Siehe Echnaton.
Basilikogrammate: Altägyptischer Beamter, königlicher Sekretär oder Schreiber.
Bechten: Mythisches fernes Königreich, eventuell in Asien, das in Ramessiden-Texten erwähnt ist, insbesondere auf der Sandsteinstele aus der Tempelanlage von Karnak, die Prisse 1846 nach Frankreich brachte.
Beni Hassan: Nekropole aus Felsgräbern in der Nähe von Al-Minya in Mittelägypten.
Bes: Gott der Zeugung und Geburt, Beschützer von Wöchnerinnen, Wächter über Schlafende.
Biban el-Muluk: Altägyptische Nekropole, bekannt unter der Bezeichnung „Tal der Könige“.
Bintanat: Altägyptische Prinzessin, Tochter von Ramses II. und seiner Frau Isisnofret, 19. Dynastie (Neues Reich).
Bukranion: Schmuckmotiv, Nachbildung eines Rinderschädels.
Bündelsäule, Lotus-Bündelsäule: Säule mit einem konvex kannelierten Schaft aus Darstellungen einzelner Lotusstängel und einem Kapitell mit zumeist geschlossenen Blütenblättern.
Caracalla: Marcus Aurelius Antoninus, genannt Caracalla (188–217 n. Chr.), römischer Kaiser der severischen Dynastie.
Chaemhat: Genannt Mahu, königlicher Schreiber und Vorsteher der beiden Scheunen von Ober- und Unterägypten, 18. Dynastie (Neues Reich), bestattet in Grab Nr. TT 57.
Chafre: Siehe Chephren.
Champollion: Jean-François Champollion (1790–1832), französischer Orientalist und Ägyptologe.
Cheker-Fries: Abschlussornament an Wandflächen, Reihung stilisierter gebündelter und geknoteter Pflanzen.
Chendjer: Thronname Userkare, Pharao der altägyptischen 13. Dynastie (Zweite Zwischenzeit).
Chenoboskion: Antike Stadt westlich des Nils in Oberägypten, heute Nag Hammadi.
Cheops: Altägyptisch Chufu, Pharao der altägyptischen 4. Dynastie (Altes Reich).
Chephren: Altägyptisch Chafre oder Chaefre, Pharao der altägyptischen 4. Dynastie (Altes Reich).
Chnum: Altägyptische Gottheit, ursprünglich assoziiert mit der Nilflut; später wurde ihr der Temple von Elephantine gewidmet.
Chons: Gott, der mit dem Neumond assoziiert ist, Sohn von Amun und Mut.
Chufu: Siehe Cheops.
Claudius: Tiberius Claudius Nero Germanicus (10 v. Chr. – 54 n. Chr.), römischer Kaiser (julisch-claudische Dynastie).
Cloisonné: Zellenschmelz, kunsthandwerkliche Technik der Emaillearbeit.
Deir el-Bersche: Ort östlich des Nils in Mittelägypten, antike Nekropole von Hermopolis Magna.
Deir el-Medina: Ruinen einer Arbeitersiedlung und einer Nekropole im antiken Theben (gegenüber von Luxor am Westufer des Nils).
Dendera: Ort westlich des Nils in Oberägypten, Stätte eines Tempels der Göttin Hathor.
Dendur: Ehemals Ort westlich des Nils in Unternubien, heute vom Nassersee überflutet.
Djedkare, Isesi: Griechisch Tancheres, Pharao der altägyptischen 5. Dynastie (Altes Reich).
Djehutihotep: Oberägyptischer Gaufürst und Hohepriester in der 12. Dynastie (Mittleres Reich).
Dromos: Gang oder Korridor, Zugang.
Dschabal as-Silsila: Altägyptischer Sandsteinbruch in Oberägypten.
Echnaton: Amenophis IV., später Echnaton, Pharao der altägyptischen 18. Dynastie (Neues Reich). Erhob die altägyptische Gottheit Aton, die in Gestalt der Sonnenscheibe verehrt wurde, zum obersten und beinahe einzigen Gott Ägyptens.
Edfu: Ort westlich des Nils in Oberägypten, Stätte eines dem Gott Horus geweihten Tempels.
Eje: Siehe Acherai.
El-Assasif: Nekropole in Theben-West.

Elephantine: Flussinsel im Nil, bei Assuan, seit prädynastischer Zeit bis in die Gegenwart bewohnt.

Epiphi: Dritter Monat der Jahreszeit Schemu nach dem altägyptischen Kalender, die der Periode Mai bis Juni nach dem gregorianischen Kalender entspricht.

Esna: Ort am westlichen Ufer des Nils in Oberägypten.

Fellache: Aus dem Arabischen übernommene Bezeichnung für einen Kleinbauern oder Angehörigen der sesshaften ländlichen Bevölkerung.

Gerf Hussein: Stätte eines Tempels von Ramses II. südlich von Assuan in Nubien; Teile des Tempels wurden bei den Rettungsgrabungen in Nubien abgetragen, da sie andernfalls vom Nassersee überflutet worden wären.

Gizeh: Ort in der Nähe des heutigen Kairo, Stätte der großen Pyramiden.

Guilloche: Muster aus ineinander verwickelten und einander überlappenden Linien.

Gynaeceum: Gynaikaion, Gemächer der Frauen in antiken griechischen Häusern.

Haremhab: Letzter Pharao der altägyptischen 18. Dynastie (Neues Reich), der seine Laufbahn als General begann und am Ende der Amarna-Zeit Pharao wurde.

Haroeris: Gott, Horus der Große oder der Alte.

Hathor: Göttin der Liebe und Schönheit sowie Herrin des Westens, Behüterin der Toten in der Unterwelt.

Hatschepsut: Altägyptische Pharaonin, Halbschwester und Gemahlin von Thutmosis II., 18. Dynastie (Neues Reich).

Heka: Personifikation der Magie, göttliche Schöpferkraft.

Hemispeos: Felsentempel, bei dem Teile außerhalb des Felsens frei stehen.

Heptanomia: Sieben Gaue (antike Verwaltungsbezirke) in Mittelägypten; Prisse' Text zu Tell el-Amarna bezieht sich auf den siebten Gau.

Herihor: General, der am Übergang von der altägyptischen 20. Dynastie zur 21. Dynastie (Neues Reich) in Theben lebte und in dieser Zeit einen Teil des Landes unter seine Herrschaft brachte.

Hermonthis: Siehe Armant.

Hermopolis Magna: Antike Stadt westlich des Nils in Mittelägypten, heute el-Aschmunein, mit der Nekropole Tuna el-Gebel.

Hor-Amun: Verbindung des Harpokrates (des kindlichen Horus) mit Amun.

Horus: Himmelsgott, Königsgott u. a.

Hypogäum: Unterirdischer Grabbau, oft mehrere Gräber.

Hypostyl: Säulensaal eines ägyptischen Tempels.

Hypselis: Altägyptischer Ort in Oberägypten, heutiges Qus.

Imiseba: Chef der Tempelschreiber des Amun, 20. Dynastie (Neues Reich), usurpierte die Grabanlage von Nebamun, Grab Nr. TT 65.

Ipet: Auch Opet, Göttin der Fruchtbarkeit, Zeugung und des Schutzes, der während des jährlichen Ipet-Festes (auch Opet-Fest) gehuldigt wurde.

Isis: Göttin der Magie, der Mutterschaft, Gemahlin des Osiris, Mutter des Horus.

Isisnofret: Große königliche Gemahlin von Ramses II.

Kadesch: Antike Stadt am Orontes, im heutigen Syrien gelegen, Schauplatz von Schlachten zwischen den Ägyptern und verschiedenen nahöstlichen Königreichen. Die berühmteste Schlacht schlug hier Ramses II.

Kafa: Ägyptische Bezeichnung für die Minoer.

Kalabscha: Stätte südlich von Assuan, im Nassersee versunken, nahe des Assuan-Staudamms wiederaufgebaut.

Kalathos: Arbeitskorb (hier antike Vasenform) aus unterschiedlichen Materialien.

Kanope: In Kanopenkrügen oder -vasen wurden die Eingeweide des mumifizierten Leichnams separat beigesetzt.

Karnak: Stätte des größten Amun-Tempels, nördlich von Luxor am Ostufer des Nils in Oberägypten; die Königsliste, die Prisse entfernte und die sich heute im Louvre befindet, stammt von hier.

Kartusche: In der Hieroglyphenschrift verwendete ovale Umrandung des Königsnamens, Symbol der Unendlichkeit.

Kaschta: Pharao der kuschitischen 25. Dynastie (Dritte Zwischenzeit).

Katarakt: Stromschnelle im Nil, besonders in Oberägypten.

Kleopatra: Kleopatra VII. (69–30 v. Chr.), Pharaonin und letzte Königin der Ptolemäer.

Kom el-Ahmar: Hierakonpolis, eine Kapitale im prädynastischen Oberägypten. Kom el-Ahmar heißen viele Stätten in Ägypten, denn der Begriff bezeichnet Hügel aus roten Scherben, die man dort gefunden hat.

Kom Ombo: Überreste einer ausgedehnten Nekropole und des Tempels von Kom Ombo in Oberägypten.

Krater: Antike Vasenform für Wein-Wasser-Gemisch.

Krummstab: Ebenso wie der Wedel Bestandteil des altägyptischen Königsornats, symbolisiert die beaufsichtigende Seite des Königs.

Kuban: Contra-Pselchis, antiker Ort bei Ad-Dakka, Unternubien.

Lambris: Wandverkleidung im unteren Bereich der Wand eines Innenraumes.

Lekythos: Vase zur Aufbewahrung von Olivenöl.

Lepsius: Karl Richard Lepsius (1810–1884), deutscher Archäologe und Ägyptologe.

Luxor: Moderne Stadt östlich des Nils in Oberägypten; ab dem Mittleren Reich religiöse Hauptstadt Ägyptens.

Lyra: Leierartiges Zupfinstrument.

Maat: Göttin der kosmischen Ordnung und Gerechtigkeit.

Maketaton: Altägyptische Prinzessin, Tochter Echnatons.

Mammisi: Kleiner Tempel in der Nähe der Front eines altägyptischen Haupttempels, auch als Geburtshaus bekannt, denn dort wurde die Geburt der Kindgottheit, generell von Horus und des Königs als Horus gefeiert.

Mastaba: Altägyptischer Grabbau in Gestalt einer Lehmziegelbank, findet sich in traditioneller Architektur.

Medinet Habu: Stätte des Totentempels von Ramses III. und anderen Herrschern von Theben.

Memnonium: Siehe Ramesseum.

Memphis: Hauptstadt des ersten Gaus von Unterägypten und während eines Großteils der altägyptischen Geschichte Verwaltungshauptstadt des Landes.

Menes: Pharao, der als Gründer der altägyptischen 1. Dynastie (auch Frühdynastische Zeit) genannt wird.

Menkare: Siehe Mykerinos.

Menkheperre: Thronname von Thutmosis III.

Mentuhotep II.: Pharao der altägyptischen 11. Dynastie (Mittleres Reich).

Merenptah, Meneptah: Pharao der altägyptischen 19. Dynastie (Neues Reich).

Merenre: Merenre II. oder Nemtiemsaef II., Sohn von Pepi II., Pharao der altägyptischen 6. Dynastie (Altes Reich).

Merire: Thronname von Pepi I., Pharao der altägyptischen 6. Dynastie (Altes Reich).

Meritaton: Altägyptische Prinzessin, Tochter Echnatons.

Merkur: Römische Gottheit, Götterbote sowie Gott der Händler und Diebe.

Meroe: Hauptstadt des historischen Reiches von Kusch (ca. 400 v. Chr. – 300 n. Chr.), im heutigen Sudan gelegen.

Mesori: Vierter Monat der Jahreszeit Schemu nach dem altägyptischen Kalender, die der Periode Juni bis Juli nach dem gregorianischen Kalender entspricht.

Metope: Raum zwischen zwei Triglyphen bei einem Fries der dorischen Ordnung. Siehe Triglyphe.

Monthherchepeschef: Altägyptischer Prinz, Sohn von Ramses II., auch Name eines Sohnes von Ramses III.

Mut: Himmelsgöttin, symbolische Mutter des Pharaos.

Mykerinos: Altägyptisch Menkare, Pharao der altägyptischen 4. Dynastie (Altes Reich).

Nacht-hor-Ammon: Hohepriester unter Pharao Eje.

Naharina: Altägyptische Bezeichnung für Nordsyrien.

Naos: Kultraum oder Kernbereich eines Tempels.

Naqa: Auch Naga, Überreste einer antiken Stadt, im heutigen Sudan, die u. a. zum Königreich Meroe gehörte.

Necho II.: Pharao der altägyptischen 26. Dynastie (Spätzeit).

Neferkare: Thronname von Pepi II., Pharao der altägyptischen 6. Dynastie (Altes Reich).

Neith: Eine der vier Schutzgöttinnen der Horussöhne.

Nektanebos: Nektanebos II., Pharao der altägyptischen 30. Dynastie (Spätzeit).

Nemes-Kopftuch: Gestreiftes dreieckiges Tuch, Bestandteil des altägyptischen Königsornats.

Nephthys: Eine der vier Schutzgöttinnen der Horussöhne.

Nilgott: Hapi, göttliche Erscheinungsform der Nilschwemme.

Nofretete: Große königliche Gemahlin (Hauptgemahlin) von Echnaton, Pharao der altägyptischen 18. Dynastie (Neues Reich).

Obelisk: Spitzsäule oder hoher, sich nach oben verjüngender Steinpfeiler mit pyramidenförmiger Spitze und quadratischem Grundriss; Gedenkmonument im Alten Ägypten.

Onager: Asiatischer Wildesel (*Equus hemionus*).

Opet: Siehe Ipet.

Orontes: In der Antike Name des Flusses, der durch den Libanon, Syrien und die Türkei fließt, heute Nahr al-Asi.

Osiris: Gott des Jenseits, Herrscher über das Totenreich.

Paser: Wesir der 19. Dynastie, diente unter Sethos I. und Ramses II. (Neues Reich).

Palmwedel-Kapitell: Kapitell, das mit Darstellungen nach außen gebogener Palmwedel verziert ist.

Pepi I.: Pharao der altägyptischen 6. Dynastie (Altes Reich).

Pepi II.: Pharao der altägyptischen 6. Dynastie (Altes Reich).

Peripteraltempel: Peripteros oder Ringhallentempel.

Petosiris: Altägyptischer Hohepriester des Thot, bestattet in Tuna el-Gebel.

Phaophi: Zweiter Monat der Jahreszeit Achet nach dem altägyptischen Kalender, die der Periode Juli bis Oktober nach dem gregorianischen Kalender entspricht.

Pharao: Bezeichnung für König mit der wörtlichen Bedeutung „großes Haus" – da der König derjenige war, der im „großen Haus", also im Palast seinen Sitz hatte. Der Begriff wurde ab dem Neuen Reich verwendet.

Pharmuti: Vierter Monat der Jahreszeit Peret nach dem altägyptischen Kalender, die der Periode November bis Februar nach dem gregorianischen Kalender entspricht.

Phre: Bedeutung „die Sonne", Sonnengott.

Pije: Auch Pianchi, Pharao der kuschitischen 25. Dynastie (Dritte Zwischenzeit).

Pronaos: Vorhalle, durch die man in den eigentlichen Kultraum (Naos) eines Tempels gelangt.

Propylon: Torbau, im Regelfall Eingangsgebäude vor einem Tempelbezirk.

Psammetich I.: Pharao und Begründer der altägyptischen 26. Dynastie (Spätzeit).

Pschent: Altägyptische Doppelkrone.

Psinaula: Siehe Tell el-Amarna.

Ptahschepses: Beamter und Hohepriester des Ptah, 5. Dynastie (Altes Reich), bestattet in einer Mastaba in Sakkara.

Ptolemäus: Claudius Ptolemäus (um 100–168 oder 178 n. Chr.), griechischer Wissenschaftler, der sich besonders mit Mathematik und Astronomie beschäftigte. Nach ihm wurde das ptolemäische Weltbild benannt.

Ptolemaios V. Epiphanes: Pharao der ptolemäischen Dynastie.

Ptolemaios VIII. Euergetes II.: Pharao der ptolemäischen Dynastie.

Ptolemaios IX. Soter II. Lathyros: Pharao der ptolemäischen Dynastie.

Punt: Eine Region, aus der die alten Ägypter wertvolle Rohstoffe wie Gold, Ebenholz und Elfenbein importierten. Die genaue geografische Lage ist noch umstritten.

Pylon: Torturmpaar mit verbindendem Torüberbau am Eingang zu Grab- oder Tempelanlagen.

Qina: Verwaltungshauptstadt des gleichnamigen Gouvernements westlich des Nils in Oberägypten, in der griechisch-römischen Antike auch Kaine genannt.

Qurna: Siehe Scheich Abd el-Qurna.

Qusair: Al-Qusair, ptolemäisch Myos Hormos, antike Stadt am Roten Meer.

Ramesseum: Tempel in Theben-West, in dem der Totenkult für Ramses II. stattfand.

Ramses I.: Pharao, Begründer der altägyptischen 19. Dynastie (Neues Reich).

Ramses II.: Pharao der altägyptischen 19. Dynastie (Neues Reich).

Ramses III.: Pharao der altägyptischen 20. Dynastie (Neues Reich).

Ramses VII.: Pharao der altägyptischen 20. Dynastie (Neues Reich).

Ramses IX.: Pharao der altägyptischen 20. Dynastie (Neues Reich).

Retjenu: Altägyptische Bezeichnung für die zwischen der Wüste Negev und dem Fluss Orontes gelegene Region.

Rhyton: Einhenkeliges Gefäß zum Ausgießen von Trankopfern.

Sagum: Römischer Wollmantel, aus einem rechteckigen Stoffstück gefertigt, in der Regel von Soldaten über der Rüstung getragen.

Sais: Altägyptische Stadt im westlichen Nildelta, Hauptstadt der 26. Dynastie.

Sakkara: Altägyptische Nekropole westlich des Nils, südlich von Kairo gelegen.

Samum: Sand- oder Staubsturm mit trockener, heißer Wüstenluft.

Satis: Göttin, Herrin von Elephantine und Spenderin des „kühlen Wassers, das aus Elephantine kommt".

Saujet el-Meitin: Ort in der Nähe der mittelägyptischen Stadt Al-Minya.

Schabaka: Pharao der kuschitischen 25. Dynastie (Dritte Zwischenzeit).

Scheich Abd el-Qurna: Auch Qurna, Ort einer bedeutenden Nekropole des Neuen Reiches westlich des Nils, gegenüber der modernen Stadt Luxor gelegen.

Scheich Said: Ort in Mittelägypten bei Deir el-Bersche, eine der antiken Nekropolen von Hermopolis Magna.

Schendit: Schurz, der bis in die Erste Zwischenzeit allein vom Pharao getragen wurde; danach übernahm auch die Oberschicht diese Art der Bekleidung.

Sebbakhin: Einheimische Bauern, die auf der Suche nach Dünger archäologische Stätten ausgruben und zerstörten.

Sedeinga: Nubische Kultstätte mit einem vermutlich der Königin Teje geweihten Tempel, im heutigen Sudan gelegen.

Sekenenra: Auch Seqenenre Tao, Sekenenre Taa, Herrscher über Theben in der 17. Dynastie (Zweite Zwischenzeit).

Sekos: Abgegrenzter Bezirk eines Heiligtums, Kultraum eines Tempels.

Selket: Göttin, die vor Skorpionstichen schützte; eine der vier Schutzgöttinnen der Horussöhne.

Semna: Altägyptische Befestigungsanlage (12. Dynastie) in Nubien, im heutigen Sudan gelegen.

Sesostris I.: Pharao der 12. Dynastie (Mittleres Reich), Sohn von Amenemhet I.

Setem: Sem-Priester, Hohepriester des Osiris.

Seth: Wüstengott, Gott des Chaos.

Sethos I.: Pharao der altägyptischen 19. Dynastie (Neues Reich).

Sethos II.: Pharao der altägyptischen 19. Dynastie (Neues Reich).

Sistrum: Handklapper, verwendet beim Isis-Kult.

Skarabäus: Heiliger Pillendreher (*Scarabaeus sacer*), Blatthornkäfer; im Alten Ägypten mit dem Sonnengott assoziiert und als Amulett oder Siegel (zumeist aus Stein oder Keramik) verwendet.

Sobek: Sonnengott in Gestalt des Nilkrokodils.

Sobekhotep: Pharao der altägyptischen 13. Dynastie (Zweite Zwischenzeit)

Sokar: Totengott, dargestellt mit Falkenkopf.

Speos: Felsentempel.

Sphinx: Statue eines männlichen Löwen, die mit einem Männer- (Androsphinx), Frauen- (Gynosphinx), Widder- (Criosphinx), Falken- oder Sperberkopf (Hierakosphinx) versehen sein kann.

Surmé: Indisches Wort für Antimonpulver, das im Alten Ägypten für Augenschminke verwendet wurde.

Sykomore: Maulbeer-Feige (*Ficus sycomorus*), im Alten Ägypten als „Himmelsbaum" verehrt, mit der Göttin Hathor assoziiert.

Taharqa: Pharao der kuschitischen 25. Dynastie (Dritte Zwischenzeit).

Takelot I.: Pharao der altägyptischen 22. Dynastie (Dritte Zwischenzeit).

Talmis: Altägyptischer Ort, heute Kalabscha.

Tanis: Altägyptischer Ort im nordöstlichen Nildelta, königliche Hauptstadt und Nekropole der 21. Dynastie.

Tausret: Große königliche Gemahlin von Pharao Sethos II.; mit ihrer Herrschaft als Pharaonin endete die 19. Dynastie (Neues Reich).

Taweret: Göttin der Geburt und Fruchtbarkeit, Schutzgöttin schwangerer Frauen, oft als Nilpferd dargestellt.

Teje: Altägyptische Königin, Gemahlin von Pharao Amenophis III., 18. Dynastie (Neues Reich).

Tell Abu-Sefeh: Altägyptisch Tjaru oder Sile; Ort im ägyptischen Ostdelta, altägyptische Festungsanlage.

Tell el-Amarna: Ort östlich des Nils in Mittelägypten. In der Nähe befinden sich die Ruinen der durch Echnaton gegründeten altägyptischen Stadt Achet-Aton.

Tell el-Maschuta: Ort im ägyptischen Ostdelta, ursprünglich Abou Kachah, nach Neugründung unter Pharao Necho II. als Per Tem Tjeku bezeichnet.

Teti: Pharao, Begründer der altägyptischen 6. Dynastie (Altes Reich).

Thebais: Gegend um die altägyptische Stadt Theben, umfasste die südlichen Gaue von Oberägypten.

Theben: Stadt am oberen Nil, mehrfach Hauptstadt Ägyptens und (dauerhafter) religiöse Hauptstadt.

Thot: Gott der Weisheit und der Schreiber, häufig mit dem Kopf eines Ibis oder eines Pavians dargestellt.

Thutmosis II.: Pharao der altägyptischen 18. Dynastie (Neues Reich).

Thutmosis III.: Pharao der altägyptischen 18. Dynastie (Neues Reich).

Thutmosis IV.: Pharao der altägyptischen 18. Dynastie (Neues Reich).

Tiberius: Tiberius Iulius Caesar Augustus (42 v. Chr. – 37 n. Chr.), römischer Kaiser der julisch-claudischen Dynastie.

Triglyphe: Dreischlitzplatte mit senkrechten vollen und halben Rillen, die in einem Fries der dorischen Ordnung zwischen den Metopen angeordnet ist (siehe Metope).

Tuna el-Gebel: Ort westlich des Nils in Mittelägypten, antike Nekropole von Hermopolis Magna.

Tutanchamun: Pharao der altägyptischen 18. Dynastie (Neues Reich).

Tympanon: Antike Handpauke.

Typhon: Griechische Gottheit und Ungeheuer, teilweise mit dem altägyptischen Gott Seth gleichgesetzt.

Unas: Letzter Pharao der altägyptischen 5. Dynastie (Altes Reich).

Userkaf: Pharao, Begründer der altägyptischen 5. Dynastie (Altes Reich).

Vitruv: Marcus Vitruvius Pollio (1. Jh. v. Chr.), römischer Architekt und Ingenieur. Er verfasste die überlieferte Schrift *De architectura libri decem (Zehn Bücher über Architektur)*.

Wadi es-Sebua: Tal der Löwen, Ort westlich des Nils in Unternubien, benannt nach den Sphingen, die den Zugang zum dortigen Tempel säumten.

Wadi Hammamat: Trockenflusstal in den Bergen der Arabischen Wüste, zentraler Abschnitt einer der wichtigsten Verbindungen zwischen Nil und Rotem Meer; hier wurde im Alten Ägypten Gold abgebaut. Auch Gesteinsvorkommen von Grauwacke, einer besonderen Art von Sandstein.

Wedel: Ebenso wie der Krummstab Bestandteil des altägyptischen Königsornats. Wedel wurden zum Korndreschen benutzt und symbolisierten die Seite des Königs, die Missetäter bestrafte und die staatliche Ordnung wahrte.

Ziborium: Gefäß, Speisekelch mit festem Deckel.

Glossaire

Aba (pat) : Sceptre, insigne de la royauté et du pouvoir divin.

Abd el-Gournah : Également connu sous le nom de Gournah, site d'une grande nécropole du Nouvel Empire, sur la rive gauche du Nil, en face de Louxor.

Abou Simbel (Abousambil, Ibsambout) : Site de deux temples taillés dans la roche, construits par le pharaon Ramsès II en Nubie, en Égypte méridionale.

Abydos : Ancienne ville et nécropole de Haute-Égypte, sur la rive gauche du Nil. Lieu supposé de la sépulture du dieu Osiris, souverain de l'autre monde.

Adytum : Chambre close, inaccessible de l'extérieur du temple, située derrière le mur du fond de la cella, la plus grande salle du temple.

Ahmès-Néfertari (Amès Nofré-Atari, Ahmès-Nofretari) : Reine, sœur et grande épouse d'Amôsis Ier et mère d'Aménophis Ier, XVIIIe dynastie (Nouvel Empire).

Aïchesi : Voir Imiseba.

Akhénaton (Khouenaten) : Aménophis IV, par la suite Akhénaton, pharaon de la XVIIIe dynastie (Nouvel Empire). Il éleva la divinité Aton, vénérée sous la forme du disque solaire, au rang de dieu principal et presque unique de l'Égypte.

Alabastron : Alabastronopolis, ville antique située près de Tell el-Amarna. Ce mot désigne également une petite jarre au corps étroit, sculptée dans de l'albâtre dans l'Égypte ancienne.

Aménardis (Aménéritès, Amnartaïs) : Nom couchite fréquemment porté par des princesses et détentrices du titre « épouse divine d'Amon », en particulier pendant la XXVe dynastie (Troisième Période Intermédiaire).

Aménophis Ier (Amounôph, Aménophis Ier) : Amenhotep Ier, pharaon de la XVIIIe dynastie (Nouvel Empire).

Aménophis II (Amounôph, Aménophis II) : Amenhotep II, pharaon de la XVIIIe dynastie (Nouvel Empire).

Aménophis III (Amounôph, Aménophis III) : Amenhotep III, pharaon de la XVIIIe dynastie (Nouvel Empire).

Amenti : « L'Occident », royaume des morts dans l'Égypte ancienne.

Amménémès Ier (Amenemhé Ier) : Pharaon de la XIIe dynastie (Moyen Empire).

Amménémès II (Amenemhé II) : Pharaon de la XIIe dynastie (Moyen Empire).

Amménémès III (Aménemhé III) : Pharaon de la XIIe dynastie (Moyen Empire).

Amon-Se-Pehôr : Voir Hérihor.

Amon, Amon-Rê (Amon-Ra) : Dieu suprême des Moyen et Nouvel Empires dont la résidence principale se trouvait à Thèbes, aujourd'hui Louxor.

Amôsis (Ahmès) : Pharaon, fondateur de la XVIIIe dynastie (Nouvel Empire) de l'Égypte ancienne.

Amphore : Grand vase au long col utilisé dans l'Antiquité pour conserver et transporter les liquides.

Anoukis (Anouké) : Déesse du Nil qui, au début de l'histoire égyptienne, était associée aux crues du Nil et à la chasse.

Anubis (Noub) : Divinité à tête de chien qui présidait aux rites funéraires, en particulier la momification.

Note : Le glossaire comprend les noms de personnes, de lieux et de concepts tels qu'ils sont écrits de nos jours. Si l'orthographe utilisée par Émile Prisse d'Avennes diverge de l'usage actuel, elle est restituée entre parenthèses.

Apophis (Apapi) : Pharaon de la XVe dynastie (Deuxième Période Intermédiaire), c'est-à-dire la période des Hyksos.

Apriès : Pharaon de la XXVIe dynastie (Dernière Période).

Assyriens : Peuple de la Mésopotamie antique.

Atef (Claft) : Couronne portée par Osiris et par le pharaon, composée d'un long chapeau central flanqué de plumes et, parfois, surmonté d'une paire de cornes.

Athlophoros (Athlophore) : En grec ancien, « victorieux » (chevaux, hommes).

Atoum (Atmou) : Premier dieu égyptien, créateur d'autres dieux et d'une divinité solaire.

Auguste : Premier empereur romain (63 av. J.-C. – 14 ap. J.-C.), né Caius Octavianus (Octavien), maître de Rome après la mort de Jules César (fondateur de la dynastie julio-claudienne).

Ay (Achéraï, Aï) : Successeur de Toutânkhamon et pharaon de la XVIIIe dynastie (Nouvel Empire).

Basilicogrammate : Personnalité officielle dans l'Égypte ancienne, secrétaire ou greffier royal.

Baskh-en-Aten (Bakh, Basch-n-Aten) : Voir Akhénaton.

Bekhten (Bischtan) : Royaume lointain et mythique, peut-être en Asie, cité dans les textes de l'époque des Ramsès, en particulier ceux de la stèle de grès prise dans le complexe du temple de Karnak et rapportée en France par Prisse en 1846.

Beni Hassan (Beni-Haçen) : Cimetière de tombes taillées dans la roche, près de Minya en Moyenne-Égypte.

Bentanat (Batianti) : Fille de Ramsès II et de son épouse Isis-Nofret, XIXe dynastie (Nouvel Empire).

Bercheh : Voir Deir el-Bercha.

Bès : Divinité de la naissance, protectrice des femmes en couches, gardienne de ceux qui dorment.

Biban el-Moulouk : Ancienne nécropole égyptienne, connue sous le nom de « Vallée des rois ».

Bokenrenef, Bocchoris (Bekenranef) : Pharaon de la XXIVe dynastie (Troisième Période Intermédiaire).

Bucrane (Bucrâne) : Motif ornemental représentant un crâne de bœuf.

Calathos : Panier (ici un ancien récipient destiné à tenir le contenu au frais), tressé avec différents matériaux.

Caracalla : Marcus Aurelius Antoninus, dit Caracalla (188–217 ap. J.-C.), empereur romain de la dynastie sévérienne.

Cartouche : Encadrement elliptique destiné à recevoir le nom d'un roi, symbole de l'infini, employé dans les inscriptions hiéroglyphiques de l'Égypte ancienne.

Cataracte : Grandes chutes d'eaux du Nil, particulièrement en Haute-Égypte.

Chabaka (Sabacon) : Pharaon de la XXVe dynastie couchite (Troisième Période Intermédiaire).

Champollion : Jean-François Champollion (1790–1832), orientaliste et égyptologue français qui fut le premier à déchiffrer correctement les hiéroglyphes égyptiens.

Chapiteau dactyliforme ou à feuilles de palmier : Chapiteau constitué de feuilles de palmier convexes.

Cheikh-Sayd : El-Cheikh Saïd, site de Moyenne-Égypte, situé près de Deir el-Bercha, où se trouve une autre ancienne nécropole dépendant d'Hermopolis Magna.

Chénoboscion : Ancienne ville de la rive gauche du Nil en Haute-Égypte, aujourd'hui Nag Hammadi.

Ciboire (Ciborion) : Récipient, verre doté d'un couvercle.

Claude Ier : Tiberius Claudius Nero Germanicus (10 av. J.-C. – 54 ap. J.-C.), empereur romain (dynastie julio-claudienne).

Cléopâtre : Cléopâtre VII (69–30 av. J.-C.), pharaonne et dernière reine ptolémaïque d'Égypte.

Cloisonné : Technique d'émaillage consistant à séparer les couleurs à l'aide de fils ou de bandes de métal.

Colonne à faisceau/en bouquet de lotus : Colonne égyptienne, composée d'un fût convexe représentant des tiges de lotus et d'un chapiteau en forme de bouton de lotus.

Cratère : Vase de la Grèce antique dans lequel on mêlait le vin et l'eau.

Dado (Lambris, Soubassement) : Partie inférieure d'un mur intérieur, entre la plinthe et la cimaise de fauteuil (dado).

Dakkah (Dakkeh) : Localité de Nubie, au sud d'Assouan.

Deir el-Bercha (Bercheh) : Village de la rive droite du Nil en Moyenne-Égypte, site de l'ancienne nécropole d'Hermopolis Magna.

Deir el-Medineh (Deyr el-Medineh) : Ruines du village et du cimetière d'artisans de l'ancienne Thèbes (rive gauche du Nil, en face de Louxor).

Dendérah (Denderah) : Ville de la rive gauche du Nil en Haute-Égypte, site d'un temple consacré à la déesse Hathor.

Dendour : Autrefois ville de la rive gauche du Nil en Basse-Nubie, aujourd'hui engloutie dans les eaux du lac Nasser.

Djedkarê (Takare) : En grec Tancharès, aussi nommé Isési, pharaon de la Ve dynastie (Ancien Empire).

Djéhutihotep (Thouthotep) : Nomarque de Haute-Égypte et grand prêtre de la XIIe dynastie (Moyen Empire).

Dromos : Couloir, entrée d'un bâtiment, d'un tombeau.

Edfou : Ville de la rive gauche du Nil en Haute-Égypte, site d'un temple consacré au dieu Horus.

Édicule : Ici : Petit sanctuaire ou périmètre sacré, encadré de deux colonnes ou plus.

El-Assacif : Nécropole de Thèbes-ouest.

Éléphantine : Île du Nil à Assouan, habitée de l'époque prédynastique à l'ère moderne.

Epiphi (Épêp) : Troisième mois de la saison Chémou dans le calendrier de l'Égypte ancienne, correspondant à la période allant de mai à juin dans le calendrier grégorien.

Ermant (Erment) : En grec ancien « Hermonthis », ville de la rive gauche du Nil en Haute-Égypte.

Esna (Esné) : Ville de la rive gauche du Nil, en Haute-Égypte.

Fellah : Mot arabe signifiant paysan ou membre d'une population rurale sédentaire.

Fléau : Élément des insignes du pharaon de l'Égypte ancienne. Outil servant à battre les céréales, le fléau symbolisait le rôle joué par le roi de redresseur de torts et de gardien de l'ordre public.

Gebel el-Silsileh, Djébel Silsilèh (Silsilis) : Carrière de grès de l'Égypte ancienne, en Haute-Égypte.

Gerf Hussein (Guirché) : Site d'un temple de Ramsès II, au sud d'Assouan en Nubie, dont des portions ont été déplacées lors de la campagne de sauvegarde des monuments de Nubie, afin d'éviter l'engloutissement du temple par les eaux du lac Nasser.

Gizeh : Ville voisine du Caire, site des grandes pyramides.

Gournah : Voir Abd el-Gournah.

Guillochis : Motif ornemental formé de bandes entrecroisées et qui paraît tressé.

Gynécée : Appartement réservé aux femmes dans une maison de l'Antiquité grecque.

Hammamat : Voir Quadi Hammamat.

Haroéris (Haroëri) : Horus l'ancien, forme du dieu Horus.

Hatchepsout (Hatasou) : Pharaonne, demi-sœur et épouse du pharaon Touthmôsis II, XVIIIe dynastie (Nouvel Empire).

Hathor : Déesse de l'amour et de la beauté, et maîtresse de l'Occident qui accueillait les morts lors de leur passage vers les enfers.

Héka (Hake) : Dieu de la magie et de la créativité.

Hémispéos : Temple, en partie taillé dans la roche et en partie construit.

Heptanomis (Heptanomide) : Sept Nomes (subdivisions de l'Égypte ancienne), circonscription de la Moyenne-Égypte ; le texte de Prisse sur Tell el-Amarna se réfère au septième nome.

Hérihor : Général qui vécut à Thèbes au cours de la transition de la XXe à la XXIe dynastie (Nouvel Empire) et régna sur une partie du pays à cette époque.

Hermonthis : Voir Ermant.

Hermopolis Magna : Ancienne ville de la rive gauche du Nil en Moyenne-Égypte, aujourd'hui al-Ashmunayn, avec le cimetière de Tounah el-Gebel.

Hor-Amon (Hor-Ammon, Horammon) : Fusion d'Horus enfant et d'Amon (Harpocrate en grec ancien).

Horemheb : Dernier pharaon de la XVIIIe dynastie (Nouvel Empire), qui fut général avant de devenir pharaon à la fin de la période amarnienne.

Horus : Dieu du Ciel, dieu de la royauté.

Hypogée : Chambre tombale taillée dans la roche, souvent destinée à recevoir plusieurs sépultures.

Hypsèle (Hypselis) **:** Ancien site de Haute-Égypte, aujourd'hui Qûs.

Imiseba (Aïchesi) **:** Chef du sanctuaire d'Amon, greffier des comptes royaux, XXe dynastie (Nouvel Empire), usurpa la tombe de Nebamon, n° TT 65.

Isési : Voir Djedkarê.

Isis : Déesse de la magie et de la maternité, épouse d'Osiris et mère d'Horus.

Isis-Nofret (Isinofré) **:** Grande épouse royale du pharaon Ramsès II.

Kachta (Kachto) **:** Pharaon couchite de la XXVe dynastie (Troisième Période Intermédiaire).

Kalabsha (Kalabché) **:** Site au sud d'Assouan, aujourd'hui englouti dans les eaux du lac Nasser, déplacé près du grand barrage d'Assouan.

Karnak (Karnac) **:** Site du plus grand temple consacré à Amon, situé au nord de Louxor sur la rive droite du Nil, en Haute-Égypte ; Prisse s'y empara de la liste des rois qui se trouve aujourd'hui au Louvre.

Keftiou (Kafa, Kéfa) **:** Nom égyptien désignant les Minoens.

Khâemhat (Chamhati, Schamthé) **:** Aussi appelé Mahou, greffier royal et gardien des greniers royaux de Haute- et Basse-Égypte, XVIIIe dynastie (Nouvel Empire), inhumé dans la tombe n° TT 57.

Khafrê : Voir Khéphren.

Kheker (Khakerou) **:** Frise composée de plantes noueuses stylisées, le long de la cimaise des murs dans l'Égypte ancienne.

Khendjer (Rentor) **:** Nom de couronnement d'Ouserkarê, pharaon de la XIIIe dynastie (Deuxième Période Intermédiaire).

Khéops (Chéops) **:** Khoufou dans l'Égypte ancienne, pharaon de la IVe dynastie (Ancien Empire).

Khéphren (Chéphren, Schafré) **:** Khafrê dans l'Égypte ancienne, pharaon de la IVe dynastie (Ancien Empire).

Khnoum (Kneph) **:** Dieu associé d'abord à la crue du Nil ; par la suite lui était dédié le temple d'Éléphantine.

Khonsou (Khons) **:** Dieu associé à la nouvelle lune, fils d'Amon et de Mout.

Khoufou (Choufou, Schoufou) **:** Voir Khéops.

Kom el-Ahmar (Koum el-Ahmar) **:** Hiérakonpolis, une des capitales de la Haute-Égypte prédynastique. Le nom de Kom el-Ahmar, « monticule rouge », désigne de nombreux sites d'Égypte où l'on trouve des amas de tessons de poterie.

Kôm Ombo (Ombos) **:** Site d'une vaste nécropole de l'Égypte ancienne et du temple de Kôm Ombo en Haute-Égypte.

Lécythe (Lekythos) **:** Jarre à huile de la Grèce antique.

Lepsius : Karl Richard Lepsius (1810–1884), archéologue et égyptologue allemand.

Louxor (Louksor) **:** Ville moderne de Haute-Égypte, sur la rive droite du Nil ; capitale religieuse de l'Égypte à partir du Moyen Empire.

Lyre : Instrument de musique de l'Antiquité grecque, à cordes pincées, ressemblant à une harpe.

Maât (Tmei) **:** Déesse de l'ordre cosmique et de la justice.

Mâkhétaton (Mak-Aten) **:** Princesse de l'Égypte ancienne, fille du pharaon Akhénaton.

Mammisi (Eimisi) **:** Petite chapelle située près de la façade d'un temple égyptien, aussi connue sous l'appellation de « maison de la naissance » car c'est là qu'était célébrée la naissance du jeune dieu, généralement Horus et le roi sous les traits d'Horus.

Mastaba : Tombeau de l'Égypte ancienne, en forme de banc de briques crues, typique de l'architecture vernaculaire.

Médinet Habou (Medineh-Tabou) **:** Site du temple érigé en mémoire de Ramsès III et d'autres souverains de Thèbes.

Memnonium : Voir Ramesséum.

Memphis : Capitale du premier nome de Basse-Égypte et capitale administrative de l'Égypte pendant la majeure partie de son histoire.

Ménès : Selon la tradition, pharaon fondateur de la

première dynastie de l'Égypte ancienne (Première Période dynastique).
Menkaourê (Menkaré) : Voir Mycérinos.
Menkhéperrê (Rementor) : Nom de couronnement de Touthmôsis III.
Mentouhotep II (Mentouôpht) : Pharaon de la XIe dynastie (Moyen Empire).
Mercure : Dieu romain, messager des dieux et divinité des marchands et des voleurs.
Mérenptah (Menephtha, Mienptah) : Pharaon de la XIXe dynastie (Nouvel Empire).
Mérenrê (Réméran) : Mérenrê II ou Nemtyemsaf II, fils de Pépi II, pharaon de la VIe dynastie (Ancien Empire).
Méroé : Capitale du royaume de Couch (vers 400 av. J.-C. – 300 ap. J.-C.), aujourd'hui au Soudan.
Méryrê (Maïré) : Nom de couronnement de Pépi Ier, pharaon de la VIe dynastie (Ancien Empire).
Mérytaton (Meri-Aten) : Princesse de l'Égypte ancienne, fille du pharaon Akhénaton.
Mésori (Mesôré) : Dans le calendrier de l'Égypte ancienne, quatrième mois de la saison de Chémou, correspondant à la période allant de juin à juillet dans le calendrier grégorien.
Métope : Espace carré séparant deux triglyphes d'une frise dans l'ordre dorique. Voir triglyphe.
Minyah : Capitale de gouvernorat sur la rive gauche du Nil en Moyenne-Égypte.
Montuherkhepeshef (Mantouhichopchf, Monthixopeshef) : Prince de l'Égypte ancienne, fils de Ramsès II et nom d'un fils de Ramsès III.
Mout (Mauth) : Déesse mère, mère symbolique des pharaons.
Mycérinos (Mykerinus) : Menkaourê de l'Égypte ancienne, pharaon de la IVe dynastie (Ancien Empire).
Naga : Site des ruines d'une ancienne ville couchite, aujourd'hui au Soudan, qui faisait partie du royaume de Méroé.
Naharin (Naharina) : Dans l'Égypte ancienne, nom désignant le nord de la Syrie.
Nakht-Hor-Amon (Nacht-Hor-Ammon) : Grand prêtre sous le règne du pharaon Ay.
Naos : Sanctuaire d'un temple.
Nectanébo : Nectanébo II, pharaon de la XXXe dynastie (Dernière Période).
Néferkarê (Nofrekaré) : Nom de couronnement de Pépi II, pharaon de la VIe dynastie (Ancien Empire).
Néfertiti (Nofre-Ati) : Grande épouse royale d'Akhénaton, pharaon de la XVIIIe dynastie (Nouvel Empire).
Neith (Netpé) : L'une des quatre déesses protectrices des quatre fils d'Horus.
Nékao II : Pharaon de la XXVIe dynastie (Dernière Période).
Némès : Coiffe à rayures, portée par les pharaons de l'Égypte ancienne.
Néphtys : L'une des quatre déesses protectrices des quatre fils d'Horus.
Nil (divinité) (dieu Nil) : Hâpy, déification de la crue annuelle du Nil.
Obélisque : Bloc de pierre fuselé de grande taille, constituant une pyramide extrêmement resserrée, sur une base carrée : monument commémoratif dans l'Égypte ancienne.
Onagre : Âne sauvage *(Equus hemonius)* des Proche et Moyen Orients.
Opet : Aussi nommée Ipet, déesse de la fertilité, procréation et protection célébrée tous les ans par la fête d'Opet.
Oronte : Fleuve traversant le Liban, la Syrie et la Turquie.
Osiris : Dans l'Égypte ancienne, dieu de l'au-delà, des enfers et des morts.
Ouadi es-Seboua (Wady Esseboua) : Vallée des lions, ainsi nommée en raison de l'alignement de sphinx qui se trouve à l'approche du temple situé sur la rive gauche du Nil, en Basse-Nubie.
Ouadi Hammamat (el-Hamamat) : Lit asséché d'une rivière du désert oriental de l'Égypte, zone d'extraction de l'or dans l'Égypte ancienne et l'une des routes les plus importantes reliant le Nil à la mer Rouge. Site où l'on trouve également une roche particulière appelée grauwacke.
Ounas : Dernier pharaon de la Ve dynastie (Ancien Empire).
Ouserkaf (Ouserchéres) : Pharaon fondateur de la Ve dynastie (Ancien Empire).

Paopi (Paôpi) : Dans le calendrier de l'Égypte ancienne, deuxième mois de la saison d'Akhet, correspondant à la période allant de juillet à octobre dans le calendrier grégorien.

Paser (Poëri) : Vizir de la XIXe dynastie, sous le règne de Séthi Ier et Ramsès II (Nouvel Empire).

Pays de Pount : Région d'où les Égyptiens importaient des matières premières précieuses comme l'or, l'ébène et l'ivoire. Sa situation précise demeure incertaine.

Pépi Ier ([Maïre-]Papi): Pharaon de la VIe dynastie (Ancien Empire).

Pépi II : Pharaon de la VIe dynastie (Ancien Empire).

Pétosiris (Pet-Osiris) : Grand prêtre de Thot dans l'Égypte ancienne, inhumé à Tounah el-Gebel.

Pharaon : « Roi » ; littéralement « grande maison », au sens de celui qui résidait dans la grande maison était le roi. C'est sous le Nouvel Empire que ce terme commence à être employé.

Pharmouthi (Parmouté) : Dans le calendrier de l'Égypte ancienne, quatrième mois de la saison de Peret, correspondant à la période allant de novembre à février dans le calendrier grégorien.

Phré : Signification « le soleil », dieu du soleil.

Piye (Piankhi) : Aussi connu sous le nom de Piânkhi, pharaon couchite de la XXVe dynastie (Troisième Période Intermédiaire).

Pronaos : Salle permettant d'accéder au sanctuaire (naos).

Propylée : Portique, généralement situé à l'entrée de l'enceinte d'un temple.

Psammétik Ier : Pharaon fondateur de la XXVIe dynastie (Dernière Période).

Pschent : Double couronne de l'Égypte ancienne.

Psinaula : Voir Tell el-Amarna.

Ptahchepsès (Ptahasès) : Vizir et grand prêtre de Ptah, V^e^ dynastie (Ancien Empire), inhumé dans un mastaba d'Abousir, près de Saqqara.

Ptolémée : Claude Ptolémée (v. 100–v. 168 ou 178), astronome et mathématicien grec. La carte du monde ptolémaïque est ainsi appelée en référence à son nom.

Ptolémée V Épiphane (Ptolémée Épiphanes) : Pharaon de la dynastie ptolémaïque.

Ptolémée VIII Évergète II (Ptolémée Évergète II) : Pharaon de la dynastie ptolémaïque.

Ptolémée IX Sôter II Lathyre (Ptolémée Sôter II) : Pharaon de la dynastie ptolémaïque.

Pylône : Structure rectangulaire en forme de tour, généralement construite de part et d'autre de la porte donnant accès à un temple.

Qadesh (Qodesh) : Ancienne ville située sur l'Oronte, aujourd'hui en Syrie, lieu de batailles livrées entre les Égyptiens et divers royaumes du Proche-Orient. Ramsès II y livra sa plus fameuse bataille.

Qena (Kéné) : Capitale de gouvernorat sur la rive droite du Nil en Haute-Égypte, appelée Kainè durant la période gréco-romaine.

Qosseyr : El-Qousseir, la Myos Hormos ptolémaïque, ancienne ville des bords de la mer Rouge.

Qouban (Koûbân) : Contra-Pselchis, site antique situé près de Dakka, en Basse-Nubie.

Ramesséum (Ramesseum) : Temple funéraire de Ramsès II à Thèbes / Louxor sur la rive gauche du Nil.

Ramsès Ier : Pharaon fondateur de la XIXe dynastie (Nouvel Empire).

Ramsès II : Pharaon de la XIXe dynastie (Nouvel Empire).

Ramsès III : Pharaon de la XXe dynastie (Nouvel Empire)

Ramsès VII : Pharaon de la XXe dynastie (Nouvel Empire).

Ramsès IX : Pharaon de la XXe dynastie (Nouvel Empire).

Rétjénou (Routen, Rothennou) : Dans l'Égypte ancienne, nom donné à la région située entre le désert du Néguev et l'Oronte.

Rhyton (Rithon) : Coupe grecque à une seule anse utilisée pour les libations.

Sagum : Vêtement militaire romain, pièce de laine carrée portée par-dessus l'armure.

Saïs : Ville de l'Égypte ancienne située dans la partie occidentale du delta du Nil, capitale de la XXVIe dynastie.

Salle hypostyle : Partie d'un temple égyptien soutenue par de nombreuses colonnes.

Saqqara (Sakkara) : Nécropole de l'Égypte ancienne, située au sud du Caire, sur la rive gauche du Nil.

Satis (Saté) : Déesse vénérée sur l'île Éléphantine, pourvoyeuse des « eaux fraîches qui viennent d'Éléphantine. »

Scarabée : Scarabée ou bousier sacré *(Scarabaeus sacer)* ; dans l'Égypte ancienne, insecte associé au dieu solaire, souvent utilisé sous la forme d'amulettes ou de sceaux en pierre ou en céramique.

Sebbakhin : Agriculteurs locaux qui, à la recherche d'engrais, ont creusé et détruit des sites archéologiques.

Sedeinga : Site d'un temple probablement consacré à la reine Tiyi de Nubie, aujourd'hui au Soudan.

Sékos : Enclos sacré, sanctuaire d'un temple.

Selket (Selk) : Déesse qui protégeait des piqûres de scorpion ; l'une des quatre protectrices des quatre fils d'Horus.

Semna (Semnech) : Ville fortifiée (XIIe dynastie) de Nubie, aujourd'hui au Soudan.

Séqénenrê (Ra-Skenn) : Séqénenrê Taâ, souverain de Thèbes et environs sous la XVIIe dynastie (Deuxième Période Intermédiaire).

Sésostris Ier (Osortasen Ier) : Pharaon de la XIIe dynastie (Moyen Empire), fils d'Amménémès Ier.

Seth : Dieu du désert, de l'orage et du désordre.

Séthi, Séti Ier : Pharaon de la XIXe dynastie (Nouvel Empire).

Séthi, Séti II : Pharaon de la XIXe dynastie (Nouvel Empire).

Shendyt (Schantie) : Pagne porté exclusivement par le roi jusqu'à la Première Période Intermédiaire, époque à laquelle l'élite l'a adopté.

Simoun (Simoon) : Vent chaud et sec du désert, qui soulève des nuages de sable et de poussière.

Sistre : Crécelle employée dans les rites d'Isis.

Sobek (Sevek) : Dieu solaire prenant l'aspect du crocodile du Nil.

Sobekhotep (Sevekôtph) : Pharaon de la XIIIe dynastie (Moyen Empire).

Sokar (Socharis) : Dieu faucon, associé à la mort et aux enfers.

Sotem (Sothem) : Mot désignant un grand prêtre.

Spéos : Temple taillé dans la roche.

Sphinx : Statue composée d'un corps de lion et d'une tête d'homme (androsphinx), de femme (gynosphinx), de bélier (criosphinx), de faucon ou d'épervier (hiréracosphinx).

Surmé : Mot d'une langue indienne signifiant « khôl » (sulfure d'antimoine), employé dans l'Égypte ancienne pour cercler les yeux de noir.

Sycomore : Figuier-mûrier *(Ficus sycomorus)* cultivé dans l'Égypte ancienne comme « arbre de vie », associé à la déesse Hathor.

Taharqa (Tahraka) : Pharaon de la XXVe dynastie couchite (Troisième Période Intermédiaire).

Takélot Ier (Takelothe Ier) : Pharaon de la XXIIe dynastie (Troisième Période Intermédiaire).

Talmis : Site de l'Égypte ancienne, aujourd'hui Nouvelle-Kalabcha.

Tanis : Ville de l'Égypte ancienne, située dans la partie nord-est du delta du Nil, capitale et sépulture royale de la XXIe dynastie.

Taouret (Taoueri) : Déesse de l'enfantement et de la fertilité, protectrice des femmes enceintes, souvent représentée sous l'aspect d'un hippopotame.

Taousert : Grande épouse royale du pharaon Séthi II et dernière pharaonne de la XIXe dynastie (Nouvel Empire).

Tell Abou Seifa (Abou-Seyfeh) : Tjarou, Silè (Selè en grec) ; localité de la partie orientale du delta du Nil, forteresse de l'Égypte ancienne.

Tell el-Amarna : Site de la rive droite du Nil en Moyenne-Égypte, où se trouvent les ruines de la capitale d'Akhetaton, fondée par le pharaon Akhénaton.

Tell el-Maskhouta (Abou-Keycheyd) : Site de Per-Atoum Tjékou, fondé par le pharaon Néchao II dans la partie orientale du delta du Nil.

Temple périptère : Temple entouré d'un rang de colonnes.

Téti (Toti) : Pharaon fondateur de la VIe dynastie (Ancien Empire).

Thébaïde : Région voisine de l'ancienne Thèbes, comprenant les nomes méridionaux de la Haute-Égypte.

Thèbes : Ville de Haute-Égypte, capitale de l'Égypte à diverses époques et, plus régulièrement, sa capitale religieuse.

Thot (Thoth) : Dieu de la sagesse et de l'écriture, souvent représenté avec une tête d'ibis ou de babouin.

Tibère : Tiberius Iulius Caesar Augustus (42 av. J.-C.–37 ap. J.-C.), empereur romain de la dynastie julio-claudienne.

Tiyi (Taïa, Tii) : Reine de l'Égypte ancienne, grande épouse royale du pharaon Aménophis III, XVIIIe dynastie (Nouvel Empire).

Tounah el-Gebel (Djébel Touneh, Toûneh el-Gebel) : Site de l'ancienne nécropole d'Hermopolis Magna, sur la rive gauche du Nil en Moyenne-Égypte.

Toutânkhamon (Amentouonkh, Onkhamoun) : Pharaon de la XVIIIe dynastie (Nouvel Empire).

Thoutmôsis II (Thoutmès II) : Pharaon de la XVIIIe dynastie (Nouvel Empire).

Thoutmôsis III (Thoutmès III) : Pharaon de la XVIIIe dynastie (Nouvel Empire).

Thoutmôsis IV (Thoutmès IV) : Pharaon de la XVIIIe dynastie (Nouvel Empire).

Triglyphe : Section d'une colonne composée de cannelures et demi-cannelures verticales, séparant les métopes (voir ce mot) dans une frise de l'ordre dorique.

Tympanon : Ancien instrument de musique tenu à la main, semblable au tambourin.

Typhon : Dans la Grèce antique, divinité et monstre, mi-homme mi-animal, parfois assimilé au dieu de l'Égypte ancienne Seth.

Vase canope : Servait à la conservation des viscères retirés pour la momification des cadavres et inhumés séparément.

Vitruve : Marcus Vitruvius Pollio (Ier siècle av. J.-C.), architecte et ingénieur romain. Auteur de *De architectura libri decem (Les dix livres d'architecture)*.

Zaouiet el-Meïtin (Zawiet / Zawyet el-Mayetin) : Village voisin du site de Minya, ville de Moyenne-Égypte.

Editorial Note

The captions accompanying the plates are taken from the writings of Émile Prisse d'Avennes (*Monuments égyptiens*, Paris, 1847, and *Histoire de l'art égyptien*, Paris, 1878/79) and are consequently informed by the intellectual attitudes and the state of scientific research of the 19th century. In some cases the names and dates used by Prisse are now obsolete or wrong. Also the spelling of many words differs from that of today.
Inserted text in parentheses originates from Prisse himself; supplementary information in square brackets has been added to this edition by the publisher for the sake of better comprehension.

Die hier veröffentlichten Tafelbeschreibungen sind den Originaltexten von Émile Prisse d'Avennes entnommen (*Monuments égyptiens*, Paris 1847, und *Histoire de l'art égyptien*, Paris 1878/79) und spiegeln daher die Weltsicht und den wissenschaftlichen Kenntnisstand des 19. Jahrhunderts. In einigen Fällen sind die von Prisse verwendeten Namen und Daten aus heutiger Sicht veraltet oder haben sich als falsch herausgestellt. Auch die Schreibweise vieler Begriffe unterscheidet sich vom heutigen Sprachgebrauch.
Texteinschübe in runden Klammern stammen von Prisse selbst; Ergänzungen in eckigen Klammern wurden der besseren Verständlichkeit halber in dieser Ausgabe vom Verlag eingefügt.

Les citations qui accompagnent les planches sont extraites des ouvrages d'Émile Prisse d'Avennes (*Monuments égyptiens*, Paris, 1847, et *Histoire de l'art égyptien*, Paris, 1878/79). Elles reflètent les attitudes intellectuelles et l'état de la recherche scientifique du XIXe siècle. Dans certains cas, les noms et les dates mentionnés par Prisse sont aujourd'hui obsolètes ou erronés. L'orthographe de nombreux termes diverge de l'usage actuel.
Les textes insérés entre parenthèses sont de Prisse ; pour une meilleure compréhension, les informations complémentaires entre crochets ont été ajoutées par l'éditeur à la présente édition. Dans les cas où l'orthographe des noms, des lieux et des concepts utilisée par Prisse diffère clairement de la forme écrite actuelle, celle-ci est restituée entre crochets dans les textes des planches françaises.

Acknowledgements

This reprint is based on the copies owned by the Niedersächsische Staats- und Universitätsbibliothek Göttingen *(Monuments égyptiens)* and by the Universitätsbibliothek Heidelberg *(Histoire de l'art égyptien)* and has been made possible through their kind permission. We are grateful to Dr Karin Zimmermann and Dr Helmut Rohlfing for their unstinting support of this project from the outset. The original was digitally reproduced by the Göttingen Digitization Center (GDZ) of the Niedersächsische Staats- und Universitätsbibliothek Göttingen. We extend our thanks to Martin Liebetruth of the GDZ for being so cooperative during all stages of this undertaking. We also wish to thank Dr Michael Herkenhoff of the Universitäts- und Landesbibliothek Bonn for his collaboration.

Der vorliegende Nachdruck erfolgte auf Grundlage der Exemplare der Niedersächsischen Staats- und Universitätsbibliothek Göttingen *(Monuments égyptiens)* und der Universitätsbibliothek Heidelberg *(Histoire de l'art égyptien)* und wurde dank deren freundlicher Genehmigung ermöglicht. Unser besonderer Dank gilt Frau Dr. Karin Zimmermann und Herrn Dr. Helmut Rohlfing, die das Projekt von Anfang an unterstützt haben. Die digitale Reproduktion des Originals führte das Göttinger Digitalisierungszentrum der Niedersächsischen Staats- und Universitätsbibliothek Göttingen durch. Für die gute Zusammenarbeit danken wir Martin Liebetruth vom GDZ. Wir danken ferner Herrn Dr. Michael Herkenhoff von der Universitäts- und Landesbibliothek Bonn für seine Unterstützung.

La présente réimpression des ouvrages a été réalisée avec l'aimable autorisation de la Niedersächsische Staats- und Universitätsbibliothek Göttingen *(Monuments égyptiens)* et de la Universitätsbibliothek Heidelberg *(Histoire de l'art égyptien)*, sur la base de leurs exemplaires. Nous remercions tout particulièrement Dr. Karin Zimmermann et Dr. Helmut Rohlfing, qui ont soutenu le projet dès son origine. La numérisation des volumes a été effectuée par le Digitalisierungszentrum de la Niedersächsische Staats- und Universitätsbibliothek Göttingen, où nous remercions chaleureusement Martin Liebetruth pour son précieux concours. Enfin, nous tenons à remercier Dr. Michael Herkenhoff de l'Universitäts- und Landesbibliothek Bonn pour sa collaboration.

Photo Credits

All plates from the *Monuments égyptiens*: Niedersächsische Staats- und Universitätsbibliothek Göttingen (except for plates on pages 183–191: Universitäts- und Landesbibliothek Bonn)

All plates from the *Histoire de l'art égyptien*: Universitätsbibliothek Heidelberg (except for plate on page 453: Universitäts- und Landesbibliothek Bonn)

©Annecy, Collection des musées de l'agglomération d'Annecy, n. inv. 2008.0751: p. 27;

© Kingston Lacy, Dorset, UK/National Trust Photographic Library/Derrick E. Witty/The Bridgeman Art Library: p. 61;

© Paris, Bibliothèque nationale de France: pp. 16/17, 36/37, 41, 42/43, 44, 46/47, 48, 51, 57;

Göttingen, Niedersächsische Staats- und Universitätsbibliothek: pp. 13, 21, 22, 23, 63;

© Paris, RMN/Hervé Lewandowski: p. 33;

© Stapleton Collection/The Bridgeman Art Library: p. 58;

Weimar, Klassik Stiftung Weimar, Herzogin Anna Amalia Bibliothek (Th C1:15[a], ArchSchr II:40): pp. 10, 24, 30, 52/53.

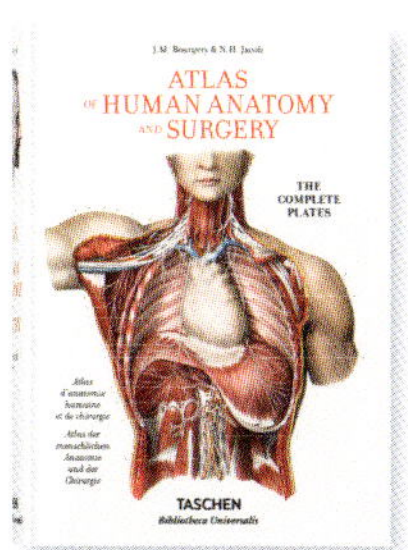
Bourgery. Atlas of Anatomy & Surgery

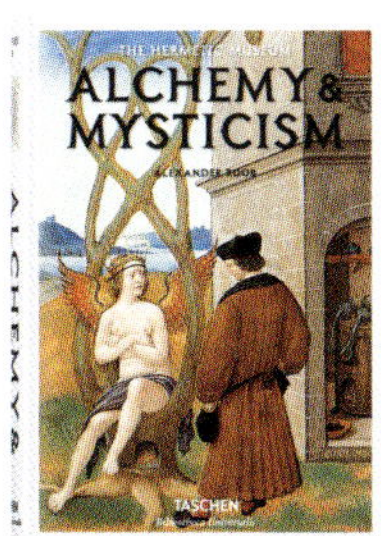
Alchemy & Mysticism

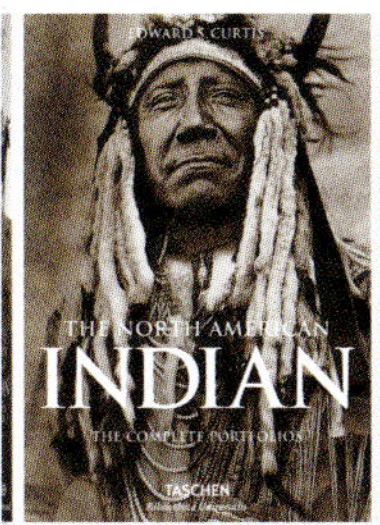
Curtis. The North American Indian

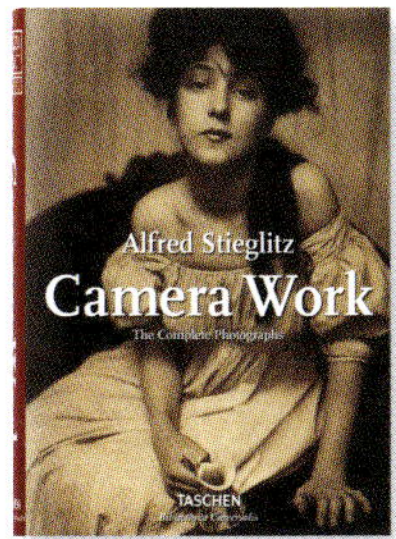
Stieglitz. Camera Work

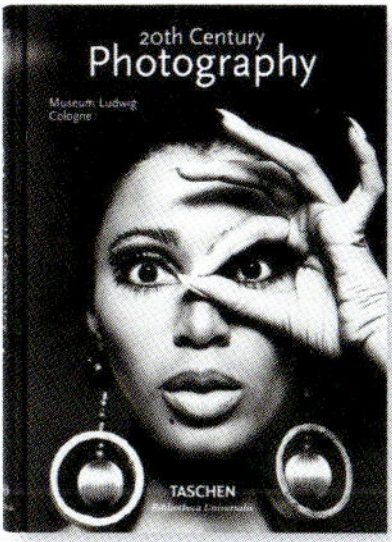
20th Century Photography

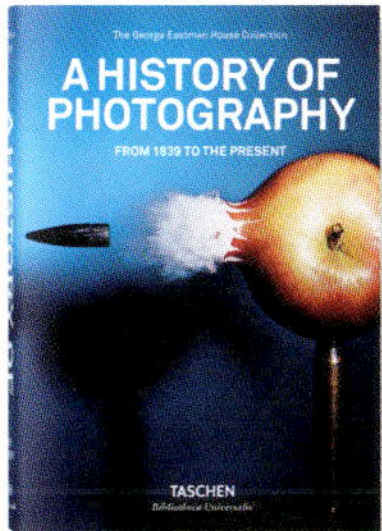
A History of Photography

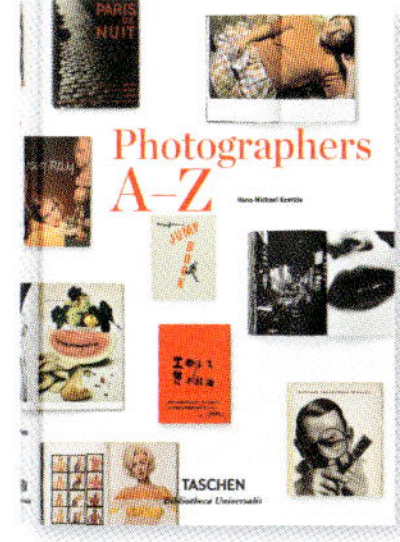
Photographers A–Z

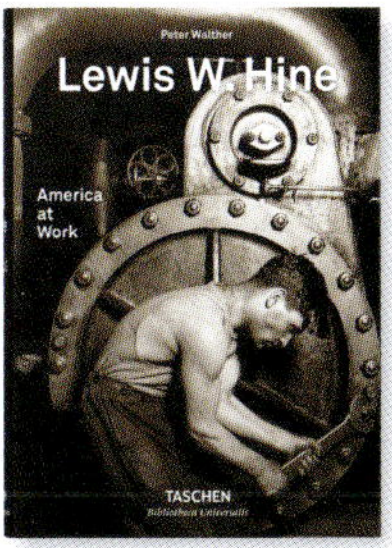
Lewis W. Hine

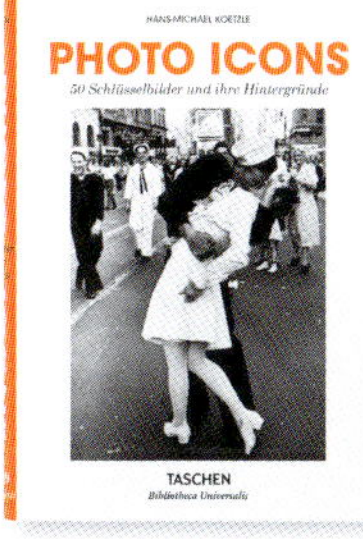
Photo Icons

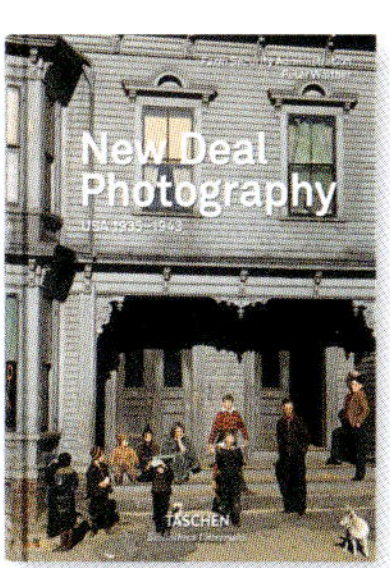
New Deal Photography

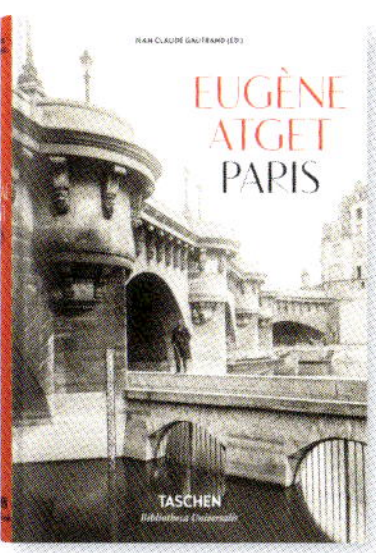
Eugène Atget. Paris

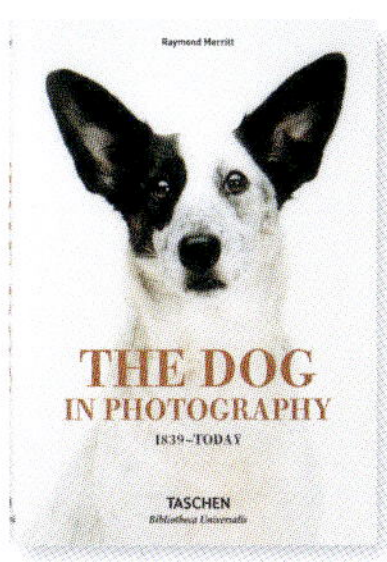
The Dog in Photography

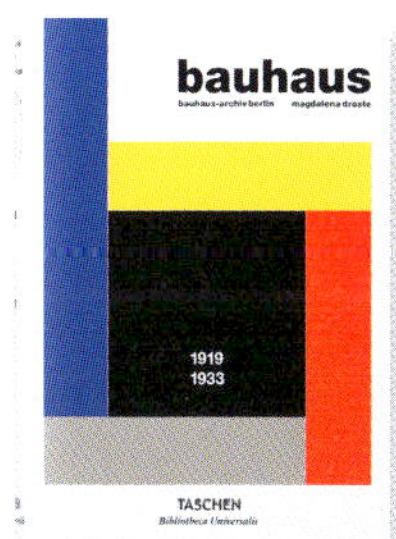
Bauhaus

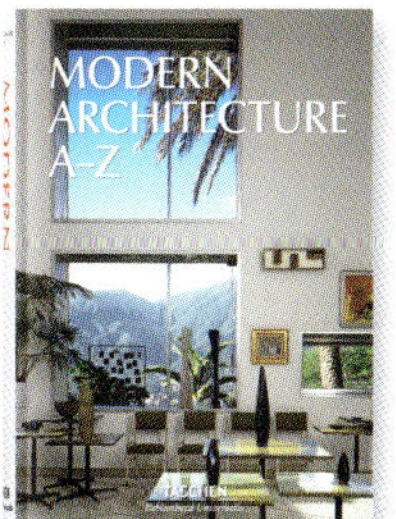
Modern Architecture A-Z

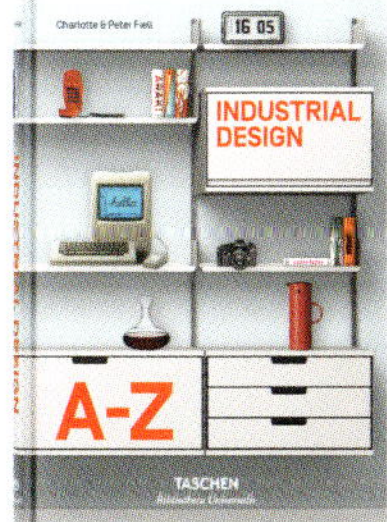
Industrial Design A–Z

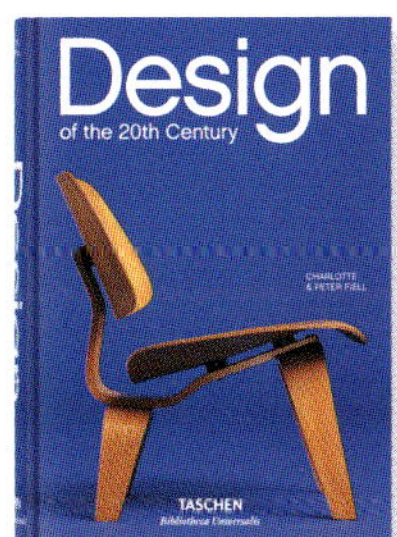
Design of the 20th Century

EACH AND EVERY TASCHEN BOOK PLANTS A SEED!
Each year, we offset our annual carbon emissions with carbon credits at the Instituto Terra, a reforestation program in Minas Gerais, Brazil, founded by Lélia and Sebastião Salgado. To find out more about this ecological partnership, please check: www.taschen.com/institutoterra.
Inspiration: unlimited. Carbon footprint: (almost) zero.

Want to see more? Visit taschen.com to view our current publications, browse our latest magazine, and subscribe to our newsletter.

Cover: Arrival of an Asiatic family in Egypt (*Histoire de l'art égyptien*)
Page 2: Renenutet, lady of the harvests (*Monuments égyptiens*, frontispiece)
Page 4: Chafre (Ranofer), scribe (*Histoire de l'art égyptien*, detail of page 403)
Pages 64/65: Criosphinx (*Histoire de l'art égyptien*, detail of page 389)
Page 591: Native of the land of Punt (*Histoire de l'art égyptien*, detail of page 447)

The author: Salima Ikram is Professor of Egyptology at the American University in Cairo. After studying History as well as Classical and Near Eastern Archaeology at Bryn Mawr College (USA), she received her PhD in Egyptian Archaeology at Cambridge University (UK). She has worked on and directed several archaeological projects in Egypt and Turkey, and has lectured around the world on subjects including ancient Egyptian food, attitudes to death, and the mummification of humans and animals. The author of several books on ancient Egypt, she has also been published in both academic and popular journals.

Hohenzollernring 53
D–50672 Köln
www.taschen.com

Project management: Mahros Allamezade, Cologne
English translation: Mary Lawson, Ashford (plate descriptions)
French translation: Jean-François Cornu, France (introduction, glossary)
German translation: Renate Heckendorf, Hamburg (plate descriptions, glossary); Helmut Roß, Krenglbach (introduction)
Design: Andy Disl, Los Angeles

Printed in Bosnia–Herzegovina
ISBN 978-3-8365-6500-4

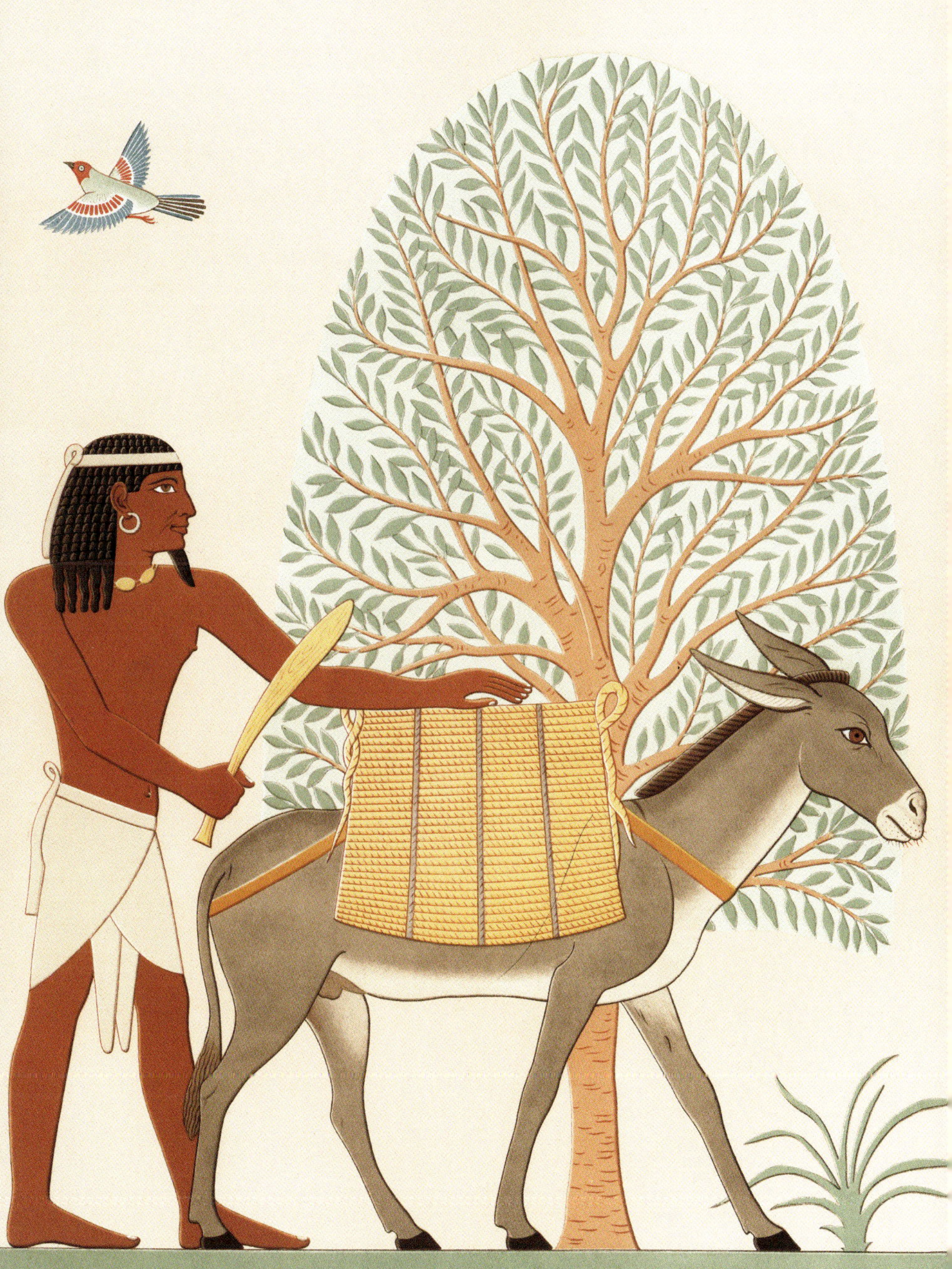

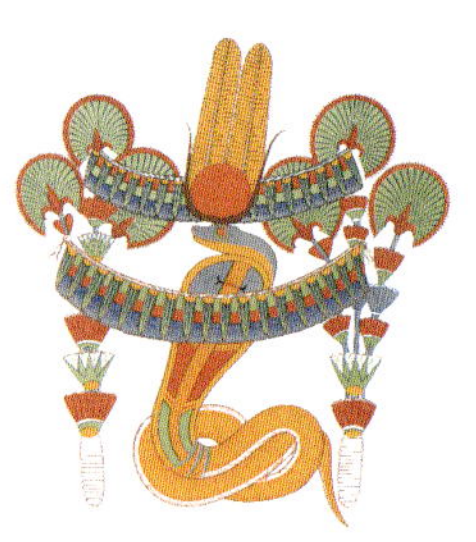